MACMILLAN LITERATURE SERIES

Introducing
Literature

Enjoying
Literature

Understanding
Literature

Appreciating
Literature

American
Literature

**English and Western
Literature**

i

General Adviser and Writer

George Kearns
Director, Expository Writing Program
English Department
Rutgers University
New Brunswick, New Jersey

Advisers

Elizabeth Ackley
Teacher
Indian Hill High School
Cincinnati, Ohio

Paula A. Calabrese
Assistant Principal, Ingomar Middle School
North Allegheny School District
Pittsburgh, Pennsylvania

Sandra A. Cavender
Teacher
Nathan Hale High School
West Allis, Wisconsin

Bernarr Paul Folta
Teacher
West Lafayette High School
West Lafayette, Indiana

Carolyn Dennis Jones
Assistant to Superintendent
Office of Manhattan High Schools
New York, New York

Judi Purvis
Department Head
Irving High School
Irving, Texas

Robert Ranta
Department Head
Lacey Township High School
Lanoka Harbor, New Jersey

Pearl Thomas
Assistant Principal, English Department
Norman Thomas High School
New York, New York

Donna Townsend
Educational Consultant
Austin, Texas

Marjory Carter Willis
Teacher
Midlothian High School
Midlothian, Virginia

Contributing Writers

Cosmo F. Ferrara
Consultant and Writer
Former English Department Head

Gale Cornelia Flynn
Poet and Writer
Former English Teacher

Barbara King
English Teacher

Philip McFarland
English Teacher

Gail Mack
Educational Writer

Julie Stone Peters
Educational Writer

Catherine Sagan
English Department Head

Brenda Weitzman
English Department Head

MACMILLAN LITERATURE SERIES

English and Western Literature

MACMILLAN PUBLISHING COMPANY

NEW YORK

COLLIER MACMILLAN PUBLISHERS

LONDON

SPECIAL ACKNOWLEDGMENTS

The Publisher is grateful for assistance and comments from the following people:

Jack V. Booch, Theater Guild, New York, New York

Mrs. Rosalie Clark, Austin High School, Decatur, Alabama

Harry James Cook, Patapsco Senior High School, Baltimore, Maryland

Mr. Albert G. Craz, Northport–East Northport High School, Northport, New York

Mrs. Doris E. R. Gilbert, Syracuse City Schools, Syracuse, New York

William Ince, Stuyvesant High School, New York, New York

Sister Edna Lutton, West Windsor–Plainsboro High School, Princeton Junction, New Jersey

Iris Gates McAnear, Austin High School, Decatur, Alabama

Macmillan Publishing Company
866 Third Avenue
New York, New York 10022
Collier Macmillan Canada, Inc.

Printed in the United States of America

ISBN 0-02-192700-6

987654321

ACKNOWLEDGMENTS

Grateful acknowledgment is given authors, publishers, and agents for permission to reprint the following copyrighted material. Every effort has been made to determine copyright owners. In the case of any omissions, the Publisher will be pleased to make suitable acknowledgments in future editions.

A. S. Barnes and Company, Inc.
VOLTAIRE: "Jeannot and Colin" from *Voltaire Shorter Writings*. The preceding selections were reprinted by permission of A. S. Barnes and Company, Inc.

The Bodley Head
GEORGE SEFERIS: "The Return of the Exile" from *Poems* translated by Rex Warner. Reprinted by permission of The Bodley Head.

John Calder (Publishers) Ltd.
SAMUEL BECKETT: "Still" from *Fizzles*. Copyright © 1976 by John Calder (Publishers) Ltd. Reprinted by permission of John Calder (Publishers) Ltd.

Jonathan Cape Ltd.
HERMANN HESSE: "The Jackdaw" from *Pictor's Metamorphoses* translated by Rika Lesser. Reprinted by permission of the Estate of Hermann Hesse, Rika Lesser, and Jonathan Cape Ltd.
JAMES JOYCE: "Araby" from *Dubliners*. Reprinted by permission of the Executors of the James Joyce Estate and Jonathan Cape Ltd.

Chatto and Windus Ltd.
EUGENIO MONTALE: "The Arno at Rovezzano" from *New Poems* translated by G. Singh. Reprinted by permission of Eugenio Montale, G. Singh, and Chatto and Windus Ltd.

VIRGIL: Extracts from *The Aeneid of Virgil* translated by C. Day Lewis. Reprinted by permission of the Executors of the Estate of C. Day Lewis and Chatto and Windus Ltd.

Toby Cole, Actors and Authors Agency
LUIGI PIRANDELLO: "War" from *The Medal and Other Stories*. Copyright 1939 by Dutton. Reprinted by permission of the Pirandello Estate and Toby Cole, agent.

Rosica Colin Limited

BOCCACCIO: "Federico's Falcon" from *The Decameron* translated by Richard Aldington. Copyright by Catherine Guillaume. Reprinted by permission of Rosica Colin Ltd.

William Collins Sons & Company Ltd.

ANNA AKHMATOVA: "Now Nobody Will Want to Listen to Songs . . ." from *Poems of Akhmatova* translated by Stanley Kunitz with Max Hayward. Reprinted by permission of the Harvill Press division of William Collins Sons & Company Ltd.

Curtis Brown Ltd., London

DORIS LESSING: "A Mild Attack of Locusts" from *The Habit of Loving*. Copyright © 1957 by Doris Lessing. Reprinted by permission of Curtis Brown Ltd., London, on behalf of Doris Lessing.

Curtis Brown Ltd., New York

SEAN O'FAOLAIN: "The Sugawn Chair" from *Selected Stories of Sean O'Faolain*. Published by Atlantic Monthly Press. Copyright © 1978 by Sean O'Faolain. Reprinted by permission of Curtis Brown Ltd., New York.

Joan Daves

HEINRICH BÖLL: "The Thrower-Away" from *18 Stories* translated by Leila Vennewitz. Copyright © 1966 by Heinrich Böll. Reprinted by permission of Joan Daves.

Andre Deutsch

GEOFFREY HILL: From "Merlin" from *Somewhere Is Such a Kingdom*. Reprinted by permission of Andre Deutsch Ltd.

Dodd, Mead & Company, Inc.

RUPERT BROOKE: "The Soldier" from *The Collected Poems of Rupert Brooke*. Copyright 1915 by Dodd, Mead & Company. Copyright renewed 1943 by Edward Marsh. Reprinted by permission of Dodd, Mead & Company, Inc.

GEORGE BERNARD SHAW: *Pygmalion*. Copyright 1913, 1914, 1916, 1930, 1941, 1944, George Bernard Shaw. Copyright 1957, The Public Trustee as Executor of the Estate of George Bernard Shaw. Copyright © 1972, The Trustees of the British Museum, The Governors and Guardians of The National Gallery of Ireland and Royal Academy of Dramatic Art. Reprinted by permission of Dodd, Mead & Company, Inc. and The Society of Authors for the Estate of George Bernard Shaw.

Doubleday & Company, Inc.

HOMER: Excerpts from *The Iliad* translated by Robert Fitzgerald. Copyright © 1974 by Robert Fitzgerald. Reprinted by permission of Doubleday & Company, Inc.

The Ecco Press

CZESLAW MILOSZ: "Encounter" from *Bells in Winter* translated by Czeslaw Milosz and Lillian Vallee. Reprinted by permission of The Ecco Press.

Faber and Faber Publishers

W. H. AUDEN: "In Memory of W. B. Yeats" and "Musée des Beaux Arts" from *Collected Poems*.

T. S. ELIOT: "Hollow Men" and "Preludes" from *Collected Poems 1909–1962*.

GOETHE: "The Pact With the Devil" and "The Prologue in Heaven" from *Goethe's Faust* translated by Louis MacNeice.

THOM GUNN: "Taylor Street" from *Touch*.

SEAMUS HEANEY: "Follower" from *Death of a Naturalist*.

TED HUGHES: "Hawk Roosting" from *Lupercal*.

ROBERT LOWELL: "Russia 1812" found in Victor Hugo's *L'Expiation* translated by Robert Lowell from *Imitations*.

LOUIS MAC NEICE: "The Park" from *The Collected Poems of Louis MacNeice*.

STEPHEN SPENDER: "I Think Continually of Those Who Were Truly Great" from *Collected Poems*.

The preceding selections were reprinted by permission of Faber and Faber Ltd.

Farrar, Straus and Giroux, Inc.

ANTON CHEKHOV: "Other People's Misfortune" from *The Unknown Chekhov* translated by Avrahm Yarmolinsky. Copyright © 1954 by Avrahm Yarmolinsky.

THOM GUNN: "Taylor Street" from *Selected Poems*. Copyright © 1957, 1958, 1961, 1967, 1971, 1973, 1974, 1975, 1976, 1979 by Thom Gunn.

SEAMUS HEANEY: "Follower" from *Poems 1965–1975*. Copyright © 1966, 1980 by Seamus Heaney.

HERMANN HESSE: "The Jackdaw" from *Pictor's Metamorphoses and Other Fantasies* translated by Rika Lesser. Translation copyright © 1981, 1982 by Farrar, Straus and Giroux, Inc.

VICTOR HUGO: "Russia 1812" from *Imitations* translated by Robert Lowell. Copyright © 1958, 1959, 1960, 1961 by Robert Lowell.

ALBERTO MORAVIA: "Doubles" from *Command, and I Will Obey You* translated by Angus Davidson. English translation © 1969 by Martin Secker & Warburg, Ltd.

The preceding selections were reprinted by permission of Farrar, Straus and Giroux, Inc.

Kimon Friar

ODYSSEUS ELÝTIS: "Drinking the Corinthian Sun" from *The Sovereign Sun* translated by Kimon Friar. Published by Temple University Press, Philadelphia, 1974. Reprinted by permission of Kimon Friar.

Grove Press, Inc.

SAMUEL BECKETT: "Still" from *Fizzles*. Translated from the original French by Samuel Beckett. Copyright © 1976 by Samuel Beckett. Reprinted by permission of Grove Press, Inc.

Hamish Hamilton Limited

ALBERT CAMUS: "The Guest" from *Exile and the Kingdom* translated by Justin O'Brien. Reprinted by permission of Hamish Hamilton Limited.

Harcourt Brace Jovanovich, Inc.

T. S. ELIOT: "The Hollow Men" and "Preludes" from *Collected Poems 1909–1962*. Copyright 1936 by Harcourt Brace Jovanovich, Inc.; copyright © 1963, 1964 by T. S. Eliot.

HEINRICH HEINE: "The Lorelei" adapted from *Heinrich Heine: Paradox and Poet, the Poems* by Louis Untermeyer. Copyright 1937 by Harcourt Brace Jovanovich, Inc.; renewed 1965 by Louis Untermeyer.

GEORGE ORWELL: "Why I Write" from *Such, Such Were the Joys*. Copyright 1945, 1952, 1953 by Sonia Brownell Orwell; renewed 1973 by Sonia Pitt-Rivers, 1980 by Sonia Brownell Orwell, 1981 by Mrs. George K. Perutz, Mrs. Miriam Gross, Dr. Michael Dickson, Executors of the Estate of Sonia Brownell Orwell.

SOPHOCLES: "The Antigone of Sophocles," an English Version trans-

CREDITS

CONTENTS

English and Western
Literature

Literary Map of Britain

This map, with current borders, identifies locales associated with many of the authors and selections included in Part One of *English and Western Literature* of the *Macmillan Literature Series*. As you read more English literature, you will be able to place other authors and literary works in correct geographic locations.

HIGHLANDS

SCOTLAND

BIRNAM WOODS

DUNSINANE

Aberdeen
Sir Patrick Spens drowns

Glasgow
Burns statue

Edinburgh
Boswell born

NORTH SEA

ATLANTIC OCEAN

NORTHERN IRELAND

IRELAND

IRISH SEA

LAKE DISTRICT POETS

Kelloe
E. B. Browning born

Whitby
Caedmon a monk

ENGLAND

York
Auden born

Winstead
Marvell born

Dublin
Beckett, Joyce, Shaw, Steele, Yeats born
Hopkins teaches
Swift preaches

Newstead Abbey
Byron home

Eastwood
Lawrence born

Kilcolman
Spenser writes *Faerie Queene*

Cork
O'Faolain born

Housman's *Shropshire Lad*

Lichfield
Dr. Johnson born

Lowestoft
Conrad lands in England

WALES

Rugby
Brooke at school

Aldwinkle
Dryden born

Stratford
Shakespeare born, lives

● OXFORD

● CAMBRIDGE

Swansea
Thomas born

● Wordsworth's
Tintern Abbey

Canterbury
Chaucer's *Tales*
Lovelace home
Marlowe born

Chalfont St. Giles
Milton writes ●

LONDON
Thames

Nether Stowey
Coleridge writes *Mariner*

Stoke Poges
Gray's Churchyard

Arnold's
Dover Beach

Tintagel
King Arthur born

WESSEX
Hardy's fiction

Bury
Galsworthy home

Sidney's
Penshurst
Place

STRAIT OF DOVER

Dean Prior
Herrick a rector

East Budleigh
Raleigh born

Portsmouth
Dickens born

West Grinstead
Pope begins *Lock*

Bournemouth
Shelley's heart buried

Maidstone
Tennyson writes

ENGLISH CHANNEL

✪ **London**
Caxton publishes Malory's tales
Bacon, Jonson, Keats, Lamb, Woolf born
Blake prints
Donne preaches
Eliot publishes periodical
Lessing, Mansfield, Pepys write
Shakespeare's Globe Theatre
Tatler and *Spectator* published

FRANCE

Part One: English Literature

This book is divided into two parts—Part One: English Literature and Part Two: Western Literature. Part One presents a chronological survey of English literature from its Anglo-Saxon beginnings in 449 to the present day.

A few basic facts about England will be helpful to you as you read. First of all, modern-day England is actually one division of the United Kingdom of Great Britain and Northern Ireland, often called simply Great Britain. The other divisions are Wales, Scotland, and Northern Ireland. When we refer to English literature in this book, however, we speak in broad terms about literature from all these areas.

The British have had a monarch, or hereditary royal sovereign, for more than a thousand years. The powers of the monarch have gradually declined over these years, and today Great Britain is a constitutional monarchy, in which the sovereign serves as the head of state but does not actually rule. A cabinet of government officials called ministers and headed by the prime minister actually rules the country. The Parliament is the lawmaking body, consisting of the House of Lords and the House of Commons. The House of Lords is composed of nobility, most of whom have inherited their titles.

Much of the literature you will be reading contains titles of royalty and nobility. Royalty includes the king (the male sovereign) and the queen (the female sovereign or the wife of the king). Other members of the royal family include princes (the sons of the sovereign, the sons of a son of the sovereign, or the husband of the queen) and princesses (the daughters of the sovereign, the daughters of a son of the sovereign, or the wives of princes). The upper nobility consists of dukes and duchesses, marquesses and marchionesses, earls and countesses, viscounts and viscountesses, and barons and baronesses.

Sovereigns of England and Great Britain

Anglo-Saxons and Danes

Kingdom of Kent
Ethelbert, 560–616

Kingdom of Northumbria
Ethelfrith, 593–617
Edwin, 617–633
Oswald, 635–642
Oswy, 642–670
Ecgfrith, 670–685

Kingdom of Mercia
Penda, 626–655
Ethelbald, 716–757
Offa II, 757–796
Cenulf, 796–821

Kingdom of Wessex
Ine, 688–726
Egbert, 802–839
Ethelwulf, 839–858
Ethelbald, 858–860
Ethelbert, 860–866
Ethelred I, 866–871
Alfred the Great, 871–899
Edward, 899–924
Athelstan, 924–939

Edmund I, 939–946
Edred, 946–955
Edwy, 955–959
Edgar, 959–975
Edward, 975–978
Ethelred II, 978–1016
Edmund II, 1016
Canute, 1016–1035
Harold I, 1035–1040
Hardecanute, 1040–1042
Edward the Confessor, 1042–1066
Harold II, 1066

Normans
William, I, 1066–1087
William II, 1087–1100
Henry I, 1100–1135
Stephen, 1135–1154

House of Plantagenet
Henry II, 1154–1189
Richard I, 1189–1199
John, 1199–1216
Henry III, 1216–1272
Edward I, 1272–1307
Edward II, 1307–1327
Edward III, 1327–1377
Richard II, 1377–1399

House of Lancaster
Henry IV, 1399–1413
Henry V, 1413–1422
Henry VI, 1422–1461

House of York
Edward IV, 1461–1483
Edward V, 1483
Richard III, 1483–1485

House of Tudor
Henry VII, 1485–1509
Henry VIII, 1509–1547
Edward VI, 1547–1553
Mary I, 1553–1558
Elizabeth I, 1558–1603

House of Stuart
James I (James VI of Scotland), 1603–1625
Charles I, 1625–1649

Interregnum (1649–1659)
Oliver Cromwell, 1653–1658
Richard Cromwell, 1658–1659

House of Stuart
Charles II, 1660–1685
James II, 1685–1688

House of Orange
William III and Mary II, 1689–1702

House of Stuart
Anne, 1702–1714

House of Hanover
George I, 1714–1727
George II, 1727–1760
George III, 1760–1820
George IV, 1820–1830
William IV, 1830–1837
Victoria, 1837–1901

House of Saxe-Coburg-Gotha (after 1917, Windsor)
Edward VII, 1901–1910
George V, 1910–1936
Edward VIII, 1936 (abdicted)
George VI, 1936–1952
Elizabeth II, 1952–

Key to Illustrations appears on page 29.

THE ANGLO-SAXON PERIOD

449–1066

What we speak of as English literature might be more accurately called British literature, for it includes the literature of Scotland, Wales, and Ireland as well as of England. The island of Britain, located twenty miles off the coast of northern Europe, was originally inhabited by primitive Celtic tribes known as Britons. This island, nearly six hundred miles from north to south and never much wider than three hundred miles, includes England, Scotland, and Wales. To its west is another island, Ireland.

Britain is a land that has had its history, culture, and literature shaped by a series of invaders from the nearby continent. Perhaps one of the reasons for the universal and lasting appeal of English literature is that it springs from a land that, in its early history, was successively invaded by people with varying languages and cultures.

Before the Anglo-Saxons

Although our study of English literature begins with the Anglo-Saxon Period, the Anglo-Saxons were not the first people, nor indeed the most civilized people, to invade Britain. Generally speaking, civilization in Europe—the development of a written language, art, religion, science, and social codes—began in Greece and in Rome, far to the south of Britain near the Mediterranean Sea.

Chesspiece from the Viking Age.

Ancient Greek civilization (see Part Two of this book) dates back to 800 B.C. For four hundred years or so this small, Aegean civilization produced, along with beautiful architecture and ordered city life, some of the most enduring works of literature that the world has ever known. The Greek influence then spread northward into what we know today as France, Germany, and Spain.

By 250 B.C. Rome had conquered the Mediterranean world. In the two hundred years between 100 B.C. and A.D. 100, Rome produced another ancient civilization, indebted to that of Greece, with a literature of its own (see Part Two). Under the Roman general Julius Caesar, the Roman empire was carried northward into what was then Gaul and is now France. Finding himself near the inviting isle of Britain in 55 B.C., Caesar himself led his army across the English Channel, bringing to England its first touch of Roman civilization.

Julius Caesar was not only a brilliant general but a noted author who composed a Latin history called *Caesar's Commentaries.* When he invaded Britain, he encountered the Celts whose life style by Roman standards was primitive and crude. Caesar remained in Britain only a short time, but in A.D. 43, during the rule of the emperor Claudius, the Romans returned to Britain in earnest and stayed for more than three hundred years.

Anglo-Saxon Invasions

The Jutes, followed by the Angles and the Saxons—all tribes of Germanic origin—invaded Britain from the European continent in 449. As they invaded, the Celts—led, stories tell us, by a Christian king named Arthur—retreated slowly into the misty uplands of present-day Wales, and the Britain that we now know began to take shape.

In the southern part of the island, the Angles and the Saxons, soon united as Anglo-Saxons, began to introduce a society that was, in a sense, democratic and order-loving. By 787 when the Danes—tribes from northern Europe, often called Vikings or Norsemen—attempted to invade England, the Anglo-Saxons had acquired a leader strong enough to repulse the invasion. He was Alfred the Great, a military leader who, like Julius Caesar before him, was also a writer and the author of a history. Alfred's history, however, was written not in Latin but in Anglo-Saxon, his native tongue.

Anglo-Saxon Civilization

If at this time you had been able to look down from the air upon Anglo-Saxon England, especially upon the southern part of the island, less mountainous and more fertile than in the north, what would have struck your eye? Perhaps first would be the legacies of Rome: the famous Roman roads, still used by the Anglo-Saxons; a few great walls; and mostly abandoned towns with baths and villas, all of stone, brick, and tile.

The Anglo-Saxons preferred their own little villages, with timber-built shelters and communal farmland (in which each family, however poor, had a strip of land). Therefore, you would see new wagon trails connecting these villages, and also winding off to an occasional castle and courtyard, to newly built Anglo-Saxon stone churches, and to monasteries, some of which dated back to Roman times. On these trails, you would see most often ox-drawn carts taking goods to market. Groups of clerics, pilgrims, or courtiers would remind you that the courts of nobles and the monasteries and cathedrals of the Roman Church formed the central institutions of the country. Warriors in unpleasantly stiff armor would remind you that Anglo-Saxon England was not only a farming so-

ciety but a heavily military society as well. It was also a seagoing society, and from the air you could see the beginning of the great city of London, a trade center for goods carried to market by ship as well as by oxcart.

Perhaps not easily distinguished from other parts of an Anglo-Saxon castle were the mead halls. People would gather in these great communal banquet halls to celebrate a battle or the return of a hero from a long journey. These meetings were the occasions for feasting and for drinking ale and mead, a malt liquor made from honey. It was in these Anglo-Saxon mead halls that English literature first began.

The Beginnings of English Literature

English literature began as oral, not written literature, with songs and poems celebrating heroes. These poems were passed on by minstrels, or **scops,** who composed many poems that praised Anglo-Saxon ideals. Probably the most important of these ideals were valor, honor, and loyalty to one's lord. This was primarily a somber time in which human destiny was believed to be ruled by fate, or _wyrd,_ as the Anglo-Saxons called it.

Through the songs of the scops, the major battles and the feats of the tribe's heroes and kings were recited and remem-

Dover Castle, constructed during the Anglo-Saxon Period.

bered. In this way heroes could win enduring fame, something that was valued highly because their religion did not acknowledge immortality through an afterlife. The scops' poems often reflect the grim, war-ridden lives of the Anglo-Saxon people. By immortalizing their heroes, the scops also brought a semblance of permanence to a world ruled by a sense of transience and fatal doom.

The earliest English story-poem to come down to us is about a hero called Beowulf. *Beowulf* was composed about 700 by an unknown minstrel, one of the many who traveled from mead hall to mead hall to entertain the courts of kings and their warriors. The poem was composed in Old English, or Anglo-Saxon, a dialect of Germanic origin that is the ancestor of our present-day English and was brought to Britain by the Anglo-Saxons. *Beowulf* is an example of an **epic,** a long narrative poem in grave and stately language about the achievements of a hero, often a national heroic

figure. Ancient Greece and Rome (see Part Two of this book) had their great epics. England itself has other epics that appear later in this book.

Few of the other poems of this period have survived. Those that have we owe to the work and learning of monks in monasteries, which, like the castles with their mead halls, dotted the landscape of Anglo-Saxon England. One of these early poems is "The Seafarer," unusual for its lyric tone and its nonreligious subject matter.

Written literature did not exist in the British Isles until about the year 700. It first comes to our attention in the work of the most famous of the Anglo-Saxon monks, the Venerable Bede, author of *Ecclesiastical History of the English People.* One of the famous people Bede wrote about in his *History* was Caedmon, a shepherd who became a monk and the first English religious poet.

Although Bede was Anglo-Saxon, he wrote his *History* in Latin. The first notable written literature actually composed in Old English came almost two centuries later when the remarkable Anglo-Saxon King Alfred the Great wrote his *Anglo-Saxon Chronicles,* also a history, in the year 892. Alfred is often considered the greatest English king. The social organization, laws, and culture that he introduced are still evident in English culture today.

TIME LINE

449   Germanic tribes cross the North Sea to England, and Anglo-Saxon rule begins

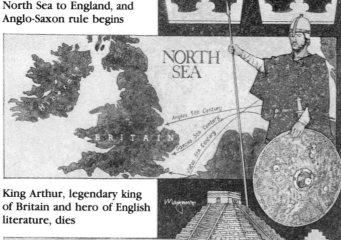

c. 537   King Arthur, legendary king of Britain and hero of English literature, dies

563   Establishment of Iona monastery, one of earliest centers of Christianity in Britain

597   St. Augustine, missionary, establishes monastery in Canterbury

c. 658   Caedmon's *Hymn*

673?   Birth of Venerable Bede, earliest English historian and earliest important prose writer

c. 700   Book of Kells, decorated manuscript of the four gospels

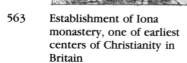

c. 460   Mexico: Peak of Mayan culture

476   End of western Roman Empire

c. 500   China: Tea brought from India

517   China: Buddhism introduced

542   Europe: Bubonic plague spreads through Europe killing about half the population

550   India: Beginnings of chess game

552   Europe: Beginning of silk industry

560   Japan: Buddhism introduced

570?   Arabia: Mohammed born, founder of Islam

630   Arabia: Cotton introduced

700   Easter eggs come into use among Christians

        China: Population explosion

700   *Beowulf* by anonymous
        author, oldest epic poem
        composed in English

787   Danish invasions

                                                         771   Charlemagne becomes ruler
                                                                 of Frankish kingdom

                                                         810   Persia: Term *algebra* coined

                                                         861   Iceland discovered by
                                                                 Vikings

871   Alfred the Great begins rule
        (until 899)

878   Alfred defeats Danish
        invaders

892   *Anglo-Saxon Chronicles*
        initiated by Alfred the Great,
        first historic record to be
        kept in English   895   Holy Land: Earliest Hebrew
                                                                 manuscript of Old Testament

                                                         900   Beginnings of Arabian tales
                                                                 "A Thousand and One
                                                                 Nights"

                                                                 Greenland discovered by
                                                                 Vikings

                                                                 Europe: Emergence of feudal
                                                                 system

975   *The Exeter Book,* group of
        short meditative poems,
        including "The Seafarer"

                                                         1000   North America discovered by
                                                                 Lief Ericson

1040   The real Macbeth kills King
        Duncan

1042   Edward the Confessor begins
        rule (until 1066), last English
        king descended from Alfred
        the Great

                                                         1045   Spain: Birth of The Cid

1066   The Norman Conquest of
        England

Anglo-Saxon Epic Poetry

English literature may be said to begin with *Beowulf,* a poem written over twelve hundred years ago. Composed around 700, it existed for future ages in only one original manuscript, made 300 years later. The poem presents the legendary history of the Anglo-Saxons, and its author would have been descended from the original tribes of Angles, Saxons, and Jutes who invaded Britain from the European continent in the fifth century. Those people spoke the Germanic language in which the poem is written.

Like the *Iliad* and the *Odyssey* of ancient Greece, *Beowulf* is an epic. An **epic** is a long narrative poem that records, in grave and stately language, the exploits of a larger-than-life hero who usually embodies national ideals. This great Anglo-Saxon epic described the achievements of their courageous ancestor, Beowulf, "the strongest man who ever lived." Beowulf had lived several hundred years earlier, at a time before the Germanic tribes had emigrated from Europe. Thus, the poem is set on the European mainland, in what is modern Denmark and Sweden.

In the primitive and harsh environment of Beowulf's world, the hero occupied a place of great importance, for his qualities of strength and wisdom and courage might save the people from the evils that threatened them. Because of the Anglo-Saxons' constant intertribal wars, life in this period was brief and strife-ridden. As a result, the Anglo-Saxons believed in the inevitability of fate (or what they called *wyrd*) as the ruling force in human destiny and in the certainty of death. The sense of fatal doom that pervaded the Anglo-Saxon world is reflected in the somber tone of *Beowulf.*

Despite life's hardships and transience, however, the Anglo-Saxon hero could attain some degree of immortality through fame—by being remembered by others for his sense of honor and his heroic deeds. Loyalty to one's lord was an important Anglo-Saxon ideal, and courage and bravery were highly valued since by demonstrating valor, fame could be achieved. Boasting was a hero's dare to destiny; and a commitment to courageous action.

Beowulf is 3,182 lines long, approximately 80 or 90 pages in book length. The story consists of two parts. The first concerns Beowulf's successful battle with the monster Grendel and with Grendel's mother. The second relates the aged Beowulf's victory over a dragon and his subsequent death and funeral. Only portions of the epic are printed here in a modern English translation.

We enter that bleak, remote world at night, at Herot, the great banquet hall of the Danish king Hrothgar [hroth′gar]. This particular evening has been spent in feasting and revels. Yet, unknown to the revelers, outside in the surrounding marshland the monster Grendel is prowling.

Carved head from a Viking
sledge unearthed with the
Oseberg Ship in Norway.

from **Beowulf**

Translated by Burton Raffel

The Battle with Grendel

   Then, when darkness had dropped, Grendel
Went up to Herot, wondering what the warriors
Would do in that hall when their drinking was done.
He found them sprawled in sleep, suspecting
5 Nothing, their dreams undisturbed. The monster's
Thoughts were as quick as his greed or his claws:
He slipped through the door and there in the silence
Snatched up thirty men, smashed them
Unknowing in their beds and ran out with their bodies,
10 The blood dripping behind him, back
To his lair, delighted with his night's slaughter.
   At daybreak, with the sun's first light, they saw
How well he had worked, and in that gray morning
Broke their long feast with tears and laments
15 For the dead. Hrothgar, their lord, sat joyless
In Herot, a mighty prince mourning
The fate of his lost friends and companions,
Knowing by its tracks that some demon had torn
His followers apart. He wept, fearing
20 The beginning might not be the end. And that night
Grendel came again, so set
On murder that no crime could ever be enough,
No savage assault quench his lust
For evil. Then each warrior tried
25 To escape him, searched for rest in different
Beds, as far from Herot as they could find,
Seeing how Grendel hunted when they slept.

Distance was safety; the only survivors
Were those who fled him. Hate had triumphed.
30   So Grendel ruled, fought with the righteous,
One against many, and won; so Herot
Stood empty, and stayed deserted for years,
Twelve winters of grief for Hrothgar, king
Of the Danes, sorrow heaped at his door
35 By hell-forged hands.

     Then Hrothgar left that hall, the Danes'
Great protector, followed by his court; the queen
Had preceded him and he went to lie at her side,
Seek sleep near his wife. It was said that God
40 Himself had set a sentinel in Herot,
Brought Beowulf as a guard against Grendel and a shield
Behind whom the king could safely rest.
And Beowulf was ready, firm with our Lord's
High favor and his own bold courage and strength.
45   He stripped off his mail[1] shirt, his helmet, his sword
Hammered from the hardest iron, and handed
All his weapons and armor to a servant,
Ordered his war-gear guarded till morning.
And then, standing beside his bed,
50 He exclaimed:
          "Grendel is no braver, no stronger
Than I am! I could kill him with my sword; I shall not,
Easy as it would be. This fiend is a bold
And famous fighter, but his claws and teeth
Scratching at my shield, his clumsy fists
55 Beating at my sword blade, would be helpless. I will meet him
With my hands empty—unless his heart
Fails him, seeing a soldier waiting
Weaponless, unafraid. Let God in His wisdom
Extend His hand where He wills, reward
60 Whom He chooses!"
            Then the Geats' great chief dropped
His head to his pillow, and around him, as ready
As they could be, lay the soldiers who had crossed the sea
At his side, each of them sure that he was lost
To the home he loved, to the high-walled towns
65 And the friends he had left behind where both he
And they had been raised. Each thought of the Danes
Murdered by Grendel in a hall where Geats
And not Danes now slept. But God's dread loom
Was woven with defeat for the monster, good fortune
70 For the Geats; help against Grendel was with them,

Gold brooch from the Viking Age.

---

1. **mail:** flexible armor made of interlinked metal rings.

And through the might of a single man
They would win. Who doubts that God in His wisdom
And strength holds the earth forever
In His hands? Out in the darkness the monster
75 Began to walk. The warriors slept
In that gabled hall where they hoped that He
Would keep them safe from evil, guard them
From death till the end of their days was determined
And the thread should be broken. But Beowulf lay wakeful,
80 Watching, waiting, eager to meet
His enemy, and angry at the thought of his coming.

    Out from the marsh, from the foot of misty
Hills and bogs, bearing God's hatred,
Grendel came, hoping to kill
85 Anyone he could trap on this trip to high Herot.
He moved quickly through the cloudy night,
Up from his swampland, sliding silently
Toward that gold-shining hall. He had visited Hrothgar's
Home before, knew the way—
90 But never, before nor after that night,
Found Herot defended so firmly, his reception
So harsh. He journeyed, forever joyless,
Straight to the door, then snapped it open,
Tore its iron fasteners with a touch
95 And rushed angrily over the threshold.
He strode quickly across the inlaid
Floor, snarling and fierce: his eyes
Gleamed in the darkness, burned with a gruesome
Light. Then he stopped, seeing the hall
100 Crowded with sleeping warriors, stuffed
With rows of young soldiers resting together.
And his heart laughed, he relished the sight,
Intended to tear the life from those bodies
By morning; the monster's mind was hot
105 With the thought of food and the feasting his belly
Would soon know. But fate, that night, intended
Grendel to gnaw the broken bones
Of his last human supper. Human
Eyes were watching his evil steps,
110 Waiting to see his swift hard claws.
Grendel snatched at the first Geat
He came to, ripped him apart, cut
His body to bits with powerful jaws,
Drank the blood from his veins and bolted
115 Him down, hands and feet; death
And Grendel's great teeth came together,
Snapping life shut. Then he stepped to another

Carved head from the Viking
Age unearthed with the
Oseberg Ship.

Silver coin from the Viking Age.

Still body, clutched at Beowulf with his claws,
Grasped at a strong-hearted wakeful sleeper
120 —And was instantly seized himself, claws
Bent back as Beowulf leaned up on one arm.
    That shepherd of evil, guardian of crime,
Knew at once that nowhere on earth
Had he met a man whose hands were harder;
125 His mind was flooded with fear—but nothing
Could take his talons and himself from that tight
Hard grip. Grendel's one thought was to run
From Beowulf, flee back to his marsh and hide there:
This was a different Herot than the hall he had emptied.
130 But Higlac's[2] follower remembered his final
Boast and, standing erect, stopped
The monster's flight, fastened those claws
In his fists till they cracked, clutched Grendel
Closer. The infamous killer fought
135 For his freedom, wanting no flesh but retreat,
Desiring nothing but escape; his claws
Had been caught, he was trapped. That trip to Herot
Was a miserable journey for the writhing monster!
    The high hall rang, its roof boards swayed,
140 And Danes shook with terror. Down
The aisles the battle swept, angry
And wild. Herot trembled, wonderfully
Built to withstand the blows, the struggling
Great bodies beating at its beautiful walls;
145 Shaped and fastened with iron, inside
And out, artfully worked, the building
Stood firm. Its benches rattled, fell
To the floor, gold-covered boards grating
As Grendel and Beowulf battled across them.
150 Hrothgar's wise men had fashioned Herot
To stand forever; only fire,
They had planned, could shatter what such skill had put
Together, swallow in hot flames such splendor
Of ivory and iron and wood. Suddenly
155 The sounds changed, the Danes started
In new terror, cowering in their beds as the terrible
Screams of the Almighty's enemy sang
In the darkness, the horrible shrieks of pain
And defeat, the tears torn out of Grendel's
160 Taut throat, hell's captive caught in the arms
Of him who of all the men on earth
Was the strongest.

---

2. **Higlac** [hig'laks]: the king of the Geats [gā'ats], Beowulf's uncle and feudal lord.

That mighty protector of men

Meant to hold the monster till its life
Leaped out, knowing the fiend was no use
165 To anyone in Denmark. All of Beowulf's
Band had jumped from their beds, ancestral
Swords raised and ready, determined
To protect their prince if they could. Their courage
Was great but all wasted: they could hack at Grendel
170 From every side, trying to open
A path for his evil soul, but their points
Could not hurt him, the sharpest and hardest iron
Could not scratch at his skin, for that sin-stained demon
Had bewitched all men's weapons, laid spells
175 That blunted every mortal man's blade.
And yet his time had come, his days
Were over, his death near; down
To hell he would go, swept groaning and helpless
To the waiting hands of still worse fiends.
180 Now he discovered—once the afflictor
Of men, tormentor of their days—what it meant
To feud with Almighty God: Grendel
Saw that his strength was deserting him, his claws
Bound fast, Higlac's brave follower tearing at
185 His hands. The monster's hatred rose higher,
But his power had gone. He twisted in pain,
And the bleeding sinews[3] deep in his shoulder
Snapped, muscle and bone split
And broke. The battle was over, Beowulf
190 Had been granted new glory: Grendel escaped,
But wounded as he was could flee to his den,
His miserable hole at the bottom of the marsh,
Only to die, to wait for the end
Of all his days. And after that bloody
195 Combat the Danes laughed with delight.
He who had come to them from across the sea,
Bold and strong-minded, had driven affliction
Off, purged Herot clean. He was happy,
Now, with that night's fierce work; the Danes
200 Had been served as he'd boasted he'd serve them; Beowulf,
A prince of the Geats, had killed Grendel,
Ended the grief, the sorrow, the suffering
Forced on Hrothgar's helpless people
By a bloodthirsty fiend. No Dane doubted
205 The victory, for the proof, hanging high
From the rafters where Beowulf had hung it, was the monster's
Arm, claw and shoulder and all.

The prow of the Oseberg
Ship. *Foreground:* silver
coin from the Viking Age.

---

3. **sinews** [sin′yūz]: tendons.

Replica of a Viking helmet from the Sutton Hoo Ship Burial, c. 625.

The Battle with the Fire-Breathing Dragon

Having mortally wounded Grendel, Beowulf is called upon to slay that creature's "monstrous hag" of a mother, who is bent on vengeance. He does so at great risk to himself, and then returns in triumph to his homeland over the seas.

Time passes and the hero Beowulf becomes king of the Geats, whom he rules wisely for fifty years. At last, having grown old, he is summoned once more to do battle against a common foe. A fire-breathing dragon, disturbed among its hoard of treasure, has emerged to molest the Geats and devastate their country. The dragon's fiery breath is soon reducing their homes to ashes.

    Vomiting fire and smoke, the dragon
Burned down their homes. They watched in horror
210 As the flames rose up: the angry monster
Meant to leave nothing alive. And the signs
Of its anger flickered and glowed in the darkness,
Visible for miles, tokens of its hate
And its cruelty, spread like a warning to the Geats
215 Who had broken its rest. Then it hurried back
To its tower, to its hidden treasure, before dawn
Could come. It had wrapped its flames around
The Geats; now it trusted in stone
Walls, and its strength, to protect it. But they would not.
220 Then they came to Beowulf, their king, and announced
That his hall, his throne, the best of buildings,
Had melted away in the dragon's burning
Breath. Their words brought misery, Beowulf's
Sorrow beat at his heart: he accused
225 Himself of breaking God's law, of bringing
The Almighty's anger down on his people.
Reproach pounded in his breast, gloomy
And dark, and the world seemed a different place.
But the hall was gone, the dragon's molten
230 Breath had licked across it, burned it
To ashes, near the shore it had guarded. The Geats
Deserved revenge; Beowulf, their leader
And lord, began to plan it, ordered
A battle-shield shaped of iron, knowing that
235 Wood would be useless, that no linden[4] shield
Could help him, protect him, in the flaming heat
Of the beast's breath. That noble prince
Would end his days on earth, soon,

---

4. **linden:** made of linden wood.

Would leave this brief life, but would take the dragon
240 With him, tear it from the heaped up treasure
It had guarded so long. And he'd go to it alone,
Scorning to lead soldiers against such
An enemy: he saw nothing to fear, thought nothing
Of the beast's claws, or wings, or flaming
245 Jaws—he had fought, before, against worse
Odds, had survived, been victorious, in harsher
Battles, beginning in Herot, Hrothgar's
Unlucky hall. He'd killed Grendel
And his mother, swept that murdering tribe
250 Away.

And Beowulf uttered his final boast:
"I've never known fear; as a youth I fought
In endless battles. I am old, now,
But I will fight again, seek fame still,
255 If the dragon hiding in his tower dares
To face me."
            Then he said farewell to his followers,
Each in his turn, for the last time:
"I'd use no sword, no weapon, if this beast
Could be killed without it, crushed to death
260 Like Grendel, gripped in my hands and torn
Limb from limb. But his breath will be burning
Hot, poison will pour from his tongue.
I feel no shame, with shield and sword
And armor, against this monster: when he comes to me
265 I mean to stand, not run from his shooting
Flames, stand till fate decides
Which of us wins. My heart is firm,
My hands calm: I need no hot
Words. Wait for me close by, my friends.
270 We shall see, soon, who will survive
This bloody battle, stand when the fighting
Is done. No one else could do
What I mean to, here, no man but me
Could hope to defeat this monster. No one
275 Could try. And this dragon's treasure, his gold
And everything hidden in that tower, will be mine
Or war will sweep me to a bitter death!"
    Then Beowulf rose, still brave, still strong,
And with his shield at his side, and a mail shirt on his breast,
280 Strode calmly, confidently, toward the tower, under
The rocky cliffs: no coward could have walked there!
And then he who'd endured dozens of desperate
Battles, who'd stood boldly while swords and shields

Clashed, the best of kings, saw
285 Huge stone arches and felt the heat
Of the dragon's breath, flooding down
Through the hidden entrance, too hot for anyone
To stand, a streaming current of fire
And smoke that blocked all passage. And the Geats'
290 Lord and leader, angry, lowered
His sword and roared out a battle cry,
A call so loud and clear that it reached through
The hoary[5] rock, hung in the dragon's
Ear. The beast rose, angry,
295 Knowing a man had come—and then nothing
But war could have followed. Its breath came first,
A steaming cloud pouring from the stone,
Then the earth itself shook. Beowulf
Swung his shield into place, held it
300 In front of him, facing the entrance. The dragon
Coiled and uncoiled, its heart urging it
Into battle. Beowulf's ancient sword
Was waiting, unsheathed, his sharp and gleaming
Blade. The beast came closer; both of them
305 Were ready, each set on slaughter. The Geats'
Great prince stood firm, unmoving, prepared
Behind his high shield, waiting in his shining
Armor. The monster came quickly toward him,
Pouring out fire and smoke, hurrying
310 To its fate. Flames beat at the iron
Shield, and for a time it held, protected
Beowulf as he'd planned; then it began to melt,
And for the first time in his life that famous prince
Fought with fate against him, with glory
315 Denied him. He knew it, but he raised his sword
And struck at the dragon's scaly hide.
The ancient blade broke, bit into
The monster's skin, drew blood, but cracked
And failed him before it went deep enough, helped him
320 Less than he needed. The dragon leaped
With pain, thrashed and beat at him, spouting
Murderous flames, spreading them everywhere.
And the Geats' ring-giver[6] did not boast of glorious
Victories in other wars: his weapon
325 Had failed him, deserted him, now when he needed it
Most, that excellent sword. Edgetho's[7]

---

5. **hoary:** grayish-white.
6. **Geats' ring-giver:** here, Beowulf. Such poetic epithets were used to refer to
good kings or lords, who rewarded their loyal followers with rings or other treasures.
7. **Edgetho's** [edj'thōz]: referring to Beowulf's father.

Famous son stared at death,
Unwilling to leave this world, to exchange it
For a dwelling in some distant place—a journey
330 Into darkness that all men must make, as death
Ends their few brief hours on earth.

        Quickly, the dragon came at him, encouraged
As Beowulf fell back; its breath flared,
And he suffered, wrapped around in swirling
335 Flames—a king, before, but now
A beaten warrior. None of his comrades
Came to him, helped him, his brave and noble
Followers; they ran for their lives, fled
Deep in a wood. And only one of them
340 Remained, stood there, miserable, remembering,
As a good man must, what kinship should mean.

        Then the monster charged again, vomiting
Fire, wild with pain, rushed out
Fierce and dreadful, its fear forgotten.
345 Watching for its chance it drove its tusks
Into Beowulf's neck; he staggered, the blood
Came flooding forth, fell like rain.

        And then when Beowulf needed him most
Wiglaf showed his courage, his strength
350 And skill, and the boldness he was born with. Ignoring
The dragon's head, he helped his lord
By striking lower down. The sword
Sank in; his hand was burned, but the shining
Blade had done its work, the dragon's
355 Belching flames began to flicker
And die away. And Beowulf drew
His battle-sharp dagger: the bloodstained old king
Still knew what he was doing. Quickly, he cut
The beast in half, slit it apart.
360 It fell, their courage had killed it, two noble
Cousins had joined in the dragon's death.
Yet what they did all men must do
When the time comes! But the triumph was the last
Beowulf would ever earn, the end
365 Of greatness and life together. The wound
In his neck began to swell and grow;
He could feel something stirring, burning
In his veins, a stinging venom, and knew
The beast's fangs had left it. He fumbled
370 Along the wall, found a slab
Of stone, and dropped down; above him he saw
Huge stone arches and heavy posts,

Holding up the roof of that giant hall.
Then Wiglaf's gentle hands bathed
375 The bloodstained prince, his glorious lord,
Weary of war, and loosened his helmet.
    Beowulf spoke, in spite of the swollen,
Livid wound, knowing he'd unwound
His string of days on earth, seen
380 As much as God would grant him; all worldly
Pleasure was gone, as life would go,
Soon:
        I've worn this crown
For fifty winters: no neighboring people
385 Have tried to threaten the Geats, sent soldiers
Against us or talked of terror. My days
Have gone by as fate willed, waiting
For its word to be spoken.

STUDY QUESTIONS

Recalling

1. With what characteristics is Grendel described in lines 122, 134, and 173?
2. With what characteristics is the hero Beowulf described in lines 44, 161–162, 278, and 284?
3. Briefly summarize how Beowulf, alone and unarmed, succeeds in mortally wounding Grendel.
4. According to lines 245–250, why is the aged hero Beowulf not afraid of fighting the dragon? In what ways, referred to at lines 263–264, does Beowulf's method of fighting the fire-breathing dragon differ from his earlier method of fighting Grendel?
5. According to lines 340–341, why does Wiglaf alone remain with Beowulf as the dragon approaches? What part does Wiglaf play in slaying the creature?

Interpreting

6. Based on the characterizations of the monster Grendel and the hero Beowulf, what universal forces might each represent? What universal struggle might their battle represent?
7. What Anglo-Saxon belief is illustrated by the reference to Grendel in lines 106–108, by the reference to Grendel in lines 106–108, by the Beowulf's statement in lines 266–267, and by the hero's awareness in lines 378–380? Find at least one other reference in the poem that illustrates this belief.
8. Based on the action of Beowulf's band in lines 165–169 and on the explanation of Wiglaf's motivation at lines 340–341, what can we infer is an important Anglo-Saxon ideal?
9. What do Beowulf's willingness to protect the Danes from Grendel and the fact that he is not afraid to fight the fire-breathing dragon tell us about the values of the Anglo-Saxons?
10. Why would the circumstances of Beowulf's death be considered an honorable and fitting end for a hero of that era?

Extending

11. What opportunities for individual heroic behavior exist in our own age?

VIEWPOINT

We can often increase our pleasure in a work of literature by consulting the opinion of an expert on the author's writing. Throughout this book in each section titled "Viewpoint," you will find a quotation about the author and selection you have read. Most of these quotations come from literary critics; some come from the authors themselves. Each quotation is followed by one or two questions that will ask you to consider the quoted opinion in light of your own reaction to the literature.

The literary historian David Daiches reminds us that the world of *Beowulf*

> is certainly not uncivilized, though the civilization it reflects is primitive enough. There is a genuine ideal of nobility underlying its adventure stories.

■ Through what evidence in the selection can we conclude that the world of *Beowulf* was primitive yet civilized? How would you distinguish between the two? Cite examples from the selection to support Daiches' claim that "a genuine ideal of nobility" underlies the story of *Beowulf*.

LITERARY FOCUS

Old English Poetry

Old English poetry was based on oral tradition. No books existed then, and scarcely anyone could read or write. The past was made known by a **scop,** or minstrel, chanting memorized poetry to an assembled group. Many devices of Old English verse serve to aid the poet's memory and make the shaping of his spoken poetry easier.

Alliteration. Like later poetry, the verse of the Anglo-Saxons makes use of repetition, but instead of repeating vowel sounds at the ends of lines (as in rhyme), Old English poetry employs **alliteration,** the repetition of identical consonant sounds at the beginning of words in the same lines. One consonant will be alliterated, or repeated, in one line, another in the next, and so on. For this reason, it is referred to as **alliterative verse.**

Caesura [si zhoor′ə]. There is a strong rhythm, or recurrence of stressed syllables, in Old English verse. A pronounced pause, or **caesura,** occurs in the middle of each line. Moreover, on either side of the caesura are always precisely two stressed syllables, though the number of unstressed syllables varies:

> When *night* came *on/ /Gren*del came *too*

Kennings. Yet another device characteristic of Old English poetry is the use of **kennings,** formalized metaphorical phrases used in place of a simple noun. Not once but many times, the sea may be referred to as the "whale-road" or the sun as "heaven's candle." In this selection the dragon's cave is an "earth-hall," and Beowulf's wound is a "life-hurt."

Thinking About Old English Poetry

1. Mark the caesura and stresses in any ten successive lines of *Beowulf.* First copy the lines, and divide the words into syllables. Then mark stressed syllables with an accent and the caesura with two diagonal lines. Also identify the different sounds that are alliterated in the passage.
2. Find three additional kennings that are repeated in the poem.

Bede *673?–735*

The Venerable Bede is considered the father of English history. During his lifetime he was without doubt the most learned scholar in all of western Europe. Bede, who was a monk, passed his days teaching in the monasteries of Wearmouth and Jarrow in northeast Britain where he had been sent at the age of seven to study. There he wrote biographies of church figures, a treatise on the physical sciences, a work on arithmetic, and his famous *Ecclesiastical History of the English People,* which he completed in 731.

The *History* is our most valuable record of the earlier Anglo-Saxon period. Composed in Latin (Bede knew Greek and Hebrew as well), it provides many fascinating glimpses of the people of the time. One such glimpse is of Caedmon, the earliest known poet in English literature. Caedmon's *Hymn,* written sometime between 658 and 680 at Whitby Abbey in Northumbria, is the oldest English poem to have been preserved. The following excerpt from Bede's *History* relates the story of Caedmon's miraculous composition of this Old English poem.

Bede

from **Ecclesiastical History of the English People**

Translated by J. A. Giles

Caedmon of Whitby

There was in this abbess's[1] monastery a certain brother, particularly remarkable for the grace of God, who was wont to make pious and religious verses, so that whatever was interpreted to him out of Scripture he soon after put the same into poetical expressions of much sweetness and humility in English, which was his native language. By his verses the minds of many were often excited to despise the world and to aspire to heaven. Others after him attempted, in the English nation, to compose religious poems, but none could ever compare with him, for he did not learn the art of poetry from men, but from God, for which reason he never could compose any trivial or vain poem, but only those which relate to religion suited his religious tongue; for having lived in a secular habit[2] till he was well advanced in years,

---

1. **abbess's:** referring to St. Hilda, who had founded the monastery in 658.

2. **secular habit:** nonreligious dress. In other words, Caedmon had been a layman, not a monk.

he had never learned anything of versifying; for which reason being sometimes at entertainments, when it was agreed for the sake of mirth that all present should sing in their turns, when he saw the instrument[3] come towards him, he rose up from table and returned home.

Having done so at a certain time, and gone out of the house where the entertainment was, to the stable, where he had to take care of the horses that night, he there composed himself to rest at the proper time; a person appeared to him in his sleep, and saluting him by his name, said, "Caedmon, sing some song to me." He answered, "I cannot sing; for that was the reason why I left the entertainment and retired to this place, because I could not sing." The other who talked to him replied, "However you shall sing." "What shall I sing?" rejoined he. "Sing the beginning of created beings," said the other. Hereupon he presently began to sing verses to the praise of God, which he had never heard, the purport whereof[4] was thus: We are now to praise the Maker of the heavenly kingdom, the power of the Creator and his counsel, the deeds of the Father of glory. How he, being the eternal God, became the author of all miracles, who first, as almighty preserver of the human race, created heaven for the sons of men as the roof of the house, and next the earth. This is the sense, but not the words in order as he sang them in his sleep; for verses, though never so well composed,[5] cannot be literally translated out of one language into another, without losing much of their beauty and loftiness. Awaking from his sleep, he remembered all that he had sung in his dream, and soon added much more to the same effect in verse worthy of the Deity.

In the morning he came to the steward, his superior, and having acquainted him with the gift he had received, was conducted to the abbess, by whom he was ordered, in the presence of many learned men, to tell his dream and repeat the verses, that they might all give their judgment what it was, and whence his verse proceeded. They all concluded that heavenly grace had been conferred on him by our Lord. They expounded to him a passage in holy writ, either historical or doctrinal,[6] ordering him, if he could, to put the same into verse. Having undertaken it, he went away, and returning the next morning, gave it to them composed in most excellent verse; whereupon the abbess, embracing the grace of God in the man, instructed him to quit the secular habit and take upon him the monastic life; which being accordingly done, she associated him to the rest of the brethren in her monastery, and ordered that he should be taught the whole series of sacred history. Thus Caedmon, keeping in mind all he heard, and as it were chewing the cud,[7] converted the same into most harmonious verse; and sweetly repeating the same, made his masters in their turn his hearers. He sang the creation of the world, the origin of man, and all the history of Genesis; and made many verses on the departure of the children of Israel out of Egypt, and their entering into the land of promise, with many other histories from holy writ; the incarnation, passion, resurrection of our Lord, and his ascension into heaven; the coming of the Holy Ghost, and the preaching of the apostles; also the terror of future judgment, the horror of the pains of hell, and the delights of heaven; besides many more about the Divine benefits and judgments, by which he endeavored to turn away all men from the love of vice, and to excite in them the love of, and application to, good actions; for he was a very religious man, and humbly submissive to regular discipline, but full of zeal against those who behaved themselves otherwise; for which reason he ended his life happily.

---

3. **instrument:** presumably a harp.
4. **purport whereof:** meaning of which.
5. **though . . . composed:** no matter how well they are written.

6. **doctrinal:** having to do with church principles or teachings.
7. **cud:** grass that a cow rechews before converting it into milk.

Caedmon's *Hymn*

Praise we the Lord
Of the heavenly kingdom,
God's power and wisdom,
The works of His hand;
5· As the Father of glory,
Eternal Lord,
Wrought the beginning
Of all His wonders! ·
Holy Creator!
10 Warden of men!
First, for a roof,
O'er the children of earth,
He stablished the heavens,
And founded the world,
15 And spread the dry land
For the living to dwell in.
Lord Everlasting!
Almighty God!

—*Translated by
Charles W. Kennedy*

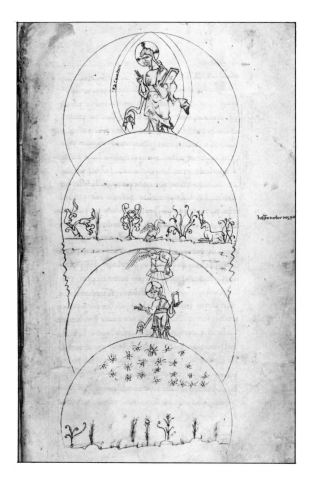

Two scenes of Creation, from the Junius Manuscript, 1025–1050.

STUDY QUESTIONS

Recalling

1. According to paragraph 1, what influence did Caedmon's religious verses have upon his listeners?
2. According to paragraph 2, where did Caedmon have his famous dream? What work did he have to do that night?
3. What did the learned men conclude had been "conferred" on Caedmon and by whom, according to paragraph 3?
4. According to Caedmon's *Hymn,* why did God create the "heavens"? Why did he create "dry land"?

Interpreting

5. What change in stature does Caedmon undergo? In light of this change, why might the place in which Caedmon had his dream be especially significant?
6. How would you characterize the kind of world God created, according to Caedmon's *Hymn*?

Extending

7. What can we conclude about Caedmon's significance to the people, and especially to the scholars, of his own time from the fact that he is included in Bede's *Ecclesiastical History of the English People*? Explain why poets of all eras may be highly esteemed by their contemporaries.

Anglo-Saxon Lyric Poetry

Only a scant 30,000 lines of the poetry of the Anglo-Saxons have survived, and more than a tenth of that is made up by *Beowulf.* Because monks were almost the only people who knew how to write then, it should not be surprising that much of the remainder is religious poetry. A few specimens of the poetry that has survived are, nevertheless, not religious, treating such subjects as a battle and a lament of a woman for her absent husband.

"The Seafarer" is another example of such secular, or nonreligious, Old English poetry. An anonymous poem included in *The Exeter Book,* a famous collection of Anglo-Saxon poetry compiled in about 975, "The Seafarer" is especially noteworthy for its lyrical nature. It expresses the emotions of an old sailor who realizes the sadness of life, its difficulties, and its brief duration. In expressing his feelings the speaker also portrays the miseries and attractions of life on the Irish and North seas. Of the 123 lines that make up the complete poem, the most representative portions follow.

Model for Active Reading

In this selection, as in one selection in each unit, you will find notes in the right-hand margin that highlight parts of the selection. These notes point out important ideas of the literary period and draw your attention to literary elements and techniques covered in the Literary Focuses. Page numbers in the notes refer you to more extensive discussions of these important ideas and elements.

Detail of Viking picture stone, eighth century.

from **The Seafarer**

Translated by Burton Raffel

This tale is true, and mine. It tells
How the sea took me, swept me back
And forth in sorrow and fear and pain,
Showed me suffering in a hundred ships,
5 In a thousand ports, and in me. It tells
Of smashing surf when I sweated in the cold
Of an anxious watch, perched in the bow
As it dashed under cliffs. My feet were cast
In icy bands, bound with frost,
10 With frozen chains, and hardship groaned
Around my heart. Hunger tore
At my sea-weary soul. No man sheltered
On the quiet fairness of earth can feel
How wretched I was, drifting through winter
15 On an ice-cold sea, whirled in sorrow,
Alone in a world blown clear of love.

. . . And yet my heart wanders away,
My soul roams with the sea, the whales'
Home, wandering to the widest corners

Alliteration (p. 18):
Alliteration was an important
tool for the Anglo-Saxon poet.
Here, the repeated *s* sounds
capture the harsh music of the
sea.

Kenning (p. 18): In the oral
literature of the Anglo-Saxons,
the sea was often called "the
whales' home" or "whale-road."

20 Of the world, returning ravenous with desire,
   Flying solitary, screaming, exciting me
   To the open ocean, breaking oaths
   On the curve of a wave.
                         Thus the joys of God
   Are fervent with life, where life itself
25 Fades quickly into the earth. The wealth
   Of the world neither reaches to Heaven nor remains.
   No man has ever faced the dawn
   Certain which of Fate's three threats
   Would fall: illness, or age, or an enemy's
30 Sword, snatching the life from his soul.

   . . . Fate is stronger
   And God mightier than any man's mind.
   Our thoughts should turn to where our home is,
   Consider the ways of coming there.

> **Anglo-Saxon idea:** Though life on earth was short and warfare was a constant danger, religion brought comfort and joy (p. 5).

STUDY QUESTIONS

Recalling

1. According to lines 4–5, where did the speaker see suffering?
2. Name three hardships that the speaker endured at sea, according to stanza 1.
3. According to stanza 2, what does the speaker's soul do?

Interpreting

4. What are the speaker's two conflicting attitudes toward the sea? Which attitude seems stronger? Why do you think this is so?
5. According to line 33, "Our thoughts should turn to where our home is." Where is home, according to the speaker? How do you know?
6. In your own words, how would you characterize the speaker's view of his life? In what tone is that view expressed?

LITERARY FOCUS

Old English

The language spoken by the Germanic tribes of Angles, Saxons, and Jutes who invaded Britain in the fifth century is called either Anglo-Saxon or Old English. While the terms are synonymous, the latter is used to distinguish that language from Middle English, which developed from it after the Norman Conquest of the eleventh century, and from modern English, which was established by the beginning of the sixteenth century.

Old English ("Angleish"), then, is the Germanic speech spoken in England before the invasion of the French-speaking Normans in 1066. The speech of the Germanic tribes that remained on the Continent developed into languages now spoken in northern Europe. Thus, the roots of English are closely intertwined with those of other modern Germanic languages: specifically, of Dutch, Danish, Swedish, Norwegian, and, especially, German.

Early Anglo-Saxons used an alphabet consisting of characters called *runes*. Runic writing was used for inscriptions carved in wood or stone. It was very common in Anglo-Saxon England until it was replaced by the Latin alphabet used by Christian missionaries and monks for writing English.

With only a little practice you can learn to read the Middle English that developed after the Norman Conquest (see page 31). Old English, however, must be learned like a foreign language, and a difficult one at that. Here, for example, are two lines of *Beowulf* in the original Old English:

þa com of móre under mist-hleóþum
Grendel gongan godes yrre bær.

They might be translated literally as: "Then came from moor under misty hills Grendel going, God's anger bore." (þ is the Old English letter *thorn,* pronounced *th.*) Compare the original with the modern translation of page 11, lines 82–84. Despite all the differences, you will recognize similarities between current English and its distant ancestor.

Old English is a highly *inflected* language—in other words, the forms of words change to indicate different meanings and usages such as tense, case, gender, and number. Over several centuries the grammar has become simpler and most inflections have been weakened.

The chart below outlines some of the inflections of the word *ship* in Old English.

	singular	plural
Subject	scip	scipu
Object	scip	scipu
Possessive	scipes	scipa
Indirect Object	scipe	scipum

Modern English has grown out of the Old English that the Anglo-Saxons spoke. Later both French and Latin were added, from the influence of the Norman invaders and the medieval Christian church, respectively. Of these three languages, Old English contributes about twenty-five percent of the vocabulary we now use, including many of our modern English connectives, pronouns, prepositions, and common nouns and verbs. While French has given English its precision and grace, the language of the Anglo-Saxons has given it much of its strength and durability.

Thinking About Old English

▨ Which words in the following passage derive from Old English? Check your guesses with a good dictionary.

Once upon a time in medieval days a poor widow lived in a little cottage standing in a dale near a grove of trees. Her life was a very simple one, with only one dog and no children. One day she was surprised by the arrival of a knight in armor. He had been wounded in battle and was far from home.

COMPOSITION

Writing About Character

▨ Write a description of the speaker of "The Seafarer." First describe his age and physical appearance as you imagine them based on information given in the poem. Then describe his personality, including evidence from the poem to support your assertions.

Writing a Description

▨ Early lines of "The Seafarer" create a sense of intense discomfort in freezing weather. Imagine a comparable discomfort from heat, cold, thirst, or hunger. Then, using vivid details, write a descriptive paragraph to convey that feeling to your reader.

COMPARING WRITERS

▨ For the Anglo-Saxons fate, or *wyrd,* was an important factor believed to rule human destiny. Compare the role of fate in the lives of two or more of the following characters: Beowulf, Caedmon, and the Seafarer. Be sure to support your assertions with specifics from the selections.

READING FOR APPRECIATION

Significant Detail

A great work of literature is made of countless details. Like a classic painting, a medieval cathedral, a symphony, or a satellite, a great story or poem is constructed with the closest attention to detail. Every element, large or small, matters.

Usually the larger elements—the characters, the plot, the setting—first attract us to a story or a narrative poem. We wonder, "Who are these characters? Where are they? What is going to happen to them?" Yet we have probably heard stories in the past that followed a similar pattern or plot line; the characters may very well be similar to others we have known; the setting or even the theme may not be particularly surprising. What then makes the work unique? What gives it its individuality, its own particular texture? The answer lies in details.

In literature a writer provides readers with a world full of details, and, as we read, we re-create that world in our imaginations. To do that imaginative work, to give body to that world, we absorb details that appeal to our senses, our minds, and our hearts. We see the color of a landscape, hear the tone of a bell, feel the warmth of a fire. We understand a motivation or an allusion; we feel an emotion.

We can of course simply enjoy the details that a writer provides; it is easy to note them and pass them by. However, we can go further and think about the *selection* of details that the writer has made. We can increase our enjoyment and appreciation of a work of literature if we think about *why* a particular detail was included and why another was not. To do so, we must look closely at every sentence, keep alert, be aware of this dimension of reading literature.

In *Beowulf,* for example, we are immediately aware of its heroic characters, harsh setting, and adventure-filled plot. Reading in this way, however, we must be sure not to overlook details. Consider the lines in which the author of *Beowulf* sings:

The high hall rang, its roof
  boards swayed,
And Danes shook with terror.
  Down
The aisles the battle swept, angry
And wild.

We hear that the benches in the hall
  . . . rattled, fell
To the floor, gold-covered
  boards grating
As Grendel and Beowulf battled
  across them.

The details in this scene are more than enough to enable us to visualize the titanic struggle taking place in the hall "of ivory and iron and wood." The hall *rang* and its roof *swayed:* As if it were a gigantic iron bell, the hall reverberates with the sound of the battle. It trembles and rocks just as the very kingdom of the Danes is trembling, rocking on its foundation, knowing it will face extinction if Grendel defeats Beowulf. The heavy wooden benches *rattled* and *fell:* We can only wonder at the stupendous crashing it would take to rattle those benches in the hall.

Later, after defeating the dragon, the fatally wounded Beowulf

  . . . fumbled
Along the wall, found a slab
Of stone, and dropped down;
  above him he saw
Huge stone arches and heavy
  posts,
Holding up the roof of that
  giant hall.

The beast is dead, but Beowulf knows that his own kingdom—the arches and posts of *his* hall, the support of *his* people—still stands. This perfectly selected, significant detail enables us to imagine one of the final satisfactions of the epic hero.

THE ENGLISH VOICE

Fate and Fame

The lives of the Anglo-Saxons were given shape and meaning by the vital ideas of *fate* and *fame*. Fate was unchangeable, universal, inescapable. Every man, woman, and child was subject to it. A hero, an artist, a common man—as we see in Beowulf, in Caedmon, and in the seafarer—all bowed down before *wyrd,* or destiny.

Fame was the only means of transcending fate, enduring it, and rising above it. Individual greatness, achievement, loyalty, or courage—the sources of fame—gave people one small measure of power over fate.

Beowulf

> . . . *I will meet him.*
> *With my hands empty—unless his heart*
> *Fails him, seeing a soldier waiting*
> *Weaponless, unafraid. Let God in His wisdom*
> *Extend His hand where He will, reward*
> *Whom He chooses!*
>
> *I've never known fear; as a youth I fought*
> *In endless battles. I am old, now,*
> *But I will fight again, seek fame still,*
> *If the dragon hiding in his tower dares*
> *To face me.*

> *My days*
> *Have gone by as fate willed, waiting*
> *For its word to be spoken.*

Bede

> *Others after him [Caedmon] attempted, in the English nation, to compose religious poems, but none could ever compare with him, for he did not learn the art of poetry from men, but from God.*

The Seafarer

> *The wealth*
> *Of the world neither reaches to Heaven nor remains.*
> *No man has ever faced the dawn*
> *Certain which of Fate's three threats*
> *Would fall: illness, or age, or an enemy's*
> *Sword, snatching the life from his soul.*
> *. . . Fate is stronger*
> *And God mightier than any man's mind.*

Slaying a dragon and composing a great poem were both heroic acts, worthy of fame. The deep underlying lament of the lonely seafarer is that he has suffered heroically without anyone knowing about it. For the Anglo-Saxons fame meant that a person would remain alive in the minds of those who came after.

Key to Illustrations on Pages 2–3.

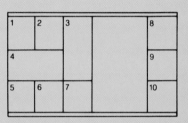

1. The Gundestrap cauldron, depicting the Celtic god Cernunnos, c. third century.

2. Detail, the Saxons, Jutes, and Angles arriving in Britain, from an English manuscript, c. 1130.

3. Detail, Viking picture stone, eighth century.

4. Detail, the Book of Kells, c. 800.

5. Viking helmet, seventh century.

6. Detail, the manuscript of Bede's *Life of St. Cuthbert,* twelfth century.

7. Roman silver coin with the head of Julius Caesar.

8. Carved head from a sledge unearthed with a Viking ship at Oseberg, Norway.

9. The Alfred Jewel, gold filigree, enamel, and rock crystal, used as either an ornament or a pointer, ninth century.

10. Detail, the Book of Lindisfarne, late seventh century.

Key to Illustrations appears on page 79.

THE MEDIEVAL PERIOD

1066–1485

In England the Medieval Period, also called the Middle Ages, began in a year that has become famous—1066. In that year the Normans, who had settled in what is now western France, defeated the Anglo-Saxons at the Battle of Hastings and earned for their leader the title William the Conqueror. Now England had a Norman king.

Norman Rule in England

William bestrode the English Channel like a colossus, with one court in England and one in Normandy. The Anglo-Saxon character and culture, solid and civilized, did not give way before the more stylized, older culture of the Norman conquerors. Instead, the two cultures seemed to blend into a truly English culture that retained—and still does—some values from each source.

Norman kings ruled England for less than a hundred years, but during that time the Normans brought England closer to the mainstream of European society. William introduced in England the European social, economic, and political system called feudalism. Under **feudalism,** land (the real wealth of the nation) was divided among noble overlords, or barons. Lesser lords, called knights, pledged their wealth and services to the overlords. The overlord, in

The murder of Thomas à Becket in 1170. Illumination from an English Psalter, or the Book of Psalms, c. 1200.

return, provided use of the land. At the lowest end of the social scale were the serfs, peasants pledged to the lord of the manor and bound to the land. William and the Norman kings who followed him (William II, Henry I, and Stephen of Blois) had feudal domains—land, lords, knights, and serfs—on the Continent, in what is now France. Similarly, some French rulers, had, or claimed to have, feudal rights in England.

The Royal Houses of Plantagenet, Lancaster, and York

In 1154 the Norman line was at an end. The royal houses, or families, of Plantagenet, Lancaster, and York would carry England through the Middle Ages.

Beginning with Henry II's reign in 1154, we find upon the throne of England a series of kings whose lives were filled with drama enough to fill the stages of the world. In fact, in Shakespeare's series of great historical dramas, they do just that. Almost all of these kings were strong, interesting people living troubled, dangerous, complex lives in their search for power.

Among the eight Plantagenet kings, Henry II has gone down in history for increasing royal power at the expense of the nobles. His desire to control the Roman Catholic Church in England led to the murder of Thomas à Becket, the Archbishop of Canterbury.

Henry's son, Richard I, called Richard the Lion-Hearted, has become a model of a true knight. Richard was away from England for all but five months of his ten-year reign, traveling across the world, giving his riches to the poor and seeking holy relics. John, Henry II's other son, who succeeded Richard I, gained a reputation as a weak, even villainous ruler. But John, too, had a moment of high drama when in 1215, a year before his death, he was forced to sign the Magna Carta (Latin for "Great Charter"). By this document he agreed not to raise taxes without the consent of the barons. Many see in this curtailment of royal power the beginning of constitutional government in England, including the right to trial by jury. Most of the remaining Plantagenet kings—Edward I, especially—provided strong leadership for England, despite family troubles over succession, trouble with Scotland, trouble with France, trouble with Ireland, and near revo-

lution at home. However, when the young Richard II took the throne, he was plagued by power-hungry relatives and was eventually forced to abdicate. The Lancaster line came to power.

The first of the three kings of the House of Lancaster, Henry IV (1399–1413), survived many crises and was succeeded by his more powerful son, Henry V, fondly known among his followers as Prince Hal. Henry V led his armies to a dramatic and memorable victory over the French in the Battle of Agincourt in 1415. It was one of the high points of the so-called Hundred Years' War with France, waged from 1337 to 1453 in England's attempt to keep its French lands. Henry V's men turned back the French army with a newly fashioned weapon, the longbow, which was able to pierce armor.

Henry VI, next in line, went insane for a brief period and left the throne in the hands of an uncle, the Duke of York. When Henry's health returned and he sought to retrieve his authority, the Duke of York rallied forces against him. Thus in 1455 began thirty years of civil strife, known as the Wars of the Roses, between the House of Lancaster (whose symbol was a red rose), and the House of York (whose symbol was a white rose). The Lancasters never returned to the throne.

Edward IV, the first of the Yorkist kings, can be thanked for encouraging William Caxton to set up a printing press with movable type, capable of printing in quantities large enough to bring the printed word to the general public. After this notable event, the drama of the Yorkist kings turns dark. When in 1483 Edward V succeeded to the throne, he was only twelve years old. At this point another storybook figure, Edward V's Uncle Richard, steps onto the stage of history. Richard had Edward V and his younger brother imprisoned in the Tower of London. He then assumed the throne as Richard III. When it was rumored that he had had the two little boys murdered in the tower, rebellion broke out. In the end, Richard III himself was killed in battle, and Henry Tudor, a distant descendant of the Lancaster kings, assumed the throne. With the beginning of Tudor rule in 1485, the story of the Middle Ages in England, so far as kings are concerned, is over.

Chivalric Life in Medieval England

The feudalism that the Normans brought to England was not just an economic and political system, a means of dividing up land and power. Feudalism was also a social system. The feudal manor—the home of the lord and the lands around it—was self-sufficient and in many ways like a small city. To the serfs in the small cottages on the estate, feudalism meant complete dependence upon the overlord. Social life, at least outside of the big towns and cities, was limited to hard work at farming or herding and a bit of amusement provided by the local church. In the royal courts and in the manor houses of the overlords, life was more sophisticated. Though the lord had responsibilities to the welfare of his estate, knights and serfs freed him from the demands of daily struggle.

The English kings and barons from 1066 to 1485 played their roles against a backdrop of glory and violence that spread from the royal courts and Roman ruins near London northward into Scotland, west into Wales and Ireland, across the English Channel into France, and southeast into what was called the Holy Land—the city of Jerusalem, then in Moslem hands. This was the period when knighthood flourished in England, when knights went on local quests, or across the sea to fight the French, or on what could be a life-time journey to the Holy

Sir Gawain. Miniature from a manuscript of Arthurian romances, c. 1400.

Land. It was also the period when knights jousted in tournaments or upon a chance meeting on the road while fair ladies watched and waited.

With feudalism and knighthood the Normans brought to England the code of chivalry. **Chivalry** was an ideal that all knights must try to attain: to be honorable, courteous, generous, brave, skillful in battle, respectful to women, and helpful to the weak. This romantic attitude would affect much of the literature of the period, especially the songs and stories.

Religious Life in Medieval England

The Roman Catholic Church was also a powerful force in the England of the Middle Ages. Never had so many people been more totally and unquestioningly at one with a single institutional church and with the faith that church professed. Kings, courts, knights, and common people down to the lowliest serf all practiced a belief in the church on earth and in the afterlife that it proclaimed. Knights were willing to die for their religious belief, as witnessed in particular by their ardent desire to join in the **Crusades,** which were military expeditions undertaken to recapture the city of Jerusalem from the Moslems.

In the years between 1096 and 1270, knights in full regalia, armor bright, with footsoldiers and all the paraphernalia that an

A view of Canterbury Cathedral, Kent, England.

army needs—almost a traveling city—plundered their way to the Holy Land. They were never successful—some never even reached Jerusalem—but they left a violent and bloody trail behind them.

Back in England the Normans strengthened the physical domain of the Church, building stone monasteries and abbeys. Like the feudal manor, each monastery or abbey was a small, self-sufficient city. They also continued to be centers of learning and of literature. Latin was the language of the Church and was known to all educated people in England. Thus, much of the literature of the time was written in Latin, particularly the more scholarly histories. The Crusaders straggling back from Jerusalem would contribute to the learning of these centers some of the more advanced knowledge that distinguished the Moslem world, including Arabic numerals, algebra, and Arab medicine.

Churches and cathedrals, perhaps the most dramatic and beautiful legacy of the period, were another product of religious faith and energy. Church bells pealed messages almost hourly, and every town, it seems, had a towering, stone cathedral. By 1200 the still-small city of London, with a population of no more than 40,000 people, had 120 churches in addition to the giant cathedral that was dedicated to the city's patron saint, St. Paul.

City Life in Medieval England

By all reports, London remained a merry town with children playing ball games in the streets and wealthy merchants, now on horseback, hunting wild boar and deer in nearby park-land. In winter when the marshes froze, people skated happily across the flats on skates of sheep bone. Sickness and death were never very far away, however. In 1348 and 1349 the dreadful Black Death, a form of the bubonic plague, killed at least a third of the English population.

In spite of plague and warfare, England prospered during the later Middle Ages. People began to move from castle towns to villages and cities, and cities had sprung up in the north as well as on the southern plains. Guilds—organizations not unlike modern-day trade unions—developed in the cities, and an apprentice moved through an elaborate hierarchy before becoming a master craftsman. Also during this time herding became more

important than farming. British wool became famous; cottages were turned into small mills; and the famous textile industry—the carding, combing, spinning, and weaving of sheep's wool—began.

Even more important than the end of knighthood (mostly due to the invention of gunpowder) and the beginning of the textile industry toward the end of the Middle Ages was the development of printing. William Caxton established his printing press in England in 1476. Up until this time literature existed in England only in manuscript, copied out by hand for the very few. When Caxton introduced to England the invention of printing that had begun to spread through Europe in the late 1400s, the written word in English began to reach a much wider audience.

Caxton was a fine editor as well as a printer. He played a very important role in bringing the two great literary works of this period—Chaucer's *Canterbury Tales* and Malory's *Morte d'Arthur*—to light.

Storytelling in the Middle Ages

Although printing was now available, it would be centuries before storytelling would take the form of novels. Nevertheless, the seeds of the novel and short story find rich ground in this period. Geoffrey Chaucer told

King Arthur. Detail from a French tapestry, c. 1450.

short stories in verse, using a bright, new kind of English poetry influenced by European models as well as hewed from his own genius. Thanks to Thomas Malory, the great English literary legend of King Arthur was printed in a version heavily influenced by the romantic notions of French storytellers. When the Anglo-Saxon soldiers at the beginning of this period marched against the Normans, they carried from England songs about King Arthur. During the Norman Period the French added their own special notes to Arthur's story and created the **romance,** a blend of chivalry with touches of love, magic, and marvels. Malory stresses the romantic aspect of the Arthur legend, but his portrait of Arthur still retains some of the real flesh-and-blood Celtic warrior-king that Arthur had once been.

The folk ballads in the pages ahead are also a form of storytelling, although, unlike the writings of Chaucer and Malory, they were still composed orally. These ballads were not the work of professional poets—minstrels who performed for the entertainment of courts—but rather stories sung by common people gathering among friends and family in their cottages in the evening. These ballads contain storytelling techniques that, centuries later, would be used by novelists; the use of dialogue to tell a story is the most important of these techniques.

Drama in the Middle Ages

Drama is a form of storytelling that seems to have a life of its own. The idea of telling a story by acting it out seems to be a very ancient one, perhaps appealing to an instinct of human nature: the desire to imitate another human being. Some of us like to act out the part. Some of us prefer to see and hear a part acted out by another. In theater (a name we give to drama that is produced on a stage) a simple, perhaps penniless baker, for example, can become for a few moments a heroic king, and his audience can lose itself in the story that unfolds.

Drama as public entertainment began in England in the Medieval Period as religious ritual, in the form of **mystery plays,** or **miracle plays,** as they are usually called. The miracle play was developed by the Church in an attempt to instruct the illiterate in the miraculous stories. To celebrate a feast day,

the Church would often have common people, members of a bakers' guild, for example, dress up like characters in the Bible. The plays were very well attended. They eventually moved from the cathedral to the village green and finally to pageant wagons, ox-drawn wagons that brought this early form of theater to neighboring towns and villages. The actors were amateurs, technically speaking, but they were paid for their work, the actor playing God getting more than the others. Rehearsals were frequent, and if one did not go well, the actors would be fined.

The miracle play was followed by a somewhat different development—the **morality play,** in which actors played the roles of virtues and vices—patience, greed, and so on. The most significant aspect of the morality play was that the conflict between virtue and vice, good and evil, was not external (a good king and a bad king, for example) but took place in the heart of a single hero.

All in all, the literature of the Medieval Period carries us back into a colorful and exciting world as reported by the poets, storytellers, and dramatists of that time and forward into other ages in which knights, crusaders, monks, and fine ladies would continue to inspire writers. Indeed, the Medieval Period is at once very far away and very close at hand.

TIME LINE

1066 Anglo-Saxons defeated by William the Conqueror of Normandy at Battle of Hastings

1086 *Domesday Book*, first official record of property owners in England

1096 Crusades, attempts to rescue Jerusalem from Moslems (until 1270)

Battle of Hastings

1151 Game of chess arrives in England

1154 House of Plantagenet rules England (until 1399)

1167 Oxford University founded

1170 Murder of Thomas à Becket, Archbishop of Canterbury

Oxford University

1215 Magna Carta, signed by King John

1265 First Parliament

1296 Wars between England and Scotland (until 1328)

King John signs the Magna Carta

1337 Beginning of Hundred Years' War, series of wars between England and France

1125 France: Beginning of troubadour music

1170 France: Chrétien de Troyes, "Lancelot"

1191 Japan: Tea arrives from China

1204 Holland: Founding of Amsterdam

1211 China: Invasion by Genghis Khan

1241 Korea: Movable metal type first used

1271 China: Exploration by Marco Polo

1307 Italy: Dante begins *Divine Comedy*

1325 Italy: Beginning of the Renaissance

Japan: Development of *No* drama

Aztec Empire: Establishment of capital on site of modern Mexico City

1348   Black Death, series of plagues

Medieval Knight

1375   Earliest part of *Sir Gawain and the Green Knight,* verse romance in English about knights at King Arthur's court

1377?   William Langland, *The Vision of Piers the Plowman,* a protest on behalf of the common people

1386   Geoffrey Chaucer, *The Canterbury Tales*

1388   John Wycliff's translation of Bible into English

1399   House of Lancaster rules England (until 1461)

1455   Beginning of thirty-year Wars of the Roses, civil war between House of York and House of Lancaster

1461   House of York rules England (until 1485)

1469   Sir Thomas Malory, *Le Morte d'Arthur*

1476   William Caxton establishes first printing press in England

1485   King Henry VII (of House of Tudor) begins reign

1341   Italy: Petrarch crowned with laurel wreath

1348   Italy: Boccaccio, *Decameron*

1368   China: Beginning of Ming Dynasty

1431   France: Joan of Arc burned at stake

1452   Italy: Birth of Leonardo da Vinci

1453   Germany: The Gutenberg Bible, thought to be the first European book printed from movable type

1462   Russia: Ivan the Great rules as first czar

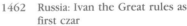

Folk Ballads

Although most people in the British Isles were unable to read or write for centuries after the Norman Conquest in 1066, they, like human beings everywhere, told stories to one another. We have inherited their **folk ballads**, the stories they told in verse and usually sang. Transmitted orally from generation to generation, most of the English and Scottish ballads we know date from the fourteenth and fifteenth centuries but were not collected and printed until the eighteenth century.

Love, adventure, courageous feats of daring, and sudden disaster are frequent topics of folk ballads. Folk ballads relate out-of-the-ordinary incidents—ones that might make headlines now, such as a shipwreck or an accidental death. Despite such tragic subjects, ballads rarely contain opinions on what has happened. The narrative usually dramatizes a single incident with little attention to characterization, background, or description. Why do the characters act as they do? How did they get into such a plight? We must read between the lines and supply our own answers, as we hear the little dramatic scenes unfold. Indeed, the ballad presents action as sparsely as possible, often through **dialogue**—the speech of the characters involved. We should not, however, think that ballads are simple or shallow. They may be brief and sparse—economic—but they contain sharp psychological portraits and much folk wisdom.

The original authors of ballads are unknown; in fact, a given ballad may exist in several versions, because many different people told and revised the ballad as it traveled from village to village. Nevertheless, when a version seemed just right, its teller would be urged to recite the story again and again without changing a thing.

It is important to remember that most ballads were originally sung. But even when read—preferably aloud—enough remains to place the best of the folk ballads among the most haunting narrative poems in British literature. After all, folk ballads have lasted this long partly because they are dramatic stories particularly well told.

Medieval gittern, an instrument similar to a guitar.

Sir Patrick Spens

The king sits in Dumferling[1] toune,
    Drinking the blude-reid[2] wine:
"O whar will I get a skilly[3] skipper,
    To sail this new schip of mine?"

5 O up and spak an eldern knicht,[4]
    Sat at the kings richt[5] kne:
"Sir Patrick Spens is the best sailor,
    That ever sailed the sea."

The king has written a braid[6] letter,
10   And sealed it wi' his hand,
And sent it to Sir Patrick Spens,
    Was walking on the strand.[7]

The first line that Sir Patrick red,
    A loud lauch[8] lauched he;
15 The next line that Sir Patrick red,
    The teir blinded his ee.[9]

"O wha[10] is this has don this deid,
    And told the king o' me,
To send us out at this time o' the yeir,
20   To sail upon the sea!

"Mak ready, mak ready, my mirry men all,
    Our guid schip sails the morne."
"Now, ever alake,[11] my master deir,
    I feir a deadlie storme.

25 "I saw the new moone late yestreen,[12]
    Wi' the auld[13] moone in hir arme,
And if we gang to sea, master,
    I feir we'll cum to harme."

O laith, laith[14] wer our guid Scots lords
30   To weet[15] their cork-heild schoone;[16]
Bot lang owre a'[17] the play was playd,
    They wat their hats aboone.[18]

O lang, lang may their ladies sit,
    Wi' their fans into their hand;
35 Before they se Sir Patrick Spens
    Cum sailing to the strand.

And lang, lang may their maidens sit,
    Wi' their gold kems[19] in their hair,
All waiting for their ain[20] deir loves,
40   For thame they'll se na mair.[21]

Haf owre, haf owre to Aberdour,[22]
    'Tis fiftie fadom[23] deip,
And thair lies guid Sir Patrick Spens,
    Wi' the Scots lords at his feit.

1. **Dumferling** [dum fur'ling]: a town in Scotland.
2. **blude-reid:** blood red.
3. **skilly:** skillful.
4. **eldern knicht:** elderly knight.
5. **richt:** right.
6. **braid:** broad (this may refer to a long sheet of paper or may mean "commanding").
7. **strand:** seashore.
8. **lauch:** laugh.
9. **ee:** eye.
10. **wha:** who.
11. **alake:** alack.
12. **yestreen:** yesterday evening.
13. **auld:** old; sailors thought that a thin crescent moon meant storms at sea.
14. **laith:** loath; very unwilling.
15. **weet:** wet.
16. **schoone:** shoes.
17. **lang owre a':** long before all.
18. **aboone:** above.
19. **kems:** combs.
20. **ain:** own.
21. **na mair:** no more.
22. **haf owre to Aberdour:** halfway over to Aberdeen (in Scotland).
23. **fadom:** fathoms. A fathom is six feet.

The Wife of Usher's Well

There lived a wife at Usher's Well,
  And a wealthy wife was she;
She had three stout[1] and stalwart sons,
  And sent them o'er the sea.

5 They hadna' been a week from her,
  A week but barely ane,[2]
When word came to the carlin[3] wife
  That her three sons were gane.[4]

They hadna' been a week from her,
10 A week but barely three,
When word came to the carlin wife
  That her sons she'd never see.

"I wish the wind may never cease,
  Nor fashes in the flood,[5]
15 Till my three sons come hame[6] to me,
  In earthly flesh and blood."

It fell about the Martinmas,[7]
  When nights are lang and mirk,[8]
The carlin wife's three sons came hame,
20 And their hats were o' the birk.[9]

It neither grew in sike[10] nor ditch,
  Nor yet in ony sheugh,[11]
But at the gates o' Paradise
  That birk grew fair eneugh.

25 "Blow up the fire, my maidens,
  Bring water from the well:
For a'[12] my house shall feast this night,
  Since my three sons are well."

And she has made to them a bed,
30 She's made it large and wide,
And she's ta'en her mantle[13] her about,
  Sat down at the bedside.

Up then crew the red, red cock,
  And up and crew the gray.
35 The eldest to the youngest said,
  " 'Tis time we were away."

The cock he hadna' crawed but once,
  And clapped his wings at a',
When the youngest to the eldest said,
40 "Brother, we must awa'.[14]

"The cock doth craw, the day doth daw,[15]
  The channerin'[16] worm doth chide:
Gin[17] we be missed out o' our place,
  A sair pain we maun bide.[18]

45 "Fare ye weel,[19] my mother dear,
  Fareweel to barn and byre.[20]
And fare ye weel, the bonny[21] lass
  That kindles my mother's fire."

---

1. **stout:** brave.
2. **ane:** one.
3. **carlin:** old.
4. **gane:** gone.
5. **fashes . . . flood:** disturbances at sea.
6. **hame:** home.
7. **Martinmas:** November 11.
8. **lang and mirk:** long and dark.
9. **o' the birk:** of the birch tree. It was believed that people who returned from the dead wore plant life on their heads.
10. **sike:** field.
11. **sheugh:** furrow.

12. **a':** all.
13. **ta'en her mantle:** taken her cloak.
14. **must awa':** must go away, leave. Spirits of the dead had to return to their graves at cockcrow.
15. **daw:** dawn.
16. **channerin':** complaining.
17. **Gin:** If.
18. **A sair . . . bide:** A sore pain we must abide; we must endure great pain.
19. **weel:** well.
20. **byre:** cow shed.
21. **bonny:** pretty.

STUDY QUESTIONS

Sir Patrick Spens

Recalling

1. According to stanza 2, what recommendation is made to the king and by whom?
2. How does Sir Patrick Spens react in stanzas 4 and 5 to the letter from his king? After reading the letter, what does he nevertheless tell his men to do?
3. According to lines 23–28, why are Sir Patrick's sailors reluctant to obey the king's order?
4. What are the king's nobles who sail on Sir Patrick's ship worried about, according to lines 29–30? What happens instead in lines 31–32?
5. Where do Sir Patrick and his nobles "lie"?

Interpreting

6. What internal conflict do you suppose Sir Patrick feels in stanzas 4 and 5?
7. What are we led to understand happens to Sir Patrick, his sailors, and the king's nobles on the voyage? Give four specific references in the ballad that support this conclusion.
8. Why is the last line fitting or just?

The Wife of Usher's Well

Recalling

1. What news of her three sons does the old wife receive in stanzas 2 and 3?
2. According to lines 20–24, what kind of hats are the sons wearing when they return to visit?
3. According to stanzas 10 and 11, when do the sons realize they must leave? What will happen to them if they don't go?

Interpreting

4. Based on the "birk" the sons are wearing, what might we surmise about the sons?
5. What might be the "place" referred to in line 43 from which the sons will be missed?
6. Why might the sons have come back to their mother's fireside?

LITERARY FOCUS

The Folk Ballad

Folk ballads are anonymous narrative verses intended to be sung and passed on by oral tradition. The folk ballad is a *popular* literary form; that is, it comes from unlettered people rather than from professional minstrels or scholarly poets. Thus, the ballad tends to express its meaning in simple language (although the centuries-old dialect of many folk ballads may make that language seem complex at first). The narrative style of the typical ballad is straightforward as well, relying heavily on dialogue and moving quickly from scene to scene.

The so-called **ballad stanza** consists of four lines (a quatrain), rhyming *abcb,* with four accented syllables within the first and third lines and three in the second and fourth lines.

a There lived a wife at Usher's Well,

b And a wealthy wife was she;

c She had three stout and stalwart sons

b And sent them o'er the sea.

Some folk ballads make use of **refrains,** repetitions of a line or lines in every stanza without variation. Refrains add emphasis and a note of continuity to the ballads.

Thinking About Folk Ballads

■ Demonstrate your understanding of the traditional ballad stanza by transcribing and marking the stress of one stanza from "Sir Patrick Spens." Indicate which lines rhyme.

COMPOSITION

Developing a Thesis About Folk Ballads

■ Develop an idea about the structure of folk ballads. Before you begin to write, review how they begin, how they develop, and how they end. State your thesis about the parts of a folk ballad. Support your idea about each part with examples. You may want to devote one paragraph to each part. *For help with this assignment, refer to Lesson 1 in the Writing About Literature Handbook at the back of this book.*

Writing a Folk Ballad

■ Try writing two or three stanzas of a folk ballad. Choose an appropriate subject and follow the form of the traditional ballad stanza (see the preceding Literary Focus). Use dialogue, repetition, and archaic (old-fashioned) diction to make your stanzas sound authentic.

Geoffrey Chaucer   1343?–1400

Geoffrey Chaucer (along with William Shakespeare and John Milton) comes to most scholars' minds when they list the three greatest poets of the English language. Chaucer's most important work, *The Canterbury Tales,* vividly demonstrated the literary potential of the English language in the 1300s. It also preserved for all future ages a realistic, detailed, and comprehensive panorama of daily life at that time.

Like the other two—Shakespeare, the actor, and Milton, the public servant—Chaucer led an extremely busy life. In fact, he was so active in public affairs that we may reasonably wonder how he found time to write as prolifically and as well as he did. The son of a wealthy London wine merchant, Chaucer had the good fortune to serve as a page in the royal household while in his early teens. Later, he married one of the queen's ladies-in-waiting, was sent as the king's emissary to France and Italy, and held various positions in the home government: controller of customs, justice of the peace, member of Parliament, clerk of the king's works, and deputy forester for a royal forest. Yet despite the demands that such responsibilities placed on him, Chaucer somehow found time to produce an astonishing body of prose and poetry. He died while still at work on his poetry and was buried in Westminster Abbey in London. Around his burial spot has grown up the famous Poets' Corner.

Chaucer's poetry is generally divided into three periods. The earliest poetry is in the artificial manner of the great French poets of the day: dream visions and allegories, which were more to the taste of medieval than of modern people. This French period was followed by an Italian period, inspired by the poet's own journeys to Italy as a royal emissary. Influenced by the vigor of three great Italian writers—Dante, Petrarch, and especially, Boccaccio (all of whom are represented in Part Two of this book)—Chaucer brought to his own verse a new strength. During this phase he produced one of his two masterpieces: *Troilus and Criseyde,* a long narrative poem based on Boccaccio's retelling of a classical love story set during the legendary Trojan War. The greatest of Chaucer's achievements—and one of the glories of all literature—was a product of his final, English period: *The Canterbury Tales.* At last Chaucer broke away from French and Italian models and fully realized his own style in his native tongue.

Chaucer's works are in Middle English, the English of London in the 1300s. Middle English did not have the prestige of the French language introduced to England by the Normans or of the Latin used by the Roman Catholic Church. Chaucer changed all that.

The Canterbury Tales is a long poem made up of general introduction ("The Prologue") and twenty-four stories, told in verse, by a cross section of English men and women. They tell their stories as they travel one April from an inn in a London suburb southeastward for fifty miles to the cathedral city of Canterbury. They are on a pilgrimage, a journey to a sacred place; Canterbury Cathedral is the site where Thomas à Becket had been murdered by order of King Henry II in 1170 to the shock of the religious world. The pilgrims' stories are framed by the narrative of the journey. That is, the tales are connected by links that relate what happens among the pilgrims traveling together. In using a frame, Chaucer borrowed from European literature such as Boccaccio's *Decameron* (see Part Two of this book).

The individual stories are of many different kinds: religious stories, legends, fables, fairy tales, sermons, and courtly romances. Short story writers in the following centuries learned much about their craft from the poet Geoffrey Chaucer.

In "The Prologue," which begins on the following page, the poet introduces us to the pilgrims who gather at the Tabard Inn at the start of the journey. The pilgrims fall into the three dominant groups that made up medieval society in England: the feudal group, the church group, and the city group. In the excerpt from "The Prologue," we will meet representatives of each group:

The Feudal Group	*The Church Group*	*The City Group*
Knight truth, honor, courage	Nun weep if saw a mouse	Merchant witty w/money, never loses$
Squire son of knight, lover	Monk lazy horseman hunter	Wife of Bath somewhat deaf
Yeoman bowman w/squire	Friar merry good man	Host (Innkeeper) giving reward for best of eaches 4 stories
Franklin ate a lot, phil. son	Cleric student, philosopher	
Plowman good worker	Parson preacher	
Miller big stout man, red hair	Summoner rode together in journeys	
Reeve old man carpenter	Pardoner both singers	

The famous opening lines of "The Prologue" appear first in the original Middle English (page 45). A modern translation of those lines and of a large excerpt from the remainder of "The Prologue" follows. The Middle English contains many words with two dots over the *e*. The dots remind us that we should pronounce every syllable in Middle English. Thus *bathëd* (line 3) has two syllables, not one as in the modern English *bathed,* and the original line of poetry consequently has the ten syllables of iambic pentameter verse.

Geoffrey Chaucer

from **The Prologue to The Canterbury Tales**

Translated by Nevill Coghill

Whan that Aprill with his shourës sootë
The droghte of March hath percëd to the rootë
And bathëd every veyne in swich licour
Of which vertu engendrëd is the flour,
5 Whan Zephirus eek with his sweetë breeth
Inspirëd hath in every holt and heeth
The tendrë croppës, and the yongë sonnë
Hath in the Ram his half cours y-ronnë,
And smalë fowelës maken melodyë
10 That slepen al the nyght with open eyë,
So priketh hem Nature in hir corages,
Than longen folk to goon on pilgrymages,
And palmeres for to seken straungë strondës,
To fernë halwës kouthe in sondry londës.
15 And specially, from every shirës endë
Of Engelond, to Caunterbury they wendë,
The holy, blisful martir for to sekë
That hem hath holpen whan that they were seekë.

When in April the sweet showers fall
And pierce the drought of March to the root, and all
The veins are bathed in liquor of such power
As brings about the engendering of the flower,
5 When also Zephyrus[1] with his sweet breath
Exhales an air in every grove and heath
Upon the tender shoots, and the young sun
His half-course in the sign of the Ram[2] has run,
And the small fowl are making melody
10 That sleep away the night with open eye
(So nature pricks them and their heart engages)
Then people long to go on pilgrimages
And palmers[3] long to seek the stranger strands[4]
Of far-off saints, hallowed in sundry lands,
15 And specially, from every shire's end
In England, down to Canterbury they wend
To seek the holy blissful martyr,[5] quick
To give his help to them when they were sick.

1 **Zephyrus** [zef′ər əs]: the west wind, which brings mild weather.

2 **Ram:** the constellation Aries and first sign of the zodiac. Evidence suggests that the pilgrimage began on April 11, 1387.

3 **palmers:** pilgrims who wore palm leaves as a sign that they had visited the Holy Land.
4 **strands:** shores.

5 **martyr:** St. Thomas à Becket, Archbishop of Canterbury, who was murdered in Canterbury Cathedral in 1170. The site of the martyrdom became the holiest place in Catholic England.

The opening lines of the *Prologue to The Canterbury Tales,* from the Ellesmere Manuscript, an original manuscript of Chaucer's work.

It happened in that season that one day
20 In Southwark,[6] at The Tabard,[7] as I lay
Ready to go on pilgrimage and start
For Canterbury, most devout at heart,
At night there came into that hostelry
Some nine and twenty in a company
25 Of sundry folk happening then to fall
In fellowship, and they were pilgrims all
That towards Canterbury meant to ride.
The rooms and stables of the inn were wide;
They made us easy, all was of the best.
30 And shortly, when the sun had gone to rest,
By speaking to them all upon the trip
I soon was one of them in fellowship
And promised to rise early and take the way
To Canterbury, as you heard me say.
35   But nonetheless, while I have time and space,
Before my story takes a further pace,
It seems a reasonable thing to say
What their condition was, the full array
Of each of them, as it appeared to me
40 According to profession and degree,
And what apparel they were riding in;
And at a Knight I therefore will begin.

There was a *Knight,* a most distinguished man,
Who from the day on which he first began
45 To ride abroad had followed chivalry,
Truth, honor, generousness and courtesy.
He had done nobly in his sovereign's war
And ridden into battle, no man more,
As well in Christian as in heathen places,
50 And ever honored for his noble graces.
    When we took Alexandria,[8] he was there.
He often sat at table in the chair
Of honor, above all nations, when in Prussia.
In Lithuania he had ridden, and Russia,
55 No Christian man so often, of his rank.
When, in Granada, Algeciras sank
Under assault, he had been there, and in
North Africa, raiding Benamarin;
In Anatolia he had been as well
60 And fought when Ayas and Attalia fell,
For all along the Mediterranean coast
He had embarked with many a noble host.
He was of sovereign value in all eyes.
And though so much distinguished, he was wise

6 **Southwark** [suth'ərk]: then a
suburb of London on the south side
of the Thames River.
7 **The Tabard** [ta'bərd]: an inn.

8 **Alexandria:** This and the place
names that immediately follow are
sites of wide-ranging campaigns and
Crusades by medieval Christians
against the Moslems.

65 And in his bearing modest as a maid.
He never yet a boorish thing had said
In all his life to any, come what might;
He was a true, a perfect gentle-knight.
　　Speaking of his equipment, he possessed
70 Fine horses, but he was not gaily dressed.
He wore a fustian⁹ tunic stained and dark
With smudges where his armor had left mark;
Just home from service, he had joined our ranks
To do his pilgrimage and render thanks.

75 　　He had his son with him, a fine young *Squire,*
A lover and cadet, a lad of fire
With locks as curly as if they had been pressed.
He was some twenty years of age, I guessed.
In stature he was of a moderate length,
80 With wonderful agility and strength.
He'd seen some service with the cavalry
In Flanders and Artois and Picardy¹⁰
And had done valiantly in little space
Of time, in hope to win his lady's grace.
85 He was embroidered like a meadow bright
And full of freshest flowers, red and white.
Singing he was, or fluting all the day;
He was as fresh as is the month of May.
Short was his gown, the sleeves were long and wide;
90 He knew the way to sit a horse and ride.
He could make songs and poems and recite,
Knew how to joust and dance, to draw and write.
He loved so hotly that till dawn grew pale
He slept as little as a nightingale.
95 Courteous he was, lowly and serviceable,
And carved to serve his father at the table.

　　There was a *Yeoman*¹¹ with him at his side,
No other servant; so he chose to ride.
This Yeoman wore a coat and hood of green,
100 And peacock-feathered arrows, bright and keen
And neatly sheathed, hung at his belt the while
—For he could dress his gear in yeoman style,
His arrows never drooped their feathers low—
And in his hand he bore a mighty bow.
105 His head was like a nut, his face was brown.
He knew the whole of woodcraft up and down.
A saucy brace¹² was on his arm to ward
It from the bow-string, and a shield and sword
Hung at one side, and at the other slipped

9 **fustian** [fus'chən]: coarse, heavy fabric of cotton and linen.

10 **Flanders . . . Picardy:** historic regions of Belgium and northern France.

11 **Yeoman** [yō'mən]: nobleman's attendant.

12 **brace:** bracelet.

110 A jaunty dirk,[13] spear-sharp and well-equipped.
A medal of Saint Christopher[14] he wore
Of shining silver on his breast, and bore
A hunting-horn, well slung and burnished clean,
That dangled from a baldric[15] of bright green.
115 He was a proper forester, I guess.

There also was a *Nun,* a Prioress,[16]
Her way of smiling very simple and coy.
Her greatest oath was only "By Saint Loy!"[17]
And she was known as Madam Eglantyne.
120 And well she sang a service,[18] with a fine
Intoning through her nose, as was most seemly,
And she spoke daintily in French, extremely,
After the school of Stratford-atte-Bowe;[19]
French in the Paris style she did not know.
125 At meat her manners were well taught withal;
No morsel from her lips did she let fall,
Nor dipped her fingers in the sauce too deep;
But she could carry a morsel up and keep
The smallest drop from falling on her breast.
130 For courtliness she had a special zest,
And she would wipe her upper lip so clean
That not a trace of grease was to be seen
Upon the cup when she had drunk; to eat,
She reached a hand sedately for the meat.
135 She certainly was very entertaining,
Pleasant and friendly in her ways, and straining
To counterfeit a courtly kind of grace,
A stately bearing fitting to her place,
And to seem dignified in all her dealings.
140 As for her sympathies and tender feelings,
She was so charitably solicitous
She used to weep if she but saw a mouse
Caught in a trap, if it were dead or bleeding.
And she had little dogs she would be feeding
145 With roasted flesh, or milk, or fine white bread.
And bitterly she wept if one were dead
Or someone took a stick and made it smart;
She was all sentiment and tender heart.
Her veil was gathered in a seemly way,
150 Her nose was elegant, her eyes glass-gray;
Her mouth was very small, but soft and red,
Her forehead, certainly, was fair of spread,
Almost a span[20] across the brows, I own;
She was indeed by no means undergrown.
155 Her cloak, I noticed, had a graceful charm.

13 **dirk:** small dagger.
14 **Saint Christopher:** patron saint of foresters and travelers.

15 **baldric:** shoulder belt.

16 **Prioress:** a nun ranking next below the abbess in an abbey.

17 **Saint Loy:** St. Eligius, patron saint of goldsmiths and courtiers, who would not swear upon holy relics.
18 **service:** daily prayers.

19 **Stratford-atte-Bowe:** a nunnery not far from London.

20 **span:** nine inches. A broad forehead was a sign of beauty.

She wore a coral trinket on her arm,
A set of beads, the gaudies[21] tricked in green,
Whence hung a golden brooch of brightest sheen
On which there first was graven a crowned *A,*
160 And lower, *Amor vincit omnia.*[22]
    Another *Nun,* the chaplain at her cell,
Was riding with her, and three *Priests* as well.

A *Monk* there was, one of the finest sort
Who rode the country; hunting was his sport.
165 A manly man, to be an Abbot able;
Many a dainty horse he had in stable.
His bridle, when he rode, a man might hear
Jingling in a whistling wind as clear,
Aye, and as loud as does the chapel bell
170 Where my lord Monk was Prior of the cell.
The Rule of good Saint Benet or Saint Maur[23]
As old and strict he tended to ignore;
He let go by the things of yesterday
And took the modern world's more spacious way.
175 He did not rate that text at a plucked hen
Which says that hunters are not holy men
And that a monk uncloistered is a mere
Fish out of water, flapping on the pier,
That is to say a monk out of his cloister.
180 That was a text he held not worth an oyster;
And I agreed and said his views were sound;
Was he to study till his head went round
Poring over books in cloisters? Must he toil
As Austin[24] bade and till the very soil?
185 Was he to leave the world upon the shelf?
Let Austin have his labor to himself.
    This Monk was therefore a good man to horse;
Greyhounds he had, as swift as birds, to course.[25]
Hunting a hare or riding at a fence
190 Was all his fun, he spared for no expense.
I saw his sleeves were garnished at the hand
With fine gray fur, the finest in the land,
And on his hood, to fasten it at his chin
He had a wrought-gold cunningly fashioned pin;
195 Into a lover's knot it seemed to pass.
His head was bald and shone like looking-glass;
So did his face, as if it had been greased.
He was a fat and personable priest;
His prominent eyeballs never seemed to settle.
200 They glittered like the flames beneath a kettle;
Supple his boots, his horse in fine condition.

21 **gaudies:** large beads used in counting prayers.

22 ***Amor vincit omnia*** [ä môr′ wink′it ōm′nē ä]: Latin for "Love conquers all."

23 **Saint Benet or Saint Maur:** French versions of Saint Benedict, who founded European monasticism in the sixth century, and Saint Maurice, one of his followers. Monastic life is governed by strict rules requiring poverty, chastity, and obedience.

24 **Austin:** English version of St. Augustine (354–430), a critic of lazy monks.

25 **to course:** for hunting.

The Knight

The Nun

The Monk

The Yeoman

He was a prelate fit for exhibition,
He was not pale like a tormented soul.
He liked a fat swan best, and roasted whole.
205 His palfrey[26] was as brown as is a berry.

There was a *Friar,* a wanton[27] one and merry,
A Limiter,[28] a very festive fellow.
In all Four Orders[29] there was none so mellow
So glib with gallant phrase and well-turned speech.
210 He'd fixed up many a marriage, giving each
Of his young women what he could afford her.
He was a noble pillar to his Order.
Highly beloved and intimate was he
With County folk within his boundary,
215 And city dames of honor and possessions;
For he was qualified to hear confessions,
Or so he said, with more than priestly scope
He had a special license from the Pope.
Sweetly he heard his penitents at shrift[30]
220 With pleasant absolution, for a gift.
He was an easy man in penance-giving
Where he could hope to make a decent living;
It's a sure sign whenever gifts are given
To a poor Order that a man's well shriven,[31]
225 And should he give enough he knew in verity
The penitent repented in sincerity.
For many a fellow is so hard of heart
He cannot weep, for all his inward smart.
Therefore instead of weeping and of prayer
230 One should give silver for a poor Friar's care.
He kept his tippet[32] stuffed with pins for curls,
And pocket-knives, to give to pretty girls.
And certainly his voice was gay and sturdy,
For he sang well and played the hurdy-gurdy.[33]
235 At sing-songs he was champion of the hour.
His neck was whiter than a lily-flower
But strong enough to butt a bruiser down.
He knew the taverns well in every town
And every innkeeper and barmaid too
240 Better than lepers, beggars and that crew,
For in so eminent a man as he
It was not fitting with the dignity
Of his position, dealing with a scum
Of wretched lepers; nothing good can come
245 Of dealings with the slum-and-gutter dwellers,
But only with the rich and victual-sellers.
But anywhere a profit might accrue

26 **palfrey:** saddle horse.

27 **wanton:** playful.

28 **Limiter:** a begging friar limited to a certain area in which to beg.
29 **Four Orders:** referring to the four orders of begging friars: Dominicans, Franciscans, Carmelites, Augustinians.

30 **shrift:** confession.

31 **well shriven:** completely forgiven of his sins through confession.

32 **tippet:** hood.

33 **hurdy-gurdy:** a stringed instrument, played by turning a hand crank.

Courteous he was and lowly of service too.
Natural gifts like his were hard to match.
250 He was the finest beggar of his batch,
And, for his begging-district, payed a rent;
His brethren did no poaching where he went.
For though a widow mightn't have a shoe,
So pleasant was his holy how-d'ye-do
255 He got his farthing from her just the same
Before he left, and so his income came
To more than he laid out. And how he romped,
Just like a puppy! He was ever prompt
To arbitrate disputes on settling days
260 (For a small fee) in many helpful ways,
Not then appearing as your cloistered scholar
With threadbare habit hardly worth a dollar,
But much more like a Doctor or a Pope.
Of double-worsted was the semi-cope[34]
265 Upon his shoulders, and the swelling fold
About him, like a bell about its mold
When it is casting, rounded out his dress.
He lisped a little out of wantonness
To make his English sweet upon his tongue.
270 When he had played his harp, or having sung,
His eyes would twinkle in his head as bright
As any star upon a frosty night.
This worthy's name was Hubert, it appeared.

There was a *Merchant* with a forking beard
275 And motley dress; high on his horse he sat,
Upon his head a Flemish[35] beaver hat
And on his feet daintily buckled boots.
He told of his opinions and pursuits
In solemn tones, and how he never lost.
280 The sea should be kept free at any cost
(He thought) upon the Harwich-Holland[36] range,
He was expert at currency exchange.
This estimable Merchant so had set
His wits to work, none knew he was in debt,
285 He was so stately in negotiation,
Loan, bargain and commercial obligation.
He was an excellent fellow all the same;
To tell the truth I do not know his name.

An *Oxford Cleric,* still a student though,
290 One who had taken logic long ago,
Was there; his horse was thinner than a rake,
And he was not too fat, I undertake,

34 **semi-cope:** cape.

35 **Flemish:** from Flanders.

36 **Harwich** [har′ich]-**Holland range:** that is, in the North Sea between England and Holland.

But had a hollow look, a sober stare;
The thread upon his overcoat was bare.
295 He had found no preferment in the church
And he was too unworldly to make search
For secular employment. By his bed
He preferred having twenty books in red
And black, of Aristotle's[37] philosophy,
300 To having fine clothes, fiddle or psaltery.[38]
Though a philosopher, as I have told,
He had not found the stone for making gold.[39]
Whatever money from his friends he took
He spent on learning or another book
305 And prayed for them most earnestly, returning
Thanks to them thus for paying for his learning.
His only care was study, and indeed
He never spoke a word more than was need,
Formal at that, respectful in the extreme,
310 Short, to the point, and lofty in his theme.
The thought of moral virtue filled his speech
And he would gladly learn, and gladly teach.

There was a *Franklin*[40] . . . it appeared;
White as a daisy-petal was his beard.
315 A sanguine man, high-colored and benign,
He loved a morning sop[41] of cake in wine.
He lived for pleasure and had always done,
For he was Epicurus'[42] very son,
In whose opinion sensual delight
320 Was the one true felicity in sight.
As noted as Saint Julian[43] was for bounty
He made his household free to all the County.
His bread, his ale were finest of the fine
And no one had a better stock of wine.
325 His house was never short of bake-meat pies,
Of fish and flesh, and these in such supplies
It positively snowed with meat and drink
And all the dainties that a man could think.
According to the seasons of the year
330 Changes of dish were ordered to appear.
He kept fat partridges in coops, beyond,
Many a bream and pike[44] were in his pond.
Woe to the cook whose sauces had no sting
Or who was unprepared in anything!
335 And in his hall a table stood arrayed
And ready all day long, with places laid.
As Justice at the Sessions[45] none stood higher;

37 **Aristotle's** [ar'is tot' əlz]:
referring to the Greek philosopher
(384–322 B.C.).
38 **psaltery** [sôl'tər ē]: an ancient
stringed musical instrument.
39 **stone . . . gold:** Medieval
alchemists believed that there existed
a "philosopher's stone" capable of
turning base metals into gold.

40 *Franklin:* wealthy landowner.

41 **sop:** piece.

42 **Epicurus** [ep'i kyoor'əs]: Greek
philosopher (341?–270 B.C.) who
held that pleasure should be one's
life goal.
43 **Saint Julian:** patron saint of
hospitality.

44 **bream and pike:** kinds of fishes.

45 **Sessions:** court sessions.

He often had been Member for the Shire.[46]
A dagger and a little purse of silk
340 Hung at his girdle, white as morning milk.
As Sheriff he checked audit, every entry.
He was a model among landed gentry.

A worthy *woman* from beside *Bath*[47] city
Was with us, somewhat deaf, which was a pity.
345 In making cloth she showed so great a bent
She bettered those of Ypres and of Ghent.[48]
In all the parish not a dame dared stir
Towards the altar steps in front of her,
And if indeed they did, so wrath was she
350 As to be quite put out of charity.
Her kerchiefs were of finely woven ground;[49]
I dared have sworn they weighed a good ten pound,
The ones she wore on Sunday, on her head.
Her hose were of the finest scarlet red
355 And gartered tight; her shoes were soft and new.
Bold was her face, handsome, and red in hue.
A worthy woman all her life, what's more
She'd had five husbands, all at the church door,
Apart from other company in youth;
360 No need just now to speak of that, forsooth.
And she had thrice been to Jerusalem,[50]
Seen many strange rivers and passed over them;
She'd been to Rome and also to Boulogne,
Saint James of Compostella and Cologne,
365 And she was skilled in wandering by the way.
She had gap-teeth, set widely, truth to say.
Easily on an ambling horse she sat
Well wimpled[51] up, and on her head a hat
As broad as is a buckler[52] or a shield;
370 She had a flowing mantle that concealed
Large hips, her heels spurred sharply under that.
In company she liked to laugh and chat
And knew the remedies for love's mischances,
An art in which she knew the oldest dances.

375 A holy-minded man of good renown
There was, and poor, the *Parson* to a town,
Yet he was rich in holy thought and work.
He also was a learned man, a clerk,
Who truly knew Christ's gospel and would preach it
380 Devoutly to parishioners, and teach it.
Benign and wonderfully diligent,
And patient when adversity was sent

46 **Member . . . Shire:** Representative to Parliament for his county.

47 **Bath:** resort city in southwestern England.

48 **Ypres** [ē′prə] . . . **Ghent** [gent]: Flemish cities known for weaving and wool making.

49 **ground:** a composite fabric.

50 **Jerusalem:** This and the place names immediately following designate famous pilgrimage sites of the Middle Ages.

51 **wimpled:** wearing a cloth covering the head, neck, and chin.
52 **buckler:** small round shield.

(For so he proved in great adversity)
He much disliked extorting tithe[53] or fee,
385 Nay rather he preferred beyond a doubt
Giving to poor parishioners round about
From his own goods and Easter offerings.
He found sufficiency in little things.
Wide was his parish, with houses far asunder,
390 Yet he neglected not in rain or thunder,
In sickness or in grief, to pay a call
On the remotest, whether great or small,
Upon his feet, and in his hand a stave.
This noble example to his sheep he gave,
395 First following the word before he taught it,
And it was from the gospel he had caught it.
This little proverb he would add thereto
That if gold rust, what then will iron do?
For a priest be foul in whom we trust
400 No wonder that a common man should rust.
The true example that a priest should give
Is one of cleanness, how the sheep should live.
He did not set his benefice to hire[54]
And leave his sheep encumbered in the mire
405 Or run to London to earn easy bread
By singing masses for the wealthy dead,
Or find some Brotherhood and get enrolled.
He stayed at home and watched over his fold
So that no wolf should make the sheep miscarry.
410 He was a shepherd and no mercenary.
Holy and virtuous he was, but then
Never contemptuous of sinful men,
Never disdainful, never too proud or fine,
But was discreet in teaching and benign.
415 His business was to show a fair behavior
And draw men thus to Heaven and their Savior,
Unless indeed a man were obstinate;
And such, whether of high or low estate,
He put to sharp rebuke to say the least.
420 I think there never was a better priest.
He sought no pomp or glory in his dealings,
No scrupulosity had spiced his feelings,
Christ and His twelve apostles and their lore
He taught, but followed it himself before.

425   There was a *Plowman* with him there, his brother
Many a load of dung one time or other
He must have carted through the morning dew.
He was an honest worker, good and true,

53 **tithe** [tīth]: one-tenth a person's income, to be paid to the church.

54 **set . . . hire:** pay someone else to perform his clerical duties.

Living in peace and perfect charity,
430 And, as the gospel bade him, so did he,
Loving God best with all his heart and mind
And then his neighbor as himself, repined
At no misfortune, slacked for no content,
For steadily about his work he went
435 To thrash his corn, to dig or to manure
Or make a ditch; and he would help the poor
For love of Christ and never take a penny
If he could help it, and, as prompt as any,
He paid his tithes in full when they were due
440 On what he owned, and on his earnings too.
He wore a tabard[55] smock and rode a mare.

The *Miller* was a chap of sixteen stone,[56]
A great stout fellow big in brawn and bone.
He did well out of them, for he could go
445 And win the ram at any wrestling show.
Broad, knotty and short-shouldered, he would boast
He could heave any door off hinge and post,
Or take a run and break it with his head.
His beard, like any sow or fox, was red
450 And broad as well, as though it were a spade;
And, at its very tip, his nose displayed
A wart on which there stood a tuft of hair
Red as the bristles in an old sow's ear.
His nostrils were as black as they were wide.
455 He had a sword and buckler at his side,
His mighty mouth was like a furnace door.
A wrangler and buffoon, he had a store
Of tavern stories, filthy in the main.
His was a master-hand at stealing grain.
460 He felt it with his thumb and thus he knew
Its quality and took three times his due—
A thumb of gold, by God, to gauge an oat!
He wore a hood of blue and a white coat.
He liked to play his bagpipes up and down
465 And that was how he brought us out of town.

The *Reeve*[57] was old and choleric and thin;
His beard was shaven closely to the skin,
His shorn hair came abruptly to a stop
Above his ears, and he was docked on top
470 Just like a priest in front; his legs were lean,
Like sticks they were, no calf was to be seen.
He kept his bins and garners[58] very trim;
No auditor could gain a point on him.

55 **tabard** [tab′ərd]: a loose jacket of heavy fabric.

56 **sixteen stone:** 224 pounds. A stone is a British unit of weight equal to 14 pounds.

57 **Reeve:** overseer or manager of a landowner's estate.

58 **garners:** buildings for storing grain.

The Merchant

The Franklin

The Wife of Bath

The Miller

And he could judge by watching drought and rain
475 The yield he might expect from seed and grain.
His master's sheep, his animals and hens,
Pigs, horses, dairies, stores and cattle pens
Were wholly trusted to his government.
And he was under contract to present
480 The accounts, right from his master's earliest years.
No one had ever caught him in arrears.
No bailiff, serf or herdsman dared to kick,
He knew their dodges, knew their every trick;
Feared like the plague he was, by those beneath.
485 He had a lovely dwelling on a heath,
Shadowed in green by trees above the sward.[59]
A better hand at bargains than his lord,
He had grown rich and had a store of treasure
Well tucked away, yet out it came to pleasure
490 His lord with subtle loans or gifts of goods,
To earn his thanks and even coats and hoods.
When young he'd learnt a useful trade and still
He was a carpenter of first-rate skill.
The stallion-cob he rode at a slow trot
495 Was dapple-gray and bore the name of Scot.
He wore an overcoat of bluish shade
And rather long; he had a rusty blade
Slung at his side. He came, as I heard tell,
From Norfolk, near a place called Baldeswell.
500 His coat was tucked under his belt and splayed.
He rode the hindmost of our cavalcade.

There was a *Summoner*[60] with us in the place
Who had a fire-red cherubinish face. . . .[61]
He and a gentle *Pardoner*[62] rode together,
505 A bird from Charing Cross of the same feather,
Just back from visiting the Court of Rome.
He loudly sang "Come hither, love, come home!"
The Summoner sang deep seconds to this song.
No trumpet ever sounded half so strong.
510 This Pardoner had hair as yellow as wax,
Hanging down smoothly like a hank of flax.
In driblets fell his locks behind his head
Down to his shoulders which they overspread;
Thinly they fell, like rat-tails, one by one.
515 He wore no hood upon his head, for fun;
The hood inside his wallet[63] had been stowed,
He aimed at riding in the latest mode;
But for a little cap his head was bare
And he had bulging eyeballs, like a hare.

59 **sward:** grassland, lawn.

60 **Summoner:** a layman charged with summoning sinners before a church court.
61 **fire-red . . . face:** In the Middle Ages the faces of cherubs, or angels, were often painted red.
62 **Pardoner:** one who is authorized to sell indulgences, or pardons from punishment from sins.

63 **wallet:** pack or knapsack.

520 He'd sewed a holy relic on his cap;
His wallet lay before him on his lap,
Brimful of pardons come from Rome all hot.
He had the same small voice a goat has got.
His chin no beard had harbored, nor would harbor,
525 Smoother than ever chin was left by barber.
I judge he was a gelding, or a mare.
As to his trade, from Berwick down to Ware[64]
There was no pardoner of equal grace,
For in his trunk he had a pillowcase
530 Which he asserted was Our Lady's veil.
He said he had a gobbet[65] of the sail
Saint Peter had the time when he made bold
To walk the waves, till Jesu Christ took hold.
He had a cross of metal set with stones
535 And, in a glass, a rubble of pigs' bones.
And with these relics, any time he found
Some poor up-country parson to astound,
On one short day, in money down, he drew
More than the parson in a month or two,
540 And by his flatteries and prevarication
Made monkeys of the priest and congregation.
But still to do him justice first and last
In church he was a noble ecclesiast.
How well he read a lesson or told a story!
545 But best of all he sang an Offertory,[66]
For well he knew that when that song was sung
He'd have to preach and tune his honey-tongue
And (well he could) win silver from the crowd.
That's why he sang so merrily and loud.

550   Now I have told you shortly, in a clause,
The rank, the array, the number and the cause
Of our assembly in this company
In Southwark, at that high-class hostelry
Known as The Tabard, close beside The Bell.[67]
555 And now the time has come for me to tell
How we behaved that evening; I'll begin
After we had alighted at the inn,
Then I'll report our journey, stage by stage,
All the remainder of our pilgrimage.
560 But first I beg of you, in courtesy,
Not to condemn me as unmannerly
If I speak plainly and with no concealings
And give account of all their words and dealings,
Using their very phrases as they fell.
565 For certainly, as you all know so well,

64 **Berwick . . . Ware:** cities in the north and south of England, respectively.

65 **gobbet:** piece.

66 **Offertory:** song accompanying the collection of the offering in church.

67 **The Bell:** another inn.

He who repeats a tale after a man
Is bound to say, as nearly as he can,
Each single word, if he remembers it,
However rudely spoken or unfit,
570 Or else the tale he tells will be untrue,
The things invented and the phrases new.
He may not flinch although it were his brother,
If he says one word he must say the other.
And Christ Himself spoke broad[68] in Holy Writ,
575 And as you know there's nothing there unfit,
And Plato[69] says, for those with power to read,
"The word should be as cousin to the deed."
Further I beg you to forgive it me
If I neglect the order and degree
580 And what is due to rank in what I've planned.
I'm short of wit[70] as you will understand.

    Our *Host* gave us great welcome; everyone
Was given a place and supper was begun.
He served the finest victuals you could think,
585 The wine was strong and we were glad to drink.
A very striking man our Host withal,
And fit to be a marshal in a hall.
His eyes were bright, his girth a little wide;
There is no finer burgess in Cheapside.[71]
590 Bold in his speech, yet wise and full of tact,
There was no manly attribute he lacked,
What's more he was a merry-hearted man.
After our meal he jokingly began
To talk of sport, and, among other things
595 After we'd settled up our reckonings,
He said as follows: "Truly, gentlemen,
You're very welcome and I can't think when
—Upon my word I'm telling you no lie—
I've seen a gathering here that looked so spry,
600 No, not this year, as in this tavern now.
I'd think you up some fun if I knew how.
And, as it happens, a thought has just occurred
And it will cost you nothing, on my word.
You're off to Canterbury—well, Godspeed!
605 Blessed Saint Thomas answer to your need!
And I don't doubt, before the journey's done
You mean to while the time in tales and fun.
Indeed, there's little pleasure for your bones
Riding along and all as dumb as stones.
610 So let me then propose for your enjoyment,
Just as I said, a suitable employment.
And if my notion suits and you agree

68 **broad:** bluntly, plainly.

69 **Plato:** a Greek philosopher (427?–347? B.C.).

70 **wit:** intelligence.

71 **Cheapside:** a district in the East End of London.

And promise to submit yourselves to me
Playing your parts exactly as I say
615 Tomorrow as you ride along the way,
Then by my father's soul (and he is dead)
If you don't like it you can have my head!
Hold up your hands, and not another word."
    Well, our consent of course was not deferred,
620 It seemed not worth a serious debate;
We all agreed to it at any rate
And bade him issue what commands he would.
"My lords," he said, "now listen for your good,
And please don't treat my notion with disdain.
625 This is the point. I'll make it short and plain.
Each one of you shall help to make things slip
By telling two stories on the outward trip
To Canterbury, that's what I intend,
And, on the homeward way to journey's end
630 Another two, tales from the days of old;
And then the man whose story is best told,
That is to say who gives the fullest measure
Of good morality and general pleasure,
He shall be given a supper, paid by all,
635 Here in this tavern, in this very hall,
When we come back again from Canterbury.
And in the hope to keep you bright and merry
I'll go along with you myself and ride
All at my own expense and serve as guide.
640 I'll be the judge, and those who won't obey
Shall pay for what we spend upon the way.
Now if you all agree to what you've heard
Tell me at once without another word,
And I will make arrangements early for it."
645   Of course we all agreed, in fact we swore it
Delightedly, and made entreaty too
That he should act as he proposed to do,
Become our Governor in short, and be
Judge of our tales and general referee,
650 And set the supper at a certain price.
We promised to be ruled by his advice
Come high, come low; unanimously thus
We set him up in judgment over us.
More wine was fetched, the business being done;
655 We drank it off and up went everyone
To bed without a moment of delay.
    Early next morning at the spring of day
Up rose our Host and roused us like a cock,
Gathering us together in a flock,

660 And off we rode at slightly faster pace
    Than walking to St. Thomas' watering-place;[72]
    And there our Host drew up, began to ease
    His horse, and said, "Now, listen if you please,
    My lords! Remember what you promised me.
665 If evensong and matins will agree[73]
    Let's see who shall be first to tell a tale.
    And as I hope to drink good wine and ale
    I'll be your judge. The rebel who disobeys,
    However much the journey costs, he pays.
670 Now draw for cut and then we can depart;
    The man who draws the shortest cut shall start."

72 **St. Thomas' watering-place:** a brook two miles from London.

73 **If evensong . . . agree:** If what you said last night is what you mean this morning. Matins are morning songs.

STUDY QUESTIONS

Recalling

1. Of the Knight, the Squire, and the Yeoman (lines 43–115), who is called the most distinguished while also being modest? Of the three, who is the youngest and freshest?

2. Give one physical characteristic of the Nun (lines 116–160), of the Monk (lines 163–205), and of the Friar (lines 206–273). Of the three, who is "solicitous" to animals? Who hunts instead of studying? Who takes money from poor widows?

3. Of the Merchant, Cleric, and Franklin (lines 274–342), who is most obsessed with food? With books?

4. Which of the following had gap-teeth and liked to laugh: the Wife of Bath, the Parson, or the Plowman (lines 343–441)?

5. Of the Miller, the Reeve, the Summoner, and the Pardoner (lines 442–549), who had eyeballs like a hare's, a voice like a goat's, and a honey-tongue?

6. After he describes the pilgrims, what does the narrator tell us his plan is (lines 555–580)?

7. What contest does the host propose in lines 626–644? How will the winner of the contest be determined? What will the prize be?

Interpreting

8. What does the narrator think of the Knight, the Parson, and of the Plowman? What do the three have in common?

9. How would you characterize the narrator's attitude toward the Nun? Toward the Friar? Toward the Pardoner? Toward whom is the narrator most bitter? Why?

10. What does the narrative gain from the narrator's explanation in lines 555–580?

Extending

11. Describe what might be the modern-day equivalents of the Merchant and of the Oxford Cleric.

VIEWPOINT

In 1809 the English poet William Blake wrote:

Every age is a Canterbury Pilgrimage; we all pass on, each sustaining one or other of these characters; nor can a child be born who is not one of these characters of Chaucer.

■ Can you think of any types of people—specifically representative of the twentieth century—whom Chaucer omits from his list of pilgrims? If not, what is your conclusion about Chaucer's powers of observation?

LITERARY FOCUS

Characterization

Chaucer describes his pilgrims so well that, after six hundred years, they still stand vividly before us as round characters, or complete and complicated people. An important technique that Chaucer uses to create round characters is the mixture of both direct and indirect characterizations. Most later writers follow Chaucer's lead. Chaucer uses **direct characterization** when the narrator explicitly tells us something about a pilgrim in a straightforward manner. For example, he explicitly says of the Squire, "Courteous he was, lowly and serviceable." He uses **indirect characterization** when he lets us see the pilgrims in motion so that we have to figure out their character traits ourselves. For example, in describing the Merchant, he makes us form our own conclusion about someone who ". . . told of his opinions and pursuits/In solemn tones, and how he never lost."

Chaucer also succeeds in presenting vivid characters by selecting **significant details**—not every detail about the characters but those details that count: the Friar's lily-white neck; the Miller's wart; the Knight's tunic, stained with rust from his chain mail.

Moreover, the details appear to be random, as when they would be remembered in real life. When we meet a group of people at a party or on the first day of school, we usually remember some details about them and forget others. Similarly, for example, Chaucer recalls where the Reeve comes from but not what his name is (although he does recall the name of the Reeve's horse). The effect is to create a sense of **verisimilitude**, a sense that what he is writing about is true, that it really happened.

In addition, Chaucer convinces us that his characters have **motivations**, reasons underlying their behavior. That is, he shows us the details of his characters' temperaments as well as the circumstances in which the characters find themselves. In this way we understand what motivates them to behave as they do. For instance, we see that the Pardoner is motivated by a love of money, and the Knight by a love of Christianity and the ideals of chivalry.

Thinking About Characterization

1. What does the narrator directly and explicitly tell us about the Oxford Cleric (lines 289–312)? What actions by the Cleric does the portrait contain to help us learn about him directly?
2. Identify two significant details about the Cleric's possessions.
3. What motivates the Cleric?

COMPOSITION

Writing a Comparison/Contrast

Compare and contrast an anonymous medieval ballad with a character portrait from Chaucer's "Prologue." First compare and contrast the poetic style of each: meter and rhyme. Then compare and contrast the completeness of character description in each, commenting on direct characterization, indirect characterization, significant detail, and motivation. Conclude by giving a reason why the ballad and Chaucer's portrait have lasted so long. *For help with this assignment, refer to Lesson 2 in the Writing About Literature Handbook at the back of this book.*

Writing a Character Portrait

Write a brief, prose character portrait about a twentieth-century intruder in Chaucer's fourteenth-century world: a musician or a student or an actor or any other character you choose to accompany the pilgrims to Canterbury. In the Chaucerian manner (1) use direct and indirect characterization, (2) select significant details that make your character come to life, and (3) make your character's motivation clear.

Were it yeven of the povereste page
Or of the povereste widwe in a village
Al sholde hir children sterve for famyne
May I nol drynke licour of the vyne
And have a ioly wenche in every toun
But herkneth lordynges in conclusioun
Youre likyng is that I shal telle a tale
Now have I dronke a draughte of corny ale
By god I hope I shal yow telle a thyng
That shal by resoun been at youre likyng
For though my self be a ful vicious man
A moral tale yet I yow telle kan
Which I am wont to preche for to wynne
Now hoold youre pees my tale I wol bigynne

Heere bigynneth the Pardoners tale

In Flaundres whilom was a compaignye
Of yonge folk that haunteden folye
As riot hasard stywes and tavernes
Wher as with harpes lutes and gyternes
They daunce and pleyen at dees bothe day and nyght
And eten also and drynken over hir myght
Thurgh which they doon the devel sacrifise
With inne that develes temple in cursed wise
By superfluytee abhomynable
Hir othes been so grete and so dampnable
That it is grisly for to heere hem swere
Oure blissed lordes body they to tere
Hem thoughte that Iewes rente hym noght ynough
And ech of hem at otheres synne lough
And right anon thanne comen tombesteres
Fetys and smale and yonge fruytesteres
Syngeres with harpes baudes wafereres
Whiche been the verray develes officeres
To kyndle and blowe the fyr of lecherye
That is annexed un to glotonye
The hooly writ take I to my witnesse
That luxurie is in wyn and dronkenesse
Lo how that dronken looth unkyndely
Lay by hise doghtres two unwityngly
So dronke he was he nyste what he wroghte
Herodes who so wel the stories soghte

The Pardoner's Tale, from the Ellesmere Manuscript.

As the pilgrims journey to Canterbury, the Knight, the Miller, the Reeve, the Nun, and the narrator each tell a tale. Then it is the Pardoner's turn.

"The Pardoner's Tale" is an *exemplum,* a concrete example or illustration within a longer sermon to illustrate the truthfulness of a moral. The tale is also full of suspense and action. In other words, this tale fulfills the Host's condition that the pilgrims' stories should give "the fullest measure/Of good morality and general pleasure" (lines 632–633 in "The Prologue").

Geoffrey Chaucer

from **The Pardoner's Tale**

　　It's of three rioters I have to tell
Who long before the morning service bell[1]
Were sitting in a tavern for a drink.
And as they sat, they heard the hand-bell clink
5　Before a coffin going to the grave;
One of them called the little tavern-knave[2]
And said "Go and find out at once—look spry!—
Whose corpse is in that coffin passing by;
And see you get the name correctly too."
10　"Sir," said the boy, "no need, I promise you;
Two hours before you came here I was told.
He was a friend of yours in days of old,
And suddenly, last night, the man was slain,
Upon his bench, face up, dead drunk again.
15　There came a privy[3] thief, they call him Death,
Who kills us all round here, and in a breath
He speared him through the heart, he never stirred.
And then Death went his way without a word.
He's killed a thousand in the present plague,[4]
20　And, sir, it doesn't do to be too vague
If you should meet him; you had best be wary.
Be on your guard with such an adversary,
Be primed to meet him everywhere you go,
That's what my mother said. It's all I know."
25　　The publican[5] joined in with, "By Saint Mary,
What the child says is right; you'd best be wary,
This very year he killed, in a large village
A mile away, man, woman, serf at tillage,[6]
Page in the household, children—all there were.

1 **long before . . . bell:** long before 9 A.M.

2 **tavern-knave:** serving boy.

3 **privy:** secretive.

4 **killed . . . plague:** In 1348 and 1349 at least a third of the population of England perished from the plague called the Black Death.

5 **publican:** tavernkeeper or innkeeper.

6 **tillage:** plowing.

30　Yes, I imagine that he lives round there.
　　It's well to be prepared in these alarms,
　　He might do you dishonor." "Huh, God's arms!"
　　The rioter said, "Is he so fierce to meet?
　　I'll search for him, by Jesus, street by street.
35　God's blessed bones! I'll register a vow!
　　Here, chaps! The three of us together now,
　　Hold up your hands, like me, and we'll be brothers
　　In this affair, and each defend the others,
　　And we will kill this traitor Death, I say!
40　Away with him as he has made away
　　With all our friends. God's dignity! To-night!"
　　　They made their bargain, swore with appetite,
　　These three, to live and die for one another
　　As brother-born might swear to his born brother.
45　And up they started in their drunken rage
　　And made towards this village which the page
　　And publican had spoken of before.
　　Many and grisly were the oaths they swore,
　　Tearing Christ's blessed body to a shred;[7]

7 **Tearing . . . shred:** Their swearing included such expressions as "God's arms" (line 32) and "God's blessed bones" (line 35).

50　"If we can only catch him, Death is dead!"
　　　When they had gone not fully half a mile,
　　Just as they were about to cross a stile,
　　They came upon a very poor old man
　　Who humbly greeted them and thus began,
55　"God look to you, my lords, and give you quiet!"
　　To which the proudest of these men of riot
　　Gave back the answer, "What, old fool? Give place!
　　Why are you all wrapped up except your face?
　　Why live so long? Isn't it time to die?"
60　　The old, old fellow looked him in the eye
　　And said, "Because I never yet have found,
　　Though I have walked to India, searching round
　　Village and city on my pilgrimage,
　　One who would change his youth to have my age.
65　And so my age is mine and must be still
　　Upon me, for such time as God may will.
　　　"Not even Death, alas, will take my life;
　　So, like a wretched prisoner at strife
　　Within himself, I walk alone and wait
70　About the earth, which is my mother's gate,[8]
　　Knock-knocking with my staff from night to noon
　　And crying, 'Mother, open to me soon!
　　Look at me, mother, won't you let me in?
　　See how I wither, flesh and blood and skin!
75　Alas! When will these bones be laid to rest?
　　Mother, I would exchange—for that were best—

8 **mother's gate:** entrance to the grave.

The wardrobe in my chamber, standing there
So long, for yours! Aye, for a shirt of hair[9]
To wrap me in!' She has refused her grace,
80 Whence comes the pallor of my withered face.
   "But it dishonored you when you began
To speak so roughly, sir, to an old man,
Unless he had injured you in word or deed.
It says in holy writ, as you may read,
85 'Thou shalt rise up before the hoary head
And honor it.' And therefore be it said
'Do no more harm to an old man than you,
Being now young, would have another do
When you are old'—if you should live till then.
90 And so may God be with you, gentlemen,
For I must go whither I have to go."
   "By God," the gambler said, "you shan't do so,
You don't get off so easy, by Saint John!
I heard you mention, just a moment gone,
95 A certain traitor Death who singles out
And kills the fine young fellows hereabout.
And you're his spy, by God! You wait a bit.
Say where he is or you shall pay for it,
By God and by the Holy Sacrament!
100 I say you've joined together by consent.
To kill us younger folk, you thieving swine!"
   "Well, sirs," he said, "If it be your design
To find out Death, turn up this crooked way
Towards that grove, I left him there today
105 Under a tree, and there you'll find him waiting.
He isn't one to hide for all your prating.
You see that oak? He won't be far to find.
And God protect you that redeemed mankind,
Aye, and amend[10] you!" Thus that ancient man.
110   At once the three young rioters began
To run, and reached the tree, and there they found
A pile of golden florins[11] on the ground,
New-coined, eight bushels of them as they thought.
No longer was it Death those fellows sought,
115 For they were all so thrilled to see the sight,
The florins were so beautiful and bright,
That down they sat beside the precious pile.
The wickedest spoke first after a while.
"Brothers," he said, "you listen to what I say.
120 I'm pretty sharp although I joke away.
It's clear that Fortune has bestowed this treasure
To let us live in jollity and pleasure.
Light come, light go! We'll spend it as we ought.

9 **shirt of hair:** usually a rough shirt worn as self-punishment; here, a shroud.

10 **amend:** improve.

11 **florins:** coins.

God's precious dignity! Who would have thought
125 This morning was to be our lucky day?
   "If one could only get the gold away,
Back to my house, or else to yours, perhaps—
For as you know, the gold is ours, chaps—
We'd all be at the top of fortune, hey?
130 But certainly it can't be done by day.
People would call us robbers—a strong gang,
So our own property would make us hang.
No, we must bring this treasure back by night
Some prudent way, and keep it out of sight.
135 And so as a solution I propose
We draw for lots and see the way it goes,
The one who draws the longest, lucky man,
Shall run to town as quickly as he can
To fetch us bread and wine—but keep things dark—
140 While two remain in hiding here to mark
Our heap of treasure. If there's no delay,
When night comes down we'll carry it away,
All three of us, wherever we have planned."
   He gathered lots and hid them in his hand
145 Bidding them draw for where the luck should fall.
It fell upon the youngest of them all,
And off he ran at once towards the town.
   As soon as he had gone the first sat down
And thus began a parley[12] with the other:
150 "You know that you can trust me as a brother;
Now let me tell you where your profit lies;
You know our friend has gone to get supplies
And here's a lot of gold that is to be
Divided equally amongst us three.
155 Nevertheless, if I could shape things thus
So that we shared it out—the two of us—
Wouldn't you take it as a friendly turn?"
   "But how?" the other said with some concern,
"Because he knows the gold's with me and you;
160 What can we tell him? What are we to do?"
   "Is it a bargain," said the first, "or no?
For I can tell you in a word or so
What's to be done to bring the thing about."
   "Trust me," the other said, "you needn't doubt
165 My word. I won't betray you, I'll be true."
   "Well," said his friend, "you see that we are two,
And two are twice as powerful as one.
Now look; when he comes back, get up in fun
To have a wrestle; then, as you attack,
170 I'll up and put my dagger through his back

12 **parley** [par′lē]: a discussion, as with an enemy.

While you and he are struggling, as in game;
Then draw your dagger too and do the same.
Then all this money will be ours to spend,
Divided equally of course, dear friend.
175 Then we can gratify our lusts and fill
The day with dicing at our own sweet will."
Thus these two miscreants[13] agreed to slay
The third and youngest, as you heard me say.

    The youngest, as he ran towards the town,
180 Kept running over, rolling up and down
Within his heart the beauty of those bright
New florins, saying, "Lord, to think I might
Have all that treasure to myself alone!
Could there be anyone beneath the throne
185 Of God so happy as I then should be?"
    And so the Fiend, our common enemy,
Was given power to put it in his thought
That there was always poison to be bought,
And that with poison he could kill his friends.
190 To men in such a state the Devil sends
Thoughts of this kind, and has a full permission
To lure them on to sorrow and perdition;[14]

For this young man was utterly content
To kill them both and never to repent.
195   And on he ran, he had no thought to tarry,
Came to the town, found an apothecary
And said, "Sell me some poison if you will,
I have a lot of rats I want to kill
And there's a polecat too about my yard
200 That takes my chickens and it hits me hard;
But I'll get even, as is only right,
With vermin that destroy a man by night."
    The chemist answered, "I've a preparation
Which you shall have, and by my soul's salvation
205 If any living creature eat or drink
A mouthful, ere he has the time to think,
Though he took less than makes a grain of wheat,
You'll see him fall down dying at your feet;
Yes, die he must, and in so short a while
210 You'd hardly have the time to walk a mile,
The poison is so strong, you understand."
    This cursed fellow grabbed into his hand
The box of poison and away he ran
Into a neighboring street, and found a man
215 Who lent him three large bottles. He withdrew
And deftly poured the poison into two.
Ke kept the third one clean, as well he might,

For his own drink, meaning to work all night
Stacking the gold and carrying it away.
220 And when this rioter, this devil's clay,
Had filled his bottles up with wine, all three,
Back to rejoin his comrades sauntered he.
   Why make a sermon of it? Why waste breath?
Exactly in the way they'd planned his death
225 They fell on him and slew him, two to one.
Then said the first of them when this was done,
"Now for a drink. Sit down and let's be merry,
For later on there'll be the corpse to bury."
And, as it happened, reaching for a sup,
230 He took a bottle full of poison up
And drank; and his companion, nothing loth,[15]
Drank from it also, and they perished both.
   There is, in Avicenna's[16] long relation
Concerning poison and its operation,
235 Trust me, no ghastlier section to transcend
What these two wretches suffered at their end.
Thus these two murderers received their due,
So did the treacherous young poisoner too.

15 **nothing loth:** very willingly.

16 **Avicenna's** [aʹvə senʹəz] **long relation:** A medieval book on medicines by the Arab physician Avicenna (980–1037) contains a chapter on poisons.

STUDY QUESTIONS

Recalling

1. About what do the tavern-knave and the publican warn the rioters? How does the rioter react in lines 32–41 to the warning?
2. Whom do the rioters meet in line 53, and how do they treat him according to line 82? What do the rioters next demand (line 98)?
3. What do the rioters find under the tree to put Death out of their minds?
4. What do the two rioters who remain by the tree plan to do to the youngest when he returns? Why? In the meantime, what is the youngest scheming to do?
5. Summarize what happens when the youngest returns.

Interpreting

6. How well do the rioters keep the vow they took in lines 36–39?
7. In what way does the old man direct the rioters to the very object they have been seeking?

8. What moral about greed or money does "The Pardoner's Tale" illustrate?

Extending

9. Review the description of the Pardoner from "The Prologue," especially lines 542–549. How does "The Pardoner's Tale" confirm Chaucer's portrait of the Pardoner?

LITERARY FOCUS

Middle English

On page 45 is an eighteen-line specimen of **Middle English,** the language that was spoken in and around London in the 1300s. By then the Old English of Germanic Angles and Saxons had merged with the Old French spoken by the Normans who had invaded the British Isles in 1066. English acquired a new stock of words from the Normans (see Vocabulary, which follows). In general, the English grammar of Chaucer's day had fewer complications than Old English (see page 26).

Most important, there were fewer inflectional endings in Middle English. As an example, notice that there were only two forms of the noun in Middle English:

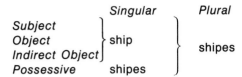

	Singular	Plural
Subject		
Object	ship	
Indirect Object		shipes
Possessive	shipes	

A number of notable features make Middle English, nevertheless, a different language from modern English. Pronunciation is the most obvious difference—especially, pronunciation of vowels. Speakers of Middle English pronounced vowels in the French manner (the letter *a* as *ah*; a long *e* as long *a*; a long *i* or *y* as long *e*; and so on).

When English people began to pronounce the vowels as we do, English experienced a phenomenon so important that it is now called the Great Vowel Shift. Another pronunciation difference of note is that speakers of Middle English pronounced every vowel, unlike speakers of modern English who acknowledge the "silent *e*." For example, in Middle English *eyë* has two syllables, whereas modern English *eye* has only one.

Thinking About Middle English

1. Looking again at the Middle English sample on page 26, what would be the plural of *breeth* in line 5?
2. How would a speaker of Middle English pronounce *breeth*?
3. From the sample find the Middle English equivalent of the modern English noun *end*. How many syllables are in the older form?

VOCABULARY

Word Origins

As the conquering Normans and their descendants established themselves in England and became a part of the life there, they lent medieval English words from Old French. Many of these French words have endured right up to the English we now speak, although their spelling and pronunciation may have changed along the way.

French importations from 1250 to the end of the Medieval Period reached astonishing proportions and affected all walks of life. For example, French gave English the words basic to government, which are now *crown*, *state*, and *prince*, among dozens of others. The words *fashion* and *dress* are French in origin as are *gown*, *veil*, *kerchief*, and *galoshes*. French also entered the English vocabularies particular to religion, the military, the arts, and medicine. In addition, adjectives from the French were very important for description in Chaucer's day and included *amiable*, *courteous*, *gentle*, *gracious*, *honest*, *rude*, *treacherous*, and nearly a thousand others.

■ Using a good dictionary, explain the changes in meaning or spelling that have occurred in each of the following words since they entered our language as Old French. The words are presented in modern English, but Chaucer used them in Middle English in *The Canterbury Tales.*

1. engender
2. tender
3. devout
4. company
5. degree
6. poison
7. chivalry
8. courtesy
9. sovereign
10. gentle

COMPOSITION

Citing Evidence

■ In a brief essay persuade your reader that "The Pardoner's Tale" has an absorbing plot. To be persuasive you will need to cite evidence—specific details to support your opinions. You may want to comment on the flow of events, suspense, foreshadowing, and outcome. *For help with this assignment, refer to Lesson 3 in the Writing About Literature Handbook at the back of this book.*

Writing a Moral Tale

■ Try your hand at writing a moral tale. Begin with the moral—some bit of popular wisdom that can be expressed in a sentence such as "The early bird gets the worm" or "Never trust flatterers" or "Better late than never." Then devise a brief story that illustrates the point. Several paragraphs should be sufficient, though you will want to include enough appropriate detail to make your story vivid and memorable.

Sir Thomas Malory   *1405–1471*

Although several Englishmen named Thomas Malory lived during the 1400s, most evidence suggests that the writer Sir Thomas Malory was the same hot-blooded Thomas Malory who had represented Warwickshire in Parliament in 1455. Those were troubled times, and the Member of Parliament had found himself supporting the wrong side—the Lancasters—in the war to determine which family would rule England, the War of the Roses. Charged with various crimes, he spent much of his later life in jail. He may have been a political prisoner rather than an actual perpetrator, but he nevertheless died in jail. It was in there that the "knyght presoner," as the author called himself, composed the great English prose work that related the heroic adventures of King Arthur and his Knights of the Round Table.

Malory's account of the legend is a reworking from English, French, and Latin sources. In this narrative Malory translated and gave order to that diverse body of Arthurian romance that had grown up in England and France since Anglo-Saxon times. William Caxton, the first English printer, published Malory's work in 1485 as *Le Morte d'Arthur,* French for "The Death of Arthur."

Did King Arthur really exist? When the Anglo-Saxons invaded Britain in the fifth century, they pushed the inhabitants of that island northward into present-day Scotland and westward into Ireland and Wales. Those older, displaced inhabitants were the Celts. Arthur was presumably a sixth-century chieftain of one of those Celtic tribes, fighting from Wales against the invading Germanic tribes. Hundreds of years later, that primitive chieftain caught the imagination of the Middle Ages. Indeed, the nonreligious literature of the Middle Ages from the twelfth century onward—on the European continent even more than in England itself—was filled with the tales of King Arthur, around whom the medieval ideal of chivalry flourished. Malory, it would seem, wanted to recapture the Arthurian romantic ideals that his age was already losing, for as he wrote, knighthood was coming to an end.

Le Morte d'Arthur chronicles Arthur's history from his mysterious birth to his dramatic death. In the adventure that follows, he is a young man mastering the skills of knighthood, guided by an older and wiser counselor, the magician Merlin.

Model for Active Reading

In this selection, as in one selection in each unit, you will find notes in the right-hand margin that highlight parts of the selection. These notes point out important ideas of the literary period and draw your attention to literary elements and techniques covered in the Literary Focuses. Page numbers in the notes refer you to more extensive discussions of these important ideas and elements.

Illustration from a medieval manuscript of Malory's *Morte d'Arthur.*

Sir Thomas Malory

from **Le Morte d'Arthur**

Modern Idiom by Keith Baines

One day a squire arrived at the court, supporting his master, Sir Myles, who had been mortally wounded. He described to Arthur how he had been attacked by King Pellinore[1] at the well, and then begged that he should be buried, and that one of Arthur's knights should avenge his death. After the burial a squire named Gryfflette pleaded with Arthur to make him a knight; he was the same age as Arthur.

"You are too young to be a knight," Arthur said gravely.

"Sire, but I beg you," said Gryfflette.

"It would be a shame," said Merlin,[2] "to lose Gryfflette. He will make an excellent knight when he is older, but at the moment he would be no match for King Pellinore."

"I will make you a knight," said Arthur, "if you will swear not to joust with King Pellinore more than once, and then return to me."

"I swear it," said Gryfflette; so Arthur dubbed[3] him.

Sir Gryfflette ran happily to his armor, and when he was clad and mounted, set off at a gallop for the well. He found there a brilliantly decorated pavilion,[4] and outside it a horse, already harnessed. A multicolored shield hung from a tree, and resting against it was a spear. Sir Gryfflette struck the shield a ringing blow, and it fell to the ground. King Pellinore appeared at the entrance to his pavilion. "Sir, why do you strike my shield?" he asked.

"Because I wish to joust with you," Sir Gryfflette replied.

"You are but newly knighted, and too young," said the king. "Tell me, where do you come from?"

"I come from the court of King Arthur, and still I mean to joust with you."

Medieval idea: Loyalty to one's master was important in the feudal hierarchy (p. 31).

---

1. **King Pellinore:** one of the many rulers of the kingdoms that made up Arthurian Britain; probably a fictitious name.
2. **Merlin:** magician and counselor to King Arthur.
3. **dubbed:** made a knight by tapping on the shoulders with a sword. Once knighted, a person is addressed as "Sir."
4. **pavilion** [pə vil′yən]: tent.

"Very well, then; but I am reluctant to do so," the king rejoined.

The two knights met at full gallop: Sir Gryfflette's spear was broken, and the shaft driven deeply into his side; he lost consciousness and fell to the ground. King Pellinore swiftly ran over to him and loosened his armor. Sir Gryfflette recovered his wind slowly, and when he had done so, King Pellinore lifted him gently onto his horse. "God's speed, young knight," he said.

At King Arthur's court Sir Gryfflette collapsed once more; however, he was placed in the hands of a surgeon by whose skillful treatment the wound was eventually healed.

Meanwhile, twelve aged ambassadors had come from Rome, and in the name of the Emperor Lucius, demanded tribute.[5] "Since you are only ambassadors," Arthur said, "we shall not put you to death for your insolent words; but tell your Emperor that if he tries to win tribute from us, that will be his fate."

The ambassadors withdrew angrily, and Arthur himself was doubly grieved: by the Emperor's message and by Sir Gryfflette's injury. He decided to avenge Sir Gryfflette secretly, so he commanded the chamberlain[6] to take his horse and armor to the outskirts of the city at dawn the following day.

When Arthur was armed and mounted, he instructed the chamberlain to await his return, and then galloped off toward the well. He had not gone far when he saw Merlin being chased by three ruffians; he galloped up to them and the ruffians fled in terror.

"Your magic did not save you that time," said Arthur.

"It could have," Merlin replied, "had I so wished, whereas your anger will certainly not save you from the superior strength of King Pellinore, whom you are about to challenge."

Merlin accompanied Arthur to the well, and when they arrived they found King Pellinore seated outside his pavilion. "Sir," said Arthur, "it would seem that no knight can pass this well without your challenging him."

"That is so," said King Pellinore.

"I have come to force you to change this custom of yours, so defend yourself!"

They jousted three times, each time breaking their spears, until the third time, when Arthur was flung from his horse. "Very well," said Arthur, "you have won the advantage jousting; now let us see what you can do on foot." King Pellinore was reluctant to dismount and lose the advantage he had won; however, when Arthur rushed at him boldly with drawn sword, he grew ashamed and did dismount.

Verisimilitude (p. 63): Malory selects details that make life in a medieval court seem real.

Motivation (p. 63): Arthur has reason for seeking King Pellinore.

---

5. **tribute:** money paid by one ruler to another to acknowledge submission or for protection.
6. **chamberlain:** officer in charge of a ruler's household.

They fought until both collapsed from pain and exhaustion; their armor was splintered and the blood flowed from their wounds. They fought again, until Arthur's sword broke in his hand. "Now," said King Pellinore, "you shall yield to me, or die."

"Not so!" Arthur shouted as he sprang at him, and grabbing him around the waist, threw him to the ground. Arthur was unlacing his helmet when, with a sudden fearful effort, King Pellinore overturned Arthur and clambered on top of him. King Pellinore had loosened Arthur's helmet and raised his sword to strike off his head when Merlin spoke.

"Hold your hand!" he said; "you will endanger the whole realm. You do not realize who it is you are about to kill."

"Who is it, then?"

"King Arthur."

Hearing this, King Pellinore feared that he would receive little mercy from Arthur if he spared him—so he raised his sword once more. Merlin adroitly put him to sleep with a magic spell.

"You have killed him with your magic," said Arthur hotly. "I would rather that my whole realm were lost, and myself killed; he was a magnificent fighter."

Medieval idea: Skill in battle was worthy of great praise (p. 33).

"He is more whole than you are," Merlin replied. "He will not only live, but serve you excellently. It is to him that you will give your sister in marriage, and she will bear two sons—Sir Percivale and Sir Lamerok—who will be two of the most famous of the Knights of the Round Table."

They mounted, and Merlin led the way to a hermit, who treated Arthur's wounds, and in whose dwelling they rested for three days. They resumed their journey, which was to the Lake of Avalon,[7] and as they were approaching the lake, Arthur said, "How sad that I broke my magic sword!"

"You shall have another one," Merlin replied.

Just then Arthur saw that in the center of the lake the surface was broken by an arm, clothed in white samite,[8] and that the hand grasped a finely jeweled sword and scabbard.

Romance (p. 35): Magic was an important element of most medieval romances.

"That is the magic sword Excalibur," said Merlin, "and it will be given to you by the Lady of the Lake, who is now crossing the water in her bark.[9] She comes from her castle, which is hewn in the rock, and more beautiful than any earthly dwelling. You must address her courteously, and do as she directs you."

The Lady of the Lake appeared before them. "My lady," said Arthur, "I beg you to make me a gift of the sword Excalibur."

"King Arthur," she replied, "Excalibur shall be yours, if you

Medieval idea: Knights were expected to treat women with respect at all times (p. 33).

---

7. **Lake of Avalon:** the lake in which is situated Avalon, the legendary rock island inhabited by a race of women who know all the world's magic.
8. **samite:** a heavy silk worn in the Middle Ages.
9. **bark:** boat.

consent now to granting me whatever gift I shall ask of you in my own time."

"I swear," said Arthur, "whatever gift is in my power to grant."

"Even so," said the Lady of the Lake. "Now use my bark and row yourself to the sword, and take it, together with the scabbard."

Arthur and Merlin tethered their horses to two trees, and boarded the bark. When Arthur had taken the sword and scabbard the arm disappeared into the water.

On the homeward journey they repassed King Pellinore's pavilion, and Arthur asked Merlin why King Pellinore was not there. "He has been fighting Sir Egglame, and has chased him nearly all the way into Caerleon,"[10] Merlin replied.

"What a pity!" said Arthur. "Because now that I have this beautiful sword I should like to fight him again, and perhaps this time have my revenge."

"That you shall not do," said Merlin. "King Pellinore is already tired from his fight with Sir Egglame. To win would bring you no honor, to lose would be to increase your shame. And lose you might, because he is still stronger than you are."

"I will do as you advise," said Arthur, as he examined his sword once more, admiring its beauty and temper. "Tell me," said Merlin, "do you prefer the sword or the scabbard?"

"The sword," said Arthur.

"You are a fool," said Merlin. "The scabbard is worth ten of the sword, because while you wear it, regardless of how seriously you are wounded, you will lose no blood."

They were drawing close to Caerleon when they passed King Pellinore; he appeared not to see them. "Why," asked Arthur, "did King Pellinore not speak to us?"

"Because he did not see us," Merlin replied. "I cast a spell over him; had he done so, you would not have escaped so lightly."

When Arthur and Merlin arrived at the court, they were questioned eagerly on all that had happened; and when the story was told, Arthur's knights rejoiced in the boldness of their king.

Medieval idea: Honor was an important part of the code of knighthood (p. 33).

---

10. **Caerleon:** Arthur's residence.

STUDY QUESTIONS

Recalling

1. On what condition does Arthur make Gryfflette a knight? What reasons does King Pellinore give for his initial reluctance to joust with Sir Gryfflette?

2. Why does Arthur decide to fight with Pellinore? How is Arthur's life saved during his combat with Pellinore?

3. After Arthur's sword is broken in the combat, how does he get his new sword and scabbard? Why is the scabbard more valuable than the sword Excalibur itself?

4. What reason does Merlin give to dissuade Arthur from fighting Pellinore again after Pellinore chases Sir Egglame? Why does King Pellinore not see Arthur and Merlin when they pass him on their way to Caerleon?

Interpreting

5. What qualities about Pellinore does King Arthur value highly? Why does Arthur react angrily when he thinks Merlin has slain Pellinore?

6. In general, what is Merlin's role in this selection? What is ironic about the knights' reaction to King Arthur at the end?

7. Besides the points noted in the margin of the selection, what medieval ideals and characteristics do the actions of Gryfflette, Merlin, and Arthur celebrate?

Extending

8. According to the modern American novelist John Steinbeck, "The myth of King Arthur continues even into the present day." He suggests that the television western, for example, bears many similarities to the world of King Arthur. What similarities do you see between the two worlds?

VIEWPOINT

The scholar Derek Brewer has noted that *Le Morte d'Arthur* expresses

the enduring contemporary need to reconcile the individual's demands with those of society, to recognize and cherish personal integrity and true love, and to create a good society.

■ Brewer is reminding us that while the knights are individuals, they are also members of a larger group to which they owe service. In this selection in what ways do the individual characters attempt to improve the society in which they live?

LITERARY FOCUS

Myth, Legend, and Literature

A **myth** is an anonymous traditional story with its roots in cultural or national folk beliefs that rely on the supernatural to explain the mysteries of the world. A **legend** is also a traditional tale handed down from generation to generation, but unlike a myth, a legend is believed to be based on history. Usually, a legend celebrates the heroic qualities of a national leader.

The world that Malory created for Arthur is far from the primitive world of the Celts and Anglo-Saxons. Rather, it is the world of chivalry—a world of elaborate courtesy and high ideals, in which the knights devote their formidable skills to making life better for the poor and oppressed, thereby ridding society of many of its dangers. Thus, the historic Arthur becomes a legendary figure.

Thinking About Myth, Legend, and Literature

■ Find at least two details in this selection that contribute to the picture of King Arthur as a legendary hero.

COMPOSITION

Writing About Character

■ Write an essay that presents Pellinore's character clearly, with his strengths as well as his defects. Consider first what we are directly told about him by Malory. Then explain what we indirectly learn from what he says and does and from what others say about him. Support each assertion with specific evidence from the selection.

Writing a Description

■ Use your imagination to describe one of Arthur and Pellinore's jousts as vividly as you can. Choose vivid details and action words to create a clear impression of the sight, sound, and movement of the struggle.

COMPARING WRITERS

1. The ballads, Chaucer, and Malory all present medieval knights and heroes. Select a knight or a hero from two of the selections in this unit, and explain in which ways the two figures are similar and in which respects they are different.

2. In "The Prologue" to *The Canterbury Tales,* the Host specifies that a good story must entertain and contain a moral. The ballads, "The Pardoner's Tale," and the excerpt from *Le Morte d'Arthur* are all examples of medieval storytelling. Which do you think comes closest to meeting the Host's conditions for a good story?

READING FOR APPRECIATION

Details of Characterization

Earlier in this book (page 62), we talked about the vital importance of details in a work of literature. Details enrich and deepen a work; they give substance to a setting, fill out the turns of a plot, lend plausibility to an action.

Details, then, are crucial to a literary work overall and especially important in characterization. Often what we remember best about a novel is a certain character whom we feel we have come to know deeply. The novelist's art has rendered that character strong, complex, fascinating—*believable.* A good deal of that believability, that art, comes from the author's selection of revealing details.

Consider for a moment some of the other arts. Good sculptors and portrait painters seek to distill and capture in a single frozen image the truth about the character of the individual being portrayed. In the same way, good writers strive for truth, depth, and distinctiveness in the characters they create. For sculptors, painters, and writers alike the most effective way to achieve this genuineness and individuality is through the imaginative and artistic choice of telling details.

In the Prologue to *The Canterbury Tales,* Chaucer introduces us to the pilgrims who will journey together to Canterbury in the course of the poem. One by one, he identifies the pilgrims, then describes them with numerous details that distinguish each portrayal.

First we meet the Knight, who, we are told at the outset, has fought hard and nobly and has lived chivalrously, honorably, and wisely: "He was a true, a perfect gentle-knight." Chaucer simply states these things, but notice how he ends this portrayal:

> . . . he possessed
> Fine horses, but he was not gaily dressed.
> He wore a fustian tunic stained and dark
> With smudges where his armor had left mark.

These details, placed near the end of the description, leave us with our sharpest impression of the Knight. Although he owns fine horses (an indication of high stature), he is himself unpretentious. Rather than fancy dress, as befits a man of his position, he chooses a rough tunic that even bears the old dark stains of the armor he used to wear. The implication in these details is that the Knight is both proud of his accomplishments and humble in the face of them.

Of course, writers are not restricted to details of physical appearance. They can also build a characterization through details of physical *action.* A little later in the Prologue we encounter the Nun, an exemplar of proper behavior and good manners:

> No morsel from her lips did she let fall,
> Nor dipped her fingers in the sauce too deep . . .
> And she would wipe her upper lip so clean
> That not a trace of grease was to be seen
> Upon the cup when she had drunk.

Through the accumulation of these amusing details, observed in a series of intense "close-ups"—from the morsel of meat to her lips to her fingers to the rim of her cup—the poet creates a picture of the Nun as a woman pristine, angelically graceful, and altogether pure. However, we can detect in this depiction of her rigorous cleanliness a certain extremism.

Why do both of these portraits leave an indelible impression? In each case Chaucer endows the characterization with precise, affectionate, revealing details, and these details help create for us a distinct and definitive image of the character.

THE ENGLISH VOICE

Order

When we think of the Middle Ages, we think of knights in shining armor. These battling lords and wandering heroes were actually a very small part of the population, but they remain the essential image of medieval adventure and romance. Yet knights were part of the complicated chivalric system just as the code of chivalry itself was part of the larger way of life called feudalism. As a part of feudalism, chivalry was not just a set of rules for good behavior: It was an *order*. Everyone—king, knight, lady, friar, squire, serf— knew his or her place. Everyone commanded and obeyed, served and was served, according to the ladder of society.

Sir Patrick Spens

"O wha is this has don this deid,
And told the king o' me,
To send us out at this time o' the yeir,
To sail upon the se!

"Mak ready, mak ready, my mirry men all,
Our guid schip sails the morne."

Chaucer

There was a Knight, a most distinguished man,
Who from the day on which he first began
To ride abroad had followed chivalry,
Truth, honor, generousness and courtesy.
He had done nobly in his sovereign's war
And ridden into battle, no man more.

He had his son with him, a fine young Squire,
A lover and cadet, a lad of fire. . . .
He'd seen some service with the cavalry
In Flanders and Artois and Picardy
And had done valiantly in little space
Of time, in hope to win his lady's grace.

Malory

"Hold your hand!" he said; you will endanger the whole realm. You do not realize who it is you are about to kill."
"Who is it, then?"
"King Arthur."

A lord's command or a lady's grace had the power to send someone into a ferocious storm at sea or into a distant desert. Any harm to the king meant harm to the whole realm—not because the king was powerful or rich or symbolic but because the king and the people were part of the vast medieval order.

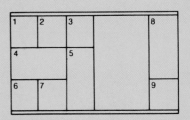
79

Key to Illustrations appears on page 197.

The Renaissance

THE ELIZABETHAN AGE

1485–1625

When Henry VII, a Tudor, became king of England in 1485, he was starting a new royal line. His defeat of Richard III and his marriage to a member of the House of York had ended the civil war known as the Wars of the Roses, and he could perhaps predict the time of peace and progress that his reign would bring to England until 1509. No one, however, could have predicted the events and forces that reshaped Henry's kingdom before the Tudor line ran out over a century later. Henry VII could not foresee his son Henry VIII marrying six wives and breaking with the Roman Catholic Church over a question of divorce and succession. Nor could Henry VII imagine his granddaughter Elizabeth's reign (1558–1603)—so long and illustrious that the whole period of history and the magnificent literature it produced came to be named for her.

The Growth of English Power

Luck, wisdom, and monumental forces were at work to produce the golden age that was to come to England by the late 1500s. To begin with, feudalism had collapsed. A new economy took shape and

Miniature of Queen Elizabeth I, after a portrait by John de Critz, seventeenth century.

brought great prosperity to the island. Money as well as land became a source of power; banking became a business. Secondly, overseas commerce helped to make the nation rich. Henry VII had been king for only seven years when Columbus landed in the New World. A few years later Englishman John Cabot sailed his ships along the coast of North America, establishing British claims to Newfoundland and New England.

During this time (the early 1500s) a religious revolution that had begun in central Europe was spreading across the Continent. It was called the Protestant Reformation, a protest against the powerful Roman Catholic Church. Until the Reformation the only form of Christianity in most of Europe was Roman Catholicism. The German monk Martin Luther and the French-born theologian John Calvin both criticized the established Church, disagreeing with its actions, its conduct, and even many of its beliefs. By the 1530s Henry VIII had reasons to align himself and England with the Protestants. He wanted his marriage to Catherine of Aragon annulled because she had not given him a male heir. When the Pope in Rome refused, Henry VIII broke with the Roman Catholic Church. He established the Church of England (the Anglican Church), and made himself its powerful head, initiating factional fighting among different religious groups that would

plague England until the end of the 1600s. It lasted even longer in Scotland and Ireland.

In 1588, during the reign of Elizabeth I, England became one of the great sea powers of the world. In that year Philip II, king of Spain and the most powerful ruler on the Continent, sent his renowned Spanish Armada to fight England's small navy. The fight seemed unequal; Philip should easily have invaded England, occupied it, and restored the supremacy of the Roman Catholic Church on the island. Yet the English navy won an amazing victory, aided by the inhospitable climate of the English seas. After this victory England forgot that it was a little island and became a great sea power. On December 31, 1599, the East India Company was chartered; world trade and colonization had begun. Nothing, not even the opening of the American frontier or our recent exploration of space, would ever match the explosion of energy in England in those days.

When Elizabeth I died in 1603, the throne of England went to her cousin James, king of Scotland and a member of the Stuart family that would rule England through most of the 1600s. Thus James VI of Scotland became James I of England, and the old island of Britain (England, Scotland, and Wales) was at last ruled by one monarch. Yet, as powerful as it became from 1485 to 1625, Great Britain, as we call it now, was still a small country, not only in area (smaller than Oregon) but also in population (probably at this time fewer than four million people).

Life in Elizabethan England

What kinds of people would you be likely to meet if you traveled along the narrow, winding, country trails of Elizabethan England? In the first place, if you were like most travelers, you would go miles without seeing anyone at all. Then you would probably get lost following the wrong trail through uncut forests. You would be fortunate if you did not meet a highwayman or two—cutthroats and robbers were numerous and dangerous—and you would most probably encounter a beggar. On the other hand, you could meet farmers and shepherds, prosperous-looking merchants, scholars, clerics, and nobles.

In London and in other cities, life was not so lonely. London was now one of the

Costume from the time of King James I.

great capitals of Europe, with a population of over 100,000. It was not free of poverty: Records indicate the presence of about 12,000 "begging poor." Nevertheless, especially when Elizabeth held her court there, the city seemed to sparkle with new wealth and energy. The Thames, and famous river that slides by London and then winds into the countryside, was both a thoroughfare for commerce and a playground for city residents. During the day it was filled with boats and barges of every size and shape; and as evening fell, pageants, music, and fireworks could be enjoyed by rich and poor alike.

The Influence of the Renaissance

While England was becoming an economic, religious, and naval power, it was also being influenced by a cultural movement, the Renaissance. Beginning in Italy with the writings of Petrarch and Boccaccio (see Part Two of this book), the **Renaissance** was a flowering of learning that swept from Italy into France and Germany and then across the Channel into England. Basically, the Renaissance was a period that saw reborn in Europe the interest in science, art, and all learning that had flourished in ancient Greece and Rome (see Part Two of this book). People became excited rather than frightened by unknown lands across the sea and by the unknown in

religion, in science, and in art. Europeans "discovered" new lands in America and the Pacific. They painted, sculpted, and composed music as never before. They tested outmoded learning in science, studied and created new forms of literature, and as explained in the discussion of the Protestant Reformation, questioned religious principles that had not been questioned for centuries.

All this flurry and creativity made its way to the court of Elizabeth I. When not involved with statecraft, the queen often occupied herself by giving new life and style to literature. She enjoyed it. She also enjoyed flattery (for chivalry was far from dead). Playwrights would dedicate their works to her, and often she was the direct subject of a piece of poetry, for writers sought her sponsorship and her favor. Responding to the new interest in learning of all kinds, the queen in 1571 reorganized and chartered the universities of Oxford and Cambridge. These

centers of learning, along with the court, the presence of printing, and the new-found wealth and consequently wider leisure for many helped to create an era of English literature that has never been surpassed. We judge its greatness not only in the works of Shakespeare but also in the new forms of literature that it explored successfully and in its abundance of talented poets and playwrights.

Elizabethan Poetry and Drama

Shakespeare and his work deserve and receive separate discussion in the pages ahead. Here we add only that he brought to its fullest flowering two new forms of written English literature: the lyric poem in sonnet form and the poetic drama.

The Elizabethan Age is an age of poetry. Except perhaps for the essayist Francis Bacon and the critic Christopher Marlowe, people were not yet writing prose of literary quality, of lasting beauty or interest. Later the translation of the Bible at the direction of King James I would do much to raise the low estate of prose writing, but, generally speaking, the literature of the age is the product of poets. Some Elizabethan writers dealt exclusively in lyric poetry, but many were also playwrights writing their plays in verse.

One new and crucial fact about these poets and play-

Globe Theatre, based on Visscher's view of London, 1616.

wrights is that almost all of them saw the writing of literature as their primary work in life and expected some financial reward for their efforts. In the Elizabethan Age there flourished three institutions that actively helped to support writing as a legitimate profession: acting companies, the universities, and the court.

An Elizabethan playwright made a very small amount of money for each play, not enough to support himself. Since actors and other members of the theatrical profession might make a better living, being a member of an acting company could give a playwright means to support himself and his work. And so, for example, Shakespeare was a professional actor. John Lyly for a short time gained control of Blackfriars Theatre, where his early plays were produced by a company in which all the actors were boys. (He later went into debt.) Thomas Kyd, author of *The Spanish Tragedy,* also earned a living in his father's business as a scrivener, by copying manuscripts by hand.

Many Elizabethan writers or their families were associated with universities or the royal court, both of which encouraged writers. Thomas Campion, a notable writer of songs and sonnets, began his career as a student at Oxford; Samuel Daniel, who often wrote patriotic verse, was the son of a well-educated music teacher. Both Edmund Spenser and Christo-

pher Marlowe wrote extensively while students at Cambridge. Sir Philip Sidney and Sir Walter Raleigh were high-born gentlemen and favorites at court.

At the same time that new and professional talent appeared, the form of poetry and drama changed. Unlike the long, storytelling poems of the Middle Ages, lyric poetry—poetry dealing with the emotions of the poet—was short, intricate, intellectual, and rigorous in form. The sonnet, which had its pedigree in Italy, was a popular form, and love was a popular topic. The poetic drama was also very different from the simple morality plays that were written in the Middle Ages.

Poetry and drama are not inseparable. To be sure, the great tragedies of ancient Greece—one of which, *Antigone,* appears in Part Two of this book—were written in verse, as were the great dramas of European countries. Most modern playwrights do not write in verse, however. The meeting of poetry and

drama in English literature—in the plays of William Shakespeare, Christopher Marlowe, John Lyly, Ben Jonson, and John Dryden, to name just a few— was glorious but relatively brief. It was glorious in its poetry and in the fact that poets produced plays that endure to this day. Yet after Shakespeare, Jonson, and Dryden, the poetic drama becomes very rare in English literature.

That the Elizabethan playwrights were skilled as poets may account for the magnificent language of their plays. It cannot account, however, for the distance covered between the medieval morality play and an Elizabethan drama such as *Macbeth.* Drama, poetic or otherwise, had obviously developed in many ways.

When we left drama in the villages of medieval England, it had by that time reached out beyond the confines of the church, both physically and intellectually. With the Renaissance, interest in ancient Greece and Rome led to the study of the works of Greek and Roman playwrights, especially the comedies of Plautus and Terence and the tragedies of Seneca. These plays often explored complex characters and themes, and they were widely imitated. Translators played a major part in the development of Elizabethan drama. It was not just coincidence that George Chapman, another famous playwright of the time, is even better known as a translator of the

William Shakespeare's home at Stratford-on-Avon.

works of the ancient Greek poet Homer.

The schools and universities contributed not only their scholarship but also an atmosphere in which drama served as entertainment. Students and teachers enjoyed working together to produce brief comedies and dialogues called **interludes** as campus entertainment. A new form of drama, of more historical than literary interest, was developing meanwhile at the court. This was the **masque,** a very stylized form of drama that involved dancing.

Ralph Roister Doister (1534) was the first true comedy of the period. It was written by Nicholas Udall, a headmaster at the Westminster School, a school for high-born boys in the borough of Westminster, within London. The comedy was about a braggart warrior whose bravery, as Alan Downer of Princeton puts it, is "purely verbal, and whose love affairs are inspired by an empty pocket rather than a warm heart." A few years later *Gammer Gurton's Needle,* a comedy by an unknown author, was produced at Cambridge University. Out of a simple comic situation

(a woman loses her sewing needle while sewing her husband's trousers and then "finds" the needle again when her husband sits down), this play stretches into a delightful entertainment, moving comedy closer to the traditional five-act form used by Shakespeare.

Meanwhile, two young playwrights, Thomas Sackville and Thomas Norton, wrote and produced *Gorboduc, or Ferrex and Porex,* a tragedy that followed the lines of an ancient Roman tragedy by Seneca. This play won the praise of Sir Phillip Sidney, and the queen herself was so inspired that she tried her own hand at translating Seneca.

These years saw a happy combination of the great literary accomplishments of ancient Greece and Rome, the soaring poetry of Elizabethan England, the young professional playwrights, and a new, cheering, theater-going public.

Queen Elizabeth I died in 1603, a convenience for historians who can end the sixteenth century more or less with her death and start talking about the Stuart kings of the seventeenth century. For the student of literature, however, 1603 is not quite so neat an end date. After all, some of the towering figures of what we think of as Elizabethan literature simply kept on writing after the queen's death. Shakespeare did not write *Macbeth* and other masterpieces in Elizabeth's lifetime, although he had the grace to retire happily to his home town, Stratford-on-Avon, soon after the turn of the century. Sir Walter Raleigh, Francis Bacon, and Ben Jonson—to name just a few "Elizabethans"—outlived and outwrote their queen. Literary historians would prefer, therefore, to give James I to the Elizabethan Age and to extend that period to 1625, the year in which King James died.

TIME LINE

1485–1625 BRITISH EVENTS

1485 Henry VII begins reign (until 1509)

King Henry VIII

1496 Scottish Parliament requires schooling for eldest sons

1503 Canterbury Cathedral (begun 1070) completed

1509 Henry VIII begins reign (until 1547)

1512 English navy builds double-deck ships with seventy guns

English seventy-gun ship

1516 Sir Thomas More, *Utopia*, statement of the ideal society

Copernicus' theory

1524 Soap first made in London

1527 Sonnet form introduced

1534 Henry VIII breaks with Roman Catholic Church

Ralph Roister Doister, first comedy of period

Sir Thomas More

1547 Edward VI begins reign (until 1553)

WORLD EVENTS 1485–1625

1492 Spain: Columbus reaches America

1497 North America: Italian John Cabot explores East Coast for the English

1501 Italy: Michelangelo begins to sculpt *David*

1503 Italy: da Vinci paints *Mona Lisa*

1512 Poland: Copernicus' theory that earth and other planets revolve around sun

1513 North America: Spaniard Balboa discovers Pacific Ocean; Spaniard Ponce de León discovers Florida

1514 Europe: Pineapples introduced

1517 Germany: Martin Luther, *Ninety-Five Theses*, declaring objections to abuses in the Church

Europe: Coffee introduced

1535 Canada: Frenchman Jacques Cartier sights St. Lawrence River, Quebec, and Montreal

1547 Russia: Ivan the Terrible crowned czar

1553 Mary I begins reign (until 1558)

1558 Elizabeth I begins reign (until 1603)

1563 Bubonic plague kills 20,000

1577 Sir Francis Drake begins sail around the world

c.1582 Sidney, *Astrophel and Stella*

Elizabeth I

1587 Marlowe, *Doctor Faustus*

1588 Defeat of Spanish Armada, by English ships

1590 First part of Spenser's *Faerie Queene*

1594 Shakespeare, *Romeo and Juliet*

1597 Bacon's first essays published

1599 Globe Theatre, home of Shakespeare's company, founded

East India Company chartered

Marlowe, "The Passionate Shepherd to His Love"

1603 James I begins reign (until 1625)

1606 Shakespeare, *Macbeth*

1611 King James Bible

Don Quixote

1623 Patent laws passed to protect inventions

1584 North America: Englishman Sir Walter Raleigh discovers Virginia

Globe Theatre

Shakespeare

1605 Spain: Cervantes, *Don Quixote, Part I*

1609 North America: Englishman Henry Hudson explores Delaware Bay and Hudson River

1615 Spain: Cervantes, *Don Quixote, Part II*

1620 North America: Pilgrims land at Plymouth

Sir Philip Sidney   *1554–1586*

A "Renaissance man" is someone who can do a variety of things exceptionally well, as so many great personalities of the Renaissance seemed able to do. The Italian Leonardo da Vinci, for example, was an architect, a scientist, and an inventor, as well as one of the world's greatest painters. Similarly, Sir Philip Sidney excelled in many ways during his brief life. Sidney was a courtier, a high-born attendant at court, and his refined, aristocratic behavior made him a particular favorite of Queen Elizabeth's. A student at Oxford, he was a great traveler who met many important teachers, writers, and statesmen during his sojourns on the Continent. Sidney was a noted patron of the arts, encouraging other writers in their work. He was also a man of convictions and a brave soldier, who gave his life on a battlefield while fighting for the Protestant cause in Holland.

Finally, Sir Philip Sidney was a gifted writer. His *Arcadia,* a story of romance, intrigue, and politics, is probably the finest imaginative prose work of the Elizabethan era, and his *Defense of Poesy* is the outstanding piece of literary criticism of the age. He is perhaps best noted, however, as the author of *Astrophel and Stella,* a sequence of mostly sonnets that began a tradition in English lyric poetry that others have followed to the present time. *Astrophel and Stella* is a series of 110 brief poems that develop a single subject, love. The poems do not tell a story. Instead, they examine love from many different perspectives. The two poems that follow are representative.

Sir Philip Sidney

Loving in Truth

Loving in truth, and fain[1] in verse my love to show,
That the dear she might take some pleasure of my pain,
Pleasure might cause her read, reading might make her know,
Knowledge might pity win, and pity grace[2] obtain,
5 I sought fit words to paint the blackest face of woe;
Studying inventions fine, her wits to entertain,
Oft turning others' leaves[3] to see if thence would flow
Some fresh and fruitful showers upon my sunburned brain.
But words came halting[4] forth, wanting Invention's stay;[5]
10 Invention, Nature's child, fled stepdame Study's blows;
And others' feet still seemed but strangers in my way.
Thus, great with child to speak, and helpless in my throes,
Biting my truant pen, beating myself for spite:
"Fool," said my Muse[6] to me, "look in thy heart, and write!"

1. **fain:** wanting, desiring.
2. **grace:** favor.
3. **leaves:** pages of books or manuscripts.
4. **halting:** limping.

5. **wanting . . . stay:** lacking the support of inspiration.
6. **Muse:** source of poetic inspiration. In Greek mythology muses presided over the various arts and sciences.

Sonnet 31

With how sad steps, Oh Moon, thou climb'st the skies!
How silently, and with how wan a face!
What, may it be that even in heavenly place
That busy archer[1] his sharp arrows tries?
5 Sure, if that long-with-love-acquainted eyes
Can judge of love, thou feel'st a lover's case,
I read it in thy looks; thy languished grace,
To me, that feel the like, thy state descries.[2]
Then, even of fellowship,[3] Oh Moon, tell me,
10 Is constant love deemed there but want of wit?[4]
Are beauties there as proud as here they be?
Do they above love to be loved, and yet
Those lovers scorn whom that love doth possess?
Do they call virtue there ungratefulness?[5]

1. **That . . . archer:** Cupid, god of love.
2. **descries:** reveals.
3. **even of fellowship:** that is, because we both know what it is to be in love.

4. **wit:** intelligence.
5. **Do . . . ungratefulness:** Is to be ungrateful to one who loves you called a virtue?

STUDY QUESTIONS

Loving in Truth

Recalling

1. According to the first two lines, what is the speaker trying to show in his poems? According to line 4, what is his ultimate goal?
2. According to lines 6–7, where does the speaker look for help? Which lines indicate that these two sources prove unsatisfactory?
3. What does the speaker's "Muse" finally tell him?

Interpreting

4. According to line 6, what sort of poem does the speaker seem to think his love will like? Do lines 2–4 reflect that kind of poem? Why or why not?
5. What does the speaker finally conclude he must write to his love? How does his conclusion contradict what he seems to think in lines 1–8?

Extending

6. Think of a difficult assignment or project that you have done in the past. Did some kind of inspiration help you to complete it? Where did you find that inspiration?

Sonnet 31

Recalling

1. How does the speaker describe the moon's "face" in line 2? What question does he ask in lines 3–4?
2. According to lines 5–9, what do the speaker and the moon have in common?
3. In your own words, tell what the speaker asks in lines 10–14.

Interpreting

4. What does the description of the moon in lines 1–8 suggest about the speaker's emotions when he is in love?
5. What do the questions that conclude the poem imply about the object of the speaker's love?

Extending

6. In Sidney's title *Astrophel and Stella* the first word is Greek for "starlover," and the second word is Latin for "star." What might Sidney be saying by thinking of himself as Astrophel and his love as Stella?

LITERARY FOCUS

The Sonnet, Meter, and Stanza Forms

Most of the brief, self-contained poems that make up Sidney's *Astrophel and Stella* are sonnets. *Astrophel and Stella* started a vogue among English poets of the time, and by the end of the sixteenth century, hundred of sonnets had appeared.

Sidney did not invent sonnet form; it was originated by the Italian poet Petrarch (see Part Two of this book). A **sonnet** (from the Italian for "little song") is a poem of fourteen lines, each containing five feet **(pentameter).** Each foot is usually an **iamb,** an unstressed syllable (marked ˘) followed by a stressed syllable (marked ʹ). This regular rhythm, or meter, is known as **iambic pentameter.**

Are beau / ties there / as proud / as they /
here be?/

Sonnet form is also characterized by its pattern of end-of-line rhyme. In analyzing a sonnet, we use letters of the alphabet to represent the end words that rhyme. Thus, we say that the **Italian,** or **Petrarchan, sonnet** is divided into two parts in which the first eight lines, or **octave,** usually follow a rhyme scheme of *abbaabba* or *abababab*. The last six lines, or **sestet,** may have one of several rhyme combinations—for example, *cdecde* or *cdcdee*. Usually, the octave asks a question or presents a problem, and the sestet answers the question or draws a conclusion.

An **English,** or **Shakespearean, sonnet** consists of three groups of four lines each, called **quatrains,** followed by two lines that rhyme with each other, called a **rhymed couplet.** The rhyme scheme is usually *abab cdcd efef gg*. Often the couplet draws a conclusion or makes an important point.

Thinking About Sonnets

1. What is the rhyme scheme of Sidney's Sonnet 31?
2. Copy one line from Sidney's Sonnet 31, and mark its division into five feet, showing the light and heavy stresses.
3. Point to the break between the octave and sestet in Sonnet 31. What is the relationship between the two parts?

Edmund Spenser *1552–1599*

Known as the "prince of poets" in his time, Edmund Spenser is generally regarded as the greatest nondramatic poet of the Elizabethan Age. He was born in London to a poor family and was educated at Cambridge on a scholarship. He studied philosophy, rhetoric, Italian, French, Latin, and Greek to prepare himself as a poet.

Spenser's most notable and ambitious poetic achievement is *The Faerie Queene,* set in the mythical world of King Arthur and his knights. Spenser had planned twelve books for *The Faerie Queene,* but he completed only six. Each book has a hero knight who performs noble deeds for a glorious fairy queen whom Spenser intentionally associates with Queen Elizabeth. The knight in each book represents a different moral virtue: justice, courtesy, and so on. Obstacles the knight enounters in the poem stand for evils and temptations that must be overcome, all in an enchanted world of dragons, giants, witches, and other marvels.

For *The Faerie Queene* Spenser invented a new stanza form, a nine-line stanza, rhyming *ababbcbcc.* The first eight lines are iambic pentameter; the last line has six iambic feet instead of five and is called an alexandrine. Known now as the Spenserian stanza, this nine-line format was used by later English poets such as Byron, Keats, Shelley, and Robert Burns.

Edmund Spenser

from The Faerie Queene

Upon a great adventure he was bond,[1]
   That greatest Gloriana to him gave,
   That greatest Glorious Queen of Faerie lond,
   To win him worship,[2] and her grace to have,
5   Which of all earthly things he most did crave;
   And ever as he rode, his heart did yearn
   To prove his puissance[3] in battle brave
   Upon his foe, and his new force to learn;
Upon his foe, a Dragon horrible and stern.

---

1. **bond:** bound.
2. **worship:** illustrious fame.
3. **puissance** [pū′ə sans]: strength, power.

Spenser did not write plays, as Shakespeare and many of his contemporaries did. Instead, he excelled in lyric and narrative poetry. Among his most famous lyrical poems are the sonnets in *Amoretti,* a sequence of "little love poems," and his moving *Astrophel,* an elegy, or death lament, for his friend and patron Sir Philip Sidney, who died at the age of thirty-two. Sonnet 75 is from Spenser's *Amoretti,* a sequence of eighty-eight sonnets recounting the courtship of a woman, possibly Elizabeth Boyle, whom he later married.

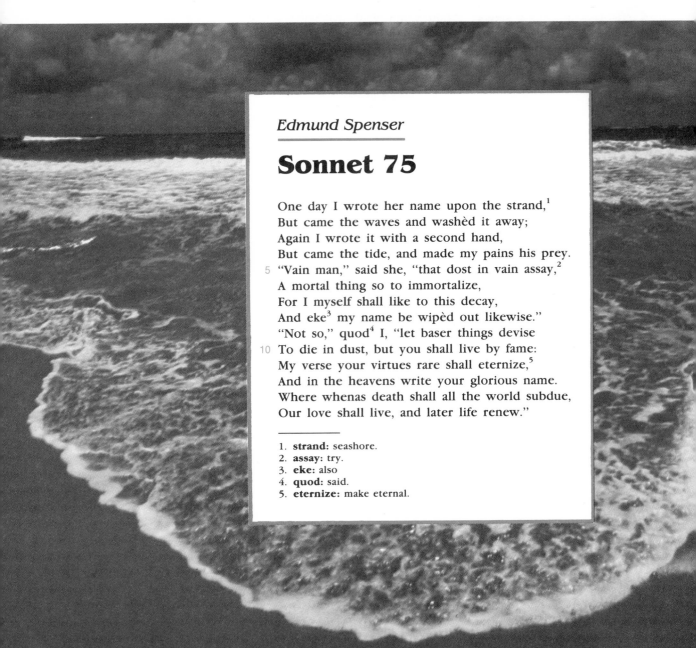

Edmund Spenser

Sonnet 75

One day I wrote her name upon the strand,[1]
But came the waves and washèd it away;
Again I wrote it with a second hand,
But came the tide, and made my pains his prey.
5 "Vain man," said she, "that dost in vain assay,[2]
A mortal thing so to immortalize,
For I myself shall like to this decay,
And eke[3] my name be wipèd out likewise."
"Not so," quod[4] I, "let baser things devise
10 To die in dust, but you shall live by fame:
My verse your virtues rare shall eternize,[5]
And in the heavens write your glorious name.
Where whenas death shall all the world subdue,
Our love shall live, and later life renew."

---

1. **strand:** seashore.
2. **assay:** try.
3. **eke:** also.
4. **quod:** said.
5. **eternize:** make eternal.

STUDY QUESTIONS

from *The Faerie Queene*

Recalling

1. According to the poem, who is Gloriana? What more than anything else on earth, does the knight want?
2. Who is the knight's foe? How will the knight prove his "puissance"?

Interpreting

3. Identify three characteristics of the knight as presented in this stanza. What is the chief characteristic of Gloriana?
4. What elements of chivalry, the important code of medieval knights, are reflected in this stanza? Consider the introduction to the preceding unit ("The Medieval Period") as well as medieval literature.

Sonnet 75

Recalling

1. Where does the speaker write the name of his love? What happens to what he has written?
2. According to lines 5–8, why does his love think him vain? What does she say will happen to her?
3. In lines 9–14, what does the speaker say his verses will do? What does he say will live after death has "subdued" all the world?

Interpreting

4. To what time is the speaker referring in the last two lines? With what belief is he therefore associating his love?

5. Is Spenser's Sonnet 75 more like an Italian sonnet or an English sonnet (see page 90)? Explain.

Extending

6. What other methods do you think could be used to "eternize" someone? Consider in particular technology that has evolved since Spenser's time.

COMPOSITION

Writing a Comparison/Contrast

■ Spenser's Sonnet 75 and Sidney's Sonnet 31 (page 89) both express the speakers' feelings about love. In a brief essay contrast the feelings of the two speakers. First state the feelings expressed in Sidney's poem, using details from the poem to support your statements. Then describe the emotions expressed in the poem by Spenser. Conclude with a short paragraph stating the differences between the two speakers' attitudes toward love. *For help with this assignment, refer to Lesson 2 in the Writing About Literature Handbook at the back of this book.*

Writing a Sonnet

■ Compose a sonnet that demonstrates your understanding of sonnet form. Though your sonnet may be unpolished, be sure it has fourteen lines of iambic pentameter and a rhyme scheme similar to that of Sidney's Sonnet 1, Sidney's Sonnet 31, or Spenser's Sonnet 75. You might write your end-rhyme words first and then fill in the rest of each line.

Christopher Marlowe *1564–1593*
Sir Walter Raleigh *1552–1618*

Christopher Marlowe.

Born in the same year as Shakespeare, Christopher Marlowe was killed in a brawl when he was just twenty-nine. Some maintain the brawl erupted from an argument over paying the bill. Others think that Marlowe was killed as a result of espionage work he had done for the government.

If Shakespeare had died at twenty-nine, his greatest plays would have remained unwritten, and we would scarcely recognize his name. Yet, Marlowe, by the time of his death had already established himself as a powerful dramatist—earning the title "father of English tragedy." His tragedies, *Tamburlaine, The Jew of Malta,* and *Dr. Faustus* place him second only to Shakespeare himself as the greatest playwright of the time.

In addition to his plays, Marlowe wrote one of the most famous of Elizabethan lyric poems, "The Passionate Shepherd to His Love." The poem is an invitation to the pastoral life, the happy peaceful life of country shepherds.

Sir Walter Raleigh.

Soldier, explorer, courtier, poet, and historian—Sir Walter Raleigh is one of the most colorful figures in English history. He founded the colony of Virginia, introduced tobacco to Europe, and fought the Spanish Armada. A famous story also has gallant Sir Walter removing his cloak and dropping it to the ground so that Queen Elizabeth could navigate a puddle without wetting her royal feet. Raleigh was also a great help to other artists of Elizabethan times. A friend of Marlowe and Spenser, he managed to obtain royal aid to help publish the first three books of Spenser's *Faerie Queene.*

James I, Elizabeth's successor, feared and distrusted Raleigh. During James's reign Raleigh was charged with treason and was convicted and sentenced to death. He was imprisoned instead in the Tower of London, where for twelve years he lived with his family and servants and wrote his *History of the World.* After a failed quest to South America for gold that was to buy his release, Raleigh was executed in 1618. Maintaining his equanimity until the end, Raleigh is said to have composed one of his best poems, "The Author's Epitaph, Made by Himself," the night before he died.

Much of Raleigh's poetry has been lost, but one gem that has survived is "The Nymph's Reply to the Shepherd," which appears on page 96. In it Raleigh's speaker, a young woman, replies to Marlowe's famous "passionate shepherd."

Christopher Marlowe

The Passionate Shepherd to His Love

Come live with me and be my love,
And we will all the pleasures prove[1]
That valleys, groves, hills, and fields,
Woods, or steepy mountain yields.

5 And we will sit upon the rocks,
Seeing the shepherds feed their flocks,
By shallow rivers to whose falls
Melodious birds sing madrigals.[2]

And I will make thee beds of roses
10 And a thousand fragrant posies,
A cap of flowers, and a kirtle[3]
Embroidered all with leaves of myrtle;

A gown made of the finest wool
Which from our pretty lambs we pull;
15 Fair lined slippers for the cold,
With buckles of the purest gold;

A belt of straw and ivy buds,
With coral clasps and amber studs:
And if these pleasures may thee move,
20 Come live with me, and be my love.

The shepherds' swains[4] shall dance and sing
For thy delight each May morning:
If these delights thy mind may move,
Then live with me and be my love.

---

1. **prove:** experience.
2. **madrigals:** here, harmonious songs.
3. **kirtle:** dress.
4. **swains:** country youths.

Sir Walter Raleigh

The Nymph's Reply to the Shepherd

If all the world and love were young,
And truth in every shepherd's tongue,
These pretty pleasures might me move
To live with thee and be thy love.

5 Time drives the flocks from field to fold[1]
When rivers rage and rocks grow cold,
And Philomel[2] becometh dumb;
The rest complains of cares to come.

The flowers do fade, and wanton[3] fields
10 To wayward winter reckoning yields;
A honey tongue, a heart of gall,[4]
Is fancy's spring, but sorrow's fall.

Thy gowns, thy shoes, thy beds of roses,
Thy cap, thy kirtle, and thy posies
15 Soon break, soon wither, soon forgotten—
In folly ripe, in reason rotten.

Thy belt of straw and ivy buds,
Thy coral clasps and amber studs,
All these in me no means can move
20 To come to thee and be thy love.

But could youth last and love still breed,[5]
Had joys no date[6] nor age no need,
Then these delights my mind might move
To live with thee and be thy love.

---

1. **fold:** enclosure or pen for sheep.
2. **Philomel:** According to Greek myth, the princess Philomela's tongue was cut out to prevent her from revealing a scandal. Later the gods turned Philomela into a nightingale.
3. **wanton:** here, profuse or ample.
4. **gall:** bitterness.
5. **still breed:** always thrive.
6. **date:** ending.

The Passionate Shepherd to His Love

Recalling

1. What does the shepherd entreat his love to do in the first stanza? What pleasures does he say he and his love will "prove"?
2. Name three things that the shepherd claims he will do for his love.

Interpreting

3. Which of the speaker's promises seem unrealistic? Why would the speaker make these promises?
4. What is the effect of the repetition of line 1 in lines 20 and 24? Does the entreaty become more or less persuasive with each repetition? Does the speaker sound more or less confident than earlier in the poem? Explain.

The Nymph's Reply to the Shepherd

Recalling

1. According to the first stanza, what would make the nymph accept the shepherd's offer?
2. What does the nymph say will happen to the flowers and fields promised by the shepherd (stanza 3)? What does she say will happen to the gown, shoes, rose beds, cap, kirtle, and posies (stanza 4)?
3. According to the last stanza, what would make the nymph accept the shepherd's offer?

Interpreting

4. What do all the predictions in stanzas 3 and 4 have in common? Basically, why does the speaker find the shepherd's offer unimpressive?
5. How are the views expressed in the first and last stanzas similar? Is the speaker saying there is a possibility she will accept the shepherd's offer, or is her answer a definite "no"? Explain.

COMPOSITION

Developing a Thesis Statement

Develop a thesis statement about what Raleigh's poem adds to your reaction to Marlowe's poem, and in a brief essay defend your thesis with examples from the two poems. Before you write, first consider what you thought of Marlowe's poem when you initially read it. Then consider your impression of Marlowe's poem after reading Raleigh's response to it. *For help with this assignment, refer to Lesson 1 in the Writing About Literature Handbook at the back of this book.*

Writing a Letter

Write your own reply in the form of a letter to the shepherd in Marlowe's poem. Like Raleigh, you might pretend to be the woman whom the shepherd addresses. Explain why you accept or refuse his offer. If you prefer, pretend to be another suitor for the lady's hand, and explain why you can offer her a better life than the shepherd can. Your letter may be serious or humorous, but it should refer to the specific promises that the shepherd makes as well as to the general picture he paints.

William Shakespeare   *1564–1616*

William Shakespeare, poet and playwright, is said to be the world's favorite author. No other writer's plays have been produced so often and read so widely in so many different countries. Shakespeare's contemporaries first admired him for his long narrative poems *Venus and Adonis* (1593) and *The Rape of Lucrece* (1594). In the latter half of the seventeenth century and in the eighteenth century, he was revered for his dramas. Poets and critics in the nineteenth century considered him the "genius of the English race," and in the twentieth century he is regarded as the greatest of all writers for the stage.

Not much is known about Shakespeare's early life. He was born in 1564, probably on April 23, in the small country town of Stratford-on-Avon. His father was a prosperous glove maker and held several important positions in the town government. His mother, Mary Arden, was the daughter of a wealthy landowner. By the age of seven, Shakespeare was probably attending the local grammar school.

In 1582 when he was eighteen, Shakespeare married Anne Hathaway, the twenty-six-year-old daughter of a farmer who lived about a mile from Stratford. Over the next three years the couple had a daughter, Susanna, and twins, Hamnet and Judith. From 1585 to 1592, a period some scholars call "the lost years," virtually nothing is known about Shakespeare's life. From 1592 on, however, the records are much fuller. Sometime during the lost years Shakespeare moved to London and became part of the city's busy theatrical life. By 1594 he was a shareholder, or part owner, in one of London's most popular acting companies, the Lord Chamberlain's Men, and at least six of his plays had been produced. (Each shareholder contributed in some way to the company. Shakespeare was both a writer and actor; he is said to have played the ghost in *Hamlet.* The more popular his plays, the larger his share of the company's income.) In 1599 the company built the Globe Theatre, the most famous of Elizabethan theaters.

After Queen Elizabeth's death in 1603, the Lord Chamberlain's Men were sponsored by King James I and became known as the King's Men. In 1608 the company acquired a second theater in Blackfriars, a fashionable district of London. Shakespeare seems to have retired from acting about this time; his name does not appear in the lists of players after 1607. Between 1608 and 1613 Shakespeare wrote his last five plays: *Pericles, Cymbeline, The Winter's Tale, The Tempest,* and *Henry VIII.* While he was writing these plays, Shakespeare lived mostly in Stratford, where he was regarded as one of the town's most important citizens. He died on April 23, 1616, and is buried in Holy Trinity Church in Stratford.

What makes Shakespeare the world's favorite author? No other writer—playwright, poet, or novelist—has seen more deeply into the many manifestations of human nature. In an uncanny way Shakespeare understands why people behave the way they do. Young and old, women and men, good and evil, beggars and kings: All live in his plays. All speak in voices so right and so true that again and again they emerge as solid as life, as much at home in our time as in Shakespeare's own.

In addition to his plays and two narrative poems, Shakespeare wrote a sequence of 154 sonnets. It was probably written in the 1590s, when Sir Philip Sidney's sequence, *Astrophel and Stella,* was so popular. Unlike the other sequences of his day, Shakespeare's cycle seems to tell a story. The plot is vague and fragmentary, involving a young nobleman, a "dark lady," a poet, and a rival poet. The sonnets that follow are addressed to the young nobleman. Shakespeare urges the man to marry and to have children, who will immortalize his virtues while time and age take their toll. The "plot" of the "story" is not as important as Shakespeare's themes regarding time, beauty, and love.

William Shakespeare

Sonnet 18

Shall I compare thee to a summer's day?
Thou art more lovely and more temperate.
Rough winds do shake the darling buds of May,
And summer's lease[1] hath all too short a date.[2]
5 Sometime too hot the eye of heaven shines,
And often is his gold complexion dimmed;
And every fair from fair[3] sometime declines,
By chance or nature's changing course untrimmed;[4]
But thy eternal summer shall not fade,
10 Nor lose possession of that fair thou ow'st,[5]
Nor shall Death brag thou wand'rest in his shade,
When in eternal lines[6] to time thou grow'st.
   So long as men can breathe or eyes can see,
   So long lives this, and this gives life to thee.

---

1. **lease:** allotted time.
2. **date:** duration.
3. **fair . . . fair:** beautiful thing from beauty.

4. **untrimmed:** stripped of beauty.
5. **thou ow'st:** you possess.
6. **lines:** lines of poetry.

William Shakespeare

Sonnet 29

When, in disgrace[1] with Fortune and men's eyes,
I all alone beweep my outcast state,
And trouble deaf heaven with my bootless[2] cries,
And look upon myself and curse my fate,
5 Wishing me like to one more rich in hope,
Featured like him, like him with friends possessed,
Desiring this man's art[3] and that man's scope,[4]
With what I most enjoy contented least;
Yet in these thoughts myself almost despising,
10 Haply[5] I think on thee, and then my state,
Like to the lark at break of day arising
From sullen earth, sings hymns at heaven's gate;
For thy sweet love rememb'red such wealth brings,
That then I scorn to change my state with kings.

1. **disgrace:** disfavor.
2. **bootless:** useless, futile.
3. **art:** skill.

4. **scope:** mental power.
5. **Haply:** by chance.

Sonnet 30

When to the sessions[1] of sweet silent thought
I summon up remembrance of things past,
I sigh the lack of many a thing I sought,
And with old woes new[2] wail my dear time's waste.
5 Then can I drown an eye, unused to flow,
For precious friends hid in death's dateless[3] night,
And weep afresh love's long since canceled[4] woe,
And moan th' expense[5] of many a vanished sight;
Then can I grieve at grievances foregone,[6]
10 And heavily from woe to woe tell[7] o'er
The sad account of fore-bemoanèd moan,
Which I new pay as if not paid before.
  But if the while I think on thee, dear friend,
  All losses are restored and sorrows end.

1. **sessions:** that is, sittings of a law court.
2. **new:** again.
3. **dateless:** endless.
4. **canceled:** that is, because paid in full.

5. **expense:** loss.
6. **grievances foregone:** earlier griefs.
7. **tell:** count.

Sonnet 55

Not marble, nor the gilded monuments
Of princes, shall outlive this pow'rful rhyme,
But you shall shine more bright in these contents
Than unswept stone, besmeared with sluttish time.[1]
5 When wasteful war shall statues overturn,
And broils[2] root out the work of masonry,
Nor Mars his sword nor[3] war's quick fire shall burn
The living record of your memory.
'Gainst death and all-oblivious enmity[4]
10 Shall you pace forth; your praise shall still find room
Even in the eyes of all posterity
That wear this world out[5] to the ending doom.
    So, till the judgment that yourself arise,[6]
    You live in this, and dwell in lovers' eyes.

---

1. **Than . . . time:** than in a stone tomb or on a memorial
tablet, worn down by time and covered with dust.
2. **broils:** skirmishes, battles.
3. **Nor Mars . . . nor:** neither the Roman war god's sword nor . . .
4. **oblivious enmity:** enmity, or hostility, that brings oblivion,
causing us to be forgotten.
5. **wear . . . out:** outlast this world.
6. **So . . . arise:** so until you rise from the dead on Judgment Day.

Sonnet 73

That time of year thou mayst in me behold
When yellow leaves, or none, or few, do hang
Upon those boughs which shake against the cold,
Bare ruined choirs,[1] where late the sweet birds sang.
5 In me thou see'st the twilight of such day
As after sunset fadeth in the west;
Which by and by black night doth take away,
Death's second self[2] that seals up all in rest.
In me thou see'st the glowing of such fire,
10 That on the ashes of his youth doth lie,
As the deathbed whereon it must expire,
Consumed with that which it was nourished by.[3]
    This thou perceiv'st which makes thy love more strong,
    To love that well which thou must leave ere long.

---

1. **choirs:** choir lofts; parts of church interiors occupied by choirs.
2. **Death's . . . self:** that is, sleep.
3. **Consumed . . . by:** choked by the ashes of the wood that previously
fueled its flame.

Model for Active Reading

In this selection, as in one selection in each unit, you will find notes in the right-hand margin that highlight parts of the selection. These notes point out important ideas of the literary period and draw your attention to literary elements and techniques covered in the Literary Focuses. Page numbers in the notes refer you to more extensive discussions of these important ideas and elements.

William Shakespeare

Sonnet 116

Let me not to the marriage of true minds
Admit impediments.[1] Love is not love
Which alters when it alteration finds
Or bends with the remover to remove.[2]
5 Oh, no, it is an ever-fixèd mark[3]
That looks on tempests and is never shaken;
It is the star to every wand'ring bark,[4]
Whose worth's unknown, although his height[5] be taken.
Love's not Time's fool,[6] though rosy lips and cheeks
10 Within his bending sickle's compass[7] come;
Love alters not with his[8] brief hours and weeks,
But bears it out even to the edge of doom.[9]
If this be error and upon[10] me proved,
I never writ, nor no man ever loved.

Sonnet (p. 90): The English, or Shakespearean, sonnet consists of three quatrains (*abab cdcd efef*) and a rhymed couplet (*gg*).

Elizabethan idea: The definition of *love* reflects the intellectual side of Elizabethan poetry (p. 83).

Figurative language (p. 104): Shakespeare uses a variety of metaphors to make the abstract *love* more concrete.

Elizabethan idea: Lyric poetry expressed human emotions as well as intellect (p. 84).

---

1. **impediments:** reasons for preventing a marriage. Compare the Marriage Service: "If any of you know cause or just impediment why these persons should not be joined together . . ."
2. **Or . . . remove:** or withdraws when the object of its love leaves.
3. **an . . . mark:** a permanent beacon.
4. **star . . . bark:** that is, the North Star, used by sailors in barks, or boats, for navigation.
5. **height:** altitude.
6. **fool:** plaything.
7. **compass:** circle, range.
8. **his:** that is, Time's.
9. **doom:** Judgment Day.
10. **upon:** against.

STUDY QUESTIONS

Sonnet 18

Recalling

1. According to lines 1–8, in what ways is the speaker's friend unlike a summer's day?
2. What will prevent the friend's eternal summer from fading, according to lines 9–12?

Interpreting

3. What does "this" refer to in the last line?
4. What is the speaker's purpose in writing his "eternal lines," and what conditions are necessary for his purpose to be carried out?

Sonnet 29

Recalling

1. List the speaker's catalogue of complaints in the first eight lines.
2. What does the speaker remember in line 10? What image describes his mood in lines 11 and 12?

Interpreting

3. Compare the speaker's thoughts in the first eight lines of the sonnet to his thoughts in the last six lines. How has his perspective changed, especially in the last two lines?

Extending

4. Is the transition in the speaker's mood realistic or insincere? Why or why not?

Sonnet 30

Recalling

1. What does the speaker think of in the first quatrain, and what does that lead him to express in the second quatrain?
2. As a result of his thoughts in the second quatrain, what does the speaker reexperience in the next quatrain?
3. Whom does the speaker think of in the final couplet? How does this affect his mood?

Interpreting

4. What do the last two lines, coming after three quatrains that express a contrasting point of view, add to the overall effect of the poem?
5. Besides the image of a court session in lines 1–2, what other image does the sonnet introduce in line 7 with "canceled" and continue in lines 10–12? Why is the image appropriate?

Sonnet 55

Recalling

1. In lines 1–4 what does the speaker say will not outlive the poem?
2. In lines 5–8 what cannot destroy the poem?
3. Therefore, what will find room "in the eyes of all posterity"?

Interpreting

4. Whose eyes is the phrase "lovers' eyes" referring to?

Extending

5. Do you think this poem has accomplished its purpose? Give reasons for your answer.

Sonnet 73

Recalling

1. The speaker associates himself with what time of year in lines 1–2? With what time of day in lines 5–6? With what kind of fire in lines 9–10?
2. What does the friend, addressed in lines 13–14, "perceiv'st"?

Interpreting

3. How does the speaker take the image in lines 1–2 and expand it in lines 3–4? Show that the speaker makes a similar expansion for the images in lines 5–6 and 9–10.
4. What do all the images in lines 1–12 symbolize?
5. According to the final couplet, for what is the speaker praising his friend? How does the couplet tie in emotionally with the first twelve lines?

Sonnet 116

Recalling

1. List three or four things that love is *not*, according to Sonnet 116.
2. List several things that love *is*, according to Sonnet 116.

Interpreting

3. What is the meaning of the image of the star in lines 7–8? How does this image apply to love?

Extending

4. Do you agree or disagree with the speaker's interpretation of love? Why or why not?

LITERARY FOCUS

Figurative Language

All words have a literal or matter-of-fact meaning. Yet words can be used in such a way that something beyond their literal meaning is implied. **Figurative language**—language using figures of speech—cannot be taken literally. For instance, Shakespeare's Sonnet 18 speaks of "the eye of heaven," but the poet does not expect us to imagine a great eye in the sky. He is using a **metaphor,** an implied comparison between two dissimilar things, in order to make us see the sun in an unusual and vivid way.

A **simile** is a figure of speech in which the comparison is made directly, most often by the use of the word *like* or *as.* If Shakespeare had written, "the sun is like the eye of heaven," his figure of speech would have been a simile.

Thinking About Figurative Language

■ Choose at least two similes and two metaphors from the Shakespeare sonnets you have read. Decide what they refer to, and explain what you think they add to the poem as a whole.

Modern English

Both the English of four hundred years ago and the English we speak and write today are referred to as **modern English.** We should discuss the pronunciation, spelling, and grammar of modern English during Elizabethan times.

Pronunciation and spelling. Three important pronunciation features of Chaucer's day had changed by Elizabethan times: (1) Elizabethans, unlike medieval Englishmen, pronounced vowels as we do. (2) Elizabethans pronounced some consonants differently from medieval Englishmen. (3) Elizabethans did *not* pronounce the final *e* at the ends of words. (For more information about Middle English, see page 70.)

The popularity of printing in the 1500s had a good deal to do with stabilizing spelling so that the English of today looks so close to Elizabethan English. But not all modern English words seem to be spelled as they are pronounced, and the reason for the discrepancy rests with the early English printers. Although pronunciations had already changed, these printers picked up and standardized medieval spellings. As a result, we have the silent consonants in *knight* and the spelling *gh* for the sound *f* in words such as *tough.*

Grammar. Elizabethan English differs from twentieth-century English in fewer ways than it differed from Middle English, but there are still enough differences in pronouns, verbs, and prepositions to remind us that all language changes over time. For one thing, Elizabethan English still uses some second-person singular pronouns that sound antiquated to our ears: *thou* for *you* in the subject position; *thee* for *you* in the object position; and *thy* for *your.* In addition, with *thou* we find certain outdated verb forms: *thou climbst, thou art.* Elizabethan English verb forms are different in another important way. We are used to using *do* with *not* as in "They do not know what they are doing." In Elizabethan English a writer would say, "They know not what they do."

One other difference between Elizabethan English and our English concerns prepositions. Old English and Middle English (see pages 26 and 70) did not rely heavily on prepositions because words had inflections, or endings, that often carried with them meanings such as "to," "for," or "by." In Shakespeare's day writers began to experiment to make up for the disappearance of inflections from words. Some of the prepositions Shakespeare used are not the ones we would use today. For example, he says, "Haply I think *on* thee," where we would say *of* or *about.* It took a while for the system of English prepositions to become polished.

Thinking About Modern English

1. From Shakespeare sonnets or from poems by Sidney, Spenser, Marlowe, or Raleigh, find one more example each of *thou, thee,* and *thy.*
2. From a Shakespeare sonnet find a verb expressing the negative without *do* before *not.*

COMPARING WRITERS

1. How is time pictured in the five sonnets by Shakespeare? What is the relationship between time, love, and art in these sonnets?
2. Compare and contrast one of Shakespeare's sonnets with Sidney's Sonnet 31. First discuss the rhyme scheme of each sonnet. Then discuss the tone of Shakespeare's speaker and of Sidney's speaker. Consider how each speaker suffers and what solace, if any, each finds in the course of the poem.
3. Of all the Elizabethan poems you have read by Sidney, Spenser, Marlowe, Raleigh, and Shakespeare, which one do you find most moving? Most humorous? Why?

Music was a popular part of Elizabethan theater, and Shakespeare's plays are filled with some of the finest songs ever written. The first of the songs that follow is from *As You Like It,* a comedy that was probably first performed in 1599; the second is from *Cymbeline,* a romance that dates from 1609.

William Shakespeare

Blow, Blow, Thou Winter Wind

Blow, blow, thou winter wind,
Thou art not so unkind
   As man's ingratitude;
Thy tooth is not so keen,
5   Because thou art not seen,
   Although thy breath be rude.[1]
Heigh-ho! sing, heigh-ho! unto the green holly:
Most friendship is feigning, most loving mere folly.
   Then, heigh-ho, the holly!
10   This life is most jolly.

Freeze, freeze, thou bitter sky,
That dost not bite so nigh
   As benefits forgot:
Though thou the waters warp,[2]
15   Thy sting is not so sharp
   As friend remembered not.
Heigh-ho! sing, heigh-ho! unto the green holly:
Most friendship is feigning, most loving mere folly.
   Then, heigh-ho, the holly!
20   This life is most jolly.

---

1. **rude:** harsh.
2. **warp:** make rough by freezing.

William Shakespeare

Fear No More the Heat o' the Sun

Fear no more the heat o' the sun,
  Nor the furious winter's rages;
Thou thy worldly task hast done,
  Home art gone, and ta'en[1] thy wages.
5 Golden lads and girls all must,
As chimney-sweepers, come to dust.

Fear no more the frown o' the great;
  Thou art past the tyrant's stroke;
Care no more to clothe and eat;
10   To thee the reed is as the oak:
The scepter,[2] learning, physic, must
All follow this, and come to dust.

Fear no more the lightning flash,
  Nor the all-dreaded thunder stone;[3]
15 Fear not slander, censure rash;
  Thou hast finished joy and moan:
All lovers young, all lovers must
Consign[4] to thee, and come to dust.

No exorciser harm thee!
20 Nor no witchcraft charm thee!
Ghost unlaid[5] forbear thee!
Nothing ill come near thee!
Quiet consummation[6] have;
And renownèd be thy grave!

---

1. **ta'en:** taken.
2. **scepter:** staff carried as a badge of royalty.
3. **thunder stone:** stone or missile once thought to be hurled to earth in a lightning's flash.
4. **consign:** give themselves over.
5. **unlaid:** troubled and wandering.
6. **consummation:** ending, completion.

STUDY QUESTIONS

Blow, Blow, Thou Winter Wind

Recalling

1. According to the song, what is more unkind than the winter wind? What has a sharper sting than the winter sky?
2. According to the refrain, what is most friendship? Most loving? What is "this life"?

Interpreting

3. Why is the metaphor about the tooth (line 4) appropriate in describing the wind? In describing human ingratitude?
4. What kind of attitude toward life is expressed in line 8? Does line 10 mean what it says? Explain.

Fear No More the Heat o' the Sun

Recalling

1. According to the first stanza, what should the person addressed "fear no more"? What has this person done (line 3)?
2. According to the song, what do all "golden lads and girls," "the scepter, learning, physic," and all lovers come to?

Interpreting

3. What has happened to the person addressed? What comforting message does the singer have for this person?

LITERARY FOCUS

Elizabethan Songs

The England of Queen Elizabeth's day was full of music. The queen herself inspired composers and musicians—as she did poets and playwrights—and was generous in rewarding their efforts. London was so full of pipers and fiddlers that an observer in 1587 notes that it was impossible for someone to enter a tavern without having "two or three of them hang at his heels, to give him a dance before he depart."

Song writing reached its peak in Elizabethan times, and lyrics often overshadowed music. Elizabethan **madrigals**—lyric poems designed to be sung without instrumental accompaniment—spoke of love and the joys of pastoral life; street jingles spread the news; ballads told exciting stories.

In Shakespeare's plays songs of all kinds augment the dramatic action by evoking emotions in the audience. The songs may make what is merry merrier or what is sad sadder. They include love songs, nonsense songs, and dirges, songs mourning a death. Although most of the original music accompanying Shakespeare's songs has been lost, traditional renditions in most modern productions of his plays probably "descend" from the original tunes.

Thinking About Elizabethan Songs

What moods or emotions do the two songs from Shakespeare's plays intensify? Which is a dirge, and why?

COMPOSITION

Analyzing the Use of Images

Write a brief essay in which you explain how Shakespeare uses images from nature in one of the songs. First describe the picture of nature he paints. Then describe the function of the natural images in the context of the song: Do they make a comparison, illustrate an idea, or what? Finally, explain how the portrait of nature is related to the mood or emotion expressed in the song.

Writing Figuratively

In the first song Shakespeare uses figurative language to express the effects of a freezing winter's day. Briefly describe another phenomenon—a rainstorm, a snowfall, or a heat wave, for example—by using figurative language. You might begin by writing a literal description of the phenomenon, using adjectives and verbs like *wet* and *rains,* and then rewrite your description with similes, metaphors, and specific verbs that make it more vivid.

SHAKESPEAREAN THEATER

Although there is no precise record of when Shakespeare wrote each of his thirty-seven plays, it is likely that by 1600 he had completed *The Taming of the Shrew, Romeo and Juliet, A Midsummer Night's Dream, The Merchant of Venice,* and *Julius Caesar,* as well as twelve or thirteen others. But even greater work lay before him: *Twelfth Night, Hamlet, Othello, King Lear, Macbeth, Antony and Cleopatra*—all masterpieces written from 1600 to 1607.

Shakespeare's plays are divided into three groups—comedies, histories, and tragedies. Most of the comedies are romantic fantasies, designed to delight and amuse their audiences. The histories illustrate the moral lessons to be learned from the crimes of ambitious and treacherous leaders of state. In his later histories he combined sober events with lively comedy. The tragedies deal with death, morality, and destruction and show how the breaking of a moral law inevitably leads to disaster.

Most of Shakespeare's plays were first performed at the Globe, a theater located across the Thames River from London in the suburb of Southwark. The Globe was an octagonal building, with a thatched roof covering only the perimeter of the area. Under the roof were three levels of galleries that surrounded a yard about sixty-five feet in diameter. The galleries looked down on the stage, a rectangular platform of twenty-seven by forty-three feet that occupied about a third of the yard at one end. The main stage had a large trap door through which actors who played the parts of ghosts and spirits could rise and disappear. At the back of the main stage was a small curtained inner stage used for indoor scenes. Above the inner stage were two galleries. The first level could be used as a balcony, bedroom, or castle wall. Musicians performed from the second level, and sound effects, such as thunder or the ringing of a bell, came from a hut on top of the stage roof.

Those who could afford it watched the plays from seats in the galleries. For a penny, less wealthy spectators, called groundlings, could stand in the yard. The yard was open to the sky, and the stage was lit by daylight. Performances were given in midafternoon before an audience of about two thousand. No curtain rose to indicate the start of the play or fell to signal the close of an act. To begin the play, actors entered by one of two doors at the rear of the stage, and when they left the stage, the scene was over. Within seconds the next scene would begin, with new actors appearing to describe the new setting.

Costumes in the Shakespearean theater were always colorful and elaborate versions of Elizabethan "modern dress," whether they were for *Macbeth,* set in the eleventh century, or for *Julius Caesar,* in 44 B.C. Scenery was almost nonexistent. One tree might signify a forest; a chair might represent a throne room. Shakespeare compensated for the lack of scenery by giving his characters beautiful descriptive passages to speak, and Elizabethan audiences listened closely to the actors' words.

The plays moved at a rapid speed, advancing from scene to scene with scarcely an interruption. Elizabethan actors probably performed much as actors do today, but they spoke their lines much more quickly than modern performers. Presenting a sixteen- to twenty-thousand-word play in about two hours left no time for dawdling.

Elizabethan audiences were accustomed to several dramatic conventions of the time. No women appeared on the stage; women's and children's roles were played by boys who, although they were apprentices to the company, were skillful and highly trained. Soliloquies and asides were two other conventions. In a **soliloquy** the actor is alone on stage, speaking to himself and revealing to the audience his inner thoughts and feelings. In an **aside** the actor speaks words that the other characters on stage are not supposed to hear.

As you read *Macbeth,* imagine from time to time that you are attending a performance at the Globe. The presentation would at first seem noisy and crude, but after a time you would get used to the trumpet calls and lack of scenery, the crowded theater, and the rapid rate of speech, and you would probably join the Elizabethan spectators who are responding to the action with displays of grief, joy, and amusement.

Model of the Globe Theatre by John Cranford Adams. Courtesy of the Folger Shakespeare Library, Washington, D.C.

Mrs. Siddons as Lady Macbeth, G. H. Harlow, early nineteenth century. (See William Hazlitt's description of Mrs. Siddons' performance as Lady Macbeth, page 394.)

The Tragedy of Macbeth

The Tragedy of Macbeth was probably written in 1606 and was performed that summer at Hampton Court Palace to celebrate the state visit of Christian IV of Denmark, King James's brother-in-law. The play touches on many topics—including witchcraft, the ideals of kingship, and special curative powers—that would have appealed to James and to other Elizabethans whose interest both in the king and in Scotland blossomed when James assumed the throne in 1603. James was already king of Scotland when he became king of England. His family was descended from a line of Scottish kings dating back to the eleventh century, when *Macbeth* takes place.

For the basic story of this play, Shakespeare turned to one of the most popular books of the times, Raphael Holinshed's *Chronicles of England, Scotland, and Ireland,* where he read about the real-life Macbeth. Shakespeare often consulted histories and stories of his own and earlier eras for the plots of his plays. He then amplified, altered, and combined incidents and personalities to serve his own dramatic purposes and to shape his own creations.

In *Macbeth,* for example, He invented the banquet scene, the ghost of Banquo, the sleepwalking scene, and the death of Lady Macbeth. History's Banquo is a traitor and an accomplice in the murder of Duncan, whereas Shakespeare's Banquo is honorable and loyal. In the *Chronicles* Duncan is a younger, feeble king, "a faint-hearted milksop," but in *Macbeth* he is an older, benevolent ruler. King James claimed Duncan, Malcolm, Banquo, and Siward as his Stuart ancestors, and they all appear in *Macbeth* as characters above reproach.

Shakespeare fashioned the story of Macbeth into one of the best-known tragic patterns—the rise and fall of a powerful but flawed individual. In Elizabethan tragedies and in earlier Greek tragedies (see Part Two) the main character, or **tragic hero,** is generally a high-ranking person, distinguished by such admirable traits as integrity, bravery, and strength. The hero's personality, however, also includes a fatal weakness, or **tragic flaw,** that causes his eventual decline from success to destruction.

Shakespeare's tragedy focuses on the downfall of Macbeth. At the start of the play, Macbeth is a brilliant and courageous general who unstintingly serves Duncan, his king. Macbeth is a noble Scot who commands great respect. As the play progresses, Macbeth's hunger for more and greater power provokes increasingly reckless and violent actions. Joined in his crimes by his wife, Macbeth rushes along a desperate course of terror and destruction, and by the play's conclusion he is a broken man.

Macbeth has always been a theatrical favorite, from Elizabethan times to the present. In many ways the faraway, dark, and murderous world of *Macbeth* is strangely current, in part because the people in the play are so vividly alive, in part because issues in the play—loyalty, fate, quenchless ambition—are timeless.

Key Ideas in *Macbeth*

As you read *Macbeth,* look for references to each of the following topics. If you keep track of what the work says about these subjects, you will grasp the most important themes of the play.

- Appearance versus reality
- Reason versus desire
- Prophecies of the future
- Attempts to control the future
- Responses by humans to supernatural powers
- Responses by nature to human actions

Key Quotations from *Macbeth*

As you read *Macbeth,* you will come across some of the most famous lines in English drama. Here are a few familiar quotations from the play.

Fair is foul, and foul is fair.
—Three Witches, Act I, Scene i, 10.

There's no art
To find the mind's construction in the face:
—Duncan, Act I, Scene iv, 11–12

Yet do I fear thy nature;
It is too full o' th' milk of human kindness
—Lady Macbeth, Act I, Scene v, 15–16

Will all great Neptune's ocean wash this blood
Clean from my hand?
—Macbeth, Act II, Scene ii, 59–60

Where we are
There's daggers in men's smiles;
—Donalbain, Act II, Scene iii, 126–127

Things without all remedy
Should be without regard: what's done is done.
—Lady Macbeth, Act III, Scene ii, 11–12

Double, double, toil and trouble;
Fire burn and caldron bubble.
—Three Witches, Act IV, Scene i, 20–21

Out, out, brief candle!
Life's but a walking shadow, a poor player
That struts and frets his hour upon the stage
And then is heard no more.
—Macbeth, Act V, Scene v, 23–26

Lady Macbeth and Macbeth.

Malcolm, Macduff, and Ross.

William Shakespeare

The Tragedy of Macbeth

CHARACTERS

DUNCAN: King of Scotland
MALCOLM: his elder son and heir to the throne
DONALBAIN: his younger son
MACBETH: Thane of Glamis, a Scottish nobleman and general in King Duncan's army
LADY MACBETH: his wife
BANQUO: Scottish nobleman and general in King Duncan's army
FLEANCE: his son
MACDUFF: Thane of Fife, a Scottish nobleman
LADY MACDUFF: his wife

LENNOX, ROSS, ANGUS, MENTEITH, CAITHNESS: noblemen of Scotland

SIWARD: Earl of Northumberland, general of the English forces
YOUNG SIWARD: his son

THREE WITCHES
A PORTER
AN OLD MAN
THREE MURDERERS
HECATE: leader of the Witches
APPARITIONS
AN ENGLISH DOCTOR
A GENTLEWOMAN: attending Lady Macbeth
SEYTON: an officer attending Macbeth

Other **LORDS, OFFICERS, SOLDIERS, ATTENDANTS, MESSENGERS**

ACT I

Scene i. *Scotland. An open place.*

[*In the midst of a great storm of thunder and lightning,* THREE WITCHES *appear in a deserted, outdoor place. They are plotting to meet* MACBETH, *a nobleman and general in* KING DUNCAN'*s army, when he returns from battle.*]

    FIRST WITCH. When shall we three meet again?
      In thunder, lightning, or in rain?

    SECOND WITCH. When the hurlyburly's[1] done,
      When the battle's lost and won.

5 **THIRD WITCH.** That will be ere the set of sun.

    FIRST WITCH. Where the place?

    SECOND WITCH   Upon the heath.

    THIRD WITCH. There to meet with Macbeth.

    FIRST WITCH. I come, Graymalkin.[2]

    SECOND WITCH. Paddock[3] calls.

    THIRD WITCH.   Anon![4]

10 **ALL.** Fair is foul, and foul is fair.
      Hover through the fog and filthy air.

      [*The* WITCHES *leave.*]

Scene ii. *A camp.*

[*The setting is a military camp near Forres, a town about a hundred miles north of Edinburgh in Scotland. From off-stage come the sounds of men fighting, weapons clashing, and trumpets blaring.* DUNCAN, *King of Scotland, enters with his two teenage sons.* MALCOLM, *the elder, who is heir to the throne, and* DONALBAIN, *the younger. With them are a Scottish nobleman,* LENNOX, *and other attendants. They meet a* CAPTAIN *bleeding from wounds received in battle between the king's army and the forces of his two rivals, Macdonwald and the Thane of Cawdor.* DUNCAN *learns of the battle's progress from the wounded sergeant.*]

    KING. What bloody[1] man is that? He can report,
      As seemeth by his plight, of the revolt
      The newest state.

    MALCOLM.   This is the sergeant[2]
      Who like a good and hardy soldier fought

1 **hurlyburly:** uproar and confusion of battle.

2 **Graymalkin:** a common name for a gray cat. In Shakespeare's time cats and toads were believed to be witches' familiars, or helpers.
3 **Paddock:** the second witch's familiar, a toad.
4 **Anon:** at once.

1 **bloody:** the atmosphere of violence and horror is increased by images of blood throughout the play. The word *blood* is used over one hundred times in *Macbeth.*
2 **sergeant:** in Shakespeare's time *sergeant* and *captain* were interchangeable.

5 'Gainst my captivity.[3] Hail, brave friend!
Say to the king the knowledge of the broil[4]
As thou didst leave it.

CAPTAIN.   Doubtful it stood,
As two spent swimmers, that do cling together
And choke their art.[5] The merciless Macdonwald—
10 Worthy to be a rebel for to that
The multiplying villainies of nature
Do swarm upon him[6]—from the Western Isles[7]
Of kerns and gallowglasses[8] is supplied;
And Fortune, on his damnèd quarrel smiling,
15 Showed like a rebel's wench:[9] but all's too weak:
For brave Macbeth—well he deserves that name—
Disdaining Fortune, with his brandished steel,
Which smoked with bloody execution,
Like valor's minion[10] carved out his passage
20 Till he faced the slave;[11]
Which nev'r shook hands, nor bade farewell to him,
Till he unseamed him from the nave to th' chops,[12]
And fixed his head upon our battlements.

KING. O valiant cousin![13] Worthy gentleman!

25 CAPTAIN. As whence the sun 'gins his reflection[14]
Shipwracking storms and direful thunders break,
So from that spring whence comfort seemed to come
Discomfort swells. Mark, King of Scotland, mark:
No sooner justice had, with valor armed,
30 Compelled these skipping kerns to trust their heels
But the Norweyan lord,[15] surveying vantage,[16]
With furbished arms and new supplies of men,
Began a fresh assault.

KING.   Dismayed not this
Our captains, Macbeth and Banquo?

CAPTAIN.   Yes;
35 As sparrows eagles, or the hare the lion.
If I say sooth,[17] I must report they were
As cannons overcharged with double cracks;[18]
So they doubly redoubled strokes upon the foe.
Except[19] they meant to bathe in reeking wounds,
40 Or memorize another Golgotha,[20]
I cannot tell—
But I am faint; my gashes cry for help.

KING. So well thy words become thee as thy wounds;
They smack of honor both. Go get him surgeons.

3 **captivity:** capture.
4 **broil:** battle.

5 **choke their art:** The image is of two exhausted swimmers, who by clinging to each other prevent each other from swimming.

6 **Worthy . . . him:** suited to be a rebel because nature has given him many evil qualities.
7 **Western Isles:** Ireland and the Hebrides, off Scotland.
8 **kerns and gallowglasses:** light-armed foot soldiers and horsemen armed with axes, both from Ireland.
9 **Fortune . . . wench:** Fortune appeared to favor the rebel Macdonwald.

10 **minion:** favorite.
11 **slave:** Macdonwald.
12 **unseamed . . . chops:** cut him open from the navel to the jaw. *Unseamed* is one of the many sewing metaphors in the play.

13 **cousin:** often a term of courtesy between noblemen. Duncan and Macbeth actually are first cousins.
14 **As . . . reflection:** as from the same place from which the sun rises.

15 **Norweyan lord:** Sweno, King of Norway.
16 **vantage:** seeing an opportunity for attack.

17 **sooth:** truth.

18 **double cracks:** double explosives.

19 **Except:** unless.

20 **memorize . . . Golgotha** [gol'gə thə]: make the place as memorable for slaughter as Golgotha, the place where Christ was crucified.

[*As the* CAPTAIN *leaves with the help of attendants, noblemen* ROSS *and* ANGUS *arrive with more news of the fighting.*]

Who comes here?

45 MALCOLM.   The worthy Thane[21] of Ross.

LENNOX. What a haste looks through his eyes! So should he
   look
That seems to[22] speak things strange.

ROSS.   God save the king!

KING. Whence cam'st thou, worthy Thane?

ROSS.   From Fife, great King;
   Where the Norweyan banners flout the sky
50 And fan our people cold.[23]
   Norway[24] himself, with terrible numbers,
   Assisted by that most disloyal traitor
   The Thane of Cawdor, began a dismal[25] conflict;
   Till that Bellona's bridegroom, lapped in proof,[26]
55 Confronted him with self-comparisons,[27]
   Point against point, rebellious arm 'gainst arm,
   Curbing his lavish[28] spirit: and, to conclude,
   The victory fell on us.

KING.   Great happiness!

ROSS.   That now
   Sweno, the Norways' king, craves composition;[29]
60 Nor would we deign him burial of his men
   Till he disbursèd, at Saint Colme's Inch,[30]
   Ten thousand dollars[31] to our general use.

KING. No more that Thane of Cawdor shall deceive
   Our bosom interest:[32] go pronounce his present[33] death,
65 And with his former title greet Macbeth.

ROSS. I'll see it done.

KING. What he hath lost, noble Macbeth hath won.

   [*They leave.*]

Scene iii. *A heath.*

[*It is thundering as the* THREE WITCHES *wait on a desolate heath for* MACBETH *and* BANQUO. *The two generals are on their way to* KING DUNCAN's *palace at Forres. As they wait, the*

21 **Thane:** a Scottish title of nobility, similar to an English earl.

22 **seems to:** seems about to.

23 **flout . . . cold:** The invading banners filled the Scots with a cold fear.
24 **Norway:** the King of Norway.
25 **dismal:** ominous.
26 **Bellona's . . . proof:** Macbeth is referred to as the mate of Bellona, Roman goddess of war, dressed in tested armor (proof).
27 **Confronted . . . self-comparisons:** faced him with equal courage and skill.
28 **lavish:** arrogant.

29 **craves composition:** desires terms of peace.

30 **Saint Colme's Inch:** Isle of St. Columbia near Edinburgh, Scotland.
31 **dollars:** Dollars were first coined in 1518, about five hundred years after Macbeth's time.
32 **bosom interest:** vital and confidential concerns.
33 **present:** immediate.

witches speak of their evil powers. They greet the two men with strange prophecies of future glory, saying that MACBETH *will ultimately be King of Scotland and that* BANQUO *will be a father of kings.*]

FIRST WITCH. Where hast thou been, sister?

SECOND WITCH. Killing swine.[1]

THIRD WITCH. Sister, where thou?

FIRST WITCH. A sailor's wife had chestnuts in her lap,
And mounched, and mounched, and mounched.
5   "Give me," quoth I.
"Aroint thee,[2] witch!" the rump-fed ronyon[3] cries.
Her husband's to Aleppo[4] gone, master o' th' Tiger:
But in a sieve I'll thither sail,
And, like a rat without a tail,[5]
10   I'll do, I'll do, and I'll do.

SECOND WITCH. I'll give thee a wind.[6]

FIRST WITCH. Th' art kind.

THIRD WITCH. And I another.

FIRST WITCH. I myself have all the other;
15   And the very ports they blow,
All the quarters that they know
I' th' shipman's card.[7]
I'll drain him dry as hay:
Sleep shall neither night nor day
20   Hang upon his penthouse lid;[8]
He shall live a man forbid:[9]
Weary sev'nights[10] nine times nine
Shall he dwindle, peak,[11] and pine:
Though his bark cannot be lost,
25   Yet it shall be tempest-tossed.
Look what I have.

SECOND WITCH. Show me, show me.

FIRST WITCH. Here I have a pilot's thumb,[12]
Wracked as homeward he did come.

[*The sound of a drum is heard offstage.*]

30 **THIRD WITCH.** A drum, a drum!
Macbeth doth come.

ALL. The weird[13] sisters, hand in hand,
Posters[14] of the sea and land,

1 **Killing swine:** It was commonly believed that witches killed or bewitched domestic animals.

2 **Aroint thee:** Go away!
3 **rump-fed ronyon:** fat-rumped, shabby creature.
4 **Aleppo:** The captain of the ship *Tiger* is sailing to Aleppo, then a city in Syria.
5 **sieve . . . tail:** According to popular belief, a witch often used a sieve as a boat and could assume the shape of any animal, but the tail would always be missing.
6 **wind:** Witches were thought to sell winds.

7 **shipman's card:** circular piece of cardboard on which the thirty-two points of the compass are marked.
8 **penthouse lid:** the eyelid, which overhangs the eye like a penthouse. A penthouse was originally a shed with a roof that sloped down from the main building.
9 **forbid:** cursed.
10 **sev'nights:** weeks.
11 **peak:** waste away.

12 **thumb:** Parts of corpses were used to create spells.

13 **weird:** As a noun this word once meant fate or destiny. As an adjective it indicates that the witches can foresee people's destinies.
14 **Posters:** swift travelers.

Thus do go about, about:
35   Thrice to thine, and thrice to mine,
And thrice again, to make up nine.
Peace! The charm's wound up.

[MACBETH *and* BANQUO *enter.*]

MACBETH. So foul and fair a day I have not seen.[15]

BANQUO. How far is 't called to Forres? What are these
40   So withered, and so wild in their attire,

15 **So . . . seen:** foul because of the storm; fair because of his victory. (Compare with Act I, scene i, line 10.)

That look not like th' inhabitants o' th' earth,
And yet are on 't? Live you, or are you aught
That man may question? You seem to understand me,
By each at once her choppy[16] finger laying
45 Upon her skinny lips. You should be women,
And yet your beards[17] forbid me to interpret
That you are so.

MACBETH.   Speak, if you can: what are you?

FIRST WITCH. All hail, Macbeth! Hail to thee, Thane of Glamis!

SECOND WITCH. All hail, Macbeth! Hail to thee, Thane of
   Cawdor!

50 THIRD WITCH. All hail, Macbeth, that shalt be King hereafter!

[MACBETH *is startled by the* WITCHES' *greeting;* BANQUO
notices and addresses him.]

BANQUO. Good sir, why do you start, and seem to fear
   Things that do sound so fair? [*To the* WITCHES.] I' th' name
      of truth,
   Are ye fantastical,[18] or that indeed
   Which outwardly ye show? My noble partner
55 You greet with present grace and great prediction
   Of noble having[19] and of royal hope,
   That he seems rapt withal:[20] to me you speak not.
   If you can look into the seeds of time,
   And say which grain will grow and which will not,
60 Speak then to me, who neither beg nor fear
   Your favors nor your hate.

FIRST WITCH. Hail!

SECOND WITCH. Hail!

THIRD WITCH. Hail!

65 FIRST WITCH. Lesser than Macbeth, and greater.

SECOND WITCH. Not so happy,[21] yet much happier.

THIRD WITCH. Thou shalt get kings, though thou be none.
   So all hail, Macbeth and Banquo!

FIRST WITCH. Banquo and Macbeth, all hail!

70 MACBETH. Stay, you imperfect[22] speakers, tell me more:
   By Sinel's[23] death I know I am Thane of Glamis;
   But how of Cawdor? The Thane of Cawdor lives,
   A prosperous gentleman; and to be King
   Stands not within the prospect of belief,
75 No more than to be Cawdor. Say from whence

16 **choppy:** chapped.

17 **beards:** According to popular belief, witches often had beards.

18 **fantastical:** imaginary.

19 **having:** possession, fortune.
20 **rapt withal:** entranced.

21 **happy:** fortunate.

22 **imperfect:** because their predictions have been so puzzling.
23 **Sinel's** [si′nəlz]: referring to Macbeth's father.

You owe this strange intelligence?[24] Or why
Upon this blasted heath you stop our way
With such prophetic greeting? Speak, I charge you.

[*The* WITCHES *vanish.*]

BANQUO. The earth hath bubbles as the water has,
80   And these are of them. Whither are they vanished?

MACBETH. Into the air, and what seemed corporal[25] melted
As breath into the wind. Would[26] they had stayed!

BANQUO. Were such things here as we do speak about?
Or have we eaten on the insane root[27]
85   That takes the reason prisoner?

MACBETH. Your children shall be kings.

BANQUO   You shall be King.

MACBETH. And Thane of Cawdor too. Went it not so?

BANQUO. To th' selfsame tune and words. Who's here?

[ROSS *and* ANGUS, *two Scottish noblemen, arrive with a
message from* KING DUNCAN.]

ROSS. The King hath happily received, Macbeth,
90   The news of thy success; and when he reads[28]
Thy personal venture in the rebels' fight,
His wonders and his praises do contend
Which should be thine or his.[29] Silenced with that,
In viewing o'er the rest o' th' selfsame day,
95   He finds thee in the stout Norweyan ranks,
Nothing afeard of what thyself didst make,
Strange images of death.[30] As thick as tale
Came post with post,[31] and every one did bear
Thy praises in his kingdom's great defense,
And poured them down before him.

100 ANGUS.   We are sent
To give thee, from our royal master, thanks;
Only to herald thee into his sight,
Not pay thee.

ROSS. And for an earnest[32] of a greater honor,
105   He bade me, from him, call thee Thane of Cawdor;
In which addition,[33] hail, most worthy Thane!
For it is thine.

BANQUO. [*Aside.*] What, can the devil speak true?

MACBETH. The Thane of Cawdor lives: why do you dress me
In borrowed robes?[34]

24 **owe . . . intelligence:** where you got this strange information.

25 **corporal** [kor′pər əl]: flesh and blood, real.
26 **Would:** I wish.

27 **insane root:** A number of plants, such as henbane and hemlock, were believed to cause insanity.

28 **reads:** thinks about.

29 **His . . . his:** His amazement at the victory struggles with his desire to praise Macbeth.

30 **Nothing . . . death:** killing, yet not afraid of dying.
31 **post with post:** message after message.

32 **earnest:** pledge.

33 **In which addition:** with this new title.

34 **why . . . robes:** The idea that Macbeth's honors are ill-fitting occurs several times in the play.

ANGUS.   Who was the thane lives yet,
110   But under heavy judgment bears that life
       Which he deserves to lose. Whether he was combined
       With those of Norway, or did line[35] the rebel   35 **line:** support, strengthen.
       With hidden help and vantage, or that with both
       He labored in his country's wrack,[36] I know not;   36 **wrack:** ruin.
115   But treasons capital, confessed and proved,
       Have overthrown him.

       MACBETH. [*Aside.*]   Glamis, and Thane of Cawdor:
       The greatest is behind.[37] [*Addressing* ROSS *and* ANGUS.]   37 **behind:** still to come.
          Thanks for your pains.
       [*Aside to* BANQUO.] Do you not hope your children shall be
          kings,
       When those that gave the Thane of Cawdor to me
       Promised no less to them?

120   BANQUO. [*Aside to* MACBETH.] That, trusted home,[38]   38 **trusted home:** fully believed.
       Might yet enkindle you unto[39] the crown,   39 **enkindle you unto:** encourage
       Besides the Thane of Cawdor. But 'tis strange: you to hope for.
       And oftentimes, to win us to our harm,
       The instruments of darkness tell us truths,
125   Win us with honest trifles, to betray's
       In deepest consequence.
       Cousins, a word, I pray you.

       [BANQUO *speaks privately to the two noblemen while* MAC-
       BETH *expresses his thoughts in an aside.*]

       MACBETH.   Two truths are told,
       As happy prologues to the swelling act
       Of the imperial theme.[40]—I thank you, gentlemen—   40 **swelling . . . theme:** stately idea
                                                                                    of becoming king.

       [MACBETH *interrupts himself to speak to* ROSS *and* BANQUO;
       he then continues his aside.]

130   This supernatural soliciting[41]   41 **supernatural soliciting:** con-
       Cannot be ill, cannot be good. If ill,   sulting the witches.
       Why hath it given me earnest of success,
       Commencing in a truth? I am Thane of Cawdor:
       If good, why do I yield to that suggestion[42]   42 **suggestion:** thought of murder-
135   Whose horrid image doth unfix my hair   ing Duncan.
       And make my seated[43] heart knock at my ribs,   43 **seated:** firmly placed.
       Against the use of nature?[44] Present fears   44 **Against . . . nature:** contrary to
       Are less than horrible imaginings.[45]   my normal state.
       My thought, whose murder yet is but fantastical,   45 **Present fears . . . imaginings:**
140   Shakes so my single state of man that function   Although Macbeth is unafraid of the
       Is smothered in surmise, and nothing is   real dangers of battle, his courage is
       But what is not.[46]   sapped by his supernatural thoughts.
                                                                                    46 **function . . . is not:** I am so
                                                                                    unnerved by my imaginings that my
                                                                                    ability to act is stifled. The only things
                                                                                    that are real to me now are unreal.

BANQUO. [*Speaking to* ROSS *about* MACBETH.] Look
    how our partner's rapt.

MACBETH. [*Aside.*] If chance will have me King, why, chance
    may crown me,
    Without my stir.[47]

BANQUO.   New honors come upon him,
145   Like our strange garments, cleave not to their mold
    But with the aid of use.[48]

MACBETH. [*Aside.*]   Come what come may,
    Time and the hour runs through the roughest day.

BANQUO. Worthy Macbeth, we stay upon your leisure.[49]

MACBETH. Give me your favor.[50] My dull brain was wrought
150   With things forgotten.[51] Kind gentlemen, your pains
    Are registered where every day I turn
    The leaf to read them. Let us toward the King.
    [*Aside to* BANQUO.] Think upon what hath chanced, and at
    more time,
    The interim having weighed it,[52] let us speak
    Our free hearts[53] each to other.

155 **BANQUO.**   Very gladly.

MACBETH. Till then, enough. Come, friends.

    [*They all leave together.*]

Scene iv. *The palace at Forres.*

[*At* KING DUNCAN's *palace at Forres, the king and his two
sons,* MALCOLM *and* DONALBAIN, *enter to a fanfare of trumpets.
They are accompanied by* LENNOX *and other attendants. They
discuss the execution of the treacherous Thane of Cawdor
and praise* MACBETH *and* BANQUO *for their valor.*]

KING. Is execution done on Cawdor? Are not
    Those in commission[1] yet returned?

MALCOLM.   My liege,
    They are not yet come back. But I have spoke
    With one that saw him die, who did report
5   That very frankly he confessed his treasons,
    Implored your Highness' pardon and set forth
    A deep repentance: nothing in his life
    Became him like the leaving it. He died
    As one that had been studied[2] in his death,
10   To throw away the dearest thing he owed[3]
    As 'twere a careless[4] trifle.

---

47 **stir:** without an effort on my part.

48 **Like . . . use:** like new clothes that do not fit comfortably until worn for awhile.

49 **we stay . . . leisure:** we are waiting for you at your convenience.

50 **Give . . . favor:** Pardon me.

51 **wrought . . . forgotten:** Macbeth pretends to be distracted by things he says he has forgotten.

52 **The interim . . . it:** having had time to consider it.

53 **Our free hearts:** our minds freely.

1 **Those in commission:** those charged with the duty of the execution.

2 **studied:** a theatrical term meaning "learned by heart." Cawdor died as if he had carefully rehearsed his execution.

3 **owed:** owned.

4 **careless:** worthless.

KING.   There's no art
To find the mind's construction in the face:[5]
He was a gentleman on whom I built
An absolute trust.

[MACBETH, BANQUO, ROSS, *and* ANGUS *join them. The* KING *addresses* MACBETH.]

                    O worthiest cousin!
15 The sin of my ingratitude even now
Was heavy on me: thou art so far before,[6]
That swiftest wing of recompense is slow
To overtake thee. Would thou hadst less deserved,
That the proportion both of thanks and payment
20 Might have been mine! Only I have left to say,
More is thy due than more than all can pay.[7]

MACBETH. The service and the loyalty I owe,
In doing it, pays itself. Your Highness' part
Is to receive our duties: and our duties
25 Are to your throne and state children and servants;
Which do but what they should, by doing every thing
Safe toward[8] your love and honor.

KING.   Welcome hither.
I have begun to plant thee, and will labor
To make thee full of growing. Noble Banquo,
30 That hast no less deserved, nor must be known
No less to have done so,[9] let me enfold thee
And hold thee to my heart.

BANQUO.   There if I grow,
The harvest is your own.

KING.   My plenteous joys,
Wanton[10] in fullness, seek to hide themselves
35 In drops of sorrow. Sons, kinsmen, thanes,
And you whose places are the nearest, know,
We will establish our estate upon
Our eldest,[11] Malcolm, whom we name hereafter
The Prince of Cumberland: which honor must
40 Not unaccompanied invest him only,
But signs of nobleness, like stars, shall shine
On all deservers. From hence to Inverness,[12]
And bind us further to you.

MACBETH. The rest is labor, which is not used for you.[13]
45 I'll be myself the harbinger,[14] and make joyful
The hearing of my wife with your approach;
So, humbly take my leave.

5 **There's . . . face:** There is no way to know what a person is thinking by looking at his face.

6 **so far before:** so far ahead.

7 **Would . . . pay:** If you had been less worthy, I could have repaid you what you deserve. You deserve more than anyone could pay.

8 **Safe toward:** with sure regard for.

9 **That . . . so:** who is just as deserving as Macbeth.

10 **Wanton:** unrestrained.

11 **establish . . . eldest:** I will settle the succession of the throne upon my oldest son. The throne of Scotland was not hereditary then. Macbeth now realizes that chance will not crown him. (Compare with Act I, Scene iii, line 143.)

12 **Inverness** [in vər nes']: Macbeth's castle, about twenty-five miles away.

13 **The rest . . . you:** Anything not done for you is a burden.
14 **harbinger** [här'bin jər]: officer who precedes royalty to arrange reception for a visit.

KING.   My worthy Cawdor!

MACBETH. [*Aside.*] The Prince of Cumberland! That is a step
On which I must fall down, or else o'erleap,
50 For in my way it lies. Stars, hide your fires;
Let not light see my black and deep desires:[15]
The eye wink at the hand;[16] yet let that be
Which the eye fears, when it is done, to see.

[MACBETH *leaves.*]

KING. True, worthy Banquo; he is full so valiant,
55 And in his commendations I am fed;
It is a banquet to me. Let's after him,
Whose care is gone before to bid us welcome.
It is a peerless kinsman.

[*They all leave to a flourish of trumpets.*]

Scene v. The castle at Inverness.

[*In* MACBETH'*s castle at Inverness,* LADY MACBETH *appears
alone, reading a letter from her husband.*]

LADY MACBETH. [*Reads.*] "They met me in the day of success; and
I have learned by the perfect'st report they have more in
them than mortal knowledge. When I burned in desire to
question them further, they made themselves air, into
5 which they vanished. Whiles I stood rapt in the wonder of
it, came missives[1] from the King, who all-hailed me 'Thane
of Cawdor'; by which title, before, these weird sisters
saluted me, and referred me to the coming on of time, with
'Hail, King that shalt be!' This have I thought good to
10 deliver thee, my dearest partner of greatness, that thou
mightst not lose the dues of rejoicing, by being ignorant of
what greatness is promised thee. Lay it to thy heart, and
farewell."

Glamis thou art, and Cawdor, and shalt be
15 What thou art promised. Yet do I fear thy nature;
It is too full o' th' milk of human kindness[2]
To catch the nearest way.[3] Thou wouldst be great,
Art not without ambition, but without
The illness[4] should attend it. What thou wouldst highly,
20 That wouldst thou holily; wouldst not play false,
And yet wouldst wrongly win. Thou'dst have, great Glamis,
That which cries "Thus thou must do" if thou have it;
And that which rather thou dost fear to do
Than wishest should be undone.[5] Hie thee hither,

15 **Stars . . . desires:** Macbeth calls on darkness to obscure his action. This is one of many images of darkness in the play.
16 **The eye . . . hand:** Let my eyes be blind to my hand's deed.

1 **missives:** messengers.

2 **th' milk . . . kindness:** sentimentality.

3 **To catch . . . way:** the quickest way to the throne—killing Duncan.

4 **illness:** wickedness.

5 **Thou'dst . . . undone:** What you want, Glamis, requires you to do certain things in order to get it. You are afraid to do these things, but you would rather do them than not get what you want.

25 That I may pour my spirits in thine ear,
And chastise[6] with the valor of my tongue
All that impedes thee from the golden round[7]
Which fate and metaphysical[8] aid doth seem
To have thee crowned withal.

[A MESSENGER *arrives.*]

What is your tidings?

MESSENGER. The King comes here tonight.

30 **LADY MACBETH.** Thou'rt mad to say it!
Is not thy master with him, who, were 't so,
Would have informed for preparation?

MESSENGER. So please you, it is true. Our thane is coming.
One of my fellows had the speed of him,[9]
35 Who, almost dead for breath, had scarcely more
Than would make up his message.

LADY MACBETH. Give him tending;
He brings great news. [*The* MESSENGER *leaves.*]
The raven[10] himself is hoarse
That croaks the fatal entrance of Duncan
Under my battlements. Come, you spirits
40 That tend on mortal[11] thoughts, unsex me here,
And fill me, from the crown to the toe, top-full
Of direst cruelty! Make thick my blood,
Stop up th' access and passage to remorse,[12]
That no compunctious visitings of nature[13]
45 Shake my fell[14] purpose, nor keep peace between
Th' effect[15] and it! Come to my woman's breasts,
And take my milk for gall,[16] you murd'ring ministers,
Wherever in your sightless substances
You wait on[17] nature's mischief! Come, thick night,
50 And pall thee in the dunnest smoke[18] of hell,
That my keen knife see not the wound it makes,
Nor heaven peep through the blanket of the dark,
To cry "Hold, hold!"

[MACBETH *enters.*]

Great Glamis! Worthy Cawdor!
Greater than both, by the all-hail hereafter!
55 Thy letters have transported me beyond
This ignorant present, and I feel now
The future in the instant.[19]

MACBETH. My dearest love,
Duncan comes here tonight.

6 **chastise:** reprimand.

7 **golden round:** the crown.

8 **metaphysical:** supernatural.

9 **had . . . him:** overtook him.

10 **raven:** traditionally a bird of ill omen.

11 **mortal:** murderous.

12 **remorse:** compassion.

13 **compunctious . . . nature:** natural feelings of pity.
14 **fell:** deadly.
15 **effect:** fulfillment.

16 **And . . . gall:** change any kindness to bitter hatred, murdering agents.
17 **in your sightless . . . on:** in your invisible forms you are ready to bring out the evil in nature.
18 **pall . . . smoke:** enshroud yourself in the darkest smoke.

19 **in the instant:** at this very moment.

LADY MACBETH.   And when goes hence?

MACBETH. Tomorrow, as he purposes.

LADY MACBETH.   O, never

60 Shall sun that morrow see!
Your face, my Thane, is as a book where men
May read strange matters. To beguile the time,
Look like the time;[20] bear welcome in your eye,
Your hand, your tongue: look like th' innocent flower,
65 But be the serpent under 't. He that's coming
Must be provided for: and you shall put
This night's great business into my dispatch;[21]
Which shall to all our nights and days to come
Give solely sovereign sway and masterdom.

MACBETH. We will speak further.

70 **MACBETH.**   Only look up clear.[22]
To alter favor ever is to fear.[23]
Leave all the rest to me.

[*They leave.*]

20 **To beguile . . . the time:** To deceive observers, imitate their expressions.

21 **my dispatch:** Lady Macbeth plans to manage the whole affair.

22 **look up clear:** appear innocent.

23 **To . . . fear:** To change your usual appearance will reveal your fear and arouse suspicion.

Scene vi. Outside the castle at Inverness.

[*Outside* MACBETH'*s castle oboes sound to announce the arrival of royalty.* KING DUNCAN *and his sons enter with a group of Scottish noblemen, including* BANQUO, LENNOX, MACDUFF, ROSS, *and* ANGUS. *It is nighttime, and they are attended by servants with torches.*]

KING. This castle hath a pleasant seat;[1] the air
Nimbly and sweetly recommends itself
Unto our gentle senses.

BANQUO.   This guest of summer,
The temple-haunting martlet, does approve
5 By his loved mansionry that the heaven's breath
Smells wooingly here.[2] No jutty,[3] frieze,
Buttress, nor coign of vantage,[4] but this bird
Hath made his pendent bed and procreant cradle.[5]
Where they most breed and haunt, I have observed
The air is delicate.

[LADY MACBETH *enters to welcome her guests.*]

10 **KING.**   See, see, our honored hostess!
The love that follows us sometime is our trouble,
Which still we thank as love.[6] Herein I teach you

1 **seat:** location.

2 **temple-haunting . . . here:** The house martin, a swallowlike bird, usually nests in churches. The presence of its nests (mansionry) at Macbeth's castle indicates that this is a pleasant place. In Shakespeare's time *martin* was a slang term for dupe.
3 **jutty:** projection.

4 **coign of vantage:** advantageous corner.
5 **procreant** [prō'krē ənt] **cradle:** nest for the young.

6 **The love . . . love:** Duncan means that since his visit to Macbeth and his wife is prompted by his love for them, they should forgive him for the great trouble he is causing.

How you shall bid God 'ield us for your pains
And thank us for your trouble.[7]

LADY MACBETH.   All our service
15   In every point twice done, and then done double,
Were poor and single business[8] to contend
Against those honors deep and broad wherewith
Your Majesty loads our house: for those of old,
And the late dignities heaped up to them,
We rest your hermits.[9]

20   KING.   Where's the Thane of Cawdor?
We coursed him at the heels,[10] and had a purpose
To be his purveyor:[11] but he rides well,
And his great love, sharp as his spur, hath holp[12] him
To his home before us. Fair and noble hostess,
We are your guest tonight.

25   LADY MACBETH.   Your servants ever
Have theirs, themselves, and what is theirs, in compt,
To make their audit at your Highness' pleasure,
Still to return your own.[13]

KING.   Give me your hand.
Conduct me to mine host: we love him highly,
30   And shall continue our graces towards him.
By your leave, hostess.

[LADY MACBETH *and the* KING *go into the castle.*]

Scene vii. The castle at Inverness.

[*In a torch-lit room in* MACBETH's *castle, music is heard. A steward, followed by other servants carrying dishes of food, crosses the stage. As they leave,* MACBETH *enters. He is trying to make up his mind about murdering* DUNCAN, *who is still in the banquet room. It is the likelihood of punishment, not the moral consequences of the crime, that discourages* MACBETH *from proceeding with the murder.*]

MACBETH. If it were done when 'tis done, then 'twere well
It were done quickly.[1] If th' assassination
Could trammel up the consequence, and catch,
With his surcease, success; that but this blow
5   Might be the be-all and the end-all—here,
But here, upon this bank and shoal of time,
We'd jump the life to come.[2] But in these cases
We still have judgment[3] here; that we but teach
Bloody instructions, which, being taught, return
10   To plague th' inventor:[4] this even-handed justice

7 **bid God 'ield us . . . trouble:** Ask God to reward me for the pains I have caused and thank me for the trouble I have caused—all has been brought about by my love for you.

8 **single business:** feeble service.

9 **We . . . hermits:** We (as hermits) will pray for you. Hermits were often paid to pray for another's soul.

10 **coursed . . . heels:** pursued him closely.

11 **purveyor:** advance supply officer.
12 **holp:** helped.

13 **Have . . . own:** Have themselves and everything that is theirs in trust for you, to be rendered to you at your wish.

1 **If . . . quickly:** If the murder itself would put an end to this whole situation, then it would be best to do it quickly.
2 **If . . . come:** If the murder could be done without consequence and if his death would achieve my objective, I would risk life in the world to come.
3 **still . . . judgment:** receive sentence.
4 **that we . . . inventor:** we teach others how to commit evil acts that they may in turn inflict on us.

Commends⁵ th' ingredients of our poisoned chalice⁶
To our own lips. He's here in double trust:
First, as I am his kinsman and his subject,
Strong both against the deed; then, as his host,
15 Who should against his murderer shut the door,
Not bear the knife myself. Besides, this Duncan
Hath borne his faculties⁷ so meek, hath been
So clear⁸ in his great office, that his virtues
Will plead like angels trumpet-tongued against
20 The deep damnation of his taking-off;
And pity, like a naked newborn babe,
Striding the blast, or heaven's cherubin⁹ horsed
Upon the sightless couriers of the air,¹⁰
Shall blow the horrid deed in every eye,
25 That tears shall drown the wind. I have no spur
To prick the sides of my intent, but only
Vaulting ambition, which o'erleaps itself
And falls on th' other—

[LADY MACBETH *joins him.*]

How now! What news?

LADY MACBETH. He has almost supped. Why have you left the
chamber?

MACBETH. Hath he asked for me?

30 **LADY MACBETH.**   Know you not he has?

MACBETH. We will proceed no further in this business:
He hath honored me of late, and I have bought¹¹
Golden opinions from all sorts of people,
Which would be worn now in their newest gloss,
Not cast aside so soon.

35 **LADY MACBETH.**   Was the hope drunk
Wherein you dressed yourself? Hath it slept since?
And wakes it now, to look so green and pale
At what it did so freely? From this time
Such I account thy love. Art thou afeard
40 To be the same in thine own act and valor
As thou art in desire? Wouldst thou have that
Which thou esteem'st the ornament of life,¹²
And live a coward in thine own esteem,
Letting "I dare not" wait upon "I would,"
Like the poor cat i' th' adage?¹³

45 **MACBETH.**   Prithee, peace!
I dare do all that may become a man;
Who dares do more is none.

5 **commends:** offers.
6 **chalice:** cup.

7 **borne . . . faculties:** used his powers.
8 **clear:** blameless, free from reproach.

9 **cherubin:** angels.
10 **sightless . . . air:** invisible runners (the wind).

11 **bought:** acquired.

12 **ornament of life:** the crown.

13 **poor . . . adage:** An old proverb tells of the cat who holds back from catching fish because it is afraid of getting its feet wet.

LADY MACBETH.   What beast was 't then
That made you break[14] this enterprise to me?
When you durst do it, then you were a man;
50 And to be more than what you were, you would
Be so much more the man. Nor time nor place
Did then adhere,[15] and yet you would make both.
They have made themselves, and that their fitness now
Does unmake you.[16] I have given suck, and know
55 How tender 'tis to love the babe that milks me:
I would, while it was smiling in my face,
Have plucked my nipple from his boneless gums,
And dashed the brains out, had I so sworn as you
Have done to this.

MACBETH.   If we should fail?

LADY MACBETH.   We fail?
60 But screw your courage to the sticking-place,[17]
And we'll not fail. When Duncan is asleep—
Whereto the rather shall his day's hard journey
Soundly invite him—his two chamberlains
Will I with wine and wassail[18] so convince,[19]
65 That memory, the warder of the brain,
Shall be a fume, and the receipt of reason
A limbeck only:[20] when in swinish sleep
Their drenchèd natures lies as in a death,
What cannot you and I perform upon
70 Th' unguarded Duncan, what not put upon
His spongy[21] officers, who shall bear the guilt
Of our great quell?[22]

MACBETH.   Bring forth men-children only;
For thy undaunted mettle[23] should compose
Nothing but males. Will it not be received,
75 When we have marked with blood those sleepy two
Of his own chamber, and used their very daggers,
That they have done 't?

LADY MACBETH.   Who dares receive it other,[24]
As[25] we shall make our griefs and clamor roar
Upon his death?

MACBETH.   I am settled, and bend up
80 Each corporal agent to this terrible feat.
Away, and mock the time[26] with fairest show:
False face must hide what the false heart doth know.

[*They leave.*]

14 **break:** disclose.

15 **Did then adhere:** was then appropriate (for murder).

16 **They . . . unmake you:** Now that time and place are right, their very convenience has made you less of a man.

17 **screw . . . sticking-place:** as in preparing a crossbow, screw the bowstring tight into the notch (sticking-place) where it will not slip before firing.

18 **wassail** [wosʹəl]: carousing, merrymaking.
19 **convince:** overpower.

20 **memory . . . only:** Memory, the guardian of the brain, shall become only a vapor, and the brain only a still (limebeck) into which the fumes pass.

21 **spongy:** sodden.

22 **quell:** murder.

23 **mettle:** spirit.

24 **receive it other:** take it otherwise.
25 **As:** seeing that.

26 **mock the time:** mislead the world; mislead all observers.

STUDY QUESTIONS

Recalling

1. After the brief Act I, Scene i, what does the captain in Scene ii tell Duncan that Macbeth did to the rebel Macdonwald? What does Ross report about Macbeth's confrontation with the Thane of Cawdor? How does Duncan reward Macbeth?

2. In Scene iii what do the witches predict for Macbeth and for Banquo? In lines 143–144 what does Macbeth decide to do about his horrible imaginings?

3. In Scene iv what obstacle does King Duncan place between Macbeth and the throne of Scotland? In lines 48–50, what does Macbeth say about the king's proclamation?

4. At the end of Scene v, how does Lady Macbeth advise Macbeth to behave toward the guests who will be arriving shortly?

5. In his speech at the beginning of Scene vii, what misgivings does Macbeth voice about killing King Duncan?

6. At the end of Scene vii, what plan does Lady Macbeth propose to Macbeth?

Interpreting

7. What kind of man is Macbeth? Base your answer on what you have learned about him from the reports of the captain and Banquo in Scene ii and from his association with the witches in Scene iii. How does Macbeth's reaction to the witches differ from Banquo's?

8. What additional character traits does Shakespeare reveal through Macbeth's aside at the end of Scene iii? How do these traits relate to the weaknesses of character that Lady Macbeth, in her speech at the beginning of Scene v, fears will prevent her husband from securing the Scottish throne?

9. What kind of woman is revealed in Lady Macbeth's speeches in Scene v? How does she feel about her husband? What motivates her to help Macbeth plan a course of action?

10. In Scene vii how does Lady Macbeth make Macbeth pledge every effort to bring about Duncan's death?

11. Reread King Duncan's speeches in Scenes ii, iv, and vi. What are several adjectives that might describe him? What kind of character is Shakespeare trying to create?

Extending

12. What do you think the witches represent? What is their effect on Macbeth? How do you think he would behave if he had never met them?

LITERARY FOCUS

Blank Verse

Shakespeare's plays are written largely in **blank verse**—unrhymed lines of iambic pentameter. Each line is divided into five units, or feet, with the stress falling on every second syllable. Blank verse is a versatile meter and comes closest of all metrical patterns to everyday speech. It can be used for description, as in the captain's report of the battle and Macbeth's bravery (Act I, Scene ii). It can be used for conversations of all kinds—for exhortation or rebuke, as in Lady Macbeth's chastisement of Macbeth (Act I, Scene vii), or for introspection, as in Macbeth's soliloquy over the murder of Duncan (Act I, Scene vii). Shakespeare is so skillful in the variation of rhythms, stresses, and caesura (page 20) in his blank verse that he can convey a speaker's every mood.

Thinking About Blank Verse

■ Read aloud Macbeth's aside at the end of Act I, Scene iii, lines 127–142. Emphasize the stresses so that you are aware of the basic iambic pattern. Analyze eight to ten lines of the passage and discuss how Shakespeare varies rhythms, stresses, and caesuras (page 20) to create a particular mood. Identify the mood you think he creates.

ACT II

Scene i. The castle at Inverness.

[*It is late at night as* BANQUO *and his son,* FLEANCE, *both guests of* MACBETH*'s, enter the courtyard of the castle.* FLEANCE *carries a torch to light the way.*]

BANQUO. How goes the night, boy?

FLEANCE. The moon is down; I have not heard the clock.

BANQUO. And she goes down at twelve.

FLEANCE.   I take't, 'tis later, sir.

BANQUO. Hold, take my sword. There's husbandry¹ in heaven.
5   Their candles are all out. Take thee that² too.
A heavy summons³ lies like lead upon me,
And yet I would not sleep. Merciful powers,
Restrain in me the cursèd thoughts that nature
Gives way to in respose!

[MACBETH *and a servant carrying a torch appear.*]

                    Give me my sword!
10   Who's there?

MACBETH. A friend.

BANQUO. What, sir, not yet at rest? The King's a-bed:
He hath been in unusual pleasure, and
Sent forth great largess to your offices:⁴
15   This diamond he greets your wife withal,
By the name of most kind hostess; and shut up⁵
In measureless content.

MACBETH.   Being unprepared,
Our will became the servant to defect,
Which else should free have wrought.⁶

BANQUO.   All's well.
20   I dreamed last night of the three weird sisters:
To you they have showed some truth.

MACBETH.   I think not of them.
Yet, when we can entreat an hour to serve,⁷
We would spend it in some words upon that business,
If you would grant the time.

BANQUO.   At your kind'st leisure.

25   **MACBETH.** If you shall cleave to my consent, when 'tis,⁸
It shall make honor for you.

1 **husbandry:** thrift. The stars are not shining.

2 **that:** probably his sword belt.

3 **summons:** weariness.

4 **largess** [lar′jis] . . . **offices:** gifts to your servants' quarters.

5 **shut up:** retired.

6 **Being . . . wrought:** Our lack of preparation hindered our will to entertain more lavishly.

7 **entreat . . . serve:** find a free hour.

8 **cleave . . . 'tis:** join my cause when the time comes.

BANQUO.   So[9] I lose none
In seeking to augment it, but still keep
My bosom franchised[10] and allegiance clear,
I shall be counseled.[11]

MACBETH.   Good repose the while!

30 **BANQUO.** Thanks, sir. The like to you!

[BANQUO *and* FLEANCE *leave.*]

MACBETH. [*To the servant.*] Go bid thy mistress, when my
    drink is ready,
She strike upon the bell. Get thee to bed.

[*The servant leaves.* MACBETH, *alone, imagines that he sees
a bloody dagger.*]

Is this a dagger which I see before me,
The handle toward my hand? Come, let me clutch thee.
35 I have thee not, and yet I see thee still.
Art thou not, fatal vision, sensible
To feeling[12] as to sight, or art thou but
A dagger of the mind, a false creation,
Proceeding from the heat-oppressèd[13] brain?
40 I see thee yet, in form as palpable
As this which now I draw.
Thou marshal'st me[14] the way that I was going;
And such an instrument I was to use.
Mine eyes are made the fools o' th' other senses,
45 Or else worth all the rest.[15] I see thee still;
And on thy blade and dudgeon[16] gouts[17] of blood,
Which was not so before. There's no such thing.
It is the bloody business which informs[18]
Thus to mine eyes. Now o'er the one half-world
50 Nature seems dead, and wicked dreams abuse
The curtained sleep;[19] witchcraft celebrates
Pale Hecate's offerings;[20] and withered murder,
Alarumed by his sentinel, the wolf,
Whose howl's his watch, thus with his stealthy pace,
55 With Tarquin's[21] ravishing strides, towards his design
Moves like a ghost.[22] Thou sure and firm-set earth,
Hear not my steps, which way they walk, for fear
Thy very stones prate of my whereabout,
And take the present horror from the time,
60 Which now suits with it.[23] Whiles I threat, he lives:
Words to the heat of deeds too cold breath gives.

[*A bell rings,* LADY MACBETH's *signal for* MACBETH *to go to*
DUNCAN's *room.*]

9 **So:** provided that.

10 **My . . . franchised:** my heart
free from guilt.
11 **I . . . counseled:** I will be ready
to listen to you.

12 **sensible . . . feeling:** capable of
being perceived by senses—in this
case, by touch.
13 **heat-oppressèd:** fevered.

14 **marshal'st me:** leads me (to King
Duncan's room).

15 **Mine eyes . . . the rest:** If the
dagger is a vision, my eyes are
misled by my other senses. If it is
real, my eyes are worth all my other
senses put together.
16 **dudgeon:** hilt, handle.
17 **gouts:** large drops.
18 **informs:** takes shape.

19 **curtained sleep:** sleeper
enclosed by the curtains of his bed.
20 **Hecate's offerings:** rituals
dedicated to Hecate, the Greek
goddess of witchcraft.
21 **Tarquin:** infamous sixth-century
Roman tyrant.
22 **withered . . . ghost:** murder,
called to action by the wolf whose
howl tells him of the progress of the
night, moves toward his victim as
silently as a ghost.

23 **take . . . it:** do not let noise
deprive this awful silence of any of its
horror.

I go, and it is done: the bell invites me.
Hear it not, Duncan, for it is a knell
That summons thee to heaven, or to hell.

[MACBETH *leaves.*]

Scene ii. *The castle at Inverness.*

[*Later the same night* LADY MACBETH *enters the empty court-yard of the castle. She is waiting for* MACBETH *to return from his murderous errand.*]

LADY MACBETH. That which hath made them drunk hath made
    me bold;
What hath quenched them hath given me fire. Hark!
    Peace!
It was the owl that shrieked, the fatal bellman,[1]
Which gives the stern'st good night. He is about it.
5   The doors are open, and the surfeited grooms[2]
Do mock their charge[3] with snores. I have drugged their
    possets,[4]
That death and nature do contend about them,
Whether they live or die.

MACBETH. [*Calling from within.*] Who's there? What, ho?

LADY MACBETH. Alack, I am afraid they have awaked
10   And 'tis not done! Th' attempt and not the deed
Confounds[5] us. Hark! I laid their daggers ready;
He could not miss 'em. Had he not resembled
My father as he slept, I had done 't.

[MACBETH *enters, his hands covered with blood.*]

                    My husband!

MACBETH. I have done the deed. Didst thou not hear a noise?

15 LADY MACBETH. I heard the owl scream and the crickets cry.
Did not you speak?

MACBETH.   When?

LADY MACBETH.   Now.

MACBETH.   As I descended?

LADY MACBETH. Ay.

MACBETH. Hark!
Who lies i' th' second chamber?

LADY MACBETH.   Donalbain.

1 **fatal bellman:** It was the custom in London for the bellman to toll the bell outside a condemned person's cell the night before his execution.
2 **surfeited grooms:** overfed servants.
3 **mock their charge:** make a mockery of their duty.
4 **possets:** hot, spiced bedtime drinks.

5 **Confounds:** ruins, destroys.

20 MACBETH. [*Looking at his hands.*] This is a sorry sight.

LADY MACBETH. A foolish thought, to say a sorry[6] sight.

MACBETH. There's one did laugh in 's sleep, and one cried
　　"Murder!"
That they did wake each other. I stood and heard them.
But they did say their prayers, and addressed them[7]
Again to sleep.

25 LADY MACBETH.　　There are two[8] lodged together.

MACBETH. One cried "God bless us!" and "Amen" the other,
As[9] they had seen me with these hangman's hands:
List'ning their fear, I could not say "Amen,"
When they did say "God bless us!"

LADY MACBETH.　　　　　　　　Consider it not so deeply.

30 MACBETH. But wherefore could not I pronounce "Amen"?
I had most need of blessing, and "Amen"
Stuck in my throat.

LADY MACBETH.　　　　These deeds must not be thought
After these ways; so,[10] it will make us mad.

MACBETH. Methought I heard a voice cry "Sleep no more!
35 Macbeth does murder sleep"—the innocent sleep,
Sleep that knits up the raveled sleave[11] of care,
The death of each day's life, sore labor's bath,
Balm of hurt minds, great nature's second course,[12]
Chief nourisher in life's feast—

LADY MACBETH.　　　　　　　What do you mean?

40 MACBETH. Still it cried "Sleep no more!" to all the house:
"Glamis hath murdered sleep, and therefore Cawdor
Shall sleep no more: Macbeth shall sleep no more."

LADY MACBETH. Who was it that thus cried? Why, worthy
　　Thane,
You do unbend[13] your noble strength, to think
45 So brainsickly of things. Go get some water,
And wash this filthy witness from your hand.
Why did you bring these daggers from the place?
They must lie there: go carry them, and smear
The sleepy grooms with blood.

MACBETH.　　　　　　　　I'll go no more.
50 I am afraid to think what I have done;
Look on 't again I dare not.

LADY MACBETH.　　　　　　Infirm of purpose!

6 **sorry:** miserable, pitiable.

7 **addressed them:** prepared themselves.

8 **two:** King Duncan's sons, Malcolm and Donalbain.

9 **As:** as if.

10 **so:** if we do so.

11 **knits . . . sleave:** straightens out the tangled threads.
12 **second course:** the main and most nourishing course of an Elizabethan feast.

13 **unbend:** relax.

Give me the daggers. The sleeping and the dead
Are but as pictures. 'Tis the eye of childhood
That fears a painted devil. If he do bleed,
55   I'll gild[14] the faces of the grooms withal,   14 **gild:** paint.
For it must seem their guilt.

[*As* LADY MACBETH *leaves, knocking is heard offstage.*]

MACBETH.   Whence is that knocking?
How is 't with me, when every noise appalls me?
What hands are here? Ha! They pluck out mine eyes!
Will all great Neptune's ocean wash this blood
60   Clean from my hand? No; this my hand will rather
The multitudinous seas incarnadine,[15]   15 **incarnadine** [in kär′nə din]:
Making the green one red.   redden, color red.

[LADY MACBETH *returns.*]

LADY MACBETH. My hands are of your color, but I shame
To wear a heart so white. [*Knocking within.*] I hear a
    knocking
65   At the south entry. Retire we to our chamber.
A little water clears us of this deed:
How easy is it then! Your constancy
Hath left you unattended.[16] [*Knock.*] Hark! more knocking.   16 **Your constancy . . .
Get on your nightgown, lest occasion call us   unattended:** Your firmness of
70   And show us to be watchers. Be not lost   purpose has deserted you.
So poorly in your thoughts.

MACBETH. To know my deed, 'twere best not know myself.[17]   17 **To . . . myself:** If I am to
    [*Knock.*]   acknowledge what I've done, it would
Wake Duncan with thy knocking! I would thou couldst!   be better for me to remain "lost" in
                                                                     my thoughts.
[*They leave.*]

Scene iii. *The castle at Inverness.*

[*The setting is the same as above, except that now it is early
morning and a drunken* PORTER, *or doorkeeper, enters. Talking to himself as he goes to open the castle gate, he imagines that he is a porter at the gates of hell who is admitting
various lost souls. Finally he lets in* MACDUFF *and* LENNOX,
two noblemen who have been staying in another part of
MACBETH's *castle.*]

PORTER. Here's a knocking indeed! If a man were porter of   1 **should have old:** old was a
    hell gate, he should have old[1] turning the key. [*Knocking*   colloquialism for "plenty of."
    is heard offstage.] Knock, knock, knock! Who's there, i'   2 **Beelzebub:** the devil's helper.
    th' name of Beelzebub?[2] Here's a farmer, that hanged   3 **Here's . . . plenty:** a farmer who
5   himself on th' expectation of plenty.[3] Come in time! Have   hoarded grain, expecting a poor
                                                                       harvest to raise prices.

napkins enow[4] about you; here you'll sweat for 't. [*Knock.*] Knock, knock! Who's there, in th' other devil's name? Faith, here's an equivocator, that could swear in both the scales against either scale;[5] who committed treason enough for God's sake, yet could not equivocate to heaven. O, come in, equivocator. [*Knock.*] Knock, knock, knock! Who's there? Faith, here's an English tailor come hither for stealing out of a French hose:[6] come in, tailor. Here you may roast your goose.[7] [*Knock.*] Knock, knock; never at quiet! What are you? But this place is too cold for hell. I'll devil-porter it no further. I had thought to have let in some of all professions that go the primrose way to th' everlasting bonfire. [*Knock.*] Anon, anon! [*The* PORTER *opens the gate.*] I pray you, remember the porter.

[MACDUFF *and* LENNOX *come in.*]

20 MACDUFF. Was it so late, friend, ere you went to bed,
That you do lie so late?

PORTER. Faith, sir, we were carousing till the second cock:[8] and drink, sir, is a great provoker.

MACDUFF. I believe drink gave thee the lie[9] last night.

25 PORTER. That it did, sir, i' the very throat on me: but I requited[10] him for his lie, and, I think, being too strong for him, though he took up my legs sometime, yet I made a shift to cast[11] him.

MACDUFF. Is thy master stirring?

[MACBETH *enters in his dressing gown.*]

30   Our knocking has awaked him; here he comes.

LENNOX. Good morrow, noble sir.

MACBETH.   Good morrow, both.

MACDUFF. Is the king stirring, worthy Thane?

MACBETH.   Not yet.

MACDUFF. He did command me to call timely[12] on him:
I have almost slipped the hour.

MACBETH.   I'll bring you to him.

35 MACDUFF. I know this is a joyful trouble to you;
But yet 'tis one.

MACBETH. The labor we delight in physics pain.[13]
This is the door.

4 **napkins enow:** handkerchiefs enough.

5 **equivocator . . . scale:** person who, under oath, can give two contradictory answers and still claim not to have violated his oath.

6 **tailor . . . hose:** He stole some cloth from the hose as he was making them.
7 **goose:** pressing iron.

8 **second cock:** 3:00 A.M.

9 **gave . . . lie:** laid you out (as in wrestling).

10 **requited:** repaid.

11 **cast:** a pun on the double meaning of the word—to throw (as in wrestling) and to vomit.

12 **timely:** early.

13 **The labor . . . pain:** The labor we enjoy cures any discomfort associated with it.

MACDUFF   I'll make so bold to call,
For 'tis my limited service.[14]

[MACDUFF *goes to wake* KING DUNCAN.]

LENNOX. Goes the king hence today?

40 **MACBETH.**   He does: he did appoint so.

LENNOX. The night has been unruly. Where we lay,
Our chimneys were blown down, and, as they say,
Lamentings heard i' th' air, strange screams of death,
And prophesying with accents terrible
45 Of dire combustion[15] and confused events
New hatched to th' woeful time: the obscure bird[16]
Clamored the livelong night. Some say, the earth
Was feverous and did shake.[17]

MACBETH.   'Twas a rough night.

LENNOX. My young remembrance cannot parallel
50 A fellow to it.

[MACDUFF *returns, appearing very shaken.*]

MACDUFF. O horror, horror, horror! Tongue nor heart
Cannot conceive nor name thee.

MACBETH and LENNOX.   What's the matter?

MACDUFF. Confusion[18] now hath made his masterpiece.
Most sacrilegious murder hath broke ope
55 The Lord's anointed temple,[19] and stole thence
The life o' th' building.

MACBETH.   What is 't you say? The life?

LENNOX. Mean you his Majesty?

MACDUFF. Approach the chamber, and destroy your sight
With a new Gorgon:[20] do not bid me speak;
60 See, and then speak yourselves. Awake, awake!

[MACBETH *and* LENNOX *rush off.* MACDUFF *comes forward, still upset and shouting.*]

Ring the alarum bell. Murder and Treason!
Banquo and Donalbain! Malcolm! Awake!
Shake off this downy sleep, death's counterfeit,
And look on death itself! Up, up, and see
65 The great doom's image![21] Malcolm! Banquo!
As from your graves rise up, and walk like sprites,[22]
To countenance[23] this horror. Ring the bell.

[*A bell begins to ring offstage as* LADY MACBETH *enters.*]

14 **limited service:** assigned duty.

15 **combustion:** confusion, especially political.

16 **obscure bird:** bird of darkness, the owl, because he is nocturnal.

17 **the earth . . . shake:** There was a popular belief that nature was unruly when there was unrest in the state.

18 **Confusion:** destruction.

19 **The Lord's anointed temple:** the King's body.

20 **Gorgon:** Medusa, a mythological monster whose appearance was so terrible that those who looked at her turned to stone.

21 **great doom's image:** likeness of Judgment Day, doomsday.

22 **sprites:** ghosts, spirits.

23 **countenance:** look upon.

LADY MACBETH. What's the business,
That such a hideous trumpet calls to parley[24]
The sleepers of the house? Speak, speak!

70 **MACDUFF.**   O gentle lady,
'Tis not for you to hear what I can speak:
The repetition, in a woman's ear,
Would murder as it fell.

[BANQUO *enters.*]

                                    O Banquo, Banquo!
Our royal master's murdered.

LADY MACBETH.   Woe, alas!
What, in our house?

75 **BANQUO.**   Too cruel anywhere.
Dear Duff, I prithee, contradict thyself,
And say it is not so.

[MACBETH *and* LENNOX *return with* ROSS.]

MACBETH. Had I but died an hour before this chance,
I had lived a blessèd time; for from this instant
80 There's nothing serious in mortality:[25]
All is but toys.[26] Renown and grace is dead,
The wine of life is drawn, and the mere lees[27]
Is left this vault[28] to brag of.

[MALCOLM *and* DONALBAIN *appear confused as they enter.*
Having just come from bed, they are still in their
nightclothes.]

DONALBAIN. What is amiss?

MACBETH.   You are, and do not know 't.
85 The spring, the head, the fountain of your blood
Is stopped; the very source of it is stopped.

MACDUFF. Your royal father's murdered.

MALCOLM.   O, by whom?

LENNOX. Those of his chamber, as it seemed, had done 't:
Their hands and faces were all badged[29] with blood;
90 So were their daggers, which unwiped we found
Upon their pillows. They stared, and were distracted.
No man's life was to be trusted with them.

MACBETH. O, yet I do repent me of my fury,
That I did kill them.

MACDUFF.   Wherefore did you so?[30]

24 **parley:** a war conference.

25 **There's . . . mortality:** There is
nothing worthwhile in human (mortal)
life.

26 **toys:** trifles, things of little value.

27 **lees:** dregs; residue.

28 **vault:** world.

29 **badged:** marked, as with a
badge.

30 **Wherefore . . . so:** Banquo is
asking Macbeth to explain why he
killed the king's grooms.

95 **MACBETH.** Who can be wise, amazed, temp'rate and furious,
Loyal and neutral, in a moment? No man.
The expedition[31] of my violent love
Outrun the pauser,[32] reason. Here lay Duncan,
His silver skin laced with his golden blood,
100 And his gashed stabs looked like a breach in nature
For ruin's wasteful entrance: there, the murderers,
Steeped in the colors of their trade, their daggers
Unmannerly breeched with gore.[33] Who could refrain,
That had a heart to love, and in that heart
Courage to make 's[34] love known?

105 **LADY MACBETH.**   Help me hence, ho!

[LADY MACBETH *faints.*]

MACDUFF. Look to the lady.

MALCOLM. [*Aside to* DONALBAIN.] Why do we hold our
    tongues,
That most may claim this argument for ours?[35]

DONALBAIN. [*Aside to* MALCOLM.] What should be spoken here,
Where our fate, hid in an auger-hole,[36]
110 May rush, and seize us? Let's away:
Our tears are not yet brewed.

MALCOLM [*Aside to* DONALBAIN.] Nor our strong sorrow
Upon the foot of motion.[37]

BANQUO.   Look to the lady.

[LADY MACBETH, *faint, is carried out.*]

And when we have our naked frailties[38] hid,
That suffer in exposure, let us meet
115 And question[39] this most bloody piece of work,
To know it further. Fears and scruples[40] shake us.
In the great hand of God I stand, and thence
Against the undivulged pretense I fight
Of treasonous malice.[41]

MACDUFF.   And so do I.

ALL.   So all.

120 **MACBETH.** Let's briefly put on manly readiness,
And meet i' th' hall together.

ALL.   Well contented.

[*Everyone leaves except* MALCOLM *and* DONALBAIN.]

MALCOLM. What will you do? Let's not consort with them.

31 **expedition:** haste.
32 **pauser:** delayer.

33 **breeched with gore:** covered with blood, as with breeches (trousers that end just below the knee).

34 **make 's:** make his.

35 **That . . . ours?:** who are the most concerned with this topic under discussion.

36 **auger-hole:** a very small hole made by a carpenter's tool. Because it is so small, an improbable hiding place.

37 **Upon . . . motion:** yet begun to express itself.

38 **naked frailties:** they are still in their nightclothes.

39 **question:** investigate.
40 **scruples:** doubts.

41 **Against . . . malice:** I fight against the reason, as yet unknown, for this treasonous act.

To show an unfelt sorrow[42] is an office[43]
Which the false man does easy. I'll to England.

125 **DONALBAIN.** To Ireland, I; our separated fortune
Shall keep us both the safer. Where we are
There's daggers in men's smiles; the near in blood,
The nearer bloody.[44]

MALCOLM.   This murderous shaft that's shot
Hath not yet lighted,[45] and our safest way
130 Is to avoid the aim. Therefore to horse;
And let us not be dainty of leave-taking,
But shift away.[46] There's warrant in that theft
Which steals itself when there's no mercy left.[47]

[*They leave.*]

Scene iv. *The castle at Inverness.*

[*The nobleman* ROSS *and an* OLD MAN *meet outside* MACBETH's
*castle. They discuss the terrible storm and other unnatural
phenomena that accompanied the murder of* DUNCAN.]

OLD MAN. Threescore and ten I can remember well:
Within the volume of which time I have seen
Hours dreadful and things strange, but this sore[1] night
Hath trifled former knowings.

ROSS.   Ha, good father,
5 Thou seest the heavens, as troubled with man's act,
Threatens his bloody stage.[2] By th' clock 'tis day,
And yet dark night strangles the traveling lamp:[3]
Is 't night's predominance, or the day's shame,
That darkness does the face of earth entomb,
When living light should kiss it?

10 **OLD MAN.**   'Tis unnatural,
Even like the deed that's done. On Tuesday last
A falcon, tow'ring in her pride of place,[4]
Was by a mousing owl hawked at and killed.

ROSS. And Duncan's horses—a thing most strange and
    certain—
15 Beauteous and swift, the minions[5] of their race,
Turned wild in nature, broke their stalls, flung out,
Contending 'gainst obedience, as they would make
War with mankind.

OLD MAN.   'Tis said they eat[6] each other.

42 **unfelt sorrow:** an indication that Malcolm and Donalbain suspect the sorrow of one of the onlookers is false.
43 **office:** duty.

44 **The near . . . bloody:** The more closely we are related to Duncan, the greater our chance of being murdered.
45 **lighted:** reached its target.

46 **And . . . away:** Let's not worry about the particulars of saying goodbye, but slip away quickly.
47 **There's . . . left:** There's justification in stealing away in these merciless times.

1 **sore:** terrible, grievous.

2 **bloody stage:** the earth.
3 **traveling lamp:** the sun.

4 **tow'ring . . . place:** soaring as high as it could before swooping down on its prey.

5 **minions:** favorites; best of their breed.

6 **eat:** ate.

ROSS. They did so, to th' amazement of mine eyes,
That looked upon 't.

[MACDUFF *enters.*]

20   Here comes the good Macduff.
How goes the world, sir, now?

MACDUFF.   Why, see you not?

ROSS. Is 't known who did this more than bloody deed?

MACDUFF. Those that Macbeth hath slain.

ROSS.   Alas, the day!
What good could they pretend?[7]

MACDUFF.   They were suborned:[8]
25   Malcolm and Donalbain, the king's two sons,
Are stol'n away and fled, which puts upon them
Suspicion of the deed.

ROSS.   'Gainst nature still.
Thriftless ambition, that will ravin up[9]
Thine own life's means! Then 'tis most like
30   The sovereignty will fall upon Macbeth.

MACDUFF. He is already named, and gone to Scone
To be invested.[10]

ROSS.   Where is Duncan's body?

MACDUFF. Carried to Colmekill,
The sacred storehouse of his predecessors
And guardian of their bones.

35 **ROSS.**   Will you to Scone?

MACDUFF. No, cousin, I'll to Fife.[11]

ROSS.   Well, I will thither.

MACDUFF. Well, may you see things well done there. Adieu,
Lest our old robes sit easier than our new![12]

ROSS. Farewell, father.

40 **OLD MAN.** God's benison[13] go with you, and with those
That would make good of bad, and friends of foes!

[*They leave.*]

7 **pretend:** intend, hope for.

8 **suborned:** bribed.

9 **ravin up:** swallow greedily.

10 **already named . . . invested:** already chosen (king) and gone to Scone, the traditional site of the coronation of Scottish kings, to be crowned.

11 **Fife:** Macduff is Thane of Fife.

12 **Lest . . . new:** Lest the old rule suits us better than the new. Another image of clothing.

13 **benison:** blessing.

STUDY QUESTIONS

Recalling

1. What does Macbeth imagine he sees as he begins his soliloquy near the end of Act II, Scene i? Where is Macbeth going at the end of the scene?
2. In Scene ii what does Lady Macbeth do with the bloody daggers that Macbeth has brought with him from the king's rooms? Why does Macbeth not deal with the daggers himself?
3. What two things does Lady Macbeth tell Macbeth to do at the end of Scene ii? What does Macbeth say when he hears the knocking at the end of the scene?
4. Why has Macduff come to Macbeth's castle in Scene iii? Who discovers the body of the king?
5. In Scene iii how does Macbeth justify his killing of the king's servants?
6. What unnatural events do the Old Man and Ross describe at the beginning of Scene iv?
7. Where is Macbeth and what is he doing as Scene iv is taking place? As the scene ends, where does Macduff tell Ross he has decided to go?

Interpreting

8. What kind of mood or atmosphere does Macbeth's soliloquy create at the end of Scene i, lines 33–64? Mention three or four images in support of your answer.
9. In Scene iii who seems more genuinely excited and troubled by the death of King Duncan, Macbeth or Macduff?
10. In Scenes ii and iii who seems better able to maintain emotional control, Macbeth or Lady Macbeth? Do you think Lady Macbeth's fainting is genuine or deliberate? Build a case for both possibilities.
11. In Scene iii what reasons do Donalbain and Malcolm give for not consorting with Banquo, Macduff, and Macbeth? Specifically, whom do they mistrust and why?

12. How do the unnatural events described by the Old Man and Ross in Scene iv relate to the violence that has taken place in Macbeth's castle?

Extending

13. For what reasons do you imagine Macbeth kills Duncan? Are his actions based on practicality or emotion? Do you think Macbeth will achieve his goals?

LITERARY FOCUS

Imagery

Through the use of **imagery,** writers expand and enhance the basic literal meaning of their words. By using devices such as similes, metaphors, symbols, and other figurative language, they engage our senses, recalling memories and associations to evoke a certain mood. Images appeal to any of the five senses and often involve more than one at a time. For example in Act I, Scene v, when Lady Macbeth says "The raven himself is hoarse/That croaks the fatal entrance of Duncan," we see a black bird of ill omen; at the same time we feel in our throats the raspy cry that rings in our ears.

Imagery that evokes a particular dramatic mood was especially important to Shakespeare because his plays were performed in daylight without benefit of elaborate scenery. The "temple-haunting martlet" soars on "heaven's breath" when the gentle, unsuspecting Duncan arrives at Macbeth's castle (Act I, Scene vi), but on the day of the king's murder "darkness does the face of the earth entomb."

Thinking About Imagery

■ Examine Macbeth's speech in Act II, Scene ii, lines 56–62. What image does he use to convey his emotion? What feelings is he expressing? What kind of mood does the image create?

ACT III

Scene i. *The palace at Forres.*

[BANQUO *is alone in a room in the royal palace at Forres. He is recalling all that the witches prophesied.*]

    BANQUO. Thou hast it now: King, Cawdor, Glamis, all,
    As the weird women promised, and I fear
    Thou play'dst most foully for 't. Yet it was said
    It should not stand¹ in thy posterity,
5   But that myself should be the root and father
    Of many kings. If there come truth from them—
    As upon thee, Macbeth, their speeches shine—
    Why, by the verities on thee made good,
    May they not be my oracles as well
10   And set me up in hope? But hush, no more!

1 **stand:** continue.

[*A trumpet sounds as* MACBETH, *the new king, and* LADY MACBETH *enter. They are accompanied by* LENNOX, ROSS, *other* LORDS, LADIES, *and attendants.*]

    MACBETH. Here's our chief guest.

    LADY MACBETH.   If he had been forgotten,
    It had been as a gap in our great feast,
    And all-thing² unbecoming.

2 **all-thing:** altogether.

    MACBETH. Tonight we hold a solemn supper,³ sir,
    And I'll request your presence.

3 **solemn supper:** formal banquet.

15 **BANQUO.**   Let your Highness
    Command upon me, to the which my duties
    Are with a most indissoluble tie
    For ever knit.

    MACBETH. Ride you this afternoon?

    BANQUO.   Ay, my good lord.

20 **MACBETH.** We should have else desired your good advice
    (Which still hath been both grave and prosperous⁴)
    In this day's council; but we'll take tomorrow.⁵
    Is 't far you ride?

4 **still . . . prosperous:** always has been weighty and profitable in its result.

5 **we'll . . . tomorrow:** tomorrow will do just as well.

    BANQUO. As far, my lord, as will fill up the time
25   'Twixt this and supper. Go not my horse the better,⁶
    I must become a borrower of the night
    For a dark hour or twain.

6 **Go . . . better:** unless my horse goes faster than I expect.

    MACBETH.   Fail not our feast.

    BANQUO. My lord, I will not.

MACBETH. We hear our bloody cousins are bestowed
30　In England and in Ireland, not confessing
Their cruel parricide, filling their hearers
With strange invention.⁷ But of that tomorrow,
When therewithal we shall have cause of state
Craving us jointly.⁸ Hie you to horse. Adieu,
35　Till you return at night. Goes Fleance with you?

BANQUO. Ay, my good lord: our time does call upon 's.⁹

MACBETH. I wish your horses swift and sure of foot,
And so I do commend you to their backs.
Farewell. [BANQUO leaves.]
40　Let every man be master of his time
Till seven at night. To make society
The sweeter welcome, we will keep ourself
Till suppertime alone. While¹⁰ then, God be with you!

[*Everyone leaves except* MACBETH *and a* SERVANT.]

Sirrah,¹¹ a word with you: attend those men
45　Our pleasure?

ATTENDANT. They are, my lord, without the palace gate.

MACBETH. Bring them before us.

[*The* SERVANT *leaves.* MACBETH, *alone, realizes that he will
never feel safe on the throne as long as* BANQUO—*promised
by the* WITCHES *to be father of kings—is alive.*]

To be thus is nothing, but to be safely thus¹²—
Our fears in Banquo stick deep,
50　And in his royalty of nature reigns that
Which would be feared. 'Tis much he dares;
And, to¹³ that dauntless temper of his mind,
He hath a wisdom that doth guide his valor
To act in safety. There is none but he
55　Whose being I do fear: and under him
My genius is rebuked,¹⁴ as it is said
Mark Antony's was by Caesar. He chid¹⁵ the sisters,
When first they put the name of King upon me,
And bade them speak to him; then prophetlike
60　They hailed him father to a line of kings.
Upon my head they placed a fruitless crown
And put a barren scepter in my gripe,¹⁶
Thence to be wrenched with an unlineal hand,
No son of mine succeeding. If 't be so,
65　For Banquo's issue have I filed¹⁷ my mind;
For them the gracious Duncan have I murdered;
Put rancors in the vessel of my peace

7 **invention:** lies.

8 **cause . . . jointly:** matters of state requiring the attention of both of us.

9 **our . . . upon 's:** time is short, urging us to depart.

10 **While:** until.

11 **Sirrah:** a form of address to an inferior.

12 **To . . . thus:** To be king is nothing, unless I can rule in safety.

13 **And, to:** in addition to.

14 **genius is rebuked:** spirit is cowed.

15 **chid:** scolded.

16 **gripe:** grip.

17 **filed:** defiled, corrupted.

Only for them, and mine eternal jewel[18]
Given to the common enemy of man,[19]
70 To make them kings, the seeds of Banquo kings!
Rather than so, come, fate, into the list,[20]
And champion me to th' utterance![21] Who's there?

[*The* SERVANT *returns with two* MURDERERS, *and* MACBETH
addresses the SERVANT.]

Now go to the door, and stay there till we call.

[*The* SERVANT *leaves.*]

Was it not yesterday we spoke together?

MURDERERS. It was, so please your Highness.

75 MACBETH.   Well then, now
Have you considered of my speeches? Know
That it was he[22] in the times past, which held you
So under fortune,[23] which you thought had been
Our innocent self: this I made good to you
80 In our last conference; passed in probation[24] with you,
How you were born in hand,[25] how crossed; the
        instruments,
Who wrought with them, and all things else that might
To half a soul[26] and to a notion[27] crazed
Say "Thus did Banquo."

FIRST MURDERER.   You made it known to us.

85 MACBETH. I did so; and went further, which is now
Our point of second meeting. Do you find
Your patience so predominant in your nature,
That you can let this go? Are you so gospeled,[28]
To pray for this good man and for his issue,
90 Whose heavy hand hath bowed you to the grave
And beggared yours for ever?

FIRST MURDERER.   We are men, my liege.

MACBETH. Ay, in the catalogue ye go for[29] men;
As hounds and greyhounds, mongrels, spaniels, curs,
Shoughs, water-rugs[30] and demi-wolves,[31] are clept[32]
95 All by the name of dogs: the valued file[33]
Distinguishes the swift, the slow, the subtle,
The housekeeper, the hunter, every one
According to the gift which bounteous nature
Hath in him closed,[34] whereby he does receive
100 Particular addition,[35] from the bill
That writes them all alike: and so of men.
Now if you have a station in the file,[36]

18 **eternal jewel:** soul.
19 **common . . . man:** devil.
20 **list:** lists, the field of combat, tournament ground.
21 **champion . . . utterance:** fight me to the very death.

22 **he:** Banquo.
23 **held . . . fortune:** thwarted your good fortune.
24 **passed in probation:** reviewed the proofs.
25 **born in hand:** deceived.

26 **half a soul:** half-wit.
27 **notion:** mind.

28 **so gospeled:** ready to forgive.

29 **go for:** pass as.

30 **Shoughs, water-rugs:** shaggy, long-haired water dogs.
31 **demi-wolves:** half-wolf, half-dog.
32 **clept:** called.
33 **valued file:** list of valuable traits that distinguish each breed.

34 **in him closed:** enclosed him.
35 **Particular addition:** a name or title that distinguishes him (from the other dogs).
36 **file:** ranks.

Not i' th' worst rank of manhood, say 't,
And I will put that business in your bosoms
105 Whose execution takes your enemy off,
Grapples you to the heart and love of us,
Who wear our health but sickly in his life,[37]
Which in his death were perfect.

SECOND MURDERER.   I am one, my liege,
Whom the vile blows and buffets of the world
110 Hath so incensed that I am reckless what
I do to spite the world.

FIRST MURDERER.   And I another
So weary with disasters, tugged with fortune,
That I would set[38] my life on any chance,
To mend it or be rid on 't.

MACBETH.   Both of you
Know Banquo was your enemy.

115 BOTH MURDERERS.   True, my lord.

MACBETH. So is he mine, and in such bloody distance[39]
That every minute of his being thrusts
Against my near'st of life:[40] and though I could
With barefaced power sweep him from my sight
120 And bid my will avouch[41] it, yet I must not,
For certain friends that are both his and mine,
Whose loves I may not drop, but wail his fall[42]
Who I myself struck down: and thence it is
That I to your assistance do make love,
125 Masking the business from the common eye
For sundry weighty reasons.

SECOND MURDERER.   We shall, my lord,
Perform what you command us.

FIRST MURDERER.   Though our lives—

MACBETH. Your spirits shine through you. Within this hour at
   most
I will advise you where to plant yourselves,
130 Acquaint you with the perfect spy o' th' time,[43]
The moment on 't; for 't must be done tonight,
And something[44] from the palace; always thought[45]
That I require a clearness:[46] and with him—
To leave no rubs[47] nor botches in the work—
135 Fleance his son, that keeps him company,
Whose absence is no less material to me[48]
Than is his father's, must embrace the fate
Of that dark hour. Resolve yourselves apart:[49]
I'll come to you anon.

37 **wear . . . life:** I am a sick man as long as he (Banquo) lives.

38 **set:** risk.

39 **distance:** disagreement.

40 **near'st of life:** most vital parts.

41 **avouch:** justify.

42 **wail his fall:** (I must) bewail his death.

43 **perfect . . . time:** exact information of the exact moment.

44 **something:** some distance.
45 **always thought:** being understood.
46 **I . . . clearness:** I must remain above suspicion.
47 **rubs:** flaws, imperfections.

48 **Whose . . . me:** whose death is no less important to me.

49 **Resolve . . . apart:** Make up your minds privately.

BOTH MURDERERS.   We are resolved, my lord.

140 MACBETH. I'll call upon you straight.⁵⁰ [*The* MURDERERS *leave.*]   50 **straight:** immediately.
　　　Abide within.
　　　It is concluded: Banquo, thy soul's flight,
　　　If it find heaven, must find it out tonight. [MACBETH
　　　　leaves.]

Scene ii. The palace at Forres.

[LADY MACBETH *and a* SERVANT *are in another room in the palace. She is concerned about what has happened and sends
for* MACBETH *to discuss recent events with him.*]

LADY MACBETH. Is Banquo gone from court?

SERVANT. Ay, madam, but returns again tonight.

LADY MACBETH. Say to the King, I would attend his leisure
　　　For a few words.

SERVANT.   Madam, I will. [*The* SERVANT *leaves to
　　　summon* MACBETH.]

LADY MACBETH.   Nought's had, all's spent,
5 Where our desire is got without content:
　　　'Tis safer to be that which we destroy
　　　Than by destruction dwell in doubtful¹ joy.   1 **doubtful:** apprehensive.

[MACBETH *enters.*]

　　　How now, my lord! Why do you keep alone,
　　　Of sorriest² fancies your companions making,   2 **sorriest:** most miserable.
10 Using those thoughts which should indeed have died
　　　With them they think on? Things without all remedy
　　　Should be without regard: what's done is done.

MACBETH. We have scorched³ the snake, not killed it: 3 **scorched:** slashed, wounded.
　　　She'll close⁴ and be herself, whilst our poor⁵ malice   4 **close:** heal.
　　　　　　　　　　　　　　　　　　　　　　　　　　　　　5 **poor:** ineffective.
15 Remains in danger of her former tooth.⁶   6 **in . . . tooth:** in as much danger
　　　But let the frame of things disjoint, both the worlds   as before.
　　　　suffer,⁷   7 **But . . . suffer:** Let the universe
　　　Ere we will eat our meal in fear, and sleep   fall apart, and let both heaven and
　　　In the affliction of these terrible dreams   earth perish.
　　　That shake us nightly: better be with the dead,
20 Whom we, to gain our peace, have sent to peace,
　　　Than on the torture of the mind to lie
　　　In restless ecstasy.⁸ Duncan is in his grave;   8 **ecstasy:** frenzy, madness.
　　　After life's fitful fever he sleeps well.
　　　Treason has done his worst: nor steel, nor poison,

25 Malice domestic, foreign levy,[9] nothing,
    Can touch him further.

LADY MACBETH.   Come on.
    Gentle my lord, sleek o'er your rugged looks;
    Be bright and jovial among your guests tonight.

MACBETH. So shall I, love; and so, I pray, be you:
30   Let your remembrance apply to Banquo;
    Present him eminence,[10] both with eye and tongue:
    Unsafe the while, that we must lave
    Our honors in these flattering[11] streams
    And make our faces vizards[12] to our hearts,
    Disguising what they are.

35 LADY MACBETH.   You must leave this.

MACBETH. O, full of scorpions is my mind, dear wife!
    Thou know'st that Banquo, and his Fleance, lives.

LADY MACBETH. But in them nature's copy's not eterne.[13]

MACBETH. There's comfort yet; they are assailable.
40   Then be thou jocund.[14] Ere the bat hath flown
    His cloistered[15] flight, ere to black Hecate's summons
    The shard-borne[16] beetle with his drowsy hums
    Hath rung night's yawning peal, there shall be done
    A deed of dreadful note.

LADY MACBETH.   What's to be done?

45 MACBETH. Be innocent of the knowledge, dearest chuck,[17]
    Till thou applaud the deed. Come, seeling[18] night,
    Scarf up[19] the tender eye of pitiful day,
    And with thy bloody and invisible hand
    Cancel and tear to pieces that great bond[20]
50   Which keeps me pale! Light thickens, and the crow
    Makes wing to th' rooky[21] wood.
    Good things of day begin to droop and drowse,
    Whiles night's black agents to their preys do rouse.
    Thou marvel'st at my words: but hold thee still;
55   Things bad begun make strong themselves by ill:
    So, prithee, go with me. [*They leave together.*]

Scene iii. *Outside the palace at Forres.*

[*About a mile from the palace, the two assassins wait to attack* BANQUO *and* FLEANCE. *They are joined by a mysterious*
THIRD MURDERER *who is probably a spy sent by* MACBETH *to
make sure the other murderers carry out his orders.*]

9 **Malice . . . levy:** civil and
foreign war.

10 **Present him eminence:** Assign
to him the highest distinction.
11 **Unsafe . . . flattering:** We are
not safe so long as we must bathe
our honors in a stream of flattery.
12 **vizards** [viz'ərdz]: masks.

13 **in . . . eterne:** they do not have
eternal life.
14 **jocund:** merry.
15 **cloistered:** Bats live in cloisters
(covered walks along the walls of a
monastery, usually built around a
courtyard) and belfries, or bell
towers.
16 **shard-borne:** borne on scaly
wings.

17 **chuck:** a term of endearment.

18 **seeling:** eye-closing. The term
comes from falconry. Night is like the
falconer who sometimes sewed his
hawk's eyes closed in order to
tame it.
19 **Scarf up:** blindfold.

20 **that great bond:** between
Banquo and fate.
21 **rooky:** black and full of rooks
(crowlike birds).

FIRST MURDERER. But who did bid thee join with us?

THIRD MURDERER.   Macbeth.

SECOND MURDERER. He needs not our mistrust; since he
     delivers
Our offices[1] and what we have to do
To the direction just.[2]

FIRST MURDERER.   Then stand with us.
5   The west yet glimmers with some streaks of day.
Now spurs the lated traveler apace[3]
To gain the timely inn,[4] and near approaches
The subject of our watch.

THIRD MURDERER.   Hark! I hear horses.

BANQUO. [*Calls from offstage.*] Give us a light there, ho!

SECOND MURDERER.   Then 'tis he. The rest
10   That are within the note of expectation[5]
Already are i' th' court.

FIRST MURDERER.   His horses go about.[6]

THIRD MURDERER. Almost a mile: but he does usually—
So all men do—from hence to th' palace gate
Make it their walk.

[BANQUO *and* FLEANCE, *carrying a torch, enter on foot.*]

SECOND MURDERER. A light, a light!

THIRD MURDERER.   'Tis he.

15 **FIRST MURDERER.**   Stand to 't.

BANQUO. It will be rain tonight.

FIRST MURDERER.   Let it come down.

[*They attack* BANQUO.]

BANQUO. O, treachery! Fly, good Fleance, fly, fly, fly!

[FLEANCE *escapes.*]

Thou mayst revenge. O slave! [BANQUO *dies.*]

THIRD MURDERER. Who did strike out the light?

FIRST MURDERER.   Was 't not the way?[7]

20 **THIRD MURDERER.** There's but one down; the son is fled.

SECOND MURDERER. We have lost best half of our affair.

1 **offices:** duties.
2 **To . . . just:** in exact detail.

3 **apace:** speedily.
4 **To gain . . . inn:** to reach an inn in good time.

5 **within . . . expectation:** on the list of the expected guests.

6 **His . . . about:** His horses have been taken around to the stable.

7 **Was 't . . . way:** Was this not the way we were told to do it?

FIRST MURDERER. Well, let's away and say how much is done.

[*The* MURDERERS *leave.*]

Scene iv. *The palace at Forres.*

[*A banquet has been prepared in a hall of the royal palace.* MACBETH *and* LADY MACBETH *enter with their guests,* ROSS, LENNOX, *and other* LORDS *and their attendants.*]

MACBETH. You know your own degrees;[1] sit down:
　At first and last, the hearty welcome.

LORDS. Thanks to your Majesty.

MACBETH. Ourself will mingle with society
5　And play the humble host.
　Our hostess keeps her state,[2] but in best time
　We will require her welcome.[3]

LADY MACBETH. Pronounce it for me, sir, to all our friends,
　For my heart speaks they are welcome.

[*The first* MURDERER *enters and stands near the door.*]

10　**MACBETH.** See, they encounter thee with their hearts' thanks.
　Both sides are even: here I'll sit i' th' midst:[4]
　Be large in mirth; anon we'll drink a measure[5]
　The table round. [*He goes to the* MURDERER *at the door.*]
　There's blood upon thy face.

MURDERER. 'Tis Banquo's then.

15　**MACBETH.** 'Tis better thee without than he within.[6]
　Is he dispatched?

MURDERER. My lord, his throat is cut; that I did for him.

MACBETH. Thou art the best o' th' cutthroats.
　Yet he's good that did the like for Fleance;
20　If thou didst it, thou art the nonpareil.[7]

MURDERER. Most royal sir, Fleance is 'scaped.

MACBETH. [*Aside.*] Then comes my fit[8] again: I had else been perfect,
　Whole as the marble, founded as the rock,
　As broad and general as the casing air:[9]
25　But now I am cabined, cribbed, confined, bound in
　To saucy[10] doubts and fears. [*To the* MURDERER.]—But
　Banquo's safe?

MURDERER. Ay, my good lord: safe in a ditch he bides,

1 **You . . . degrees:** You know your ranks. At state banquets guests were seated according to rank.

2 **keeps her state:** sits apart on her throne.
3 **in . . . welcome:** When the proper time comes, we will ask her to join us.

4 **Both . . . midst:** There are equal numbers on both sides of the table, and Macbeth sits at the head.

5 **measure:** toast.

6 **'Tis better . . . within:** It is better on your face than in his body.

7 **nonpareil** [non′pə rel′]: one without equal.

8 **my fit:** my torment.

9 **As . . . air:** as free and unrestrained as the surrounding air.

10 **saucy:** insolent.

With twenty trenchèd gashes[11] on his head,
The least a death to nature.[12]

MACBETH.   Thanks for that.
30 [*Aside.*] There the grown serpent lies; the worm that's fled
Hath nature that in time will venom breed,
No teeth for th' present. [*To the* MURDERER.]—Get thee gone. Tomorrow
We'll hear ourselves[13] again. [*The* MURDERER *leaves.*]

LADY MACBETH.   My royal lord,
You do not give the cheer.[14] The feast is sold
35 That is not often vouched, while 'tis a-making,
'Tis given with welcome.[15] To feed were best at home;
From thence, the sauce to meat is ceremony;[16]
Meeting were bare without it.

[*The* GHOST OF BANQUO *enters and sits in* MACBETH'*s place.*]

MACBETH.   Sweet remembrancer!
Now good digestion wait on appetite,
And health on both!

40 LENNOX.   May 't please your Highness sit.

MACBETH. Here had we now our country's honor roofed,[17]
Were the gracèd person of our Banquo present—
Who may I rather challenge for unkindness
Than pity for mischance![18]

ROSS.   His absence, sir,
45 Lays blame upon his promise. Please 't your Highness
To grace us with your royal company?

[MACBETH *looks at his chair and sees the* GHOST.]

MACBETH. The table's full.

LENNOX.   Here is a place reserved, sir.

MACBETH. Where?

LENNOX. [*Indicating the empty place where* MACBETH *sees the* GHOST.] Here, my good lord. What is 't that moves your Highness?

MACBETH. Which of you have done this?

50 LORDS.   What, my good lord?

MACBETH. Thou canst not say I did it. Never shake
Thy gory locks at me.

ROSS. Gentlemen, rise, his Highness is not well.

LADY MACBETH. Sit, worthy friends. My lord is often thus,

11 **trenchèd gashes:** deep cuts.
12 **death to nature:** enough to kill a man.

13 **hear ourselves:** talk it over.

14 **cheer:** make the company welcome.
15 **The feast . . . welcome:** A feast where guests are not made welcome is no more than a tavern-bought meal.
16 **To feed . . . ceremony:** When not eating at home, ceremony adds a pleasant flavor to the meal.

17 **our . . . roofed:** the most honorable men in the country under one roof.

18 **I . . . mischance:** I would rather reproach him for being absent due to discourtesy than because of some accident.

55 And hath been from his youth. Pray you, keep seat.
The fit is momentary; upon a thought[19]
He will again be well. If much you note him,
You shall offend him and extend his passion.[20]
Feed, and regard him not. [*To* MACBETH.]—Are you a man?

60 MACBETH. Ay, and a bold one, that dare look on that
Which might appall the devil.

LADY MACBETH.   O proper stuff![21]
This is the very painting of your fear.
This is the air-drawn dagger which, you said,
Led you to Duncan. O, these flaws[22] and starts,
65 Impostors to true fear, would well become
A woman's story at a winter's fire,
Authorized by her grandam.[23] Shame itself!
Why, do you make such faces? Whan all's done,
You look but on a stool.

MACBETH.   Prithee, see there!
70 Behold! Look! Lo! [*To the* GHOST.] How say you?
Why, what care I? If thou canst nod, speak too.
If charnel houses[24] and our graves must send
Those that we bury back, our monuments
Shall be the maws of kites.[25] [*The* GHOST *vanishes.*]

LADY MACBETH.   What, quite unmanned in folly?

MACBETH. If I stand here, I saw him.

75 LADY MACBETH.   Fie, for shame!

MACBETH. Blood hath been shed ere now, i' th' olden time,
Ere humane statute purged the gentle weal;[26]
Ay, and since too, murders have been performed
Too terrible for the ear. The times has been
80 That, when the brains were out, the man would die,
And there an end; but now they rise again,
With twenty mortal murders on their crowns,[27]
And push us from our stools. This is more strange
Than such a murder is.

LADY MACBETH.   My worthy lord,
Your noble friends do lack you.

85 MACBETH.   I do forget.
Do not muse at me, my most worthy friends;
I have a strange infirmity, which is nothing
To those that know me. Come, love and health to all!
Then I'll sit down. Give me some wine, fill full.

[*The* GHOST *reappears, but* MACBETH *does not notice him at once.*]

19 **upon a thought:** in a moment.

20 **passion:** suffering.

21 **proper stuff!:** Nonsense!

22 **flaws:** literally, sudden gusts of wind; outbursts of emotion.

23 **Authorized . . . grandam:** given on the authority of her grandmother.

24 **charnel houses:** buildings where bones dug up from old graves were stored.
25 **our . . . kites:** our tombs will be the bellies of birds of prey.

26 **Ere . . . weal:** before human laws civilized the state and made it peaceful.

27 **mortal . . . crowns:** deadly wounds on their heads.

90　I drink to th' general joy o' th' whole table,
　　And to our dear friend Banquo, whom we miss;
　　Would he were here! To all and him we thirst,[28]
　　And all to all.

　　LORDS.　　　　　Our duties, and the pledge.

　　MACBETH. [*To the* GHOST.] Avaunt![29] and quit my sight! Let
　　　the earth hide thee!
95　Thy bones are marrowless, thy blood is cold;
　　Thou hast no speculation[30] in those eyes
　　Which thou dost glare with.

　　LADY MACBETH.　　　　Think of this, good peers,
　　But as a thing of custom; 'tis no other.
　　Only it spoils the pleasure of the time.

100　MACBETH. What man dare, I dare.
　　Approach thou like the rugged Russian bear,
　　The armed rhinoceros, or th' Hyrcan tiger;[31]
　　Take any shape but that,[32] and my firm nerves
　　Shall never tremble. Or be alive again,
105　And dare me to the desert[33] with thy sword.
　　If trembling I inhabit then, protest me
　　The baby of a girl.[34] Hence, horrible shadow!
　　Unreal mock'ry, hence! [*The* GHOST *vanishes again.*]
　　　　　　　Why, so: being gone,
　　I am a man again. Pray you, sit still.

　　LADY MACBETH. You have displaced the mirth, broke the good
110　　meeting,
　　With most admired disorder.[35]

　　MACBETH.　　　　　Can such things be,
　　And overcome us[36] like a summer's cloud,
　　Without our special wonder? You make me strange
　　Even to the disposition that I owe,[37]
115　When now I think you can behold such sights,
　　And keep the natural ruby of your cheeks,
　　When mine is blanched with fear.

　　ROSS.　　　　　　What sights, my lord?

　　LADY MACBETH. I pray you, speak not: he grows worse and
　　　worse;
　　Question enrages him: at once, good night.
120　Stand not upon the order of your going,[38]
　　But go at once.

　　LENNOX.　　　Good night; and better health
　　Attend his Majesty!

28 **thirst:** drink.

29 **Avaunt!:** Be gone!

30 **speculations:** sights.

31 **Hyrcan** [hûr′kən] **tiger:** Hyrcania was located south of the Caspian Sea in ancient Asia. Hercules was said to have killed the Hyrcan tiger.
32 **that:** Banquo's shape.

33 **desert:** inescapable place.

34 **If . . . girl:** If I tremble, then call me a baby girl.

35 **admired disorder:** amazing lack of self-control.

36 **overcome us:** come over us.

37 **disposition . . . owe:** my own nature, myself.

38 **Stand . . . going:** Do not wait to leave in order of your rank.

LADY MACBETH.   A kind good night to all!

[*Everyone leaves except* MACBETH *and* LADY MACBETH.]

MACBETH. It will have blood, they say: blood will have blood.
Stones have been known to move and trees to speak;
125 Augures and understood relations[39] have
By maggot-pies and choughs[40] and rooks brought forth[41]
The secret'st man of blood.[42] What is the night?

LADY MACBETH. Almost at odds[43] with morning, which is
which.

MACBETH. How say'st thou, that Macduff denies his person
At our great bidding?

130 **LADY MACBETH.**   Did you send to him, sir?

MACBETH. I hear it by the way, but I will send:
There's not a one of them but in his house
I keep a servant fee'd.[44] I will tomorrow,
And betimes[45] I will, to the weird sisters:
135 More shall they speak, for now I am bent[46] to know
By the worst means the worst. For mine own good
All causes shall give way. I am in blood
Stepped in so far that, should I wade no more,
Returning were as tedious as go o'er.
140 Strange things I have in head that will to hand,
Which must be acted ere they may be scanned.[47]

LADY MACBETH. You lack the season of all natures,[48] sleep.

MACBETH. Come, we'll to sleep. My strange and self-abuse[49]
Is the initiate fear that wants hard use.[50]
145 We are yet but young in deed.

[*They leave.*]

Scene v. A heath.

[*There is thunder and lightning on a heath as the* THREE
WITCHES *enter and meet* HECATE, *the goddess of witchcraft.*]

FIRST WITCH. Why, how now, Hecate! you look angerly.

HECATE. Have I not reason, beldams[1] as you are,
Saucy and overbold? How did you dare
To trade and traffic with Macbeth
5 In riddles and affairs of death;
And I, the mistress of your charms,

---

39 **Augures . . . relations:** omens and the relationship between the omens and what they signify.
40 **maggot-pies and choughs** [chufs]: magpies and crows.
41 **brought forth:** revealed.
42 **man of blood:** murderer.

43 **at odds:** disputing (it is almost midnight).

44 **fee'd:** in my pay as a spy.
45 **betimes:** early in the morning.
46 **bent:** eager.

47 **scanned:** examined.

48 **season . . . natures:** that which keeps fresh all living things.
49 **My . . . self-abuse:** my strange delusion.
50 **initiate . . . use:** beginner's fear that will toughen with more experience.

1 **beldams:** old hags.

The close contriver[2] of all harms,
Was never called to bear my part,
Or show the glory of our art?

10 And, which is worse, all you have done
Hath been but for a wayward son,
Spiteful and wrathful; who, as others do,
Loves for his own ends, not for you.
But make amends now: get you gone,

15 And at the pit of Acheron[3]
Meet me i' th' morning: thither he
Will come to know his destiny.
Your vessels and your spells provide,
Your charms and everything beside.

20 I am for th' air; this night I'll spend
Unto a dismal[4] and a fatal end:
Great business must be wrought ere noon.
Upon the corner of the moon
There hangs a vap'rous drop profound;

25 I'll catch it ere it come to ground:
And that distilled by magic sleights[5]
Shall raise such artificial sprites[6]
As by the strength of their illusion
Shall draw him on to his confusion.[7]

30 He shall spurn fate, scorn death, and bear
His hopes 'bove wisdom, grace, and fear:
And you all know security[8]
Is mortals' chiefest enemy.

[*Music and a song are heard offstage.* HECATE *is called
away.*]

Hark! I am called; my little spirit,[9] see,
35 Sits in a foggy cloud and stays for me.

[HECATE *leaves.*]

FIRST WITCH. Come, let's make haste; she'll soon be back
again.

[*The* WITCHES *leave quickly.*]

Scene vi. The palace at Forres.

[LENNOX *and another* LORD *enter a room in the palace and
discuss the recent deaths of* DUNCAN *and* BANQUO *and* MAC-
DUFF'S *mission to the court of King Edward of England to enlist the king's aid against* MACBETH.]

LENNOX. My former speeches have but hit[1] your thoughts,
Which can interpret farther.[2] Only I say

2 **close contriver:** secret inventor.

3 **Acheron** [ak'ə ron']: hell; in Greek
mythology, a river of Hades.

4 **dismal:** disastrous.

5 **sleights:** devices, arts.
6 **artificial sprites:** spirits created by
magic.
7 **confusion:** ruin, destruction.

8 **security:** overconfidence.

9 **my little spirit:** her familiar, or
helper.

1 **hit:** agreed with.
2 **Which . . . farther:** from which
you can draw your own conclusions.

Things have been strangely borne.[3] The gracious Duncan
Was pitied of Macbeth: marry,[4] he was dead.
5 And the right-valiant Banquo walked too late;
Whom, you may say, if 't please you, Fleance killed,
For Fleance fled. Men must not walk too late.
Who cannot want the thought,[5] how monstrous
It was for Malcolm and for Donalbain
10 To kill their gracious father? Damnèd fact![6]
How it did grieve Macbeth! Did he not straight,
In pious rage, the two delinquents tear,
That were the slaves of drink and thralls[7] of sleep?
Was not that nobly done? Ay, and wisely too;
15 For 'twould have angered any heart alive
To hear the men deny 't. So that I say
He has borne all things well:[8] and I do think
That, had he Duncan's sons under his key—
As, an 't[9] please heaven, he shall not—they should find
20 What 'twere to kill a father. So should Fleance.
But, peace! for from broad words,[10] and 'cause he failed
His presence at the tyrant's feast, I hear,
Macduff lives in disgrace. Sir, can you tell
Where he bestows himself?

LORD.   The son of Duncan,
25 From whom this tyrant holds the due of birth,[11]
Lives in the English court, and is received
Of the most pious Edward[12] with such grace
That the malevolence of fortune nothing
Takes from his high respect.[13] Thither Macduff
30 Is gone to pray the holy King, upon his aid[14]
To wake Northumberland and warlike Siward;[15]
That by the help of these, with Him above
To ratify the work, we may again
Give to our tables meat, sleep to our nights,
35 Free from our feasts and banquets bloody knives,
Do faithful homage and receive free honors:[16]
All which we pine for now. And this report
Hath so exasperate the King that he
Prepares for some attempt of war.

LENNOX.   Sent he to Macduff?

40 **LORD.** He did: and with an absolute "Sir, not I,"
The cloudy[17] messenger turns me his back,
And hums, as who should say "You'll rue the time
That clogs[18] me with this answer."

LENNOX.   And that well might
Advise him to a caution, t' hold what distance
45 His wisdom can provide. Some holy angel

3 **strangely borne:** oddly managed.

4 **marry:** indeed; a mild oath, originally, "By the Virgin Mary!"

5 **Who . . . thought:** who cannot help thinking.

6 **fact:** act, deed.

7 **thralls:** slaves.

8 **He . . . well:** He has managed things cunningly.

9 **an 't:** if it.

10 **broad words:** free, unguarded speaking.

11 **holds . . . birth:** withholds his birthright—that is, the throne.

12 **Edward:** Edward the Confessor, King of England 1042–1066.

13 **That . . . respect:** His misfortune does not lessen the high respect he is given.
14 **his aid:** on Malcolm's behalf.
15 **To wake . . . Siward:** to call to arms the Earl of Northumberland, general of the English forces, and his son, Siward. Northumberland is a part of England close to the Scottish border.

16 **free honors:** honors given to free men.

17 **cloudy:** disturbed.

18 **clogs:** burdens.

Fly to the court of England and unfold
His message ere he come, that a swift blessing
May soon return to this our suffering country
Under a hand accursed!

LORD.   I'll send my prayers with him.

[*They leave.*]

STUDY QUESTIONS

Recalling

1. In Act III, Scene i, just before the murderers enter, what reasons does Macbeth give for wanting to have Banquo killed? At the end of Scene i, whom else does Macbeth tell the murderers to kill?
2. At the beginning of Scene ii, what does Lady Macbeth say that reveals her feelings about being queen of Scotland?
3. What happens to Banquo and Fleance in Scene iii?
4. In Scene iv why does Macbeth refuse to sit at the table with his guests? What explanation do Lady Macbeth and Macbeth give for his strange behavior?
5. At the end of Scene iv, why does Macbeth decide to seek the advice of the weird sisters?
6. At the end of her speech in Scene v, what effect does Hecate say the witches' predictions will have on Macbeth?
7. In Scene vi what reason are we given for Macduff's trip to the king of England? What does Macbeth do when he learns of Macduff's mission?

Interpreting

8. In Scene i how does Macbeth manipulate the murderers into doing what he wants them to do?
9. How has Macbeth's attitude toward murder changed? Compare his state of mind as he arranges Banquo's assassination in Act III, Scene i, with his emotional state in Act II, Scene i, as he prepares to murder King Duncan.

10. Examine Macbeth's speeches in Scene ii. What do they show about how his relationship with his wife has changed?
11. In what ways do the events in Scene iv change Macbeth's personality? At this point could he stop killing even if he wanted to?
12. What are your impressions of Macduff from what you learn about him in Scene vi? What importance do you think he will have in Acts IV and V?

Extending

13. Imagine that you are a guest at Macbeth's banquet. How would you react to the new king's behavior? How would you explain it?

VIEWPOINT

According to Mark Van Doren, the world of *Macbeth*

can be most easily described as "strange." The word, like the witches, is always somewhere doing its work. Even in the battle which precedes the play the Thane of Glamis [Macbeth] has made "strange images of death" (Act I, Scene iii, line 97), and when he comes home to his lady his face is "as a book where men may read strange matters" (Act I, Scene v, lines 61 – 62). . . . . Nothing is as it should be in such a world. . . . There is a drift of disorder in all events, and the air is murky with unwelcome miracles.

■ What "unwelcome miracles" can you cite in support of Van Doren's observation? What else seems strange about the world the play creates? Is the word *strange* used elsewhere?

ACT IV

Scene i. *A deserted place.*

[*It is thundering as the* THREE WITCHES *enter and stand around a large caldron, or pot, in their deserted meeting place.*]

FIRST WITCH. Thrice the brinded[1] cat hath mewed.

SECOND WITCH. Thrice and once the hedge-pig[2] whined.

THIRD WITCH. Harpier[3] cries. 'Tis time, 'tis time.

FIRST WITCH. Round about the caldron go:
5   In the poisoned entrails throw.

[*The* WITCHES *circle the caldron, and as each mentions an item, she throws it into the pot.*]

Toad, that under cold stone
Days and nights has thirty-one
Swelt'red venom sleeping got,[4]
Boil thou first i' th' charmèd pot.

10 ALL. Double, double, toil and trouble;
   Fire burn and caldron bubble.

SECOND WITCH. Fillet of a fenny snake,[5]
   In the caldron boil and bake;
   Eye of newt and toe of frog,
15   Wool of bat and tongue of dog,
   Adder's fork[6] and blindworm's[7] sting,
   Lizard's leg and howlet's[8] wing,
   For a charm of pow'rful trouble,
   Like a hell-broth boil and bubble.

20 ALL. Double, double, toil and trouble;
   Fire burn and caldron bubble.

THIRD WITCH. Scale of dragon, tooth of wolf,
   Witch's mummy, maw and gulf[9]
   Of the ravined[10] salt-sea shark,
25   Root of hemlock digged i' th' dark,
   Slivered in the moon's eclipse,
   Nose of Turk and Tartar's lips,
   Finger of birth-strangled babe
   Ditch-delivered[11] by a drab,
30   Make the gruel thick and slab:[12]
   Add thereto a tiger's chaudron,[13]
   For th' ingredients of our caldron.

1 **brinded** [brin′did]: striped.

2 **hedge-pig:** hedgehog, a witch's familiar, like the brinded cat.

3 **Harpier:** one of the familiar spirits attending the witches. Harpier is derived from *harpy,* a birdlike monster of classical mythology.

4 **Swelt'red . . . got:** sweated out poison while sleeping.

5 **fenny snake:** a snake from the fens, or marshes.

6 **fork:** forked tongue.
7 **blindworm:** small, harmless, limbless lizard, once believed to be poisonous.
8 **howlet:** small owl.

9 **maw and gulf:** stomach and gullet.
10 **ravined:** ravenous.

11 **Ditch-delivered:** born in a ditch.

12 **slab:** sticky.

13 **chaudron** [shô′drən]: entrails.

ALL. Double, double, toil and trouble;
Fire burn and caldron bubble.

35 **SECOND WITCH.** Cool it with a baboon's blood,
Then the charm is firm and good.

[HECATE, *goddess of witches, enters and addresses the other* THREE WITCHES.]

HECATE. O, well done! I commend your pains;
And everyone shall share i' th' gains:
And now about the caldron sing,
40 Like elves and fairies in a ring,
Enchanting all that you put in.

[*Music and a song are heard offstage.* HECATE *leaves.*]

SECOND WITCH. By the pricking of my thumbs,
Something wicked this way comes:
    Open, locks,
45   Whoever knocks!

[MACBETH *enters.*]

MACBETH. How now, you secret, black, and midnight hags!
What is 't you do?

ALL.   A deed without a name.

MACBETH. I conjure you, by that which you profess,[14]
Howe'er you come to know it, answer me:
50 Though you untie the winds and let them fight
Against the churches; though the yesty[15] waves
Confound[16] and swallow navigation up;
Though bladed corn be lodged[17] and trees blown down;
Though castles topple on their warders' heads;
55 Though palaces and pyramids do slope[18]
Their heads to their foundations; though the treasure
Of nature's germens[19] tumble all together,
Even till destruction sicken, answer me
To what I ask you.[20]

FIRST WITCH.   Speak.

SECOND WITCH.   Demand.

THIRD WITCH.   We'll answer.

60 **FIRST WITCH.** Say, if th' hadst rather hear it from our mouths,
Or from our masters?

MACBETH.   Call 'em, let me see 'em.

FIRST WITCH. Pour in sow's blood, that hath eaten

14 **that . . . profess:** witchcraft.

15 **yesty:** foamy.

16 **Confound:** destroy.
17 **lodged:** beaten down.

18 **slope:** bend.

19 **germens:** seeds of all life.

20 **Though you untie . . . I ask you:** Macbeth must know the truth, whatever the cost.

Her nine farrow;[21] grease that's sweaten
From the murderer's gibbet[22] throw
Into the flame.

65 **ALL.**   Come, high or low,
Thyself and office[23] deftly show!

[*The* THREE APPARITIONS, *or ghosts—an Armored Head, a
Bloody Child, and a Child Crowned—that appear in turn
here are symbolic of the stages of* MACBETH'S *downfall.
Their significance is unknown to* MACBETH *at this time.
Thunder is heard as the* FIRST APPARITION, *the armored head
of a warrior, appears. This head symbolizes* MACBETH'S *future battle with* MACDUFF.]

MACBETH. Tell me, thou unknown power—

FIRST WITCH.   He knows thy thought:
Hear his speech, but say thou nought.

FIRST APPARITION. Macbeth! Macbeth! Macbeth! Beware
    Macduff!
70 Beware the Thane of Fife. Dismiss me: enough.

[*The* FIRST APPARITION *disappears.*]

MACBETH. Whate'er thou art, for thy good caution thanks:
Thou has harped[24] my fear aright. But one word more—

FIRST WITCH. He will not be commanded. Here's another,
More potent than the first.

[*More thunder as the* SECOND APPARITION, *a Bloody Child,
appears. The Bloody Child symbolizes* MACDUFF *at birth.*]

75 **SECOND APPARITION.** Macbeth! Macbeth! Macbeth!

MACBETH. Had I three ears, I'd hear thee.

SECOND APPARITION. Be bloody, bold, and resolute! Laugh to
    scorn
The pow'r of man, for none of woman born
Shall harm Macbeth.

[*The* SECOND APPARITION *disappears.*]

80 **MACBETH.** Then live, Macduff: what need I fear of thee?
But yet I'll make assurance double sure,
And take a bond of fate.[25] Thou shalt not live;
That I may tell pale-hearted fear it lies,
And sleep in spite of thunder.

[*Thunder sounds as the* THIRD APPARITION, *a Crowned Child
with a tree in his hand, appears. This child symbolizes*
MALCOLM, KING DUNCAN'*s elder son.*]

21 **farrow:** young pigs.
22 **gibbet** [jib'it]: gallows.

23 **office:** your function.

24 **harped:** guessed.

25 **take . . . fate:** get a guarantee
from fate that he will be safe.

What is this,
85 That rises like the issue of a king,
And wears upon his baby-brow the round
And top of sovereignty?²⁶

26 **top of sovereignty:** crown.

ALL.   Listen, but speak not to 't.

THIRD APPARITION. Be lion-mettled, proud, and take no care
Who chafes, who frets, or where conspirers are:
90 Macbeth shall never vanquished be until
Great Birnam Wood to high Dunsinane Hill
Shall come against him.²⁷

[*The* THIRD APPARITION *disappears.*]

27 **Macbeth . . . him:** Macbeth will never be conquered unless the forest of Great Birnam marches twelve miles to his castle on Dunsinane Hill.

MACBETH.   That will never be.
Who can impress²⁸ the forest, bid the tree
Unfix his earth-bound root? Sweet bodements,²⁹ good!
95 Rebellious dead, rise never, till the Wood
Of Birnam rise, and our high-placed Macbeth
Shall live the lease of nature, pay his breath
To time and mortal custom.³⁰ Yet my heart
Throbs to know one thing. Tell me, if your art
100 Can tell so much: shall Banquo's issue ever
Reign in this kingdom?

28 **impress:** force into service.

29 **bodements:** prophecies.

30 **live . . . custom:** live and die a natural death.

ALL.   Seek to know no more.

MACBETH. I will be satisfied. Deny me this,
And an eternal curse fall on you! Let me know
Why sinks that caldron? And what noise is this?

[*Oboes are heard.*]

105 FIRST WITCH. Show!

SECOND WITCH. Show!

THIRD WITCH. Show!

ALL. Show his eyes, and grieve his heart;
Come like shadows, so depart!

[*A pantomime passes across the stage. In the show are the apparitions of eight kings, representing the eight Stuart kings of Scotland. The eighth king represents James I of England, also known as King James IV of Scotland. He was a descendant of* BANQUO *and reigned at the time* MACBETH *was written. The last king has a mirror in his hand so that* MACBETH *can look into the future.* BANQUO'S GHOST *appears at the end of the procession.*]

110 MACBETH. Thou art too like the spirit of Banquo. Down!
Thy crown does sear mine eyelids. And thy hair,

Thou other gold-bound brow, is like the first.
A third is like the former. Filthy hags!
Why do you show me this? A fourth! Start, eyes!
115 What, will the line stretch out to th' crack of doom?
Another yet! A seventh! I'll see no more.
And yet the eighth appears, who bears a glass
Which shows me many more; and some I see
That twofold balls and treble scepters[31] carry:
120 Horrible sight! Now I see 'tis true;
For the blood-boltered[32] Banquo smiles upon me,
And points at them for his.

[*The* APPARITIONS *in the pantomime vanish.*]

What, is this so?

FIRST WITCH. Ay, sir, all this is so. But why
Stands Macbeth thus amazedly?[33]
125 Come, sisters, cheer we up his sprites,[34]
And show the best of our delights:
I'll charm the air to give a sound,
While you perform your antic round,[35]
That this great king may kindly say
130 Our duties did his welcome pay.

[*Music plays as the* WITCHES *dance and vanish.*]

MACBETH. Where are they? Gone? Let this pernicious hour
Stand aye accursed in the calendar![36]
Come in, without there!

[LENNOX *enters.*]

LENNOX.   What's your Grace's will?

MACBETH. Saw you the weird sisters?

LENNOX.   No, my lord.

MACBETH. Came they not by you?

135 **LENNOX.**   No indeed, my lord.

MACBETH. Infected be the air whereon they ride,
And damned all those that trust them! I did hear
The galloping of horse. Who was 't came by?

LENNOX. 'Tis two or three, my lord, that bring you word
Macduff is fled to England.

140 **MACBETH.**   Fled to England?

LENNOX. Ay, my good lord.

MACBETH. [*Aside.*] Time, thou anticipat'st[37] my dread exploits.

31 **twofold . . . scepters:** coronation emblems and insignia of the kingdoms of England, Scotland, and Ireland, united in 1603.
32 **blood-boltered:** hair matted with blood.

33 **amazedly:** entranced.
34 **sprites:** spirits.

35 **antic round:** grotesque circle dance.

36 **Stand . . . calendar:** be forever cursed.

37 **anticipat'st:** foretold.

The flighty purpose never is o'ertook
Unless the deed go with it.[38] From this moment
145 The very firstlings of my heart[39] shall be
The firstlings of my hand. And even now,
To crown my thoughts with acts, be it thought and done:
The castle of Macduff I will surprise;
Seize upon Fife; give to th' edge o' th' sword
150 His wife, his babes, and all unfortunate souls
That trace[40] him in his line. No boasting like a fool;
This deed I'll do before this purpose cool:
But no more sights!—Where are these gentlemen?
Come, bring me where they are.

[MACBETH *leaves with* LENNOX.]

Scene ii. MACDUFF'S *castle at Fife.*

[*In Fife, on the southeast coast of Scotland,* LADY MACDUFF, *her son, and* ROSS *enter a room in* MACDUFF'S *castle.* LADY MACDUFF *is upset and angry with her husband for leaving Scotland.*]

LADY MACDUFF. What had he done, to make him fly the land?

ROSS. You must have patience, madam.

LADY MACDUFF.   He had none:
His flight was madness. When our actions do not,
Our fears do make us traitors.[1]

ROSS.   You know not
5 Whether it was his wisdom or his fear.

LADY MACDUFF. Wisdom! To leave his wife, to leave his babes,
His mansion and his titles,[2] in a place
From whence himself does fly? He loves us not;
He wants the natural touch:[3] for the poor wren,
10 The most diminutive of birds, will fight,
Her young ones in her nest, against the owl.
All is the fear and nothing is the love;
As little is the wisdom, where the flight
So runs against all reason.

ROSS.   My dearest coz,[4]
15 I pray you, school[5] yourself. But, for your husband,
He is noble, wise, judicious, and best knows
The fits o' th' season.[6] I dare not speak much further:
But cruel are the times, when we are traitors
And do not know ourselves;[7] when we hold rumor
20 From what we fear,[8] yet know not what we fear,
But float upon a wild and violent sea

38 **The flighty . . . it:** The fleeting plan is never fulfilled unless it is carried out at once.
39 **firstlings . . . heart:** first thoughts and impulses.

40 **trace:** succeed.

1 **When . . . traitors:** Although we may not be traitors, displaying our fears gives us the appearance of guilt.

2 **his titles:** all he is entitled to, his possessions.

3 **wants . . . touch:** lacks the feeling of natural affection.

4 **coz** [kuz]: an affectionate shortening of *cousin.* (Macduff and Ross are cousins.)
5 **school:** control.
6 **fits . . . season:** violent disorders of the time.
7 **we . . . ourselves:** we are treated as traitors but do not know of any treason.
8 **hold . . . fear:** interpret rumors based on our fears.

Each way and move. I take my leave of you.
Shall not be long but I'll be here again.
Things at the worst will cease, or else climb upward
25 To what they were before. [*He addresses* MACDUFF's *son.*]
My pretty cousin,
Blessing upon you!

LADY MACDUFF. Fathered he is, and yet he's fatherless.

ROSS. I am so much a fool, should I stay longer,
It would be my disgrace and your discomfort.[9]
I take my leave at once.

[ROSS *leaves.*]

30 **LADY MACDUFF.**   Sirrah, your father's dead:
And what will you do now? How will you live?

SON. As birds do, mother.

LADY MACDUFF.   What, with worms and flies?

SON. With what I get, I mean; and so do they.

LADY MACDUFF. Poor bird! thou'dst never fear the net nor
lime,[10]
35 The pitfall nor the gin.[11]

SON. Why should I, mother? Poor birds they are not set for.
My father is not dead, for all your saying.

LADY MACDUFF. Yes, he is dead: how wilt thou do for a
father?

SON. Nay, how will you do for a husband?

40 **LADY MACDUFF.** Why, I can buy me twenty at any market.

SON. Then you'll buy 'em to sell[12] again.

LADY MACDUFF. Thou speak'st with all thy wit, and yet, i'
faith,
With wit enough for thee.[13]

SON. Was my father a traitor, mother?

45 **LADY MACDUFF.** Ay, that he was.

SON. What is a traitor?

LADY MACDUFF. Why, one that swears and lies.[14]

SON. And be all traitors that do so?

LADY MACDUFF. Every one that does so is a traitor, and must
be hanged.

50 **SON.** And must they all be hanged that swear and lie?

9 **It . . . discomfort:** I would disgrace myself and embarrass you by weeping.

10 **lime:** birdlime, a sticky substance smeared on branches to catch birds.
11 **pitfall . . . gin:** traps or snares.

12 **sell:** betray.

13 **for thee:** for a child.

14 **swears and lies:** takes an oath and breaks it.

LADY MACDUFF. Every one.

SON. Who must hang them?

LADY MACDUFF. Why, the honest men.

SON. Then the liars and swearers are fools; for there are liars
55   and swearers enow[15] to beat the honest men and hang up
    them.

LADY MACDUFF. Now, God help thee, poor monkey! But how
    wilt thou do for a father?

SON. If he were dead, you'd weep for him. If you would not,
60   it were a good sign that I should quickly have a new
    father.

LADY MACDUFF. Poor prattler, how thou talk'st!

    [*A* MESSENGER *comes in.*]

MESSENGER. Bless you, fair dame! I am not to you known,
    Though in your state of honor I am perfect.[16]
65   I doubt[17] some danger does approach you nearly:
    If you will take a homely[18] man's advice,
    Be not found here; hence, with your little ones.
    To fright you thus, methinks I am too savage;
    To do worse to you were fell[19] cruelty,
70   Which is too nigh your person. Heaven preserve you!
    I dare abide no longer.

    [*The* MESSENGER *leaves quickly.*]

LADY MACDUFF.   Whither should I fly?
    I have done no harm. But I remember now
    I am in this earthly world, where to do harm
    Is often laudable, to do good sometime
75   Accounted dangerous folly. Why then, alas,
    Do I put up that womanly defense,
    To say I have done no harm?—What are these faces?

    [*The* MURDERERS *hired by* MACBETH *enter.*]

MURDERER. Where is your husband?

LADY MACDUFF. I hope, in no place so unsanctified
    Where such as thou mayst find him.

80 **MURDERER.**   He's a traitor.

SON. Thou li'st, thou shag-eared[20] villain!

MURDERER.   What, you egg!

    [*The* MURDERER *stabs the child.*]

15 **enow:** enough.

16 **in . . . perfect:** I know of your honorable rank.
17 **I doubt:** I fear.
18 **homely:** simple.

19 **fell:** fierce.

20 **shag-eared:** with shaggy hair about his ears.

Young fry of treachery!²¹

SON.   He has killed me, mother:
Run away, I pray you!

[*The* BOY *dies as* LADY MACDUFF *runs off crying, "Murder!"*
The MURDERERS *pursue her.*]

Scene iii. *The palace of the King of England.*

[MACDUFF *has come to England in an attempt to ally himself*
with MALCOLM, KING DUNCAN*'s elder son and rightful heir to*
the Scottish crown. He meets MALCOLM *in front of the palace*
of Edward the Confessor, the devoutly religious King of Eng-
land.]

MALCOLM. Let us seek out some desolate shade, and there
Weep our sad bosoms empty.

MACDUFF.   Let us rather
Hold fast the mortal¹ sword, and like good men
Bestride our down-fall'n birthdom.² Each new morn
5   New widows howl, new orphans cry, new sorrows
Strike heaven on the face, that it resounds
As if it felt with Scotland and yelled out
Like syllable of dolor.³

MALCOLM.   What I believe, I'll wail;
What know, believe; and what I can redress,
10   As I shall find the time to friend,⁴ I will.
What you have spoke, it may be so perchance.
This tyrant, whose sole⁵ name blisters our tongues,
Was once thought honest:⁶ you have loved him well;
He hath not touched you yet. I am young; but something
15   You may deserve of him through me;⁷ and wisdom⁸
To offer up a weak, poor, innocent lamb
T' appease an angry god.

MACDUFF. I am not treacherous.

MALCOLM.   But Macbeth is.
A good and virtuous nature may recoil
20   In an imperial charge.⁹ But I shall crave your pardon;
That which you are, my thoughts cannot transpose:¹⁰
Angels are bright still, though the brightest¹¹ fell:
Though all things foul would wear the brows of grace,
Yet grace must still look so.¹²

MACDUFF.   I have lost my hopes.¹³

21 **Young . . . treachery:** child spawned by a traitor.

1 **mortal:** deadly.

2 **Bestride . . . birthdom:** stand over, protect, our native land, which has been beaten down.

3 **Like . . . dolor:** a similar cry.

4 **to friend:** friendly.

5 **sole:** very.

6 **honest:** good.

7 **something . . . me:** you may benefit by betraying me to Macbeth.
8 **and wisdom:** and it is wise.

9 **recoil . . . charge:** reverse itself by royal command.
10 **transpose:** change; my suspicions alone cannot make you a traitor.
11 **the brightest:** Lucifer.
12 **Though . . . so:** Even if all foul things looked gracious, grace would not change its appearance.
13 **my hopes:** my hopes of saving Scotland from Macbeth.

MALCOLM. Perchance even there where I did find my

25   doubts.[14]
    Why in that rawness[15] left you wife and child,
    Those precious motives, those strong knots of love,
    Without leave-taking? I pray you,
    Let not my jealousies[16] be your dishonors,
30   But mine own safeties.[17] You may be rightly just
    Whatever I shall think.

MACDUFF.   Bleed, bleed, poor country:
    Great tyranny, lay thou thy basis sure,
    For goodness dare not check thee: wear thou thy wrongs;
    The title is affeered.[18] Fare thee well, lord:
35   I would not be the villain that thou think'st
    For the whole space that's in the tyrant's grasp
    And the rich East to boot.

MALCOLM.   Be not offended:
    I speak not as in absolute fear of you.
    I think our country sinks beneath the yoke;
40   It weeps, it bleeds, and each new day a gash
    Is added to her wounds. I think withal
    There would be hands uplifted in my right;[19]
    And here from gracious England[20] have I offer
    Of goodly thousands: but, for all this,
45   When I shall tread upon the tyrant's head,
    Or wear it on my sword, yet my poor country
    Shall have more vices than it had before,
    More suffer, and more sundry ways than ever,
    By him that shall succeed.

MACDUFF.   What should he be?[21]

50 MALCOLM. It is myself I mean, in whom I know
    All the particulars of vice so grafted[22]
    That, when they shall be opened,[23] black Macbeth
    Will seem as pure as snow, and the poor state
    Esteem him as a lamb, being compared
55   With my confineless harms.[24]

MACDUFF.   Not in the legions
    Of horrid hell can come a devil more damned
    In evils to top Macbeth.

MALCOLM.   I grant him bloody,
    Luxurious,[25] avaricious, false, deceitful,
    Sudden, malicious, smacking of every sin
60   That has a name: but there's no bottom, none,
    In my voluptuousness: your wives, your daughters,
    Your matrons and your maids, could not fill up

14 **Perchance . . . doubts:** Malcolm is suspicious of Macduff's desertion of his wife and children.
15 **rawness:** unprotected condition.

16 **jealousies:** suspicions.
17 **safeties:** protections.

18 **affeered:** confirmed by law.

19 **in my right:** on behalf of my claim.
20 **England:** the King of England, Edward the Confessor.

21 **What . . . be:** Who could be worse than Macbeth?

22 **grafted:** implanted.
23 **opened:** in bloom.

24 **confineless harms:** boundless evils.

25 **Luxurious:** lecherous.

The cistern of my lust, and my desire
All continent impediments[26] would o'erbear,
65   That did oppose my will. Better Macbeth
Than such an one to reign.

MACDUFF.   Boundless intemperance
In nature[27] is a tyranny; it hath been
Th' untimely emptying of the happy throne,
And fall of many kings. But fear not yet
70   To take upon you what is yours: you may
Convey[28] your pleasures in a spacious plenty,
And yet seem cold, the time you may so hoodwink.
We have willing dames enough. There cannot be
That vulture in you, to devour so many
75   As will to greatness dedicate themselves,
Finding it so inclined.

MALCOLM.   With this there grows
In my most ill-composed affection[29] such
A stanchless avarice[30] that, were I King,
I should cut off the nobles for their lands,
80   Desire his[31] jewels and this other's house:
And my more-having would be as a sauce
To make me hunger more, that I should forge
Quarrels unjust against the good and loyal,
Destroying them for wealth.

MACDUFF.   This avarice
85   Sticks deeper, grows with more pernicious root
Than summer-seeming[32] lust, and it hath been
The sword of our slain kings.[33] Yet do not fear.
Scotland hath foisons[34] to fill up your will
Of your mere own.[35] All these are portable,[36]
90   With other graces weighed.[37]

MALCOLM. But I have none: the king-becoming graces,
As justice, verity, temp'rance, stableness,
Bounty, perseverance, mercy, lowliness,
Devotion, patience, courage, fortitude,
95   I have no relish of them, but abound
In the division of each several crime,[38]
Acting it many ways. Nay, had I pow'r, I should
Pour the sweet milk of concord into hell,
Uproar the universal peace, confound[39]
All unity on earth.

100 MACDUFF.   O Scotland, Scotland!

MALCOLM. If such a one be fit to govern, speak:
I am as I have spoken.

26 **continent impediments:**
restraints.

27 **nature:** man's nature.

28 **Convey:** secretly manage.

29 **affection:** personality.
30 **stanchless avarice:** never-
ending, insatiable greed.

31 **his:** that man's.

32 **summer-seeming:** summerlike.
33 **The . . . kings:** The sword that
killed our kings.
34 **foisons** [foi′zənz]: plenty,
abundance.
35 **mere own:** own property.
36 **portable:** bearable.
37 **weighed:** counterbalanced.

38 **division . . . crime:** variations of
each kind of crime.

39 **confound:** destroy.

MACDUFF.   Fit to govern!
No, not to live. O nation miserable!
With an untitled[40] tyrant bloody-sceptered,
105 When shalt thou see thy wholesome days again,
Since that the truest issue of thy throne[41]
By his own interdiction[42] stands accursed,
And does blaspheme his breed?[43] Thy royal father
Was a most sainted king: the queen that bore thee,
110 Oft'ner upon her knees than on her feet,
Died every day she lived.[44] Fare thee well!
These evils thou repeat'st upon thyself
Hath banished me from Scotland. O my breast,
Thy hope ends here!

MALCOLM.   Macduff, this noble passion,
115 Child of integrity, hath from my soul
Wiped the black scruples, reconciled my thoughts
To thy good truth and honor. Devilish Macbeth
By many of these trains[45] hath sought to win me
Into his power; and modest wisdom[46] plucks me
120 From over-credulous haste: but God above
Deal between thee and me! For even now
I put myself to thy direction, and
Unspeak mine own detraction;[47] here abjure
The taints and blames I laid upon myself,
125 For[48] strangers to my nature. I am yet
Unknown to woman, never was forsworn,[49]
Scarcely have coveted what was mine own,
At no time broke my faith, would not betray
The devil to his fellow, and delight
130 No less in truth than life. My first false speaking
Was this upon myself. What I am truly,
Is thine and my poor country's to command:
Whither indeed, before thy here-approach,
Old Siward, with ten thousand warlike men,
135 Already at a point,[50] was setting forth.
Now we'll together, and the chance of goodness
Be like our warranted quarrel![51] Why are you silent?

MACDUFF. Such welcome and unwelcome things at once
'Tis hard to reconcile.

[*An* ENGLISH DOCTOR *enters.*]

MALCOLM. Well, more anon. Comes the King forth, I pray
140 you?

DOCTOR. Ay, sir. There are a crew of wretched souls
That stay his cure:[52] their malady convinces

---

40 **untitled:** having no right to the throne.

41 **truest . . . throne:** child of the true king.
42 **interdiction:** exclusion.
43 **blaspheme . . . breed:** slander his ancestry.

44 **Died . . . lived:** lived every day always prepared for death.

45 **trains:** enticements.
46 **modest wisdom:** prudence.

47 **detraction:** slander.

48 **For:** as.
49 **was forsworn:** broke my oath.

50 **Old Siward . . . at a point:** Old Siward was the general of the English forces, and his troops were prepared.
51 **the chance . . . quarrel:** may our chance of success be as good as our cause is just.

52 **stay his cure:** wait for him to heal them. It was believed that King Edward could heal by touch—a power James I felt he had inherited.

The great assay of art;[53] but at his touch,
Such sanctity hath heaven given his hand,
They presently amend.[54]

145 MALCOLM.   I thank you, doctor.

[*The* DOCTOR *leaves.*]

MACDUFF. What's the disease he means?

MALCOLM.   'Tis called the evil:[55]
A most miraculous work in this good King,
Which often since my here-remain in England
I have seen him do. How he solicits heaven,
150 Himself best knows: but strangely visited people,
All swoll'n and ulcerous, pitiful to the eye,
The mere[56] despair of surgery, he cures,
Hanging a golden stamp[57] about their necks,
Put on with holy prayers: and 'tis spoken,
155 To the succeeding royalty he leaves
The healing benediction. With this strange virtue
He hath a heavenly gift of prophecy,
And sundry blessings hang about his throne
That speak him full of grace.

[ROSS *enters.*]

MACDUFF.   See, who comes here?

160 MALCOLM. My countryman; but yet I know him not.

MACDUFF. My ever gentle[58] cousin, welcome hither.

MALCOLM. I know him now: good God, betimes[59] remove
The means that makes us strangers!

ROSS.   Sir, amen.

MACDUFF. Stands Scotland where it did?

ROSS.   Alas, poor country!
165 Almost afraid to know itself! It cannot
Be called our mother but our grave, where nothing[60]
But who knows nothing is once[61] seen to smile;
Where sighs and groans, and shrieks that rent the air,
Are made, not marked; where violent sorrow seems
170 A modern ecstasy.[62] The dead man's knell
Is there scarce asked for who, and good men's lives
Expire before the flowers in their caps,
Dying or ere[63] they sicken.

MACDUFF.   O, relation
Too nice,[64] and yet too true!

53 **convinces . . . art:** defies the best efforts of medical science.

54 **presently amend:** recover at once.

55 **the evil:** scrofula [skrof′yə lə], a skin disease called "the King's evil" because it was believed that the King's touch would cure it.

56 **mere:** utter.
57 **stamp:** coin.

58 **gentle:** noble.

59 **betimes:** quickly.

60 **nothing:** no one.
61 **once:** at any time.

62 **modern ecstasy:** common emotion.

63 **ere:** before.

64 **nice:** exact.

MALCOLM.   What's the newest grief?

175 **ROSS.** That of an hour's age doth hiss the speaker;[65]
Each minute teems[66] a new one.

MACDUFF.   How does my wife?

ROSS. Why, well.

MACDUFF.   And all my children?

ROSS.   Well too.

MACDUFF. The tyrant has not battered at their peace?

ROSS. No; they were well at peace when I did leave 'em.

180 **MACDUFF.** Be not a niggard of your speech: how goes 't?

ROSS. When I came hither to transport the tidings,
Which I have heavily borne, there ran a rumor
Of many worthy fellows that were out;[67]
Which was to my belief witnessed the rather,[68]
185 For that I saw the tyrant's power[69] afoot.
Now is the time of help. Your eye in Scotland
Would create soldiers, make our women fight,
To doff[70] their dire distresses.

MALCOLM.   Be 't their comfort
We are coming thither. Gracious England[71] hath
190 Lent us good Siward and ten thousand men;
An older and a better soldier none
That Christendom gives out.

ROSS.   Would I could answer
This comfort with the like! But I have words
That would be howled out in the desert air,
Where hearing should not latch[72] them.

195 **MACDUFF.**   What concern they?
The general cause or is it a fee-grief[73]
Due to some single breast?

ROSS.   No mind that's honest
But in it shares some woe, though the main part
Pertains to you alone.

MACDUFF.   If it be mine,
200 Keep it not from me, quickly let me have it.

ROSS. Let not your ears despise my tongue for ever,
Which shall possess them with the heaviest sound
That ever yet they heard.

MACDUFF.   Humh! I guess at it.

65 **That . . . speaker:** There are so many new griefs that hour-old news is hissed because it is out of date.
66 **teems:** gives birth to.

67 **out:** in open rebellion.
68 **witnessed the rather:** confirmed.
69 **power:** army.

70 **doff:** put off.

71 **Gracious England:** the King of England.

72 **latch:** catch.

73 **fee-grief:** a personal grief.

ROSS. Your castle is surprised; your wife and babes
205   Savagely slaughtered. To relate the manner,
      Were, on the quarry[74] of these murdered deer,
      To add the death of you.

MALCOLM.   Merciful heaven!
      What, man! Ne'er pull your hat upon your brows;
      Give sorrow words. The grief that does not speak
210   Whispers the o'er-fraught[75] heart, and bids it break.

MACDUFF. My children too?

ROSS.   Wife, children, servants, all
      That could be found.

MACDUFF.   And I must be from thence!
      My wife killed too?

ROSS.   I have said.

MALCOLM.   Be comforted.
      Let's make us med'cines of our great revenge,
215   To cure this deadly grief.

MACDUFF. He[76] has no children. All my pretty ones?
      Did you say all? O hell-kite![77] All?
      What, all my pretty chickens and their dam[78]
      At one fell swoop?

MALCOLM. Dispute it[79] like a man.

220 **MACDUFF.**   I shall do so;
      But I must also feel it as a man.
      I cannot but remember such things were,
      That were most precious to me. Did heaven look on,
      And would not take their part? Sinful Macduff,
225   They were all struck for thee! Naught[80] that I am,
      Not for their own demerits but for mine
      Fell slaughter on their souls. Heaven rest them now!

MALCOLM. Be this the whetstone of your sword. Let grief
      Convert to anger; blunt not the heart, enrage it.

230 **MACDUFF.** O, I could play the woman with mine eyes,
      And braggart with my tongue! But, gentle heavens,
      Cut short all intermission; front to front[81]
      Bring thou this fiend of Scotland and myself;
      Within my sword's length set him. If he 'scape,
      Heaven forgive him too!

235 **MALCOLM.**   This time goes manly.
      Come, go we to the King. Our power is ready;

74 **quarry:** heap of game slain in a hunt.

75 **o'er-fraught:** overburdened.

76 **He:** may refer to Malcolm or Macbeth.
77 **hell-kite:** bird of prey.
78 **dam:** mother.

79 **Dispute it:** resist your grief.

80 **Naught:** wicked.

81 **front to front:** face to face.

Our lack is nothing but our leave.[82] Macbeth
Is ripe for shaking, and the pow'rs above
Put on their instruments.[83] Receive what cheer you may.
240 The night is long that never finds the day.

[*They all leave.*]

82 **Our . . . leave:** We have everything except permission to go.

83 **Put . . . instruments:** urge us onward as their agents.

STUDY QUESTIONS

Recalling

1. In Act IV, Scene i, what does Macbeth learn from each of the three apparitions? What additional question does he ask the witches, and by what means do they answer him?
2. At the end of Scene i, what does Macbeth vow to do to Macduff's family?
3. At the beginning of Scene iii, how does Malcolm test Macduff's loyalty? How does Macduff finally convince Malcolm that he is not on Macbeth's side?
4. What awful news does Ross bring Macduff? At the end of Scene iii, what action do Malcolm and Macduff plan?

Interpreting

5. What does Macbeth's final speech in Scene i reveal about his state of mind?

6. Describe the characters of Lady Macduff and her son, and explain your reaction to them. How does their fate color your opinion of Macbeth?
7. How do you react to the portion of Scene iii where Macduff is told his family's fate? What do you learn about Macduff's character from this scene?
8. Assess the state of Scotland under Macbeth's rule. Who supports Macbeth at this point in the play?
9. How does Scene iii advance the action of the play?

Extending

10. If Macbeth were to seek your advice about how he should react to the witches' latest prophecies, how would you respond to him? What would you advise him to do?

ACT V

Scene i. MACBETH'*s castle at Dunsinane.*

[*It is late at night in* MACBETH'*s castle at Dunsinane. A* GEN-TLEWOMAN *who serves* LADY MACBETH *enters with a* SCOTTISH PHYSICIAN. *They have come to observe* LADY MACBETH, *who has recently begun to sleepwalk.*]

DOCTOR. I have two nights watched with you, but can perceive no truth in your report. When was it she last walked?

GENTLEWOMAN. Since his Majesty went into the field,[1] I have
5   seen her rise from her bed, throw her nightgown upon
her, unlock her closet,[2] take forth paper, fold it, write
upon 't, read it, afterwards seal it, and again return to
bed; yet all this while in a most fast sleep.

DOCTOR. A great perturbation in nature,[3] to receive at once
10   the benefit of sleep and do the effects of watching![4] In
this slumb'ry agitation, besides her walking and other
actual performances, what, at any time, have you heard
her say?

GENTLEWOMAN. That, sir, which I will not report after her.

15 DOCTOR. You may to me, and 'tis most meet[5] you should.

GENTLEWOMAN. Neither to you nor anyone, having no witness
to confirm my speech.

[LADY MACBETH *enters, carrying a candlestick.*]

Lo you, here she comes! This is her very guise,[6] and,
upon my life, fast asleep! Observe her; stand close.[7]

20 DOCTOR. How came she by that light?

GENTLEWOMAN. Why, it stood by her. She has light by her
continually. 'Tis her command.

[LADY MACBETH *moves across the stage, unaware that others
are watching her.*]

DOCTOR. You see, her eyes are open.

GENTLEWOMAN. Ay, but their sense[8] are shut.

25 DOCTOR. What is it she does now? Look, how she rubs her
hands.

GENTLEWOMAN. It is an accustomed action with her, to seem
thus washing her hands: I have known her continue in
this a quarter of an hour.

---

1 **into the field:** joined the army on the battlefield to repress rebellious subjects.

2 **closet:** a chest or box.

3 **perturbation in nature:** disorder of the body and mind.
4 **effects of watching:** actions of one awake.

5 **meet:** suitable.

6 **guise:** custom.
7 **close:** hidden.

8 **their sense:** power of sight.

30 **LADY MACBETH.** Yet here's a spot.

DOCTOR. Hark! she speaks. I will set down what comes from her, to satisfy[9] my remembrance the more strongly.

LADY MACBETH. [*She sets down the candlestick and rubs her hands as if she were washing them.*] Out, damned spot! Out, I say! One: two: why, then 'tis time to do 't.[10] Hell
35 is murky. Fie, my lord, fie! A soldier, and afeard? What need we fear who knows it, when none can call our pow'r to accompt?[11] Yet who would have thought the old man to have had so much blood in him?

DOCTOR. Do you mark that?

40 **LADY MACBETH.** The Thane of Fife had a wife. Where is she now? What, will these hands ne'er be clean? No more o' that, my lord, no more o' that! You mar all with this starting.

DOCTOR. Go to,[12] go to! You have known what you should not.

45 **GENTLEWOMAN.** She has spoke what she should not, I am sure of that. Heaven knows what she has known.

LADY MACBETH. Here's the smell of the blood still. All the perfumes of Arabia will not sweeten this little hand. Oh, oh, oh!

50 **DOCTOR.** What a sigh is there! The heart is sorely charged.[13]

GENTLEWOMAN. I would not have such a heart in my bosom for the dignity[14] of the whole body.

DOCTOR. Well, well, well—

GENTLEWOMAN. Pray God it be, sir.

55 **DOCTOR.** This disease is beyond my practice. Yet I have known those which have walked in their sleep who have died holily in their beds.

LADY MACBETH. Wash your hands; put on your nightgown; look not so pale! I tell you yet again, Banquo's buried. He
60 cannot come out on 's[15] grave.

DOCTOR. Even so?

LADY MACBETH. To bed, to bed! There's knocking at the gate. Come, come, come, come, give me your hand! What's done cannot be undone. To bed, to bed, to bed!

[LADY MACBETH *leaves.*]

65 **DOCTOR.** Will she go now to bed?

9 **satisfy:** support.

10 **One . . . do 't:** She thinks she hears the clock strike and is reminded of the night of Duncan's murder.

11 **call . . . accompt:** call to account anyone so powerful as we.

12 **Go to:** an exclamation, "Enough!" addressed to Lady Macbeth.

13. **charged:** burdened.

14 **dignity:** worth.

15 **on 's:** of his.

GENTLEWOMAN. Directly.

DOCTOR. Foul whisp'rings[16] are abroad. Unnatural deeds
    Do breed unnatural troubles. Infected minds
    To their deaf pillows will discharge their secrets.
70   More needs she the divine than the physician.
    God, God forgive us all! Look after her;
    Remove from her the means of all annoyance,[17]
    And still[18] keep eyes upon her. So good night.
    My mind she has mated[19] and amazed my sight:
    I think, but dare not speak.

75 GENTLEWOMAN.   Good night, good doctor.

    [*They leave.*]

Scene ii. *Near Dunsinane.*

[*In the countryside near Dunsinane soldiers enter with the
Scottish noblemen* MENTEITH, CAITHNESS, ANGUS, *and* LENNOX.
*The soldiers are carrying drums and flags. They are all on
the way to join forces with an approaching English army to
rebel against Macbeth.*]

MENTEITH. The English pow'r[1] is near, led on by Malcolm,
    His uncle Siward and the good Macduff.
    Revenges burn in them; for their dear causes
    Would to the bleeding and the grim alarm
    Excite the mortified man.[2]

5 ANGUS.   Near Birnam Wood
    Shall we well[3] meet them; that way are they coming.

CAITHNESS. Who knows if Donalbain be with his brother?

LENNOX. For certain, sir, he is not. I have a file[4]
    Of all the gentry: there is Siward's son,
10   And many unrough[5] youths that even now
    Protest[6] their first of manhood.

MENTEITH.   What does the tyrant?

CAITHNESS. Great Dunsinane he strongly fortifies.
    Some say he's mad; others, that lesser hate him,
    Do call it valiant fury: but, for certain,
15   He cannot buckle his distempered cause
    Within the belt of rule.[7]

ANGUS.   Now does he feel
    His secret murders sticking on his hands;
    Now minutely revolts upbraid his faith-breach.[8]

16 **Foul whisp'rings:** evil rumors.

17 **annoyance:** injury.
18 **still:** always.
19 **mated:** bewildered.

1 **pow'r:** army.

2 **alarm . . . man:** would call to
arms even the dead.

3 **well:** probably.

4 **file:** list.

5 **unrough:** beardless.
6 **Protest:** assert.

7 **Within . . . rule:** under self-
control.

8 **minutely . . . faith-breach:** Every
minute revolts reproach his disloyalty.

Those he commands move only in command,
20 Nothing in love. Now does he feel his title
Hang loose about him, like a giant's robe
Upon a dwarfish thief.

MENTEITH.   Who then shall blame
His pestered[9] senses to recoil and start,
When all that is within him does condemn
Itself for being there?

25 CAITHNESS.   Well, march we on,
To give obedience where 'tis truly owed.
Meet we the med'cine of the sickly weal,[10]
And with him pour we, in our country's purge,
Each drop of us.[11]

LENNOX.   Or so much as it needs
30 To dew the sovereign flower and drown the weeds.[12]
Make we our march towards Birnam.

[*They march off.*]

Scene iii. *The castle at Dunsinane.*

[MACBETH, *the* DOCTOR, *and attendants enter a room in Dunsinane Castle.* MACBETH *has heard reports of the approaching English and rebel Scottish forces, but he disregards them. He feels secure in his knowledge of the* WITCHES' *predictions: that no one born of a woman will be able to harm him and that he will be unconquered until Birnam Wood marches twelve miles to his castle on Dunsinane Hill.*]

MACBETH. Bring me no more reports; let them fly all![1]
Till Birnam Wood remove to Dunsinane
I cannot taint[2] with fear. What's the boy Malcolm?
Was he not born of woman? The spirits that know
5 All mortal consequences[3] have pronounced me thus:
"Fear not, Macbeth; no man that's born of woman
Shall e'er have power upon thee." Then fly, false thanes,
And mingle with the English epicures.[4]
The mind I sway[5] by and the heart I bear
10 Shall never sag with doubt nor shake with fear.

[*A* SERVANT *enters.*]

The devil damn thee black, thou cream-faced loon![6]
Where got'st thou that goose look?

SERVANT. There is ten thousand—

MACBETH.   Geese, villain?

9 **pestered:** tormented.

10 **the med'cine . . . weal:** Malcolm and his supporters will heal the sickly community.
11 **pour . . . us:** spill our blood to cleanse our country.

12 **To . . . weeds:** to water the royal flower (Malcolm) and drown the evil (Macbeth).

1 **let . . . all:** let the noblemen who are deserting us go.

2 **taint:** be infected.

3 **mortal consequences:** the events of human fate.

4 **epicures** [ep'i kyoorz']: gluttons. The Scots, who ate plain food, believed that the English dined on rich food.
5 **sway:** move.

6 **loon:** rogue, worthless rascal.

SERVANT. Soldiers, sir.

MACBETH. Go prick thy face and over-red thy fear,

15 Thou lily-livered boy. What soldiers, patch?[7]
Death of thy soul! Those linen[8] cheeks of thine
Are counselors to fear.[9] What soldiers, whey-face?

SERVANT. The English force, so please you.

MACBETH. Take thy face hence.

[*The* SERVANT *leaves, and* MACBETH *calls for* SEYTON, *his trusted officer.*]

Seyton!—I am sick at heart,
20 When I behold—Seyton, I say!—This push[10]
Will cheer me ever, or disseat[11] me now.
I have lived long enough. My way of life
Is fall'n into the sear,[12] the yellow leaf,
And that which should accompany old age,
25 As honor, love, obedience, troops of friends,
I must not look to have; but, in their stead,
Curses not loud but deep, mouth-honor,[13] breath,
Which the poor heart would fain deny, and dare not.
Seyton!

[SEYTON *enters.*]

SEYTON. What's your gracious pleasure?

30 **MACBETH.** What news more?

SEYTON. All is confirmed, my lord, which was reported.

MACBETH. I'll fight, till from my bones my flesh be hacked.
Give me my armor.

SEYTON. 'Tis not needed yet.

MACBETH. I'll put it on.
35 Send out moe[14] horses, skirr[15] the country round.
Hang those that talk of fear. Give me mine armor.
How does your patient, doctor?

DOCTOR. Not so sick, my lord,
As she is troubled with thick-coming fancies
That keep her from her rest.

MACBETH. Cure her of that.
40 Canst thou not minister to a mind diseased,
Pluck from the memory a rooted sorrow,
Raze out[16] the written troubles of the brain,
And with some sweet oblivious antidote
Cleanse the stuffed bosom of that perilous stuff
Which weighs upon the heart?

7 **patch:** fool.

8 **linen:** pale as linen.

9 **Are . . . fear:** prompt others to fear.

10 **push:** effort in battle.

11 **disseat:** unthrone.

12 **the sear:** a withered state.

13 **mouth-honor:** honor from the lips, not from the heart.

14 **moe:** more.
15 **skirr:** scour.

16 **Raze out:** erase.

45 **DOCTOR.** Therein the patient
Must minister to himself.

MACBETH. Throw physic[17] to the dogs, I'll none of it.
Come, put mine armor on. Give me my staff.
Seyton, send out—Doctor, the thanes fly from me—
50 Come, sir, dispatch. If thou couldst, doctor, cast
The water[18] of my land, find her disease
And purge it to a sound and pristine health,
I would applaud thee to the very echo,
That should applaud again—Pull 't off,[19] I say—
55 What rhubarb, senna, or what purgative drug,
Would scour these English hence? Hear'st thou of them?

DOCTOR. Ay, my good lord; your royal preparation
Makes us hear something.

MACBETH. Bring it[20] after me.
I will not be afraid of death and bane[21]
60 Till Birnam Forest come to Dunsinane.

DOCTOR. [*Aside.*] Were I from Dunsinane away and clear,
Profit again should hardly draw me here.

[*They leave.*]

Scene iv. Near Birnam Wood.

[*In the countryside near Birnam Wood, not far from Dunsinane, the English and the rebel Scottish troops have joined forces. A group of soldiers and noblemen enter marching. Among them are a drummer, flagbearer,* MALCOLM, MACDUFF, MENTEITH, CAITHNESS, ANGUS, *and* SIWARD, *the general sent by the King of England, and his son,* YOUNG SIWARD.]

MALCOLM. Cousins, I hope the days are near at hand
That chambers will be safe.[1]

MENTEITH. We doubt it nothing.

SIWARD. What wood is this before us?

MENTEITH. The Wood of Birnam.

MALCOLM. Let every soldier hew him down a bough
5 And bear 't before him. Thereby shall we shadow[2]
The numbers of our host, and make discovery[3]
Err in report of us.

SOLDIERS. It shall be done.

SIWARD. We learn no other but the confident tyrant
Keeps still in Dunsinane, and will endure
Our setting down[4] before 't.

17 **physic:** medicine.

18 **cast the water:** diagnose the illness.

19 **Pull 't off:** remove the piece of armor.

20 **it:** his armor.
21 **bane:** destruction.

1 **That chambers . . . safe:** when we can sleep in our beds without fear of being murdered.

2 **shadow:** conceal.

3 **discovery:** these who see us.

4 **setting down:** laying siege to it.

10 **MALCOLM.**   'Tis his main hope,
    For where there is advantage to be given
    Both more and less have given him the revolt,[5]
    And none serve with him but constrainèd things
    Whose hearts are absent too.

5 **more . . . revolt:** People of high and low rank have turned against him.

    MACDUFF.   Let our just censures
15 Attend the true event,[6] and put we on
    Industrious soldiership.

6 **our . . . event:** Let our true judgment wait until the battle is over.

    SIWARD.   The time approaches,
    That will with due decision make us know
    What we shall say we have and what we owe.[7]
    Thoughts speculative their unsure hopes relate,
20 But certain issue strokes must arbitrate:[8]
    Towards which advance the war.[9]

7 **owe:** own.

8 **strokes must arbitrate:** battle must decide.
9 **war:** army.

    [*They march off.*]

Scene v. *The castle at Dunsinane.*

[*Inside Dunsinane Castle,* MACBETH, SEYTON, *and other soldiers, including a drummer and flagbearer, prepare for battle.*]

    MACBETH. Hang out our banners on the outward walls.
    The cry is still "They come!" Our castle's strength
    Will laugh a siege to scorn. Here let them lie
    Till famine and the ague[1] eat them up.
5   Were they not forced[2] with those that should be ours,
    We might have met them dareful,[3] beard to beard,
    And beat them backward home.

1 **ague:** fever.
2 **forced:** reinforced.
3 **dareful:** boldly.

    [*A cry is heard within the castle.*]

                              What is that noise?

    SEYTON. It is the cry of women, my good lord.

    [SEYTON *leaves.*]

    MACBETH. I have almost forgot the taste of fears:
10 The time has been, my senses would have cooled
    To hear a night-shriek, and my fell[4] of hair
    Would at a dismal treatise[5] rouse and stir
    As life were in 't. I have supped full with horrors.
    Direness, familiar to my slaughterous thoughts,
    Cannot once start[6] me.

4 **fell:** scalp.
5 **dismal treatise:** ominous story.

6 **start:** startle.

    [SEYTON *returns, and as* MACBETH *learns of his wife's death, he reveals his attitude toward life and time.*]

15   Wherefore was that cry?

SEYTON. The Queen, my lord, is dead.

MACBETH. She should have died hereafter;[7]
There would have been a time for such a word.[8]
Tomorrow, and tomorrow, and tomorrow
20 Creeps in this petty pace from day to day,
To the last syllable of recorded time;
And all our yesterdays have lighted fools
The way to dusty death. Out, out, brief candle!
Life's but a walking shadow, a poor player
25 That struts and frets his hour upon the stage
And then is heard no more. It is a tale
Told by an idiot, full of sound and fury
Signifying nothing.

[*A messenger comes in.*]

Thou com'st to use thy tongue; thy story quickly!

30 **MESSENGER.** Gracious my lord,
I should report that which I say I saw,
But know not how to do 't.

MACBETH.   Well, say, sir.

MESSENGER. As I did stand my watch upon the hill,
I looked toward Birnam, and anon, methought,
The wood began to move.

35 **MACBETH.**   Liar and slave!

MESSENGER. Let me endure your wrath, if 't be not so.
Within this three mile may you see it coming;
I say a moving grove.

MACBETH.   If thou speak'st false,
Upon the next tree shalt thou hang alive,
40 Till famine cling[9] thee. If thy speech be sooth,[10]
I care not if thou dost for me as much.
I pull in resolution, and begin
To doubt th' equivocation of the fiend[11]
That lies like truth: "Fear not, till Birnam Wood
45 Do come to Dunsinane!" And now a wood
Comes toward Dunsinane. Arm, arm, and out!
If this which he avouches[12] does appear,
There is nor flying hence nor tarrying here.
I 'gin to be aweary of the sun,
50 And wish th' estate o' th' world were now undone.
Ring the alarum bell! Blow wind, come wrack!
At least we'll die with harness[13] on our back.

[*They all leave.*]

182 *English Literature: The Elizabethan Age*

---

7 **She . . . hereafter:** It would have been better if she had died at some other time.
8 **word:** message ("The queen is dead").

9 **cling:** wither.
10 **sooth:** truth.

11 **equivocation** [i kwiv′ə kā′shən] **. . . fiend:** double talk of the weird sisters.

12 **avouches:** affirms, asserts.

13 **harness:** armor.

Scene vi. *Near the castle at Dunsinane.*

[MALCOLM, SIWARD, MACDUFF, *and their soldiers, hidden by the tree boughs they are carrying, advance toward Dunsinane Castle.*]

MALCOLM. Now near enough. Your leavy[1] screens throw
   down,
  And show like those you are. You, worthy uncle,[2]
  Shall, with my cousin, your right noble son,
  Lead our first battle.[3] Worthy Macduff and we
5 Shall take upon 's what else remains to do,
  According to our order.[4]

SIWARD.   Fare you well.
  Do we but find the tyrant's power[5] tonight,
  Let us be beaten, if we cannot fight.

MACDUFF. Make all our trumpets speak; give them all breath,
10 Those clamorous harbingers[6] of blood and death.

    [*Blaring trumpets and the sounds of battle are heard as they leave.*]

1 **leavy:** leafy.

2 **uncle:** Siward, general of the English forces.

3 **battle:** battalion.

4 **order:** plan.

5 **power:** forces.

6 **harbingers:** messengers.

Scene vii. *Near the castle at Dunsinane.*

[*On another part of the battlefield outside the castle,* MACBETH *enters.*]

MACBETH. They have tied me to a stake; I cannot fly,
  But bearlike I must fight the course.[1] What's he
  That was not born of woman? Such a one
  Am I to fear, or none.

    [YOUNG SIWARD *enters and challenges* MACBETH.]

YOUNG SIWARD. What is thy name?

5 MACBETH.   Thou'lt be afraid to hear it.

YOUNG SIWARD. No; though thou call'st thyself a hotter name
  Than any is in hell.

MACBETH.   My name's Macbeth.

YOUNG SIWARD. The devil himself could not pronounce a title
  More hateful to mine ear.

MACBETH.   No, nor more fearful.

10 YOUNG SIWARD. Thou liest, abhorrèd tyrant; with my sword
  I'll prove the lie thou speak'st.

1 **bearlike . . . course:** Like a bear tied to a stake, I must fight until the end. In Elizabethan sport a bear was chained to a stake and attacked by dogs.

[They fight, and YOUNG SIWARD *is slain.]*

MACBETH.   Thou wast born of woman.
But swords I smile at, weapons laugh to scorn,
Brandished by man that's of a woman born.

*[*MACBETH *leaves as the sounds of battle mount.* MACDUFF *enters.]*

MACDUFF. That way the noise is. Tyrant, show thy face!
15   If thou be'st slain and with no stroke of mine,
My wife and children's ghosts will haunt me still.
I cannot strike at wretched kerns,[2] whose arms
Are hired to bear their staves.[3] Either thou, Macbeth,
Or else my sword, with an unbattered edge,
20   I sheathe again undeeded.[4] There thou shouldst be;
By this great clatter, one of greatest note
Seems bruited.[5] Let me find him, Fortune!
And more I beg not.

[More battle sounds are heard as MACDUFF *leaves.* MALCOLM *and* OLD SIWARD *enter.]*

SIWARD. This way, my lord. The castle's gently rend'red:[6]
25   The tyrant's people on both sides do fight;
The noble thanes do bravely in the war;
The day almost itself professes yours,
And little is to do.

MALCOLM.   We have met with foes
That strike beside us.[7]

SIWARD.   Enter, sir, the castle.

[They leave as the sounds of battle continue.]

Scene viii. *Near the castle at Dunsinane.*

*[*MACBETH *enters in another part of the battlefield, still ready to fight to the end despite overwhelming opposition.]*

MACBETH. Why should I play the Roman fool, and die
On mine own sword?[1] Whiles I see lives,[2] the gashes
Do better upon them.

*[*MACDUFF *enters.]*

MACDUFF.   Turn, hell-hound, turn!

MACBETH. Of all men else I have avoided thee.
5   But get thee back! My soul is too much charged
With blood of thine already.

2 **kerns:** hired Irish soldiers.

3 **staves:** spears.

4 **undeeded:** unused.

5 **bruited:** proclaimed, reported.

6 **gently rend'red:** easily surrendered.

7 **strike . . . us:** deliberately miss us.

1 **play . . . sword:** die like Brutus or Cassius, who killed themselves with their own swords rather than face defeat.
2 **Whiles . . . lives:** so long as I see living men.

184   *English Literature: The Elizabethan Age*

MACDUFF.   I have no words:
  My voice is in my sword, thou bloodier villain
  Than terms can give thee out!³

  [*They fight.*]

MACBETH.   Thou losest labor:
  As easy mayst thou the intrenchant air
10   With thy keen sword impress as make me bleed:⁴

3 **Than . . . out:** than words can describe you.

4 **as easy . . . me bleed:** You will have no more success in making me bleed than you would in making the air bleed.

Let fall thy blade on vulnerable crests;
I bear a charmèd life, which must not yield
To one of woman born.

MACDUFF.   Despair thy charm,
And let the angel⁵ whom thou still hast served
15   Tell thee, Macduff was from his mother's womb
Untimely ripped.⁶

MACBETH. Accursèd be that tongue that tells me so,
For it hath cowed my better part of man!⁷
And be these juggling fiends no more believed,
20   That palter⁸ with us in a double sense;
That keep the word of promise to our ear,
And break it to our hope. I'll not fight with thee.

MACDUFF. Then yield thee, coward,
And live to be the show and gaze o' th' time:⁹
25   We'll have thee, as our rarer monsters are,
Painted upon a pole,¹⁰ and underwrit,
"Here may you see the tyrant."

MACBETH.   I will not yield,
To kiss the ground before young Malcolm's feet,
And to be baited with the rabble's curse.
30   Though Birnam Wood be come to Dunsinane,
And thou opposed, being of no woman born,
Yet I will try the last.¹¹ Before my body
I throw my warlike shield. Lay on, Macduff;
And damned be him that first cries "Hold, enough!"

[*They leave, fighting. More trumpet blasts and battle cries
are heard. They reenter fighting, and* MACBETH *is slain.*
MACDUFF *removes* MACBETH's *body. After he leaves,* MALCOLM,
OLD SIWARD, ROSS, *various thanes and soldiers, including a
drummer and flagbearer, enter.*]

35   **MALCOLM.** I would the friends we miss were safe arrived.

SIWARD. Some must go off;¹² and yet, by these I see,
So great a day as this is cheaply bought.

MALCOLM. Macduff is missing, and your noble son.

ROSS. Your son, my lord, has paid a soldier's debt:
40   He only lived but till he was a man;
The which no sooner had his prowess confirmed
In the unshrinking station¹³ where he fought,
But like a man he died.

SIWARD.   Then he is dead?

---

5 **angel:** fallen angel, fiend.

6 **Macduff . . . ripped:** Macduff's mother died before giving birth to him; therefore he was not "of woman born."
7 **better . . . man:** courage.

8 **palter:** deal deceitfully.

9 **o' th' time:** spectacle of the age.

10 **We'll . . . pole:** Like a freak (monster) in a sideshow, we will paint your face on a post and place it outside a showman's booth.

11 **I . . . last:** I will fight to the end.

12 **go off:** die (in battle).

13 **unshrinking station:** place where he stood firm.

ROSS. Ay, and brought off the field. Your cause of sorrow
45 Must not be measured by his worth, for then
    It hath no end.

SIWARD.   Had he his hurts before?

ROSS. Ay, on the front.

SIWARD.   Why then, God's soldier be he!
    Had I as many sons as I have hairs,
    I would not wish them to a fairer death:
    And so his knell is knolled.

50 MALCOLM.   He's worth more sorrow,
    And that I'll spend for him.

SIWARD.   He's worth no more:
    They say he parted well and paid his score:
    And so God be with him! Here comes newer comfort.

    [MACDUFF *enters with* MACBETH's *head.*]

    MACDUFF. Hail, King! for so thou art: behold, where stands
55 Th' usurper's cursèd head. The time is free.¹⁴
    I see thee compassed with thy kingdom's pearl,¹⁵
    That speak my salutation in their minds,
    Whose voices I desire aloud with mine:
    Hail, King of Scotland!

ALL.   Hail, King of Scotland!

    [*There is a trumpet flourish.*]

60 MALCOLM. We shall not spend a large expense of time
    Before we reckon with your several loves,¹⁶
    And make us even with you.¹⁷ My thanes and kinsmen,
    Henceforth be earls, the first that ever Scotland
    In such an honor named. What's more to do,
65 Which would be planted newly with the time¹⁸—
    As calling home our exiled friends abroad
    That fled the snares of watchful tyranny,
    Producing forth the cruel ministers
    Of this dead butcher and his fiendlike queen,
70 Who, as 'tis thought, by self and violent hands
    Took off her life—this, and what needful else
    That calls upon us, by the grace of Grace¹⁹
    We will perform in measure, time, and place:²⁰
    So thanks to all at once and to each one,
75 Whom we invite to see us crowned at Scone.

    [*They all leave to a flourish of trumpets.*]

14 **The . . . free:** Our country is free.

15 **compassed . . . pearl:** surrounded by the noblest in the kingdom.

16 **reckon . . . loves:** reward each of you for your loyalty.

17. **make . . . you:** pay what we owe you.

18 **What's . . . time:** What remains to be done at the beginning of this new era.

19 **Grace:** God.

20 **in . . . place:** with decorum at the appropriate time and place.

STUDY QUESTIONS

Recalling

1. At the beginning of Act V, Scene i, why are the doctor and gentlewoman observing Lady Macbeth?

2. As she is sleepwalking in Scene i, what prior incidents does Lady Macbeth refer to? List four or five such incidents. Whom is Lady Macbeth talking about when she says, "The Thane of Fife had a wife. Where is she now?"

3. In Scene ii what do Caithness and Angus say Macbeth is doing to prepare for the upcoming war? How do they describe Macbeth's state of mind?

4. What prophecy from Act IV, Scene i, is Malcolm fulfilling in Act V, Scene iv, when he gives his men orders as they reach the wood of Birnam?

5. What does Macbeth learn has happened to his wife in Scene v? Where is Macbeth going at the end of Scene v?

6. Which of the witches' prophecies does Macduff fulfill in Scene viii? What is Macbeth's first reaction to Macduff's statement? Does he change his mind?

7. Who finally kills Macbeth? Who becomes the King of Scotland?

Interpreting

8. Compare Lady Macbeth's behavior in Act V, Scene i, with her actions in Act II, Scene iii. How has she changed, and to what do you attribute the changes? What is different about her relationship with Macbeth?

9. In Scene iii where is Macbeth? What does he say and do that corresponds to the description of him given by Caithness and Angus in Scene ii?

10. In Scene v, lines 17–28, how does Macbeth express his attitude toward life after he learns of his wife's fate?

11. How is Macbeth's behavior in Scene viii reminiscent of accounts of him given in Act I, Scene ii?

Extending

12. How do you think Scotland will fare under Malcolm's rule? Base your answer on his final speech. Does he share any of the characteristics of the play's other kings, Duncan and Macbeth?

VIEWPOINT

For three and a half centuries critics have tried to explain Shakespeare's universal popularity. To Samuel Johnson, whose own writings appear on page 290, Shakespeare is

> the poet that holds up to his readers a faithful mirror of manners and of life. His characters are not modified by the customs of particular places, unpracticed by the rest of the world; . . . they are the genuine progeny [children] of common humanity, such as the world will always supply. . . .

■ Do you agree or disagree with Johnson's observations? Choose examples of Macbeth's, Lady Macbeth's, and Banquo's behavior to support your answer.

LITERARY FOCUS

The Total Effect

Before putting on a play, a director must have a clear idea of how the various elements will work together to make the performance a success. For instance, in *Macbeth* a director would want to emphasize plot, character, setting and atmosphere, irony, and theme in an effort to convey to the audience the total effect of the play.

Thinking About Plot

The **plot** of a literary work is a sequence of related incidents that revolve around a **conflict,** or struggle. The conflict may be **internal** (within the character) or **external** (between the character and another person, society, fate, or environment). A playwright generally presents the essential information about the characters and their lives in the first act. This background information is called **exposition.** As the play proceeds, **rising action** builds the conflict to a **climax,** a decisive turning point and a moment of great tension. In a tragedy the climax is usually in the middle of the play, when something that will lead to the downfall of the tragic hero takes place. Following the crisis, the **falling action** depicts the disastrous reversal of the tragic hero's fortunes and leads to the **resolution,** when the conflict ends and the outcome of the play is made known.

1. Give examples of internal and external conflict from Act I.

2. Make a list of important background information given in Act I. What happens at the end

of Act I that begins the rising action of the play?

3. Identify the rising action in Acts II and III.
4. Where in Act III do you think the climax—the moment of greatest intensity—occurs?
5. What falling action in Acts IV and V signals the downfall of Macbeth?
6. What is the resolution of the play?

Thinking About Character

We learn about a character in a play by seeing how the character looks and acts. Through speeches the character reveals what he or she thinks and feels. The speeches of the others let us know how they regard the character. Some characters remain static, or unchanged, throughout the course of the story or drama. These characters, who are generally minor, are called **flat characters.** Others, dynamic, or **round characters,** are a mix of many changing qualities that grow and develop as the story unfolds.

1. Which characters in Macbeth would you consider to be flat? Give several examples of static behavior in support of your decisions.
2. How does Shakespeare use soliloquies and asides to reveal character? Give examples from the speeches of two or three characters.
3. Analyze the personality of one of the leading characters in *Macbeth.* How is the character's personality revealed? Cite examples of the reactions of others and the character's own actions and conversations.

Thinking About Setting and Atmosphere

The **setting,** or locale, is the place and time in which the action of a dramatic or literary work occurs. Descriptions of the setting often enhance the overall mood or **atmosphere**.

1. What mood does the setting of Act I, Scene i, create? What impressions of the play to come does the setting inspire?
2. What is the significance of darkness and light in *Macbeth*? How does it contribute to the overall atmosphere of the play?

Thinking About Irony

Irony involves a contrast between appearance and reality. In **verbal** irony there is a contrast between what is stated and what is actually meant— when a person says one thing but means the opposite. **Dramatic** irony occurs when the audience or reader of a play knows something a character does not and therefore understands the speech or action more fully than the character does.

1. Find an example of verbal irony in the conversation between Banquo and Macbeth at the beginning of Act III, Scene i.
2. Find an example of dramatic irony in the beginning of Act I, Scene vi.
3. What is ironical about Macbeth's entrance in Act I, Scene iv?

Thinking About Theme

All the preceding elements work together to point to the play's **themes,** or general statements about life.

1. Explain how *Macbeth* is a story of one man's attempts to control the future.
2. Explain the importance of the witches and their prophecies. To what extent do they control Macbeth's destiny? To what extent does he govern his own free will?
3. Discuss the impact of Macbeth's actions on nature. Why do storms occur? Why is time upset? Why is Macbeth himself unable to sleep "naturally" during the course of the play?

COMPOSITION

Writing About the Total Effect

■ Describe the total effect of *Macbeth*. That is, what was the impact of the play on you after you finished reading it? Support your statement by explaining how Shakespeare uses the following literary elements to achieve this effect: plot, character, setting and atmosphere, imagery, irony, and theme. *For help with this assignment, refer to Lesson 8 in the Writing About Literature Handbook at the back of this book.*

Writing a Speech

■ Imagine that Malcolm has asked you to give a speech for him at his coronation at Scone. Scots are coming from great distances to see the new king. They are weary of the turmoil of Macbeth's reign, and they are looking for assurances from Malcolm that his rule will restore peace. Malcolm is your friend, and you have been with him ever since his father, Duncan, was killed. In your speech, explain why you think he will be an effective king. Support your opinions with examples of his behavior and actions that you have recently observed.

Sir Francis Bacon   *1561–1626*

As a young man Francis Bacon wrote, "I have taken all knowledge to be my province." His accomplishments would seem to support this extraordinary claim: *The Advancement of Learning* sets down nothing less than the progress of human knowledge up to his own time; his *Essays and Counsels* were a landmark in English prose composition; and his ideas about the importance of observation and experiment (empiricism) form the basis of the modern scientific method.

Bacon was born in London, the son of a government minister in Queen Elizabeth's court. After attending Trinity College, Cambridge, and training as a lawyer, he held a series of government posts and was knighted in 1603. A supporter of King James I, he rose to the position of Lord Chancellor of England, the highest honor in the legal profession. In 1621 he was convicted of taking bribes by James's enemies and was forced to retire from public life. Thereafter he pursued his interests in science and philosophy. Scientists today owe their reliance on the inductive method of reasoning to Bacon. That is, he promoted the idea that generalizations should be made only after careful consideration of facts. As obvious as this idea is to us, it was revolutionary during Bacon's lifetime, when scholars still preferred deductive reasoning—moving from generalizations to specifics instead of vice versa. In addition, Bacon introduced the concept of hypotheses to scientists, arguing that scientists needed to make initial assumptions before beginning their experiments. Bacon even died in the service of science: He developed bronchitis after collecting snow to study refrigeration of a chicken.

Of all Bacon's writings the most popular remain his *Essays and Counsels,* which he began publishing in 1597. The **essay,** a brief prose composition exploring a single subject, was a development of the Renaissance, and Bacon was the first English writer to make use of this new literary form and shape it to his own taste. Unlike the warm, personal essays of Bacon's European contemporaries, the Baconian essay is objective, compact, and logical.

Bacon packs his essays full of meaning and omits specific examples or illustrations to make the general comments clearer. Nevertheless, their author's shrewd judgments about human nature make them worth the effort required to read them, for much of what Bacon writes about his own age applies equally well to ours. "Of Ambition" may relate to Shakespeare's character Macbeth and to others, fictional and real.

Detail, *Portrait of a Young Man,* Agnolo Bronzino, c. 1550.

Francis Bacon

Of Ambition

Ambition is like choler; which is a humor[1] that maketh men active, earnest, full of alacrity, and stirring, if it be not stopped. But if it be stopped, and cannot have his way, it becometh adust,[2] and thereby malign and venomous. So ambitious men, if they find the way open for their rising, and still get forward, they are rather busy than dangerous; but if they be checked in their desires, they become secretly discontent, and look upon men and matters with an evil eye, and are best pleased when things go backward; which is the worst property in a servant of a prince or state. Therefore, it is good for princes, if they use ambitious men, to handle it so as they be still progressive and not retrograde:[3] which because it cannot be without inconvenience, it is good not to use such natures at all. For if they rise not with their service, they will take order[4] to make their service fall with them.

But since we have said it were good not to use men of ambitious natures, except it be upon necessity, it is fit we speak in what cases they are of necessity. Good commanders in the wars must be taken, be they never so ambitious:[5] for the use of their service dispenseth with the rest; and to take a soldier without ambition is to pull off his spurs. There is also great use of ambitious men in being screens to princes in matters of danger and envy: for no

---

1. **humor:** Elizabethans believed that the body contained four humors, or fluids, that combined in different ways from individual to individual to determine temperament. The fluids were blood, phlegm, black bile (melancholy), and red bile (*choler,* or irritability; hot temperedness).
2. **adust:** overheated, scorched.

3. **still . . . retrograde:** always moving forward rather than backward.
4. **take order:** proceed.
5. **be . . . ambitious:** no matter how ambitious they are.

man will take that part, except he be like a seeled[6] dove, that mounts and mounts because he cannot see about him. There is use also of ambitious men in pulling down the greatness of any subject that overtops: as Tiberius used Macro in the pulling down of Sejanus.[7]

Since therefore they must be used in such cases, there resteth[8] to speak how they are to be bridled, that they may be less dangerous. There is less danger of them if they be of mean[9] birth than if they be noble; and if they be rather harsh of nature than gracious and popular; and if they be rather new raised[10] than grown cunning and fortified in their greatness. It is counted by some a weakness in princes to have favorites; but it is of all others the best remedy against ambitious great ones. For when the way of pleasuring and displeasuring lieth by the favorite, it is impossible any other should be overgreat. Another means to curb them is to balance them by others as proud as they. But then there must be some middle counselors to keep things steady; for without that ballast the ship will roll too much. At the least, a prince may animate and inure[11] some meaner persons to be, as it were, scourges[12] to ambitious men.

As for the having of them obnoxious[13] to ruin, if they be of fearful natures, it may do well; but if they be stout and daring, it may precipitate their designs and prove dangerous. As for the pulling of them down, if the affairs require it, and that[14] it may not be done with safety suddenly, the only way is the interchange continually of favors and disgraces;[15] whereby they may not know what to expect, and be, as it were, in a wood.[16] Of ambitions, it is less harmful, the ambition to prevail in great things than that other, to appear in everything; for that breeds confusion and mars business. But yet it is less danger to have an ambitious man stirring in business than great in dependences.[17]

He that seeketh to be eminent amongst able men hath a great task; but that is ever good for the public. But he that plots to be the only figure amongst ciphers[18] is the decay of a whole age. Honor[19] hath three things in it: the vantage ground to do good; the approach to kings and principal persons; and the raising of a man's own fortunes. He that hath the best of these intentions, when he aspireth, is an honest man; and that prince that can discern of these intentions in another that aspireth is a wise prince. Generally, let princes and states choose such ministers as are more sensible of duty than of rising; and such as love business rather upon conscience than upon bravery:[20] and let them discern[21] a busy nature from a willing mind.

---

6. **seeled:** with eyelids sewn together. Falcons were seeled in order to train them to fly in high circles to hunt before returning to their trainers.

7. **Tiberius** [tī bēr′ē əs] . . . **Sejanus** [sa jā′nəs]: For many years Sejanus was chief aide and confidant to the Roman emperor Tiberius. The emperor grew suspicious of him and had him put to death in A.D. 31.

8. **resteth:** remains.

9. **mean:** lowly, humble.

10. **new raised:** recently elevated to greatness.

11. **inure:** accustom.

12. **scourges:** whips (to keep them on good behavior).

13. **obnoxious:** liable.

14. **that:** presuming.

15. **disgraces:** dismissals from (royal) favor.

16. **in a wood:** that is, lost in the woods; confused.

17. **stirring . . . dependences:** working to advance himself rather than waiting and expecting advancement automatically.

18. **ciphers:** people of no importance; nonentities.

19. **Honor:** exalted rank or position.

20. **bravery:** ostentation, show.

21. **discern:** distinguish.

STUDY QUESTIONS

Recalling

1. What does the first paragraph advise princes to do about using ambitious men?
2. According to the second paragraph, in what three specific cases must princes use ambitious men? In such cases, what characteristics itemized in paragraph 3 will make the men less dangerous?
3. What are the three advantages of a position of honor, according to the last paragraph? How does Bacon define an honest man?
4. Generally, what kind of ministers should princes and states choose, according to the last paragraph?

Interpreting

5. According to Bacon, in what or whom are ambitious people interested? In what or whom should a good public servant be interested?
6. Describe the kind of writer that Bacon seems to be. For example, is he perceptive? Is he naive? Support your answers with details from the essay.

Extending

7. How, according to Bacon's essay, might Duncan have dealt with the threat of Macbeth's ambition?

VOCABULARY STUDY

Synonyms

A **synonym** is a word that has the same or nearly the same meaning as another word. *Begin* and *start* are synonyms. The words in capitals are from "Of Ambition." Choose the word that is *nearest* the meaning of the word in capitals, *as the word is used in the selection.* Write the number of each item and the letter of your choice on a separate sheet.

1. ALACRITY: (a) eagerness (b) agitation (c) firmness (d) cleverness
2. VENOMOUS: (a) dishonest (b) malicious (c) mischievous (d) contagious
3. BRIDLED: (a) saddled (b) restrained (c) tamed (d) angered
4. BALLAST: (a) sails (b) steering device (c) captain (d) stabilizer
5. ANIMATE: (a) proclaim (b) harden (c) inspire (d) dehumanize
6. PRECIPITATE: (a) indicate (b) hasten (c) condense (d) foreshadow
7. MARS: (a) impairs (b) disfigures (c) battles (d) ends
8. EMINENT: (a) haughty (b) competent (c) lowly (d) prominent

COMPOSITION

Writing About Nonfiction

▨ Explain the purpose of Bacon's essay "On Ambition." First discuss the various techniques that Bacon uses, such as facts, examples, and opinion. Be sure to cite examples of each technique from the selection. Then tell how these techniques help Bacon accomplish the purpose you have identified. *For help with this assignment, refer to Lesson 4 in the Writing About Literature Handbook at the back of this book.*

Writing an Essay

▨ Try writing a brief composition using Bacon's essay as a model. Choose a topic, and jot down your thoughts about it. (Among the topics Bacon himself wrote about are truth, envy, travel, friendship, riches, studies, and beauty.) Concentrate on a few general observations regarding the topic: (1) how it affects people, (2) when it is necessary, (3) how to use it. Avoid emotional language and personal anecdotes. Polish your prose into three coherent paragraphs that express your thoughts as clearly and logically as possible.

The King James Bible

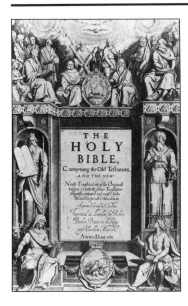

What has been called "the noblest monument of English prose" appeared in 1611, during Shakespeare's lifetime. It was the result of seven years of labor by a group of notable scholars and clergymen under orders of King James I. Many other translations of the Bible are in existence, but the King James Bible, as it came to be called, was the first English-language translation to receive widespread, lasting acceptance among English-speaking people.

Bible means "books." The Christian Bible consists of the books of the Old Testament, originally in Hebrew, and the New Testament, originally in Greek. Before the Protestant Reformation the Bible was ordinarily read in Latin, though an early English translation of the complete Holy Scriptures was made by the Wycliffites, or Lollards, unsuccessful religious reformers of Chaucer's day. With the Reformation came many translations into the **vernacular**, the language of the people.

William Tyndale's 1525 translation of the New Testament was the first English translation to be printed, but Tyndale's work on the Old Testament ended abruptly with his execution in 1535 during the religious turmoil of the period. Other English translations appeared soon after, notably the Great Bible of Miles Coverdale; the Geneva Bible, translated by English Calvinists living in Switzerland; and the Rheims Bible, translated by English Catholics living in France. However, it was to Tyndale's masterful prose that the King James translators turned when they began their efforts in 1604.

The resulting King James, or Authorized, Version of the Holy Bible was for centuries not only the most widely read English Bible, but the most widely read English book. Thus it exerted an enormous stabilizing influence on the English language, which had been changing steadily since the Norman Conquest.

The King James Bible is written chiefly in prose, but some portions use **free verse**, poetry without rhyme or regular rhythm but poetry nevertheless. This is true of the Book of Psalms, perhaps the most frequently read book of the Old Testament. The **psalms**, or songs of praise, are most commonly attributed to David, king of Israel in 1000 B.C.

Psalm 8

O Lord our Lord,
How excellent is thy name in all the earth!
Who hast set thy glory above the heavens.
Out of the mouths of babes and sucklings hast thou ordained
    strength because of thine enemies,
5 That thou mightest still the enemy and the avenger.
When I consider thy heavens, the work of thy fingers,
The moon and the stars, which thou hast ordained;
What is man, that thou art mindful of him?
And the son of man, that thou visitest him?
10 For thou hast made him a little lower than the angels,
And hast crowned him with glory and honor.
Thou madest him to have dominion over the works of thy hands;
Thou hast put all things under his feet:
All sheep and oxen,
15 Yea, and the beasts of the field;
The fowl of the air, and the fish of the sea,
And whatsoever passeth through the paths of the seas.
O Lord our Lord,
How excellent is thy name in all the earth!

Psalm 23

The Lord is my shepherd; I shall not want.[1]
He maketh me to lie down in green pastures: he leadeth me be-
    side the still waters.
He restoreth my soul:[2] he leadeth me in the paths of righteous-
    ness for his name's sake.
Yea, though I walk through the valley of the shadow of death,
    I will fear no evil: for thou art with me; thy rod and thy staff
    they comfort me.
5 Thou preparest a table before me in the presence of mine
    enemies: thou anointest my head with oil; my cup runneth over.
Surely goodness and mercy shall follow me all the days of my
    life: and I will dwell in the house of the Lord forever.[3]

---

1. **want:** be in need.
2. **soul:** here, vitality.

3. **dwell . . . forever:** worship in the temple
as long as I live.

READING FOR APPRECIATION

Sound in Drama

We think of drama as literature; yet it is important to remember when we read a play that the author wrote it to be staged and performed. Reading a play is a very different experience from that of actually seeing and hearing it in performance. Nevertheless, if we read carefully and *imaginatively,* we will find that the experience can be just as rewarding.

We can make a play come to life for us in several ways. First, we must place ourselves in the theater; we must imagine ourselves among the real theater audience for which the play was created. Further, as we read, we should carefully note and imaginatively *respond to* the stage directions, which will evoke in our mind's eye the particulars of the setting; the lighting of each scene; and the costumes, physical appearance, and gestures of the performers.

Stage directions can help us to summon up another vital dimension of the play in performance: its *sound.* Just as you should try to picture the particular actor, so you must try to "hear" the music, the natural sounds, and even the inflections of voice that the playwright has imagined.

Consider, for example, the opening stage direction of *Macbeth.* We are somewhere in the midst of Scotland:

In the midst of a great storm of thunder and lightning, THREE WITCHES *appear in a deserted, outdoor place.*

We are given at the outset not only a stunning visual image but also a component of sound that sets a tone and a mood for the entire play. While three witches confer, a violent storm rages and swirls. The violence of the setting foreshadows and symbolizes the turbulence—psychological and emotional as well as physical—that courses through much of the play. The sound of the storm also evokes a sense of elemental terror: The characters in this play will encounter and contend with mysterious and awesome forces. We should "hear" this storm not only at the beginning but *throughout* the opening scene. By truly hearing the storm, we hear a good deal more that may enlighten us about the play as a whole.

Vocal inflections are another important sound element that we must listen for as we read a play. Often these variations in the tone or pitch of a character's voice are not indicated in stage directions. Nevertheless, we can hear them if we keep the character and the situation in mind—and our ears open.

Thus, in Act I, Scene vii, Macbeth has second thoughts about murdering Duncan. Lady Macbeth urges him on, however, scolding him for his sudden meekness. Angry and defiant, knowing that his decision might go either way—but sensing that he will decide against his better self—Macbeth responds. He is terrified at the thought of murder; yet he understands at the same time that he cannot resist the idea. If we read these lines sensitively, we can hear the fear and frustration engendered by this awful conflict:

[*with clenched teeth, almost hissing*] Prithee, PEACE!
[*boldly*] I dare do ALL that may become a MAN;
[*subsiding to a frightened whisper*] Who dares do MORE is none.

Hearing these inflections as we read, we gain a clearer impression of Macbeth's psychological state at this moment. It is a critical moment: Macbeth must decide whether or not to murder his king, and the *way* he speaks is at least as revealing as what he says. By paying attention to vocal inflections—and to the whole dimension of sound in the drama—we give ourselves a richer and more illuminating experience in reading.

THE ENGLISH VOICE

Love and Poetry

The Elizabethan love lyrics are one of the glories of literature. Within the strict conventions of their time, these sonnets and songs succeed time after time in giving love a voice. Descending from the courtly love tradition of the Middle Ages, in which a man worshiped a highborn lady from afar, Elizabethan lyrics brilliantly blend passion and elegance, body and mind. They escape the negative effects of artificiality, though they abound with cleverness and wit. They escape because the Elizabethans knew perfectly well that such "love" was a convention, an accepted poetic device. These poems triumph because they accept artifice and step beyond it: They unite the timeless power of love and the life-giving power of poetry itself.

Sidney

Loving in truth, and fain in verse my love to show
That the dear she might take some pleasure in my pain, . . .
Biting my truant pen, beating myself for spite:
"Fool," said my Muse to me, "look in thy heart, and write!"

Spenser

"My verse your virtues rare shall eternize,
And in the heavens write your glorious name.
Where whenas death shall all the world subdue,
Our love shall live, and later life renew."

Marlowe

If these delights thy mind may move,
Then live with me and be my love.

Shakespeare

So long as men can breathe or eyes can see,
So long lives this, and this gives life to thee.

Not marble, nor the gilded monuments
Of princes, shall outlive this pow'rful rhyme, . . .
'Gainst death and all-oblivious enmity
Shall you pace forth; your praise shall still find room
Even in the eyes of all posterity.

In Elizabethan lyrics love is celebrated in all its aspects. We still marvel at the ability of many of the poems to evoke a love that is both real and ideal, earthly and heavenly. The conventions of the time—and faith in the power of poetry—enabled Elizabethan poets to sing of love as both a mortal delight and an immortal possibility.

Key to Illustrations on Pages 80–81.

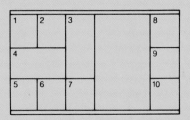

1. Portrait of Sir Francis Bacon, Paul van Somer (c. 1576–1621).
2. Detail, engraving of Macbeth and Banquo meeting the Three Witches, from Raphael Holinshed's *Chronicles*, 1577.
3. *A Young Man*, miniature by Nicholas Hilliard (1537–1619).
4. Detail, design for a tapestry depicting the defeat of the Spanish Armada.
5. Costume from the time of James I.
6. Portrait of Sir Philip Sidney (1544–1586), artist unknown.
7. Detail, title page to *The Mariners Mirrour*, an Elizabethan book.
8. Coat of arms of Elizabeth I.
9. Monument to William Shakespeare, erected in 1740 in Westminster Abbey, London.
10. Detail, *The Tower of London*, etching by Wenceslaus Hollar (1607–1677).

197

Key to Illustrations appears on page 249.

THE SEVENTEENTH CENTURY

1625–1700

Political and Religious Upheaval

In England the seventeenth century was a time of political and religious turmoil punctuated with violence that surprised and shocked England's neighbors on the Continent. The disputes in part resulted from the struggle for power between Parliament, which wanted more authority, and the throne, which held the theory that kings ruled by a "divine right" bestowed by God, not by the consent of Parliament.

Parliamentary power versus a self-righteous monarchy was not the only cause of dissension in this period, however. Religion was also an important factor. The ruler of England was also the head of the Church of England, or Anglican Church, which Henry VIII had established in 1534.

Charles I, who came to the throne in 1625, proved to be politically stubborn and untrustworthy. He continued to alienate Parliament, many of whose members were Puritans, fervent Protestant critics of both the Roman Catholic Church and the Church of England. These Puritans disliked Charles's insistence on the divine right of kings, his continuation of restrictions on Puritan preaching, and his several attempts to do without Parliament altogether. In 1642

Replica of Isaac Newton's reflecting telescope, 1671.

civil war broke out between the royalists—the king and his supporters—and the supporters of Parliament. The landed aristocrats supported the royalist cause. They were noted for their long hair and their gallant and witty manner and were thus often called Cavaliers. The plainly dressed Parliamentary forces were recognized by their closely cropped hair and grim determination. They were called Roundheads.

Oliver Cromwell—a Puritan member of Parliament and a military genius as well as a religious fanatic—brought victory to the Parliamentary forces and temporarily ended the monarchy in 1649. The Parliamentarians attempted to make the end of the monarchy permanent: After having ruled for almost a quarter of a century, Charles I was beheaded.

The stern Puritans frowned on all forms of frivolity, including the theater and even the lovely lyrics of the court poets. Yet despite their solemn and often gloomy attitudes, the Puritans became extremely powerful, chiefly because Cromwell proved a strong and efficient leader. (It was twenty years earlier that a group of Puritans—the Pilgrims—left England for the New World in search of religious freedom. Now, however, Puritans in England wielded power enough to have the king deposed and Cromwell installed at the head of the government.) However, Cromwell was a dictator. In an effort to control the

nation's morals, he enacted laws that invaded and severely restricted personal liberties. Theaters were shut down; Catholics and Anglicans were denied freedom of worship; and massacres were conducted against those Irish forces that challenged England's Puritan rule.

Oliver Cromwell—England's first nonroyal ruler—headed England as Lord Protector of the Commonwealth for nine violent years until his death in 1658. When his son Richard attempted to fill his shoes, he failed. By 1660 the English people had had their fill of Puritanism and were happy to restore the monarchy to a Stuart king. At the invitation of Parliament, the eldest son of Charles I returned to London from his exile in France and Holland and assumed the throne as Charles II. His return in 1660 is called the Restoration, and the term is also used to describe Charles II's entire reign, a lively period that saw a rebirth in the theater and in literature.

Equally important during the

Restoration was the scientific and philosophical growth to which Englishmen were contributing. London at this time was the center of new theories in both science and philosophy, and Charles II had a serious interest in the progress of science. In 1660 the Royal Society of London was established to promote scientific research, and in 1662 it was officially chartered by Charles II. Of the many scientific contributions, perhaps the most outstanding were those of the great English mathematician and astronomer Sir Isaac Newton, who formulated, among a great many other things, the law of gravity.

Charles II's reign was followed by the brief, unhappy reign of his brother James II, who came to the throne in 1685. James's Roman Catholicism and his stiff-headedness did not ingratiate him with the English people. In the so-called Glorious Revolution of 1688–1689—a revolution without violence or bloodshed—Parliament invited James's Protestant daughter Mary and her Dutch husband, Prince William of Orange, to accept the British crown. James II fled to permanent exile in France. In 1689 a Bill of Rights that limited a monarch's powers was enacted. No longer would an absolute monarch reign above the law. Now the propertied classes would rule through a Parliament elected by them. Thus, during the reign of William and Mary, Parliamentary government was firmly estab-

Costumes of the mid-seventeenth century.

lished in England. The century closed near the end of their reign.

Life in Seventeenth-Century England

Any statement about the quality of seventeenth-century English life depends on which part of the century is under discussion. In the early years of the century, most things were very much as they had been in Queen Elizabeth's day. The years during the Cromwellian revolution and Protectorate were a time darkened by fear, violence, and soul searching. The years following the Restoration were merry, and the end of the century saw signs of England's becoming an industrial nation.

When the first Stuart king, James I, came down from Scotland to ascend the English throne in 1603, he observed great houses and large estates along the way and expressed surprise at the richness of the country he was to govern. Toward the end of the century, the nation's wealth might better have been judged by observing London's increased commercial activity and size. By 1700 the greater metropolitan area of London included over 600,000 inhabitants, 200,000 of whom lived within the city proper. Furthermore, Bristol and Norwich were now cities of about 30,000 people. Still, other English cities were very small, usually with populations under 10,000.

In 1665 the Great Plague swept through London, leaving over 68,000 dead. After the city was devastated by the Great Fire in 1666, the famous architect Christopher Wren oversaw its rebuilding. According to one record, the fire consumed 13,200 houses, 400 streets, and almost 90 of London's 101 churches. Directed by Wren, the rebuilding of 51 churches was completed by 1700.

The English textile industry was growing throughout the century, but it was still a "cottage industry," carried on chiefly in the homes of the poor—and, to a surprising extent, by children. Young children spent their days darning woolen socks, and the profits from their labors would make some London or Bristol merchant rich. These were the children of the poor, of course, but all children in those days were kept well occupied in one way or another, and children of the well-to-do spent their time studying. It was not too unusual for a child of five to be able to write and translate both Latin and Greek (a fact that may explain the preponderance of young, well-educated playwrights and poets in that day).

At least children were not in the coal mines as they would be later, although in the seventeenth century coal was beginning to be an important English commodity. It was shipped from the town of Newcastle, for example, to London and even abroad. *Shipped* is exactly the word, for it was transported by ships traveling down the eastern coast of England and up the Thames River to London docks. Transporting goods of any kind in any substantial quantity over land for long distances was seldom thought of, for most roads were rutty, boggy, or concealed in whirls of dust, and bridges were so poorly built that they were a danger to life and limb.

A traveler along the English roads during the late seventeenth century might, nevertheless, come across the beginnings of overland travel—perhaps a market-bound "long-wagon," pulled by as many as eight huge dray horses, or a pack-horse train not unlike those used in the American West. After 1637, at least on the best roads, a traveler on foot might have to step aside for a public mail coach carrying paying passengers as well as the mail. Later in the century mail service was improved with the introduction of the "penny post" and hourly pickups of mail in London during daytime hours.

Detail, *Nell Gwyn,* from the studio of Sir Peter Lely, c. 1675.

Poetry in Seventeenth-Century England

Up to and through the period of Queen Elizabeth I, only a few Englishmen, it appears, had enough learning or talent or interest to write prose literature. On the other hand, even common people could compose ballads and put on plays. In Elizabeth's time, verse was the dominant form of literature.

Poetry again dominates the literature of the early seventeenth century. John Donne and his followers wrote what would later be called metaphysical poetry—complex, highly intellectual verse filled with intricate and far-fetched metaphors. Ben Jonson, the forerunner of English neoclassicism, and his disciples, called the Sons of Ben or the Tribe of Ben, were responsible for a second main style of poetry. They wrote in a more conservative, restrained fashion and on more limited subjects than the metaphysical poets. Above all, Jonson strove for clarity and precision. Some of the Sons of Ben are known as Cavaliers because their verses often take the form of witty, elegant, and gentlemanly compliments or trifles.

A great poet of the century, John Milton had a style of his own, and he remained outside both Donne's and Jonson's influence. His epic, *Paradise Lost,* a work of over ten thousand lines, takes its place in western literature along with Homer's *Odyssey* and *Iliad,* Virgil's *Aeneid,* and Dante's *Divine Comedy* (see Part Two of this book) and in English literature with *Beowulf* and Spenser's *Faerie Queene* (see pages 9 and 91).

Drama in Seventeenth-Century England

We left drama in the last unit at its height—in the hands of Shakespeare, Marlowe, and others, with acting companies formed and playhouses built and filled with appreciative audiences. As the seventeenth century progresses into the reign of Charles I, the new plays are neither bone-shaking tragedies, like those of Shakespeare and Marlowe, nor the traditional, rather simple-minded comedies that grew out of medieval morality plays and Roman comedies. Rather, early seventeenth-century theater saw satiric comedies by Ben Jonson, tragicomedies, and a kind of melodrama. As the terms *satiric comedy, tragicomedy,* and *comedy of manners* suggest, comedy was becoming more sophisticated, less dependent upon stock situations—like mistaken identity—and on pratfalls and other sight gags. The manners of the English upper class became the source of situations and of humor. Also, the introduction of a new element, called wit, reflected the influence—to some degree, at least—of the masterfully inventive, witty French playwright Molière (see Part Two of this book).

At the beginning of the civil war in 1642, the Puritans, who regarded drama as frivolous, made theater illegal in England. Plays were still produced, of course, in private houses and even in playhouses until the hoofbeats of mounted law enforcers signaled the evening raid.

If the theater lost its momentum in the years of the Cromwell Commonwealth, it sprang to life joyfully when, in 1660, young King Charles II restored the easygoing, theater-loving monarchy. Women actresses, like the famous Nell Gwynn, began to play female roles. The drama that came to life in the last half of the seventeenth century has been called, aptly enough, Restoration comedy. To be sure, a few tragicomedies from the past were popular on the newly lighted stages. However, during the later seventeenth century French-influenced playwrights created more sophisticated plays, still based on the manners of upper-class society but sharpened with wit and satire.

Izaak Walton, whose classic, *The Compleat Angler*, has taught many the joys of fishing.

Then as the seventeenth century came to a close, the witty frivolity of Restoration comedy fell into disfavor. Playwrights turned to sentimental comedy, in which the heroine attempts to reform the hero.

Prose in Seventeenth-Century England

Generally speaking, the prose of the seventeenth century was not used for imaginative literature. When John Milton wrote his great narrative, *Paradise Lost,* he turned, as his predecessors had, to poetry. With one interesting exception, the prose works that we are concerned with in seventeenth-century literature are works of nonfiction—essays and histories, works about religion and science, and works reflecting a new interest in what was going on, in London as well as in a country trout stream. Toward the end of the century, essays on literary criticism began to appear, and criticism became a kind of literature in itself.

The fiction exception mentioned above is John Bunyan's *Pilgrim's Progress.* This is, in fact, a long prose work in which imaginary characters tell a story. Bunyan, like Oliver Cromwell and like John Milton, was a Puritan. He was also a preacher. *The Pilgrim's Progress* drew upon the medieval morality play for its approach and for the kind of character it invents. It is the story of a hero named Christian, who, carrying Sin on his shoulders and a Bible in one hand,

with the help of another character called Helpful, overcomes obstacles such as Vanity on his journey, or pilgrimage, to heaven. *The Pilgrim's Progress,* its prose modeled on that of the King James Bible (page 194), was written to provide uplifting entertainment for the poor. No other book in the seventeenth century reached a greater number of people.

The bulk of seventeenth-century prose—nonfiction—developed because of several influences, not the least of which was the continuing marvel of Caxton's printing press. Some writers created prose for the growing bureaucracy that demanded a large body of legal and governmental writings. Some writers produced prose in response to the spirit of scientific inquiry that was sweeping England. Some relied on prose to persuade wide audiences to adopt certain religious and political convictions. And yet other writers turned to prose for their own eccentric reasons: Robert Burton wrote a brilliant, gloomy,

undefinable work called *The Anatomy of Melancholy.* Izaak Walton wrote a fascinating manual on fishing (and many an angler since has been playfully called an Izaak Walton). Samuel Pepys kept a private, coded diary, an act quite different from setting out to write a prose work with the intent of informing or persuading a large body of readers. Whatever their purposes, one thing is clear: Just as we had professional minstrels or poets in the mead halls during Anglo-Saxon times and professional playwrights in the London of Queen Elizabeth, so the seventeenth century saw the emergence of serious, professional prose writers.

Prose style in the seventeenth century developed in two distinct directions. Early in the century, we find an ornate though often majestic style. Religious leaders including John Donne wrote sermons and other works that were complex and richly seeded with images. After the Restoration the Royal Society declared that its members should use a plainer, more efficient prose style. John Dryden was the leading prose writer of the last third of the century, and his writing attempted to move closer to the rhythms and spirit of actual speech. The development of more modern-sounding prose reminds us that the seventeenth century was in all ways a period of continuing exploration and experimentation—in politics, in religion, in science, and in language.

TIME LINE

1625 Charles I becomes king

First fire engine in England

1628 William Harvey publishes treatise on the circulation of blood

1630 America: John Winthrop, Puritan leader, founds Boston

1633 John Donne, *Poems*

1635 Public mail service set up

1637 Public mail coaches carry passengers

Ben Jonson dies

1637 Japan: European contacts prohibited

Europe: Ferdinand III becomes Holy Roman Emperor

1638 America: Harvard, first college, established

1640 Holland: Rembrandt Van Rijn, *Self-Portrait*

1642 Outbreak of civil war

All theaters closed by order of the Puritans

1642 America: Education becomes compulsory in Massachusetts

1644 John Milton, *Areopagitica,* on freedom of the press

1644 China: Ming dynasty ends; Manchu dynasty begins

1647 First newspaper advertisement appears

1648 Robert Herrick, "The Argument of His Book"

1649 Charles I beheaded; Oliver Cromwell becomes Lord Protector of England

Richard Lovelace, "To Lucasta"

1650 Tea first drunk in England

1650 America: Anne Bradstreet, *The Tenth Muse Lately Sprung up in America*

1651 Thomas Hobbes, *Leviathan,* political philosophy in support of monarchy

1651 Africa: Dutch settle at Cape of Good Hope

1653 Andrew Marvell, "Bermudas"

Izaak Walton, *The Compleat Angler*

1654 France: Coronation of Louis XIV at Rheims

Molière

1655 Cromwell dissolves Parliament, prohibits Anglican services

1656 Opening of first London opera house

1657 Drinking chocolate introduced in London

1657 France: First stockings and fountain pens manufactured

1658 Oliver Cromwell dies; his son Richard succeeds him

1659 France: Molière, "The Flying Doctor"

1660 End of the Protectorate; Charles II restored to throne

1660 Denmark: Danish crown becomes hereditary

The Royal Society of London established to promote scientific research

1661 Coronation of Charles II

1664 America: English capture New Amsterdam from the Dutch

1665 Isaac Newton experiments on gravitation

1665 America: First theatrical performance takes place in Virginia

Great Plague kills over 68,000 in London

1666 Great Fire of London

1666 Italy: Antonio Stradivari labels his first violin

1667 John Milton, *Paradise Lost*

1668 John Dryden, *Essay of Dramatic Poesy*

Coronation of Charles II

1674 John Bunyan, *The Pilgrim's Progress*

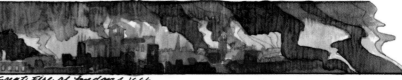

Great Fire of London 1666

1685 Charles II dies; James II succeeds his brother

1685 China: All ports opened to foreign trade

1687 John Dryden, "A Song for Saint Cecilia's Day"

1688 Glorious Revolution: Overthrow of James II, and accession of William and Mary

1689 Bill of Rights ensures freedoms for Parliament

1690 John Locke, *Essay Concerning Human Understanding*, influential work describing human mental processes

1690 America: *New England Primer*, a textbook for colonial youth

John Dryden

John Donne   *1572–1631*

The life of John Donne is filled with contradictions. Born into a Roman Catholic family, he left that faith in his young manhood. Later, he returned to religion, ending his days as Dean of St. Paul's Cathedral. That position, the presiding official of the cathedral, is one of the highest offices in the Church of England, which had been established by Henry VIII after his break with the Catholic Church. Donne acquired the reputation as perhaps the greatest preacher of his age. He was a vivid, dramatic, and spellbinding speaker, and many of his sermons survive as testimony to his enormous popularity. Yet this is the same man who had been a worldly and sophisticated youth in London, a welcome visitor at Elizabeth's court, a soldier and adventurer, and an author of some of the most appreciated love poetry in the language.

Although John Donne lived most of his life during the reigns of Queen Elizabeth I and King James I, his poetry is not like Elizabethan verse. Donne does not always present harmonious images and predictable meters. Rather, he often startles us with his images. Therefore, Donne is most often grouped with writers who come slightly later in the 1600s, a group known from the 1700s on as the metaphysical poets. Donne and the other **metaphysical poets** (such as George Herbert, Andrew Marvell, and Henry Vaughn) wrote very intellectual verse, speculating about the realms of philosophy. They wrote both love lyrics and religious, or meditative, poems in this highly intellectual style, showing off their wit and learning, demanding that readers become immersed in each poem. In fact, in the 1700s and the 1800s literary critics considered Donne's poetry too intellectual, but in the 1900s Donne has found favor again. Now critics applaud Donne's style: the conversational tone of his poetry, the rigorous and often witty pursuit of an argument, the sturdy sound of the verse, and the extraordinary imagery drawn from unusual sources. All these elements tend to give Donne's poetry a distinctly modern flavor. John Donne now generally ranks as the finest English poet between William Shakespeare and John Milton (page 226).

Introducing A Valediction: Forbidding Mourning

The poem that appears on the following page is one of Donne's most celebrated verses, and the figure at the end of the poem is one of the most famous in all of English poetry. In order to begin to understand this poem, however, it helps to know a bit about the circumstances under which Donne wrote it; to learn something about how he, as a man in the early 1600s, viewed the universe; and to review beforehand the central image of the last three stanzas.

Donne was addressing his wife in this poem, according to Izaak Walton (1593–1683), the English writer who was Donne's biographer. Donne was about to leave his wife to go to France. Already he himself was feeling forebodings at the separation, and indeed his misgivings were confirmed later when his wife gave birth to a stillborn child during his absence abroad. Nevertheless, he was determined to still his and his wife's tears upon parting by writing this valediction, which is a statement made as a farewell.

Donne gleaned his images for lines 5–16 of this poem from what he and other intelligent men thought about the universe. During this period in England and on the Continent, people believed that the earth was the center of the universe. Around the earth in concentric spheres were situated the other heavenly bodies. God and the angels were in control of the entire system. People generally believed that all existence below the sphere of the moon—including existence on the earth—was inferior. Only in the heavenly spheres beyond the moon was there a perfect existence.

At the end of the poem (lines 25–36), Donne introduces and develops the image of a compass, the instrument used for drawing arcs or circles. Also called a pair of compasses, this instrument consists of two pointed legs connected at one end by a pivot. Keeping in mind how this instrument works will help with an appreciation of not only the last three stanzas but of the poem as a whole.

John Donne

A Valediction: Forbidding Mourning

As virtuous men pass mildly away,
   And whisper to their souls to go,
Whilst some of their sad friends do say
   The breath goes now, and some say, No;

5 So let us melt,[1] and make no noise,
   No tear-floods, nor sigh-tempests move,
'Twere profanation[2] of our joys
   To tell the laity[3] our love.

Moving of th' earth brings harms and fears,
10   Men reckon what it did and meant;
But trepidation of the spheres,
   Though greater far, is innocent.[4]

Dull sublunary[5] lovers' love
   (Whose soul is sense)[6] cannot admit
15 Absence, because it doth remove
   Those things which elemented it.[7]

But we by a love so much refined
   That our selves know not what it is,
Inter-assurèd[8] of the mind,
20   Care less, eyes, lips, and hands to miss.

Our two souls therefore, which are one,
   Though I must go, endure not yet
A breach, but an expansion,
   Like gold to airy thinness beat.[9]

25 If they be two, they are two so
   As stiff twin compasses[10] are two;
Thy soul, the fixed foot, makes no show
   To move, but doth, if th' other do.

And though it in the center sit,
30   Yet when the other far doth roam,
It leans and hearkens after it,
   And grows erect, as it comes home.

Such wilt thou be to me, who must
   Like th' other foot, obliquely run;
35 Thy firmness makes my circle just,[11]
   And makes me end where I begun.

---

1. **melt:** part, change state. This line may also refer to the quietness with which pure gold melts.
2. **profanation:** debasement; violation.
3. **laity:** laymen; nonclergy. Here, the speaker is implying he and his beloved are like priest and priestess as opposed to the laity.
4. **Moving . . . innocent:** Earthquakes are harmful and dangerous, whereas the much greater movements of the celestial spheres are harmless.
5. **sublunary** [sub loo′ner′ē]: under the moon, or earthly. Everything under the moon's sphere, including the earth, was considered subject to change; all beyond that sphere was permanent and perfect.
6. **Whose . . . sense:** whose essence is the senses, not the mind.
7. **which elemented it:** which constituted its essential nature.

8. **Inter-assurèd:** mutually assured.
9. **Like . . . beat:** Gold leaf is made by beating gold into tissue-thin pieces. Baser metals would break up under the beating. "Airy" in this line refers to the buoyancy of gold leaf.
10. **twin compasses:** the two legs of a geometrical compass.
11. **just:** true, accurate.

STUDY QUESTIONS

Recalling

1. According to lines 1–4, how do virtuous men die, and, in contrast, how do observers of dying men sometimes react?
2. What kind of behavior mentioned in lines 1–4 does the speaker in lines 5–6 recommend he and his beloved follow? What, according to lines 7–8, would happen if the lovers cried out and told everyone of their love?
3. What is the difference between earthquakes and "trepidation of the spheres," as stated in lines 9–12?
4. When sublunary lovers are absent from each other, what does the absence cause to be removed, according to lines 13–16? What attitude toward absence do such lovers feel?
5. In contrast to the sublunary lovers of lines 13–16, what kind of love does the speaker claim he and his beloved share (lines 17–20)? Consequently, what happens to their souls upon parting, according to lines 21–24?
6. Paraphrase the last three stanzas of the poem, explaining what happens to the two feet of a compass as one moves away and then returns.

Interpreting

7. What effect is achieved by the speaker's associating himself and his beloved with the spheres (line 11)?
8. What, if anything, is startling about the speaker's comparing himself and his beloved to the two feet of a compass? Why? What is appropriate about the image?
9. Why should the parting of the lovers not be a cause for mourning? What is true love, according to this poem? How persuasive is the speaker?

Extending

10. How would you describe this poem to someone? What would you say about its complexity? Does its complexity add to or distract from its impact on you?

VIEWPOINT

According to one critic, Donne's love poetry *speaks* to the beloved rather than *sings* to her. It even argues with her; and in doing so,

the poet's passionate argument does not allow for those stately, self-contained lines whose perfection redeems many a lifeless sonnet. There is hardly a line in Donne's poem which makes sense by itself . . . . The unit is not the line . . . and not even the stanza but the entire poem in its serpentine swerving from one excitement to another.

—Mario Praz

▪ Examine Donne's "Valediction." Does Praz's insight on the poem's structure seem to be accurate? Support your answer with specifics.

LITERARY FOCUS

Conceit

A **conceit** (from the Italian *concetto,* meaning "concept") is an elaborate metaphor or simile that makes a comparison between two significantly different things. The comparison may seem far-fetched at first but, when examined, gains clarity and persuasion. The conceit not only brings together two entirely different images or ideas but then develops the comparison in detail, so as to highlight the similarities.

Donne and the other so-called metaphysical poets used conceits frequently. Of all the conceits they devised, none is more famous than the example developed through the final three stanzas of "A Valediction: Forbidding Mourning." As we have seen, there the souls of the two lovers are compared to the two legs of a geometrical compass—a startling image at first but one that becomes clearer the more we think about it.

Thinking About Conceit

▪ Another unusual image in the poem—extravagant enough to be thought of as a conceit—compares the parting of lovers with a process of working gold. Explain and justify the conceit.

Donne's love poetry was written in his youth. Later in life he concentrated on religious subjects. Composed after the death of his wife in 1617, Donne's *Holy Sonnets,* nineteen in all, reveal his complex thoughts on divine love and on death. In Sonnet 10, which follows, Donne addresses the subject of death.

John Donne

Sonnet 10

Death, be not proud, though some have callèd thee
Mighty and dreadful, for thou art not so;
For those whom you think'st thou dost overthrow
Die not, poor Death, nor yet canst thou kill me.
5 From rest and sleep, which but thy pictures[1] be,
Much pleasure, then from thee much more must flow,
And soonest our best men with thee do go,
Rest of their bones and souls' delivery.[2]
Thou art slave to fate, chance, kings, and desperate men,
10 And dost with poison, war, and sickness dwell,
And poppy,[3] or charms can make us sleep as well,
And better than thy stroke; why swell'st[4] thou then?
One short sleep past, we wake eternally,
And Death shall be no more; Death, thou shalt die.

---

1. **pictures:** images.
2. **And . . . delivery:** Our best men die willingly, in order to rest their bones and free their souls. (Compare the opening of "A Valediction.")
3. **poppy:** opium.
4. **swell'st:** swell with pride.

By 1623 Donne was a distinguished minister in the Church of England. In that year he fell seriously ill. He recovered, and the illness provoked a group of private prose meditations, or thoughts, on his mortality. One of the most famous, Meditation XVII, draws its central image from the custom of sounding the village bell to signal that someone was about to die. Others in the village, hearing the death knells, would offer prayers for the dying person's soul. The following selection is an excerpt from Meditation XVII.

from Meditation XVII

Nunc lento sonitu dicunt, Morieris
Now this bell, tolling softly for another,
      says to me, Thou must die

Perchance he for whom this bell tolls may be so ill as that he knows not it tolls for him; and perchance I may think myself so much better than I am, as that they who are about me and see my state, may have caused it to toll for me, and I know not that. . . .

All mankind is of one author, and is one volume. When one man dies, one chapter is not torn out of the book, but translated into a better language, and every chapter must be so translated. God employs several translators. Some pieces are translated by age, some by sickness, some by war, some by justice. But God's hand is in every translation; and his hand shall bind up all our scattered leaves again for that library where every book shall lie open to one another. As therefore the bell that rings to a sermon calls not upon the preacher only, but upon the congregation to come, so this bell calls us all; but how much more me, who am brought so near the door by this sickness. . . .

The bell doth toll for him that thinks it doth; and though it intermit[1] again, yet from that minute that that occasion wrought[2] upon him, he is united to God. Who casts not up his eye to the sun when it rises? But who takes off his eye from a comet when that breaks out? Who bends not his ear to any bell which upon any occasion rings? But who can remove it from that bell which is passing a piece of himself out of this world?

No man is an island, entire of itself; every man is a piece of the continent, a part of the main.[3] If a clod be washed away by the sea, Europe is the less, as well as if a promontory were, as well as if a manor of thy friend's or of thine own were. Any man's death diminishes me, because I am involved in mankind, and therefore never send to know for whom the bell tolls; it tolls for thee.

---

1. **intermit:** stop for a time.
2. **wrought:** made an impression.
3. **main:** mainland.

STUDY QUESTIONS

Sonnet 10

Recalling

1. According to the first two lines of the sonnet, what characteristics have some people mistakenly given to Death?
2. In line 5 what are the "pictures" of Death? What do they offer people?
3. According to lines 9–12, to what things is Death actually a slave? With what disagreeable things is Death associated?
4. According to lines 13–14, when will Death himself die?

Interpreting

5. What is the relationship of sleep and Death in this sonnet?
6. What is paradoxical about the last two lines? That is, what seeming contradiction is introduced?
7. What standard portrait of Death is the speaker negating in this poem? Instead, what does the speaker think about the dominion of death?
8. What does the poet achieve by personifying Death, that is, by giving human characteristics to it?

Extending

9. Based on the earlier descriptions of sonnets (page 90), explain how Sonnet 10's octave and sestet relate to each other.

from Meditation XVII

Recalling

1. According to the opening paragraph, why might the person the bell is tolling for be unaware that it is ringing for him?
2. What is humankind compared to in the beginning of the second paragraph? What are the "several translators" that Donne refers to in the second paragraph?

3. According to the beginning of the last paragraph, what is each person part of?

Interpreting

4. Who is the author of the "volume" of all humankind? Into what "better language" will the volume be "translated," or carried over?
5. What images in the final paragraph contribute to the idea that human beings cannot exist in isolation? Why does the bell always toll for "thee"?

Extending

6. Ernest Hemingway took the title for a major American novel from this meditation. *For Whom the Bell Tolls* (1940) is about an American fighting in the Spanish Civil War of 1936 to 1939, which immediately preceded World War II. What is the significance of Hemingway's title in that context?

COMPOSITION

Writing About a Quotation

Donne's statement "No man is an island, entire of itself" is very famous. Discuss its significance in Meditation XVII. First explain what Donne means by the statement. Then demonstrate how that particular statement is the essence of the entire piece. That is, show how other statements by Donne lead to the conclusion that "no man is an island." *For help with this assignment, refer to Lesson 5 in the Writing About Literature Handbook at the back of this book.*

Writing a Letter

Write a letter to John Donne responding to his statement "No man is an island, entire of itself." Begin by telling him whether you agree or disagree with his view. Then defend your position by citing instances from current events or your own experience.

Andrew Marvell *1621–1678*

Andrew Marvell is now recognized as a fine and influential poet, but during his life he was known first and foremost as a public servant and member of Parliament. After graduating from Cambridge University in 1638, Andrew Marvell spent several years traveling in Europe before returning to England. Around 1650 he began tutoring the daughter of the Lord General of the Parliamentary army, and it was in this position, in the early 1650s, that he wrote most of his poetry.

In 1657 Marvell was appointed assistant to the Latin Secretary of Oliver Cromwell's Puritan Commonwealth. That high public official was John Milton, the greatest poet of his age, and his job was to prepare government documents in Latin, still considered the language of state affairs at that time. Thus Milton and Marvell were colleagues, both supporters of the Puritan cause.

However, the Commonwealth was doomed. Cromwell, its leader, died in 1658. Soon afterward the people moved to restore the monarchy, summoning the son of the murdered King Charles I to the throne as Charles II. At that time, Milton's life was in danger. He was saved (to write his greatest poetry) by the intervention of his former assistant Marvell, then a member of Parliament representing his home town of Hull. Marvell, unlike some others who had supported the Puritan cause, had managed to survive the Restoration and went on to serve in Parliament until his death in 1678, nearly two decades later.

Only then, in 1681, was his lyric poetry published, and only gradually did it attract the attention and the high regard that it now enjoys. Marvell's poetry ingeniously presents serious, sometimes harsh and satiric, sentiments behind graceful, often witty, verse. Marvell's apparent lightness and even rhythms stand him apart from Donne, but the depth of his concerns justifies placing him in the same school of poetry.

The poem that follows may have been inspired by an incident that had occurred about forty years earlier. In 1609 an English ship on its way to Virginia was wrecked near an island in the Atlantic Ocean. The survivors stepped ashore onto a place of extraordinary beauty; we know it as Bermuda. Shakespeare learned of the shipwreck, and opened his play *The Tempest* with just such an event. Some decades later Marvell wrote this poem about discovery through shipwreck. Marvell's interest in Bermuda may also have developed through his acquaintance with John Oxenbridge, a minister there at some point before Marvell wrote this poem around 1653.

Andrew Marvell

Bermudas

Where the remote Bermudas[1] ride
In the ocean's bosom unespied,[2]
From a small boat that rowed along
The listening winds received this song:

5 "What should we do but sing His praise
That led us through the watery maze
Unto an isle so long unknown,
And yet far kinder than our own?

Where He the huge sea-monsters wracks[3]
10 That lift the deep upon their backs,
He lands us on a grassy stage,
Safe from the storms' and prelates'[4] rage.
He gave us this eternal spring
Which here enamels everything,
15 And sends the fowls to us in care
On daily visits through the air.
He hangs in shades the orange bright

---

1. **Bermudas:** Bermuda is actually made up
of several islands; therefore, the poet uses
the plural here.
2. **unespied:** unseen.

3. **wracks:** overthrows.
4. **prelates'** [prel′its]: high church
officials'; bishops'.

Like golden lamps in a green night,
And does in the pomegranates close
20 Jewels more rich than Ormus[5] shows.
He makes the figs our mouths to meet
And throws the melons at our feet;
But apples[6] plants of such a price,
No tree could ever bear them twice.
25 With cedars chosen by His hand
From Lebanon[7] He stores the land;
And makes the hollow seas that roar
Proclaim the ambergris[8] on shore.

———————

5. **Ormus** [ôr′muz]: city in the Persian
Gulf famous for jewel trading.
6. **apples**: pineapples.
7. **Lebanon**: country on eastern shore of
Mediterranean Sea.
8. **ambergris** [am′ber grēs′]: substance
from whales, used to make perfume.

He cast (of which we rather boast)
30 The Gospel's pearl upon our coast;
And in these rocks for us did frame
A temple where to sound His name.
Oh, let our voice His praise exalt
Till it arrive at heaven's vault,
35 Which thence, perhaps, rebounding may
Echo beyond the Mexique bay!"[9]

Thus sung they in the English boat
A holy and a cheerful note;
And all the way, to guide their chime,[10]
40 With falling oars they kept the time.

———————

9. **Mexique** [mex′ēk] **bay**: Gulf of
Mexico.
10. **chime**: rhythm or melody.

STUDY QUESTIONS

Recalling

1. What scene do the first four lines of the poem set up?
2. What have the mariners been saved from, according to lines 9–12?
3. Based on lines 13–28, what is the new island's climate? What kinds of food are in ample supply?
4. What will the mariners do in the temple fashioned out of rocks (line 32)?
5. According to lines 38–39, in what tone of voice are the mariners speaking as they approach the island?

Interpreting

6. How would you categorize the song that the shipwrecked mariners wish to sing? How do the mariners feel about arriving at this new land?
7. What are the specific differences that we can assume exist between the new island and the island the mariners are setting out from (see lines 8 and 12)?

Extending

8. What may be an advantage and a disadvantage of building a fictional account (such as this poem) on a real-life event (such as the 1609 shipwreck)?

COMPOSITION

Writing About Poetry

■ Discuss the overall meaning of "Bermudas," and indicate the techniques that the author uses to reveal that meaning. Discuss in particular rhythm, rhyme, similes, metaphors, and individual word choice. *For help with this assignment, refer to Lesson 7 in the Writing About Literature Handbook at the back of this book.*

Writing a Description

■ Marvell, who had not been to Bermuda, was imagining the scene he described. Imagine a scene of great beauty and wonderment—an awesome view from a mountain, a spectacular sunset at sea, or a giant waterfall. Describe the scene in prose or poetry as specifically and appealingly as you can.

Andrew Marvell 215

Ben Jonson   *1572–1637*

Reared to the bricklayer's trade and without the benefit of a formal university education, Ben Jonson, by force of will, made himself a great scholar of the classics and consequently affected English literature for nearly two hundred years. He was an active and hot-tempered man—a soldier, a duelist, and a brawler—who mellowed only in middle age.

Jonson's major contribution to poetry was to adapt the poetic forms that had been used by the classic writers of ancient Rome (see Part Two of this book). Whether writing terse satire or lyrical songs, Jonson was influenced by poets who had composed centuries before in Latin. As a result, Jonson disciplined English, ridding it of floweriness and overwhelming metaphors. He introduced to English specific and strong language, great order and balance, plainness and restraint. He was the forerunner of English **neoclassicism**, a revival of the style and attitude of classical literature.

As Donne had his imitators—poets of the so-called metaphysical school, who wrote in his manner—so Ben Jonson inspired a host of imitators and followers, collectively known as the Tribe of Ben, or the Sons of Ben. These followers, generally aristocrats who had also been supporters of the doomed Charles I, were, in addition, the founders of the Cavalier school of English poets. Robert Herrick, Richard Lovelace, and others who formed this group aspired to write the clear, deftly turned lyrics that Jonson had mastered. Indeed, the influence of Ben Jonson was felt during the entire century—through example, through critical pronouncements, and through the memory of the poet's formidable personality. It was felt most strongly at the century's end in the work of John Dryden, who passed on Jonson's return to classicism as the dominant literary manner of the eighteenth century.

Jonson was also an excellent playwright. His first dramatic success, *Every Man in His Humor,* was performed by Shakespeare's acting company in 1598, with Shakespeare himself playing a prominent role. From 1605 on, Jonson produced elaborate dramatic spectacles in the court of King James I, who then in 1616 made Jonson the poet laureate (the official poet of the nation). However, Jonson's once vast reputation as a dramatist suffered by constant comparison with his peerless contemporary, for what writer could stand to be compared continually with Shakespeare? During Shakespeare's lifetime Jonson resented such persistent comparisons, and even spoke slightingly of his competitor. Yet after the greater playwright's death in 1616, when friends were assembling Shakespeare's plays for publication, they turned to the rival dramatist Ben Jonson to write the dedication. What he wrote appeared in the opening pages of the collected plays in 1623. It is a tribute by one playwright to another and is as eloquent and generous as it is fair-minded.

Ben Jonson

To the Memory of My Beloved Master, William Shakespeare

To draw no envy, Shakespeare, on thy name,
Am I thus ample[1] to thy book and fame;
While I confess thy writings to be such
As neither man, nor muse, can praise too much.
5 'Tis true, and all men's suffrage.[2] But these ways
Were not the paths I meant unto thy praise;
For silliest[3] ignorance on these may light,
Which, when it sounds at best, but echoes right;
Or blind affection, which doth ne'er advance
10 The truth, but gropes, and urgeth all by chance;
Or crafty malice might pretend this praise,
And think to ruin, where it seemed to raise. . . .
But thou art proof against them, and, indeed,
Above the ill fortune of them, or the need.
15 I therefore will begin. Soul of the age!
The applause, delight, the wonder of our stage!
My Shakespeare, rise! I will not lodge thee by
Chaucer, or Spenser, or bid Beaumont[4] lie
A little further, to make thee a room;
20 Thou art a monument without a tomb,
And art alive still while thy book doth live
And we have wits to read and praise to give.
That I not mix thee so, my brain excuses,
I mean with great, but disproportioned[5] Muses;
25 For if I thought my judgment were of years,
I should commit thee surely with thy peers,
And tell how far thou didst our Lyly outshine,
Or sporting Kyd, or Marlowe's[6] mighty line.
And though thou hadst small[7] Latin and less Greek
30 From thence to honor thee, I would not seek
For names; but call forth thundering Aeschylus,

---

1. **ample:** liberal, unstinted in praise.
2. **suffrage:** agreement.
3. **silliest:** simplest.
4. **Beaumont:** Francis Beaumont (1584–1616), playwright who was
a contemporary of Shakespeare. Chaucer, Spenser, and Beaumont
were buried in Westminster Abbey in London; Shakespeare was
buried in Stratford.
5. **disproportioned:** not comparable.
6. **Lyly . . . Kyd . . . Marlowe:** English playwrights, contemporaries
of Shakespeare.
7. **small:** a limited knowledge of.

Euripides, and Sophocles[8] to us;
Pacuvius, Accius,[9] him of Cordova[10] dead,
To life again, to hear thy buskin[11] tread,
35 And shake a stage; or, when thy socks[12] were on,
Leave thee alone for the comparison
Of all that insolent Greece or haughty Rome
Sent forth, or since did from their ashes come.
Triumph, my Britain, thou hast one to show
40 To whom all scenes[13] of Europe homage owe.
He was not of an age, but for all time!
And all the Muses still were in their prime,
When, like Apollo,[14] he came forth to warm
Our ears, or like a Mercury[15] to charm!
45 Nature herself was proud of his designs
And joyed to wear the dressing of his lines!
Which were so richly spun, and woven so fit,[16]
As,[17] since, she will vouchsafe no other wit.
The merry Greek, tart Aristophanes,
50 Neat Terence, witty Plautus,[18] now not please,
But antiquated and deserted lie,
As they were not of Nature's family.
Yet must I not give Nature all; thy art,
My gentle Shakespeare, must enjoy a part.
55 For though the poet's matter nature be,
His art doth give the fashion; and, that he
Who casts[19] to write a living line, must sweat
(Such as thine are) and strike the second heat
Upon the Muses' anvil; turn the same
60 (And himself with it) that he thinks to frame,
Or, for the laurel,[20] he may gain a scorn;
For a good poet's made, as well as born.
And such wert thou! Look how the father's face
Lives in his issue; even so the race
65 Of Shakespeare's mind and manners brightly shines

---

8. **Aeschylus** [es′kə ləs], **Euripides** [yoo rip′ə dēz′], **and Sophocles** [sof′ə klēz′]: classical Greek tragic dramatists.
9. **Pacuvius** [pə koo′vē əs], **Accius** [ak′ē əs]: Roman tragic playwrights.
10. **him of Cordova** [kôr dō′və]: Seneca, Roman dramatist born in Cordova, Spain.
11. **buskin:** high boot, worn by tragic actors.
12. **socks:** worn by comic actors.
13. **scenes:** stages.
14. **Apollo:** in classical mythology the god of music and poetry; also, god of the sun.
15. **Mercury:** Roman messenger of the gods, and god of cleverness.
16. **fit:** appropriately.
17. **As:** that.
18. **Aristophanes,** [ar′is tof′ə nēz′] . . . **Terence,** [ter′əns]. . . . **Plautus** [plô′təs]: classical comic playwrights, the first Greek, the other two Roman.
19. **casts:** sets out.
20. **laurel:** fame or distinction.

In his well turnèd, and true filèd[21] lines;
In each of which he seems to shake a lance,[22]
As brandished at the eyes of ignorance.
Sweet Swan of Avon![23] what a sight it were
70 To see thee in our waters yet appear,
And make those flights upon the banks of Thames,
That so did take Eliza, and our James![24]
But stay, I see thee in the hemisphere
Advanced, and made a constellation there!
75 Shine forth, thou Star of poets, and with rage[25]
Or influence, chide or cheer the drooping stage,
Which, since thy flight from hence, hath mourned like night,
And despairs day, but for thy volume's light.[26]

---

21. **true filèd:** accurately refined; polished.
22. **shake a lance:** pun on the name *Shake-speare.*
23. **Avon:** Shakespeare was born and died in Stratford, on the Avon River.
24. **Eliza . . . James:** Queen Elizabeth and King James I, before
whom Shakespeare's plays were performed.
25. **rage:** rapture, poetic imagination.
26. **thy volume's light:** that is, this present (1623) publication of your plays.

STUDY QUESTIONS

Recalling

1. What does Jonson say in lines 1–12 are the wrong motivations for praising Shakespeare?
2. What does Jonson say in lines 17–22 about a burial place for Shakespeare?
3. How does Shakespeare compare to his contemporary playwrights, according to lines 27–28?
4. Whom does Jonson call forth in lines 30–34 to appreciate Shakespeare's tragedies? What does Jonson say in lines 35–38 about comparing Shakespeare's comedies to others'?
5. According to lines 53–62, what are the two influences that account for Shakespeare's great achievement?
6. What does Jonson wish for in lines 69–72? How has the "drooping stage" reacted since Shakespeare's death? According to the end of the poem, what will help remedy this situation?

Interpreting

7. According to Jonson, why was Shakespeare "not of an age, but for all time"?

8. What can we learn from this poem about Jonson's intellect? His attitude toward literature as a profession? His attitude toward Shakespeare's accomplishments? Cite specific examples.

Extending

9. Several of Shakespeare's sonnets (see pages 99–102) proclaim that the beloved is immortalized by poetry. How does Ben Jonson reinforce the idea of art as a route to eternity in his poem?

VIEWPOINT

The literary critic Edmund Wilson says of Ben Jonson:

The one thing he really loved was literature, and, having served it as well as he could, no touchiness of personal pride could keep him from honoring one who had been fitted to serve it better . . . .

■ Examine lines 45–48. For what specific poetic talent does Jonson praise Shakespeare most?

The delicacy and polish of Jonson's verse are exemplified most clearly in the following lines, which have served as the lyrics of an abidingly popular song.

Ben Jonson

Song: to Celia

Drink to me only with thine eyes,
    And I will pledge[1] with mine;
Or leave a kiss but in the cup,
    And I'll not look for wine.
5 The thirst that from the soul doth rise
    Doth ask a drink divine;
But might I of Jove's[2] nectar[3] sup,
    I would not change for thine.

I sent thee late[4] a rosy wreath,
10   Not so much honoring thee
As giving it a hope, that there
    It could not withered be.
But thou thereon didst only breathe,
    And sent'st it back to me;
15 Since when it grows, and smells, I swear,
    Not of itself, but thee.

---

1. **pledge:** drink a toast.
2. **Jove's:** Jupiter's; referring to the Roman ruler of the gods.
3. **nectar:** the drink of the gods.
4. **late:** recently.

STUDY QUESTIONS

Recalling

1. What signs is the speaker looking for in lines 1–4?
2. What would the speaker prefer over Jove's divine nectar?
3. According to lines 10–13, why did the speaker send a wreath of roses to his beloved? What did she do with it?

Interpreting

4. With what qualities does the speaker endow his beloved?
5. What proof does the poem offer that the speaker will be persistent in his love?

Robert Herrick   *1591–1674*

Born and raised in a middle-class London family, Robert Herrick was not quite the aristocratic gentleman pictured when referring to the Cavalier school of poetry. However, Herrick's poetry is perhaps the finest example of the kind of lyrics for which the Cavaliers have become known—playful, delicate, witty verses.

After earning his university degrees and being ordained in the Church of England, the young Herrick spent a number of years in London as one of the Tribe of Ben. Ben Jonson's verse and classical interests were vital in forming Herrick's own tastes. Then, in his late thirties, the younger writer was compelled to support himself by accepting a church appointment that sent him far from London, to Devonshire in southwest England. In his new surroundings the transplanted Londoner was for a long time miserable, though gradually he did learn to love the calmer ways of country life. Indeed, the charm of much of his poetry derives from his sophisticated treatment of simple country pleasures. Herrick's poems, like many of Jonson's, are modest in scope, crystal clear, but rich and polished. Herrick's father and uncle were goldsmiths, and Herrick the poet has been called "a goldsmith and jeweler of language." Three of his poems appear on the following pages.

Detail, *King George Spaniel*, G. Sheridan Knowles, 1907.

Robert Herrick

Upon His Spaniel Tracy

Now thou art dead, no eye shall ever see,
For shape and service, spaniel like to thee.
This shall my love do, give thy sad death one
Tear, that deserves of me a milliòn.

Robert Herrick

The Argument of His Book

I sing of brooks, of blossoms, birds, and bowers,[1]
Of April, May, of June, and July flowers.
I sing of Maypoles, hock carts, wassails, wakes,[2]
Of bridegrooms, brides, and of their bridal cakes.
5 I write of youth, of love, and have access
By these to sing of cleanly wantonness.[3]
I sing of dews, of rains, and, piece by piece,
Of balm, of oil, of spice, and ambergris.[4]
I sing of times trans-shifting, and I write
10 How roses first came red and lilies white.
I write of groves, of twilights, and I sing
The court of Mab[5] and of the fairy king.
I write of hell; I sing (and ever shall)
Of heaven, and hope to have it after all.

1. **bowers:** arbors; shaded recesses.
2. **Maypoles . . . wakes:** All relate to festive rural
occasions: The hock cart brings in the last of the
harvest; wassails [wos′əlz] are assemblies for drink
and song; and wakes, here, are annual festivities
associated with a parish church.
3. **cleanly wantonness:** clean playfulness.
4. **ambergris** [am′ber grēs]: substance from whales,
used to make perfume.
5. **Mab:** queen of the fairies; their king was Oberon.

His Prayer to Ben Jonson

When I a verse shall make,
　　Know I have prayed thee,
For old religion's sake,
　　Saint Ben, to aid me.

5 Make the way smooth for me,
　　When I, thy Herrick,
Honoring thee, on my knee
　　Offer my lyric.

Candles I'll give to thee,
10 　　And a new altar;
And thou, Saint Ben, shalt be
　　Writ in my psalter.[1]

---

1. **psalter** [sôl′tər]: psalm book.

STUDY QUESTIONS

Upon His Spaniel Tracy

Recalling

1. According to line 2, what are the two specific traits that the poet most admired about Tracy?
2. How many tears will the poet shed for Tracy? How many tears does he think he should shed?

Interpreting

3. How does Herrick feel about Tracy's death?
4. What justification can you offer for the brevity and simplicity of the poem?

The Argument of His Book

Recalling

1. What daylight subjects does the poet mention? Evening subjects? What seasons does the poet concentrate on?

Interpreting

2. By "argument" Herrick means "subject matter." Where in a volume of Herrick's poetry would this particular poem be likely to appear?
3. What are some of the things that the poet will *not* sing about?

His Prayer to Ben Jonson

Recalling

1. As a poet, why does Herrick pray to "Saint Ben"?

2. How will the poet honor Jonson?

Interpreting

3. What might be the significance of being entered in Herrick's psalm book?
4. Why is a "prayer" an appropriate form for Herrick to use? Consider his profession and his relationship to Jonson.

COMPOSITION

Writing About Structure

▪ "The Argument of His Book" celebrates rural pleasures by listing many details. Analyze the order in which Herrick presents the details. Begin by explaining what the first three sentences call attention to. Then discuss the shift of topic in each of the next three sentences. Finally, comment on the subject matter of Herrick's last sentence, noting the progression of his ideas.

Writing a Letter

▪ Poets often respond to one another's work. For example, reading Marlowe's poem "The Passionate Shepherd to His Love," Sir Walter Raleigh was led to answer it in the voice of the "nymph" herself (page 96). Assume a similar, realistic voice in prose—perhaps that of a city dweller—and discuss some of the things Herrick has omitted from "The Argument of His Book." Make your observations good-natured and even humorous, and try to convey the voice of a character other than yourself.

Richard Lovelace   *1618–1657*

Richard Lovelace was the perfect model of a seventeenth-century court favorite. On a visit to Oxford University in 1636, the king and queen of England were so favorably impressed by the student Lovelace that they arranged for a degree to be awarded to him on the spot. The elegant young man was committed to aristocratic values. His interests were those considered appropriate for a gentleman and included literature, languages, painting, music, and falconry—the sport of training and hunting with hawks.

Lovelace is the most notable of those literary descendants of Ben Jonson known as the Cavalier poets—polished, gallant, and worldly supporters of King Charles I. Like the others, he remained loyal to the king throughout the turbulent civil war of the 1640s. That support led to the poet's imprisonment by the Puritan government and his death in poverty at the early age of thirty-nine.

Lovelace's poetry is graceful and witty and, in true Cavalier fashion, often addresses the themes of love, war, and loyalty to the king. Cavalier lyrics in general are much quieter, less exuberant, than Elizabethan poetry.

Richard Lovelace

To Lucasta, Going to the Wars

Tell me not, sweet, I am unkind,
   That from the nunnery[1]
Of thy chaste breast and quiet mind
   To war and arms I fly.

5 True, a new mistress now I chase,
   The first foe in the field;
And with a stronger faith embrace
   A sword, a horse, a shield.

Yet this inconstancy[2] is such
10   As you too shall adore;
I could not love thee, dear, so much,
   Loved I not honor more.

---

1. **nunnery:** convent; cloister.
2. **inconstancy:** fickleness.

To Althea, from Prison

When Love with unconfinèd wings
  Hovers within my gates,
And my divine Althea brings
  To whisper at the grates;
5 When I lie tangled in her hair
  And fettered[1] to her eye,
The gods[2] that wanton[3] in the air
  Know no such liberty.

When flowing cups run swiftly round,
10 With no allaying Thames,[4]
Our careless heads with roses bound,
  Our hearts with loyal flames;
When thirsty grief in wine we steep,
  When healths[5] and draughts[6] go free,
15 Fishes that tipple in the deep
  Know no such liberty.

When, like committed linnets,[7] I
  With shriller throat shall sing
The sweetness, mercy, majesty,
20 And glories of my King;
When I shall voice aloud how good
  He is, how great should be,
Enlargèd[8] winds that curl the flood
  Know no such liberty.

25 Stone walls do not a prison make,
  Nor iron bars a cage:
Minds innocent and quiet take
  That for an hermitage.[9]
If I have freedom in my love,
30 And in my soul am free,
Angels alone, that soar above,
  Enjoy such liberty.

---

1. **fettered:** bound.
2. **gods:** In some versions of the poem, the word is *birds* instead of *gods*.
3. **wanton:** sport; play.
4. **cups . . . Thames** [temz]: wine with no diluting water. (The Thames is a river.)
5. **healths:** toasts.
6. **draughts** [drafts]: drinks.

7. **committed linnets:** caged songbirds.
8. **Enlargèd:** released, as from imprisonment.
9. **hermitage:** secluded dwelling place; private retreat.

STUDY QUESTIONS

To Lucasta, Going to the Wars

Recalling
1. After deserting Lucasta, what new "mistress" does the speaker pursue?
2. What things does the speaker embrace now that he has left Lucasta?
3. Who or what does the speaker love more than Lucasta?

Interpreting
4. What contrasts does the speaker cite between the two "mistresses"?
5. What is the meaning of the last two lines of the poem? Why will Lucasta adore the speaker's inconstancy?

To Althea, from Prison

Recalling
1. Where is the speaker?
2. With what three occasions does he associate liberty?
3. Identify the images of freedom that appear at the end of each of the four stanzas.
4. What does the prison offer the speaker, according to the last stanza? What conditions may enable him to enjoy the kind of liberty that angels have?

Interpreting
5. What is ironical about the words "tangled" and "fettered" in lines 5 and 6?
6. In what way is the speaker really free despite his imprisonment?

John Milton   *1608–1674*

As Chaucer towers over the literary world of medieval England, and as Shakespeare is the supreme writer of the Elizabethan Age, so John Milton is the outstanding English poet of the seventeenth century.

At an early age this citizen of London realized his purpose: "By labor and intent study (which I take to be my portion in this life) joined with the strong propensity of nature, I might perhaps leave something so witten to aftertimes as they should not willingly let it die." Milton's labor and study extended from his years as a student at St. Paul's School in London, through university years at Cambridge, through five years of reading day and night in English, Latin, Greek, Hebrew, French, and Italian, and on through two more years of travel abroad that ended in 1639, when he was over thirty. Already that long period of study had combined with the "strong propensity of nature"—his poetic gifts and inclinations—to produce distinguished poetry, including *Lycidas,* the finest elegy in English, written upon the death of a close friend.

Despite this extensive preparation, Milton's poetic performance was interrupted by the outbreak of civil war in England. Milton was a Puritan. As a staunch supporter of the Parliamentary cause against the Royalists, the poet devoted twenty years out of the prime of his life, from 1640 to 1660, to defending the Puritan Commonwealth against its enemies and detractors. During that long interlude he wrote primarily prose pamphlets on matters relating to the new government; what little poetry Milton managed during these years was inspired by current events. Indeed, as Latin Secretary in Cromwell's government, he labored so diligently in preparing documents in the official language of the state that his eyesight began to fail him. By 1652 he was blind.

When the Royalists managed finally, in 1660, to triumph over Cromwell's followers and restore the monarchy, the poet found himself also in figurative darkness, with all that he had worked for repudiated by the English people. For a while his very life was in danger, but through the help of men like Andrew Marvell (page 213) in time he was pardoned for his earlier activities in support of antimonarchy elements. He survived with a fine and with a substantial loss of property.

In poverty, Milton then moved to a village west of London where he began his masterpiece, conceiving and memorizing portions of it at night, and dictating what he had created to secretaries in the morning. In that laborious way he wrote *Paradise Lost,* a work of over ten thousand lines, the greatest epic in our language.

The two sonnets that follow were written before *Paradise Lost.* They are deeply personal expressions of Milton's belief in the existence of a divine order to which he subordinates his own ambition.

John Milton

How Soon Hath Time

How soon hath Time, the subtle thief of youth,
   Stolen on his wing my three-and twentieth year!
   My hasting days fly on with full career,[1]
   But my late spring no bud or blossom shew'th.[2]
5 Perhaps my semblance[3] might deceive[4] the truth
   That I to manhood am arrived so near;
   And inward ripeness doth much less appear,
   That some more timely-happy spirits endu'th.[5]
   Yet, be it less or more, or soon or slow,
10   It shall be still[6] in strictest measure even[7]
   To that same lot,[8] however mean or high,
Toward which Time leads me, and the will of Heaven.
   All is, if I have grace to use it so,
   As ever in my great Task-Master's eye.

---

1. **career:** speed.
2. **shew'th:** shows.
3. **semblance:** appearance.
4. **deceive:** prove false.
5. **endu'th:** endows.
6. **still:** always.
7. **even:** equal or adequate.
8. **lot:** fate.

STUDY QUESTIONS

Recalling

1. How does Milton refer to time in the first line of the poem?
2. According to line 4, what has the poet's "late spring" not yet shown?
3. According to lines 10–12, in what does the poet place his faith?

Interpreting

4. What is appropriate about the personification of time in lines 1–2?
5. What do the "bud" and "blossom" of line 4 represent? How does Milton extend the plant imagery in line 7?
6. In line 13, "All" may refer to time or to talent. What is the meaning of lines 13–14 in each case?

In this sonnet, also referred to as "On His Blindness," Milton uses **allusions**, or references to other works the reader is supposed to know. He refers to the Parable of the Talents from Matthew 25:14–30, where a servant is scolded by his master for hiding his one talent—fifteen years' wages—instead using it for profit. Thus Milton gives *talent* a double meaning in the sonnet.

John Milton

When I Consider How My Light Is Spent

When I consider how my light is spent
   Ere[1] half my days in this dark world and wide,
   And that one talent which is death to hide
   Lodged with me useless, though my soul more bent
5 To serve there with my Maker, and present
   My true account, lest He returning chide,
   "Doth God exact day-labor, light denied?"
   I fondly[2] ask. But Patience, to prevent
That murmur, soon replies, "God doth not need
10   Either man's work or His own gifts. Who best
   Bear His mild yoke, they serve Him best. His state
Is kingly: thousands[3] at His bidding speed,
   And post[4] o'er land and ocean without rest;
   They also serve who only stand and wait."

1. **Ere:** before.
2. **fondly:** foolishly.
3. **thousands:** that is, of angels.
4. **post:** hasten.

STUDY QUESTIONS

Recalling

1. What is the speaker lamenting in lines 1–2?
2. What happens if the talent is hidden, according to line 3? What does the speaker want to do with the talent?
3. What does the speaker ask in line 7?
4. What does Patience say God asks for?

Interpreting

5. What two meanings does *talent* have?
6. What is the speaker's mood in lines 1–8?
7. What are the two kinds of activity pictured in lines 9–14? In what category does the speaker place himself?
8. Does the speaker find consolation? Explain.

Extending

9. Are the themes of Milton's sonnets alike?

Introducing **Paradise Lost**

Paradise Lost is an epic divided into twelve books, or chapters. An **epic** is a long narrative poem that records, in grave and stately language, heroic exploits and majestic events. Other than the Anglo-Saxon *Beowulf* (page 9), Milton's *Paradise Lost* is *the* epic in English literature.

Steeped in both classical and biblical scholarship, Milton set out to write a Christian epic as spacious and universal as the major epics of ancient Greek and Roman days, such as the *Odyssey* and the *Iliad* by Homer and the *Aeneid* by Virgil (see Part Two of this book). Milton selected as his subject matter the fall of man—that is, the story in which Satan tempts Adam and Eve to commit the original sin (eating the forbidden fruit) and they fall from God's grace (being exiled from Paradise, or the Garden of Eden). In working with this subject matter, Milton wanted to "justify the ways of God to men." In addition, Milton wanted his readers to focus on the individual—on Adam—and his particular relationship with God, for religion as an individual act was extremely important to Milton the Puritan.

In addition to drawing relentlessly on his familiarity with the classics and with the Bible, Milton created his own poetic style—different from both Donne's conceits and Jonson's restraint. Milton was an innovator, introducing a new style to English poetry. For one thing he wrote formally, using stiff sentence patterns (based on Latin) and extensive metaphors. For another, he wrote in blank verse—until Milton's attempt not used for writing other than drama. Yet in spite of its unusualness and difficulty, *Paradise Lost* has always been considered a supreme masterpiece of English literature.

In order to help seventeenth-century readers with the poem, Milton provided, at the suggestion of his printer, for each book a prose "argument" that summarized the action of the poem. We have provided brief introductions and marginal notes for the excerpts from Books I, III, and XII, which begin on the following page.

Angel playing a rebec,
a medieval instrument,
German, c. 1500.

John Milton

from **Paradise Lost**

from **Book I**

*Book I begins, as classical epics do, with an **invocation**, a call to a muse (in this case, a heavenly muse) to inspire the poet at the outset of his ambitious task.*

After the invocation the poet recounts how the angel Lucifer led a revolt against God's sovereignty in heaven, how he and his followers were cast into hell, and how from that place they plotted revenge by traveling to Earth and tempting Adam and Eve—God's creatures in the Garden of Eden—to sin. In the first of the two extracts that follow the invocation, Lucifer, now renamed Satan (the "Adversary"), attempts to rally his forces after their fall from heaven. In the second excerpt he considers his new domain, its mournful gloom contrasting with his memories of the celestial light of heaven.

Of man's first disobedience, and the fruit
Of that forbidden tree whose mortal[1] taste
Brought death into the world, and all our woe,
With loss of Eden, till one greater Man[2]
5 Restore us, and regain the blissful seat,
Sing, Heavenly Muse, that, on the secret top
Of Oreb, or of Sinai, didst inspire
That shepherd who first taught the chosen seed[3]
In the beginning how the Heavens and Earth
10 Rose out of Chaos: or, if Sion[4] hill
Delight thee more, and Siloa's brook[5] that flowed
Fast[6] by the oracle of God, I thence
Invoke thy aid to my adventurous song,
That with no middle flight intends to soar
15 Above th' Aonian mount,[7] while it pursues
Things unattempted yet in prose or rhyme.
And chiefly thou, O Spirit,[8] that dost prefer
Before all temples th' upright heart and pure,
Instruct me, for thou know'st; thou from the first
20 Wast present, and, with mighty wings outspread,
Dovelike sat'st brooding[9] on the vast abyss,
And mad'st it pregnant: what in me is dark
Illumine; what is low, raise and support;
That, to the height of this great argument,[10]
25 I may assert[11] Eternal Providence,
And justify the ways of God to men.

"Fallen cherub,[12] to be weak is miserable,
Doing or suffering:[13] but of this be sure,
To do aught[14] good never will be our task,
30 But ever to do ill our sole delight,
As being the contrary to his high will
Whom we resist. If then his providence
Out of our evil seek to bring forth good,
Our labor must be to pervert that end,
35 And out of good still[15] to find means of evil;
Which oft times may succeed, so as perhaps
Shall grieve him, if I fail not,[16] and disturb
His inmost counsels from their destined aim.
But see! the angry Victor[17] hath recalled
40 His ministers of vengeance and pursuit
Back to the gates of Heaven; the sulphurous hail,
Shot after us in storm, o'erblown hath laid
The fiery surge that from the precipice
Of Heaven received us falling; and the thunder,
45 Winged with red lightning and impetuous rage,

1 **mortal:** deadly.

2 **greater Man:** Christ.

3 **Heavenly Muse . . . chosen seed:**
The poet is asking for inspiration from
the spirit that inspired Moses ("That
shepherd"), who taught the Israelites
("the chosen seed") the laws as God
pronounced them on Oreb, or Sinai,
a mountain in the Holy Land. Moses
is also traditionally regarded as the
author of the first five books of the
Bible, including Genesis, on which
Paradise Lost is based.
4 **Sion** [sī′ ən]: hill in Jerusalem on
which stood the Temple ("the oracle
of God").
5 **Siloa's** [si lō′ əz] **brook:** stream
near Jerusalem.
6 **Fast:** close.
7 **Aonian** [ā ō′ nē ən] **mount:** Mount
Helicon, in Greek mythology, home of
the Muses.
8 **Spirit:** Holy Spirit.

9 **brooding:** as a bird on a nest.

10 **argument:** subject matter; theme.
11 **assert:** defend; champion.

12 **cherub:** Beëlzebub [bē el′ zə
bub′], the fallen angel whom Satan is
addressing.
13 **Doing or suffering:** whether
active or passive.
14 **aught:** anything.

15 **still:** always.

16 **if I fail not:** if I am not mistaken.

17 **Victor:** God.

Perhaps hath spent his shafts, and ceases now
To bellow through the vast and boundless deep.
Let us not slip[18] th' occasion, whether scorn
Or satiate[19] fury yield it from our Foe.
50 Seest thou yon dreary plain, forlorn and wild,
The seat of desolation, void of light.
Save[20] what the glimmering of these livid flames
Casts pale and dreadful? Thither let us tend
From off the tossing of these fiery waves;
55 There rest, if any rest can harbor there;
And, reassembling our afflicted powers,[21]
Consult how we may henceforth most offend[22]
Our enemy, our own loss how repair,
How overcome this dire calamity,
60 What reinforcement we may gain from hope,
If not, what resolution from despair."

"Is this the region, this the soil, the clime,"
Said then the lost archangel, "this the seat
That we must change[23] for Heaven? this mournful gloom
65 For that celestial light? Be it so, since he
Who now is sovereign can dispose and bid
What shall be right: farthest from him is best,
Whom reason hath equaled, force hath made supreme
Above his equals. Farewell, happy fields,
70 Where joy forever dwells! Hail, horrors! hail,
Infernal world! and thou, profoundest Hell,
Receive thy new possessor, one who brings
A mind not to be changed by place or time.
The mind is its own place, and in itself
75 Can make a Heaven of Hell, a Hell of Heaven.
What matter where, if I be still the same,
And what I should be, all but less than[24] he
Whom thunder hath made greater? Here at least
We shall be free; th' Almighty hath not built
80 Here for his envy, will not drive us hence:
Here we may reign secure; and, in my choice,
To reign is worth ambition, though in Hell:
Better to reign in Hell than serve in Heaven.
But wherefore[25] let we then our faithful friends,
85 Th' associates and co-partners of our loss,
Lie thus astonished[26] on th' oblivious[27] pool,
And call them not to share with us their part
In this unhappy mansion, or once more
With rallied arms to try what may be yet
90 Regained in Heaven, or what more lost in Hell?"

18 **slip:** fail to take advantage of.
19 **satiate** [sã′shē ãt]: satisfied.

20 **Save:** except.

21 **afflicted powers:** overthrown armies.
22 **offend:** take the offensive against.

23 **change:** exchange.

24 **all . . . than:** almost equal to.

25 **wherefore:** why.

26 **astonished:** thunderstruck, stunned.
27 **oblivious:** causing oblivion or forgetfulness.

from **Book III**

Determined to tempt Adam and Eve, Satan rises from the gloom of hell toward the light of the universe in which the Earth is placed. At the begining of Book III, the blind poet Milton rises in imagination from hell's darkness to the radiance his own eyes will never see again. The book opens with his famous Hymn to Light.

Hail, holy Light, offspring of Heaven first-born![1]
Or of th' Eternal co-eternal beam,
May I express thee unblamed?[2] since God is light,
And never but in unapproachèd light
5 Dwelt from eternity, dwelt then in thee,
Bright effluence of bright essence increate![3]
Or hear'st thou rather[4] pure ethereal stream,
Whose fountain who shall tell?[5] Before the sun,
Before the heavens, thou wert, and at the voice
10 Of God, as with a mantle, didst invest[6]
The rising world of waters dark and deep,
Won from the void and formless infinite!
Thee I revisit now with bolder wing,
Escaped the Stygian pool,[7] though long detained
15 In that obscure sojourn, while in my flight,
Through utter[8] and through middle darkness borne,
With other notes than to th' Orphean[9] lyre
I sung of Chaos and eternal Night;
Taught by the Heavenly Muse to venture down
20 The dark descent, and up to reascend,
Though hard and rare. Thee I revisit safe,
And feel thy sovereign vital lamp; but thou
Revisit'st not these eyes, that roll in vain
To find thy piercing ray, and find no dawn;
25 So thick a drop serene[10] hath quenched their orbs,
Or dim suffusion veiled. Yet not the more
Cease I to wander where the Muses haunt
Clear spring, or shady grove, or sunny hill,
Smit[11] with the love of sacred song; but chief[12]
30 Thee, Sion, and the flowery brooks beneath,
That wash thy hallowed feet, and warbling flow,
Nightly I visit: nor sometimes forget[13]
Those other two equaled with me in fate,[14]
So were I equaled with them in renown,
35 Blind Thamyris and blind Maeonides,
And Tiresias and Phineus, prophets old:[15]
Then feed on thoughts that voluntary move[16]
Harmonious numbers;[17] as the wakeful bird[18]

1 **first-born:** the first thing God created (Genesis 1 : 1–5).

2 **Or . . . unblamed?:** Or may I, without being faulted, describe light as co-eternal with God?

3 **increate:** uncreated.
4 **hear'st . . . rather:** would you prefer to be called.
5 **Whose . . . tell?:** whose origin is unknown?

6 **invest:** cover, envelop.

7 **Stygian** [stij′ē ən] **pool:** in classical mythology, the river Styx, in the Underworld.
8 **utter:** outer.

9 **Orphean** [ôr′fē ən]: referring to Orpheus, the poet-musician in classical mythology, who visited the Underworld seeking his wife.

10 **drop serene:** refers to medical theory regarding blindness (like "suffusion" in the next line).

11 **Smit:** smitten, struck.
12 **chief:** chiefly.

13 **nor . . . forget:** that is, and never forget.
14 **equaled . . . fate:** also blind.
15 **Blind . . . old:** classical Greek figures; Thamyris [tham′ə ris] and Maeonides [mē on′ə dēz], a name referring to Homer, were blind poets; Tiresias [tī rē′sē əs] and Phineus [fin′ē əs], blind prophets.
16 **voluntary move:** freely utter.
17 **nùmbers:** verses.
18 **wakeful bird:** the nightingale.

Sings darkling,[19] and, in shadiest covert hid,

40   Tunes her nocturnal note. Thus with the year
Seasons return; but not to me returns
Day, or the sweet approach of even or morn,
Or sight of vernal[20] bloom, or summer's rose,
Or flocks, or herds, or human face divine;

45   But cloud instead and ever-during[21] dark
Surrounds me, from the cheerful ways of men
Cut off, and, for the book of knowledge fair,
Presented with a universal blank[22]
Of Nature's works, to me expunged and rased,[23]

50   And wisdom at one entrance quite shut out.
So much the rather thou, Celestial Light,
Shine inward, and the mind through all her powers
Irradiate; there plant eyes; all mist from thence
Purge and disperse, that I may see and tell

55   Of things invisible to mortal sight.

19 **darkling:** in the dark.

20 **vernal:** referring to springtime.

21 **ever-during:** always enduring.

22 **universal blank:** the grayness ever before the poet's blind eyes.
23 **rased:** erased.

from Book XII

Paradise Lost *concludes with the expulsion of Adam and Eve from Paradise. They are expelled only after the angel Michael has given them new hope by revealing the destiny that awaits their children, up to and including the arrival on Earth of the son of God to redeem humankind for committing the original sin.*

He[1] ended, and they both descend the hill.
Descended, Adam to the bower where Eve
Lay sleeping ran before, but found her waked;
And thus with words not sad she him received:

5   "Whence thou return'st and whither went'st, I know;
For God is also in sleep, and dreams advise,
Which he hath sent propitious,[2] some great good
Presaging,[3] since, with sorrow and heart's distress
Wearied, I fell asleep. But now lead on;

10   In me is no delay; with thee to go
Is to stay here; without thee here to stay
Is to go hence unwilling; thou to me
Art all things under Heaven, all places thou,
Who for my willful crime art banished hence.

15   This further consolation yet secure
I carry hence: though all by me is lost,
Such favor I unworthy am vouchsafed,[4]
By me the Promised Seed shall all restore."
    So spake our mother Eve; and Adam heard

20   Well pleased, but answered not; for now too nigh
Th' archangel stood, and from the other hill
To their fixed station, all in bright array,

1 **He:** the angel Michael.

2 **propitious** [prə pish′əs]: presenting favorable conditions.
3 **Presaging** [pres′ij ing]: foretelling.

4 **vouchsafed:** granted.

The cherubim descended; on the ground
Gliding meteorous,[5] as evening mist
25 Risen from a river o'er the marish[6] glides,
And gathers ground fast at the laborer's heel
Homeward returning. High in front advanced,
The brandished sword of God before them blazed,
Fierce as a comet; which with torrid heat,
30 And vapor as the Libyan[7] air adust,[8]
Began to parch that temperate clime; whereat
In either hand the hastening angel caught
Our lingering parents, and to th' eastern gate
Led them direct, and down the cliff as fast
35 To the subjected[9] plain; then disappeared.
They, looking back, all th' eastern side beheld
Of Paradise, so late their happy seat,[10]
Waved over by that flaming brand;[11] the gate
With dreadful faces thronged and fiery arms.
40 Some natural tears they dropped, but wiped them soon;
The world was all before them, where to choose
Their place of rest, and Providence their guide.
They, hand in hand, with wandering steps and slow,
Through Eden took their solitary way.

5 **meteorous:** high above, like a meteor.
6 **marish:** marsh.

7 **Libyan** [lib'ē ən]: referring to Libya, a country in northern Africa, which is largely desert.
8 **adust:** burnt; scorched.

9 **subjected:** lying below.

10 **seat:** home.
11 **brand:** sword.

STUDY QUESTIONS

Recalling

1. According to the opening five lines of Book I, what does Milton want the muse to help him portray? As stated in line 26, what is the poet's chief purpose in writing the poem?

2. According to line 30, what is Satan's "sole delight"? What matters, discussed in lines 57–61, will Satan and his cohorts consider on "yon dreary plain"?

3. According to lines 50–54, 64–65, and 69–71, in what physical ways does hell differ from heaven?

4. What arguments does Satan give in the final excerpt from Book I (at lines 74–80) to reconcile his followers to hell?

5. According to Book III, lines 51–55, what things will be revealed to the poet when the Celestial Light shines inward?

6. According to Book XII, lines 10–14, what reasons does Eve give for her willingness to leave Paradise with Adam? According to line 41, what lies before Adam and Eve as they leave Paradise?

Interpreting

7. In the invocation to the sacred muse at the opening of Book I, Milton announces his intention "to soar / Above th' Aonian mount." What does the figurative language reveal about the poet's ambitions?

8. What does Satan mean in Book I, line 35, when he says that he and his cohorts will labor "out of good still to find means of evil"? Which line at the end of the last extract from Book I tells us most about Satan's nature?

9. What is the "sovereign vital lamp" referred to in Book III, line 22? What is Milton's literal meaning when he then says, in lines 27–28, that he wanders nightly "where the Muses haunt / Clear spring, or shady grove, or sunny hill"?

10. According to Eve's speech (Book XII, lines 15–18) and Milton's final picture of the expelled couple, what hope do they now have?

Extending

11. Figuratively, how may the following part of Satan's argument be applied to situations outside the poem: "The mind is its own place, and in itself / Can make a Heaven of Hell, a Hell of Heaven"?

VIEWPOINT

The critic Douglas Bush reminds us that

in writing an epic, above all an epic on such a theme as his, Milton naturally wished to raise the reader's mind above mundane affairs, to create a world and an atmosphere befitting his divine and superhuman characters . . . . Milton's elevation of style has the effect of keeping action and scene and characters at a requisite aesthetic distance; everything must have recognizable reality, but not too much. A realistic treatment of Adam and Eve would be quite fatal; as it is, they are both human and superhuman . . .

—*Major British Writers*

■ What is "recognizable reality" in Milton's description of hell? What in the description places hell beyond our grasp?

LITERARY FOCUS

Milton's Elevated Style

Epics are long narrative poems that illustrate exalted themes through heroic action. A dignified style is required to express the superhuman action and the grave and consequential themes. Everyday language would be inappropriate, for it would fatally diminish the epic effect. Thus, both Milton's language and his theme in the epic *Paradise Lost* are elevated above what we usually encounter in our reading. Milton elevates his language in specific ways.

Blank verse. First, he abandons prose in favor of a particular kind of poetry: **blank verse**— unrhymed lines of iambic pentameter. He has purposely abandoned rhyme, choosing instead what he calls "English heroic verse without rhyme, as that of Homer in Greek and Virgil in

Latin." This verse form is in imitation of the classical epics.

Sentence length. Milton's extravagant sentences—too long to fit into a line of verse—also give a grandness to the poem.

Allusions. Milton relies heavily on **allusions,** references to people and places with which the reader is expected to be familiar. Milton's allusions are most often to classical and biblical matters, with which modern readers are less familiar than were the poet's contemporaries. Nevertheless, the effect of those allusions is to give his poetry a spaciousness and universality and an extension of meaning beyond its immediate context.

Thinking About Milton's Style

1. Mark the stresses of the first two lines of the poem to demonstrate that the meter is iambic pentameter. (See page 90 for instruction in marking meter if necessary.)
2. How many sentences do the first sixteen lines of Book I contain? What are the principal verbs? How does Milton emphasize them?
3. Explain in your own words how the allusions in Book I, lines 6–10, help to elevate Milton's invocation.

COMPOSITION

Writing About Theme

■ Show how Milton illuminates his theme, or main idea, in *Paradise Lost*. First write a sentence or two that express Milton's theme. Then explain how he develops that theme through title, plot, characterization, setting, and tone. *For help with this assignment, refer to Lesson 6 in the Writing About Literature Handbook at the back of this book.*

Writing a Narrative

■ Imagine that Adam and Eve have just completed the first day after their expulsion from paradise. Narrate the events of the day. What have they done? Have they found food and shelter? How do they react to their new surroundings?

John Dryden   *1631–1700*

John Dryden was the outstanding English poet from the Restoration in 1660 to the end of the century. He was born to a Puritan family in London and was graduated from Cambridge University in 1654. His earliest successful poem, *Heroic Stanzas,* extolled the virtues of Oliver Cromwell, the leader of the movement to rid England of a monarchy. Yet with Cromwell's death and the return of the monarchy, Dryden (like many others in search of order) immediately gave his allegiance to Charles II, the new Stuart king. That allegiance to Charles and later to his Catholic brother James II never faltered, even after the Stuarts had been driven into exile in 1688 and Dryden himself had been deprived of the title poet laureate that they had bestowed on him twenty years earlier.

Dryden wrote verse in several forms: odes, poetic drama, biting satires, and translations of classical authors. Unlike many of his predecessors, Dryden wrote in celebration of noteworthy occasions more often than in response to more personal experiences. Among Dryden's most important legacy to the poets of the next century was his mastery of the **heroic couplet,** paired lines of rhyming iambic pentameter. Another major contribution is Dryden's dignified, unaffected, and always musical language. Both of Dryden's poetic hallmarks are evident in these lines from *Absalom and Achitophel,* a poem written in support of King Charles II, whom he compared to King David from the Bible:

> Now what relief can righteous David bring?
> How fatal 'tis to be too good a king!
> Friends he has few, so high the madness grows:
> Who dare be such, must be the people's foes:
> Yet some there were, even in the worst of days;
> Some let me name, and naming is to praise.

Dryden wrote notable prose as well, including literary criticism of Shakespeare, Chaucer, and others that is as sound in judgment now as when he conceived it. In fact, he is sometimes considered the father of English criticism. His prose is the first that strikes us as modern: It is written in a manner that resembles speech.

Dryden wrote "A Song for St. Cecilia's Day," which begins on the following page, in memory of a Roman woman and Christian martyr who has traditionally been regarded as the patron saint of music and the inventor of the organ. He composed the poem in the form of an ode for a celebration in her memory on November 22, 1687. Originally a Greek choral song in honor of gods and goddesses, the **ode** as developed by Dryden is a lyric poem of irregular line lengths and stanzas, addressing a serious subject, and written in a dignified style. In 1739 the composer George Frederick Handel composed a score to accompany this ode.

In this selection, as in one selection in each unit, you will find notes in the right-hand margin that highlight parts of the selection. These notes point out important ideas of the literary period and draw your attention to literary elements and techniques covered in the Literary Focuses. Page numbers in the notes refer you to more extensive discussions of these important ideas and elements.

John Dryden

A Song for St. Cecilia's Day

1

From harmony, from heavenly harmony
    This universal frame[1] began;
    When Nature underneath a heap
      Of jarring atoms[2] lay,
5   And could not heave her head,
The tuneful voice was heard from high,
      "Arise, ye more than dead."
Then cold and hot and moist and dry[3]
    In order to their stations leap,
10   And music's power obey.
From harmony, from heavenly harmony
    This universal frame began:
     From harmony to harmony
Through all the compass of the notes it ran,
15 The diapason[4] closing full in man.

Imagery (p. 141): Dryden enhances his meaning by appealing to the sense of sound.

2

What passion cannot music raise and quell?
    When Jubal struck the corded shell,
    His listening brethren stood around,
     And, wondering, on their faces fell
20   To worship that celestial sound:

Allusion (p. 236): The poet assumes readers are familiar with Jubal, the biblical father of music (Genesis 4 : 21), whose harp is here described as made from tortoise shell ("corded shell").

1. **universal frame:** the structure of the universe.
2. **jarring atoms:** chaos preceding the arrangement of the universe.
3. **cold . . . dry:** describes earth, fire, water, and air, of which it was thought everything was composed.
4. **diapason** [dī′ə pā′zən]: range of tones of a musical scale; also complete harmony. Dryden is also thinking of the Chain of Being, a view that ordered creation from inanimate nature up through humankind.

Less than a god they thought there could not dwell
    Within the hollow of that shell,
    That spoke so sweetly and so well.
What passion cannot music raise and quell?

3

25   The trumpet's loud clangor
      Excites us to arms
    With shrill notes of anger
      And mortal[5] alarms.
    The double, double, double beat
30   Of the thund'ring drum
    Cries, "Hark, the foes come;
Charge, charge, 'tis too late to retreat."

4

    The soft complaining flute
In dying notes discovers[6]
35   The woes of hopeless lovers,
Whose dirge is whispered by the warbling lute.

Stanza form (p. 90): The poet uses a variety of line lengths and varies the number of lines in the stanzas to accommodate his meaning.

5

    Sharp violins proclaim
Their jealous pangs and desperation,
Fury, frantic indignation,
40 Depth of pains and height of passion,
    For the fair, disdainful dame.

6

    But Oh! What art can teach,
    What human voice can reach,
    The sacred organ's praise?
45   Notes inspiring holy love,
Notes that wing their heavenly ways
    To mend the choirs above.

Seventeenth-century idea: Religion was an overriding concern (p. 199).

7

Orpheus could lead the savage race,
And trees unrooted left their place,
50   Sequacious of[7] the lyre;
But bright Cecilia raised the wonder higher;
When to her organ vocal breath was given,
An angel heard and straight appeared,
    Mistaking earth for heaven.

Allusion (p. 236): Here Dryden alludes to the musician who, in Greek mythology, enchanted trees and stones and tamed wild beasts with his music.

---

5. **mortal:** preceding or accompanying death.
6. **discovers:** reveals.
7. **Sequacious of:** following.

Grand Chorus

55　As from the power of sacred lays[8]
　　　The spheres began to move,
　　And sung the great Creator's praise
　　　To all the blest above;
　　So when the last and dreadful hour
60　This crumbling pageant[9] shall devour,
　　The trumpet[10] shall be heard on high,
　　The dead shall live, the living die,
　　And music shall untune the sky.

　　8. **lays:** songs.
　　9. **pageant:** universe and the spectacle it represents.
　　10. **trumpet:** the last trumpet, which announces the
biblical Judgment Day, or end of the universe
(I Corinthians 15 : 52).

Seventeenth-century idea: It was believed that heavenly bodies were set in transparent, spherical shells revolving around the earth, put in motion by angelic songs (p. 207).

STUDY QUESTIONS

Recalling

1. From what, according to the first stanza, did the universe begin?
2. According to lines 21–23, why did the listeners worship the sound of Jubal's instrument?
3. What musical instruments are referred to in the poem?
4. According to lines 52–54, why did an angel pay a visit to earth?
5. With what sound will the world end, according to the Grand Chorus?

Interpreting

6. Based on an understanding of the Chain of Being, (see footnote 4), what is the relationship between notes of a musical scale and all natural things? What does man represent in line 15?
7. What passions are stirred by different instruments in stanzas 3–6? What relationship exists in each of the stanzas between the sound of the words and the instrument that is being described?
8. Of all the musical instruments mentioned throughout the poem, which receives the highest praise? Why?

9. What puzzle or paradox do the last two lines of the Grand Chorus present?

Extending

10. On what occasions in our daily lives does music reflect or heighten our emotions?

COMPOSITION

Writing About a Quotation

■ Show how Dryden centers his poem around the line "What passion cannot music raise and quell?" Demonstrate how each of stanzas 3–7 expands on that line. Conclude by explaining how the Grand Chorus relates to that line. *For help with this assignment, refer to Lesson 5 in the Writing About Literature Handbook at the back of this book.*

Writing a Description

■ Read stanzas 3–6 aloud to appreciate the effect of sound on meaning. Think of two contrasting situations—such as climbing up a steep mountain through brush and coasting down a slide into a pool. Describe the two experiences, choosing language with sounds that help convey the difficulty of one situation and the ease of the other.

Samuel Pepys   *1633–1703*

In a century known for remarkable offerings in poetry, Samuel Pepys is one of the most important contributors of prose. The fifth child of a well-to-do tailor, Samuel Pepys (pronounced "Peeps") was born in London and studied on scholarships at Cambridge University. Having no independent means, he initially relied on the patronage of his wealthy and influential relatives, the Montagus. With their assistance, he was appointed to his first position in the navy office in 1660.

Through hard work and loyalty, Pepys received additional appointments and rose quickly in the navy office. In 1672 he was appointed Secretary of the Admiralty, or navy department, and under his watchful direction the British navy regained its efficiency and reputation as a major power on the seas. However, his successful public career came to an end with the Glorious Revolution of 1688, and Pepys spent his remaining years in leisurely retirement.

More impressive even than the contributions he made to England in his role as a high public official is the extraordinary private legacy that Pepys left to future generations. On New Year's Day 1660, the then twenty-seven-year-old Pepys began in shorthand a diary that he would keep faithfully for the next nine years, until his failing eyesight forced him to stop. Consisting of six volumes, the diary was not completely deciphered and published until 1825. It is now considered the most famous and valuable diary in English.

Pepys's diary is an endlessly fascinating document, partly because its author was such an important official in the British Admiralty and thus had access to the king and to many other significant Englishmen of the period. In part, the six volumes of diary manuscript are riveting because Pepys was such an enthusiastic and curious individual, full of vitality, willing to see everything and go everywhere, and able to report his experiences and observations fully and honestly. The diary also holds our attention because in the period and place he wrote of there was so much to see: the pageantry of King Charles's ascent to the throne, a horrible plague that ran through London, and the Great Fire of 1666 that destroyed a third of the city, to mention just some of the drama. Finally, the diary reveals the domestic and personal details of one man's life. In fact, no other source gives so vivid a sense of what being alive in London would have been like in the second half of the seventeenth century. Two excerpts from the diary begin on the following page.

Samuel Pepys

from **The Diary**

The Coronation of Charles II

April 23, 1661. Coronation Day. About four I rose and got to the Abbey, where I followed Sir J. Denham,[1] the Surveyor, with some company that he was leading in. And with much ado, by the favor of Mr. Cooper, his man, did get up into a great scaffold across the north end of the Abbey, where with a great deal of patience I sat from past four till eleven before the King came in. And a great pleasure it was to see the Abbey raised in the middle, all covered with red, and a throne (that is a chair) and footstool on the top of it; and all the officers of all kinds, so much as the very fiddlers, in red vests.

At last comes in the Dean and Prebends[2] of Westminster, with the Bishops (many of them in cloth-of-gold copes),[3] and after them the Nobility, all in their Parliament robes, which was a most magnificent sight. Then the Duke, and the King with a scepter (carried by my Lord Sandwich) and sword and mond[4] before him, and the crown too. The King in his robes, bare-headed, which was very fine. And after all had placed themselves, there was a sermon and the service; and then in the Choir at the high altar, the King passed through all the ceremonies of the Coronation, which to my great grief I and most in the Abbey could not see. The crown being put upon his head, a great shout began, and he came forth to the throne; and there passed more ceremonies: as taking the oath, and having things read to him by the Bishop; and his Lords (who put on their caps as soon as the King put on his crown) and bishops came and kneeled before him. And three times the King at Arms[5] went to the three open places on the scaffold and proclaimed that if anyone could show any reason why Charles Stuart should not be King of England, that now he should come and speak. And a General Pardon also was read by the Lord Chancellor, and medals flung up and down by my Lord Cornwallis, of silver, but I could not come by any. But so great a noise that I could make but little of the music; and indeed, it was lost to everybody.

I went out a little while before the King had done all his ceremonies, and went round the Abbey to Westminster Hall, all the way within rails, and ten thousand people, with the ground covered with blue cloth; and scaffolds all the way. Into the Hall I got, where it was very fine with hangings and scaffolds one upon another full of brave[6] ladies; and my wife in one little one, on the right hand. Here I stayed walking up and down, and at last, upon one of the side stalls, I stood and saw the King come in with all the persons (but the soldiers) that were yesterday in the cavalcade; and a most pleasant sight it was to see them in their several robes. And the King came in with his crown on, and his scepter in his hand, under a canopy borne up by six silver staves, carried by Barons of the Cinque Ports,[7] and little bells at every end.

And after a long time, he got up to the farther end, and all set themselves down at their several tables; and that was also a brave sight; and the King's first course carried up by the Knights of the Bath. And many fine ceremonies there was of the herald's leading up people before him, and bowing; and my Lord of Albe-

---

1. **Sir J. Denham:** Sir John Denham (1615–1669), English poet and architect.
2. **Prebends** [preb'əndz]: high church officials.
3. **copes:** mantles or capes.
4. **mond:** ceremonial orb or ball of gold or other precious material, representing the globe of the earth.

5. **King at Arms:** chief herald.
6. **brave:** finely dressed.
7. **Cinque** [singk] **Ports:** five English Channel ports.

marle's going to the kitchen and eat[8] a bit of the first dish that was to go to the King's table. But, above all, was these three Lords, Northumberland, and Suffolk, and the Duke of Ormond, coming before the courses on horseback, and staying so all dinnertime, and at last to bring up [Dymock] the King's champion,[9] all in armor on horseback, with his spear and target carried before him. And a herald proclaims, "That if any dare deny Charles Stuart to be lawful King of England, here was a champion that would fight with him"; and with these words, the champion flings down his gauntlet, and all this he do three times in his going up toward the King's table. At last when he is come, the King drinks to him and then sends him the cup, which is of gold, and he drinks it off and then rides back again with the cup in his hand. I went from table to table to see the bishops and all others at their dinner, and was infinitely pleased with it. And at the Lords' table, I met with William Howe, and he spoke to my Lord[10] for me, and he did give me four rabbits and a pullet, and so I got it and Mr. Creed and I got Mr. Michell to give us some bread, and so we at a stall eat it, as everybody else did what they could get. I took a great deal of pleasure to go up and down, and look upon the ladies, and to hear the music of all sorts, but above all, the twenty-four violins.

The London Fire

September 2, 1666.   (Lord's Day.) Some of our maids sitting up late last night to get things ready against our feast today, Jane called us up about three in the morning, to tell us of a great fire they saw in the city. So I rose and slipped on my nightgown, and went to her window, and thought it to be on the back side of Mark Lane at the farthest; but, being unused to such fires as followed, I thought it far enough off; and so went to bed again and to sleep. About seven rose again to dress myself, and there looked out at the window, and saw the fire not so much as it was and farther off. So to my closet to set things to rights after yesterday's cleaning.

By and by Jane comes and tells me that she hears that above 300 houses have been burned down tonight by the fire we saw, and that it is now burning down all Fish Street, by London Bridge. So I made myself ready presently, and walked to the Tower,[1] and there got up upon one of the high places, Sir J. Robinson's little son going up with me; and there I did see the houses at the end of the bridge all on fire, and an infinite great fire on this and the other side the end of the bridge; which, among other people, did trouble me for poor little Michell and our Sarah on the bridge.[2] So down, with my heart full of trouble, to the Lieutenant of the Tower, who tells me that it begun this morning in the King's baker's house in Pudding Lane, and that it hath burned St. Magnus Church and most part of Fish Street already. So I down to the waterside, and there got a boat and through bridge,[3] and there saw a lamentable fire. Poor Michell's house, as far as the Old Swan, already burned that way, and the fire running farther, that in a very little time it got as far as the Steel Yard, while I was there. Everybody endeavoring to remove their goods, and flinging into the river or bringing them into lighters[4] that lay off; poor people staying in their houses as long as till the very fire touched them, and then running into boats, or clambering from one pair of stairs by the waterside to another. And among other things, the poor pigeons, I perceive, were loath to leave their houses, but hovered about the windows and balconies till they were, some of them

8. **eat** [et]: past tense.
9. **King's champion:** a ceremonial office at the coronation; the office had been held by the Dymock family since the coronation of Richard II in 1377.
10. **my Lord:** Pepys's lifelong patron, the Earl of Sandwich.

1. **Tower:** the Tower of London.
2. **on the bridge:** London Bridge, the only bridge over the Thames River at that time; its sides were lined with shops and houses.
3. **through bridge:** under the arches.
4. **lighters:** barges.

burned, their wings, and fell down. Having stayed, and in an hour's time seen the fire rage every way, and nobody, to my sight, endeavoring to quench it, but to remove their goods, and leave all to the fire, and having seen it get as far as the Steel Yard, and the wind mighty high and driving it into the City;[5] and everything, after so long a drought, proving combustible, even the very stones of churches. I to Whitehall, and there up to the King's closet[6] in the Chapel, where people come about me, and I did give them an account dismayed them all, and word was carried in to the King. So I was called for and did tell the King and Duke of York[7] what I saw, and that unless his Majesty did command houses to be pulled down nothing could stop the fire. They seemed much troubled, and the King commanded me to go to my Lord Mayor from him and command him to spare no houses, but to pull down before the fire every way. The Duke of York bid me tell him that if he would have any more soldiers he shall; and so did my Lord Arlington afterward, as a great secret. Here meeting with Captain Cocke, I in his coach, which he lent me, and Creed with me to Paul,[8] and there walked along Watling Street, as well as I could, every creature coming away laden with goods to save, and here and there sick people carried away in beds. Extraordinary good goods carried in carts and on backs. At last met my Lord Mayor in Canning Street, like a man spent, with a handkerchief about his neck. To the King's message he cried, like a fainting woman, "Lord! what can I do? I am spent: people will not obey me. I have been pulling down houses; but the fire overtakes us faster than we can do it." That he needed no more soldiers and that, for himself, he must go and refresh himself, having been up all night.

---

5. **City:** the commercial center of London, the part that lay within what had been the medieval city walls.
6. **closet:** room for private devotion.
7. **Duke of York:** King Charles' brother, later James II.
8. **Paul:** St. Paul's Cathedral. The original St. Paul's was destroyed in the fire.

So he left me, and I him, and walked home, seeing people all almost distracted, and no manner of means used to quench the fire. The houses, too, so very thick thereabouts and full of matter for burning, as pitch and tar, in Thames Street; and warehouses of oil, and wines, and brandy, and other things. Here I saw Mr. Issake Houblon, the handsome man, prettily dressed and dirty, at his door at Dowgate, receiving some of his brothers' things, whose houses were on fire; and, as he says, have been removed twice already; and he doubts (as it soon proved) that they must be in a little time removed from his house also which was a sad consideration. And to see the churches all filling with goods by people who themselves should have been quietly there at this time.

By this time it was about twelve o'clock; and so home. Soon as dined, away, and walked through the city, the streets full of nothing but people and horses and carts laden with goods, ready to run over one another, and removing goods from one burned house to another. They now removing out of Canning Street (which received goods in the morning) into Lombard Street, and farther; and among others I now saw my little goldsmith, Stokes, receiving some friend's goods, whose house itself was burned the day after. We parted at Paul's; he home, and I to Paul's Wharf, where I had appointed a boat to attend me, and took in Mr. Carcasse and his brother, whom I met in the street, and carried them below and above bridge, to and again to see the fire, which was now got farther, both below and above, and no likelihood of stopping it. Met with the King and Duke of York in their barge, and with them to Queenhithe, and there called Sir Richard Browne to them. Their order was only to pull down houses apace,[9] and so below bridge at the waterside; but little was or could be done, the fire coming upon them so fast. Good hopes there was of stopping it at the Three Cranes above, and at Buttolph's Wharf below bridge, if

---

9. **apace:** swiftly.

Detail, *The Great Fire of London*, Dutch School, c. 1666.

care be used; but the wind carries it into the City, so as we know not by the waterside what it do there. River full of lighters and boats taking in goods, and good goods swimming in the water, and only I observed that hardly one lighter or boat in three that had the goods of a house in, but there was a pair of virginals[10] in it.

_____
10. **pair of virginals:** type of harpsichord.

Having seen as much as I could now, I away to Whitehall by appointment and there walked to St. James's Park, and there met my wife and Creed and walked to my boat; and there upon the water again, and to the fire up and down, it still increasing, and the wind great. So near the fire as we could for smoke; and all over the Thames, with one's face in the wind, you were almost burned with a shower of firedrops. This is very true; so as houses were burned by these drops and flakes of fire, three or four, nay, five or six houses, one from another. When we could endure no more upon the water, we to a little alehouse on the Bankside, over against the Three Cranes, and there stayed till it was dark almost, and saw the fire grow; and, as it grew darker, appeared more and more, and in corners and upon steeples, and between churches and houses, as far as we could see up the hill of the City, in a most horrid malicious bloody flame not like the fine flame of an ordinary fire. Barbary and her husband away before us. We stayed till, it being darkish, we saw the fire as only one entire arch of fire from this to the other side of the bridge and in a bow up the hill for an arch of above a mile long: it made me weep to see it. The churches, houses, and all on fire and flaming at once; and a horrid noise the flames made, and the crackling of houses at their ruin.

So home with a sad heart, and there find everybody discoursing and lamenting the fire; and poor Tom Hater come with some few of his goods saved out of his house, which is burned upon Fish Street Hill. I invited him to lie at my house, and did receive his goods, but was deceived in his lying there, the news coming every moment of the growth of the fire; so as we were forced to begin to pack up our own goods and prepare for their removal; and did by moonshine (it being brave dry, and moonshine, and warm weather) carry much of my goods into the garden, and Mr. Hater and I did remove my money and iron chests into my cellar, as thinking that the safest place. And got my bags of gold into my office, ready to carry away, and my chief papers of accounts also there, and my tallies into a box by themselves. So great was our fear, as Sir W. Batten hath carts come out of the country to fetch away his goods this night. We did put Mr. Hater, poor man, to bed a little; but he got but very little rest, so much noise being in my house, taking down of goods.

3rd. About four o'clock in the morning, my Lady Batten sent me a cart to carry away all my money, and plate, and best things, to Sir W. Rider's at Bednall Green. Which I did, riding myself in my nightgown in the cart; and, Lord! to see how the streets and the highways are crowded with people running and riding, and getting of carts at any rate to fetch away things. I find Sir W. Rider tired with being called up all night, and receiving things from several friends. His house full of goods, and much of Sir W. Batten's and Sir W. Pen's. I am eased at my heart to have my treasure so well secured. Then home, with much ado to find a way, nor any sleep all this night to me nor my poor wife.

STUDY QUESTIONS

Recalling

1. How does the crowd react when the crown is placed upon the king's head? What further ceremonies occur in the Abbey after the king is crowned?
2. On what day and hour does news of the Great Fire of London first reach Pepys? Who is the first to tell him of it? What had been planned in the Pepys household for that day?
3. Why does Pepys, along with his wife and Creed, find it difficult to remain on the river?

4. When the Pepys household is forced to begin packing up its own goods, why does the diarist take his money and iron chests into his cellar? How does Pepys ultimately carry his money and valuables away from his house?

Interpreting

5. In what mood does the diarist witness the coronation proceedings? How much can you infer from his behavior at the coronation? Does he like crowds, music, and pretty women?
6. What evidence from the diary entry on the London fire would lead you to conclude that Pepys is civic-minded?

Extending

7. The crowning of an English monarch partakes of a long tradition. What aspects of the banquet ceremony seem particularly medieval, out of the mythical court of Malory's King Arthur?

VIEWPOINT

It has been said that Pepys's diary

is so intimate that we feel closer to Pepys than we do to almost any [other] man who has ever written.

—A. C. Baugh

■ Do you agree or disagree with that assessment? What would cause you to identify with a writer?

LITERARY FOCUS

Diaries and Journals

Diaries are personal, day-by-day accounts of impressions and events kept by an individual. Most diaries are private and if published at all are generally not published until after the death of the author. While journals also chronicle daily thoughts and events, they are usually less intimate than diaries.

Diaries bring us directly into contact with another person going about his daily business. Pepys's diary is full of the kind of details that would never find their way into an epic poem or a tragic drama: for example, his delight in purchasing a new knife, his irritation at a household servant, his jealousies, and his domestic triumphs and disappointments. These are not the stuff of heroic literature, but they agree with the scale on which most of us lead our lives.

Thinking About Diaries and Journals

■ From the excerpts reprinted here from Pepys's diary, find at least two other reactions or incidents that are appropriate to a diary but not to an epic.

VOCABULARY

Word Origins

Excerpts from Pepys's diary allow us a firsthand view of the English spoken and written by ordinary Englishmen in the seventeenth century. Many of the common nouns that Pepys uses have been in the English language since Old English days. They have developed from Anglo-Saxon or Germanic origins. Many other common nouns in the Pepys excerpts have other histories, however. As explained on page 71, French has had a large impact on the English vocabulary. So, too, have other Latin-based languages such as Italian. Using a good dictionary, look up each of the following words from Pepys's diary, and indicate whether the word came into English from French or from Italian.

1. coronation
2. cavalcade
3. scepter
4. gauntlet
5. violins
6. balconies
7. herald
8. scaffolds
9. champion
10. treasure

COMPOSITION

Citing Evidence and Documenting

■ Write an essay arguing, first, that Pepys was an efficient, businesslike man and, then, that he was a fun-loving, lively man. In order to defend your two portraits of Pepys, cite phrases and sentences from the diary entries. *For help with citing evidence and documenting your sources, see Lesson 3 in the Writing About Literature Handbook at the back of this book.*

Writing a Diary Entry

■ In the form of a diary entry describe an unusual event that your personal observation enables you to write about confidently. Include specific details to let your reader experience the event fully.

COMPARING WRITERS

■ Reconsider all the poems you have read by Donne, Marvell, Jonson, Herrick, Lovelace, Milton, and Dryden in terms of the overall tone, or attitude, of the speaker. What generalization can you make about the tone with which the poems end? That is, do the speakers sound angry? Resigned? Hopeful? Faithful? Consoled? Based on the individual poems, what seems to make the speaker feel the way he does?

READING FOR APPRECIATION

Sound in Poetry

The sound of a poem contributes greatly to the effect that it has on us as readers. Ideally, we should read a poem aloud to appreciate fully its impact.

Poets seek to create an overall pattern or quality of sound that is *appropriate to* the particular mood and meaning of a poem. In order to accomplish this goal, poets manipulate and experiment with the *form* of poetry—for instance, with the various techniques of rhythm, rhyme, alliteration, assonance, consonance, and so on. In all great poems and in any poem that we would call successful, the poet has managed to discover not only the proper words and the proper structure but also exactly the right *sound* needed to convey the sense.

The nineteenth-century English poet Gerard Manley Hopkins (page 436) underscored the importance of sound in poetry when he defined poetry as "speech framed . . . to be heard for its own sake and interest even over and above its interest of meaning." This is perhaps an exaggeration. We should not consider the sound of a poem— no matter how lovely or thrilling it is—to be *more* important than its meaning. We should not even regard the two elements as separable. In any good poem sound and meaning are intertwined and interdependent: Each supports and in turn relies upon the other. If when reading a poem we discount or devalue either element, then we diminish the poem as a whole—and, hence, our *experience* of it. Nevertheless, Hopkins' statement shows just how crucial the component of sound was to *him.*

Poets attempt, then, to produce a special fabric of sound through which meaning can be communicated more directly and forcefully. Consider, for example, Dryden's "Song for St. Cecilia's Day," in which he marvels at the power of music to move us in countless ways. He examines the different effects of musical instruments:

The double, double, double beat
  Of the thund'ring drum . . .
  The soft complaining flute
  In dying notes discovers
  The woes of hopeless lovers.

To emphasize the rousing, rhythmic, pounding qualities of the drum, the poet twice repeats the word *double.* He mainly uses heavy, percussive consonant sounds: "*Th*e," "*dou*ble," "*b*eat," "thun*d*'ring," "*d*rum." Moreover, the very words *drum* and *beat* sound their meanings; they are, in short, *onomatopoetic* words. One result of these choices is that when we read these lines, we hear the strong, steady beat of a drum. In contrast, Dryden uses quieter, softer consonants and combinations of letters to evoke the gentle, wistful, and sometimes mournful sound of the flute. Notice, for instance, the repetition of light, breathy *f* sounds and delicate *l* sounds: "so*f*t," "comp*l*aining," "*f*lute," "hope*l*ess," "*l*overs." Notice, too, the repetition of *o* sounds: "The w*o*es *o*f h*o*peless l*o*vers." We hear the lonely, plaintive flute in the distance somewhere and, perhaps, even feel some of the sadness it expresses.

When sound and sense are merged, as they are in Dryden's poem, the impact can be emotional as well as intellectual. The poem can reach us and move us with surprising immediacy— much like music can.

THE ENGLISH VOICE

A Sense of Place

A keen awareness of place has always marked the finest writers. Certainly the *Beowulf* poet, Chaucer, and Shakespeare possessed to a high degree this sense of their surroundings, their environment, the physical reality of their worlds. In the same way, the sense of place gave solidity to seventeenth-century writing.

Journeys and geography took on a new interest after the discoveries made by Elizabethan explorers. This was the century of sailing to America; establishing settlements; trading with India, China, Japan, and Africa. In literature, no matter how metaphysical or unearthly the vision, the concrete sense of place brought it home.

Donne

No man is an island, entire of itself; every man is a piece of the continent, a part of the main.

Marvell

He makes the figs our mouths to meet
And throws the melons at our feet
But apples plants of such a price,
No tree could ever bear them twice.

Jonson

But stay, I see thee in the hemisphere
Advanced, and made a constellation there!
Shine forth, thou Star of poets.

Pepys

It is now burning down Fish Street. So I . . . walked to the Tower and did see the houses at the end of the bridge all on fire. . . . It begun this morning in the King's baker's house in Pudding Lane. . . . It hath burned St. Magnus Church.

Milton

"Is this the region, this the soil, the clime,"
Said then the lost archangel, "this the seat
That we must change for Heaven?" . . .
The world was all before them, where to choose
Their place of rest, and Providence their guide.

Geography, history, metaphysics, and poetry unite in these voices. Donne saw a human "continent." Jonson transformed a poet into a guiding star. Pepys made a city seem as wide as a world. Milton vivified a lost paradise, even as Marvell celebrated the discovery of a new one.

Key to Illustrations on Pages 198–199.

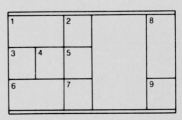

1. Detail, *The Great Fire of London*, engraving by Wenceslaus Hollar, (1607–1677).
2. Portrait of Ben Jonson, Isaac Oliver.
3. Portrait of John Donne (1572–1631), after Isaac Oliver.
4. Detail, nineteenth-century engraving of Sir Isaac Newton dispersing sunlight through a prism.
5. Seventeenth-century penny-post envelope.
6. Detail, *Charles II of England in the Bay of Dordrecht During His Journey from Mordyk to Delft in 1660*, Willem II van de Velde (1633–1707).
7. Detail, map of London showing London Bridge, 1650.
8. Detail from a seventeenth-century engraving of St. Paul's Cathedral.
9. Portrait of John Milton (1608–1674), artist unknown.

Key to Illustrations appears on page 317.

THE EIGHTEENTH CENTURY

1700–1798

Political and Economic Developments

As the bells of London rang in the year 1700, William III sat alone on the throne. His wife Mary had died six years before. Two years later William himself died and was succeeded by Mary's sister Anne.

The Glorious Revolution that brought William and Mary to England in 1688 had put limitations on the monarchy that would lead, over the centuries, to real democracy. Yet the legitimacy of their rule was not agreed upon by all. Irish Catholics rallied behind the deposed James II; after their rebellion was crushed, penal laws robbed them of political and religious freedom for over a century. Many Scots, too, were Jacobites—supporters of James II and his son James Stuart. However, with the Act of Union of 1707, England and Scotland were politically joined as Great Britain, and in 1745 the last Jacobite rebellion in Scotland was quelled.

Louis XIV, King of France, had also backed James II, but the centuries-old battle for supremacy between England and France went beyond the matter of the monarchy. As it had been in the time of Elizabeth I, the question was really who would lead Europe as a commercial and colonial power. Throughout the eighteenth century periodic wars with France disturbed the English peace.

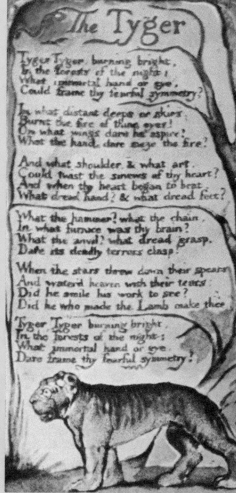

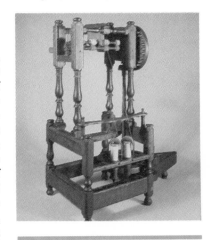

Spinning machine invented by Sir Thomas Arkwright (1732–1792).

During Queen Anne's reign, Parliament—composed of the House of Lords and the House of Commons—found itself dominated by two rival political parties. These parties—the Whigs and the Tories—went on to form the fundamental opposition within the Parliament for the rest of the century. The Tories included most of the British nobility, represented in the House of Lords, and the lesser landowners, known as the "squirearchy" or landed gentry. They sought to advance agricultural interests and preferred an end to the continuing conflicts with France. The Whigs were chiefly from the growing merchant class and represented urban, commercial interests. They sought to promote war with France, which they hoped would lead to British dominance in trade.

Queen Anne favored the Tories. However, Anne outlived all her children, and when she became ill in 1713, many Tories threw support to the Catholic James Stuart, hoping he would convert to the Church of England. He would not, and since by law the crown could not go to a Catholic, it went to the next Protestant in line, a distant relative, the Elector of Hanover, Germany, who in 1714 came to Britain's throne as George I. This marks the beginning of Georgian England, for the first four kings of the new House of Hanover were all named George.

George I spoke no English and was easily guided by politi-cians in Parliament. He favored the Whigs, since the Tories at first had not supported him. During his reign the Whig-dominated House of Commons—to which members were elected—grew in importance, while the hereditary House of Lords lost some of its superior status. The new power of the House of Commons was another milestone on the road to democracy, although only a small percentage of the population was allowed to vote.

Beginning in the reign of George I, the king's cabinet of ministers, or advisers, were chosen from Parliament. The greatest or "prime" minister of the time was Robert Walpole, a clever Whig who made himself indispensable to the newcomer from Hanover and his successor, George II. During one of the many wars with France—called the Seven Years' War (1756–1763) in Europe and the French and Indian War in America—another Whig leader took center stage. His name was William Pitt. More than any other politician, Pitt saw the need for naval supremacy if Britain were to end commercial competition from France once and for all. His plans were thwarted in 1760 when George II died and was succeeded by his grandson, George III.

Unlike George I and George II, George III believed that the king should play an active role in politics. The costly Seven Years' War had grown unpopular among the Tory squirearchy, with whom the new king was in sympathy. In 1761 George forced Pitt to resign, and two years later an inconclusive peace treaty with the French was signed.

At about this time Britain was undergoing something that would have overwhelming effects on the future of the world. We now call it the Industrial Revolution, but it was not a revolution in the sense of something that happened suddenly. Rather, it was a gradual process of change from "cottage industries," where workers produced goods in their homes, to factory manufacturing, in which goods were produced in far greater quantities and in far less time with the help of newly invented machinery.

The Industrial Revolution, even in its infancy, made factory owners very influential. It became their policy to keep industry from spreading to the colonies. The colonies, they felt, should not be allowed to rival

Britain as producers of finished goods, but should be kept subordinate as suppliers of raw materials and markets for British goods. This policy infuriated many colonists in America. Nor were they pleased when, after the Seven Years' War, their mother country attempted to refill her emptied coffers with a number of irregular taxes. In a series of disastrous decisions, King George III and the now-Tory government pushed the colonists into rebellion, and George III earned for himself the name of tyrant in most American history books.

Naturally, France came to the aid of the Americans. Help also came from the Whig party, which grew critical of Tory policies in America. The American Revolution, as a result, divided British public opinion. Furthermore, poor communications between Britain and the American colonies made it difficult for Britain to conduct the war. After their defeat at Yorktown, the British were forced to sign a treaty setting an amazing precedent: In 1783, Britain recognized America as an independent nation.

Beginning in 1783 a son of William Pitt, also named William, rose on the political scene. Unlike his father, he was able to work with the king, and he soon became the leader of a restructured Tory party. Pitt came to power hoping to solve domestic problems neglected during the almost constant warfare of pre-

Detail, *Covent Garden Market,* John Collet, c. 1760.

ceding decades. When in 1789 the French Revolution broke out, assisting the French monarchy was the last thing in Pitt's mind. Ironically, it was the French revolutionaries who declared war on England, putting an end to Pitt's peacetime plans and eventually sweeping Britain into war against the French dictator Napoleon. That conflict, however, was resolved in the nineteenth century.

Life in the Eighteenth Century

The eighteenth century has been called the **Age of Reason,** for it was a time when prevailing philosophy argued that almost anything could be achieved through the calm workings of the human mind. It has been called the **Age of Classicism,** for it saw in all the arts a fascination with ancient Greece and Rome. It has been called the **Age of Elegance,** for it displayed among the upper classes an elegant style of life, a style

that ended when the effects of the Industrial Revolution became pronounced and the French Revolution destroyed the belief in an orderly hierarchy in society.

If we look at the hierarchy of eighteenth-century English society, we find first the nobility, then the landed gentry, then the merchants and professionals like doctors and lawyers, and finally the bulk of the population—the poor. For the small group who were not poor, life was very pleasant. The center of social activity was London, to which the nobility and all political families flocked during the social season, the spring session of Parliament. The chief resort was the city of Bath, an architectural gem built over mineral waters thought to be healthful.

The City of London bustled with commerce. In the coffee and chocolate houses, Tories and Whigs argued politics, exchanged gossip, and perused the latest journals.

Whatever the state of Anglo-French relations, British dress was decidedly influenced by fashions in France. Men wore colorful knee breeches and equally colorful coats, vests, and stockings; women wore lavish costumes and laced themselves into corsets so tight that breathing was difficult. Both sexes wore wigs or powdered their hair until a 1790s hair powder tax led to "natural" hairdos.

The arts in this Age of Elegance lack the simplicity of, for example, Elizabethan music. The

Commode made by Thomas Chippendale, 1771–1773.

music of George Frederick Handel dominated the first half of the century, for the German-born composer enjoyed the patronage of the Hanover kings. In architecture we see the Classical influence in the magnificent homes designed by the Adam brothers, with their columns, porticoes, and tall, wide windows that—for the first time in those centuries without electricity—let in the sunlight. Elegant, too, are the grounds of Georgian estates, with landscapes by Lancelot "Capability" Brown, and the interiors of Georgian homes, with their Chippendale, Hepplewhite, and Sheridan furniture and family portraits by Joshua Reynolds and Thomas Gainsborough. Another eighteenth-century painter, William Hogarth, is more famous for satirical sketches of upper-class absurdity and lower-class poverty.

Scientific and technological advances went hand-in-hand with the Industrial Revolution. Especially important were James Watt's steam engine (1769), which provided an efficient means of harnessing power, and James Hargreaves' spinning jenny (1770), which revolutionized the textile industry. The mid-century development of vaccinations helped end the epidemics of earlier centuries, though practices such as bloodletting to reduce fevers still caused many untimely deaths. Coach accidents were also a common cause of death, for with the new prosperity more people traveled,

and though roadside inns grew more splendid, the roads themselves remained muddy and dangerous.

Nevertheless, beginning in about 1760 England experienced a population boom, due in part to the new vaccinations and in part to farming improvements that increased England's food supply. This population explosion in turn swelled the ranks of the new labor force that would be an important factor in the century to come.

Literature in the Eighteenth Century

Eighteenth-century literature reflects the ideas and interests of the Age of Reason, the Age of Classicism, the Age of Elegance. Works show a sense of order and moderation; writers display their "wit," or cleverness, but usually not their heart and soul. Prose arguments are calm and logical; poems are carefully structured and often make classical allusions. Many writers sat-

irize "elegant" society or politics, but even when their humor grows bitter, they never abandon the detached, urbane tone of the eighteenth-century wit.

Eighteenth-century England is often called the **Augustan Age,** a reference to the prosperous Rome of Emperor Augustus, when commerce and great literature also thrived. Augustan literature is sometimes divided into two periods, each named for its most influential man of letters—the **Age of Pope** and, after 1750, the **Age of Johnson.**

Alexander Pope was the leading literary figure of Queen Anne's day, the greatest of the so-called Queen Anne Wits. In the work of Pope and his colleagues, the idea of an orderly, hierarchic society modeled on that of "the ancients" is most pronounced. Pope portrays this **Classical**—or **neoclassical**—thinking in long poems such as *Essay on Man,* while in *The Rape of the Lock* he mocks the foibles of "elegant" society.

Pope's fellow Tory Jonathan Swift wrote satire with a sharper edge. In *Gulliver's Travels* he lampoons the events of the day; but this forerunner of the modern novel is delightful even to readers today who know nothing of the politics of the age. Swift is also famous for satiric poems and essays.

Samuel Johnson was the great man of letters of midcentury Georgian England. He is noted not only for what he wrote—the first great English *Dictionary,*

Detail, *A Scene from the Beggar's Opera,*
William Hogarth, 1728.

among other things—but for what he believed and said. His witty ideas and conversation are captured by his friend James Boswell in *The Life of Samuel Johnson,* the first modern biography in English.

In addition to Pope and Swift, talented Augustan poets include Matthew Prior, John Gay, Oliver Goldsmith, and William Cowper. Cowper is noted for religious verse with traces of the strong emotion that marks the late eighteenth-century reaction to Classicism known as **Romanticism,** which is described in the next unit. Even more important poets who marked the transition to Romanticism are Thomas Gray, Robert Burns, and William Blake.

Drama in the Eighteenth Century

Most eighteenth-century drama continues the traditions of Restoration playwrights, although tragedies were not as fine as in the preceding century. **Sentimental tragedies** were popular with the growing audience from the merchant class, and the interest in classical literature prompted many **classical tragedies** modeled on those of ancient Rome.

The Augustan comedies are far more memorable than Augustan tragedies. They include John Gay's *Beggar's Opera,* a play with ballads; Oliver Goldsmith's *She Stoops to Conquer;* and Richard Brinsley Sheridan's *Ri-*

vals and *School for Scandal,* satires that gave the stage such famous characters as Mrs. Malaprop.

Prose and the Novel in the Eighteenth Century

The greatest achievements of Augustan literature were not in poetry or drama, however, but in prose. The age gave us not only Johnson's *Dictionary* and Boswell's biography but England's first major literary magazines, *The Tatler* and *The Spectator.* These journals, produced by Joseph Addison and Richard Steele, contain serious essays like those of Francis Bacon and less formal essays known for their satiric humor.

Literary letters flourish in the hands of Lord Chesterfield, while in the area of literary criticism, the outstanding figures are Pope and Johnson. Notable contributions in history and philosophy include the writings of David Hume; Charles E. Gib-

bon's *Decline and Fall of the Roman Empire (1776–1788);* Adam Smith's *Wealth of Nations* (1776); and Edmund Burke's *Reflections on the Revolution in France* (1790).

However, no prose achievement can outshine the development of the long fictional prose work known as the **novel.** Whether we name Daniel Defoe's *Robinson Crusoe* (1719) as the first true novel or reserve that privilege for Samuel Richardson's *Pamela* (1740), we can number among the best eighteenth-century novels Henry Fielding's *Tom Jones* (1749), Laurence Sterne's *Tristram Shandy* (1759–1767), and Oliver Goldsmith's *Vicar of Wakefield* (1776). Popular types of early novels include the **picaresque novel,** a series of loosely strung episodes about an adventurer or a lovable rogue, best represented by the works of Tobias Smollett; the **novel of sentiment,** a moral tale of romance and tears, such as Richardson's *Clarissa* (1747–1748); the **gothic novel,** pioneered in English by Horace Walpole and best illustrated by Anne Radcliffe's *Mysteries of Udolpho* (1794); and the **novel of manners,** witty society tales such as those by Fanny Burney and Maria Edgeworth. The novel as we know it began to take shape in the eighteenth century; in the nineteenth and twentieth centuries it would evolve into one of the crowning glories of English literature.

TIME LINE

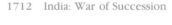

1702 William III dies; Queen Anne's reign begins

1707 Union of England and Scotland as Great Britain

1709 Addison and Steele, *The Tatler*

1710 Christopher Wren completes St. Paul's Cathedral

1712 Alexander Pope, *The Rape of the Lock*

1714 George I begins reign

1719 Daniel Defoe, *Robinson Crusoe*

1720 Wallpaper becomes fashionable

1721 Sir Robert Walpole becomes Prime Minister

1726 Jonathan Swift, *Gulliver's Travels*

1727 George II becomes king

1732 Covent Garden Opera House opens

1741 Handel composes *The Messiah*

1749 Henry Fielding, *Tom Jones*

1751 Thomas Gray, *Elegy Written in a Country Churchyard*

1752 David Hume, *Political Discourses*

1755 Samuel Johnson, *Dictionary of the English Language*

1701 Japan: Hakuseki writes history of feudal lords

1703 Russia: Peter the Great lays foundations of St. Petersburg

1709 Italy: Invention of pianoforte

1712 India: War of Succession

1714 Holland: Fahrenheit devises mercury thermometer

1721 Germany: Bach composes *Brandenburg Concertos*

1727 Brazil: Coffee first planted

1733 America: Benjamin Franklin, *Poor Richard's Almanack*

1741 Germany: First translation of Shakespeare published

1742 Sweden: Celsius devises the centigrade thermometer

1749 Portugal: Sign language for deaf invented

1756	The Seven Years' War begins
1760	George III begins reign
	Josiah Wedgwood founds his pottery works
1765	Parliament passes the Stamp Act
1769	Painter Joshua Reynolds knighted
	James Watt patents steam engine
1772	Thomas Chippendale produces furniture
1774	Lord Chesterfield, *Letters to His Son*
1775	Richard Sheridan, *The Rivals*
1783	William Pitt made Prime Minister by George III
1786	Robert Burns, *Poems Chiefly in the Scottish Dialect*
1789	William Blake, *Songs of Innocence*
1791	James Boswell, *Life of Samuel Johnson*
	Thomas Paine, *The Rights of Man*
1794	Mrs. Ann Radcliffe, *The Mysteries of Udolpho*

George III

Watt's steam engine

Chippendale furniture

Songs of Innocence by William Blake

Rosetta Stone

1756	France: Sèvres porcelain factory founded
1759	France: Voltaire writes *Candide*
1762	France: Rousseau writes *The Social Contract*
1765	Europe: Potato becomes popular food
1769	France: Shakespeare's *Hamlet* produced
1773	America: Boston Tea Party
1774	Austria: F. A. Mesmer develops hypnosis
1775	America: Revolutionary War begins
1783	America: Treaty of Paris ends the Revolutionary War
1786	Austria: Mozart composes *The Marriage of Figaro*
1789	France: French Revolution begins as mob storms the Bastille
1799	Egypt: Rosetta Stone found

English Literature: The Eighteenth Century **257**

Jonathan Swift   *1667–1745*

Jonathan Swift is generally thought to be the greatest prose writer of the eighteenth century. He was a man whom many considered a misanthrope (one who hates humankind) because his writings were deeply critical of humanity. It was, however, his deep love for humanity that caused him to criticize it, and his great dream was to cure the ills of his age through humor.

Swift was born of English parents in Ireland and was educated at Trinity College, Dublin. In 1689, with hopes of beginning a political career, he traveled to England to become private secretary to Sir William Temple, a wealthy aristocrat, essayist, and former ambassador to Holland. Swift hoped that Temple, a trusted friend of King William, would return to political life. However, Temple was content to be an occasional adviser to the king, and a few years later a disappointed Swift returned to Ireland to become a minister. After a short, unhappy time in a country parish, Swift returned to Temple's employment and served as his secretary until Temple's death in 1699.

It was in Temple's house that Swift began to write. He first composed awkward odes in the ancient, classical style of Pindar (see Part Two of this book), but soon realized that he had a gift for humorous prose on religious and political themes. By 1697 he had written *A Tale of a Tub,* a comic piece that ridiculed the extravagances of religion, literature, and academia. It was published in 1704 together with *The Battle of the Books,* a mock debate between ancient and modern authors. *A Tale of a Tub* established Swift's position as a great wit and genius of the age, and he began a short collaboration with Joseph Addison and Richard Steele (page 268) on their popular journal, *The Tatler.*

After Temple's death, Swift returned to Ireland to be a pastor in a small Protestant parish. In 1710 he became a powerful advocate of the new Tory government, and in 1713, in recognition of his skillful articles and pamphlets in defense of Tory policies, Queen Anne appointed Swift dean of St. Patrick's Cathedral in Dublin. For the more than thirty years until his death, Swift served as dean of St. Patrick's and as champion of the Irish cause. He wrote many pamphlets to protest the suffering of the Irish under their British rulers, and he taught the Irish the power of the boycott when he encouraged them to refuse to accept English goods that competed with their own industries. In his later years Swift underwent a mental decline to which he finally succumbed in 1745. His friends stayed loyal to him, and the Irish people continue to this day to celebrate him as a hero. The generosity of spirit, deep learning, and harsh but humane humor that informed his writing were a great gift to the literary tradition.

Introducing Gulliver's Travels

Gulliver's Travels (1726) is Swift's greatest achievement, earning him a place among the few who have been able to write a book so wide in its appeal that it becomes known throughout the world. He fashioned his observations of the ways of men and women, kings and queens, courts and ministers, into a **parody**, or humorous imitation, of a travel book, one of the most popular kinds of literature in the early eighteenth century. In *Gulliver's Travels* Swift used the form to expose the inadequacies of British politics and society. Captain Gulliver is a ship's surgeon who is washed up on a number of imaginary shores. In each country he makes observations about society in general, and the perspective he gains leaves him sadly disillusioned. He finally returns to England with a painful recognition of his own country's flaws.

Gulliver's first voyage takes him to the island of Lilliput [lil′ə put′], inhabited by people who are only six inches tall. The Lilliputians [lil′ə pū′shənz] find Gulliver asleep, shipwrecked and exhausted by his long swim to shore, and they immobilize him by fastening him to the earth with threads and tiny stakes.

Jonathan Swift

from Gulliver's Travels

A Voyage to Lilliput

When I awaked, it was just daylight. I attempted to rise, but was not able to stir: for as I happened to lie on my back, I found my arms and legs were strongly fastened on each side to the ground; and my hair, which was long and thick, tied down in the same manner. I likewise felt several slender ligatures across my body, from my armpits to my thighs. I could only look upwards; the sun began to grow hot, and the light offended my eyes. I heard a confused noise about me, but in the posture I lay, could see nothing except the sky.

In a little time I felt something alive moving on my left leg, which advancing gently forward over my breast, came almost up to my chin; when bending my eyes downwards as much as I could, I perceived it to be a human creature not six inches high, with a bow and arrow in his hands, and a quiver at his back. In the meantime, I felt at least forty more of the same kind (as I conjectured) following the first. . . .

I a little loosened the strings that tied down my hair on the left side; so that I was just able to turn my head about two inches. But the creatures ran off a second time, before I could seize them; whereupon there was a great shout in a very shrill accent; and after it ceased, I heard one of them cry aloud, *Tolgo Phonac;* when in an instant I felt above a hundred arrows discharged on my left hand, which

Engraving from an early edition of *Gulliver's Travels.*

pricked me like so many needles; and besides, they shot another flight into the air, as we do bombs in Europe. . . .

I had reason to believe I might be a match for the greatest armies they could bring against me, if they were all of the same size with him that I saw. But fortune disposed otherwise of me. When the people observed I was quiet, they discharged no more arrows; but, by the noise increasing, I knew their numbers were greater; and about four yards from me, over against my right ear, I heard a knocking for above an hour, like people at work; when turning my head that way, as well as the pegs and strings would permit me, I saw a stage erected about a foot and a half from the ground, capable of holding four of the inhabitants, with two or three ladders to mount it: from whence one of them, who seemed to be a person of quality,[1]

made me a long speech, whereof I understood not one syllable. . . .

He appeared to be of a middle age, and taller than any of the other three who attended him; whereof one was a page,[2] who held up his train,[3] and seemed to be somewhat longer than my middle finger; the other two stood one on each side to support him. He acted every part of an orator; and I could observe many periods of threatenings, and others of promises, pity, and kindness.

I answered in a few words, but in the most submissive manner, lifting up my left hand and both my eyes to the sun, as calling him for a witness; and being almost famished with hunger, having not eaten a morsel for some hours before I left the ship, I found the demands of nature so strong upon me that I could not for-

---

1. **person of quality:** nobleman.

2. **page:** court servant.
3. **train:** long part of his robe that would otherwise trail on the ground.

bear showing my impatience (perhaps against the strict rules of decency) by putting my finger frequently on my mouth, to signify that I wanted food. The *Hurgo* (for so they call a great lord, as I afterwards learned) understood me very well. He descended from the stage, and commanded that several ladders should be applied to my sides, on which above a hundred of the inhabitants mounted, and walked towards my mouth, laden with baskets full of meat, which had been provided and sent thither by the King's orders upon the first intelligence he received of me. I observed there was the flesh of several animals, but could not distinguish them by the taste. There were shoulders, legs, and loins shaped like those of mutton, and very well dressed, but smaller than the wings of a lark. I eat them by two or three at a mouthful; and took three loaves at a time, about the bigness of musket bullets. They supplied me as fast as they could, showing a thousand marks of wonder and astonishment at my bulk and appetite. . . .

I took up the two officers in my hands, put them first into my coat pockets, and then into every other pocket about me, except my two fobs,[4] and another secret pocket which I had no mind should be searched, wherein I had some little necessaries of no consequence to any but myself. In one of my fobs there was a silver watch, and in the other a small quantity of gold in a purse. These gentlemen, having pen, ink, and paper about them, made an exact inventory of every thing they saw; and when they had done, desired I would set them down, that they might deliver it to the Emperor. This inventory I afterwards translated into English, and is word for word as follows.

Imprimis.[5] In the right coat pocket of the *Great Man-Mountain* (for so I interpret the words *Quinbus Flestrin*) after the strictest search, we found only one great piece of coarse cloth, large enough to be a footcloth[6]

for your Majesty's chief room of state. In the left pocket, we saw a huge silver chest, with a cover of the same metal, which we, the searchers, were not able to lift. We desired it should be opened; and one of us stepping into it, found himself up to the mid-leg in a sort of dust, some part whereof flying up to our faces set us both a-sneezing for several times together. In his right waistcoat[7] pocket, we found a prodigious bundle of white thin substances, folded one over another, about the bigness of three men, tied with a strong cable, and marked with black figures, which we humbly conceive to be writings, every letter almost half as large as the palm of our hands. In the left, there was a sort of engine,[8] from the back of which were extended twenty long poles, resembling the pallisado's[9] before your Majesty's court, wherewith we conjecture the Man-Mountain combs his head, for we did not always trouble him with questions, because we found it a great difficulty to make him understand us. In the large pocket on the right side of his middle cover (so I translate the word *ranfu-lo,* by which they meant my breeches), we saw a hollow pillar of iron, about the length of a man, fastened to a strong piece of timber, larger than the pillar; and upon one side of the pillar were huge pieces of iron sticking out, cut into strange figures, which we know not what to make of. In the left pocket, another engine of the same kind. In the smaller pocket on the right side were several round flat pieces of white and red metal, of different bulk: some of the white, which seemed to be silver, were so large and heavy that my comrade and I could hardly lift them. In the left pocket were two black pillars irregularly shaped: we could not, without difficulty, reach the top of them as we stood at the bottom of his pocket. One of them was covered, and seemed all of a piece; but at the upper end of the other, there appeared a white round substance, about twice the bigness of our heads.

---

4. **fobs:** small pockets for watches.
5. *Imprimis* [im pri′mis]: in the first place.
6. **footcloth:** rug.

7. **waistcoat** [wes′kət]: vest.
8. **engine:** device.
9. **pallisado's** [pal′sa′doz]: fence poles.

Within each of these was enclosed a prodigious plate of steel, which, by our orders, we obliged him to show us, because we apprehended they might be dangerous engines. He took them out of their cases, and told us that in his own country his practice was to shave his beard with one of these and to cut his meat with the other. There were two pockets which we could not enter: these he called his fobs; they were two large slits cut into the top of his middle cover, but squeezed close by the pressure of his belly. Out of the right fob hung a great silver chain, with a wonderful kind of engine at the bottom. We directed him to draw out whatever was at the end of that chain, which appeared to be a globe, half silver, and half of some transparent metal; for on the transparent side we saw certain strange figures circularly drawn, and thought we could touch them, until we found our fingers stopped with that lucid substance. He put this engine to our ears, which made an incessant noise like that of a water mill. And we conjecture it is either some unknown animal, or the god that he worships; but we are more inclined to the latter opinion, because he assured us (if we understood him right, for he expressed himself very imperfectly) that he seldom did any thing without consulting it. He called it his oracle,[10] and said it pointed out the time for every action of his life. From the left fob he took out a net almost large enough for a fisherman, but contrived to open and shut like a purse, and served him for the same use: we found therein several massy pieces of yellow metal, which if they be of real gold, must be of immense value.

Having thus, in obedience to your Majesty's commands, diligently searched all his pockets, we observed a girdle[11] about his waist made of the hide of some prodigious animal, from which, on the left side, hung a sword of the length of five men and on the right, a bag or pouch divided into two cells, each cell capable of holding three of your Majesty's subjects. In one of these cells were several globes or balls of a most ponderous metal, about the bigness of our heads, and required a strong hand to lift them: the other cell contained a heap of certain black grains, but of no great bulk or weight, for we could hold about fifty of them in the palms of our hands.

This is an exact inventory of what we found about the body of the Man-Mountain, who used us with great civility and due respect to your Majesty's commission. Signed and sealed on the fourth day of the eighty-ninth moon of your Majesty's auspicious reign. . . .

I had sent so many memorials and petitions for my liberty that his Majesty at length mentioned the matter first in the cabinet, and then in a full council. . . .

Because the reader may perhaps be curious to have some idea of the style and manner of expression peculiar to that people, as well as to know the articles upon which I recovered my liberty, I have made a translation of the whole instrument, word for word, as near as I was able, which I here offer to the public.

GOLBASTO MOMAREN EVLAME GURDILO SHEFIN MULLY ULLY GUE, most mighty Emperor of Lilliput, delight and terror of the universe, whose dominions extend five thousand *blustrugs* (about twelve miles in circumference), to the extremities of the globe; monarch of all monarchs, taller than the sons of men; whose feet press down to the center, and whose head strikes against the sun; at whose nod the princes of the earth shake their knees; pleasant as the spring, comfortable as the summer, fruitful as autumn, dreadful as winter. His most sublime Majesty proposeth to the Man-Mountain, lately arrived at our celestial dominions, the following articles, which by a solemn oath he shall be obliged to perform.

First, The Man-Mountain shall not depart from our dominions, without our license under our great seal.

Secondly, he shall not presume to come into our metropolis, without our express order; at which time, the inhabitants shall have two

---

10. **oracle:** prophet; infallible guide.
11. **girdle:** belt.

hours warning, to keep within their doors.

Thirdly, The said Man-Mountain shall confine his walks to our principal high roads; and not offer to walk or lie down in a meadow, or field of corn.

Fourthly, As he walks the said roads, he shall take the utmost care not to trample upon the bodies of any of our loving subjects, their horses, or carriages; nor take any of our said subjects into his hands, without their own consent.

Fifthly, If an express require extraordinary dispatch, the Man-Mountain shall be obliged to carry in his pocket the messenger and horse, a six days journey once in every moon, and return the said messenger back (if so required) safe to our Imperial Presence.

Sixthly, He shall be our ally against our enemies in the island of *Blefuscu,* and do his utmost to destroy their fleet, which is now preparing to invade us.

Seventhly, That the said Man-Mountain shall, at his times of leisure, be aiding and assisting to our workmen, in helping to raise certain great stones, towards covering the wall of the principal park and other our royal buildings.

Eighthly, That the said Man-Mountain shall, in two moons time, deliver in an exact survey of the circumference of our dominions, by a computation of his own paces round the coast.

Lastly, That upon his solemn oath to observe all the above articles, the said Man-Mountain shall have a daily allowance of meat and drink, sufficient for the support of 1728 of our subjects, with free access to our Royal Person, and other marks of our favor. Given at our Palace at Belfaborac the twelfth day of the ninety-first moon of our reign.

I swore and subscribed to these articles with great cheerfulness and content, although some of them were not so honorable as I could have wished. . . .

Gulliver's second voyage takes him to the island of Brobdingnag [brob′ding nag′], somewhere in the Pacific Ocean in the vicinity of *Alaska. In this adventure the tables are turned, for the Brobdingnagians [brob′ding nag′e ənz] are twelve times as tall as Gulliver. Eventually Gulliver finds himself in the court of the king and queen of Brobdingnag, learning the ways of another strange and remote society.*

A Voyage to Brobdingnag

Every Wednesday (which, as I have before observed, was their Sabbath), the King and Queen, with the royal issue of both sexes, dine together in the apartment of his Majesty; to whom I was now become a favorite; and at these times my little chair and table were placed at his left hand before one of the saltcellars. This prince took a pleasure in conversing with me, inquiring into the manners, religion, laws, government, and learning of Europe, wherein I gave him the best account I was able. His apprehension was so clear, and his judgment so exact, that he made very wise reflections and observations upon all I said. But, I confess, that after I had been a little too copious in talking of my own beloved country; of our trade, and wars by sea and land, of our schisms in religion, and parties in the state; the prejudices of his education prevailed so far, that he could not forbear taking me up in his right hand, and stroking me gently with the other; after a hearty fit of laughing, asked me whether I were a Whig or a Tory.[12] Then turning to his first minister, who waited behind him with a white staff, near as tall as the mainmast of the Royal *Sovereign,* he observed how contemptible a thing was human grandeur, which could be mimicked by such diminutive insects as I. "And yet," said he, "I dare engage, those creatures have their titles and distinctions of honor; they contrive little nests and burrows, that they call houses and cities; they make a figure in dress and equipage;[13] they

---

12. **Whig . . . Tory:** the two principal British political parties.
13. **equipage** [ek′wə pij]: horses and carriages.

love, they fight, they dispute, they cheat, they betray." And thus he continued on, while my color came and went several times, with indignation to hear our noble country, the mistress of arts and arms, the scourge of France, the arbitress of Europe, the seat of virtue, piety, honor and truth, the pride and envy of the world, so contemptuously treated. . . .

I one day took the freedom to tell his Majesty that the contempt he discovered towards Europe, and the rest of the world, did not seem answerable to those excellent qualities of mind that he was master of, that, reason did not extend itself with the bulk of the body. On the contrary, we observed in our country that the tallest persons were usually least provided with it. That among other animals, bees and ants had the reputation of more industry, art, and sagacity than many of the larger kinds. And that, as inconsiderable as he took me to be, I hoped I might live to do his Majesty some signal service. The King heard me with attention, and began to conceive a much better opinion of me than he had ever before. He desired I would give him as exact an account of the government of England as I possibly could, because, as fond as princes commonly are of their own customs (for so he conjectured of other monarchs by my former discourses), he should be glad to hear of any thing that might deserve imitation.

Imagine with thy self, courteous reader, how often I then wished for the tongue of Demosthenes or Cicero,[14] that might have enabled me to celebrate the praise of my own dear native country in a style equal to its merits and felicity. . . .

This conversation was not ended under five audiences, each of several hours, and the King heard the whole with great attention, frequently taking notes of what I spoke, as well as memorandums of what questions he intended to ask me.

When I had put an end to these long discourses, his Majesty in a sixth audience, consulting his notes, proposed many doubts, queries, and objections, upon every article. He asked what methods were used to cultivate the minds and bodies of our young nobility, and in what kind of business they commonly spent the first and teachable part of their lives. What course was taken to supply that assembly, when any noble family became extinct. What qualifications were necessary in those who are to be created new lords:[15] whether the humor of the prince, a sum of money to a court lady or a prime minister, or a design of strengthening a party opposite to the public interest ever happened to be motives in those advancements. What share of knowledge these lords had in the laws of their country, and how they came by it, so as to enable them to decide the properties of their fellow subjects in the last resort. Whether they were always so free from avarice, partialities, or want that a bribe, or some other sinister view, could have no place among them. Whether those holy lords I spoke of were constantly promoted to that rank upon account of their knowledge in religious matters, and the sanctity of their lives; had never been compliers with the times, while they were common priests; or slavish chaplains to some nobleman, whose opinions they continued servilely to follow after they were admitted into that assembly.

He then desired to know what arts were practiced in electing those whom I called commoners.[16] Whether a stranger with a strong purse[17] might not influence the vulgar voters to choose him before their own landlords or the most considerable gentleman in the neighborhood. How it came to pass that people were so violently bent upon getting into this assembly, which I allowed to be a great trouble and expense, often to the ruin of their fam-

---

14. **Demosthenes** [də mos′thə nēz′] . . . **Cicero** [sis′ə ro′]: ancient Greek orator (384?–322 B.C.) and Roman orator (106–43 B.C.), respectively.

15. **lords:** English nobles and high-ranking clergy who comprised the upper branch of Parliament, the House of Lords.
16. **commoners:** elected representatives who comprise the lower branch of Parliament.
17. **a strong purse:** much money.

ilies, without any salary or pension: because this appeared such an exalted strain of virtue and public spirit that his Majesty seemed to doubt it might possibly not be always sincere. And he desired to know whether such zealous gentlemen could have any views of refunding themselves for the charges and trouble they were at, by sacrificing the public good to the designs of a weak and vicious prince, in conjunction with a corrupted ministry. He multiplied his questions, and sifted me thoroughly upon every part of this head; proposing numberless inquiries and objections, which I think it not prudent or convenient to repeat.

Upon what I said in relation to our courts of justice, his Majesty desired to be satisfied in several points. And this I was the better able to do, having been formerly almost ruined by a long suit in chancery,[18] which was decreed for me with costs. He asked what time was usually spent in determining between right and wrong; and what degree of expense. Whether advocates and orators had liberty to plead in causes manifestly known to be unjust, vexatious, or oppressive. Whether party in religion or politics were observed to be of any weight in the scale of justice. Whether those pleading orators were persons educated in the general knowledge of equity; or only in provincial, national, and other local customs. Whether they or their judges had any part in penning those laws, which they assumed the liberty of interpreting and glossing[19] upon at their pleasure. Whether they had ever at different times pleaded for and against the same cause, and cited precedents to prove contrary opinions. Whether they were a rich or a poor corporation. Whether they received any pecuniary reward for pleading or delivering their opinions. And particularly whether they were ever admitted as members in the lower senate.[20]

He fell next upon the management of our

---

18. **chancery:** British court that handles equity and common-law cases. Gulliver won his suit but lost all his money in paying the lawyers.
19. **glossing:** commenting.
20. **senate:** here, house of Parliament, referring to the House of Commons.

treasury, and said he thought my memory had failed me, because I computed our taxes at about five or six million a year; and when I came to mention the issues, he found they sometimes amounted to more than double; for, the notes he had taken were very particular in this point; because he hoped, as he told me, that the knowledge of our conduct might be useful to him; and he could not be deceived in his calculations. But, if what I told him were true, he was still at a loss how a kingdom could run out of its estate like a private person. He asked me who were our creditors and where we found money to pay them. He wondered to hear me talk of such chargeable and extensive wars; that, certainly we must be a quarrelsome people, or live among very bad neighbors; and that our generals must needs be richer than our kings. He asked what business we had out of our own islands, unless upon the score of trade or treaty, or to defend the coasts with our fleet. Above all, he was amazed to hear me talk of a mercenary standing army in the midst of peace, and among a free people. He said if we were governed by our own consent in the persons of our representatives, he could not imagine of whom we were afraid, or against whom we were to fight, and would hear my opinion, whether a private man's house might not better be defended by himself, his children, and family than by half a dozen rascals picked up at a venture in the streets, for small wages, who might get a hundred times more by cutting their throats.

He laughed at my odd kind of arithmetic (as he was pleased to call it) in reckoning the numbers of our people by a computation drawn from the several sects among us in religion and politics. He said he knew no reason why those who entertain opinions prejudicial to the public should be obliged to change or should not be obliged to conceal them. And, as it was tyranny in any government to require the first, so it was weakness not to enforce the second; for, a man may be allowed to keep poisons in his closet, but not to vend them about as cordials.

He observed that among the diversions of

our nobility and gentry[21] I had mentioned gaming.[22] He desired to know at what age this entertainment was usually taken up, and when it was laid down. How much of their time it employed; whether it ever went so high as to affect their fortunes. Whether mean vicious people, by their dexterity in that art, might not arrive at great riches, and sometimes keep our very nobles in dependence, as well as habituate them to vile companions; wholly take them from the improvement of their minds, and force them by the losses they received, to learn and practice that infamous dexterity upon others.

He was perfectly astonished with the historical account I gave him of our affairs during the last century, protesting it was only a heap of conspiracies, rebellions, murders, massacres, revolutions, banishments, the very worst effects that avarice, faction, hypocrisy, perfidiousness, cruelty, rage, madness, hatred, envy, lust, malice, and ambition could produce.

His Majesty in another audience was at the pains to recapitulate the sum of all I had spoken; compared the questions he made with the answers I had given; then taking me into his hands, and stroking me gently, delivered himself in these words, which I shall never forget, nor the manner he spoke them in. My little friend *Grildrig,* you have made a most admirable panegyric[23] upon your country. You have clearly proved that ignorance, idleness, and vice are the proper ingredients for qualifying a legislator. That laws are best explained, interpreted, and applied by those whose interest and abilities lie in perverting, confounding, and eluding them. I observe among you some lines of an institution, which in its original might have been tolerable; but these half erased, and the rest wholly blurred and blotted by corruptions. It doth not appear from all you have said how any one perfection is required towards the procurement of any one station among you; much less that men are ennobled on account of their virtue, that priests are advanced for their piety or learning, soldiers for their conduct or valor, judges for their integrity, senators for the love of their country, or counselors for their wisdom. As for yourself (continued the King) who have spent the greatest part of your life in traveling, I am well disposed to hope you may hitherto have escaped many vices of your country. But, by what I have gathered from your own relation, and the answers I have with much pains wringed and extorted from you, I cannot but conclude the bulk of your natives to be the most pernicious race of little odious vermin that nature ever suffered to crawl upon the surface of the earth. . . .

Nothing but an extreme love of truth could have hindered me from concealing this part of my story. It was in vain to discover my resentments, which were always turned into ridicule; and I was forced to rest with patience, while my noble and most beloved country was so injuriously treated. I am heartily sorry as any of my readers can possibly be that such an occasion was given; but this prince happened to be so curious and inquisitive upon every particular that it could not consist either with gratitude or good manners to refuse giving him what satisfaction I was able. Yet thus much I may be allowed to say in my own vindication that I artfully eluded many of his questions and gave to every point a more favorable turn by many degrees than the strictness of truth would allow. For I have always born that laudable partiality to my own country, which Dionysius Halicarnassensis[24] with so much justice recommends to an historian. I would hide the frailties and deformities of my political mother, and place her virtues and beauties in the most advantageous light. This was my sincere endeavor in those many discourses I had with that mighty monarch, although it unfortunately failed of success.

---

21. **gentry:** landowners ranking just below the nobility.
22. **gaming:** gambling.
23. **panegyric** [pan'ə jir′ik]: speech of praise.

---

24. **Dionysius** [dī′ə nish′əs] **Halicarnassensis**
[hal′ə kär na sen′sis]: Greek writer who lived in Rome and tried to persuade the conquered Greeks to submit to the Romans. Swift is being ironic.

STUDY QUESTIONS

Recalling

1. Why do the Lilliputians stop attacking Gulliver?
2. What does Gulliver convince the Lilliputians that he needs? How does he make his wishes clear?
3. What two things do the Lilliputians think Gulliver's watch might be? Why do they think it might be the latter?
4. Name four services that the "Man-Mountain" agrees to provide for the Lilliputians in exchange for his liberty.
5. Why does the king of Brobdingnag ask Gulliver to give an exact account of the government of England? What does Gulliver say the king did as he listened to the account?
6. List five topics that the king questions in the sixth audience with Gulliver.
7. In the second-to-last paragraph, what conclusion does the king draw about the rest of Gulliver's race?

Interpreting

8. What aspects of human nature does Swift seem to be satirizing through Gulliver's huge size in Lilliput? Why is this contrast effective?
9. Reread the final paragraph of "A Voyage to Brobdingnag." How does Gulliver's statement that he gave "every point a more favorable turn by many degrees" affect your opinion of the king and of Gulliver?

Extending

10. Do you think Swift's technique of ridicule is more or less effective than simple, direct criticism? Why?

VIEWPOINT

The late renowned scholar Samuel Holt Monk reminds us that Gulliver

is *not* Jonathan Swift. . . . He is a fully rendered, objective, dramatic character.

Monk goes on to suggest not only that Swift's and Gulliver's perspectives are different but that Swift created a character who is far from the perfect hero.

■ In what ways is Gulliver a dramatic fictional character? In what ways is he a less than perfect hero?

LITERARY FOCUS

Satire

A **satire** exposes the vices and follies of individuals or societies in such a way that they appear ridiculous. Satire ranges from gentle mockery to violent condemnation. It may take any literary shape—poetry, drama, novel, or essay. Whatever the form, the satirist's intent is always to set a moral standard for society and, through the use of humor and wit, to inspire readers to see a particular point of view. As Swift wrote of himself, "His satire points at no defect, / But what all mortals may correct."

Thinking About Satire

■ What are some elements of society that Swift exposes as ridiculous in *Gulliver's Travels*? Is the satire "gentle" or "violent"?

VOCABULARY

Synonyms

A **synonym** is a word that has the same or nearly the same meaning as another word. For example, *love* and *adore* are synonyms. The words in capital letters come from *Gulliver's Travels*. Choose the word that is *nearest* the meaning of the word in capitals, *as the word is used in the selection.*

1. PRODIGIOUS: (a) expensive (b) enormous (c) glorious (d) profound
2. CONJECTURE: (a) guess (b) scribble (c) explore (d) devise
3. CONTRIVE: (a) decorate (b) conceal (c) explore (d) devise
4. SAGACITY: (a) cleverness (b) wisdom (c) talent (d) power
5. FELICITY: (a) pride (b) wealth (c) happiness (d) consistency
6. SANCTITY: (a) sanity (b) cleanliness (c) poverty (d) holiness
7. VEXATIOUS: (a) annoying (b) delirious (c) detrimental (d) lethal
8. PERFIDIOUSNESS: (a) discomfort (b) treachery (c) persuasiveness (d) evil
9. PERNICIOUS: (a) destructive (b) tasteless (c) ill-mannered (d) stingy
10. ODIOUS: (a) condescending (b) loathsome (c) ugly (d) putrid

Joseph Addison.

Richard Steele.

Joseph Addison   *1672–1719*
Richard Steele   *1672–1729*

One of the most famous literary collaborations of all time was that of Joseph Addison and Richard Steele. Their friendship began when they were classmates at the Charterhouse School in London, and it continued through their years at Oxford University. After receiving their degrees, the two went their separate ways for a time. Steele headed straight for London, where he captured much notoriety for his charm and gallantry. He was an officer in the army; the editor of the *London Gazette,* an official newspaper of the Whig party; a member of Parliament; and a theater manager. Addison became known as an excellent Latin scholar, and his long poem *The Campaign* (1704) won him considerable fame. From 1704 to 1710, he served in a variety of government positions.

The two men had very different personalities. Addison was a man of vast learning, serious, prudent, and, although charming with his close friends, reserved in public. His writing is considered to have the better style of the pair. Steele, on the other hand, was buoyant and witty, playful, energetic, and a bit irresponsible; his writing is more creative and inventive than Addison's. The two balanced each other and worked well together, for they shared the same values. Their mutual goal was to improve the manners, morals, and minds of their readers. In 1709 Steele began to publish *The Tatler,* a periodical focusing on news, poetry, learning, philosophy, and general London gossip, and he asked his friend Joseph Addison to contribute notes and articles. Through their short essays the two attempted to reform the manners of the age, refine its tastes, and provide topics of discussion at the popular coffee houses of London. *The Tatler* was discontinued in 1711 for political reasons, but Addison and Steele quickly started a new journal, *The Spectator,* which was issued daily except Sundays from 1711 to 1712.

The Spectator was to be nonpolitical and was to "bring philosophy out of the closets and libraries, schools and colleges, to dwell in the clubs and assemblies, at tea-tables and in coffee-houses." The essays that Addison and Steele wrote were of two types: serious essays on such well-known topics as marriage, education, and friendship; and "occasional essays" that, according to Addison, dealt with "the folly, extravagance, and caprice of the present age." Their venture was highly successful.

Despite their success, Addison and Steele again went their separate ways in 1712. The two unfortunately quarreled over a political matter in 1717, and Addison died in 1719. Nonetheless, their friendship resulted in a great literary achievement, the creation of the periodical essay.

Steele's vibrant personality made him uniquely suited for involvement in the theater. His gifts to the London stage, as playwright, critic, and theater manager, were rewarded as Steele quickly became a favorite among the best London actors of his day. His devotion to the stage, however, was not simply that of a playful and affectionate man; it also involved a more serious approach that is often reflected in his writing. Steele was one of the foremost practitioners of "sensibility," a literary manner that reveals a sympathetic heart and a quickness to respond to the joys and sorrows of others. Although it is most often used in comedy, Steele maintains the values of sensibility in his more serious philosophical essays. The following essay from *The Tatler* discusses the death of Thomas Betterton, the famous Shakespearean actor of the early eighteenth century.

Richard Steele

from **The Tatler**

The Funeral of Thomas Betterton

Having received notice that the famous actor Mr. Betterton was to be interred this evening in the cloisters[1] near Westminster Abbey,[2] I was resolved to walk thither, and see the last office done to a man whom I had always very much admired, and from whose action I had received more strong impressions of what is great and noble in human nature than from the arguments of the most solid philosophers, or the descriptions of the most charming poets I had ever read. As the rude and untaught multitude are no way wrought upon more effectually than by seeing public punishments and executions, so men of letters and education feel their humanity most forcibly exercised when they attend the obsequies of men who had arrived at any perfection in liberal accomplishments. Theatrical action is to be esteemed as such, except it be objected that we cannot call that an art which cannot be attained by art. Voice, stature, motion, and other gifts must be very bountifully bestowed by nature, or labor and industry will but push the unhappy endeavorer, in that way, the further off his wishes.

Such an actor as Mr. Betterton ought to be recorded with the same respect as Roscius[3] among the Romans. The greatest orator[4] has thought fit to quote his judgment, and celebrate his life. Roscius was the example to all that would form themselves into proper and winning behavior. His action was so well adapted to the sentiments he expressed that the youth of Rome thought they wanted only to be virtuous to be as graceful in their appearance as Roscius. The imagination took a

1. **cloisters:** covered walk.
2. **Westminster Abbey:** great gothic cathedral in London where many distinguished citizens are buried.

3. **Roscius** [rō′shəs]: greatest Roman actor of his day (126–62 B.C.).
4. **greatest orator:** Cicero, sometimes called Tully (106–43 B.C.), Roman speaker and writer.

lovely impression of what was great and good; and they who never thought of setting up for the art of imitation became themselves imitable characters.

There is no human invention so aptly calculated for the forming of a free-born people as that of a theater. Tully reports that the celebrated player of whom I am speaking used frequently to say, "The perfection of an actor is only to become what he is doing." Young men, who are too unattentive to receive lectures, are irresistibly taken with performances. Hence it is that I extremely lament the little relish the gentry of this nation have at present for the just and noble representations in some of our tragedies. The operas, which are of late introduced, can leave no trace behind them that can be of service beyond the present moment. To sing and to dance are accomplishments very few have any thoughts of practicing; but to speak justly, and move gracefully, is what every man thinks he does perform, or wishes he did.

I have hardly a notion that any performer of antiquity could surpass the action of Mr. Betterton in any of the occasions in which he has appeared on our stage. The wonderful agony which he appeared in, when he examined the circumstance of the handkerchief in *Othello;*[5] the mixture of love that intruded upon his mind upon the innocent answers Desdemona makes, betrayed in his gesture such a variety and vicissitude of passions as would admonish a man to be afraid of his own heart, and perfectly convince him that it is to stab it, to admit that worst of daggers, jealousy. Whoever reads in his closet this admirable scene will find that he cannot, except he has as warm an imagination as Shakespeare himself, find any but dry, incoherent, and broken sentences; but a reader that has seen Betterton act it observes there could not be a word added;

that longer speeches had been unnatural, nay impossible, in Othello's circumstances. The charming passage in the same tragedy, where he tells the manner of winning the affection of his mistress, was urged with so moving and graceful an energy that while I walked in the cloisters, I thought of him with the same concern as if I waited for the remains of a person who had in real life done all that I had seen him represent. The gloom of the place, and faint lights before the ceremony appeared, contributed to the melancholy disposition I was in; and I began to be extremely afflicted that Brutus and Cassius[6] had any difference; that Hotspur's[7] gallantry was so unfortunate; and that the mirth and good humor of Falstaff[8] could not exempt him from the grave. Nay, this occasion in me, who look upon the distinctions amongst men to be merely scenical, raised reflections upon the emptiness of all human perfection and greatness in general; and I could not but regret that the sacred heads which lie buried in the neighborhood of this little portion of earth in which my poor old friend is deposited are returned to dust as well as he, and that there is no difference in the grave between the imaginary and the real monarch. This made me say of human life itself with *Macbeth:*

Tomorrow, tomorrow, and tomorrow,
Creeps in a stealing pace from day to day,
To the last moment of recorded time!
And all our yesterdays have lighted fools
To their eternal night! Out, out short candle
Life's but a walking shadow, a poor player
That struts and frets his hour upon the stage,
And then is heard no more.[9]

---

5. **handkerchief in *Othello*:** Shakespeare's Othello demanded to see the handkerchief he had given to his wife, Desdemona, believing she had given it to another man and was thus unfaithful to him.

6. **Brutus . . . Cassius:** In Shakespeare's *Julius Caesar,* the co-conspirators quarrel after Caesar's death.
7. **Hotspur:** Sir Henry Percy in Shakespeare's *Henry IV* insisted on facing young Prince Hal alone in battle and died in the combat.
8. **Falstaff:** Sir John Falstaff, the lovable old coward in Shakespeare's *Henry IV* and *Henry V.*
9. **Tomorrow . . . heard no more:** Steele quotes, not completely accurately, from an early and somewhat different edition of *Macbeth.*

The famous eighteenth-century critic Samuel Johnson (page 289) recommended that "whoever wishes to attain an English style, familiar but not coarse, and elegant but not ostentatious, must give his days and nights to the volumes of Addison." Addison perfected his famous style in the person of the Spectator, a fictional character whose observations of London life were recorded in *The Spectator*. He is learned, thoughtful, and serious yet has a good sense of humor. In their journal *The Spectator,* Addison and Steele printed many letters in response to the Spectator's essays, some of which were real, but most of which were invented by Addison himself. By printing these fictional letters, Addison could create a dialogue between the Spectator and his supposed readers. The following letter from Ralph Crotchet gives an excellent example of Addison's ironic yet acute observations of London life and the character of his fellow human beings.

Model for Active Reading

In this selection, as in one selection in each unit, you will find notes in the right-hand margin that highlight parts of the selection. Those notes point out important ideas of the literary period and draw your attention to literary elements and techniques covered in the Literary Focuses. Page numbers in the notes will refer you to more extensive discussions of these important ideas and elements.

Joseph Addison

from The Spectator

The Cries of London

There is nothing which more astonishes a foreigner, and frights a country squire,[1] than the cries of London. My good friend Sir Roger often declares that he cannot get them out of his head, or go to sleep for them, the first week that he is in town. On the contrary, Will Honeycomb[2] calls them the *ramage de la ville,*[3] and prefers them to the sounds of larks and nightingales, with all the music of the fields and woods. I have lately received a letter from some very odd fellow upon this subject, which I shall leave with my reader, without saying anything further of it.

> **Informal essay** (p. 275): The personal nature and rambling structure of an informal essay allow its author to introduce fictional characters and even a letter in its midst.

---

1. **country squire:** gentleman landowner in the country.
2. **Sir Roger . . . Will Honeycomb:** fictional friends of the Spectator.
3. *ramage de la ville* [rä mäzh′də lä vēl′]: French for "chirping of the town."

.r,—

I am a man of all business, and would willingly turn my head to anything for an honest livelihood. I have invented several projects for raising many millions of money without burthening[4] the subject, but I cannot get the Parliament to listen to me, who look upon me, forsooth, as a crack and a projector;[5] so that despairing to enrich either myself or my country by this public spiritedness, I would make some proposals to you relating to a design which I have very much at heart, and which may procure me a handsome subsistence, if you will be pleased to recommend it to the cities of London and Westminster.[6]

The post I would aim at is to be Comptroller General of the London Cries, which are at present under no manner of rules or discipline. I think I am pretty well qualified for this place, as being a man of very strong lungs, of great insight into all the branches of our British trades and manufactures, and of a competent skill in music.

The cries of London may be divided into vocal and instrumental. As for the latter, they are at present under a very great disorder. A freeman[7] of London has the privilege of disturbing a whole street for an hour together, with the twanking of a brass kettle or a frying pan. The watchman's thump at midnight startles us in our beds, as much as the breaking in of a thief. The sowgelder's[8] horn has indeed something musical in it, but this is seldom heard within the liberties. I would therefore propose, that no instrument of this nature should be made use of, which I have not tuned and licensed, after having carefully examined in what manner it may affect the ears of her Majesty's liege subjects.

Vocal cries are of a much larger extent, and, indeed, so full of incongruities and barbarisms, that we appear a distracted city to foreigners, who do not comprehend the meaning of such enormous outcries. Milk is generally sold in a note above *cla*,[9] and in sounds so exceeding shrill, that it often sets our teeth on edge. The chimney sweeper is confined to no certain pitch; he sometimes utters himself in the deepest bass, and sometimes in the sharpest treble, sometimes in the highest, and sometimes in the lowest note of the gamut.[10] The same observation might be made on the retailers of small coal, not to mention broken glasses or brick dust. In these, therefore, and the like cases, it should be my care to sweeten and mellow the voices of these itinerant tradesmen, before they make

Eighteenth-century idea: Classifying things into categories is common in Neoclassical literature (p. 254), for the practice follows the scientific method of Aristotle, the Greek philosopher. Here, of course, the categories are not very philosophical or scientific.

Eighteenth-century idea: The urbane eighteenth-century writer displays his wit, or cleverness (p. 254).

---

4. **burthening:** burdening.
5. **projector:** one who invents outrageous business schemes.
6. **Westminster:** a borough of London.
7. **freeman:** merchant.
8. **sowgelder:** one who neuters pigs.
9. ***cla:*** the highest note in the musical register.
10. **gamut:** the whole series of notes used by musicians.

Cries of London, "Green-Vegetable Seller" (left) and "Shrimp Girl" (right), P. Sandby (1725–1809).

their appearance in our streets, as also to accommodate their cries to their respective wares; and to take care in particular that those may not make the most noise who have the least to sell, which is very observable in the venders of card matches, to whom I cannot but apply that old proverb of "Much cry, but little wool."

Some of these last mentioned musicians are so very loud in the sale of these trifling manufactures, that an honest splenetic[11] gentleman of my acquaintance bargained with one of them never to come into the street where he lived. But what was the effect of this contract? Why, the whole tribe of card matchmakers which frequent that quarter passed by his door the very next day, in hopes of being bought off after the same manner.

It is another great imperfection in our London cries, that there is no just time nor measure observed in them. Our news should, indeed, be published in a very quick time, because it is a commodity that will not keep cold. It should not, however, be cried with the same precipitation as fire: yet this is generally the case. A bloody battle alarms the town from one end to another in an instant. Every motion of the French is published in so great a hurry, that one would think the enemy were at our gates.[12] This likewise I would take upon me to regulate in such a manner, that there should be some distinction made between the spreading of a victory, a march, or an encampment, a Dutch, a Portugal, or a Spanish mail.[13] Nor must I omit, under this head, those excessive alarms with which several boisterous rustics infest our streets in turnip season; and which are more inexcusable, because these are wares which are in no danger of cooling upon their hands.

There are others who affect a very slow time, and are, in my opinion, much more tunable than the former; the cooper,[14] in particular, swells his last note in a hollow voice, that is not without its harmony; nor can I forbear being inspired with a most agreeable melancholy, when I hear that sad and solemn air with which the

Verbal irony (p. 189): The contrast between what is stated ("musicians") and what is meant (quite the reverse) is an example of verbal irony, a common tool of the eighteenth-century wit.

---

11. **splenetic:** afflicted with low spirits.
12. **Every motion . . . gates:** England and France had been at war, although peace negotiations were in progress.
13. **Dutch . . . mail:** Mail coaches brought letters and news from abroad.
14. **cooper:** one who makes wooden containers, barrels.

_e_ are very often asked if they have any chairs to mend. Your _a_ memory may suggest to you many other lamentable ditties of _e_ same nature, in which the music is wonderfully languishing and melodious.

I am always pleased with that particular time of the year which is proper for the pickling of dill and cucumbers; but, alas, this cry, like the song of the nightingale, is not heard above two months. It would therefore be worthwhile to consider whether the same air might not in some cases be adapted to other words.

It might likewise deserve our most serious consideration, how far, in a well-regulated city, those humorists are to be tolerated, who, not contented with the traditional cries of their forefathers, have invented particular songs and tunes of their own; such as was, not many years since, the pastry man, commonly known by the name of the colly-molly-puff; and such as is at this day the vender of powder and washballs,[15] who, if I am rightly informed, goes under the name of Powder Watt.

Simile (p. 104): The farfetched comparison between the cry of the pickler and the song of the nightingale adds to the wit of the piece.

I must not here omit one particular absurdity which runs through this whole vociferous generation, and which renders their cries very often not only incommodious, but altogether useless to the public; I mean that idle accomplishment, which they all of them aim at, of crying so as not to be understood. Whether or no they have learned this from several of our affected singers, I will not take upon me to say; but most certain it is, that people know the wares they deal in rather by their tunes than by their words; insomuch, that I have sometimes seen a country boy run out to buy apples of a bellows-mender, and gingerbread from a grinder of knives and scissors. Nay, so strangely infatuated are some very eminent artists of this particular grace in a cry, that none but their acquaintance are able to guess at their profession; for who else can know that "Work if I had it" should be the signification of a corn-cutter?

Forasmuch therefore, as persons of this rank are seldom men of genius or capacity, I think it would be very proper, that some man of good sense and sound judgment should preside over these public cries, who should permit none to lift up their voices in our streets, that have not tunable throats, and are not only able to overcome the noise of the crowd, and the rattling of coaches, but also to vend their respective merchandises in apt phrases, and in the most distinct and agreeable sounds. I do therefore humbly recommend myself as a person rightly qualified for this post; and if I meet with fitting encouragement, shall communicate some other projects which I have by me, that may no less conduce to the emolument of the public.

I am, Sir, etc.

Ralph Crotchet

Satire (p. 267): The entire essay ridicules the abundance of cries on London's streets, though the satire here is mild rather than bitter.

---

15. **powder and washballs:** talcum powder and soap.

STUDY QUESTIONS

The Funeral of Thomas Betterton

Recalling

1. At the beginning of his essay, what does Steele say he has learned from Betterton's acting?
2. In the third paragraph how does Steele say the theater helps to form "a free-born people"? What advantages do the theater's tragedies have over the opera's?

Interpreting

3. Express in your own words Steele's final reflections on Betterton's death at the end of the last paragraph.
4. Why is the quotation from *Macbeth* an appropriate ending for this essay?

Extending

5. Do you agree with Steele's observations about the influence of actors on the general public? Why or why not?

The Cries of London

Recalling

1. According to the first paragraph of Addison's essay, what is the subject of Crotchet's letter?
2. What post does Crotchet propose for himself? What are his three qualifications for this post?
3. In the fourth and fifth paragraphs what duties does he propose for himself with regard to "instrumental cries" and "vocal cries," respectively?
4. List four of Crotchet's complaints about the cries of London.
5. At the end of his letter, what does Crotchet say he will do if he is considered rightly qualified for the post?

Interpreting

6. How would you characterize the tone of Crotchet's letter?
7. How do you think the Spectator views Crotchet's proposals? What evidence do you find in the selection to support this opinion?
8. What is *your* opinion of Crotchet?

Extending

9. In what ways do modern city street sounds differ from those of eighteenth-century London?

LITERARY FOCUS

The Essay

An **essay** is generally a short prose composition that discusses a single subject. First used by the French writer Michel de Montaigne, the word comes from the French *essai,* meaning "attempt," and is an apt description of the loose and highly personal thoughts Montaigne recorded. Francis Bacon (page 190) wrote more structured, philosophical discourses. He was the first Englishman to introduce the term *essay* and the first English essayist.

The difference between Montaigne's and Bacon's essays reveals the range and flexibility of the form and points to a standard distinction often made between essay styles. Bacon's type of essay, the **formal essay,** often argues a single point of view in an impersonal, structured, and logical way and usually uses highly serious language. Montaigne's type of essay, the **informal essay,** is more free-form and rambling and is usually highly personal. An informal essay sometimes employs character and description and often uses a fluid, colloquial, and even humorous language.

Thinking About the Essay

■ What qualities make Steele's essay "The Funeral of Thomas Betterton" formal or informal? Support your answer with specific examples from the essay.

COMPOSITION

Writing About Nonfiction

■ In a brief composition on either "The Funeral of Sir Thomas Betterton" or "The Cries of London," state the author's purpose in writing. Then cite with examples the particular techniques that the author uses, such as facts, statistics, examples, and opinion, to accomplish the purpose of the essay. *For help with this assignment, refer to Lesson 4 in the Writing About Literature Handbook at the back of this book.*

Writing an Informal Essay

■ Write either a brief descriptive essay (like Addison's) or a brief meditative essay (like Steele's) in which you try to convey the feeling of a place or person. The essay should be free form, in fluid or even humorous language.

Alexander Pope   *1688–1744*

In an age of satire, Alexander Pope was the greatest verse satirist. His achievements are especially notable in light of the hardships he had to overcome. Born a Catholic, he was therefore barred from attending a university or receiving a government post, the source of income on which many writers of the day depended. In addition, he had contracted tuberculosis of the spine in childhood and was permanently crippled, never growing beyond four feet six inches tall and suffering from severe pain throughout his life.

Pope recognized his own limitations, and from an early age he labored to overcome them. He began by giving himself the strict classical education that most other young men received at school, and at the age of twenty-one he published a group of pastoral, or nature, poems. Almost immediately he was hailed as a literary prodigy and brought into a tight London literary circle that included Swift, Addison, Steele, and the poets John Gay and John Arbuthnot. His *Essay on Criticism* (1711) impressed Londoners with its evidence of learning and good judgment, and by the age of twenty-five Pope was acknowledged England's greatest living poet. By 1718 he was the first English author to support himself solely by his writings.

Pope's poems rapidly developed from the gentle lyrics of his earlier years into biting satires of English society and politics. Like his friend Jonathan Swift, he saw the age as one badly in need of the correction that satire could offer. Unfortunately, his satires gained him many enemies, who brutally attacked not only his poetry but also his religion and his physical deformities. When he was not busy writing poems and cultivating the magnificent garden at his estate at Twickenham [twit′nam], he was busy defending himself from his enemies, who had labeled him "the wicked wasp of Twickenham," a title that unfairly portrays him as a mean-spirited man who lashed out at all around him. Fortunately, the loyalty of his friends attests to the fact that he was more gentle and generous than his critics liked to portray.

Pope believed that moral and artistic correctness went hand-in-hand and that one could best practice this correctness by following the models of the ancient Greek and Roman authors (see Part Two of this book). He felt that many of the ills of society could be cured by looking back to classical civilization. All of his poetry reflects these values, whether it be the informative *Essay on Criticism; The Dunciad,* his sparkling satire of literary pretension; or the philosophical *Essay on Man.* It is not Pope's philosophy, however, but the brilliance of his poetic art that qualifies him as one of the greatest poets in the English language. The compression of his language, its clarity, glitter, exactness, and beauty, lyrical by turns, satiric by turns—all these qualities unite to form verses that only a master craftsman could create.

Pope's *Rape of the Lock,* one of his greatest comic poems, was based on an actual event. A wealthy baron named Lord Petre had cut a lock of hair from the beautiful Arabella Fermor's head and refused to give it back. A great scandal ensued. At the urging of his friend John Caryll, to whom he addresses the poem, Pope created a miniature masterpiece of satire out of the event.

Although Pope was certainly mocking the extravagance of the drawing room society that is his subject, his careful observation of the details of that society shows that he also had an appreciation of its beauties. Belinda, the heroine of the poem, is a fully developed character, and her world, despite its frivolity, is a complete one.

Pope wrote two versions of *The Rape of the Lock.* In 1712 he published a two-canto version, a tremendously popular poem that Joseph Addison considered to be perfect. In 1713 Pope began a second, expanded version of five cantos, which included supernatural characters and an elaborate card game. In 1717 he made his final revisions by adding a speech on good humor. The original two-canto version Addison so admired is presented here.

Alexander Pope

The Rape of the Lock

Canto I

What dire offense from amorous causes springs,
What mighty quarrels rise from trivial things,
I sing—This verse to C—l,[1] Muse![2] is due;
This, even Belinda may vouchsafe to view:
5 Slight is the subject, but not so the praise,
If she inspire, and he approve my lays.
    Say what strange motive, goddess! could compel
A well-bred lord t'assault a gentle belle?[3]
Oh say what stranger cause, yet unexplored,
10 Could make a gentle belle reject a lord?
And dwells such rage in softest bosoms then?
And lodge such daring souls in little men?
    Sol[4] through white curtains did his beams display,

---

1. **C——l:** Pope's friend, John Caryll, who suggested the subject of the poem.
2. **Muse:** the poet's inspiring goddess.
3. **belle:** young lady, in this case Belinda, the heroine of the poem.
4. **Sol:** the sun.

And oped those eyes which brighter shine than they;
15 Shock[5] just had given himself the rousing shake,
And nymphs prepared their chocolate[6] to take;
Thrice the wrought slipper knocked against the ground,[7]
And striking watches the tenth hour resound.
Belinda rose, and 'midst attending dames
20 Launched on the bosom of the silver Thames:[8]

> *The lovely, lively Belinda awakes and then takes a boat trip on the Thames River (lines 19–20).*

A train of well dressed youths around her shone,
And every eye was fixed on her alone;
Her lively looks a sprightly mind disclose,
Quick as her eyes, and as unfixed as those:
25 Favors to none, to all she smiles extends;
Oft she rejects, but never once offends.
Bright as the sun her eyes the gazers strike,
And, like the sun, they shine on all alike.
Yet graceful ease, and sweetness void of pride,
30 Might hide her faults, if belles had faults to hide:
If to her share some female errors fall,
Look on her face, and you'll forgive them all.
    This nymph, to the destruction of mankind,
Nourished two locks, which graceful hung behind

> *Belinda has two curls resting on her neck (lines 33–35).*

35 In equal curls, and well conspired to deck
With shining ringlets her smooth ivory neck.
Love in these labyrinths his slaves detains,
And mighty hearts are held in slender chains.
With hairy sprindges[9] we the birds betray,
40 Slight lines of hair surprise the finny prey,[10]
Fair tresses man's imperial race ensnare,
And beauty draws us with a single hair.
    Th' adventrous Baron the bright locks admired,
He saw, he wished, and to the prize aspired:

> *The Baron admires them and resolves to obtain them (lines 43–45).*

45 Resolved to win, he meditates the way,
By force to ravish, or by fraud betray;
For when success a lover's toil attends,
Few ask, if fraud or force attained his ends.
    For this, ere Phoebus[11] rose, he had implored
50 Propitious heaven, and every power adored,
But chiefly Love—to Love an altar built,

---

5. **Shock:** one of Belinda's dogs.
6. **chocolate:** hot cocoa, a morning beverage.
7. **Thrice . . . ground:** Belinda is banging her slipper on the ground to call her maid.
8. **Thames:** the river that passes through London.
9. **sprindges** [sprin′jəz]: traps containing nooses. Pope is detailing the uses of hair for entrapment.
10. **finny prey:** fish, which are caught with hairlike fishline.
11. **Phoebus** [fē′bəs]: the sun; Phoebus Apollo was god of the sun.

Of twelve vast French romances, neatly gilt.
There lay the sword-knot[12] Sylvia's hands had sown,
With Flavia's[13] busk[14] that oft had rapped his own:
55 A fan, a garter, half a pair of gloves;
And all the trophies of his former loves.
With tender billet-doux[15] he lights the pyre,
And breaths three amorous sighs to raise the fire.
Then prostrate falls, and begs with ardent eyes
60 Soon to obtain, and long possess the prize:
The powers gave ear, and granted half his prayer,
The rest, the winds dispersed in empty air.
   Close by those meads[16] for ever crowned with flowers,
Where Thames with pride surveys his rising towers,
65 There stands a structure of majestic frame,[17]
Which from the neighboring Hampton takes its name.
Here Britain's statesmen oft the fall foredoom
Of foreign tyrants, and of nymphs at home;
Here thou, great Anna![18] whom three realms obey,
70 Dost sometimes counsel take—and sometimes tea.
   Hither our nymphs and heroes did resort,
To taste awhile the pleasures of a court;
In various talk the cheerful hours they passed,
Of, who was bitt, or who capotted[19] last:
75 This speaks the glory of the British Queen,
And that describes a charming Indian screen;
A third interprets motions, looks, and eyes;
At every word a reputation dies.
Snuff, or the fan, supply each pause of chat,
80 With singing, laughing, ogling, and all that.
   Now, when declining from the noon of day,
The sun obliquely shoots his burning ray;
When hungry judges soon the sentence sign,
And wretches hang that jury men may dine;
85 When merchants from th' Exchange[20] return in peace,
And the long labors of the toilette[21] cease—

The fashionable people—including Belinda and the Baron—gather at Hampton Court to take tea (lines 63–72).

---

12. **sword-knot:** ribbon tied to the hilt of a sword.
13. **Sylvia's . . . Flavia's:** referring to young ladies who had flirted with the Baron in the past.
14. **busk:** a strip used to support a corset.
15. **billet-doux** [bil′ē dōō′]: love letter.
16. **meads:** wet, grassy lands.
17. **structure . . . frame:** Hampton Court, the royal palace.
18. **Anna:** Queen Anne, who ruled Great Britain and Ireland, and claimed to rule France: thus, "whom three Realms obey."
19. **bitt . . . capotted:** card-playing terms for "cheated" and "scored all the tricks," respectively.
20. **Exchange:** the place where merchants traded their goods.
21. **toilette** [twä let′]: the process of washing and grooming oneself.

The board's with cups and spoons, alternate, crowned;[22]
The berries crackle, and the mill turns round;
On shining altars of Japan they raise
90 The silver lamp, and fiery spirits blaze;
From silver spouts the grateful liquors glide,
And China's earth receives the smoking tide;
At once they gratify their smell and taste,
While frequent cups prolong the rich repast.
95 Coffee (which makes the politician wise,
And see through all things with his half-shut eyes),
Sent up in vapors to the Baron's brain
New stratagems, the radiant lock to gain.
Ah cease rash youth! desist ere 'tis too late,
100 Fear the just gods, and think of Scylla's fate![23]
Changed to a bird, and sent to flit in air,
She dearly pays for Nisus' injured hair!
　　But when to mischief mortals bend their mind,
How soon fit instruments of ill they find?
105 Just then, Clarissa[24] drew with tempting grace
A two-edged weapon from her shining case;
So ladies in romance assist their knight,
Present the spear, and arm him for the fight.
He takes the gift with reverence, and extends

The Baron snips off one of Belinda's curls—the rape of the lock (lines 109–116).

110 The little engine[25] on his fingers' ends,
This just behind Belinda's neck he spread,
As o'er the fragrant steams she bends her head:
He first expands the glittering forfex[26] wide
T'inclose the lock; then joins it, to divide;
115 One fatal stroke the sacred hair does sever
From the fair head, forever, and forever!
　　The living fires come flashing from her eyes,
And screams of horror rend th' affrighted skies.
Not louder shrieks by dames to Heaven are cast,
120 When husbands die, or lap dogs breath their last,
Or when rich china vessels fallen from high,
In glittering dust and painted fragments lie!
　　Let wreaths of triumph[27] now my temples twine
(The victor cried), the glorious prize is mine!

As Belinda laments, the victorious Baron rejoices (lines 117–124).

---

22. **board's . . . crowned:** tray on which coffee will be served. Lines 87–94 describe the preparation and serving of coffee. The beans ("berries") crackle when they are roasted and then are ground in the mill. The "altars of Japan" are lacquered tables. Coffee ("the smoking tide") is poured into Chinese porcelain cups ("China's earth").
23. **Scylla's** [sil′əz] **fate:** Scylla plucked out one of her father Nisus' hairs, on which the safety of the kingdom depended. As punishment, she was turned into a bird.
24. **Clarissa:** a young lady who disapproves of Belinda's vanity.
25. **engine:** device.
26. **forfex:** scissors.
27. **wreaths of triumph:** Ancient Greek victors wore wreaths on their heads.

A portrait by Thomas Gainsborough, 1775.

125   While fish in streams, or birds delight in air,
      Or in a coach and six[28] the British fair,
      As long as *Atalantis*[29] shall be read,
      Or the small pillow grace a lady's bed,
      While visits[30] shall be paid on solemn days,
130   When numerous wax-lights in bright order blaze,
      While nymphs take treats, or assignations give,
      So long my honor, name and praise shall live!
        What time would spare, from steel receives its date,
      And monuments, like men, submit to fate!
135   Steel did the labor of the gods destroy,
      And strike to dust th'aspiring towers of Troy;[31]
      Steel could the works of mortal pride confound,
      And hew triumphal arches to the ground.
      What wonder then, fair nymph! thy hairs should feel
140   The conquering force of unresisted steel?

---

28. **coach and six:** a prestigious carriage with six horses.
29. *Atalantis:* a popular gossipy romance in which real society people were
thinly disguised as fictional characters.
30. **visits:** The regular evening visit was a serious ritual for the society lady,
who was accompanied by servants carrying candles ("wax-lights").
31. **And strike . . . Troy:** According to legend, the swords of the Ancient Greeks
conquered Troy.

Alexander Pope   **281**

Canto II

But anxious cares the pensive nymph oppressed,
And secret passions labored in her breast.
Not youthful kings in battle seized alive,
Not scornful virgins who their charms survive,
5 Not ardent lover robbed of all his bliss,
Not ancient lady when refused a kiss,
Not tyrants fierce that unrepenting die,
Not Cynthia[32] when her manteau's[33] pinned awry,
E'er felt such rage, resentment, and despair,
10 As thou, sad virgin! for they ravished hair.

    While her racked soul repose and peace requires,
The fierce Thalestris[34] fans the rising fires.
O wretched maid (she spreads her hands, and cried,
And Hampton's echoes, wretched maid! replied)
15 Was it for this you took such constant care,
Combs, bodkins, leads, pomatums,[35] to prepare?
For this your locks in paper durance[36] bound,
For this with torturing irons wreathed around?
Oh had the youth but been content to seize
20 Hairs less in sight—or any hairs but these!

Belinda and her friends are furious that the Baron has cut the lock (line 20).

Gods! shall the ravisher display this hair,
While the fops envy, and the ladies stare!
Honor forbid! at whose unrivaled shrine
Ease, pleasure, virtue, all, our sex resign.
25 Methinks already I your tears survey,
Already hear the horrid things they say,
Already see you a degraded toast,[37]
And all your honor in a whisper lost!
How shall I, then, your helpless fame defend?
30 'Twill then be infamy to seem your friend!
And shall this prize, th' inestimable prize,
Exposed through crystal to the gazing eyes,
And heightened by the diamond's circling rays,
On that rapacious hand forever blaze?

The Baron intends to encase Belinda's lock in a ring and wear it (lines 31–34).

35 Sooner shall grass in Hyde Park Circus[38] grow,
And wits take lodgings in the sound of Bow;[39]
Sooner let earth, air, sea, to chaos fall,
Men, monkeys, lap dogs, parrots, perish all!

---

32. **Cynthia:** any young lady.
33. **manteau** [man tō′]: a loose cloak worn by women.
34. **Thalestris:** [thə les′tris]: Belinda's friend, named for the Queen of the Amazons, a nation of women warriors.
35. **bodkins . . . pomatums:** beauty aids and concoctions.
36. **durance:** forced confinement.
37. **toast:** a woman whom men praise and make toasts to.
38. **Hyde Park Circus:** a crowded circular drive.
39. **Bow:** a mercantile area where no fashionable wit would live.

She said; then raging to Sir Plume[40] repairs,
40 And bids her beau demand the precious hairs:
(Sir Plume, of amber snuffbox justly vain,
And the nice conduct of a clouded cane[41])
With earnest eyes, and round unthinking face,
He first the snuffbox opened, then the case,
45 And thus broke out—"My Lord, why, what the devil?
"Z—ds! d—the lock! 'fore Gad, you must be civil!
"Plague on't! 'tis past a jest—nay prithee, pox![42]
"Give her the hair"—he spoke, and rapped his box.
"It grieves me much" (replied the peer again)
50 "Who speaks so well should ever speak in vain.
But by this lock, this sacred lock I swear,
(Which never more shall join its parted hair,
Which never more its honors shall renew,
Clipped from the lovely head where once it grew)
55 That while my nostrils draw the vital air,
This hand, which won it, shall forever wear."
He spoke, and speaking in proud triumph spread
The long-contended honors of her head.
But see! the nymph in sorrow's pomp appears,
60 Her eyes half languishing, half drowned in tears;
Now livid pale her cheeks, now glowing red;
On her heaved bosom hung her drooping head,
Which, with a sigh, she raised; and thus she said,
"For ever cursed be this detested day,
65 Which snatched my best, my favorite curl away!
Happy! ah ten times happy, had I been,
If Hampton Court these eyes had never seen!
Yet am not I the first mistaken maid,
By love of courts to numerous ills betrayed.
70 Oh had I rather unadmired remained
In some lone isle, or distant northern land;
Where the gilt chariot never marked the way,
Where none learn ombre,[43] none e'er taste bohea![44]
There kept my charms concealed from mortal eye,
75 Like roses that in deserts bloom and die.
What moved my mind with youthful lords to roam?
O had I stayed, and said my prayers at home!
'Twas this, the morning omens did foretell;
Thrice from my trembling hand the patchbox[45] fell;

Despite Sir Plume's entreaties, the Baron swears he will always wear the ring (lines 39–56).

In a soliloquy Belinda mourns her fate and the fate of her curl. She wishes she had heeded the morning's omens (her silent parrot and unkind dog), and she finds no comfort in the lock that remains because she fears its fate will be the same as that of the one already lost (lines 63–89).

40. **Sir Plume:** Thalestris' "beau."
41. **amber . . . cane:** Most fashionable men took snuff and carried canes. Sir Plume's accessories are particularly fine.
42. **Z——ds . . . pox:** common oaths.
43. **ombre** [om′bər]: a fashionable card game.
44. **bohea** [bō hē′]: a popular kind of tea.
45. **patchbox:** box in which Belinda keeps her patches, or small pieces of black silk used to cover facial blemishes.

80 The tottering china shook without a wind,
Nay, Poll[46] sat mute, and Shock was most unkind!
See the poor remnants of this slighted hair!
My hands shall rend what even thy own did spare.
This, in two sable ringlets taught to break,
85 Once gave new beauties to the snowy neck.
The sister lock now sits uncouth, alone,
And in its fellow's fate foresees its own;
Uncurled it hangs! the fatal shears demands;
And tempts once more thy sacrilegious hands."

90   She said: the pitying audience melt in tears,
But Fate and Jove[47] had stopped the Baron's ears.
In vain Thalestris with reproach assails,
For who can move when fair Belinda fails?
Not half so fixed the Trojan could remain,
95 While Anna begged and Dido[48] raged in vain.
To arms, to arms! the bold Thalestris cries,
And swift as lightning to the combat flies.
All side in parties, and begin th' attack;
Fans clap, silks rustle, and tough whalebones[49] crack;
100 Heroes' and heroines' shouts confusedly rise,
And base, and treble voices strike the skies.
No common weapons in their hands are found,
Like gods they fight, nor dread a mortal wound.
    So when bold Homer makes the gods engage,[50]
105 And heavenly breasts with human passions rage;
'Gainst Pallas, Mars, Latona, Hermes[51] arms;
And all Olympus[52] rings with loud alarms.
Jove's thunder roars, heaven trembles all around;
Blue Neptune[53] storms, the bellowing deeps resound;
110 Earth shakes her nodding towers, the ground gives way,
And the pale ghosts start at the flash of day!
    While through the press enraged Thalestris flies,
And scatters deaths around from both her eyes,
A beau and Witling perished in the throng,
115 One died in metaphor, and one in song.
O cruel nymph! a living death I bear,
Cried Dapperwit, and sunk beside his chair.

Belinda's friends help her try to convince the Baron to return the lock (lines 90–111).

The battle rages between the wits—the Baron's forces—and the hairs— Belinda's forces (lines 112–129).

---

46. **Poll:** parrot.
47. **Jove:** God.
48. **Trojan . . . Dido:** In Virgil's *Aeneid,* the Trojan Aeneas was unmoved by Dido's great passion for him and the pleas of Dido's sister Anna on her behalf.
49. **whalebones:** Whalebones were used for support in corsets.
50. **Homer . . . engage:** In Homer's *Iliad* the gods are involved in the battle.
51. **Pallas . . . Hermes:** gods involved in the Trojan War, according to Homer's *Iliad.*
52. **Olympus:** mountain home of the Greek gods.
53. **Neptune:** god of the sea.

A mournful glance Sir Fopling[54] upwards cast,
Those eyes are made so killing—was his last:
120 Thus on Meander's[55] flowery margin lies
Th' expiring swan, and as he sings he dies.

As bold Sir Plume had drawn Clarissa down,
Chloë stepped in, and killed him with a frown;
She smiled to see the doughty hero slain,
125 But at her smile, the beau revived again.

Now Jove suspends his golden scales in air,
Weighs the men's wits against the lady's hair;
The doubtful beam long nods from side to side;
At length the wits mount up, the hairs subside.

130 See fierce Belinda on the Baron flies,
With more than usual lightning in her eyes;
Nor feared the chief th' unequal fight to try,
Who sought no more than on his foe to die.
But this bold lord, with manly strength endued,

Belinda throws snuff at the Baron, and he sneezes (lines 130–139).

135 She with one finger and a thumb subdued:
Just where the breath of life his nostrils drew,
A charge of snuff the wily virgin threw;
Sudden, with starting tears each eye o'erflows,
And the high dome re-echoes to his nose.

140 "Now meet thy fate," th'incensed virago[56] cried,
And drew a deadly bodkin[57] from her side.
"Boast not my fall," he said, "insulting foe!
Thou by some other shalt be laid as low.
Nor think, to die dejects my lofty mind;
145 All that I dread, is leaving you behind!
Rather than so, ah let me still survive,
And still burn on, in Cupid's flames, alive."

"Restore the lock!" she cries; and all around
"Restore the lock!" the vaulted roofs rebound.
150 Not fierce Othello in so loud a strain
Roared for the handkerchief that caused his pain.[58]
But see! how oft ambitious aims are crossed,
And chiefs contend 'till all the prize is lost!
The lock, obtained with guilt, and kept with pain,
155 In every place is sought, but sought in vain:
With such a prize no mortal must be blessed,
So Heaven decrees! with Heaven who can contest?

The lock cannot be found, and there is speculation about what happened to it (lines 153–167).

---

54. **Witling . . . Dapperwit . . . Fopling:** conventional names in
Restoration comedy for silly, vain men.
55. **Meander:** river that passed through Troy.
56. **virago** [vi rä′go]: female warrior, in this case Belinda.
57. **bodkin:** dagger.
58. **Othello . . . pain:** Shakespeare's Othello demands to see the
handkerchief he had given his wife, believing her to have given it to
another man and thus to be unfaithful to him.

Some thought it mounted to the lunar sphere,
Since all that man ever lost, is treasured there.
160 There Hero's wits are kept in pondrous vases,
And beau's in snuffboxes and tweezer cases.[59]
There broken vows, and deathbed alms are found,
And lovers' hearts with ends of riband[60] bound;
The courtier's promises, and sick man's prayers,
165 The smiles of harlots, and the tears of heirs,
Cages for gnats, and chains to yoke a flea;
Dried butterflies, and tomes of casuistry.
     But trust the Muse—she saw it upward rise,
Though marked by none but quick poetic eyes:
170 (Thus Rome's great founder to the heavens withdrew,[61]
To Proculus[62] alone confessed in view.)
A sudden star, it shot through liquid air,
And drew behind a radiant trail of hair.
Not Berenice's[63] locks first rose so bright,
175 The skies bespangling with disheveled light.
This, the beau monde[64] shall from the mall[65] survey,
As through the moonlight shade they nightly stray,
And hail with music its propitious ray.
This Partridge[66] soon shall view in cloudless skies,
180 When next he looks through Galileo's[67] eyes;
And hence th' egregious wizard shall foredoom
The fate of Louis, and the fall of Rome.
     Then cease, bright nymph! to mourn the ravished hair
Which adds new glory to the shining sphere!
185 Not all the tresses that fair head can boast
Shall draw such envy as the lock you lost.
For, after all the murders of your eye,
When, after millions slain, your self shall die;
When those fair suns shall set, as set they must,
190 And all those tresses shall be laid in dust;
This lock, the Muse shall consecrate to fame,
And midst the stars inscribe Belinda's name!

The star will be an eternal tribute to Belinda (lines 188–191).

---

59. **tweezer cases:** elaborate cases with grooming aids.
60. **riband** [rib'ənd]: decorative ribbon.
61. **Rome's . . . withdrew:** Rome's founder, according to legend, is Romulus, who was snatched up into heaven.
62. **Proculus:** a Roman who claimed to have seen Romulus being taken up to heaven.
63. **Berenice's:** referring to the Queen of Ancient Cyrene and Egypt (c. 273–221 B.C.), whose husband named a comet after her, "Berenice's Hair."
64. **beau monde** [bō mond']: fashionable world.
65. **mall:** fashionable place for walking.
66. **Partridge:** the astrologer John Partridge (1644–1715), who every year mistakenly predicted the downfall of the King of France ("Louis") and of the Pope ("Rome").
67. **Galileo:** Galileo Galilei (1564–1642), the great Italian astronomer who vastly improved the newly invented telescope.

STUDY QUESTIONS

Recalling

1. From what do mighty quarrels often rise, according to line 2?
2. According to line 20, where is Belinda at the opening of Canto I?
3. In lines 63–70 of Canto I, where is she and what is she doing when the baron cuts her hair? Who aids the baron in his quest?
4. According to lines 136–137 of Canto II, what does Belinda throw at the baron? What happens to the lock in the end, according to lines 172–178? What does the Muse do with the lock and with Belinda's name?

Interpreting

5. Reread lines 23–32 and lines 49–62 in Canto I. From the details Pope presents, describe the characters of Belinda and the Baron.
6. In Canto I, lines 103–122, how does Pope use tone and diction to satirize the rape of the lock?
7. In Canto II, lines 185–192, compare Belinda's fate to the fate of her lock. Does Pope offer adequate consolation for her loss?

VIEWPOINT

Critic Cleanth Brooks does not believe that Pope is simply satirizing Belinda. He argues

that Belinda's dressing table does glow with a special radiance and charm, and that Pope, though amused by the vanity which it represents, is at the same time thoroughly alive to a beauty which it actually possesses.

■ Do you agree that Pope both appreciates Belinda's beauty and satirizes it? Point to specific passages to explain your answer.

LITERARY FOCUS

The Mock-Epic

The **mock-epic** is exactly what the word implies: an imitation epic, or long narrative poem, that makes fun of a society that cannot live up to the standards of the classical heroic epic. The mock-heroic style makes a trivial subject appear ridiculous by using elevated language to describe a mundane event. The mock-epic uses epic con-

ventions to imitate in a comic way the characters, events, and linguistic structures that had become traditional in such classical epics as Homer's *Iliad* and Virgil's *Aeneid* (see Part Two of this book). Some of the most important **epic conventions** are a hero whose bravery allows him to overcome great trials, a major battle scene, a discussion of the hero's weapon, gods who participate in or direct the action, and epic similes in which the things compared are each elaborately and lengthily described.

Thinking About the Mock-Epic

1. What in *The Rape of the Lock* corresponds to the epic hero, battle scene, and description of the weapon, which were conventional in classical epics?
2. Find one example of a mock-epic simile.
3. Find one specific example of lines in which Pope uses elevated language to describe something trivial. Explain how the language makes the thing described appear ridiculous.

COMPOSITION

Writing About Irony

■ Throughout *The Rape of the Lock* Pope juxtaposes (places side by side) for ironic effect both grand and ridiculous ideas, events, and images. Write a brief essay in which you first describe and explain these ironic juxtapositions. Then discuss the way in which they relate to the larger purpose of the poem. You might want to look especially at some of the following lines: Canto I, lines 69–70, 75–76, 77–78, 85–86, 107–110, 121–124, 136–140; Canto II, lines 3–8, 35–38, 160–167.

Writing a Mock-Heroic Description

■ Think of a trivial quarrel, and write a brief prose description of it using the most inflated language you can. Try to include a battle scene and an epic hero.

COMPARING WRITERS

■ Compare and contrast the satire in *Gulliver's Travels* and *The Rape of the Lock*. In discussing the techniques of satire that Swift and Pope use, consider their tone, word choice, and treatment of plot, setting, character, and theme.

Much of Pope's genius lay in his use of the **heroic couplet** (two rhymed lines in iambic pentameter) that was the basis of his poetry. Where in other poets the form, with its regular rhythms and insistent rhymes, seems heavy and labored, in Pope it seems light and effortless. The compact way in which he phrased old ideas into **epigrams** (brief philosophical sayings) makes him one of the most frequently quoted poets today.

Alexander Pope

Epigrams

T'is education forms the common mind:
Just as the twig is bent the tree's inclined.
    —Moral Essays, Epistle IV, lines 247–248

A little learning is a dangerous thing;
Drink deep, or taste not the Pierian spring.[1]
    —Essay on Criticism, Part II, lines 15–16

To err is human, to forgive divine.
    —Ibid., line 325

True wit is Nature to advantage dressed,
What oft was thought, but ne'er so well
    expressed.
    —Ibid., lines 97–98

Be not the first by whom the new are tried,
Nor yet the last to lay the old aside.
    —Ibid., lines 135–136

For fools rush in where angels fear to tread.
    —Ibid., Part III, line 66

Hope springs eternal in the human breast
Man never is, but always to be blessed.
    —Essay on Man, Epistle I, lines 95–96

Know then thyself, presume not God to scan;
The proper study of mankind is man.
    —Ibid., Epistle II, lines 1–2

---

1. **Pierian** [pī ēr′ē ən] **spring:** a spring in Macedonia, supposedly sacred to the Muses and an inspiration to poets and artists.

STUDY QUESTIONS

Recalling

1. What is Pope's definition of "true wit"?
2. What, according to Pope, should people know? What does Pope believe people should study?

Interpreting

3. What does Pope's definition of true wit suggest about originality?
4. Find at least two epigrams in which Pope recommends moderation and carefulness. Explain his recommendations.
5. Which of the epigrams are heroic couplets?

Samuel Johnson   *1709–1784*

The second half of the eighteenth century, the period between Pope (page 276) and Wordsworth (page 326), is often called the **Age of Johnson**. It was so named after Samuel Johnson—critic, poet, playwright, lexicographer, essayist, and biographer—the period's most learned, versatile, and influential literary figure. He was renowned as a superb conversationalist and respected as a moralist with a special insight into human experience. Johnson may not have been the greatest writer of his time, but his conservative values and his deep sensibility reflected the age and had a profound impact on it.

Johnson was born in the northern cathedral town of Litchfield, where his father ran a small bookstore. The family was poor, and his father's lack of money forced Johnson to leave Oxford University without taking a degree. Success for Johnson, as for Pope, came only with hardship, and for most of his life Johnson struggled against poverty. After he left Oxford, he supported himself and his new wife with a number of teaching and journalism jobs, none of which were a financial success and none of which could satisfy his literary ambitions. By the 1740s, however, he began to produce works of considerable importance, including the essays for his popular periodicals, *The Rambler* and *The Idler,* which critics praised as equal if not superior to Addison and Steele's *Spectator.* With the publication of the great *Dictionary of the English Language* (1755), his reputation was secure. *Lives of the Poets* (1779–1781), ten volumes of critical biographies written in his later years, had a deep influence on the critics who followed him. Unlike earlier biographers, Johnson insisted on the truth in his biographies, including the subjects' shortcomings.

In all his writings Dr. Johnson (so-called because of the honorary degrees bestowed upon him by Oxford and Dublin) held to a few general principles: A writer must both please and instruct; he must not offend against morality or religion; he must neither copy others nor attempt anything so original as to be odd. Even those who do not agree with these principles must admit to the wit and grace with which Johnson elaborated them.

In 1746 Johnson published the *Plan* of his *Dictionary,* dedicating it to Lord Chesterfield, at that time an important secretary of state. Although Chesterfield showed some initial interest and made several suggestions, he offered no patronage, or monetary assistance, and Johnson was forced to proceed without Chesterfield's help. After the *Dictionary* was completed, Chesterfield published two articles praising it (perhaps hoping that Johnson would, even after Chesterfield's neglect, dedicate the work to him). Johnson responded with a famous letter, which appears on the following page.

Samuel Johnson

Letter to Lord Chesterfield

To the Right Honorable the Earl of Chesterfield

February 7, 1755

My Lord:

I have been lately informed by the proprietor of the *World*[1] that two papers in which my *Dictionary* is recommended to the public were written by your Lordship. To be so distinguished is an honor which, being very little accustomed to favors from the great, I know not well how to receive, or in what terms to acknowledge.

When upon some slight encouragement I first visited your Lordship, I was overpowered like the rest of mankind by the enchantment of your address,[2] and I could not forbear to wish that I might boast myself *"le vainqueur du vainqueur de la terre"*;[3] that I might obtain that regard for which I saw the world contending; but I found my attendance so little encouraged that neither pride nor modesty would suffer me to continue it. When I had once addressed your Lordship in public, I had exhausted all the art of pleasing which a retired and uncourtly scholar can possess. I had done all that I could; and no man is well pleased to have his all neglected, be it ever so little.

Seven years, my Lord, have now passed since I waited in your outward rooms or was repulsed from your door, during which time I have been pushing on my work through difficulties of which it is useless to complain, and have brought it at last to the verge of publication without one act of assistance, one word of encouragement, or one smile of favor. Such treatment I did not expect, for I never had a patron before.

The shepherd in Virgil grew at last acquainted with Love, and found him a native of the rocks.[4]

Is not a patron, my Lord, one who looks with unconcern on a man struggling for life in the water and, when he has reached ground, encumbers him with help? The notice which you have been pleased to take of my labors, had it been early, had been kind; but it has been delayed till I am indifferent and cannot enjoy it; till I am solitary and cannot impart it; till I am known and do not want it. I hope it is no very cynical asperity not to confess obligations where no benefit has been received, or to be unwilling that the public should consider me as owing that to a patron which Providence has enabled me to do for myself.

Having carried on my work thus far with so little obligation to any favorer of learning, I shall not be disappointed though I should conclude it, if less be possible, with less; for I have been long wakened from that dream of hope in which I once boasted myself with so much exultation, my Lord,

your Lordship's most humble,
most obedient servant,
Sam: Johnson

---

1. ***World:*** newspaper in which Lord Chesterfield had praised Johnson.
2. **address:** conversation.
3. *le vainqueur . . . terre* [lə van kər′ dyo͞o van kər′ də lä ter′]: French for "the conqueror of the conqueror of the earth."

4. **The shepherd . . . rocks:** In a work by the Roman poet Virgil (70–19 B.C.) a shepherd complains that love was born among jagged rocks.

Johnson's great *Dictionary of the English Language,* published in 1755, was a truly exceptional accomplishment for one individual. To complete a similar French dictionary, over forty members of the French Academy had labored for over forty years. Yet Johnson, working alone in impoverished circumstances and frequently plagued by illness, produced in only seven years a dictionary that none had matched and that none would match for many years to come. It seemed a miracle, and Johnson was justly proud.

In his Preface to the *Dictionary,* Johnson talks about his reasons for undertaking the project and his feelings on its completion. The definitions reprinted here show both the straightforwardness of most of the definitions and the author's occasional turns into wit and satire.

Samuel Johnson

from The Preface to A Dictionary of the English Language

In hope of giving longevity to that which its own nature forbids to be immortal, I have devoted this book, the labor of years, to the honor of my country that we may no longer yield the palm of philology without a contest to the nations of the continent. The chief glory of every people arises from its authors. Whether I shall add anything by my own writings to the reputation of English literature must be left to time. Much of my life has been lost under the pressures of disease; much has been trifled away; and much has always been spent in provision for the day that was passing over me; but I shall not think my employment useless or ignoble, if by my assistance foreign nations and distant ages gain access to the propagators of knowledge and understand the teachers of truth; if my labors afford light to the repositories of science and add celebrity to Bacon, to Hooker, to Milton, and to Boyle.[1]

When I am animated by this wish, I look with pleasure on my book, however defective, and deliver it to the world with the spirit of a man that has endeavored well. That it will immediately become popular I have not promised to myself. A few wild blunders and risible absurdities, from which no work of such multiplicity was ever free, may for a time furnish folly with laughter and harden ignorance into contempt; but useful diligence will at last prevail, and there never can be wanting some who distinguish desert; who will consider that no

---

1. **Bacon . . . Boyle:** writers whom Johnson quotes throughout the *Dictionary.*

dictionary of a living tongue ever can be perfect, since while it is hastening to publication, some words are budding and some falling away; that a whole life cannot be spent upon syntax and etymology, and that even a whole life would not be sufficient; that he whose design includes whatever language can express must often speak of what he does not understand; that a writer will sometimes be hurried by eagerness to the end and sometimes faint with weariness under a task which Scaliger[2] compares to the labors of the anvil and the mine; that what is obvious is not always known and what is known is not always present; that sudden fits of inadvertency will surprise vigilance, slight avocations will seduce attention, and casual eclipses of the mind will darken learning; and that the writer shall often in vain trace his memory at the moment of need for that which yesterday he knew with intuitive readiness and which will come uncalled into his thoughts tomorrow.

In this work, when it shall be found that much is omitted, let it not be forgotten that much likewise is performed; and though no book was ever spared out of tenderness to the author and the world is little solicitous to know whence proceeded the faults of that which it condemns, yet it may gratify curiosity to inform it that the English Dictionary was written with little assistance of the learned and without any patronage of the great; not in the soft obscurities of retirement or under the shelter of academic bowers, but amidst inconvenience and distraction, in sickness and in sorrow. It may repress the triumph of malignant criticism to observe that if our language is not here fully displayed, I have only failed in an attempt which no human powers have hitherto completed. If the lexicons of ancient tongues, now immutably fixed and comprised in a few volumes, be yet, after the toil of successive ages, inadequate and delusive; if the aggregated knowledge and co-operating diligence of the Italian academicians did not secure them from the censure of Beni;[3] if the embodied critics of France, when fifty years had been spent upon their work, were obliged to change its economy[4] and give their second edition another form, I may surely be contented without the praise of perfection, which, if I could obtain in this gloom of solitude, what would it avail me? I have protracted my work till most of those whom I wished to please have sunk into the grave and success and miscarriage are empty sounds. I therefore dismiss it with frigid tranquillity, having little to fear or hope from censure or from praise.

---

2. **Scaliger:** J. J. Scaliger (1540–1609) suggested that criminals be sentenced to writing dictionaries.

3. **Beni:** Paola Beni severely criticized the Italian Academy's dictionary.
4. **economy:** organization.

from **A Dictionary of the English Language**

anthology *n.*   A collection of flowers.

club *n.*   An assembly of good fellows, meeting under certain conditions.

> What right has any man to meet in factious *clubs* to vilify the government?
> Dryden, *Medal, Dedication.*

imagination *n.*   **1.** Fancy; the power of forming ideal pictures; the power of representing things absent to one's self or others.   **2.** Conception; image in the mind; idea.   **3.** Contrivance; scheme.

kind *adj.*   Benevolent; filled with general good-will.

> By the *kind* gods, 'tis most ignobly done
> To pluck me by the beard.
> Shakespeare, *King Lear.*

lexicographer *n.*   A writer of dictionaries; a harmless drudge that busies himself in tracing the original, and detailing the signification of words.

man *n.*   **1.** Human being.

> The king is but a *man* as I am; the violet smells to him as it doth to me; the element shows to him as it doth to me, all his senses have but human conditions.
> Shakespeare.

2. Not a woman.   **3.** Not a boy.   **4.** A word of familiarity bordering on contempt.   **5.** Not a beast.

nature *n.*   **1.** An imaginary being supposed to preside over the material and animal world.   **2.** The constitution of an animated body.

> We're not ourselves.
> When *nature,* being oppressed, commands the mind
> To suffer with the body.
> Shakespeare, *King Lear.*

3. Disposition of mind; temper.   **4.** The regular course of things.   **5.** Natural affection, or reverence; native sensations.   **6.** Sort; species.   **7.** Physics; the science which teaches the qualities of things.

oats *n.*   A grain, which in England is generally given to horses, but in Scotland supports the people.[1]

pastern[2] *n.*   The knee of a horse.

> I will not change my horse with any that treads on four *pasterns.*
> Shakespeare, *Henry V.*

patron *n.*   One who countenances, supports, or protects. Commonly a wretch who supports with insolence, and is paid with flattery.

pension *n.*   An allowance made to anyone without an equivalent. In England it is generally understood to mean pay given to a state hireling for treason to his country.

peppermint *n.*   Mint eminently hot.

slothful *adj.*   Idle; lazy; sluggish; inactive; indolent; dull of motion.

> The desire of the *slothful* killeth him; for his hands refuse to labor. Proverbs, *xxi: 25.*

smoke *n.*   The visible effluvium,[3] or sooty exhalation from anything burning.

sneeze *n.*   Emission of wind audibly by the nose.

wit *n.*   **1.** The powers of the mind; the mental faculties; the intellects. This is the original signification.   **2.** Imagination; quickness of fancy.   **3.** Sentiments produced by quickness of fancy.   **4.** A man of fancy.   **5.** A man of genius.   **6.** Sense and judgment.   **7.** In the plural. Sound mind; intellect not crazed.   **8.** Contrivance; strategem; power of expedients.

yawn *v.*   **1.** To gape; to oscitate; to have the mouth opened involuntarily by fumes, as in sleepiness.

youth *n.*   The part of life succeeding to childhood and adolescence; the time from fourteen to twenty-eight.

---

2. **pastern:** actually part of a horse's foot. When an acquaintance asked Johnson why he had defined it as a knee, instead of making an elaborate defense, he answered, "Ignorance, Madam, pure ignorance."
3. **effluvium:** disagreeable vapor.

---

1. **in Scotland . . . people:** Johnson's disdain for the Scottish was well known.

STUDY QUESTIONS

Letter to Lord Chesterfield

Recalling

1. According to paragraphs 1 and 2, why is Johnson writing this letter?
2. Why did Johnson first visit Lord Chesterfield? Summarize his impression of Chesterfield and treatment by him.
3. How many years passed between that first meeting and Johnson's writing of this letter? What did Johnson do in the interim?
4. What is Johnson's definition of a patron, according to paragraph 5?

Interpreting

5. In what specific ways does Johnson's definition of a patron relate to his situation with Lord Chesterfield?
6. In your own words explain how Johnson feels about the notice Lord Chesterfield has taken of his work.
7. What appears to be the real purpose of Johnson's letter?

from Preface; from Dictionary

Recalling

1. According to paragraph 1, why has Johnson written the *Dictionary*?
2. Give four reasons why no dictionary can ever be perfect.
3. According to the last paragraph, under what conditions was the *Dictionary* written?

Interpreting

4. What argument against the *Dictionary* does Johnson anticipate and address in the Preface? Is his justification convincing? Why or why not?
5. What does Johnson's definition of *lexicographer* suggest about his presentation of himself? Compare the tone of this definition with the tone in the Preface.
6. Which definitions seem especially sarcastic or satiric? Explain.

Extending

7. Look up in a modern dictionary two of the words Johnson defines. How do the modern definitions differ from Johnson's? What do the differences suggest about the changes in the meaning of the word?

VOCABULARY

Antonyms

Antonyms are words that have opposite or nearly opposite meanings. For example, *bright* and *dim* are antonyms. The words in capital letters are from "Letter to Lord Chesterfield" and the Preface to *A Dictionary of the English Language*. Choose the word that is *most nearly the opposite* of each word in capitals, *as the word is used in the selection.*

1. ENCUMBERS: (a) burdens (b) surrounds (c) relieves (d) lavishes
2. ASPERITY: (a) courtesy (b) compliment (c) hope (d) bitterness
3. RISIBLE: (a) ridiculous (b) invisible (c) serious (d) hostile
4. INADVERTENCY: (a) caution (b) error (c) singlemindedness (d) flawlessness
5. VIGILANCE: (a) precision (b) violence (c) carelessness (d) humility

COMPOSITION

Developing a Thesis Statement

■ Develop a thesis statement about Samuel Johnson's "Letter to Lord Chesterfield," and in a brief essay defend your thesis with examples from the letter. To develop your statement, you may wish to consider Johnson's use of events, point of view, or tone. *For help with this assignment, refer to Lesson 1 in the Writing About Literature Handbook at the back of this book.*

Writing Definitions

■ Write four definitions in the style of Samuel Johnson. You may define any words of your own choosing, but some possibilities are *friendship, education, politics.* Illustrate your definitions with brief quotations from literature.

COMPARING WRITERS

■ Show how the writings of Addison and Steele, Boswell, and Johnson are typical of the eighteenth century. Discuss four characteristics of the period, and cite quotations and specific details in support of each from the works you have read.

James Boswell   *1740–1795*

The modern art of biography would not be what it is today were it not for James Boswell, author of *The Life of Samuel Johnson* (1791), considered the world's greatest biography. For many years he was known only as Johnson's biographer. Now Boswell is known to be a fascinating literary personality in his own right due to the unexpected discovery from the 1920s through 1940s of an abundance of his personal papers (in such odd places as an abandoned croquet box and a disused barn at a castle in Ireland).

Boswell was a gentleman in the full eighteenth-century meaning of the word. He came from a wealthy and ancient Scottish family and was heir to a large estate, circumstances that helped him gain entry into the upper circles of London society. In addition, he was charming, personable, an excellent listener, and somehow able to make people feel they could share their deepest secrets with him. Yet these qualities alone did not make him a natural biographer; Boswell also had a lifelong habit of keeping a diary and observing and remembering an event or conversation until he had time to write it down. He developed an outstanding memory for detail and a style of writing that could capture and interpret in a few sentences the character of an individual.

Boswell's first important literary work, *An Account of Corsica,* was published in 1768. As part of a tour of Europe, he had visited the island. His journal documents his experiences and includes an account of his visit to the Corsican patriot General Pascal Paoli.

Boswell's natural habitat, however, was intellectual and socially vigorous London. Although he spent some time in Scotland establishing a successful law practice and raising a family, he could not stay away from London for long. Because of his social status and personal charm, he was able to mingle with such men as the painter Sir Joshua Reynolds, the playwright and novelist Oliver Goldsmith, and of course the great sage, scholar, and critic Dr. Johnson.

In 1763, when he was twenty-two, Boswell met the fifty-three-year-old Johnson. The two were friends until Johnson's death in 1784, and Boswell devoted close to thirty years to collecting information for his monumental biography of over 500,000 words. He scrutinized Johnson's every move and questioned him on any topic, even asking him, "What would you do, sir, if you were locked up in a tower with a baby?" In 1773 the two traveled to the Scottish highlands and the Hebrides Islands. Boswell described the events of the trip in his *Journal of a Tour to the Hebrides,* which he published a year after Johnson's death. Eight years later he published his *Life of Johnson.* Thanks to Boswell's vast descriptive and interpretive skill, the account of their friendship allows us a glimpse into the life and relationship of two great eighteenth-century minds.

Detail, *Dr. Johnson in Anteroom of Lord Chesterfield, Waiting for an Audience,* E. M. Ward, 1748.

James Boswell

from **The Life of Samuel Johnson**

To write the life of him who excelled all mankind in writing the lives of others,[1] and who, whether we consider his extraordinary endowments, or his various works, has been equalled by few in any age, is an arduous and may be reckoned in me a presumptuous task.

Had Dr. Johnson written his own life, in conformity with the opinion which he has given that every man's life may be best written by himself; had he employed in the preservation of his own history that clearness of narration and elegance of language in which he has embalmed so many eminent persons, the world would probably have had the most perfect example of biography that was ever exhibited. But although he at different times, in a desultory manner, committed to writing many particulars of the progress of his mind and fortunes, he never had persevering diligence enough to form them into a regular composition. Of these memorials a few have been preserved; but the greater part was consigned by him to the flames, a few days before his death.

As I had the honor and happiness of enjoying his friendship for upwards of twenty years; as I had the scheme of writing his life constantly in view; as he was well apprised of this circumstance, and from time to time obligingly satisfied my inquiries, by communicating to me the incidents of his early years; as I acquired a facility in recollecting, and was very assiduous in recording, his conversation, of which the extraordinary vigor and vivacity constituted one of the first features of his character; and as I have spared no pains in obtaining materials concerning him, from every quarter where I could discover that they were to be found, and

---

1. **writing . . . others:** Johnson wrote a series of biographical essays entitled *The Lives of the Poets.*

have been favored with the most liberal communications by his friends; I flatter myself that few biographers have entered upon such a work as this, with more advantages, independent of literary abilities, in which I am not vain enough to compare myself with some great names who have gone before me in this kind of writing.

Had his other friends been as diligent and ardent as I was, he might have been almost entirely preserved. As it is, I will venture to say that he will be seen in this work more completely than any man who has ever yet lived.

What I consider as the peculiar value of the following work is the quantity that it contains of Johnson's conversation, which is universally acknowledged to have been eminently instructive and entertaining, and of which the specimens that I have given upon a former occasion have been received with so much approbation that I have good grounds for supposing that the world will not be indifferent to more ample communications of a similar nature.

Of one thing I am certain, that considering how highly the small portion which we have of the table talk and other anecdotes of our celebrated writers is valued, and how earnestly it is regretted that we have not more, I am justified in preserving rather too many of Johnson's sayings, than too few; especially as from the diversity of dispositions it cannot be known with certainty beforehand, whether what may seem trifling to some, and perhaps to the collector himself, may not be most agreeable to many; and the greater number that an author can please in any degree, the more pleasure does there arise to a benevolent mind.

1763. This is to me a memorable year; for in it I had the happiness to obtain the acquaintance of that extraordinary man whose memoirs I am now writing; an acquaintance which I shall ever esteem as one of the most fortunate circumstances in my life. Though then but two-and-twenty, I had for several years read his works with delight and instruction, and had the highest reverence for their author, which had grown up in my fancy into a kind of mysterious veneration, by figuring to myself a state of solemn elevated abstraction, in which I supposed him to live in the immense metropolis of London. Mr. Gentleman,[2] a native of Ireland, who passed some years in Scotland as a player, and as an instructor in the English language, a man whose talents and worth were depressed by misfortunes, had given me a representation of the figure and manner of Dictionary Johnson as he was then generally called; and during my first visit to London, which was for three months in 1760, Mr. Derrick[3] the poet, who was Gentleman's friend and countryman, flattered me with hopes that he would introduce me to Johnson, an honor of which I was very ambitious. But he never found an opportunity; which made me doubt that he had promised to do what was not in his power; till Johnson some years afterwards told me, "Derrick, Sir, might very well have introduced you. I had a kindness for Derrick, and am sorry he is dead."

In the summer of 1761 Mr. Thomas Sheridan was at Edinburgh, and delivered lectures upon the English Language and Public Speaking to large and respectable audiences. I was often in his company, and heard him frequently expatiate upon Johnson's extraordinary knowledge, talents, and virtues, repeat his pointed sayings, describe his particularities, and boast of his being his guest sometimes till two or three in the morning. At his house I hoped to have many opportunities of seeing the sage, as Mr. Sheridan obligingly assured me I should not be disappointed. . . .

Mr. Thomas Davies[4] the actor, who then kept a bookseller's shop in Russel Street, Covent Garden,[5] told me that Johnson was very much his friend, and came frequently to his house, where he more than once invited me to meet him: but by some unlucky accident or other he was prevented from coming to us.

---

2. **Mr. Gentleman:** Francis Gentleman (1728–1784), actor and dramatist.
3. **Mr. Derrick:** Samuel Derrick (1724–1769), author.
4. **Mr. Thomas Davies:** actor, bookseller, and author (1712–1785).
5. **Covent Garden:** area of London with many booksellers.

At last, on Monday the 16th of May, when I was sitting in Mr. Davies's back parlor, after having drunk tea with him and Mrs. Davies, Johnson unexpectedly came into the shop; and Mr. Davies having perceived him through the glass door in the room in which we were sitting, advancing towards us—he announced his awful approach to me, somewhat in the manner of an actor in the part of Horatio, when he addresses Hamlet on the appearance of his father's ghost,[6] "Look, my Lord, it comes." I found that I had a very perfect idea of Johnson's figure, from the portrait of him painted by Sir Joshua Reynolds[7] soon after he had published his Dictionary, in the attitude of sitting in his easy chair in deep meditation; which was the first picture his friend did for him, which Sir Joshua very kindly presented to me, and from which an engraving has been made for this work. Mr. Davies mentioned my name, and respectfully introduced me to him. I was much agitated; and recollecting his prejudice against the Scotch, of which I had heard much, I said to Davies, "Don't tell where I come from."

"From Scotland," cried Davies, roguishly. "Mr. Johnson (said I), I do indeed come from Scotland, but I cannot help it."

I am willing to flatter myself that I meant this as light pleasantry to soothe and conciliate him, and not as an humiliating abasement at the expense of my country. But however that might be, this speech was somewhat unlucky; for with that quickness of wit for which he was so remarkable, he seized the expression "come from Scotland," which I used in the sense of being of that country; and, as if I had said that I had come away from it, or left it, retorted, "That, Sir, I find, is what a very great many of your countrymen cannot help."

This stroke stunned me a good deal; and when we had sat down, I felt myself not a little embarrassed, and apprehensive of what might come next. He then addressed himself to Davies: "What do you think of Garrick?[8] He has refused me an order for the play for Miss Williams,[9] because he knows the house will be full, and that an order would be worth three shillings."

Eager to take any opening to get into conversation with him, I ventured to say, "O, Sir, I cannot think Mr. Garrick would grudge such a trifle to you."

"Sir, (said he, with a stern look), I have known David Garrick longer than you have done: and I know no right you have to talk to me on the subject."

Perhaps I deserved this check; for it was rather presumptuous in me, an entire stranger, to express any doubt of the justice of his animadversion[10] upon his old acquaintance and pupil. I now felt myself much mortified, and began to think, that the hope which I had long indulged of obtaining his acquaintance was blasted. And, in truth, had not my ardor been uncommonly strong, and my resolution uncommonly persevering, so rough a reception might have deterred me forever from making any further attempts. Fortunately, however, I remained upon the field not wholly discomfited; and was soon rewarded by hearing some of his conversation, of which I preserved the following short minute, without marking the questions and observations by which it was produced.

Speaking of one who with more than ordinary boldness attacked public measures and the royal family, he said, "I think he is safe from the law, but he is an abusive scoundrel; and instead of applying to my Lord Chief Justice to punish him, I would send half a dozen footmen and have him well ducked."[11] . . .

I was highly pleased with the extraordinary vigor of his conversation, and regretted that I was drawn away from it by an engagement at another place. I had, for a part of the evening, been left alone with him, and had ventured to

---

6. **Horatio . . . ghost:** Shakespeare's Hamlet is told of his father's ghost by his friend Horatio.
7. **Sir Joshua Reynolds:** great portrait painter.
8. **Garrick:** the great actor David Garrick (1717–1779).

9. **Miss Williams:** Garrick gave a benefit performance for his impoverished friend, the blind poet Anna Williams (1706–1783), also a friend of Johnson's.
10. **animadversion** [an'ə mad'vur'zhən]: unfavorable comments.
11. **ducked:** thrown into a body of water.

make an observation now and then, which he received very civilly; so that I was satisfied that though there was a roughness in his manner, there was no ill nature in his disposition. Davies followed me to the door, and when I complained to him a little of the hard blows which the great man had given me, he kindly took upon him to console me by saying, "Don't be uneasy. I can see he likes you very well."

A few days afterwards I called on Davies, and asked him if he thought I might take the liberty of waiting on Mr. Johnson at his chambers in the Temple. He said I certainly might, and that Mr. Johnson would take it as a compliment. So on Tuesday the 24th of May, after having been enlivened by the witty sallies of Messieurs Thornton, Wilkes, Churchill, and Lloyd,[12] with whom I had passed the morning, I boldly repaired to Johnson. His chambers were on the first floor of No. 1, Inner Temple Lane, and I entered them with an impression given me by the Reverend Dr. Blair,[13] of Edinburgh, who had been introduced to him not long before, and described his having "found the Giant in his den," an expression which, when I came to be pretty well acquainted with Johnson, I repeated to him, and he was diverted at this picturesque account of himself. Dr. Blair had been presented to him by Dr. James Fordyce.[14] At this time the controversy concerning the pieces published by Mr. James Macpherson,[15] as translations of Ossian, was at its height. Johnson had all along denied their authenticity; and, what was still more provoking to their admirers, maintained that they had no merit. The subject having been introduced by Dr. Fordyce, Dr. Blair, relying on the internal evidence of their antiquity, asked Dr. John-son whether he thought any man of a modern age could have written such poems. Johnson replied, "Yes, Sir, many men, many women, and many children." . . .

He received me very courteously: but, it must be confessed, that his apartment, and furniture, and morning dress, were sufficiently uncouth. His brown suit of clothes looked very rusty: he had on a little old shriveled unpowdered wig, which was too small for his head; his shirtneck and knees of his breeches were loose; his black worsted stockings ill drawn up; and he had a pair of unbuckled shoes by way of slippers. But all these slovenly particularities were forgotten the moment that he began to talk. Some gentlemen, whom I do not recollect, were sitting with him; and when they went away, I also rose; but he said to me, "Nay, don't go."

"Sir (said I), I am afraid that I intrude upon you. It is benevolent to allow me to sit and hear you."

He seemed pleased with this compliment, which I sincerely paid him, and answered, "Sir, I am obliged to any man who visits me."

I have preserved the following short minute of what passed this day. . . .

Talking of Garrick, he said, "He is the first man in the world for sprightly conversation."

When I rose a second time, he again pressed me to stay, which I did.

He told me that he generally went abroad at four in the afternoon, and seldom came home till two in the morning. I took the liberty to ask if he did not think it wrong to live thus, and not make more use of his great talents. He owned it was a bad habit.

Before we parted, he was so good as to promise to favor me with his company one evening at my lodgings: and, as I took my leave, shook me cordially by the hand. It was almost needless to add that I felt no little elation at having now so happily established an acquaintance of which I had been so long ambitious.

My readers will, I trust, excuse me for being thus minutely circumstantial, when it is considered that the acquaintance of Dr. John-

12. **Thornton . . . Lloyd:** Bonnell Thornton, journalist; Charles Churchill, satirist; Robert Lloyd, poet and essayist; John Wilkes, political radical.
13. **Reverend Dr. Blair:** Hugh Blair (1718–1800), Professor at the University of Edinburgh.
14. **Dr. James Fordyce:** a preacher in Scotland (1720–1796).
15. **Mr. James Macpherson:** Macpherson (1736–1796) had published a group of poems which he claimed were translations of a Gaelic epic, "Ossian." The work was probably partly authentic and partly of Macpherson's own composition.

son was to me a most valuable acquisition, and laid the foundation of whatever instruction and entertainment they may receive from my collections concerning the great subject of the work which they are now perusing. . . .

On Friday, March 31, I supped with him and some friends at a tavern. One of the company attempted, with too much forwardness, to rally him on his late appearance at the theater; but had reason to repent of his temerity.

"Why, Sir, did you go to Mrs. Abington's[16] benefit? Did you see?"

JOHNSON. "No, Sir."

"Did you hear?"

JOHNSON. "No, Sir."

"Why, then, Sir, did you go?"

JOHNSON. "Because, Sir, she is a favorite of the public; and when the public cares the thousandth part for you that it does for her, I will go to your benefit too."

Next morning I won a small bet from Lady Diana Beauclerk,[17] by asking him as to one of his particularities, which her Ladyship laid I durst not do. It seems he had been frequently observed at the club to put into his pocket the Seville oranges, after he had squeezed the juice of them into the drink which he made for himself. Beauclerk and Garrick talked of it to me, and seemed to think that he had a strange unwillingness to be discovered. We could not divine what he did with them; and this was the bold question to be put. I saw on his table the spoils of the preceding night, some fresh peels nicely scraped and cut into pieces.

"O, Sir (said I), I now partly see what you do with the squeezed oranges which you put into your pocket at the Club."

JOHNSON. "I have a great love for them."

BOSWELL. "And pray, Sir, what do you do with them? You scrape them it seems, very neatly, and what next?"

JOHNSON. "Let them dry, Sir."

BOSWELL. "And what next?"

JOHNSON. "Nay, Sir, you shall know their fate no further."

BOSWELL. "Then the world must be left in the dark. It must be said (assuming a mock solemnity), he scraped them and let them dry, but what he did with them next, he never could be prevailed upon to tell."

JOHNSON. "Nay. Sir, you should say it more emphatically:—he could not be prevailed upon, even by his dearest friends, to tell. . . ."

Talking of biography, I said, in writing a life, a man's peculiarities should be mentioned, because they mark his character.

JOHNSON. "Sir, there is no doubt as to peculiarities: the question is, whether a man's vices should be mentioned. . . ."

When Lord Hailes and he sat one morning calmly conversing in my house at Edinburgh, I well remember that Dr. Johnson maintained that, "If a man is to write a panegyric,[18] he may keep vices out of sight; but if he professes to write a life, he must represent it really as it was. . . ."

He sometimes could not bear being teased with questions. I was once present when a gentleman asked so many, as, "What did you do, Sir?" "What did you say, Sir?" that he at last grew enraged, and said, "I will not be put to the *question*. Don't you consider, Sir, that these are not the manners of a gentleman? I will not be baited with *what* and *why*; what is this? what is that? why is a cow's tail long? why is a fox's tail bushy?"

The gentleman, who was a good deal out of countenance, said, "Why, Sir, you are so good, that I venture to trouble you."

JOHNSON. "Sir, my being so *good* is no reason why you should be so *ill*. . . ."

The gentleman who had dined with us at Dr. Percy's[19] came in. Johnson attacked the Americans with intemperate vehemence of abuse. I said something in their favor; and added, that I was always sorry, when he talked on that subject. This, it seems, exasperated

16. **Mrs. Abington's:** referring to Frances Abington (1737–1815), actress.
17. **Lady Diana Beauclerk:** amateur artist (1734–1808).

18. **panegyric:** poem or other work of praise.
19. **Dr. Percy's:** referring to Thomas Percy (1729–1811), editor.

him; though he said nothing at the time. The cloud was charged with sulfurous vapor, which was afterwards to burst in thunder. We talked of a gentleman who was running out his fortune in London; and I said, "We must get him out of it. All his friends must quarrel with him, and that will soon drive him away."

JOHNSON. "Nay, Sir, we'll send *you* to him. If your company does not drive a man out of his house, nothing will."

This was a horrible shock, for which there was no visible cause. I afterwards asked him why he had said so harsh a thing.

JOHNSON. "Because, Sir, you made me angry about the Americans."

BOSWELL. "But why did you not take your revenge directly?"

JOHNSON (smiling). "Because, Sir, I had nothing ready. A man cannot strike till he has his weapons."

This was a candid and pleasant confession.

STUDY QUESTIONS

Recalling

1. Name three advantages that Boswell cites as qualifications for being Johnson's biographer.
2. What peculiar value does Boswell feel his biography has? What justifies Boswell in "preserving rather too many of Johnson's sayings, than too few"?
3. Briefly summarize the circumstances of Boswell's first encounter with Johnson.
4. What compliment does Johnson pay Boswell at the end of the anecdote about the Seville oranges?

Interpreting

5. Describe and explain one instance of Johnson's wit.
6. On the whole, how does Johnson regard Boswell? Are his emotions consistent or do they vary? Refer to specific conversations in the selection.

LITERARY FOCUS

Biography and Autobiography

A **biography** is an account of a person's life and character. As the form has developed, biographies have become more personal, conveying more of the subject's day-to-day life, ideas, and relationship to society. The modern biography often has a psychological orientation and attempts to describe the subconscious motivations of its subject.

When Dr. Johnson suggested that each person's life is best related by that individual, he was recommending **autobiography,** a person's narrative of his or her own life. Autobiographies are not always the most accurate accounts; a person may forget events or wish to hide certain facts. They can, however, offer intricate insights into a person's self-concept.

Thinking About Biography and Autobiography

1. Do you agree that a biographer should be absolutely truthful? Why or why not?
2. How would you describe Boswell's attitude toward Johnson? Do you think he presents Johnson with an unbiased point of view?
3. In what ways might *The Life of Johnson* have been different had it been an autobiography?

COMPOSITION

Citing Evidence

▧ Write a brief essay in which you describe Johnson. Begin with a physical description, then discuss his character traits, and then his beliefs. Be sure to cite as evidence for your points specific details from Boswell's work. *For help with this assignment, refer to Lesson 3 in the Writing About Literature Handbook at the back of this book.*

Writing a Biographical Sketch

▧ Write a brief biographical sketch, using specific situations to portray the character of a person. Use some of Boswell's techniques, such as including dialogue, using detail to describe surroundings, and recording your own reactions.

Thomas Gray   *1716–1771*

Although Thomas Gray wrote few poems during his lifetime, his place in eighteenth-century literature is distinctive and assured primarily because of one poem, "Elegy Written in a Country Churchyard." Gray is also perhaps the most important transitional figure between the neoclassical writers of the seventeenth and eighteenth centuries (those who applied the literary standards and forms of ancient Greece and Rome to their writing) and the Romantic poets of the early nineteenth century. While Gray used many traditional neoclassical techniques—personified concepts such as Fame and Fate, elevated poetic language, and classical forms—his love of nature and belief in the common man anticipated important ideals of the Romantic poets.

Gray was, before anything else, a scholar. He studied Greek and Latin intensively and eventually became a professor at Cambridge University. However, like some other professors of his day, he never gave a single lecture. Rather than teaching, he spent his time advising students and exploring the libraries, where his studies led him to discover the little-known beauties of English and Scottish ballads and Welsh and Norse literature that would later become important to the Romantics.

Gray was not eager to have his poetry published. In 1748 a friend sponsored the anonymous publication of Gray's first three poems. In 1751 Gray allowed his "Elegy Written in a Country Churchyard" to be printed only because he had heard that an imperfect version was about to be published without his consent. Because he felt that a gentleman should not accept payment for writing poetry, he let his publisher keep all the profits. In 1757 he was offered the position of poet laureate (poet to the royal family), an honor he declined. He published several more small volumes of poetry before his death in 1771.

Gray's poetic output was small because he composed each poem with painstaking care, phrasing and rephrasing until he felt that each was perfect. Despite the fact that his language is often artificial (he believed that "the language of the age is never the language of poetry"), his poems are clear and genuine expressions of deep feeling.

Gray's "Elegy Written in a Country Churchyard," which was begun after the death of his close friend Richard West, took Gray nine years to complete. The "Elegy" remains his best-known and most beloved poem. Even Samuel Johnson, who in general did not admire Gray's work, wrote, "The Churchyard abounds with images which find a mirror in every mind, and with sentiments to which every bosom returns an echo." Indeed, the "Elegy" is one of the world's most famous poems and has been translated into many languages.

Thomas Gray

Elegy Written in a Country Churchyard

The curfew tolls the knell of parting day,
   The lowing herd wind slowly o'er the lea,[1]
The plowman homeward plods his weary way,
   And leaves the world to darkness and to me.

5 Now fades the glimmering landscape on the sight,
   And all the air a solemn stillness holds,
Save where the beetle wheels his droning flight,
   And drowsy tinklings lull the distant folds;

Save that from yonder ivy-mantled tower
10   The moping owl does to the moon complain
Of such, as wandering near her secret bower,
   Molest her ancient solitary reign.

Beneath those rugged elms, that yew-tree's shade,
   Where heaves the turf in many a moldering heap,
15 Each in his narrow cell forever laid,
   The rude[2] forefathers of the hamlet sleep.

The breezy call of incense-breathing Morn,
   The swallow twittering from the straw-built shed,
The cock's shrill clarion, or the echoing horn,[3]
20   No more shall rouse them from their lowly bed.

For them no more the blazing hearth shall burn,
   Or busy housewife ply her evening care;
No children run to lisp their sire's return,
   Or climb his knees the envied kiss to share.

25 Oft did the harvest to their sickle yield,
   Their furrow oft the stubborn glebe[4] has broke;
How jocund did they drive their team afield!
   How bowed the woods beneath their sturdy stroke!

Let not Ambition mock their useful toil,
30   Their homely joys, and destiny obscure;

---

1. **lea:** meadow.
2. **rude:** uneducated.
3. **horn:** hunter's horn.
4. **glebe:** soil.

Nor Grandeur hear, with a disdainful smile
    The short and simple annals of the poor.

The boast of heraldry,[5] the pomp of power,
    And all that beauty, all that wealth e'er gave,
35 Awaits alike the inevitable hour.
    The paths of glory lead but to the grave.

Nor you, ye proud, impute to these the fault,
    If Memory o'er their tomb no trophies[6] raise,
Where through the long-drawn aisle and fretted vault[7]
40   The pealing anthem swells the note of praise.

Can storied urn[8] or animated[9] bust
    Back to its mansion call the fleeting breath?
Can Honor's voice provoke[10] the silent dust,
    Or Flattery soothe the dull cold ear of Death?

45 Perhaps in this neglected spot is laid
    Some heart once pregnant with celestial fire;
Hands that the rod of empire might have swayed,
    Or waked to ecstasy the living lyre.

But Knowledge to their eyes her ample page
50   Rich with the spoils of time did ne'er unroll;
Chill Penury repressed their noble rage,
    And froze the genial current of the soul.

Full many a gem of purest ray serene,
    The dark unfathomed caves of ocean bear:
55 Full many a flower is born to blush unseen,
    And waste its sweetness on the desert air.

Some village Hampden,[11] that with dauntless breast
    The little tyrant of his fields withstood;

---

5. **heraldry:** coat of arms; noble birth.
6. **trophies:** pictures or figures symbolizing the
achievements of the dead person.
7. **fretted vault:** church ceiling decorated with
a pattern of intersecting straight lines.
8. **storied urn:** funeral urn bearing a story of
the deceased in pictures.
9. **animated:** lifelike.
10. **provoke:** move to life.
11. **Hampden:** John Hampden (1594–1643), a
heroic statesman who fought against unfair
taxation.

Some mute inglorious Milton[12] here may rest,
60   Some Cromwell[13] guiltless of his country's blood.

The applause of listening senates to command,
    The threats of pain and ruin to despise,
To scatter plenty o'er a smiling land,
    And read their history in a nation's eyes,
65 Their lot forbade: nor circumscribed alone
    Their growing virtues, but their crimes confined;
Forbade to wade through slaughter to a throne,
    And shut the gates of mercy on mankind,

The struggling pangs of conscious truth to hide,
70   To quench the blushes of ingenuous shame,
Or heap the shrine of Luxury and Pride
    With incense kindled at the Muse's flame.

Far from the madding[14] crowd's ignoble strife,
    Their sober wishes never learned to stray;
75 Along the cool sequestered vale of life
    They kept the noiseless tenor of their way.

Yet ev'n these bones from insult to protect
    Some frail memorial still erected nigh,
With uncouth[15] rhymes and shapeless sculpture decked,
80   Implores the passing tribute of a sigh.

Their name, their years, spelt by the unlettered Muse,
    The place of fame and elegy supply:
And many a holy text around she strews,
    That teach the rustic moralist to die.

85 For who to dumb Forgetfulness a prey,
    This pleasing anxious being e'er resigned,
Left the warm precincts of the cheerful day,
    Nor cast one longing, lingering look behind?

On some fond breast the parting soul relies,
90   Some pious drops the closing eye requires;

12. **Milton:** John Milton (1608–1674), one of the
greatest English poets.
13. **Cromwell:** Oliver Cromwell (1599–1658),
great English statesman and general who was
nonetheless responsible for much bloodshed.
14. **madding:** frenzied.
15. **uncouth:** innocently artless.

Ev'n from the tomb the voice of Nature cries,
Ev'n in our ashes live their wonted fires.

For thee,[16] who mindful of the unhonored dead
Dost in these lines their artless tale relate;
95 If chance, by lonely contemplation led,
Some kindred spirit shall inquire thy fate,

Haply[17] some hoary-headed[18] swain may say,
"Oft have we seen him at the peep of dawn
Brushing with hasty steps the dews away
100   To meet the sun upon the upland lawn.

"There at the foot of yonder nodding beech
That wreathes its old fantastic roots so high,
His listless length at noontide would he stretch,
And pore upon the brook that babbles by.

105 "Hard by yon wood, now smiling as in scorn,
Muttering his wayward fancies he would rove,
Now drooping, woeful wan, like one forlorn,
Or crazed with care, or crossed in hopeless love.

"One morn I missed him on the customed hill,
110   Along the heath, and near his favorite tree;
Another came; nor yet beside the rill,
Nor up the lawn, nor at the wood was he;

"The next with dirges due in sad array
Slow through the churchway path we saw him borne.
115 Approach and read (for thou canst read) the lay,
Graved on the stone beneath yon aged thorn."[19]

The Epitaph[20]

Here rests his head upon the lap of Earth
   A youth to Fortune and to Fame unknown.
Fair Science frowned not on his humble birth,
120   *And Melancholy marked him for her own.*

---

16. **thee:** Gray is addressing himself.
17. **Haply:** perhaps.
18. **hoary-headed:** white-haired.
19. **thorn:** hawthorn tree.
20. **Epitaph:** an inscription on a tombstone; a
brief poem composed in memory of someone
who has died.

Large was his bounty, and his soul sincere,
  Heaven did a recompense as largely send:
He gave to Misery all he had, a tear,
  He gained from Heaven ('twas all he wished) a friend.

No farther seek his merits to disclose,
  Or draw his frailties from thier dread abode
(There they alike in trembling hope repose),
  The bosom of his Father and his God.

STUDY QUESTIONS

Recalling

1. According to lines 13–16, what lies beneath the rugged elms and the yew-tree's shade?
2. Name five of the "homely joys" from lines 17–30 that will no longer be experienced.
3. In lines 33–36 what do heraldry, power, beauty, and wealth all await? What path will they all follow?
4. In lines 45–48 and lines 57–60 what does Gray speculate that some of the country people might have had the potential to become? In lines 73–76 what does he say the country people did?
5. To whom is Gray referring in lines 93–116? What observations does the swain make in lines 97–116?

Interpreting

6. What kind of person is described in the epitaph? What does this person have in common with the other kinds of people mentioned in the elegy?
7. What kinds of life does Gray refer to in the elegy? How do they differ? Which does Gray seem to prefer?
8. What truths common to all humankind do you think Gray is expressing?

Extending

9. In what ways are Gray's statements about human nature still valid in today's world?

LITERARY FOCUS

The Elegy

Although the **elegy** has a long tradition dating from Latin and Greek literature, it was only in the sixteenth century that it gained its modern definition: a serious poem lamenting the death of an individual or a group of individuals. The elegy is a poem of mourning, but the poet often finds consolation in contemplation of a common human truth. The **elegiac stanza,** a form often but not always used in the elegy, consists of four iambic pentameter lines rhyming *abab.*

Thinking About the Elegy

▨ What does Gray's "Elegy" mourn? Is it just the death of one individual or does it go beyond? Cite evidence from the poem.

VOCABULARY

Expressive Verbs and Adjectives

▨ In "Elegy Written in a Country Churchyard" Thomas Gray uses a rich variety of strong, expressive verbs and adjectives. Select five verbs and five adjectives from the following list of words from Gray's poem, and write five sentences of your own, using a different combination of verb and adjective for each one.

Verbs	*Adjectives*
plods	glimmering
wheels	droning
lull	moldering
heaves	breezy
rouse	jocund
ply	fleeting
drive	serene
impute	dauntless
implores	sequestered
strews	artless

Robert Burns   *1759–1796*

Robert Burns, still celebrated as a Scottish national hero, wrote simple lyrics that continue to capture the imagination of readers around the world. Although dignified literary circles immediately recognized Burns's genius, his poetic voice was that of the Scottish peasant. Even when he was fully accepted by Edinburgh high society, he never lost his connection to the land and to the simple people who inspired his poetry.

Burns, the son of a poor farmer, spent his childhood reading not only the great body of English literature but also all the traditional Scottish poets. Although he liked to portray himself as an artist whose work was the spontaneous overflow of natural feeling, he was actually quite well educated by the time he began to write, and his work reflects his wide reading. Songs that seem naive are actually elaborately crafted lyrics based on a long Scottish tradition. Poems that appear to be simple commentaries on day-to-day life are in reality subtle satires in the best neoclassical tradition. Burns was not altogether unaware of the conflict between his image as poet of the common people and the reality of his acceptance by high society. Although he spent much time in Edinburgh after the brilliant success of his first volume of poems, he soon realized that once the novelty of being the "peasant-poet" wore off, the upper classes with whom he mingled might lose interest. In 1788 he returned to farming and became a devoted father and family man, but he continued to write and edit several collections of Scottish songs.

Burns wrote many poems in standard English, but his best work is in Scottish dialect that, if difficult to understand today, nonetheless evokes the true spirit of the Scottish peasant. There is a heartiness to his language, a generosity that is underscored by a tenderness for both the natural and the human worlds. Burns was a great believer in the values of the American and French revolutions: democracy, equality, and justice. These values infuse both his long lyrics and his more than three hundred songs. The songs, on which his reputation rests, celebrate the joy of being human, of loving, working, laughing with friends, or standing up for one's country. On the basis of his songs, which talk of common people in common language, Burns is often called a pre-Romantic, a precursor to Wordsworth (page 326).

Sadly enough, Burns's devotion to his country and to the peasant life was the cause of his early death. He had developed a heart disease from overly strenuous work on his father's farm as a boy, and he finally succumbed to it at the age of thirty-seven. But Burns the poet lives on in spirit when every year on New Year's Eve people join hands and sing his beautiful song, "Auld Lang Syne."

Robert Burns

A Man's a Man for A' That

Is there, for honest poverty,
  That hangs his head, and a' that?
The coward slave, we pass him by,
  We dare be poor for a' that!
5   For a' that, and a' that,
      Our toils obscure, and a' that;
    The rank is but the guinea's stamp,[1]
    The man's the gowd[2] for a' that.

What tho' on hamely fare we dine,
10 Wear hodden-gray,[3] and a' that;
Gie fools their silks, and knaves their wine,
  A man's a man for a' that:
    For a' that, and a' that,
      Their tinsel show, and a' that;
15   The honest man, though e'er sae poor,
    Is king o' men for a' that.

Ye see yon birkie,[4] ca'd a lord,
  Wha struts, and stares, and a' that;
Though hundreds worship at his word,

20 He's but a coof[5] for a' that:
    For a' that, and a' that,
      His riband, star, and a' that
    The man of independent mind,
    He looks and laughs at a' that.

25 A prince can mak a belted knight,
  A marquis, duke, and a' that;
But an honest man's aboon[6] his might,
  Guid faith he mauna fa'[7] that!
    For a' that, and a' that,
30   Their dignities, and a' that,
    The pith o' sense, and pride o' worth,
    Are higher rank than a' that.

Then let us pray that come it may,
  As come it will for a' that,
35 That sense and worth, o'er a' the earth,
  May bear the gree,[8] an' a' that.
    For a' that, and a' that,
      It's coming yet, for a' that,
    That man to man, the warld o'er
40   Shall brothers be for a' that.

1. **guinea's stamp:** picture stamped superficially on a coin to show its value.
2. **gowd:** gold.
3. **hodden-gray:** the coarse gray cloth of the poor.
4. **birkie:** young man.

5. **coof:** fool.
6. **aboon:** above.
7. **mauna fa':** must not get.
8. **bear the gree:** get the reward.

STUDY QUESTIONS

Recalling

1. In stanza 2 who does Burns say is the king?
2. How does the independent man respond to the lord who struts, according to stanza 3?
3. Name three qualities that place the honest man above the marquis and duke, according to stanza 4.
4. In the last stanza for what does Burns pray? What does he say is yet to come?

Interpreting

5. Which characteristics does Burns suggest belong only to the rich? Only to the poor?
6. Which does Burns seem to favor, the rich or the poor? Support your answer.
7. Explain the views of brotherhood that Burns expresses in the poem.

Extending

8. Do you think Burns's views of the rich in any way contradict his idea of brotherhood?

Robert Burns

To a Mouse

*On Turning Her up in Her Nest with
the Plow, November, 1785*

Wee, sleekit, cow'rin, tim'rous beastie,
O, what a panic's in thy breastie!
Thou need na start awa sae hasty
  Wi' bickering brattle![1]
5 I wad be laith[2] to rin an' chase thee
  Wi' murd'ring pattle![3]

I'm truly sorry man's dominion
Has broken Nature's social union,
An' justifies that ill opinion
10 Which makes thee startle
At me, thy poor, earth-born companion,
  An' fellow-mortal!

I doubt na, whiles,[4] but thou may thieve;
What then? poor beastie, thou maun[5] live!
15 A daimen-icker in a thrave[6]
  'S a sma' request:
I'll get a blessin wi' the lave,[7]
  An' never miss 't!

Thy wee-bit housie, too, in ruin!
20 Its silly wa's the win's are strewin'!
An' naething, now, to big[8] a new ane,
  O' foggage[9] green!

An' bleak December's winds ensuin',
  Baith snell[10] an' keen!

25 Thou saw the fields laid bare and waste,
An' weary winter comin' fast,
An' cozie here, beneath the blast,
  Thou thought to dwell,
Till crash! the cruel coulter[11] passed
30 Out-through thy cell.

That wee-bit heap o' leaves an' stibble,
Hast cost thee mony a weary nibble!
Now thou's turned out, for a' thy trouble,
  But[12] house or hald,[13]
35 To thole[14] the winter's sleety dribble,
  An' cranreuch[15] cauld!

But Mousie, thou art no thy lane,[16]
In proving foresight may be vain:
The best-laid schemes o' mice an' men
40 Gang aft a-gley,[17]
An' lea'e us nought but grief an' pain,
  For promised joy.

Still thou art blest, compared wi' me!
The present only toucheth thee:
45 But och! I backward cast my e'e
  On prospects drear!
An' forward though I canna see,
  I guess an' fear!

---

1. **Wi' . . . brattle:** in sudden flight.
2. **wad be laith:** would be loath.
3. **pattle:** paddle used to clean a plow.
4. **whiles:** sometimes.
5. **maun:** must.
6. **daimen . . . thrave:** an occasional ear of
grain from a shock.
7. **lave:** rest.
8. **big:** build.
9. **foggage:** rough grass.

---

10. **snell:** sharp.
11. **coulter:** cutter on a plow.
12. **But:** without.
13. **hald:** home.
14. **thole:** withstand.
15. **cranreuch:** frost.
16. **no thy lane:** not alone.
17. **Gang . . . a-gley:** go often awry.

John Anderson My Jo

John Anderson my jo,[1] John,
 When we were first acquent,
Your locks were like the raven,
 Your bonie[2] brow was brent;[3]
5 But now your brow is beld,[4] John,
 Your locks are like the snow;
But blessings on your frosty pow,[5]
 John Anderson my Jo.

John Anderson my jo, John,
10 We clamb[6] the hill thegither;
And mony[7] a canty[8] day, John,
 We've had wi' ane anither:
Now we maun[9] totter down, John,
 And hand in hand we'll go,
15 And sleep thegither at the foot,
 John Anderson, my Jo.

1. **jo:** joy (friendly address).
2. **bony:** beautiful
3. **brent:** unwrinkled.
4. **beld:** bald.
5. **pow:** head.

6. **clamb:** climbed.
7. **mony:** many.
8. **canty:** cheerful, merry.
9. **maun:** must.

STUDY QUESTIONS

To a Mouse

Recalling

1. According to stanza 2, what has man's dominion broken? Who are fellow-mortals?
2. What has happened to the mouse's house, according to stanza 4?
3. According to stanza 7, what often happens to the "best-laid schemes"? What are we left with in the end?
4. Why is the mouse blessed compared with Burns, according to the last stanza?

Interpreting

5. What is Burns's view of the mouse's misfortune? What does this view suggest about his attitude toward nature?
6. What do Burns's comments about the mouse's plight reveal about his own personality?

John Anderson My Jo

Recalling

1. Describe John Anderson as he is depicted in stanza 1. Describe him as depicted in stanza 2.
2. According to stanza 2, what did John Anderson and the speaker do together?

Interpreting

3. What is the main difference in John Anderson from stanza 1 to stanza 2?
4. What might the hill and the foot of the hill each represent?
5. What does the poem suggest about Burns's attitude toward old age?

Extending

6. Why do you think Burns's poems appealed so much to Scottish peasants?

William Blake   *1757–1827*

William Blake was a poet, artist, and mystic—a transitional figure in English literature who followed no style but his own. Blake grew up in the middle of London, surrounded by the grit and poverty of the new industrial age. His family was poor, and Blake received virtually no education as a child. When he was ten, however, his father was able to send him to drawing school, and at fourteen he was apprenticed to an engraver. As an apprentice he had time to read widely and began to write the first of his poetry, realizing early that he was not content to follow the artistic and literary values of the day.

In 1778, when he had completed his apprenticeship, Blake became a professional engraver and earned a living over the next twenty years by supplying booksellers and publishers with copperplate engravings. In 1789 he published a volume of lyrical poems called *Songs of Innocence. Songs of Experience,* a companion volume to *Songs of Innocence,* meant to be read in conjunction with it, followed in 1794. The two works contrast with each other: One deals with good, passivity, and reason; the other, with evil, violence, and emotion. They were the first of Blake's books to be illustrated, engraved, and printed on copperplates by a process of his own. Blake's engravings and paintings are an important part of his artistic expression, for the verbal and visual work together to evoke one unified impression. Blake himself manufactured all his poems that appeared during his lifetime.

As Blake grew older, he became more and more caught up in his mystical faith and his visions of a heavenly world. As a child he was fascinated by the Bible and by the ideas of the German mystic Jacob Boehme. Blake's heavily symbolic later works, including *The Marriage of Heaven and Hell* (1790), *The Gates of Paradise* (1793), and *Jerusalem* (1804), reflect his ever-deepening reflections about God and man. His interest in the supernatural and his imaginative experimentation with his art and verse classify him, like Robert Burns, as a pre-Romantic. During the last twenty years of his life, Blake's genius as an artist, especially evident in his illustrations of Chaucer's Canterbury pilgrims, Dante's *Divine Comedy,* and the Book of Job, overshadowed his work as a poet.

Toward the end of his life, Blake had a small group of devoted followers, but when he died at seventy his work was virtually unknown. The Romantics praised his *Songs of Innocence* and *Songs of Experience,* but the full extent of his creative genius went largely unrecognized for over half a century after his death. Although scholars today continue to puzzle over the complex philosophical symbolism of his later works, all readers can appreciate the delicate lyricism of his *Songs of Innocence* and *Songs of Experience.*

William Blake

The Lamb

Little Lamb, who made thee?
　　Dost thou know who made thee?
Gave thee life and bid thee feed,
By the stream and o'er the mead;[1]
5　Gave thee clothing of delight,
Softest clothing woolly bright;
Gave thee such a tender voice,
Making all the vales rejoice!
　　Little Lamb who made thee?
10　　Dost thou know who made thee?

　　Little Lamb I'll tell thee,
　　Little Lamb I'll tell thee!
He is callèd by thy name,
For he calls himself a Lamb,
15 He is meek and he is mild,
He became a little child:
I a child and thou a lamb,
We are callèd by his name.
　　Little Lamb God bless thee.
20　　Little Lamb God bless thee.

———————

1. **mead:** wet, grassy land.

The Tiger

Tiger! Tiger! burning bright
In the forests of the night,
What immortal hand or eye
Could frame thy fearful symmetry?

5　In what distant deeps or skies
Burnt the fire of thine eyes?
On what wings dare he aspire?
What the hand, dare seize the fire?

And what shoulder and what art,
10 Could twist the sinews of thy heart?
And when thy heart began to beat,
What dread hand? and what dread feet?

What the hammer? what the chain?
In what furnace was thy brain?
15 What the anvil? what dread grasp
Dare its deadly terrors clasp?

When the stars threw down their spears,
And water'd heaven with their tears,
Did he smile his work to see?
20 Did he who made the Lamb make thee?

Tiger! tiger! burning bright
In the forests of the night,
What immortal hand or eye
Dare frame thy fearful symmetry?

The title page from *Songs of Innocence,* a
volume of poetry written, illustrated, and
printed by William Blake.

William Blake

A Poison Tree

I was angry with my friend:
I told my wrath, my wrath did end.
I was angry with my foe:
I told it not, my wrath did grow.

5 And I watered it in fears,
Night and morning with my tears;
And I sunnèd it with smiles,
And with soft deceitful wiles.

And it grew both day and night,
10 Till it bore an apple bright.
And my foe beheld it shine,
And he knew that it was mine,

And into my garden stole,
When the night had veiled the pole;[1]
15 In the morning glad I see
My foe outstretched beneath the tree.

---

1. **pole:** sky; heavens.

The Sick Rose

O Rose, thou art sick.
The invisible worm
That flies in the night
In the howling storm

5 Has found out thy bed
Of crimson joy,
And his dark secret love
Does thy life destroy.

STUDY QUESTIONS

The Lamb

Recalling

1. In stanza 1 what does the speaker ask the lamb? What three things does the speaker say were given to the lamb?
2. What adjectives describe the lamb? What adjectives describe his maker?
3. According to stanza 2, what does the maker call himself? What did he become?

Interpreting

4. Who does the poem suggest made the lamb? By what name are the speaker and the lamb called?
5. What do you think the lamb represents? Cite evidence from the poem to support your answer.
6. Describe the overall tone of the poem. Which details contribute to this tone?

The Tiger

Recalling

1. What question does the speaker ask at the end of the first stanza? What question does he ask at the end of the last stanza? How is the wording of the questions different?
2. In stanza 4 what does the speaker suggest has shaped the tiger's "fearful symmetry"?
3. What two questions does the speaker ask in stanza 5?

Interpreting

4. What central metaphor does the speaker use to describe the tiger's maker?
5. What might the tiger represent? Explain your answer.
6. How do you think the speaker would answer the question, "Did he who made the lamb make thee?"
7. How is the meaning of the question in the first and last stanzas changed by the change in wording? What lines in the poem seem to inspire the change in wording?

A Poison Tree

Recalling

1. What happened to the anger the speaker felt for his friend? Why? What happened to the anger he felt for his foe? Why?

2. How did the speaker nurture his anger? What was finally produced?
3. What did the foe do, and what was his fate? How did the speaker react?

Interpreting

4. Do you think the foe's death in the fourth stanza is literal or symbolic? Explain your answer.
5. What does the poem say about human nature? Which way of dealing with anger seems more sensible?

The Sick Rose

Recalling

1. What adjective is used to describe the rose in line 1? What adjective describes the worm in line 2?
2. What specifically destroys the rose's life?

Interpreting

3. Write a sentence describing the literal, or exact, meaning of the poem.
4. Write a sentence or two describing a more symbolic interpretation of the poem. What words and details suggest that something more than the literal meaning is intended?

VIEWPOINT

In a discussion of Blake's *Songs of Innocence* and *Songs of Experience,* the critic Robert F. Gleckner writes that the point of view of the speaker

is unobtrusive [does not call attention to itself], but many times a faithful interpretation of the poem depends upon a correct determination of the speaker and perspective.

▨ What different points of view can you find in the four Blake poems you have read? How does each relate to the meaning of the poem? Do you agree that the speaker's point of view is unobtrusive?

LITERARY FOCUS

Symbolism

A **symbol** is an object, person, place, or experience that stands for something more than itself. Symbols are more complex than metaphors,

for they often carry a wide range of connotations. For instance, a stop sign is not a symbol because it means only one specific thing: The motorist must stop. An American flag is a symbol, for it suggests not only the United States, but also the values of freedom, justice, and equality.

The use of symbols in a literary work is called **symbolism.** Writers vary a great deal in their use of symbols. To one, the sun might be a symbol of monarchy and power, yet to another it might represent the benevolent forces of nature. A symbol intensifies and elevates the meaning of what is being symbolized far beyond the importance of the individual item itself.

Thinking About Symbolism

▨ In "The Sick Rose" what might the rose symbolize? What other qualities does the rose suggest? What might the worm symbolize?

COMPOSITION

Writing About a Symbol

▨ Choose a symbol from one of Blake's poems other than "The Sick Rose." First explain the specific meaning of the symbol in the poem. Then discuss the significance of the symbol to the poem as a whole, and explain how it relates to the theme of the poem. *For help with this assignment, see Lesson 5 in the Writing About Literature Handbook at the back of this book.*

Writing a Description

▨ On the basis of their imagery, visualize two of Blake's poems as paintings, and write a description of each. Specify the colors, style, and images in each painting as well as its overall mood. You may wish, instead, to make the actual paintings.

COMPARING WRITERS

▨ Both Burns and Blake are considered pre-Romantics. Romantic writers were experimental and imaginative. They used spontaneous, natural diction to describe ordinary situations involving common people living in rural settings. Discuss why Burns and Blake can be considered pre-Romantics. Cite examples from their poems to support your points.

READING FOR APPRECIATION

Implication and Inference

When we read, as when we listen, we can deepen our appreciation of what is being said by looking for implications and making inferences. Be careful not to confuse these two terms: Remember that the writer or speaker *implies* and the reader or listener *infers.* Drawing the proper inference, understanding the writer's implication, is illuminating and often pleasurable and is an important part of what makes literature an experience of *discovery.*

In general, we can say that more intelligence, more precision, more subtlety, more grace—in short, more artistry—are needed to imply a thought or an idea than to stand up, open wide one's mouth, and bellow it forth. A simple line drawing by a skillful artist can catch a person's essence as well as or better than a copiously detailed painting. A gesture or a look can speak volumes. An implication can tell more than a bald statement and can tell it more directly and more powerfully.

Why is an implication more *powerful?* Rather than being told an idea, we discover it for ourselves. Arriving at a conclusion on our own, we understand it better and remember it longer. Because the idea has in a sense come to us from "within" (we have *inferred* it), its impact is immeasurably greater.

Look, for example, at Samuel Johnson's "Letter to Lord Chesterfield." Despite its brevity, this document expresses a great deal. It is a remarkable instance of the *penetrating* power of implication. The author begins respectfully enough and harmlessly, but the second sentence already indicates that the letter will be no mere note of complacent thanks:

. . . To be so distinguished is an honor which, being very little accustomed to favors from the great, I know not well how to receive, or in what terms to acknowledge.

Johnson acknowledges that he has been honored, but at the same time he observes that such "favors from the great" have been few—so few, indeed, that he has no idea even how to react. He *implies* that the matter extends far beyond gratefulness for this particular favor. Lord Chesterfield is in for something more.

With extraordinary conciseness, Johnson demonstrates the essential falseness of the patronage system. After all, Johnson explains that he has the arduous task of compiling the *Dictionary* without the least assistance from Chesterfield, who now wants to consider himself Johnson's patron. Chesterfield has not given "one act of assistance, one word of encouragement, or one smile of favor."

Johnson seems to say, "So *this* is what patrons do—nothing! So *this* is what patronage is all about: *Now* I know!"

To reinforce these sentiments, he then alludes to Virgil's eighth *Eclogue:*

The shepherd in Virgil grew at last acquainted with Love, and found him a native of the rocks.

The shepherd bitterly laments that love must have been born among barren rocks. By way of analogy, Johnson implies that at last he has learned the true meaning of patronage, and it proves most cold and hard, dry and unyielding.

Samuel Johnson showed great skill in writing a letter bristling with implications. A careful reader must use skills to untangle, or infer, Johnson's meaning and tone.

THE ENGLISH VOICE

A Human Perspective

The eighteenth century—the age of reason, neoclassicism, order, and elegance—was a time particularly conscious of perspective. In literary and cultural terms perspective is a sense of proportion, of the relationship of one thing to another, of one person or class or idea or attitude to another. It was a sense of perspective that gave rise to a century of reasoned essays, objective criticism, and elegant satire.

The eighteenth century demanded not only a balanced perspective but a human one. People were the gauge of what was important or what was trivial, of what was possible and what was not.

Swift

He observed, how contemptible a thing was human grandeur, which could be mimicked by such diminutive insects as I.

Steele

The imagination took a lovely impression of what was great and good; and they who never thought of setting up for the art of imitation, became themselves imitable characters.

Addison

It should be my care . . . in particular that those may not make the most noise who have the least to sell.

Pope

Know then thyself, presume not God to scan;
The proper study of mankind is man.

Johnson

In this work, when it shall be found that much is omitted, let it not be forgotten that much likewise is performed.

Gray

The paths of glory lead but to the grave.

Burns

The best-laid schemes o' mice an' men,
Gang aft agley.

Addison and Steele put English society into perspective for their readers. Swift and Pope did more: They put the whole human race into perspective. In the preface to his *Dictionary,* Johnson used the model of a great literary endeavor to put all of human endeavor into perspective. Gray and Burns used nature to achieve the same vision: a human perspective, neither too high nor too low, neither too large nor too small, but balanced, ordered, reasoned.

Key to Illustrations on Pages 250–251.

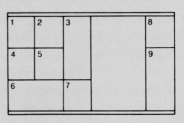

1. Portrait of Robert Burns, Nasmyth Alexander (1758–1840).
2. Detail, *Cries of London,* "*Mop Sellers,*" an eighteenth-century watercolor, Paul Sandby (1725–1809).
3. Detail, portrait, Thomas Gainsborough, 1775.
4. Detail, *Coffee House,* eighteenth-century, artist unknown.
5. Portrait of Jonathan Swift, Charles Gervas.
6. Detail, engraving depicting London and London Bridge from the Surrey side of the Thames, 1707.
7. *Dr. Johnson,* Sir Joshua Reynolds (1732–1792).
8. Pulteney Bridge, Bath, England.
9. Poem from *Songs of Experience,* written, illustrated and printed by William Blake, 1794.

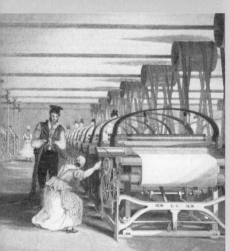

Key to Illustrations appears on page 401.

THE ROMANTIC AGE

1798–1837

The intellectuals who lived from 1798 to about 1837 knew there was something unique and dramatic about their times, even if no one officially named the period the Romantic Age until much later in the 1800s. Said one of them, the great essayist William Hazlitt, "There was a mighty ferment in the heads of statesmen and poets, kings and people. . . . It was a time of promise, a renewal of the world—and of letters." During this period much of Europe including England—and eventually America—experienced a monumental upheaval in political, economic, social, and philosophical systems. Revolutionary attitudes crashed across the Old World, and out of the new energy came a new literature.

The Political Background

During the early 1800s the French situation dominated England's foreign policy. The French Revolution had begun in 1789 as a protest against royal despotism, an assertion of the equality of people. In its early phases the French Revolution had seemed to offer great hope for common people. At the outbreak of the French Revolution, most enlightened people in Great Britain had felt sympathy for the democratic ideals of the revolutionaries in France. Yet once the rev-

Detail, *The Battle of Trafalgar, 21 October 1805*, J. M. W. Turner, 1823.

olutionary government in France had achieved power, it resorted to brutality. The violence—notably, the massacres of imprisoned nobility; the execution of King Louis XVI and his wife, Marie Antoinette; and the guillotining of thousands during the Reign of Terror (1793–1794) under Robespierre—made continued English sentiment in favor of the French Revolution difficult, if not completely impossible.

Furthermore, in 1793 revolutionary France declared war on England. From that point until 1815, with no more than a brief respite, England and France were engaged in the Napoleonic Wars. Napoleon Bonaparte—a brilliant young Corsican, one of the most successful military strategists the world has ever known, and originally a champion of the French Revolution—gained control of France and became emperor in 1804.

The British fought Napoleon on land and sea. Admiral Horatio Nelson became a British national hero by completely annihilating French naval power at the Battle of Trafalgar (1805) off the coast of Spain. Napoleon remained victorious on land until another British hero, the Duke of Wellington, beat Napoleon's armies in Spain and then, in the fatal blow, at the Battle of Waterloo, in 1815. Subsequently, the peace conference, the Congress of Vienna, restored the absolute monarchies to France and to other European nations whose

royalty Napoleon had overthrown in his attempt to dominate Europe. With the return of France to its prerevolutionary condition, the hopes of democratic idealists were crushed.

During this period of conflict with France, England had severe domestic political problems as well. To begin with, England's Hanoverian king, George III, was on the throne (from 1760 to 1820), but in 1811 he was declared permanently and incurably insane. His son George, the Prince of Wales, was made regent, or stand-in ruler, until the father's death in 1820. Then he was crowned George IV and began a ten-year reign. He became a fiercely intolerant foe of the liberal minority.

Domestic repression against political reformers and agitators grew severe as the Napoleonic Wars with France continued. Measures were enacted to restrict freedoms of assembly, of speech, and of the press.

After Napoleon's defeat, dissent and agitation for reform

continued, but during the years 1815 to 1820, the conservative Tory party exhibited an unyieldingly repressive attitude toward the call for reform from England's liberals. Workers had no legal recourse, for labor unions were illegal, nor did workers have a vote, and the government maintained a policy of *laissez faire,* or noninterference.

In 1830 George IV died and was succeeded by his more liberal brother, William IV. During William's reign the growing need for parliamentary reform was finally addressed when the Parliament passed the historic First Reform Bill of 1832. This bill extended the right to vote—not to the working class but at least to much of the newly well-to-do middle class. In 1800 less than 5 percent of adult males in England had the right to vote for Parliament. Finally, in 1832, more Englishmen for the first time gained the right to elect their leaders.

Life in England During the Romantic Age

The Industrial Revolution had begun in the 1760s, and certainly by the end of the Romantic Age its effects had produced drastic social and economic changes. New machines and power tools replaced hand tools, transforming an agricultural nation into an urbanized, industrialized one. In rural England home industry was destroyed, agricultural laborers were paid

The Factory Children from *The Costume of Yorkshire,* George Walker, 1814.

less than subsistence wages, and land fell into fewer, more powerful hands. In the cities a large new working class developed. Most of these people were poor factory workers who faced a life of drudgery, squalor, long hours, harsh treatment, and bad health. Children suffered exploitation because they were a cheap source of labor, easy to discipline and easy to recruit.

For the rich, the Regency (1811–1820) was a time of extravagance and lavish social display. In fashion, men's styles were influenced by the tastes of George "Beau" Brummel, who introduced the practices of stiffening cravats and wearing dark clothing instead of the formerly colorful knee britches, vests, and coats. Women abandoned tight bodices and stiff corsets in favor of high-waisted, flowing gowns such as those worn by Napoleon's empress, Josephine. Beginning in the 1790s, hairpowder and wigs were largely discarded. Men and women wore their hair in classical curls —as can be seen in portraits of Lord Byron.

However, it would be a mistake to assume that all Englishmen of comfortable means were oblivious to the plight of the poor. Among liberal intellectuals, like the poet Lord Byron and the social philosopher William Godwin, and among reform-minded members of the Church of England, there was a growing humanitarian feeling. Slave trade in the British colo-

nies was made illegal in 1807, and slavery itself was abolished throughout Britain's overseas colonies in 1833. On the whole, though, the rich were largely indifferent to the deprivation and suffering of the poor.

Scientific achievements in the areas of geology, chemistry, physics, and astronomy flourished during the Romantic Age. The drop in the country's death rate was attributable to some limited advances in medicine including the reduction of smallpox, the increase of hospitals, and better medical treatment in childbirth. However, the general state of medicine was still poor, and people did not clearly understand the relationship between dirt and disease.

In sum, the Romantic Age in England saw excruciating living conditions as well as the possibility for relief and improvement. The strength of the common working people and the promise of freedom from oppression were keenly felt by the Romantic poets.

Poetry and Essays in the Romantic Age

The literary movement called Romanticism represented a renewal of progressive thought and emotion, which had existed before the 1700s and which had never totally died out. While Romanticism in the 1800s signaled a new mood, the world had witnessed earlier cultural movements that also merit the name *Romanticism.* Specifically, the ancient Greek epics (see Part Two of this book) can be called Romantic, as can much literature of the Medieval Period (page 31) and of the Renaissance, or Elizabethan Age (page 81). All these writings—and the writings of the English Romantic Age under study here— emphasize human adventure, passion, delight, love of splendor, of extravagance, and of the supernatural. The Romantic tradition in all these periods can be viewed in contrast to another main literary tradition—Classicism or neoclassicism. The pendulum of literary taste seems to swing between the two traditions.

Examine the following lists, which contrast elements, outlooks, and concerns associated with the neoclassicism of the 1700s and the Romanticism of the early 1800s. Keep in mind also that although earlier literary periods can indeed be seen as typically Romantic, the period discussed here (1798–1837) is considered *the* Romantic Age.

Neoclassical	Romantic
tradition	experiment
society	individual
urban	rural
artificial	nature loving
intellect, reason	imagination, emotion
public	private, subjective
logical, solid	mysterious, supernatural
aristocratic	common
cultivated	primitive
conformist	independent
constraint	spontaneity
formal diction	natural diction

Three notable poets of the 1700s—Thomas Gray, William Blake, and Robert Burns—were in many respects as "romantic" as any poets of the Romantic Age, but the work of these three was isolated. Why did English literature change its views and philosophies, its aims and subject matter, so decisively at just the turn of the century?

Certainly, the historical issues and developments of the time played a major role in provoking and shaping the new literary movement of Romanticism: One critic has said, "The French Revolution and Napoleon made a clean sweep; after them it was no longer possible to think, act, or write as if the old forms still had life." Also, the Industrial Revolution, its urban-ization of English life, and its abuses against the working class called for a change in literary concerns and style. The Romantic poets in England also owed much to the Swiss-born French philosopher, Jean Jacques Rousseau (1712–1787). In his philosophies Rousseau rebelled against the cold logic of the 1700s and championed freedom and experimentation. He believed that man was most perfect in a state of nature, free from artificial societal restraints.

The Romantic Age in English literature begins in 1798 with the publication of *Lyrical Ballads,* the product of a great creative collaboration between the poets William Wordsworth and Samuel Taylor Coleridge. This volume revolutionized poetry—both in its theory and its subject matter.

In the Preface accompanying the second edition of *Lyrical Ballads,* Wordsworth enunciated his aims, among which was his belief that poetry should reflect spontaneity and emotion rather than the more sedate, or-dered tones of the previous generation. Wordsworth also stressed a desire to depict commonplace situations involving common people living in natural settings. Coleridge chose to concentrate his efforts on the supernatural. But both poets intended that their work—whether a treatment of the ordinary or of the mysterious—would stimulate an awareness of the workings of the human mind and personality. With respect to poetic form, they advocated using natural, ordinary speech over the formal, stylized diction of the 1700s.

Perhaps it is in their view of nature and natural phenomena and in their treatment of the supernatural and mysterious that the Romantics differed most profoundly from the neoclassicists. Partly as a reaction against the urbanizing, dehumanizing effects of the Industrial Revolution, the Romantic poets regarded nature in a fresh light and abandoned the well-tended gardens of the 1700s for the wilderness.

Though Romanticism shared with neoclassicism an interest in the past, Romanticism emphasized Ancient Greece over Ancient Rome. Furthermore, the Romantic concern with the past encompassed a renewed interest in the Middle Ages. Finally, the Romantics paid greater attention to the works of Shakespeare, Spenser, and Milton than had literary critics of the neoclassical era.

The essence of the English

Mary Shelley (1797–1851), Richard Rothwell, 1841.

Romantic Age is contained in the works of five poets—Wordsworth and Coleridge constituting the so-called first generation of Romantic poets, and Percy Bysshe Shelley, Lord Byron, and John Keats composing the second generation. These poets also wrote essays and letters explaining their ideas about poetry. In addition, Charles Lamb, William Hazlitt, and Thomas de Quincey wrote personal and subjective essays on a wide range of subjects.

Drama in the Romantic Age

Drama did not flourish during the Romantic Age. Only two theaters—Drury Lane and Covent Garden—were licensed to produce spoken drama. Audiences at both theaters were usually boisterous and unrefined. Thus, the main type of drama produced was simplistic, extreme melodrama in which all the poor are good and all the rich are evil.

Still, some of the leading Romantic poets wrote so-called **closet drama,** poetic drama written to be read rather than produced. Among the better known plays of this type are Shelley's tragedy *The Cenci,* Byron's *Manfred,* and Coleridge's *Remorse.*

The Novel in the Romantic Age

The **gothic novel** became increasingly popular during the Romantic Age. This kind of novel often involved the supernatural and was set against foreboding backgrounds such as haunted castles and gloomy ruins. Perhaps the most famous gothic novel published during this time was *Frankenstein,* written by Mary Shelley, the wife of the Romantic poet Percy Bysshe Shelley. *Frankenstein* goes beyond the gothic interest in the supernatural to explore the nature of evil and the possible consequences of mechanization in the new industrial age.

Two of the most popular and respected novelists in English literature wrote during the Romantic Age. One, the Scottish Sir Walter Scott (1771–1832), wrote novels of adventure. He was immensely popular during his lifetime and is now considered the father of the historical novel. Reflecting the Romantic interest in the past, he set many of his novels in England and Scotland of old. For example, Scott wrote about thirteenth-century England in *Ivanhoe,* a complex romance. Like Rousseau, Scott believed there was more to life than reason alone and incorporated his fascination with the marvelous and uncommon into his work. In this and in his love of nature and of a legendary past, Scott was a true product of the Romantic Age.

The other major novelist writing during the Romantic Age was Jane Austen. Austen's novels were drastically different from Scott's. Though she wrote during the height of this period, she remained remarkably unaffected by Romantic literary influences. Her plots concerned domestic situations, with sensitivity and manners dominant. Her most famous novel, *Pride and Prejudice,* is about a genteel eighteenth-century family in an English country town. Realistic in tone, graceful, and deliberately decorous in the fashion of the **novel of manners,** Austen's novels usually revolve around the business of finding appropriate husbands for marriageable daughters. Much of the plot unfolds through brilliant conversations, as in the dialogue of a play. This dialogue reveals character and directs plot in a stylish, "modern" way. Austen had a keen ear for conversation and a wit tuned to satire. She was truly more representative of the neoclassical tradition of eighteenth-century literature than of the Romantic Period. Although she received little public recognition during her lifetime, Austen is now one of the best-loved English novelists and one who—in her use of dialogue—helped to develop the modern novel.

TIME LINE

1798   William Wordsworth and Samuel Coleridge, *Lyrical Ballads*

1801   Act of Union of Great Britain and Ireland

1800   America: Washington, D.C., becomes the new capital

1804   France: Napoleon crowns himself emperor

JANE AUSTEN

1805   Battle of Trafalgar; Admiral Nelson defeats Napoleon

1807   First gaslights on London streets

      Charles and Mary Lamb, *Tales from Shakespeare*

1808   Austria: German composer Ludwig van Beethoven, *Symphony No. 5*

1809   America: Washington Irving, *Rip Van Winkle*

1811   Regency period begins

1812   New Drury Lane Theatre erected in London

1812   America: War declared on Great Britain

      Germany: The Brothers Grimm, *Fairy Tales*

LORD BYRON

1813   Jane Austen, *Pride and Prejudice*

1813   Mexico: Independence is declared

1814   First practical steam locomotive constructed

1814   America: British forces burn Washington, D.C.

1815   Duke of Wellington leads final defeat of Napoleon at Waterloo

1815   Austria: Congress of Vienna

      France: Bourbons restored to throne

1816   Samuel Taylor Coleridge, "Kubla Khan"

1817   William Hazlitt, *The Characters of Shakespeare's Plays*

1818   George Gordon, Lord Byron begins *Don Juan*

      Mary Wollstonecraft Shelley, *Frankenstein or the Modern Prometheus*

1818   Germany: Friederich W. Bessel, catalog of 3,222 stars

1820 John Keats, "Ode to a Nightingale"

Sir Walter Scott, *Ivanhoe*

Percy Bysshe Shelley, *Prometheus Unbound*

Charles Lamb begins *Essays of Elia*

George III dies; George IV becomes king

1825 Workers are allowed to form labor unions

1826 First railroad tunnel built for Liverpool–Manchester Railway

Royal Zoological Society is founded

1829 Metropolitan police force established in London by Sir Robert Peel

1830 William IV ascends the throne

1832 Britain occupies the Falkland Islands

1834 Two-wheeled, one horse hansom cabs introduced

1835 W. H. Fox Talbot takes the earliest negative photograph

1837 Victoria ascends the throne

First railway telegraph installed in London

JOHN KEATS

PERCY BYSSHE SHELLEY

1820 Greece: *Discovery of Venus de Milo,* classical statue carved about 150 B.C.

America: Missouri Compromise

1825 Russia: Bolshoi Ballet established in Moscow

1826 America: James Fenimore Cooper, *The Last of the Mohicans*

1828 America: First passenger and freight railroad constructed

America: Noah Webster, *American Dictionary of the English Language*

1829 Austria: Frédéric Chopin's debut in Vienna

1831 Germany: Johann Wolfgang von Goethe completes *Faust*

1832 America: First horse-drawn trolleys in New York

1834 America: Cyrus McCormick patents reaper

France: Louis Braille perfects system of characters enabling the blind to read

1835 Denmark: Hans Christian Andersen, *Fairy Tales*

America: Phineas T. Barnum holds his first exhibition

1836 America: Davy Crockett killed at the Alamo

William Wordsworth   *1770–1850*

William Wordsworth in collaboration with his friend and colleague Samuel Taylor Coleridge (page 339) was the first poet to announce the literary ideals of the English Romantic Age. Wordsworth was born in England's Lake District, a land of breathtaking scenery, and the most beautiful region in the entire country. His mother died when he was eight, and he, along with his three brothers, was sent to study at the excellent grammar school at Hawkshead, also in the Lake District. There he grew up, free to wander through the countryside, hiking and skating. As we shall see, these early opportunities to commune with nature would have a profound effect on much of Wordsworth's poetry. He received a fine education, both at the grammar school and at Cambridge University, from which he was graduated in 1791.

While in France during 1791 and 1792, he became an ardent supporter of the French Revolution, which he (and many other liberal Englishmen) enthusiastically interpreted as championing the cause of human liberty. During this time he also fell passionately in love with a French girl, Annette Vallon. Though he wished to remain in France because of the revolution and because of his love for Annette, lack of money forced his departure for England. The outbreak of war between England and France in 1793 prevented Wordsworth's immediate return to France, and his conscience plagued him, his loyalties divided between the two countries. Then he grew ever more disillusioned with the course of the French Revolution as events there became increasingly violent and the revolution departed drastically from the original democratic ideals he had so admired. Guilt over his inability to marry Annette, unhappiness at not finding suitable employment, and the growing certainty that the French Revolution was not the example for humankind that he had once thought it could be brought Wordsworth to the brink of mental collapse. He fell into a period of deep depression.

In 1795, almost three years after returning from a second visit to France, he came into enough money to move into a small cottage with his sister, Dorothy, who was his close friend and confidant. Soon afterward, he met Coleridge, and this meeting resulted in what is certainly the most significant friendship in all of English literature. With the companionship and support of Dorothy and Coleridge, who deeply admired Wordsworth's poetry and convinced him of its worth, Wordsworth recovered from the despair that had engulfed him for several years.

"All good poetry is the spontaneous overflow of powerful feelings." This remark occurs in the course of Wordsworth's Preface to *Lyrical Ballads* of 1800. Spontaneity, excess, power, and emotion:

Those are the traits of Romanticism, subscribed to by Wordsworth in that slim volume of poems entitled *Lyrical Ballads,* first published in 1798, written jointly by him and Coleridge. That book is the cornerstone of English Romanticism. Late in the eighteenth century other poets—Gray and Burns and Blake—had reacted against the strict demands of neoclassicism. Yet none rebelled as consciously, as consistently, and as influentially as did Wordsworth, working closely with his friend Coleridge. Wordsworth's Preface, written for the second edition of *Lyrical Ballads* in 1800, explains the principles underlying his and Coleridge's new approach to poetry and may thus serve as the formal announcement of a new literary age.

Dryden, Pope, and Johnson—giants of neoclassicism—had seen poetry as an aristocratic pursuit, calculated rather than spontaneous, more a matter of wit than power, an endeavor more of the mind than the heart. Through poetry, aristocrats spoke to aristocrats. To Wordsworth, however, and to Coleridge, poetry was more properly regarded as people speaking to people—and not in heroic couplets but in whatever form might be suitable to a particular occasion. Wordsworth, in particular, called for the use of natural, commonplace diction in literary works.

Unlike the neoclassicists, Wordsworth was convinced of the importance of subjectivity in poetry. He believed that poetry "takes its origin from emotion recollected in tranquillity." In other words, true poetry, conceived in spontaneous emotion, takes on meaning and shape as the poet contemplates the subject. Thus poetry reflects the poet's subjective reactions and reasoned reflections. Nor should poets choose for their subjects lords and ladies, with all their courtly affectations. Instead, they should write, so Wordsworth felt, of "humble and rustic" people, whose feelings were genuine and unspoiled, living out their lives close to nature. Clearly nature, which had been a major element of the poet's youth, had a substantial influence on Wordsworth's poetic inspiration. The response of the individual human mind to the simple, universal truths and beauty revealed in nature fascinated Wordsworth. He focused on the natural and ordinary in an attempt to explore the relationship between nature and our inner life.

Wordsworth spent most of his long life back in the beautiful Lake District with his wife, Mary (who had been a childhood friend), and his beloved sister, Dorothy. Although he continued to compose poetry into old age, his greatest poems had been written by then, most of them done in a single remarkable decade—between 1797 and 1807—while he and Coleridge were consciously altering the direction of English literature.

"One afternoon in 1801," Wordsworth recalled, "my sister read to me the sonnets of Milton. I had long been well acquainted with them, but I was particularly struck on that occasion with the dignified simplicity and majestic harmony that runs through most of them. . . ." The experience was so inspiring that the poet proceeded to write three sonnets of his own that same day. In the course of his lifetime, Wordsworth went on to write more than 130 sonnets—including some of the very best in the language. He returned the sonnet form to the prestigious position from which it had fallen during the eighteenth century. Wordsworth wrote the greatest of his sonnets by 1807, when he published his collected *Poems in Two Volumes.*

William Wordsworth

The World Is Too Much with Us

The world is too much with us; late and soon,
Getting and spending, we lay waste our powers;
Little we see in Nature that is ours;
We have given our hearts away, a sordid boon![1]
5 This sea that bares her bosom to the moon,
The winds that will be howling at all hours,
And are up-gathered now like sleeping flowers,
For this, for everything, we are out of tune;
It moves us not.—Great God! I'd rather be
10 A Pagan suckled in a creed outworn;
So might I, standing on this pleasant lea,[2]
Have glimpses that would make me less forlorn;
Have sight of Proteus[3] rising from the sea;
Or hear old Triton[4] blow his wreathèd horn.

---

1. **boon:** gift, favor.
2. **lea** [lē]: meadow.
3. **Proteus** [prō′tē′əs]: in classical mythology, a sea god who could assume various forms.
4. **Triton** [trīt′ən]: in classical mythology, a figure who was half man and half fish and blew upon a conch-shell horn.

London, 1802

Milton! thou shouldst be living at this hour:
England hath need of thee: she is a fen[1]
Of stagnant waters: altar, sword, and pen,
Fireside, the heroic wealth of hall and bower,
5 Have forfeited their ancient English dower[2]
Of inward happiness. We are selfish men;
Oh! raise us up, return to us again;
And give us manners, virtue, freedom, power.
Thy soul was like a Star, and dwelt apart;
10 Thou hadst a voice whose sound was like the sea:
Pure as the naked heavens, majestic, free,
So didst thou travel on life's common way,
In cheerful godliness; and yet thy heart
The lowliest duties on herself did lay.

---

1. **fen:** swamp, bog.
2. **dower:** gift, endowment.

It Is a Beauteous Evening, Calm and Free

It is a beauteous evening, calm and free,
The holy time is quiet as a Nun
Breathless with adoration; the broad sun
Is sinking down in its tranquility;
5 The gentleness of heaven broods o'er the Sea:
Listen! the mighty Being is awake,
And doth with his eternal motion make
A sound like thunder—everlastingly.
Dear Child! dear Girl! that walkest with me here,
10 If thou appear untouched by solemn thought,
Thy nature is not therefore less divine:
Thou liest in Abraham's bosom[1] all the year,
And worship'st at the Temple's inner shrine,
God being with thee when we know it not.

---

1. **Abraham's bosom:** heaven (Luke 16 : 22).

William Wordsworth

Composed upon Westminster Bridge, September 3, 1802

Earth has not anything to show more fair:
Dull would he be of soul who could pass by
A sight so touching in its majesty;
This City now doth, like a garment, wear
5 The beauty of the morning; silent, bare,
Ships, towers, domes, theaters, and temples lie
Open unto the fields, and to the sky;
All bright and glittering in the smokeless air.
Never did sun more beautifully steep[1]
10 In his first splendor, valley, rock, or hill;
Ne'er saw I, never felt, a calm so deep!
The river glideth at his own sweet will:
Dear God! the very houses seem asleep;
And all that mighty heart is lying still!

---

1. **steep:** saturate.

The Houses of Parliament, Winslow Homer, 1881.

STUDY QUESTIONS

The World Is Too Much with Us

Recalling

1. What do we do that causes us to "lay waste our powers" (line 2)?
2. According to lines 5–7, with what, specifically, are we "out of tune"?
3. Beginning in the middle of line 9 (in the sestet of the sonnet), what kind of life and what kinds of sights would make the speaker "less forlorn"?

Interpreting

4. What aspect of the world "is too much with us," according to this poem? In general terms, what does the speaker suggest we turn to instead?
5. In the context of the poem, what do Proteus and Triton represent? How might an older, pagan creed enable the speaker to have a greater feeling of identity with nature?
6. What emotion can you attribute to this poem's speaker? Explain your reasoning.

Extending

7. Explain why this poem remains relevant.

London, 1802

Recalling

1. Why should Milton, the seventeenth-century poet, be living during Wordsworth's day, according to line 2?
2. According to lines 5–6, what have the English forfeited?
3. What Miltonic characteristics, listed in line 8, are longed for by the poet (recently returned from France and struck by "the vanity and parade" of England)?

Interpreting

4. What is conveyed about English society of the time by the image of England as "a fen/Of stagnant waters"?
5. What do altar, sword, pen, and fireside stand for?

6. Based on the second part of the sonnet (lines 9–14), what do you think Wordsworth most admires about Milton?

Extending

7. Compare the pictures of London in "Composed upon Westminster Bridge" and in "London, 1802." How can the pictures be so different?

It Is a Beauteous Evening, Calm and Free

Recalling

1. What adjectives and nouns in lines 1–5 describe the mood of the evening?
2. What does the speaker hear in lines 6–8?
3. With whom does the speaker walk, and how does that person appear?

Interpreting

4. How does Wordsworth give nature a spiritual significance in the sonnet's first eight lines?
5. What contrast exists between the sonnet's first eight lines and its last six?
6. What is the speaker's feeling about childhood, implicit in the final four lines of this sonnet?

Composed upon Westminster Bridge

Recalling

1. What two statements of praise for London does the speaker offer in lines 1–3?
2. At what time of day is London being described in this poem, which Wordsworth later said was "composed on the roof of a coach, on my way to France"? What specific elements of the London landscape does the speaker applaud in lines 5–8?
3. According to line 11, what is the dominant atmosphere of London at this time?

Interpreting

4. What is the city being likened to in lines 4–5? What is the city being compared to in lines 9–10? Explain the personification in lines 12–14.
5. What is surprising about the picture of the city in this poem? Consider in your answer the contrast between "touching" and "majesty" (line 3).

This is one of five poems on a similar subject, written during the winter of 1798–1799 while Wordsworth was in Germany with his sister, Dorothy, and his friend Coleridge, who was studying German philosophy at the University of Gottingen. They are known as the Lucy poems—the name mentioned in three of them.

William Wordsworth

A Slumber Did My Spirit Seal

A slumber did my spirit seal;
  I had no human fears:
She seemed a thing that could not feel
  The touch of earthly years.

5 No motion has she now, no force;
  She neither hears nor sees;
Rolled round in earth's diurnal[1] course,
  With rocks, and stones, and trees.

---

1. **diurnal** [dī urn′əl]: daily.

Detail, *Near Dunkeld*, John Samuel Raven (1829–1877).

"No poem of mine," writes Wordsworth, "was composed under circumstances more pleasant for me to remember than this." He had brought his sister to visit a beautiful rural landscape—complete with an abbey, or church building—just over the Welsh border. Five years earlier, in 1793, the poet had passed through the same region alone. Now, under these pleasant circumstances, he began composing verses in his head, completing a poem in the course of this second walking tour. "Not a line of it was altered, and not any part of it written down till I reached Bristol."

Lines Composed a Few Miles Above Tintern Abbey

Five years have passed; five summers, with the length
Of five long winters! and again I hear
These waters, rolling from their mountain springs
With a soft inland murmur. Once again
5 Do I behold these steep and lofty cliffs,
That on a wild secluded scene impress
Thoughts of more deep seclusion; and connect
The landscape with the quiet of the sky.
The day is come when I again repose
10 Here, under this dark sycamore, and view
These plots of cottage ground, these orchard tufts,
Which at this season, with their unripe fruits,
Are clad in one green hue, and lose themselves
'Mid groves and copses.[1] Once again I see
15 These hedgerows, hardly hedgerows, little lines
Of sportive wood run wild; these pastoral farms,
Green to the very door; and wreaths of smoke
Sent up, in silence, from among the trees!
With some uncertain notice, as might seem
20 Of vagrant dwellers in the houseless woods,
Or of some Hermit's cave, where by his fire
The Hermit sits alone.
          These beauteous forms,
Through a long absence, have not been to me

---

1. **copses** [kops′əz]: grove of small trees or bushes.

As is a landscape to a blind man's eye;
25 But oft, in lonely rooms, and 'mid the din
Of towns and cities, I have owed to them,
In hours of weariness, sensations sweet,
Felt in the blood, and felt along the heart;
And passing even into my purer mind,
30 With tranquil restoration—feelings too
Of unremembered pleasure; such, perhaps,
As have no slight or trivial influence
On that best portion of a good man's life,
His little, nameless, unremembered acts
35 Of kindness and of love. Nor less, I trust,
To them I may have owed another gift,
Of aspect more sublime; that blessed mood,
In which the burthen[2] of the mystery,
In which the heavy and the weary weight
40 Of all this unintelligible world,
Is lightened—that serene and blessed mood,
In which the affections gently lead us on—
Until, the breath of this corporeal frame[3]
And even the motion of our human blood
45 Almost suspended, we are laid asleep
In body, and become a living soul;
While with an eye made quiet by the power
Of harmony, and the deep power of joy,
We see into the life of things.
                                            If this
50 Be but a vain belief, yet, oh! how oft—
In darkness and amid the many shapes
Of joyless daylight; when the fretful stir
Unprofitable, and the fever of the world,
Have hung upon the beatings of my heart—
55 How oft, in spirit, have I turned to thee,
O sylvan[4] Wye![5] thou wanderer through the woods,
How often has my spirit turned to thee!

   And now, with gleams of half-extinguished thought
With many recognitions dim and faint,
60 And somewhat of a sad perplexity,
The picture of the mind revives again;
While here I stand, not only with the sense
Of present pleasure, but with pleasing thoughts
That in this moment there is life and food

---

2. **burthen:** burden.
3. **corporeal** [kôr pôr′ē əl] **frame:** physical body.
4. **sylvan** [sil′vən]: wooded.
5. **Wye** [wī]: river that runs near Tintern Abbey.

Detail, *Tintern Abbey,* Henry Harris
(c. 1805–1865).

65 For future years. And so I dare to hope,
Though changed, no doubt, from what I was when first
I came among these hills; when like a roe[6]
I bounded o'er the mountains, by the sides
Of the deep rivers, and the lonely streams,
70 Wherever nature led—more like a man
Flying from something that he dreads than one
Who sought the thing he loved. For nature then
(The coarser pleasures of my boyish days,
And their glad animal movements all gone by)
75 To me was all in all.—I cannot paint
What then I was. The sounding cataract[7]
Haunted me like a passion; the tall rock,
The mountain, and the deep and gloomy wood,
Their colors and their forms, were then to me
80 An appetite; a feeling and a love,
That had no need of a remoter charm,
By thought supplied, nor any interest
Unborrowed from the eye.—That time is past,
And all its aching joys are now no more,
85 And all its dizzy raptures. Nor for this
Faint[8] I, nor mourn nor murmur; other gifts
Have followed; for such loss, I would believe,
Abundant recompense. For I have learned
To look on nature, not as in the hour
90 Of thoughtless youth; but hearing oftentimes
The still, sad music of humanity,
Nor harsh nor grating, though of ample power
To chasten and subdue. And I have felt
A presence that disturbs me with the joy
95 Of elevated thoughts; a sense sublime
Of something far more deeply interfused,
Whose dwelling is the light of setting suns,
And the round ocean and the living air,
And the blue sky, and in the mind of man:
100 A motion and a spirit, that impels
All thinking things, all objects of all thought,
And rolls through all things. Therefore am I still
A lover of the meadows and the woods,
And mountains; and of all that we behold
105 From this green earth; of all the mighty world
Of eye, and ear—both what they half create,
And what perceive; well pleased to recognize
In nature and the language of the sense

---

6. **roe:** kind of deer.
7. **cataract:** waterfall.
8. **Faint:** lose heart or courage; become depressed.

The anchor of my purest thoughts, the nurse,
110 The guide, the guardian of my heart, and soul
Of all my moral being.
                         Nor perchance,
If I were not thus taught, should I the more
Suffer[9] my genial[10] spirits to decay:
For thou art with me here upon the banks
115 Of this fair river; thou my dearest Friend,[11]
My dear, dear Friend; and in thy voice I catch
The language of my former heart, and read
My former pleasures in the shooting lights
Of thy wild eyes. Oh! yet a little while
120 May I behold in thee what I was once,
My dear, dear Sister! and this prayer I make,
Knowing that Nature never did betray
The heart that loved her; 'tis her privilege,
Through all the years of this our life, to lead
125 From joy to joy: for she can so inform[12]
The mind that is within us, so impress
With quietness and beauty, and so feed
With lofty thoughts, that neither evil tongues,
Rash judgments, nor the sneers of selfish men,
130 Nor greetings where no kindness is, nor all
The dreary intercourse of daily life,
Shall e'er prevail against us, or disturb
Our cheerful faith, that all which we behold
Is full of blessings. Therefore let the moon
135 Shine on thee in thy solitary walk;
And let the misty mountain winds be free
To blow against thee: and, in after years,
When these wild ecstasies shall be matured
Into a sober pleasure; when thy mind
140 Shall be a mansion for all lovely forms,
Thy memory be as a dwelling place
For all sweet sounds and harmonies; oh! then,
If solitude, or fear, or pain, or grief
Should be thy portion, with what healing thoughts
145 Of tender joy wilt thou remember me,
And these my exhortations! Nor, perchance—
If I should be where I no more can hear
Thy voice, nor catch from thy wild eyes these gleams
Of past existence—wilt thou then forget

---

9. **Suffer:** allow.
10. **genial:** relating to "genius" (natural disposition or powers).
11. **Friend:** Dorothy Wordsworth, the poet's sister.
12. **inform:** inspire.

150 That on the banks of this delightful stream
We stood together; and that I, so long
A worshiper of Nature, hither came
Unwearied in that service: rather say
With warmer love—oh! with far deeper zeal
155 Of holier love. Nor wilt thou then forget
That after many wanderings, many years
Of absence, these steep woods and lofty cliffs,
And this green pastoral landscape, were to me
More dear, both for themselves and for thy sake!

STUDY QUESTIONS

A Slumber Did My Spirit Seal

Recalling

1. Into what state did the speaker's spirit seal him? While in that state, why, according to lines 3 and 4, did the speaker have no earthly fears?
2. In the second stanza what has happened to the "she" of the poem?

Interpreting

3. What does the speaker learn by the second stanza?
4. Is the language of the poem complex or simple? What is the effect of such diction in this context?

Lines Composed a Few Miles Above Tintern Abbey

Recalling

1. What is impressed "on a wild secluded scene" (lines 6–7), and what does the speaker notice now that five years have passed?
2. In lines 25–26 where does the speaker say he spent the five years? According to lines 26–41, in what two ways has this scene of nature influenced the speaker during the five years since he first viewed it?
3. What thoughts, described in lines 63–65, does the poet experience in addition to his "sense of present pleasure" while standing at the Wye river?
4. According to line 75, what role did nature play for the speaker in his adolescence? In place of his earlier view of nature, what does the speaker now see in nature (lines 93–111)?
5. What does the speaker wish for his sister in lines 116–120? In lines 134–146?
6. Why does the speaker consider nature dear to him, according to the last line?

Interpreting

7. In what terms would you describe the opening scene of the poem? What effect is suggested by the speaker's "repose" (line 9)? Based on lines 12–13, in what season would you say the speaker is revisiting the Wye valley?
8. How does the speaker convey the impression that he first hears and then sees the scene described in lines 2–5?
9. What do you suppose is that "something" the speaker refers to in line 96 when looking on nature?
10. In the context of the poem, what is the meaning of "Nature never did betray/The heart that loved her" (lines 122–123)?

Extending

11. Can you think of temporary enthusiasms—fads or interests—that, unlike Nature, might "betray" their adherents because of their impermanence or lack of real value?

VIEWPOINT

Matthew Arnold (page 433) wrote of Wordsworth's poetry:

The cause of its greatness is simple, and may be told quite simply. Wordsworth's poetry is great because of the extraordinary power with which Wordsworth feels the joy offered to us in nature, the joy offered to us in the simple primary affections and duties; and because of the extraordinary powers with which, in case after case, he shows us this joy, and renders it so as to make us share it.

■ Which of Wordsworth's poems presented here best convey that sense of joy? What specific phrases impart joy so vividly that we are led to share it?

LITERARY FOCUS

Structure

Structure refers to the units of thought that make up a literary work—the building blocks by means of which the work is put together in an organized and meaningful fashion. Thus, structure involves far more than the poem's verse form and arrangement: It is the sequence of thoughts and images that work together to impart the meaning of the poem. Perceiving the structure, or organizing principle, of a literary work helps us to understand it better—all the more so when the work is long and complex.

The structure of "A Slumber Did My Spirit Seal" (page 332) is as simple as the poem itself, and this simplicity contributes enormously to the power of the poem. In that poem the structure coincides with the stanzas: two units of thought, one in the past ("did," "had," "seemed") and one in the present ("now" and the present tense). All of stanza 1 refers to what "She" was; all of stanza 2 refers to what "She" is now.

"Tintern Abbey" is made more accessible if we follow the larger units of thought by means of which the poem moves forward. Wordsworth believed that poetry "takes its origin from emotion recollected in tranquillity." Two emotional responses to a particular scene are reported in "Tintern Abbey," and these responses serve as the poem's organizing principle.

Clearly the first twenty-two lines of the poem are grouped around a single idea, or purpose: to describe a natural scene. The end of that description is signaled by the gathering together of the various details in the summarizing phrase "These

beauteous forms" (line 22). What follows, for a number of lines, concerns the recollection of this same scene during the past five years: where that recollection has taken place and what its effect has been. Then Wordsworth presents a related thought, which, paraphrased, suggests, "Whether the memory of this beautiful landscape has been all I think it has or not, it is true that I have thought about it often." "And now . . ." (line 58) signals the commencement of yet another unit of thought—back to the present.

We must be alert to language that signals such thought shifts in a work. "Therefore" is one such word (lines 102, 134), drawing a conclusion from what has gone before. "Nor" (lines 111 and 146) is another. By becoming more sensitive to larger blocks of meaning—to the structure of a poem or story—we are better able to understand details within and related to those meanings.

Thinking About Structure

1. Line 111 introduces to the poem a new element that continues through to its conclusion. What is that new element?
2. That unit of thought from line 111 to the end of the poem might be subdivided at line 134. How do the two parts of the larger unit relate to each other? How do they differ?

COMPOSITION

Writing About Literature and Its Period

■ Write a brief essay that begins with this statement: "'Lines Composed a Few Miles Above Tintern Abbey' typifies Romantic poetry." Identify at least three aspects of the poem that mark it as Romantic, perhaps dealing with each aspect in a paragraph of its own. Support each point with quotations and specific details from the poem. *For help with this assignment, refer to Lesson 10 in the Writing About Literature Handbook at the back of this book.*

Describing a Scene

■ Think of a scene that awakens a strong emotion: of delighted awe, as in "Tintern Abbey," or of fright or exhilaration or disgust. In a paragraph or two describe the scene by choosing details that awaken the appropriate emotion in your reader, without mentioning specifically what that emotion is. You may begin with details of sound and work up to details of sight.

Samuel Taylor Coleridge
1772–1834

Samuel Taylor Coleridge is the other great figure besides Wordsworth in what is known as the first generation of Romantics. These two poets (distinguished from the so-called second generation: Byron, Shelley, and Keats) were close friends and collaborators, though their personal lives were in marked contrast and their literary accomplishments explored quite different areas of human experience.

Coleridge was born in England's Devonshire countryside. His father was a clergyman, and when he died, Samuel, then nine years old, was sent to school in London. While he was still quite young, tales such as *Robinson Crusoe* and the *Arabian Nights* enthralled Coleridge, and from an early age he enjoyed the worlds of fantasy and the exotic. At school he was an outstandingly brilliant student and, in 1791, went on to study at Cambridge University. There, however, he became increasingly unhappy and disillusioned with university life. In 1793 he left school to enlist in the army under the alias Silas Tomkyn Comberbacke, a pseudonym whose first initials were the same as his real ones. It was immediately apparent that Coleridge was completely and hopelessly unfit for army service, and, through the intervention of his brothers, he was discharged. Though he returned to Cambridge, he left the university in 1794 without obtaining a degree.

As a young man Coleridge was quite an idealist—in particular about the French Revolution. Only later, as the course of the revolution changed undeniably, did his idealism give way to disillusionment and disappointment.

In 1795 Coleridge met Wordsworth for the first time. The meeting proved momentous, and Wordsworth and his sister, Dorothy, soon moved to Somerset to be near Coleridge, who lived in the neighborhood with his wife, Sara. The two poets spent endless hours in each other's company and began their famous poetic collaboration. For Coleridge this period—leading up to their publication of *Lyrical Ballads* in 1798—was the happiest and most fulfilling of his life.

While Wordsworth's life was in its broadest outlines serene, Coleridge's was tormented, in part because early in life he developed rheumatism. Opium was then a standard medical treatment for such a painful malady, and in the course of persistent attacks, Coleridge became dependent on the drug. "Yet to my fellow men," he wrote, "I may say that I was seduced into the *accursed* Habit ignorantly."

Despite a life filled with illness and depression, Coleridge did a prodigious amount of work. He was the greatest literary critic of his age and one of the two or three greatest critics in the history of English literature; no one has more acute things to say on Shakespeare than does Coleridge. According to the testimony of many who heard him, he was also the finest conversationalist since Samuel Johnson. He was a noted lecturer, an influential philosopher, a theologian, and a journalist as well. The collected work of this towering figure (who faulted himself for not doing more) fills twenty volumes and seven notebooks. Included in that work are several poems supreme of their kind in the whole range of English literature.

The direction in which Coleridge's imagination led him resulted in a kind of Romantic poetry with notable differences from Wordsworth's. Wordsworth wrote poetry that strove "to give the charm of novelty to things of every day." Coleridge, on the other hand, directed his attention to "persons and characters supernatural, or at least romantic," but in a way that made them credible, that gave them "a semblance of truth sufficient to procure for these shadows of imagination that willing suspension of disbelief . . . which constitutes poetic faith." One poet dealt with the familiar; the other, with the strange and unfamiliar. Yet both exulted in expressing the sense of wonder that delights Romantics, whether found far off or close at hand.

Introducing **Kubla Khan**

Coleridge apparently had two explanations for the composition of this poem. On the one hand, he testifies that he devised this fragment under the influence of a painkiller (opium), prescribed for him "in consequence of a slight indisposition." According to this account, he had been reading about Kubla Khan [ko͞o′blə kän]—the thirteenth-century founder of the Mongol dynasty in China—in a travel book when, due to the drug's influence, he fell asleep. Upon waking from a three-hour dream, he found himself possessed of some two to three hundred lines of vivid poetry, which he began immediately to set down—only to be interrupted by "a person on business from Porlock," a nearby town. By the time the visitor had left, he had forgotten the rest of the poem. According to the other, more likely account of Coleridge's composition of "Kubla Khan," the poem was conceived during a daydream and did not come to him as a finished product after a dream.

Regardless of which account of Coleridge's inspiration is accurate, we should realize that the poem is a product of the poet's imagination and thus could be composed only because of his previous conscious and diligent work. The poem is a haunting elaboration of the passage Coleridge had been reading when he either fell asleep or into a daydream, specifically these words (as he recalled them) from *Purchas His Pilgrimage* (1613): "Here the Khan Kubla commanded a palace to be built, and a stately garden thereunto. And thus ten miles of fertile ground were enclosed with a wall."

Samuel Taylor Coleridge

Kubla Khan

In Xanadu[1] did Kubla Khan
A stately pleasure dome decree:[2]
Where Alph,[3] the sacred river, ran
Through caverns measureless to man
5   Down to a sunless sea.
So twice five miles of fertile ground
With walls and towers were girdled round:
And there were gardens bright with sinuous rills,[4]
Where blossomed many an incense-bearing tree;
10 And here were forests ancient as the hills,
Enfolding sunny spots of greenery.

But oh! that deep romantic[5] chasm which slanted
Down the green hill athwart[6] a cedarn[7] cover!
A savage place! as holy and enchanted
15 As e'er beneath a waning moon was haunted
By woman wailing for her demon lover!
And from this chasm, with ceaseless turmoil seething,
As if this earth in fast thick pants were breathing,
A mighty fountain momently[8] was forced:
20 Amid whose swift half-intermitted burst
Huge fragments vaulted like rebounding hail,
Or chaffy grain beneath the thresher's flail:
And 'mid these dancing rocks at once and ever
It flung up momently the sacred river.
25 Five miles meandering with a mazy motion
Through wood and dale the sacred river ran,
Then reached the caverns measureless to man,
And sank in tumult to a lifeless ocean:
And 'mid this tumult Kubla heard from far
30 Ancestral voices prophesying war!
    The shadow of the dome of pleasure
    Floated midway on the waves;

---

1. **Xanadu** [zan′ə dōō′]: an indefinite region in Asia and Europe.
2. **decree:** order to be built.
3. **Alph:** probably the Greek river, Alpheus, or a reference to the classical Greek river god of that name.
4. **rills:** small streams, brooks.
5. **romantic:** having imaginative appeal.
6. **athwart:** across.
7. **cedarn:** made of cedar.
8. **momently:** from moment to moment.

Where was heard the mingled measure
From the fountain and the caves.
35 It was a miracle of rare device,[9]
A sunny pleasure dome with caves of ice!

A damsel with a dulcimer[10]
In a vision once I saw:
It was an Abyssinian[11] maid,
40 And on her dulcimer she played,
Singing of Mount Abora.[12]
Could I revive within me
Her symphony and song,
To such a deep delight 'twould win me,
45 That with music loud and long,
I would build that dome in air,
That sunny dome! those caves of ice!
And all who heard should see them there,
And all should cry, Beware! Beware!
50 His flashing eyes, his floating hair!
Weave a circle round him thrice,
And close your eyes with holy dread,
For he on honeydew hath fed,
And drunk the milk of Paradise.

---

9. **device:** design.
10. **dulcimer** [dul′sə mər]: stringed musical instrument played by striking the strings with light hammers.
11. **Abyssinian** [ab′ə sin′ē ən]: from Ethiopia in Africa.
12. **Mount Abora:** probably Mount Amara in Abyssinia.

STUDY QUESTIONS

Recalling

1. What are the distinctive details of the pleasure dome in Xanadu, as described in the first eleven lines?
2. What images in the second stanza then emphasize that the world outside the dome is "A savage place" (line 14)?
3. What do the "Ancestral voices" (in line 30) predict?
4. What vision is introduced at line 37? What aspect of the vision does the speaker long to recover? What does he want to build?

Interpreting

5. To which different senses does the poem's opening description appeal?
6. What or whom do you suppose the damsel of the vision represents to the speaker?

Extending

7. "Kubla Khan" presents an exotic world—one that is strange and distant. How does the exotic continue to have an appeal? What current books or movies focus on mysterious, alien, or magical settings, characters, or situations?

Initially Wordsworth collaborated with Coleridge on the composition of "The Rime of the Ancient Mariner." Before dropping out of the joint venture, Wordsworth suggested several memorable details, including the shooting of the albatross and the ship's navigation by dead men. "The Rime" is an account of a sea voyage to distant places, with crime, death, and inhuman suffering as parts of the ghastly adventure. Some years after completing the poem, Coleridge himself wrote prose explanations for the margins to help the reader follow the movement of the narrative.

Samuel Taylor Coleridge

The Rime of the Ancient Mariner

ARGUMENT

How a Ship having passed the Line was driven by storms to the cold Country towards the South Pole, and how from thence she made her course to the tropical Latitude of the Great Pacific Ocean, and of the strange things that befell: and in what manner the Ancyent Marinere came back to his own Country.

PART I

It is an ancient Mariner,
And he stoppeth one of three.
—"By the long gray beard and glittering eye,
Now wherefore stopp'st thou me?

An ancient Mariner meeteth three Gallants bidden to a wedding feast, and detaineth one.

5 "The Bridegroom's doors are opened wide,
And I am next of kin,
The guests are met, the feast is set:
May'st hear the merry din."

He holds him with his skinny hand;
10 "There was a ship," quoth he.
"Hold off! unhand me, graybeard loon!"
Eftsoons[1] his hand dropped he.

He holds him with his glittering eye—
The Wedding Guest stood still,
15 And listens like a three years' child:
The Mariner hath his will.

The Wedding Guest is spellbound by the eye of the old seafaring man and constrained to hear his tale.

---

1. **Eftsoons:** at once.

The Wedding Guest sat on a stone:
He cannot choose but hear;
And thus spake on that ancient man,
20 The bright-eyed Mariner.

"The ship was cheered, the harbor cleared,
Merrily did we drop
Below the kirk,² below the hill,
Below the lighthouse top.

25 "The Sun came up upon the left,
Out of the sea came he!
And he shone bright, and on the right
Went down into the sea.

*The Mariner tells how
the ship sailed
southward with a good
wind and fair weather,
till it reached the Line.³*

"Higher and higher every day,
30 Till over the mast at noon⁴—"
The Wedding Guest here beat his breast,
For he heard the loud bassoon.

The bride hath paced into the hall,
Red as a rose is she;
35 Nodding their heads before her goes
The merry minstrelsy.

*The Wedding Guest
heareth the bridal music;
but the Mariner
continueth his tale.*

The Wedding Guest he beat his breast,
Yet he cannot choose but hear;
And thus spake on that ancient man,
40 The bright-eyed Mariner.

"And now the Storm-blast came, and he
Was tyrannous and strong;
He struck with his o'ertaking wings,
And chased us south along.

*The ship driven by a
storm toward the South
Pole.*

45 "With sloping masts and dipping prow,
As who pursued with yell and blow
Still treads the shadow of his foe,
And forward bends his head,
The ship drove fast, loud roared the blast,
50 And southward aye⁵ we fled.

"And now there came both mist and snow,
And it grew wondrous cold:
And ice, mast-high, came floating by,
As green as emerald.

---

2. **kirk:** Scottish for "church."
3. **Line:** equator.
4. **over . . . noon:** Sun's position indicates that ship has reached equator.
5. **aye:** ever.

55   "And through the drifts the snowy clifts
Did send a dismal sheen:
Nor shapes of men nor beasts we ken[6]—
The ice was all between.

"The ice was here, the ice was there,
60 The ice was all around:
It cracked and growled, and roared and howled,
Like noises in a swound![7]

"At length did cross an Albatross,
Thorough[8] the fog it came;
65 As if it had been a Christian soul,
We hailed it in God's name.

"It ate the food it ne'er had eat,[9]
And round and round it flew.
The ice did split with a thunder-fit;
70 The helmsman steered us through!

"And a good south wind sprung up behind;
The Albatross did follow,
And every day, for food or play,
Came to the mariners' hollo!

75 "In mist or cloud, on mast or shroud,[10]
It perched for vespers[11] nine;
Whiles all the night, through fog-smoke white,
Glimmered the white Moon-shine."

"God save thee, ancient Mariner!
80 From the fiends, that plague thee thus!—
Why look'st thou so?"[12]—"With my crossbow
I shot the Albatross!"

The land of ice, and of fearful sounds, where no living thing was to be seen.

Till a great sea bird, called the Albatross, came through the snow-fog, and was received with great joy and hospitality.

And lo! the Albatross proveth a bird of good omen, and followeth the ship as it returned northward through fog and floating ice.

The ancient Mariner inhospitably killeth the pious bird of good omen.

PART II

"The Sun now rose upon the right:[13]
Out of the sea came he,
85 Still hid in mist, and on the left
Went down into the sea.

---

6. **ken:** Scottish for "saw"; "knew."
7. **swound:** fainting fit, swoon.
8. **Thorough:** through.
9. **eat** [et]: old form of past participle of eat.
10. **shroud:** rope supporting the mast.
11. **vespers:** evenings.
12. **"God . . . so?":** spoken by the Wedding Guest.
13. **The Sun . . . right:** The sun's position indicates that ship is traveling north.

"And the good south wind still blew behind,
But no sweet bird did follow,
Nor any day for food or play
90 Came to the mariners' hollo!

"And I had done a hellish thing,
And it would work 'em woe:
For all averred, I had killed the bird
That made the breeze to blow.
95 Ah, wretch! said they, the bird to slay,
That made the breeze to blow!

"Nor dim nor red, like God's own head,
The glorious Sun uprist:[14]
Then all averred, I had killed the bird
100 That brought the fog and mist.
'Twas right, said they, such birds to slay,
That bring the fog and mist.

"The fair breeze blew, the white foam flew,
The furrow[15] followed free;
105 We were the first that ever burst
Into that silent sea.

"Down dropped the breeze, the sails dropped down,
'Twas sad as sad could be;
And we did speak only to break
110 The silence of the sea!

"All in a hot and copper sky,
The bloody Sun, at noon,
Right up above the mast did stand,
No bigger than the Moon.

115 "Day after day, day after day,
We stuck, nor breath nor motion;
As idle as a painted ship
Upon a painted ocean.

"Water, water, everywhere,
120 And all the boards did shrink;
Water, water, everywhere,
Nor any drop to drink.

*His shipmates cry out
against the ancient
Mariner for killing the
bird of good luck.*

*But when the fog cleared
off they justify the same,
and thus make
themselves accomplices
in the crime.*

*The fair breeze
continues; the ship
enters the Pacific Ocean,
and sails northward,
even till it reaches the
Line.*

*The ship hath been
suddenly becalmed.*

*And the Albatross begins
to be avenged.*

---

14. **uprist:** uprose.
15. **furrow:** ship's wake.

Engraving by Gustave Doré (1832–1883).

"The very deep did rot: O Christ!
That ever this should be!
125 Yea, slimy things did crawl with legs
Upon the slimy sea.

"About, about, in reel and rout[16]
The death-fires[17] danced at night;
The water, like a witch's oils,
130 Burned green, and blue and white.

"And some in dreams assurèd were
Of the Spirit that plagued us so;
Nine fathom[18] deep he had followed us
From the land of mist and snow.

135 "And every tongue, through utter drought,
Was withered at the root;
We could not speak, no more than if
We had been choked with soot.

"Ah! well-a-day! what evil looks
140 Had I from old and young!
Instead of the cross, the Albatross
About my neck was hung.

A Spirit had followed them; one of the invisible inhabitants of this planet, neither departed souls nor angels. They are very numerous, and there is no climate or element without one or more.

The shipmates, in their sore distress, would fain throw the whole guilt on the ancient Mariner: in sign whereof they hang the dead sea bird round his neck.

PART III

"There passed a weary time. Each throat
Was parched, and glazed each eye.
145 A weary time! a weary time!
How glazed each weary eye,
When looking westward, I beheld
A something in the sky.

"At first it seemed a little speck,
150 And then it seemed a mist;
It moved and moved, and took at last
A certain shape, I wist.[19]

"A speck, a mist, a shape, I wist!
And still it neared and neared:
155 As if it dodged a water sprite,
It plunged and tacked and veered.

The ancient Mariner beholdeth a sign in the element afar off.

---

16. **rout:** disorderly crowd.
17. **death-fires:** St. Elmo's fire, an electrical effect lighting masts
of ships; believed by seamen to be a portent of disaster.
18. **fathom:** unit of measure equal to six feet.
19. **wist:** knew.

"With throats unslaked, with black lips baked,
We could nor laugh nor wail;
Through utter drought all dumb we stood!
160 I bit my arm, I sucked the blood,
And cried, A sail! a sail!

At its nearer approach, it seemeth him to be a ship; and at a dear ransom he freeth his speech from the bonds of thirst.

"With throats unslaked, with black lips baked,
Agape they heard me call:
Gramercy![20] they for joy did grin,
165 And all at once their breath drew in,
As they were drinking all.

A flash of joy;

"See! see! (I cried) she tacks no more!
Hither to work us weal;[21]
Without a breeze, without a tide,
170 She steadies with upright keel!

And horror follows. For can it be a ship that comes onward without wind or tide?

"The western wave was all aflame,
The day was well nigh done!
Almost upon the western wave
Rested the broad bright Sun;
175 When that strange shape drove suddenly
Betwixt us and the Sun.

"And straight the Sun was flecked with bars,
(Heaven's Mother send us grace!)
As if through a dungeon grate he peered
180 With broad and burning face.

It seemeth him but the skeleton of a ship.

"Alas! (thought I, and my heart beat loud)
How fast she nears and nears!
Are those *her* sails that glance in the Sun,
Like restless gossameres?[22]

185 "Are those her ribs through which the Sun
Did peer, as through a grate?
And is that Woman all her crew?
Is that a Death? and are there two?
Is Death that woman's mate?

And its ribs are seen as bars on the face of the setting Sun. The Specter-Woman and her Death mate, and no other on board the skeleton ship.

190 "*Her* lips were red, *her* looks were free,
Her locks were yellow as gold:
Her skin was as white as leprosy,
The Nightmare Life-in-Death was she,
Who thicks man's blood with cold.

Like vessel, like crew!

---

20. **Gramercy** [grə mur′sē]: great thanks.
21. **work us weal:** do us good, benefit us.
22. **gossameres:** spiderwebs.

195 "The naked hulk alongside came,
And the twain were casting dice;
'The game is done! I've won! I've won!'
Quoth she, and whistles thrice.

"The Sun's rim dips; the stars rush out:
200 At one stride comes the dark;
With far-heard whisper, o'er the sea,
Off shot the specter bark.

"We listened and looked sideways up!
Fear at my heart, as at a cup,
205 My lifeblood seemed to sip!
The stars were dim, and thick the night,
The steersman's face by his lamp gleamed white;
From the sails the dew did drip—
Till clomb²³ above the eastern bar
210 The hornèd²⁴ Moon, with one bright star
With the nether²⁵ tip.

"One after one, by the star-dogged Moon,²⁶
Too quick for groan or sigh,
Each turned his face with a ghastly pang,
215 And cursed me with his eye.

"Four times fifty living men,
(And I heard nor sigh nor groan)
With heavy thump, a lifeless lump,
They dropped down one by one.

220 "The souls did from their bodies fly—
They fled to bliss or woe!
And every soul, it passed me by
Like the whizz of my crossbow!"

PART IV

"I fear thee, ancient Mariner!
225 I fear thy skinny hand!
And thou art long, and lank, and brown,
As is the ribbed sea-sand.

"I fear thee and thy glittering eye,
And thy skinny hand, so brown."—

Death and Life-in-Death have diced for the ship's crew, and she (the latter) winneth the ancient Mariner.

No twilight, within the courts of the Sun.

At the rising of the Moon,

One after another,

His shipmates drop down dead.

But Life-in-Death begins her work on the ancient Mariner.

The Wedding Guest feareth that a Spirit is talking to him;

---

23. **clomb:** climbed.
24. **hornèd:** crescent.
25. **nether:** lower.
26. **star-dogged Moon:** sign of impending evil.

230 "Fear not, fear not, thou Wedding Guest!
This body dropped not down.

"Alone, alone, all, all alone,
Alone on a wide wide sea!
And never a saint took pity on
235 My soul in agony.

"The many men, so beautiful!
And they all dead did lie:
And a thousand thousand slimy things
Lived on; and so did I.

240 "I looked upon the rotting sea,
And drew my eyes away;
I looked upon the rotting deck,
And there the dead men lay.

"I looked to heaven, and tried to pray;
245 But or²⁷ ever a prayer had gushed,
A wicked whisper came, and made
My heart as dry as dust.

"I closed my lids, and kept them close,
And the balls like pulses beat;
250 For the sky and sea, and the sea and the sky
Lay like a load on my weary eye,
And the dead were at my feet.

"The cold sweat melted from their limbs,
Nor rot nor reek did they:
255 The look with which they looked on me
Had never passed away.

"An orphan's curse would drag to hell
A spirit from on high;
But oh! more horrible than that
260 Is a curse in a dead man's eye!
Seven days, seven nights, I saw that curse,
And yet I could not die.

"The moving Moon went up the sky,
And nowhere did abide:
265 Softly she was going up,
And a star or two beside—

But the ancient Mariner assureth him of his bodily life, and proceedeth to relate his horrible penance.

He despiseth the creatures of the calm.

And envieth that they should live, and so many lie dead.

But the curse liveth for him in the eye of the dead men.

In his loneliness and fixedness he yearneth towards the journeying Moon, and the stars that still move onward; and everywhere the blue sky belongs to them, and is their appointed rest, and their native country and their own natural homes, which they enter unannounced, as lords that are certainly expected, and yet there is a silent joy at their arrival.

---

27. **or:** before.

"Her beams bemocked the sultry main,
Like April hoar-frost spread;
But where the ship's huge shadow lay,
270 The charmèd water burned alway
A still and awful red.

"Beyond the shadow of the ship,
I watched the water snakes:
They moved in tracks of shining white,
And when they reared, the elfish light
Fell off in hoary flakes.

*By the light of the Moon
he beholdeth God's
creatures of the great
calm.*

"Within the shadow of the ship
I watched their rich attire:
Blue, glossy green, and velvet black,
280 They coiled and swam; and every track
Was a flash of golden fire.

"O happy living things! no tongue
Their beauty might declare:
A spring of love gushed from my heart,
285 And I blessed them unaware;
Sure my kind saint took pity on me,
And I blessed them unaware.

*Their beauty and their
happiness.*

*He blesseth them in his
heart.*

"The selfsame moment I could pray;
And from my neck so free
290 The Albatross fell off, and sank
Like lead into the sea."

*The spell begins to
break.*

PART V

"Oh sleep! it is a gentle thing,
Beloved from pole to pole!
To Mary Queen the praise be given!
295 She sent the gentle sleep from Heaven,
That slid into my soul.

"The silly²⁸ buckets on the deck,
That had so long remained,
I dreamed that they were filled with dew;
300 And when I awoke it rained.

*By grace of the holy
Mother, the ancient
Mariner is refreshed with
rain.*

"My lips were wet, my throat was cold,
My garments all were dank;

---

28. **silly:** plain, simple.

Sure I had drunken in my dreams,
And still my body drank.

305 "I moved, and could not feel my limbs:
I was so light—almost
I thought that I had died in sleep,
And was a blessed ghost.

"And soon I heard a roaring wind:
310 It did not come anear;
But with its sound it shook the sails,
That were so thin and sere.

*He heareth sounds and
seeth strange sights and
commotions in the sky
and the elements.*

"The upper air burst into life!
And a hundred fire-flags[29] sheen,[30]
315 To and fro they were hurried about!
And to and fro, and in and out,
The wan stars danced between.

"And the coming wind did roar more loud,
And the sails did sigh like sedge;[31]
320 And the rain poured down from one black cloud;
The Moon was at its edge.

"The thick black cloud was cleft, and still
The Moon was at its side:
Like waters shot from some high crag,
325 The lightning fell with never a jag,
A river steep and wide.

"The loud wind never reached the ship,
Yet now the ship moved on!
Beneath the lightning and the Moon
330 The dead men gave a groan.

*The bodies of the ship's
crew are inspired,[32] and
the ship moves on;*

"They groaned, they stirred, they all uprose,
Nor spake, nor moved their eyes;
It had been strange, even in a dream,
To have seen those dead men rise.

335 "The helmsman steered, the ship moved on;
Yet never a breeze up-blew;
The mariners all 'gan work the ropes,

---

29. **fire-flags:** the aurora australis, or southern lights.
30. **sheen:** shone.
31. **sedge:** marsh grass.
32. **inspired:** filled with a spirit.

Where they were wont[33] to do;
They raised their limbs like lifeless tools—
340 We were a ghastly crew.

"The body of my brother's son
Stood by me, knee to knee:
The body and I pulled at one rope,
But he said nought to me."

345 "I fear thee, ancient Mariner!"
"Be calm, thou Wedding Guest!
'Twas not those souls that fled in pain,
Which to their corses[34] came again,
But a troop of spirits blessed:

But not by the souls of the men, nor by demons of earth or middle air, but by a blessed troop of angelic spirits, sent down by the invocation of the guardian saint.

350 "For when it dawned—they dropped their arms,
And clustered round the mast;
Sweet sounds rose slowly through their mouths,
And from their bodies passed.

"Around, around, flew each sweet sound,
355 Then darted to the Sun;
Slowly the sounds came back again,
Now mixed, now one by one.

"Sometimes a-dropping from the sky
I heard the skylark sing;
360 Sometimes all little birds that are,
How they seemed to fill the sea and air
With their sweet jargoning![35]

"And now 'twas like all instruments,
Now like a lonely flute;
365 And now it is an angel's song,
That makes the heavens be mute.

"It ceased; yet still the sails made on
A pleasant noise till noon,
A noise like of a hidden brook
370 In the leafy month of June,
That to the sleeping woods all night
Singeth a quiet tune.

---

33. **wont:** accustomed.
34. **corses:** corpses.
35. **jargoning:** warbling.

"Till noon we quietly sailed on,
Yet never a breeze did breathe:
375 Slowly and smoothly went the ship,
Moved onward from beneath.

"Under the keel nine fathom deep,
From the land of mist and snow,
The Spirit slid: and it was he
380 That made the ship to go.
The sails at noon left off their tune,
And the ship stood still also.

"The Sun, right up above the mast,
Had fixed her to the ocean:
385 But in a minute she 'gan stir,
With a short uneasy motion—
Backwards and forwards half her length
With a short uneasy motion.

"Then like a pawing horse let go,
390 She made a sudden bound:
It flung the blood into my head,
And I fell down in a swound.

"How long in that same fit I lay,
I have not[36] to declare;
395 But ere my living life returned,
I heard, and in my soul discerned,
Two voices in the air.

"'Is it he?' quoth one, 'Is this the man?
By him who died on cross,
400 With his cruel bow he laid full low
The harmless Albatross.

"'The Spirit who bideth by himself
In the land of mist and snow,
He loved the bird that loved the man
405 Who shot him with his bow.'

"The other was a softer voice,
As soft as honeydew:
Quoth he, 'The man hath penance done,
And penance more will do.' "

*The lonesome Spirit
from the South Pole
carries on the ship as
far as the Line, in
obedience to the angelic
troop, but still requireth
vengeance.*

*The Polar Spirit's fellow
demons, the invisible
inhabitants of the
element, take part in his
wrong; and two of them
relate, one to the other,
that penance long and
heavy for the ancient
Mariner hath been
accorded to the Polar
Spirit, who returneth
southward.*

---

36. **have not:** have not the ability or knowledge.

PART VI

FIRST VOICE

410 "'But tell me, tell me! speak again,
Thy soft response renewing—
What makes that ship drive on so fast?
What is the ocean doing?'

SECOND VOICE

"'Still as a slave before his lord,
415 The ocean hath no blast;
His great bright eye most silently
Up to the Moon is cast—

"'If he may know which way to go;
For she guides him smooth or grim.
420 See, brother, see! how graciously
She looketh down on him.'

FIRST VOICE

"'But why drives on that ship so fast,
Without or wave or wind?'

SECOND VOICE

"'The air is cut away before,
425 And closes from behind.'

The Mariner hath been cast into a trance; for the angelic power causeth the vessel to drive northward faster than human life could endure.

"'Fly, brother, fly! more high, more high!
Or we shall be belated:[37]
For slow and slow that ship will go,
When the Mariner's trance is abated.'

430 "I woke, and we were sailing on
As in a gentle weather:
'Twas night, calm night, the moon was high;
The dead men stood together.

The supernatural motion is retarded; the Mariner awakes, and his penance begins anew.

"All stood together on the deck,
435 For a charnel-dungeon[38] fitter:
All fixed on me their stony eyes,
That in the Moon did glitter.

"The pang, the curse, with which they died,
Had never passed away:

---

37. **belated:** made late.
38. **charnel-dungeon:** vault to hold bones of the dead.

440 I could not draw my eyes from theirs,
Nor turn them up to pray.

"And now this spell was snapped: once more
I viewed the ocean green,
And looked far forth, yet little saw
445 Of what had else been seen—

"Like one, that on a lonesome road
Doth walk in fear and dread,
And having once turned round walks on,
And turns no more his head;
450 Because he knows, a frightful fiend
Doth close behind him tread.

"But soon there breathed a wind on me,
Nor sound nor motion made:
Its path was not upon the sea,
455 In ripple or in shade.

"It raised my hair, it fanned my cheek
Like a meadow-gale of spring—
It mingled strangely with my fears,
Yet it felt like a welcoming.

460 "Swiftly, swiftly flew the ship,
Yet she sailed softly too:
Sweetly, sweetly blew the breeze—
On me alone it blew.

"Oh! dream of joy! is this indeed
465 The lighthouse top I see?
Is this the hill? is this the kirk?
Is this mine own countree?

"We drifted o'er the harbor bar,
And I with sobs did pray—
470 O let me be awake, my God!
Or let me sleep alway.

"The harbor bay was clear as glass,
So smoothly it was strewn!⁴⁰
And on the bay the moonlight lay,
475 And the shadow of the Moon.

"The rock shone bright, the kirk no less,
That stands above the rock:

*The curse is finally expiated.*³⁹

And the ancient Mariner beholdeth his native country.

---

39. **expiated:** paid for, made amends for.
40. **strewn:** spread.

The moonlight steeped in silentness
The steady weathercock.

480 "And the bay was white with silent light
Till, rising from the same,
Full many shapes, that shadows were,
In crimson colors came.

*The angelic spirits leave
the dead bodies,*

"A little distance from the prow
485 Those crimson shadows were:
I turned my eyes upon the deck—
Oh, Christ! what saw I there!

"Each corse lay flat, lifeless and flat,
And, by the holy rood!⁴¹
490 A man all light, a seraph⁴² man,
On every corse there stood.

*And appear in their own
forms of light.*

"This seraph band, each waved his hand:
It was a heavenly sight!
They stood as signals to the land,
495 Each one a lovely light;

"This seraph band, each waved his hand,
No voice did they impart—
No voice; but oh! the silence sank
Like music on my heart.

500 "But soon I heard the dash of oars,
I heard the Pilot's cheer;
My head was turned perforce⁴³ away,
And I saw a boat appear.

"The Pilot and the Pilot's boy,
505 I heard them coming fast:
Dear Lord in Heaven! it was a joy
The dead men could not blast.

"I saw a third—I heard his voice:
It is the Hermit good!
510 He singeth loud his godly hymns
That he makes in the wood.
He'll shrieve⁴⁴ my soul, he'll wash away
The Albatross's blood."

---

41. **rood:** cross.
42. **seraph:** highest in the rank of angels.
43. **perforce:** of necessity.
44. **shrieve** [shrēv]: hear confession, grant forgiveness, impose penance.

PART VII

"This Hermit good lives in that wood

515 Which slopes down to the sea.
How loudly his sweet voice he rears!
He loves to talk with mariners
That come from a far countree.

"He kneels at morn, and noon, and eve—

520 He hath a cushion plump:
It is the moss that wholly hides
The rotted old oak stump.

"The skiff boat neared: I heard them talk,
'Why, this is strange, I trow!⁴⁵

525 Where are those lights so many and fair,
That signal made but now?'

"'Strange, by my faith!' the Hermit said—
'And they answered not our cheer!
The planks looked warped! and see those sails,

530 How thin they are and sere!
I never saw aught like to them,
Unless perchance it were

"'Brown skeletons of leaves that lag
My forest-brook along;

535 When the ivy tod⁴⁶ is heavy with snow,
And the owlet whoops to the wolf below,
That eats the she-wolf's young.'

"'Dear Lord! it hath a fiendish look,'
(The Pilot made reply)

540 'I am a-feared'—'Push on, push on!'
Said the Hermit cheerily.

"The boat came closer to the ship,
But I nor spake nor stirred;
The boat came close beneath the ship,

545 And straight⁴⁷ a sound was heard.

"Under the water it rumbled on,
Still louder and more dread:
It reached the ship, it split the bay;
The ship went down like lead.

The Hermit of the wood.

Approacheth the ship with wonder.

The ship suddenly sinketh.

---

45. **trow:** believe.
46. **ivy tod:** ivy bush.
47. **straight:** straightaway, immediately.

550 "Stunned by that loud and dreadful sound,
Which sky and ocean smote,
Like one that hath been seven days drowned
My body lay afloat;
But swift as dreams, myself I found
555 Within the Pilot's boat.

The ancient Mariner is saved in the Pilot's boat.

"Upon the whirl, where sank the ship,
The boat spun round and round;
And all was still, save that the hill
Was telling of the sound.

560 "I moved my lips—the Pilot shrieked
And fell down in a fit;
The holy Hermit raised his eyes,
And prayed where he did sit.

"I took the oars: the Pilot's boy,
565 Who now doth crazy go,
Laughed loud and long, and all the while
His eyes went to and fro.
'Ha! ha!' quoth he, 'full plain I see,
The Devil knows how to row.'

570 "And now, all in my own countree,
I stood on the firm land!
The Hermit stepped forth from the boat,
And scarcely he could stand.

"'O shrieve me, shrieve me, holy man!'
575 The Hermit crossed his brow.⁴⁸
'Say quick,' quoth he, 'I bid thee say—
What manner of man art thou?'

The ancient Mariner earnestly entreateth the Hermit to shrieve him; and the penance of life falls on him.

"Forthwith this frame of mine was wrenched
With a woeful agony,
580 Which forced me to begin my tale;
And then it left me free.

"Since then, at an uncertain hour,
That agony returns;
And till my ghastly tale is told,
585 This heart within me burns.

And ever and anon throughout his future life an agony constraineth him to travel from land to land,

"I pass, like night, from land to land;
I have strange power of speech;
That moment that his face I see,

---

48. **crossed his brow:** made the sign of the cross on his forehead.

I know the man that must hear me:
590 To him my tale I teach.

"What loud uproar bursts from that door!
The wedding guests are there:
But in the garden-bower the bride
And bridemaids singing are:
595 And hark the little vesper bell,
Which biddeth me to prayer!

"O Wedding Guest! this soul hath been
Alone on a wide, wide sea:
So lonely 'twas, that God himself
600 Scarce seemèd there to be.

"Oh sweeter than the marriage feast,
'Tis sweeter far to me,
To walk together to the kirk
With a goodly company!—

605 "To walk together to the kirk,
And all together pray,
While each to his great Father bends,
Old men, and babes, and loving friends,
And youths and maidens gay!

610 "Farewell, farewell! but this I tell
To thee, thou Wedding Guest!
He prayeth well, who loveth well
Both man and bird and beast.

And to teach by his own example love and reverence to all things that God made and loveth.

"He prayeth best, who loveth best
615 All things both great and small;
For the dear God who loveth us,
He made and loveth all."

The Mariner, whose eye is bright,
Whose beard with age is hoar,
620 Is gone: and now the Wedding Guest
Turned from the bridegroom's door.

He went like one that hath been stunned,
And is of sense forlorn:[49]
A sadder and a wiser man,
625 He rose the morrow morn.

----

49. **forlorn:** bereft, stripped of.

STUDY QUESTIONS

Recalling

1. In Part I what happens to the wedding guest? Summarize the voyage as described by the ancient Mariner in Part I, noting his admission in lines 81–82.

2. In the beginning of Part II, explain the immediate consequence of the crime, and then tell what happens to the ship in the loneliness of the Pacific. How do the ancient Mariner's fellow crewmen single him out for punishment?

3. Who are the two people aboard the strange vessel in Part III, and what are they doing? What is the outcome of their activity?

4. In Part IV what happens when the Mariner prays?

5. What reasons are given at lines 402–405 for the actions of the lonesome Polar Spirit? What is the Mariner's fate, according to lines 408–409?

6. By what miraculous means, detailed in Part VI, does the Mariner's ship return home? What does the Mariner hope for in lines 512–513?

7. According to lines 572–590, what has been the fate of the Mariner since returning to shore? What, according to lines 612–617, is the moral of the Mariner's story?

Interpreting

8. What do you think is meant by the term "Life-in-Death," introduced in Part III when Death wins all the crew except for one? How does the phrase "Life-in-Death" describe the Mariner's life subsequently?

9. Identify at least three vivid details and images that help Coleridge succeed in making the reader willingly "suspend disbelief" and accept the possibility of the story.

10. How do we know that the Mariner's penance is for his act of contempt against a living creature? How is this illustrated throughout the poem?

Extending

11. Coleridge here is imitating the ballad form that "Sir Patrick Spens" (page 39) exemplifies. What similarities—in stanza form, in diction, in subject matter, and in style—do you see between the two? What variations on the basic four-line stanza does Coleridge allow

himself? How do you account for the variations?

VIEWPOINT

Robert Penn Warren has explained "The Rime of the Ancient Mariner" is in part a statement about sin, punishment, repentance, and redemption:

> The Mariner shoots the bird; suffers various pains, the greatest of which is loneliness and spiritual anguish; upon recognizing the beauty of the foul sea snakes experiences a gush of love for them and is able to pray; is returned miraculously to his home port, where he discovers the joy of human communion in God, and utters the moral, "He prayeth best who loveth best. . . ."

■ What evidence can you point to that supports Warren's assertion concerning the Mariner's greatest pain? What relation do you see between the sea snakes and the albatross? How does the Mariner bear his burden of repentance?

LITERARY FOCUS

Sound in Poetry

To be appreciated fully, a poem should be read aloud, for its very sound contributes to its effectiveness and brings pleasure. Much of that pleasure comes from repetition of sound.

Rhyme is the repetition of similar or identical vowels and succeeding consonants in words of a poem. If the words in question occur at the ends of lines, we have **end rhyme,** as when *Khan, ran,* and *man* rhyme in lines 1, 3, and 4 of "Kubla Khan." If the rhyme occurs within a line, we have **internal rhyme** as in this example from "The Ancient Mariner":

The guests are *met,* the feast is *set.*

There are still other agreeable repetitions in poetry. Repetition of initial consonant sounds is called (as explained with "Beowulf") **alliteration:** *K*ubla *K*han, *d*ome, *d*ecree, *r*iver *r*an, measure-less to *m*an, and *s*unless *s*ea.

Assonance is the repetition in two or more nearby words of similar vowel sounds: for example, the first vowel sound in "pleasure" and "measureless" and the vowels in "tw*i*ce f*i*ve miles." **Consonance** is the repetition in two or more nearby words of similar consonant sounds within the words: for example, the consonants in "*A*lone, *a*lone, *a*ll, *a*ll, *a*lone."

A final important sound effect in poetry is **onomatopoeia,** which refers to a word whose sound suggests its meaning. *Buzz* and *hum* are obvious examples of words with sounds that suggest their meaning. In addition, sometimes a whole line of poetry may be onomatopoeic:

Five miles meandering with a mazy motion

The very sound of the line imitates what is being described, a river flowing leisurely in the words.

Thinking About Sound in Poetry

1. Find at least two other examples of internal rhyme in "The Rime of the Ancient Mariner."
2. What example of alliteration do you find in the remaining lines of the first stanza of "Kubla Khan" (lines 6–11)?
3. What other examples of assonance do you find in "Kubla Khan"?
4. Find an example of onomatopoeia in lines 59–62 of "The Rime of the Ancient Mariner."

VOCABULARY

Archaic Words

Coleridge used words that were already out of date by the late eighteenth century, when he wrote "The Rime of the Ancient Mariner." We use the term **archaic** to describe words that are old-fashioned or that belong to an earlier period. For example, Coleridge used *eftsoons* (line 12), *swound* (line 62), and *rood* (line 489). In particular, he used old past-tense forms of verbs.

1. Find the archaic past-tense verb in each of the following lines, and explain its meaning: line 19, line 98, line 152, line 209.
2. Suggest why Coleridge chose to use archaic words. What effect do they create?

COMPOSITION

Writing About a Symbol

Discuss the symbolism of the albatross in "The Rime of the Ancient Mariner." Begin by report-ing what the bird first represents (lines 63–78). Then describe what its murder causes and the possible meaning of hanging the dead bird around the Mariner's neck. Conclude by explaining when and why the albatross fell from the Mariner, and then briefly give the meaning of the expression *an albatross around one's neck. For help with this assignment, refer to Lesson 5 in the Writing About Literature Handbook at the back of this book.*

Describing a Journey

Consider the progress of the ship's journey in "The Rime of the Ancient Mariner." Describe the journey accurately in two or three paragraphs that cite relevant lines from the poem. In writing your paragraphs consider the following questions: How accurate is the description of the voyage? To begin with, why does the Mariner mention kirk, hill, and lighthouse top in that order in lines 23–24? Compare the order with that in the stanza beginning at line 464. What language in line 466 indicates that the ship is sailing from Scotland? In what direction is the ship going when the sun comes up upon the left (line 25)? Where is it when the sun is directly over the mast at noon (line 30)? What other lines in the poem help you to follow the progress of the ship?

COMPARING WRITERS

1. It has been said that although Coleridge's subject matter is so different from Wordsworth's the two poets create similar effects; that is, they both convey the Romantic spirit of wonder. What spirit, or sense, of wonder can you find in "The Rime of the Ancient Mariner"? In the poems included here by Wordsworth?
2. While acknowledging that Wordsworth and Coleridge created worlds of wonder, comment on the realism in the poems by both these writers. Find examples of each poet's realism of detail as he develops a picture or a mood.
3. Find examples of Wordsworth's turning to nature as a source of inspiration and assurance. Based on "Kubla Khan," when or how does nature offer comfort to Coleridge?

George Gordon, Lord Byron
1788–1824

Though his poetry is now regarded as the least representative of the Romantic movement with which he is identified, the image that his contemporaries had of George Gordon, Lord Byron was of the arch-Romantic, extraordinary in almost every way. Byron was uncommonly handsome; Coleridge said he had scarcely ever seen "so beautiful a countenance." However, Byron had a handicap—a club foot—that both physically and psychologically distressed him all his life. To compensate for this impairment he became an outstanding athlete: a masterful swimmer, horseman, boxer, cricket player, and fencer.

A descendant of two aristocratic but flamboyant and violent families, Byron unexpectedly inherited his title at the age of ten when his great-uncle, known as the Wicked Lord, died. Thereupon he was sent to Harrow, a famous private school. Later, as a student at Cambridge University, he was known for his lavish and fashionable life style and flamboyant behavior; he even kept a tame bear as a pet. After graduating from Cambridge, he embarked upon an adventurous journey, traveling on horseback across Portugal and Spain and on to distant lands that few Englishmen had visited, including such unfamiliar places as Asia Minor and mountainous Albania. Returning, he effortlessly wrote a poem in Spenserian stanzas, *Childe Harold's Pilgrimage*—a travelogue, narrated by an eloquent but emotional fictitious tourist—that made him the toast of London society. In his own words, "I awoke one morning and found myself famous." That was when he was twenty-four. In addition, Byron the poet was also a champion of liberal political causes, and, as a member of the House of Lords, he became an active spokesman for the extreme liberal faction of the Whig party. In this capacity he bravely defended the rebelling Nottingham weavers whose jobs had been threatened by new textile machines.

Soon, however, his fame had turned to notoriety, as the dashing young poet became the center of scandals, including an early and much publicized separation from his very proper young wife. In 1816, when he was twenty-eight, Byron went into self-imposed exile, never to return to England. The rest of his brief life was lived on the Continent, mostly in Italy. During his travels he befriended the poet Percy Bysshe Shelley (page 371), with whom he developed a productive intellectual relationship. Always an outspoken defender of personal and political freedom, Byron died shortly after his thirty-sixth birthday, having exhausted his energies training Greek troops fighting for independence from Turkey.

His life is assuredly a romantic one: His scandalous behavior, idealism, attractiveness, defiance of conventionality, and superlative gifts all contribute to our notion of Byron as the quintessential

Romantic. Yet in literary terms he now seems the least Romantic of the five great poets who best exemplify that movement of the early nineteenth century. While Byron wrote about the connection between nature and the individual, his treatment of this theme, unlike Wordsworth's, focused on nature as a refuge for the human soul stricken with melancholy and alienation. Furthermore, he did not approve of any of his Romantic contemporaries except for Shelley. He believed that he, himself, and the other Romantics, were "upon a wrong revolutionary poetical system." Byron's love poems seem reminiscent of the Cavalier poets of the seventeenth century—easy and graceful compliments in the manner of a Richard Lovelace (page 224). His greatest literary achievements seem more in the spirit of Alexander Pope and John Dryden, two neoclassicist poets whom Byron himself acknowledged as his masters. In short, Byron—that arch-Romantic in life—in literature is deeply indebted to neoclassicism for his most impressive poetry.

Why then is Byron considered a Romantic poet? The answer to this question lies in his chief contribution to his age, namely the creation of the so-called Byronic hero, a character who embodied the yearnings of all Romantics. Readers knew enough about Byron's life— the scandals associated with his name, his passionate nature, his fierce hatred of oppression, and his self-imposed exile from England—to assume that the characters he created were all self-portraits. In most ways they were not; for Byron was usually a witty, gregarious, generous, and loyal man of the world. Nonetheless, that hardly mattered; what mattered was the extraordinary influence the Byronic hero had on the poet's contemporaries and on successive generations of English and American writers. Ahab, the obsessed sea captain in the American novelist Herman Melville's great whaling novel *Moby-Dick,* is a nineteenth-century Byronic hero. In the twentieth century Ernest Hemingway developed his own version of the same character type.

What, or who, is a Byronic hero? In the poet's own words, he is one in whom there is mixed much to love and to hate, one whose "silences formed a theme for other's prate," or chatter. The Byronic hero was an aloof wanderer, a moody, smoldering individual, isolated from the common run of humanity. An outsider, silent, passionate, gloomy, and mysterious: He seemed to be something new in literature. Actually Byron did not invent this character who scorned convention; in some ways he is a descendant of Milton's Satan in *Paradise Lost.* Yet it was Byron who ineradicably impressed the character on the world's imagination: the restless, doom-driven, alien spirit, harboring some nameless, mysterious guilt from the past as he moves with quiet scorn and defiant individualism through the present.

This poem, written for music, was inspired by the sight of the poet's cousin by marriage, the beautiful Lady Wilmot Horton, who appeared at a party dressed in a black mourning gown scattered with spangles, or bits of sparkling material.

George Gordon, Lord Byron

She Walks in Beauty

1

She walks in beauty, like the night
   Of cloudless climes and starry skies;
And all that's best of dark and bright
   Meet in her aspect and her eyes:
5 Thus mellowed to that tender light
   Which heaven to gaudy day denies.

2

One shade the more, one ray the less,
   Had half impaired the nameless grace
Which waves in every raven tress,
10   Or softly lightens o'er her face;
Where thoughts serenely sweet express
   How pure, how dear their dwelling place.

3

And on that cheek, and o'er that brow,
   So soft, so calm, yet eloquent,
15 The smiles that win, the tints that glow,
   But tell of days in goodness spent,
A mind at peace with all below,
   A heart whose love is innocent!

Stanzas Written on the Road Between Florence and Pisa

Oh, talk not to me of a name great in story—
The days of our youth are the days of our glory;
And the myrtle[1] and ivy[2] of sweet two-and-twenty
Are worth all your laurels,[3] though ever so plenty.

5 What are garlands and crowns to the brow that is wrinkled?
'Tis but as a dead-flower with May-dew besprinkled:
Then away with all such from the head that is hoary!
What care I for the wreaths that can *only* give glory!

Oh Fame!—if I e'er took delight in thy praises,
10 'Twas less for the sake of thy high-sounding phrases,
Than to see the bright eyes of the dear one discover,
She thought that I was not unworthy to love her.

There chiefly I sought thee, *there* only I found thee;
Her glance was the best of the rays that surround thee;
15 When it sparkled o'er aught that was bright in my story,
I knew it was love, and I felt it was glory.

---

1. **myrtle:** a plant sacred to Venus, goddess of love in classical mythology.
2. **ivy:** a plant sacred to Bacchus, god of wine in classical mythology.
3. **laurels:** foliage of the laurel tree, an emblem of honor or distinction.

STUDY QUESTIONS

She Walks in Beauty

Recalling

1. How clearly does the poem picture its subject? What do her eyes look like? What color is her hair? What expression does she wear?

Interpreting

2. To what in the poem's opening lines does the black gown worn by the beautiful woman correspond? To what do the spangles scattered on her dress correspond?
3. Why is day described as "gaudy"?
4. How are the woman's mind and heart reflected in her appearance?

Stanzas Written on the Road Between Florence and Pisa

Recalling

1. In the first stanza, with what does the speaker equate glory?
2. According to lines 5–9, what can give someone glory?
3. By the last stanza what does the speaker consider to be glory and to be worth more than fame?

Interpreting

4. What is the only delight that fame has provided the speaker?

Byron was in Venice when he was moved to write this poem, which is based on the refrain of a Scottish song. Carnival season had just passed and the twenty-nine-year-old poet found himself in a period of reflection.

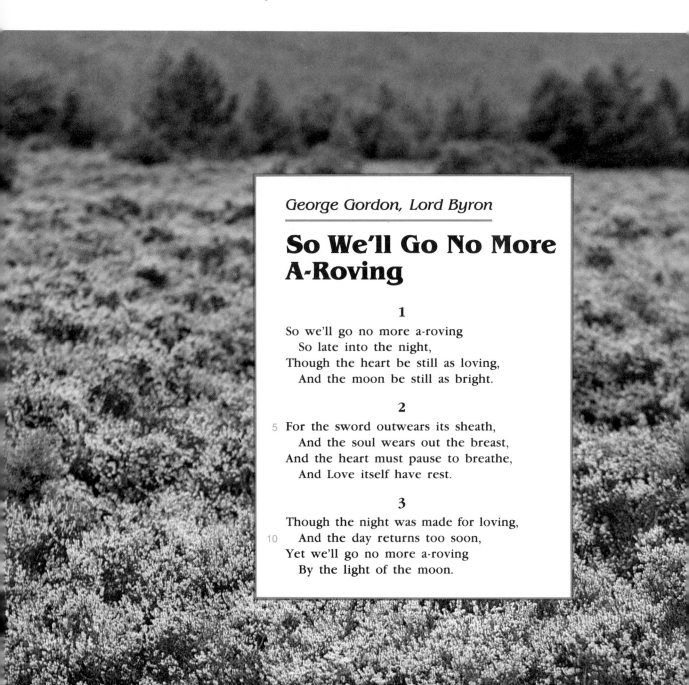

George Gordon, Lord Byron

So We'll Go No More A-Roving

1

So we'll go no more a-roving
    So late into the night,
Though the heart be still as loving,
    And the moon be still as bright.

2

5 For the sword outwears its sheath,
    And the soul wears out the breast,
And the heart must pause to breathe,
    And Love itself have rest.

3

Though the night was made for loving,
10   And the day returns too soon,
Yet we'll go no more a-roving
    By the light of the moon.

The achievement of Byron's that has best stood the test of time is the long, unfinished mock epic, *Don Juan*. The work, considered Byron's masterpiece, is written in **ottava rima**, a stanzaic form consisting of eight iambic pentameter lines, rhyming *ababacc*. The English poet thoroughly mastered this Italian form in the nearly two thousand stanzas that make up *Don Juan*.

Based loosely on the character of a legendary fourteenth-century Spaniard, Byron's Juan (pronounced jōō′un) wanders from Spain to Greece, Russia, and England. The true delight of the work lies less in the story itself than in the speaker's commentary, as often off the subject as on. Here, for example, are five stanzas in which the speaker abandons the hero to talk about himself.

Self-Portrait from **Don Juan**

But now at thirty years my hair is gray
   (I wonder what it will be like at forty?
I thought of a peruke[1] the other day)—
   My heart is not much greener; and, in short, I
5 Have squandered my whole summer while 'twas May,
   And feel no more the spirit to retort; I
Have spent my life, both interest and principal,
And deem not, what I deemed, my soul invincible.

No more—no more—Oh! never more on me
10   The freshness of the heart can fall like dew,
Which out of all the lovely things we see
   Extracts emotions beautiful and new;
Hived in our bosoms like the bag o' the bee:
   Think'st thou the honey with those objects grew?
15 Alas! 'twas not in them, but in thy power
To double even the sweetness of a flower.

No more—no more—Oh! never more, my heart,
   Canst thou be my sole world, my universe!
Once all in all, but now a thing apart,
20   Thou canst not be my blessing or my curse:
The illusion's gone for ever, and thou art
   Insensible, I trust, but none the worse,
And in thy stead I've got a deal of judgment,
Though heaven knows how it ever found a lodgment.[2]

---

1. **peruke** [pə rōōk′]: wig.
2. **lodgment**: dwelling place.

25 My days of love are over; me no more
    The charms of maid, wife, and still less of widow,
Can make the fool of which they made before—
    In short, I must not lead the life I did do;
The credulous hope of mutual minds is o'er,
30   The copious use of claret is forbid too,
So for a good old-gentlemanly vice,
I think I must take up with avarice. . . .
Ambition was my idol, which was broken
    Before the shrines of Sorrow, and of Pleasure;
35 And the two last have left me many a token
    O'er which reflection may be made at leisure;
Now, like Friar Bacon's brazen head,[3] I've spoken,
    "Time is, Time was, Time's past:"—a chymic[4] treasure
Is glittering youth, which I have spent betimes[5]—
40 My heart in passion, and my head on rhymes.

---

3. **Friar . . . head:** The reference is to a play in which the medieval philosopher Roger Bacon is represented as having fashioned of brass a head that could speak.
4. **chymic** [kim′ik]: alchemic; of counterfeit gold.
5. **betimes:** early.

STUDY QUESTIONS

So We'll Go No More A-Roving

Recalling
1. Despite what three things mentioned in the first and last stanzas will the speaker "go no more a-roving"?
2. The sheath covers the sword, as the body covers the soul. In each case, which wears out first, according to stanza 2?

Interpreting
3. Why must the heart "pause to breathe"?
4. In what tone of voice do you imagine the speaker would speak these simple words? Explain your answer.

Extending
5. Can you think of other metaphors, besides the sheath and the sword that Byron uses, to convey the relationship that exists between body and soul?

Don Juan

Recalling
1. Why does the speaker think of getting a wig?
2. What power is attributed to the heart in lines 15–16? In stanza 3 what has come to take the place of the illusions once fostered in the poet's heart but now gone forever?
3. What, according to the fourth stanza, must the "aging poet" give up? Which "good old-gentle-manly vice" does he plan to take up?
4. According to the last lines of this excerpt, on what was the speaker's heart fixed before his youth had been consumed?

Interpreting
5. What do you imagine the speaker's mood is in this self-portrait? Discuss the content and tone, considering the rhymes and their effect.

Extending
6. What aspects of *Don Juan* remind you of Pope's poetry (page 276)?

Percy Bysshe Shelley   *1792–1822*

His belief in human perfectability, his conviction that beauty and love could guide life's meaning, and his radical but perceptive social and political philosophies distinguish Percy Bysshe Shelley as the greatest idealist among the Romantic poets. Although his ancestors were wealthy and conventional members of the Sussex aristocracy, Shelley proved to be a nonconformist throughout his life. As a young student at Sion House Academy and then at the famous private school of Eton, he developed attractions to science and especially to gothic romances that were to influence his adult preoccupations and writing. While attending Eton Shelley began to read radical literature and decided to devote his life to opposing hypocrisy and injustice. Shortly after entering Oxford University he was expelled for refusing to deny authorship of a pamphlet entitled "The Necessity of Atheism." His expulsion created a breach with his father that was never mended.

Shelley then went to London, where his sisters were in school. There he met young Harriet Westbrooke, a classmate of his sisters, whom he soon married in order to rescue her from what he regarded as her father's tyranny. In keeping with Shelley's interest in humanitarian causes, they spent their honeymoon in Ireland, participating in the movement for the reform of government and Catholic emancipation. Returning to London, Shelley met the radical philosopher William Godwin, whose theories had already influenced him as a student. Having drifted apart from Harriet, Shelley fell in love with the philosopher's daughter, Mary Wollstonecraft Godwin, who was to be his second wife. (Mary Godwin, while still in her teens, wrote the novel *Frankenstein,* a work that proved more popular during the poet's lifetime than anything he himself had written.)

Shelley's was in many ways an unhappy life. His health was poor, and, in spite of his sensitive and inquisitive nature, his motives were often misunderstood. He himself acknowledged that his good impulses often backfired on him and were "the source of all sorts of mischief." He was regarded by most of his contemporaries—those who did not know him personally—as scarcely less than a monster. It was known that his controversial views had led to his expulsion from Oxford, that his father had disinherited him, that his first wife had apparently committed suicide in despair, and that the courts had taken custody of his children from that marriage.

As a result of his strong commitment to unconventional social views, Shelley was considered a revolutionary and was treated like a pariah. In 1818 he, like his fellow poet Byron, exiled himself from England in disgust. Before he was thirty, he was drowned in a boating accident during a violent storm off the coast of Italy, and his body was found washed ashore with a volume of Keats and another of Sophocles in his pockets. He was cremated on the beach, and his ashes were buried in the Protestant cemetery in Rome, near the grave of the poet John Keats (page 379). At his death Shelley's volumes of poetry remained for the most part unsold, his public undiscovered.

Despite financial difficulties and personal worries of his own, Shelley had always been singularly generous to others. After Shelley's death the poet Lord Byron wrote to his London publisher, "You were all brutally mistaken about Shelley." In Switzerland and Italy Byron had come to know the younger poet well. He was, so the lord insisted, "the best and least selfish man I ever knew. I never knew one who was not a beast in comparison."

Now Shelley—who had almost no audience when he died—is justly regarded as one of the greatest of the English Romantics, a fierce idealist whose verses illustrate his hope for the future and his devotion to human betterment. William Wordsworth believed that "Shelley is one of the best *artists* of us all: I mean in workmanship of style." Furthermore, Shelley wrote an impressive amount of poetry, and in an outstanding number of forms. *Adonais,* an elegy on the death of John Keats, is one of his finest works, and *Prometheus Unbound,* a dramatic poem in the manner of Greek tragedy, is another masterpiece. He also wrote sonnets, satires, odes, allegories, hymns, a splendid play in the Elizabethan manner—and, in prose, marvelous travel letters and a wonderful though uncompleted piece of literary criticism ("A Defense of Poetry"). At his death he was in the midst of a poem, *The Triumph of Life,* that might well have developed into the greatest work in a charged and compressed career.

Ozymandias [ōz i man′dē əs] was the Greek name for Ramses II, the pharaoh who ruled Egypt during the thirteenth century B.C. During his rule Ramses II conducted an extensive building program and was responsible for the largest statue in Egypt, which bore the inscription: "I am Ozymandias, king of kings; if anyone wishes to know what I am and where I lie, let him surpass me in some of my exploits."

Ramses II was also known as the pharaoh who oppressed the Israelites. Shelley—always an ardent challenger of oppression—depicts the ironical outcome of the pharaoh's legacy in this sonnet, a favorite poetic form of the Romantics.

Percy Bysshe Shelley

Ozymandias

I met a traveler from an antique land
Who said: Two vast and trunkless legs of stone
Stand in the desert . . . Near them, on the sand,
Half sunk, a shattered visage lies, whose frown,
5 And wrinkled lip, and sneer of cold command,
Tell that its sculptor well those passions read
Which yet survive, stamped on these lifeless things,
The hand that mocked them,[1] and the heart[2] that fed:
And on the pedestal these words appear:
10 "My name is Ozymandias, king of kings:
Look on my works, ye Mighty, and despair!"
Nothing beside remains. Round the decay
Of that colossal wreck, boundless and bare
The lone and level sands stretch far away.

---

1. **The hand . . . them:** the sculptor's hand that
"mocked" (imitated and ridiculed) the ruler's passions.
2. **heart:** the king's heart; "hand" and "heart" are both
direct objects of "survive" (line 7).

Painting by Elihu Vedder (1836–1923).

Percy Bysshe Shelley

To ——

Music, when soft voices die,
Vibrates in the memory—
Odors, when sweet violets sicken,
Live within the sense they quicken.
5 Rose leaves, when the rose is dead,
Are heaped for the belovèd's[1] bed;
And so thy thoughts,[2] when thou art gone,
Love itself shall slumber on.

---

1. **the belovèd's:** the rose's.
2. **thy thoughts:** thoughts of thee.

A Dirge

Rough wind, that moanest loud
  Grief too sad for song;
Wild wind, when sullen cloud
  Knells all the night long;
5 Sad storm, whose tears are vain,
Bare woods, whose branches strain,
Deep caves and dreary main[1]—
  Wail, for the world's wrong!

---

1. **main:** the open sea.

STUDY QUESTIONS

Ozymandias

Recalling

1. What has happened to the statue, according to lines 3–4?
2. Which facial expressions recording Ozymandias' passions still survive, according to lines 4–5?
3. What words appear on the pedestal of the statue? What else, besides the statue, remains of Ozymandias' vast achievements, his "works"?

Interpreting

4. Based on how the sculptor captured Ozymandias, what were the pharaoh's passions, or emotions? In what sense do those emotions survive?
5. What might Ozymandias have wanted onlookers to despair of? At the time of the traveler's report, what should the mighty despair of, given the condition of the statue and its surroundings? Explain the poem's irony.

Extending

6. What effect does Shelley achieve by putting the poem in the words of "a traveler from an antique land"?

To ——

Recalling

1. What three images of loveliness that can disappear are mentioned in lines 1–6? What happens after each kind of loveliness sickens or dies?
2. In line 7 what is the fourth image of loveliness?

Interpreting

3. In what way do the first six lines help explain the meaning and tone of the last two lines?

A Dirge

Recalling

1. What natural elements are represented as wailing forth the dirge (a funeral song, a song of mourning)?
2. For what are they mourning?

Interpreting

3. Based on what you know about history and Shelley, what do you understand by the phrase "the world's wrong" (line 8)? Give examples to explain your answer.
4. Why would a Romantic poet expect nature to mourn the world's wrong?

This poem was written in a forest near Florence, Italy, "on a day," says Shelley, "when that tempestuous wind, whose temperature is at once mild and animating [invigorating], was collecting the vapors which pour down the autumnal rains."

Ode to the West Wind

1

O wild West Wind, thou breath of Autumn's being,
Thou, from whose unseen presence the leaves dead
Are driven, like ghosts from an enchanter fleeing,

Yellow, and black, and pale, and hectic[1] red,
5 Pestilence-stricken multitudes: O thou,
Who chariotest to their dark wintry bed

The wingèd seeds, where they lie cold and low,
Each like a corpse within its grave, until
Thine azure sister of the Spring[2] shall blow

10 Her clarion[3] o'er the dreaming earth, and fill
(Driving sweet buds like flocks to feed in air)
With living hues and odors plain and hill:

Wild Spirit, which art moving everywhere;
Destroyer and preserver; hear, oh, hear!

2

15 Thou on whose stream, mid the steep sky's commotion,
Loose clouds like earth's decaying leaves are shed,
Shook from the tangled boughs of Heaven and Ocean,[4]

---

1. **hectic:** relating to the reddening of the face caused by hectic fever, which accompanies wasting diseases.
2. **sister . . . Spring:** the wind that will accompany spring.
3. **clarion:** sound of a trumpet.
4. **tangled . . . Ocean:** a metaphorical representation of the manner in which clouds are formed by a suspension of water ("Ocean") in air ("Heaven").

Angels[5] of rain and lightning: there are spread
On the blue surface of thine aëry surge,
20 Like the bright hair uplifted from the head

Of some fierce Maenad,[6] even from the dim verge
Of the horizon to the zenith's height,
The locks of the approaching storm. Thou dirge

Of the dying year, to which this closing night
25 Will be the dome of a vast sepulcher,
Vaulted with all thy congregated might

Of vapors, from whose solid atmosphere
Black rain, and fire, and hail will burst: oh, hear!

3

Thou who didst waken from his summer dreams
30 The blue Mediterranean, where he lay,
Lulled by the coil of his crystàlline streams,

Beside a pumice[7] isle in Baiae's bay,[8]
And saw in sleep old palaces and towers
Quivering within the wave's intenser day,

35 All overgrown with azure moss and flowers
So sweet, the sense faints picturing them! Thou
For whose path the Atlantic's level powers

Cleave themselves into chasms, while far below
The sea-blooms and the oozy woods which wear
40 The sapless foliage of the ocean, know

---

5. **Angels:** messengers.
6. **Maenad** [mē′nad]: a female worshiper of Bacchus, classical mythological god of wine and revelry.
7. **pumice** [pum′is]: volcanic rock.
8. **Baiae's** [bā′yēz] **bay:** an ancient resort in Italy.

Thy voice, and suddenly grow gray with fear,
And tremble and despoil themselves: oh, hear!

4

If I were a dead leaf thou mightest bear,
If I were a swift cloud to fly with thee;
45 A wave to pant beneath thy power, and share

The impulse of thy strength, only less free
Than thou, O uncontrollable! If even
I were as in my boyhood, and could be

The comrade of thy wanderings over Heaven,
50 As then, when to outstrip thy skyey speed
Scarce seemed a vision; I would ne'er have striven

As thus with thee in prayer in my sore need.
Oh, lift me as a wave, a leaf, a cloud!
I fall upon the thorns of life! I bleed!

55 A heavy weight of hours has chained and bowed
One too like thee: tameless, and swift, and proud.

5

Make me thy lyre,[9] even as the forest is:
What if my leaves are falling like its own!
The tumult of thy mighty harmonies

60 Will take from both a deep, autumnal tone,
Sweet though in sadness. Be thou, Spirit fierce,
My spirit! Be thou me, impetuous one!

Drive my dead thoughts over the universe
Like withered leaves to quicken a new birth!
65 And, by the incantation of this verse,

Scatter, as from an unextinguished hearth
Ashes and sparks, my words among mankind!
Be through my lips to unawakened earth

The trumpet of a prophecy! O Wind,
70 If Winter comes, can Spring be far behind?

---

9. **lyre:** refers to the aeolian [ē ō′lē ən] harp, a stringed instrument
that produces musical sounds when the wind passes over it.

STUDY QUESTIONS

Recalling

1. From line 1 on, whom or what is being addressed in this poem? What does the speaker ask of the addressee at the very end of stanzas 1, 2, and 3?
2. On what natural object does the wind's power show itself in stanza 1? In stanza 2? In stanza 3? Find these objects again in stanza 4, which serves as a summary of stanzas 1–3.
3. What is the speaker's present situation, as revealed in lines 54 and 55–56?
4. What does the speaker ask for in line 57? What does he ask the wind to do with his thoughts and words (lines 63–67)?

Interpreting

5. Why, at the end of stanza 1, is the west wind referred to as "Destroyer and preserver"? That is, what does winter, which the west wind brings, destroy? What does it preserve? What is the poet's final vision of winter in line 70?
6. How does the speaker in stanza 4 compare himself to the wind in terms of power and freedom? What might be the literal meaning of the "thorns of life" (line 54)?
7. By stanza 5 how has the speaker's attitude progressed? In your own words explain what the speaker hopes to accomplish.
8. In what way are nature and imagination related, according to this poem? Consider what this poem says about the effect that each can have. By examining word choice, rhythms, and the rhyme scheme, consider also how imagination captures nature in this very poem. (The rhyme scheme of the first twelve lines of each stanza is **terza rima,** composed of interlocking groups of three lines: *aba bcb cdc ded.*)

LITERARY FOCUS

Personification and Apostrophe

The more our emotions are involved, the more likely we are to use **figurative language,** writing that contains one or more figures of speech such as metaphor, personification, and apostrophe.

Metaphor, we recall, involves an implied comparison between two dissimilar things. Shelley's words at line 67 of "Ode to the West Wind" are metaphorically compared to ashes and sparks. **Personification** is a specific kind of metaphor, in which an inanimate object, an animal, or an abstraction is compared to a person and endowed with human characteristics. In lines 29–31, the Mediterranean Sea is compared to a person—a "he" who wakens "from his summer dreams." This picture stirs our emotions more than a sea that remained simply a body of water.

When a personification is addressed directly, the result is called **apostrophe.** Thus, Shelley apostrophizes the west wind throughout the poem, addressing it from first to last as though it could hear and respond, being the "Wild Spirit" that it is. Similarly, the same poet apostrophizes natural objects or phenomena in "A Dirge."

Apostrophe may also involve directly addressing an absent person as though he or she were present. Wordsworth apostrophizes the dead poet Milton when he invokes that poet's aid by writing "Milton! thou shouldst be living at this hour" (page 329). The effect of this kind of apostrophe is still the same: By speaking directly and emotionally, the poet heightens the reader's involvement.

Thinking About Personification and Apostrophe

1. How is love personified in Shelley's "To _____"?
2. How is "heart" personified in "Ozymandias"?
3. What is apostrophized in Byron's "Stanzas Written on the Road Between Florence and and Pisa" (page 367)?

COMPOSITION

Analyzing the Structure of a Poem

■ "Ode to the West Wind" is a highly structured poem. In an essay discuss the structure of the poem in ways that will enlarge your reader's appreciation of Shelley's achievement. Begin by explaining how the first three stanzas resemble each other. Be sure to discuss what single idea holds those stanzas together. Then show how stanzas 4 and 5 differ from the first three and how they move the poem forward.

Writing a Personification

■ In a prose paragraph or two personify one element of nature. You may choose as your subject the ocean, the sun, a brook, a simple tree, or any other element of nature you think will lend itself well to personification. Describe the object by showing it sounding, moving, and otherwise appearing human.

John Keats   *1795–1821*

All three of the great "second generation" of Romantic poets died young. Byron (page 364) died at the age of thirty-six, Shelley (page 371) died when he was twenty-nine. But John Keats was only twenty-five when he died. Moreover, he had not been precocious; his earliest poems, written in his late teens, are conventional and unpromising, and, in fact, most of Keats's great work was done in a single year, 1819, when he was twenty-three. Thereafter, the debilitating effects of tuberculosis made writing impossible. Yet already, in that short time, the young man had composed poetry that places him among the five or six greatest English poets—work far superior to anything Chaucer or Shakespeare or Milton had done at a comparable age.

Keats's ancestry and background would have seemed hardly conducive to forming a poet. Byron was an aristocrat, educated at the best schools. Shelley, too, was born into an old, aristocratic family, which assured him leisure to pursue the life of the mind. Keats's father, however, was a hostler, grooming horses at a London livery stable. The elder Keats died from a fall from a horse when his son John was eight; Keats's mother, the daughter of the stable's proprietor and also of modest origins, died when he was fourteen. As a boy Keats was sent to a nearby private school where the headmaster's son, who was one of his teachers, encouraged his literary interests. After the death of Keats's mother, however, the young man's guardian took him out of school. There was to be no Cambridge or Oxford in the life of this orphan but rather an apprenticeship to a surgeon and apothecary, or druggist, at a time when medicine enjoyed none of the prestige as a profession that it does now.

Nonetheless, Keats the humble medical student was soon to meet various literary personalities in London. Leigh Hunt—an editor who was a political radical and a friend of Shelley and Byron—was among them. Hunt encouraged the young man in the writing that he had already begun, and Keats soon abandoned medicine in favor of poetry. As noted, those early efforts at verse were not impressive. Keats had not even started to write until he was eighteen. Suddenly, at twenty-one, he produced his first great poem (and one of the greatest sonnets in the language): "On First Looking into Chapman's Homer."

From that time on, Keats consciously and triumphantly fashioned himself into a major poet, growing almost month by month in ability. His letters reveal that growth less as a miracle than as something worked for, something brought about. The result was that in the space of nine months in 1819, from January through September, he was able to produce a dazzling succession of outstanding poems: *The*

Eve of St. Agnes, "La Belle Dame sans Merci," six superlative odes, and more astonishing sonnets. Then, soon after this period of intense creative activity, illness made the poet set down his pen.

During the fall of 1818, Keats had fallen deeply in love with Fanny Brawne, an attractive and lively girl who was devoted to the poet. Although they became engaged, Keats's extreme commitment to his poetry, his lack of money, and, especially, his increasingly poor health made it impossible for them to marry. His mother and youngest brother had died of tuberculosis. Keats himself contracted the disease—a terrifying and dreadful nineteenth-century malady. Friends took him to Italy, in hopes that the warmer climate would prolong his life, but his condition was hopeless. He died in Rome early in 1821 and was buried there, in the same cemetery where Shelley's remains would be placed the following year.

Keats's poetry is distinctive for its unusual physical concreteness and its rich appeal to all of the senses. While many Romantic poets—including Wordsworth and Shelley—describe objects, Keats actually *presents* them. In this way he is able to stimulate the reader's senses as though the object were actually present. Furthermore, Keats believed that the poet should subordinate his own identity in order to enable the poem's subject to emerge fully. His ability to capture his subject's unique characteristics often allows the reader to experience a feeling of direct identification and participation. Finally, though Keats is known as a sensuous poet, his greatness also lies in the fact that he was an outstanding philosophical poet whose works portray experience as a complexity of unavoidable, inherent contradictions and opposites.

The first two Keats poems presented are sonnets and provide us with an opportunity to examine Keats's use of both the Petrarchan (Italian) and Shakespearean (English) sonnet forms. Keats composed "On First Looking into Chapman's Homer" after his friend and former schoolteacher, Charles Cowden Clarke, introduced him to a translation of the Greek poet Homer. The translation was by George Chapman, an Elizabethan poet. The two friends read the translation together through the night. Keats returned home at dawn, and Cowden received this sonnet with the morning mail.

John Keats

On First Looking into Chapman's Homer

Much have I traveled in the realms of gold,
   And many goodly states and kingdoms seen;
   Round many western islands have I been
Which bards[1] in fealty[2] to Apollo[3] hold.
5 Oft of one wide expanse had I been told
   That deep-browed Homer ruled as his demesne;[4]
   Yet did I never breathe its pure serene[5]
Till I heard Chapman speak out loud and bold:
Then felt I like some watcher of the skies
10   When a new planet swims into his ken;[6]
Or like stout Cortez[7] when with eagle eyes
   He stared at the Pacific—and all his men
Looked at each other with a wild surmise—
   Silent, upon a peak in Darien.[8]

---

1. **bards:** poets.
2. **fealty** [fē′əl tē]: loyalty owed by a feudal tenant to his lord.
3. **Apollo:** in classical mythology, the god of poetry and music.
4. **demesne** [di mān′]: realm, domain; feudal possession.
5. **serene:** clear, calm air.
6. **ken:** view.
7. **Cortez** [kôr tez′]: Hernando Cortez (1485–1547) Spanish conquistador of Mexico, whom Keats erroneously credits with the discovery of the Pacific Ocean, which was discovered by Balboa in 1513.
8. **Darien** [dār′ē en′]: the Isthmus of Panama.

STUDY QUESTIONS

Recalling

1. What was the "one wide expanse," described in lines 5–7, that the speaker had not explored in his reading? By what means, according to line 8, was he admitted into that literary region?
2. According to lines 9–14, what events did the speaker's experience resemble?

Interpreting

3. What, literally, are "the realms of gold" referred to in the first line of this poem?
4. What do the Pacific, the planet, and Homer's poetry have in common with respect to the effects on their beholders?
5. What is appropriate about Keats's choice of metaphors for this sonnet? In answering, comment on the division of thought between the octave (lines 1–8) and the sestet (lines 9–14).

Extending

6. What is your reaction to learning of Keats's celebrated mistake in line 11?

John Keats

When I Have Fears That I May Cease to Be

When I have fears that I may cease to be
    Before my pen has gleaned my teeming brain,
Before high-pilèd books, in charact'ry,[1]
    Hold like rich garners[2] the full-ripened grain;
5 When I behold, upon the night's starred face.
    Huge cloudy symbols of high romance,
And think that I may never live to trace
    Their shadows, with the magic hand of chance;
And when I feel, fair creature of an hour!
10   That I shall never look upon thee more,
Never have relish in the fairy power
    Of unreflecting love!—then on the shore
Of the wide world I stand alone, and think
Till Love and Fame to nothingness do sink.

---

1. **charact'ry:** written characters; letters of the alphabet.
2. **garners:** storehouses for grain.

STUDY QUESTIONS

Recalling

1. In lines 1–4 what is the speaker afraid he will not have time to do? In lines 5–8? In lines 9 through the middle of line 12?
2. How, according to the last two lines, does he cope with his fears?

Interpreting

3. How is an agricultural image developed in the opening four lines? How is the brain like a field ready to be harvested? What, literally, is the grain? What tool will do the harvesting? Where will the "harvest" be put?
4. How would the poet "trace" the visions that he beholds?
5. How do the nouns "Love" and "Fame" in the final line sum up the three quatrains of the poem? What is the speaker's attitude at the end of the poem?

COMPOSITION

Writing About Poetry

■ Discuss the overall meaning of one of Keats's preceding sonnets, and indicate the techniques that the poet uses to reveal that meaning. Discuss in particular rhythm, rhyme, similes or metaphors, and individual word choice. *For help with this assignment, refer to Lesson 7 in the Writing About Literature Handbook at the back of this book.*

Writing a Personal Reaction

■ Like Keats in "On First Looking into Chapman's Homer," offer a personal reaction to a reading experience. Begin, like Keats, by telling how you came to have the experience. Then go on to state the effect that the work of literature had on you. Obviously, your reaction will be more interesting to your audience if you tell about a strongly positive reading experience.

In the spring of 1819, when he was twenty-three, Keats wrote five great odes. (For more on odes, see page 388.) He wrote a sixth ode, "To Autumn," that September after seeing the harvest fields. Three of these six odes follow.

Ode to a Nightingale

1

My heart aches, and a drowsy numbness pains
   My sense, as though of hemlock[1] I had drunk,
Or emptied some dull opiate to the drains
   One minute past, and Lethe-wards[2] had sunk:
5 'Tis not through envy of thy happy lot,
   But being too happy in thine happiness—
      That thou, light-wingèd Dryad[3] of the trees,
        In some melodious plot
   Of beechen green, and shadows numberless,
10   Singest of summer in full-throated ease.

2

O, for a draught[4] of vintage! that hath been
   Cooled a long age in the deep-delvèd earth,
Tasting of Flora[5] and the country green,
   Dance, and Provençal[6] song, and sunburned mirth!
15 O for a beaker full of the warm South,
   Full of the true, the blushful Hippocrene,[7]
      With beaded bubbles winking at the brim,
        And purple-stainèd mouth;
   That I might drink, and leave the world unseen,
20   And with thee fade away into the forest dim:

---

1. **hemlock:** a poison herb.
2. **Lethe** [lē'thē]-**wards:** toward Lethe—in classical mythology, river of forgetfulness in the underworld.
3. **Dryad** [drī'əd]: in classical mythology, a nymph or deity of the woods.
4. **draught** [draft]: drink.
5. **Flora:** in classical mythology, goddess of flowers; the flowers themselves.
6. **Provençal** [prov'ən säl']: pertaining to Provence, in southern France, where troubadours, or singing poets, flourished in the Middle Ages.
7. **Hippocrene** [hip'ə krēn']: in classical mythology, a spring on Mount Helicon; its waters were regarded as a source of poetic inspiration.

3

Fade far away, dissolve, and quite forget
 What thou among the leaves hast never known,
The weariness, the fever, and the fret
 Here, where men sit and hear each other groan;
25 Where palsy shakes a few, sad, last gray hairs,
 Where youth grows pale, and specter-thin, and dies;
  Where but to think is to be full of sorrow
   And leaden-eyed despairs,
 Where Beauty cannot keep her lustrous eyes,
30   Or new Love pine at them beyond tomorrow.

4

Away! away! for I will fly to thee,
 Not charioted by Bacchus[8] and his pards,
But on the viewless[9] wings of Poesy,
 Though the dull brain perplexes and retards:
35 Already with thee! tender is the night,
 And haply[10] the Queen-Moon is on her throne,
  Clustered around by all her starry Fays;[11]
   But here there is no light,
Save what from heaven is with the breezes blown
40   Through verdurous[12] glooms and winding mossy ways.

5

I cannot see what flowers are at my feet,
 Nor what soft incense hangs upon the boughs,
But, in embalmèd[13] darkness, guess each sweet
 Wherewith the seasonable month endows

---

8. **Bacchus** [bak'əs]: in classical mythology, the god of wine, who was
commonly portrayed in a chariot drawn by leopards ("pards").
9. **viewless:** invisible.
10. **haply:** perhaps.
11. **Fays:** fairies.
12. **verdurous:** green with vegetation.
13. **embalmèd:** perfumed.

45 The grass, the thicket, and the fruit-tree wild;
   White hawthorn, and the pastoral eglantine;[14]
     Fast fading violets covered up in leaves;
       And mid-May's eldest child,
   The coming musk-rose, full of dewy wine,
50   The murmurous haunt of flies on summer eves.

6

Darkling[15] I listen; and, for many a time,
   I have been half in love with easeful Death,
Called him soft names in many a musèd rhyme,
   To take into the air my quiet breath;
55 Now more than ever seems it rich to die,
   To cease upon the midnight with no pain,
     While thou art pouring forth thy soul abroad
       In such an ecstasy!
   Still wouldst thou sing, and I have ears in vain—
60   To thy high requiem become a sod.

7

Thou wast not born for death, immortal Bird!
   No hungry generations tread thee down;
The voice I hear this passing night was heard
   In ancient days by emperor and clown:
65 Perhaps the selfsame song that found a path
   Through the sad heart of Ruth,[16] when, sick for home,
     She stood in tears amid the alien corn;
       The same that ofttimes hath
Charmed magic casements, opening on the foam
70   Of perilous seas, in fairylands forlorn.

8

Forlorn! the very word is like a bell
   To toll me back from thee to my sole self,
Adieu! the fancy cannot cheat so well
   As she is famed[17] to do, deceiving elf.
75 Adieu! adieu! thy plaintive anthem[18] fades
   Past the near meadows, over the still stream,
     Up the hillside; and now 'tis buried deep
       In the next valley-glades:
   Was it a vision, or a waking dream?
80   Fled is that music:—Do I wake or sleep?

---

14. **eglantine** [egʹlən tīnʹ]: sweetbrier or honeysuckle.
15. **Darkling:** in the dark.
16. **Ruth:** in the Bible, a young widow who left her homeland and went with her mother-in-law to work in the fields of Judah (Ruth 2 : 1–23).
17. **famed:** reported.
18. **anthem:** hymn.

John Keats

Ode on a Grecian Urn

1

Thou still unravished bride of quietness,
   Thou foster child of silence and slow time,
Sylvan[1] historian, who canst thus express
   A flowery tale more sweetly than our rhyme:
5 What leaf-fringed legend haunts about thy shape
   Of deities or mortals, or of both,
     In Tempe[2] or the dales of Arcady?[3]
   What men or gods are these? What maidens loath?[4]
What mad pursuit? What struggle to escape?
10   What pipes and timbrels?[5] What wild ecstasy?

2

Heard melodies are sweet, but those unheard
   Are sweeter; therefore, ye soft pipes, play on;
Not to the sensual[6] ear, but, more endeared,
   Pipe to the spirit ditties of no tone:
15 Fair youth, beneath the trees, thou canst not leave
   Thy song, nor ever can those trees be bare;
     Bold Lover, never, never canst thou kiss,
Though winning near the goal—yet, do not grieve;
     She cannot fade, though thou hast not thy bliss,
20   Forever wilt thou love, and she be fair!

3

Ah, happy, happy boughs! that cannot shed
   Your leaves, nor ever bid the Spring adieu;
And, happy melodist, unwearièd,
   Forever piping songs forever new.
25 More happy love! more happy, happy love!
   Forever warm and still to be enjoyed,
     Forever panting, and forever young;
All breathing human passion far above,
   That leaves a heart high-sorrowful and cloyed,
30   A burning forehead, and a parching tongue.

---

1. **Sylvan:** rustic, of the woods or forest.
2. **Tempe** [tem′pē]: a valley in Greece; also, any beautiful rural spot.
3. **Arcady** [är′kə dē]: Arcadia, a region of Greece, considered to embody the ideal in rural contentment.
4. **loath:** unwilling.
5. **timbrels:** tambourines or similar instruments.
6. **sensual:** pertaining to the physical senses, in this case, hearing.

4

Who are these coming to the sacrifice?
  To what green altar, O mysterious priest,
Lead'st thou that heifer lowing at the skies,
  And all her silken flanks with garlands dressed?
35 What little town by river or seashore,
  Or mountain-built with peaceful citadel,
    Is emptied of this folk, this pious morn?
And, little town, thy streets forevermore
  Will silent be; and not a soul to tell
40   Why thou art desolate, can e'er return.

5

O Attic[7] shape! Fair attitude! with brede[8]
  Of marble men and maidens overwrought,[9]
With forest branches and the trodden weed;
  Thou, silent form! dost tease us out of thought
45 As doth eternity: Cold Pastoral!
  When old age shall this generation waste,
    Thou shalt remain, in midst of other woe
Than ours, a friend to man, to whom thou say'st,
"Beauty is truth, truth beauty,"—that is all
50   Ye know on earth, and all ye need to know.

---

7. **Attic:** displaying the simple, graceful style characteristic of Attica, or Athens.
8. **brede:** a braided or intertwined design.
9. **overwrought:** with the surface decorated.

STUDY QUESTIONS

Ode to a Nightingale

Recalling

1. What three sensations does the speaker feel in the poem's opening "scene"—a garden in the morning (stanza 1)? What does he hear?
2. What specific griefs, from which the poet wishes to escape into the melodious world of the nightingale, are mentioned in lines 23–30? After rejecting wine as a means of escape from a grief-filled world, how does the poet determine to fly to the enchanted world that the bird inhabits?
3. What expressions in stanza 4 announce the next "scene"—the imagined world at night?

What, according to lines 38–50, is this world like?
4. In the nightingale's world of stanza 6, what does the speaker feel about the prospect of death (line 55)? With what realization is that thought qualified at lines 59–60? Is the nightingale's song subject to death, according to stanza 7?
5. In the last stanza, as the speaker realizes that imagination cannot deceive "so well / As she is famed to do," what happens to the nightingale? What is the speaker's final question?

Interpreting

6. What are the differences between the speaker's world and the natural world (the nightingale's world)?

7. What examples does the speaker cite to convince us of the nightingale's, or nature's power and influence in stanza 7?

8. What role does the word "forlorn" play in bringing the poet back to reality by the end of the poem? How does the speaker feel toward the nightingale and its world at the end of the poem?

Extending

9. What other images—of sound, sight, smell, taste, or touch—have led you on a journey of the imagination, perhaps back to some remembered past occurrence?

Ode on a Grecian Urn

Recalling

1. Identify details of the scene (assumed by some to be a wedding procession) that is described in stanza 1 as the first "flowery tale" or "leaf-fringed legend" pictured on the Grecian urn.

2. In the second stanza identify the next two picture groups on the urn by telling who is doing—or not doing—what.

3. In stanza 4 what other scene—perhaps on the other side of the urn—is presented?

4. When the speaker stands back and looks at the urn as a whole in stanza 5, what does he say will happen to the urn? What, according to him, does the urn say as "a friend to man"?

Interpreting

5. What does the speaker think about the changelessness of art, which is made clear by the piper who cannot sound his tune, by the trees that cannot shed their leaves, and by the lover who cannot kiss his beloved? How does actual human life compare to life as captured by art?

6. Explain the note of sadness introduced in stanza 4. How does the effect of art here contrast with the effect of art in stanzas 2 and 3?

7. When the speaker calls the urn a "Cold Pastoral" in stanza 5, what does he mean?

8. In spite of some negative qualities, what about art is so appealing to the speaker? In

spite of our human limitations, why should we seek an ideal?

9. Some critics claim that the quotation marks beginning in line 49 should not end until the last word in line 50. What difference in meaning would that punctuation cause?

Extending

10. Both odes have related themes but different images. What does "Ode to a Nightingale" suggest as superior to human experience? "Ode on a Grecian Urn"?

LITERARY FOCUS

The Ode

An **ode** is a long lyric poem, serious and dignified in subject, tone, and style, often written to celebrate an event, person, being, or power—or to provide a vehicle for private meditation. Sometimes an ode may have an elaborate stanzaic structure. Almost all odes are poems of address, in which the poet uses apostrophe (see page 378). This definition notwithstanding, we must explain that the ode is perhaps the most freely defined of poetical forms, and odes vary markedly.

The ode was originally a Greek form used in dramatic poetry, in which a chorus would follow the movements of a dance while singing the words of the ode. Those odes often celebrated a public occasion of consequence such as a military victory. (See Part Two of this book.) From those ancient Greek beginnings the form has descended through western culture to appear in English divested of dance and song.

In English poetry the ode exists in one of two manifestations. Irregular odes have no set rhyme scheme and no set stanza pattern. Dryden's ode on page 238 is an example of the irregular ode form. By contrast, the Horatian ode, named for the Roman poet Horace, follows a regular stanza pattern and rhyme scheme, as does the ode by Shelley (page 375) and these by Keats.

Thinking About the Ode

1. What is the serious theme of Shelley's "Ode to the West Wind"? Of Keats's "Ode on a Grecian Urn" and "Ode to a Nightingale"?

2. Does Keats follow the same stanza form in his odes?

Model for Active Reading

In this selection, as in one selection in each unit, you will find notes in the right-hand margin that highlight parts of the selection. These notes point out important ideas of the literary period and draw your attention to literary elements and techniques covered in the Literary Focuses. Page numbers in the notes will refer you to more extensive discussions of these important ideas and elements.

John Keats

To Autumn

1

Season of mists and mellow fruitfulness,
  Close bosom-friend of the maturing sun;
Conspiring with him how to load and bless
  With fruit the vines that round the thatch-eaves run;
5 To bend with apples the mossed cottage-trees,
  And fill all fruit with ripeness to the core;
    To swell the gourd, and plump the hazel shells
  With a sweet kernel; to set budding more,
And still more, later flowers for the bees,
10 Until they think warm days will never cease,
    For Summer has o'er-brimmed their clammy cells.

2

Who hath not seen thee oft amid thy store?
  Sometimes whoever seeks abroad may find
Thee sitting careless on a granary floor,
15 Thy hair soft-lifted by the winnowing[1] wind;
Or on a half-reaped furrow sound asleep,
  Drowsed with the fume of poppies, while thy hook
    Spares the next swath and all its twinèd flowers:
And sometime like a gleaner thou dost keep
20 Steady thy laden head across a brook;
  Or by a cider-press, with patient look,
    Thou watchest the last oozings, hours by hours.

Romantic idea: This poem reflects the Romantic habit of relating the natural, rustic world to personal concerns (p. 322).

Alliteration, Assonance, Consonance (p. 362): The melodious repetition of initial *m*, of internal *o*, of final *l*, and of *s* creates a mood.

Personification, Apostrophe (p. 378): The entire poem is addressed to autumn, but the apostrophe becomes obvious in stanza 2, where Keats also gives human qualities to the season. **Onomatopoeia** (p. 363): The *z* and *s* sounds along with the vowels in the last part of line 22 imitate the action of the cider-press.

---

1. **winnowing:** blowing; also, the fanning process by which the wheat chaff is separated from the grain.

3

Where are the songs of Spring? Ay, where are they?
Think not of them, thou hast thy music too—
25 While barred clouds bloom the soft-dying day,
And touch the stubble-plains with rosy hue;
Then in a wailful choir the small gnats mourn
Among the river sallows,[2] borne aloft
Or sinking as the light wind lives or dies;
30 And full-grown lambs loud bleat from hilly bourn;[3]
Hedge crickets sing; and now with treble soft
The redbreast whistles from a garden croft,[4]
And gathering swallows twitter in the skies.

Romantic idea: A description, the poem shows the poet's subjectivity (p. 322) in line 23.

---

2. **sallows:** willow trees.
3. **bourn** [bōrn]: region.
4. **croft:** enclosed plot of ground.

STUDY QUESTIONS

Recalling

1. Name at least four things that autumn and the sun are conspiring to do in stanza 1. How may autumn confuse the bees?
2. Cite three instances in which the spirit of autumn is personified as a farm girl.
3. What sights are evoked at lines 25–26 to picture autumn's beauty? What autumn sounds are mentioned in the last seven lines of the final stanza?

Interpreting

4. What does Keats suggest about autumn's beauty and about the cyclic pattern of nature? Is this poem mainly descriptive, or does the poet intrude his moods on the poem?
5. What examples of tactile imagery—imagery that appeals to the sense of touch—do you find in "To Autumn"?

VIEWPOINT

"Poetry is either something that lives like fire inside of you," wrote the celebrated American novelist F. Scott Fitzgerald,

. . . or else it is nothing, an empty, formalized bore around which pedants can endlessly drone their notes and explanations.

"The Grecian Urn" is unbearably beautiful . . . or it's just something you don't understand. . . . I suppose I've read it a hundred times. About the tenth time I began to know what it is about, and caught the chime in it and the exquisite inner mechanics. Likewise with the "Nightingale," which I can never read through without tears in my eyes. . . .

■ Based on your reading of Keats's odes, what do you suppose Fitzgerald means by "the chime" of the poems? What do you think he means by their "exquisite inner mechanics"?

COMPARING WRITERS

1. For each of the Romantic poets in the preceding pages, find at least one example of fascination with the remote—the remote in place or the remote in time. You may cite entire poems and themes or specific lines or images.
2. Demonstrate how each Romantic poet was seeking an ideal of one kind or another. You may look for the poets' attention to nature, to feminine beauty and love, or to art.
3. Citing examples, explain how the Romantic writers represented here were similar or different in their view of the state of the world and in their view of the future. Based on these poems, were the writers hopeful or despondent, accepting or critical?

William Hazlitt   *1778–1830*

The essay, the prose form that Francis Bacon had introduced into English literature, thrived throughout the eighteenth century in the hands of such practitioners as Addison and Steele. In the nineteenth century the form continued to appeal, for the Romantic temperament, with its stress on the individual, relished the essay as a vehicle for subjective, personal feeling.

One of the best of the Romantic essayists was William Hazlitt. Hazlitt had been among the first to recognize the greatness of young Keats's poetic talents. He was a friend of Wordsworth's and of Coleridge's as well and had an especially close, lifelong friendship with Charles Lamb—the other outstanding essayist among the Romantics.

When Hazlitt was five years old, his father, a Unitarian minister with strong liberal views, took his family to America and founded the first Unitarian Church in Boston. Four years later they returned to England and settled in Shropshire. Between the ages of fifteen and eighteen, Hazlitt attended college in London, where he vigorously pursued philosophical studies. In 1802 he decided to become a portrait painter. Not until he was in his mid-thirties did he discover his true calling, as a contributor of essays on a wide variety of subjects to various English periodicals. As a popular lecturer on English poetry and drama and as a skilled writer, Hazlitt also became, along with Coleridge, one of the two most important critics of his time.

Hazlitt was a moody and often quarrelsome man, and his domestic life was not a happy one, both of his marriages ending in separation. He maintained very liberal political and religious views throughout his lifetime even though many of his former liberal friends and contemporaries became increasingly conservative. As a result of his vehemence, he alienated at one time or another many of his acquaintances. Yet Hazlitt was admired, both personally and professionally, for his honesty and intensity of feeling.

In his prose Hazlitt employs an energetic, forceful, and natural style in which his subjective opinion is prominent. His writing includes the expression of thought on such diverse concerns as philosophy, economics, politics, painting, prizefighting, the theater, and literature. In the following essay he presents his views on *Macbeth,* awakened by attending a performance of the play in London.

William Hazlitt

Macbeth

The poet's eye in a fine frenzy rolling
Doth glance from heaven to earth, from earth
to heaven;
And as imagination bodies forth
The forms of things unknown, the poet's pen
Turns them to shape, and gives to airy
nothing
A local habitation and a name.[1]

Macbeth and *Lear*, *Othello* and *Hamlet*, are usually reckoned Shakespeare's four principal tragedies. *Lear* stands first for the profound intensity of the passion; *Macbeth* for the wildness of the imagination and the rapidity of the action; *Othello* for the progressive interest and powerful alternations of feeling; *Hamlet* for the refined development of thought and sentiment. If the force of genius shown in each of these works is astonishing, their variety is not less so. They are like different creations of the same mind, not one of which has the slightest reference to the rest. This distinctness and originality is indeed the necessary consequence of truth and nature. Shakespeare's genius alone appeared to possess the resources of nature. He is "your only *tragedy maker*." His plays have the force of things upon the mind. What he represents is brought home to the bosom as a part of our experience, implanted in the memory as if we had known the places, persons, and things of which he treats. *Macbeth* is like a record of a preternatural[2] and tragical event. It has the rugged severity of an old chronicle with all that the imagination of the poet can engraft upon traditional belief. The castle of Macbeth, round which "the air smells wooingly," and where "the temple-haunting martlet builds," has a real subsistence in the mind; the Weird Sisters meet us in person on "the blasted heath"; the "air-drawn dagger" moves slowly before our eyes; the "gracious Duncan," the "blood-boltered Banquo" stand before us; all that passed through the mind of Macbeth passes, without the loss of a tittle,[3] through ours. All that could actually take place, and all that is only possible to be conceived, what was said and what was done, the workings of passion, the spells of magic, are brought before us with the same absolute truth and vividness.

Shakespeare excelled in the openings of his plays: that of Macbeth is the most striking of any. The wildness of the scenery, the sudden shifting of the situations and characters, the bustle, the expectations excited, are equally extraordinary. From the first entrance of the Witches and the description of them when they meet Macbeth:

What are these
So withered and so wild in their attire,
That look not like th' inhabitants o' th' earth
And yet are on 't?

the mind is prepared for all that follows.

This tragedy is alike distinguished for the lofty imagination it displays, and for the tumultuous vehemence of the action; and the one is made the moving principle of the other. The overwhelming pressure of preternatural agency urges on the tide of human passion with redoubled force. Macbeth himself appears driven along by the violence of his fate like a vessel drifting before a storm: he reels to and fro like a drunken man; he staggers under the weight of his own purposes and the suggestions of

---

1. **"The poet's eye . . . name"**: from Shakespeare's *A Midsummer Night's Dream*, Act V, scene i.
2. **preternatural** [prē′tər nach′ər əl]: beyond or differing from what is natural; extraordinary or abnormal.

3. **tittle:** very small part or quantity.

others; he stands at bay with his situation; and from the superstitious awe and breathless suspense into which the communications of the Weird Sisters throw him is hurried on with daring impatience to verify their predictions, and with impious and bloody hand to tear aside the veil which hides the uncertainty of the future. He is not equal to the struggle with fate and conscience. He now "bends up each corporal instrument to the terrible feat"; at other times his heart misgives him, and he is cowed and abashed by his success. "The deed, no less than the attempt, confounds him." His mind is assailed by the stings of remorse, and full of "preternatural solicitings." His speeches and soliloquies are dark riddles on human life, baffling solution, and entangling him in their labyrinths. In thought he is absent and perplexed, sudden and desperate in act, from a distrust of his own resolution. His energy springs from the anxiety and agitation of his mind. His blindly rushing forward on the objects of his ambition and revenge or his recoiling from them equally betrays the harassed state of his feelings. This part of his character is admirably set off by being brought in connection with that of Lady Macbeth, whose obdurate strength of will and masculine firmness give her the ascendancy over her husband's faltering virtue. She at once seizes on the opportunity that offers for the accomplishment of all their wished-for greatness, and never flinches from her object till all is over. The magnitude of her resolution almost covers the magnitude of her guilt. She is a great bad woman, whom we hate but whom we fear more than we hate. She does not excite our loathing and abhorrence like Regan and Goneril.[4] She is only wicked to gain a great end and is perhaps more distinguished by her commanding presence of mind and inexorable self-will, which do not suffer her to be diverted from a bad purpose, when once formed, by weak and womanly regrets, than by the hardness of her heart or want of natural affections. The impression which her lofty determination of character makes on the mind of Macbeth is well described where he exclaims:

> Bring forth men-children only;
> For thy undaunted mettle should compose
> Nothing but males.

Nor do the pains she is at to "screw his courage to the sticking-place," the reproach to him not to be "lost so poorly in himself," the assurance that "a little water clears them of this deed," show anything but her greater consistency in depravity. Her strong-nerved ambition furnishes ribs of steel to "the sides of his intent"; and she is herself wound up to the execution of her baneful project with the same unshrinking fortitude in crime that in other circumstances she would probably have shown patience in suffering. The deliberate sacrifice of all other considerations to the gaining "for their future days and nights sole sovereign sway and masterdom," by the murder of Duncan, is gorgeously expressed in her invocation on hearing of "his fatal entrance under her battlements":

> *Come, you spirits*
> *That tend on mortal thoughts, unsex me*
>   *here,*
> *And fill me, from the crown to the toe, top-*
>   *full*
> *Of direst cruelty! Make thick my blood,*
> *Stop up th' access and passage to remorse,*
> *That no compunctious visitings of nature*
> *Shake my fell purpose, nor keep peace*
>   *between*
> *Th' effect and it! Come to my woman's*
>   *breasts,*
> *And take my milk for gall, you murd'ring*
>   *ministers,*
> *Wherever in your sightless substances*
> *You wait on nature's mischief! Come, thick*
>   *night,*
> *And pall thee in the dunnest smoke of hell,*

---

4. **Regan . . . Goneril:** Lear's evil daughters in Shakespeare's *King Lear.*

*That my keen knife see not the wound it
    makes,
Nor heaven peep through the blanket of the
    dark,
To cry, "Hold, hold!"*

When she first hears that "Duncan comes there to sleep," she is so overcome by the news, which is beyond her utmost expectations, that she answers the messenger, "Thou 'rt mad to say it": and on receiving her husband's account of the predictions of the Witches, conscious of his instability of purpose, and that her presence is necessary to goad him on to the consummation of his promised greatness, she exclaims:

> *Hie thee hither,*
> *That I may pour my spirits in thine ear,*
> *And chastise with the valor of my tongue*
> *All that impedes thee from the golden round*
> *Which fate and metaphysical aid doth seem*
> *To have thee crowned withal.*

This swelling exultation and keen spirit of triumph, this uncontrollable eagerness of anticipation, which seems to dilate her form and take possession of all her faculties, this solid, substantial flesh-and-blood display of passion, exhibit a striking contrast to the cold, abstracted, gratuitous, servile malignity of the Witches, who are equally instrumental in urging Macbeth to his fate for the mere love of mischief and from a disinterested delight in deformity and cruelty. They are hags of mischief, obscene panders to iniquity, malicious from their impotence of enjoyment, enamored of destruction, because they are themselves unreal, abortive, half-existences, and who become sublime from their exemption from all human sympathies and contempt for all human affairs, as Lady Macbeth does by the force of passion! Her fault seems to have been an excess of that strong principle of self-interest and family aggrandizement, not amenable to the common feelings of compassion and justice, which is so marked a feature in barbarous nations and times. A passing reflection of this kind, on the resemblance of the sleeping king to her father, alone prevents her from slaying Duncan with her own hand.

In speaking of the character of Lady Macbeth, we ought not to pass over Mrs. Siddons's[5] manner of acting that part. We can conceive of nothing grander. It was something above nature. It seemed almost as if a being of a superior order had dropped from a higher sphere to awe the world with the majesty of her appearance. Power was seated on her brow, passion emanated from her breast as from a shrine; she was tragedy personified. In coming on in the sleeping scene, her eyes were open, but their sense was shut. She was like a person bewildered and unconscious of what she did. Her lips moved involuntarily—all her gestures were involuntary and mechanical. She glided on and off the stage like an apparition. To have seen her in that character was an event in everyone's life, not to be forgotten.

Macbeth (generally speaking) is done upon a stronger and more systematic principle of contrast than any other of Shakespeare's plays. It moves upon the verge of an abyss, and is a constant struggle between life and death. The action is desperate, and the reaction is dreadful. It is a huddling together of fierce extremes, a war of opposite natures which of them shall destroy the other. There is nothing but what has a violent end or violent beginnings. The lights and shades are laid on with a determined hand; the transitions from triumph to despair, from the height of terror to the repose of death, are sudden and startling; every passion brings in its fellow-contrary, and the thoughts pitch and jostle against each other as in the dark. The whole play is an unruly chaos of strange and forbidden things, where the ground rocks under our feet. Shakespeare's genius here took its full swing, and trod upon the furthest bounds of nature and passion.

---

5. **Mrs. Siddons's:** Sarah Siddons (1755–1831), celebrated British actress.

STUDY QUESTIONS

Recalling

1. In the opening paragraph, what general praise does Hazlitt heap on Shakespeare as a "tragedy maker"? On *Macbeth* specifically?
2. After Hazlitt analyzes the character Macbeth in the long third paragraph, which character does he next take up? Why does that character move us to hatred, but not to loathing? What are the character's principal faults?
3. What does Hazlitt think of the portrayal of Lady Macbeth in the performance he saw?
4. According to the last paragraph, what principle does Hazlitt conclude is at work through the play as a whole? What examples does the essayist mention to make that point clear?

Interpreting

5. What are the outstanding personality differences between the characters of Macbeth and Lady Macbeth, as analyzed by Hazlitt?

Extending

6. To what modern journalistic form does this essay correspond?

LITERARY FOCUS

Literary Criticism

Hazlitt's remarks on Macbeth provide a good example of **literary criticism:** the analysis or interpretation of a literary work in order to enlarge a reader's appreciation or comprehension. This celebrated essayist adopts two devices in this piece of literary criticism.

First, Hazlitt uses the present tense to discuss his subject. "When she first *hears* that 'Duncan comes there to sleep,' " he writes, "she *is* so overcome by the news. . . ." Not *heard;* not *was.* The past sounds finished and dead, but *Macbeth* comes to new life each time it is read or performed. That vitality is conveyed through Hazlitt's use of the present tense.

Second, Hazlitt quotes extensively from the play. The effect is to bring us close to what he is

considering and to reassure us that he is testing what he says against the text. It takes more time to check the text and then write "the 'gracious Duncan,' the 'blood-boltered Banquo' stand before us," but that phrasing is much more effective than a general statement such as, "The various characters stand before us." Quoting from the play focuses the imagery and supports points that might otherwise be in doubt.

Thinking About Literary Criticism

1. Why does Hazlitt switch to past tense in the next-to-the-last paragraph?
2. Find an instance in which Hazlitt quotes from the play to support his analysis of Lady Macbeth. Explain why the quotations he has chosen are effective.

COMPOSITION

Developing a Thesis Statement

▉ Choose the selection in this unit that most stirred your interest and enthusiasm. (You will write literary criticism more effectively if you care about your subject.) In an essay of three or four paragraphs discuss an aspect of that selection in ways that will heighten your reader's appreciation of the writer's achievement. You may want to concentrate on imagery, word choice, structure, or sound. State your thesis about this aspect of the selection, and support your thesis with examples from the text. *For help with this assignment, refer to Lesson 1 in the Writing About Literature Handbook at the back of this book.*

Writing a Review

▉ Select a play, movie, or television show you have recently enjoyed. Write a review of the performance. Begin by commenting on the work's overall theme. Then discuss two characters—their strengths, their weaknesses, and their relationship to each other. Go on to evaluate the actors' portrayals of the characters. Conclude with a statement of your reaction to the experience of watching the performance.

Charles Lamb   *1775–1834*

Charles Lamb is the master of what is called the familiar essay, a personal type of informal essay that, in a casual style and conversational tone, reveals the writer's own personality and feelings. The figure who emerges through this essayist's writings is genial, knowledgeable, and altogether appealing. Yet Lamb himself had a difficult, even tragic life.

He was the friend of Wordsworth, Hazlitt, and Keats—and was Coleridge's oldest friend, the two having met when they were students at Christ's Hospital School in London. At the age of seventeen, Lamb began working as a clerk in the East India Company, an immense commercial establishment where he was employed until his retirement to the country thirty-three years later. Lamb began to write in several forms early in his career in order to supplement his salary at the company.

One evening when he was twenty-two, Lamb watched in horror as his beloved older sister Mary, temporarily insane, stabbed their mother; the murder was committed before he could get the knife from her hands. For the rest of his life, the writer looked after Mary, who for much of the time was able to lead a normal life. Mary shared her brother's interests in the theater, London art galleries, and old books, and both brother and sister were outgoing and friendly. The Lambs entertained their friends and acquaintances (including many important writers and artists of the day) at weekly Wednesday or Thursday night gatherings at their home. However—and the image is extremely poignant—Mary's symptoms would return periodically, and the two of them would set out together in tears for the asylum, carrying a straight jacket with them. Thus they got through life together, and together wrote *Tales from Shakespeare,* the famous prose version for children of Shakespeare's plays.

Eventually, this writer of poems, farces, and melodramatic plays began to submit essays to periodicals. By his forties he wrote for the newly formed *London Magazine,* to which he contributed under the pen name Elia. *Essays of Elia* and *Last Essays of Elia* established a prose genre: the familiar essay, an entertaining way of writing that thousands have imitated since, though few with the grace and deftness of Lamb himself.

Charles Lamb

Playhouse Memoranda

I once sat in the pit[1] of Drury Lane Theatre[2] next to a blind man, who, I afterwards learned, was a street musician, well known about London. The play was *Richard the Third,*[3] and it was curious to observe the interest which he took in every successive scene, so far more lively than could be perceived in any of the company around him. At those pathetic interviews between the Queen and Duchess of York, after the murder of the children, his eyes (or rather the places where eyes should have been) gushed out tears in torrents, and he sat entranced in attention, while everyone about him was tittering, partly at him, and partly at the grotesque figures and wretched action of the women, who had been selected by managerial taste to personate[4] those royal mourners. Having no drawback of sight to impair his sensibilities, he simply attended to the scene, and received its unsophisticated impression. *So much the rather her celestial light shone inward.*[5] I was pleased with an observation which he made, when I asked him how he liked Kemble,[6] who played Richard. I should have thought (said he) that that man had been reading something out of a book, if I had not known that I was in a playhouse.

I was once amused in a different way by a knot of country people who had come to see a play at that same Theatre. They seemed perfectly inattentive to all the best performers for the first act or two, though the piece was ad-mirably played, but kept poring in the playbill,[7] and were evidently watching for the appearance of one, who was to be the source of supreme delight to them that night. At length the expected actor arrived, who happened to be in possession of a very insignificant part, not much above a mute. I saw their faint attempt at raising a clap on his appearance, and their disappointment at not being seconded by the audience in general. I saw them try to admire and to find out something very wonderful in him, and wondering all the while at the moderate sensation he produced. I saw their pleasure and their interest subside at last into flat mortification, when the riddle was at once unfolded by my recollecting that this performer bore the same name with an actor, then in the acme of his celebrity, at Covent Garden,[8] but who lately finished his theatrical and mortal career on the other side of the Atlantic. They had come to see Mr. C., but had come to the wrong house.

Is it a stale remark to say that I have constantly found the interest excited at a playhouse to bear an exact inverse proportion to the price paid for admission? Formerly, when my sight and hearing were more perfect, and my purse a little less so, I was a frequenter of the upper gallery[9] in the old theaters. The eager attention, the breathless listening, the anxiety not to lose a word, the quick anticipation of the significance of the scene (every sense kept as it were upon a sharp lookout), which are exhibited by the occupiers of those higher and now almost out-of-sight regions (who, going seldom to a play, cannot afford to lose anything by inattention), suffer some little dim-

---

1. **pit:** section of the theater at ground level.
2. **Drury Lane Theatre:** one of the major London theaters of the time.
3. ***Richard the Third:*** one of Shakespeare's history plays.
4. **personate:** play the part of.
5. ***So much . . . inward:*** slight alteration of lines from Milton's "Hymn to Light" in *Paradise Lost*.
6. **Kemble:** John Philip Kemble (1757–1823), an English actor.

7. **playbill:** theatrical program, giving names of the actors.
8. **Covent Garden:** another major London theater.
9. **upper gallery:** uppermost section of the theater, with the cheapest seats.

inution as you descend to the lower or two-shilling ranks; but still the joy is lively and un-allayed, save that by some little *incursion* of *manners*, the expression of it is expected to abate somewhat of its natural liveliness. The oaken plaudits of the trunk maker would *here* be considered as going a little beyond the line.

In the pit first begins that accursed critical faculty, which, making a man the judge of his own pleasures, too often constitutes him the executioner of his own and others! You may see the *jealousy of being unduly pleased*, the *suspicion of being taken in to admire;* in short, the vile critical spirit, creeping and diffusing itself, and spreading from the wrinkled brows and cloudy eyes of the front row sages and newspaper reporters (its proper residence), till it infects and clouds over the thoughtless, vacant countenance of John Bull tradesmen and clerks of countinghouses, who, but for that approximation, would have been contented to have grinned without rule, and to have been pleased without asking why.

The sitting next a critic is contagious. Still now and then, a *genuine spectator* is to be found among them, a shopkeeper and his family, whose honest titillations of mirth and generous chucklings of applause cannot wait or be at leisure to take the cue from the sour judging faces about them. Haply[10] they never dreamed that there were such animals in nature as critics or reviewers; even the idea of an author may be a speculation they never entered into; but they take the mirth they find as a pure effusion of the actor-folks, set there on purpose to make them fun. I love the uninquiring gratitude of such spectators.

As for the boxes,[11] I never can understand what brings the people there. I see such frigid indifference, such unconcerned spectatorship, such impenetrability to pleasure or its contrary, such being *in the house* and yet not *of it,* certainly they come far nearer the nature of *the Gods,* upon the system of Lucretius[12] at least, than those honest, hearty, well-pleased, unindifferent mortals above,[13] who, from time immemorial, have had that name, upon no other ground than situation, assigned them.

Take the playhouse altogether, there is a less sum of enjoyment than used to be. Formerly you might see something like the effect of a novelty upon a citizen, his wife and daughters, in the pit—their curiosity upon every new face that entered upon the stage. The talk of how they got in at the door, and how they were crowded upon some former occasion, made a topic till the curtain drew up. People go too often nowadays to make their ingress or egress of consequence. Children of seven years of age will talk as familiarly of the performers, aye and as knowingly (according to the received opinion) as grown persons—more than the grown persons in my time.

Oh when shall I forget first seeing a play, at the age of five or six? It was *Artaxerxes.*[14] Who played, or who sang in it, I know not. Such low ideas as actors' names, or actors' merits, never entered my head. The mystery of delight was not cut open and dissipated for me by those who took me there. It was Artaxerxes and Arbaces and Mandane that I saw, not Mr. Beard or Mr. Leoni or Mrs. Kennedy. It was all enchantment and a dream. No such pleasure has since visited me but in dreams. I was in Persia for the time, and the burning idol of their devotion in the temple almost converted me into a worshiper. I was awestruck, and believed those significations to be something more than elemental fires. I was, with Uriel, in the body of the sun.

What should I have gained by knowing (as I should have done, had I been born thirty years later) that that solar representation was a

---

10. **Haply:** perhaps.
11. **boxes:** compartments to accommodate a small number of seats.

12. **Lucretius** [lōō krē′shəs]: Roman poet and philosopher of the first century B.C.
13. **mortals above:** those in the topmost galleries were called, ironically, "gods."
14. *Artaxerxes* [är tə zurk′sēz]: play set in ancient Persia. The name is that of a Persian king of the fifth century B.C.

mere painted scene that had neither fire nor light in itself, and that the royal phantoms, which passed in review before me, were but such common mortals as I could see every day out of my father's window? We crush the faculty of delight and wonder in children by explaining everything. We take them to the source of the Nile, and show them the scanty runnings, instead of letting the beginnings of that seven-fold stream remain in impenetrable darkness, a mysterious question of wonderment and delight to ages.

STUDY QUESTIONS

Recalling

1. According to Lamb's first "memorandum," why did the blind man enjoy the performance of *Richard III* more than the others around him?
2. In the second "memorandum" what factor confused the knot of country people who clapped for the actor with the minor part?
3. In the last and longest "memorandum" who, among the various types who attend the theater, seems to enjoy a play most? Who enjoys it least? What sort of theater-goer does Lamb like best? Why?

Interpreting

4. In what ways is this essay familiar? Consider its point of view and the writer's involvement in the topics under discussion.

VOCABULARY

Analogies

Analogies are comparisons stated as double relationships: "*A* is to *B* as *C* is to *D*." On tests analogies are printed as "*A* : *B* : : *C* : *D*." You may be given the first pair and asked to find a second pair that has the same kind of relationship as the first pair. See the following example:

CAR : MOTOR : : person : heart

Here the first word in each pair can operate only with the second word in each pair.

Each of the following numbered items begins with two related words in capital letters. The first word in each capitalized pair comes from the excerpt by Lamb. First decide how these two capitalized words relate to each other. Then choose the pair with the relationship most like the relationship between the pair in capital letters.

1. PATHETIC : PITY : :
   (a) emotional : happy
   (b) humorous : amusement
   (c) expressive : sorrow
   (d) amusing : sadness

2. ACME : LOWEST POINT : :
   (a) summit : highest point
   (b) abyss : highest point
   (c) peak : pinnacle
   (d) zenith : nadir

3. DIMINUTION : LESS : :
   (a) addition : more
   (b) multiplication : division
   (c) reduction : more
   (d) multiplication : less

4. DISSIPATED : PRESERVED : :
   (a) dispersed : scattered
   (b) eroded : conserved
   (c) squandered : wasted
   (d) weakened : strengthened

5. SCANTY : ADEQUATE : :
   (a) meager : sufficient
   (b) plenty : abundant
   (c) spare : empty
   (d) sparse : inadequate

COMPARING WRITERS

▉ Given Hazlitt's reaction to the actress's portrayal of Lady Macbeth and given Lamb's memories of his earliest experiences in the theater, what thoughts do the two essayists seem to share regarding performances of drama? Specifically, what do both seem to appreciate greatly? Which of their emotions do they seem to want tapped by a performance?

Charles Lamb **399**

READING FOR APPRECIATION

Criticism and Critical Reading

Literature at its best serves a dual purpose: It provides pleasure and diversion, and it offers stimulation and even enlightenment. Sometimes we read for pleasure only, just as sometimes we listen to music for relaxation or go to a movie for entertainment. Good and great literature, however, makes us work a little harder. It demands more because in the end it has more to give. It compels us to read actively and alertly. It insists that while reading we question and think hard. In short, good literature asks that we read *critically.*

Although one definition of *criticism* is "the act of finding fault," when we speak of literary criticism or criticism of the arts in general, we should bear in mind the original meaning of the term. The word *criticize* derives from the Greek *krinein,* which means "to discern or to separate." Criticism in this sense implies observing, recognizing, categorizing, making distinctions, and making judgments. To read critically, then, is to clarify a work, to know and understand it more profoundly, to evaluate its merit and the author's achievement.

William Hazlitt's essay on *Macbeth,* because it exemplifies the basic principles of literary criticism, reminds us how to read critically. Consider, for instance, a few of Hazlitt's thoughts on the character of Lady Macbeth:

. . . She at once seizes on the opportunity that offers for the accomplishment of all their wished-for greatness, and never flinches from her object till all is over. The magnitude of her resolution almost covers the magnitude of her guilt. She is a great bad woman, whom we hate but whom we fear more than we hate.

In these three sentences alone, Hazlitt encompasses a description and an analysis of the character and penetrates to several truths about her. Lady Macbeth does *seize* the opportunity that arises and does remain resolute throughout. There is a kind of grandeur in her overwhelming determination that almost surpasses even the enormity of her guilt. She *is* "a great bad woman." Hazlitt gives us an insight into ourselves as well, for

we do fear Lady Macbeth even more than we hate her. Further, Hazlitt implies his admiration of Shakespeare, who imagined this character and brought her fully and splendidly to life.

Hazlitt can only have reached this level of understanding by reading the play carefully, by closely observing Lady Macbeth's words and actions, by formulating a sense of her patterns and assessing their truth or falseness, and by reacting honestly to the character. By doing all of these things—that is, by reading critically—he clarified a vital aspect of *Macbeth* for himself and for us.

The kind of elucidation that Hazlitt achieves here is the aim of all true criticism, but it is not always so gracefully attained. Yet the effort itself is valuable, regardless of the outcome. For by reading critically we learn to make important distinctions. We learn to *separate* and to compare. We learn to determine what is good, better, best—and poor—in literature. And we learn *why.* In the process, too, we learn more about ourselves—our tastes, our preferences, our standards.

THE ENGLISH VOICE

"Nature Never Did Betray"

We live in nature. It has always been the context of our experience. Yet in the nineteenth century, as cities grew and industry prospered, human experiences seemed to grow more and more remote from nature. The Romantics resisted that alienation: They made nature the central force in their lives and their literature.

Most great writers have expressed a deep love and understanding of nature. However, it was not until the Romantic poets that nature became almost exclusively the subject of poetry. The Romantics gave nature the qualities of the sublime; they gave the experience of nature the power of religious devotion. Comforting and awe-inspiring in all its cycles of life, death, and rebirth, nature was celebrated as source of delight, image of love, and model of moral perfection. The Romantics strove to make their creative lives images of nature itself.

Wordsworth

For I have learned
To look on nature, not as in
*   the hour*
Of thoughtless youth; but hear-
*   ing oftentimes*
The still, sad music of human-
*   ity. . . .*
In nature and the language of
*   the sense*

The anchor of my purest
*   thoughts, the nurse,*
The guide, the guardian of my
*   heart, and soul*
Of all my moral being. . . .
And this prayer I make,
Knowing that Nature never did
*   betray*
The heart that loved her.

Byron

She walks in beauty, like the
*   night*
Of cloudless climes and starry
*   skies;*
And all that's best of dark and
*   bright*
Meet in her aspect and her eyes.

Shelley

*   Be thou, Spirit fierce,*
My spirit! Be thou me, impetu-
*   ous one!*

Keats

Who hath not seen thee oft
*   amid thy store?*
Sometimes   whoever   seeks
*   abroad may find*
Thee sitting careless on a gran-
*   ary floor,*
Thy hair soft-lifted by the win-
*   nowing wind.*

It was nature that was honest, without artifice. Nature was the ultimate source of truth and beauty, and the greatest human joy was to imitate nature, absorb it, and be absorbed by it.

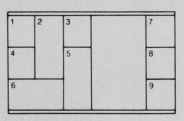

Key to Illustrations appears on page 449.

THE VICTORIAN AGE

1837–1901

Queen Victoria and the Empire

Queen Victoria was only eighteen when she ascended the throne, and she ruled not only the world's most powerful nation but also an empire extending to Canada, Australia, India, and parts of Africa. After the death of her uncle, William IV, the young Princess Victoria was awakened from a sound sleep and brought downstairs in her dressing gown. Her diary for that day records that on the staircase that morning she had felt quite prepared to be queen. She remained queen until her death sixty-four years later at the age of eighty-two. Her long reign was a period of progress and prosperity for the nation.

Victoria's personal life was rich also. She married her cousin Prince Albert of Saxe-Coburg Gotha (a name that their successors would eventually change to the more British-sounding Windsor). Victoria and Albert had a happy family life with four sons and five daughters, and they traveled often to visit royal relatives on the Continent, especially in Germany. The queen's exemplary personal life, along with her famous honesty, sense of morality, and propriety, won a new respect for the monarchy.

The Victorian Age did contain conflict, inevitable in an empire that spanned the globe, an empire upon

Detail, *The Triumph of Steam and Electricity*, 1897, a lithograph celebrating the diamond jubilee of Queen Victoria.

which the sun literally never set. A dispute between Upper and Lower Canada led to union between the two and the beginning of self-government. In the Crimean War (1853–1856) Britain joined France in an effort to prevent Russia from gaining a Mediterranean port. Mutiny in India in 1857 caused the British government to take control of the entire Indian subcontinent from the East India Company, which besides handling trade had always shared the responsibility of governing the colony. Britain was also economically involved in the American Civil War because factories in northern England depended upon raw cotton from the Confederate states.

British interests in China were threatened in 1900 by the Boxer Rebellion against foreign influence. In addition, British troops were fighting in Africa to defend British possessions there. The Boer War, a destructive war against Dutch settlers in South Africa, had begun in 1889. Its end, in 1902, marked the end of British empire building, but by that time the Empress of India (as Parliament had dubbed Victoria in 1877) had died.

Although she was a successful and well-loved monarch, Victoria's powers were only advisory, and she was fortunate to have an array of distinguished ministers. Wellington, the hero who had defeated Napoleon at Waterloo, was a statesman as well as a military leader. Sir

Robert Peel served the queen well in domestic affairs; he initiated the practice of unarmed police officers, nicknamed bobbies after him. The British political scene was dominated, however, by the dramatic rivalry between Liberal Party (Whig) leader W. E. Gladstone, a "Little Englander" opposed to the expansion of the empire, and Conservative (Tory) Benjamin Disraeli. Disraeli was the queen's favorite and prevailed. Later, however, the "Little England" philosophy would become an inevitable reality because of world events in the years after Victoria's death.

Life in Victorian Times

Victoria's reign saw important developments in transportation, manufacturing, and commerce. The queen herself became a patron of the growing railways when she took her first train trip in 1842 from Windsor Castle, west of London, into the city. According to reports, the

queen's coachman insisted that duty called for him to drive the engine. Steamship lines also grew during this period, facilitating trade with colonies and with the United States. British commerce flourished as raw materials were imported and manufactured goods were exported.

Newly powerful industrialists and merchants rapidly expanded the British middle class, a group whose attitudes increasingly came to represent the age. Their values included hard work, strict morality, social reform, and pragmatism. Progress inspired self-assurance and optimism. At the same time, however, new ideas in government, science, and economics fostered curiosity, doubt, and controversy.

One innovative and positive aspect of the Victorian Age was that many people, including the lower classes, could share in the great events of the time. News, sent by train, steamship, and telegraph, traveled faster than ever before, and there was good news to be shared. In spite of their lack of political influence, their long working hours and inadequate wages, in spite of the danger of poor sanitary conditions and disease (even the plague returned in 1849 and 1853), the working class enthusiastically cheered reports of overseas victories and domestic advances. They flocked to London for the Great Exhibition of 1851. This display of British industrial success was held in the Crystal Palace, a construction of glass that continued to symbolize Britain's triumphs until destroyed by fire in 1936.

Although the lives of British workers remained difficult, major steps were taken to correct abuses against the working class. Women and children no longer worked in coal mines and could not be expected to work more than ten hours a day in factories. Workers in the textile industry were granted a half-day holiday on Saturday.

Although diseases like the plague could still remind people of the limits of science, progress was made in sanitation and medicine. Adequate sewers were becoming a reality, and people were using the clean water now being piped into cities instead of contaminated wells and springs. The use of anesthetics in hospital operating rooms became widespread; Victoria herself aided their acceptance by agreeing to an anesthetic during the birth of her seventh child. During the plague in London, bystanders were surprised to see an elegant, wealthy woman working as a nurse in the makeshift hospital rooms that were set up on the city's streets. Florence Nightingale would later win fame in the same role in hospital tents on the Crimean front.

Life in England, especially in London, changed in other ways. Parliament prohibited the use of "climbing boys" to clean chimneys in 1840, more than ten years after William Blake's death.

Detail, wallpaper designed by the Englishman William Morris, 1896.

Debtors' prisons were abolished in 1869. The first underground railroad in London was completed in 1884, and in the first year of the twentieth century, horses in the streets began to grow accustomed to the few steam-driven cars that sped about the city at more than four miles an hour.

Poetry in the Victorian Age

The Romantic poets—Wordsworth, Coleridge, Shelley, Byron, and Keats—were revolutionary poets. They wrote when they were young and, except for Wordsworth, died young. William Wordsworth (1770–1850) survived into the Victorian Age, turned away from rebellion, and became Queen Victoria's poet laureate, the official poet writing verse custom-made for state occasions. When he died, Wordsworth was succeeded as poet laureate by Alfred, Lord Tennyson, then in the midst of a long and illustrious poetic career. Un-

like the poetry of the Romantic Age, Tennyson's poems demonstrate the conservatism, optimism, and self-assurance that marked the Victorian Age. The Brownings—Robert Browning and his wife, Elizabeth Barrett Browning—were not rebels either; they too were positive poets for a positive time.

Other original poetic geniuses of the period include Matthew Arnold, who was also an educator and essayist, and Gerard Manley Hopkins, who was also a scholar and priest. Dante Gabriel Rossetti, a poet and painter, was at the center of a group that called themselves the **Pre-Raphaelites** because they sought to bring to their poetry the simplicity and directness notable in medieval Italian art before the Renaissance painter Raphael came on the scene. Toward the end of the nineteenth century, Victorian optimism began to wane. Even Tennyson and Browning had acknowledged the darker side of life in some of their best verses, but now A. E. Housman and Thomas Hardy added distinguished and pessimistic poetry to the Victorian Age. Both at its patriotic height and during the end-of-century reaction to mainstream optimism, the Victorian Age gave us memorable poetry by Rudyard Kipling (1865–1936), Algernon Swinburne (1837–1909), and Oscar Wilde (1854–1900), writers who—like Thomas Hardy—achieved fame for work in other genres as well.

Alice and the Mock Turtle, Sir John Tenniel, 1866. Illustration for *Alice's Adventures in Wonderland,* by Lewis Carroll.

Drama in the Victorian Age

Drama did not thrive during the Victorian Age. Although Tennyson and Browning tried to create poetic dramas, the real theater celebrities of the age were actors—William Macready, Henry Irving, and Ellen Terry—rather than playwrights. When the Victorians finally produced great drama, the age was approaching its close. An accomplished critic, novelist, and poet, Oscar Wilde also wrote several comic plays that satirize upper-class manners and morals. *Lady Windermere's Fan* (1892) and *The Importance of Being Earnest* (1895)—considered by many to be a perfect comedy—still delight audiences today. Arthur Wing Pinero (1855–1934) represents a movement toward the well-made play, a play with carefully crafted plot, characters, and setting; *The Second Mrs. Tanqueray* (1893) is an example. For audiences of Victoria's day, the high point of theatrical enjoyment was a series of light comic operas by William Gilbert (1836–1911) and Arthur Sullivan (1842–1900), including *The Pirates of Penzance* (1880) and *The Mikado* (1885).

Prose in the Victorian Age

A highly imaginative and satirical masterpiece of the Victorian Age was written as a children's story. Charles Dodgson, using the pen name Lewis Carroll (1832–1898), wrote *Alice's Ad-ventures in Wonderland* (1865) and its companion piece, *Through the Looking Glass* (1871), for the entertainment of a friend's daughter. John Ruskin (1819–1900) achieved fame with books about art such as *Stones of Venice* (1851–1853). The era also produced great historical works. Thomas Babington Macaulay (1800–1859) was the most popular historian of his day; publication of his five-volume *History of England* was completed after his death. The Scottish philosopher Thomas Carlyle (1795–1881) wrote a major history of the French Revolution. In his philosophical work Carlyle decried the materialism and lack of purpose of his day. Another philosopher, John Stuart Mill (1806–1873), championed individual liberty and the power of reason. John Henry Newman (1801–1890) wrote a series of essays intended to inspire religious reform, and Walter Pater (1839–1894) wrote impressionistic essays on Romantic poets.

The Novel in the Victorian Age

During the reign of Queen Victoria, the English novel came of age suddenly, swiftly, and dramatically. One innovation of Victorian novelists was **Realism,** which presented a detailed portrait of life in nineteenth-century England. The novel dominates the literary scene of the period; even Prime Minister Benjamin Disraeli was a novelist. Many of the great novels of the day were also rousing popular successes, making authors like Charles Dickens celebrated public figures. Some of these novels were published in installments in weekly magazines. This style of presentation often affected the content of the work, as popular novels were stretched out to prolong their success and unpopular works were altered in attempts to win the public's affection.

Among the most popular and productive Victorian novelists is Charles Dickens, whose work combined social criticism with comedy and sentiment to create a tone that the world identifies as Victorian. Like Chaucer and Shakespeare before him, Dickens enjoyed inventing a vast array of memorable characters in novels such as *Oliver Twist* (1837–1839), *A Tale of Two Cities* (1859), and *Great Expectations* (1860–1861). His heartfelt criticism helped to change British institutions that badly needed reform, especially prisons and

Traveling inkstand, 1814–1815, belonging to Charles Dickens.

schools. William Makepeace Thackeray (1811–1863), like Dickens a journalist of humble background, was a satirist of the morality, the hypocricies, and the manners of the English middle class. Thackeray is best remembered today as the creator of Becky Sharp, heroine of *Vanity Fair* (1847–1848). Becky is a schemer who prettily but cold-heartedly plots her way from poverty to social success. Anthony Trollope (1815–1882), the third major midcentury novelist, set much of his fiction—for example, *Barchester Towers* (1857)—against a background of Anglican Church life. By focusing on British institutions, these three novelists dissected an age as well as entertained their readers and commented on life itself.

George Eliot was the pen name of Mary Ann Evans (1819–1880). Her novels include *The Mill on the Floss* (1860), *Silas Marner* (1861), and *Middlemarch* (1871–1872). Charlotte (1816–1855) and Emily (1818–1848) Brontë made literary history while living in almost complete seclusion in a Yorkshire village. From their pens came two particularly remarkable and well-loved novels, Charlotte's *Jane Eyre* and Emily's *Wuthering Heights,* both published in 1847.

A fascination with history is revealed in novels like Benjamin Disraeli's *Sybil* (1845), Edward George Bulwer-Lytton's *Last Days of Pompeii* (1834), Charles Reade's *Cloister and the Hearth* (1861), and Charles Kingsley's *Westward Ho!* (1855). The Scottish author Robert Louis Stevenson (1850–1894) created a remarkable series of adventure novels with exotic, historical settings. Best known are *Treasure Island* (1882), *The Strange Case of Doctor Jekyll and Mister Hyde* (1886), and *Kidnapped* (1886). Another famous storyteller was Rudyard Kipling, whose novels include *Captains Courageous* (1897) and *Kim* (1901). Wilkie Collins (1824–1889) wrote what may be the first widely admired mystery novel, *The Moonstone* (1858). Toward the end of the era, two of the best-known characters in literature came into being when Arthur Conan Doyle (1859–1930) created his master detective, Sherlock Holmes, and Bram Stoker (1847–1912) created Count Dracula.

The novels of Thomas Hardy are set in the lonely farm country of Wessex, and they slice pessimistically through manners and social customs to touch on the nature of life itself. They include *Far from the Madding Crowd* (1874), *Return of the Native* (1878), *Tess of the D'Urbervilles* (1891), and *Jude the Obscure* (1896). Samuel Butler (1835–1902) also satirized his own time; his novel *The Way of All Flesh* (1903) was such a strong attack on Butler's own Victorian family that it was not published until after his death.

In an age when literature was a major form of popular entertainment, British novelists provided a remarkably diverse body of work that appealed to a mass audience. Today many of these novels are still read and enjoyed, and they also provide us with much of our knowledge of life and thought during the age of Queen Victoria.

TIME LINE

1837 Victoria becomes queen

1838 Dickens' *Oliver Twist* and *Nicholas Nickleby* best sellers

1839 First bicycle made in Scotland

1840 Queen Victoria marries Prince Albert

Construction begins on Houses of Parliament

1841 Robert Browning, *Pippa Passes*

Punch, a humorous weekly magazine, begins publication

Scottish surgeon James Braid discovers hypnosis

1842 Queen Victoria makes her first railway journey

Alfred, Lord Tennyson, "Ulysses"

1845 Failure of the potato crop causes famine in Ireland

1847 Charlotte Brontë, *Jane Eyre*

Emily Brontë, *Wuthering Heights*

1848 William Makepeace Thackeray, *Vanity Fair*

1850 Elizabeth Barrett Browning, *Sonnets from the Portuguese*

1854 England enters the Crimean War

1855 Robert Browning, *Men and Women*

1856 "Big Ben," fourteen-ton bell at Houses of Parliament, cast

1859 John Stuart Mill, *On Liberty*

Charles Darwin, *Origin of Species*

QUEEN VICTORIA

CHARLES DICKENS

CHARLOTTE BRONTE

1838 Sweden: Opera singer Jenny Lind debuts

1839 Switzerland: First electric clock built

1840 France: Artists Monet, Renoir, and Rodin born

Canada: Upper and Lower Canada united

1841 China: Hong Kong comes under British sovereignty

America: Ralph Waldo Emerson, *Essays*

1842 South Africa: Boers set up Orange Free State

1845 America: Edgar Allan Poe, "The Raven"

1847 Italy: Verdi's opera *Macbeth* premières

1848 Belgium: Marx and Engels, *The Communist Manifesto*

1850 America: Nathaniel Hawthorne, *The Scarlet Letter*

1855 Russia: Florence Nightingale applies hygienic standards in Crimean War hospitals

1856 France: Gustave Flaubert, *Madame Bovary*

1859 Egypt: Work on Suez Canal begins

British Events	World Events
1863 Construction begins on first London underground railway	1863 Mexico: French troops proclaim Maximilian of Austria emperor
1866 Algernon Charles Swinburne, *Poems and Ballads*	1866 Austria: Gregor Mendel presents laws of heredity
1867 Matthew Arnold, "Dover Beach"	
1868 Politics dominated by rivalry between Gladstone and Disraeli	
1869 Debtors' prisons abolished	1869 India: Mahatma Gandhi born
1870 Charles Dickens dies	1870 Italy: Rome made capital of newly unified nation
1871 Lewis Carroll, *Through the Looking Glass*	1871 French defeated in Franco-Prussian War
1874 Thomas Hardy, *Far from the Madding Crowd*	1874 France: First Impressionist exhibit in Paris
1875 First swim across English Channel	1875 Germany: Heinrich Schliemann, *Troy and Its Remains*
1877 Queen Victoria proclaimed Empress of India	1877 India: Famine in Bengal
1880 Gilbert and Sullivan, *The Pirates of Penzance*	1880 France: Auguste Rodin sculpts *The Thinker*
1882 Robert Louis Stevenson, *Treasure Island*	1882 Norway: Henrik Ibsen, *An Enemy of the People*
1891 Arthur Conan Doyle, *The Adventures of Sherlock Holmes*	1891 French artist Paul Gauguin settles in Tahiti
1894 Rudyard Kipling, *The Jungle Book*	
1895 H. G. Wells, *The Time Machine*	1895 Cuba: Fight for independence from Spain
William Butler Yeats, *Poems*	Italy: Marconi invents the wireless telegraph
Oscar Wilde, *The Importance of Being Earnest*	
1896 A. E. Housman, *A Shropshire Lad*	1896 Sweden: Five Nobel Prizes established
1897 Bram Stoker, *Dracula*	
	1899 South Africa: Boer War begins
1900 Joseph Conrad, *Lord Jim*	1900 China: Boxer Rebellion against foreign influence
1901 Queen Victoria dies	

MATTHEW ARNOLD

SHERLOCK HOLMES

MARCONI

WILLIAM BUTLER YEATS

Alfred, Lord Tennyson   *1809–1892*

Alfred, Lord Tennyson, was the most eminent and most revered of the Victorian poets; his poems found their way into almost every Victorian home. In the words of writer Thomas Carlyle, his contemporary, Tennyson was "one of the finest looking men in the world," and he possessed "a right valiant, true-fighting, victorious heart; strong as a lion's, yet gentle, loving, and full of music."

One of twelve children of a country minister, Tennyson grew up in the quiet village of Somersby in Lincolnshire, an area in eastern England known for its beautiful countryside. His father had an excellent library where the young Tennyson began his study of the English classics. He also began writing poetry at a very early age, producing a six-thousand-line epic by the age of twelve; at eighteen he published an anonymous collection of poetry with two of his brothers. Tennyson learned classical and modern languages from his gifted father in preparation for the university. His father also made the young Tennyson memorize and recite all of the odes of the Roman poet Horace before allowing him to leave for Cambridge University.

At Cambridge Tennyson joined a circle of young intellectuals whose center was the brilliant student Arthur Henry Hallam. Hallam and Tennyson developed a close friendship, as Hallam encouraged Tennyson's interest in poetry and became engaged to Tennyson's sister. While still at the university Tennyson made a promising debut as a young poet with the publication *Poems, Chiefly Lyrical* (1830). Then calamity shadowed Tennyson's life. His father's fatal illness forced Tennyson to leave Cambridge without finishing his degree. His next publication, *Poems,* met with stinging criticism early in 1833. And in that same grim year his friend Hallam died unexpectedly in Vienna at the age of twenty-three.

Hallam's death threw Tennyson into a deep and long depression. Nearly a decade passed before he published any poetry, and some of his friends believed that grief had caused him to abandon poetry forever. In fact, he was working out his grief by perfecting his craft during what he later called his "ten years' silence."

He broke that silence in 1842 by publishing new work that soon established him as the leading poet of his time. And in 1850, after years of intermittent labor, he published his great elegy to Hallam, *In Memoriam A. H. H.,* recording the shattering effect on his spirit of Hallam's death seventeen years before. He also married in that year and was named Wordsworth's successor as poet laureate.

Tennyson continued to write throughout his long and productive life, experimenting with a great variety of poetic forms. Among his most popular works is *The Idylls of the King,* a series of poems celebrating the legend of King Arthur. Tennyson worked on the dozen poems that make up *The Idylls* over a period that spanned fifty years, beginning the work shortly after Hallam's death and publishing the last poem in the series in 1885.

Toward the end of his career, Tennyson was knighted by Queen Victoria; this honor, never before given to a writer, indicates the enormous esteem in which Tennyson was held by the people of his country. To his contemporaries Tennyson was the great consoling voice of their age, a prophet who managed through suffering to reconcile the upheavals of the nineteenth century with an abiding belief in God and in human worth. Modern readers turn to Tennyson's poetry less for its reassurances than for its heartbreaking beauty, its musicality, and its haunting sense of the transitory nature of life.

As we learn in Homer's epic the *Iliad* (see Part Two of this book), the Greek hero Ulysses fought for ten years in the siege of Troy. With the war finally won, he set out for his home in Ithaca, a voyage Homer recounts in the *Odyssey*. Adventures along the way delayed Ulysses' return for another decade. At last, the warrior reestablished himself as king of Ithaca and was reunited with his faithful wife, Penelope, and son, Telemachus [tə lem′ə kəs]. Tennyson's "Ulysses" carries the story further, presenting the thoughts of the aging hero long after the joys of welcome have faded.

Third-century Roman mosaic showing Ulysses and his companions sailing past the Isle of the Sirens.

Alfred, Lord Tennyson **411**

Alfred, Lord Tennyson

Ulysses

It little profits that an idle king,
By this still hearth, among these barren crags,
Matched with an aged wife, I mete and dole[1]
Unequal[2] laws unto a savage race,
5 That hoard, and sleep, and feed, and know not me.
    I cannot rest from travel; I will drink
Life to the lees.[3] All times I have enjoyed
Greatly, have suffered greatly, both with those
That loved me, and alone; on shore, and when
10 Through scudding drifts[4] the rainy Hyades[5]
Vexed the dim sea. I am become a name:
For always roaming with a hungry heart
Much have I seen and known—cities of men
And manners, climates, councils, governments,
15 Myself not least, but honored of them all—
And drunk delight of battle with my peers,
Far on the ringing plains of windy Troy.
I am a part of all that I have met;
Yet all experience is an arch wherethrough
20 Gleams that untraveled world whose margin fades
Forever and forever when I move.
How dull it is to pause, to make an end,
To rust unburnished, not to shine in use!
As though to breathe were life! Life piled on life
25 Were all too little, and of one to me
Little remains; but every hour is saved
From that eternal silence, something more,
A bringer of new things; and vile it were
For some three suns to store and hoard myself,
30 And this gray spirit yearning in desire
To follow knowledge like a sinking star,
Beyond the utmost bound of human thought.

---

1. **mete . . . dole:** portion out.
2. **Unequal:** unjust, unfair.
3. **lees:** dregs, sediment.
4. **scudding drifts:** wind-driven rain or spray.
5. **Hyades** [hī′ə dēz′]: group of stars whose rising with the sun was thought to bring rain.

Draped Warrior, bronze, late sixteenth century B.C.

This is my son, mine own Telemachus,
To whom I leave the scepter and the isle[6]—
35 Well-loved of me, discerning to fulfill
This labor, by slow prudence to make mild
A rugged people, and through soft degrees
Subdue them to the useful and the good.
Most blameless is he, centered in the sphere
40 Of common duties, decent not to fail
In offices of tenderness, and pay
Meet[7] adoration to my household gods,
When I am gone. He works his work, I mine.

There lies the port; the vessel puffs her sail;
45 There gloom the dark, broad seas. My mariners,
Souls that have toiled, and wrought, and thought with me—
That ever with a frolic welcome took
The thunder and the sunshine, and opposed
Free hearts, free foreheads—you and I are old;
50 Old age hath yet his honor and his toil.
Death closes all; but something ere the end,
Some work of noble note, may yet be done,
Not unbecoming men that strove with gods.
The lights begin to twinkle from the rocks;
55 The long day wanes; the slow moon climbs; the deep
Moans round with many voices. Come, my friends.
'Tis not too late to seek a newer world.
Push off, and sitting well in order smite
The sounding furrows;[8] for my purpose holds
60 To sail beyond the sunset, and the baths
Of all the western stars, until I die.
It may be that the gulfs will wash us down;
It may be we shall touch the Happy Isles,[9]
And see the great Achilles,[10] whom we knew.
65 Though much is taken, much abides; and though
We are not now that strength which in old days
Moved earth and heaven, that which we are, we are—
One equal temper of heroic hearts,
Made weak by time and fate, but strong in will
70 To strive, to seek, to find, and not to yield.

_____

6. **isle:** Ithaca, an island off the coast of Greece.
7. **Meet:** appropriate.
8. **sounding furrows:** ocean waves.
9. **Happy Isles:** Elysium; in classical mythology, the place to which heroes
and virtuous people were thought to go after death.
10. **Achilles** [ə kil′ēz]: Greek hero and companion of Ulysses, killed in
the Trojan War.

Tennyson's long narrative poem *The Princess,* about women's emancipation and education, is not often read today. However, the songs that Tennyson added to later editions of the work are some of his finest and most familiar poems. "The Splendor Falls on Castle Walls" and "Tears, Idle Tears" are among the most famous of these lyrics.

Alfred, Lord Tennyson

The Splendor Falls on Castle Walls

The splendor falls on castle walls
   And snowy summits old in story;
The long light shakes across the lakes,
   And the wild cataract[1] leaps in glory.
5 Blow, bugle, blow, set the wild echoes flying,
  Blow, bugle; answer, echoes, dying, dying, dying.

O hark, O hear! how thin and clear,
   And thinner, clearer, farther going!
O sweet and far from cliff and scar[2]
10   The horns of Elfland faintly blowing!
  Blow, let us hear the purple glens replying,
  Blow, bugle; answer, echoes, dying, dying, dying.

O love, they die in yon rich sky,
   They faint on hill or field or river;
15 Our echoes roll from soul to soul,
   And grow forever and forever.
  Blow, bugle, blow, set the wild echoes flying,
  And answer, echoes, answer, dying, dying, dying.

1. **cataract:** waterfall.
2. **scar:** steep face of a mountainside.

Tears, Idle Tears

Tears, idle[1] tears, I know not what they mean,
Tears from the depth of some divine despair
Rise in the heart, and gather to the eyes,
In looking on the happy autumn-fields,
5 And thinking of the days that are no more.

Fresh as the first beam glittering on a sail,
That brings our friends up from the underworld,
Sad as the last which reddens over one
That sinks with all we love below the verge;[2]
10 So sad, so fresh, the days that are no more.

Ah, sad and strange as in dark summer dawns
The earliest pipe of half-awakened birds
To dying ears, when unto dying eyes
The casement[3] slowly grows a glimmering square;
15 So sad, so strange, the days that are no more.

Dear as remembered kisses after death,
And sweet as those by hopeless fancy feigned[4]
On lips that are for others; deep as love,
Deep as first love, and wild with all regret;
20 O Death in Life, the days that are no more!

---

1. **idle:** useless, pointless.
2. **verge:** edge or rim; here, the horizon.
3. **casement:** type of window.
4. **feigned:** imagined.

Like Milton's *Lycidas* and Shelley's *Adonais,* Tennyson's *In Memoriam A. H. H.* commemorates the death of a gifted young man at the threshold of his life. *In Memoriam* differs from the earlier elegies in that it is not a single poem written in a short period of time but rather a series of 131 lyrics written over a period of seventeen years to express the poet's reaction to Arthur Hallam's death. Together the lyrics form a spiritual autobiography tracing Tennyson's shifting emotions as the years pass. The poet moves from desolation, despair, and grief to reconciliation and hope. The lyric that follows, also known as "Ring out, Wild Bells," occurs late in the sequence. It is a response on New Year's Eve to the end of yet another year.

Alfred, Lord Tennyson

from **In Memoriam A. H. H.**

Ring out, wild bells, to the wild sky,
  The flying cloud, the frosty light:
  The year is dying in the night;
Ring out, wild bells, and let him die.

5 Ring out the old, ring in the new,
  Ring, happy bells, across the snow:
  The year is going, let him go;
Ring out the false, ring in the true.

Ring out the grief that saps the mind,
10   For those that here we see no more;
  Ring out the feud of rich and poor,
Ring in redress to all mankind.

Ring out a slowly dying cause,
  And ancient forms of party strife;
15   Ring in the nobler modes of life,
With sweeter manners, purer laws.

Ring out the want, the care, the sin,
  The faithless coldness of the times;
  Ring out, ring out my mournful rhymes,
20 But ring the fuller minstrel in.

Ring out false pride in place and blood,
  The civic slander and the spite;
  Ring in the love of truth and right,
Ring in the common love of good.

25 Ring out old shapes of foul disease;
  Ring out the narrowing lust of gold;
  Ring out the thousand wars of old,
Ring in the thousand years of peace.

Ring in the valiant man and free,
30   The larger heart, the kindlier hand;
  Ring out the darkness of the land,
Ring in the Christ that is to be.[1]

---

1. **the Christ . . . be:** reference to the New Testament account in the Book of Revelations of the second coming of Christ.

At eighty-one Tennyson wrote the following poem, and just a few days before his death he asked that it be placed at the end of every edition of his work.

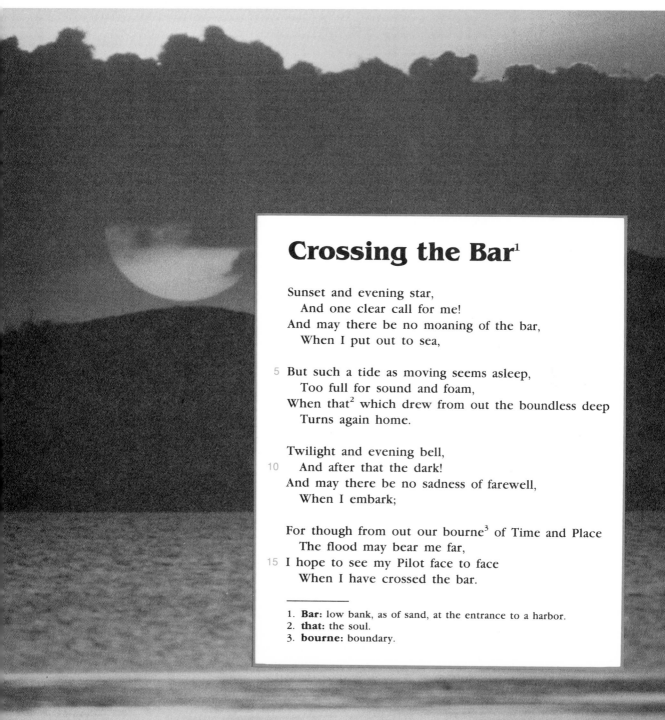

Crossing the Bar[1]

Sunset and evening star,
    And one clear call for me!
And may there be no moaning of the bar,
    When I put out to sea,

5 But such a tide as moving seems asleep,
    Too full for sound and foam,
When that[2] which drew from out the boundless deep
    Turns again home.

Twilight and evening bell,
10   And after that the dark!
And may there be no sadness of farewell,
    When I embark;

For though from out our bourne[3] of Time and Place
    The flood may bear me far,
15 I hope to see my Pilot face to face
    When I have crossed the bar.

---

1. **Bar:** low bank, as of sand, at the entrance to a harbor.
2. **that:** the soul.
3. **bourne:** boundary.

STUDY QUESTIONS

Ulysses

Recalling

1. What is Ulysses' present situation as he describes it in lines 1–5? What past experiences does he recall in lines 7–17?
2. What does Ulysses say in lines 22–24 about making an end? What does his "gray spirit" (line 30) yearn to do?
3. To whom is Ulysses leaving the scepter and the isle? In lines 35–38 what two things does he say his successor will do for those he rules? In lines 39–43 how does Ulysses further describe his successor?
4. Whom is Ulysses addressing? In lines 51–53 what does he say may yet be done?
5. In lines 57–61, what does he ask his friends to seek with him? According to lines 65–70, what qualities do Ulysses and his friends still possess, despite the passage of time?

Interpreting

6. Contrast Ulysses' present life with his earlier days. What is his attitude toward each part of his life?
7. Describe Ulysses' personality from his comments about his present and past as well as his hopes for the future. What view of life does he advocate? What is he actually seeking in leaving Ithaca?

Extending

8. Why might people feel as Ulysses does? What human need does Ulysses' speech express?

The Splendor Falls on Castle Walls

Recalling

1. What setting is described in the first stanza? What visual details make up this setting? What does the bugle set flying?
2. In the second stanza what blows from "cliff and scar"? What words in lines 7–10 describe these sounds?
3. In lines 13–14 where do the echoes die? What other echoes are mentioned in lines 15–16? Where do they roll, and for how long will they grow?

Interpreting

4. What do you think Tennyson means by "Elfland" in line 10?

5. What is meant by "our echoes" in line 15? In what ways are these echoes different from the "wild echoes" made by the horns of Elfland?

Extending

6. What "splendor" might have been fading from the world that Tennyson knew? Has it faded completely from *our* world? Explain.

Tears, Idle Tears

Recalling

1. According to the first stanza, from what do the tears rise? When do they rise?
2. Where do the friends mentioned in line 7 come from? Where do they go?
3. In lines 10 and 15, what various qualities does the speaker ascribe to "the days that are no more"? With what does the last line associate these days?

Interpreting

4. Why is the speaker weeping, and why are the tears "idle"?
5. What view of memory does the poem express? Do you agree with this view?

Extending

6. Why do you think pleasant sights often make people sad?

from In Memoriam A. H. H.

Recalling

1. What does the speaker say about the old year in lines 3–4?
2. Make a list of things the speaker wants the wild bells to ring out.
3. What things does he want the bells to ring in?

Interpreting

4. Which of these wishes pertain only to the speaker? To whom or what do the others apply?
5. What overall hope do the wishes express?

Extending

6. Which of the poem's hopes can be applied to the world today?

Crossing the Bar

Recalling

1. What requests does the speaker make in lines 3–4 and 11–12? According to line 8, where is the tide going?

2. What does the speaker hope to see when he has crossed the bar, according to line 15?

Interpreting
3. What does Tennyson actually mean by "crossing the bar"?
4. In what way does the poem express a consolation to those the speaker leaves behind?
5. What can you infer about Tennyson's attitude toward death from this poem?

LITERARY FOCUS

Rhythm and Meter

Rhythm, which comes from the Greek word meaning "flow," is any recurring pattern of movement. In poetry **rhythm** refers to the alternation between accented and unaccented syllables in the lines of a poem. **Meter** is a type of rhythm in which the alternation between stressed and unstressed syllables is predictable and regular. For example, the last line of Keats's "To Autumn" has a definite meter. The unstressed syllables are marked ˘, and the stressed syllables are marked ′.

And gathering swallows twitter in the skies.

This line follows **iambic pentameter,** a meter in which unstressed and stressed syllables alternate in lines that are ten syllables long.

In reading a poem that has a definite meter, we need to pay attention to the pattern of stresses. However, we should not allow that pattern to take over the poem and turn it into singsong. Rather, we need to pay attention to the meaning and sound of individual words, occasionally changing the regularity of the meter by lengthening or pausing after certain words for emphasis or emotional effect.

Thinking About Rhythm and Meter

Read "Ulysses" aloud, and describe the pattern of stressed and unstressed syllables in each line. What meter does the poem use? Give three or four examples of points at which a sensitive reader might alter that meter for emphasis or emotional effect.

VOCABULARY

Analogies

An **analogy** is a comparison. Analogy items appear on vocabulary tests as double comparisons between two pairs of words. You may be given the first pair of words and asked to find or complete a second pair that have the same relationship to each other as the first pair. For example, you would complete the analogy TOP : BOTTOM : : _____ : _____ with the pair HIGH : LOW, since both pairs of words are antonyms, or opposites. In other cases, the paired words may be related as synonyms, as different grammatical forms of the same word, as a part and a whole, or as different degrees of the same quality.

The first capitalized word in each of the following items comes from one of the poems by Tennyson. Choose the letter of the pair of words that best completes the analogy.

1. STRIFE : CONFLICT : :
   (a) home : residence   (c) love : hate
   (b) song : dance   (d) light : dark
2. BARREN : BARRENNESS : :
   (a) night : fortnight   (c) bold : bolt
   (b) hungry : hunger   (d) red : blue
3. UNBURNISHED : FILTHY : :
   (a) amusing : hilarious   (c) quiet : noisy
   (b) bright : shiny   (d) read : write
4. SLANDER : PRAISE : :
   (a) street : road   (c) snow : rain
   (b) ugliness : beauty   (d) shout : yell
5. VESSEL : DECK : :
   (a) boat : ship   (c) wave : storm
   (b) house : floor   (d) land : sky

COMPOSITION

Writing About a Symbol

Discuss Tennyson's use of the tide as a symbol in "Crossing the Bar." First explain the symbolic meaning of the tide in line 5. Then discuss its significance for the poem as a whole. Be sure to explain how the symbol of the tide is related to the other images in the poem and its overall theme. *For help with this assignment, refer to Lesson 5 in the Writing About Literature Handbook at the back of this book.*

Creating a Symbol

Write a poem about an object that could represent a particular time or part of your life—for example, your years in high school. Describe the object clearly in your poem, and show why it has a larger meaning for you.

Robert Browning   *1812–1889*

Robert Browning is one of the two great pillars on which Victorian poetry rests, the other being Alfred, Lord Tennyson. These two towering figures could not have been more different, both as men and as poets. Tennyson was introverted, withdrawn, and often melancholy; Browning was open, social, and generally optimistic. Tennyson's poetry is melodic and beautifully polished; Browning's is intentionally harsh and "unpoetic," echoing the language of lively conversation. Tennyson's work sounds the true Victorian note of noble sentiment, deep melancholy, and almost mystical exaltation. In contrast, Browning strikes twentieth-century readers as the more modern writer, not only because of his colloquial and quirky diction, but also because of his interest in human psychology and his use of sensational subject matter.

Browning was raised in a household of modest but genteel means on the outskirts of London. His father, a bank official, pursued scholarship as a hobby, collecting a library of six thousand books. Educated at home, young Browning developed unusually broad knowledge in the classics, painting, poetry, and the theater.

After writing lyrical verse that imitated Byron and Shelley, Browning began to find his own poetic voice with the dramatic, psychological *Paracelsus* (1835). After making an unsuccessful foray into drama in *Strafford* (1837) and spending two years in Italy, Browning wrote his long, difficult *Sordello* (1840), a poem that English readers found obscure and that made its author unpopular. Browning followed this work with a series of poems and dramas entitled *Bells and Pomegranates,* published from 1841 to 1846. This series includes the play *Pippa Passes* (1841) and other dramatic works, but it is most notable for a series of short dramatic monologues in which interesting, complex characters reveal themselves in informal and seemingly offhand remarks. Browning found in this combination of poetry, drama, and colloquial language a new and congenial style for himself.

When he was still largely unknown, Browning came across a volume of poetry by the popular Elizabeth Barrett, a semi-invalid who was six years older than he. He fell in love with the poems and then with the poet herself. Despite her father's strenuous disapproval, the two poets eloped in 1846. Their happy life together in Italy revived Mrs. Browning. She remained much more famous than her husband, who was chiefly known as Mrs. Browning's devoted partner in an idyllically romantic marriage.

After his wife's death in 1861, Browning returned to England with their son. It was only then, in his fifties, that Browning established his own reputation as a poet with additional collections of dramatic monologues such as *Dramatis Personae* (1866). His masterpiece in this vein is *The Ring and the Book* (1869), a novel-length series of dramatic monologues presenting a dozen different views of a murder that actually took place in seventeenth-century Italy.

Although delayed, Browning's eventual fame was bountiful. He nearly became the beloved Tennyson's equal among Victorian readers; later, Browning's feeling for the unruliness of life and human psychology and his experimentation with discordant, prosaic diction would make him seem a modern poet before his time.

Pippa, the young girl who speaks in this poem, works exhausting hours in the silk mills and endures the full range of hardships associated with industrial life. Yet her optimism eventually triumphs. This poem contains the most famous lines written by Browning, and yet they are not typical of his poetry.

Robert Browning

from **Pippa Passes**

The year's at the spring
And day's at the morn;
Morning's at seven;
The hillside's dew-pearled;

5 The lark's on the wing;
The snail's on the thorn;
God's in his heaven—
All's right with the world!

STUDY QUESTIONS

Recalling

1. During what time of year and day does the poem take place?
2. What other details of the setting does Pippa mention? What opinion does she express in lines 7–8?

Interpreting

3. What qualities or attributes of the world does Pippa stress in her song?
4. What does she leave out and why? Why do you suppose Pippa's song does not reflect the difficult conditions of her own life?

Extending

5. Do people in real life ever feel as Pippa does?

The Brownings spent their married life happily in Italy, where the warm climate eased Mrs. Browning's health. However, in the springtime especially, moments of homesickness would visit them.

Robert Browning

Home-Thoughts, from Abroad

1

Oh, to be in England
Now that April's there,
And whoever wakes in England
Sees, some morning, unaware,
5 That the lowest boughs and the brushwood sheaf
Round the elm-tree bole[1] are in tiny leaf,
While the chaffinch sings on the orchard bough
In England—now!

2

And after April, when May follows,
10 And the whitethroat builds, and all the swallows!
Hark, where my blossomed peartree in the hedge
Leans to the field and scatters on the clover
Blossoms and dewdrops—at the bent spray's edge—
That's the wise thrush; he sings each song twice over,
15 Lest you should think he never could recapture
The first fine careless rapture!
And though the fields look rough with hoary dew,
All will be gay when noontide wakes anew
The buttercups, the little children's dower[2]
20 —Far brighter than this gaudy melon-flower![3]

---

1. **bole:** tree trunk.
2. **dower:** endowment, gift.
3. **melon-flower:** large, trumpet-shaped yellow bloom from a melon plant (such as a cantaloupe or pumpkin). Browning contrasts this flower, which is native to a warm climate, with the smaller buttercups seen in early spring in England.

The time is the sixteenth century. The place is a castle in Ferrara, a province in northern Italy. The duke who owns the castle is negotiating with an emissary from a count over his possible betrothal to the count's daughter. The two men pause before the painting of a beautiful young woman, the duke's first wife.

My Last Duchess

Ferrara

That's my last Duchess painted on the wall,
Looking as if she were alive. I call
That piece a wonder, now: Frà Pandolf's[1] hands
Worked busily a day, and there she stands.
5 Will't please you sit and look at her? I said
"Frà Pandolf" by design,[2] for never read
Strangers like you that pictured countenance,
The depth and passion of its earnest glance,
But to myself they turned (since none puts by
10 The curtain I have drawn for you, but I)
And seemed as they would ask me, if they durst,[3]
How such a glance came there; so, not the first
Are you to turn and ask thus. Sir, 'twas not
Her husband's presence only, called that spot
15 Of joy into the Duchess' cheek: perhaps
Frà Pandolf chanced to say, "Her mantle laps
Over my lady's wrist too much," or "Paint
Must never hope to reproduce the faint
Half-flush that dies along her throat": such stuff
20 Was courtesy, she thought, and cause enough
For calling up that spot of joy. She had
A heart—how shall I say?—too soon made glad,
Too easily impressed; she liked whate'er
She looked on, and her looks went everywhere.
25 Sir, 'twas all one! My favor at her breast,
The dropping of the daylight in the West,

---

1. **Frà Pandolf's:** Brother Pandolf's; refers to the work of a fictitious painter who is also a friar.
2. **by design:** intentionally.
3. **durst:** dared.

The bough of cherries some officious fool
Broke in the orchard for her, the white mule
She rode with round the terrace—all and each
30 Would draw from her alike the approving speech,
Or blush, at least. She thanked men—good! but thanked
Somehow—I know not how—as if she ranked
My gift of a nine-hundred-years-old name
With anybody's gift. Who'd stoop to blame
35 This sort of trifling? Even had you skill
In speech—(which I have not)—to make your will
Quite clear to such an one, and say, "Just this
Or that in you disgusts me; here you miss,
Or there exceed the mark"—and if she let
40 Herself be lessoned so, nor plainly set
Her wits to yours, forsooth,[4] and made excuse,
—E'en then would be some stooping; and I choose
Never to stoop. Oh sir, she smiled, no doubt,
Whene'er I passed her; but who passed without
45 Much the same smile? This grew; I gave commands;
Then all smiles stopped together. There she stands
As if alive. Will't please you rise? We'll meet
The company below, then. I repeat,
The Count your master's known munificence[5]
50 Is ample warrant that no just pretense[6]
Of mine for dowry[7] will be disallowed;
Though his fair daughter's self, as I avowed
At starting, is my object. Nay, we'll go
Together down, sir! Notice Neptune,[8] though,
55 Taming a sea horse, thought a rarity,
Which Claus of Innsbruck[9] cast in bronze for me!

---

4. **forsooth:** in truth.
5. **munificence:** generosity.
6. **just pretense:** legitimate claim.
7. **dowry:** financial settlement given to the groom by the bride's father.
8. **Neptune:** in classical mythology, the god of the sea.
9. **Claus of Innsbruck:** fictitious sculptor from Innsbruck, Austria.

STUDY QUESTIONS

Home-Thoughts, from Abroad

Recalling

1. During what season does the poem take place? Where does the speaker want to be?
2. According to lines 3–6 what might someone in the speaker's homeland notice when he wakes one morning? What might he hear in line 7?
3. What does the speaker's peartree do, according to the second stanza?
4. What two flowers does the speaker compare in lines 19–20? What words does he apply to each?

Interpreting

5. Where is the speaker? How do you know?
6. What picture of his present surroundings does the image in line 20 create? What contrast between his homeland and present surroundings does the speaker suggest?

My Last Duchess

Recalling

1. How does the duke describe his wife in lines 22–23? Name four of the things that all drew "approving speech" from her. What "gift" did he give his wife, and how did she rank this gift?
2. How does the duke explain why he never told his wife about his feelings? What did he do instead, and what happened (line 46)?
3. To what does the duke call the emissary's attention as they go downstairs?

Interpreting

4. What are the duke's feelings about his late wife? How do you know? Do you think they are justified?
5. Contrast the personality of the duke with that of his first wife.
6. What do you think really happened to the duke's first wife?
7. In what way might the duke's reference in the last three lines to the sea horse be related to his account of his marriage?

Extending

8. What report do you think the emissary should make to the count about the proposed marriage of his daughter to the duke?

LITERARY FOCUS

Dramatic Monologue

A **dramatic monologue** is a poem that resembles a speech from a play; spoken by someone who differs markedly from the poet, the dramatic monologue consists entirely of the words that this person utters on a single occasion, usually to a silent listener. A dramatic monologue usually presents the speaker at a crucial point in his or her life, often a moment of conflict. Unlike a play, the dramatic monologue does not directly portray the action that leads up to the character's speech. However, through the speaker's words, we come to understand the situation that prompts

the speech and, more important, the speaker's own personality. In most dramatic monologues the speaker reveals more than he or she realizes.

A number of Victorian poets experimented with dramatic monologues. For example, Tennyson's "Ulysses" presents a complex speaker who defines his attitude toward life as he speaks. However, no poet used the form of the dramatic monologue as often or as successfully as Robert Browning. The dramatic monologue allowed Browning to explore human psychology without commenting directly on it. Browning's dramatic monologues move from one emotion to another and seem improvised from moment to moment, like everyday speech; they often manage to capture the changing, quicksilver quality of life itself.

Thinking About Dramatic Monologues

1. What personality traits does the duke reveal in his monologue? What traits does he reveal without fully realizing that he is doing so? Explain, using specific lines from the poem.
2. In "My Last Duchess" find three examples of contractions, interrupted sentences, parenthetical expressions, or other aspects of a conversational style.
3. What different emotions does the duke convey during the monologue? When do you think he is most intense, and why?

COMPOSITION

Writing a Comparison/Contrast

◼ Compare and contrast Browning's "My Last Duchess" with Tennyson's "Ulysses." First point out the traits that these two dramatic monologues have in common. Then explain the ways in which they differ, both in the personalities of the speakers and the ways in which these personalities are revealed. End by indicating which poem you prefer and the reasons for your preference. *For help with this assignment, refer to Lesson 2 in the Writing About Literature Handbook at the back of this book.*

Writing a Dramatic Monologue

◼ Invent a character quite unlike yourself, and write a dramatic monologue for this character. Before writing, decide on the situation in which the character is speaking and the person whom he or she is addressing. Try to make the character's words both natural and revealing. Your monologue may be in prose or poetry.

Elizabeth Barrett Browning

1806–1861

When she met Robert Browning in 1845, Elizabeth Barrett had already established her name as a poet with four highly popular volumes of poetry. Her work was characterized by enthusiasm, directness, and a warmly felt sense of social responsibility. Yet the author of what were often passionate poems lived a fragile and sheltered life, having suffered a series of illnesses in her adolescence. The favorite daughter of a possessive and tyrannical father, she was enduring the life of an invalid and recluse when Robert Browning read her poems and fell in love with her.

To Elizabeth Barrett's father, Browning looked like a failure. Despite this strong opposition Browning persisted, and the couple managed to elope to Italy. There, for several years, Elizabeth Barrett Browning wrote a series of sonnets expressing her love for her husband. She published them in 1850 under the title *Sonnets from the Portuguese,* to make them appear to be translated from Portuguese, thereby disguising their deeply personal nature.

Elizabeth Barrett Browning

If Thou Must Love Me

If thou must love me, let it be for naught
Except for love's sake only. Do not say
"I love her for her smile—her look—her way
Of speaking gently—for a trick of thought
5 That falls in well with mine, and certes[1] brought
A sense of pleasant ease on such a day"—
For these things in themselves, Beloved, may
Be changed, or change for thee—and love, so wrought,[2]
May be unwrought so. Neither love me for
10 Thine own dear pity's wiping my cheeks dry—
A creature might forget to weep, who bore
Thy comfort long, and lose thy love thereby!
But love me for love's sake, that evermore
Thou mayst love on, through love's eternity.

---

1. **certes** [sur′tēz]: certainly, truly.
2. **wrought:** fashioned.

How Do I Love Thee?

How do I love thee? Let me count the ways.
I love thee to the depth and breadth and height
My soul can reach, when feeling out of sight
For the ends of Being and ideal Grace.
5 I love thee to the level of everyday's
Most quiet need, by sun and candle light.
I love thee freely, as men strive for Right;
I love thee purely, as they turn from Praise.
I love thee with the passion put to use
10 In my old griefs, and with my childhood's faith.
I love thee with a love I seemed to lose
With my lost saints—I love thee with the breath,
Smiles, tears, of all my life!—and, if God choose,
I shall but love thee better after death.

STUDY QUESTIONS

If Thou Must Love Me

Recalling

1. Why does the speaker want to be loved?
2. According to lines 2–6, for what four things does the speaker not want her beloved to love her? What reasons does she give?
3. What additional reasons for loving her does she mention? Why does she reject these?
4. For how long does she hope to be loved?

Interpreting

5. What kind of love does the speaker not want? From what is she trying to protect her love?
6. What kind of love does the speaker want?

How Do I Love Thee?

Recalling

1. How many different ways does the speaker love her beloved, according to this poem?
2. To what depth, breadth, and height does the speaker love her beloved? To what level?
3. With what sort of faith does she love him?
4. What will she do "if God choose"?

Interpreting

5. In what sense is the type of love mentioned in lines 2–4 different from that mentioned in lines 5–6? Explain how these types of love show the range of the speaker's feeling.
6. What feeling is the speaker describing when she refers to "a love I seemed to lose/With my lost saints"? What is she saying that her beloved means to her?

Extending

7. This sonnet is probably the most-quoted love poem in the English language. What qualities, both in its content and its style, make "How Do I Love Thee?" memorable?

COMPARING WRITERS

1. Compare the use of rhyme, rhythm, and other sound devices in poems by two or more of the Victorian poets presented here. What effects does each poet produce through the use of these devices? Which poem is more striking in its use of sound, and why?
2. Compare the speakers in poems by two or more of these writers. Do you identify the speaker with the poet, or is the speaker someone clearly different from the poet? How do you know? In each case briefly describe the speaker, and identify the emotions he or she expresses in the poem.

Charles Dickens   *1812–1870*

Charles Dickens was the most popular British author of the Victorian Age, and more than a hundred years after his death, his work is still popular both in print and in dramatic and musical versions. The magic that millions still find in Dickens' novels can be traced, at least in part, to the eccentric, colorful array of characters that he created: the gullible Pickwick of *The Pickwick Papers* (1836–1837), the villainous Fagin of *Oliver Twist* (1837–1839), the pathetic Little Nell of *The Old Curiosity Shop* (1840–1841), the miserly Scrooge of *A Christmas Carol* (1843), the shiftless Micawber of *David Copperfield* (1849–1850), the honorable Sydney Carton of *A Tale of Two Cities* (1859), the bitter Miss Havisham of *Great Expectations* (1860–1861).

The basis for many of these characters lies in Dickens' own experience. In fact, many people believe that his father was the model for Micawber and that his mother inspired Mrs. Nickleby in *Nicholas Nickleby* (1838–1839). Dickens was born in Portsmouth in southern England, the second of eight children. His father was a clerk who worked for the navy. The family repeatedly moved in order to escape creditors. When his father was finally sent to a debtors' prison, Charles, then twelve, began working in a warehouse pasting labels on pots of shoe blacking. After a sudden inheritance improved the family's fortunes, Charles found work as a lawyer's clerk and then as a reporter. His literary career began with the success of *Sketches by Boz,* a collection of vignettes about life in the city that he wrote for a London newspaper. *Boz* led to *The Pickwick Papers,* his first novel.

While Dickens has entertained millions with his novels, he also intended them as a means of social reform. Human welfare could not keep pace with the technological advances of his time, and Dickens did much to expose evil by-products of industrialization: child labor, debtors' prisons, ruinous financial speculation, inhuman legal procedures, and mismanagement of schools, orphanages, prisons, and hospitals.

Dickens' many novels add up to a vast panorama of human nature and specifically of Victorian life. One excerpt from one novel is a very small sample indeed. The following selection from *Oliver Twist,* however, can be read as a serial installment. An excerpt from the second chapter, the selection introduces Oliver, an orphan who must depend on the mercies of public support. When he turns nine, Oliver becomes too old for the orphanage. He is brought by Mr. Bumble, a parish official, to a workhouse, a kind of prison where the poor must work for a meager upkeep. When we meet him, Oliver has been given a slice of bread so that he will not look hungry when he appears before the parish board of directors to be introduced formally to his new home.

Charles Dickens

from **Oliver Twist**

Oliver had not been within the walls of the workhouse a quarter of an hour, and had scarcely completed the demolition of a second slice of bread, when Mr. Bumble, who had handed him over to the care of an old woman, returned; and, telling him it was a board night, informed him that the board had said he was to appear before it forthwith.

Not having a very clearly defined notion of what a live board was, Oliver was rather astounded by this intelligence, and was not quite certain whether he ought to laugh or cry. He had no time to think about the matter, however; for Mr. Bumble gave him a tap on the head with his cane, to wake him up, and another on the back to make him lively, and bidding him follow, conducted him into a large whitewashed room, where eight or ten fat gentlemen were sitting round a table. At the top of the table, seated in an armchair rather higher than the rest, was a particularly fat gentleman, with a very round, red face.

"Bow to the board," said Bumble. Oliver brushed away two or three tears that were lingering in his eyes; and seeing no board but the table, fortunately bowed to that.

"What's your name, boy?" said the gentleman in the high chair.

Oliver was frightened at the sight of so many gentlemen, which made him tremble; and the beadle[1] gave him another tap behind, which made him cry. These two causes made him answer in a very low and hesitating voice; whereupon a gentleman in a white waistcoat[2] said he was a fool. Which was a capital way of raising his spirits, and putting him quite at his ease.

"Boy," said the gentleman in the high chair, "listen to me. You know you're an orphan, I suppose?"

"What's that, sir?" inquired poor Oliver.

"The boy *is* a fool—I though he was," said the gentleman in the white waistcoat.

"Hush!" said the gentleman who had spoken first. "You know you've got no father or mother, and that you were brought up by the parish, don't you?"

"Yes sir," replied Oliver, weeping bitterly.

"What are you crying for?" inquired the gentleman in the white waistcoat. And to be sure it was very extraordinary. What *could* the boy be crying for?

"I hope you say your prayers every night," said another gentleman in a gruff voice; "and pray for the people who feed you, and take care of you—like a Christian."

"Yes, sir," stammered the boy. The gentleman who spoke last was unconsciously right. It would have been *very* like a Christian, and a marvelously good Christian too, if Oliver had prayed for the people who fed and took care of *him.* But he hadn't, because nobody had taught him.

"Well! You have come here to be educated, and taught a useful trade," said the red-faced gentleman in the high chair.

"So you'll begin to pick oakum[3] tomorrow morning at six o'clock," added the surly one in the white waistcoat.

For the combination of both these blessings in the one simple process of picking oakum, Oliver bowed low, by the direction of the beadle, and was hurried away to a large ward: where, on a rough hard bed, he sobbed himself to sleep. What a noble illustration of the tender laws of England! They let the paupers go to sleep!

Poor Oliver! He little thought, as he lay sleeping in happy unconsciousness of all around him, that the board had that very day arrived at a decision which would exercise the

---

1. **beadle:** minor officer of a parish, or church district.
2. **waistcoat** [wes′kət]: vest.

3. **pick oakum:** tear apart old rope for the stringy fiber that was used in sealing the seams of boats.

most material influence over all his future fortunes. But they had. And this was it:

The members of this board were very sage, deep, philosophical men; and when they came to turn their attention to the workhouse, they found out at once, what ordinary folks would never have discovered—the poor people like it! It was a regular place of public entertainment for the poorer classes; a tavern where there was nothing to pay; a public breakfast, dinner, tea, and supper all the year round; a brick and mortar elysium, where it was all play and no work. "Oho!" said the board, looking very knowing; "we are the fellows to set this to rights; we'll stop it all, in no time." So, they established the rule, that all poor people should have the alternative (for they would compel nobody, not they) of being starved by a gradual process in the house, or by a quick one out of it. With this view, they contracted with the waterworks to lay on an unlimited supply of water; and with a corn factor to supply periodically small quantities of oatmeal; and issued three meals of thin gruel a day, with an onion twice a week, and half a roll on Sundays. They made a great many other wise and humane regulations, having reference to the ladies, which it is not necessary to repeat; kindly undertook to divorce poor married people, in consequence of the great expense of a suit in Doctors' Commons; and, instead of compelling a man to support his family, as they had theretofore done, took his family away from him, and made him a bachelor! There is no saying how many applicants for relief, under these last two heads, might have started up in all classes of society, if it had not been coupled with the workhouse; but the board were long-headed men, and had provided for this difficulty. The relief was inseparable from the workhouse and the gruel; and that frightened people.

For the first six months after Oliver Twist was removed, the system was in full operation. It was rather expensive at first, in consequence of the increase in the undertaker's bill, and the necessity of taking in the clothes of all the paupers, which fluttered loosely on their wasted, shrunken forms, after a week or two's gruel.

But the number of workhouse inmates got thin as well as the paupers; and the board were in ecstasies.

The room in which the boys were fed was a large stone hall, with a copper[4] at one end: out of which the master, dressed in an apron for the purpose, and assisted by one or two women, ladled the gruel at mealtimes. Of this festive composition, each boy had one porringer,[5] and no more—except on occasions of great public rejoicing, when he had two ounces and a quarter of bread besides. The bowls never wanted washing. The boys polished them with their spoons till they shone again; and when they had performed this operation (which never took very long, the spoons being nearly as large as the bowls), they would sit staring at the copper, with such eager eyes, as if they could have devoured the very bricks of which it was composed; employing themselves, meanwhile, in sucking their fingers most assiduously, with the view of catching up any stray splashes of gruel that might have been cast thereon. Boys have generally excellent appetites. Oliver Twist and his companions suffered the tortures of slow starvation for three months: at last they got so voracious and wild with hunger that one boy, who was tall for his age, and hadn't been used to that sort of thing (for his father had kept a small cook's shop), hinted darkly to his companions, that unless he had another basin of gruel *per diem,* he was afraid he might some night happen to eat the boy who slept next him, who happened to be a weakly youth of tender age. He had a wild, hungry eye; and they implicitly believed him. A council was held, lots were cast who should walk up to the master after supper that evening and ask for more; and it fell to Oliver Twist.

The evening arrived; the boys took their places. The master, in his cook's uniform, stationed himself at the copper; his pauper assistants ranged themselves behind him; the gruel

---

4. **copper:** large container, originally but not necessarily made of copper.
5. **porringer** [pôr′in jər]: small, shallow bowl.

was served out; and a long grace was said over the short commons.[6] The gruel disappeared; the boys whispered each other, and winked at Oliver, while his next neighbors nudged him. Child as he was, he was desperate with hunger, and reckless with misery. He rose from the table; and advancing to the master, basin and spoon in hand, said, somewhat alarmed at his own temerity:

"Please, sir, I want some more."

The master was a fat, healthy man; but he turned very pale. He gazed in stupefied astonishment on the small rebel for some seconds; and then clung for support to the copper. The assistants were paralyzed with wonder; the boys with fear.

"What!" said the master at length, in a faint voice.

"Please, sir," replied Oliver, "I want some more."

The master aimed a blow at Oliver's head with the ladle, pinioned him in his arms, and shrieked aloud for the beadle.

The board were sitting in solemn conclave,[7] when Mr. Bumble rushed into the room in great excitement, and addressing the gentleman in the high chair, said:

"Mr. Limbkins, I beg your pardon, sir! Oliver Twist has asked for more!"

There was a general start. Horror was depicted on every countenance.

"For *more!*" said Mr. Limbkins. "Compose yourself, Bumble, and answer me distinctly. Do I understand that he asked for more, after he had eaten the supper allotted by the dietary?"[8]

"He did, sir," replied Bumble.

"That boy will be hung," said the gentleman in the white waistcoat. "I know that boy will be hung."

Nobody controverted the prophetic gentleman's opinion. An animated discussion took place. Oliver was ordered into instant confinement; and a bill was next morning pasted on the outside of the gate, offering a reward of five pounds to anybody who would take Oliver Twist off the hands of the parish. In other words, five pounds and Oliver Twist were offered to any man or woman who wanted an apprentice,[9] to any trade, business, or calling.

"I never was more convinced of anything in my life," said the gentleman in the white waistcoat, as he knocked at the gate and read the bill next morning: "I never was more convinced of anything in my life, than I am that that boy will come to be hung."

---

6. **commons:** ration or allowance of food.
7. **conclave:** private meeting.
8. **dietary** [dī'ə ter'ē]: daily ration or allowance of food.

9. **apprentice** [ə pren'tis]: trainee who works in return for instruction in a trade.

STUDY QUESTIONS

Recalling

1. Describe the gentlemen of the board. Relate the circumstances that lead the gentlemen of the board to think Oliver a fool.
2. What is the weekly menu at the workhouse? Give two new workhouse regulations, and describe the results.
3. Briefly outline the events that lead to the prediction that Oliver will be hung some day.
4. What is the message on the bill that is pasted on the workhouse gate?

Interpreting

5. Compare the physical description of the board with the physical description of the boys. What does the comparison imply?
6. What is the official attitude toward the poor? What does the board think of its own efforts on behalf of the poor?
7. Explain what is implied by the prediction that Oliver will be hung and by the bill that is posted on the gate.

Extending

8. What insights into human nature do you find in the behavior of Oliver and of the board?

VIEWPOINT

One critic explained Dickens' style of characterization as an ability to view all people as children see adults. To children adults are

odd, arbitrary, incomprehensible, sometimes absurdly comic, sometimes terrifying, sometimes both at once. Scarcely ever are they ordinary.

—W. Allen, *The English Novel*

■ Which adjectives in the quotation apply to the adults in the excerpt? Why? Why is a child's view of adults important to this scene?

LITERARY FOCUS

The Novel

The **novel** is a long work of narrative prose fiction. In England the form developed during the eighteenth century with such early contributions as Daniel Defoe's *Robinson Crusoe* (1719), Samuel Richardson's *Pamela* (1740), and Henry Fielding's *Tom Jones* (1749). The nineteenth century, however, saw the novel come of age as a literary genre and as a form of entertainment for the new middle class, and the works of Charles Dickens exemplify that success.

Because of its length, the novel usually has a complicated plot. **Plot** is the sequence of events in a narrative, each event causing or leading to the next. A novel usually has several subplots in addition to its central plot. A **subplot** is a less important plot that is somehow related to the main action of the narrative. A novel also has many characters, major and minor, and often has a variety of settings. **Setting** is the time and place of a narrative, and a novel can take place in a number of locations and over a long period of time. Because a novel may contain many subplots, characters, and settings, it can also have more than one **theme,** or general statement about life.

Many Victorian novels were written in installments for magazines; as a result, they are often very long. They present a detailed, richly populated world that offers the reader a high level of involvement and an impressive record of British life and thought in the 1800s.

Thinking About the Novel

■ What theme is implied by the excerpt from *Oliver Twist*? Explain how the elements in the excerpt suggest the theme.

COMPOSITION

Writing About Literature and Its Period

■ Write an essay to demonstrate how Dickens, as represented by the excerpt from *Oliver Twist,* exemplifies his era in the ideas he explores and the literary techniques he uses. First identify the period. Then state several characteristics of the time; include popular literary techniques as well as prevalent ideas and achievements. For each characteristic of the period, give examples from the excerpt from *Oliver Twist. For help with this assignment, refer to Lesson 10 in the Writing About Literature Handbook at the back of this book.*

Continuing the Story

■ The excerpt from *Oliver Twist* comes very early in the novel. Imagine your own continuation of the novel, and write a short excerpt that would come near the end. Try to relate your excerpt to details in the portion you have read. Use details in your excerpt that imply events in Oliver's life up to that point.

Matthew Arnold *1822–1888*

The nineteenth century brought enormous changes to England. In the midst of whatever had been gained by these changes, many wrote of what had been lost. No one expressed this sense of loss more eloquently than Matthew Arnold.

Arnold grew up as the son of the most renowned educator in early Victorian England, the headmaster of the famous Rugby School. However, to his somber father's dismay, the young Arnold turned himself into a flamboyant dandy, dressing in eccentric clothes and cultivating bright, witty speech. Then in his mid-twenties Arnold surprised his family and friends by publishing a volume of melancholy and profoundly serious verse, *The Strayed Reveller, and Other Poems* (1849). This work and its successor, *Empedocles on Etna, and Other Poems* (1852), both reflect Arnold's lifelong love of classical Greek culture. Arnold produced only a few more volumes of poetry, but the work is of so high a quality that he is regarded as the greatest Victorian poet after Tennyson and Browning.

Marrying in 1851, and unable to support a family by writing poetry, Arnold took a job as an inspector of elementary schools. For thirty-five years he traveled over England's wretched roads and stayed at dreary inns in order to inspect the dismal schools of the period. The labor was exhausting, but Arnold performed it with skill and good cheer. He also wrote extensive and valuable reports about European education in his capacity as foreign assistant commissioner on education.

Arnold became known first as a poet, but he achieved equal success with his prose works. Besides being an expert in the field of education, Arnold wrote brilliant criticism of literature and of all other aspects of culture, eventually becoming perhaps the most influential critic in all of English literature. His masterful works in this vein include *Essays in Criticism* (1865–1881), *On Translating Homer* (1861), *Culture and Anarchy* (1869), and *Literature and Dogma* (1873). These commentaries set a high ethical standard for art, invoking what Arnold refers to as the "high seriousness" of any artistic undertaking.

Arnold's prose, especially that written late in his life, tends to reassure readers by looking toward the noblest aspects of experience and underlining the purposefulness of human endeavor. In his poetry, however, Arnold often addresses the deep sense of loss and futility felt by many over the economic and social changes that swept across nineteenth-century England. Of all his poems, "Dover Beach" is the most famous. Dover is on Britain's southeast coast, on a narrow strait of water that separates England from France, only twenty miles away. Lights on the French coast can be seen from the beach, which stretches beneath the famous white cliffs—huge chalk peaks that line the English shore.

Matthew Arnold

Dover Beach

The sea is calm tonight.
The tide is full, the moon lies fair
Upon the straits[1]—on the French coast the
    light
Gleams and is gone; the cliffs of England
    stand,
5 Glimmering and vast, out in the tranquil bay.
Come to the window, sweet is the night air!
Only, from the long line of spray
Where the sea meets the moon-blanched
    land,
Listen! you hear the grating roar
10 Of pebbles which the waves draw back, and
    fling,
At their return, up the high strand,[2]
Begin, and cease, and then again begin,
With tremulous cadence slow, and bring
The eternal note of sadness in.

15 Sophocles[3] long ago
Heard it on the Aegean,[4] and it brought
Into his mind the turbid ebb and flow
Of human misery; we

Find also in the sound a thought,
20 Hearing it by his distant northern sea.

The Sea of Faith
Was once, too, at the full, and round earth's
    shore
Lay like the folds of a bright girdle[5] furled.
But now I only hear
25 Its melancholy, long, withdrawing roar,
Retreating, to the breath
Of the night wind, down the vast edges
    drear
And naked shingles[6] of the world.

Ah, love, let us be true
30 To one another! for the world, which seems
To lie before us like a land of dreams,
So various, so beautiful, so new,
Hath really neither joy, nor love, nor light,
Nor certitude, nor peace, nor help for pain;
35 And we are here as on a darkling[7] plain
Swept with confused alarms of struggle and
    flight,
Where ignorant armies clash by night.

---

1. **straits:** Strait of Dover, between England and France.
2. **strand:** shore.
3. **Sophocles** [sof′ə klēz]: Sophocles (496?–406 B.C.) was a Greek tragic dramatist, the author of *Oedipus Rex* and *Antigone*.
4. **Aegean** [i jē′ən]: arm of the Mediterranean Sea between Greece and Turkey.

5. **girdle:** garment such as a belt or sash, worn about the waist; anything that encircles or confines.
6. **shingles:** beach gravel composed of water-worn stones or pebbles.
7. **darkling:** lying in darkness.

STUDY QUESTIONS

Recalling

1. What does the speaker see from the window in lines 1–6? What does he hear in lines 9–14? In line 14 what does the sea bring in?
2. According to the second stanza, what did this sound bring to Sophocles' mind?
3. What, according to the speaker, was once "at the full"? How has it changed, according to lines 24–28?
4. In lines 29–30 what plea does the speaker address to his listener? How does he describe the world in lines 30–34? In the poem's last three lines, to what does he compare the world in which he and his listener live?

Interpreting

5. Describe the mood of the opening lines of the poem. Where and why does the mood shift?
6. In what way has the world not changed since the time of Sophocles, according to Arnold?
7. What does Arnold mean by the "Sea of Faith"? Why does he say it was once full but is now withdrawing?
8. According to the last stanza of the poem, how does this withdrawal affect human affairs? What does Arnold suggest is the only refuge from this state of things?

Extending

9. Do you think the view of human life presented in "Dover Beach" is applicable to today's world? Why or why not?

VIEWPOINT

The American critic Lionel Trilling saw Arnold as the Victorian most ahead of his time:

Perhaps more than any other man of his time and nation he perceived the changes that were taking place in the conditions of life and in the minds of men to bring into being the world we now know. In certain respects he was, of all the intellectual figures of his period, the most modern.

■ To what changes "in the conditions of life and in the minds of men" was Arnold responding in "Dover Beach"? Referring to specific lines, describe the attitude of the poem toward these changes. Does "Dover Beach" seem more in tune with the modern world than the other Victorian poems you have read so far? Why or why not?

COMPOSITION

Writing About Poetry

■ Discuss the meaning of "Dover Beach," and show how Arnold uses the techniques of poetry to express this meaning. Begin by stating the theme of the poem in one sentence. Then show how Arnold illuminates this theme through his speaker, use of sound, tone, imagery, and figurative language. *For help with this assignment, refer to Lesson 7 in the Writing About Literature Handbook at the back of this book.*

Writing About a Scene

■ Write a poem that describes a particular scene in details and language that evoke a definite mood. You may want to describe a serene lake or unruly street scene, but be sure that you use concrete images that allow your reader to see and hear what you are describing and to feel the mood that you want to convey.

Gerard Manley Hopkins   *1844–1889*

Through much of his brief life, Gerard Manley Hopkins was a Jesuit priest. Brought up an Anglican, he was influenced by the religious reformer John Henry Newman and converted to Roman Catholicism while studying at Oxford University. A devout and scholarly man, Hopkins worked briefly among the poor in the slums of Liverpool but fled from the dirt and the vice that he saw there. He was then given a church in Oxford and eventually became a professor of Greek at the University of Dublin. Hopkins had no interest in worldly fame and was uneasy about reconciling his poetry with his priestly duties. In fact, his poems were not published until 1918, long after his death.

Hopkins wrote much of his poetry while studying for the priesthood. The subject of his poems is usually religious; their musical patterns are often elaborate. Had the poems appeared during Hopkins' own lifetime, they may not have been accepted because the verse is worlds away from the work of most Victorians. The twentieth century, however, responded with enthusiasm to what sounded amazingly modern both in diction and in melody.

Gerard Manley Hopkins

Pied[1] Beauty

Glory be to God for dappled things—
   For skies of couple-color as a brinded[2] cow;
     For rose-moles all in stipple[3] upon trout that swim;
Fresh-firecoal chestnut-falls;[4] finches' wings;
5   Landscape plotted and pieced—fold, fallow, and plow;
     And áll trádes, their gear and tackle and trim.

All things counter,[5] original, spare, strange;
   Whatever is fickle, freckled (who knows how?)
     With swift, slow; sweet, sour; adazzle, dim;
10 He fathers-forth whose beauty is past change:
     Praise him.

---

1. **Pied:** spotted.
2. **brinded:** streaked.
3. **in stipple:** dotted with tiny spots.
4. **Fresh-firecoal chestnut-falls:** roasted chestnuts.
5. **counter:** contrary, contrasting.

God's Grandeur

The world is charged with the grandeur of God.
　　It will flame out, like shining from shook foil;[1]
　　It gathers to a greatness, like the ooze of oil
Crushed.[2] Why do men then now not reck his rod?[3]
5 Generations have trod, have trod, have trod;
　　And all is seared with trade; bleared, smeared with toil;
　　And wears man's smudge and shares man's smell: the soil
Is bare now, nor can foot feel, being shod.

And for all this, nature is never spent;
10　　There lives the dearest freshness deep down things;
And though the last lights off the black West went,
　　Oh, morning, at the brown brink eastward, springs—
Because the Holy Ghost over the bent
　　World broods[4] with warm breast and with ah! bright wings.

---

1. **foil:** gold leaf, which is gold hammered into a thin sheet, or tinsel.
2. **Crushed:** squeezed from olives.
3. **reck his rod:** heed his power.
4. **broods:** hovers protectively like a bird on eggs.

Spring and Fall

To a Young Child

Márgarét, are you gríeving
Over Goldengrove unleaving?[1]
Leáves, líke the things of man, you
With your fresh thoughts care for, can you?
5 Ah! ás the heart grows older
It will come to such sights colder
By and by, nor spare a sigh
Though worlds of wanwood[2] leafmeal[3] lie;
And yet you wíll weep and know why.
10 Now no matter, child, the name:
Sórrow's spríngs áre the same,
Nor mouth had, no nor mind, expressed
What heart heard of, ghost[4] guessed:
It ís the blight man was born for,
15 It is Margaret you mourn for.

---

1. **unleaving:** losing its leaves.
2. **wanwood** [won′wood]: pale wood.
3. **leafmeal:** crushed decomposed leaves.
4. **ghost:** spirit.

STUDY QUESTIONS

Pied Beauty

Recalling

1. Name four dappled things for which the speaker gives glory to God in the first stanza.
2. List at least five adjectives that are used to describe creation in the second stanza.
3. What advice does the speaker give to the reader in the second stanza?

Interpreting

4. Why do you think Hopkins uses pied, or spotted, things as proof of the greatness of creation?
5. Explain your interpretation of line 10. What contrast is implied in the phrase "past change"?

God's Grandeur

Recalling

1. Based on the first three lines, name three qualities of God's grandeur.
2. According to lines 4–8, in what ways has humanity changed the world?
3. Give two examples that the speaker uses to show that "nature is never spent." What reason does the speaker give for this?

Interpreting

4. Find three examples of alliteration in the poem. Find two examples of internal rhyme.
5. What is the rhyme scheme of the poem? Give two examples of how the rhyme affects line breaks in the poem.
6. According to the poem, what is nature's relationship with God? With humanity?

Spring and Fall

Recalling

1. At the beginning of the poem, what emotion does Margaret feel? Why?
2. In what way does the heart change as it gets older?
3. According to the last three lines, what has the heart heard of and the ghost, or Margaret's soul, guessed?

Interpreting

4. What do the following word coinages suggest to you: Goldengrove, unleaving, and leafmeal?

5. Explain the comparison that the poem makes between the seasons of the year and a human life.
6. According to line 11, all sorrow comes from the same source. Explain how the poem's final two lines suggest the nature of that source.

LITERARY FOCUS

Sprung Rhythm

The sound of a poem by Gerard Manley Hopkins is unique because of a technique for which the poet created the term *sprung rhythm*. **Sprung rhythm** is a kind of meter in which each foot contains one stressed syllable, usually the first, and any number of unstressed syllables. Hopkins believed this to be the rhythm of natural speech. Study the following lines:

Már ga / ret are / you / griev ing

Notice that the number of unstressed syllables may vary from foot to foot. Also, in sprung rhythm two accented syllables may occur together as in the fifth and sixth syllables of the example.

Thinking About Sprung Rhythm

■ Scan the first stanza of "Pied Beauty." Mark each accented syllable, and divide each line into feet. Choose one line, and count the unaccented syllables in each foot on that line.

VOCABULARY

Antonyms

Antonyms are words that have opposite or nearly opposite meanings. *Long* and *short* are antonyms. The words in capitals are from Hopkins' poems. Choose the word that is *most nearly the opposite* of each word in capitals, *as the word is used in the selections.*

1. SEARED: (a) moist (b) withered (c) visible (d) consumed
2. BLEARED: (a) exhausted (b) blind (c) illusory (d) lucid
3. DAPPLED: (a) juicy (b) handsome (c) uniform (d) spotted
4. FICKLE: (a) courteous (b) loyal (c) obedient (d) cooperative
5. BLIGHT: (a) destiny (b) well-being (c) truth (d) disease

Thomas Hardy *1840–1928*

Thomas Hardy was born in Dorsetshire in southwestern England. He was educated locally and was apprenticed to an ecclesiastical architect. For much of his early life, Hardy wavered between careers in architecture and in literature, winning prizes in architecture and design while also composing poems, essays, and short stories. The success of his writing caused him finally to abandon architecture in his early thirties.

Hardy's home and the surrounding districts played an important role in his literary career. The region is agricultural, and across its rugged surface stand monuments of the past: Saxon and Roman ruins and the great boulders of Stonehenge, which extend back into prehistory. Before the Norman invasion of 1066, the area had been the Anglo-Saxon kingdom of Wessex. Hardy revived the name to describe the setting for a long string of novels, among them *Far from the Madding Crowd* (1874), his first popular success; *The Return of the Native* (1878); *The Mayor of Casterbridge* (1886); and *Tess of the D'Urbervilles* (1891). The novels all set a harsh vision of life against the bleakly beautiful landscape that Hardy knew well. His characters are subject to a blind fate that, like the landscape, is indifferent to human pain and suffering.

The failure of Hardy's most pessimistic—and possibly his greatest—novel, *Jude the Obscure* (1895), angered him and contributed to his decision to abandon the form of the novel. Hardy felt that he had expressed his philosophy of life as well as he could within a novel, and after 1896 he turned to verse exclusively.

Hardy wrote *The Dynasts* (1904–1908), a patriotic verse play about the Napoleonic Wars. He then turned his attention to lyric poems that combine strict form and musical patterns with everyday, nonpoetic language. This poetry represents a second literary career for Hardy, already ranked among the greatest Victorian novelists. This last of the great Victorians, as Hardy has been called, died in 1928. His ashes are buried in Westminster Abbey, but, because of his lasting relationship with his home district, his heart is buried in Wessex.

Thomas Hardy

A Thunderstorm in Town

(A Reminiscence: 1893)

She wore a new "terra-cotta"[1] dress,
And we stayed, because of the pelting storm,
Within the hansom's[2] dry recess,
Though the horse had stopped; yea, motionless
5   We sat on, snug and warm.

Then the downpour ceased, to my sharp sad pain,
And the glass that had screened our forms before
Flew up, and out she sprang to her door:
I should have kissed her if the rain
10   Had lasted a minute more.

---

1. **"terra-cotta":** rust-colored.
2. **hansom:** horse-drawn carriage.

Rainy Day, Boston 1885, Childe Hassam.

The Man He Killed

"Had he and I but met
By some old ancient inn,
We should have sat us down to wet
Right many a nipperkin!¹

5　"But ranged as infantry,
And staring face to face,
I shot at him as he at me,
And killed him in his place.

"I shot him dead because—
10　Because he was my foe,

Just so—my foe of course he was;
That's clear enough; although

"He thought he'd 'list,² perhaps,
Off-hand like—just as I—
15　Was out of work—had sold his traps—
No other reason why.

"Yes; quaint and curious war is!
You shoot a fellow down
You'd treat if met where any bar is,
20　Or help to half-a-crown."³

----

1. **nipperkin:** small glass for ale, beer, or wine.

2. **'list:** enlist (in the military).
3. **half-a-crown:** coin.

STUDY QUESTIONS

A Thunderstorm in Town

Recalling

1. Describe what happens in the first eight lines of the poem.
2. According to the last two lines, what might the speaker have done? What prevented him?

Interpreting

3. What words in the first stanza describe the mood inside the cab?
4. Explain why the speaker feels pain over the end of the storm.
5. Does fate play a role in the poem, or is the speaker responsible for his unhappiness?

The Man He Killed

Recalling

1. According to the first stanza, what would have happened if the two men had met in an inn?

2. Based on the second stanza, describe the circumstances under which the two men actually meet.
3. In the third stanza what reason does the speaker give for shooting?
4. In what ways does the speaker compare the dead man to himself in the fourth stanza?

Interpreting

5. Explain the irony of line 17 and of the poem in general.
6. Hardy's novels deal pessimistically with the power of fate. In what sense is "The Man He Killed" similarly pessimistic?

Extending

7. Why do you think Hardy chose the title he did instead of something like "The Victor"? What details in the poem would be left out if the poem's attitude toward war were more positive?

In this selection, as in one selection in each unit, you will find notes in the right-hand margin that highlight parts of the selection. These notes point out important ideas of the literary period and draw your attention to literary elements and techniques covered in the Literary Focuses. Page numbers in the notes refer you to more extensive discussions of these important ideas and elements.

Thomas Hardy

The Darkling[1] Thrush

I leant upon a coppice gate[2]
   When Frost was specter-gray,
And Winter's dregs made desolate
   The weakening eye of day.
5 The tangled bine[3] stems scored the sky
   Like strings of broken lyres,
And all mankind that haunted nigh
   Had sought their household fires.

The land's sharp features seemed to be
10   The Century's corpse[4] outleant,[5]
His crypt the cloudy canopy,
   The wind his death lament.
The ancient pulse of germ[6] and birth
   Was shrunken hard and dry,
15 And every spirit upon earth
   Seemed fervorless as I.

At once a voice arose among
   The bleak twigs overhead
In a full-hearted evensong
20   Of joy illimited;

Rhythm (p. 419): Lines of four beats alternate with lines of three beats. Each three-beat line achieves a note of finality in keeping with the gloomy mood of the poem.

Victorian idea: End-of-century pessimism was a reaction to the optimism that preceded it (p. 405).

---

1. **Darkling:** in the dark.
2. **coppice** [kop′is] **gate:** gate leading to a coppice, which is a thicket, or small wood.
3. **bine:** a twining stem.
4. **Century's corpse:** The poem was written on December 31, 1900, the last of the nineteenth century.
5. **outleant:** outstretched.
6. **germ:** seed or bud.

An aged thrush, frail, gaunt, and small,
In blast-beruffled plume,
Had chosen thus to fling his soul
Upon the growing gloom.

25 So little cause for carolings
Of such ecstatic sound
Was written on terrestrial things
Afar or nigh around,
That I could think there trembled through
30 His happy good-night air
Some blessed Hope, whereof he knew
And I was unaware.

> **Realism** (p. 405): The thrush, is described realistically, rather than with the idealism of the Romantic poet (p. 321).

> **Rhyme** (p. 362): The end rhymes alternate to form a pattern that is followed throughout the poem.

STUDY QUESTIONS

Recalling

1. What words or phrases in the first stanza tell us the season of the year and the time of day?
2. To what does the speaker compare the land, the sky, and the wind in the second stanza?
3. Describe the sound that the speaker hears in the third stanza and its source.
4. According to the fourth stanza, what does the speaker think as a result of the sound?

Interpreting

5. Explain how imagery and diction create a grim mood in the first stanza.
6. Why is death an appropriate image in the second stanza?
7. Why is it more effective for the thrush to be old and frail than young and strong?

VIEWPOINT

Hardy's poetry is unlike that of most Victorians. One critic, however, does compare Hardy's work to that of Browning:

> . . . like Browning, the only Victorian poet by whom he was strongly influenced, . . . he [Hardy] was trying to produce a dramatic rather than a pictorial or musical effect. He differed from Browning, however, in avoiding the romantic and the picturesque, and in his deliberate use of commonplace and contemporary subject matter.
>
> —V. de Sola Pinto, *Crisis in English Poetry, 1880–1940*

■ In what sense is Hardy's poetry dramatic, commonplace, and contemporary? Do you agree that Hardy avoids the pictorial, the musical, and the romantic?

COMPOSITION

Writing About Poetry

■ Select one of the following poems by Hardy: "The Man He Killed," "A Thunderstorm in Town," or "The Darkling Thrush." First explain the meaning of the poem. Then explain what techniques Hardy uses to reveal his meaning. You may want to consider: (a) speaker, (b) rhythm and rhyme, (c) imagery, and (d) figurative language. *For help with this assignment, refer to Lesson 7 in the Writing About Literature Handbook at the back of this book.*

Writing a Description

■ Descriptive details in "The Darkling Thrush" reinforce the speaker's bleak mood. Describe a scene of your choice, and limit descriptive details to those that convey a specific mood. Do not state the mood directly, but allow it to come across through your description.

A. E. Housman   *1859–1936*

Alfred Edward Housman was born a little north of Hardy country in the far west of England. He spent his youth in and around Shropshire, an agricultural region like Hardy's Wessex. As a gifted young man Housman was enrolled at Oxford University, where he was expected to excel. Four years later, however, he astounded his friends by failing his final examinations. As a result, Housman took a job in the patent office in London to support himself while continuing his classical studies independently.

Housman's private pursuit of knowledge was so successful that, on the basis of articles he published in scholarly journals, he was eventually awarded a professorship at the University of London. In 1911 he was appointed professor of Latin at Cambridge University, a prestigious position that he held for a quarter of a century until his death. During his long lifetime he became known as one of the greatest classical scholars of his age.

Housman's output as a poet is small; he wrote little more than a hundred poems. In 1896 he published *A Shropshire Lad,* a slim volume of verse that made him famous. Twenty-six years passed before his next slim volume, *Last Poems,* appeared. Because of the reputation of the first book, *Last Poems* was an instant success. A third book, *More Poems,* was compiled by his brother and published after Housman's death.

Housman's poems are mournful and pessimistic statements about the transient nature of love and youth, about nature's savage beauty, and about human vanity. Many are written in the voice of a country boy stranded in London. The language is direct; the rhythm is pronounced. Housman traced his inspiration to Scottish folk ballads and the songs of Shakespeare. His poems resemble those earlier works in their simplicity, their clarity, and their haunting power, a power that comes from the poet's ability to say a great deal in a small space and to imply even more.

La Primavera (Spring), Jean François Millet (1814–1875).

A. E. Housman

Loveliest of Trees

Loveliest of trees, the cherry now
Is hung with bloom along the bough,
And stands about the woodland ride
Wearing white for Eastertide.

5 Now, of my threescore years and ten,[1]
Twenty will not come again,
And take from seventy springs a score,
It only leaves me fifty more.

And since to look at things in bloom
10 Fifty springs are little room,
About the woodlands I will go
To see the cherry hung with snow.

---

1. **threescore . . . ten:** seventy years, the human life span according to the Bible.

When I Was One-and-Twenty

When I was one-and-twenty
  I heard a wise man say,
"Give crowns and pounds and guineas[1]
  But not your heart, away;
5 Give pearls away and rubies
  But keep your fancy free."[2]
But I was one-and-twenty—
  No use to talk to me.

When I was one-and-twenty
10   I heard him say again,
"The heart out of the bosom
  Was never given in vain;
'Tis paid with sighs a plenty
  And sold for endless rue."[3]
15 And I am two-and-twenty,
  And oh, 'tis true, 'tis true.

---

1. **crowns . . . guineas:** denominations of money.
2. **keep . . . free:** stay free of the power of love.
3. **rue:** sorrow, remorse.

A. E. Housman

To an Athlete Dying Young

The time you won your town the race
We chaired you through the market place;
Man and boy stood cheering by,
And home we brought you shoulder-high.

5 Today, the road all runners come,
Shoulder-high we bring you home,
And set you at your threshold down,
Townsman of a stiller town.

Smart lad, to slip betimes[1] away
10 From fields where glory does not stay
And early though the laurel[2] grows
It withers quicker than the rose.

Eyes the shady night has shut
Cannot see the record cut,
15 And silence sounds no worse than cheers
After earth has stopped the ears:
Now you will not swell the rout[3]
Of lads that wore their honors out,
Runners whom renown outran
20 And the name died before the man.

So set, before its echoes fade,
The fleet foot on the sill of shade,
And hold to the low lintel[4] up
The still-defended challenge cup.

25 And round that early-laureled head
Will flock to gaze the strengthless dead,
And find unwithered on its curls
The garland briefer than a girl's.

---

1. **betimes:** early.
2. **laurel:** symbol of victory or distinction.
3. **rout:** crowd.
4. **lintel:** horizontal piece over a door or window.

STUDY QUESTIONS

Loveliest of Trees

Recalling

1. Based on the first stanza, describe the loveliest tree. At what time of year is this poem set?
2. How old is the speaker of the poem? In the last stanza what does the speaker say that he or she will do?

Interpreting

3. According to lines 5–10, what is the speaker's attitude about his or her age?
4. Do you think the snow in the last two lines is meant to be literal? Why or why not?

When I Was One-and-Twenty

Recalling

1. According to the first stanza, what should a person not give away? What should be given away instead? What is the speaker's reaction to this advice?
2. According to the second stanza, what is the price that is paid for one's heart? What is the speaker's reaction to the advice in the second stanza?

Interpreting

3. Explain the effect of the repetition in the poem's last line.
4. What happens in the speaker's life in the time between the two stanzas? Explain how we know this from the poem.
5. In what ways would the impact of the poem be different if the speaker were much older in the second stanza?

Extending

6. Explain what the poem implies about the relationship between the old and the young.

To an Athlete Dying Young

Recalling

1. At what sport did the athlete excel? Describe the scene that is detailed in the first stanza.
2. What is the second occasion on which the athlete is carried shoulder-high? What words or phrases are used in the second stanza to describe death?
3. What is likely to happen to "glory" in the third

stanza, "the record" in the fourth stanza, "honors" and "the name" in the fifth stanza?

4. According to the third stanza, what happens to the laurel? Describe the garland in the last stanza.

Interpreting

5. Explain why the speaker says that the athlete is smart to die young.

Extending

6. What does the poem imply about problems that most successful athletes must face?

LITERARY FOCUS

Lyric Poetry

Poetry is traditionally classified into three types: **Narrative poetry** tells a story; Chaucer's "Pardoner's Tale" is an example. **Dramatic poetry** is verse in the form of a monologue by one character (Robert Browning's "My Last Duchess") or dialogue between two or more characters (Shakespeare's *Macbeth*). **Lyric poetry** is a speaker's expression of personal thoughts and feelings. Tennyson's "Tears, Idle Tears," Browning's "Home Thoughts, from Abroad," and Hardy's "Darkling Thrush" are all lyrics.

A lyric poem may describe an object, a person, or an event, but the central concern of the poem is the emotion that is awakened by the subject of the description. Therefore, we read lyric poetry to consider a poet's ideas and to share the feelings that are associated with them. The emotions that are expressed may remind us of our own emotional experiences, or they may cause us to imagine how we would respond to circumstances like those in the poem.

Lyric poetry is usually brief and can take many shapes. For example, the ode and the sonnet are two types of lyric. Most lyric poetry is very musical. The name itself comes from *lyre,* the guitar-like instrument that was originally used to accompany the recitation of such poetry. We still use the word *lyric* to refer to the words of songs, and most songs are expressions of emotion.

Thinking About Lyric Poetry

■ Choose one of the following poems by Housman, and explain why it is considered a lyric poem: "Loveliest of Trees," "When I Was One-and-Twenty," and "To an Athlete Dying Young." First explain the basic situation be-

hind the poem. Then tell what thoughts this situation arouses in the speaker. Finally explain what emotions are associated with these thoughts.

COMPOSITION

Applying a Statement About Literature

■ One concern of Housman's poetry is that so much in life is transient and does not last. Choose one of the poems by Housman that are presented here, and explain how this statement applies to the poem. First explain the statement in your own words. Then demonstrate how the statement fits the poem. Give examples from the poem to support your opinion. *For help with this assignment, refer to Lesson 9 in the Writing About Literature Handbook at the back of this book.*

Conveying an Emotional Response

■ In "Loveliest of Trees" Housman says that fifty years is hardly enough time to appreciate the beauty of a cherry orchard. Choose a natural phenomenon that you think deserves similar enthusiasm, and describe it in poetry or in prose. Use details that are vivid enough to convey your own emotional response.

COMPARING WRITERS

1. Compare two or more of the following works: the excerpt from *Oliver Twist,* "Dover Beach," "God's Grandeur," "A Thunderstorm in Town," and "To an Athlete Dying Young." For each work tell what emotion the author conveys, and explain what techniques the author uses to capture that emotion.

2. Great authors can suggest much in a few words. Compare two or more of the following works: the excerpt from *Oliver Twist,* "Dover Beach," "Spring and Fall," "The Man He Killed," and "When I Was One-and-Twenty." For each work tell what the author implies about what has happened to the speaker or central character. Then explain what details in the work provide the suggestions.

3. Choose and compare one work each by two or more of the following authors: Arnold, Hopkins, Hardy, and Housman. For each poem explain how the poet expresses the typical pessimism and adopts the Realism of the late Victorian Age.

READING FOR APPRECIATION

Active, Imaginative Reading

A fabulous wealth of literature is available to us as a rich source of pleasure and knowledge, for literature opens up an infinite variety of *experience*. To make the most of the experience, however, we must in turn open ourselves up: That is, we must read actively and *imaginatively*.

Active, imaginative reading means several things. It means reading alertly and inquisitively. If something confuses us or strikes us as obscure, we should not pass by it but should question it, think it through, turn it over in our minds until we can make sense of it. We should drop all preconceptions and familiar ways of seeing and feeling. We must read with open minds and hearts, for to resist automatically what seems strange is to cheat ourselves of much knowledge and pleasure. We must accept—at least for a while—what the author gives us and try to understand it on its own terms.

Truly imaginative reading also means giving ourselves up to the language of a work, to its particular rhythm and sound. We must read carefully and very slowly at first, until we can naturally "feel" the flow of the words and allow it to carry us out of ourselves and into the world of the characters and the vision of the writer.

For example, we might read Tennyson's poem "Ulysses" (page 412) from a distance, saying to ourselves, "This is just a poem after all; this is just someone's idea of what Ulysses might have felt when he grew old." We would understand the poem this way and perhaps even come to admire it, but we probably would not truly *feel* the sentiments it expresses. On the other hand, we might read the poem from "the inside." We might, first of all, remember what we know about Ulysses—his story, his character, his time. Then we might try to enter fully and deeply into his thoughts and feelings. We might try to submerge ourselves in his situation: Here is a great and accomplished man and a tireless spirit. Although old and weary, he still yearns "to strive, to seek, to find, and not to yield." Also, if we read with an awareness of the somber, stately rhythm of the language, we will appreciate the poem on an even profounder level. We will realize the hero's pride and dignity and expansiveness of vision, and we will comprehend the true majesty of his feelings.

We must use our imaginations in a somewhat different way when we read Hopkins' poem "God's Grandeur" (page 437). Here it is less a matter of entering into a character's consciousness and mood than of reacting as openly as we can to the emotions and inspirations of the poet. We must try to see what the poet sees, think what he thinks, feel what he feels. We must, like the poet, lose ourselves momentarily in nature. If we can, then we will have a truer idea of what the poet means by God's "grandeur." We will have a clearer sense of what he means by "the dearest freshness deep down things." We will ourselves recognize the exquisite joy that impels the poet to utter that surprising and wonderfully expressive "ah!" that interrupts the final ecstatic line.

By observing more closely, we not only see more but also understand more thoroughly. By attempting to know all that a character knows, we obtain more profound insight into that character's mind and heart and being. Through closer involvement *inside* a work, we derive greater pleasure and, moreover, give ourselves a richer, more poignant, more meaningful experience.

THE ENGLISH VOICE

Losses

Victorian literature describes an era of empire, progress, self-assurance, and optimism. Yet close readings of Victorian poetry and prose reveal something more: an undercurrent of regret, a tone of nostalgia, a haunting sense of loss.

Tennyson

*Though much is taken, much
   abides; and though
We are not now that strength
   which in old days
Moved earth and heaven, that
   which we are, we are.*

*Deep as first love, and wild
   with all regret;
O Death in Life, the days that
   are no more!*

*Ring out the grief that saps the
   mind,
For those that here we see no
   more.*

Robert Browning

*Oh, to be in England
Now that April's there.*

Elizabeth Barrett Browning

*I love thee with the passion put
   to use
In my old griefs, and with my
   childhood's faith.
I love thee with a love I seemed
   to lose
With my lost saints.*

Arnold

*Ah, love, let us be true
To one another! for the world,
   which seems
To lie before us like a land of
   dreams,
So various, so beautiful, so
   new,
Hath really neither joy, nor
   love, nor light,
Nor certitude, nor peace, nor
   help for pain.*

Hopkins

*It is the blight man was born
   for,
It is Margaret you mourn for.*

Hardy

*I should have kissed her if the
   rain
      Had lasted a minute more.*

Housman

*Now, of my threescore years
   and ten,
Twenty will not come again,
And take from seventy springs
   a score,
It only leaves me fifty more.*

The deaths of loved ones, the passing of time, emptiness of spirit, even homesickness—these too are Victorian subjects. Beneath Victorian assertions of life, love, and moral fervor, flow currents of unease.

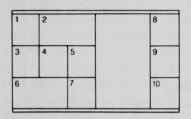
449

Key to Illustrations appears on page 645.

THE TWENTIETH CENTURY

(1900—Present)

Challenge and Change

During the nineteenth century Britons proudly believed that the sun never set on the British Empire. The twentieth century, however, brought enormous changes to England, a nation that has always taken pride in its stability and its solid traditions. Both internally and externally, England found it had to achieve a new identity.

Queen Victoria, the very symbol of empire for more than sixty years, died in 1901. As the twentieth century progressed, that empire gradually became the British Commonwealth, a federation of independent nations united under the merely symbolic power of the British crown. The national wealth and international influence that had been a way of life during the days of empire were quickly becoming things of the past. In addition, the relationships among the long-established classes of English society began to break down as the power of the common people increased.

While its empire was shrinking, Britain—now officially known as the United Kingdom of Great Britain and Northern Ireland—made great changes affecting the everyday life of English men, women, and children. In 1928 universal suffrage was finally achieved, more than seven hundred years after the Magna Carta. Labor unions were formed to protect industrial workers and miners. After

Victoria Station, R. Jack, 1916. The painting depicts English soldiers waiting to leave for France during World War I.

World War II the government assumed responsibility for public housing, pensions, unemployment, and the nation's railroads and mines. The state guaranteed every child an education, and a national health program made medical care available to everyone.

Queen Victoria had symbolized nineteenth-century England—a strict moral code, prosperity, contentment, and an unquestioning attitude toward authority. The Edwardian era, however—the reign of Edward VII (1901–1910)—saw those characteristics begin to break down, especially with widespread questioning of authority in politics, social matters, religion, and art. Later, through the reigns of George V and George VI and into the time of Elizabeth II, who assumed the throne in 1953, the British Commonwealth began to acquire an image different from that of the empire under authoritarian Victoria. The image is not that of the king but the commoner, not the queen but the prime minister, not the royalist but the rebel. Of course England still reveres its royal family. However, the modern English identity seems to have been shaped more by people who wore no crowns—people like Prime Minister Winston Churchill and opponents of the empire like Indian leader Mohandas Gandhi and Irish nationalist Charles Stewart Parnell.

The "troubles" in Ireland are themselves a large part of Britain's image in the modern world. In 1920 six predominantly Protestant counties in the north of Ireland became a separate entity known as Northern Ireland. Two years later the rest of Ireland broke with Great Britain to form the Irish Free State. Anxiety and violence accompanied Irish nationalism and independence, and continue to do so even in our own decade.

The greatest changes, however, in England's identity resulted from the two world wars that scar our century. Their cost in life and property contributed greatly to the decline of British power and resources, forced a redefinition of the British world view, and brought forth a great outpouring of literature.

The Great War

Britain was largely unprepared when World War I began in 1914. This was the first war to involve modern weapons—tanks planes, and poison gas. In four years of combat, most of it endured in trenches across the face of Europe, one million Britons were killed.

The Great War, as it was called, had an effect on British and European attitudes that was unparalleled. It is important to remember that the people who fought in World War I were Victorians: They had grown up with a set of ideals and attitudes that were about to be shattered by the gruesome reality of modern warfare. One English officer, typical of the gentlemen who went to Europe to fight, gave four soccer balls to his men and offered a reward to the one who would kick the ball through the German lines during an attack. The officer and many of his men were killed, never surviving to feel the skepticism and bitterness that marked the postwar generation.

Those who fought never forgot what it was like to live in the trenches. It seemed to many as if the whole world had simply become a place made of mud. Poets Siegfried Sassoon and Rupert Brooke, among others, recorded the agony and courage of those who lost their lives and those who, though still alive, had lost their spirit.

Contemporary Britain

The twenties in England saw the same disillusion and breakdown of values that afflicted America after the war. Political commitment and a spirit of reform set

Winston S. Churchill (1874–1965).

in with the thirties, but this new spirit bowed before the onslaught of Adolf Hitler. Winston Churchill, a courageous and inspiring prime minister, led Britain through the dark days of World War II. From 1939 to 1945 England desperately needed that inspiration, for the Battle of Britain was fought not only by soldiers but by the British people at home. German aircraft tried to bomb England to its knees. Children were evacuated from cities; all Britons grew familiar with food shortages, air raids, and underground shelters. A fire-tested Britain emerged into the postwar world.

After the war the Labor Party created programs to meet Britain's enormous economic problems, aware that the sun was indeed setting on the empire. More British colonies achieved home rule, including India and Palestine. In 1957 Prime Minister Anthony Eden was forced to resign when his military effort to keep the Suez Canal open met with international protest. The Irish troubles continued to be one of the greatest causes of British anxiety. In 1982, however, Prime Minister Margaret Thatcher prevented Argentina from annexing one of the remnants of the empire, the Falkland Islands.

Britain helped to create the modern world, and the modern world has created a new Britain. The national identity is still a subject of controversy among British writers. There is no doubt, however, of the quantity and quality of literature that Britain produced in our time.

Twentieth-Century British Literature

The achievement of modern British literature lies in the outpouring of literature from Ireland, the development of the short story, new movements in poetry, exciting experiments in fiction, and drama worthy of the nation that bred Shakespeare. In each field, however, we need first to ask ourselves what makes that literature *modern*.

Modern literature is characterized by great differences from the past in both form and content. The literary changes that took place early in our century were more extreme than at any other time in literary history. Writers and other artists were creating a new way of seeing the world, of listening to it, of expressing feelings about it.

Spurred on by Ezra Pound's outcry, "Make it new!" poets in England and America broke out of established forms and meters. New rhythms were invented, especially in free verse, an approach that emphasized matching rhythm to meaning rather than remaining confined to arbitrary meters.

The development of psychology brought psychological realism into literature: Writers attempted to show not only what their characters thought but *how* they thought. The stream-of-consciousness technique, and various modifications of it, created a new attitude toward writing and reading.

The subject matter of literature changed too. With the shocks of the wars, technological advances, and greater social freedom, writers realized that they could and should write about *anything*. No subject was too dignified or undignified, too familiar or remote, to appear in a modern poem or novel.

Modern Poetry

No poet better demonstrates the range of modern poetic possibilities than the Irishman William Butler Yeats. Yeats also provides a bridge from the Victorian Age into the twentieth century. His early Romantic work, produced before the century turned, gradually became more realistic and direct, personal yet politically committed, and finally mystical and visionary. Yeats remains, in the opinion of many readers, the finest poet of our time.

Scene from a recent Abbey Theatre (Dublin) production of a Sean O'Casey play.

T. S. Eliot, an American expatriate, responded to the horror of World War I and the confusion of modern life with *The Waste Land* (1922). *The Waste Land* is a fragmented poem of disillusion and the difficulty of human communication in the modern world. With its portrayal of "hollow" people, its unconnected images, and its use of myths of the past to describe the present, it is perhaps the single most influential poem of the century.

W. H. Auden, Stephen Spender, and Louis MacNeice—important poets of the 1930s—suggested that the world could be improved. A liberal spirit of reform moves through their work. The Welshman Dylan Thomas, on the other hand, did not burden his poems with social or political ideas. His affirmation of life and his overpowering love of language make his poems sing with a musical quality surpassed only by William Butler Yeats.

After decades of innovation, poets since World War II have been free to develop in many different directions. The tradition of British poetry offers today's poets a wealth of sources to learn from or to react against. As a result, contemporary poetry ranges from Thom Gunn's use of nonpoetic language and subject matter to Ted Hughes's fascination with animals, from Charles Tomlinson's abstract images to Geoffrey Hill's new uses of myths.

Modern Drama

Drama in modern Britain thrives. Several major playwrights and theatrical movements, many accomplished actors, and innovative directors have established Britain's theaters as models for the world.

William Butler Yeats started the trend to poetic drama with plays based on Irish folklore, including *On Baile's Strand* (1904). Yeats helped found the Irish National Theater, a company that produced two remarkable playwrights and plays that are inescapably Irish in mood and content, mixing cynical comedy with stark realism. John Millington Synge's masterpiece is *The Playboy of the Western World* (1907), and Sean O'Casey is best known for *Juno and the Paycock* (1925) and *The Plough and the Stars* (1926).

Another Irish-born playwright left Ireland when he was twenty to become an Englishman and an entire theatrical movement in himself—George

Bernard Shaw. Shaw had a satiric wit and an almost Puritanical concern for setting things right. He applied his satirical approach to such contemporary and eternal themes as war, religion, and women's rights. *Pygmalion* is one of Shaw's most popular plays, a box-office success as well as a biting satire on male-female relationships and British class distinctions.

British dramatists of the twentieth century cover a broad spectrum of styles. Some followed the nineteenth-century convention of the "well-made play" with its carefully developed plot, characters, and setting. J. M. Barrie, for example, continued the tradition with *The Admirable Crichton* (1902) and *Peter Pan* (1904).

The well-made plot is less important than mood and character in the plays of T. S. Eliot and Harold Pinter. Eliot wrote several verse plays, including *Murder in the Cathedral* (1935) and several philosophical "comedies" including *The Cocktail Party* (1950). Harold Pinter's dramas, like *The Birthday Party* (1958), seem realistic but all have a sinister undercurrent beneath his characters' seemingly ordinary conversation. No playwright has been more experimental than Samuel Beckett, whose most famous play is *Waiting for Godot* (1952). Combinations of philosophy and comedy, reason and absurdity, Beckett's plays continue to be controversial and influential.

Illustration from an early edition of Joseph Conrad's *Lord Jim*.

Modern Prose

With the exceptions of Yeats and Eliot, Britain's greatest writers in this century have been novelists. In British fiction daring innovation produced a stunning string of achievements.

Virginia Woolf said, "On or about December 1910 human nature changed." Woolf knew perfectly well that it was not human nature that had changed but the ways human beings perceived one another. She reflected this enormous change in her elegant, intellectual, and introspective novels. Her use of stream of consciousness, lyric imagery, and sophisticated wit made modern masterpieces of *Mrs. Dalloway* (1922) and *To the Lighthouse* (1927).

Polish-born Joseph Conrad, for whom English was a second language, wrote lush and vivid adventures like *Lord Jim* (1900) that explored such themes as honor, fate, identity, and disillusion. The novels of D. H. Lawrence offered new definitions of human relationships and intense psychological insight into the working classes.

Woolf, Conrad, and Lawrence explored new territory for fiction. In this respect, however, no writer can match Irish novelist James Joyce. Joyce took the stream-of-consciousness technique to its limits in *Ulysses* (1922), creating a book that is simultaneously realistic, symbolic, poetic, didactic, comic, ironic, and mythic. In 1939 he published *Finnegans Wake*, a book that takes language itself to its limits. After Joyce every writer of fiction in our time has had to think differently about the nature of the novel.

These novelists and others—among them E. M. Forster, John Galsworthy, Aldous Huxley, Ford Madox Ford, C. P. Snow, Graham Greene, Doris Lessing, and Evelyn Waugh—also produced short stories. The short story is a recent development in fiction although its roots go back to Chaucer. The genre was developed in America, notably by Edgar Allan Poe (1809–1849), who described the short story as a fiction written to be read in one sitting and intended to create a single effect. The short story came late to Britain, possibly because the great novelists of the nineteenth century like Dickens and Thackeray found public favor with long works. In this century, however, Britain's best novelists have also written superb short stories. In fact, some authors—like Katherine Mansfield, Sean O'Faolain, and Nadine Gordimer—established their literary reputations largely through short stories.

In the space age, with all its advances in technology, the world seems to be a smaller place. Nevertheless, literature remains a major source of understanding and entertainment, just as it was in the time of Chaucer, Shakespeare, and Keats. Throughout this worldwide community, the global village, people continue to look to British literature for a glorious tradition that is still growing and seeking new directions.

TIME LINE

1901	Edward VII becomes king
1902	Joseph Conrad, *Heart of Darkness*
1905	First motor buses in London
1910	D. H. Lawrence, "Goose Fair"
1911	Rupert Brooke, *Poems*
1912	George Bernard Shaw, *Pygmalion*
1913	Suffragette demonstrations in London
1914	World War I begins
1917	Siegfried Sassoon, *Counter-Attack and Other Poems*
	W. B. Yeats, "The Wild Swans at Coole"
1918	Women over thirty are allowed to vote
1919	Lady Astor elected as first woman in Parliament
1920	Parliament passes Government of Ireland Act
1922	Katherine Mansfield, *The Garden Party and Other Stories*
	James Joyce, *Ulysses*
1925	T. S. Eliot, "The Hollow Men"
1929	Virginia Woolf, *A Room of One's Own*
1936	King Edward VIII abdicates, succeeded by George VI
1939	James Joyce, *Finnegans Wake*

KING EDWARD VII

T. S. ELIOT

VIRGINA WOOLF

JAMES JOYCE

1901	China: Boxer uprising ends
	Africa: Boer War begins
1902	Egypt: Aswan Dam opens
1910	France: Marie Curie, *Treatise on Radiography*
1911	China: Manchu dynasty falls; republic proclaimed
1913	Africa: Albert Schweitzer opens hospital in French Congo
1914	Panama Canal opens
1917	Russia: Revolution forces the czar from power
	Austria: Sigmund Freud, *Introduction to Psychoanalysis*
1918	Italy: Luigi Pirandello, *Six Characters in Search of an Author*
1920	Belgium: First postwar Olympic games held
1922	India: Gandhi sentenced to prison for civil disobedience
	Soviet states form U.S.S.R.
1925	Germany: Franz Kafka, *The Trial*
1929	Worldwide economic crisis after New York stock market crashes
1936	Spain: Civil war begins
1939	World War II begins when Germany invades Poland

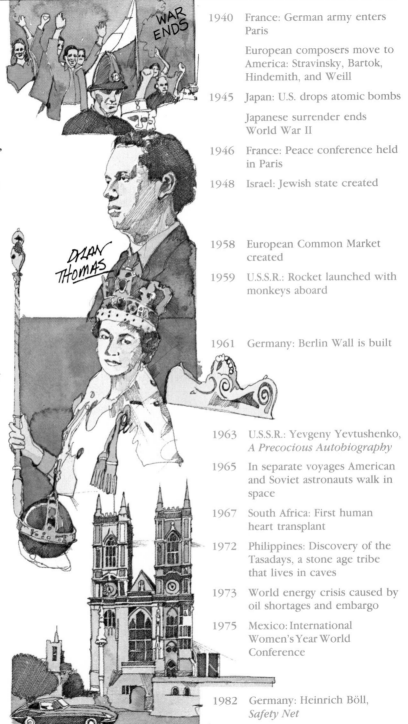

1940	Winston Churchill becomes prime minister
	W. H. Auden, "Musée des Beaux Arts"
1945	War ends in Europe
	Dylan Thomas, "Fern Hill"
1946	George Orwell, "Why I Write"
1948	Wartime bread rationing ends
1952	Elizabeth II becomes queen
1957	Samuel Beckett, *Endgame*
1958	First parking meters in London
1959	Robert Graves, *Collected Poems*
	Geoffrey Hill, *For the Unfallen*
1961	Louis MacNeice, *Eighty-five Poems*
	Sean O'Faolain, *I Remember, I Remember*
1962	Doris Lessing, *The Golden Notebook*
1965	Westminster Abbey is nine hundred years old
1967	Elizabeth II takes part in Canadian centennial
1972	Forty-seven-day coal strike cripples Britain
1973	Great Britain joins the Common Market
1979	Margaret Thatcher first woman to become prime minister

1940	France: German army enters Paris
	European composers move to America: Stravinsky, Bartok, Hindemith, and Weill
1945	Japan: U.S. drops atomic bombs
	Japanese surrender ends World War II
1946	France: Peace conference held in Paris
1948	Israel: Jewish state created
1958	European Common Market created
1959	U.S.S.R.: Rocket launched with monkeys aboard
1961	Germany: Berlin Wall is built
1963	U.S.S.R.: Yevgeny Yevtushenko, *A Precocious Autobiography*
1965	In separate voyages American and Soviet astronauts walk in space
1967	South Africa: First human heart transplant
1972	Philippines: Discovery of the Tasadays, a stone age tribe that lives in caves
1973	World energy crisis caused by oil shortages and embargo
1975	Mexico: International Women's Year World Conference
1982	Germany: Heinrich Böll, *Safety Net*

DRAMA

George Bernard Shaw   *1856–1950*

George Bernard Shaw ranks next to Shakespeare among English playwrights, and yet he did not begin to write drama until he was middle-aged. He made up for lost time with an amazing output of forty-seven plays during a creative life that spanned the Victorian and modern eras. A brilliant and opinionated man, Shaw was essentially self-educated, and he did a splendid job of teaching himself what he needed to know. Above all else, he was always vigorously engaged with the world around him; his long, productive life bristled with vitality, intelligence, and a consuming passion for ideas.

Irish by birth, Shaw came to England at the age of twenty and lived in and near London throughout the rest of his life. After writing several unsuccessful novels, the young Shaw turned to reviewing books and paintings in order to earn a living. He first became known as a music critic; from his mother, an aspiring singer, he had learned much about music, and he combined this knowledge with excellent taste and a sparkling prose style to become the most influential music critic of his day.

Shaw's lively intelligence did not confine itself to art, fiction, and music. At an early age he became committed to the cause of social reform. He joined the Fabian movement, a type of socialism founded in England in the 1880s to reform the social, economic, and political systems gradually through peaceful, democratic measures. Although he was shy by nature, Shaw turned himself into an outstanding public speaker. He continued to participate actively in politics the rest of his life. However, he found a particularly satisfying forum for his ideas in reviewing drama and, eventually, in writing plays of his own.

In the 1890s Shaw became recognized as London's wittiest and most stimulating drama critic. He took drama very seriously; in particular, he idolized the Norwegian dramatist Henrik Ibsen, whose unsparing critique of middle-class life revealed to Shaw the potential impact of drama upon society. After writing his influential essay "The Quintessence of Ibsenism" (1891), Shaw began to try his own hand at writing plays. The result, *Widowers' Houses* (produced in 1892), proved to be the first of many plays to come in the years ahead.

At first Shaw's plays were too controversial for English theatergoers, who were accustomed to light or sentimental entertainments but not to provocative examinations of moral and social issues. However, Shaw continued to write and publish his plays, usually accompanying them with lengthy and argumentative prefaces that expressed his ideas on a wide range of subjects. Eventually he established himself as the leading English playwright of the modern period with such works as *Arms and the Man* (1894),

Candida (1895), *Caesar and Cleopatra* (1898), *Man and Superman* (1903), *Major Barbara* (1907), *Pygmalion* (1912), *Heartbreak House* (1917), and *Saint Joan* (1923). For those achievements the playwright was awarded the Nobel Prize for Literature in 1925.

For the most part, Shaw's plays are **comedies of ideas,** works that present complex and often controversial themes within the framework of entertaining plots, appealing and unpredictable characters, and witty dialogue. Shaw's works are insistently rational, coolly ridiculing the conventions and prejudices of his time.

Pygmalion [pig māl′yən], written in 1912 and first produced in England in 1914, remains one of his most popular works. The title refers to a mythological king of Cyprus named Pygmalion, who carved a statue of a woman so beautiful that he fell in love with her. Aphrodite, the goddess of love, answered the lovesick king's prayers by bringing his statue, Galatea, to life. Shaw's play concerns a professor of phonetics (the study of the sounds of speech) who attempts to remold a cockney flower seller from the London slums into a refined lady by teaching her how to speak proper English.

Pygmalion gave Shaw a platform for many of his concerns. He was passionately interested in the English language and the varieties of ways in which people spoke (and misspoke) it. Shaw longed to simplify and reform English; he once pointed out that the rules of spelling in English are so inconsistent and confusing that the word *fish* could conceivably be spelled "ghoti" if the speller used the sound of *gh* in *enough,* the sound of *o* in *women,* and the sound of *ti* in the suffix *-tion.* The text of *Pygmalion* reflects some of his efforts at simplifying English usage—principally his omission of apostrophes in contractions such as *Ive* and *dont. Pygmalion* also allowed Shaw to present ideas about other topics that concerned him—such matters as social equality, male and female roles, and the relationship between what people seem to be and what they really are. Like his other successful plays, *Pygmalion* wins us over with its charm and then startles us out of our preconceptions with its keen intelligence.

Key Ideas in *Pygmalion*

As you read *Pygmalion,* look for references to each of the following. If you keep track of what Shaw says about these topics, you will begin to grasp the play's most important themes.

- Social equality
- The rights and social position of women
- Relationships between men and women
- Appearance and reality
- Language and individual identity

PREFACE TO PYGMALION

A Professor of Phonetics

The English have no respect for their language, and will not teach their children to speak it. They cannot spell it because they have nothing to spell it with but an old foreign alphabet of which only the consonants—and not all of them—have any agreed speech value. Consequently no man can teach himself what it should sound like from reading it; and it is impossible for an Englishman to open his mouth without making some other Englishman despise him. Most European languages are now accessible in black and white to foreigners: English and French are not thus accessible even to Englishmen and Frenchmen. The reformer we need most today is an energetic phonetic enthusiast: that is why I have made such a one the hero of a popular play.

There have been heroes of that kind crying in the wilderness for many years past. When I became interested in the subject towards the end of the eighteen-seventies, the illustrious Alexander Melville Bell, the inventor of Visible Speech, had emigrated to Canada, where his son invented the telephone; but Alexander J. Ellis[1] was still a London Patriarch, with an impressive head always covered by a velvet skull cap, for which he would apologize to public meetings in a very courtly manner. He and Tito Pagliardini,[2] another phonetic veteran, were men whom it was impossible to dislike. Henry Sweet,[3] then a young man, lacked their sweetness of character: he was about as conciliatory to conventional mortals as Ibsen[4] or Samuel Butler.[5] His great ability as a phonetician (he was, I think, the best of them all at his job) would have entitled him to high official recognition, and perhaps enabled him to popularize his subject, but for his Satanic contempt for all academic dignitaries and persons in general who thought more of Greek than of phonetics. Once, in the days when the Imperial Institute rose in South Kensington, and Joseph Chamberlain[6] was booming the Empire, I induced the editor of a leading monthly review to commission an article from Sweet on the imperial importance of his subject. When it arrived, it contained nothing but a savagely derisive attack on a professor of language and literature

---

1. **Alexander J. Ellis** (1814–1890): English philologist and mathematician.

2. **Tito Pagliardini** [tē′tō pal yär dē′ nē]
3. **Henry Sweet** (1845–1912): English grammarian and philologist.
4. **Ibsen:** Henrik Ibsen (1828–1906), Norwegian playwright, admired by Shaw for his portrayals of society.
5. **Samuel Butler** (1835–1902): English novelist.
6. **Joseph Chamberlain** (1836–1914): British statesman, known as the greatest orator of his time.

whose chair Sweet regarded as proper to a phonetic expert only. The article, being libellous, had to be returned as impossible; and I had to renounce my dream of dragging its author into the limelight. When I met him afterwards, for the first time for many years, I found to my astonishment that he, who had been a quite tolerably presentable young man, had actually managed by sheer scorn to alter his personal appearance until he had become a sort of walking repudiation of Oxford and all its traditions. It must have been largely in his own despite that he was squeezed into something called a Readership[7] of phonetics there. The future of phonetics rests probably with his pupils, who all swore by him; but nothing could bring the man himself into any sort of compliance with the university to which he nevertheless clung by divine right in an intensely Oxonian[8] way. I daresay his papers, if he has left any, include some satires that may be published without too destructive results fifty years hence. He was, I believe, not in the least an ill-natured man: very much the opposite, I should say; but he would not suffer fools gladly; and to him all scholars who were not rabid phoneticians were fools.

Those who knew him will recognize in my third act the allusion to the Current Shorthand in which he used to write postcards. It may be acquired from a four and sixpenny manual published by the Clarendon Press. The postcards which Mrs Higgins describes are such as I have received from Sweet. I would decipher a sound which a cockney would represent by *zerr,* and a Frenchman by *seu,* and then write demanding with some heat what on earth it meant. Sweet, with boundless contempt for my stupidity, would reply that it not only meant but obviously was the word Result, as no other word containing that sound, and capable of making sense with the context, existed in any language spoken on earth. That less expert mortals should require fuller indications was beyond Sweet's patience. Therefore, though the whole point of his Current Shorthand is that it can express every sound in the language perfectly, vowels as well as consonants, and that your hand has to make no stroke except the easy and current ones with which you write m, n, and u, l, p, and q, scribbling them at whatever angle comes easiest to you, his unfortunate determination to make this remarkable and quite legible script serve also as a shorthand reduced it in his own practice to the most inscrutable of cryptograms.[9] His true objective was the provision of a full, accurate, legible script for our language; but he was led past that by his contempt for the popular Pitman system of shorthand, which he called the Pitfall system. The triumph of Pitman was a triumph of business organization: there was a weekly paper to persuade you to learn Pitman: there were cheap textbooks and exercise books and transcripts of speeches for you to copy, and schools where experienced teachers coached you up to the necessary proficiency. Sweet could not organize his market in that fashion. He might as well have been the Sybil[10] who tore up the leaves of prophecy that nobody would attend to. The four and sixpenny manual, mostly in his lithographed handwriting, that was never vulgarly advertized, may perhaps some day be taken up by a syndicate and pushed upon the public as The Times pushed the Encyclopaedia Britannica; but until then it will certainly not prevail against Pitman. I have bought three copies of it during my lifetime; and I am informed by the publishers that its cloistered existence is still a steady and healthy one. I actually learned the system two several times; and yet the shorthand in which I am writing these lines is Pitman's. And the reason is, that my secretary cannot transcribe Sweet, having been perforce taught in the schools of Pitman. In America I could use the commercially organized Gregg shorthand, which has taken a hint from Sweet by making its letters writable (current, Sweet would have called them) instead of having to be geometrically

---

7. **Readership:** type of teaching position.
8. **Oxonian:** pertaining to Oxford University.

9. **cryptograms:** words written in code.
10. **Sybil:** prophetess in Greek and Roman mythology.

drawn like Pitman's; but all these systems, including Sweet's, are spoilt by making them available for verbatim reporting, in which complete and exact spelling and word division are impossible. A complete and exact phonetic script is neither practicable nor necessary for ordinary use; but if we enlarge our alphabet to the Russian size, and make our spelling as phonetic as Spanish, the advance will be prodigious.

Pygmalion Higgins is not a portrait of Sweet, to whom the adventure of Eliza Doolittle would have been impossible; still, as will be seen, there are touches of Sweet in the play. With Higgins's physique and temperament Sweet might have set the Thames on fire. As it was, he impressed himself professionally on Europe to an extent that made his comparative personal obscurity, and the failure of Oxford to do justice to his eminence, a puzzle to foreign specialists in his subject. I do not blame Oxford, because I think Oxford is quite right in demanding a certain social amenity from its nurslings (heavens knows it is not exorbitant in its requirement!); for although I well know how hard it is for a man of genius with a seriously underrated subject to maintain serene and kindly relations with the men who underrate it, and who keep all the best places for less important subjects which they profess without originality and sometimes without much capacity for them, still, if he overwhelms them with wrath and disdain, he cannot expect them to heap honors on him.

Of the later generations of phoneticians I know little. Among them towered Robert Bridges, to whom perhaps Higgins may owe his Miltonic sympathies, though here again I must disclaim all portraiture. But if the play makes the public aware that there are such people as phoneticians, and that they are among the most important people in England at present, it will serve its turn.

I wish to boast that Pygmalion has been an extremely successful play, both on stage and screen, all over Europe and North America as well as at home. It is so intensely and deliberately didactic, and its subject is esteemed so dry, that I delight in throwing it at the heads of the wiseacres[11] who repeat the parrot cry that art should never be didactic. It goes to prove my contention that great art can never be anything else.

Finally, and for the encouragement of people troubled with accents that cut them off from all high employment, I may add that the change wrought by Professor Higgins in the flower-girl is neither impossible nor uncommon. The modern concierge's[12] daughter who fulfills her ambition by playing the Queen of Spain in Ruy Blas[13] at the Théâtre Français is only one of many thousands of men and women who have sloughed off their native dialects and acquired a new tongue. Our West End shop assistants and domestic servants are bilingual. But the thing has to be done scientifically, or the last state of the aspirant may be worse than the first. An honest slum dialect is more tolerable than the attempts of phonetically untaught persons to imitate the plutocracy.[14] Ambitious flower-girls who read this play must not imagine that they can pass themselves off as fine ladies by untutored imitation. They must learn their alphabet over again, and different, from a phonetic expert. Imitation will only make them ridiculous.

NOTE FOR TECHNICIANS. A complete representation of the play as printed in this edition is technically possible only on the cinema screen or on stages furnished with exceptionally elaborate machinery. For ordinary theatrical use the scenes separated by rows of asterisks are to be omitted.

In the dialogue an e upside down indicates the indefinite vowel, sometimes called obscure or neutral, for which, though it is one of the commonest sounds in English speech, our wretched alphabet has no letter.

---

11. **wiseacres:** smart alecks.
12. **concierge's:** A concierge [kon′ sē urzh′] is the caretaker of a building.
13. **Ruy Blas** [r$\overline{oo}$ ē′ blas′]: poetic drama by French writer Victor Hugo (1802–1885).
14. **plutocracy:** the wealthy.

Eliza Doolittle.   Alfred Doolittle.   Henry Higgins.

George Bernard Shaw

Pygmalion

CHARACTERS

HENRY HIGGINS	MRS EYNSFORD HILL	TAXIMEN
COLONEL PICKERING	MISS EYNSFORD HILL	COUNT NEPOMMUCK
FREDDY EYNSFORD HILL	CONSTABLES	HOST
ALFRED DOOLITTLE	MRS HIGGINS	HOSTESS
BYSTANDERS	MRS PEARCE	FOOTMEN
ELIZA DOOLITTLE	PARLORMAID	

ACT ONE

London at 11.15 P.M. Torrents of heavy summer rain. Cab whistles blowing frantically in all directions. Pedestrians running for shelter into the portico of St Paul's church (not Wren's cathedral but Inigo Jones's church in Covent Garden vegetable market), among them a lady and her daughter in evening dress. All are peering out gloomily at the rain, except one man with his back turned to the rest, wholly preoccupied with a notebook in which he is writing.

The church clock strikes the first quarter.[1]

THE DAUGHTER [*in the space between the central pillars, close to the one on her left*] I'm getting chilled to the bone. What can Freddy be doing all this time? He's been gone twenty minutes.

THE MOTHER [*on her daughter's right*] Not so long. But he ought to have got us a cab by this.

A BYSTANDER [*on the lady's right*] He wont get no cab not until half-past eleven, missus, when they come back after dropping their theatre fares.

THE MOTHER. But we must have a cab. We cant stand here until half-past eleven. It's too bad.

---

1. **first quarter:** fifteen minutes after the hour.

THE BYSTANDER. Well, it ain't my fault, missus.

THE DAUGHTER. If Freddy had a bit of gumption, he would have got one at the theatre door.

THE MOTHER. What could he have done, poor boy?

THE DAUGHTER. Other people got cabs. Why couldnt he?

FREDDY *rushes in out of the rain from the Southampton Street side, and comes between them closing a dripping umbrella. He is a young man of twenty, in evening dress, very wet round the ankles.*

THE DAUGHTER. Well, havnt you got a cab?

FREDDY. Theres not one to be had for love or money.

THE MOTHER. Oh, Freddy, there must be one. You cant have tried.

THE DAUGHTER. It's too tiresome. Do you expect us to go and get one ourselves?

FREDDY. I tell you theyre all engaged. The rain was so sudden: nobody was prepared; and everybody had to take a cab. Ive been to Charing Cross one way and nearly to Ludgate Circus the other; and they were all engaged.

THE MOTHER. Did you try Trafalgar Square?

FREDDY. There wasnt one at Trafalgar Square.

THE DAUGHTER. Did you try?

FREDDY. I tried as far as Charing Cross Station. Did you expect me to walk to Hammersmith?

THE DAUGHTER. You havnt tried at all.

THE MOTHER. You really are very helpless, Freddy. Go again; and dont come back until you have found a cab.

FREDDY. I shall simply get soaked for nothing.

THE DAUGHTER. And what about us? Are we to stay here all night in this draught,[2] with next to nothing on? You selfish pig—

FREDDY. Oh, very well: I'll go, I'll go. [*He opens*

his *umbrella and dashes off Strandwards, but comes into collision with a flower girl who is hurrying in for shelter, knocking her basket out of her hands. A blinding flash of lightning, followed instantly by a rattling peal of thunder, orchestrates the incident*].

THE FLOWER GIRL. Nah then, Freddy: look wh' y' gowin, deah.[3]

FREDDY. Sorry [*he rushes off*].

THE FLOWER GIRL [*picking up her scattered flowers and replacing them in the basket*] Theres menners f' yer! Tə-oo banches o voylets trod into the mad.[4] [*She sits down on the plinth[5] of the column sorting her flowers, on the lady's right. She is not at all a romantic figure. She is perhaps eighteen, perhaps twenty, hardly older. She wears a little sailor hat of black straw that has long been exposed to the dust and soot of London and has seldom if ever been brushed. Her hair needs washing rather badly: its mousy color can hardly be natural. She wears a shoddy black coat that reaches nearly to her knees and is shaped to her waist. She has a brown skirt with a coarse apron. Her boots are much the worse for wear. She is no doubt as clean as she can afford to be; but compared to the ladies she is very dirty. Her features are no worse then theirs; but their condition leaves something to be desired; and she needs the services of a dentist*].

THE MOTHER. How do you know that my son's name is Freddy, pray?

THE FLOWER GIRL. Ow, eez yə-ooa san, is e? Wal, fewd dan y' də-ooty bawmz a mather should, eed now bettern to spawl a pore gel's flahrzn than ran awy athaht pyin. Will ye-oo py me f'them?[6] [*Here, with apologies, this desperate*

---

2. **draught** [draft]: draft.

3. **Nah . . . deah:** "Now then, Freddy: look where you're going, dear."
4. **Theres . . . mad:** "There's manners for you! Two bunches of violets trod into the mud."
5. **plinth:** block at the bottom of a column.
6. **Ow . . . them?** "Oh, he's your son, is he? Well, if you'd done your duty by him as a mother should, he'd know better than to spoil a poor girl's flowers and then run away without paying. Will you pay me for them?"

attempt to represent her dialect without a phonetic alphabet must be abandoned as unintelligible outside London].

THE DAUGHTER. Do nothing of the sort, mother. The idea!

THE MOTHER. Please allow me, Clara. Have you any pennies?

THE DAUGHTER. No. Ive nothing smaller than sixpence.

THE FLOWER GIRL [*hopefully*] I can give you change for a tanner,[7] kind lady.

THE MOTHER [*to* CLARA] Give it to me. [CLARA *parts reluctantly*]. Now [*to the* GIRL] This is for your flowers.

THE FLOWER GIRL. Thank you kindly, lady.

THE DAUGHTER. Make her give you the change. These things are only a penny a bunch.

THE MOTHER. Do hold your tongue, Clara. [*To the* GIRL] You can keep the change.

THE FLOWER GIRL. Oh, thank you, lady.

THE MOTHER. Now tell me how you know that young gentleman's name.

THE FLOWER GIRL. I didnt.

THE MOTHER. I heard you call him by it. Dont try to deceive me.

THE FLOWER GIRL [*protesting*] Who's trying to deceive you? I called him Freddy or Charlie same as you might yourself if you was talking to a stranger and wished to be pleasant.

THE DAUGHTER. Sixpence thrown away! Really, mamma, you might have spared Freddy that. [*She retreats in disgust behind the pillar*].

An elderly gentleman of the amiable military type rushes into the shelter, and closes a dripping umbrella. He is in the same plight as FREDDY, *very wet above the ankles. He is in evening dress, with a light over-coat. He takes the place left vacant by the* DAUGHTER.

THE GENTLEMAN. Phew!

THE MOTHER [*to the* GENTLEMAN] Oh, sir, is there any sign of its stopping?

THE GENTLEMAN. I'm afraid not. It started worse than ever about two minutes ago [*he goes to the plinth beside the* FLOWER GIRL; *puts up his foot on it; and stoops to turn down his trouser ends*].

THE MOTHER. Oh dear! [*She retires sadly and joins her daughter*].

THE FLOWER GIRL [*taking advantage of the military gentleman's proximity to establish friendly relations with him*] If it's worse, it's a sign it's nearly over. So cheer up, Captain; and buy a flower off a poor girl.

THE GENTLEMAN. I'm sorry. I havnt any change.

THE FLOWER GIRL. I can give you change, Captain.

THE GENTLEMAN. For a sovereign?[8] Ive nothing less.

THE FLOWER GIRL. Garn! Oh do buy a flower off me, Captain. I can change half-a-crown. Take this for tuppence.

THE GENTLEMAN. Now dont be troublesome: theres a good girl. [*Trying his pockets*] I really havnt any change—Stop: heres three hapence, if thats any use to you [*he retreats to the other pillar*].

THE FLOWER GIRL [*disappointed, but thinking three half-pence better than nothing*] Thank you, sir.

THE BYSTANDER [*to the* GIRL] You be careful: give him a flower for it. Theres a bloke[9] here behind taking down every blessed word youre saying. [*All turn to the man who is taking notes*].

---

7. **tanner:** slang for *sixpence.*

8. **sovereign:** English coin, as are *half-a-crown* and *tuppence* (two pence) in the lines that follow.
9. **bloke:** slang for man or fellow.

THE FLOWER GIRL [*springing up terrified*] I aint done nothing wrong by speaking to the gentleman. Ive a right to sell flowers if I keep off the kerb. [*Hysterically*] I'm a respectable girl: so help me, I never spoke to him except to ask him to buy a flower off me.

> *General hubbub, mostly sympathetic to the* FLOWER GIRL, *but deprecating her excessive sensibility. Cries of* Dont start hollerin. Who's hurting you? Nobody's going to touch you. Whats the good of fussing? Steady on. Easy, easy, etc., *come from the elderly staid spectators, who pat her comfortingly. Less patient ones bid her shut her head, or ask her roughly what is wrong with her. A remoter group, not knowing what the matter is, crowd in and increase the noise with question and answer:* Whats the row?[10] What-she do? Where is he? A tec[11] taking her down. What! him? Yes: him over there: Took money off the gentleman, etc.

THE FLOWER GIRL [*breaking through them to the* GENTLEMAN, *crying wildly*] Oh, sir, dont let him charge me. You dunno what it means to me. Theyll take away my character and drive me on the streets for speaking to gentlemen. They—

THE NOTE TAKER [*coming forward on her right, the rest crowding after him*] There! there! there! there! who's hurting you, you silly girl? What do you take me for?

THE BYSTANDER. It's aw rawt: e's a genleman: look at his bə-oots.[12] [*Explaining to the* NOTE TAKER] She thought you was a copper's nark, sir.

THE NOTE TAKER [*with quick interest*] Whats a copper's nark?

THE BYSTANDER [*inapt at definition*] It's a— well, it's a copper's nark, as you might say. What else would you call it? A sort of informer.

THE FLOWER GIRL [*still hysterical*] I take my Bible oath I never said a word—

THE NOTE TAKER [*overbearing but good-humored*] Oh, shut up, shut up. Do I look like a policeman?

THE FLOWER GIRL [*far from reassured*] Then what did you take down my words for? How do I know whether you took me down right? You just shew[13] me what youve wrote about me. [*The* NOTE TAKER *opens his book and holds it steadily under her nose, though the pressure of the mob trying to read it over his shoulders would upset a weaker man*]. Whats that? That aint proper writing. I cant read that.

THE NOTE TAKER. I can. [*Reads, reproducing her pronunciation exactly*] "Cheer ap, Keptin; n' baw ya flahr orf a pore gel."[14]

THE FLOWER GIRL [*much distressed*] It's because I called him Captain. I meant no harm. [*To the* GENTLEMAN] Oh, sir, dont let him lay a charge agen me for a word like that. You—

THE GENTLEMAN. Charge! I make no charge. [*To the* NOTE TAKER] Really, sir, if you are a detective, you need not begin protecting me against molestation by young women until I ask you. Anybody could see that the girl meant no harm.

THE BYSTANDERS GENERALLY [*demonstrating against police espionage*] Course they could. What business is it of yours? You mind your own affairs. He wants promotion, he does. Taking down people's words! Girl never said a word to him. What harm if she did? Nice thing a girl cant shelter from the rain without being insulted, etc., etc., etc. [*She is conducted by the more sympathetic demonstrators back to her plinth, where she resumes her seat and struggles with her emotion*].

THE BYSTANDER. He aint a tec. He's a blooming

---

10. **row** [rou]: trouble, disturbance.
11. **tec**: slang abbreviation for detective.
12. **It's . . . bə-oots**: "It's all right; he's a gentleman: look at his boots."

13. **shew** [shō]: archaic spelling of *show*.
14. **Cheer . . . gel**: "Cheer up, Captain; and buy a flower off a poor girl."

busybody: thats what he is, I tell you, look at his bə-oots.

THE NOTE TAKER [*turning on him genially*] And how are all your people down at Selsey?

THE BYSTANDER [*suspiciously*] Who told you my people come from Selsey?

THE NOTE TAKER. Never you mind. They did. [*To the* GIRL] How do you come to be up so far east? You were born in Lisson Grove.

THE FLOWER GIRL [*appalled*] Oh, what harm is there in my leaving Lisson Grove? It wasnt fit for a pig to live in; and I had to pay four-and-six[15] a week. [*In tears*] Oh, boo-hoo-oo—

THE NOTE TAKER. Live where you like; but stop that noise.

THE GENTLEMAN [*to the* GIRL] Come, come! he cant touch you: you have a right to live where you please.

A SARCASTIC BYSTANDER [*thrusting himself between the* NOTE TAKER *and the* GENTLEMAN] Park Lane, for instance. I'd like to go into the Housing Question with you, I would.

THE FLOWER GIRL [*subsiding into a brooding melancholy over her basket, and talking very low-spiritedly to herself*] I'm a good girl, I am.

THE SARCASTIC BYSTANDER [*not attending to her*] Do you know where I come from?

THE NOTE TAKER [*promptly*] Hoxton.

Titterings. Popular interest in the NOTE TAK-ER'S *performance increases.*

THE SARCASTIC ONE [*amazed*] Well, who said I didnt? Bly me! you know everything, you do.

THE FLOWER GIRL [*still nursing her sense of injury*] Aint no call to meddle with me, he aint.

THE BYSTANDER [*to her*] Of course he aint. Dont you stand it from him. [*To the* NOTE TAKER] See here: what call have you to know about people what never offered to meddle with you?

THE FLOWER GIRL. Let him say what he likes. I dont want to have no truck with him.

THE BYSTANDER. You take us for dirt under your feet, dont you? Catch you taking liberties with a gentleman!

THE SARCASTIC BYSTANDER. Yes: tell him where he come from if you want to go fortune-telling.

THE NOTE TAKER. Cheltenham, Harrow, Cambridge, and India.

THE GENTLEMAN. Quite right.

Great laughter. Reaction in the NOTE TAKER'S *favor. Exclamations of* He knows all about it. Told him proper. Hear him tell the toff[16] where he come from? *etc.*

THE GENTLEMAN. May I ask, sir, do you do this for your living at a music hall?

THE NOTE TAKER. I've thought of that. Perhaps I shall some day.

The rain has stopped; and the persons on the outside of the crowd begin to drop off.

THE FLOWER GIRL [*resenting the reaction*] He's no gentleman, he aint, to interfere with a poor girl.

THE DAUGHTER [*out of patience, pushing her way rudely to the front and displacing the* GENTLEMAN, *who politely retires to the other side of the pillar*] What on earth is Freddy doing? I shall get pneumownia if I stay in this draught any longer.

THE NOTE TAKER [*to himself, hastily making a note of her pronunciation of "monia"*] Earls-court.

THE DAUGHTER [*violently*] Will you please keep your impertinent remarks to yourself.

THE NOTE TAKER. Did I say that out loud? I didnt mean to. I beg your pardon. Your mother's Epsom, unmistakeably.

THE MOTHER [*advancing between the* DAUGHTER

---

15. **four-and-six:** four shillings six pence, then $1.50.

16. **toff:** slang for fashionable gentleman.

and the NOTE TAKER] How very curious! I was brought up in Largelady Park, near Epsom.

THE NOTE TAKER [*uproariously amused*] Ha! ha! What a devil of a name! Excuse me. [*To the* DAUGHTER] You want a cab, do you?

THE DAUGHTER. Dont dare speak to me.

THE MOTHER. Oh please, please, Clara. [*Her daughter repudiates her with an angry shrug and retires haughtily*] We should be so grateful to you, sir, if you found us a cab. [*The* NOTE TAKER *produces a whistle*] Oh, thank you. [*She joins her daughter*].

    The NOTE TAKER *blows a piercing blast.*

THE SARCASTIC BYSTANDER. There! I knowed he was a plainclothes copper.

THE BYSTANDER. That aint a police whistle: thats a sporting whistle.

THE FLOWER GIRL [*still preoccupied with her wounded feelings*] He's no right to take away my character.[17] My character is the same to me as any lady's.

THE NOTE TAKER. I dont know whether youve noticed it; but the rain stopped about two minutes ago.

THE BYSTANDER. So it has. Why didnt you say so before? and us losing our time listening to your silliness! [*He walks off towards the Strand*].

THE SARCASTIC BYSTANDER. I can tell where you come from. You come from Anwell. Go back there.

THE NOTE TAKER [*helpfully*] Hanwell.

THE SARCASTIC BYSTANDER [*affecting great distinction of speech*] Thenk you, teacher. Haw haw! So long [*he touches his hat with mock respect and strolls off*].

THE FLOWER GIRL. Frightening people like that! How would he like it himself?

THE MOTHER. It's quite fine now, Clara. We can walk to a motor bus. Come. [*She gathers her skirts above her ankles and hurries off towards the Strand*].

THE DAUGHTER. But the cab—[*her mother is out of hearing*]. Oh, how tiresome! [*She follows angrily*].

    All the rest have gone except the NOTE TAKER, *the* GENTLEMAN, *and the* FLOWER GIRL, *who sits arranging her basket, and still pitying herself in murmurs.*

THE FLOWER GIRL. Poor girl! Hard enough for her to live without being worried and chivied.[18]

THE GENTLEMAN [*returning to his former place on the* NOTE TAKER'S *left*] How do you do it, if I may ask?

THE NOTE TAKER. Simply phonetics. The science of speech. Thats my profession: also my hobby. Happy is the man who can make a living by his hobby! You can spot an Irishman or a Yorkshireman by his brogue. *I* can place any man within six miles. I can place him within two miles in London. Sometimes within two streets.

THE FLOWER GIRL. Ought to be ashamed of himself, unmanly coward.

THE GENTLEMAN. But is there a living in that?

THE NOTE TAKER. Oh yes. Quite a fat one. This is an age of upstarts. Men begin in Kentish Town with £80 a year, and end in Park Lane with a hundred thousand. They want to drop Kentish Town; but they give themselves away every time they open their mouths. Now I can teach them—

THE FLOWER GIRL. Let him mind his own business and leave a poor girl—

THE NOTE TAKER [*Explosively*] Woman: cease this detestable boohooing instantly; or else seek the shelter of some other place of worship.

---

17. **character:** reputation.

18. **worried and chivied:** worried and tormented.

THE FLOWER GIRL [*with feeble defiance*] Ive a right to be here if I like, same as you.

THE NOTE TAKER. A woman who utters such depressing and disgusting sounds has no right to be anywhere—no right to live. Remember that you are a human being with a soul and the divine gift of articulate speech: that your native language is the language of Shakespear and Milton and The Bible; and dont sit there crooning like a bilious pigeon.

THE FLOWER GIRL [*quite overwhelmed, looking up at him in mingled wonder and deprecation without daring to raise her head*] Ah-ah-ah-ow-ow-ow-oo!

THE NOTE TAKER [*whipping out his book*] Heavens! what a sound! [*He writes; then holds out the book and reads, reproducing her vowels exactly*] Ah-ah-ah-ow-ow-ow-oo!

THE FLOWER GIRL [*tickled by the performance, and laughing in spite of herself*] Garn![19]

THE NOTE TAKER. You see this creature with her kerbstone English: the English that will keep

---

19. **Garn!:** "Go on!"

her in the gutter to the end of her days. Well, sir, in three months I could pass that girl off as a duchess at an ambassador's garden party. I could even get her a place as lady's maid or shop assistant, which requires better English.

THE FLOWER GIRL. What's that you say?

THE NOTE TAKER. Yes, you squashed cabbage leaf, you disgrace to the noble architecture of these columns, you incarnate insult to the English language: I could pass you off as the Queen of Sheba. [*To the* GENTLEMAN] Can you believe that?

THE GENTLEMAN. Of course I can. I am myself a student of Indian dialects; and—

THE NOTE TAKER [*eagerly*] Are you? Do you know Colonel Pickering, the author of Spoken Sanscrit?

THE GENTLEMAN. I am Colonel Pickering. Who are you?

THE NOTE TAKER. Henry Higgins, author of Higgins's Universal Alphabet.

PICKERING [*with enthusiasm*] I came from India to meet you.

HIGGINS. I was going to India to meet you.

PICKERING. Where do you live?

HIGGINS. 27A Wimpole Street. Come and see me tomorrow.

PICKERING. I'm at the Carlton. Come with me now and lets have a jaw[20] over some supper.

HIGGINS. Right you are.

THE FLOWER GIRL [*to* PICKERING, *as he passes her*] Buy a flower, kind gentleman. I'm short for my lodging.

PICKERING. I really havnt any change. I'm sorry [*he goes away*].

HIGGINS [*shocked at the* GIRL'*s mendacity*[21]] Liar. You said you could change half-a-crown.

THE FLOWER GIRL [*rising in desperation*] You ought to be stuffed with nails, you ought. [*Flinging the basket at his feet*] Take the whole blooming basket for sixpence.

The church clock strikes the second quarter.

HIGGINS [*hearing in it the voice of God, rebuking him for his Pharisaic*[22] *want of charity to the poor girl*] A reminder. [*He raises his hat solemnly; then throws a handful of money into the basket and follows* PICKERING].

THE FLOWER GIRL [*picking up a half-crown*] Ah-ow-ooh! [*Picking up a couple of florins*] Aaah-ow-ooh! [*Picking up several coins*] Aaaaah-ow-ooh! [*Picking up a half-sovereign*] Aaaaaaaaaaaah-ow-ooh!!!

FREDDY [*springing out of a taxicab*] Got one at last. Hallo! [*To the* GIRL] Where are the two ladies that were here?

THE FLOWER GIRL. They walked to the bus when the rain stopped.

FREDDY. And left me with a cab on my hands! Damnation!

THE FLOWER GIRL [*with grandeur*] Never mind, young man. *I'm going home in a taxi.* [*She sails off to the cab. The driver puts his hand behind him and holds the door firmly shut against her. Quite understanding his mistrust, she shews him her handful of money*]. A taxi fare aint no object to me, Charlie. [*He grins and opens the door*]. Here. What about the basket?

THE TAXIMAN. Give it here. Tuppence extra.

LIZA. No: I dont want nobody to see it. [*She crushes it into the cab and gets in, continuing the conversation through the window*] Goodbye, Freddy.

FREDDY [*dazedly raising his hat*] Goodbye.

TAXIMAN. Where to?

LIZA. Bucknam Pellis [Buckingham Palace].

TAXIMAN. What d'ye mean—Bucknam Pellis?

LIZA. Dont you know where it is? In the Green Park, where the King lives. Goodbye, Freddy. Dont let me keep you standing there. Goodbye.

FREDDY. Goodbye. [*He goes*].

TAXIMAN. Here? Whats this about Bucknam Pellis? What business have you at Bucknam Pellis?

LIZA. Of course I havnt none. But I wasnt going to let him know that. You drive me home.

TAXIMAN. And wheres home?

LIZA. Angel Court, Drury Lane, next Meiklejohn's oil shop.

TAXIMAN. That sounds more like it, Judy. [*He drives off*].

* * * * * *

Let us follow the taxi to the entrance to Angel Court, a narrow little archway between two shops, one of them Meiklejohn's oil shop. When it stops there, Eliza gets out, dragging her basket with her.

---

20. **jaw**: slang for *chat*.
21. **mendacity**: lying.
22. **Pharisaic** [far'ə sā'ik]: alluding to the Pharisees, a group among the ancient Jews known for their strictness.

LIZA. How much?

TAXIMAN [*indicating the taximeter*] Cant you read? A shilling.

LIZA. A shilling for two minutes!!

TAXIMAN. Two minutes or ten: it's all the same.

LIZA. Well, I dont call it right.

TAXIMAN. Ever been in a taxi before?

LIZA [*with dignity*] Hundreds and thousands of times, young man.

TAXIMAN [*laughing at her*] Good for you, Judy. Keep the shilling, darling, with best love from all at home. Good luck! [*He drives off*].

LIZA [*humiliated*] Impidence!

She picks up the basket and trudges up the alley with it to her lodging: a small room with very old wall paper hanging loose in the damp places. A broken pane in the window is mended with paper. A portrait of a popular actor and a fashion plate of ladies' dresses, all wildly beyond poor ELIZA's *means, both torn from newspapers, are pinned up on the wall. A birdcage hangs in the window; but its tenant died long ago: it remains as a memorial only.*

These are the only visible luxuries: the rest is the irreducible minimum of poverty's needs: a wretched bed heaped with all sorts of coverings that have any warmth in them, a draped packing case with a basin and jug on it and a little looking glass over it, a chair and table, the refuse of some suburban kitchen, and an American alarum clock on the shelf above the unused fireplace: the whole lighted with a gas lamp with a penny in the slot meter. Rent: four shillings a week.

Here Eliza, chronically weary, but too excited to go to bed, sits, counting her new riches and dreaming and planning what to do with them, until the gas goes out, when she enjoys for the first time the sensation of being able to put in another penny without grudging it. This prodigal[23] mood does not extinguish her gnawing sense of the need for economy sufficiently to prevent her from calculating that she can dream and plan in bed more cheaply and warmly than sitting up without a fire. So she takes off her shawl and skirt and adds them to the miscellaneous bedclothes. Then she kicks off her shoes and gets into bed without any further change.

---

23. **prodigal:** extravagant, spendthrift.

STUDY QUESTIONS

Recalling
1. What is Higgins writing down when he first appears? What is Liza's reaction to his activities?
2. Why is the crowd suspicious of Higgins at first? What skill does he demonstrate to win them over? How does he make his living?
3. Why is Higgins offended by Liza? What does he say will keep her in the gutter all her life? What boasts does he make about her?
4. Describe Liza's mood when she goes to bed.

Interpreting
5. Explain how Liza's speech and behavior show that she comes from a different class from the mother and daughter she meets in the beginning of Act I.
6. What are your impressions of Liza and of Higgins in Act I? What seems most important to each? How does each treat other people? In what other ways are they different?
7. What effect does Shaw create by using labels rather than names for the characters through most of Act I?

Extending
8. Why do you think people often base their impressions of others on the way they speak? Why might it be difficult to change one's accent?

ACT TWO

Next day at 11 A.M. HIGGINS's *laboratory in Wimpole Street. It is a room on the first floor, looking on the street, and was meant for the drawing room. The double doors are in the middle of the back wall; and persons entering find in the corner to their right two tall file cabinets at right angles to one another against the walls. In this corner stands a flat writing-table, on which are a phonograph, a laryngoscope,[1] a row of tiny organ pipes with a bellows, a set of lamp chimneys for singing flames with burners attached to a gas plug in the wall by an indiarubber tube, several tuning-forks of different sizes, a life-size image of half a human head, shewing in section the vocal organs, and a box containing a supply of wax cylinders for the phonograph.*

Further down the room, on the same side, is a fireplace, with a comfortable leather-covered easy-chair at the side of the hearth nearest the door, and a coal-scuttle. There is a clock on the mantlepiece. Between the fireplace and the phonograph table is a stand for newspapers.

On the other side of the central door, to the left of the visitor, is a cabinet of shallow drawers. On it is a telephone and the telephone directory. The corner beyond, and most of the side wall, is occupied by a grand piano, with the keyboard at the end furthest from the door, and a bench for the players extending the full length of the keyboard. On the piano is a dessert dish heaped with fruit and sweets, mostly chocolates.

The middle of the room is clear. Besides the easy-chair, the piano bench, and two chairs at the phonograph table, there is one stray chair. It stands near the fireplace. On the walls, engravings: mostly Piranesi[2] and mezzotint[3] portraits. No paintings.

PICKERING *is seated at the table, putting down some cards and a tuning-fork which he has been using.* HIGGINS *is standing up near him, closing two or three file drawers which are hanging out. He appears in the morning light as a robust, vital, appetizing sort of man of forty or thereabouts, dressed in a professional-looking black frock-coat with a white linen collar and black silk tie. He is of energetic, scientific type, heartily, even violently interested in everything that can be studied as a scientific subject, and careless about himself and other people, including their feelings. He is, in fact, but for his years and size, rather like a very impetuous baby "taking notice" eagerly and loudly, and requiring almost as much watching to keep him out of unintended mischief. His manner varies from genial bullying when he is in a good humor to stormy petulance when anything goes wrong; but he is so entirely frank and void of malice that he remains likeable even in his least reasonable moments.*

HIGGINS [*as he shuts the last drawer*] Well, I think thats the whole show.

PICKERING. It's really amazing. I havnt taken half of it in, you know.

HIGGINS. Would you like to go over any of it again?

PICKERING [*rising and coming to the fireplace, where he plants himself with his back to the fire*] No, thank you: not now. I'm quite done up for this morning.

HIGGINS [*following him, and standing beside him on his left*] Tired of listening to sounds?

PICKERING. Yes. It's a fearful strain. I rather fancied myself because I can pronounce twenty-four distinct vowel sounds; but your hundred

---

1. **laryngoscope** [lə rin′ gə skōp]: instrument for examining the throat.
2. **Piranesi** [pēr′ ə nā′zēz]: works of the Italian artist Giambattista Piranesi (1720–1778).

3. **mezzotint** [met′sō tint]: engraving made from a metal plate, producing an effect of light and shade.

and thirty beat me. I cant hear a bit of difference between most of them.

HIGGINS [*chuckling, and going over to the piano to eat sweets*] Oh, that comes with practice. You hear no difference at first; but you keep on listening, and presently you find theyre all as different as A from B. [MRS PEARCE *looks in: she is* HIGGINS's *housekeeper*]. Whats the matter?

MRS PEARCE [*hesitating, evidently perplexed*] A young woman asks to see you, sir.

HIGGINS. A young woman! What does she want?

MRS PEARCE. Well, sir, she says youll be glad to see her when you know what she's come about. She's quite a common girl, sir. Very common indeed. I should have sent her away, only I thought perhaps you wanted her to talk into your machines. I hope Ive not done wrong; but really you see such queer people sometimes—youll excuse me, I'm sure, sir—

HIGGINS. Oh, thats all right, Mrs Pearce. Has she an interesting accent?

MRS PEARCE. Oh, something dreadful, sir, really. I dont know how you can take an interest in it.

HIGGINS [*to* PICKERING] Lets have her up. Shew her up, Mrs Pearce [*he rushes across to his working table and picks out a cylinder to use on the phonograph*].

MRS PEARCE [*only half resigned to it*] Very well, sir. It's for you to say. [*She goes downstairs*].

HIGGINS. This is rather a bit of luck. I'll shew you how I make records. We'll set her talking; and I'll take it down first in Bell's Visible Speech; then in broad Romic; and then we'll get her on the phonograph so that you can turn her on as often as you like with the written transcript before you.

MRS PEARCE [*returning*] This is the young woman, sir.

The FLOWER GIRL *enters in state. She has a hat with three ostrich feathers, orange, sky-blue, and red. She has a nearly clean apron, and the shoddy coat has been tidied a little. The pathos of this deplorable figure, with its innocent vanity and consequential air, touches* PICKERING, *who has already straightened himself in the presence of* MRS PEARCE. *But as to* HIGGINS, *the only distinction he makes between men and women is that when he is neither bullying nor exclaiming to the heavens against some feather-weight cross,[4] he coaxes women as a child coaxes its nurse when it wants to get anything out of her.*

HIGGINS [*brusquely, recognizing her with unconcealed disappointment, and at once, babylike, making an intolerable grievance of it*] Why, this is the girl I jotted down last night. She's no use: Ive got all the records I want of the Lisson Grove lingo; and I'm not going to waste another cylinder on it. [*To the* GIRL] Be off with you: I dont want you.

THE FLOWER GIRL. Dont you be so saucy. You aint heard what I come for yet. [*To* MRS PEARCE, *who is waiting at the door for further instructions*] Did you tell him I come in a taxi?

MRS PEARCE. Nonsense, girl! What do you think a gentleman like Mr Higgins cares what you came in?

THE FLOWER GIRL. Oh, we are proud! He aint above giving lessons, not him: I heard him say so. Well, I aint come here to ask for any compliment; and if my money's not good enough I can go elsewhere.

HIGGINS. Good enough for what?

THE FLOWER GIRL. Good enough for yə-oo. Now you know, dont you? I'm come to have lessons, I am. And to pay for em tə-oo: make no mistake.

HIGGINS [*stupent[5]*] Well!!! [*Recovering his breath with a gasp*] What do you expect me to say to you?

---

4. **feather-weight cross**: a very minor burden to bear.
5. **stupent**: amazed.

THE FLOWER GIRL. Well, if you was a gentleman, you might ask me to sit down, I think. Dont I tell you I'm bringing you business?

HIGGINS. Pickering: shall we ask this baggage to sit down, or shall we throw her out of the window?

THE FLOWER GIRL [*running away in terror to the piano, where she turns at bay*] Ah-ah-oh-ow-ow-ow-oo! [*Wounded and whimpering*] I wont be called a baggage when Ive offered to pay like any lady.

Motionless, the two men stare at her from the other side of the room, amazed.

PICKERING [*gently*] But what is it you want?

THE FLOWER GIRL. I want to be a lady in a flower shop stead of sellin at the corner of Tottenham Court Road. But they wont take me unless I can talk more genteel. He said he could teach me. Well, here I am ready to pay him—not asking any favor—and he treats me zif[6] I was dirt.

MRS PEARCE. How can you be such a foolish ignorant girl as to think you could afford to pay Mr Higgins?

THE FLOWER GIRL. Why shouldnt I? I know what lessons cost as well as you do; and I'm ready to pay.

HIGGINS. How much?

THE FLOWER GIRL [*coming back to him, triumphant*] Now youre talking! I thought youd come off it when you saw a chance of getting back a bit of what you chucked at me last night. [*Confidentially*] Youd had a drop in,[7] hadnt you?

HIGGINS [*peremptorily*] Sit down.

THE FLOWER GIRL. Oh, if youre going to make a compliment of it—

HIGGINS [*thundering at her*] Sit down.

MRS PEARCE [*severely*] Sit down, girl. Do as youre told.

THE FLOWER GIRL. Ah-ah-ah-ow-ow-oo! [*She stands, half rebellious, half bewildered*].

PICKERING [*very courteous*] Wont you sit down? [*He places the stray chair near the hearthrug between himself and* HIGGINS].

LIZA [*coyly*] Dont mind if I do. [*She sits down.* PICKERING *returns to the hearthrug*].

HIGGINS. Whats your name?

THE FLOWER GIRL. Liza Doolittle.

HIGGINS [*declaiming gravely*]
  Eliza, Elizabeth, Betsy and Bess,
  They went to the woods to get a bird's nes':

PICKERING. They found a nest with four eggs in it:

HIGGINS. They took one apiece, and left three in it.

They laugh heartily at their own fun.

LIZA. Oh, dont be silly.

MRS PEARCE [*placing herself behind* ELIZA's *chair*] You mustnt speak to the gentleman like that.

LIZA. Well, why wont he speak sensible to me?

HIGGINS. Come back to business. How much do you propose to pay me for the lessons?

LIZA. Oh, I know whats right. A lady friend of mine gets French lessons for eighteenpence an hour from a real French gentleman. Well, you wouldnt have the face to ask me the same for teaching me my own language as you would for French; so I wont give more than a shilling.[8] Take it or leave it.

HIGGINS [*walking up and down the room, rattling his keys and his cash in his pockets*] You know, Pickering, if you consider a shilling, not as a simple shilling, but as a percentage of this

---

6. **zif:** "as if."
7. **had a drop in:** been drinking.

8. **a shilling:** equivalent to about thirty cents.

girl's income, it works out as fully equivalent to sixty or seventy guineas[9] from a millionaire.

PICKERING. How so?

HIGGINS. Figure it out. A millionaire has about £150 a day. She earns about half-a-crown.

LIZA [*haughtily*] Who told you I only—

HIGGINS [*continuing*] She offers me two-fifths of her day's income for a lesson. Two-fifths of a millionaire's income for a day would be somewhere about £60. It's handsome. By George, it's enormous! it's the biggest offer I ever had.

LIZA [*rising, terrified*] Sixty pounds! What are you talking? I never offered you sixty pounds. Where would I get—

HIGGINS. Hold your tongue.

LIZA [*weeping*] But I aint got sixty pounds. Oh—

MRS PEARCE. Dont cry, you silly girl. Sit down. Nobody is going to touch your money.

HIGGINS. Somebody is going to touch you, with a broomstick, if you dont stop snivelling. Sit down.

LIZA [*obeying slowly*] Ah-ah-ah-ow-oo-o! One would think you was my father.

HIGGINS. If I decide to teach you, I'll be worse than two fathers to you. Here [*he offers her his silk handkerchief*]!

LIZA. Whats this for?

HIGGINS. To wipe your eyes. To wipe any part of your face that feels moist. Remember: thats your handkerchief; and thats your sleeve. Dont mistake the one for the other if you wish to become a lady in a shop.

LIZA, *utterly bewildered, stares helplessly at him.*

MRS PEARCE. It's no use talking to her like that, Mr Higgins: she doesnt understand you. Besides, youre quite wrong: she doesnt do it that

way at all [*she takes the handkerchief*].

LIZA [*snatching it*] Here! You give me that handkerchief. He gev it to me, not to you.

PICKERING [*laughing*] He did. I think it must be regarded as her property, Mrs Pearce.

MRS PEARCE [*resigning herself*] Serve you right, Mr Higgins.

PICKERING. Higgins: I'm interested. What about the ambassador's garden party? I'll say youre the greatest teacher alive if you make that good. I'll bet you all the expenses of the experiment you cant do it. And I'll pay for the lessons.

LIZA. Oh, you are real good. Thank you, Captain.

HIGGINS [*tempted, looking at her*] It's almost irresistible. She's so deliciously low—so horribly dirty—

LIZA [*protesting extremely*] Ah-ah-ah-ah-ow-ow-oo-oo!!! I aint dirty: I washed my face and hands afore I come, I did.

PICKERING. Youre certainly not going to turn her head with flattery, Higgins.

MRS PEARCE [*uneasy*] Oh, dont say that, sir: theres more ways than one of turning a girl's head; and nobody can do it better than Mr Higgins, though he may not always mean it. I do hope, sir, you wont encourage him to do anything foolish.

HIGGINS [*becoming excited as the idea grows on him*] What is life but a series of inspired follies? The difficulty is to find them to do. Never lose a chance: it doesnt come every day. I shall make a duchess of this draggletailed guttersnipe.

LIZA [*strongly deprecating this view of her*] Ah-ah-ah-ow-ow-oo!

HIGGINS [*carried away*] Yes: in six months—in three if she has a good ear and a quick tongue—I'll take her anywhere and pass her off as anything. We'll start today: now! this

---

9. **sixty . . . guineas:** equivalent to about $250.

moment! Take her away and clean her, Mrs Pearce. Monkey Brand,[10] if it wont come off any other way. Is there a good fire in the kitchen?

MRS PEARCE [*protesting*] Yes; but—

HIGGINS [*storming on*] Take all her clothes off and burn them. Ring up Whitely or somebody for new ones. Wrap her up in brown paper til they come.

LIZA. Youre no gentleman, youre not, to talk of such things. I'm a good girl, I am; and I know what the like of you are, I do.

HIGGINS. We want none of your Lisson Grove prudery here, young woman. Youve got to learn to behave like a duchess. Take her away, Mrs Pearce. If she gives you any trouble, wallop her.

LIZA [*springing up and running between* PICKERING *and* MRS PEARCE *for protection*] No! I'll call the police, I will.

MRS PEARCE. But Ive no place to put her.

HIGGINS. Put her in the dustbin.[11]

LIZA. Ah-ah-ah-ow-ow-oo!

PICKERING. Oh come, Higgins! be reasonable.

MRS PEARCE [*resolutely*] You must be reasonable, Mr Higgins: really you must. You cant walk over everybody like this.

HIGGINS, *thus scolded, subsides. The hurricane is succeeded by a zephyr of amiable surprise.*

HIGGINS [*with professional exquisiteness of modulation*] I walk over everybody! My dear Mrs Pearce, my dear Pickering, I never had the slightest intention of walking over anyone. All I propose is that we should be kind to this poor girl. We must help her to prepare and fit herself for her new station in life. If I did not express myself clearly it was because I did not wish to hurt her delicacy, or yours.

---

10. **Monkey Brand:** harsh cleaning agent.
11. **dustbin:** garbage can.

LIZA, *reassured, steals back to her chair.*

MRS PEARCE [*to* PICKERING] Well, did you ever hear anything like that, sir?

PICKERING [*laughing heartily*] Never, Mrs Pearce: never.

HIGGINS [*patiently*] Whats the matter?

MRS PEARCE. Well, the matter is, sir, that you cant take a girl up like that as if you were picking up a pebble on the beach.

HIGGINS. Why not?

MRS PEARCE. Why not! But you dont know anything about her. What about her parents? She may be married.

LIZA. Garn!

HIGGINS. There! As the girl very properly says, Garn! Married indeed! Dont you know that a woman of that class looks a worn out drudge of fifty a year after she's married?

LIZA. Whood marry me?

HIGGINS [*suddenly resorting to the most thrillingly beautiful low tones in his best elocutionary style*] By George, Eliza, the streets will be strewn with the bodies of men shooting themselves for your sake before Ive done with you.

MRS PEARCE. Nonsense, sir. You mustnt talk like that to her.

LIZA [*rising and squaring herself determinedly*] I'm going away. He's off his chump, he is. I dont want no balmies teaching me.

HIGGINS [*wounded in his tenderest point by her insensibility to his elocution*] Oh, indeed! I'm mad, am I? Very well, Mrs Pearce: you neednt order the new clothes for her. Throw her out.

LIZA [*whimpering*] Nah-ow. You got no right to touch me.

MRS PEARCE. You see now what comes of being saucy. [*Indicating the door*] This way, please.

LIZA [*almost in tears*] I didnt want no clothes.

I wouldnt have taken them [*she throws away the handkerchief*]. I can buy my own clothes.

HIGGINS [*deftly retrieving the handkerchief and intercepting her on her reluctant way to the door*] Youre an ungrateful wicked girl. This is my return for offering to take you out of the gutter and dress you beautifully and make a lady of you.

MRS PEARCE. Stop, Mr Higgins. I wont allow it. It's you that are wicked. Go home to your parents, girl; and tell them to take better care of you.

LIZA. I aint got no parents. They told me I was big enough to earn my own living and turned me out.

MRS PEARCE. Wheres your mother?

LIZA. I aint got no mother. Her that turned me out was my sixth stepmother. But I done without them. And I'm a good girl, I am.

HIGGINS. Very well, then, what on earth is all this fuss about? The girl doesnt belong to anybody—is no use to anybody but me. [*He goes to* MRS PEARCE *and begins coaxing*]. You can adopt her, Mrs Pearce: I'm sure a daughter would be a great amusement to you. Now dont make any more fuss. Take her downstairs; and—

MRS PEARCE. But whats to become of her? Is she to be paid anything? Do be sensible, sir.

HIGGINS. Oh, pay her whatever is necessary: put it down in the housekeeping book. [*Impatiently*] What on earth will she want with money? She'll have her food and her clothes. She'll only drink if you give her money.

LIZA [*turning on him*] Oh you are a brute. It's a lie: nobody ever saw the sign of liquor on me. [*To* PICKERING] Oh, sir: youre a gentleman: dont let him speak to me like that.

PICKERING [*in good-humored remonstrance*] Does it occur to you, Higgins, that the girl has some feelings?

HIGGINS [*looking critically at her*] Oh no, I dont think so. Not any feelings that we need bother about. [*Cheerily*] Have you, Eliza?

LIZA. I got my feelings same as anyone else.

HIGGINS [*to* PICKERING, *reflectively*] You see the difficulty?

PICKERING. Eh? What difficulty?

HIGGINS. To get her to talk grammar. The mere pronunciation is easy enough.

LIZA. I dont want to talk grammar. I want to talk like a lady in a flower-shop.

MRS PEARCE. Will you please keep to the point, Mr Higgins. I want to know on what terms the girl is to be here. Is she to have any wages? And what is to become of her when youve finished your teaching? You must look ahead a little.

HIGGINS [*impatiently*] Whats to become of her if I leave her in the gutter? Tell me that, Mrs Pearce.

MRS PEARCE. Thats her own business, not yours, Mr Higgins.

HIGGINS. Well, when Ive done with her, we can throw her back into the gutter; and then it will be her own business again; so thats all right.

LIZA. Oh, youve no feeling heart in you: you dont care for nothing but yourself. [*She rises and takes the floor resolutely*]. Here! Ive had enough of this. I'm going [*making for the door*]. You ought to be ashamed of yourself, you ought.

HIGGINS [*snatching a chocolate cream from the piano, his eyes suddenly beginning to twinkle with mischief*] Have some chocolates, Eliza.

LIZA [*halting, tempted*] How do I know what might be in them? Ive heard of girls being drugged by the like of you.

HIGGINS *whips out his penknife; cuts a chocolate in two; puts one half into his mouth and bolts it; and offers her the other half.*

HIGGINS. Pledge of good faith, Eliza. I eat one half: you eat the other. [LIZA *opens her mouth to retort: he pops the half chocolate into it*]. You shall have boxes of them, barrels of them, every day. You shall live on them. Eh?

LIZA [*who has disposed of the chocolate after being nearly choked by it*] I wouldnt have ate it, only I'm too ladylike to take it out of my mouth.

HIGGINS. Listen, Eliza. I think you said you came in a taxi.

LIZA. Well, what if I did? Ive as good a right to take a taxi as anyone else.

HIGGINS. You have, Eliza; and in future you shall have as many taxis as you want. You shall go up and down and round the town in a taxi every day. Think of that, Eliza.

MRS PEARCE. Mr Higgins: youre tempting the girl. It's not right. She should think of the future.

HIGGINS. At her age! Nonsense! Time enough to think of the future when you havnt any future to think of. No, Eliza: do as this lady does: think of other people's futures; but never think of your own. Think of chocolates, and taxis, and gold, and diamonds.

LIZA. No: I dont want no gold and no diamonds. I'm a good girl, I am. [*She sits down again, with an attempt at dignity*].

HIGGINS. You shall remain so, Eliza, under the care of Mrs Pearce. And you shall marry an officer in the Guards, with a beautiful moustache: the son of a marquis, who will disinherit him for marrying you, but will relent when he sees your beauty and goodness—

PICKERING. Excuse me, Higgins; but I really must interfere. Mrs Pearce is quite right. If this girl is to put herself in your hands for six months for an experiment in teaching, she must understand thoroughly what she's doing.

HIGGINS. How can she? She's incapable of understanding anything. Besides, do any of us understand what we are doing? If we did, would we ever do it?

PICKERING. Very clever, Higgins; but not to the present point. [*To* ELIZA] Miss Doolittle—

LIZA [*overwhelmed*] Ah-ah-ow-oo!

HIGGINS. There! Thats all youll get out of Eliza. Ah-ah-ow-oo! No use explaining. As a military man you ought to know that. Give her her orders: thats enough for her. Eliza: you are to live here for the next six months, learning how to speak beautifully, like a lady in a florist's shop. If youre good and do whatever youre told, you shall sleep in a proper bedroom, and have lots to eat, and money to buy chocolates and take rides in taxis. If youre naughty and idle you will sleep in the back kitchen among the black beetles, and be walloped by Mrs Pearce with a broomstick. At the end of six months you shall go to Buckingham Palace in a carriage, beautifully dressed. If the King finds out youre not a lady, you will be taken by the police to the Tower of London, where your head will be cut off as a warning to other presumptuous flower girls. If you are not found out, you shall have a present of seven-and-sixpence to start life with as a lady in a shop. If you refuse this offer you will be a most ungrateful wicked girl; and the angels will weep for you. [*To* PICKERING] Now are you satisfied, Pickering? [*To* MRS PEARCE] Can I put it more plainly and fairly, Mrs Pearce?

MRS PEARCE [*patiently*] I think youd better let me speak to the girl properly in private. I dont know that I can take charge of her or consent to the arrangement at all. Of course I know you dont mean her any harm; but when you get what you call interested in people's accents, you never think or care what may happen to them or you. Come with me, Eliza.

HIGGINS. Thats all right. Thank you, Mrs Pearce. Bundle her off to the bath-room.

LIZA [*rising reluctantly and suspiciously*] Youre a great bully, you are. I wont stay here if I dont like. I wont let nobody wallop me. I never asked to go to Bucknam Palace, I didnt. I was never in trouble with the police, not me. I'm a good girl—

MRS PEARCE. Dont answer back, girl. You dont understand the gentleman. Come with me. [*She

leads the way to the door, and holds it open for ELIZA].

LIZA [as she goes out] Well, what I say is right. I wont go near the King, not if I'm going to have my head cut off. If I'd known what I was letting myself in for, I wouldnt have come here. I always been a good girl; and I never offered to say a word to him; and I dont owe him nothing; and I dont care; and I wont be put upon; and I have my feelings the same as anyone else—

MRS PEARCE shuts the door; and ELIZA's plaints are no longer audible.

* * * * * *

Eliza is taken upstairs to the third floor greatly to her surprise; for she expected to be taken down to the scullery.[12] There Mrs Pearce opens a door and takes her into a spare bedroom.

MRS PEARCE. I will have to put you here. This will be your bedroom.

LIZA. O-h, I couldnt sleep here, missus. It's too good for the likes of me. I should be afraid to touch anything. I aint a duchess yet, you know.

MRS PEARCE. You have got to make yourself as clean as the room: then you wont be afraid of it. And you must call me Mrs Pearce, not missus. [She throws open the door of the dressing-room, now modernized as a bathroom].

LIZA. Gawd! whats this? Is this where you wash clothes? Funny sort of copper[13] I call it.

MRS PEARCE. It is not a copper. This is where we wash ourselves, Eliza, and where I am going to wash you.

LIZA. You expect me to get into that and wet myself all over! Not me. I should catch my death. I knew a woman did it every Saturday night; and she died of it.

---

12. **scullery:** workroom adjoining a kitchen, used for cleaning utensils and other rough kitchen work.

13. **copper:** large tub for washing clothes.

MRS PEARCE. Mr Higgins has the gentlemen's bathroom downstairs; and he has a bath every morning, in cold water.

LIZA. Ugh! He's made of iron, that man.

MRS PEARCE. If you are to sit with him and the Colonel and be taught you will have to do the same. They wont like the smell of you if you dont. But you can have the water as hot as you like. There are two taps: hot and cold.

LIZA [*weeping*] I couldnt. I dursnt. Its not natural: it would kill me. Ive never had a bath in my life: not what youd call a proper one.

MRS PEARCE. Well, dont you want to be clean and sweet and decent, like a lady? You know you cant be a nice girl inside if youre a dirty slut outside.

LIZA. Boohoo!!!!

MRS PEARCE. Now stop crying and go back into your room and take off all your clothes. Then wrap yourself in this [*Taking down a gown from its peg and handing it to her*] and come back to me. I will get the bath ready.

LIZA [*all tears*] I cant. I wont. I'm not used to it. Ive never took off all my clothes before. It's not right: it's not decent.

MRS PEARCE. Nonsense, child. Dont you take off all your clothes every night when you go to bed?

LIZA [*amazed*] No. Why should I? I should catch my death. Of course I take off my skirt.

MRS PEARCE. Do you mean that you sleep in the underclothes you wear in the daytime?

LIZA. What else have I to sleep in?

MRS PEARCE. You will never do that again as long as you live here. I will get you a proper nightdress.

LIZA. Do you mean change into cold things and lie awake shivering half the night? You want to kill me, you do.

MRS PEARCE. I want to change you from a frowzy slut to a clean respectable girl fit to sit with the gentlemen in the study. Are you going to trust me and do what I tell you or be thrown out and sent back to your flower basket?

LIZA. But you dont know what the cold is to me. You dont know how I dread it.

MRS PEARCE. Your bed won't be cold here: I will put a hot water bottle in it. [*Pushing her into the bedroom*] Off with you and undress.

LIZA. Oh, if only I'd known what a dreadful thing it is to be clean I'd never have come. I didnt know when I was well off. I— [MRS PEARCE *pushes her through the door, but leaves it partly open lest her prisoner should take to flight*].

MRS PEARCE *puts on a pair of white rubber sleeves, and fills the bath, mixing hot and cold, and testing the result with the bath thermometer. She perfumes it with a handful of bath salts and adds a palmful of mustard. She then takes a formidable looking long handled scrubbing brush and soaps it profusely with a ball of scented soap.*

ELIZA *comes back with nothing on but the bath gown huddled tightly round her, a piteous spectacle of abject terror.*

MRS PEARCE. Now come along. Take that thing off.

LIZA. Oh I couldnt, Mrs Pearce: I reely couldnt. I never done such a thing.

MRS PEARCE. Nonsense. Here: step in and tell me whether it's hot enough for you.

LIZA. Ah-oo! Ah-oo! It's too hot.

MRS PEARCE [*deftly snatching the gown away and throwing* ELIZA *down on her back*]. It wont hurt you. [*She sets to work with the scrubbing brush*].

ELIZA's *screams are heartrending.*

* * * * * *

Meanwhile the Colonel has been having it out with Higgins about Eliza. Pickering has come from the hearth to the chair and seated himself astride of it with his arms on the back to cross-examine him.

PICKERING. Excuse the straight question, Higgins. Are you a man of good character where women are concerned?

HIGGINS [*moodily*] Have you ever met a man of good character where women are concerned?

PICKERING. Yes: very frequently.

HIGGINS [*dogmatically, lifting himself on his hands to the level of the piano, and sitting on it with a bounce*] Well, I havnt. I find that the moment I let a woman make friends with me, she becomes jealous, exacting, suspicious, and a damned nuisance. I find that the moment I let myself make friends with a woman, I become selfish and tyrannical. Women upset everything. When you let them into your life, you find that the woman is driving at one thing and youre driving at another.

PICKERING. At what, for example?

HIGGINS [*coming off the piano restlessly*] Oh, Lord knows! I suppose the woman wants to live her own life; and the man wants to live his; and each tries to drag the other on to the wrong track. One wants to go north and the other south; and the result is that both have to go east, though they both hate the east wind. [*He sits down on the bench at the keyboard*]. So here I am, a confirmed old bachelor, and likely to remain so.

PICKERING [*rising and standing over him gravely*] Come, Higgins! You know what I mean. If I'm to be in this business I shall feel responsible for that girl. I hope it's understood that no advantage is to be taken of her position.

HIGGINS. What! That thing! Sacred, I assure you. [*Rising to explain*] You see, she'll be a pupil; and teaching would be impossible unless pupils were sacred. Ive taught scores of American millionairesses how to speak English: the best looking women in the world. I'm seasoned.

They might as well be blocks of wood. *I* might as well be a block of wood. It's—

MRS PEARCE *opens the door. She has* ELIZA's *hat in her hand.* PICKERING *retires to the easy-chair at the hearth and sits down.*

HIGGINS [*eagerly*] Well, Mrs Pearce: is it all right?

MRS PEARCE [*at the door*] I just wish to trouble you with a word, if I may, Mr Higgins.

HIGGINS. Yes, certainly. Come in. [*She comes forward*]. Dont burn that, Mrs Pearce. I'll keep it as a curiosity. [*He takes the hat*].

MRS PEARCE. Handle it carefully, sir, please. I had to promise her not to burn it; but I had better put it in the oven for a while.

HIGGINS [*putting it down hastily on the piano*] Oh! thank you. Well, what have you to say to me?

PICKERING. Am I in the way?

MRS PEARCE. Not in the least, sir. Mr Higgins: will you please be very particular what you say before the girl?

HIGGINS [*sternly*] Of course. I'm always particular about what I say. Why do you say this to me?

MRS PEARCE [*unmoved*] No, sir: youre not at all particular when youve mislaid anything or when you get a little impatient. Now it doesnt matter before me: I'm used to it. But you really must not swear before the girl.

HIGGINS [*indignantly*] I swear! [*Most emphatically*] I never swear. I detest the habit. What the devil do you mean?

MRS PEARCE [*stolidly*] Thats what I mean, sir. You swear a great deal too much. I dont mind your damning and blasting, and what the devil and where the devil and who the devil—

HIGGINS. Mrs Pearce: this language from your lips! Really!

MRS PEARCE [*not to be put off*]—but there is a

certain word[14] I must ask you not to use. The girl used it herself when she began to enjoy the bath. It begins with the same letter as bath. She knows no better: she learnt it at her mother's knee. But she must not hear it from your lips.

HIGGINS [*loftily*] I cannot charge myself with having ever uttered it, Mrs Pearce. [*She looks at him steadfastly. He adds, hiding an uneasy conscience with a judicial air*] Except perhaps in a moment of extreme and justifiable excitement.

MRS PEARCE. Only this morning, sir, you applied it to your boots, to the butter, and to the brown bread.

HIGGINS. Oh, that! Mere alliteration, Mrs Pearce, natural to a poet.

MRS PEARCE. Well, sir, whatever you choose to call it, I beg you not to let the girl hear you repeat it.

HIGGINS. Oh, very well, very well. Is that all?

MRS PEARCE. No, sir. We shall have to be very particular with this girl as to personal cleanliness.

HIGGINS. Certainly. Quite right. Most important.

MRS PEARCE. I mean not to be slovenly about her dress or untidy in leaving things about.

HIGGINS [*going to her solemnly*] Just so. I intended to call your attention to that. [*He passes on to* PICKERING, *who is enjoying the conversation immensely*]. It is these little things that matter, Pickering. Take care of the pence and the pounds will take care of themselves is as true of personal habits as of money. [*He comes to anchor on the hearthrug, with the air of a man in an unassailable position*].

MRS PEARCE. Yes, sir. Then might I ask you not to come down to breakfast in your dressing-gown, or at any rate not to use it as a napkin to the extent you do, sir. And if you would be so good as not to eat everything off the same plate, and to remember not to put the porridge saucepan out of your hand on the clean table-cloth, it would be a better example to the girl. You know you nearly choked yourself with a fishbone in a jam only last week.

HIGGINS [*routed from the hearthrug and drifting back to the piano*] I may do these things sometimes in absence of mind; but surely I dont do them habitually. [*Angrily*] By the way: my dressing-gown smells most damnably of benzine.

MRS PEARCE. No doubt it does, Mr Higgins. But if you will wipe your fingers—

HIGGINS [*yelling*] Oh very well, very well: I'll wipe them in my hair in future.

MRS PEARCE. I hope youre not offended, Mr Higgins.

HIGGINS [*shocked at finding himself thought capable of an unamiable sentiment*] Not at all, not at all. Youre quite right, Mrs Pearce: I shall be particularly careful before the girl. Is that all?

MRS PEARCE. No, sir. Might she use some of those Japanese dresses you brought from abroad? I really cant put her back into her old things.

HIGGINS. Certainly. Anything you like. Is that all?

MRS PEARCE. Thank you, sir. Thats all. [*She goes out*].

HIGGINS. You know, Pickering, that woman has the most extraordinary ideas about me. Here I am, a shy, diffident sort of man. Ive never been able to feel really grown-up and tremendous, like other chaps. And yet she's firmly persuaded that I'm an arbitrary overbearing bossing kind of person. I cant account for it.

MRS PEARCE *returns*.

MRS PEARCE. If you please, sir, the trouble's be-

---

14. **certain word:** The word is *bloody*, in England much stronger profanity early in the century than it is now.

ginning already. Theres a dustman[15] downstairs, Alfred Doolittle, wants to see you. He says you have his daughter here.

PICKERING [*rising*] Phew! I say!

HIGGINS [*promptly*] Send the blackguard[16] up.

MRS PEARCE. Oh, very well, sir. [*She goes out*].

PICKERING. He may not be a blackguard, Higgins.

HIGGINS. Nonsense. Of course he's a blackguard.

PICKERING. Whether he is or not, I'm afraid we shall have some trouble with him.

HIGGINS [*confidently*] Oh no: I think not. If theres any trouble he shall have it with me, not I with him. And we are sure to get something interesting out of him.

PICKERING. About the girl?

HIGGINS. No. I mean his dialect.

PICKERING. Oh!

MRS PEARCE [*at the door*] Doolittle, sir. [*She admits* DOOLITTLE *and retires*].

ALFRED *is an elderly but vigorous dustman, clad in the costume of his profession, including a hat with a back brim covering his neck and shoulders. He has well marked and rather interesting features, and seems equally free from fear and conscience. He has a remarkably expressive voice, the result of a habit of giving vent to his feelings without reserve. His present pose is that of wounded honor and stern resolution.*

DOOLITTLE [*at the door, uncertain which of the two gentlemen is his man*] Professor Iggins?

HIGGINS. Here. Good morning. Sit down.

DOOLITTLE. Morning, Governor. [*He sits down magisterially*]. I come about a very serious matter, Governor.

---

15. **dustman**: garbage collector.
16. **blackguard** [blag′ərd]: rascal, scoundrel.

HIGGINS [*to* PICKERING] Brought up in Hounslow. Mother Welsh, I should think. [DOOLITTLE *opens his mouth, amazed.* HIGGINS *continues*] What do you want, Doolittle?

DOOLITTLE [*menacingly*] I want my daughter: thats what I want. See?

HIGGINS. Of course you do. Youre her father, arnt you? You dont suppose anyone else wants her, do you? I'm glad to see you have some spark of family feeling left. She's upstairs. Take her away at once.

DOOLITTLE [*rising, fearfully taken aback*] What!

HIGGINS. Take her away. Do you suppose I'm going to keep your daughter for you?

DOOLITTLE [*remonstrating*] Now, now, look here, Governor. Is this reasonable? Is it fairity to take advantage of a man like this? The girl belongs to me. You got her. Where do I come in? [*He sits down again*].

HIGGINS. Your daughter had the audacity to come to my house and ask me to teach her how to speak properly so that she could get a place in a flower-shop. This gentleman and my housekeeper have been here all the time. [*Bullying him*] How dare you come here and attempt to blackmail me? You sent her here on purpose.

DOOLITTLE [*protesting*] No, Governor.

HIGGINS. You must have. How else could you possibly know that she is here?

DOOLITTLE. Don't take a man up like that, Governor.

HIGGINS. The police shall take you up. This is a plant—a plot to extort money by threats. I shall telephone for the police [*he goes resolutely to the telephone and opens the directory*]

DOOLITTLE. Have I asked you for a brass farthing? I leave it to the gentleman here: have I said a word about money?

HIGGINS [*throwing the book aside and marching down on* DOOLITTLE *with a poser*] What else did you come for?

DOOLITTLE [*sweetly*] Well, what would a man come for? Be human, Governor.

HIGGINS [*disarmed*] Alfred: did you put her up to it?

DOOLITTLE. So help me, Governor. I never did. I take my Bible oath I aint seen the girl these two months past.

HIGGINS. Then how did you know she was here?

DOOLITTLE [*"most musical, most melancholy"*] I'll tell you, Governor, if youll only let me get a word in. I'm willing to tell you. I'm wanting to tell you. I'm waiting to tell you.

HIGGINS. Pickering: this chap has a certain natural gift of rhetoric. Observe the rhythm of his native woodnotes wild. "I'm willing to tell you: I'm wanting to tell you: I'm waiting to tell you." Sentimental rhetoric! thats the Welsh strain in him. It also accounts for his mendacity and dishonesty.

PICKERING. Oh, please, Higgins: I'm west country myself. [*To* DOOLITTLE] How did you know the girl was here if you didnt send her?

DOOLITTLE. It was like this, Governor. The girl took a boy in the taxi to give him a jaunt. Son of her landlady, he is. He hung about on the chance of her giving him another ride home. Well, she sent him back for her luggage when she heard you was willing for her to stop here. I met the boy at the corner of Long Acre and Endell Street.

HIGGINS. Public house. Yes?

DOOLITTLE. The poor man's club, Governor: why shouldnt I?

PICKERING. Do let him tell his story, Higgins.

DOOLITTLE. He told me what was up. And I ask you, what was my feelings and my duty as a father? I says to the boy, "You bring me the luggage," I says—

PICKERING. Why didnt you go for it yourself?

DOOLITTLE. Landlady wouldnt have trusted me with it, Governor. She's that kind of woman: you know. I had to give the boy a penny afore he trusted me with it, the little swine. I brought it to her just to oblige you like, and make myself agreeable. Thats all.

HIGGINS. How much luggage?

DOOLITTLE. Musical instrument, Governor. A few pictures, a trifle of jewelry, and a birdcage. She said she didnt want no clothes. What was I to think from that, Governor? I ask you as a parent what was I to think?

HIGGINS. So you came to rescue her from worse than death, eh?

DOOLITTLE [*appreciatively: relieved at being so well understood*] Just so, Governor. That's right.

PICKERING. But why did you bring her luggage if you intended to take her away?

DOOLITTLE. Have I said a word about taking her away? Have I now?

HIGGINS [*determinedly*] Youre going to take her away, double quick. [*He crosses to the hearth and rings the bell*].

DOOLITTLE [*rising*] No, Governor. Dont say that. I'm not the man to stand in my girl's light. Heres a career opening for her, as you might say; and—

MRS PEARCE *opens the door and awaits orders.*

HIGGINS. Mrs Pearce: this is Eliza's father. He has come to take her away. Give her to him. [*He goes back to the piano, with an air of washing his hands of the whole affair*].

DOOLITTLE. No. This is a misunderstanding. Listen here—

MRS PEARCE. He cant take her away. Mr. Higgins: how can he? You told me to burn her clothes.

DOOLITTLE. Thats right. I cant carry the girl

through the streets like a blooming monkey, can I? I put it to you.

HIGGINS. You have put it to me that you want your daughter. If she has no clothes go out and buy her some.

DOOLITTLE [*desperate*] Wheres the clothes she come in? Did I burn them or did your missus here?

MRS PEARCE. I am the housekeeper, if you please. I have sent for some clothes for your girl. When they come you can take her away. You can wait in the kitchen. This way, please.

DOOLITTLE, much troubled, accompanies her to the door; then hesitates; finally turns confidentially to HIGGINS.

DOOLITTLE. Listen here, Governor. You and me is men of the world, aint we?

HIGGINS. Oh! Men of the world, are we? Youd better go, Mrs Pearce.

MRS PEARCE. I think so, indeed, sir. [*She goes, with dignity*].

PICKERING. The floor is yours, Mr Doolittle.

DOOLITTLE [*to* PICKERING] I thank you, Governor. [*To* HIGGINS, *who takes refuge on the piano bench, a little overwhelmed by the proximity of his visitor; for* DOOLITTLE *has a professional flavour of dust about him*]. Well, the truth is, Ive taken a sort of fancy to you, Governor; and if you want the girl, I'm not so set on having her back home again but what I might be open to an arrangement. Regarded in the light of a young woman, she's a fine handsome girl. As a daughter she's not worth her keep; and so I tell you straight. All I ask is my rights as a father; and youre the last man alive to expect me to let her go for nothing; for I can see youre one of the straight sort, Governor. Well, whats a five-pound note to you? and whats Eliza to me? [*He turns to his chair and sits down judicially*].

PICKERING. I think you ought to know, Doolittle, that Mr Higgins's intentions are entirely honorable.

DOOLITTLE. Course they are, Governor. If I thought they wasnt, I'd ask fifty.

HIGGINS [*revolted*] Do you mean to say that you would sell your daughter for £50?

DOOLITTLE. Not in a general way I would; but to oblige a gentleman like you I'd do a good deal, I do assure you.

PICKERING. Have you no morals, man?

DOOLITTLE [*unabashed*] Cant afford them, Governor. Neither could you if you was as poor as me. Not that I mean any harm, you know. But if Liza is going to have a bit out of this, why not me too?

HIGGINS [*troubled*] I dont know what to do, Pickering. There can be no question that as a matter of morals it's a positive crime to give this chap a farthing. And yet I feel a sort of rough justice in his claim.

DOOLITTLE. Thats it, Governor. Thats all I say. A father's heart, as it were.

PICKERING. Well, I know the feeling; but really it seems hardly right—

DOOLITTLE. Dont say that, Governor. Dont look at it that way. What am I, Governors both? I ask you, what am I? I'm one of the undeserving poor: thats what I am. Think of what that means to a man. It means that he's up agen middle class morality all the time. If theres anything going, and I put in for a bit of it, it's always the same story: "Youre undeserving; so you cant have it." But my needs is as great as the most deserving widows' that ever got money out of six different charities in one week for the death of the same husband. I dont need less than a deserving man: I need more. I dont eat less hearty than him; and I drink a lot more. I want a bit of amusement, cause I'm a thinking man. I want cheerfulness and a song and a band when I feel low. Well, they charge me just the same for everything as they charge the deserving. What is middle class morality? Just an excuse for never giving me anything. Therefore, I ask you, as two gentlemen, not to play that game on me. I'm playing straight with you. I aint pretending to be deserving. I'm undeserving; and I mean to go on being undeserving. I like it; and thats the truth. Will you take advantage of a man's nature to do him out of the price of his own daughter what he's brought up and fed and clothed by the sweat of his brow until she's growed big enough to be interesting to you two gentlemen? Is five pounds unreasonable? I put it to you; and I leave it to you.

HIGGINS [*rising, and going over to* PICKERING] Pickering: if we were to take this man in hand for three months, he could choose between a seat in the Cabinet and a popular pulpit in Wales.

PICKERING. What do you say to that, Doolittle?

DOOLITTLE. Not me, Governor, thank you kindly. Ive heard all the preachers and all the prime ministers—for I'm a thinking man and game for politics or religion or social reform same as all the other amusements—and I tell you it's a dog's life any way you look at it. Undeserving poverty is my line. Taking one station in society with another, it's—it's—well, it's the only one that has any ginger in it, to my taste.

HIGGINS. I suppose we must give him a fiver.

PICKERING. He'll make a bad use of it, I'm afraid.

DOOLITTLE. Not me, Governor, so help me I wont. Dont you be afraid that I'll save it and spare it and live idle on it. There wont be a penny of it left by Monday: I'll have to go to work same as if I'd never had it. It wont pauperize me, you bet. Just one good spree for myself and the missus, giving pleasure to ourselves and employment to others, and satisfaction to you to think it's not been throwed away. You couldnt spend it better.

HIGGINS [*taking out his pocket book and coming between* DOOLITTLE *and the piano*] This is irresistible. Lets give him ten. [*He offers two notes to the* DUSTMAN].

DOOLITTLE. No, Governor. She wouldnt have the heart to spend ten; and perhaps I shouldnt neither. Ten pounds is a lot of money: it makes a man feel prudent like; and then goodbye to happiness. You give me what I ask you, Governor: not a penny more, and not a penny less.

PICKERING. Why dont you marry that missus of yours? I rather draw the line at encouraging that sort of immorality.

DOOLITTLE. Tell her so, Governor: tell her so. I'm willing. It's me that suffers by it. Ive no hold on her. I got to be agreeable to her. I got to give her presents. I got to buy her clothes something sinful. I'm a slave to that woman, Governor, just because I'm not her lawful husband. And she knows it too. Catch her marrying me! Take my advice, Governor: marry Eliza while she's young and dont know no better. If you dont youll be sorry for it after. If you do, she'll be sorry for it after; but better her than you, because youre a man, and she's only a woman and dont know how to be happy anyhow.

HIGGINS. Pickering: if we listen to this man another minute, we shall have no convictions left. [*To* DOOLITTLE] Five pounds I think you said.

DOOLITTLE. Thank you kindly, Governor.

HIGGINS. Youre sure you wont take ten?

DOOLITTLE. Not now. Another time, Governor.

HIGGINS [*handing him a five-pound note*] Here you are.

DOOLITTLE. Thank you, Governor. Good morning. [*He hurries to the door, anxious to get away with his booty. When he opens it he is confronted with a dainty and exquisitely clean young* JAPANESE LADY *in a simple blue cotton kimono printed cunningly with small white jasmine blossoms.* MRS PEARCE *is with her. He gets out of her way deferentially and apologizes*]. Beg pardon, miss.

THE JAPANESE LADY. Garn! Dont you know your own daughter?

DOOLITTLE	[*exclaiming*	Bly me! it's Eliza!
HIGGINS	*simul-*	Whats that? This!
PICKERING	*taneously*]	By Jove!

LIZA. Dont I look silly?

HIGGINS. Silly?

MRS PEARCE [at the door] Now, Mr Higgins, please dont say anything to make the girl conceited about herself.

HIGGINS [conscientiously] Oh! Quite right, Mrs Pearce. [To ELIZA] Yes: damned silly.

MRS PEARCE. Please, sir.

HIGGINS [correcting himself] I mean extremely silly.

LIZA. I should look all right with my hat on. [She takes up her hat; puts it on; and walks across the room to the fireplace with a fashionable air].

HIGGINS. A new fashion, by George! And it ought to look horrible!

DOOLITTLE [with fatherly pride] Well, I never thought she'd clean up as good looking as that, Governor. She's a credit to me, aint she?

LIZA. I tell you, it's easy to clean up here. Hot and cold water on tap, just as much as you like, there is. Woolly towels, there is; and a towel horse[17] so hot, it burns your fingers. Soft brushes to scrub yourself, and a wooden bowl of soap smelling like primroses. Now I know why ladies is so clean. Washing's a treat for them. Wish they could see what it is for the like of me!

HIGGINS. I'm glad the bathroom met with your approval.

LIZA. It didnt: not all of it; and I dont care who hears me say it. Mrs Pearce knows.

HIGGINS. What was wrong, Mrs Pearce?

MRS PEARCE [blandly] Oh, nothing, sir. It doesnt matter.

LIZA. I had a good mind to break it. I didnt know which way to look. But I hung a towel over it, I did.

_____
17. **towel horse:** towel rack; this one is heated to dry the towels.

HIGGINS. Over what?

MRS PEARCE. Over the looking-glass, sir.

HIGGINS. Doolittle: you have brought your daughter up too strictly.

DOOLITTLE. Me! I never brought her up at all, except to give her a lick of a strap now and again. Dont put it on me, Governor. She aint accustomed to it, you see: thats all. But she'll soon pick up your free-and-easy ways.

LIZA. I'm a good girl, I am; and I wont pick up no free-and-easy ways.

HIGGINS. Eliza: if you say again that youre a good girl, your father shall take you home.

LIZA. Not him. You dont know my father. All he come here for was to touch you for some money to get drunk on.

DOOLITTLE. Well, what else would I want money for? To put into the plate in church, I suppose. [She puts out her tongue at him. He is so incensed by this that PICKERING presently finds it necessary to step between them]. Dont you give me none of your lip; and dont let me hear you giving this gentleman any of it neither, or youll hear from me about it. See?

HIGGINS. Have you any further advice to give her before you go, Doolittle? Your blessing, for instance.

DOOLITTLE. No, Governor: I aint such a mug as to put up my children to all I know myself. Hard enough to hold them in without that. If you want Eliza's mind improved, Governor, you do it yourself with a strap. So long, gentlemen. [He turns to go].

HIGGINS [impressively] Stop. Youll come regularly to see your daughter. It's your duty, you know. My brother is a clergyman; and he could help you in your talks with her.

DOOLITTLE [evasively] Certainly, I'll come, Governor. Not just this week, because I have a job at a distance. But later on you may depend on me. Afternoon, gentlemen. Afternoon, maam. [He touches his hat to MRS PEARCE, who disdains the salutation and goes out. He winks *at* HIGGINS, *thinking him probably a fellow-sufferer from* MRS PEARCE'*s difficult disposition, and follows her*].

LIZA. Don't you believe the old liar. He'd as soon you set a bulldog on him as a clergyman. You wont see him again in a hurry.

HIGGINS. I dont want to, Eliza. Do you?

LIZA. Not me. I dont want never to see him again, I dont. He's a disgrace to me, he is, collecting dust,[18] instead of working at his trade.

PICKERING. What is his trade, Eliza?

LIZA. Talking money out of other people's pockets into his own. His proper trade's a navvy;[19] and he works at it sometimes too—for exercise—and earns good money at it. Aint you going to call me Miss Doolittle any more?

PICKERING. I beg your pardon, Miss Doolittle. It was a slip of the tongue.

LIZA. Oh, I dont mind; only it sounded so genteel. I should just like to take a taxi to the corner of Tottenham Court Road and get out there and tell it to wait for me, just to put the girls in their place a bit. I wouldnt speak to them, you know.

PICKERING. Better wait til we get you something really fashionable.

HIGGINS. Besides, you shouldnt cut your old friends now that you have risen in the world. Thats what we call snobbery.

LIZA. You dont call the like of them my friends now, I should hope. Theyve took it out of me often enough with their ridicule when they had the chance; and now I mean to get a bit of my own back. But if I'm to have fashionable clothes, I'll wait. I should like to have some. Mrs Pearce says youre going to give me some to wear in bed at night different to what I wear in the daytime; but it do seem a waste of money when you could get something to shew.

Besides, I never could fancy changing into cold things on a winter night.

MRS PEARCE [*coming back*] Now, Eliza. The new things have come for you to try on.

LIZA. Ah-ow-oo-ooh! [*She rushes out*].

MRS PEARCE [*following her*] Oh, dont rush about like that, girl. [*She shuts the door behind her*].

HIGGINS. Pickering: we have taken on a stiff job.

PICKERING [*with conviction*] Higgins: we have.

* * * * * *

There seems to be some curiosity as to what Higgins's lessons to Eliza were like. Well, here is a sample: the first one.

Picture Eliza, in her new clothes, and feeling her inside put out of step by a lunch, dinner, and breakfast of a kind to which it is unaccustomed, seated with Higgins and the Colonel in the study, feeling like a hospital out-patient at a first encounter with the doctors.

Higgins, constitutionally unable to sit still, discomposes her still more by striding restlessly about. But for the reassuring presence and quietude of her friend the Colonel she would run for her life, even back to Drury Lane.

HIGGINS. Say your alphabet.

LIZA. I know my alphabet. Do you think I know nothing? I dont need to be taught like a child.

HIGGINS [*thundering*] Say your alphabet.

PICKERING. Say it, Miss Doolittle. You will understand presently. Do what he tells you; and let him teach you in his own way.

LIZA. Oh well, if you put it like that—Ahyee, bəyee, cəyee, dəyee—

HIGGINS [*with the roar of a wounded lion*] Stop. Listen to this, Pickering. This is what we pay for as elementary education. This unfortunate animal has been locked up for nine years in school at our expense to teach her to speak

---

18. **collecting dust:** picking up garbage.
19. **navvy** [nav′ē]: unskilled laborer, ditchdigger.

and read the language of Shakespear and Milton. And the result is Ahyee, Bə-yee, Cə-yee, Dəyee. [*To* ELIZA] Say A, B, C, D.

LIZA [*almost in tears*] But I'm sayin it. Ahyee, Bəyee, Cəyee—

HIGGINS. Stop. Say a cup of tea.

LIZA. A cappətə-ee.

HIGGINS. Put your tongue forward until it squeezes against the top of your lower teeth. Now say cup.

LIZA. C-c-c—I cant. C-Cup.

PICKERING. Good. Splendid, Miss Doolittle.

HIGGINS. By Jupiter, she's done it the first shot. Pickering: we shall make a duchess of her. [*To* ELIZA] Now do you think you could possibly say tea? Not tə-yee, mind: if you ever say bə-yee cə-yee də-yee again you shall be dragged round the room three times by the hair of your head. [*Fortissimo*] T, T, T, T.

LIZA [*weeping*] I cant hear no difference cep that it sounds more genteel-like when you say it.

HIGGINS. Well, if you can hear the difference, what the devil are you crying for? Pickering: give her a chocolate.

PICKERING. No, no. Never mind crying a little, Miss Doolittle: you are doing very well; and the lessons wont hurt. I promise you I wont let him drag you round the room by your hair.

HIGGINS. Be off with you to Mrs Pearce and tell her about it. Think about it. Try to do it by yourself: and keep your tongue well forward in your mouth instead of trying to roll it up and swallow it. Another lesson at half-past four this afternoon. Away with you.

ELIZA, *still sobbing, rushes from the room.*

And that is the sort of ordeal Eliza has to go through for months before we meet her again on her first appearance in London society of the professional class.

STUDY QUESTIONS

Recalling

1. What proposition does Liza offer Higgins when she first comes to his study? Why is he impressed?

2. What bet does Colonel Pickering offer Higgins? Summarize the plan that results from this bet.

3. What new experiences is Liza exposed to at Higgins' house? Describe her reactions to these experiences.

4. What various concerns about the experiment with Liza are expressed by Mrs. Pearce and Colonel Pickering? What answers does Higgins give them?

5. Why does Doolittle visit Higgins? Why does he not recognize Liza at first?

Interpreting

6. In what ways must Liza change if Higgins is to pass her off as a lady?

7. Describe Higgins' attitude toward Liza, and contrast it with Colonel Pickering's treatment of her. What does this contrast reveal about the two men?

8. What qualities does Liza reveal by coming to Higgins for lessons? What qualities does she show in her various responses to Higgins and to Pickering? What traits in her character indicate that she is not just an ordinary flower girl?

9. What does Doolittle mean by calling himself a member of the "undeserving poor" and by his complaints about "middle class morality"? What serious point does Shaw make in Doolittle's statement that he cannot afford to have morals?

Extending

10. Is proper speech still as important as it seems to Liza in *Pygmalion*? Why or why not?

ACT THREE

It is MRS HIGGINS's *at-home day.*[1] *Nobody has yet arrived. Her drawing room, in a flat on Chelsea Embankment, has three windows looking on the river; and the ceiling is not so lofty as it would be in an older house of the same pretension. The windows are open, giving access to a balcony with flowers in pots. If you stand with your face to the windows, you have the fireplace on your left and the door in the right-hand wall close to the corner nearest the windows.*

MRS HIGGINS *was brought up on Morris and Burne Jones;*[2] *and her room, which is very unlike her son's room in Wimpole Street, is not crowded with furniture and little tables and nicknacks. In the middle of the room there is a big ottoman; and this, with the carpet, the Morris wall-papers, and the Morris chintz window curtains and brocade covers of the ottoman and its cushions, supply all the ornament, and are much too handsome to be hidden by odds and ends of useless things. A few good oil-paintings from the exhibitions in the Grosvenor Gallery thirty years ago (the Burne Jones, not the Whistler*[3] *side of them) are on the walls. The only landscape is a Cecil Lawson*[4] *on the scale of a Rubens.*[5] *There is a portrait of* MRS HIGGINS *as she was when she defied the fashion in her youth in one of the beautiful Rossettian*[6] *costumes which, when caricatured by people who did not understand, led to the absurdities of popular estheticism in the eighteen-seventies.*

In the corner diagonally opposite the door MRS HIGGINS, *now over sixty and long past taking the trouble to dress out of the fashion sits writing at an elegantly simple writing-table with a bell button within reach of her hand. There is a Chippendale chair further back in the room between her and the window nearest her side. At the other side of the room, further forward, is an Elizabethan chair roughly carved in the taste of Inigo Jones.*[7] *On the same side a piano in a decorated case. The corner between the fireplace and the window is occupied by a divan cushioned in Morris chintz.*

It is between four and five in the afternoon.

The door is opened violently; and HIGGINS *enters with his hat on.*

MRS HIGGINS [*dismayed*] Henry! [*Scolding him*] What are you doing here today? It is my at-home day; you promised not to come. [*As he bends to kiss her, she takes his hat off, and presents it to him*].

HIGGINS. Oh bother! [*He throws the hat down on the table*].

MRS HIGGINS. Go home at once.

HIGGINS [*kissing her*] I know, mother. I came on purpose.

MRS HIGGINS. But you mustnt. I'm serious, Henry. You offend all my friends: they stop coming whenever they meet you.

HIGGINS. Nonsense! I know I have no small talk; but people dont mind. [*He sits on the settee*].

MRS HIGGINS. Oh! dont they? Small talk indeed! What about your large talk? Really, dear, you mustnt stay.

HIGGINS. I must. Ive a job for you. A phonetic job.

---

1. **at-home day:** specified day of the week when a lady regularly receives visitors, who need no invitation.
2. **Morris, Burne Jones:** William Morris (1834–1896) and Sir Edward Coley Burne Jones (1833–1898), Victorian artists who influenced interior decoration in ways of which Shaw approved.
3. **Whistler:** James Abbott McNeill Whistler (1834–1903), popular American painter who lived in England.
4. **Cecil Lawson:** Cecil Gordon Lawson (1851–1882), English landscape painter.
5. **Rubens:** Flemish painter Peter Paul Rubens (1577–1640), famous for his monumental paintings.
6. **Rossettian:** referring to the stylized work of Dante Gabriel Rossetti (1828–1882), painter and poet.
7. **Inigo Jones** (1573–1652): English architect and stage designer.

MRS HIGGINS. No use, dear. I'm sorry; but I cant get round your vowels; and though I like to get pretty postcards in your patent shorthand, I always have to read the copies in ordinary writing you so thoughtfully send me.

HIGGINS. Well, this isnt a phonetic job.

MRS HIGGINS. You said it was.

HIGGINS. Not your part of it. Ive picked up a girl.

MRS HIGGINS. Does that mean that some girl has picked you up?

HIGGINS. Not at all. I dont mean a love affair.

MRS HIGGINS. What a pity!

HIGGINS. Why?

MRS HIGGINS. Well, you never fall in love with anyone under forty-five. When will you discover that there are some rather nice-looking young women about?

HIGGINS. Oh, I cant be bothered with young women. My idea of a lovable woman is somebody as like you as possible. I shall never get into the way of seriously liking young women: some habits lie too deep to be changed. [*Rising abruptly and walking about, jingling his money and his keys in his trouser pockets*] Besides, theyre all idiots.

MRS HIGGINS. Do you know what you would do if you really loved me, Henry?

HIGGINS. Oh bother! What? Marry, I suppose.

MRS HIGGINS. No. Stop fidgeting and take your hands out of your pockets. [*With a gesture of despair, he obeys and sits down again*]. Thats a good boy. Now tell me about the girl.

HIGGINS. She's coming to see you.

MRS HIGGINS. I dont remember asking her.

HIGGINS. You didnt. *I* asked her. If youd known her you wouldnt have asked her.

MRS HIGGINS. Indeed! Why?

HIGGINS. Well, it's like this. She's a common flower girl. I picked her off the kerbstone.

MRS HIGGINS. And invited her to my at-home!

HIGGINS [*rising and coming to her to coax her*] Oh, thatll be all right. Ive taught her to speak properly; and she has strict orders as to her behavior. She's to keep to two subjects: the weather and everybody's health—Fine day and How do you do, you know—and not to let herself go on things in general. That will be safe.

MRS HIGGINS. Safe! To talk about our health! about our insides! perhaps about our outsides! How could you be so silly, Henry?

HIGGINS [*impatiently*] Well, she must talk about something. [*He controls himself and sits down again*]. Oh, she'll be all right: dont you fuss. Pickering is in it with me. Ive a sort of bet on that I'll pass her off as a duchess in six months. I started on her some months ago; and she's getting on like a house on fire. I shall win my bet. She has a quick ear; and she's easier to teach than my middle-class pupils because she's had to learn a complete new language. She talks English almost as you talk French.

MRS HIGGINS. Thats satisfactory, at all events.

HIGGINS. Well, it is and it isnt.

MRS HIGGINS. What does that mean?

HIGGINS. You see, Ive got her pronunciation all right; but you have to consider not only how a girl pronounces, but what she pronounces; and thats where—

They are interrupted by the PARLORMAID, *announcing guests.*

THE PARLORMAID. Mrs and Miss Eynsford Hill. [*She withdraws*].

HIGGINS. Oh Lord! [*He rises; snatches his hat from the table; and makes for the door; but before he reaches it his mother introduces him*].

MRS *and* MISS EYNSFORD HILL *are the mother and daughter who sheltered from the rain in Covent Garden. The mother is well bred, quiet, and has the habitual anxiety of straitened means. The daughter has acquired a gay air of being very much at home in society: the bravado of genteel poverty.*

MRS EYNSFORD HILL [*to* MRS HIGGINS] How do you do? [*They shake hands*].

MISS EYNSFORD HILL. How d'you do? [*She shakes*].

MRS HIGGINS [*introducing*] My son Henry.

MRS EYNSFORD HILL. Your celebrated son! I have so longed to meet you, Professor Higgins.

HIGGINS [*glumly, making no movement in her direction*] Delighted. [*He backs against the piano and bows brusquely*].

MISS EYNSFORD HILL [*going to him with confident familiarity*] How do you do?

HIGGINS [*staring at her*] Ive seen you before somewhere. I havnt the ghost of a notion where; but Ive heard your voice. [*Drearily*] It doesnt matter. Youd better sit down.

MRS HIGGINS. I'm sorry to say that my celebrated son has no manners. You mustnt mind him.

MISS EYNSFORD HILL [*gaily*] I dont. [*She sits in the Elizabethan chair*].

MRS EYNSFORD HILL [*a little bewildered*] Not at all. [*She sits on the ottoman between her daughter and* MRS HIGGINS, *who has turned her chair away from the writing-table*].

HIGGINS. Oh, have I been rude? I didnt mean to be.

He goes to the central window, through which, with his back to the company, he contemplates the river and the flowers in Battersea Park on the opposite bank as if they were a frozen desert.

The PARLORMAID *returns, ushering in* Pickering.

THE PARLORMAID. Colonel Pickering. [*She withdraws*].

PICKERING. How do you do, Mrs Higgins?

MRS HIGGINS. So glad youve come. Do you know Mrs Eynsford Hill—Miss Eynsford Hill? [*Exchange of bows. The* COLONEL *brings the Chippendale chair a little forward between* MRS HILL *and* MRS HIGGINS, *and sits down*].

PICKERING. Has Henry told you what weve come for?

HIGGINS [*over his shoulder*] We were interrupted: damn it!

MRS HIGGINS. Oh, Henry, Henry, really!

MRS EYNSFORD HILL [*half rising*] Are we in the way?

MRS HIGGINS [*rising and making her sit down again*] No, no. You couldnt have come more fortunately: we want you to meet a friend of ours.

HIGGINS [*turning hopefully*] Yes, by George! We want two or three people. You'll do as well as anybody else.

The PARLORMAID *returns, ushering* FREDDY.

THE PARLORMAID. Mr Eynsford Hill.

HIGGINS [*almost audibly, past endurance*] God of Heaven! another of them.

FREDDY [*shaking hands with* MRS HIGGINS] Ahdedo?[8]

MRS HIGGINS. Very good of you to come. [*Introducing*] Colonel Pickering.

FREDDY [*bowing*] Ahdedo?

MRS HIGGINS. I dont think you know my son, Professor Higgins.

FREDDY [*going to* HIGGINS] Ahdedo?

HIGGINS [*looking at him much as if he were a pickpocket*] I'll take my oath Ive met you before somewhere. Where was it?

FREDDY. I dont think so.

HIGGINS [*resignedly*] It dont matter, anyhow. Sit down.

---

8. **Ahdedo:** "How do you do?"

He shakes FREDDY's *hand, and almost slings him on to the ottoman with his face to the window; then comes round to the other side of it.*

HIGGINS. Well, here we are, anyhow! [*He sits down on the ottoman next* MRS EYNSFORD HILL, *on her left*] And now, what the devil are we going to talk about until Eliza comes?

MRS HIGGINS. Henry: you are the life and soul of the Royal Society's soirées;[9] but really youre rather trying on more commonplace occasions.

HIGGINS. Am I? Very sorry. [*Beaming suddenly*] I suppose I am, you know. [*Uproariously*] Ha, ha!

MISS EYNSFORD HILL [*who considers* HIGGINS *quite eligible matrimonially*] I sympathize. *I* havnt any small talk. If people would only be frank and say what they really think!

HIGGINS [*relapsing into gloom*] Lord forbid!

MRS EYNSFORD HILL [*taking up her daughter's cue*] But why?

HIGGINS. What they think they ought to think is bad enough, Lord knows; but what they really think would break up the whole show. Do you suppose it would be really agreeable if I were to come out now with what *I* really think?

MISS EYNSFORD HILL [*gaily*] Is it so very cynical?

HIGGINS. Cynical! Who the dickens said it was cynical? I mean it wouldnt be decent.

MRS EYNSFORD HILL [*seriously*] Oh! I'm sure you dont mean that, Mr Higgins.

HIGGINS. You see, we're all savages, more or less. We're supposed to be civilized and cultured—to know all about poetry and philosophy and art and science, and so on; but how many of us know even the meanings of these names? [*To* MISS HILL] What do you know of poetry? [*To* MRS HILL] What do you know of science? [*Indicating* FREDDY] What does he know

of art or science or anything else? What the devil do you imagine I know of philosophy?

MRS HIGGINS [*warningly*] Or of manners, Henry?

THE PARLORMAID [*opening the door*] Miss Doolittle. [*She withdraws*].

HIGGINS [*rising hastily and running to* MRS HIGGINS] Here she is, mother. [*He stands on tiptoe and makes signs over his mother's head to* ELIZA *to indicate to her which lady is her hostess*].

ELIZA, *who is exquisitely dressed, produces an impression of such remarkable distinction and beauty as she enters that they all rise, quite fluttered. Guided by* HIGGINS's *signals, she comes to* MRS HIGGINS *with studied grace.*

LIZA [*speaking with pedantic correctness of pronunciation and great beauty of tone*] How do you do, Mrs Higgins? [*She gasps slightly in making sure of the H in Higgins, but is quite successful*]. Mr Higgins told me I might come.

MRS HIGGINS [*cordially*] Quite right: I'm very glad indeed to see you.

PICKERING. How do you do, Miss Doolittle?

LIZA [*shaking hands with him*] Colonel Pickering, is it not?

MRS EYNSFORD HILL. I feel sure we have met before, Miss Doolittle. I remember your eyes.

LIZA. How do you do? [*She sits down on the ottoman gracefully in the place just left vacant by* HIGGINS].

MRS EYNSFORD HILL [*introducing*] My daughter Clara.

LIZA. How do you do?

CLARA [*impulsively*] How do you do? [*She sits down on the ottoman beside* ELIZA, *devouring her with her eyes*].

FREDDY [*coming to their side of the ottoman*] Ive certainly had the pleasure.

---

9. **soirées:** social gatherings held in the evening.

MRS EYNSFORD HILL [*introducing*] My son Freddy.

LIZA. How do you do?

FREDDY *bows and sits down in the Elizabethan chair, infatuated.*

HIGGINS [*suddenly*] By George, yes: it all comes back to me! [*They stare at him*]. Covent Garden! [*Lamentably*] What a damned thing!

MRS HIGGINS. Henry, please! [*He is about to sit on the edge of the table*] Dont sit on my writing-table: youll break it.

HIGGINS [*sulkily*] Sorry.

He goes to the divan, stumbling into the fender[10] *and over the fire-irons on his way; extricating himself with muttered imprecations; and finishing his disastrous journey by throwing himself so impatiently on the divan that he almost breaks it.* MRS HIGGINS *looks at him, but controls herself and says nothing.*

A long and painful pause ensues.

MRS HIGGINS [*at last, conversationally*] Will it rain, do you think?

LIZA. The shallow depression in the west of these islands is likely to move slowly in an easterly direction. There are no indications of any great change in the barometrical situation.

FREDDY. Ha! ha! how awfully funny!

LIZA. What is wrong with that, young man? I bet I got it right.

FREDDY. Killing!

MRS EYNSFORD HILL. I'm sure I hope it wont turn cold. Theres so much influenza about. It runs right through our whole family regularly every spring.

LIZA [*darkly*] My aunt died of influenza: so they said.

MRS EYNSFORD HILL [*clicks her tongue sympathetically*]!!!

LIZA [*in the same tragic tone*] But it's my belief they done the old woman in.

MRS HIGGINS [*puzzled*] Done her in?

LIZA. Y-e-e-e-es, Lord love you! Why should she die of influenza? She come through diphtheria right enough the year before. I saw her with my own eyes. Fairly blue with it, she was. They all thought she was dead; but my father he kept ladling gin down her throat til she came to so sudden that she bit the bowl off the spoon.

MRS EYNSFORD HILL [*startled*] Dear me!

LIZA [*piling up the indictment*] What call would a woman with that strength in her have to die of influenza? What become of her new straw hat that should have come to me? Somebody pinched it; and what I say is, them as pinched it done her in.

MRS EYNSFORD HILL. What does doing her in mean?

HIGGINS [*hastily*] Oh, thats the new small talk. To do a person in means to kill them.

MRS EYNSFORD HILL [*to* ELIZA, *horrified*] You surely dont believe that your aunt was killed?

LIZA. Do I not! Them she lived with would have killed her for a hat-pin, let alone a hat.

MRS EYNSFORD HILL. But it cant have been right for your father to pour spirits down her throat like that. It might have killed her.

LIZA. Not her. Gin was mother's milk to her. Besides, he'd poured so much down his own throat that he knew the good of it.

MRS EYNSFORD HILL. Do you mean that he drank?

LIZA. Drank! My word! Something chronic.

MRS EYNSFORD HILL. How dreadful for you!

LIZA. Not a bit. It never did him no harm what I could see. But then he did not keep it up regular. [*Cheerfully*] On the burst, as you might say, from time to time. And always more agreeable when he had a drop in. When he was

---

10. **fender:** metal guard before a fireplace.

out of work, my mother used to give him fourpence and tell him to go out and not come back until he'd drunk himself cheerful and loving-like. Theres lots of women has to make their husbands drunk to make them fit to live with. [*Now quite at her ease*] You see, it's like this. If a man has a bit of conscience, it always takes him when he's sober; and then it makes him low-spirited. A drop of booze just takes that off and makes him happy. [*To* FREDDY, *who is in convulsions of suppressed laughter*] Here! what are you sniggering at?

FREDDY. The new small talk. You do it so awfully well.

LIZA. If I was doing it proper, what was you laughing at? [*To* HIGGINS] Have I said anything I oughtnt?

MRS HIGGINS [*interposing*] Not at all, Miss Doolittle.

LIZA. Well, thats a mercy, anyhow. [*Expansively*] What I always say is—

HIGGINS [*Rising and looking at his watch*] Ahem!

LIZA [*looking round at him; taking the hint; and rising*] Well: I must go. [*They all rise.* FREDDY *goes to the door*]. So pleased to have met you. Goodbye. [*She shakes hands with* MRS HIGGINS].

MRS HIGGINS. Goodbye.

LIZA. Goodbye, Colonel Pickering.

PICKERING. Goodbye, Miss Doolittle. [*They shake hands*].

LIZA [*nodding to the others*] Goodbye, all.

FREDDY [*opening the door for her*] Are you walking across the Park, Miss Doolittle? If so—

LIZA [*with perfectly elegant diction*] Walk! Not bloody likely. [*Sensation*]. I am going in a taxi. [*She goes out*].

PICKERING *gasps and sits down.* FREDDY *goes out on the balcony to catch another glimpse of* ELIZA.

MRS EYNSFORD HILL [*suffering from shock*] Well, I really cant get used to the new ways.

CLARA [*throwing herself discontentedly into the Elizabethan chair*] Oh, it's all right, mamma, quite right. People will think we never go anywhere or see anybody if you are so old-fashioned.

MRS EYNSFORD HILL. I daresay I am very old-fashioned; but I do hope you wont begin using that expression, Clara. I have got accustomed to hear you talking about men as rotters, and calling everything filthy and beastly; though I do think it horrible and unladylike. But this last is really too much. Dont you think so, Colonel Pickering?

PICKERING. Dont ask me. Ive been away in India for several years; and manners have changed so much that I sometimes dont know whether I'm at a respectable dinnertable or in a ship's forecastle.

CLARA. It's all a matter of habit. Theres no right or wrong in it. Nobody means anything by it. And it's so quaint, and gives such a smart emphasis to things that are not in themselves very witty. I find the new small talk delightful and quite innocent.

MRS EYNSFORD HILL [*rising*] Well, after that, I think it's time for us to go.

PICKERING *and* HIGGINS *rise.*

CLARA [*rising*] Oh yes: we have three at-homes to go to still. Goodbye, Mrs Higgins. Goodbye, Colonel Pickering. Goodbye, Professor Higgins.

HIGGINS [*coming grimly at her from the divan, and accompanying her to the door*] Goodbye. Be sure you try on that small talk at the three at-homes. Dont be nervous about it. Pitch it in strong.

CLARA [*all smiles*] I will. Goodbye. Such nonsense, all this early Victorian prudery!

HIGGINS [*tempting her*] Such damned nonsense!

CLARA. Such bloody nonsense!

MRS EYNSFORD HILL [*convulsively*] Clara!

CLARA. Ha! ha! [*She goes out radiant, conscious of being thoroughly up to date, and is heard descending the stairs in a stream of silvery laughter*].

FREDDY [*to the heavens at large*] Well, I ask you— [*He gives it up, and comes to* MRS HIGGINS]. Goodbye.

MRS HIGGINS [*shaking hands*] Goodbye. Would you like to meet Miss Doolittle again?

FREDDY [*eagerly*] Yes, I should, most awfully.

MRS HIGGINS. Well, you know my days.[11]

FREDDY. Yes. Thanks awfully. Goodbye. [*He goes out*].

MRS EYNSFORD HILL. Goodbye, Mr Higgins.

HIGGINS. Goodbye. Goodbye.

MRS EYNSFORD HILL [*to* PICKERING] It's no use. I shall never be able to bring myself to use that word.

PICKERING. Dont. It's not compulsory, you know. Youll get on quite well without it.

MRS EYNSFORD HILL. Only, Clara is so down on me if I am not positively reeking with the latest slang. Goodbye.

PICKERING. Goodbye [*They shake hands*].

MRS EYNSFORD HILL [*to* MRS HIGGINS] You mustnt mind Clara. [PICKERING, *catching from her lowered tone that this is not meant for him to hear, discreetly joins* HIGGINS *at the window*]. We're so poor! and she gets so few parties, poor child! She doesnt quite know. [MRS HIGGINS, *seeing that her eyes are moist, takes her hand sympathetically and goes with her to the door*]. But the boy is nice. Dont you think so?

MRS HIGGINS. Oh, quite nice. I shall always be delighted to see him.

MRS EYNSFORD HILL. Thank you, dear. Goodbye. [*She goes out*].

HIGGINS [*eagerly*] Well? Is Eliza presentable [*he swoops on his mother and drags her to the ottoman, where she sits down in* ELIZA's *place with her son on her left*]?

PICKERING *returns to his chair on her right.*

MRS HIGGINS. You silly boy, of course she's not presentable. She's a triumph of your art and of her dressmaker's; but if you suppose for a moment that she doesnt give herself away in every sentence she utters, you must be perfectly cracked about her.

PICKERING. But dont you think something might be done? I mean something to eliminate the sanguinary[12] element from her conversation.

MRS HIGGINS. Not as long as she is in Henry's hands.

HIGGINS [*aggrieved*] Do you mean that my language is improper?

MRS HIGGINS. No, dearest: it would be quite proper—say on a canal barge; but it would not be proper for her at a garden party.

HIGGINS [*deeply injured*] Well I must say—

PICKERING [*interrupting him*] Come, Higgins: you must learn to know yourself. I havnt heard such language as yours since we used to review the volunteers in Hyde Park twenty years ago.

HIGGINS [*sulkily*] Oh, well, if you say so, I suppose I dont always talk like a bishop.

MRS HIGGINS [*quieting* HENRY *with a touch*] Colonel Pickering: will you tell me what is the exact state of things in Wimpole Street?

PICKERING [*cheerfully: as if this completely changed the subject*] Well, I have come to live there with Henry. We work together at my Indian Dialects; and we think it more convenient—

---

11. **my days:** the days on which she receives visitors.

12. **sanguinary:** bloody. Pickering is alluding to Eliza's use of the slang term *bloody*.

MRS HIGGINS. Quite so. I know all about that: it's an excellent arrangement. But where does this girl live?

HIGGINS. With us, of course. Where should she live?

MRS HIGGINS. But on what terms? Is she a servant? If not, what is she?

PICKERING [*slowly*] I think I know what you mean, Mrs Higgins.

HIGGINS. Well, dash me if *I* do! Ive had to work at the girl every day for months to get her to her present pitch. Besides, she's useful. She knows where my things are, and remembers my appointments and so forth.

MRS HIGGINS. How does your housekeeper get on with her?

HIGGINS. Mrs Pearce? Oh, she's jolly glad to get so much taken off her hands; for before Eliza came, she used to have to find things and remind me of my appointments. But she's got some silly bee in her bonnet about Eliza. She keeps saying "You dont think, sir": doesnt she, Pick?

PICKERING. Yes: thats the formula. "You dont think, sir." Thats the end of every conversation about Eliza.

HIGGINS. As if I ever stop thinking about the girl and her confounded vowels and consonants. I'm worn out, thinking about her, and watching her lips and her teeth and her tongue, not to mention her soul, which is the quaintest of the lot.

MRS HIGGINS. You certainly are a pretty pair of babies, playing with your live doll.

HIGGINS. Playing! The hardest job I ever tackled: make no mistake about that, mother. But you have no idea how frightfully interesting it is to take a human being and change her into a quite different human being by creating a new speech for her. It's filling up the deepest gulf that separates class from class and soul from soul.

PICKERING [*drawing his chair closer to* MRS HIGGINS *and bending over to her eagerly*] Yes: it's enormously interesting. I assure you, Mrs Higgins, we take Eliza very seriously. Every week—every day almost—there is some new change. [*Closer again*] We keep records of every stage—dozens of gramophone disks and photographs—

HIGGINS [*assailing her at the other ear*] Yes, by George: it's the most absorbing experiment I ever tackled. She regularly fills our lives up: doesnt she, Pick?

PICKERING. We're always talking Eliza.

HIGGINS. Teaching Eliza.

PICKERING. Dressing Eliza.

MRS HIGGINS. What!

HIGGINS. Inventing new Elizas.

HIGGINS.	[*speaking together*]	You know, she has the most extraordinary quickness of ear:
PICKERING.		I assure you, my dear Mrs Higgins, that girl
HIGGINS.		just like a parrot. Ive tried her with every
PICKERING.		is a genius. She can play the piano quite beautifully.
HIGGINS.		possible sort of sound that a human being can make—
PICKERING.		We have taken her to classical concerts and to music
HIGGINS.		Continental dialects, African dialects, Hottentot
PICKERING.		halls; and it's all the same to her: she plays everything

HIGGINS. | clicks, things it took me years to get hold of; and

PICKERING. | she hears right off when she comes home, whether it's

HIGGINS. *[speaking together]* | she picks them up like a shot, right away, as if she had

PICKERING. | Beethoven and Brahms or Lehar and Lionel Monckton;

HIGGINS. | been at it all her life.

PICKERING. | though six months ago, she'd never as much as touched a piano—

MRS HIGGINS [*putting her fingers in her ears, as they are by this time shouting one another down with an intolerable noise*] Sh-sh-sh—sh! [*They stop*].

PICKERING. I beg your pardon. [*He draws his chair back apologetically*].

HIGGINS. Sorry. When Pickering starts shouting nobody can get a word in edgeways.

MRS HIGGINS. Be quiet, Henry. Colonel Pickering: dont you realize that when Eliza walked in Wimpole Street, something walked in with her?

PICKERING. Her father did. But Henry soon got rid of him.

MRS HIGGINS. It would have been more to the point if her mother had. But as her mother didnt something else did.

PICKERING. But what?

MRS HIGGINS [*unconsciously dating herself by the word*] A problem.

PICKERING. Oh, I see. The problem of how to pass her off as a lady.

HIGGINS. I'll solve that problem. Ive half solved it already.

MRS HIGGINS. No, you two infinitely stupid male creatures: the problem of what is to be done with her afterwards.

HIGGINS. I dont see anything in that. She can go her own way, with all the advantages I have given her.

MRS HIGGINS. The advantages of that poor woman who was here just now! The manners and habits that disqualify a fine lady from earning her own living without giving her a fine lady's income! Is that what you mean?

PICKERING [*indulgently, being rather bored*] Oh, that will be all right, Mrs Higgins. [*He rises to go*].

HIGGINS [*rising also*] We'll find her some light employment.

PICKERING. She's happy enough. Dont you worry about her. Goodbye. [*He shakes hands as if he were consoling a frightened child, and makes for the door*].

HIGGINS. Anyhow, theres no good bothering now. The thing's done. Goodbye, mother. [*He kisses her, and follows* PICKERING].

PICKERING [*turning for a final consolation*] There are plenty of openings. We'll do whats right. Goodbye.

HIGGINS [*to* PICKERING *as they go out together*] Lets take her to the Shakespear exhibition at Earls Court.

PICKERING. Yes: lets. Her remarks will be delicious.

HIGGINS. She'll mimic all the people for us when we get home.

PICKERING. Ripping.[13] [*Both are heard laughing as they go downstairs*].

MRS HIGGINS [*rises with an impatient bounce, and returns to her work at the writing-table. She sweeps a litter of disarranged papers out of the way; snatches a sheet of paper from her*

---

13. **Ripping:** "Splendid!"

stationery case; and tries resolutely to write. At the third time she gives it up; flings down her pen; grips the table angrily and exclaims] Oh, men! men!! men!!!

* * * * * *

Clearly Eliza will not pass as a duchess yet; and Higgins's bet remains unwon. But the six months are not yet exhausted and just in time Eliza does actually pass as a princess. For a glimpse of how she did it imagine an Embassy in London one summer evening after dark. The hall door has an awning and a carpet across the sidewalk to the kerb, because a grand reception is in progress. A small crowd is lined up to see the guests arrive.

A Rolls-Royce car drives up. Pickering in evening dress, with medals and orders, alights, and hands out Eliza, in opera cloak, evening dress, diamonds, fan, flowers and all accessories. Higgins follows. The car drives off; and the three go up the steps and into the house, the door opening for them as they approach.

Inside the house they find themselves in a spacious hall from which the grand staircase rises. On the left are the arrangements for the gentlemen's cloaks. The male guests are depositing their hats and wraps there.

On the right is a door leading to the ladies' cloakroom. Ladies are going in cloaked and coming out in splendor. Pickering whispers to Eliza and points out the ladies' room. She goes into it. Higgins and Pickering take off their overcoats and take tickets for them from the attendant.

One of the guests, occupied in the same way, has his back turned. Having taken his ticket, he turns round and reveals himself as an important looking young man with an astonishingly hairy face. He has an enormous moustache, flowing out into luxuriant whiskers. Waves of hair cluster on his brow. His hair is cropped closely at the back, and glows with oil. Otherwise he is very smart. He wears several worthless orders. He is ev-idently a foreigner, guessable as a whiskered Pandour[14] from Hungary; but in spite of the ferocity of his moustache he is amiable and genially voluble.

Recognizing Higgins, he flings his arms wide apart and approaches him enthusiastically.

WHISKERS. Maestro, maestro [*he embraces* HIGGINS *and kisses him on both cheeks*]. You remember me?

HIGGINS. No I dont. Who the devil are you?

WHISKERS. I am your pupil: your first pupil, your best and greatest pupil. I am little Nepommuck, the marvellous boy. I have made your name famous throughout Europe. You teach me phonetic. You cannot forget ME.

HIGGINS. Why dont you shave?

NEPOMMUCK. I have not your imposing appearance, your chin, your brow. Nobody notice me when I shave. Now I am famous: they call me Hairy Faced Dick.

HIGGINS. And what are you doing here among all these swells?

NEPOMMUCK. I am interpreter. I speak 32 languages. I am indispensable at these international parties. You are great cockney specialist: you place a man anywhere in London the moment he open his mouth. I place any man in Europe.

A FOOTMAN *hurries down the grand staircase and comes to* NEPOMMUCK.

FOOTMAN. You are wanted upstairs. Her Excellency cannot understand the Greek gentleman.

NEPOMMUCK. Thank you, yes, immediately.

The FOOTMAN *goes and is lost in the crowd.*

NEPOMMUCK [*to* HIGGINS] This Greek diplomatist pretends he cannot speak nor understand English. He cannot deceive me. He is the

---

14. **Pandour:** bodyguard or servant of a Hungarian nobleman.

son of a Clerkenwell watchmaker. He speaks English so villainously that he dare not utter a word of it without betraying his origin. I help him to pretend; but I make him pay through the nose. I make them all pay. Ha ha! [*He hurries upstairs*].

PICKERING. Is this fellow really an expert? Can he find out Eliza and blackmail her?

HIGGINS. We shall see. If he finds her out I lose my bet.

    ELIZA *comes from the cloakroom and joins them.*

PICKERING. Well, Eliza, now for it. Are you ready?

LIZA. Are you nervous, Colonel?

PICKERING. Frightfully. I feel exactly as I felt before my first battle. It's the first time that frightens.

LIZA. It is not the first time for me, Colonel. I have done this fifty times—hundreds of times—in my little piggery in Angel Court in my day-dreams. I am in a dream now. Promise me not to let Professor Higgins wake me; for if he does I shall forget everything and talk as I used to in Drury Lane.

PICKERING. Not a word, Higgins. [*To* ELIZA] Now, ready?

LIZA. Ready.

PICKERING. Go.

    They mount the stairs, HIGGINS *last.* PICKERING *whispers to the* FOOTMAN *on the first landing.*

FIRST LANDING FOOTMAN. Miss Doolittle, Colonel Pickering, Professor Higgins.

SECOND LANDING FOOTMAN. Miss Doolittle, Colonel Pickering, Professor Higgins.

    At the top of the staircase the AMBASSADOR *and his* WIFE, *with* NEPOMMUCK *at her elbow, are receiving.*

HOSTESS [*taking* Eliza's *hand*] How d'ye do?

HOST [*same play*] How d'ye do? How d'ye do, Pickering?

LIZA [*with a beautiful gravity that awes her hostess*] How do you do? [*She passes on to the drawingroom*].

HOSTESS. Is that your adopted daughter, Colonel Pickering? She will make a sensation.

PICKERING. Most kind of you to invite her for me. [*He passes on*].

HOSTESS [*to* NEPOMMUCK] Find out all about her.

NEPOMMUCK [*bowing*] Excellency—[*he goes into the crowd*].

HOST. How d'ye do, Higgins? You have a rival here tonight. He introduced himself as your pupil. Is he any good?

HIGGINS. He can learn a language in a fortnight—knows dozens of them. A sure mark of a fool. As a phonetician, no good whatever.

HOSTESS. How d'ye do, Professor?

HIGGINS. How do you do? Fearful bore for you this sort of thing. Forgive my part in it. [*He passes on*].

In the drawing room and its suite of salons the reception is in full swing. Eliza passes through. She is so intent on her ordeal that she walks like a somnambulist[15] in a desert instead of a débutante in a fashionable crowd. They stop talking to look at her, admiring her dress, her jewels, and her strangely attractive self. Some of the younger ones at the back stand on their chairs to see.

    The Host and Hostess come in from the staircase and mingle with their guests. Higgins, gloomy and contemptuous of the whole business, comes into the group where they are chatting.

HOSTESS. Ah, here is Professor Higgins: he will tell us. Tell us all about the wonderful young lady, Professor.

---

15. **somnambulist:** sleepwalker.

HIGGINS [*almost morosely*] What wonderful young lady?

HOSTESS. You know very well. They tell me there has been nothing like her in London since people stood on their chairs to look at Mrs Langtry.[16]

NEPOMMUCK *joins the group, full of news.*

HOSTESS. Ah, here you are at last, Nepommuck. Have you found out all about the Doolittle lady?

NEPOMMUCK. I have found out all about her. She is a fraud.

HOSTESS. A fraud! Oh no.

NEPOMMUCK. YES, yes. She cannot deceive me. Her name cannot be Doolittle.

HIGGINS. Why?

NEPOMMUCK. Because Doolittle is an English name. And she is not English.

HOSTESS. Oh, nonsense! She speaks English perfectly.

NEPOMMUCK. Too perfectly. Can you shew me any English woman who speaks English as it should be spoken? Only foreigners who have been taught to speak it speak it well.

HOSTESS. Certainly she terrified me by the way she said How d'ye do. I had a schoolmistress who talked like that; and I was mortally afraid of her. But if she is not English what is she?

NEPOMMUCK. Hungarian.

ALL THE REST. Hungarian!

NEPOMMUCK. Hungarian. And of royal blood. I am Hungarian. My blood is royal.

HIGGINS. Did you speak to her in Hungarian?

NEPOMMUCK. I did. She was very clever. She said "Please speak to me in English: I do not understand French." French! She pretends not to know the difference between Hungarian and French. Impossible: she knows both.

HIGGINS. And the blood royal? How did you find that out?

NEPOMMUCK. Instinct, maestro, instinct. Only the Magyar races can produce that air of the divine right, those resolute eyes. She is a princess.

HOST. What do you say, Professor?

HIGGINS. I say an ordinary London girl out of

---

16. **Mrs. Langtry:** Lily Langtry (1852–1929), celebrated English actress and beauty.

the gutter and taught to speak by an expert. I place her in Drury Lane.

NEPOMMUCK. Ha ha ha! Oh, maestro, maestro, you are mad on the subject of cockney dialects. The London gutter is the whole world for you.

HIGGINS [*to the* HOSTESS] What does your Excellency say?

HOSTESS. Oh, of course I agree with Nepommuck. She must be a princess at least.

HOST. Not necessarily legitimate, of course. Morganatic[17] perhaps. But that is undoubtedly her class.

HIGGINS. I stick to my opinion.

---

17. **Morganatic** [mör′gə nat′ik]: referring to a marriage between royalty and a commoner. Although such a marriage is valid, the children do not inherit titles.

HOSTESS. Oh, you are incorrigible.

The group breaks up, leaving HIGGINS *isolated.* PICKERING *joins him.*

PICKERING. Where is Eliza? We must keep an eye on her.

ELIZA *joins them.*

LIZA. I dont think I can bear much more. The people all stare so at me. An old lady has just told me that I speak exactly like Queen Victoria. I am sorry if I have lost your bet. I have done my best; but nothing can make me the same as these people.

PICKERING. You have not lost it, my dear. You have won it ten times over.

HIGGINS. Let us get out of this. I have had enough of chattering to these fools.

PICKERING. Eliza is tired; and I am hungry. Let us clear out and have supper somewhere.

STUDY QUESTIONS

Recalling
1. What does Liza discuss at Mrs. Higgins' gathering? How does Higgins explain her to the guests, and how do they react to her?
2. According to Mrs. Higgins, what "problem" walked in the door with Liza? What answer do Higgins and Pickering give Mrs. Higgins?
3. Whom do Higgins and Liza meet at the ambassador's party? What conclusion regarding Liza does this person draw and why?
4. How is Pickering's bet with Higgins resolved?

Interpreting
5. At Mrs. Higgins' gathering, in what way does Liza "give herself away in every sentence"? Why do you think the Eynsford Hills accept Higgins' explanation of Liza's conversation?
6. Contrast Mrs. Higgins with her son. Why do his and Pickering's attitude toward Liza prompt Mrs. Higgins' outburst on page 499?
7. Describe the change in Liza from her tea in Mrs. Higgins' parlor to the embassy ball.

LITERARY FOCUS

Dramatic Conventions
Dramatic conventions are practices that we accept on stage but that differ from real-life behavior. In Shakespeare's plays, for instance, we accept the conventions of blank verse, soliloquies, and asides.

One very important function of dramatic conventions is to portray shifts in time. The passage of days, months, even years is presented on stage through such conventions as breaks in the action, variations in the set, and, most important, changes in the characters. Similarly, dramatic action operates within the convention that time on stage is often *telescoped,* or speeded up—Liza's bath takes much less time than an actual bath would. Such dramatic conventions help to bridge the gap between stage life and real life.

Thinking About Dramatic Conventions
■ In what ways is the passage of time signaled from Act II to Act III of *Pygmalion* and from the first to the second part of Act III?

ACT FOUR

The Wimpole Street laboratory. Midnight. Nobody in the room. The clock on the mantelpiece strikes twelve. The fire is not alight: it is a summer night.

Presently HIGGINS *and* PICKERING *are heard on the stairs.*

HIGGINS [*calling down to* PICKERING] I say, Pick: lock up, will you? I shant be going out again.

PICKERING. Right. Can Mrs Pearce go to bed? We dont want anything more, do we?

HIGGINS. Lord, no!

ELIZA *opens the door and is seen on the lighted landing in all the finery in which she has just won* HIGGINS'*s bet for him. She comes to the hearth, and switches on the electric lights there. She is tired: her pallor contrasts strongly with her dark eyes and hair; and her expression is almost tragic. She takes off her cloak; puts her fan and gloves on the piano; and sits down on the bench, brooding and silent.* HIGGINS, *in evening dress, with overcoat and hat, comes in, carrying a smoking jacket which he has picked up downstairs. He takes off the hat and overcoat; throws them carelessly on the newspaper stand; disposes of his coat in the same way; puts on the smoking jacket; and throws himself wearily into the easy-chair at the hearth.* PICKERING, *similarly attired, comes in. He also takes off his hat and overcoat, and is about to throw them on* HIGGINS'*s when he hesitates.*

PICKERING. I say: Mrs Pearce will row if we leave these things lying about in the drawing room.

HIGGINS. Oh, chuck them over the bannisters into the hall. She'll find them there in the morning and put them away all right. She'll think we were drunk.

PICKERING. We are, slightly. Are there any letters?

HIGGINS. I didnt look. [PICKERING *takes the overcoats and hats and goes downstairs.* HIGGINS *begins half singing half yawning an air from* La Fanciulla del Golden West.[1] *Suddenly he stops and exclaims*] I wonder where the devil my slippers are!

ELIZA *looks at him darkly; then rises suddenly and leaves the room.*

HIGGINS *yawns again, and resumes his song.*

PICKERING *returns, with the contents of the letter-box in his hand.*

PICKERING. Only circulars, and this coroneted billet-doux[2] for you. [*He throws the circulars into the fender, and posts himself on the hearthrug, with his back to the grate*].

HIGGINS [*glancing at the billet-doux*] Money-lender. [*He throws the letter after the circulars*].

ELIZA *returns with a pair of large down-at-heel slippers. She places them on the carpet before* HIGGINS, *and sits as before without a word.*

HIGGINS [*yawning again*] Oh Lord! What an evening! What a crew! What a silly tomfoolery! [*He raises his shoe to unlace it, and catches sight of the slippers. He stops unlacing and looks at them as if they had appeared there of their own accord*]. Oh! theyre there, are they?

PICKERING [*stretching himself*]. Well, I feel a bit tired. It's been a long day. The garden party, a dinner party, and the reception! Rather too much of a good thing. But youve won your bet, Higgins. Eliza did the trick, and something to spare, eh?

HIGGINS [*fervently*] Thank God it's over!

ELIZA *flinches violently; but they take no no-*

---

1. **La Fanciulla** [la fan cho͞o′la] **del Golden West:** *The Girl of the Golden West,* opera by Italian composer Giacomo Puccini (1858–1924).
2. **coroneted billet-doux** [bil′ā do͞o′]: love letter decorated with a small crown.

tice of her; and she recovers herself and sits stonily as before.

PICKERING. Were you nervous at the garden party? *I* was. Eliza didnt seem a bit nervous.

HIGGINS. Oh, she wasnt nervous. I knew she'd be all right. No: it's the strain of putting the job through all these months that has told on me. It was interesting enough at first, while we were at the phonetics; but after that I got deadly sick of it. If I hadnt backed myself to do it I should have chucked the whole thing up two months ago. It was a silly notion: the whole thing has been a bore.

PICKERING. Oh come! the garden party was frightfully exciting. My heart began beating like anything.

HIGGINS. Yes, for the first three minutes. But when I saw we were going to win hands down, I felt like a bear in a cage, hanging about doing nothing. The dinner was worse: sitting gorging there for over an hour, with nobody but a damned fool of a fashionable woman to talk to! I tell you, Pickering, never again for me. No more artificial duchesses. The whole thing has been simple purgatory.

PICKERING. Youve never been broken in properly to the social routine. [*Strolling over to the piano*] I rather enjoy dipping into it occasionally myself: it makes me feel young again. Anyhow, it was a great success: an immense success. I was quite frightened once or twice because Eliza was doing it so well. You see, lots of the real people cant do it at all: theyre such fools that they think style comes by nature to people in their position; and so they never learn. Theres always something professional about doing a thing superlatively well.

HIGGINS. Yes: thats what drives me mad: the silly people dont know their own silly business. [*Rising*] However, it's over and done with; and now I can go to bed at last without dreading tomorrow.

ELIZA'*s beauty becomes murderous.*

PICKERING. I think I shall turn in too. Still, it's been a great occasion: a triumph for you. Goodnight. [*He goes*].

HIGGINS [*following him*] Goodnight. [*Over his shoulder, at the door*] Put out the lights, Eliza; and tell Mrs Pearce not to make coffee for me in the morning: I'll take tea. [*He goes out*].

ELIZA *tries to control herself and feel indifferent as she rises and walks across to the hearth to switch off the lights. By the time she gets there she is on the point of screaming. She sits down in* HIGGINS'*s chair and holds on hard to the arms. Finally she gives way and flings herself furiously on the floor, raging.*

HIGGINS [*in despairing wrath outside*] What the devil have I done with my slippers? [*He appears at the door*].

LIZA [*snatching up the slippers, and hurling them at him one after the other with all her force*] There are your slippers. And there. Take your slippers; and may you never have a day's luck with them!

HIGGINS [*astounded*] What on earth—! [*He comes to her*]. Whats the matter? Get up. [*He pulls her up*] Anything wrong?

LIZA [*breathless*] Nothing wrong—with you. Ive won your bet for you, havnt I? Thats enough for you. *I* dont matter, I suppose.

HIGGINS. You won my bet! You! Presumptuous insect! *I* won it. What did you throw those slippers at me for?

LIZA. Because I wanted to smash your face. I'd like to kill you, you selfish brute. Why didnt you leave me where you picked me out of—in the gutter? You thank God it's all over, and that now you can throw me back again there, do you? [*She crisps her fingers[3] frantically*].

HIGGINS [*looking at her in cool wonder*] The creature is nervous, after all.

---

3. **crisps her fingers:** clenches them into fists.

LIZA [*gives a suffocated scream of fury, and instinctively darts her nails at his face*]!!

HIGGINS [*catching her wrists*] Ah! would you? Claws in, you cat. How dare you shew your temper to me? Sit down and be quiet. [*He throws her roughly into the easy-chair*].

LIZA [*crushed by superior strength and weight*] Whats to become of me? Whats to become of me?

HIGGINS. How the devil do I know whats to become of you? What does it matter what becomes of you?

LIZA. You dont care. I know you dont care. You wouldnt care if I was dead. I'm nothing to you—not so much as them slippers.

HIGGINS [*thundering*] Those slippers.

LIZA [*with bitter submission*] Those slippers. I didnt think it made any difference now.

A pause. ELIZA *hopeless and crushed.* HIGGINS *a little uneasy.*

HIGGINS [*in his loftiest manner*] Why have you begun going on like this? May I ask whether you complain of your treatment here?

LIZA. No.

HIGGINS. Has anybody behaved badly to you? Colonel Pickering? Mrs Pearce? Any of the servants?

LIZA. No.

HIGGINS. I presume you dont pretend that *I* have treated you badly?

LIZA. No.

HIGGINS. I am glad to hear it. [*He moderates his tone*]. Perhaps youre tired after the strain of the day. Will you have a glass of champagne? [*He moves towards the door*].

LIZA. No. [*Recollecting her manners*] Thank you.

HIGGINS [*good-humored again*] This has been coming on you for some days. I suppose it was natural for you to be anxious about the garden party. But thats all over now. [*He pats her kindly on the shoulder. She writhes*]. Theres nothing more to worry about.

LIZA. No. Nothing more for you to worry about. [*She suddenly rises and gets away from him by going to the piano bench, where she sits and hides her face*]. Oh God! I wish I was dead.

HIGGINS [*staring after her in sincere surprise*] Why? In heaven's name, why? [*Reasonably, going to her*] Listen to me, Eliza. All this irritation is purely subjective.

LIZA. I dont understand. I'm too ignorant.

HIGGINS. It's only imagination. Low spirits and nothing else. Nobody's hurting you. Nothing's wrong. You go to bed like a good girl and sleep it off. Have a little cry and say your prayers: that will make you comfortable.

LIZA. I heard your prayers. "Thank God it's all over!"

HIGGINS [*impatiently*] Well, dont you thank God it's all over? Now you are free and can do what you like.

LIZA [*pulling herself together in desperation*] What am I fit for? What have you left me fit for? Where am I to go? What am I to do? Whats to become of me?

HIGGINS [*enlightened, but not at all impressed*] Oh, thats whats worrying you, is it? [*He thrusts his hands into his pockets, and walks about in his usual manner, rattling the contents of his pockets, as if condescending to a trivial subject out of pure kindness*]. I shouldnt bother about it if I were you. I should imagine you wont have much difficulty in settling yourself somewhere or other, though I hadnt quite realized that you were going away. [*She looks quickly at him: he does not look at her, but examines the dessert stand on the piano and decides that he will eat an apple*]. You might marry, you know. [*He bites a large piece out of the apple and munches it noisily*]. You see,

Eliza, all men are not confirmed old bachelors like me and the Colonel. Most men are the marrying sort (poor devils!); and youre not bad-looking: it's quite a pleasure to look at you sometimes—not now, of course, because youre crying and looking as ugly as the very devil; but when youre all right and quite yourself, youre what I should call attractive. That is, to the people in the marrying line, you understand. You go to bed and have a good nice rest; and then get up and look at yourself in the glass; and you wont feel so cheap.

ELIZA *again looks at him, speechless, and does not stir.*

The look is quite lost on him: he eats his apple with a dreamy expression of happiness, as it is quite a good one.

HIGGINS [*a genial afterthought occurring to him*] I daresay my mother could find some chap or other who would do very well.

LIZA. We were above that at the corner of Tottenham Court Road.

HIGGINS [*waking up*] What do you mean?

LIZA. I sold flowers. I didnt sell myself. Now youve made a lady of me I'm not fit to sell anything else. I wish youd left me where you found me.

HIGGINS [*slinging the core of the apple decisively into the grate*] Tosh, Eliza. Dont you insult human relations by dragging all this cant[4] about buying and selling into it. You neednt marry the fellow if you dont like him.

LIZA. What else am I to do?

HIGGINS. Oh, lots of things. What about your old idea of a florist's shop? Pickering could set you up in one: he has lots of money. [*Chuckling*] He'll have to pay for all those togs you have been wearing today; and that, with the hire of the jewellery, will make a big hole in

two hundred pounds. Why, six months ago you would have thought it the millennium to have a flower shop of your own. Come! youll be all right. I must clear off to bed: I'm devilish sleepy. By the way, I came down for something: I forgot what it was.

LIZA. Your slippers.

HIGGINS. Oh yes, of course. You shied them at me. [*He picks them up, and is going out when she rises and speaks to him*].

LIZA. Before you go, sir—

HIGGINS [*dropping the slippers in his surprise at her calling him Sir*] Eh?

LIZA. Do my clothes belong to me or to Colonel Pickering?

HIGGINS [*coming back into the room as if her question were the very climax of unreason*] What the devil use would they be to Pickering?

LIZA. He might want them for the next girl you pick up to experiment on.

HIGGINS [*shocked and hurt*] Is that the way you feel towards us?

LIZA. I dont want to hear anything more about that. All I want to know is whether anything belongs to me. My own clothes were burnt.

HIGGINS. But what does it matter? Why need you start bothering about that in the middle of the night?

LIZA. I want to know what I may take away with me. I dont want to be accused of stealing.

HIGGINS [*now deeply wounded*] Stealing! You shouldnt have said that, Eliza. That shews a want of feeling.

LIZA. I'm sorry. I'm only a common ignorant girl; and in my station I have to be careful. There cant be any feelings between the like of you and the like of me. Please will you tell me what belongs to me and what doesnt?

HIGGINS [*very sulky*] You may take the whole damned houseful if you like. Except the jewels.

---

4. **cant:** hollow words and borrowed phrases, repeated without thought.

Theyre hired.[5] Will that satisfy you? [*He turns on his heel and is about to go in extreme dudgeon[6]*].

LIZA [*drinking in his emotion like nectar,[7] and nagging him to provoke a further supply*] Stop, please. [*She takes off her jewels*]. Will you take these to your room and keep them safe? I dont want to run the risk of their being missing.

HIGGINS [*furious*] Hand them over. [*She puts them into his hands*]. If these belonged to me instead of to the jeweller, I'd ram them down your ungrateful throat. [*He perfunctorily thrusts them into his pockets, unconsciously decorating himself with the protruding ends of the chains*].

LIZA [*taking a ring off*]. This ring isnt the jeweller's: it's the one you bought me in Brighton. I dont want it now. [HIGGINS *dashes the ring violently into the fireplace, and turns on her so threateningly that she crouches over the piano with her hands over her face, and exclaims*] Dont you hit me.

HIGGINS. Hit you! You infamous creature, how dare you accuse me of such a thing? It is you who have hit me. You have wounded me to the heart.

LIZA [*thrilling with hidden joy*] I'm glad. Ive got a little of my own back, anyhow.

HIGGINS [*with dignity, in his finest professional style*] You have caused me to lose my temper: a thing that has hardly ever happened to me before. I prefer to say nothing more tonight. I am going to bed.

LIZA [*pertly*] Youd better leave a note for Mrs Pearce about the coffee; for she wont be told by me.

HIGGINS [*formally*] Damn Mrs Pearce; and damn the coffee; and damn you; and [*wildly*] damn my own folly in having lavished my hard-

---

5. **hired:** rented.
6. **dudgeon:** anger.
7. **nectar:** in mythology, the drink of the gods.

earned knowledge and the treasure of my regard and intimacy on a heartless guttersnipe. [*He goes out with impressive decorum, and spoils it by slamming the door savagely*].

ELIZA *goes down on her knees on the hearthrug to look for the ring. When she finds it she considers for a moment what to do with it. Finally she flings it down on the dessert stand and goes upstairs in a tearing rage.*

*   *   *   *   *   *

The furniture of Eliza's room has been increased by a big wardrobe and a sumptuous dressing-table. She comes in and switches on the electric light. She goes to the wardrobe; opens it; and pulls out a walking dress, a hat, and a pair of shoes, which she throws on the bed. She takes off her evening dress and shoes; then takes a padded hanger from the wardrobe; adjusts it carefully in the evening dress; and hangs it in the wardrobe, which she shuts with a slam. She puts on her walking shoes, her walking dress, and hat. She takes her wrist watch from the dressing-table and fastens it on. She pulls on her gloves; takes her vanity bag; and looks into it to see that her purse is there before hanging it on her wrist. She makes for the door. Every movement expresses her furious resolution.

She takes a last look at herself in the glass.

She suddenly puts out her tongue at herself; then leaves the room, switching off the electric light at the door.

Meanwhile, in the street outside, Freddy Eynsford Hill, lovelorn, is gazing up at the second floor, in which one of the windows is still lighted.

The light goes out.

FREDDY. Goodnight, darling, darling, darling.

ELIZA *comes out, giving the door a considerable bang behind her.*

LIZA. Whatever are you doing here?

FREDDY. Nothing. I spend most of my nights here. It's the only place where I'm happy. Dont laugh at me, Miss Doolittle.

LIZA. Dont you call me Miss Doolittle, do you hear? Liza's good enough for me. [*She breaks down and grabs him by the shoulders*] Freddy: you dont think I'm a heartless guttersnipe, do you?

FREDDY. Oh no, no, darling: how can you imagine such a thing? You are the loveliest, dearest—

He loses all self-control and smothers her with kisses. She, hungry for comfort, responds. They stand there in one another's arms.

An elderly police constable arrives.

CONSTABLE [*scandalized*] Now then! Now then!! Now then!!!

They release one another hastily.

FREDDY. Sorry, constable. Weve only just become engaged.

They run away.

The constable shakes his head, reflecting on his own courtship and on the vanity of human hopes. He moves off in the opposite direction with slow professional steps.

The flight of the lovers takes them to Cavendish Square. There they halt to consider their next move.

LIZA [*out of breath*] He didnt half give me a fright, that copper. But you answered him proper.

FREDDY. I hope I havnt taken you out of your way. Where were you going?

LIZA. To the river.

FREDDY. What for?

LIZA. To make a hole in it.

FREDDY [*horrified*] Eliza, darling. What do you mean? What's the matter?

LIZA. Never mind. It doesnt matter now. There's nobody in the world now but you and me, is there?

FREDDY. Not a soul.

They indulge in another embrace, and are

again surprised by a much younger constable.

SECOND CONSTABLE. Now then, you two! What's this? Where do you think you are? Move along here, double quick.

FREDDY. As you say, sir, double quick.

They run away again, and are in Hanover Square before they stop for another conference.

FREDDY. I had no idea the police were so devilishly prudish.

LIZA. It's their business to hunt girls off the streets.

FREDDY. We must go somewhere. We cant wander about the streets all night.

LIZA. Cant we? I think it'd be lovely to wander about for ever.

FREDDY. Oh, darling.

They embrace again, oblivious of the arrival of a crawling taxi. It stops.

TAXIMAN. Can I drive you and the lady anywhere, sir?

They start asunder.

LIZA. Oh, Freddy, a taxi. The very thing.

FREDDY. But, damn it, I've no money.

LIZA. I have plenty. The Colonel thinks you should never go out without ten pounds in your pocket. Listen. We'll drive about all night; and in the morning I'll call on old Mrs Higgins and ask her what I ought to do. I'll tell you all about it in the cab. And the police wont touch us there.

FREDDY. Righto! Ripping. [*To the* TAXIMAN] Wimbledon Common. [*They drive off*].

STUDY QUESTIONS

Recalling

1. What do Higgins and Pickering talk about when they return to Wimpole Street? What does Higgins say when Pickering congratulates him? How does Liza react to Higgins?
2. Describe Liza's behavior to Higgins after Pickering leaves. How does she reply to his comment that she can do anything she likes now?
3. What various futures does Higgins outline for Liza? How does she answer his suggestion that his mother might find her a husband?
4. What does Freddy tell Liza when she meets him? What do they do?

Interpreting

5. Describe Liza's feelings after the party. Why might she feel as she does?
6. What does Higgins reveal about his personality in his treatment of Liza after the party? Why do you think he is wounded by Liza's behavior?
7. What new sides do Liza and Higgins both reveal in their argument?

Extending

8. What are the risks of changing a human being "into quite a different human being"? Under what circumstances might such an undertaking be justified?

ACT FIVE

MRS HIGGINS's *drawing room. She is at her writing-table as before. The* PARLORMAID *comes in.*

THE PARLORMAID [*at the door*] Mr Henry, maam, is downstairs with Colonel Pickering.

MRS HIGGINS. Well, shew them up.

THE PARLORMAID. Theyre using the telephone, maam. Telephoning to the police, I think.

MRS HIGGINS. What!

THE PARLORMAID [*coming further in and lowering her voice*] Mr Henry is in a state, maam. I thought I'd better tell you.

MRS HIGGINS. If you had told me that Mr Henry was not in a state it would have been more surprising. Tell them to come up when theyve finished with the police. I suppose he's lost something.

THE PARLORMAID. Yes, maam [*going*].

MRS HIGGINS. Go upstairs and tell Miss Doolittle that Mr Henry and the Colonel are here. Ask her not to come down til I send for her.

THE PARLORMAID. Yes, maam.

> HIGGINS *bursts in. He is, as the* PARLORMAID *has said, in a state.*

HIGGINS. Look here, mother: heres a confounded thing!

MRS HIGGINS. Yes, dear. Good morning. [*He checks his impatience and kisses her, whilst the* PARLORMAID *goes out*]. What is it?

HIGGINS. Eliza's bolted.[1]

MRS HIGGINS [*calmly continuing her writing*] You must have frightened her.

HIGGINS. Frightened her! nonsense! She was left last night, as usual, to turn out the lights and all that; and instead of going to bed she changed her clothes and went right off: her bed wasnt slept in. She came in a cab for her things before seven this morning; and that fool Mrs Pearce let her have them without telling me a word about it. What am I to do?

MRS HIGGINS. Do without, I'm afraid, Henry. The girl has a perfect right to leave if she chooses.

HIGGINS [*wandering distractedly across the room*] But I cant find anything. I dont know what appointments Ive got. I'm—[PICKERING *comes in.* MRS HIGGINS *puts down her pen and turns away from the writing-table*].

PICKERING [*shaking hands*] Good morning, Mrs Higgins. Has Henry told you? [*He sits down on the ottoman*].

HIGGINS. What does that ass of an inspector say? Have you offered a reward?

MRS HIGGINS [*rising in indignant amazement*] You dont mean to say you have set the police after Eliza.

HIGGINS. Of course. What are the police for? What else could we do? [*He sits in the Elizabethan chair*].

PICKERING. The inspector made a lot of difficulties. I really think he suspected us of some improper purpose.

MRS HIGGINS. Well, of course he did. What right have you to go to the police and give the girl's name as if she were a thief, or a lost umbrella, or something? Really! [*She sits down again, deeply vexed*].

HIGGINS. But we want to find her.

PICKERING. We cant let her go like this, you know, Mrs Higgins. What were we to do?

MRS HIGGINS. You have no more sense, either of you, than two children. Why—

> The PARLORMAID *comes in and breaks off the conversation.*

THE PARLORMAID. Mr Henry: a gentleman wants

---

1. **bolted:** run away.

to see you very particular. He's been sent on from Wimpole Street.

HIGGINS. Oh, bother! I cant see anyone now. Who is it?

THE PARLORMAID. A Mr Doolittle, sir.

PICKERING. Doolittle! Do you mean the dustman?

THE PARLORMAID. Dustman! Oh no, sir: a gentleman.

HIGGINS [springing up excitedly] By George, Pick, it's some relative of hers that she's gone to. Somebody we know nothing about. [To the PARLORMAID] Send him up, quick.

THE PARLORMAID. Yes, sir. [She goes].

HIGGINS [eagerly, going to his mother] Genteel relatives! now we shall hear something. [He sits down in the Chippendale chair].

MRS HIGGINS. Do you know any of her people?

PICKERING. Only her father: the fellow we told you about.

THE PARLORMAID [announcing] Mr Doolittle. [She withdraws].

DOOLITTLE enters. He is resplendently dressed as for a fashionable wedding, and might, in fact, be the bridegroom. A flower in his buttonhole, a dazzling silk hat, and patent leather shoes complete the effect. He is too concerned with the business he has come on to notice MRS HIGGINS. He walks straight to HIGGINS, and accosts him with vehement reproach.

DOOLITTLE [indicating his own person] See here! Do you see this? You done this.

HIGGINS. Done what, man?

DOOLITTLE. This, I tell you. Look at it. Look at this hat. Look at this coat.

PICKERING. Has Eliza been buying you clothes?

DOOLITTLE. Eliza! not she. Why would she buy me clothes?

MRS HIGGINS. Good morning, Mr Doolittle. Wont you sit down?

DOOLITTLE [taken aback as he becomes conscious that he has forgotten his hostess] Asking your pardon, maam. [He approaches her and shakes her proffered hand]. Thank you. [He sits down on the ottoman, on PICKERING's right]. I am that full of what has happened to me that I cant think of anything else.

HIGGINS. What the dickens has happened to you?

DOOLITTLE. I shouldnt mind if it had only happened to me: anything might happen to anybody and nobody to blame but Providence, as you might say. But this is something that you done to me: yes, you, Enry Iggins.

HIGGINS. Have you found Eliza?

DOOLITTLE. Have you lost her?

HIGGINS. Yes.

DOOLITTLE. You have all the luck, you have. I aint found her; but she'll find me quick enough now after what you done to me.

MRS HIGGINS. But what has my son done to you, Mr Doolittle?

DOOLITTLE. Done to me! Ruined me. Destroyed my happiness. Tied me up and delivered me into the hands of middle class morality.

HIGGINS [rising intolerantly and standing over DOOLITTLE] Youre raving. Youre drunk. Youre mad. I gave you five pounds. After that I had two conversations with you, at half-a-crown an hour. Ive never seen you since.

DOOLITTLE. Oh! Drunk am I? Mad am I? Tell me this. Did you or did you not write a letter to an old blighter in America that was giving five millions to found Moral Reform Societies all over the world, and that wanted you to invent a universal language for him?

HIGGINS. What! Ezra D. Wannafeller! He's dead. [He sits down again carelessly].

DOOLITTLE. Yes: he's dead; and I'm done for. Now did you or did you not write a letter to him to say that the most original moralist at present in England, to the best of your knowledge, was Alfred Doolittle, a common dustman?

HIGGINS. Oh, after your first visit I remember making some silly joke of the kind.

DOOLITTLE. Ah! You may well call it a silly joke. It put the lid on me right enough. Just give him the chance he wanted to shew that Americans is not like us: that they reckonize and respect merit in every class of life, however humble. Them words is in his blooming will, in which, Henry Higgins, thanks to your silly joking, he leaves me a share in his Pre-digested Cheese Trust worth three thousand a year on condition that I lecture for his Wannafeller Moral Reform World League as often as they ask me up to six times a year.

HIGGINS. The devil he does! Whew! [*Brightening suddenly*] What a lark!

PICKERING. A safe thing for you, Doolittle. They wont ask you twice.

DOOLITTLE. It aint the lecturing I mind. I'll lecture them blue in the face, I will, and not turn a hair. It's making a gentleman of me that I object to. Who asked him to make a gentleman of me? I was happy. I was free. I touched pretty nigh everybody for money when I wanted it, same as I touched you, Enry Iggins. Now I am worrited; tied neck and heels; and everybody touches me for money. It's a fine thing for you, says my solicitor. Is it? says I. You mean it's a good thing for you, I says. When I was a poor man and had a solicitor[2] once when they found a pram[3] in the dust cart, he got me off, and got shut of me and got me shut of him as quick as he could. Same with the doctors: used to shove me out of the hospital before I could hardly stand on my legs, and nothing to pay. Now they finds out that I'm not a healthy man and cant live unless they looks after me twice a day. In the house I'm not let do a hand's turn for myself: somebody else must do it and touch me for it. A year ago I hadnt a relative in the world except two or three that wouldnt speak

to me. Now Ive fifty, and not a decent week's wages among the lot of them. I have to live for others and not for myself: that middle class morality. You talk of losing Eliza. Dont you be anxious: I bet she's on my doorstep by this: she that could support herself easy by selling flowers if I wasnt respectable. And the next one to touch me will be you, Enry Iggins. I'll have to learn to speak middle class language from you, instead of speaking proper English. Thats where youll come in; and I daresay thats what you done it for.

MRS HIGGINS. But, my dear Mr Doolittle, you need not suffer all this if you are really in earnest. Nobody can force you to accept this bequest. You can repudiate it. Isnt that so, Colonel Pickering?

PICKERING. I believe so.

DOOLITTLE [*softening his manner in deference to her sex*] Thats the tragedy of it, maam. It's easy to say chuck it; but I havnt the nerve. Which of us has? We're all intimidated. Intimidated, maam: thats what we are. What is there for me if I chuck it but the workhouse in my old age? I have to dye my hair already to keep my job as a dustman. If I was one of the deserving poor, and had put by a bit, I could chuck it; but then why should I, acause the deserving poor might as well be millionaires for all the happiness they ever has. They dont know what happiness is. But I, as one of the undeserving poor, have nothing between me and the pauper's uniform but this here blasted three thousand a year that shoves me into the middle class. (Excuse the expression, maam; youd use it yourself if you had my provocation.) Theyve got you every way you turn: it's a choice between the Skilly of the workhouse and the Char Bydis[4] of the middle class; and I

_____

2. **solicitor:** type of lawyer.
3. **pram:** baby carriage.

4. **Skilly, Char Bydis:** alluding to Scylla [sil′ə] and Charybdis [kə rib′ dis], a treacherous rock and whirlpool on either side of the narrow passage between Italy and Sicily. Represented by the Greeks as two monsters, Scylla and Charybdis have come to stand for any two dangers neither of which can be avoided without risking the other.

havnt the nerve for the workhouse. Intimidated: thats what I am. Broke. Bought up. Happier men than me will call for my dust, and touch me for their tip; and I'll look on helpless, and envy them. And thats what your son has brought me to. [*He is overcome by emotion*].

MRS HIGGINS. Well, I'm very glad youre not going to do anything foolish, Mr Doolittle. For this solves the problem of Eliza's future. You can provide for her now.

DOOLITTLE [*with melancholy resignation*] Yes, maam: I'm expected to provide for everyone now, out of three thousand a year.

HIGGINS [*jumping up*] Nonsense! he cant provide for her. He shant provide for her. She doesnt belong to him. I paid him five pounds for her. Doolittle: either youre an honest man or a rogue.

DOOLITTLE [*tolerantly*] A little of both, Henry, like the rest of us: a little of both.

HIGGINS. Well, you took that money for the girl; and you have no right to take her as well.

MRS HIGGINS. Henry: dont be absurd. If you want to know where Eliza is, she is upstairs.

HIGGINS [*amazed*] Upstairs!!! Then I shall jolly soon fetch her downstairs. [*He makes resolutely for the door*].

MRS HIGGINS [*rising and following him*] Be quiet, Henry. Sit down.

HIGGINS. I—

MRS HIGGINS. Sit down, dear; and listen to me.

HIGGINS. Oh very well, very well, very well. [*He throws himself ungraciously on the ottoman, with his face towards the windows*]. But I think you might have told us this half an hour ago.

MRS HIGGINS. Eliza came to me this morning. She told me of the brutal way you two treated her.

HIGGINS [*bounding up again*] What!

PICKERING [*rising also*] My dear Mrs Higgins, she's been telling you stories. We didnt treat her brutally. We hardly said a word to her; and we parted on particularly good terms. [*Turning on* HIGGINS] Higgins: did you bully her after I went to bed?

HIGGINS. Just the other way about. She threw my slippers in my face. She behaved in the most outrageous way. I never gave her the slightest provocation. The slippers came bang into my face the moment I entered the room— before I had uttered a word. And used perfectly awful language.

PICKERING [*astonished*] But why? What did we do to her?

MRS HIGGINS. I think I know pretty well what you did. The girl is naturally rather affectionate, I think. Isnt she, Mr Doolittle?

DOOLITTLE. Very tender-hearted, maam. Takes after me.

MRS HIGGINS. Just so. She had become attached to you both. She worked very hard for you, Henry. I dont think you quite realize what anything in the nature of brain work means to a girl of her class. Well, it seems that when the great day of trial came, and she did this wonderful thing for you without making a single mistake, you two sat there and never said a word to her, but talked together of how glad you were that it was all over and how you had been bored with the whole thing. And then you were surprised because she threw your slippers at you! *I* should have thrown the fire-irons at you.

HIGGINS. We said nothing except that we were tired and wanted to go to bed. Did we, Pick?

PICKERING [*shrugging his shoulders*] That was all.

MRS HIGGINS [*ironically*] Quite sure?

PICKERING. Absolutely. Really, that was all.

MRS HIGGINS. You didnt thank her, or pet her, or admire her, or tell her how splendid she'd been.

HIGGINS [*impatiently*] But she knew all about that. We didnt make speeches to her, if thats what you mean.

PICKERING [*conscience stricken*] Perhaps we were a little inconsiderate. Is she very angry?

MRS HIGGINS [*returning to her place at the writing-table*] Well, I'm afraid she wont go back to Wimpole Street, especially now that Mr Doolittle is able to keep up the position you have thrust on her; but she says she is quite willing to meet you on friendly terms and to let bygones be bygones.

HIGGINS [*furious*] Is she, by George? Ho!

MRS HIGGINS. If you promise to behave yourself, Henry, I'll ask her to come down. If not, go home; for you have taken up quite enough of my time.

HIGGINS. Oh, all right. Very well. Pick: you behave yourself. Let us put on our best Sunday manners for this creature that we picked out of the mud. [*He flings himself sulkily into the Elizabethan chair*].

DOOLITTLE [*remonstrating*] Now, now, Enry Iggins! Have some consideration for my feelings as a middle class man.

MRS HIGGINS. Remember your promise, Henry. [*She presses the bell-button on the writing-table*]. Mr Doolittle: will you be so good as to step out on the balcony for a moment. I dont want Eliza to have the shock of your news until she has made it up with these two gentlemen. Would you mind?

DOOLITTLE. As you wish, lady. Anything to help Henry to keep her off my hands. [*He disappears through the window*].

The PARLORMAID *answers the bell.* PICKERING *sits down in* DOOLITTLE's *place.*

MRS HIGGINS. Ask Miss Doolittle to come down, please.

THE PARLORMAID. Yes, maam. [*She goes out*].

MRS HIGGINS. Now, Henry: be good.

HIGGINS. I am behaving myself perfectly.

PICKERING. He is doing his best, Mrs Higgins.

A pause. HIGGINS *throws back his head; stretches out his legs; and begins to whistle.*

MRS HIGGINS. Henry, dearest, you dont look at all nice in that attitude.

HIGGINS [*pulling himself together*] I was not trying to look nice, mother.

MRS HIGGINS. It doesnt matter, dear. I only wanted to make you speak.

HIGGINS. Why?

MRS HIGGINS. Because you cant speak and whistle at the same time.

HIGGINS *groans. Another very trying pause.*

HIGGINS [*springing up, out of patience*] Where the devil is that girl? Are we to wait here all day?

ELIZA *enters, sunny, self-possessed, and giving a staggeringly convincing exhibition of ease of manner. She carries a little work-basket, and is very much at home.* PICKERING *is too much taken aback to rise.*

LIZA. How do you do, Professor Higgins? Are you quite well?

HIGGINS [*choking*] Am I— [*He can say no more*].

LIZA. But of course you are: you are never ill. So glad to see you again, Colonel Pickering. [*He rises hastily; and they shake hands*]. Quite chilly this morning, isnt it? [*She sits down on his left. He sits beside her*].

HIGGINS. Dont you dare try this game on me. I taught it to you; and it doesnt take me in. Get up and come home; and dont be a fool.

ELIZA *takes a piece of needlework from her basket, and begins to stitch at it, without taking the least notice of this outburst.*

MRS HIGGINS. Very nicely put, indeed, Henry. No woman could resist such an invitation.

HIGGINS. You let her alone, mother. Let her speak for herself. You will jolly soon see whether she has an idea that I havnt put into her head or a word that I havnt put into her mouth. I tell you I have created this thing out of the squashed cabbage leaves of Covent Garden; and now she pretends to play the fine lady with me.

MRS HIGGINS [*placidly*] Yes, dear; but youll sit down, wont you?

HIGGINS *sits down again, savagely.*

LIZA [*to* PICKERING, *taking no apparent notice of* HIGGINS, *and working away deftly*] Will you drop me altogether now that the experiment is over, Colonel Pickering?

PICKERING. Oh dont. You mustnt think of it as an experiment. It shocks me, somehow.

LIZA. Oh, I'm only a squashed cabbage leaf—

PICKERING [*impulsively*] No.

LIZA [*continuing quietly*]—but I owe so much to you that I should be very unhappy if you forgot me.

PICKERING. It's very kind of you to say so, Miss Doolittle.

LIZA. It's not because you paid for my dresses. I know you are generous to everybody with money. But it was from you that I learnt really nice manners; and that is what makes one a lady, isnt it? You see it was so very difficult for me with the example of Professor Higgins always before me. I was brought up to be just like him, unable to control myself, and using bad language on the slightest provocation. And I should never have known that ladies and gentlemen didnt behave like that if you hadnt been there.

HIGGINS. Well!!

PICKERING. Oh, thats only his way, you know. He doesnt mean it.

LIZA. Oh, *I* didnt mean it either, when I was a flower girl. It was only my way. But you see I did it; and thats what makes the difference after all.

PICKERING. No doubt. Still, he taught you to speak; and I couldnt have done that, you know.

LIZA [*trivially*] Of course: that is his profession.

HIGGINS. Damnation!

LIZA [*continuing*] It was just like learning to dance in the fashionable way: there was nothing more than that in it. But do you know what began my real education?

PICKERING. What?

LIZA [*stopping her work for a moment*] Your calling me Miss Doolittle that day when I first came to Wimpole Street. That was the beginning of self-respect for me. [*She resumes her stitching*] And there were a hundred little things you never noticed, because they came naturally to you. Things about standing up and taking off your hat and opening doors—

PICKERING. Oh, that was nothing.

LIZA. Yes: things that shewed you thought and felt about me as if I were something better than a scullery-maid; though of course I know you would have been just the same to a scullery-maid if she had been let into the drawing room. You never took off your boots in the dining room when I was there.

PICKERING. You mustnt mind that. Higgins takes off his boots all over the place.

LIZA. I know. I am not blaming him. It is his way, isnt it? But it made such a difference to me that you didnt do it. You see, really and truly, apart from the things anyone can pick up (the dressing and the proper way of speaking, and so on), the difference between a lady and a flower girl is not how she behaves, but how she's treated. I shall always be a flower girl to Professor Higgins, because he always treats me as a flower girl, and always will; but I know I can be a lady to you, because you always treat me as a lady, and always will.

MRS HIGGINS. Please dont grind your teeth, Henry.

PICKERING. Well, this is really very nice of you, Miss Doolittle.

LIZA. I should like you to call me Eliza, now, if you would.

PICKERING. Thank you. Eliza, of course.

LIZA. And I should like Professor Higgins to call me Miss Doolittle.

HIGGINS. I'll see you damned first.

MRS HIGGINS. Henry! Henry!

PICKERING [laughing] Why dont you slang back at him? Dont stand it. It would do him a lot of good.

LIZA. I cant. I could have done it once; but now I cant go back to it. You told me, you know, that when a child is brought to a foreign country, it picks up the language in a few weeks, and forgets its own. Well, I am a child in your country. I have forgotten my own language, and can speak nothing but yours. Thats the real break-off with the corner of Tottenham Court Road. Leaving Wimpole Street finishes it.

PICKERING [much alarmed] Oh! but youre coming back to Wimpole Street, arnt you? Youll forgive Higgins?

HIGGINS [rising] Forgive! Will she, by George! Let her go. Let her find out how she can get on without us. She will relapse into the gutter in three weeks without me at her elbow.

DOOLITTLE appears at the centre window. With a look of dignified reproach at HIGGINS, he comes slowly and silently to his daughter, who, with her back to the window, is unconscious of his approach.

PICKERING. He's incorrigible, Eliza. You wont relapse, will you?

LIZA. No: not now. Never again. I have learnt my lesson. I dont believe I could utter one of the old sounds if I tried. [DOOLITTLE touches her on the left shoulder. She drops her work, losing her self-possession utterly at the spectacle of her father's splendor] A-a-a-a-ah-ow-ooh!

HIGGINS [with a crow of triumph] Aha! Just so. A-a-a-a-ahowooh! A-a-a-a-ahowooh! A-a-a-a-aho-wooh! Victory! Victory! [He throws himself on the divan, folding his arms, and spraddling arrogantly].

DOOLITTLE. Can you blame the girl? Dont look at me like that, Eliza. It aint my fault. Ive come into some money.

LIZA. You must have touched a millionaire this time, dad.

DOOLITTLE. I have. But I'm dressed something special today. I'm going to St George's, Hanover Square. Your stepmother is going to marry me.

LIZA [angrily] Youre going to let yourself down to marry that low common woman!

PICKERING [quietly] He ought to, Eliza. [To DOOLITTLE] Why has she changed her mind?

DOOLITTLE [sadly] Intimidated, Governor. Intimidated. Middle class morality claims its victim. Wont you put on your hat, Liza, and come and see me turned off?

LIZA. If the Colonel says I must, I—I'll [almost sobbing] I'll demean myself. And get insulted for my pains, like enough.

DOOLITTLE. Dont be afraid: she never comes to words with anyone now, poor woman! respectability has broke all the spirit out of her.

PICKERING [squeezing ELIZA's elbow gently] Be kind to them, Eliza. Make the best of it.

LIZA [forcing a little smile for him through her vexation] Oh well, just to shew theres no ill feeling. I'll be back in a moment. [She goes out].

DOOLITTLE [sitting down beside PICKERING] I feel uncommon nervous about the ceremony, Colonel. I wish youd come and see me through it.

PICKERING. But youve been through it before, man. You were married to Eliza's mother.

DOOLITTLE. Who told you that, Colonel?

PICKERING. Well, nobody told me. But I concluded—naturally—

DOOLITTLE. No: that aint the natural way, Colonel: it's only the middle class way. My way was always the undeserving way. But dont say nothing to Eliza. She dont know: I always had a delicacy about telling her.

PICKERING. Quite right. We'll leave it so, if you dont mind.

DOOLITTLE. And youll come to the church, Colonel, and put me through straight?

PICKERING. With pleasure. As far as a bachelor can.

MRS HIGGINS. May I come, Mr Doolittle? I should be very sorry to miss your wedding.

DOOLITTLE. I should indeed be honored by your condescension, maam; and my poor old woman would take it as a tremenjous compliment. She's been very low, thinking of the happy days that are no more.

MRS HIGGINS [*rising*] I'll order the carriage and get ready. [*The men rise, except* HIGGINS]. I shant be more than fifteen minutes. [*As she goes to the door* ELIZA *comes in, hatted and buttoning her gloves*]. I'm going to the church to see your father married, Eliza. You had better come in the brougham[5] with me. Colonel Pickering can go on with the bridegroom.

MRS HIGGINS *goes out.* ELIZA *comes to the middle of the room between the centre window and the ottoman.* PICKERING *joins her.*

DOOLITTLE. Bridegroom. What a word! It makes a man realize his position, somehow. [*He takes up his hat and goes towards the door*].

PICKERING. Before I go, Eliza, do forgive Higgins and come back to us.

---

5. **brougham** [broom]: a kind of carriage.

LIZA. I dont think dad would allow me. Would you, dad?

DOOLITTLE [*sad but magnanimous*] They played you off very cunning, Eliza, them two sportsmen. If it had been only one of them, you could have nailed him. But you see, there was two; and one of them chaperoned the other, as you might say. [*To* PICKERING] It was artful of you, Colonel; but I bear no malice: I should have done the same myself. I been the victim of one woman after another all my life, and I dont grudge you two getting the better of Liza. I shant interfere. It's time for us to go, Colonel. So long, Henry. See you in St George's, Eliza. [*He goes out*].

PICKERING [*coaxing*] Do stay with us, Eliza. [*He follows* DOOLITTLE].

ELIZA *goes out on the balcony to avoid being alone with* HIGGINS. *He rises and joins her there. She immediately comes back into the room and makes for the door; but he goes along the balcony and gets his back to the door before she reaches it.*

HIGGINS. Well, Eliza, youve had a bit of your own back, as you call it. Have you had enough? and are you going to be reasonable? Or do you want any more?

LIZA. You want me back only to pick up your slippers and put up with your tempers and fetch and carry for you.

HIGGINS. I havnt said I wanted you back at all.

LIZA. Oh, indeed. Then what are we talking about?

HIGGINS. About you, not about me. If you come back I shall treat you just as I have always treated you. I cant change my nature; and I dont intend to change my manners. My manners are exactly the same as Colonel Pickering's.

LIZA. Thats not true. He treats a flower girl as if she was a duchess.

HIGGINS. And I treat a duchess as if she was a flower girl.

LIZA. I see [*She turns away composedly, and sits on the ottoman, facing the window*]. The same to everybody.

HIGGINS. Just so.

LIZA. Like father.

HIGGINS [*grinning, a little taken down*] Without accepting the comparison at all points, Eliza, it's quite true that your father is not a snob, and that he will be quite at home in any station of life to which his eccentric destiny may call him. [*Seriously*] The great secret, Eliza, is not having bad manners or good manners or any other particular sort of manners, but having the same manner for all human souls: in short, behaving as if you were in Heaven, where there are no third-class carriages, and one soul is as good as another.

LIZA. Amen. You are a born preacher.

HIGGINS [*irritated*] The question is not whether I treat you rudely, but whether you ever heard me treat anyone else better.

LIZA [*with sudden sincerity*] I dont care how you treat me. I dont mind your swearing at me. I shouldnt mind a black eye: Ive had one before this. But [*standing up and facing him*] I wont be passed over.

HIGGINS. Then get out of my way; for I wont stop for you. You talk about me as if I were a motor bus.

LIZA. So you are a motor bus: all bounce and go, and no consideration for anyone. But I can do without you: dont think I cant.

HIGGINS. I know you can. I told you you could.

LIZA [*wounded, getting away from him to the other side of the ottoman with her face to the hearth*] I know you did, you brute. You wanted to get rid of me.

HIGGINS. Liar.

LIZA. Thank you. [*She sits down with dignity*]

HIGGINS. You never asked yourself, I suppose, whether *I* could do without you.

LIZA [*earnestly*] Dont you try to get round me. Youll have to do without me.

HIGGINS [*arrogant*] I can do without anybody. I have my own soul: my own spark of divine fire. But [*with sudden humility*] I shall miss you, Eliza. [*He sits down near her on the ottoman*] I have learnt something from your idiotic notions: I confess that humbly and gratefully. And I have grown accustomed to your voice and appearance. I like them, rather.

LIZA. Well, you have both of them on your gramophone and in your book of photographs. When you feel lonely without me, you can turn the machine on. It's got no feelings to hurt.

HIGGINS. I cant turn your soul on. Leave me those feelings; and you can take away the voice and the face. They are not you.

LIZA. Oh, you are a devil. You can twist the heart in a girl as easy as some could twist her arms to hurt her. Mrs Pearce warned me. Time and again she has wanted to leave you; and you always got round her at the last minute. And you dont care a bit for her. And you dont care a bit for me.

HIGGINS. I care for life, for humanity; and you are a part of it that has come my way and been built into my house. What more can you or anyone ask?

LIZA. I wont care for anybody that doesnt care for me.

HIGGINS. Commercial principles, Eliza. Like [*reproducing her Covent Garden pronunication with professional exactness*] s'yollin voylets [*selling violets*], isnt it?

LIZA. Dont sneer at me. It's mean to sneer at me.

HIGGINS. I have never sneered in my life. Sneering doesnt become either the human face or the human soul. I am expressing my righteous contempt for Commercialism. I dont and wont trade in affection. You call me a brute because you couldnt buy a claim on me by fetching my slippers and finding my spectacles. You were a fool: I think a woman fetching a man's slippers is a disgusting sight: did I ever fetch your slippers? I think a good deal more of you for throwing them in my face. No use slaving for me and then saying you want to be cared for: who cares for a slave? If you come back, come back for the sake of good fellowship; for youll get nothing else. Youve had a thousand times as much out of me as I have out of you; and if you dare to set up your little dog's tricks of fetching and carrying slippers against my creation of a Duchess Eliza, I'll slam the door in your silly face.

LIZA. What did you do it for if you didnt care for me?

HIGGINS [*heartily*] Why, because it was my job.

LIZA. You never thought of the trouble it would make for me.

HIGGINS. Would the world ever have been made if its maker had been afraid of making trouble? Making life means making trouble. Theres only one way of escaping trouble; and thats killing things. Cowards, you notice, are always shrieking to have troublesome people killed.

LIZA. I'm no preacher: I dont notice things like that. I notice that you dont notice me.

HIGGINS [*jumping up and walking about intolerantly*] Eliza: youre an idiot. I waste the treasures of my Miltonic mind by spreading them before you. Once for all, understand that I go my way and do my work without caring twopence what happens to either of us. I am not intimidated, like your father and your stepmother. So you can come back or go to the devil: which you please.

LIZA. What am I to come back for?

HIGGINS [*bouncing up on his knees on the ottoman and leaning over it to her*] For the fun of it. Thats why I took you on.

LIZA [*with averted face*] And you may throw me out tomorrow if I dont do everything you want me to?

HIGGINS. Yes; and you may walk out tomorrow if I dont do everything you want me to.

LIZA. And live with my stepmother?

HIGGINS. Yes, or sell flowers.

LIZA. Oh, if I only could go back to my flower basket! I should be independent of both you and father and all the world! Why did you take my independence from me? Why did I give it up? I'm a slave now, for all my fine clothes.

HIGGINS. Not a bit. I'll adopt you as my daughter and settle money on you if you like. Or would you rather marry Pickering?

LIZA [*looking fiercely round at him*] I wouldnt marry you if you asked me; and youre nearer my age than what he is.

HIGGINS [*gently*] Than he is: not "than what he is."

LIZA [*losing her temper and rising*] I'll talk as I like. Youre not my teacher now.

HIGGINS [*reflectively*] I dont suppose Pickering would, though. He's as confirmed an old bachelor as I am.

LIZA. Thats not what I want; and dont you think it. I've always had chaps enough wanting me that way. Freddy Hill writes to me twice and three times a day, sheets and sheets.

HIGGINS [*disagreeably surprised*] Damn his impudence! [*He recoils and finds himself sitting on his heels*].

LIZA. He has a right to if he likes, poor lad. And he does love me.

HIGGINS [*getting off the ottoman*] You have no right to encourage him.

LIZA. Every girl has a right to be loved.

HIGGINS. What! By fools like that?

LIZA. Freddy's not a fool. And if he's weak and poor and wants me, may be he'd make me happier than my betters that bully me and dont want me.

HIGGINS. Can he make anything of you? Thats the point.

LIZA. Perhaps I could make something of him. But I never thought of us making anything of one another; and you never think of anything else. I only want to be natural.

HIGGINS. In short, you want me to be as infatuated about you as Freddy? Is that it?

LIZA. No I dont. Thats not the sort of feeling I want from you. And dont you be too sure of yourself or of me. I could have been a bad girl if I'd liked. Ive seen more of some things than you, for all your learning. Girls like me can drag gentlemen down to make love to them easy enough. And they wish each other dead the next minute.

HIGGINS. Of course they do. Then what in thunder are we quarrelling about?

LIZA [*much troubled*] I want a little kindness. I know I'm a common ignorant girl, and you a book-learned gentleman; but I'm not dirt under your feet. What I done (*correcting herself*) what I did was not for the dresses and the taxis: I did it because we were pleasant together and I come—came—to care for you; not to want you to make love to me, and not forgetting the difference between us, but more friendly like.

HIGGINS. Well, of course. Thats just how I feel. And how Pickering feels. Eliza: youre a fool.

LIZA. Thats not a proper answer to give me [*she sinks on the chair at the writing-table in tears*].

HIGGINS. It's all youll get until you stop being a common idiot. If youre going to be a lady, youll have to give up feeling neglected if the men you know dont spend half their time snivelling over you and the other half giving you black eyes. If you cant stand the coldness of my sort of life, and the strain of it, go back to the gutter. Work til youre more a brute than a human being; and then cuddle and squabble and drink til you fall asleep. Oh, it's a fine life, the life of the gutter. It's real: it's warm: it's violent: you can feel it through the thickest skin: you can taste it and smell it without any training or any work. Not like Science and Literature and Classical Music and Philosophy and Art. You find me cold, unfeeling, selfish, dont you? Very well: be off with you to the sort of people you like. Marry some sentimental hog or other with lots of money, and a thick pair of lips to kiss you with and a thick pair of boots to kick you with. If you cant appreciate what youve got, youd better get what you can appreciate.

LIZA [*desperate*] Oh, you are a cruel tyrant. I cant talk to you: you turn everything against me: I'm always in the wrong. But you know very well all the time that youre nothing but a bully. You know I cant go back to the gutter, as you call it, and that I have no real friends in the world but you and the Colonel. You know well I couldnt bear to live with a low common man after you two; and it's wicked and cruel of you to insult me by pretending I could. You think I must go back to Wimpole Street because I have nowhere else to go but father's. But dont you be too sure that you have me under your feet to be trampled on and talked down. I'll marry Freddy, I will, as soon as I'm able to support him.

HIGGINS [*thunderstruck*] Freddy!!! that young fool! That poor devil who couldnt get a job as an errand boy even if he had the guts to try for it! Woman: do you not understand that I have made you a consort for a king?

LIZA. Freddy loves me: that makes him king enough for me. I dont want him to work: he wasnt brought up to it as I was. I'll go and be a teacher.

HIGGINS. Whatll you teach, in heaven's name?

LIZA. What you taught me. I'll teach phonetics.

HIGGINS. Ha! ha! ha!

LIZA. I'll offer myself as an assistant to that hairyfaced Hungarian.

HIGGINS [*rising in a fury*] What! That impostor! that humbug! that toadying ignoramus! Teach him my methods! my discoveries! You take one step in his direction and I'll wring your neck. [*He lays hands on her*]. Do you hear?

LIZA [*defiantly non-resistant*] Wring away. What do I care? I knew youd strike me some day. [*He lets her go, stamping with rage at having forgotten himself, and recoils so hastily that he stumbles back into his seat on the ottoman*]. Aha! Now I know how to deal with you. What a fool I was not to think of it before! You cant take away the knowledge you gave me. You said I had a finer ear than you. And I can be civil and kind to people, which is more than you can. Aha! [*Purposely dropping her aitches to annoy him*] Thats done you, Enry Iggins, it az. Now I dont care that [*snapping her fingers*] for your bullying and your big talk. I'll advertize it in the papers that your duchess is only a flower girl that you taught, and that she'll teach anybody to be a duchess just the same in six months for a thousand guineas. Oh, when I think of myself crawling under your feet and being trampled on and called names, when all the time I had only to lift up my finger to be as good as you, I could just kick myself.

HIGGINS [*wondering at her*] You damned impudent slut, you! But it's better than snivelling; better than fetching slippers and finding spectacles, isnt it? [*Rising*] By George, Eliza. I said I'd make a woman of you; and I have. I like you like this.

LIZA. Yes: you turn round and make up to me now that I'm not afraid of you, and can do without you.

HIGGINS. Of course I do, you little fool. Five minutes ago you were like a millstone round my neck. Now youre a tower of strength: a consort battleship. You and I and Pickering will be three old bachelors instead of only two men and a silly girl.

MRS HIGGINS *returns dressed for the wedding.* ELIZA *instantly becomes cool and elegant.*

MRS HIGGINS. The carriage is waiting, Eliza. Are you ready?

LIZA. Quite. Is the Professor coming?

MRS HIGGINS. Certainly not. He cant behave himself in church. He makes remarks out loud all the time on the clergyman's pronunciation.

LIZA. Then I shall not see you again, Professor. Goodbye. [*She goes to the door*].

MRS HIGGINS [*coming to* HIGGINS] Goodbye, dear.

HIGGINS. Goodbye, mother. [*He is about to kiss her, when he recollects something*]. Oh, by the way, Eliza, order a ham and a Stilton cheese, will you? And buy me a pair of reindeer gloves, number eights, and a tie to match that new suit of mine. You can choose the color. [*His cheerful, careless, vigorous voice shews that he is incorrigible*].

LIZA [*disdainfully*] Number eights are too small for you if you want them lined with lamb's wool. You have three new ties that you have forgotten in the drawer of your washstand. Colonel Pickering prefers double Gloucester to Stilton; and you dont notice the difference. I telephoned Mrs Pearce this morning not to forget the ham. What you are to do without me I cannot imagine. [*She sweeps out*].

MRS HIGGINS. I'm afraid youve spoilt that girl, Henry. I should be uneasy about you and her if she were less fond of Colonel Pickering.

HIGGINS. Pickering! Nonsense; she's going to marry Freddy. Ha ha! Freddy! Freddy!! Ha ha ha ha ha!!!!! [*He roars with laughter as the play ends*].

EPILOGUE

The rest of the story need not be shewn in action, and indeed, would hardly need telling if our imaginations were not so enfeebled by their lazy dependence on the ready-mades and reach-me-downs of the ragshop in which Romance keeps its stock of "happy endings" to misfit all stories. Now, the history of Eliza Doolittle, though called a romance because the transfiguration it records seems exceedingly improbable, is common enough. Such transfigurations have been achieved by hundreds of resolutely ambitious young women since Nell Gwynne[1] set them the example by playing queens and fascinating kings in the theatre in which she began by selling oranges. Nevertheless, people in all directions have assumed, for no other reason than that she became the heroine of a romance, that she must have married the hero of it. This is unbearable, not only because her little drama, if acted on such a thoughtless assumption, must be spoiled, but because the true sequel is patent to anyone with a sense of human nature in general, and of feminine instinct in particular.

Eliza, in telling Higgins she would not marry him if he asked her, was not coquetting:[2] she was announcing a well-considered decision. When a bachelor interests, and dominates, and teaches, and becomes important to a spinster, as Higgins with Eliza, she always, if she has character enough to be capable of it, considers very seriously indeed whether she will play for becoming that bachelor's wife, especially if he is so little interested in marriage that a determined and devoted woman might capture him if she set herself resolutely to do it. Her decision will depend a good deal on whether she is really free to choose; and that, again, will depend on her age and income. If she is at the end of her youth, and has no security for her livelihood, she will marry him because she must marry anybody who will provide for her. But at Eliza's age a good-looking girl does not feel that pressure: she feels free to pick and choose. She is therefore guided by her instinct in the matter. Eliza's instinct tells her not to marry Higgins. It does not tell her to give him up. It is not in the slightest doubt as to his remaining one of the strongest personal interests in her life. It would be very sorely strained if there was another woman likely to supplant her with him. But as she feels sure of him on that last point, she has no doubt at all as to her course, and would not have any, even if the difference of twenty years in age, which seems so great to youth, did not exist between them.

As our own instincts are not appealed to by her conclusion, let us see whether we cannot discover some reason in it. When Higgins excused his indifference to young women on the ground that they had an irresistible rival in his mother, he gave the clue to his inveterate old-bachelordom. The case is uncommon only to the extent that remarkable mothers are uncommon. If an imaginative boy has a sufficiently rich mother who has intelligence, personal grace, dignity of character without harshness, and a cultivated sense of the best art of her time to enable her to make her house beautiful, she sets a standard for him against which very few women can struggle, besides effecting for him a disengagement of his affections, his sense of beauty, and his idealism from his specifically sexual impulses. This makes him a standing puzzle to the huge number of uncultivated people who have been brought up in tasteless homes by commonplace or disagreeable parents, and to whom, consequently, literature, painting, sculpture, music, and affectionate personal relations come as modes of sex if they come at all. The word passion means nothing else to them; and that Higgins could have a passion for phonetics and idealize his mother instead of Eliza, would seem to them absurd and unnatural. Nevertheless, when

---

1. **Nell Gwynne** (1650–1687): actress and favorite of Charles II. From being a peddler of oranges, she rose to the heights of late seventeenth-century English society.
2. **coquetting:** being flirtatiously coy.

we look round and see that hardly anyone is too ugly or disagreeable to find a wife or a husband if he or she wants one, whilst many old maids and bachelors are above the average in quality and culture, we cannot help suspecting that the disentanglement of sex from the associations with which it is so commonly confused, a disentanglement which persons of genius achieve by sheer intellectual analysis, is sometimes produced or aided by parental fascination.

Now, though Eliza was incapable of thus explaining to herself Higgins's formidable powers of resistance to the charm that prostrated Freddy at the first glance, she was instinctively aware that she could never obtain a complete grip of him, or come between him and his mother (the first necessity of the married woman). To put it shortly, she knew that for some mysterious reason he had not the makings of a married man in him, according to her conception of a husband as one to whom she would be his nearest and fondest and warmest interest. Even had there been no mother-rival, she would still have refused to accept an interest in herself that was secondary to philosophic interests. Had Mrs Higgins died, there would still have been Milton and the Universal Alphabet. Landor's[3] remark that to those who have the greatest power of loving, love is a secondary affair, would not have recommended Landor to Eliza. Put that along with her resentment of Higgins's domineering superiority, and her mistrust of his coaxing cleverness in getting round her and evading her wrath when he had gone too far with his impetuous bullying, and you will see that Eliza's instinct had good grounds for warning her not to marry her Pygmalion.

And now, whom did Eliza marry? For if Higgins was a predestinate old bachelor, she was most certainly not a predestinate old maid. Well, that can be told very shortly to those who have not guessed it from the indications she has herself given them.

Almost immediately after Eliza is stung into proclaiming her considered determination not to marry Higgins, she mentions that fact that young Mr Frederick Eynsford Hill is pouring out his love for her daily through the post. Now Freddy is young, practically twenty years younger than Higgins: he is a gentleman (or, as Eliza would qualify him, a toff), and speaks like one. He is nicely dressed, is treated by the Colonel as an equal, loves her unaffectedly, and is not her master, nor ever likely to dominate her in spite of his advantage of social standing. Eliza has no use for the foolish romantic tradition that all women love to be mastered, if not actually bullied and beaten. "When you go to women" says Nietzsche[4] "take your whip with you." Sensible despots have never confined that precaution to women: they have taken their whips with them when they have dealt with men, and been slavishly idealized by the men over whom they have flourished the whip much more than by women. No doubt there are slavish women as well as slavish men; and women, like men, admire those that are stronger than themselves. But to admire a strong person and to live under that strong person's thumb are two different things. The weak may not be admired and hero-worshipped; but they are by no means disliked or shunned; and they never seem to have the least difficulty in marrying people who are too good for them. They may fail in emergencies; but life is not one long emergency: it is mostly a string of situations for which no exceptional strength is needed, and with which even rather weak people can cope if they have a stronger partner to help them out. Accordingly, it is a truth everywhere in evidence that strong people, masculine or feminine, not only do not marry stronger people, but do not shew any preference for them in selecting their friends. When a lion meets another with a louder roar "the first lion thinks the last a bore." The man or

---

3. **Landor's:** referring to English writer Walter Savage Landor (1775–1864).

4. **Nietzsche** [nē′chə]: Friedrich Wilhelm Nietzsche (1844–1900), influential German philosopher.

woman who feels strong enough for two, seeks for every other quality in a partner than strength.

The converse is also true. Weak people want to marry strong people who do not frighten them too much; and this often leads them to make the mistake we describe metaphorically as "biting off more than they can chew." They want too much for too little; and when the bargain is unreasonable beyond all bearing, the union becomes impossible: it ends in the weaker party being either discarded or borne as a cross, which is worse. People who are not only weak, but silly or obtuse as well, are often in these difficulties.

This being the state of human affairs, what is Eliza fairly sure to do when she is placed between Freddy and Higgins? Will she look forward to a lifetime of fetching Higgins's slippers or to a lifetime of Freddy fetching hers? There can be no doubt about the answer. Unless Freddy is biologically repulsive to her, and Higgins biologically attractive to a degree that overwhelms all her other instincts, she will, if she marries either of them, marry Freddy.

And that is just what Eliza did.

Complications ensued; but they were economic, not romantic. Freddy had no money and no occupation. His mother's jointure,[5] a last relic of the opulence of Largelady Park, had enabled her to struggle along in Earlscourt with an air of gentility, but not to procure any serious secondary education for her children, much less give the boy a profession. A clerkship at thirty shillings a week was beneath Freddy's dignity, and extremely distasteful to him besides. His prospects consisted of a hope that if he kept up appearances somebody would do something for him. The something appeared vaguely to his imagination as a private secretaryship or a sinecure[6] of some sort. To his mother it perhaps appeared as a marriage to some lady of means who could not resist her boy's niceness. Fancy her feelings when he married a flower girl who had become disclassed under extraordinary circumstances which were now notorious!

It is true that Eliza's situation did not seem wholly ineligible. Her father, though formerly a dustman, and now fantastically disclassed, had become extremely popular in the smartest society by a social talent which triumphed over every prejudice and every disadvantage. Rejected by the middle class, which he loathed, he had shot up at once into the highest circles by his wit, his dustmanship (which he carried like a banner), and his Nietzschean transcendence of good and evil. At intimate ducal dinners he sat on the right hand of the Duchess; and in country houses he smoked in the pantry and was made much of by the butler when he was not feeding in the dining room and being consulted by cabinet ministers. But he found it almost as hard to do all this on [three] thousand a year as Mrs Eynsford Hill to live in Earlscourt on an income so pitiably smaller that I have not the heart to disclose its exact figure. He absolutely refused to add the last straw to his burden by contributing to Eliza's support.

Thus Freddy and Eliza, now Mr and Mrs Eynsford Hill, would have spent a penniless honeymoon but for a wedding present of £500 from the Colonel to Eliza. It lasted a long time because Freddy did not know how to spend money, never having had any to spend, and Eliza, socially trained by a pair of old bachelors, wore her clothes as long as they held together and looked pretty, without the least regard to their being many months out of fashion. Still, £500 will not last two young people for ever; and they both knew, and Eliza felt as well, that they must shift for themselves in the end. She could quarter herself on Wimpole Street because it had come to be her home; but she was quite aware that she ought not to quarter Freddy there, and that it would not be good for his character if she did.

Not that the Wimpole Street bachelors objected. When she consulted them, Higgins de-

---

5. **jointure:** widow's inheritance, payable only during her lifetime; surviving children do not benefit.
6. **sinecure** [sin′ə kyoor′]: salaried position requiring little or no work.

clined to be bothered about her housing problem when that solution was so simple. Eliza's desire to have Freddy in the house with her seemed of no more importance than if she had wanted an extra piece of bedroom furniture. Pleas as to Freddy's character, and the moral obligation on him to earn his own living, were lost on Higgins. He denied that Freddy had any character, and declared that if he tried to do any useful work some competent person would have the trouble of undoing it: a procedure involving a net loss to the community, and great unhappiness to Freddy himself, who was obviously intended by Nature for such light work as amusing Eliza, which, Higgins declared, was a much more useful and honorable occupation than working in the city. When Eliza referred again to her project of teaching phonetics, Higgins abated not a jot of his violent opposition to it. He said she was not within ten years of being qualified to meddle with his pet subject; and as it was evident that the Colonel agreed with him, she felt she could not go against them in this grave matter, and that she had no right, without Higgins's consent, to exploit the knowledge he had given her; for his knowledge seemed to her as much his private property as his watch: Eliza was no communist. Besides, she was superstitiously devoted to them both, more entirely and frankly after her marriage than before it.

It was the Colonel who finally solved the problem, which had cost him much perplexed cogitation. He one day asked Eliza, rather shyly, whether she had quite given up her notion of keeping a flower shop. She replied that she had thought of it, but had put it out of her head, because the Colonel had said, that day at Mrs Higgins's, that it would never do. The Colonel confessed that when he said that, he had not quite recovered from the dazzling impression of the day before. They broke the matter to Higgins that evening. The sole comment vouchsafed by him very nearly led to a serious quarrel with Eliza. It was to the effect that she would have in Freddy an ideal errand boy.

Freddy himself was next sounded on the subject. He said he had been thinking of a shop himself; though it had presented itself to his pennilessness as a small place in which Eliza should sell tobacco at one counter whilst he sold newspapers at the opposite one. But he agreed that it would be extraordinarily jolly to go early every morning with Eliza to Covent Garden and buy flowers on the scene of their first meeting: a sentiment which earned him many kisses from his wife. He added that he had always been afraid to propose anything of the sort, because Clara would make an awful row about a step that must damage her matrimonial chances, and his mother could not be expected to like it after clinging for so many years to that step of the social ladder on which retail trade is impossible.

This difficulty was removed by an event highly unexpected by Freddy's mother. Clara, in the course of her incursions into those artistic circles which were the highest within her reach, discovered that her conversational qualifications were expected to include a grounding in the novels of Mr H. G. Wells.[7] She borrowed them in various directions so energetically that she swallowed them all within two months. The result was a conversion of a kind quite common today. A modern Acts of the Apostles would fill fifty whole Bibles if anyone were capable of writing it.

Poor Clara, who appeared to Higgins and his mother as a disagreeable and ridiculous person, and to her own mother as in some inexplicable way a social failure, had never seen herself in either light; for, though to some extent ridiculed and mimicked in West Kensington like everybody else there, she was accepted as a rational and normal—or shall we say inevitable?—sort of human being. At worst they called her The Pusher; but to them no more than to herself had it ever occurred that she was pushing the air, and pushing it in a wrong direction. Still, she was not happy. She

---

7. **H. G. Wells:** Herbert George Wells (1866–1946), English novelist, historian, and social reformer.

was growing desperate. Her one asset, the fact that her mother was what the Epsom greengrocer called a carriage lady, had no exchange value, apparently. It had prevented her from getting educated, because the only education she could have afforded was education with the Earlscourt greengrocer's daughter. It had led her to seek the society of her mother's class; and that class simply would not have her, because she was much poorer than the greengrocer, and, far from being able to afford a maid, could not afford even a housemaid, and had to scrape along at home with an illiberally treated general servant. Under such circumstances nothing could give her an air of being a genuine product of Largelady Park. And yet its tradition made her regard a marriage with anyone within her reach as an unbearable humiliation. Commercial people and professional people in a small way were odious to her. She ran after painters and novelists; but she did not charm them; and her bold attempts to pick up and practise artistic and literary talk irritated them. She was, in short, an utter failure, an ignorant, incompetent, pretentious, unwelcome, penniless, useless little snob; and though she did not admit these disqualifications (for nobody ever faces unpleasant truths of this kind until the possibility of a way out dawns on them) she felt their effects too keenly to be satisfied with her position.

Clara had a startling eyeopener when, on being suddenly awakened to enthusiasm by a girl of her own age who dazzled her and produced in her a gushing desire to take her for a model, and gain her friendship, she discovered that this exquisite apparition had graduated from the gutter in a few months time. It shook her so violently, that when Mr H. G. Wells lifted her on the point of his puissant[8] pen, and placed her at the angle of view from which the life she was leading and the society to which she clung appeared in its true relation to real human needs and worthy social structure, he effected a conversion and a conviction of sin

comparable to the most sensational feats of General Booth[9] or Gypsy Smith. Clara's snobbery went bang. Life suddenly began to move with her. Without knowing how or why, she began to make friends and enemies. Some of the acquaintances to whom she had been a tedious or indifferent or ridiculous affliction, dropped her: others became cordial. To her amazement she found that some "quite nice" people were saturated with Wells, and that this accessibility to ideas was the secret of their niceness. People she had thought deeply religious, and had tried to conciliate on that tack with disastrous results, suddenly took an interest in her, and revealed a hostility to conventional religion which she had never conceived possible except among the most desperate characters. They made her read Galsworthy; and Galsworthy exposed the vanity of Largelady Park and finished her. It exasperated her to think that the dungeon in which she had languished for so many unhappy years had been unlocked all the time, and that the impulses she had so carefully struggled with and stifled for the sake of keeping well with society, were precisely those by which alone she could have come into any sort of sincere human contact. In the radiance of these discoveries, and the tumult of their reaction, she made a fool of herself as freely and conspicuously as when she so rashly adopted Eliza's expletive in Mrs Higgins's drawing room; for the new-born Wellsian had to find her bearings almost as ridiculously as a baby; but nobody hates a baby for its ineptitudes, or thinks the worse of it for trying to eat the matches; and Clara lost no friends by her follies. They laughed at her to her face this time; and she had to defend herself and fight it out as best she could.

When Freddy paid a visit to Earlscourt (which he never did when he could possibly help it) to make the desolating announcement that he and his Eliza were thinking of black-

<hr>

8. **puissant** [pwis′ənt]: powerful.

9. **General Booth:** William Booth (1829–1912), founder of the Salvation Army.

ening the Largelady scutcheon[10] by opening a shop, he found the little household already convulsed by a prior announcement from Clara that she also was going to work in an old furniture shop in Dover Street, which had been started by a fellow Wellsian. This appointment Clara owed, after all, to her old social accomplishment of Push. She had made up her mind that, cost what it might, she would see Mr Wells in the flesh; and she had achieved her end at a garden party. She had better luck than so rash an enterprise deserved. Mr Wells came up to her expectations. Age had not withered him, nor could custom stale his infinite variety in half an hour. His pleasant neatness and compactness, his small hands and feet, his teeming ready brain, his unaffected accessibility, and a certain fine apprehensiveness which stamped him as susceptible from his topmost hair to his tipmost toe, proved irresistible. Clara talked of nothing else for weeks and weeks afterwards. And as she happened to talk to the lady of the furniture shop, and that lady also desired above all things to know Mr Wells and sell pretty things to him, she offered Clara a job on the chance of achieving that end through her.

And so it came about that Eliza's luck held, and the expected opposition to the flower shop melted away. The shop is in the arcade of a railway station not very far from the Victoria and Albert Museum; and if you live in that neighborhood you may go there any day and buy a buttonhole from Eliza.

Now here is a last opportunity for romance. Would you not like to be assured that the shop was an immense success, thanks to Eliza's charms and her early business experience in Covent Garden? Alas! the truth is the truth: the shop did not pay for a long time, simply because Eliza and her Freddy did not know how to keep it. True, Eliza had not to begin at the very beginning: she knew the names and prices of the cheaper flowers; and her elation was unbounded when she found that Freddy, like all youths educated at cheap, pretentious, and thoroughly inefficient schools, knew a little Latin. It was very little, but enough to make him appear to her a Porson or Bentley,[11] and to put him at his ease with botanical nomenclature. Unfortunately he knew nothing else; and Eliza, though she could count money up to eighteen shillings or so, and had acquired a certain familiarity with the language of Milton from her struggles to qualify herself for winning Higgins's bet, could not write out a bill without utterly disgracing the establishment. Freddy's power of stating in Latin that Balbus built a wall and that Gaul was divided into three parts[12] did not carry with it the slightest knowledge of accounts or business: Colonel Pickering had to explain to him what a cheque book and a bank account meant. And the pair were by no means easily teachable. Freddy backed up Eliza in her obstinate refusal to believe that they could save money by engaging a bookkeeper with some knowledge of the business. How, they argued, could you possibly save money by going to extra expense when you already could not make both ends meet? But the Colonel, after making the ends meet over and over again, at last gently insisted; and Eliza, humbled to the dust by having to beg from him so often, and stung by the uproarious derision of Higgins, to whom the notion of Freddy succeeding at anything was a joke that never palled, grasped the fact that business, like phonetics, has to be learned.

On the piteous spectacle of the pair spending their evenings in shorthand schools and polytechnic classes, learning bookkeeping and typewriting with incipient junior clerks, male and female, from the elementary schools, let me not dwell. There were even classes at the London School of Economics, and a humble personal appeal to the director of that institution to recommend a course bearing on the

---

10. **scutcheon** [skuch′ən]: coat of arms.

11. **Porson, Bentley:** celebrated Latin scholars.
12. **Balbus . . . parts:** alluding to elementary Latin exercises. Caesar's *Gallic Wars* begins with the latter statement.

flower business. He, being a humorist, explained to them the method of the celebrated Dickensian essay on Chinese Metaphysics by the gentleman who read an article on China and an article on Metaphysics and combined the information. He suggested that they should combine the London School with Kew Gardens. Eliza, to whom the procedure of the Dickensian gentleman seemed perfectly correct (as in fact it was) and not in the least funny (which was only her ignorance), took the advice with entire gravity. But the effort that cost her the deepest humiliation was a request to Higgins, whose pet artistic fancy, next to Milton's verse, was calligraphy and who himself wrote a most beautiful Italian hand, that he would teach her to write. He declared that she was congenitally incapable of forming a single letter worthy of the least of Milton's words; but she persisted; and again he suddenly threw himself into the task of teaching her with a combination of stormy intensity, concentrated patience, and occasional bursts of interesting disquisition on the beauty and nobility, the august mission and destiny, of human handwriting. Eliza ended by acquiring an extremely uncommercial script which was a positive extension of her personal beauty, and spending three times as much on stationery as anyone else because certain qualities and shapes on paper became indispensable to her. She could not even address an envelope in the usual way because it made the margins all wrong.

Their commercial schooldays were a period of disgrace and despair for the young couple. They seemed to be learning nothing about flower shops. At last they gave it up as hopeless, and shook the dust of the shorthand schools, and the polytechnics, and the London School of Economics from their feet for ever. Besides, the business was in some mysterious way beginning to take care of itself. They had somehow forgotten their objections to employing other people. They came to the conclusion that their own way was the best, and that they had really a remarkable talent for business. The Colonel, who had been compelled for some years to keep a sufficient sum on current account at his bankers to make up their deficits, found that the provision was unnecessary: the young people were prospering. It is true that there was not quite fair play between them and their competitors in trade. Their week-ends in the country cost them nothing, and saved them the price of their Sunday dinners; for the motor car was the Colonel's; and he and Higgins paid the hotel bills. Mr F. Hill, florist and greengrocer (they soon discovered that there was money in asparagus; and asparagus led to other vegetables), had an air which stamped the business as classy; and in private life he was still Frederick Eynsford Hill, Esquire. Not that there was any swank[13] about him: nobody but Eliza knew that he had been christened Frederick Chaloner. Eliza herself swanked like anything.

That is all. That is how it has turned out. It is astonishing how much Eliza still manages to meddle in the housekeeping at Wimpole Street in spite of the shop and her own family. And it is notable that though she never nags her husband, and frankly loves the Colonel as if she were his favorite daughter, she has never got out of the habit of nagging Higgins that was established on the fatal night when she won his bet for him. She snaps his head off on the faintest provocation, or on none. He no longer dares to tease her by assuming an abysmal inferiority of Freddy's mind to his own. He storms and bullies and derides; but she stands up to him so ruthlessly that the Colonel has to ask her from time to time to be kinder to Higgins; and it is the only request of his that brings a mulish expression into her face. Nothing but some emergency or calamity great enough to break down all likes and dislikes, and throw them both back on their common humanity—and may they be spared any such trial!—will ever alter this. She knows that Higgins does not need her, just as her father did not need her. The very scrupulousness with

---

13. **swank:** ostentatious swagger.

which he told her that day that he had become used to having her there, and dependent on her for all sorts of little services, and that he should miss her if she went away (it would never have occurred to Freddy or the Colonel to say anything of the sort) deepens her inner certainty that she is "no more to him than them slippers"; yet she has a sense, too, that his indifference is deeper than the infatuation of commoner souls. She is immensely interested in him. She has even secret mischievous moments in which she wishes she could get him alone, on a desert island, away from all ties and with nobody else in the world to consider, and just drag him off his pedestal and see him making love like any common man. We all have private imaginations of that sort. But when it comes to business, to the life that she really leads as distinguished from the life of dreams and fancies, she likes Freddy and she likes the Colonel; and she does not like Higgins and Mr Doolittle. Galatea never does quite like Pygmalion: his relation to her is too godlike to be altogether agreeable.

STUDY QUESTIONS

Recalling

1. Explain the reasons for Doolittle's changed appearance. How does he feel about his new life in comparison to his old life? Why?
2. For what does Liza express gratitude to Pickering? What does she say is the real difference between a lady and a flower girl?
3. What does Higgins tell Liza is "the great secret" about handling other people?
4. What sort of feeling does Liza deny that she wants from Higgins? What does she want?
5. What two things does Liza say she will do with her life? How does Higgins react to her?

Interpreting

6. Why would Doolittle's money become a burden to him? What relationship does Shaw present among social position, wealth, morality, and happiness through the character of Doolittle?
7. What has Liza gained as a result of Higgins' experiment? What has she lost?
8. Why do you think Higgins refuses to let Liza go?
9. What does Liza want that Higgins is unwilling to give? In one sentence state the position of each in their final debate. With whom do you agree?

Extending

10. Were you satisfied with Shaw's account of Liza's future in the Epilogue? Why or why not?

VIEWPOINT

Critic I. Wardle argues that Shaw's most important theme is the liberation of the human mind:

Whenever [Shaw's plays] record a victory, it is the victory of *Pygmalion*—the release of a free, autonomous creature from the petrified forest of unexamined values and social conditioning.

"The Plays," in *The Genius of Shaw*

■ From what "unexamined values and social conditioning" does Shaw seek to free people in *Pygmalion*? Do you agree that Liza is more free at the end of the play than at the beginning? Why or why not?

LITERARY FOCUS

The Total Effect

In staging a play like *Pygmalion,* a director should pay attention to the individual elements of plot, character, setting, tone, symbol, and theme, and should keep in mind the total effect that these elements will produce on an audience when they come together in a performance.

Thinking About Plot

1. What are the major conflicts in *Pygmalion?* Keep in mind conflicts that occur within characters, between characters, and between characters and external forces such as the social system. How are these various conflicts resolved?

Thinking About Character

2. Describe the various changes that occur in Liza over the course of the play. Higgins says that he created the Liza we see at the end of the play. To what extent is this true?

3. Name several of Higgins' most outstanding shortcomings. What appealing qualities does he also reveal?

Thinking About Setting

4. Most of the play takes place in pleasant rooms of upper-class society. In what ways do these rooms contrast with the rainy street scene and Liza's lodgings of Act I?

5. Describe the social setting of the play, particularly the contrast between the upper and lower classes.

Thinking About Tone

6. The tone of *Pygmalion* mixes the serious and the comic. Choose one purely comic moment, and explain why it is funny. Find one moment when Shaw is absolutely earnest. What point is being made?

Thinking About Symbol

7. Keeping in mind who Pygmalion was in Greek legend, explain the symbolic implications of the title *Pygmalion*.

Thinking About Theme

8. According to *Pygmalion*, what is the relationship between language and class? Between the way a person speaks and his identity?

9. What various views concerning women's social position are presented in *Pygmalion*?

10. Why would aspects of appearance such as clothes, manners, and speech have such a profound effect on someone's life? What does *Pygmalion* suggest about the relationship between appearance and reality?

VOCABULARY

Dialect

In Act I of *Pygmalion,* Henry Higgins demonstrates his ability to identify a person's background purely on the basis of dialect. A **dialect** is a type of speech that differs from the standard form of a language; the difference occurs mostly in pronunciation but also in vocabulary and grammar. Speakers of English in the United States use many different regional dialects, some of the most recognizable being those heard in New England, New York City, and the South.

In Britain people also speak in many different dialects, some of which differ so much from the English we know that we would probably not be able to understand them. In the first two acts of *Pygmalion,* Liza Doolittle speaks a dialect known as **cockney,** which is common among people of the lower class who live in London's East End. Shaw attempts to reproduce the exact sound of this dialect in Liza's first three speeches in the play and again in Act II in her attempt to say the alphabet in Higgins' study. Besides affecting her pronunciation, Liza's cockney dialect includes numerous lapses from standard grammar (such as using present tense for past tense) and special vocabulary words—such as ''garn,'' which actually means ''go on,'' and might be translated into the common American expression ''You've got to be kidding.''

■ Look at Liza's first three speeches in Act I, and list all the differences you can find between her pronunciation and grammar and standard English.

COMPOSITION

Writing About the Total Effect

■ Explain the total effect that you think makes *Pygmalion* popular on stage as well as on film and television and in its musical version. First describe the impact that the play had on you. Then explain how Shaw uses the following elements to achieve this effect: (a) plot, (b) character, (c) setting, (d) theme, and (e) tone. *For help with this assignment, refer to Lesson 8 in the Writing About Literature Handbook at the back of this book.*

Writing About a Play's Ending

■ In the Epilogue to *Pygmalion*, Shaw explains why Liza cannot marry Higgins. On the other hand, the film and musical versions of *Pygmalion* both end with Liza's return to Higgins. Indicate which ending you find the more logical and satisfying outcome to the play. Then use evidence from the play such as the characters' behavior and statements to support your choice of ending.

POETRY

William Butler Yeats   *1865–1939*

Considered by many to be the greatest poet writing in English in this century, William Butler Yeats remained a productive author throughout his lifetime. While many poets produce their finest work during their early years, Yeats was one of those rare poets who create their greatest poems after the age of fifty.

The son of a painter, Yeats was born in Sandymount, Ireland, and attended school in Dublin. He loved to read and daydream, especially during his summers at his grandparents' home in the wild country of County Sligo on Ireland's northwest coast.

Yeats studied painting but soon abandoned his studies to become a professional writer. His interest in Irish culture led him to collect and publish Irish legends and write poems and plays based on Irish myths. As a result of this work, Yeats soon became a central figure in the Irish Renaissance, a turn-of-the-century movement to revive an Irish national language and celebrate Celtic traditions. In 1889 Yeats published his first volume of poems. Later, with his friend Lady Augusta Gregory, he founded the Irish National Theatre Society, and he began to write plays based on Irish legends.

However, Yeats's interest in Ireland was not merely literary and linguistic. Inspired by the beautiful Maud Gonne, a leader of the Irish National Movement, which sought to free Ireland from British rule, Yeats developed an interest in Irish politics. Gonne was his Joan of Arc, his Helen of Troy, and he courted her unsuccessfully for over thirteen years. After her marriage to another Irish political leader, Yeats finally admitted defeat in love and turned his full attention to his work. He himself eventually married years later.

During the 1920s Yeats gained even more prominence in both political and literary circles. He became a senator in the Irish Free State in 1922 and received the Nobel Prize for Literature in 1923. In 1925 Yeats published his major philosophical and historical prose work, *A Vision*.

Yeats began his poetic career as a Romantic and finished it as a poet of the modern world. His early work was strongly influenced by Blake and Shelley, the Pre-Raphaelites (see page 405), the French Symbolists (see Part Two of this book), and Irish mythology. These early poems were often simple, musical, romantic, and dreamlike. In the middle of his career, his poetry became less dreamlike and more direct and realistic; his imagery became more economical and his tone more conversational. In the last stages of his poetic career, his interest in a universal system of historical cycles dominated his work. Although some of his later works are obscure and complex, the best of these poems touch universal concerns and demonstrate a brilliant balance between emotion and intellect.

"Down by the Salley Gardens" is a good example of Yeats's early poetry. Like the other poems he wrote early in his career, it is simply structured, Romantic, musical, and based on traditional Irish lore. By his own account, the poem is an expansion of "three lines imperfectly remembered" from an Irish folk song that he once heard an old peasant woman sing in Sligo.

William Butler Yeats

Down by the Salley Gardens[1]

Down by the salley gardens my love and I did meet;
She passed the salley gardens with little snow-white feet.
She bid me take love easy, as the leaves grow on the tree;
But I, being young and foolish, with her would not agree.

5 In a field by the river my love and I did stand,
And on my leaning shoulder she laid her snow-white hand.
She bid me take life easy, as the grass grows on the weirs;[2]
But I was young and foolish, and now am full of tears.

---

1. **Salley Gardens:** willow gardens. *Salley* is a variant of *sallow,* which means "willow."
2. **weirs** [wĕrz]: earth piled in river or stream beds to back up or change the course of the water.

STUDY QUESTIONS

Recalling
1. In line 3 what does the speaker's love advise him to do? What is his response?
2. What suggestion does his love make in line 7?
3. How does he describe himself in each stanza?

Interpreting
4. Find four specific changes from the first to the second stanza. How and why does the speaker's emotional state change?

5. In the long run, does his sweetheart's advice prove to be correct or incorrect? How do you know?
6. Where in the poem does Yeats use repetition and parallelism? Explain how these techniques add to the poem's meaning and emotional impact.

Extending
7. Why do you think advice often seems more sensible in retrospect than at the time it is offered?

It is believed that Yeats wrote this poem for Major Robert Gregory, the son of his friend Lady Augusta Gregory. Major Gregory, an artist and aviator, was killed in action over Italy during World War I while flying for England's Royal Flying Corps.

An Irish Airman Foresees His Death

I know that I shall meet my fate
Somewhere among the clouds above;
Those that I fight I do not hate,
Those that I guard I do not love;[1]
5 My country is Kiltartan[2] Cross,
My countrymen Kiltartan's poor,
No likely end could bring them loss
Or leave them happier than before

Nor law, nor duty bade me fight,
10 Nor public men, nor cheering crowds,
A lonely impulse of delight
Drove to this tumult in the clouds;
I balanced all, brought all to mind,
The years to come seemed waste of breath,
15 A waste of breath the years behind
In balance with this life, this death.

---

1. **Those . . . love:** Many Irish volunteered to fight on the side of the English in World War I in spite of Ireland's technical neutrality and ongoing struggle for independence from England.
2. **Kiltartan:** village near the estate of the Gregory family.

STUDY QUESTIONS

Recalling

1. Who is the speaker of the poem? How does he feel about the people he fights for and against?
2. In contrast, who are *his* people? What effect does he think his fate will have on them?
3. According to the second stanza, what things did not motivate the speaker to fight? What drove him "to this tumult in the clouds"?
4. With what phrase does the speaker characterize both past and future? In the last line what does he balance against the past and future?

Interpreting

5. What is the speaker's attitude toward the war and toward his own survival? How do you know?
6. Why would *delight* be an unusual word for someone in the speaker's circumstances to use? What does it reveal about the speaker?
7. What do the words *this life, this death* mean? Why might "this life, this death" be more valuable to him than the rest of his life?

Extending

8. Why do you think people in grave danger are often calm in their acceptance of death?

William Butler Yeats

The Lake Isle of Innisfree

I will arise and go now, and go to Innisfree,
And a small cabin build there, of clay and wattles[1] made:
Nine bean-rows will I have there, a hive for the honeybee,
And live alone in the bee-loud glade.

5   And I shall have some peace there, for peace comes dropping
      slow,
Dropping from the veils of the morning to where the cricket
      sings;
There midnight's all a glimmer, and noon a purple glow,
And evening full of the linnet's[2] wings.

I will arise and go now, for always night and day
10 I hear lake water lapping with low sounds by the shore;
While I stand on the roadway, or on the pavements gray,
I hear it in the deep heart's core.

---

1. **wattles:** networks of woven twigs used for walls, roofs, and crude huts.
2. **linnet's:** referring to a European singing bird.

The Wild Swans at Coole

The trees are in their autumn beauty,
The woodland paths are dry,
Under the October twilight the water
Mirrors a still sky;
5 Upon the brimming water among the stones
Are nine and fifty swans.

The nineteenth autumn has come upon me
Since I first made my count;
I saw, before I had well finished,
10 All suddenly mount
And scatter wheeling in great broken rings
Upon their clamorous wings.

I have looked upon those brilliant creatures,
And now my heart is sore.
15 All's changed since I, hearing at twilight,
The first time on this shore,
The bell beat of their wings above my head,
Trod with a lighter tread.

Unwearied still, lover by lover,
20 They paddle in the cold
Companionable streams or climb the air;
Their hearts have not grown old;
Passion or conquest, wander where they will,
Attend upon them still.

25 But now they drift on the still water,
Mysterious, beautiful;
Among what rushes will they build,
By what lake's edge or pool
Delight men's eyes when I awake some day
30 To find they have flown away?

STUDY QUESTIONS

The Lake Isle of Innisfree

Recalling

1. According to the first stanza, where does the speaker intend to go, what will he do there, and how will he live?
2. From the second stanza list three physical characteristics of the place to which the speaker wants to go.
3. Where is the speaker now, according to line 11?
4. What does the speaker hear, and how does he hear this sound, according to the third stanza?

Interpreting

5. Contrast the speaker's present location with the place that beckons him. What is the emotional effect of this contrast?
6. Describe the speaker's current emotional state. Is he contented or frustrated? Is this mood momentary or ongoing? How do you know?
7. Instead of actually going to Innisfree, what is the speaker doing in the poem? How does hearing something "in the deep heart's core" differ from hearing it with one's ears?
8. Explain how Yeats uses sound images to heighten the emotional effect of the poem.

The Wild Swans at Coole

Recalling

1. For how many years has the speaker been observing the swans? What did they do the first year that the speaker counted them? What are they doing now?
2. According to line 14, how does the speaker feel now? According to line 18, how did he react the first time he heard the "bell beat" of the swans' wings?
3. According to stanza 4, in what ways have the swans remained the same?
4. What does the speaker anticipate that he will find when he awakes "some day"?

Interpreting

5. Point out the various contrasts the speaker might be drawing in the fourth stanza between the swans and himself.
6. Why might the passage of time change the speaker's response to the swans?

7. What do you think the swans symbolize to the speaker?

Extending

8. In what ways can seeing a beautiful scene in nature be a painful experience?

VIEWPOINT

"The Lake Isle of Innisfree" was influenced by Yeats's reading of *Walden,* a book in which the nineteenth-century American writer Henry David Thoreau describes his retreat from the city into a simple cabin by a forest pond. Yeats wrote his poem after the sight of a small fountain in a shop window in London brought the sound of Sligo's lake water lapping back into his consciousness. However, the poem is more than an exercise in escapism, as critic Thomas L. Byrd, Jr., notes:

> In the first place, the poem is grounded in reality. Innisfree is as real as Walden Pond. . . . If Innisfree represents escape, it is the escape of the seeking hermit.
> —*The Early Poetry of W. B. Yeats*

■ What specific concrete details help to ground "The Lake Isle of Innisfree" in reality? What is the poem's speaker escaping, and what is he seeking?

COMPOSITION

Writing About Form in Poetry

■ In a paragraph or two, describe the effect of Yeats's use of different line lengths in "The Lake Isle of Innisfree." Begin by describing the various patterns of line length in the poem—in particular, Yeats's combination of longer and shorter lines. Then analyze the visual, rhythmic, and other effects of these different line lengths. End by explaining how these different line lengths add to the poem's overall meaning and emotional impact.

Imitating a Poet's Style

■ Write a poem of at least two stanzas that expresses a longing for a particular place. Try to imitate several aspects of Yeats's style in "The Lake Isle of Innisfree." Begin with the words "I will arise and go now, and go to _____." Use vivid, specific images of sight and sound to describe and contrast your special place with your present location.

"The Second Coming" is based on Yeats's special theory of history. According to his theory, cycles of history and nature occur every two thousand years. During this time one civilization grows, improves, decays, and dissolves, and then a new civilization takes its place. The title of the poem refers to the New Testament prediction of the return of Jesus Christ to the earth at the end of the world.

William Butler Yeats

The Second Coming

Turning and turning in the widening gyre[1]
The falcon cannot hear the falconer;
Things fall apart; the center cannot hold;
Mere anarchy is loosed upon the world,
5 The blood-dimmed tide is loosed, and everywhere
The ceremony of innocence is drowned;
The best lack all conviction, while the worst
Are full of passionate intensity.

Surely some revelation[2] is at hand;
10 Surely the Second Coming is at hand.
The Second Coming! Hardly are those words out
When a vast image out of *Spiritus Mundi*[3]
Troubles my sight: somewhere in sands of the desert
A shape with lion body and the head of a man,[4]
15 A gaze blank and pitiless as the sun,
Is moving its slow thighs, while all about it
Reel shadows of the indignant desert birds.
The darkness drops again; but now I know
That twenty centuries[5] of stony sleep
20 Were vexed to nightmare by a rocking cradle,
And what rough beast, its hour come round at last,
Slouches toward Bethlehem to be born?

---

1. **gyre** [jīr]: circular or spiral form or motion, which Yeats uses as the symbol for the winding up and winding down of cycles of history.
2. **revelation:** disclosure; in Christian teaching, God's unfolding of His will to the human race.
3. ***Spiritus Mundi*** [spir′i təs mo͞on′dē]: world soul or spirit that, according to Yeats's theories, acts as a universal memory for all people.
4. **A shape . . . man:** the sphinx.
5. **twenty centuries:** Yeats's cycles each lasted two thousand years.

Byzantium was the name of the eastern Roman Empire and also designated the Greek Christian civilization. During Europe's Dark Ages its capital, Constantinople, now Istanbul, was a great artistic center, containing several magnificent churches decorated with mosaics of holy men portrayed in the stylized, two-dimensional manner that typified Byzantine art. Yeats wrote several poems about Byzantium, which he regarded as a kind of holy city of the imagination, a place where the spiritual and the artistic came together.

William Butler Yeats

Sailing to Byzantium

1

That is no country[1] for old men. The young
In one another's arms, birds in the trees
—Those dying generations—at their song,
The salmon falls, the mackerel-crowded seas,
5 Fish, flesh, or fowl, commend all summer long
Whatever is begotten, born, and dies.
Caught in that sensual music all neglect
Monuments of unaging intellect.

2

An aged man is but a paltry thing,
10 A tattered coat upon a stick, unless
Soul clap its hands and sing, and louder sing
For every tatter in its mortal dress,
Nor is there singing school but studying
Monuments of its own magnificence;
15 And therefore I have sailed the seas and come
To the holy city of Byzantium.

---

1. **That . . . country:** the sensual world where time passes and death is certain to occur.

O sages standing in God's holy fire
As in the gold mosaic of a wall,[2]
Come from the holy fire, perne in a gyre,[3]
20 And be the singing masters of my soul.
Consume my heart away; sick with desire
And fastened to a dying animal
It knows not what it is; and gather me
Into the artifice of eternity.

4

25 Once out of nature I shall never take
My bodily form from any natural thing,
But such a form as Grecian goldsmiths make
Of hammered gold and gold enameling
To keep a drowsy Emperor awake;
30 Or set upon a golden bough to sing[4]
To lords and ladies of Byzantium
Of what is past, or passing, or to come.

---

2. **sages . . . wall:** wise old men (sages) depicted on the mosaic walls of Byzantine churches.
3. **perne in a gyre:** descend or spin with a whirling, spiral motion.
4. **To keep . . . sing:** Byzantine Emperor Theophilus is said to have ordered his artisans to make him a gold and silver tree in which mechanical birds perched and sang.

STUDY QUESTIONS

The Second Coming

Recalling

1. Describe the behavior of the falcon in lines 1–2.
2. What two things are loosed upon the world, and what is drowned?
3. What contrast do lines 7–8 draw between "the best" and "the worst"?
4. Describe the creature that the speaker envisions crawling through the desert.
5. Where is the "rough beast" going, and why is it going there?

Interpreting

6. What picture of human affairs is created in stanza 1?

7. Explain what seems to be happening in stanza 2, and describe the speaker's attitude toward this event. Use examples from the poem.
8. This poem was written in 1919, shortly after the end of World War I, which had devastated much of Europe. What relationship can you see between war and the events of this poem?

Sailing to Byzantium

Recalling

1. What do the inhabitants of the country described in stanza 1 "commend"? What do they "neglect"?
2. In what terms does the speaker describe old age in lines 9–10?
3. List three requests that the speaker addresses to the sages, or wise men, in the third stanza.

4. Describe the bodily form that the speaker wants to assume when he is "out of nature," and list two of the things the speaker says he would do.

Interpreting

5. In the country described in stanza 1, what aspect of life seems most important?

6. In what ways does Byzantium differ from the first country? Why might the speaker prefer Byzantium?

7. Explain how the golden bird described in stanza 4 differs from the birds mentioned in stanza 1. Why might the speaker choose the form of the golden bird over that of "any natural thing"?

8. What is the speaker's attitude toward aging and death? What does the poem say about the relationship between body and soul? Nature and art?

LITERARY FOCUS

Yeats and Symbolism

A **symbol** is a figure of speech in which a person, object, or situation represents something in addition to its literal meaning. A symbol usually creates a correspondence between something concrete and something abstract: For example, a growing plant might symbolize life itself.

The **Symbolist** movement in literature was begun in France around 1885 by a group of poets that included Baudelaire [bōd'əl är'], Rimbaud [ram bō'], and Mallarmé [ma lär mä']. The poems of the French Symbolists are richly musical and include vivid symbols whose larger meanings are suggested rather than directly stated. (See Part Two of this book.) The Symbolist movement had a profound effect on Yeats and a group of younger English and American poets, including T. S. Eliot.

Yeats was especially aware of the power of symbols because of his interest in visionary and mystical experiences. From the writings of mystics, Yeats borrowed the idea that all human beings share in one great reservoir of experience and emotion, a reservoir that can be tapped through the use of symbols. Yeats repeatedly used in his poems certain symbols, such as the sun, moon, bird, rose, and tower, because he believed that these symbols had the power to evoke common human feelings and experiences.

Thinking About Yeats and Symbolism

■ Choose a symbol in "Sailing to Byzantium," and explain what it represents. What qualities in the symbol suggest its larger meaning?

VOCABULARY

Synonyms

A **synonym** is a word that has the same or nearly the same meaning as another word. *Walk* and *stroll* are synonyms. The words in capitals are from Yeats's poems. Choose the word that is *nearest* the meaning of the word in capitals, *as the word is used in the selection.*

1. TUMULT: (a) somersault (b) tranquillity (c) sandwich (d) uproar

2. BRIMMING: (a) full (b) wide (c) overflowing (d) stupendous

3. CLAMOROUS: (a) noisy (b) grateful (c) loving (d) ingenious

4. REVELATION: (a) recognition (b) disclosure (c) homecoming (d) alteration

5. ANARCHY: (a) chaos (b) ignorance (c) brutality (d) injustice

COMPOSITION

Writing a Comparison/Contrast

■ Compare and contrast Yeats's "Second Coming" and "Sailing to Byzantium." Begin by pointing out the similarities between the content and literary techniques of the two poems. Then note the differences between them. In particular, compare and contrast Yeats's use of symbols to express his ideas in the two poems. *For help with this assignment, refer to Lesson 2 in the Writing About Literature Handbook at the back of this book.*

Writing a Poem About a Transformation

■ Write a brief poem expressing a wish to be transformed into someone or something else. Your poem should use precise images to describe the person or creature you would like to become. You should also make clear the reasons that you desire such a transformation.

T. S. Eliot   *1888–1965*

Thomas Stearns Eliot was one of the most influential writers of his time and a pioneer among the first modern poets, who are now referred to as Modernist. These poets belonged to and wrote for a generation whose view of life was radically altered by World War I, which has undermined many people's faith in the systems that had once ordered human existence. Eliot sought to make sense of modern life. He was determined, as he put it, "to see both beauty and ugliness, to see the boredom, the horror and the glory."

Eliot was born in St. Louis, Missouri, where his grandfather had founded Washington University. His family was strict, religious, and literary. Shy and frail as a boy, Eliot studied literature and philosophy at Harvard University, wrote for college magazines, and took boxing lessons at night. After receiving his Master's degree in 1910, he studied at Oxford and at the Sorbonne in Paris.

Eliot moved permanently to England in 1915 and became a British subject seven years later. Still, he remained American in many ways. He sometimes signed his name Thomas (Missouri) Eliot, and he loved American folk songs, comic strips, and the movies of the Marx Brothers. Marrying in 1915, Eliot eventually became a successful partner in a publishing firm.

T. S. Eliot's early poems capture the alienation and spiritual bankruptcy felt by many writers of his time. He returned frequently to these matters in his first volume of poetry, *Prufrock and Other Observations* (1917), as well as in his subsequent works, *The Waste Land* (1922) and "The Hollow Men" (1925). After these works, however, Eliot's poetry began to show the stirrings of religious faith. "Ash-Wednesday" (1930), written after his conversion to the Church of England, portrays his climb from despair to hope and from disillusionment to belief. In his masterpiece, the *Four Quartets* (1943), he affirms his belief in spiritual values in the midst of war.

Eliot's poems are known for their concrete images, irregular rhythms, shifting moods, and "patchwork" presentation of religious, historical, mythological, and literary references. His poetry also mixes elevated language with slang and colloquial expressions. Eliot believed that poetry should not state emotions directly; rather, the poet should select images that trigger these emotions in the reader. According to his theory of art, the poet's personal emotions are of no artistic worth in themselves. What matters is the art that reworks these emotions into universal patterns and symbols.

In 1948 Eliot was awarded the Nobel Prize for Literature, becoming the first American-born poet to be so honored. However, Eliot found success with other forms of writing besides poetry. He published influential literary criticism, and, like Yeats, wrote poetic dramas. Among his best-known plays are *Murder in the Cathedral* (1935), *The Family Reunion* (1939), and *The Cocktail Party* (1950).

In "Preludes" a speaker offers what seem to be random observations on his surroundings. A prelude is any performance or act that leads up to a main event; in particular, a musical prelude is a short piece based on a repeated phrase.

T. S. Eliot

Preludes

1

The winter evening settles down
With smell of steaks[1] in passageways.
Six o'clock.
The burned-out ends of smoky days.
5 And now a gusty shower wraps
The grimy scraps
Of withered leaves about your feet
And newspapers from vacant lots;
The showers beat
10 On broken blinds and chimney pots,
And at the corner of the street
A lonely cab horse steams and stamps.
And then the lighting of the lamps.

2

The morning comes to consciousness
15 Of faint stale smells of beer
From the sawdust-trampled street
With all its muddy feet that press
To early coffee stands.
With the other masquerades
20 That time resumes,
One thinks of all the hands
That are raising dingy shades
In a thousand furnished rooms.

3

You tossed a blanket from the bed,
25 You lay upon your back, and waited;
You dozed, and watched the night revealing
The thousand sordid images

Of which your soul was constituted;
They flickered against the ceiling.
30 And when all the world came back
And the light crept up between the shutters
And you heard the sparrows in the gutters,
You had such a vision of the street
As the street hardly understands;
35 Sitting along the bed's edge, where
You curled the papers from your hair,
Or clasped the yellow soles of feet
In the palms of both soiled hands.

4

His soul stretched tight across the skies
40 That fade behind a city block,
Or trampled by insistent feet
At four and five and six o'clock;
And short square fingers stuffing pipes,
And evening newspapers, and eyes
45 Assured of certain certainties,
The conscience of a blackened street
Impatient to assume the world.

I am moved by fancies that are curled
Around these images, and cling:
50 The notion of some infinitely gentle
Infinitely suffering thing.

Wipe your hand across your mouth,
and laugh;
The worlds revolve like ancient women
Gathering fuel in vacant lots.

---

1. **steaks:** When this poem was composed, steak was a common meal of the lower classes.

"The Hollow Men" is one of Eliot's most dramatic and powerful poems. It is an example of his "patchwork" style of writing, which juxtaposes various literary, mythological, religious, historical, and cultural references as well as different styles of speech. In "The Hollow Men" Eliot joins to his own poetic voice the echoes of other voices—literary works, prayers, even nursery rhymes—to create a uniquely modern lament for his own time.

The Hollow Men

Mistah Kurtz[1]—he dead.

A penny for the Old Guy[2]

1

We are the hollow men
We are the stuffed men
Leaning together
Headpiece filled with straw. Alas!
5 Our dried voices, when
We whisper together
Are quiet and meaningless
As wind in dry grass
Or rats' feet over broken glass
10 In our dry cellar

Shape without form, shade without color,
Paralyzed force, gesture without motion;

Those who have crossed
With direct eyes, to death's other Kingdom[3]
15 Remember us—if at all—not as lost
Violent souls, but only
As the hollow men
The stuffed men.

2

Eyes I dare not meet in dreams
20 In death's dream kingdom
These do not appear:
There, the eyes are
Sunlight on a broken column
There, is a tree swinging
25 And voices are
In the wind's singing
More distant and more solemn
Than a fading star.

---

1. **Mistah Kurtz:** character in Joseph Conrad's short novel *Heart of Darkness.* Kurtz sets out to civilize the natives in Africa and instead becomes one of them and dies in the jungle. He is described as being "hollow to the core."

2. **A penny . . . Old Guy:** traditional expression used by English children on Guy Fawkes Day, November 5. Guy Fawkes (1570–1606) tried and failed to blow up the Houses of Parliament and was subsequently hanged. On Guy Fawkes Day children burn straw dummies representing him.

3. **Those . . . Kingdom:** the virtuous who have gone to Heaven, according to Dante's *Paradiso.* The *Paradiso,* which is the final section of the *Divine Comedy,* describes the soul's union with God in Heaven (page 737).

Let me be no nearer

30 In death's dream kingdom
Let me also wear
Such deliberate disguises
Rat's coat, crowskin, crossed staves[4]
In a field

35 Behaving as the wind behaves
No nearer—

Not that final meeting
In the twilight kingdom

3

This is the dead land

40 This is the cactus land
Here the stone images
Are raised, here they receive
The supplication[5] of a dead man's hand
Under the twinkle of a fading star.

45 Is it like this
In death's other kingdom
Waking alone
At the hour when we are
Trembling with tenderness

50 Lips that would kiss
Form prayers to broken stone.

4

The eyes are not here
There are no eyes here
In this valley of dying stars

55 In this hollow valley
This broken jaw of our lost kingdoms

In this last of meeting places
We grope together
And avoid speech

60 Gathered on this beach of the tumid river[6]

Sightless, unless
The eyes reappear
As the perpetual star
Multifoliate rose[7]

65 Of death's twilight kingdom
The hope only
Of empty men.

5

Here we go round the prickly pear[8]
Prickly pear prickly pear

70 *Here we go round the prickly pear*
At five o'clock in the morning.

Between the idea
And the reality
Between the motion

75 And the act[9]
Falls the Shadow
For Thine is the Kingdom[10]

Between the conception
And the creation

80 Between the emotion
And the response
Falls the Shadow
Life is very long[11]

Between the desire

85 And the spasm
Between the potency[12]
And the existence

---

4. **staves:** wood strips, rods, or staffs. Crossed staves suggest scarecrows.
5. **supplication:** a humble prayer or plea.
6. **tumid river:** swollen river; in Dante's *Inferno,* the condemned must cross the River Acheron in order to pass from the world of the living into Hell.

7. **star . . . rose:** The star and the rose are traditional symbols for Christ and the Virgin Mary. Dante described Paradise as a "multifoliate rose"—a rose with many leaves.
8. **Here . . . pear:** version of a well-known nursery rhyme; prickly pear is a desert cactus.
9. **Between . . . act:** reference to *Julius Caesar,* Act II, Scene i, 63–65: "Between the acting of a dreadful thing/And the first motion, all the interim is/Like a phantasma or a hideous dream."
10. **For . . . Kingdom:** These words come from the ending of the Lord's Prayer.
11. **Life . . . long:** quotation from another Joseph Conrad novel, *An Outcast of the Islands;* these words are spoken to a character who, like Kurtz, is "hollow."
12. **potency:** power; in this case, to procreate.

Between the essence
And the descent
90 Falls the Shadow
                    For Thine is the Kingdom

For Thine is
Life is
For Thine is the

95 *This is the way the world ends*
This is the way the world ends
This is the way the world ends
Not with a bang but a whimper.

STUDY QUESTIONS

Preludes

Recalling

1. List five specific images of evening and morning presented in sections 1 and 2.
2. In section 3 what does the person described by the speaker see? What does night reveal to this person, according to lines 26–28?
3. In section 4 what does the speaker find moving? To what does the speaker compare the revolving worlds?

Interpreting

4. What is the mood of "Preludes"? Choose four images, one in each section, and explain how each of them conveys this mood.
5. Is the laughter referred to in line 52 good or bad? How do you know? Describe the vision of the universe that the poem ends with.
6. What images in the poem might be particularly associated with twentieth-century existence? Point out the aspects of modern life that Eliot emphasizes most. Summarize the view of modern life that the poem expresses.

Extending

7. Do you think this poem paints an accurate picture of modern life? If not, what alternative images would you offer?

The Hollow Men

Recalling

1. What words and phrases do the hollow men use to describe their heads and voices in part 1?
2. List four images of "death's dream kingdom" in part 2. What disguise does the hollow man want to wear in this place?
3. What adjectives describe the land of the hollow men in part 3?
4. What four lines are repeated throughout part 5? How does the world end, according to line 95?

Interpreting

5. Describe the life of the hollow men. What do they seem to lack?
6. Lines 13–14 refer to those who have had faith, led good lives, and gone to Paradise. In what ways are the hollow men different from these people?
7. What do you think Eliot means by the Shadow? What effect does the Shadow seem to have on human action, according to the hollow men?
8. Explain how the repetitions in part 5 add to the power of the poem. Is it fitting that the world of the hollow men ends as it does? Why or why not?

9. Why do you think Eliot portrays modern people as hollow men? What qualities in modern life does Eliot lament in this poem?

Extending
10. Do you think the poem is equally applicable to our own time as it was to the period after World War I? Why or why not?

LITERARY FOCUS

Allusion

An **allusion** is a reference in a work to something outside the work, usually to another piece of literature or to a well-known person, place, or event from history, religion, or mythology. Writers who use allusions do not often explain or elaborate on such references, because they expect their audiences to recognize the sources to which they refer. The most common sources of allusions are the Bible and the Greek and Roman myths.

An allusion serves as a kind of shorthand reference to a larger picture or idea, thereby adding to the meaning of a work. It can also widen the scope of a work to include other historical periods and cultures.

T. S. Eliot relies heavily on allusions to add depth, create surprise, point out contrasts, or make his modern subjects universal in scope. His allusions come from many different sources, often patching together such diverse materials as the Bible, works of literature, myths, and even nursery rhymes and popular jingles. By referring to many different historical periods, types of works, styles of speech, and even languages, Eliot creates a complex and varying tone in his own works. Eliot's special use of allusions often creates a picture of modern life as a kind of grab bag full of broken fragments of the past, with no wholeness or order of its own.

Thinking About Allusion
1. What lines in "The Hollow Men" contain allusions? From what kinds of sources (biblical, historical, literary, and so on) does Eliot draw these allusions?
2. What is the effect of the allusions in part 5 of "The Hollow Men"? In the poem as a whole? Explain how these allusions add to the depth and impact of the poem.

VIEWPOINT

According to the modern American author Delmore Schwartz, the poetry of T. S. Eliot

has a direct relationship to modern life. The width and the height and the depth of modern life are exhibited in his poetry; the agony and the horror of modern life are represented as inevitable to any human being who does not wish to deceive himself with systematic lies.

—*Literary Modernism*

■ What evidence of "the agony and the horror of modern life" can you find in "Preludes"? Where in the poem does Eliot suggest the idea of inevitability? Are there any hints of hope in the poem, and if so, where?

COMPOSITION

Writing About Tone
■ The tone of a work is the attitude its author expresses toward his or her subject. In a brief essay analyze the tone of "Preludes." First identify the emotion or emotions the poem conveys, explaining how Eliot's choices of words and images create this tone. Then point out any changes in the tone, and explain how these changes reveal the poem's meaning.

Writing a Collage Poem
■ Write a free-verse poem that is a stream of related images. These images do not need to be connected into a single story or scene. However, they should be vivid and concrete, as Eliot's are in "Preludes," and they should eventually add up to a dominant impression, conveying a definite emotion of some kind.

COMPARING WRITERS

1. What symbols do Yeats and Eliot use in their poetry to represent modern life? What overall view of modern life does each poet express?
2. Yeats and Eliot both attempted to show the relationship between their time and universal human problems. Compare each poet's use of symbolism, allusion, and other techniques to add a universal dimension to his poetry.

Siegfried Sassoon *1886–1967*

Siegfried Sassoon is chiefly known as one of the poets who voiced their generation's anger over the futility and suffering of World War I. Born to a wealthy and prominent family, Sassoon spent his youth living the life of an English country gentleman. After leaving school he moved to London, where he published several slim volumes of verse celebrating the beauties of nature and English country life. At this stage his work was typical of the so-called Georgian poets, whose pastoral, patriotic poems were published between 1911 and 1922, during the early part of the reign of King George V.

However, Sassoon's poetry changed drastically after he entered the British Army to fight in World War I. His battle experiences made him bitter and angry about the horrors of war. After the war ended, Sassoon worked as the literary editor of a newspaper and continued to write poetry. In addition to poetry, Sassoon wrote stories and novels, and his later works include memoirs, satire, meditations, and love lyrics. His *Collected Poems* was finally published in 1947.

Sassoon's poem "Everyone Sang" does not directly describe the fighting and suffering on the western front, but it does concern World War I. Sassoon wrote the poem in response to the welcome news of the armistice on November 11, 1918, when people all over the world rejoiced that the "war to end all wars" was finally over.

Siegfried Sassoon

Everyone Sang

Everyone suddenly burst out singing;
And I was filled with such delight
As prisoned birds must find in freedom,
Winging wildly across the white
5 Orchards and dark green fields;
     on—on—and out of sight.

Everyone's voice was suddenly lifted;
And beauty came like the setting sun:
My heart was shaken with tears; and horror
Drifted away . . . O, but Everyone
10 Was a bird; and the song was wordless;
     the singing will never be done.

Rupert Brooke   *1887–1915*

Rupert Brooke was handsome, charming, intelligent, privileged, and beloved—a "golden young Apollo," as one of his friends described him. Because of his early, tragic death in World War I, he has remained that golden young poet forever, and it is partly because of his early death that his reputation as a poet survives.

Brooke began to write for pleasure at an early age and won a prize for his verse while still in school. Popular and energetic, he played football and cricket and edited the school magazine. His early published poems are associated with Georgian poetry: traditional verse that sings of country life and patriotic ideals—a kind of poetry in keeping with Brooke's happy, sheltered youth.

In his mid-twenties Brooke left his native England to travel extensively in Europe, America, and the South Seas. It was in Tahiti in 1913 that he wrote some of his most famous poems.

He returned to England and enlisted in the wartime navy. During the last year of his life, he wrote his series of war sonnets, which are traditional, formal, and patriotic in tone. "The Soldier" is the most famous of these poems. Unlike so many of his contemporaries, Brooke never wrote angry or bitter descriptions of battle, possibly because he spent so little time in the trenches. He died on his way to battle: While traveling to Turkey, he was stricken with blood poisoning and died on a Greek island. Ironically, his death brought him almost immediate fame as both a poet and a symbol of innocent youth struck down by war.

Rupert Brooke

The Soldier

If I should die, think only this of me:
    That there's some corner of a foreign field
That is for ever England. There shall be
    In that rich earth a richer dust concealed;
5 A dust whom England bore, shaped, made aware,
    Gave, once, her flowers to love, her ways to roam,
A body of England's, breathing English air,
    Washed by the rivers, blessed by suns of home.

And think, this heart, all evil shed away,
10   A pulse in the eternal mind, no less
      Gives somewhere back the thoughts by England given;
Her sights and sounds; dreams happy as her day;
    And laughter, learned of friends; and gentleness,
      In hearts at peace, under an English heaven.

Stephen Spender   *born 1909*

For over fifty years Stephen Spender has remained a prominent voice among British authors. The son of a journalist and Oxford lecturer, he showed an early interest in literature. The year before he entered Oxford he began his own printing press, printing up a volume of his own poems along with a batch of chemical labels. While still in college, he published a second volume of poems and became associated with a small circle of poets led by W. H. Auden.

The publication in 1933 of his *Poems* firmly established Spender's place among a circle of poets that included Auden, Louis MacNeice, and Cecil Day Lewis. These poets had all been deeply affected by World War I. They blamed the decline of England in the 1920s and 1930s on the loss of faith in humanity and the social order as a result of the war. The work of these poets reflected the economic and political turbulence of the 1930s: the worldwide Depression, the rise of fascism and Nazism, and the Spanish civil war. However, unlike Eliot, they did not condemn modern society or regard social injustice as evidence of civilization's collapse. Instead they chose positive protest, political involvement, and artistic expression as healthy ways of confronting an ailing world.

Spender has had a varied career. He has taught at several British and American universities and edited the artistic magazines *Encounters* and *Horizon.* He has remained active in literary circles, writing criticism, short stories, and a novel in addition to poetry. Among his recent work is *The Thirties and After: Poetry, Politics, People, 1933–1970* (1979).

Spender's poetry is somewhat more romantic and direct in its tone than that of the other poets in his circle. His work is less satiric and more lyrical than Auden's, more personal than MacNeice's. In addition, Spender did more than the others to turn the machine and the technological society it eventually produced into legitimate subjects for poetry. "I Think Continually of the Truly Great," however, draws much of its impact from Spender's intensely lyrical use of nature images.

Stephen Spender

I Think Continually of Those Who Were Truly Great

I think continually of those who were truly great.
Who, from the womb, remembered the soul's history
Through corridors of light where the hours are suns,
Endless and singing. Whose lovely ambition
5 Was that their lips, still touched with fire,
Should tell of the Spirit, clothed from head to foot in song.
And who hoarded from the Spring branches
The desires falling across their bodies like blossoms.

What is precious, is never to forget
10 The essential delight of the blood drawn from ageless springs
Breaking through rocks in worlds before our earth.
Never to deny its pleasure in the simple morning light
Nor its grave evening demand for love.
Never to allow gradually the traffic to smother
15 With noise and fog, the flowering of the Spirit.

Near the snow, near the sun, in the highest fields,
See how these names are feted[1] by the waving grass
And by the streamers of white cloud
And whispers of wind in the listening sky.
20 The names of those who in their lives fought for life,
Who wore at their hearts the fire's center.
Born of the sun, they traveled a short while toward the sun
And left the vivid air signed with their honor.

---

1. **feted** [fāt′əd]: honored or commemorated with a fete, or celebration.

STUDY QUESTIONS

Everyone Sang (Sassoon)

Recalling

1. What does the speaker feel when everyone bursts out singing? To what does he compare this feeling?
2. In the second stanza what happens to the speaker's heart? What "Drifted away"?
3. How long will the singing last, according to line 10?

Interpreting

4. Why is everyone singing? Explain why the simile in the first stanza is appropriate to the situation in the poem.
5. In the second stanza why might beauty come like the "setting" rather than rising sun?
6. What different emotions does the speaker express from the beginning to the end of the poem? What causes his emotions to change?

Extending

7. Why might we be powerfully moved when a large group of people suddenly respond in unison to something? Can you think of instances when such a response is exhilarating? When it is frightening?

The Soldier (Brooke)

Recalling

1. What does the speaker want people to think of him if he should die?
2. According to lines 5–8, what did England do for the speaker?
3. What will his heart become? What sorts of thoughts will his heart give back?

Interpreting

4. What is the speaker's attitude toward England? What words and images in the poem convey this emotion?
5. What is the speaker's attitude toward death? In what sense can life win out over death?
6. In what ways is "The Soldier" more than simply an English soldier's poem about his homeland? What might be its more universal theme and appeal?

Extending

7. How would you define the word *patriot*? What different meanings might the word have for different people?

I Think Continually . . . (Spender)

Recalling

1. What is the ambition of the "truly great"?
2. According to the second stanza, what things should not be forgotten? What should not be denied? What should not be allowed to happen?
3. According to lines 22–23, of what were the truly great born, and what did they do?
4. Point out five nature images in lines 8–19.

Interpreting

5. Describe the personal qualities of the "truly great." What does Spender mean when he says that great people "fought for life"?
6. Why do you think Spender describes these special people with terms like *Spirit, fire,* and *the sun*?
7. Why might Spender turn to nature for imagery to salute great human beings?

COMPOSITION (Brooke)

Writing About a Quotation

■ Discuss the meaning of the lines "That there's some corner of a foreign field / That is for ever England." First explain the specific meaning of these lines at the point at which they occur in "The Soldier." Then explain the significance of the lines in relation to the overall meaning of the poem. *For help with this assignment, refer to Lesson 5 in the Writing About Literature Handbook at the back of this book.*

Writing a Poem About a Person

■ In a short poem list and describe those characteristic articles that you might place in a time capsule to represent yourself or some famous person for all time.

COMPARING WRITERS

1. What similarities in outlook can you find in the poems of Sassoon, Brooke, and Spender? Are their poems positive, neutral, or negative in their descriptions of human life?
2. All three poets use nature imagery in describing human affairs and problems. In at least two of these poems, relate the feelings evoked by these images of nature. What differences can you detect in each poet's view of nature?

Louis MacNeice   *1907–1963*

Louis MacNeice was a member of the group of English poets that included Stephen Spender, W. H. Auden, and Cecil Day Lewis. He has come to be regarded as one of the most original and least typical writers in this group.

The son of a Protestant bishop, MacNeice was born and reared in Belfast, Ireland. After graduating from Oxford, he taught at several universities, combining his teaching career with a heavy writing schedule. From serious poetry he branched out into writing light verse, criticism, poetic drama, and travel literature. MacNeice and his friend and fellow poet W. H. Auden collaborated in recording their observations and feelings during a trip to Iceland in *Letters from Iceland* (1937), a mixture of poetry and prose.

During the 1940s MacNeice worked for the British Broadcasting Corporation as a producer and feature writer, changing jobs in 1950 to direct the British Institute in Athens. He also continued to teach from time to time, always leaving time for his two greatest passions—writing and tennis.

Although MacNeice's early association with Auden, Spender, and other poets of the 1930s is important, his work deviated from theirs in some significant ways. While the others believed that poetry truly could change the world, MacNeice was more cautious about poetry's impact on society. He saw the poet not as an engineer of social change but rather as an entertainer, a commentator, a broadcaster of the truth, whose message was made up of both fact and emotion. His poetry was less political and more literary than that of his associates, and his style was often colloquial, or drawn from everyday speech.

During World War II MacNeice's poetry darkened and became more introspective and philosophical than his earlier work. However, his later poems regained the lyricism for which he is now known and which is demonstrated in "The Park."

Louis MacNeice

The Park

Through a glass greenly[1] men as trees walking[2]
Led by their dogs, trees as torrents
Loosed by the thaw, tulips as shriekmarks
(Yelps of delight), lovers as coracles[3]
5 Riding the rapids: Spring as a spring
Releasing the jack-in-a-box of a fanfare.

Urban enclave[4] of lawns and water,
Lacquered ducks and young men sculling,[5]
Children who never had seen the country
10 Believing it this while those who had once
Known real country ignore the void
Their present imposes, their past exposes.

South and east lie the yellowed terraces
Grandiose, jerrybuilt,[6] ghosts of gracious
15 Living, and north those different terraces
Where great white bears with extensile[7]
        necks,
Convicted sentries, lope their beat,
No rest for their paws till the day they die.

Fossils of flesh, fossils of stucco:
20 Between them the carefully labeled flower
        beds
And the litter baskets, but also between
        them
Through a grille gaily men as music
Forcing the spring to loose the lid,
To break the bars, to find the world.

---

1. **Through . . . greenly:** a playful version of the
Biblical quotation "We see through a glass, darkly" (I
Corinthians, 13 : 12).
2. **men . . . walking:** a reference to the New
Testament episode in which Jesus cured a blind man,
who then said that he saw "men as trees walking."
3. **coracles** [kôr′ə kəlz]: small boats made with wicker
frames covered with hides.
4. **enclave:** self-contained unit within a foreign
community.
5. **sculling:** rowing with large oars.
6. **jerrybuilt:** cheaply or hastily made.
7. **extensile:** able to be extended or stretched.

Robert Graves   *born 1895*

Robert Graves is one of the most prolific writers in the twentieth century. He is famous as a scholar and novelist as well as a poet, and his varied literary output of over one hundred books includes biographical and autobiographical works, translations, works of literary criticism, and studies of such subjects as anthropology and psychology.

Graves was born in Wimbledon, England; his father was a poet with a passion for Irish folklore. In 1914 Graves left school to enlist in the Royal Welsh Fusiliers, serving alongside Siegfried Sassoon. Badly wounded early in the war, Graves began writing poetry during his recovery. In 1916 his first two volumes of poetry, *Over the Brazier* and *Goliath and David,* established his reputation as an antiwar poet. After the war Graves married, resumed his education at Oxford, and later pursued his interests in writing, scholarship, and teaching. Although he taught at Oxford for many years, he has not always lived in England. As a young man, he taught in Cairo, Egypt, and in more recent years he has made his home in Majorca [mə yôr′kə], an island off the coast of Spain.

Graves's work is a mixture of the traditional and the modern, of traditional forms and modern sensibilities. Even his historical novels, which are based on ancient history and myth and include the popular works *I, Claudius* and *Claudius, the God,* use the idiom of the twentieth century. Graves's earliest poetry reflects the traditional style of the Georgian poets. As he developed as a poet, his subject matter shifted first to philosophy and later to personal and romantic relationships. Regardless of period, however, all of his best poems combine irony and sensitivity with a smoothly lyrical style. As he says of his own poetic standards, "My minimum requirement of a poem is that it should make prose sense as well as poetic sense," a rule that he obeys in "Song: Sullen Moods."

Robert Graves

Song: Sullen Moods

Love, never count your labor lost
    Though I turn sullen or retired
Even at your side; my thought is crossed
    With fancies by no evil fired.

5 And when I answer you, some days,
    Vaguely and wildly, never fear
That my love walks forbidden ways,
    Snapping the ties that hold it here.

If I speak gruffly, this mood is
10   Mere indignation at my own
Shortcomings, plagues, uncertainties:
    I forget the gentler tone.

You, now that you have come to be
    My one beginning, prime and end,
15 I count at last as wholly me,
    Lover no longer nor yet friend.

Help me to see you as before
    When overwhelmed and dead, almost,
I stumbled on that secret door
20   Which saves the live man from the ghost.

Be once again the distant light,
    Promise of glory, not yet known
In full perfection—wasted quite
    When on my imperfection thrown.

STUDY QUESTIONS

The Park (MacNeice)

Recalling

1. In the first stanza to what does MacNeice compare the men walking in the park? List three other comparisons that MacNeice makes in this stanza.
2. What term in line 7 describes the park? What do the children in lines 9–10 believe the park to be? What must be ignored by the people mentioned in lines 10–12?
3. For what three reasons are the men in the park "forcing the spring," according to lines 23–24?

Interpreting

4. What conflict is expressed in the image of "Lacquered ducks" in line 8? What might this image have in common with the images of the bears in the zoo and the "carefully labeled flower beds" in line 20?
5. What do you think MacNeice means by the word *void* in line 11? Is the park part of the void or a refuge from it? Defend your answer.
6. To what is the park superior? To what is it inferior? By the end of the poem, does the park seem more a positive place or a negative place? Why?
7. What is MacNeice saying about the relationship between the works of human beings and the works of nature?

Extending

8. What needs does a park satisfy for people who live in a city? How important do you think such needs are to the quality of human life?

Song: Sullen Moods (Graves)

Recalling

1. In line 7 what does the speaker say his love should never fear? What explanation does the speaker give in the third stanza for his own gruffness?
2. In the fourth stanza what does the speaker say

his love has now come to be?
3. In the last stanza what does the speaker ask his love to become again?

Interpreting

4. Restate in your own words the various requests, stated or implied, that the speaker makes of his love in the first three stanzas. What do these requests show about the speaker's attitude toward his love and toward himself?
5. What view of love does the fourth stanza suggest?
6. In what ways is the speaker's former feeling for his love different from his present feeling? Why do you think he now wants to see his love as he saw her before?

Extending

7. Why do you think people often take those they love for granted?

COMPOSITION (MacNeice)

Writing About a Symbol

▓ Discuss MacNeice's use of the bears as a symbol in "The Park." Begin by explaining the symbolic meaning of the bears when they first appear in the third stanza. Then discuss the significance of the bears to the poem as a whole, showing how MacNeice uses the bears to help reveal the theme of "The Park." *For help with this assignment, refer to Lesson 5 in the Writing About Literature Handbook at the back of this book.*

Writing with Imagery

▓ Write either a pair of stanzas or a pair of paragraphs in which you use contrasting images. Your first stanza or paragraph should use imagery from nature to describe an industrial or mechanical object or scene (for example, a lawn mower, an assembly line, a traffic jam). Your second stanza or paragraph should use technological imagery to describe an animal, a plant, or a scene from the natural world.

W. H. Auden *1907–1973*

Photograph © 1982 by Jill Krementz

After Yeats and Eliot, Wystan Hugh Auden is the most influential English poet in the modern period. Auden spent the first thirty-two years of his life in England and most of the remainder in the United States. Like T. S. Eliot, whose life followed the opposite pattern, Auden is often regarded as both an English and an American writer.

The young Auden had no particular literary ambitions; his father was a respected physician, his mother a nurse, and Auden himself originally planned to become a mining engineer. Auden studied at Oxford University, where he became the leader of the group that included Stephen Spender, Louis MacNeice, and Cecil Day Lewis. He shared their disenchantment with the modern world as well as their determination to provide political and poetic alternatives to its ills. In 1928 Spender published twenty-six of Auden's poems, and in that same year Auden went to Germany to study politics and psychology.

During the 1930s Auden was something of a romantic radical who delighted in shocking both readers and friends with his language and opinions; by his own admission he loved to show off. However, his life and his work became more subdued after 1940. In 1937 he married the daughter of German novelist Thomas Mann so that she could leave Nazi Germany. In that same year Auden also set off to aid the Loyalists in the Spanish civil war. On returning to England, he received the King's Poetry Medal. Perhaps the greatest change in Auden's work came from his return to the practice of Christianity.

In 1939 Auden moved to the United States, giving frequent lectures at American universities. Seven years after his arrival in America, he became a U.S. citizen, and the following year he won the Pulitzer Prize. In addition to poetry, Auden wrote drama, criticism, blues music, musical librettos, and nonsense verse. Among his best-known works are *On This Island* (1937), *For the Time Being* (1944), and *The Age of Anxiety* (1947).

Auden's early work was somewhat obscure. His language was difficult, his symbolism borrowed, and his subject matter primarily that of a world rushing toward disaster. As his poetic career progressed, however, his poems became clearer and less angry. His work shows the influence of Eliot, Yeats, German poetry, and German cabaret lyrics, which lent a dark wit and potential violence to his poetry. As his friend Stephen Spender once said, Auden's poetry has a "vitality, an explosive violence that leaves his contemporaries dazed." Still, above the impulse to shock and show off, Auden's work preserved a strict morality, a vision of humanity's responsibility to create a more humane world.

W. B. Yeats died in January, 1939. Nine months later World War II erupted in Europe. Soon after, Auden wrote this tribute, reflecting also on the state of the world Yeats had left behind.

W. H. Auden

In Memory of W. B. Yeats

1

He disappeared in the dead of winter:
The brooks were frozen, the airports almost deserted,
And snow disfigured the public statues;
The mercury sank in the mouth of the dying day.
5 O all the instruments agree
The day of his death was a dark cold day.

Far from his illness
The wolves ran on through the evergreen forests,
The peasant river was untempted by the fashionable quays;[1]
10 By mourning tongues
The death of the poet was kept from his poems.

But for him it was his last afternoon as himself,
An afternoon of nurses and rumors;
The provinces of his body revolted,
15 The squares of his mind were empty,
Silence invaded the suburbs,
The current of his feeling failed: he became his admirers.

Now he is scattered among a hundred cities
And wholly given over to unfamiliar affections;
20 To find his happiness in another kind of wood
And be punished under a foreign code of conscience.
The words of a dead man
Are modified in the guts of the living.

But in the importance and noise of tomorrow
When the brokers are roaring like beasts on the floor of the
    Bourse,[2]
25 And the poor have the sufferings to which they are fairly
    accustomed,
And each in the cell of himself is almost convinced of his freedom;
A few thousand will think of this day
As one thinks of a day when one did something slightly unusual.
30 O all the instruments agree
The day of his death was a dark cold day.

---

1. **quays** [kēz]: loading docks or banks beside a waterway.
2. **Bourse** [bōŏrs]: the Paris Stock Exchange.

2

You were silly like us: your gift survived
    it all;
The parish of rich women, physical decay,
Yourself; mad Ireland hurt you into
    poetry.
35 Now Ireland has her madness and her
    weather still,
For poetry makes nothing happen:
    it survives
In the valley of its saying where
    executives
Would never want to tamper; it flows
    south
From ranches of isolation and the busy
    griefs,
40 Raw towns that we believe and die in;
    it survives,
A way of happening, a mouth.

3

Earth, receive an honored guest;
William Yeats is laid to rest:
Let the Irish vessel lie
45 Emptied of its poetry.

Time that is intolerant
Of the brave and innocent,
And indifferent in a week
To a beautiful physique,

50 Worships language and forgives
Everyone by whom it lives;
Pardons cowardice, conceit,
Lays its honors at their feet.

55 Time that with this strange excuse
Pardoned Kipling and his views,[3]
And will pardon Paul Claudel,[4]
Pardons him for writing well.

In the nightmare of the dark
60 All the dogs of Europe bark,
And the living nations wait,
Each sequestered[5] in its hate;

Intellectual disgrace
Stares from every human face,
And the seas of pity lie
65 Locked and frozen in each eye.

Follow, poet, follow right
To the bottom of the night,
With your unconstraining voice
Still persuade us to rejoice;

70 With the farming of a verse
Make a vineyard of the curse,
Sing of human unsuccess
In a rapture of distress;

In the deserts of the heart
75 Let the healing fountain start,
In the prison of his days
Teach the free man how to praise.

---

3. **Kipling . . . views:** English writer Rudyard
Kipling (1865–1936) was criticized for supporting
imperialism.
4. **pardon Paul Claudel** [klō del′]: French poet,
dramatist, and statesman Paul Claudel (1868–1955)
was attacked for his antidemocratic views, which
Yeats to some extent shared.
5. **sequestered:** set apart. Lines 60–61 refer to
World War II, then in progress.

STUDY QUESTIONS

Recalling

1. What happens to the words of the dead, according to lines 22–23?
2. What of Yeats survived, according to line 32? What various things did it survive?
3. What three things does time care nothing about? What does time worship, and whom does it forgive?
4. List the six requests that Auden makes of the dead Yeats in the last three stanzas.

Interpreting

5. What, according to this poem, are the various differences between Yeats's life and his poetry? Between any poet's life and his or her poetry?
6. When Auden says in line 36 that "poetry makes nothing happen," what things is he actually talking about? What *can* poetry do, according to this poem?
7. Explain how Auden's references to world affairs are related to his views on poetry.

Extending

8. What do you think is the value of poetry? Can poetry make the world better in any way?

LITERARY FOCUS

Paradox

A **paradox** is a statement or situation that at first seems impossible or self-contradictory but may be true in fact or in a figurative sense. For example, Wordsworth's metaphor "the child is father to the man" is a paradox that expresses a figurative truth about the relationship between a child's imagination and that of the adult he becomes. The word *paradox* comes from a Greek expression meaning "contrary to popular opinion or expectation."

As a literary device, paradox can serve many functions. It can attract attention to a difficult idea and persuade readers to accept it. Paradox can also dramatize the fact that experience is full of apparent contradictions.

Sometimes paradox is one literary technique among many used in a poem; at other times, however, paradox can be the basis for an entire poem. The seventeenth-century poet John Donne, for example, is famous for his frequent and extended use of paradox. Modern poets—Auden among them—also find paradox a particularly apt way of expressing the contradictions of their own time.

Thinking About Paradox

1. Point out the paradoxes in the lines "Sing of human unsuccess / In a rapture of distress." What truth might lie behind those apparent contradictions? Find two other seeming contradictions in the last twelve lines of the poem, and explain them as well.
2. Would you have preferred these lines if they had been more straightforward and less paradoxical? Why or why not?

COMPOSITION

Writing About Sound in a Poem

▪ Write an essay about the effect of sound in Auden's "In Memory of W. B. Yeats." Using examples, describe the change in the poem's rhythm and rhyme that occurs in section 3. Then explain how this change affects the emotional impact of the poem.

Writing a Poem of Tribute

▪ Write a short poem in which you pay tribute to someone whom you admire. Be sure to include that person's character traits as well as his or her achievements and effect on you.

In "Musée des Beaux Arts" Auden uses the work of the great painters—the "Old Masters"—as a backdrop for comments about human nature. In particular, he refers to "The Fall of Icarus," a work by the sixteenth-century Flemish painter, Pieter Brueghel [broi′gəl]. Icarus is a figure from Greek mythology who tried to fly but fell to his death when his man-made wings melted in the sun.

W. H. Auden

Musée des Beaux Arts

About suffering they were never wrong,
The Old Masters: how well they understood
Its human position; how it takes place
While someone else is eating or opening a window or just
    walking dully along;
5 How, when the aged are reverently, passionately waiting
For the miraculous birth, there always must be
Children who did not specially want it to happen, skating
On a pond at the edge of the wood:
They never forgot
10 That even the dreadful martyrdom must run its course
Anyhow in a corner, some untidy spot
Where the dogs go on with their doggy life and the torturer's
    horse
Scratches its innocent behind on a tree.

In Brueghel's *Icarus,* for instance: how everything turns away
15 Quite leisurely from the disaster; the ploughman may
Have heard the splash, the forsaken cry,
But for him it was not an important failure; the sun shone
As it had to on the white legs disappearing into the green
Water; and the expensive delicate ship that must have seen
20 Something amazing, a boy falling out of the sky,
Had somewhere to get to and sailed calmly on.

Opposite page: The Fall of Icarus, Pieter Brueghel the Elder, sixteenth century.

STUDY QUESTIONS

Recalling

1. What, according to lines 3–4, did the Old Masters understand about suffering?
2. What disaster occurs in the second stanza?
3. How does "everything" react to this disaster? Give two of the examples of such behavior listed in that stanza.

Interpreting

4. What is the place of suffering, miraculous birth, and martyrdom within human affairs?
5. What contrast can you see between expressions like "doggy life" and "forsaken cry"? Relate this contrast in Auden's diction to the two views of life he presents in this poem.
6. Does Auden sympathize with or condemn the behavior he describes? How do you know?

Extending

7. Explain why people often react as they do in this poem. Do you think these reactions show human nature in a positive or negative light?

VIEWPOINT

The speaker of a "typical" Auden poem often views human experience with an overseeing eye. According to critic Richard Hoggart, the best picture of Auden's writing would portray

> a landscape and a wanderer. . . . The Wanderer . . . is physically isolated and surveys from a great height the interesting but muddled life of those below; he can see a possible order in the muddle which they do not see, and he would like to help it emerge. He is detached and slightly clinical. He is compassionate but also rather coldly reformative.

> —Auden, A Collection of Critical Essays

■ In what ways does the speaker in "Musée des Beaux Arts" seem isolated high above those he describes? What overall order does he see in these events? At what points in the poem does the speaker seem compassionate? Clinical?

Dylan Thomas   *1914–1953*

Dylan Thomas' ardent romanticism and passion for language have made him one of the most popular poets in the twentieth century. Thomas was born in South Wales, where he was formally educated only through grammar school. He knew as a young boy that he wanted to be a writer, and he vigorously read and wrote throughout his youth. By the age of twenty, he had published his first volume of poetry, *Eighteen Poems,* for which he received instant critical acclaim. After serving as an antiaircraft gunner during World War II, Thomas became a commentator on poetry for the British Broadcasting Corporation.

In 1949 he began visiting the United States for poetry-reading tours; he quickly became a celebrity on American college campuses, developing a reputation as one of the best performers of poetry in modern times. Between these visits Thomas would return to his wife and children in the Welsh village of Laugharne, where his personal life was always stormy. While on tour in New York, he died suddenly of pneumonia.

Not long before his death, Thomas' *Collected Poems* was published, along with his now-famous radio play, *Under Milk Wood.* Besides these works Thomas wrote essays, reminiscences, short stories, scripts for documentary films, and one novel. Still, Dylan Thomas remains best known for his radiant poetry. Thomas saw himself as a modern-day descendant of the English Romantic poets. His writing was not intellectual and restrained like that of Eliot; unlike Auden, Spender, and their colleagues, he had little interest in righting social wrongs. Instead, Thomas was fascinated with the inner workings of the mind and enchanted with the potency of language.

At first glance, many of Thomas' poems seem to be disorderly, overwhelming outpourings of language. However, although the sheer sound of words does sometimes overpower sense in his early poetry, Thomas' mature poems are neither dizzy with sound nor chaotic. Influenced by the oral tradition of the ancient Welsh bards, Thomas wrote unconventional and intensely musical poems, but his work was highly disciplined and was often based on elaborate patterns. As Thomas himself once said, " . . . a poem of mine is, or should be, a watertight section of the stream that is flowing all ways, all warring images within it should be reconciled for that small stop of time."

Thomas' Welsh childhood provides material for much of his poetry. Other major themes in his work include wartime London, religion, his own emotional life, and the relationship of life to death. His poems are full of brooding, and in the course of his career they became increasingly preoccupied with death. Yet his poetry is often intricately laced with wit and hope and above all blazes with the joy of using language.

Dylan Thomas

Do Not Go Gentle into That Good Night

Do not go gentle into that good night,
Old age should burn and rave at close of day;
Rage, rage against the dying of the light.

Though wise men at their end know dark is right,
5 Because their words had forked no lightning they
Do not go gentle into that good night.

Good men, the last wave by, crying how bright
Their frail deeds might have danced in a green bay,
Rage, rage against the dying of the light.

10 Wild men who caught and sang the sun in flight,
And learn, too late, they grieved it on its way,
Do not go gentle into that good night.

Grave men, near death, who see with blinding sight
Blind eyes could blaze like meteors and be gay,
15 Rage, rage against the dying of the light.

And you, my father, there on the sad height,
Curse, bless, me now with your fierce tears, I pray.
Do not go gentle into that good night.
Rage, rage against the dying of the light.

STUDY QUESTIONS

Recalling

1. What does the speaker tell the person he is addressing not to do? What does he want that person to do instead?
2. What do wise men know? What do they do in spite of this knowledge, and why?
3. Whom is the speaker addressing? Where is this person, according to line 16?

Interpreting

4. How would you interpret the words *good night* and *the dying of the light*? What might dark and light symbolize in the poem?
5. For what reasons might the different men mentioned in the poem refuse to "go gentle"?
6. What is actually happening to the person whom the speaker addresses? How does the speaker feel about it, and how do you know?
7. Describe the emotional impact of the poem and the view of life and death it expresses.

LITERARY FOCUS

Villanelle

The **villanelle** is a poetic form that consists of nineteen lines divided into five three-line stanzas called **tercets** and a final four-line stanza called a **quatrain**. All of the lines in the villanelle use only two end rhymes, with the rhyme scheme following the pattern: *aba aba aba aba aba abaa.* In addition, almost half of the poem is made up of repeated lines: Line 1 is repeated in lines 6, 12, and 18, while line 3 is repeated in lines 9, 15, and 19.

This careful and intricate arrangement of lines is meant to appear simple and spontaneous. Based on an Italian word, *villanello,* which means "rural" or "rustic," the villanelle was invented by French poets as a pastoral poem with a light, lyric tone. Poets in the nineteenth and twentieth centuries took up this form and removed the original restrictions on its subject matter and tone. Today villanelles are written on many different subjects in a wide variety of tones. "Do Not Go Gentle into That Good Night" is perhaps the most famous modern example of the form.

Thinking About the Villanelle

1. Does Thomas' poem exactly follow the formal requirements of the villanelle with respect to number of lines, repetition, stanza form, and rhyme scheme? In what ways is it different from the original villanelles?
2. Explain how the repeated lines add to the meaning and emotional impact of this poem.

COMPARING WRITERS

1. Referring to at least one of the poems by W. H. Auden and by Dylan Thomas that you have read, compare the attitudes of these poets toward suffering and death. Which seems more accepting of suffering and mortality?
2. Which poet, Auden or Thomas, touches you more? Explain.

"Fern Hill," Dylan Thomas' famous poem about childhood, first appeared in 1945 and is considered one of his best works. Written during a highly creative, productive year of his life, it captures an "Eden-like memory" for all time. The poem is also a fine example of Thomas' characteristic uses of original images, rich symbols, and dazzling language.

Dylan Thomas

Fern Hill

Now as I was young and easy under the apple boughs
About the lilting house and happy as the grass was green,
   The night above the dingle[1] starry,
    Time let me hail and climb
5   Golden in the heydays[2] of his eyes,
And honored among wagons I was prince of the apple towns
And once below a time I lordly had the trees and leaves
    Trail with daisies and barley
   Down the rivers of the windfall light.

10   And as I was green and carefree, famous among the barns
About the happy yard and singing as the farm was home,
   In the sun that is young once only,
    Time let me play and be
   Golden in the mercy of his means,
15 And green and golden I was huntsman and herdsman, the calves
Sang to my horn, the foxes on the hills barked clear and cold,
    And the sabbath rang slowly
   In the pebbles of the holy streams.

All the sun long it was running, it was lovely, the hay
20 Fields high as the house, the tunes from the chimneys, it was air
    And playing, lovely and watery
     And fire green as grass.
    And nightly under the simple stars
As I rode to sleep the owls were bearing the farm away,

---

1. **dingle:** small, wooded valley nestled between steep hills.
2. **heydays:** periods of one's greatest vitality.

25 All the moon long I heard, blessed among stables, the nightjars[3]
     Flying with the ricks,[4] and the horses
       Flashing into the dark.

And then to awake, and the farm, like a wanderer white
With the dew, come back, the cock on his shoulder: it was all
30   Shining, it was Adam and maiden,
      The sky gathered again
      And the sun grew round that very day.
So it must have been after the birth of the simple light
In the first, spinning place, the spellbound horses walking warm
35   Out of the whinnying green stable
      On to the fields of praise.

And honored among foxes and pheasants by the gay house
Under the new made clouds and happy as the heart was long,
    In the sun born over and over,
40   I ran my heedless ways,
      My wishes raced through the house high hay
And nothing I cared, at my sky blue trades, that time allows
In all his tuneful turning so few and such morning songs
    Before the children green and golden
45   Follow him out of grace,

Nothing I cared, in the lamb white days, that time would
      take me
Up to the swallow thronged loft by the shadow of my hand,
    In the moon that is always rising,
      Nor that riding to sleep
50   I should hear him fly with the high fields
And wake to the farm forever fled from the childless land.
Oh as I was young and easy in the mercy of his means,
    Time held me green and dying
    Though I sang in my chains like the sea.

---

3. **nightjars:** grayish-brown birds that sing at night.
4. **ricks:** stacks of hay in the open air.

STUDY QUESTIONS

Recalling

1. According to lines 10–11, what is the setting of the poem? List five details of the setting mentioned in the poem.
2. In the first two stanzas what four things does time let the speaker do? List five words that the speaker uses to describe himself in these stanzas.
3. In the fifth stanza what does the speaker say he cared nothing about? What words does the speaker use to describe himself in stanza 6 as time held him?

Interpreting

4. What mood predominates for most of the poem? Point out four or five images, and explain how they help to create this mood.
5. In what way does the mood of the poem shift, and what causes this shift?
6. Why do you think Thomas refers so often to the colors green and gold? What do these colors seem to symbolize in the poem? What combination of ideas does he suggest at the end, when he says he was "green and dying"?
7. Of what are children not aware, according to the poem? What does the poem seem to be saying about childhood? About time?

Extending

8. Why do you think time seems to move differently for children and for adults?

LITERARY FOCUS

Diction

Diction is another term for word choice. Good writers choose their words carefully and precisely so that these words express exactly what the writer intends. In choosing their words writers are mindful of three things in particular: the word's **denotation,** or dictionary definition, its various **connotations,** or suggested meanings and associations, and its *sound.* When choosing among several words with similar denotations, a writer can usually sense which word sounds best and brings the most appropriate associations into a given text.

Styles change in diction, and what sounds appropriate to the writers of one century might sound barbaric or pompous to the writers of another time. If Dr. Samuel Johnson (page 289) were to visit us, he might be offended by our casual way of speaking and writing. We, in turn, might find his diction rather stiff and unnatural.

Individual writers can often be recognized by their word choices from one work to the next. Some may characteristically prefer plain words of one syllable, while others prefer to spangle their writing with more colorful or unusual words. Some may like to jar their readers with odd combinations of words, while others write in a seamlessly graceful style. Dylan Thomas is one writer whose diction is as characteristic and recognizable as his signature. For example, in "Fern Hill" notice his playful phrase "once below a time" and his adverb "lordly" (line 7).

Thinking About Diction

1. Find other illustrations of Thomas' use of unusual or playful diction in "Fern Hill," and explain the effect of these word choices.
2. Based on your reading of "Fern Hill," make up a list of qualities you would expect to see in the diction of a Dylan Thomas poem. Give examples from "Fern Hill."

COMPOSITION

Writing About Poetry

■ Explain the meaning of "Fern Hill," and show how Thomas uses poetic techniques to illuminate this meaning. In particular, explain how Thomas uses speaker, sound, imagery, and figurative language to present his visions of childhood and time. Point out the various changes in these elements throughout the poem, and relate these changes to the poem's meaning. *For help with this assignment, see Lesson 7 in the Writing About Literature Handbook at the back of this book.*

Writing a Poem About Childhood

■ Write a lyrical, colorful, image-packed poem depicting a childhood scene as Thomas has done in "Fern Hill." Your choice of details should convey emotion about the subject.

Charles Tomlinson   *born 1927*

According to English critic David Davie, Charles Tomlinson is the "most original and accomplished of all our postwar poets." However, Tomlinson has also been criticized for leaving the human element out of his work.

Born at Staffordshire in England, Tomlinson graduated from Cambridge University and took a secretarial job in northern Italy. Since that time he has divided his time between writing and teaching. He teaches at the University of Bristol and has also been a visiting professor at several American universities as well as a translator of French, Italian, and German poetry.

In "Suggestions for the Improvement of a Sunset" Tomlinson characteristically focuses on the natural, rather than the human, world. Nevertheless, he claims that even in those poems that do not contain humans his "theme is relationship."

Charles Tomlinson

Suggestions for the Improvement of a Sunset

Darkening the edges of the land,
Imperceptibly it must drain out colors
Drawing all light into its center.

Six points of vantage[1] provide us with six sunsets.

5 The sea partakes of the sky. It is less
Itself than the least pool which, if threatened,
Prizes lucidity.

The pond is lime green, an enemy
Of gold, bearing no change but shadow.

10 Seen from above, the house would resemble
A violin, abandoned, and lost in its own darkness;

Diminished, through the wrong end of a glass,
A dice ambushed by lowering greens;

Accorded its true proportions,
15 The stone would give back the light
Which, all day, it has absorbed.

The afterglow, broken by leaves and windows,
Confirms green's triumph[2] against yellow.

---

1. **points of vantage:** positions from which something is viewed.
2. **afterglow . . . green's triumph:** In the last instant of
sunset a green flash appears at the rim of the sinking sun.

Thom Gunn   *born 1929*

Thomson William Gunn is associated with "The Movement" of the 1950s, which consisted of a group of poets who met at Oxford University and who wrote poems about ordinary life in a deliberately conversational style. Born in England, Gunn has spent much of his time in the United States. He has studied at both Cambridge and Stanford universities and taught at the University of California at Berkeley from 1957 to 1966. As he does in "Taylor Street," Gunn writes poems that anchor ideas in concrete physical details.

Thom Gunn

Taylor Street

The small porch of imitation
marble is never sunny, but
outside the front door he
sits on his kitchen chair facing
5 the street. In the bent yellowish
face, from under the brim
of a floppy brown hat,
his small eyes watch what
he is not living. But he
10 lives what he can:
watches without a smile, with
a certain strain, the warmth
of his big crumpled
body anxiously cupped
15 by himself in himself, as
he leans over himself not
over the cold railing, unmoving but carefully getting
a little strength from the sight of the
20 passers-by. He has it
all planned: he will live
here morning by morning.

STUDY QUESTIONS

Suggestions for Improvement . . . (Tomlinson)

Recalling

1. Of the six "points of vantage" that the speaker presents, list the two described in lines 5–9.
2. From what "point of vantage" would the house resemble a violin? From what "point of vantage" would it resemble dice?
3. List the two "points of vantage" described in the final two stanzas.
4. What does the "afterglow" confirm?

Interpreting

5. In your own words, describe each of the six sunsets portrayed in the poem.
6. What various spatial relationships does the speaker experiment with? What color relationships does the poem establish?
7. What tone does the title lend the poem? Is it possible to improve a sunset? What do the speaker's six vantage points actually do?

Extending

8. Suggest five more ways of "improving" a sunset.

Taylor Street (Gunn)

Recalling

1. Where is the subject of the poem sitting? Point out three of the physical details Gunn uses to describe this man.
2. What, according to lines 8–9, does he watch? How does he watch it, according to lines 11–18?
3. What does he get from the passers-by? What is his plan for living his life?

Interpreting

4. In your own words describe the life of the man in the poem. What is his attitude toward life?
5. What is the speaker's attitude toward the man? Does the speaker admire him, pity him, ridicule him? How do you know?
6. What is the significance of the fact that the title of the poem does not mention the man on whom the poem focuses?
7. In what sense might the meaning of the poem extend beyond this one man?

Extending

8. Why do you think inactive people often like to watch busy city streets?

LITERARY FOCUS (Gunn)

Elements of Style in Modern Poetry

Modern poetry, a term referring to poems written since 1914, is as complex and diverse as the world that has given rise to it. Unlike earlier poets, modern poets recognize no limits on content, writing about any subject, no matter how seemingly unworthy.

Modern poetry draws on all types and levels of language. Rather than being confined to traditional poetic diction, much modern poetry actually uses "antipoetic" diction: jarring combinations of apparently incompatible words. Furthermore, modern poetry often replaces strict meter, rhyme, and traditional poetic form with the freer rhythms of ordinary "unpoetic" speech. As a result, the line between poetry and prose has become difficult to draw, and word placement, line length, and other visual effects have become especially important in modern poetry. When modern poets do use traditional poetic forms such as couplets, quatrains, ballads, and sonnets, they usually ring unexpected, experimental twists on these old forms. In short, modern poets have changed poetry so that it can speak of and to their time.

Thinking About Modern Poetry

■ Using specific examples, discuss the ways in which "Taylor Street" represents the tendencies of modern poetry. Consider in particular the poet's subject matter, diction, imagery, figurative language, form, and organization.

COMPOSITION (Tomlinson)

Writing About Literature and Its Period

■ Write an essay showing how "Suggestions for the Improvement of a Sunset" exemplifies the poetry of the modern period. Begin by listing the most important characteristics of modern poetry. Then give examples of these characteristics in the poem. *For help with this assignment, see Lesson 10 in the Writing About Literature Handbook at the back of this book.*

Writing a Series of Related Poems

■ Write three or four poems, of no more than five lines each, presenting different views of the same subject. For example, you may vary your spatial perspective, or you may want to describe the same thing at different times or from the point of view of different speakers.

Ted Hughes   *born 1930*

Ted Hughes is known chiefly for his unflinching portrayal of the violence and fierce beauty of the natural world. He spent his childhood roaming the farms and moors of his native Yorkshire and showed a passion for capturing and studying animals. From the time he began to write poetry at fifteen, this fascination with the animal world has found its way into his work.

After serving in the Royal Air Force as a mechanic, Hughes attended Cambridge University, where he learned all of the works in Yeats's *Collected Poems* by heart. His first volume of poetry, *Hawk in the Rain* (1957), brought him instant acclaim—a rare occurrence that permitted him to devote the bulk of his time to teaching and writing. During the late 1950s Hughes spent several years in the United States with his first wife, the American poet Sylvia Plath (who died in 1963), but since that time he has resided in England.

Hughes admits that one of the early influences on his writing was Dylan Thomas. Although Hughes's poetry tends to be more compact than Thomas', both poets use urgent rhythms, record a wild inner music, and return again and again to the theme of death in life. Throughout his poetry Hughes portrays nature as a violent, vivid, gripping force. He often focuses on the similarities and differences between predatory animals and human beings, sympathizing more often with the former than with the latter. His creatures are powerful, watchful, and spontaneous. Like Aesop, Hughes portrays animals in terms that carry messages about human nature. However, Hughes's messages are seldom moralistic, predictable, or reassuring, as can be seen in "Hawk Roosting," one of his most characteristic poems.

Ted Hughes

Hawk Roosting

I sit in the top of the wood, my eyes closed.
Inaction, no falsifying dream
Between my hooked head and hooked feet:
Or in sleep rehearse perfect kills and eat.

5 The convenience of the high trees!
The air's buoyancy and the sun's ray
Are of advantage to me;
And the earth's face upward for my inspection.

My feet are locked upon the rough bark.
10 It took the whole of Creation
To produce my foot, my each feather:
Now I hold Creation in my foot

Or fly up, and revolve it all slowly—
I kill where I please because it is all mine.
15 There is no sophistry[1] in my body:
My manners are tearing off heads—

The allotment of death.
For the one path of my flight is direct
Through the bones of the living.
20 No arguments assert my right:

The sun is behind me.
Nothing has changed since I began.
My eye has permitted no change.
I am going to keep things like this.

---

1. **sophistry:** false but clever and believable reasoning or argument.

STUDY QUESTIONS

Recalling
1. Where does the speaker sit? What does he rehearse in his sleep?
2. What does he say he holds in his foot? Of what do his manners consist?
3. Why has nothing changed, according to the speaker? What does he plan to do?

Interpreting
4. Who is the speaker? What traits make him seem human? Inhuman?
5. Describe the speaker's image of himself and of the world. How valid do you find his view of life?
6. What do you think the speaker means by "no falsifying dream"? What does he mean by lines 18–19?
7. Describe the emotional effect of the poem—is it amusing, frightening, moving, or something else altogether? Explain how Hughes creates that effect.
8. What does the poet's view of nature seem to be? Do you think the poem also portrays an aspect of *human* nature? Explain.

COMPOSITION

Writing About Poetry
■ Discuss the meaning of "Hawk Roosting," and explain how Hughes's poetic techniques develop this meaning. In particular, explain how his choice of speaker, diction, tone, and imagery reveal the meaning of the poem. *For help with this assignment, refer to Lesson 7 in the Writing About Literature Handbook at the back of this book.*

Writing from Another Point of View
■ Write a poem from the point of view of an animal, as Hughes does in "Hawk Roosting." Your animal speaker should describe the way in which it looks at the world and then explain its motivation for some act. As Hughes does, use concrete, gripping, and precise images.

Geoffrey Hill   *born 1932*

Geoffrey Hill's impersonal, historical, and extremely formal poetry departs sharply from the work of his contemporaries. Born in Worcestershire, England, he was educated at Oxford University. Since his graduation he has served as professor of English and senior lecturer at the University of Leeds in northern England.

Hill's style is highly controlled and often adheres to strict patterns of meter and rhyme. His subject matter is often significant—death, love, suffering, war, God—and his tone is intensely serious. Because his lines and poems are short, Hill has been called "a poet of pain and economy."

In "Merlin" Hill demonstrates his taste for history, legend, and serious subject matter. Using Arthurian legend as his backdrop, he writes from the point of view of Merlin, the famous sorcerer who was well acquainted with both past and future.

Geoffrey Hill

Merlin

I will consider the outnumbering dead:
For they are the husks of what was rich seed.
Now, should they come together to be fed,
They would outstrip the locusts' covering tide.

5 Arthur, Elaine, Mordred;[1] they are all gone
Among the raftered galleries of bone.
By the long barrows of Logres[2] they are made one,
And over their city stands the pinnacled corn.

---

1. **Arthur, Elaine, Mordred:** references to the legend of King Arthur. According to some versions of this legend, Elaine was an innocent young woman who died for her love of Arthur's chief knight, Sir Lancelot, and Mordred was Arthur's evil nephew who ultimately destroyed the order of the Round Table and killed Arthur in battle.
2. **Logres:** that part of Britain now known as England.

Seamus Heaney *born 1939*

Seamus [shā′məs] Heaney was born in County Derry, Ireland, and his Irish heritage has remained at the center of his writing. The eldest of nine children, Heaney grew up on his father's farm. He became aware at a very early age of the difficult and violent history of his homeland. Educated at Queens University in Belfast, he worked first as a secondary school teacher; later he taught at Queens University and the University of California at Berkeley, as well as at other universities in Ireland and America.

Beginning with his first volume of poems, *Death of a Naturalist* (1966), Heaney has written about both modern and ancient Ireland. His work depicts the people, landscape, crafts, politics, history, and myths of his native land, particularly the bitter conflicts between Ireland and England over the independence and unification of the divided Irish state. In addition, Heaney's fascination with archaic lore extends beyond Irish forebears to Danes, Normans, and Vikings.

Heaney's work is known for its phrasing, which is fresh and striking, and for its vivid imagery, which is often tactile, energetic, and violent. His sense of history is personal as well as political and mythic. In "Follower" he reveals in intimate and clear-eyed detail his need to acknowledge both the gifts and the burdens of the past.

Seamus Heaney

Follower

My father worked with a horse plough,
His shoulders globed like a full sail strung
Between the shafts and the furrow.
The horses strained at his clicking tongue.

5 An expert. He would set the wing
And fit the bright steel-pointed sock.
The sod rolled over without breaking.
At the headrig, with a single pluck

Of reins, the sweating team turned round
10 And back into the land. His eye
Narrowed and angled at the ground,
Mapping the furrow exactly.

I stumbled in his hobnailed[1] wake,
Fell sometimes on the polished sod;
15 Sometimes he rode me on his back
Dipping and rising to his plod.

I wanted to grow up and plough,
To close one eye, stiffen my arm.
All I ever did was follow
20 In his broad shadow round the farm.

I was a nuisance, tripping, falling,
Yapping always. But today
It is my father who keeps stumbling
Behind me, and will not go away.

---

1. **hobnailed:** marked by the short, hard-headed nails used as studs in shoes.

STUDY QUESTIONS

Merlin (Hill)

Recalling

1. Whom does the speaker say he will consider? What would happen if these people should "come together"?
2. What people does he mention in stanza 2? Where does he say they are?
3. What now stands over their city?

Interpreting

4. Whom do the dead outnumber? How can the numerous dead be "made one"?
5. What might the figures of Arthur, Elaine, and Mordred symbolize? In what figurative sense were they once "rich seed"? What might be absent from a land and time from which these figures are "all gone"?
6. What might Merlin himself symbolize?
7. What view of life, death, and time does the poem express?

Extending

8. In what senses is this a modern poem? In what ways does it differ from modern poetry?

Follower (Heaney)

Recalling

1. From the first three stanzas, list four details of the father's activities.
2. What did the speaker want to do when he grew up? What did he do while his father worked?
3. What does the speaker say about his father today?

Interpreting

4. Prove that the speaker admires his father's activities in stanzas 1–3. In what senses is his father "expert"?
5. Since the poem is autobiographical, the speaker became a poet, not a farmer like his father. Do you think the speaker has any regrets about his decision not to work the land? How can you tell?

6. What do you think the last sentence of the poem means? What might the "stumbling" father who "will not go away" symbolize?

Extending

7. In what way can the past be both a gift and a burden?

COMPOSITION (Hill)

Writing About a Symbol

■ Briefly discuss the harvest as a symbol in "Merlin." First point out the specific images and stages of the harvest presented in the poem. Then indicate the symbolic meaning of the harvest in the poem, and explain how this symbol is related to the theme of the poem as a whole. *For help with this assignment, see Lesson 5 in the Writing About Literature Handbook at the back of this book.*

Writing as a Historical Character

■ Choose a figure from legend or history (for example, King Arthur, Paul Bunyan, Cleopatra), and write a short poem from that character's point of view, describing his or her views of life and the world. Be sure to choose language and ideas appropriate to your speaker.

COMPARING WRITERS

1. Compare at least two of the following contemporary poets: Gunn, Hughes, Heaney, Tomlinson, and Hill. What similarities in content and style can you find among them, particularly in their portrayal of the workings of the mind? What major differences can you find?
2. Consider all of the following twentieth-century English poets that you have studied: Yeats, Eliot, Sassoon, Brooke, Spender, MacNeice, Graves, Auden, Thomas, Gunn, Hughes, Heaney, Tomlinson, and Hill. Based on your knowledge of these poets, if you had to provide a character sketch of a "typical" twentieth-century poet, what characteristics would you include?

PROSE

Joseph Conrad *1857–1924*

Joseph Conrad was one of the first truly modern British novelists. In 1878 when he first arrived in England at the age of twenty, he spoke virtually no English. Yet he wrote his first novel, *Almayer's Folly* (1895), in English and continued to use his adopted language to create a string of great novels including *Lord Jim* (1900), *Nostromo* (1904), and *Victory* (1915).

Conrad was born Josef Teodor Conrad Nalecz Korzeniowski in Russian-occupied Poland. His father was exiled to northern Russia because of activities on behalf of Polish independence, and both his parents died before Conrad was ten. Conrad left Poland at the age of sixteen and, inspired by books about the sea, became an apprentice seaman first for France and then for England. He sailed to Asia, South America, and Africa, exotic locales that would later become settings for his fiction. In 1886 he became a British subject and a ship's captain. After the publication of his first book, Conrad married, left the sea, and devoted himself to his family and to his literary career.

Conrad wrote fiction about the sea and the "mysterious corners" of the world that had captivated his youth. His stories and novels convey the glamour and terror of the nomadic life of a nineteenth-century seaman. Yet they are much more than adventure stories. Dark seas, winding inlets, and dense jungles serve as backdrop and symbol for Conrad's real concerns—the contrast between individuality and human communication, between illusion and reality. Life at sea provides a model for Conrad's ideal of human interdependence; exotic ports-of-call represent the dark, unknown areas of human experience where characters wrestle with moral choices that will shape their lives. Conrad experimented with unusual, sometimes multiple, points of view to demonstrate the complexity of experience and the difficulty of human communication. His first-person storytellers are often intermediate narrators, characters who are not directly involved in the action and, therefore, can provide both first-hand information and objective detachment. At his dramatic climaxes characters and readers alike arrive at what Conrad called a "moral discovery [that] should be the object of every tale."

The sea, the jungle, and the moral tug-of-war that they represent are all present in "The Lagoon." As with all of Conrad's best work, this story requires that the reader patiently follow the seemingly pointless turns and the seemingly unrelated events that are the scattered clues to Conrad's vision of reality. Gradually patience is rewarded as the various pieces fall into a pattern and the reader is faced with a moment of discovery.

Joseph Conrad

The Lagoon

The white man, leaning with both arms over the roof of the little house in the stern of the boat, said to the steersman—

"We will pass the night in Arsat's clearing. It is late."

The Malay[1] only grunted, and went on looking fixedly at the river. The white man rested his chin on his crossed arms and gazed at the wake of the boat. At the end of the straight avenue of forests cut by the intense glitter of the river, the sun appeared unclouded and dazzling, poised low over the water that shone smoothly like a band of metal. The forests, somber and dull, stood motionless and silent on each side of the broad stream. At the foot of big, towering trees, trunkless nipa palms rose from the mud of the bank, in bunches of leaves enormous and heavy, that hung unstirring over the brown swirl of eddies. In the stillness of the air every tree, every leaf, every bough, every tendril of creeper and every petal of minute blossoms seemed to have been bewitched into an immobility perfect and final. Nothing moved on the river but the eight paddles that rose flashing regularly, dipped together with a single splash; while the steersman swept right and left with a periodic and sudden flourish of his blade describing a glinting semicircle above his head. The churned-up water frothed alongside with a confused murmur. And the white man's canoe, advancing upstream in the short-lived disturbance of its own making, seemed to enter the portals of a land from which the very memory of motion had forever departed.

The white man, turning his back upon the setting sun, looked along the empty and broad expanse of the sea-reach.[2] For the last three miles of its course the wandering, hesitating river, as if enticed irresistibly by the freedom of an open horizon, flows straight into the sea, flows straight to the east—to the east that harbors both light and darkness. Astern of the boat the repeated call of some bird, a cry discordant and feeble, skipped along over the smooth water and lost itself, before it could reach the other shore, in the breathless silence of the world.

The steersman dug his paddle into the stream, and held hard with stiffened arms, his body thrown forward. The water gurgled aloud; and suddenly the long straight reach seemed to pivot on its center, the forests swung in a semicircle, and the slanting beams of sunset touched the broadside of the canoe with a fiery glow, throwing the slender and distorted shadows of its crew upon the streaked glitter of the river. The white man turned to look ahead. The course of the boat had been altered at right angles to the stream, and the carved dragon-head of its prow was pointing now at a gap in the fringing bushes of the bank. It glided through, brushing the overhanging twigs, and disappeared from the river like some slim and amphibious creature leaving the water for its lair in the forests.

The narrow creek was like a ditch: tortuous, fabulously deep; filled with gloom under the thin strip of pure and shining blue of the heaven. Immense trees soared up, invisible behind the festooned draperies of creepers. Here and there, near the glistening blackness of the water, a twisted root of some tall tree showed amongst the tracery of small ferns, black and dull, writhing and motionless, like an arrested snake. The short words of the paddlers reverberated loudly between the thick and somber walls of vegetation. Darkness oozed out from between the trees, through the tangled maze of the creepers, from behind the great fantastic and unstirring leaves; the darkness, mysterious

---

1. **Malay** [mā′lā]: inhabitant of the Malay peninsula in Southeast Asia.
2. **sea-reach:** straight course of a river when it approaches the sea.

and invincible; the darkness scented and poisonous of impenetrable forests.

The men poled in the shoaling[3] water. The creek broadened, opening out into a wide sweep of a stagnant lagoon. The forests receded from the marshy bank, leaving a level strip of bright green, reedy grass to frame the reflected blueness of the sky. A fleecy pink cloud drifted high above, trailing the delicate coloring of its image under the floating leaves and the silvery blossoms of the lotus. A little house, perched on high piles, appeared black in the distance. Near it, two tall nibong palms, that seemed to have come out of the forests in the background, leaned slightly over the ragged roof, with a suggestion of sad tenderness and care in the droop of their leafy and soaring heads.

The steersman, pointing with his paddle, said, "Arsat is there. I see his canoe fast between the piles."

The polers ran along the sides of the boat glancing over their shoulders at the end of the day's journey. They would have preferred to spend the night somewhere else than on this lagoon of weird aspect and ghostly reputation. Moreover, they disliked Arsat, first as a stranger, and also because he who repairs a ruined house, and dwells in it, proclaims that he is not afraid to live amongst the spirits that haunt the places abandoned by mankind. Such a man can disturb the course of fate by glances or words; while his familiar ghosts are not easy to propitiate by casual wayfarers upon whom they long to wreak the malice of their human master. White men care not for such things, being unbelievers and in league with the Father of Evil, who leads them unharmed through the invisible dangers of this world. To the warnings of the righteous they oppose an offensive pretense of disbelief. What is there to be done?

So they thought, throwing their weight on the end of their long poles. The big canoe glided on swiftly, noiselessly, and smoothly, toward Arsat's clearing, till, in a great rattling of poles thrown down, and the loud murmurs of "Allah[4] be praised!" it came with a gentle knock against the crooked piles below the house.

The boatmen with uplifted faces shouted discordantly, "Arsat! O Arsat!" Nobody came. The white man began to climb the rude ladder giving access to the bamboo platform before the house. The juragan[5] of the boat said sulkily, "We will cook in the sampan, and sleep on the water."

"Pass my blankets and the basket," said the white man, curtly.

He knelt on the edge of the platform to receive the bundle. Then the boat shoved off, and the white man, standing up, confronted Arsat, who had come out through the low door of his hut. He was a man young, powerful, with broad chest and muscular arms. He had nothing on but his sarong.[6] His head was bare. His big, soft eyes stared eagerly at the white man, but his voice and demeanor were composed as he asked, without any words of greeting—

"Have you medicine, Tuan?"[7]

"No," said the visitor in a startled tone. "No. Why? Is there sickness in the house?"

"Enter and see," replied Arsat, in the same calm manner, and turning short round, passed again through the small doorway. The white man, dropping his bundles, followed.

In the dim light of the dwelling he made out on a couch of bamboos a woman stretched on her back under a broad sheet of red cotton cloth. She lay still, as if dead; but her big eyes, wide open, glittered in the gloom, staring upward at the slender rafters, motionless and unseeing. She was in a high fever, and evidently

3. **shoaling** [shō′ling]: shallow water difficult to navigate.

4. **Allah** [al′ə]: name for God in the Moslem religion.
5. **juragan** [jōō ä′gän]: master of a sampan [sam′pan′], or flat-bottomed boat with a cabin made of mats.
6. **sarong** [sə rông′]: brightly colored cloth worn as a skirt.
7. **Tuan** [twän]: Malayan for "sir," usually applied to Europeans.

unconscious. Her cheeks were sunk slightly, her lips were partly open, and on the young face there was the ominous and fixed expression—the absorbed, contemplating expression of the unconscious who are going to die. The two men stood looking down at her in silence.

"Has she been long ill?" asked the traveler.

"I have not slept for five nights," answered the Malay, in a deliberate tone. "At first she heard voices calling her from the water and struggled against me who held her. But since the sun of today rose she hears nothing—she hears not me. She sees nothing. She sees not me—me!"

He remained silent for a minute, then asked softly—

"Tuan, will she die?"

"I fear so," said the white man, sorrowfully. He had known Arsat years ago, in a far country in times of trouble and danger, when no friendship is to be despised. And since his Malay friend had come unexpectedly to dwell in the hut on the lagoon with a strange woman, he had slept many times there, in his journeys up and down the river. He liked the man who knew how to keep faith in council and how to fight without fear by the side of his white friend. He liked him—not so much perhaps as a man likes his favorite dog—but still he liked him well enough to help and ask no questions, to think sometimes vaguely and hazily in the midst of his own pursuits, about the lonely man and the long-haired woman with audacious face and triumphant eyes, who lived together hidden by the forests—alone and feared.

The white man came out of the hut in time to see the enormous conflagration of sunset put out by the swift and stealthy shadows that, rising like a black and impalpable vapor above the tree tops, spread over the heaven, extinguishing the crimson glow of floating clouds and the red billiance of departing daylight. In a few moments all the stars came out above the intense blackness of the earth and the great lagoon gleaming suddenly with reflected lights resembled an oval patch of night sky flung down into the hopeless and abysmal night of the wilderness. The white man had some supper out of the basket, then collecting a few sticks that lay about the platform, made up a small fire, not for warmth, but for the sake of the smoke, which would keep off the mosquitoes. He wrapped himself in the blankets and sat with his back against the reed wall of the house, smoking thoughtfully.

Arsat came through the doorway with noiseless steps and squatted down by the fire. The white man moved his outstretched legs a little.

"She breathes," said Arsat in a low voice, anticipating the expected question. "She breathes and burns as if with a great fire. She speaks not; she hears not—and burns!"

He paused for a moment, then asked in a quiet, incurious tone—

"Tuan . . . will she die?"

The white man moved his shoulders uneasily and muttered in a hesitating manner—

"If such is her fate."

"No, Tuan," said Arsat, calmly. "If such is my fate. I hear, I see, I wait. I remember . . . Tuan, do you remember the old days? Do you remember my brother?"

"Yes," said the white man. The Malay rose suddenly and went in. The other, sitting still outside, could hear the voice in the hut. Arsat said: "Hear me! Speak!" His words were succeeded by a complete silence. "O Diamelen!" he cried, suddenly. After that cry there was a deep sigh. Arsat came out and sank down again in his old place.

They sat in silence before the fire. There was no sound within the house, there was no sound near them; but far away on the lagoon they could hear the voices of the boatmen ringing fitful and distinct on the calm water. The fire in the bows of the sampan shone faintly in the distance with a hazy red glow. Then it died out. The voices ceased. The land and the water slept invisible, unstirring and mute. It was as though there had been nothing left in the world but the glitter of stars streaming, ceaseless and vain, through the black stillness of the night.

The white man gazed straight before him into the darkness with wide-open eyes. The fear and fascination, the inspiration and the wonder of death—of death near, unavoidable, and unseen, soothed the unrest of his race and stirred the most indistinct, the most intimate of his thoughts. The ever-ready suspicion of evil, the gnawing suspicion that lurks in our hearts, flowed out into the stillness round him—into the stillness profound and dumb, and made it appear untrustworthy and infamous, like the placid and impenetrable mask of an unjustifiable violence. In that fleeting and powerful disturbance of his being the earth enfolded in the starlight peace became a shadowy country of inhuman strife, a battlefield of phantoms terrible and charming, august or ignoble, struggling ardently for the possession of our helpless hearts. An unquiet and mysterious country of inextinguishable desires and fears.

A plaintive murmur rose in the night; a murmur saddening and startling, as if the great solitudes of surrounding woods had tried to whisper into his ear the wisdom of their immense and lofty indifference. Sounds hesitating and vague floated in the air round him, shaped themselves slowly into words; and at last flowed on gently in a murmuring stream of soft and monotonous sentences. He stirred like a man waking up and changed his position slightly. Arsat, motionless and shadowy, sitting with bowed head under the stars, was speaking in a low and dreamy tone—

". . . for where can we lay down the heaviness of our trouble but in a friend's heart? A man must speak of war and of love. You, Tuan, know what war is, and you have seen me in time of danger seek death as other men seek life! A writing may be lost; a lie may be written; but what the eye has seen is truth and remains in the mind!"

"I remember," said the white man, quietly. Arsat went on with mournful composure—

"Therefore I shall speak to you of love. Speak in the night. Speak before both night and love are gone—and the eye of day looks upon my sorrow and my shame; upon my blackened face; upon my burned-up heart."

A sigh, short and faint, marked an almost imperceptible pause, and then his words flowed on, without a stir, without a gesture.

"After the time of trouble and war was over and you went away from my country in the pursuit of your desires, which we, men of the islands, cannot understand, I and my brother became again, as we had been before, the sword bearers of the Ruler. You know we were men of family, belonging to a ruling race, and more fit than any to carry on our right shoulder the emblem of power. And in the time of prosperity Si Dendring showed us favor, as we, in time of sorrow, had showed to him the faithfulness of our courage. It was a time of peace. A time of deer hunts and cock fights; of idle talks and foolish squabbles between men whose bellies are full and weapons are rusty.

But the sower watched the young rice shoots grow up without fear, and the traders came and went, departed lean and returned fat into the river of peace. They brought news, too. Brought lies and truth mixed together, so that no man knew when to rejoice and when to be sorry. We heard from them about you also. They had seen you here and had seen you there. And I was glad to hear, for I remembered the stirring times, and I always remembered you, Tuan, till the time came when my eyes could see nothing in the past, because they had looked upon the one who is dying there—in the house."

He stopped to exclaim in an intense whisper, "O Mara bahia!⁸ O Calamity!" then went on speaking a little louder:

"There's no worse enemy and no better friend than a brother, Tuan, for one brother knows another, and in perfect knowledge is strength for good or evil. I loved my brother. I went to him and told him that I could see nothing but one face, hear nothing but one voice. He told me: 'Open your heart so that she can see what is in it—and wait. Patience is wisdom. Inchi Midah may die or our Ruler may throw off his fear of a woman!' . . . I waited! . . . You remember the lady with the veiled face, Tuan, and the fear of our Ruler before her cunning and temper. And if she wanted her servant, what could I do? But I fed the hunger of my heart on short glances and stealthy words. I loitered on the path to the bath houses in the daytime, and when the sun had fallen behind the forest I crept along the jasmine hedges of the women's courtyard. Unseeing, we spoke to one another through the scent of flowers, through the veil of leaves, through the blades of long grass that stood still before our lips; so great was our prudence, so faint was the murmur of our great longing. The time passed swiftly . . . and there were whispers amongst women—and our enemies watched—my brother was gloomy, and I began to think of killing and of a fierce death. . . . We are of a people who take what they want—

like you whites. There is a time when a man should forget loyalty and respect. Might and authority are given to rulers, but to all men is given love and strength and courage. My brother said, 'You shall take her from their midst. We are two who are like one.' And I answered, 'Let it be soon, for I find no warmth in sunlight that does not shine upon her.' Our time came when the Ruler and all the great people went to the mouth of the river to fish by torchlight. There were hundreds of boats, and on the white sand, between the water and the forests, dwellings of leaves were built for the households of the Rajahs.⁹ The smoke of cooking fires was like a blue mist of the evening, and many voices rang in it joyfully. While they were making the boats ready to beat up the fish, my brother came to me and said, 'Tonight!' I looked to my weapons, and when the time came our canoe took its place in the circle of boats carrying the torches. The lights blazed on the water, but behind the boats there was darkness. When the shouting began and the excitement made them like mad we dropped out. The water swallowed our fire, and we floated back to the shore that was dark with only here and there the glimmer of embers. We could hear the talk of slave girls amongst the sheds. Then we found a place deserted and silent. We waited there. She came. She came running along the shore, rapid and leaving no trace, like a leaf driven by the wind into the sea. My brother said gloomily, 'Go and take her; carry her into our boat.' I lifted her in my arms. She panted. Her heart was beating against my breast. I said, 'I take you from those people. You came to the cry of my heart, but my arms take you into my boat against the will of the great!' 'It is right,' said my brother. 'We are men who take what we want and can hold it against many. We should have taken her in daylight.' I said, 'Let us be off'; for since she was in my boat I began to think of our Ruler's many men. 'Yes. Let us be off,' said my brother. 'We are cast out and this boat is our country now—and the sea is our refuge.' He lingered

---

8. **O Mara bahia!** [ō′mä′rä bä hī′ä]

9. **Rajahs** [rä′jɔz]: Malayan chiefs.

with his foot on the shore, and I entreated him to hasten, for I remembered the strokes of her heart against my breast and thought that two men cannot withstand a hundred. We left, paddling downstream close to the bank; and as we passed by the creek where they were fishing, the great shouting had ceased, but the murmur of voices was loud like the humming of insects flying at noonday. The boats floated, clustered together, in the red light of torches, under a black roof of smoke; and men talked of their sport. Men that boasted, and praised, and jeered—men that would have been our friends in the morning, but on that night were already our enemies. We paddled swiftly past. We had no more friends in the country of our birth. She sat in the middle of the canoe with covered face; silent as she is now; unseeing as she is now—and I had no regret at what I was leaving because I could hear her breathing close to me—as I can hear her now."

He paused, listened with his ear turned to the doorway, then shook his head and went on:

"My brother wanted to shout the cry of challenge—one cry only—to let the people know we were freeborn robbers who trusted our arms and the great sea. And again I begged him in the name of our love to be silent. Could I not hear her breathing close to me? I knew the pursuit would come quick enough. My brother loved me. He dipped his paddle without a splash. He only said, 'There is half a man in you now—the other half is in that woman. I can wait. When you are a whole man again, you will come back with me here to shout defiance. We are sons of the same mother.' I made no answer. All my strength and all my spirit were in my hands that held the paddle—for I longed to be with her in a safe place beyond the reach of men's anger and of women's spite. My love was so great that I thought it could guide me to a country where death was unknown, if I could only escape from Inchi Midah's fury and from our Ruler's sword. We paddled with haste, breathing through our teeth. The blades bit deep into the smooth water. We passed out of the river; we flew in clear channels amongst the shallows. We skirted the

black coast; we skirted the sand beaches where the sea speaks in whispers to the land; and the gleam of white sand flashed back past our boat, so swiftly she ran upon the water. We spoke not. Only once I said, 'Sleep, Diamelen, for soon you may want all your strength.' I heard the sweetness of her voice, but I never turned my head. The sun rose and still we went on. Water fell from my face like rain from a cloud. We flew in the light and heat. I never looked back, but I knew that my brother's eyes, behind me, were looking steadily ahead, for the boat went as straight as a bushman's dart, when it leaves the end of the sumpitan. There was no better paddler, no better steersman than my brother. Many times, together, we had won races in that canoe. But we never had put out our strength as we did then—then, when for the last time we paddled together! There was no braver or stronger man in our country than my brother. I could not spare the strength to turn my head and look at him, but every moment I heard the hiss of his breath getting louder behind me. Still he did not speak. The sun was high. The heat clung to my back like a flame of fire. My ribs were ready to burst, but I could no longer get enough air into my chest. And then I felt I must cry out with my last breath, 'Let us rest!' . . . 'Good!' he answered; and his voice was firm. He was strong. He was brave. He knew not fear and no fatigue . . . My brother!"

A murmur powerful and gentle, a murmur vast and faint; the murmur of trembling leaves, of stirring boughs, ran through the tangled depths of the forests, ran over the starry smoothness of the lagoon, and the water between the piles lapped the slimy timber once with a sudden splash. A breath of warm air touched the two men's faces and passed on with a mournful sound—a breath loud and short like an uneasy sigh of the dreaming earth.

Arsat went on in an even, low voice.

"We ran our canoe on the white beach of a little bay close to a long tongue of land that seemed to bar our road; a long wooded cape going far into the sea. My brother knew that place. Beyond the cape a river has its entrance, and through the jungle of that land there is a narrow path. We made a fire and cooked rice. Then we lay down to sleep on the soft sand in the shade of our canoe, while she watched. No sooner had I closed my eyes than I heard her cry of alarm. We leaped up. The sun was half-way down the sky already, and coming in sight in the opening of the bay we saw a prau[10] manned by many paddlers. We knew it at once; it was one of our Rajah's praus. They were watching the shore, and saw us. They beat the gong, and turned the head of the prau into the bay. I felt my heart become weak within my breast. Diamelen sat on the sand and covered her face. There was no escape by sea. My brother laughed. He had the gun you had given him, Tuan, before you went away, but there was only a handful of powder. He spoke to me quickly: 'Run with her along the path. I shall keep them back, for they have no firearms, and landing in the face of a man with a gun is certain death for some. Run with her. On the other side of that wood there is a fisherman's house—and a canoe. When I have fired all the shots I will follow. I am a great runner, and before they can come up we shall be gone. I will hold out as long as I can, for she is but a woman—that can neither run nor fight, but she has your heart in her weak hands.' He dropped behind the canoe. The prau was coming. She and I ran, and as we rushed along the path I heard shots. My brother fired—once—twice—and the booming of the gong ceased. There was silence behind us. That neck of land is narrow. Before I heard my brother fire the third shot I saw the shelving shore, and I saw the water again; the mouth of a broad river. We crossed a grassy glade. We ran down to the water. I saw a low hut above the black mud, and a small canoe hauled up. I heard another shot behind me. I thought, 'That is his last charge.' We rushed down to the canoe; a man came running from the hut, but I leaped on him, and we rolled together in the mud. Then I got up, and he lay still at my feet. I don't

know whether I had killed him or not. I and Diamelen pushed the canoe afloat. I heard yells behind me, and I saw my brother run across the glade. Many men were bounding after him, I took her in my arms and threw her into the boat, then leaped in myself. When I looked back I saw that my brother had fallen. He fell and was up again, but the men were closing round him. He shouted, 'I am coming!' The men were close to him. I looked. Many men. Then I looked at her. Tuan, I pushed the canoe! I pushed it into deep water. She was kneeling forward looking at me, and I said, 'Take your paddle,' while I struck the water with mine. Tuan, I heard him cry. I heard him cry my name twice; and I heard voices shouting, 'Kill! Strike!' I never turned back. I heard him calling my name again with a great shriek, as when life is going out together with the voice—and I never turned my head. My own name! . . . My brother! Three times he called—but I was not afraid of life. Was she not there in that canoe? And could I not with her find a country where death is forgotten—where death is unknown!"

The white man sat up. Arsat rose and stood, an indistinct and silent figure above the dying embers of the fire. Over the lagoon a mist drifting and low had crept, erasing slowly the glittering images of the stars. And now a great expanse of white vapor covered the land: it flowed cold and gray in the darkness, eddied in noiseless whirls round the tree trunks and about the platform of the house, which seemed to float upon a restless and impalpable illusion of a sea. Only far away the tops of the trees stood outlined on the twinkle of heaven, like a somber and forbidding shore—a coast deceptive, pitiless and black.

Arsat's voice vibrated loudly in the profound peace.

"I had her there! I had her! To get her I would have faced all mankind. But I had her—and—"

His words went out ringing into the empty distances. He paused, and seemed to listen to them dying away very far—beyond help and

---

10. **prau** [prou]: fast Malayan boat with a large sail.

beyond recall. Then he said quietly—

"Tuan, I loved my brother."

A breath of wind made him shiver. High above his head, high above the silent sea of mist the drooping leaves of the palms rattled together with a mournful and expiring sound. The white man stretched his legs. His chin rested on his chest, and he murmured sadly without lifting his head—

"We all love our brothers."

Arsat burst out with an intense whispering violence—

"What did I care who died? I wanted peace in my own heart."

He seemed to hear a stir in the house—listened—then stepped in noiselessly. The white man stood up. A breeze was coming in fitful puffs. The stars shone paler as if they had retreated into the frozen depths of immense space. After a chill gust of wind there were a few seconds of perfect calm and absolute silence. Then from behind the black and wavy line of the forests a column of golden light shot up into the heavens and spread over the semicircle of the eastern horizon. The sun had risen. The mist lifted, broke into drifting patches, vanished into thin flying wreaths; and the unveiled lagoon lay, polished and black, in the heavy shadows at the foot of the wall of trees. A white eagle rose over it with a slanting and ponderous flight, reached the clear sunshine and appeared dazzlingly brilliant for a moment, then soaring higher, became a dark and motionless speck before it vanished into the blue as if it had left the earth forever. The white man, standing gazing upward before the doorway, heard in the hut a confused and broken murmur of distracted words ending with a loud groan. Suddenly Arsat stumbled out with outstretched hands, shivered, and stood still for some time with fixed eyes. Then he said—

"She burns no more."

Before his face the sun showed its edge above the tree tops rising steadily. The breeze freshened; a great brilliance burst upon the lagoon, sparkled on the rippling water. The forests came out of the clear shadows of the morning, became distinct, as if they had rushed nearer—to stop short in a great stir of leaves, of nodding boughs, of swaying branches. In the merciless sunshine the whisper of unconscious life grew louder, speaking in an incomprehensible voice round the dumb darkness of that human sorrow. Arsat's eyes wandered slowly, then stared at the rising sun.

"I can see nothing," he said half aloud to himself.

"There is nothing," said the white man, moving to the edge of the platform and waving his hand to his boat. A shout came faintly over the lagoon and the sampan began to glide toward the abode of the friend of ghosts.

"If you want to come with me, I will wait all the morning," said the white man, looking away upon the water.

"No, Tuan," said Arsat, softly. "I shall not eat or sleep in this house, but I must first see my road. Now I can see nothing—see nothing! There is no light and no peace in the world; but there is death—death for many. We are sons of the same mother—and I left him in the midst of enemies; but I am going back now."

He drew a long breath and went on in a dreamy tone:

"In a little while I shall see clear enough to strike—to strike. But she has died, and . . . now . . . darkness."

He flung his arms wide open, let them fall along his body, then stood still with unmoved face and stony eyes, staring at the sun. The white man got down into his canoe. The polers ran smartly along the sides of the boat, looking over their shoulders at the beginning of a weary journey. High in the stern, his head muffled up in white rags, the juragan sat moody, letting his paddle trail in the water. The white man, leaning with both arms over the grass roof of the little cabin, looked back at the shining ripple of the boat's wake. Before the sampan passed out of the lagoon into the creek he lifted his eyes. Arsat had not moved. He stood lonely in the searching sunshine; and he looked beyond the great light of a cloudless day into the darkness of a world of illusions.

STUDY QUESTIONS

Recalling

1. Find details of the openness and brightness of the river and of the narrowness and darkness of the creek and lagoon. What does the story's last sentence say about light and dark?
2. Why do the polers dislike Arsat? Why does the white man like him?
3. Why did Arsat not court and marry the woman in the standard way? What finally happens to the woman?
4. Briefly explain how Arsat and his brother take the woman away. Tell what happens to Arsat's brother.
5. At the end of the story, what does Arsat intend to do?

Interpreting

6. What illusions about love and death did Arsat once hold? In what ways are his illusions related to the story's contrast between light and dark?
7. In what ways is Arsat an outcast? Why has the lagoon been a fitting place for him to live?
8. Explain Arsat's decision to leave the lagoon. What do you think he is looking for?

Extending

9. Use "The Lagoon" as an example, and explain why people—even those who consider themselves loners—must relate to a larger community.

LITERARY FOCUS

The Short Story

The major elements of the short story are plot, characterization, setting, point of view, and theme. When analyzing a story, we can examine each element separately, but in a good story these elements interact to form one total effect, the impact on the reader.

Plot is the sequence of events in a story, each event causing or leading to the next. A **conflict,** or struggle between opposing forces, is at the center of every plot.

Characterization is the personality of a character in a story and the method by which the author reveals that personality. Characters are influenced by events of the plot and can affect events also.

Setting is the place and time in which a story happens. Setting can contribute to plot and to our understanding of characters.

Point of view is the relationship of the storyteller to the story. An author's choice of narrator can sometimes reveal his or her opinion of events and characters in a story.

Theme is a story's main idea. A theme usually extends beyond the confines of a story to form a general statement about life. A story's theme is usually implied through the title, through the outcome of the plot, through changes in character or setting, or through the author's choice of point of view. A theme should be stated as a sentence.

Thinking About the Short Story

1. Identify a conflict that Arsat faces in "The Lagoon." Explain the effect of the conflict on his personality.
2. Explain how the setting of "The Lagoon" adds to the plot and to the personalities of the characters.
3. "The Lagoon" has two different narrators. Identify them. In what sense does the story's point of view demonstrate Arsat's alienation?
4. What do you think is Conrad's attitude about the individual's responsibility to the community? What is the theme of "The Lagoon"?

COMPOSITION

Developing a Thesis Statement

■ Develop a thesis statement about "The Lagoon," and in a brief essay defend your thesis with examples from the story. To develop your statement, you may wish to consider one of the following elements of the story: (a) the use of figurative language, (b) the internal lives of characters, or (c) the setting. *For help with this assignment, refer to Lesson 1 in the Writing About Literature Handbook at the back of this book.*

Writing a Letter

■ Imagine that you are the white man of Conrad's story. Write a letter about Arsat to a friend. First explain what you know of Arsat. Then describe your feelings both while Arsat was telling his story and later after you had time to think about the experience. Conclude your letter by telling what you think finally happened to Arsat.

John Galsworthy *1867–1933*

John Galsworthy is best known for his realistic depictions of contemporary upper-class British society. His characters are born to privilege; his settings include elegant drawing rooms and manicured gardens. Galsworthy himself was a member of the wealthy and intellectual class he wrote about.

Born in Surrey in southern England, Galsworthy attended New College, Oxford. He trained as a lawyer but never practiced. Instead, he traveled throughout the world, and at thirty he began to write. The novel that established his reputation was *The Man of Property* (1906). This was the first in a series of novels later brought together as *The Forsyte Saga,* a study of several generations in one wealthy family. These novels were so popular that when the hero, Soames Forsyte, died in one novel, his death was announced in the *London Times.* In 1929 Galsworthy was awarded the British Order of Merit, and in 1933 he received the Nobel Prize for Literature.

"The Japanese Quince" is representative Galsworthy. In one brief, seemingly plotless incident, the author provides a rich insight into an individual and, perhaps, into an entire social class.

John Galsworthy

The Japanese Quince

As Mr. Nilson, well known in the City,[1] opened the window of his dressing room on Campden Hill, he experienced a peculiar sweetish sensation in the back of his throat, and a feeling of emptiness just under his fifth rib. Hooking the window back, he noticed that a little tree in the Square Gardens had come out in blossom, and that the thermometer stood at sixty. "Perfect morning," he thought; "spring at last!"

Resuming some meditations on the price of Tintos, he took up an ivory-backed handglass and scrutinized his face. His firm, well-colored cheeks, with their neat brown moustaches, and his round, well-opened, clear gray eyes, wore a

---

1. **the City:** financial district of London.

reassuring appearance of good health. Putting on his black frock coat, he went downstairs.

In the dining room his morning paper was laid out on the sideboard. Mr. Nilson had scarcely taken it in his hand when he again became aware of that queer feeling. Somewhat concerned, he went to the French window and descended the scrolled iron steps into the fresh air. A cuckoo clock struck eight.

"Half an hour to breakfast," he thought; "I'll take a turn in the Gardens."

He had them to himself, and proceeded to pace the circular path with his morning paper clasped behind him. He had scarcely made two revolutions, however, when it was borne in on him that, instead of going away in the fresh air, the feeling had increased. He drew several deep breaths, having heard deep breathing recommended by his wife's doctor; but they augmented rather than diminished the sensation—as of some sweetish liquor in course within him, together with a faint aching just above his heart. Running over what he had eaten the night before, he could recollect no unusual dish, and it occurred to him that it might possibly be some smell affecting him. But he could detect nothing except a faint sweet lemony scent, rather agreeable than otherwise, which evidently emanated from the bushes budding in the sunshine. He was on the point of resuming his promenade, when a blackbird close by burst into song, and, looking up, Mr. Nilson saw at a distance of perhaps five yards a little tree, in the heart of whose branches the bird was perched. He stood staring curiously at this tree, recognizing it for that which he had noticed from his window. It was covered with young blossoms, pink and white, and little bright green leaves both round and spiky; and on all this blossom and these leaves the sunlight glistened. Mr. Nilson smiled; the little tree was so alive and pretty! And instead of passing on, he stayed there smiling at the tree.

"Morning like this!" he thought; "and here I am the only person in the Square who has the—to come out and—!" But he had no sooner conceived this thought than he saw quite near him a man with his hands behind him, who was also staring up and smiling at the little tree. Rather taken aback, Mr. Nilson ceased to smile, and looked furtively at the stranger. It was his next-door neighbor, Mr. Tandram, well known in the City, who had occupied the adjoining house for some five years. Mr. Nilson perceived at once the awkwardness of his position, for, being married, they had not yet had occasion to speak to one another. Doubtful as to his proper conduct, he decided at last to murmur: "Fine morning!" and was passing on, when Mr. Tandram answered: "Beautiful, for the time of year!" Detecting a slight nervousness in his neighbor's voice, Mr. Nilson was emboldened to regard him openly. He was of about Mr. Nilson's own height, with

firm, well-colored cheeks, neat brown moustaches, and round, well-opened, clear gray eyes; and he was wearing a black frock coat. Mr. Nilson noticed that he had his morning paper clasped behind him as he looked up at the little tree. And, visited somehow by the feeling that he had been caught out, he said abruptly:
"Er—can you give me the name of that tree?"
Mr. Tandram answered:
"I was about to ask you that," and stepped toward it. Mr. Nilson also approached the tree.
"Sure to have its name on, I should think," he said.
Mr. Tandram was the first to see the little label, close to where the blackbird had been sitting. He read it out.
"Japanese quince!"
"Ah!" said Mr. Nilson, "thought so. Early flowerers."
"Very," assented Mr. Tandram, and added: "Quite a feelin' in the air today."
Mr. Nilson nodded.
"It was a blackbird singin'," he said.
"Blackbirds," answered Mr. Tandram. "I prefer them to thrushes myself; more body in the note." And he looked at Mr. Nilson in an almost friendly way.
"Quite," murmured Mr. Nilson. "These exotics, they don't bear fruit. Pretty blossom!" and he again glanced up at the blossom, thinking: "Nice fellow, this, I rather like him."
Mr. Tandram also gazed at the blossom. And the little tree, as if appreciating their attention, quivered and glowed. From a distance the blackbird gave a loud, clear call. Mr. Nilson dropped his eyes. It struck him suddenly that Mr. Tandram looked a little foolish; and, as if he had seen himself, he said: "I must be going in. Good morning!"
A shade passed over Mr. Tandram's face, as if he, too, had suddenly noticed something about Mr. Nilson.
"Good morning," he replied, and clasping their journals to their backs they separated.
Mr. Nilson retraced his steps toward his garden window, walking slowly so as to avoid

arriving at the same time as his neighbor. Having seen Mr. Tandram mount his scrolled iron steps, he ascended his own in turn. On the top step he paused.

With the slanting spring sunlight darting and quivering into it, the Japanese quince seemed more living than a tree. The blackbird had returned to it, and was chanting out his heart.

Mr. Nilson sighed; again he felt that queer sensation, that choky feeling in his throat.

The sound of a cough or sigh attracted his attention. There, in the shadow of his French window, stood Mr. Tandram, also looking forth across the Gardens at the little quince tree.

Unaccountably upset, Mr. Nilson turned abruptly into the house, and opened his morning paper.

STUDY QUESTIONS

Recalling

1. Describe the unusual sensation that Mr. Nilson feels in the morning.
2. Describe the appearance of Mr. Nilson and of Mr. Tandram.
3. What circumstances lead to the conversation between the two men?
4. Describe the manner in which Mr. Nilson walks home from the garden.

Interpreting

5. What do you think is the explanation for Mr. Nilson's unusual sensation?
6. In what ways are Mr. Nilson and Mr. Tandram alike? Why is the similarity significant?
7. Explain why Mr. Nilson becomes "unaccountably upset." What does the story imply about his way of life?
8. Explain the symbolism of the quince and of the names *Nilson* and *Tandram*.

Extending

9. What do you think Mr. Nilson will do during the rest of his day? Do you think he will think of the Japanese quince again? Why or why not?

LITERARY FOCUS

Conflict

A **conflict,** or a struggle between opposing forces, exists at the center of every plot and is a frame on which the plot is structured. Conflicts can be internal or external. An **internal conflict** occurs within a character who, for example, struggles to accept reality or to understand a new idea. Because modern fiction often deals with emotional and psychological states, the internal conflict is common in modern stories. An **external conflict** is a struggle between two characters or between a character and nature, society, or fate. Because the opponents are more readily identifiable, an external conflict is usually more obvious than an internal conflict.

Thinking About Conflict

1. What forces within Mr. Nilson are in conflict?
2. Is the conflict in "The Japanese Quince" resolved? Explain your opinion.

COMPOSITION

Writing a Comparison/Contrast

Compare and contrast Conrad's "Lagoon" and Galsworthy's "Japanese Quince." To do this, point out similarities and differences in content and literary technique. You may wish to consider the following elements of the stories: (a) the relationships between major characters and their communities, (b) the internal lives of characters, and (c) the settings. *For help with this assignment, refer to Lesson 2 in the Writing About Literature Handbook at the back of this book.*

Writing a Character Sketch

Galsworthy tells us a great deal about Mr. Nilson with just a few carefully chosen details. Write a brief sketch of a person who is walking alone through a park. Describe your character's appearance and manner. Include just enough details to suggest the character's personality, career, and daily life.

James Joyce *1882–1941*

James Joyce, an Irish novelist who experimented with language, plot, and characterization, earned a place as one of the most influential writers of the modern period. Joyce was concerned with inner reality, the psychological reactions people have to their surroundings. Many "events" in his fiction take place in the minds of the characters. These events, not action in the typical sense of the word, may be suggestions or realizations inspired by an outside stimulus. Certainly Joyce's characters move and act in the world, but the author directs our attention inside, to the mind and its response to external happenings.

Joyce was born into a large family in Dublin, Ireland, and attended school and college there. A fine student, he was an avid reader of classical and modern literature, and he mastered a number of languages, including Latin. Feeling stifled by his surroundings, Joyce left his homeland permanently and spent most of his time in Trieste, Paris, Zurich, and Rome. For a time he supported himself by teaching languages.

Much of Joyce's fiction is autobiographical. *Dubliners* (1914) is a collection of stories dealing with the life and the character of Dublin, the city he called "the center of paralysis." In fact, Joyce set all of his work in Dublin and uses the city as a microcosm, or miniature model, of the world. *A Portrait of the Artist as a Young Man* (1916) is based on Joyce's life up to 1902. It is a moving account of an adolescent's struggle for maturity and independence as well as a statement on the meaning of art. *Ulysses* (1922) is the story of a day in the lives of three Dubliners, including Stephen Dedalus, the hero of *Portrait*. The novel makes frequent allusions to Homer's *Odyssey* and observes parallels between the ancient and modern worlds. The cyclical nature of history is explored again in *Finnegans Wake*, in which one Dublin family represents humanity throughout history.

The psychological aspect of Joyce's work and his experiments with literary form often challenge his readers. For this reason and because of his frankness, Joyce had great difficulty getting his work published. *Dubliners* was rejected by twenty-two publishers before being printed; *Ulysses* was banned for many years in England and America. As a result, Joyce did not make money from his writing. He died penniless in Switzerland after fleeing German-occupied France during World War II.

"Araby" is one story from *Dubliners*. It is not as difficult as some of Joyce's other work. It is typical, however, because much of the plot takes place within the mind of the main character. Like most of Joyce's best fiction, the story has for a climax a stunning realization that changes a character's way of looking at life.

James Joyce

Araby

North Richmond Street, being blind,[1] was a quiet street except at the hour when the Christian Brothers' School set the boys free. An uninhabited house of two stories stood at the blind end, detached from its neighbors in a square ground. The other houses of the street, conscious of decent lives within them, gazed at one another with brown imperturbable faces.

The former tenant of our house, a priest, had died in the back drawing room. Air, musty from having been long enclosed, hung in all the rooms, and the waste room behind the kitchen was littered with old useless papers. Among these I found a few paper-covered books, the pages of which were curled and damp: *The Abbot*, by Walter Scott, *The Devout Communicant* and *The Memoirs of Vidocq.*[2] I liked the last best because its leaves were yellow. The wild garden behind the house contained a central apple tree and a few straggling bushes under one of which I found the late

---

1. **blind:** dead end.

2. ***The Abbot . . . Vidocq*** [vē dôk′]: historical tale, a manual of religious instruction, and the recollections of a French adventurer, respectively.

tenant's rusty bicycle pump. He had been a very charitable priest; in his will he had left all his money to institutions and the furniture of his house to his sister.

When the short days of winter came dusk fell before we had well eaten our dinners. When we met in the street the houses had grown somber. The space of sky above us was the color of ever-changing violet and toward it the lamps of the street lifted their feeble lanterns. The cold air stung us and we played till our bodies glowed. Our shouts echoed in the silent street. The career of our play brought us through the dark muddy lanes behind the houses where we ran the gantlet of the rough tribes from the cottages, to the back doors of the dark dripping gardens where odors arose from the ashpits, to the dark odorous stables where a coachman smoothed and combed the horse or shook music from the buckled harness. When we returned to the street, light from the kitchen windows had filled the areas. If my uncle was seen turning the corner we hid in the shadow until we had seen him safely housed. Or if Mangan's sister came out on the doorstep to call her brother in to his tea we watched her from our shadow peer up and down the street. We waited to see whether she would remain or go in and, if she remained, we left our shadow and walked up to Mangan's steps resignedly. She was waiting for us, her figure defined by the light from the half-opened door. Her brother always teased her before he obeyed and I stood by the railings looking at her. Her dress swung as she moved her body and the soft rope of her hair tossed from side to side.

Every morning I lay on the floor in the front parlor watching her door. The blind was pulled down to within an inch of the sash so that I could not be seen. When she came out on the doorstep my heart leaped. I ran to the hall, seized my books and followed her. I kept her brown figure always in my eye and, when we came near the point at which our ways diverged, I quickened my pace and passed her. This happened morning after morning. I had never spoken to her, except for a few casual words, and yet her name was like a summons to all my foolish blood.

Her image accompanied me even in places the most hostile to romance. On Saturday evenings when my aunt went marketing I had to go to carry some of the parcels. We walked through the flaring streets, jostled by drunken men and bargaining women, amid the curses of laborers, the shrill litanies of shopboys who stood on guard by the barrels of pigs' cheeks, the nasal chanting of street singers, who sang a *come-all-you* about O'Donovan Rossa,[3] or a ballad about the troubles in our native land. These noises converged in a single sensation of life for me: I imagined that I bore my chalice safely through a throng of foes. Her name sprang to my lips at moments in strange prayers and praises which I myself did not understand. My eyes were often full of tears (I could not tell why) and at times a flood from my heart seemed to pour itself out into my bosom. I thought little of the future. I did not know whether I would ever speak to her or not or, if I spoke to her, how I could tell her of my confused adoration. But my body was like a harp and her words and gestures were like fingers running upon the wires.

One evening I went into the back drawing room in which the priest had died. It was a dark rainy evening and there was no sound in the house. Through one of the broken panes I heard the rain impinge upon the earth, the fine incessant needles of water playing in the sodden beds. Some distant lamp or lighted window gleamed below me. I was thankful that I could see so little. All my senses seemed to desire to veil themselves and, feeling that I was about to slip from them, I pressed the palms of my hands together until they trembled, murmuring: *"O love! O love!"* many times.

At last she spoke to me. When she addressed the first words to me I was so confused that I did not know what to answer. She asked me was I going to *Araby.* I forget

3. *come-all-you . . .* **Rossa:** ballad about an Irish hero.

whether I answered yes or no. It would be a splendid bazaar, she said; she would love to go.

"And why can't you?" I asked.

While she spoke she turned a silver bracelet round and round her wrist. She could not go, she said, because there would be a retreat[4] that week in her convent.[5] Her brother and two other boys were fighting for their caps and I was alone at the railings. She held one of the spikes, bowing her head toward me. The light from the lamp opposite our door caught the white curve of her neck, lit up her hair that rested there and, falling, lit up the hand upon the railing. It fell over one side of her dress and caught the white border of a petticoat, just visible as she stood at ease.

"It's well for you," she said.

"If I go," I said, "I will bring you something."

What innumerable follies laid waste my waking and sleeping thoughts after that evening! I wished to annihilate the tedious intervening days. I chafed against the work of school. At night in my bedroom and by day in the classroom her image came between me and the page I strove to read. The syllables of the word *Araby* were called to me through the silence in which my soul luxuriated and cast an Eastern enchantment over me. I asked for leave to go to the bazaar on Saturday night. My aunt was surprised and hoped it was not some Freemason[6] affair. I answered few questions in class. I watched my master's face pass from amiability to sternness; he hoped I was not beginning to idle. I could not call my wandering thoughts together. I had hardly any patience with the serious work of life which, now that it stood between me and my desire, seemed to me child's play, ugly monotonous child's play.

On Saturday morning I reminded my uncle that I wished to go to the bazaar in the evening. He was fussing at the hallstand, looking for the hat brush, and answered me curtly:

"Yes, boy, I know."

As he was in the hall I could not go into the front parlor and lie at the window. I left the house in bad humor and walked slowly toward the school. The air was pitilessly raw and already my heart misgave me.

When I came home to dinner my uncle had not yet been home. Still it was early. I sat staring at the clock for some time and, when its ticking began to irritate me, I left the room. I mounted the staircase and gained the upper part of the house. The high cold empty gloomy rooms liberated me and I went from room to room singing. From the front window I saw my companions playing below in the street. Their cries reached me weakened and indistinct and, leaning my forehead against the cool glass, I looked over at the dark house where she lived. I may have stood there for an hour, seeing nothing but the brown-clad figure cast by my imagination, touched discreetly by the lamplight at the curved neck, at the hand upon the railings and at the border below the dress.

When I came downstairs again I found Mrs. Mercer sitting at the fire. She was an old garrulous woman, a pawnbroker's widow, who collected used stamps for some pious purpose. I had to endure the gossip of the tea table. The meal was prolonged beyond an hour and still my uncle did not come. Mrs. Mercer stood up to go: she was sorry she couldn't wait any longer, but it was after eight o'clock and she did not like to be out late, as the night air was bad for her. When she had gone I began to walk up and down the room, clenching my fists. My aunt said:

"I'm afraid you may put off your bazaar for this night of Our Lord."

At nine o'clock I heard my uncle's latchkey in the hall door. I heard him talking to himself and heard the hallstand rocking when it had received the weight of his overcoat. I could interpret these signs. When he was midway through his dinner I asked him to give me the money to go to the bazaar. He had forgotten.

---

4. **retreat:** seclusion of a group for prayer, meditation, and religious study.
5. **convent:** school run by an order of nuns.
6. **Freemason:** international secret service society, also called the Free and Accepted Masons.

"The people are in bed and after their first sleep now," he said.

I did not smile. My aunt said to him energetically:

"Can't you give him the money and let him go? You've kept him late enough as it is."

My uncle said he was very sorry he had forgotten. He said he believed in the old saying: *All work and no play makes Jack a dull boy.* He asked me where I was going and, when I had told him a second time he asked me did I know *The Arab's Farewell to His Steed.*[7] When I left the kitchen he was about to recite the opening lines of the piece to my aunt.

I held a florin[8] tightly in my hand as I strode down Buckingham Street toward the station. The sight of the streets thronged with buyers and glaring with gas recalled to me the purpose of my journey. I took my seat in a third-class carriage of a deserted train. After an intolerable delay the train moved out of the station slowly. It crept onward among ruinous houses and over the twinkling river. At Westland Row Station a crowd of people pressed to the carriage doors; but the porters moved them back, saying that it was a special train for the bazaar. I remained alone in the bare carriage. In a few minutes the train drew up beside an improvised wooden platform. I passed out onto the road and saw by the lighted dial of a clock that it was ten minutes to ten. In front of me was a large building which displayed the magical name.

I could not find any sixpenny entrance and, fearing that the bazaar would be closed, I passed in quickly through a turnstile, handing a shilling to a weary-looking man. I found myself in a big hall girdled at half its height by a gallery. Nearly all the stalls were closed and the greater part of the hall was in darkness. I recognized a silence like that which pervades a church after a service. I walked into the center of the bazaar timidly. A few people were gathered about the stalls which were still open. Before a curtain, over which the words *Café Chantant*[9] were written in colored lamps, two men were counting money on a salver.[10] I listened to the fall of the coins.

Remembering with difficulty why I had come I went over to one of the stalls and examined porcelain vases and flowered tea sets. At the door of the stall a young lady was talking and laughing with two young gentlemen. I remarked their English accents and listened vaguely to their conversation.

"O, I never said such a thing!"

"O, but you did!"

"O, but I didn't!"

"Didn't she say that?"

"Yes. I heard her."

"O, there's a . . . fib!"

Observing me the young lady came over and asked me did I wish to buy anything. The tone of her voice was not encouraging; she seemed to have spoken to me out of a sense of duty. I looked humbly at the great jars that stood like Eastern guards at either side of the dark entrance to the stall and murmured:

"No, thank you."

The young lady changed the position of one of the vases and went back to the two young men. They began to talk of the same subject. Once or twice the young lady glanced at me over her shoulder.

I lingered before her stall, though I knew my stay was useless, to make my interest in her wares seem the more real. Then I turned away slowly and walked down the middle of the bazaar, I allowed the two pennies to fall against the sixpence in my pocket. I heard a voice call from one end of the gallery that the light was out. The upper part of the hall was now completely dark.

Gazing up into the darkness I saw myself as a creature driven and derided by vanity; and my eyes burned with anguish and anger.

---

7. *The Arab's . . . Steed:* popular nineteenth-century poem.
8. **florin:** a former two-shilling coin. At the time of the story one shilling was worth approximately twenty-five American cents.

9. *Café Chantant:* café with musical entertainment.
10. **salver** [sal′vər]: tray, usually used for serving food.

STUDY QUESTIONS

Recalling
1. At what times of day does the boy usually see Mangan's sister? When does he think of her?
2. What promise does the boy make to the girl?
3. Why is the boy late for the bazaar? Describe the bazaar.
4. How does the boy feel at the end of the story?

Interpreting
5. Contrast the boy's expectations of the bazaar with his usual surroundings.
6. Explain how the boy reveals to the reader his infatuation with the girl. Give two examples of his inexperience with girls.
7. Why does the bazaar become a negative experience for the boy? What do you think the experience teaches him about dreams as opposed to reality?

VIEWPOINT

The famous literary critic Edmund Wilson compared what happens in Joyce's fiction to what goes on in the mind just before sleep:

> Images or words in the conscious mind take on an ominous significance . . . incidents swell with meaning. . . .
> —*Axel's Castle*

■ Find at least two significant images in "Araby." Explain how the incident at the bazaar swells with meaning.

LITERARY FOCUS

Plot

Plot is the sequence of events in a story, each event causing or leading to the next. The author of a story arranges and orders events of a plot to capture, hold, and heighten our interest as the story progresses. To accomplish this involvement, the development of a plot generally includes the following points: The **exposition,** usually at the beginning of the story, introduces characters, settings, and situations that are important to the story. The **narrative hook** is the point at which the conflict begins. The **rising action** adds complications to the conflict and increases our interest. The **climax** is the point of our highest interest and emotional involvement in

the story, the point at which we know how the conflict will be resolved. The **falling action** shows the result of the climax and ends with the **resolution,** the denouement, or final outcome.

Because modern fiction often experiments with plot, many modern stories have unusual plot structures: The information usually presented in the exposition may be gradually revealed throughout the story instead. A story may end at the climax, leaving the reader at the peak of emotional involvement. Another story may not have a dramatic climax, and the reader may be free to form a personal interpretation of the outcome. James Joyce created his own innovation for the climax of a story. His stories often end with an **epiphany,** a sudden realization—by the reader as well as a character—of the true nature of a person, place, object, or situation.

Thinking About Plot
1. List the points in the plot of "Araby" that are the story's exposition, narrative hook, rising action, climax, and, if any, falling action and resolution.
2. Is the climax of "Araby" an epiphany?

COMPOSITION

Citing Evidence
■ A good short story is particular and universal. That is, a good story is specific in its plot, characters, and setting but has concerns that are common to all people. Cite evidence from the story to show that "Araby" is particular and universal. To do this, cite examples from the story—verbatim and in paraphrase—to show that the story has a specific plot, characters, and setting. Then, still citing evidence from the story, explain how the story represents an experience that is common to most people. *For help with this assignment, refer to Lesson 3 in the Writing About Literature Handbook at the back of this book.*

Writing a Journal Entry
■ Imagine that you are the boy in "Araby" twenty years later, and write a journal entry about your memories of the events in the story. In writing your entry, consider the following questions: Does the adult remember the events with joy or sadness? Did these events have a lasting effect on the boy? What became of the boy's infatuation with Mangan's sister?

Katherine Mansfield   *1888–1923*

In a relatively short career Katherine Mansfield exerted a major influence on the modern short story. Mansfield was born in New Zealand and spent most of her childhood there, but she attended Queens College in London. By the age of nineteen, she had published a few short vignettes and was determined to achieve fame as a writer. Back in New Zealand after college, she felt that her homeland restricted her, and she returned to London in 1908. Mansfield wrote short stories, poetry, literary criticism, and a journal. Ironically the stories inspired by her early life in New Zealand brought her first success. Always plagued by poor health, she died of tuberculosis at the age of thirty-five.

Mansfield's *Journal* (1927) affords an insight into her personality and explains her literary goals and methods, but she is best known for her short stories. The stories—collected in volumes such as *In a German Pension* (1911) and *The Garden Party* (1922)—reflect the complexity and confusion of the modern age. Mansfield writes about ordinary events, quiet moments that gradually reveal their significance.

"The Singing Lesson" illustrates Mansfield's talent for characterization. By eavesdropping on the thoughts racing through Miss Meadows' mind, the reader forms a finely etched portrait of a complicated woman.

Katherine Mansfield

The Singing Lesson

With despair—cold, sharp despair—buried deep in her heart like a wicked knife, Miss Meadows, in cap and gown and carrying a little baton, trod the cold corridors that led to the music hall. Girls of all ages, rosy from the air, and bubbling over with that gleeful excitement that comes from running to school on a fine autumn morning, hurried, skipped, fluttered by; from the hollow classrooms came a quick drumming of voices; a bell rang; a voice like a bird cried, "Muriel." And then there came from the staircase a tremendous knock-knock-knocking. Someone had dropped her dumbbells.

The Science Mistress stopped Miss Meadows.

"Good mor-ning," she cried, in her sweet, affected drawl. "Isn't it cold? It might be winter."

Miss Meadows, hugging the knife, stared in hatred at the Science Mistress. Everything about her was sweet, pale, like honey. You would not have been surprised to see a bee caught in the tangles of that yellow hair.

"It is rather sharp," said Miss Meadows, grimly.

The other smiled her sugary smile.

"You look fro-zen," said she. Her blue eyes opened wide; there came a mocking light in them. (Had she noticed anything?)

"Oh, not quite as bad as that," said Miss Meadows, and she gave the Science Mistress, in exchange for her smile, a quick grimace and passed on. . . .

Forms[1] Four, Five, and Six were assembled in the music hall. The noise was deafening. On the platform, by the piano, stood Mary Beazley, Miss Meadows' favorite, who played accompaniments. She was turning the music stool. When she saw Miss Meadows she gave a loud, warning "Sh-sh! girls!" and Miss Meadows, her hands thrust in her sleeves, the baton under her arm, strode down the center aisle, mounted the steps, turned sharply, seized the brass music stand, planted it in front of her, and gave two sharp taps with her baton for silence.

"Silence, please! Immediately!" and, looking at nobody, her glance swept over that sea of colored flannel blouses, with bobbing pink faces and hands, quivering butterfly hair bows, and music books outspread. She knew perfectly well what they were thinking. "Meady is in a wax."[2] Well, let them think it! Her eyelids quivered; she tossed her head, defying them. What could the thoughts of those creatures matter to someone who stood there bleeding to death, pierced to the heart, to the heart, by such a letter—

. . . "I feel more and more strongly that our marriage would be a mistake. Not that I do not love you. I love you as much as it is possible for me to love any woman, but, truth to tell, I have come to the conclusion that I am not a marrying man, and the idea of settling down fills me with nothing but—" and the word "disgust" was scratched out lightly and "regret" written over the top.

Basil! Miss Meadows stalked over to the piano. And Mary Beazley, who was waiting for this moment, bent forward; her curls fell over her cheeks while she breathed, "Good morning, Miss Meadows," and she motioned toward rather than handed to her mistress a beautiful yellow chrysanthemum. This little ritual of the flower had been gone through for ages and ages, quite a term and a half. It was as much part of the lesson as opening the piano. But this morning, instead of taking it up, instead of tucking it into her belt while she leaned over Mary and said, "Thank you, Mary. How very nice! Turn to page thirty-two," what was Mary's horror when Miss Meadows totally ignored the chrysanthemum, made no reply to her greeting, but said in a voice of ice, "Page fourteen, please, and mark the accents well."

Staggering moment! Mary blushed until the tears stood in her eyes, but Miss Meadows was gone back to the music stand; her voice rang through the music hall.

"Page fourteen. We will begin with page fourteen. 'A Lament.'[3] Now, girls, you ought to know it by this time. We shall take it all together; not in parts, all together. And without expression. Sing it, though, quite simply, beating time with the left hand."

She raised the baton; she tapped the music stand twice. Down came Mary on the opening chord; down came all those left hands, beating the air, and in chimed those young, mournful voices:—

Fast! Ah, too Fast Fade the Ro-o-ses of Pleasure;
Soon Autumn yields unto Wi-i-nter Drear.
Fleetly! Ah, Fleetly Mu-u-sic's Gay Measure
Passes away from the Listening Ear.

Good Heavens, what could be more tragic than that lament! Every note was a sigh, a sob, a groan of awful mournfulness. Miss Meadows lifted her arms in the wide gown and began conducting with both hands. ". . . I feel more and more strongly that our marriage would be a mistake. . . ." she beat. And the voices cried: *Fleetly! Ah, Fleetly.* What could have possessed him to write such a letter! What could have

---

1. **Forms:** grades in British schools.
2. **in a wax:** in a rage; angry.

3. **'A Lament':** song expressing sorrow or grief.

I feel more marriage ... I do not love ... to love any conclusion that the idea of but regret disgust—

led up to it! It came out of nothing. His last letter had been all about a fumed-oak bookcase he had bought for "our" books, and a "natty little hall stand" he had seen, "a very neat affair with a carved owl on a bracket, holding three hat brushes in its claws." How she had smiled at that! So like a man to think one needed three hat brushes! *From the Listening Ear,* sang the voices.

"Once again," said Miss Meadows. "But this time in parts. Still without expression." *Fast! Ah, too Fast.* With the gloom of the contraltos[4] added, one could scarcely help shuddering. *Fade the Roses of Pleasure.* Last time he had come to see her, Basil had worn a rose in his buttonhole. How handsome he had looked in that bright blue suit, with that dark red rose! And he knew it, too. He couldn't help knowing it. First he stroked his hair, then his moustache; his teeth gleamed when he smiled.

"The headmaster's wife keeps on asking me to dinner. It's a perfect nuisance. I never get an evening to myself in that place."

"But can't you refuse?"

"Oh, well, it doesn't do for a man in my position to be unpopular."

Music's Gay Measure, wailed the voices. The willow trees, outside the high, narrow windows, waved in the wind. They had lost half their leaves. The tiny ones that clung wriggled like fishes caught on a line. ". . . I am not a marrying man. . . ." The voices were silent; the piano waited.

"Quite good," said Miss Meadows, but still in such a strange, stony tone that the younger girls began to feel positively frightened. "But now that we know it, we shall take it with expression. As much expression as you can put into it. Think of the words, girls. Use your imaginations. *Fast! Ah, too Fast,*" cried Miss Meadows. "That ought to break out—a loud, strong *forte*[5]—a lament. And then in the second line, *Winter Drear,* make that *Drear* sound as if a cold wind were blowing through it. *Dre-ear!*" said she so awfully that Mary Beazley, on the music stool, wriggled her spine. "The third line should be one crescendo.[6] *Fleetly! Ah, Fleetly Music's Gay Measure.* Breaking on the first word of the last line, *Passes.* And then on the word, *Away,* you must begin to die . . . to fade . . . until *The Listening Ear* is nothing more than a faint whisper. . . . You can slow down as much as you like almost on the last line. Now, please."

Again the two light taps; she lifted her arms again. *Fast! Ah, too Fast.* ". . . and the idea of settling down fills me with nothing but disgust—" Disgust was what he had written. That was as good as to say their engagement was definitely broken off. Broken off! Their engagement! People had been surprised enough that she had got engaged. The Science Mistress would not believe it at first. But nobody had been as surprised as she. She was thirty. Basil was twenty-five. It had been a miracle, simply a miracle, to hear him say, as they walked home from church that very dark night. "You know, somehow or other, I've got fond of you." And he had taken hold of the end of her ostrich feather boa. *Passes away from the Listening Ear.*

"Repeat! Repeat!" said Miss Meadows. "More expression, girls! Once more!"

---

4. **contraltos** [kən tral′tōz]: singers with the lowest female singing voice.

5. *forte* [fôr′tā]: increase in volume.

6. **crescendo** [kri shen′dō]: increase in volume.

Fast! Ah, too Fast. The older girls were crimson; some of the younger ones began to cry. Big spots of rain blew against the windows, and one could hear the willows whispering, ". . . not that I do not love you. . . ."

"But, my darling, if you love me," thought Miss Meadows, "I don't mind how much it is. Love me as little as you like." But she knew he didn't love her. Not to have cared enough to scratch out that word "disgust," so that she couldn't read it! *Soon Autumn yields unto Winter Drear.* She would have to leave the school, too. She could never face the Science Mistress or the girls after it got known. She would have to disappear somewhere. *Passes away.* The voices began to die, to fade, to whisper . . . to vanish. . . .

Suddenly the door opened. A little girl in blue walked fussily up the aisle, hanging her head, biting her lips, and twisting the silver bangle on her red little wrist. She came up the steps and stood before Miss Meadows.

"Well, Monica, what is it?"

"Oh, if you please, Miss Meadows," said the little girl, gasping, "Miss Wyatt wants to see you in the mistress's room."

"Very well," said Miss Meadows. And she called to the girls, "I shall put you on your honor to talk quietly while I am away." But they were too subdued to do anything else. Most of them were blowing their noses.

The corridors were silent and cold; they echoed to Miss Meadows' steps. The head mistress sat at her desk. For a moment she did not look up. She was as usual disentangling her eyeglasses, which had got caught in her lace tie. "Sit down, Miss Meadows," she said very kindly. And then she picked up a pink envelope from the blotting pad. "I sent for you just now because this telegram has come for you."

"A telegram for me, Miss Wyatt?"

Basil! He had committed suicide, decided Miss Meadows. Her hand flew out, but Miss Wyatt held the telegram back a moment. "I hope it's not bad news," she said, so more than kindly. And Miss Meadows tore it open.

"Pay no attention to letter, must have been mad, bought hat stand today—Basil," she read.

She couldn't take her eyes off the telegram.

"I do hope it's nothing very serious," said Miss Wyatt, leaning forward.

"Oh, no, thank you, Miss Wyatt," blushed Miss Meadows. "It's nothing bad at all. It's"— and she gave an apologetic little laugh—"it's from my *fiancé* saying that . . . saying that—" There was a pause. "I *see*," said Miss Wyatt. And another pause. Then—"You've fifteen minutes more of your class, Miss Meadows, haven't you?"

"Yes, Miss Wyatt." She got up. She half ran toward the door.

"Oh, just one minute, Miss Meadows," said Miss Wyatt. "I must say I don't approve of my teachers having telegrams sent to them in school hours, unless in case of very bad news, such as death," explained Miss Wyatt, "or a very serious accident, or something to that effect. Good news, Miss Meadows, will always keep, you know."

On the wings of hope, of love, of joy, Miss Meadows sped back to the music hall, up the aisle, up the steps, over to the piano.

"Page thirty-two, Mary," she said, "page thirty-two," and, picking up the yellow chrysanthemum, she held it to her lips to hide her smile. Then she turned to the girls, rapped

with her baton: "Page thirty-two, girls. Page thirty-two."

We come here To-day with Flowers o'erladen,
With Baskets of Fruit and Ribbons to boot,
To-oo Congratulate. . . .

"Stop! Stop!" cried Miss Meadows. "This is awful. This is dreadful." And she beamed at her girls. "What's the matter with you all? Think, girls, think of what you're singing. Use your imaginations. *With Flowers o'erladen. Baskets of Fruit and Ribbons to boot. And Congratulate.*" Miss Meadows broke off. "Don't look so doleful, girls. It ought to sound warm, joyful, eager. *Congratulate.* Once more. Quickly. All together. Now then!"

And this time Miss Meadows' voice sounded over all the other voices—full, deep, glowing with expression.

STUDY QUESTIONS

Recalling

1. At the beginning of the story, what is Miss Meadows' mood? To what object is her mood compared?
2. Explain the contents of the letter that Miss Meadows thinks about during her lesson.
3. In what way does Miss Meadows cause Mary Beazley "horror"?
4. Describe the incident that interrupts the singing lesson.
5. What fault does Miss Meadows find with the class when she returns?

Interpreting

6. Describe Miss Meadows' manner in class before and after the interruption. Use details from the story to show which type of behavior is more typical for Miss Meadows.
7. Relate Miss Meadows' treatment of other people and the songs she chooses to her emotional states.
8. Describe Basil's personality, and explain his relationship with Miss Meadows.

Extending

9. Do you think that Miss Meadows should be as happy as she is about Basil's telegram?

LITERARY FOCUS

Point of View

Point of view is the relationship of the **narrator,** or storyteller, to the story. The author's choice of narrator influences the information and the emotional involvement that the story provides.

A story told in the **first-person point of view** is narrated by a character in the story. A first-person narrator relates personal experience, using the pronoun *I.* Because we are reading a personal account, we sympathize with the narrator and become emotionally involved in the story. The first-person narrator, however, may tell only one side of a story and may actually deceive the reader either deliberately or because he or she does not know the truth.

A story told in the **limited third-person point of view** is narrated by the author but from the limited viewpoint of only one character. The narrator is detached from the action and uses the pronoun *he* or *she.* Because we read the thoughts of only one character, we sympathize with him or her. The character, however, may not completely understand a situation, and therefore we too are denied full information.

A story told in the **omniscient point of view** is narrated by the author who reveals the thoughts and feelings of *all* the characters. An omniscient narrator uses the third person—*he* or *she*—and stands completely outside the story. Because the narrator is detached, he can always be trusted.

Thinking About Point of View

1. What is the point of view of "The Singing Lesson"? Explain your answer.
2. Explain how the point of view of "The Singing Lesson" keeps complete information from the reader but still inspires sympathy for Miss Meadows.

D. H. Lawrence   1885–1930

D. H. Lawrence helped to define modern literature with his carefully constructed, highly original, and socially conscious novels and short stories. David Herbert Lawrence was born in a small coal mining town in Nottinghamshire, England. Lawrence left school at an early age, held a number of jobs, and then completed his education. His life was marred by poor health, and he traveled extensively—to Italy, Australia, and Mexico—to improve his condition. Besides fiction, Lawrence wrote poetry and travel books; he was also a talented painter. He died of tuberculosis in southern France.

A recurring concern in Lawrence's fiction is the effect of the Industrial Revolution. Lawrence felt that the scientific-industrial age both separated people from their own feelings and estranged them from nature. In his stories and especially in novels like *Sons and Lovers* (1913), *The Rainbow* (1915), and *Women in Love* (1921), he wrote of the need for harmony with nature and for integration of the individual's body and spirit.

"Goose Fair" demonstrates Lawrence's concern with the influence of industrialization. He exemplifies the differences between classes by contrasting two young women of very dissimilar backgrounds. In just a few pages the story parades before the reader a wide array of characters who embody the struggles that filled Lawrence's work and changed England.

D. H. Lawrence

Goose Fair

1

Through the gloom of evening, and the flare of torches of the night before the fair, through the still fogs of the succeeding dawn came paddling the weary geese, lifting their poor feet that had been dipped in tar for shoes, and trailing them along the cobblestones into the town. Last of all, in the afternoon, a country girl drove in her dozen birds, disconsolate because she was so late. She was a heavily built girl, fair, with regular features, and yet unprepossessing. She needed chiseling down, her contours were brutal. Perhaps it was weariness that hung her eyelids a little lower than was

pleasant. When she spoke to her clumsily lagging birds it was in a snarling nasal tone. One of the silly things sat down in the gutter and refused to move. It looked very ridiculous, but also rather pitiful, squat there with its head up, refusing to be urged on by the ungentle toe of the girl. The latter swore heavily, then picked up the great complaining bird, and fronting her road stubbornly, drove on the lamentable eleven.

No one had noticed her. This afternoon the women were not sitting chatting on their doorsteps, seaming up the cotton hose, or swiftly passing through their fingers the piled white lace; and in the high dark house the song of the hosiery frames was hushed: "Shackety-boom, Shackety-shackety-boom, Z—zzz!" As she dragged up Hollow Stone, people returning from the fair chaffed her and asked her what o'clock it was. She did not reply, her look was sullen. The Lace Market was quiet as the Sabbath: even the great brass plates on the doors were dull with neglect. There seemed an afternoon atmosphere of raw discontent. The girl stopped a moment before the dismal prospect of one of the great warehouses that had been gutted with fire. She looked at the lean, threatening walls and watched her white flock waddling in reckless misery below, and she would have laughed out loud had the wall fallen flat upon them and relieved her of them. But the wall did not fall, so she crossed the road, and walking on the safe side, hurried after her charge. Her look was even more sullen. She remembered the state of trade—Trade, the invidious[1] enemy; Trade, which thrust out its hand and shut the factory doors, and pulled the stockingers[2] off their seats, and left the web half-finished on the frame; Trade, which mysteriously choked up the sources of the rivulets of wealth, and blacker and more secret than a pestilence, starved the town. Through this morose atmosphere of bad trade, in the afternoon of the first day of the fair, the girl strode down to the Poultry with eleven sound geese and one lame one to sell.

The Frenchmen were at the bottom of it! So everybody said, though nobody quite knew how. At any rate, they had gone to war with the Prussians and got beaten, and trade was ruined in Nottingham!

A little fog rose up, and the twilight gathered around. Then they flared abroad their torches in the fair, insulting the night. The girl still sat in the Poultry, and her weary geese unsold on the stones, illuminated by the hissing lamp of a man who sold rabbits and pigeons and such-like assorted livestock.

---

1. **invidious** [in vid′ē əs]: offensively unfair.
2. **stockingers:** hosiery knitters or weavers.

2

In another part of the town, near Sneinton Church, another girl came to the door to look at the night. She was tall and slender, dressed with the severe accuracy which marks the girl of superior culture. Her hair was arranged with simplicity about the long, pale, cleanly cut face. She leaned forward very slightly to glance down the street, listening. She very carefully preserved the appearance of having come quite casually to the door, yet she lingered and lingered and stood very still to listen when she heard a footstep, but when it proved to be only a common man, she drew herself up proudly and looked with a small smile over his head. He hesitated to glance into the open hall, lighted so spaciously with a scarlet-shaded lamp, and at the slim girl in brown silk lifted up before the light. But she, she looked over his head. He passed on.

Presently she started and hung in suspense. Somebody was crossing the road. She ran down the steps in a pretty welcome, not effuse,[3] saying in quick but accurately articulated words: "Will! I began to think you'd gone to the fair. I came out to listen to it. I felt almost sure you'd gone. You're coming in, aren't you?" She waited a moment anxiously. "We expect you to dinner, you know," she added wistfully.

The man, who had a short face and spoke with his lip curling up on one side, in a drawling speech with ironically exaggerated intonation, replied after a short hesitation:

"I'm awfully sorry, I am, straight,[4] Lois. It's a shame. I've got to go round to the biz. Man proposes—the devil disposes." He turned aside with irony in the darkness.

"But surely, Will!" remonstrated the girl, keenly disappointed.

"Fact, Lois!—I feel wild about it myself. But I've got to go down to the works. They may be getting a bit warm down there, you know"—he jerked his head in the direction of the fair. "If the Lambs get frisky!—they're a bit off about the work, and they'd just be in their

---

3. **effuse** [i fūz′]: poured out freely.
4. **straight:** honestly.

element if they could set a lighted match to something——"

"Will, you don't think——!" exclaimed the girl, laying her hand on his arm in the true fashion of romance, and looking up at him earnestly.

"Dad's not sure," he replied, looking down at her with gravity. They remained in this attitude for a moment, then he said:

"I might stop a bit. It's all right for an hour, I should think."

She looked at him earnestly, then said in tones of deep disappointment and of fortitude: "No, Will, you must go. You'd better go——"

"It's a shame!" he murmured, standing a moment at a loose end. Then, glancing down the street to see he was alone, he put his arm round her waist and said in a difficult voice: "How goes it?"

She let him keep her for a moment, then he kissed her as if afraid of what he was doing. They were both uncomfortable.

"Well——!" he said at length.

"Good night!" she said, setting him free to go.

He hung a moment near her, as if ashamed. Then "Good night," he answered, and he broke away. She listened to his footsteps in the night, before composing herself to turn indoors.

"Helloa!" said her father, glancing over his paper as she entered the diningroom. "What's up, then?"

"Oh, nothing," she replied, in her calm tones. "Will won't be here to dinner tonight."

"What, gone to the fair?"

"No."

"Oh! What's got him then?"

Lois looked at her father, and answered:

"He's gone down to the factory. They are afraid of the hands."

Her father looked at her closely.

"Oh, aye!" he answered, undecided, and they sat down to dinner.

3

Lois retired very early. She had a fire in her bedroom. She drew the curtains and stood holding aside a heavy fold, looking out at the night. She could see only the nothingness of the fog; not even the glare of the fair was evident, though the noise clamored small in the distance. In front of everything she could see her own faint image. She crossed to the dressing table, and there leaned her face to the mirror, and looked at herself. She looked a long time, then she rose, changed her dress for a dressing jacket, and took up *Sesame and Lilies.*[5]

Late in the night she was roused from sleep by a bustle in the house. She sat up and heard a hurrying to and fro and the sound of anxious voices. She put on her dressing gown and went out to her mother's room. Seeing her mother at the head of the stairs, she said in her quick clean voice:

"Mother, what is it?"

"Oh, child, don't ask me! Go to bed, dear, do! I shall surely be worried out of my life."

"Mother, what is it?" Lois was sharp and emphatic.

"I hope your father won't go. Now I do hope your father won't go. He's got a cold as it is."

"Mother, tell me what it is?" Lois took her mother's arm.

"It's Selby's. I should have thought you would have heard the fire engine, and Jack isn't in yet. I hope we're safe!" Lois returned to her bedroom and dressed. She coiled her plaited[6] hair, and having put on a cloak, left the house.

She hurried along under the fog-dripping trees toward the meaner part of the town. When she got near, she saw a glare in the fog, and closed her lips tight. She hastened on till she was in the crowd. With peaked, noble face she watched the fire. Then she looked a little wildly over the fire-reddened faces in the crowd, and catching sight of her father, hurried to him.

"Oh, Dadda—is he safe? Is Will safe——?"

"Safe, aye, why not? You've no business

---

5. *Sesame and Lilies:* book by English writer John Ruskin (1819–1900).
6. **plaited** [plā′tid]: braided.

here. Here, here's Sampson, he'll take you home. I've enough to bother me; there's my own place to watch. Go home now, I can't do with you here."

"Have you seen Will?" she asked.

"Go home—Sampson, just take Miss Lois home—now!"

"You don't really know where he is—father?"

"Go home now—I don't want you here——" her father ordered peremptorily.

The tears sprang to Lois' eyes. She looked at the fire and the tears were quickly dried by fear. The flames roared and struggled upward. The great wonder of the fire made her forget even her indignation at her father's light treat-ment of herself and of her lover. There was a crashing and bursting of timber, as the first floor fell in a mass into the blazing gulf, splash-ing the fire in all directions, to the terror of the crowd. She saw the steel of the machines growing white-hot and twisting like flaming let-ters. Piece after piece of the flooring gave way, and the machines dropped in red ruin as the wooden framework burned out. The air be-came unbreathable; the fog was swallowed up; sparks went rushing up as if they would burn the dark heavens; sometimes cards of lace went whirling into the gulf of the sky, waving with wings of fire. It was dangerous to stand near this great cup of roaring destruction.

Sampson, the gray old manager of Buxton

and Co.'s, led her away as soon as she would turn her face to listen to him. He was a stout, irritable man. He elbowed his way roughly through the crowd, and Lois followed him, her head high, her lips closed. He led her for some distance without speaking, then at last, unable to contain his garrulous irritability, he broke out:

"What do they expect? What can they expect? They can't expect to stand a bad time. They spring up like mushrooms as big as a house side, but there's no stability in 'em. I remember William Selby when he'd run on my errands. Yes, there's some as can make much out of little, and there's some as can make much out of nothing, but they find it won't last. William Selby's sprung up in a day, and he'll vanish in a night. You can't trust to luck alone. Maybe he thinks it's a lucky thing this fire has come when things are looking black. But you can't get out of it as easy as that. There's been a few too many of 'em. No, indeed, a fire's the last thing I should hope to come to—the very last!"

Lois hurried and hurried, so that she brought the old manager panting in distress up the steps of her home. She could not bear to hear him talking so. They could get no one to open the door for some time. When at last Lois ran upstairs, she found her mother dressed, but all unbuttoned again, lying back in the chair in her daughter's room, suffering from palpitation of the heart, with *Sesame and Lilies* crushed beneath her. Lois administered brandy, and her decisive words and movements helped largely to bring the good lady to a state of recovery sufficient to allow of her returning to her own bedroom.

Then Lois locked the door. She glanced at her fire-darkened face, and taking the flattened Ruskin out of the chair, sat down and wept. After a while she calmed herself, rose and sponged her face. Then once more on that fatal night she prepared for rest. Instead, however, of retiring, she pulled a silk quilt from her disordered bed and, wrapping it round her, sat miserably to think. It was two o'clock in the morning.

4

The fire was sunk to cold ashes in the grate, and the gray morning was creeping through the half-opened curtains like a thing ashamed, when Lois awoke. It was painful to move her head: her neck was cramped. The girl awoke in full recollection. She sighed, roused herself and pulled the quilt closer about her. For a little while she sat and mused. A pale, tragic resignation fixed her face like a mask. She remembered her father's irritable answer to her question concerning her lover's safety—"Safe, aye—why not?" She knew that he suspected the factory of having been purposely set on fire. But then, he had never liked Will. And yet—and yet—Lois' heart was heavy as lead. She felt her lover was guilty. And she felt she must hide her secret of his last communication to her. She saw herself being cross-examined—"When did you last see this man?" But she would hide what he had said about watching at the works. How dreary it was—and how dreadful. Her life was ruined now, and nothing mattered any more. She must only behave with dignity, and submit to her own obliteration. For even if Will were never accused, she knew in her heart he was guilty. She knew it was over between them.

It was dawn among the yellow fog outside, and Lois, as she moved mechanically about her toilet, vaguely felt that all her days would arrive slowly struggling through a bleak fog. She felt an intense longing at this uncanny hour to slough the body's trammeled weariness and to issue at once into the new bright warmth of the far Dawn where a lover waited transfigured; is it so easy and pleasant in imagination to step out of the chill gray dampness of another terrestrial daybreak, straight into the sunshine of the eternal morning? And who can escape his hour? So Lois performed the meaningless routine of her toilet,[7] which at last she made meaningful when she took her black dress, and fastened a black jet brooch at her throat.

---

7. **toilet** [toi′lit]: act of dressing and grooming oneself.

Then she went downstairs and found her father eating a mutton chop. She quickly approached and kissed him on the forehead. Then she retreated to the other end of the table. Her father looked tired, even haggard.

"You are early," he said, after a while. Lois did not reply. Her father continued to eat for a few moments, then he said:

"Have a chop—here's one! Ring for a hot plate. Eh, what? Why not?"

Lois was insulted, but she gave no sign. She sat down and took a cup of coffee, making no pretense to eat. Her father was absorbed, and had forgotten her.

"Our Jack's not come home yet," he said at last.

Lois stirred faintly. "Hasn't he?" she said.

"No." There was silence for a time. Lois was frightened. Had something happened also to her brother? This fear was closer and more irksome.

"Selby's was cleaned out, gutted. We had a near shave of it——"

"You have no loss, Dadda?"

"Nothing to mention." After another silence, her father said:

"I'd rather be myself than William Selby. Of course it may merely be bad luck—you don't know. But whatever it was, I wouldn't like to add one to the list of fires just now. Selby was at the 'George' when it broke out—I don't know where the lad was——!"

"Father," broke in Lois, "why do you talk like that? Why do you talk as if Will had done it?" She ended suddenly. Her father looked at her pale, mute face.

"I don't talk as if Will had done it," he said. "I don't even think it."

Feeling she was going to cry, Lois rose and left the room. Her father sighed, and leaning his elbows on his knees, whistled faintly into the fire. He was not thinking about her.

Lois went down to the kitchen and asked Lucy, the parlor maid, to go out with her. She somehow shrank from going alone, lest people should stare at her overmuch: and she felt an overpowering impulse to go to the scene of the tragedy, to judge for herself.

The churches were chiming half-past eight when the young lady and the maid set off down the street. Nearer the fair, swarthy, thin-legged men were pushing barrels of water toward the market place, and the gypsy women, with hard brows, and dressed in tight velvet bodices, hurried along the pavement with jugs of milk, and great brass water ewers and loaves and breakfast parcels. People were just getting up, and in the poorer streets was a continual splash of tea leaves, flung out on to the cobblestones. A teapot came crashing down from an upper story just behind Lois, and she, starting round and looking up, thought that the trembling, drink-bleared man at the upper window, who was stupidly staring after his pot, had had designs on her life; and she went on her way shuddering at the grim tragedy of life.

In the dull October morning the ruined factory was black and ghastly. The window frames were all jagged, and the walls stood gaunt. Inside was a tangle of twisted debris, the iron, in parts red with bright rust, looking still hot; the charred wood was black and satiny; from disheveled heaps, sodden with water, a faint smoke rose dimly. Lois stood and looked. If he had done that! He might even be dead there, burned to ash and lost forever. It was almost soothing to feel so. He would be safe in the eternity which now she must hope in.

At her side the pretty, sympathetic maid chatted plaintively. Suddenly, from one of her lapses into silences, she exclaimed:

"Why if there isn't Mr. Jack!"

Lois turned suddenly and saw her brother and her lover approaching her. Both looked soiled, untidy and wan. Will had a black eye, some ten hours old, well colored. Lois turned very pale as they approached. They were looking gloomily at the factory, and for a moment did not notice the girls.

"I'll be jiggered if there ain't our Lois!" exclaimed Jack, the reprobate,[8] swearing under his breath.

---

8. **reprobate** [rep′rə bāt′]: unprincipled person.

"Oh, God!" exclaimed the other in disgust.

"Jack, where have you been?" said Lois sharply, in keen pain, not looking at her lover. Her sharp tone of suffering drove her lover to defend himself with an affectation of comic recklessness.

"In quod,"[9] replied her brother, smiling sickly.

"Jack!" cried his sister very sharply.

"Fact."

Will Selby shuffled on his feet and smiled, trying to turn away his face so that she should not see his black eye. She glanced at him. He felt her boundless anger and contempt, and with great courage he looked straight at her, smiling ironically. Unfortunately his smile would not go over his swollen eye, which remained grave and lurid.

"So I look pretty?" he inquired with a hateful twist of his lip.

"Very!" she replied.

"I thought I did," he replied. And he turned to look at his father's ruined works, and he felt miserable and stubborn. The girl standing there so clean and out of it all! Oh, God, he felt sick. He turned to go home.

The three went together, Lois silent in anger and resentment. Her brother was tired and overstrung, but not suppressed. He chattered on, blindly.

"It was a lark we had! We met Bob Osborne and Freddy Mansell coming down Poultry. There was a girl with some geese. She looked a tanger sitting there, all like statues, her and the geese. It was Will who began it. He offered her threepence and asked her to begin the show. She called him a—she called him something, and then somebody poked an old gander to stir him up, and somebody squirted him in the eye. He upped and squawked and started off with his neck out. Laugh! We nearly killed ourselves, keeping back those old birds with squirts and teasers. Oh, Lum! Those old geese, oh, scrimmy, they didn't know where to turn, they fairly went off their dots, coming at

<hr>

9. **quod** [kwäd]: British slang for "prison."

us right an' left, and such a row—it was fun, you never knew? Then the girl she got up and knocked somebody over the jaw, and we were right in for it. Well, in the end. Billy here got hold of her round the waist——"

"Oh, dry it up!" exclaimed Will bitterly.

Jack looked at him, laughed mirthlessly, and continued: "An' we said we'd buy her birds. So we got hold of one goose apiece—an' they took some holding. I can tell you—and off we set round the fair, Billy leading with the girl. The bloomin' geese squawked an' pecked. Laugh—I thought I should a' died. Well, then we wanted the girl to have her birds back—and then she fired up. She got some other chaps on her side, and there was a proper old row. The girl went tooth and nail for Will there—she was dead set against him. She gave him a black eye, by gum, and we went at it, I can tell you. It was a free fight, a beauty, an' we got run in. I don't know what became of the girl."

Lois surveyed the two men. There was no glimmer of a smile on her face, though the maid behind her was sniggering. Will was very bitter. He glanced at his sweetheart and at the ruined factory.

"How's dad taken it?" he asked, in a biting, almost humble tone.

"I don't know," she replied coldly. "Father's in an awful way. I believe everybody thinks you set the place on fire."

Lois drew herself up. She had delivered her blow. She drew herself up in cold condemnation and for a moment enjoyed her complete revenge. He was despicable, abject in his disheveled, disfigured, unwashed condition.

"Aye, well, they made a mistake for once," he replied, with a curl of the lip.

Curiously enough, they walked side by side as if they belonged to each other. She was his conscience-keeper. She was far from forgiving him, but she was still farther from letting him go. And he walked at her side like a boy who has to be punished before he can be exonerated. He submitted. But there was a genuine bitter contempt in the curl of his lip.

STUDY QUESTIONS

Recalling

1. Describe the country girl and Lois. What is each doing when she first appears?
2. According to the narrator, what is "the state of trade" at the time of the story?
3. What reason does Will give Lois for not joining her for dinner?
4. What news does Lois learn late at night from her mother? In what way does Lois think Will is involved in this event?
5. Briefly outline the pranks that cause Jack and Will to be arrested.

Interpreting

6. What connection does the story imply between trade, agriculture, and manufacturing?
7. In what ways does the story show an antagonism between classes? Between people and nature?
8. Describe the relationship between Lois and Will. In what ways does Lois show that she does not understand her own feelings for Will?
9. Why do you think Lawrence titled the story "Goose Fair"?

Extending

10. Who do you think started the fire? Why does Lawrence not tell us who started it?

LITERARY FOCUS

Characterization

Characterization is the personality of a character in a short story; it is also the method by which the author reveals that personality. Characters can be many-sided and changing, as surprising as real people, or they can be simple and one dimensional. They must, however, seem true to life and act in believable ways. To make characters credible, the author must supply **motivation,** stated or implied reasons for their behavior.

Characterization can be direct or indirect. With **direct characterization** the author directly states facts about a character's personality; with **indirect characterization** the author reveals a character's personality indirectly through the character's physical appearance, words, thoughts, and actions or through what other characters say about that character. In addition, the author may present a **flat character**—one with only one personality trait—or a **round,** or **complex, character**—one with many different, even contradictory, traits. A character can also be dynamic or static. **Dynamic characters** change in the course of a story because of the influence of events or other people. **Static characters** remain primarily the same throughout a story.

Thinking About Characterization

1. What motivation does the story imply for Jack and Will in their argument with the country girl?
2. What personality traits of the country girl do we learn through direct characterization? Through indirect characterization?
3. Explain how Lois is a realistic character, both round and dynamic.

COMPOSITION

Writing About a Symbol

■ Many objects, characters, and actions in Lawrence's fiction are symbolic. Write a brief essay about one symbol in "Goose Fair." First identify the symbol, and explain its meaning. Then discuss the significance of the symbol in the story as a whole, explaining how it relates to the theme of the story. *For help with this assignment, refer to Lesson 5 in the Writing About Literature Handbook at the back of this book.*

Writing a Sequel to the Story

■ Write a short continuation of "Goose Fair" in which Lois and the country girl meet. Write in omniscient point of view (page 000), and include narration, description, and dialogue. Be sure to explain the circumstances of their meeting and to demonstrate the fact that they come from very different backgrounds.

Virginia Woolf   *1882–1941*

In her critical essays Virginia Woolf set standards for modern fiction, and she met those standards in a string of finely detailed introspective novels and stories. Woolf grew up in a home where famous intellectuals and artists were frequent guests. Her father, Sir Leslie Stephen, was the first editor of the *Dictionary of National Biography,* and he introduced his children to great minds and great books. As an adult Woolf founded the Hogarth Press with her husband, Leonard Woolf, who was also a writer. They published much of their own work and became the center of the Bloomsbury Group, a circle of famous artists, writers, and philosophers that was named for a London neighborhood.

Woolf began her writing career as a literary critic. She used her reviews and essays to promote her strong opinions about what fiction should be. For example, she thought that writers could get close to real life only by basing their work in their own feelings. In 1915 she began to put her theories into practice in her first novel, *The Voyage Out.* She continued to refine her style in eight other novels—among them *Mrs. Dalloway* (1925) and *To the Lighthouse* (1927)—and four collections of short stories.

Woolf's work was a deliberate attempt to break the conventions of fiction. She saw life not as a series of carefully arranged bright lights but as "a luminous halo, a semi-transparent envelope surrounding us from the beginning of consciousness to the end." In other words, life is not a neatly arranged series of major events but a process we live every day. To be faithful to this idea, her fiction avoids plot as we know it and instead swirls through the consciousness of characters, revealing the essence of their lives. With James Joyce, Woolf was among the first to use this stream-of-consciousness technique. Her stories are quiet episodes seen through the minds of the characters. The intention was to "examine for a moment an ordinary mind on an ordinary day," to uncover people as they really are. By pouring out one thought after another in a steady stream, characters reveal who they are and what they feel. Mabel Waring is such a character, and in "The New Dress" she reveals herself to us through a constant stream of memories, thoughts, and observations.

Virginia Woolf

The New Dress

Mabel had her first serious suspicion that something was wrong as she took her cloak off and Mrs. Barnet, while handing her the mirror and touching the brushes and thus drawing her attention, perhaps rather markedly, to all the appliances for tidying and improving hair, complexion, clothes, which existed on the dressing table, confirmed the suspicion—that it was not right, not quite right, which growing stronger as she went upstairs and springing at her with conviction as she greeted Clarissa Dalloway, she went straight to the far end of the room, to a shaded corner where a looking glass hung and looked. No! It was not *right*. And at once the misery which she always tried to hide, the profound dissatisfaction—the sense she had had, ever since she was a child, of being inferior to other people—set upon her, relentlessly, remorselessly, with an intensity which she could not beat off, as she would when she woke at night at home, by reading Borrow[1] or Scott;[2] for oh these men, oh these women, all were thinking—"What's Mabel wearing? What a fright she looks! What a hideous new dress!"—their eyelids flickering as they came up and then their lids shutting rather tight. It was her own appalling inadequacy; her cowardice; her mean, water-sprinkled blood that depressed her. And at once the whole of the room where, for ever so many hours, she had planned with the little dressmaker how it was to go, seemed sordid, repulsive; and her own drawing room so shabby, and herself, going out, puffed up with vanity as she touched the letters on the hall table and said, "How dull!" to show off— all this now seemed unutterably silly, paltry, and provincial. All this had been absolutely de-stroyed, shown up, exploded, the moment she came into Mrs. Dalloway's drawing room.

What she had thought that evening when, sitting over the teacups, Mrs. Dalloway's invitation came, was that, of course, she could not be fashionable. It was absurd to pretend it even—fashion meant cut, meant style, meant thirty guineas at least—but why not be original? Why not be herself, anyhow? And, getting up, she had taken that old fashion book of her mother's, a Paris fashion book of the time of the Empire, and had thought how much prettier, more dignified, and more womanly they were then, and so set herself—oh, it was foolish—trying to be like them, pluming herself in fact, upon being modest and old-fashioned and very charming, giving herself up, no doubt about it, to an orgy of self-love, which deserved to be chastised, and so rigged herself out like this.

But she dared not look in the glass. She could not face the whole horror—the pale yellow, idiotically old-fashioned silk dress with its long skirt and its high sleeves and its waist and all the things that looked so charming in the fashion book, but not on her, not among all these ordinary people. She felt like a dressmaker's dummy standing there, for young people to stick pins into.

"But, my dear, it's perfectly charming!" Rose Shaw said, looking her up and down with that little satirical pucker of the lips which she expected—Rose herself being dressed in the height of the fashion, precisely like everybody else, always.

We are all like flies trying to crawl over the edge of the saucer, Mabel thought, and repeated the phrase as if she were crossing herself, as if she were trying to find some spell to annul this pain, to make this agony endurable. Tags of Shakespeare, lines from books she had read ages ago, suddenly came to her when she

---

1. **Borrow:** George Borrow (1803–1881). English traveler and novelist.
2. **Scott:** Sir Walter Scott (1771–1827), Scottish poet, novelist, journalist.

was in agony, and she repeated them over and over again. "Flies trying to crawl," she repeated. If she could say that over often enough and make herself see the flies, she would become numb, chill, frozen, dumb. Now she could see flies crawling slowly out of a saucer of milk with their wings stuck together; and she strained and strained (standing in front of the looking glass, listening to Rose Shaw) to make herself see Rose Shaw and all the other people there as flies, trying to hoist themselves out of something, or into something, meager, insignificant, toiling flies. But she could not see them like that, not other people. She saw herself like that—she was a fly, but the others were dragonflies, butterflies, beautiful insects, dancing, fluttering, skimming, while she alone dragged herself up out of the saucer. (Envy and spite, the most detestable of the vices, were her chief faults.)

"I feel like some dowdy, decrepit, horribly dingy old fly," she said, making Robert Haydon stop just to hear her say that, just to reassure herself by furbishing up a poor weak-kneed phrase and so showing how detached she was, how witty, that she did not feel in the least out of anything. And, of course, Robert Haydon answered something quite polite, quite insincere, which she saw through instantly, and said to herself, directly he went (again from some book), "Lies, lies, lies!" For a party makes things either much more real, or much less real, she thought; she saw in a flash to the bottom of Robert Haydon's heart; she saw through everything. She saw the truth. *This* was true, this drawing room, this self, and the other false. Miss Milan's little workroom was really terribly hot, stuffy, sordid. It smelled of clothes and cabbage cooking; and yet, when Miss Milan put the glass in her hand, and she looked at herself with the dress on, finished, an extraordinary bliss shot through her heart. Suffused with light, she sprang into existence. Rid of cares and wrinkles, what she had dreamed of herself was there—a beautiful woman. Just for a second (she had not dared look longer, Miss Milan wanted to know about the length of the skirt), there looked at her, framed in the scrolloping mahogany, a gray-white, mysteriously smiling, charming girl, the core of herself, the soul of herself; and it was not vanity only, not only self-love that made her think it good, tender, and true. Miss Milan said that the skirt could not well be longer; if anything the skirt, said Miss Milan, puckering her forehead, considering with all her wits about her, must be shorter; and she felt, suddenly, honestly, full of love for Miss Milan, much, much fonder of Miss Milan than of anyone in the whole world, and

could have cried for pity that she should be crawling on the floor with her mouth full of pins, and her face red and her eyes bulging— that one human being should be doing this for another, and she saw them all as human beings merely, and herself going off to her party, and Miss Milan pulling the cover over the canary's cage, or letting him pick a hempseed from between her lips, and the thought of it, of this side of human nature and its patience and its endurance and its being content with such miserable, scanty, sordid little pleasures filled her eyes with tears.

And now the whole thing had vanished. The dress, the room, the love, the pity, the scrolloping looking glass, and the canary's cage—all had vanished, and here she was in a corner of Mrs. Dalloway's drawing room, suffering tortures, woken wide awake to reality.

But it was all so paltry, weak-blooded, and petty-minded to care so much at her age with two children, to be still so utterly dependent on people's opinions and not have principles or convictions, not to be able to say as other people did, "There's Shakespeare! There's death! We're all weevils in a captain's biscuit"—or whatever it was that people did say.

She faced herself straight in the glass; she pecked at her left shoulder; she issued out into the room, as if spears were thrown at her yellow dress from all sides. But instead of looking fierce or tragic, as Rose Shaw would have done—Rose would have looked like Boadicea[3] —she looked foolish and self-conscious, and simpered like a schoolgirl and slouched across the room, positively slinking, as if she were a beaten mongrel, and looked at a picture, an engraving. As if one went to a party to look at a picture! Everybody knew why she did it—it was from shame, from humiliation.

"Now the fly's in the saucer," she said to herself, "right in the middle, and can't get out,

and the milk," she thought, rigidly staring at the picture, "is sticking its wings together."

"It's so old-fashioned," she said to Charles Burt, making him stop (which by itself he hated) on his way to talk to someone else.

She meant, or she tried to make herself think that she meant, that it was the picture and not her dress that was old-fashioned. And one word of praise, one word of affection from Charles would have made all the difference to her at the moment. If he had only said, "Mabel, you're looking charming tonight!" it would have changed her life. But then she ought to have been truthful and direct. Charles said nothing of the kind, of course. He was malice itself. He always saw through one, especially if one were feeling particularly mean, paltry, or feeble-minded.

"Mabel's got a new dress!" he said, and the poor fly was absolutely shoved into the middle of the saucer. Really, he would like her to drown, she believed. He had no heart, no fundamental kindness, only a veneer of friendliness. Miss Milan was much more real, much kinder. If only one could feel that and stick to it always. "Why," she asked herself—replying to Charles much too pertly, letting him see that she was out of temper, or "ruffled" as he called it ("Rather ruffled?" he said and went on to laugh at her with some woman over there)—"Why," she asked herself, "can't I feel one thing always, feel quite sure that Miss Milan is right, and Charles wrong and stick to it, feel sure about the canary and pity and love and not be whipped all round in a second by coming into a room full of people?" It was her odious, weak, vacillating character again, always giving at the critical moment and not being seriously interested in conchology, etymology, botany, archaeology, cutting up potatoes and watching them fructify[4] like Mary Dennis, like Violet Searle.

Then Mrs. Holman, seeing her standing there, bore down upon her. Of course a thing

<hr />

3. **Boadicea** [bō ad′ə sē′ə]: queen in ancient Britain who led a revolt against the Romans, was defeated, and poisoned herself in A.D. 62.

<hr />

4. **fructify**: bear fruit.

like a dress was beneath Mrs. Holman's notice, with her family always tumbling downstairs or having the scarlet fever. Could Mabel tell her if Elmthorpe was ever let for August and September? Oh, it was a conversation that bored her unutterably!—it made her furious to be treated like a house agent or a messenger boy, to be made use of. Not to have value, that was it, she thought, trying to grasp something hard, something real, while she tried to answer sensibly about the bathroom and the south aspect and the hot water to the top of the house; and all the time she could see little bits of her yellow dress in the round looking glass which made them all the size of boot buttons or tadpoles; and it was amazing to think how much humiliation and agony and self-loathing and effort and passionate ups and downs of feeling were contained in a thing the size of a threepenny bit. And what was still odder, this thing, this Mabel Waring, was separate, quite disconnected; and though Mrs. Holman (the black button) was leaning forward and telling her how her eldest boy had strained his heart running, she could see her, too, quite detached in the looking glass, and it was impossible that the black dot, leaning forward, gesticulating, should make the yellow dot, sitting solitary, self-centered, feel what the black dot was feeling, yet they pretended.

"So impossible to keep boys quiet"—that was the kind of thing one said.

And Mrs. Holman, who could never get enough sympathy and snatched what little there was greedily, as if it were her right (but she deserved much more for there was her little girl who had come down this morning with a swollen kneejoint), took this miserable offering and looked at it suspiciously, grudgingly, as if it were a halfpenny when it ought to have been a pound and put it away in her purse, must put up with it, mean and miserly though it was, times being hard, so very hard; and on she went, creaking, injured Mrs. Holman, about the girl with the swollen joints. Ah, it was tragic, this greed, this clamor of human beings, like a row of cormorants,[5] barking and flapping their wings for sympathy—it was tragic, could one have felt it and not merely pretended to feel it!

But in her yellow dress tonight she could not wring out one drop more; she wanted it all, all for herself. She knew (she kept on looking into the glass, dipping into that dreadfully showing up blue pool) that she was condemned, despised, left like this in a backwater, because of her being like this a feeble, vacillating creature; and it seemed to her that the yellow dress was a penance which she had deserved, and if she had been dressed like Rose Shaw, in lovely, clinging green with a ruffle of swansdown, she would have deserved that; and she thought that there was no escape for her—none whatever. But it was not her fault altogether, after all. It was being one of a family of ten; never having money enough, always skimping and paring; and her mother carrying great cans, and the linoleum worn on the stair edges, and one sordid little domestic tragedy after another—nothing catastrophic, the sheep farm failing, but not utterly; her eldest brother marrying beneath him but not very much—there was no romance, nothing extreme about them all. They petered out respectably in seaside resorts; every watering place had one of her aunts even now asleep in some lodging with the front windows not quite facing the sea. That was so like them—they had to squint at things always. And she had done the same—she was just like her aunts. For all her dreams of living in India, married to some hero like Sir Henry Lawrence,[6] some empire builder (still the sight of a native in a turban filled her with romance), she had failed utterly. She had married Hubert, with his safe, permanent underling's job in the Law Courts, and they managed tolerably in a smallish house without proper

---

5. **cormorants:** large swimming and diving birds with webbed feet and voracious appetites. Greedy people are sometimes referred to as cormorants.
6. **Sir Henry Lawrence:** English general and administrator in India (1806–1857).

maids and hash when she was alone or just bread and butter, but now and then—Mrs. Holman was off, thinking her the most dried up, unsympathetic twig she had ever met, absurdly dressed, too, and would tell everyone about Mabel's fantastic appearance—now and then, thought Mabel Waring, left alone on the blue sofa, punching the cushion in order to look occupied, for she would not join Charles Burt and Rose Shaw, chattering like magpies and perhaps laughing at her by the fireplace—now and then, there did come to her delicious moments, reading the other night in bed, for instance, or down by the sea on the sand in the sun at Easter—let her recall it—a great tuft of pale sand grass standing all twisted like a shock of spears against the sky, which was blue like a smooth china egg, so firm, so hard, and then the melody of the waves—"Hush, hush," they said, and the children's shouts paddling—yes, it was a divine moment, and there she lay, she felt, in the hand of the Goddess who was the world; rather a hard-hearted, but very beautiful Goddess, a little lamb laid on the altar (one did think these silly things, and it didn't matter so long as one never said them). And also with Hubert sometimes she had quite unexpectedly—carving the mutton for Sunday lunch, for no reason, opening a letter, coming into a room—divine moments, when she said to herself (for she would never say this to anybody else), "This is it. This has happened. This is it!" And the other way about it was equally surprising—that is, when everything was arranged—music, weather, holidays, every reason for happiness was there—then nothing happened at all. One wasn't happy. It was flat, just flat, that was all.

Her wretched self again, no doubt! She had always been a fretful, weak, unsatisfactory mother, a wobbly wife, lolling about in a kind of twilight existence with nothing very clear or very bold, or more one thing than another, like all her brothers and sisters, except perhaps Herbert—they were all the same poor water-veined creatures who did nothing. Then in the midst of this creeping, crawling life, suddenly she was on the crest of a wave. That wretched fly—where had she read the story that kept coming into her mind about the fly and the saucer?—struggled out. Yes, she had those moments. But now that she was forty, they might come more and more seldom. By degrees she would cease to struggle any more. But that was deplorable! That was not to be endured! That made her feel ashamed of herself!

She would go to the London Library tomorrow. She would find some wonderful, helpful, astonishing book, quite by chance, a book by a clergyman, by an American no one had ever heard of; or she would walk down the Strand and drop, accidentally, into a hall where a miner was telling about the life in the pit, and suddenly she would become a new person. She would be absolutely transformed. She would wear a uniform; she would be called Sister Somebody; she would never give a thought to clothes again. And forever after she would be perfectly clear about Charles Burt and Miss Milan and this room and that room; and it would be always, day after day, as if she were lying in the sun or carving the mutton. It would be it!

So she got up from the blue sofa, and the yellow button in the looking glass got up too, and she waved her hand to Charles and Rose to show them she did not depend on them one scrap, and the yellow button moved out of the looking glass, and all the spears were gathered into her breast as she walked toward Mrs. Dalloway and said, "Good night."

"But it's too early to go," said Mrs. Dalloway, who was always so charming.

"I'm afraid I must," said Mabel Waring. "But," she added in her weak, wobbly voice which only sounded ridiculous when she tried to strengthen it, "I have enjoyed myself enormously."

"I have enjoyed myself," she said to Mr. Dalloway, whom she met on the stairs.

"Lies, lies, lies!" she said to herself, going downstairs, and "Right in the saucer!" she said to herself as she thanked Mrs. Barnet for helping her and wrapped herself round and round and round in the Chinese cloak she had worn these twenty years.

STUDY QUESTIONS

Recalling

1. How long has Mabel had feelings of inferiority? What brings out these feelings at the party?
2. Find at least three flaws that Mabel sees in her own personality.
3. Briefly outline Mabel's family background and marriage.
4. Give at least three examples of what Mabel considers happy moments from her everyday life.

Interpreting

5. What do we learn about Mabel from her reasons for choosing the new dress?
6. What kinds of activity and people does Mabel most and least enjoy? Explain how her preferences relate to her upbringing.
7. Explain how Mabel's plan to become a new person reveals a cause of her unhappiness.
8. In what ways does her sense of inferiority become a barrier between Mabel and other people?

Extending

9. In what ways can self-criticism be helpful? In what ways can it be harmful?

LITERARY FOCUS

Stream of Consciousness

Stream of consciousness is a term originated by American psychologist William James to describe human thought as a continuous flow of observation and reflection. Our minds jump without apparent logic and without rest from one thought to another. In literature **stream of consciousness** is a method of writing that imitates human thought with a continuous and formless flow of ideas, feelings, observations, and memories. Unlike stories with conventional plots, stream-of-consciousness stories may change topic suddenly and illogically in order to imitate the way the mind suddenly shifts from one thought to another. The author seldom speaks directly to the reader but allows characters to reveal themselves through their thoughts. Stream of consciousness can be written in first or third person. The technique was

pioneered by James Joyce in his first novel, *A Portrait of the Artist as a Young Man.*

Thinking About Stream of Consciousness

1. In what sense is "The New Dress" a stream-of-consciousness story?
2. Find at least two examples of sudden shifts in the narrative that imitate the way that the mind jumps from one thought to another.

COMPOSITION

Writing About Character

■ Because "The New Dress" is a stream-of-consciousness story, we learn about Mabel indirectly from her own thoughts and actions. Describe your impressions of Mabel's personality, and explain how the story gave you the impressions. To do this, identify at least four personality traits; be sure that at least two traits are positive traits that Mabel herself may not be aware of. For each trait explain what specific thoughts or actions in the story revealed the trait to you.

Writing with Stream-of-Consciousness Technique

■ Write a short sketch of a person whose problem is the opposite of Mabel's, a superiority complex. Use the stream-of-consciousness technique, and be sure that everything in your sketch is in the form of your character's thoughts. First record your character's impressions of a setting in which other people are present. Then give the character's impressions of other people and of himself or herself.

COMPARING WRITERS

■ Choose two or more of the stories in this section: "The Lagoon," "The Japanese Quince," "Araby," "The Singing Lesson," "Goose Fair," and "The New Dress." Compare the ways in which the stories delve into the minds of their characters. To what extent is external reality pictured in each story? How deeply does each story delve into a character's thoughts? How much sympathy is created for the character by revealing that character's thoughts?

George Orwell   *1903–1950*

George Orwell wrote fiction and nonfiction that was inspired by a strong social conscience. He was born Eric Blair in Bengal, India. His father was a minor customs official who sacrificed to send his son to preparatory schools in England. Eric felt inferior among his wealthier schoolmates, and human relationships were always difficult for him. The class distinctions that he learned at school also made him sympathetic to the working class and to victims of injustice. Such attitudes later influenced some of his most successful writing, which includes novels, essays, and autobiographical nonfiction.

Instead of going to college, Orwell joined the Indian Imperial Police in Burma in southeast Asia. He worked there five years and developed a permanent distaste for imperialism, or the maintenance of a colonial empire such as the colonies England had in Asia. This experience also provided the material for *Burmese Days* (1934), his first novel, and the well-known essay "Shooting an Elephant." After returning to Europe, Orwell held a number of menial jobs that kept him on the edge of poverty. From this experience he wrote *Down and Out in Paris and London* (1933). In 1936 he was wounded while fighting for the Loyalists (those fighting against military dictatorship) in the Spanish civil war. He recorded his observations of the war and his disillusionment with the infighting of the Loyalists in *Homage to Catalonia* (1938).

Orwell was inspired by his experiences in Spain and by World War II to write the novels for which he is best known. *Animal Farm* (1945) is a fable and a satire on dictatorships. *Nineteen Eighty-Four* (1949) is Orwell's prophetic warning about the spread of totalitarianism. Both novels demonstrate his chief concern as a writer: to alert humanity to the evils of political tyranny.

"Why I Write" is an excerpt from Orwell's autobiographical work, *Such, Such Were the Joys* (1945). The essay recounts the various influences on the author's youth and on his writing career. Orwell's statements about writing reveal a great deal about the craft. They also show us a sensitive, solitary man who felt a unique sense of responsibility as a writer.

George Orwell

Why I Write

From a very early age, perhaps the age of five or six, I knew that when I grew up I should be a writer. Between the ages of about seventeen and twenty-four I tried to abandon this idea, but I did so with the consciousness that I was outraging my true nature and that sooner or later I should have to settle down and write books.

I was the middle child of three, but there was a gap of five years on either side, and I barely saw my father before I was eight. For this and other reasons I was somewhat lonely, and I soon developed disagreeable mannerisms which made me unpopular throughout my school days. I had the lonely child's habit of making up stories and holding conversations with imaginary persons, and I think from the very start my literary ambitions were mixed up with the feeling of being isolated and undervalued. I knew that I had a facility with words and a power of facing unpleasant facts, and I felt that this created a sort of private world in which I could get my own back for my failure in everyday life. Nevertheless the volume of serious—*i.e.* seriously intended—writing which I produced all through my childhood and boyhood would not amount to half a dozen pages. I wrote my first poem at the age of four or five, my mother taking it down to dictation. I cannot remember anything about it except that it was about a tiger and the tiger had "chairlike teeth"—a good enough phrase, but I fancy the poem was a plagiarism of Blake's "Tiger, Tiger." At eleven, when the war of 1914–18 broke out, I wrote a patriotic poem which was printed in the local newspaper, as was another, two years later, on the death of Kitchener.[1] From time to time, when I was a bit older, I wrote bad and usually unfinished "nature poems" in the Georgian style.[2] I also, about twice, attempted a short story which was a ghastly failure. That was the total of the would-be serious work that I actually set down on paper during all those years.

However, throughout this time I did in a sense engage in literary activities. To begin with there was the made-to-order stuff which I produced quickly, easily and without much pleasure to myself. Apart from school work, I wrote *vers d'occasion,*[3] semicomic poems which I could turn out at what now seems to me astonishing speed—at fourteen I wrote a whole rhyming play, in imitation of Aristophanes,[4] in about a week—and helped to edit school magazines, both printed and in manuscript. These magazines were the most pitiful burlesque[5] stuff that you could imagine, and I took far less trouble with them than I now would with the cheapest journalism. But side by side with all this, for fifteen years or more, I was carrying out a literary exercise of a quite different kind: this was the making up of a continuous "story" about myself, a sort of diary existing only in the mind. I believe this is a common habit of children and adolescents. As a very small child I used to imagine that I was, say, Robin Hood, and picture myself as the hero of thrilling adventures, but quite soon my "story" ceased to be narcissistic in a crude way and became more and more a mere description of what I was doing and the things I saw. For minutes at a time this kind of thing would be running through my head: "He pushed the

---

1. **Kitchener:** Horatio Herbert Kitchener (1850–1916), British statesman and military officer, who drowned when his ship was torpedoed during World War I.

2. **Georgian style:** traditional style of poetry characteristic of the first decade in the reign of King George V, who ruled from 1910 to 1936.
3. *vers d'occasion* [vãr′dō kä zyōn′]: verses for special occasions.
4. **Aristophanes** [ar′is tof′ə nēz′] (448?–385 B.C.): Greek comic dramatist.
5. **burlesque** [bər lesk′]: comic or satirical imitation of serious written work.

door open and entered the room. A yellow beam of sunlight, filtering through the muslin curtains, slanted on to the table, where a matchbox, half open, lay beside the inkpot. With his right hand in his pocket he moved across to the window. Down in the street a tortoiseshell cat was chasing a dead leaf," etc., etc. This habit continued till I was about twenty-five, right through my nonliterary years. Although I had to search, and did search, for the right words, I seemed to be making this descriptive effort almost against my will, under a kind of compulsion from outside. The "story" must, I suppose, have reflected the styles of the various writers I admired at different ages, but so far as I remember it always had the same meticulous descriptive quality.

When I was about sixteen I suddenly discovered the joy of mere words, *i.e.* the sounds and associations of words. The lines from *Paradise Lost*[6]—

So hee with difficulty and labour hard
Moved on: with difficulty and labour hee,

which do not now seem to me so very wonderful, sent shivers down my backbone; and the spelling "hee" for "he" was an added pleasure. As for the need to describe things, I knew all about it already. So it is clear what kind of books I wanted to write, in so far as I could be said to want to write books at that time. I wanted to write enormous naturalistic novels with unhappy endings, full of detailed descriptions and arresting similes, and also full of purple passages in which words were used partly for the sake of their sound. And in fact my first completed novel, *Burmese Days,* which I wrote when I was thirty but projected much earlier, is rather that kind of book.

I give all this background information because I do not think one can assess a writer's motives without knowing something of his early development. His subject matter will be determined by the age he lives in—at least this is true in tumultuous, revolutionary ages like our own—but before he ever begins to write he will have acquired an emotional attitude from which he will never completely escape. It is his job, no doubt, to discipline his temperament and avoid getting stuck at some immature stage, or in some perverse mood: but if he escapes from his early influences altogether, he will have killed his impulse to write. Putting aside the need to earn a living, I think there are four great motives for writing, at any rate for writing prose. They exist in different degrees in every writer, and in any one writer the proportions will vary from time to time, according to the atmosphere in which he is living. They are:

(1) Sheer egoism. Desire to seem clever, to be talked about, to be remembered after death, to get your own back on grownups who snubbed you in childhood, etc., etc. It is humbug to pretend that this is not a motive, and a strong one. Writers share this characteristic with scientists, artists, politicians, lawyers, soldiers, successful businessmen—in short, with the whole top crust of humanity. The great mass of human beings are not acutely selfish. After the age of about thirty they abandon individual ambition—in many cases, indeed, they almost abandon the sense of being individuals at all—and live chiefly for others, or are simply smothered under drudgery. But there is also the minority of gifted, willful people who are determined to live their own lives to the end, and writers belong in this class. Serious writers, I should say, are on the whole more vain and self-centered than journalists, though less interested in money.

(2) Aesthetic enthusiasm. Perception of beauty in the external world, or, on the other hand, in words and their right arrangement. Pleasure in the impact of one sound on another, in the firmness of good prose or the rhythm of a good story. Desire to share an experience which one feels is valuable and ought not to be missed. The aesthetic motive is very feeble in a lot of writers, but even a pamphleteer or a writer of textbooks will have pet words and phrases which appeal to him for

------

6. *Paradise Lost:* major work by English poet John Milton (1608–1674). See page 226.

nonutilitarian reasons; or he may feel strongly about typography, width of margins, etc. Above the level of a railway guide, no book is quite free from aesthetic considerations.

(3) Historical impulse. Desire to see things as they are, to find out true facts and store them up for the use of posterity.

(4) Political purpose—using the word "political" in the widest possible sense. Desire to push the world in a certain direction, to alter other people's idea of the kind of society that they should strive after. Once again, no book is genuinely free from political bias. The opinion that art should have nothing to do with politics is itself a political attitude.

It can be seen how these various impulses must war against one another, and how they must fluctuate from person to person and from time to time. By nature—taking your "nature" to be the state you have attained when you are first adult—I am a person in whom the first three motives would outweigh the fourth. In a peaceful age I might have written ornate or merely descriptive books, and might have remained almost unaware of my political loyalties. As it is I have been forced into becoming a sort of pamphleteer. First I spent five years in an unsuitable profession (the Indian Imperial Police, in Burma), and then I underwent poverty and the sense of failure. This increased my natural hatred of authority and made me for the first time fully aware of the existence of the working classes, and the job in Burma had given me some understanding of the nature of imperialism: but these experiences were not enough to give me an accurate political orientation. Then came Hitler,[7] the Spanish civil war,[8] etc. By the end of 1935 I had still failed to reach a firm decision. I remember a little poem that I wrote at that date, expressing my dilemma:

A happy vicar I might have been
Two hundred years ago,
To preach upon eternal doom
And watch my walnuts grow;

But born, alas, in an evil time,
I missed that pleasant haven,
For the hair has grown on my upper lip
And the clergy are all clean-shaven.

And later still the times were good,
We were so easy to please,
We rocked our troubled thoughts to sleep
On the bosoms of the trees.

All ignorant we dared to own
The joys we now dissemble;
The greenfinch on the apple bough
Could make my enemies tremble.

But girls' bellies and apricots,
Roach in a shaded stream,
Horses, ducks in flight at dawn,
All these are a dream.

It is forbidden to dream again;
We maim our joys or hide them;
Horses are made of chromium steel
And little fat men shall ride them.

I am the worm who never turned,
The eunuch without a harem;
Between the priest and the commissar[9]
I walk like Eugene Aram,[10]

And the commissar is telling my fortune
While the radio plays,
But the priest has promised an Austin
    Seven,[11]
For Duggie always pays.[12]

7. **Hitler:** Adolf Hitler (1889–1945), dictator of Germany (1933–1945).
8. **Spanish civil war:** war in Spain (1936–1939) between the right-wing nationalists, who were led by General Francisco Franco and supported by the fascist governments of Germany and Italy, and the Loyalists, who included liberals, Communists, and other left-wing groups.

9. **commissar:** Communist party official responsible for enforcing party loyalty.
10. **Eugene Aram** (1704–1759): English scholar who was convicted of murder and executed. He is remembered in the novel of the same name by Edward Bulwer-Lytton.
11. **Austin Seven:** early, popular model of automobile manufactured by the Austin Motor Company of England.
12. **Duggie . . . pays:** advertisement of Doug Stewart, whose bet-taking business was widely known.

I dreamed I dwelt in marble halls,
And woke to find it true;
I wasn't born for an age like this;
Was Smith? Was Jones? Were you?

The Spanish war and other events in 1936–37 turned the scale and thereafter I knew where I stood. Every line of serious work that I have written since 1936 has been written, directly or indirectly, *against* totalitarianism and *for* democratic socialism, as I understand it. It seems to me nonsense, in a period like our own, to think that one can avoid writing of such subjects. Everyone writes of them in one guise or another. It is simply a question of which side one takes and what approach one follows. And the more one is conscious of one's political bias, the more chance one has of acting politically without sacrificing one's aesthetic and intellectual integrity.

What I have most wanted to do throughout the past ten years is to make political writing into an art. My starting point is always a feeling of partisanship, a sense of injustice. When I sit down to write a book, I do not say to myself, "I am going to produce a work of art." I write it because there is some lie that I want to expose, some fact to which I want to draw attention, and my initial concern is to get a hearing. But I could not do the work of writing a book, or even a long magazine article, if it were not also an aesthetic experience. Anyone who cares to examine my work will see that even when it is downright propaganda it contains much that a full-time politician would consider irrelevant. I am not able, and I do not want, completely to abandon the world-view that I acquired in childhood. So long as I remain alive and well I shall continue to feel strongly about prose style, to love the surface of the earth, and to take a pleasure in solid objects and scraps of useless information. It is no use trying to suppress that side of myself. The job is to reconcile my ingrained likes and dislikes with the essentially public, nonindividual activities that this age forces on all of us.

It is not easy. It raises problems of construction and of language, and it raises in a new way the problem of truthfulness. Let me give just one example of the cruder kind of difficulty that arises. My book about the Spanish civil war, *Homage to Catalonia,* is, of course, a frankly political book, but in the main it is written with a certain detachment and regard for form. I did try very hard in it to tell the whole truth without violating my literary instincts. But among other things it contains a long chapter, full of newspaper quotations and the like, defending the Trotskyists[13] who were accused of plotting with Franco. Clearly such a chapter, which after a year or two would lose its interest for any ordinary reader, must ruin the book. A critic whom I respect read me a lecture about it. "Why did you put in all that stuff?" he said. "You've turned what might have been a good book into journalism." What he said was true, but I could not have done otherwise. I happened to know what very few people in England had been allowed to know, that innocent men were being falsely accused. If I had not been angry about that I should never have written the book.

In one form or another this problem comes up again. The problem of language is subtler and would take too long to discuss. I will only say that of late years I have tried to write less picturesquely and more exactly. In any case I find that by the time you have perfected any style of writing, you have always outgrown it. *Animal Farm*[14] was the first book in which I tried, with full consciousness of what I was *doing,* to fuse political purpose and artistic purpose into one whole. I have not written a novel for seven years, but I hope to write another fairly soon. It is bound to be a failure, every book is a failure, but I do know with some clarity what kind of book I want to write. Looking back through the last page or two,

---

13. **Trotskyists:** adherents to the radically leftist Communist politics of Leon Trotsky (1879–1940), a Russian revolutionary leader, who advocated world revolution.
14. ***Animal Farm:*** political satire directed against totalitarian governments.

I see that I have made it appear as though my motives in writing were wholly public-spirited. I don't want to leave that as the final impression. All writers are vain, selfish and lazy, and at the very bottom of their motives there lies a mystery. Writing a book is a horrible, exhausting struggle, like a long bout of some painful illness. One would never undertake such a thing if one were not driven on by some demon whom one can neither resist nor understand. For all one knows that demon is simply the same instinct that makes a baby squall for attention. And yet it is also true that one can write nothing readable unless one constantly struggles to efface one's own personality. Good prose is like a window pane. I cannot say with certainty which of my motives are the strongest, but I know which of them deserve to be followed. And looking back through my work, I see that it is invariably where I lacked a *political* purpose that I wrote lifeless books and was betrayed into purple passages, sentences without meaning, decorative adjectives and humbug generally.

STUDY QUESTIONS

Recalling

1. Why was Orwell a lonely and unpopular child? Explain how he relates his childhood loneliness to his desire to write.
2. Describe the diary that Orwell created in his mind as a youth.
3. According to Orwell, what are the four great motives for writing?
4. What has Orwell's aim been for "the last ten years"? What is his purpose when he sits down to write a book?
5. What adjectives does Orwell use to describe writers in the last paragraph of the essay?

Interpreting

6. In what way has the young Orwell's diary of the mind influenced his adult career?
7. According to Orwell's poem, which motive for writing is strongest? Why?
8. Explain Orwell's blend of political purpose and aesthetic enthusiasm.
9. What is Orwell's opinion of writers?

Extending

10. Based on your own favorite books, explain which motive for writing you most respect.

VIEWPOINT

As "Why I Write" demonstrates, much of Orwell's work is autobiographical. One author wrote that Orwell was a young man who suffered a good many torments of mind and spirit.

—R. Rovere, *The Orwell Reader*

■ What torments of childhood and adulthood are revealed in the essay? Based on Orwell's discussion of his writing, explain how these torments can be found in his work.

COMPOSITION

Writing About Nonfiction

■ Any essay must be written with a purpose in mind. The purpose is the central idea that the author tries to convey in the essay. Explain the purpose of "Why I Write." First describe Orwell's stated purpose for writing in general and his specific purpose for writing this essay. Then explain how he uses personal recollections to achieve this purpose. *For help with this assignment, refer to Lesson 4 in the Writing About Literature Handbook at the back of this book.*

Writing an Expository Essay

■ Orwell lists four motives that inspire a writer. Explain at least three motives that drive a person in any specific career. If you wish, you may use one of the following: (a) a student, (b) a professional athlete, (c) an actor, or (d) a newspaper reporter. First identify the occupation, and give the motives. Then explain how each motive is a driving force, giving reasons and examples.

Samuel Beckett *born 1906*

Some twentieth-century writers focus on the minds of their characters to find the essence of reality and truth. Samuel Beckett differs from them because he denies the existence of absolute, universal reality. According to Beckett, the only thing that humankind can be sure of is that it exists. His work is free of abstractions like truth and beauty, goodness and evil. Beckett aims to communicate an experience instead of a message. His readers try to feel that experience, not find meaning in it.

The lack of meaning in his work stems from Beckett's belief that life itself has no meaning that we can discover with any certainty. To him life consists of intellectual games that we create to pass the time. The games, the way we pass the time, are the essence of life for Beckett, and they make up the action in his plays, novels, stories, and film scripts.

Samuel Beckett was born in Dublin, Ireland, and attended Trinity College there. He taught literature at colleges in Ireland and France, settling for a time in Paris, where he was a friend of James Joyce. Beckett often helped Joyce, who was nearly blind, by taking dictation and copying out portions of Joyce's books. During World War II Beckett worked for a time with the French resistance to German occupation. He also served with the Irish Red Cross.

After the war Beckett wrote his most famous play, *Waiting for Godot* (1953). The play is a cornerstone of what is called **theater of the absurd**, a kind of drama that illustrates life's supposed futility with formless, plotless plays. The first line of *Godot* is "Nothing to be done," and nothing happens in the play. Two people await the arrival of someone who never appears. To Beckett this pointless waiting is an experience that captures life's essence.

"Still" is a short prose work describing a concrete experience. Read it carefully in order to live the experience that Beckett is communicating. Then decide for yourself whether the author is also implying a message.

Samuel Beckett

Still

Bright at last close of a dark day the sun shines out at last and goes down. Sitting quite still at valley window normally turn head now and see it the sun low in the southwest sinking. Even get up certain moods and go stand by western window quite still watching it sink and then the afterglow. Always quite still some reason some time past this hour at open window facing south in small upright wicker chair with armrests. Eyes stare out unseeing till first movement some time past close though unseeing still while still light. Quite still again then all quite quiet apparently till eyes open again while still light though less. Normally turn head now ninety degrees to watch sun which if already gone then fading afterglow. Even get up certain moods and go stand by western window till quite dark and even some evenings some reason long after. Eyes then open again while still light and close again in what if not quite a single movement almost. Quite still again then at open window facing south over the valley in this wicker chair though actually close inspection not still at all but trembling all over. Close inspection namely detail by detail all over to add up finally to this whole not still at all but trembling all over. But casually in this failing light impression dead still even the hands clearly trembling and the breast faint rise and fall. Legs side by side broken right angles at the knees as in that old statue some old god twanged at sunrise and again at sunset. Trunk likewise dead plumb right up to top of skull seen from behind including nape clear of chairback. Arms likewise broken right angles at the elbows forearms along armrests just right length forearms and rests for hands clenched lightly to rest on ends. So quite still again then all quite quiet apparently eyes closed which to anticipate when they open again if they do in time then dark or some degree of starlight or moonlight or both. Normally watch night fall however long from this narrow chair or standing by western window quite still either case. Quite still namely staring at some one thing alone such as tree or bush a detail alone if near if far the whole if far enough till it goes. Or by eastern window certain moods staring at some point on the hillside such as that beech in whose shade once quite still till it goes. Chair some reason always same place same position facing south as though clamped down whereas in reality no lighter no more movable imaginable. Or anywhere any ope staring out at nothing just failing light quite still till quite dark though of course no such thing just less light still when less did not seem possible. Quite still then all this time eyes open when discovered then closed then opened and closed again no other movement any kind though of course not still at all when suddenly or so it looks this movement impossible to follow let alone describe. The right hand slowly opening leaves the armrest taking with it the whole forearm complete with elbow and slowly rises opening further as it goes and turning a little deasil[1] till midway to the head it hesitates and hangs half open trembling in mid air. Hangs there as if half inclined to return that is sink back slowly closing as it goes and turning the other way till as and where it began clenched lightly on end of rest. Here because of what comes now not midway to the head but almost there before it hesitates and hangs there trembling as if half inclined etc. Half no but on the verge when in its turn the head moves from its place forward and down among the ready fingers where no sooner received and held it weighs on down till elbow meeting armrest brings this last movement to an end and all still once more. Here back a little way to that suspense before head to rescue as if hand's

---

1. **deasil** [dē′zəl]: clockwise.

need the greater and on down in what if not quite a single movement almost till elbow against rest. All quite still again then head in hand namely thumb on outer edge of right socket index ditto left and middle on left cheekbone plus as the hours pass lesser contacts each more or less now more now less with the faint stirrings of the various parts as night wears on. As if even in the dark eyes closed not enough and perhaps even more than ever necessary against that no such thing the further shelter of the hand. Leave it so all quite still or try listening to the sounds all quite still head in hand listening for a sound.

STUDY QUESTIONS

Recalling

1. In a few words describe the scene that the watcher is looking at.
2. From what two vantage points does the watcher observe this scene?
3. Find at least four descriptive details that are added to the basic scene as the selection continues.
4. Find at least three details that describe the watcher's movements as the selection continues.

Interpreting

5. Explain two different meanings of the word *still* that the selection implies.
6. What is "trembling all over"? Why?
7. "Close inspection namely detail by detail all over to add up finally to this whole. . . ." In what sense does this quotation from "Still" apply to the entire selection?
8. What quality of human experience does Beckett illustrate by gradually adding details to one basic scene?
9. Do you think "Still" has a message, or is it simply the description of an experience? Explain your opinion.

Extending

10. In what sense does "Still" represent typical human behavior?

LITERARY FOCUS

Elements of Style in Modern Prose

Style is made up of an author's choice and arrangement of words to convey both an idea and the author's individuality. Elements of style include subject, diction, and structure.

Subject is the topic of a literary work, the experience or idea being written about. Modern authors have responded to the rapid expansion of human knowledge by exploring new topics for literature, for example, the effects of technology on life or the working of the human mind.

Diction is the author's use of appropriate words to convey a particular meaning. The choice of words should suit the situation and subject being written about and should also reflect the author's personality. Modern authors have experimented with diction to create startling effects. They may use technical scientific language; they may sacrifice meaning and use words purely for their sound.

Structure is the framework or general plan of a piece of literature. The structure of an essay is its outline, or the scheme of its thesis statement and topic sentences. The structure of a short story is its plot and the arrangement of events in the plot. An example of a modern innovation in structure is the stream-of-consciousness story, which dispenses with plot and imitates the continuous flow of human thought.

Thinking About Elements of Style

1. What subject is Beckett writing about in "Still"? What does his choice of subject reveal about Beckett?
2. In what sense does Beckett's diction—the use of simple vocabulary and repetition—fit his subject?
3. Describe the structure of "Still." In what way does the structure of the selection match its subject?

Sean O'Faolain   *born 1900*

Sean O'Faolain [shôn′ ō fā′lin] is an Irish author whose homeland
supplies themes, settings, and characters for his short stories and
novels. He has also written travel books, biographies, critical studies,
and an autobiography. Born John Whelan in Cork, Ireland, he
changed his name to its Gaelic variant when he was sixteen. He was
educated in Ireland and at Harvard University. After fighting in the
Irish Revolution (1918–1921), O'Faolain lectured at colleges in the
United States and in England. He discovered what would become the
subject of his fiction while attending a play in his home town: "Here
was a most moving play about Irish peasants, shopkeeping and
farming folk, men and women who could have been anyone of my
uncles and aunts down the country. It brought me strange and
wonderful news—that writers could also write books and plays about
the common everyday reality of Irish life."

"The Sugawn Chair," a small cameo of Irish life, is about the kind
of people O'Faolain knows best. He portrays them honestly but with
warmth and compassion, and the mood established early in the story
casts a glow throughout.

Sean O'Faolain

The Sugawn Chair

Every autumn I am reminded of an abandoned sugawn chair that languished for years,
without a seat, in the attic of my old home. It
is associated in my mind with an enormous
sack which the carter used to dump with a
thud on the kitchen floor around every October. I was a small kid then, and it was as high
as myself. This sack had come "up from the
country," a sort of diplomatic messenger from
the fields to the city. It smelled of dust and
hay and apples, for the top half of it always
bulged with potatoes, and, under a layer of
hay, the bottom half bulged with apples. Its arrival always gave my mother great joy and a little sorrow, because it came from the farm
where she had been born. Immediately she saw
it she glowed with pride in having a "back," as
she called it—meaning something behind her
more solid and permanent than city streets,

though she was also saddened by the memories
that choked her with this smell of hay and potatoes from the home farm, and apples from
the little orchard near the farmhouse. My father, who had also been born on a farm, also
took great pleasure in these country fruits, and
as the two of them stood over the sack, in the
kitchen, in the middle of the humming city,
everything that their youth had meant to them
used to make them smile and laugh and use
words that they had never used during the rest
of the year, and which I thought magical:
words like *late sowing, clover crop, inch field,
marl bottom, headlands, tubers,* and the
names of potatoes, British Queens or Arran
Banners, that sounded to me like the names of
regiments. For those moments my father and
mother became a young, courting couple again.
As they stood over that sack, as you might say

warming their hands to it, they were intensely happy, close to each other, in love again. To me they were two very old people. Counting back now, I reckon that they were about forty-two or forty-three.

One autumn evening after the sack arrived, my father went up to the attic and brought down the old sugawn chair. I suppose he had had it sent up from his home farm. It was the only thing of its kind in our house, which they had filled—in the usual peasants' idea of what constitutes elegance—with plush chairs, gold-framed pictures of Stags at Bay, and exotic tropical birds, pelmets[1] on the mantelpieces, Delft shepherdesses, Chinese mandarins[2] with nodding heads, brass bedsteads with mighty knobs and mother-of-pearl escutcheons[3] set with bits of mirror, vast mahogany chiffoniers,[4] and so on. But the plush-bottomed chairs, with their turned legs and their stiff backs, were for show, not for comfort, whereas in the old country sugawn chair my da could tilt and squeak and rock to his behind's content.

It had been in the place for years, rockety, bockety, chipped and well polished, and known simply as "your father's chair," until the night when, as he was reading the *Evening Echo* with his legs up on the kitchen range, there was a sudden rending noise, and down he went through the seat of it. There he was then, bending over, with the chair stuck on to him, and my mother and myself in the splits of laughter, pulling it from him while he cursed like a trooper. This was the wreck that he now suddenly brought down from the dusty attic.

The next day, he brought in a great sack of straw from the Cornmarket, a half-gallon of porter[5] and two old buddies from the street—an ex-soldier known to the kids around as "Tear-'em-and-ate-'em" and a little dwarf of a man who guarded the stage door at the Opera House when he was not behind the sacristan[6] at the chapel. I was enchanted when I heard what they were going to do. They were going to make ropes of straw—a miracle I had never heard of—and reseat the chair. Bursting with pride in my da, I ran out and brought in my best pal, and the two of us sat quiet as cats on the kitchen table, watching the three men filling the place with dust, straw, and loud arguments as they began to twist the ropes for the bottom of the chair.

More strange words began to float in the air with the dust: *scallops,*[7] *flat tops, bulrushes, cipeens,*[8] *fields in great heart . . .* And when the three sat down for a swig of porter, and looked at the old polished skeletons in the middle of the floor, they began to rub the inside of their thighs and say how there was no life at all like the country life, and my mother poured out more porter for them, and laughed happily when my da began to talk about horses, and harrows,[9] and a day after the plough, and how, for *that* much, he'd throw up this blooming city life altogether and settle down on a bit of a farm for the heel of his days.

This was a game of which he, she and I never got tired, a fairy tale that was so alluring it did not matter that they had not enough money to buy a window box, let alone a farm of land.

"Do you remember that little place," she would say, "that was going last year down at Nantenan?"[10]

When she said that, I could see the little reedy fields of Limerick that I knew from hol-

---

1. **pelmets** [pel′məts]: horizontal moldings.
2. **Delft . . . mandarins:** small sculptured figurines.
3. **escutcheons** [es kuch′ənz]: shield shapes displaying a coat of arms.
4. **chiffoniers** [shif′ə nērz′]: large, heavy chests of drawers.
5. **porter:** bitter, heavy beer.

6. **sacristan** [sak′ris tən]: official in charge of the sacristy, the room in a church were ceremonial robes and sacred objects are kept.
7. *scallops* [skôl′əps]: long wooden rods from salley trees, used in making thatched roofs and baskets.
8. *cipeens* [kip′ēnz]: small twigs often used for starting fires.
9. **harrows:** implements used to break up and level plowed land.
10. **Nantenan** [nan′ti nən]: town in County Limerick in southwestern Ireland.

idays with my uncle, and the crumbling stone walls of old demesnes[11] with the moss and saffron lichen on them, and the willow sighing softly by the Deel,[12] and I could smell the wet turf rising in the damp air, and, above all, the tall wildflowers of the mallow, at first cabbage-leaved, then pink and coarse, then gossamery, then breaking into cakes that I used to eat—a rank weed that is the mark of ruin in so many Irish villages, and whose profusion and color is for me the sublime emblem of Limerick's loneliness, loveliness and decay.

"Ah!" my da would roar. "You and your blooming old Limerick! That bog of a place! Oh, but why didn't I grab that little farm I was looking at two years ago there below Emo!"[13]

"Oho, ho, ho!" she would scoff. "The Queen's! The Lousy Queen's! I'd live like a tiger and die like a Turk for Limerick. For one patch of good old Limerick. Oh, Limerick, my love, and it isn't alike! Where would you get spuds and apples the like of them in the length and breadth of the Queen's County?"

And she grabbed a fist of hay from the bag and buried her face in it, and the tears began to stream down her face, and me and my pal screaming with laughter at her, and the sacristan lauding Tipperary,[14] and the voices rose as Tear-'em-and-ate-'em brought up the River Barrow[15] and the fields of Carlow, until my da jumped up with:

"Come on, lads, the day is dyin' and acres wide before us!"

For all that, the straw rope was slow in emerging. Their arguments about it got louder and their voices sharper. At first all their worry had been whether the kitchen was long enough for the rope; but so far, only a few, brief

worms of straw lay on the red tiles. The sacristan said: "That bloody straw is too moist." When he was a boy in Tipp he never seen straw the like o' that. Tear-'em-and-ate-'em said that straw was old straw. When he was a lad in Carlow they never used old straw. Never! Under no possible circumstances! My dad said: "What's wrong with that straw is it's too bloomin' short!" And they began to kick the bits with their toes, and grimace at the heap on the floor, and pick up bits and fray them apart and throw them aside until the whole floor was like a stable. At last they put on their coats, and gave the straw a final few kicks, and my pal jumped down and said he was going back to his handball and, in my heart, I knew that they were three imposters.

The kitchen was tidy that evening when I came back with the *Evening Echo*. My da was standing by the sack of potatoes. He had a spud in his fist, rubbing off the dust of its clay with his thumb. When he saw me he tossed it back in the sack, took the paper, took one of the plush-bottom chairs and sat on it with a little grimace. I did not say anything, but young as I was, I could see that he was not reading what he was looking at. Who knows what he was seeing at that moment.

For years the anatomy of the chair stood in one of the empty attics. It was there for many years after my father died. When my mother died and I had to sell out the few bits of junk that still remained from their lives, the dealer would not bother to take the useless frame, so that when, for the last time, I walked about the echoing house, I found it standing alone in the middle of the bare attic. As I looked at it I smelled apples, and the musk of Limerick's dust, and the turf-tang[16] from its cottages, and the mallows among the limestone ruins, and I saw my mother and my father again as they were that morning—standing over the autumn sack, their arms about one another, laughing foolishly, and madly in love again.

---

11. **demesnes** [di mānz']: large estates or land holdings that were usually enclosed by walls.
12. **Deel:** river in County Limerick.
13. **Emo:** town in County Laois [lēsh], once known as Queen's County, southwest of Dublin.
14. **Tipperary:** inland county in the south having the richest agricultural region in Ireland.
15. **River Barrow:** river flowing through County Carlow, southwest of Dublin.

16. **turf-tang:** the smell of burning peat.

STUDY QUESTIONS

Recalling

1. What association does the sugawn chair hold for the narrator?
2. Where is the chair kept? Where does the narrator suppose the chair came from? Why is it no longer used?
3. What do the father and his friends plan to do with the chair? What is the narrator's original opinion of this plan?
4. What do the father and his friends actually do instead? What is the narrator's opinion of them?
5. What finally happens to the chair?

Interpreting

6. Explain the effect of the sack on the mother and father. Why did it have this effect?
7. Explain the symbolism of the chair and of the father's inability to repair it.

Extending

8. At the end of the story, what do you think the narrator did with the chair? Why?

LITERARY FOCUS

Atmosphere

Atmosphere is the mood of a story. It is created through (1) the story's **setting,** or time and place and (2) the author's **tone,** or attitude toward the subject of the story. The result is a frame of mind in which the story places the reader. The setting is usually described in the story's exposition and establishes the mood. For example, the description of a vast deserted tropical beach may set a mood of mystery or isolation. Atmosphere is reinforced by tone, through which the author reveals an attitude toward the events and characters of a story through the choice of particular words and details. The tone of a story—which may be comic, tragic, nostalgic, eerie, and so on—will help to create its overall mood.

Thinking About Atmosphere

1. Explain why setting—the story's actual setting and the farm setting that we never see—is important to the impact of "The Sugawn Chair." What atmosphere is established by the difference between the two settings?
2. What is the author's tone in the story? Give at least three examples of words or details that convey the tone. Explain how this tone contributes to the atmosphere of the story.

COMPOSITION

Writing About Theme

■ Write a brief essay about the theme of "The Sugawn Chair." First identify the theme of the story. Then show how O'Faolain illuminates this theme through the following elements of the story: (a) plot, (b) characterization, (c) setting, (d) point of view, (e) tone, and (f) symbolism. *For help with this assignment, refer to Lesson 6 in the Writing About Literature Handbook at the back of this book.*

Writing a Journal Entry

■ Write a fictional journal entry in which you describe an object that awakens associations for you, as the sack or the sugawn chair does for the narrator of the story. First describe an ordinary object. Then narrate an event or describe a setting associated with the object.

Doris Lessing *born 1919*

Doris Lessing's varied career has encompassed realistic novels, psychological novels, and science fiction. Unsatisfied with the lack of humanity in the fiction writers of the 1950s, Lessing turned for inspiration to older novels such as Tolstoy's *War and Peace* and Stendhal's *Red and the Black*. "I was looking," she wrote, "for the warmth, the compassion, the humanity, the love of people which illuminates the literature of the nineteenth century and which makes all these old novels a statement of faith in man himself."

Lessing was born in Iran of British parents. When she was five, the family moved to Rhodesia in southern Africa. She grew up in a sparsely populated district, and being alone much of the time, she read a great deal. Lessing moved to England in 1949. A year later she published her first novel, *The Grass Is Singing,* a story that takes place in Rhodesia.

In her early work Lessing chose a direct, traditional style of narrative. Her subjects were her African experiences and various social issues, especially the problems of women in modern society. With *The Golden Notebook* (1962) she began to experiment with the psychological novel, a form she continued in *Briefing for a Descent into Hell* (1971). Over a period of years, Lessing also produced *Children of Violence,* a multivolume work about the harsh realities and the effects of war.

"I hold the view," Lessing has said, "that the realist novel, the realist story, is the highest form of prose writing." "A Mild Attack of Locusts" illustrates Lessing's realism. The story interweaves a deep knowledge of the Rhodesian farmlands with a sensitive portrayal of complex human beings.

Model for Active Reading

In this selection you will find notes in the right-hand margin that highlight parts of the selection. These notes point out important ideas of the literary period and draw your attention to literary elements and techniques covered in the Literary Focuses. Page numbers in the notes refer you to more extensive discussions of these important ideas and elements.

Doris Lessing

A Mild Attack of Locusts

The rains that year were good; they were coming nicely just as the crops needed them—or so Margaret gathered when the men said they were not too bad. She never had an opinion of her own on matters like the weather, because even to know about what seems a simple thing like the weather needs experience. Which Margaret had not got. The men were Richard, her husband, and old Stephen, Richard's father, a farmer from way back; and these two might argue for hours whether the rains were ruinous or just ordinarily exasperating. Margaret had been on the farm three years. She still did not understand how they did not go bankrupt altogether, when the men never had a good word for the weather, or the soil, or the government. But she was getting to learn the language. Farmers' language. And they neither went bankrupt nor got very rich. They jogged along doing comfortably.

Their crop was maize.[1] Their farm was three thousand acres on the ridges that rise up toward the Zambesi escarpment[2]—high, dry, wind-swept country, cold and dusty in winter, but now, in the wet season, steamy with the heat rising in wet soft waves off miles of green foliage. Beautiful it was, with the sky blue and brilliant halls of air, and the bright green folds and hollows of country beneath, and the mountains lying sharp and bare twenty miles off across the rivers. The sky made her eyes ache; she was not used to it. One does not look so much at the sky in the city she came from. So that evening when Richard said: "The government is sending out warnings that locusts are expected, coming down from the breeding grounds up North," her instinct was to look about her at the trees. Insects—swarms of them—horrible! But Richard and the old man had raised their eyes and were looking up over the mountain. "We haven't had locusts in seven years," they said. "They go in cycles, locusts do." And then: "There goes our crop for this season!"

But they went on with the work of the farm just as usual until one day they were coming up the road to the homestead for the midday break, when old Stephen stopped, raised his finger and pointed: "Look, look, there they are!"

Out ran Margaret to join them, looking at the hills. Out came the servants from the kitchen. They all stood and gazed. Over the rocky levels of the mountain was a streak of rust-colored air. Locusts. There they came.

At once Richard shouted at the cookboy. Old Stephen yelled at

Exposition (p. 597): The first two paragraphs provide background information, introduce the characters, and establish the **limited-third-person point of view** (p. 602).

Setting (p. 630): The story is set on a farm in Africa. The steamy, beautiful landscape also supplies an **atmosphere** (p. 630).

Narrative hook (p. 597): The conflict begins when the threat of locusts is introduced.

Modern idea: Short sentences capture the characters' thoughts, a major concern of modern literature (p. 453).

---

1. **maize** [māz]: corn.
2. **Zambesi** [zam bē′zē] **escarpment:** steep cliffs along the Zambesi River in southern Africa.

the houseboy. The cookboy ran to beat the old plowshare hanging from a tree branch, which was used to summon the laborers at moments of crisis. The houseboy ran off to the store to collect tin cans, any old bit of metal. The farm was ringing with the clamor of the gong; and they could see the laborers come pouring out of the compound, pointing at the hills and shouting excitedly. Soon they had all come up to the house, and Richard and old Stephen were giving them orders—Hurry, hurry, hurry.

And off they ran again, the two white men with them, and in a few minutes Margaret could see the smoke of fires rising from all around the farmlands. Piles of wood and grass had been prepared there. There were seven patches of bared soil, yellow and oxblood color and pink, where the new mealies were just showing, making a film of bright green; and around each drifted up thick clouds of smoke. They were throwing wet leaves onto the fires now, to make it acrid and black. Margaret was watching the hills. Now there was a long, low cloud advancing, rust-color still, swelling forward and out as she looked. The telephone was ringing. Neighbors—quick, quick, there come the locusts. Old Smith had had his crop eaten to the ground. Quick, get your fires started. For of course, while every farmer hoped the locusts would overlook his farm and go on to the next, it was only fair to warn each other; one must play fair. Everywhere, fifty miles over the countryside, the smoke was rising from myriads[3] of fires. Margaret answered the telephone calls, and between calls she stood watching the locusts. The air was darkening. A strange darkness, for the sun was blazing—it was like the darkness of a veldt[4] fire, when the air gets thick with smoke. The sunlight comes down distorted, a thick, hot orange. Oppressive it was, too, with the heaviness of a storm. The locusts were coming fast. Now half the sky was darkened. Behind the reddish veils in front, which were the advance guards of the swarm, the main swarm showed in dense black cloud, reaching almost to the sun itself.

Margaret was wondering what she could do to help. She did not know. Then up came old Stephen from the lands. "We're finished, Margaret, finished! Those beggars can eat every leaf and blade off the farm in half an hour! And it is only early afternoon—if we can make enough smoke, make enough noise till the sun goes down, they'll settle somewhere else perhaps. . . ." And then: "Get the kettle going. It's thirsty work, this."

So Margaret went to the kitchen, and stoked up the fire, and boiled the water. Now, on the tin roof of the kitchen she could hear the thuds and bangs of falling locusts, or a scratching slither as one skidded down. Here were the first of them. From down on the lands came the beating and banging and clanging of a hundred

Conflict (p. 591): The story's **external conflict** pits the farmers against nature—the locusts.

Style (p. 626): Vivid word choice allows us to picture the locust attack.

---

3. **myriads** [mir′ē ədz]: countless numbers.
4. **veldt** [velt]: region of rolling grassland in southern Africa.

gasoline cans and bits of metal. Stephen impatiently waited while one gasoline can was filled with tea, hot, sweet and orange-colored, and the other with water. In the meantime, he told Margaret about how twenty years back he was eaten out, made bankrupt, by the locust armies. And then, still talking, he hoisted up the gasoline cans, one in each hand, by the wood pieces set cornerwise across each, and jogged off down to the road to the thirsty laborers. By now the locusts were falling like hail onto the roof of the kitchen. It sounded like a heavy storm. Margaret looked out and saw the air dark with a crisscross of the insects, and she set her teeth and ran out into it—what the men could do, she could. Overhead the air was thick, locusts everywhere. The locusts were flopping against her, and she brushed them off, heavy red-brown creatures, looking at her with their beady old-men's eyes while they clung with hard, serrated legs. She held her breath with disgust and ran through into the house. There it was even more like being in a heavy storm. The iron roof was reverberating, and the clamor of iron from the lands was like thunder. Looking out, all the trees were queer and still, clotted with insects, their boughs weighed to the ground. The earth seemed to be moving, locusts crawling everywhere, she could not see the lands at all, so thick was the swarm. Toward the mountains it was like looking into driving rain—even as she watched, the sun was blotted out with a fresh onrush of them. It was a half-night, a perverted blackness. Then came a sharp crack from the bush—a branch had snapped off. Then another. A tree down the slope leaned over and settled heavily to the ground. Through the hail of insects a man came running. More tea, more water was needed. She supplied them. She kept the fires stoked and filled cans with liquid, and then it was four in the afternoon, and the locusts had been pouring across overhead for a couple of hours. Up came old Stephen again, crunching locusts underfoot with every step, locusts clinging all over him; he was cursing and swearing, banging with his old hat at the air. At the doorway he stopped briefly, hastily pulling at the clinging insects and throwing them off, then he plunged into the locust-free living room.

"All the crops finished. Nothing left," he said.

But the gongs were still beating, the men still shouting, and Margaret asked: "Why do you go on with it, then?"

"The main swarm isn't settling. They are heavy with eggs. They are looking for a place to settle and lay. If we can stop the main body settling on our farm, that's everything. If they get a chance to lay their eggs, we are going to have everything eaten flat with hoppers[5] later on." He picked a stray locust off his shirt and split it down with his thumbnail—it was clotted inside with eggs. "Imagine that multiplied by millions. You ever seen a hopper swarm on the march? Well, you're lucky."

Internal conflict (p. 591): Margaret struggles to overcome her revulsion of the locusts in order to help.

Setting (p. 630): Time is an important part of setting as the farmers battle against the clock.

Rising action (p. 597): The locust attack and the human reactions carry the story toward its climax. The possibility that the locusts will lay eggs adds a complication to the plot.

---

5. **hoppers:** slang for baby locusts.

Margaret thought an adult swarm was bad enough. Outside now the light on the earth was a pale, thin yellow, clotted with moving shadows; the clouds of moving insects thickened and lightened like driving rain. Old Stephen said, "They've got the wind behind them, that's something."

"Is it very bad?" asked Margaret fearfully, and the old man said emphatically: "We're finished. This swarm may pass over, but once they've started, they'll be coming down from the North now one after another. And then there are the hoppers—it might go on for two or three years."

Margaret sat down helplessly, and thought: Well, if it's the end, it's the end. What now? We'll all three have to go back to town. . . . But at this, she took a quick look at Stephen, the old man who had farmed forty years in this country, been bankrupt twice, and she knew nothing would make him go and become a clerk in the city. Yet her heart ached for him, he looked so tired, the worry lines deep from nose to mouth. Poor old man. . . . He had lifted up a locust that had got itself somehow into his pocket, holding it in the air by one leg. "You've got the strength of a steel spring in those legs of yours," he was telling the locust, good-humoredly. Then, although he had been fighting locusts, squashing locusts, yelling at locusts, sweeping them in great mounds into the fires to burn for the last three hours, nevertheless he took this one to the door and carefully threw it out to join its fellows, as if he would rather not harm a hair of its head. This comforted Margaret; all at once she felt irrationally cheered. She remembered it was not the first time in the last three years the man had announced their final and irremediable ruin.

"Get me a drink, lass," he then said, and she set the bottle of whisky by him.

In the meantime, out in the pelting storm of insects, her husband was banging the gong, feeding the fires with leaves, the insects clinging to him all over—she shuddered. "How can you bear to let them touch you?" she asked. He looked at her, disapproving. She felt suitably humble—just as she had when he had first taken a good look at her city self, hair waved and golden, nails red and pointed. Now she was a proper farmer's wife, in sensible shoes and a solid skirt. She might even get to letting locusts settle on her— in time.

Having tossed back a whisky or two, old Stephen went back into the battle, wading now through glistening brown waves of locusts.

Five o'clock. The sun would set in an hour. Then the swarm would settle. It was as thick overhead as ever. The trees were ragged mounds of glistening brown.

Margaret began to cry. It was all so hopeless—if it wasn't a bad season, it was locusts; if it wasn't locusts, it was army worm[6] or

Characterization (p. 610): We are told **directly** of Margaret's helplessness, but we see Stephen **indirectly** through his actions and through Margaret's impressions.

Theme (p. 632): Lessing uses Stephen's ability to recover from hardship as an example of the power of the human spirit.

Modern idea: Margaret's "city self" is an important part of her character. Modern literature is often concerned with urban life (p. 453).

Modern idea: Despair is a frequent reaction to problems in modern literature (p. 453).

---

6. **army worm:** larvae of certain moths that destroy crops.

veldt fires. Always something. The rustling of the locust armies was like a big forest in the storm; their settling on the roof was like the beating of the rain; the gound was invisible in a sleek, brown, surging tide—it was like being drowned in locusts, submerged by the loathsome brown flood. It seemed as if the roof might sink in under the weight of them, as if the door might give in under their pressure and these rooms fill with them—and it was getting so dark . . . she looked up. The air was thinner; gaps of blue showed in the dark, moving clouds. The blue spaces were cold and thin— the sun must be setting. Through the fog of insects she saw figures approaching. First old Stephen, marching bravely along, then her husband, drawn and haggard with weariness. Behind them the servants. All were crawling all over with insects. The sound of the gongs had stopped. She could hear nothing but the ceaseless rustle of a myriad wings.

The two men slapped off the insects and came in.

"Well," said Richard, kissing her on the cheek, "the main swarm has gone over."

"For heaven's sake," said Margaret angrily, still half crying, "what's here is bad enough, isn't it?" For although the evening air was no longer black and thick, but a clear blue, with a pattern of insects whizzing this way and that across it, everything else—trees, buildings, bushes, earth—was gone under the moving brown masses.

"If it doesn't rain in the night and keep them here—if it doesn't rain and weight them down with water, they'll be off in the morning at sunrise."

"We're bound to have some hoppers. But not the main swarm— that's something."

Margaret roused herself, wiped her eyes, pretended she had not been crying, and fetched them some supper, for the servants were too exhausted to move. She sent them down to the compound to rest.

She served the supper and sat listening. There is not one maize plant left, she heard. Not one. The men would get the planters out the moment the locusts had gone. They must start all over again.

But what's the use of that, Margaret wondered, if the whole farm was going to be crawling with hoppers? But she listened while they discussed the new government pamphlet that said how to defeat the hoppers. You must have men out all the time, moving over the farm to watch for movement in the grass. When you find a patch of hoppers, small lively black things, like crickets, then you dig trenches around the patch or spray them with poison from pumps supplied by the government. The government wanted them to cooperate in a world plan for eliminating this plague forever. You should attack locusts at the source. Hoppers, in short. The men were talking as if they were planning a war, and Margaret listened, amazed.

Round character (p. 610): We see Margaret's hopelessness, anger, courage, and kindness.

In the night it was quiet; no sign of the settled armies outside, except sometimes a branch snapped, or a tree could be heard crashing down.

Margaret slept badly in the bed beside Richard, who was sleeping like the dead, exhausted with the afternoon's fight. In the morning she woke to yellow sunshine lying across\ the bed—clear sunshine, with an occasional blotch of shadow moving over it. She went to the window. Old Stephen was ahead of her. There he stood outside, gazing down over the bush. And she gazed, astounded—and entranced, much against her will. For it looked as if every tree, every bush, all the earth, were lit with pale flames. The locusts were fanning their wings to free them of the night dews. There was a shimmer of red-tinged gold light everywhere.

She went out to join the old man, stepping carefully among the insects. They stood and watched. Overhead the sky was blue, blue and clear.

"Pretty," said old Stephen, with satisfaction.

Well, thought Margaret, we may be ruined, we may be bankrupt, but not everyone has seen an army of locusts fanning their wings at dawn.

Over the slopes, in the distance, a faint red smear showed in the sky, thickened and spread. "There they go," said old Stephen. "There goes the main army, off south."

And now from the trees, from the earth all round them, the locusts were taking wing. They were like small aircraft, maneuvering for the takeoff, trying their wings to see if they were dry enough. Off they went. A reddish-brown steam was rising off the miles of bush, off the lands, the earth. Again the sunlight darkened.

And as the clotted branches lifted, the weight on them lightening, there was nothing but the black spines of branches, trees. No green left, nothing. All morning they watched, the three of them, as the brown crust thinned and broke and dissolved, flying up to mass with the main army, now a brownish-red smear in the southern sky. The lands which had been filmed with green, the new tender mealie plants, were stark and bare. All the trees stripped. A devastated landscape. No green, no green anywhere.

By midday the reddish cloud had gone. Only an occasional locust flopped down. On the ground were the corpses and the wounded. The African laborers were sweeping these up with branches and collecting them in tins.

"Ever eaten sun-dried locust?" asked old Stephen. "That time twenty years ago, when I went broke, I lived on mealie meal and dried locusts for three months. They aren't bad at all—rather like smoked fish, if you come to think of it."

But Margaret preferred not even to think of it.

After the midday meal the men went off to the lands. Everything was to be replanted. With a bit of luck another swarm would not come traveling down just this way. But they hoped it would

Modern idea: The beauty of the locusts contrasts with the destruction they cause. Such paradoxes are common in modern literature (p. 453).

Climax (p. 597): The locusts fly away, and the tension reaches a peak. The climax is followed by the **falling action.**

Modern idea: The description of the dead locusts uses images of war. Such imagery is common in modern literature (p. 453).

rain very soon, to spring some new grass, because the cattle would die otherwise—there was not a blade of grass left on the farm. As for Margaret, she was trying to get used to the idea of three or four years of locusts. Locusts were going to be like bad weather, from now on, always imminent. She felt like a survivor after war—if this devastated and mangled countryside was not ruin, well, what then was ruin?

But the men ate their supper with good appetites.

"It could have been worse," was what they said. "It could be much worse."

> **Resolution** (p. 597): The falling action ends. The ending is typically modern because the problem is not completely solved.

STUDY QUESTIONS

Recalling

1. How long has Margaret lived on the farm? Give two examples of her lack of experience.
2. Name three actions the farmers take to ward off the locusts.
3. Explain why the farmers want to keep the locusts from settling.
4. What do the locusts actually do to the farm?
5. What plans do the farmers make? In what way do they assess the attack of locusts?

Interpreting

6. The events of the story are narrated through the consciousness of Margaret, a novice on the farm. What effect does this point of view have on the impact of the story?
7. Find examples of Stephen's pessimism and of his optimism. Explain the contradiction.

LITERARY FOCUS

Theme

Theme is a story's main idea, a general statement about life. A theme goes beyond the specific details of a story to some universal meaning. For example, although Joyce's "Araby" is about a particular young Irishman at a bazaar in Dublin, the theme of the story should be applicable to the life of anyone, anywhere. In addition, a theme is always expressed as a sentence. For example, the theme of "Araby" may be stated as "Unrealistic expectations lead to disappointment."

A theme can be directly **stated** or **implied**, and all the elements of a story point in some way

to the theme. The title may imply an opinion of what happens in the story. The outcome of the plot may suggest a lesson about life. Characterization may reveal the author's ideas about people in general, and setting may suggest an attitude about the world. Point of view may tell us how the author wants us to react to the story. Symbols represent abstract ideas and, therefore, direct us to the author's concerns.

Thinking About Theme

■ State the theme of "A Mild Attack of Locusts." Explain how this theme develops out of the story and how it is universally applicable.

VOCABULARY

Antonyms

Antonyms are words that have opposite or nearly opposite meanings. *Quiet* and *loud* are antonyms. The words in capitals are from "A Mild Attack of Locusts." Choose the word that is *most nearly the opposite* of each word in capitals, *as the word is used in the selection.*

1. RUINOUS: (a) optimistic (b) constructive (c) calamitous (d) disastrous
2. EXASPERATING: (a) tiresome (b) hopeful (c) pleasing (d) necessary
3. ACRID: (a) mild (b) bitter (c) brilliant (d) melodious
4. SERRATED: (a) jagged (b) fashionable (c) smooth (d) peculiar
5. REVERBERATING: (a) musical (b) anxious (c) still (d) quaking

Nadine Gordimer   *born 1923*

Nadine Gordimer has written novels and short stories, and her work has appeared regularly in periodicals such as the *New Yorker* and the *Atlantic*. Born in Springs, near Johannesburg, South Africa, she was educated there at private schools and—for one year—at the University of Witwatersrand. She has lectured extensively and was a visiting professor to the United States.

Gordimer's fiction reflects the concern with racial problems that has dominated life in South Africa in this century. Her themes include the political and social consequences of apartheid, South Africa's policy of strict racial segregation. The stories, however, are more than sociological journalism. While they grow out of the South African scene, they have universal application and appeal.

The settings of Nadine Gordimer's fiction range from sophisticated South African suburbs to huts with thatched roofs and mud floors. She is equally adept at writing about society matrons, native peddlers, and professional hunters. The stories focus on the observed moment, the brief but revealing incident.

"The Train from Rhodesia" is a sad but beautiful story demonstrating Gordimer's ability to arrest the reader's attention with a telling moment of reality.

Nadine Gordimer

The Train from Rhodesia

The train came out of the red horizon and bore down toward them over the single straight track.

The stationmaster came out of his little brick station with its pointed chalet roof, feeling the creases in his serge uniform in his legs as well. A stir of preparedness rippled through the squatting native vendors waiting in the dust; the face of a carved wooden animal, eternally surprised, stuck out of a sack. The stationmaster's barefoot children wandered over. From the gray mud huts with the untidy heads that stood within a decorated mud wall, chickens, and dogs with their skin stretched like parchment over their bones, followed the piccanins[1] down to the track. The flushed and perspiring west cast a reflection, faint, without heat, upon the station, upon the tin shed marked "Goods," upon the walled kraal,[2] upon the gray tin house of the stationmaster and upon the sand, that lapped all around, from sky

---

1. **piccanins:** native children.
2. **kraal** [kräl]: in southern Africa, a fenced enclosure for livestock; corral.

to sky, cast little rhythmical cups of shadow, so that the sand became the sea, and closed over the children's black feet softly and without imprint.

The stationmaster's wife sat behind the mesh of her veranda. Above her head the hunk of a sheep's carcass moved slightly, dangling in a current of air.

They waited.

The train called out, along the sky; but there was no answer; and the cry hung on: I'm coming . . . I'm coming . . .

The engine flared out now, big, whisking a dwindling body behind it; the track flared out to let it in.

Creaking, jerking, jostling, gasping, the train filled the station.

Here, let me see that one—the young woman curved her body further out of the corridor window. Missus? smiled the old boy, looking at the creatures he held in his hand. From a piece of string on his gray finger hung a tiny woven basket; he lifted it, questioning. No, no, she urged, leaning down toward him, across the height of the train, toward the man in the piece of old rug; that one, that one, her hand commanded. It was a lion, carved out of soft dry wood that looked like spongecake; heraldic, black and white, with impressionistic detail burnt in. The old man held it up to her still smiling, not from the heart, but at the cus-

tomer. Between its Vandyke teeth, in the mouth opened in an endless roar too terrible to be heard, it had a black tongue. Look, said the young husband, if you don't mind! And round the neck of the thing, a piece of fur (rat? rabbit? meerkat?); a real mane, majestic, telling you somehow that the artist had delight in the lion.

All up and down the length of the train in the dust the artists sprang, walking bent, like performing animals, the better to exhibit the fantasy held toward the faces on the train. Buck, startled and stiff, staring with round black and white eyes. More lions, standing erect, grappling with strange, thin, elongated warriors who clutched spears and showed no fear in their slits of eyes. How much, they asked from the train, how much?

Give me penny, said the little ones with nothing to sell. The dogs went and sat, quite still, under the dining car, where the train breathed out the smell of meat cooking with onion.

A man passed beneath the arch of reaching arms meeting gray-black and white in the exchange of money for the staring wooden eyes, the stiff wooden legs sticking up in the air; went along under the voices and the bargaining, interrogating the wheels. Past the dogs; glancing up at the dining car where he could stare at the faces, behind glass, drinking beer, two by two, on either side of a uniform railway

vase with its pale dead flower. Right to the end, to the guard's van, where the stationmaster's children had just collected their mother's two loaves of bread; to the engine itself, where the stationmaster and the driver stood talking against the steaming complaint of the resting beast.

The man called out to them, something loud and joking. They turned to laugh, in a twirl of steam. The two children careered over the sand, clutching the bread, and burst through the iron gate and up the path through the garden in which nothing grew.

Passengers drew themselves in at the corridor windows and turned into compartments to fetch money, to call someone to look. Those sitting inside looked up: suddenly different, caged faces, boxed in, cut off, after the contact of outside. There was an orange a piccanin would like. . . . What about that chocolate? It wasn't very nice. . . .

A young girl had collected a handful of the hard kind, that no one liked, out of the chocolate box, and was throwing them to the dogs, over at the dining car. But the hens darted in, and swallowed the chocolates, incredibly quick and accurate, before they had even dropped in the dust, and the dogs, a little bewildered, looked up with their brown eyes, not expecting anything.

—No, leave it, said the girl, don't take it. . . .

Too expensive, too much, she shook her head and raised her voice to the old boy, giving up the lion. He held it up where she had handed it to him. No, she said, shaking her head. Three-and-six?[3] insisted her husband, loudly. Yes baas! laughed the boy. *Three-and-six?*—the young man was incredulous. Oh leave it—she said. The young man stopped. Don't you want it? he said, keeping his face closed to the boy. No, never mind, she said, leave it. The old native kept his head on one side, looking at them sideways, holding the lion. Three-and-six, he murmured, as old people repeat things to themselves.

The young woman drew her head in. She went into the coupe[4] and sat down. Out of the window, on the other side, there was nothing; sand and bush; a thorn tree. Back through the open doorway, past the figure of her husband in the corridor, there was the station, the voices, wooden animals waving, running feet. Her eye followed the funny little valance of scrolled wood that outlined the chalet roof of the station; she thought of the lion and smiled. That bit of fur round the neck. But the wooden buck, the hippos, the elephants, the baskets that already bulked out of their brown paper under the seat and on the luggage rack! How will they look at home? Where will you put them? What will they mean away from the places you found them? Away from the unreality of the last few weeks? The man outside. But he is not part of the unreality; he is for good now. Odd . . . somewhere there was an idea that he, that living with him, was part of the holiday, the strange places.

Outside, a bell rang. The stationmaster was leaning against the end of the train, green flag rolled in readiness. A few men who had got down to stretch their legs sprang onto the train, clinging to the observation platforms, or perhaps merely standing on the iron step, holding the rail; but on the train, safe from the one

---

3. **Three-and-six:** three shillings and a sixpence, the equivalent of approximately thirty-four American cents when the story takes place.
4. **coupe** [k$\overline{oo}$ pā′]: in British trains, a half-compartment at the end of a passenger car with only one row of seats.

dusty platform, the one tin house, the empty sand.

There was a grunt. The train jerked. Through the glass the beer drinkers looked out, as if they could not see beyond it. Behind the flyscreen, the stationmaster's wife sat facing back at them beneath the darkening hunk of meat.

There was a shout. The flag drooped out. Joints not yet coordinated, the segmented body of the train heaved and bumped back against itself. It began to move; slowly the scrolled chalet moved past it, the yells of the natives, running alongside, jetted up into the air, fell back at different levels. Staring wooden faces waved drunkenly, there, then gone, questioning for the last time at the windows. Here, one-and-six baas!—As one automatically opens a hand to catch a thrown ball, a man fumbled wildly down his pocket, brought up the shilling and sixpence and threw them out; the old native, gasping, his skinny toes splaying the sand, flung the lion.

The piccanins were waving, the dogs stood, tails uncertain, watching the train go: past the mud huts, where a woman turned to look, up from the smoke of the fire, her hand pausing on her hip.

The stationmaster went slowly in under the chalet.

The old native stood, breath blowing out the skin between his ribs, feet tense, balanced in the sand, smiling and shaking his head. In his opened palm, held in the attitude of receiving, was the retrieved shilling and sixpence.

The blind end of the train was being pulled helplessly out of the station.

The young man swung in from the corridor, breathless. He was shaking his head with laughter and triumph. Here! he said. And waggled the lion at her. One-and-six!

What? she said.

He laughed. I was arguing with him for fun, bargaining—when the train had pulled out already, he came tearing after. . . . One-and-six baas! So there's your lion.

She was holding it away from her, the head with the open jaws, the pointed teeth, the black tongue, the wonderful ruff of fur facing her. She was looking at it with an expression of not seeing, of seeing something different. Her face was drawn up, wryly, like the face of a discomforted child. Her mouth lifted nervously at the corner. Very slowly, cautious, she lifted her finger and touched the mane, where it was joined to the wood.

But how could you, she said. He was shocked by the dismay of her face.

Good heavens, he said, what's the matter?

If you wanted the thing, she said, her voice rising and breaking with the shrill impotence of anger, why didn't you buy it in the first place? If you wanted it, why didn't you pay for it? Why didn't you take it decently, when he offered it? Why did you have to wait for him to run after the train with it, and give him one-and-six? One-and-six!

She was pushing it at him, trying to force him to take it. He stood astonished, his hands hanging at his sides.

But you wanted it! You liked it so much?

—It's a beautiful piece of work, she said fiercely, as if to protect it from him.

You liked it so much! You said yourself it was too expensive—

Oh *you*—she said, hopeless and furious. *You*. . . . She threw the lion onto the seat.

He stood looking at her.

She sat down again in the corner and, her face slumped in her hand, stared out of the window. Everything was turning round inside her. One-and-six. One-and-six. One-and-six for the wood and the carving and the sinews of the legs and the switch of the tail. The mouth open like that and the teeth. The black tongue, rolling, like a wave. The mane round the neck. To give one-and-six for that. The heat of shame mounted through her legs and body and sounded in her ears like the sound of sand pouring. Pouring, pouring. She sat there, sick. A weariness, a tastelessness, the discovery of a void made her hands slacken their grip, atrophy emptily, as if the hour was not worth their grasp. She was feeling like this again. She had thought it was something to do with single-ness, with being alone and belonging too much to oneself.

She sat there not wanting to move or speak, or to look at anything, even; so that the mood should be associated with nothing, no object, word or sight that might recur and so recall the feeling again. . . . Smuts[5] blew in grittily,

_____
5. **smuts:** black grimy particles; soot.

settled on her hands. Her back remained at exactly the same angle, turned against the young man sitting with his hands drooping between his sprawled legs, and the lion, fallen on its side in the corner.

The train had cast the station like a skin. It called out to the sky, I'm coming, I'm coming; and again, there was no answer.

STUDY QUESTIONS

Recalling
1. Describe the station and the people there at the beginning of the story.
2. Give three examples of the activity that begins when the train arrives at the station.
3. What are the woman's thoughts about the souvenirs of her "holiday" and about her husband?
4. Explain the steps that lead to the purchase of the carved lion. Describe the woman's reaction to the purchase.

Interpreting
5. What does the arrival of the train mean to the people at the station?
6. What does the incident with the lion tell us about the relationship between the woman and her husband?
7. In what sense does the station symbolize the woman's psychological condition?

Extending
8. Use the story as an example to explain the difference between being alone and being lonely.

COMPOSITION

Writing About Significant Details
▪ Explain the use of significant detail in "The Train from Rhodesia." First choose at least two details from the story. Then explain the inferences that can be made from each detail. Finally explain how the use of such details adds to the richness of the story. Although you may use any details from the story you wish, you may want to consider one or more of the following: (a) the woman's thoughts about her souvenirs and what they say about her personality, (b) the description of the station and what it symbolizes, and (c) the description of the lion and why the author itemizes its features.

Writing a Friendly Letter
▪ Imagine that you are traveling by train through an empty landscape like the one depicted in the story. Write a letter to a friend describing the land through which you are traveling and the feelings that the landscape inspires in you.

COMPARING WRITERS

1. Twentieth-century fiction often concentrates on the psychological conditions of characters. Because such topics are abstract, authors sometimes use concrete objects to symbolize characters' mental states. Compare two or more of the following stories: "Still," "A Mild Attack of Locusts," "The Sugawn Chair," and "The Train from Rhodesia." For each story explain how a concrete object or scene helps us to understand the mental state of a character.
2. In "Why I Write" Orwell explains that the motivating forces behind his work are both political and aesthetic. Compare Orwell's essay to one or more of the following stories: "Still," "A Mild Attack of Locusts," "The Sugawn Chair," and "The Train from Rhodesia." In what sense is each story political and aesthetic? What might Orwell's opinion of each story be?

READING FOR APPRECIATION

Sound in Prose

Earlier in this book we looked at how poets try to create patterns of sound in poetry. We saw that these patterns are built up not only through word choice but also through rhythm, rhyme, alliteration, and other techniques of sound. We saw that in poetry sound can help to evoke moods and emotions and express meanings.

In prose we cannot always point so readily to this kind of use of sound. Yet all good writers are sensitive to the effects of particular rhythms and special combinations of sounds. For example, the novelist James Joyce was acutely aware of the special effects of sound in prose. Consider the following passage from his story "Araby" (page 593), in which he describes the lively activity of children outdoors just before dark:

When the short days of winter came dusk fell before we had well eaten our dinners. When we met in the street the houses had grown somber. The space of sky above us was the color of ever-changing violet and toward it the lamps of the street lifted their feeble lanterns. The cold air stung us and we played till our bodies glowed. Our shouts echoed in the silent street. The career of our play brought us through the dark muddy lanes behind the houses where we ran the gantlet of the rough tribes from the cottages, to the back doors of the dark dripping gardens where odors arose from the ashpits, to the dark odorous stables where a coachman smoothed and combed the horse or shook music from the buckled harness.

Joyce gives us the scene and the actions. Moreover, he calls up a rich, lovely combination of impressions and moods: the children's excitement, the darkening light, the sharp cold, the hushed quiet in the streets, the sense of bustling play, the momentum of spontaneous motion. How does Joyce achieve these marvelous effects? One answer lies in his selection of wonderful details and images; a second answer lies in the very rhythm and sound of the prose.

Thus, to convey some of the children's excitement and hurry, Joyce writes with monosyllabic words primarily—for instance, "*When the short days of* winter *came dusk fell* before *we had well* eaten *our* dinners." To quicken the pace, he omits all internal punctuation, so that the first half of the passage must be read almost without pause. Also, by including a variety of soft consonant and vowel sounds, he gives the passage the quality of an eager, rapid whisper: "*When the sh*ort days *of w*inter came dusk *fell.* . . ."

In the second through fifth sentences, Joyce even captures something of what we feel when nightfall approaches, with its greater stillness and deeper darkness and silence. He now uses longer, more resonant, more somber vowel sounds: ". . . the h*ou*ses had gr*ow*n somber . . . the c*o*lor of ever-changing v*io*let . . . *ou*r bodies gl*ow*ed. . . . *Ou*r sh*ou*ts ech*oe*d. . . ."

Then, to suggest the feeling of rushing, cascading physical movement, Joyce lets the last sentence of the passage run on and on—in contrast to the preceding sentences. He adds punctuation and clause upon clause, so as to carry us along *rhythmically,* as well as through images. Thus, we "see" and "feel" the children's escapades through "the dark muddy lanes" to "the dark dripping gardens" to "the dark odorous stables."

Try to imagine this extraordinary passage without these nuances of sound and rhythm. We would have the scene and the actions, and the story would proceed. However, the whole imaginative texture—what is unstated yet touches our senses, our emotions, and perhaps even our memories—would be lost.

THE ENGLISH VOICE

The Artist's View

The writers of the past, on the rare occasions when they paid any attention to their own roles, identified themselves as chroniclers or singers, entertainers or sonneteers, lexicographers or moralists, rhapsodists or seers. The modern writer, on the other hand, emphasizes that he or she is, above all, an *artist*.

Usually in celebration, though sometimes in self-defense, the voice of the modern artist insists: I am a maker, a creator, an artificer. I wield imagination as my weapon, my shield, my tool for reshaping reality.

Shaw

Yes, you squashed cabbage leaf, you disgrace to the noble architecture of these columns, you incarnate insult to the English language: I could pass you off as the Queen of Sheba.

Yeats

. . . Gather me
Into the artifice of eternity.

Eliot

I am moved by fancies that are
  curled
Around these images.

Auden

Follow, poet, follow right
To the bottom of the night,

With your unconstraining voice
Still persuade us to rejoice.

Thomas

. . . It was all
Shining, it was Adam and
  maiden,
  The sky gathered again
And the sun grew round that
  very day.

Hughes

I sit in the top of the wood, my
  eyes closed. . . .
Now I hold Creation in my
  foot.

Tomlinson

Suggestions for the Improve-
  ment of a Sunset

Joyce

I imagined that I bore my chalice safely through a throng of foes. Her name sprang to my lips at moments in strange prayers and praises which I myself did not understand.

Woolf

But why not be original? Why not be herself, anyhow?

The modern artist never tires of celebrating creation, imagination, originality. The lesson of this celebration is clear: Reality is what the artists in all of us make of it.

Key to Illustrations on Pages 450–451.

1. Wedding of Prince Charles and Lady Diana Spencer, St. Paul's Cathedral, London, July 29, 1981.
2. Virginia Woolf (1882–1941).
3. Detail, *Still Life with Spots*, Ben Nicolson (1884–1980).
4. The Houses of Parliament and Westminster Bridge, London.
5. William Butler Yeats (1865–1939).
6. *Working Model for Standing Figure: Knife Edge*, Henry Moore, bronze, 1961.
7. Joseph Conrad (1857–1924).
8. Detail, French cartoon depicting a suffragette rally in London, 1908.
9. Scene from 1938 film version of George Bernard Shaw's *Pygmalion*.

Literary Map of Europe

This map, with current borders, identifies locales associated
with the authors and selections included in Part Two of
English and Western Literature of the *Macmillan Literature Series.*
All place names are modern; older names appear in parentheses.
As you read more European literature, you will be able
to place other authors and literary works in correct
geographic locations.

SCOTLAND

NORTHERN
IRELAND

NORTH
SEA

BALTIC
SEA

SWEDEN

FINLAND

NORWAY

DENMARK

UNITED KINGDOM

IRELAND

ENGLAND

WALES

Lübeck ●
Mann born

ATLANTIC
OCEAN

NETHERLANDS

WEST
GERMANY

EAST
GERMANY

POLAND

Warsaw ●
Milosz works, writes

BELGIUM

Düsseldorf ●
Heine born

Goderville ●
Maupassant's "Piece of String"

Cologne ●
Böll born

Weimar ●
Goethe writes

LUX.

Charleville ●
Rimbaud born

Frankfurt ●
Goethe born

Prague ●
Rilke, Kafka born

Paris ●
Molière, Baudelaire born
Heine writes, buried
Verlaine studies, writes
Maupassant, Milosz write

Metz ●
Verlaine born

Calw ●
Hesse born

CZECHOSLOVAKIA

Besançon ●
Hugo born

Baden ●
Hesse's "Jackdaw"

Vienna ●
Walther's early career

Ferney ●
Voltaire's
last years

SWITZERLAND

VALAIS
Rilke's last years

AUSTRIA

HUNGARY

ROMAN

FRANCE

ITALY

YUGOSLAVIA

Sète ●
Valéry born

PROVENCE
Troubadours

Rovezzano
Montale's "Arno"

SPAIN

PORTUGAL

Madrid ●
Cervantes born

Florence ●
Boccaccio's
"Federigo's Falcon"
Dante born

Arno

ADRIATIC
SEA

BU

ALBANIA

LA MANCHA
Don Quixote

Rome ●
Virgil, Ovid, Petrarch write
Moravia born

GREECE

● **Moguer**
Jiménez born

● **Granada**
García Lorca born, writes, dies

A

Thebes
Sophocles' *Antigone*
Pindar born ●

MEDITERRANEAN   SEA

Athens
Aesop lives

SICILY
Pirandello born

Corinth
Elytis' "Sun"

MOROCCO

ALGERIA
Camus born; location of "The Guest"

TUNISIA

CR
Elyt

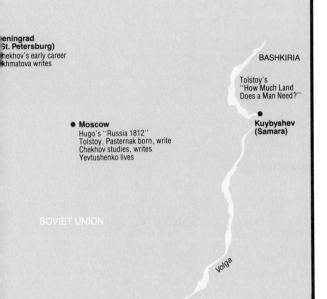

eningrad
St. Petersburg)
hekhov's early career
khmatova writes

BASHKIRIA

Tolstoy's
"How Much Land
Does a Man Need?"

● Moscow
Hugo's "Russia 1812"
Tolstoy, Pasternak born, write
Chekhov studies, writes
Yevtushenko lives

● Kuybyshev
(Samara)

SOVIET UNION

Volga

Constanta
(Tomis)
Ovid's exile

BLACK SEA

Troy
Homer's *Iliad*
Virgil's *Aeneid* begins

Mytilene
Sappho born, writes

URKEY

Izmir (Smyrna)
Seferis born

Part Two:
Western Literature

Part Two of this book presents works by
significant authors of western literature
from its beginnings with the Ancient Greeks
and Ancient Romans to the present day.
This overview shows what the writers of Europe
were producing as English writers were at
work on their masterpieces. The literature is
organized chronologically and divided into
units that generally correspond to those for
the English literature in Part One. In the
following pages you will encounter authors
from various European countries including
Greece, Italy, France, Spain, Russia,
Germany, Poland, and Czechoslovakia.
The accompanying map shows these countries
with current borders. Remember, however, that
some did not always exist as countries or did
not always have the same boundaries as they
have today. For example, there was no such
place called Italy when the Ancient Romans were
writing; these writers lived in Rome, which was
the center of the Roman Empire.

Key to Illustrations appears on page 922.

THE CLASSICAL HERITAGE

C. 800 B.C. to A.D. 500

If you were to leave twentieth-century London and fly southeastward—over the English Channel, across France and the majestic Swiss Alps—you would sense a different world approaching. You would be drawing near the birthplace of western civilization.

The warm, golden world that surrounds the Mediterranean Sea stretches from the southern tip of Spain eastward to the Middle East. Africa forms its southern shoreline; the beaches of France and Italy lie along its northern border. In the mountainous, island-dotted northeast corner, washed by the Aegean Sea, lies Greece. As we move geographically to Greece, we will also move back in time, thousands of years back to the beginnings of what we now call western literature. The glorious tradition of British literature, we will see, is one part of an even more glorious tradition.

In classical Greece and Rome, so many of our ideas, forms, and uses of language were born and developed. They continued to be transformed as they moved through different countries and different centuries, through Europe, toward us. In the following pages of Part Two, we will travel from Ancient Greece and Rome up the Italian peninsula into the heartland of medieval and Renaissance Europe. We will move across Europe toward the Atlantic, traveling through both space and time, approaching our own modern period once more.

ANCIENT GREECE

Apollo with dolphins, Athenian amphora, or vase, fifth century B.C.

The civilization of the Greeks goes back to about 6500 B.C., when nomad farmers crossed into the European continent from the fertile river valleys of Mesopotamia in the Middle East. By 3000 B.C. these settlers had fortified cities on the European mainland and on the nearby islands in the Mediterranean that would become the isles of Greece. About 1900 B.C. an Indo-European people called the Achaeans migrated to the area, founded their own towns, and brought with them a language that became Greek.

The Greek land itself is a blend of green olive orchards and rugged mountains. Mountains run down to the sea and form ragged and treacherous coastlines. The soil, though poor, is rich enough to pasture cattle, which in ancient days were served up on the tables of the rich or sacrificed on the altars of the gods. The surrounding sea has always been vital to the Greeks, especially for trade and travel. Yet they invested their greatest energy and powers of invention in building their own cities. In fact as early as 1600 B.C. the city of Knossos on the island of Crete had running water in its spectacular royal palace.

To understand both the Greek experience and its literature, it is helpful to divide ancient times into three periods. The eighth century B.C. can be called the *epic age,* when aristocratic families ruled and Homer wrote of noble heroes. The seventh and sixth centuries B.C. were a *lyric age,* when many social and political changes occurred and individuals began to think for themselves. The fifth century B.C. is often considered the high point of Greece, the *dramatic age* that reflected the achievement of the city-state and the growth of democracy. When we speak of the Golden Age of Greece, we are referring approximately to the fifth century B.C.

The Epic Age

The epic age is the age of Homer, the poet whose *Iliad* and *Odyssey* preserve for us a brilliant and well-rounded picture of the time. Greek legend—and some archaeological evidence—indicates that about 1200 B.C. the Greeks attacked the city of Troy in Asia Minor. In the eighth century B.C., building on centuries of oral tradition, Homer composed the *Iliad,* probably to be recited for a group of wealthy nobles. He told the story of the Trojan War, filling out the tale of the Greek King Menelaus and his attempt to reclaim his wife Helen who had been abducted by a Trojan named Paris. The *Iliad* shows us several different worlds: the quarreling gods on Mount Olympus, the warring Greek and Trojan camps, the loving family of Hector. Above all, however, we see an aristocratic society in action, where noble kings and lords fight for honor and pride, where reputation is paramount, and where the greatest fighter was the greatest hero.

The *Odyssey* is more of a personal epic than the *Iliad,* an adventure that follows Odysseus as he attempts to return home after the ten-year Trojan conflict. His skill and cunning enable him to outwit monsters and witches, survive storms, and even visit the dead in the underworld. Yet the *Iliad* and the *Odyssey* are much more than stories of war and adventure. When we see Hector playing with his infant son before he goes out to meet his death at the hands of Achilles, we see a human, domestic side of the ancient world that would otherwise have been lost to us. In the same way we feel the human touch of a poetic genius when we read of Homer's herdsmen, Odysseus' family dogs, his wife Penelope's weaving, the tools and clothes and foods and wines of daily life. Homer's great gift was in revealing both the brutal and the beautiful during the epic age.

One major element in this portrait of the time is religion. Although by the eighth century B.C. the Greeks had stopped believing in the gods and goddesses as real spirits ruling the universe, Homer gives them vivid personalities and treats them as characters, as real as Hector or Helen. The religion of the Greeks had developed from an early belief in an anthropomorphic (human-shaped) earth goddess to the worship of a large family of gods and goddesses, each with distinct powers and qualities. Many of these gods and goddesses have come down to us in other sources of Greek myths, but it is Homer's re-creations that are unforgettable: gray-eyed Athena, Hera the divine consort, Poseidon the god of the sea, Zeus the wielder of thunderbolts.

Homer dominates the epic age, although many fragments of other epics survive, written by poets trying to imitate Homer's grandeur. Of those, only Hesiod's *Works and Days* seems to possess any genuine poetic force. Hesiod sang his song about 750 B.C., a song that presents a different perspective on the Greek world. Hesiod drew his material from experience on his farm in the Greek province of Boeotia. He relates with compassion the lives of the peasants who worked the land, the nonaristocrats for whom kings and lords were merely "gift-devouring tyrants."

The Lyric Age

In the seventh and sixth centuries B.C. Greece underwent many changes on its way to forming the democratic city-states of the fifth century. Old ways were challenged: The rule of the few was becoming the rule of the many. Social and religious traditions were changed; individualism grew. A person might be judged more on his or her own merits than on slavish devotion to a king. In this age of increasing freedom, lyric poetry was born.

Lyric poetry was originally poetry sung to the accompaniment of the lyre, a plucked harplike instrument. It was not poetry that told long tales of warring countries or related the deeds of national heroes. It was poetry that revealed personal feelings, individual human emotions, simple and complex—love, hate, dreams, ambition. Eventually, lyric poetry came to include the elegy, although originally an elegy was a sad poem sung to the accompaniment of a flute.

The development of lyric poetry was accomplished over a long period of time, and we will never even know the names of many of those whose songs have been lost. We do, however, have ample evidence of two of the greatest lyric singers—Sappho and Pindar. Sappho's grace and charm are still the model for many writers of lyric poems. Pindar wrote a special kind of lyric poem, the ode, honoring the winners of athletic competitions. His dazzling images and emotional intensity are matched by an extraordinary willingness to experiment with meters: Of all his forty-five odes, only two are written in the same meter.

The Dramatic Age

The fifth century B.C. in Greece was a golden age in more ways than one. In politics, architecture, philosophy, history, and drama, achievements were unparalleled. This period, sometimes called the Classical Period in Greek culture, was marked by the flourishing of the city-state of Athens. After a defeat by Persia in 479 B.C., the Athenians formed the Delian League as a defense. To the resentment of the other city-states, Athens dominated the league, leading to the Peloponnesian War (431–404 B.C.). The war was tragic for Athens and for the Greek world; it pitted Athens and other city-states, including Sparta, against each other. Even under the leadership of Pericles, a brilliant statesman and general, Athens was eventually defeated. Sparta and later Thebes took over leadership until the Greek world gave way to the Macedonians from the north about 350 B.C.

Until its downfall, however, Athens in this period was the center of the most exciting, beautiful, and thoughtful civilization the western world has known. The beauty of its architecture can still be seen in its ruins. Its sculpture still strikes viewers as sublime. Its thinkers—including Socrates, Plato, and Aristotle—are the fathers of philosophy, psychology, and literary criticism. Herodotus, Thucydides, and Xenophon recorded some of the most literate histories ever written.

This was a period of participation, when most Athenians took an active role as citizens in the daily life of their city. Citizens took part in political discussions and debates, celebrated at public religious festivals, and sent all male children to school to learn grammar, music, gymnastics, Homer, Hesiod, and the fables of Aesop.

One of the greatest glories of the Periclean Age was its drama. Beginning as religious ritual, the Greeks developed a complete form of literature—secular drama, tragedy, and comedy. Thousands of plays were produced at great public drama festivals with prizes going to the playwright who produced the best trilogy, or series of three plays. The first of the great dramatists was Aeschylus, who achieved his first festival victory in 484 B.C. Aeschylus probably wrote about ninety plays, of which seven have survived, including the finest of the trilogies, the *Oresteia.* Stately language, noble and dignified imagery, and a profound interest in the relationship between the human and the divine mark the masterpieces of Aeschylus.

Sophocles, whose play *Antigone* appears in the pages ahead, was one of the most successful of the Greek dramatists, winning the tragedy competition twenty times. Only seven of his 125 plays survive, but they are among the world's greatest dramatic masterpieces. In *Oedipus the King,* the classic example of dramatic irony, Sophocles asserts the courage and enduring value of humanity even in the face of catastrophe.

Euripides won the tragedy contests only four times, probably because his ideas seemed rather unorthodox to his audiences. His plays, however, like *Medea* and *Alcestis,* are complex and profound studies of character. Because of the penetration of his psychology and his ability to show human beings caught up in events, Euripides is generally considered to have had a greater impact on the history of drama than any other Greek playwright.

The Greeks had separate contests for tragedy and comedy, and the greatest of the comic writers was Aristophanes. Producing his first comedy when he was eighteen, Aristophanes became enormously successful, though we do not know how many of his forty plays won first prizes. His comedies overflow with brilliant wit, imaginative situations, and biting satire. It has been said that only an age that was supremely self-confident could produce and enjoy the mockery and satire of Aristophanes.

When we read the literature of ancient Greece, we can understand how the English Romantic poet John Keats felt when he first read George Chapman's translation of Homer:

> Then felt I like some watcher of the skies
> When a new planet swims into his ken.

It was not only the beauty of Homer's words that amazed Keats. It was the vision of a brilliant civilization that existed some thousand years before the Anglo-Saxons invaded Britain.

Homer *c. 850 B.C.*

As discussed in "The Anglo-Saxon Period" (pages 3–5), before written literature evolved, myths, legends, customs, and history were preserved orally by professional traveling storytellers. No permanent version of a story existed; therefore, the storyteller, although bound to the outline of the original story, could still shape his own version imaginatively through description, similes, and emphasis.

Out of the multitude of unknown storytellers stretching back centuries before the Anglo-Saxon scops (page 5), in another part of the world, emerged the genius Homer in the eighth century B.C. Homer, the first known poet of western literature, could neither read nor write. Singing to the accompaniment of a lyre, a small stringed instrument, he composed his poetry orally; an authoritative edition of his poems was not published until about 150 B.C., hundreds of years after his death, by scholars at the Alexandrian library in Egypt.

Little is known about Homer's life, though his authorship of the two great epic poems, the *Iliad* [il′ē əd] and the *Odyssey* [od′ə sē], is established by tradition. Some scholars believe Homer lived in a city on the eastern shore of the Aegean; others doubt he ever existed. The Greek historian Herodotus, who lived in the fifth century B.C., was one of several who wrote early biographies of Homer, but the "facts" presented in these works are largely deduced from passages in the poems credited to Homer. According to legend, Homer was a poor, old, blind poet of great wisdom, who wandered from city to city singing his verse.

By 400 B.C. Homer's epics had become classics, as well as a vital part of Greek life. They were recited as part of the great religious festivals, and Greeks revered them as a source of guidance in religious and moral matters. Every child who learned to read studied Homer, for he was regarded as a master of literature and rhetoric, too. The Greek philosophers Plato and Aristotle often referred to the epics in their own writing, and the Greek playwrights Sophocles (page 678) and Euripides based their dramas on characters and plots set down by Homer. Homer's influence gradually spread throughout the world, and he remains today one of the most widely read authors in western literature. Much of the literary heritage of the western world is rooted in his epics, and many generations of writers have been so inspired by his heroes and themes that they have created their own works around them. In this book alone we have three such works: Keats's "On First Looking into Chapman's Homer" (page 381), Tennyson's "Ulysses" (page 411), and Valéry's "Helen" (page 857).

Introducing the Iliad

Four hundred years after the Trojan War, a great conflict between the Greeks and the Trojans that occurred about 1200 B.C., Homer selected material from the many tales told about its causes, battles, and heroes. Using this material he fashioned the *Iliad* and the *Odyssey,* both of which present an awesome sweep of human experience. They deal with individual thoughts and feelings, the political and military actions of two societies, and the relationship of humanity to the universe.

The name of the *Iliad* comes from the word *Ilion,* another name for the city of Troy, which was located in what is now Turkey. It was watered by the river Scamandros [skə man′drōs] and guarded by the Scaean [sē′än] gate. The *Iliad* tells the story of the Trojan War and sets the stage for the *Odyssey.* In the *Odyssey,* which takes place after the events of the *Iliad,* Homer tells of the cunning and victorious hero Odysseus' [ō dis′ ē ə s]* long and adventurous journey home from Troy to Greece after the Trojan War and of the resumption of his domestic and political life.

In the *Iliad* Homer tells us that the war began when Paris, a Trojan prince, abducted Helen, the queen of Sparta in Greece. For nine years the irate Greeks attacked Troy, and for nine years the Trojans successfully resisted them. As the epic begins, a plague is ravaging the Greek camp. Agamemnon [ag′ə mem′non], leader of the Greek forces, has angered the god Apollo by insulting one of Apollo's priests. Apollo had rewarded Agamemnon by giving him the priest's daughter. When the priest tried to bargain for her return, Agamemnon sent him away, and the plague began. The gods agree to end the devastation only if Agamemnon returns the prize. He obeys, but demands to be given a captive of Achilles' [ə kil′ēz], the greatest of Greek warriors, to take her place. Achilles is outraged.

While the gods watch and take sides, Achilles withdraws his powerful troops, the Myrmidons, and sulks in his camp. Without Achilles' support, the Greeks are sufficiently weakened to allow the Trojans, led by Hector, the son of King Priam [prī′əm] of Troy, to venture from the safety of their city and very nearly destroy the Greek fleet. Although Achilles cannot be persuaded to help, his friend Patroclus [pə trō′kləs] dons Achilles' armor intending to frighten the Trojans. The Trojan Hector kills him and strips his body of the armor. Infuriated, Achilles remains idle no longer, waiting only to receive new armor from his mother, the goddess Thetis, before setting out to avenge Patroclus' death on Hector and the Trojans.

---

*In Greek names *ch* is always pronounced like the English *k; c* and *g* are hard sounds except before *e, i, y,* and *ae,* when the *c* is pronounced *s* and the *g, j.* An *e* at the end of names is always sounded like the long *e.*

Homer

from the **Iliad**

Translated by Robert Fitzgerald

CHARACTERS

Trojans

ANDROMACHE [an drom′ə kē]: Hector's wife

HECUBA: Priam's wife

HECTOR: Priam's eldest son; leader of the Trojan warriors

PARIS: also called Alexander; Priam's son who abducted Helen, thereby causing the war

PRIAM [prī′əm]: Troy's king

ASTYANAX [as tī′ə naks′]: baby son of Hector and Andromache

Greeks

ACHAEANS [ə kē′ənz]: Greeks (the name comes from a section of northeastern Greece); also called Danaans and Argives

ACHILLES [ə kil′ēz]: leader of the Myrmidons, greatest of the Greek warriors

HELEN: Greek queen abducted by Paris

PATROCLUS [pə trō′kləs]: best friend of Achilles

Gods

APOLLO [ə pol′ō]: son of Zeus and protector of Troy, which he helped to build

ATHENA [ə thē′nə]: also called Pallas Athena; daughter of Zeus, protector of Achilles

ZEUS [zo͞os]: king of the gods

from Book 6, Hector and Andromache

Hector whirled and left his hall,
taking the same path he had come by,
along byways, walled lanes, all through the town
until he reached the Scaean Gates, whereby
5 before long he would issue on the field.
There his warmhearted lady
came to meet him, running: Andromache,
whose father, Eetion, once had ruled
the land under Mount Placus, dark with forest,
10 at Thebe under Placus—lord and king
of the Cilicians. Hector was her lord now,
head to foot in bronze; and now she joined him.
Behind her came the maid, who held the child
against her breast, a rosy baby still,
15 Hectorides,[1] the world's delight, as fresh
as a pure shining star. Scamandrius
his father named him; other men would say
Astyanax, "Lord of the Lower Town,"
as Hector singlehandedly guarded Troy.
20 How brilliantly the warrior smiled, in silence,
his eyes upon the child! Andromache
rested against him, shook away a tear,
and pressed his hand in both her own, to say:

"Oh, my wild one, your bravery will be
25 your own undoing! No pity for our child,
poor little one, or me in my sad lot—
soon to be deprived of you! soon, soon
Achaeans as one man will set upon you
and cut you down! Better for me, without you,
30 to take cold earth for mantle.[2] No more comfort,
no other warmth, after you meet your doom,
but heartbreak only. Father is dead, and Mother.
My father great Achilles killed when he
besieged and plundered Thebes, our high town,
35 citadel of Cilicians. He killed him,
but, reverent at least in this, did not
despoil him. Body, gear, and weapons forged
so handsomely, he burned, and heaped a barrow
over the ashes. Elms were planted round
40 by mountain-nymphs of him who bears the stormcloud.[3]

---

1. **Hectorides** [hek'tər ē'dez]: Greek form for the son of Hector, Astyanax.
2. **for mantle:** as a cover.
3. **him . . . stormcloud:** Zeus.

Then seven brothers that I had at home
in one day entered Death's dark place. Achilles,
prince and powerful runner, killed all seven
amid their shambling cattle and silvery sheep.
45 Mother, who had been queen of wooded Placus,
he brought with other winnings home, and freed her,
taking no end of ransom. Artemis
the Huntress[4] shot her in her father's house.
Father and mother—I have none but you,
50 nor brother, Hector; lover none but you!
Be merciful! Stay here upon the tower!
Do not bereave your child and widow me!
Draw up your troops by the wild fig tree; that way
the city lies most open, men most easily
55 could swarm the wall where it is low:
three times, at least, their best men tried it there
in company of the two called Ajax,[5] with
Idomeneus, the Atreidai, Diomedes[6]—
whether someone who had it from oracles[7]
60 had told them, or their own hearts urged them on."

Great Hector in his shimmering helmet answered:

"Lady, these many things beset my mind
no less than yours. But I should die of shame
before our Trojan men and noblewomen
65 if like a coward I avoided battle,
nor am I moved to. Long ago I learned
how to be brave, how to go forward always
and to contend for honor, Father's and mine.
Honor—for in my heart and soul I know
70 a day will come when ancient Ilion falls,
when Priam and the folk of Priam perish.
Not by the Trojans' anguish on that day
am I so overborne in mind—the pain
of Hecuba herself, or Priam king,
75 or of my brothers, many and valorous,
who will have fallen in dust before our enemies—
as by your own grief, when some armed Achaean
takes you in tears, your free life stripped away.

---

4. **Artemis** [är′tə mis] **the Huntress:** Greek goddess of hunting
and chastity.
5. **two called Ajax:** Ajax the Great and Ajax the Lesser, unrelated,
heroic Greek warriors.
6. **Idomeneus** [ī dom′ə nōōs′], **the Atreidai** [a trē′i dī], **Diomedes**
[dī′ə mē′dēz]: brave hero and leader of the Cretans, the sons of Atreus
(Agamemnon and Menelaus), and a Greek warrior, respectively.
7. **oracles:** prophesying priests, believed to have been inspired by
the gods.

Before another woman's loom in Argos
80 it may be you will pass, or at Messeis
or Hypereia fountain, carrying water,
against your will—iron constraint upon you.
And seeing you in tears, a man may say:
'There is the wife of Hector, who fought best
85 of Trojan horsemen when they fought at Troy.'
So he may say—and you will ache again
for one man who could keep you out of bondage.
Let me be hidden dark down in my grave
before I hear your cry or know you captive!"

90 As he said this, Hector held out his arms
to take his baby. But the child squirmed round
on the nurse's bosom and began to wail,
terrified by his father's great war helm—
the flashing bronze, the crest with horsehair plume
95 tossed like a living thing at every nod.
His father began laughing, and his mother
laughed as well. Then from his handsome head
Hector lifted off his helm and bent
to place it, bright with sunlight, on the ground.
100 When he had kissed his child and swung him high
to dandle him, he said this prayer:

                              "O Zeus
and all immortals, may this child, my son,
become like me a prince among the Trojans.
Let him be strong and brave and rule in power
105 at Ilion; then someday men will say
'This fellow is far better than his father!'
seeing him home from war, and his arms
the bloodstained gear of some tall warrier slain—
making his mother proud."

                         After this prayer,
110 into his dear wife's arms he gave his baby,
whom on her fragrant breast
she held and cherished, laughing through her tears.
Hector pitied her now. Caressing her,
he said:

              "Unquiet soul, do not be too distressed
115 by thoughts of me. You know no man dispatches me
into the undergloom against my fate;
no mortal, either, can escape his fate,
coward or brave man, once he comes to be.
Go home, attend to your own handiwork

120 at loom and spindle, and command the maids
to busy themselves, too. As for the war,
that is for men, all who were born at Ilion,
to put their minds on—most of all for me."

He stooped now to recover his plumed helm
125 as she, his dear wife, drew away, her head
turned and her eyes upon him, brimming tears.
She made her way in haste then to the ordered
house of Hector and rejoined her maids,
moving them all to weep at sight of her.
130 In Hector's home they mourned him, living still
but not, they feared, again to leave the war
or be delivered from Achaean fury.

Neither his wife Andromache's entreaties nor his own foreboding can prevent Hector, leader of the Trojans, from confronting Achilles, the great Greek warrior. Before their battle takes place, however, Hector fights and kills Patroclus, Achilles' best friend. Achilles, in terrible rage over Patroclus' death, kills many Trojans and captures twelve Trojan youths to sacrifice at Patroclus' funeral. The gods, greatly angered by the excesses of Achilles' fury, enter the action to rebuke him. Meanwhile, all the Trojans withdraw into the walled city of Troy; only Hector remains outside, determined to confront Achilles despite his family's pleas.

from Book 22, Achilles and Hector

Hector stood firm, as huge Achilles neared.
The way a serpent, fed on poisonous herbs,
coiled at his lair upon a mountainside,
with all his length of hate awaits a man
5 and eyes him evilly: so Hector, grim
and narrow-eyed, refused to yield. He leaned
his brilliant shield against a spur of wall
and in his brave heart bitterly reflected:
"Here I am badly caught. If I take cover,
10 slipping inside the gate and wall, the first
to accuse me for it will be Polydamas,
he who told me I should lead the Trojans
back to the city on that cursed night
Achilles joined the battle. No, I would not,
15 would not, wiser though it would have been.
Now troops have perished for my foolish pride,
I am ashamed to face townsmen and women.
Someone inferior to me may say:
'He kept his pride and lost his men, this Hector!'
20 So it will go. Better, when that time comes,

that I appear as he who killed Achilles
man to man, or else that I went down
fighting him to the end before the city.
Suppose, though, that I lay my shield and helm
25 aside, and prop my spear against the wall,
and go to meet the noble Prince Achilles,
promising Helen, promising with her
all treasures that Alexander brought home
by ship to Troy—the first cause of our quarrel—
30 that he may give these things to the Atreidai?
Then I might add, apart from these, a portion
of all the secret wealth the city owns.
Yes, later I might take our counselors' oath
to hide no stores, but share and share alike
35 to halve all wealth our lovely city holds,
all that is here within the walls. Ah, no,
why even put the question to myself?
I must not go before him and receive
no quarter, no respect! Aye, then and there
40 he'll kill me, unprotected as I am,
my gear laid by, defenseless as a woman.
No chance, now, for charms from oak or stone
in parley with him—charms a girl and boy
might use when they enchant each other talking!
45 Better we duel, now at once, and see
to whom the Olympian[8] awards the glory."

These were his shifts of mood. Now close at hand
Achilles like the implacable god of war
came on with blowing crest, hefting the dreaded
50 beam of Pelian ash[9] on his right shoulder.
Bronze light played around him, like the glare
of a great fire or the great sun rising,
and Hector, as he watched, began to tremble.
Then he could hold his ground no more. He ran,
55 leaving the gate behind him, with Achilles
hard on his heels, sure of his own speed.
When that most lightning-like of birds, a hawk
bred on a mountain, swoops upon a dove,
the quarry dips in terror, but the hunter,
60 screaming, dips behind and gains upon it,
passionate for prey. Just so, Achilles
murderously cleft the air, as Hector

---

8. **the Olympian:** Zeus.
9. **beam of Pelian** [pē′lē ən] **ash:** a spear originally received by Achilles' father
Peleus as a wedding gift from the kind centaur Chiron [kī′ron], in whose cave
on Mount Pelion Peleus and Achilles' mother Thetis were married. The spear was
made of the hard wood of an ash tree from Mount Pelion.

ran with flashing knees along the wall.
They passed the lookout point, the wild fig tree
65 with wind in all its leaves, then veered away
along the curving wagon road, and came
to where the double fountains well, the source
of eddying Scamander. One hot spring
flows out, and from the water fumes arise
70 as though from fire burning; but the other
even in summer gushes chill as hail
or snow or crystal ice frozen on water.
Near these fountains are wide washing pools
of smooth-laid stone, where Trojan wives and daughters
75 laundered their smooth linen in the days
of peace before the Achaeans came. Past these
the two men ran, pursuer and pursued,
and he who fled was noble, he behind
a greater man by far. They ran full speed,
80 and not for bull's hide or a ritual beast
or any prize that men compete for: no,
but for the life of Hector, tamer of horses.

*While Achilles pursues Hector around the walls of Troy, the
gods debate the outcome of their confrontation. Despite Hector's
lifelong respect for the gods, Zeus cannot save him from his fate.
While Athena assures Achilles of his victory, Apollo, who had previously aided Hector, abandons him. Quite alone now, Hector realizes he has no choice but to stand and fight Achilles.*

And when at last the two men faced each other,
Hector was the first to speak. He said:

85 "I will no longer fear you as before,
son of Peleus, though I ran from you
round Priam's town three times and could not face you.
Now my soul would have me stand and fight,
whether I kill you or am killed. So come,
90 we'll summon gods here as our witnesses,
none higher, arbiters of a pact: I swear
that, terrible as you are,
I'll not insult your corpse should Zeus allow me
victory in the end, your life as prize.
95 Once I have your gear, I'll give your body
back to Achaeans. Grant me, too, this grace."

But swift Achilles frowned at him and said:

"Hector, I'll have no talk of pacts with you,
forever unforgiven as you are.
100 As between men and lions there are none,

no concord between wolves and sheep, but all
hold one another hateful through and through,
so there can be no courtesy between us,
no sworn truce, till one of us is down
105 and glutting with his blood the war god Ares.
Summon up what skills you have. By god,
you'd better be a spearman and a fighter!
Now there is no way out. Pallas Athena
will have the upper hand of you. The weapon
110 belongs to me. You'll pay the reckoning
in full for all the pain my men have borne,
who met death by your spear."

He twirled and cast
his shaft with its long shadow. Splendid Hector,
keeping his eye upon the point, eluded it
115 by ducking at the instant of the cast,
so shaft and bronze shank passed him overhead
and punched into the earth. But unperceived
by Hector, Pallas Athena plucked it out
and gave it back to Achilles. Hector said:

120 "A clean miss. Godlike as you are,
you have not yet known doom for me from Zeus.
You thought you had, by heaven. Then you turned
into a word-thrower, hoping to make me lose
my fighting heart and head in fear of you.
125 You cannot plant your spear between my shoulders
while I am running. If you have the gift,
just put it through my chest as I come forward.
Now it's for you to dodge my own. Would god
you'd give the whole shaft lodging in your body!
130 War for the Trojans would be eased
if you were blotted out, bane that you are."

With this he twirled his long spearshaft and cast it,
hitting his enemy mid-shield, but off
and away the spear rebounded. Furious
135 that he had lost it, made his throw for nothing,
Hector stood bemused. He had no other.
Then he gave a great shout to Deiphobus
to ask for a long spear. But there was no one
near him, not a soul. Now in his heart
140 the Trojan realized the truth and said:

"This is the end. The gods are calling deathward.
I had thought
a good soldier, Deiphobus, was with me.

He is inside the walls. Athena tricked me.
145 Death is near, and black, not at a distance,
not to be evaded. Long ago
this hour must have been to Zeus's liking
and to the liking of his archer son.
They have been well disposed before, but now
150 the appointed time's upon me. Still, I would not
die without delivering a stroke,
or die ingloriously, but in some action
memorable to men in days to come.''

With this he drew the whetted blade that hung
155 upon his left flank, ponderous and long,
collecting all his might the way an eagle
narrows himself to dive through shady cloud
and strike a lamb or cowering hare: so Hector
lanced ahead and swung his whetted blade.
160 Achilles with wild fury in his heart
pulled in upon his chest his beautiful shield—
his helmet with four burnished metal ridges
nodding above it, and the golden crest
Hephaestus[10] locked there tossing in the wind.
165 Conspicuous as the evening star that comes,
amid the first in heaven, at fall of night,
and stands most lovely in the west, so shone
in sunlight the fine-pointed spear
Achilles poised in his right hand, with deadly
170 aim at Hector, at the skin where most
it lay exposed. But nearly all was covered
by the bronze gear he took from slain Patroclus,
showing only, where his collarbones
divided neck and shoulders, the bare throat
175 where the destruction of a life is quickest.
Here, then, as the Trojan charged, Achilles
drove his point straight through the tender neck,
but did not cut the windpipe, leaving Hector
able to speak and to respond. He fell
180 aside into the dust. And Prince Achilles
now exulted:

        "Hector, had you thought
that you could kill Patroclus and be safe?
Nothing to dread from me; I was not there.
All childishness. Though distant then, Patroclus'
185 comrade in arms was greater far than he—

---

10. **Hephaestus** [hi fes′təs]: Greek god of fire and divine blacksmith.

and it is I who had been left behind
that day beside the deep-sea ships who now
have made your knees give way. The dogs and kites
will rip your body. His will lie in honor
190 when the Achaeans give him funeral."

Hector, barely whispering, replied:

"I beg you by your soul and by your parents,
do not let the dogs feed on me
in your encampment by the ships. Accept
195 the bronze and gold my father will provide
as gifts, my father and her ladyship
my mother. Let them have my body back,
so that our men and women may accord me
decency of fire when I am dead."

200 Achilles the great runner scowled and said:

"Beg me no beggary by soul or parents,
whining dog! Would god my passion drove me
to slaughter you and eat you raw, you've caused
such agony to me! No man exists
205 who could defend you from the carrion pack[11]—
not if they spread for me ten times your ransom,
twenty times, and promise more as well;
aye, not if Priam, son of Dardanus,
tells them to buy you for your weight in gold!
210 You'll have no bed of death, nor will you be
laid out and mourned by her who gave you birth.
Dogs and birds will have you, every scrap."

Then at the point of death Lord Hector said:

"I see you now for what you are. No chance
215 to win you over. Iron in your breast
your heart is. Think a bit, though: this may be
a thing the gods in anger hold against you
on that day when Paris and Apollo
destroy you at the Gates, great as you are."

220 Even as he spoke, the end came, and death hid him;
spirit from body fluttered to undergloom,
bewailing fate that made him leave his youth
and manhood in the world. And as he died
Achilles spoke again. He said:

---

11. **carrion pack:** birds of prey.

225 "Die, make an end. I shall accept my own
whenever Zeus and the other gods desire."

At this he pulled his spearhead from the body,
laying it aside, and stripped
the bloodstained shield and cuirass[12] from his shoulders.
230 Other Achaeans hastened round to see
Hector's fine body and his comely face,
and no one came who did not stab the body.
Glancing at one another they would say:

"Now Hector has turned vulnerable, softer
235 than when he put the torches to the ships!"

And he who said this would inflict a wound.
When the great master of pursuit, Achilles,
had the body stripped, he stood among them,
saying swiftly:

"Friends, my lords and captains
240 of Argives, now that the gods at last have let me
bring to earth this man who wrought
havoc among us—more than all the rest—
come, we'll offer battle around the city,
to learn the intentions of the Trojans now.
245 Will they give up their strong point at this loss?
Can they fight on, though Hector's dead?

But wait:
why do I ponder, why take up these questions?
Down by the ships Patroclus' body lies
unwept, unburied. I shall not forget him
250 while I can keep my feet among the living.
If in the dead world they forget the dead,
I say there, too, I shall remember him,
my friend. Men of Achaea, lift a song!
Down to the ships we go, and take this body,
255 our glory. We have beaten Hector down,
to whom as to a god the Trojans prayed."

Indeed, he had in mind for Hector's body
outrage and shame. Behind both feet he pierced
the tendons, heel to ankle. Rawhide cords
260 he drew through both and lashed them to his chariot,
letting the man's head trail. Stepping aboard,
bearing the great trophy of the arms,

---

12. **cuirass** [kwi ras′]: breastplate.

he shook the reins, and whipped the team ahead
into a willing run. A dustcloud rose
265 above the furrowing body; the dark tresses
flowed behind, and the head so princely once
lay back in dust. Zeus gave him to his enemies
to be defiled in his own fatherland. . . .

*Priam, seeing his son slain, futilely begs Achilles to return
Hector's body. Achilles returns to his camp to conduct funeral
rites for Patroclus. Protecting Hector's body from decay and des-
ecration, the gods send their messenger, Hermes, to lead Priam to
Achilles so that Priam can retrieve the body. Achilles recognizes
the will of the gods and yields the body to Priam, who carries it
back to Troy for Hector's burial rites.*

from Book 24, Hector's Funeral

Now, at the sight of Hector, all gave way
to loss and longing, and all crowded down
to meet the escort and body near the gates,
till no one in the town was left at home.
5 There Hector's lady and his gentle mother
tore their hair for him, flinging themselves
upon the wagon to embrace his person
while the crowd groaned. All that long day
until the sun went down they might have mourned
10 in tears before the gateway. But old Priam
spoke to them from his chariot:

           "Make way,
let the mules pass. You'll have your fill of weeping
later, when I've brought the body home."

They parted then, and made way for the wagon,
15 allowing Priam to reach the famous hall.
They laid the body of Hector in his bed,
and brought in minstrels, men to lead the dirge.
While these wailed out, the women answered, moaning.
Andromache of the ivory-white arms
20 held in her lap between her hands
the head of Hector who had killed so many.
Now she lamented:

           "You've been torn from life,
my husband, in young manhood, and you leave me
empty in our hall. The boy's a child
25 whom you and I, poor souls, conceived; I doubt
he'll come to manhood. Long before, great Troy
will go down plundered, citadel and all,

now that you are lost, who guarded it
and kept it, and preserved its wives and children.
30 They will be shipped off in the murmuring hulls
one day, and I along with all the rest.
You, my little one, either you come with me
to do some grinding labor, some base toil
for a harsh master, or an Achaean soldier
35 will grip you by the arm and hurl you down
from a tower here to a miserable death—
out of his anger for a brother, a father,
or even a son that Hector killed. Achaeans
in hundreds mouthed black dust under his blows.
40 He was no moderate man in war, your father,
and that is why they mourn him through the city.
Hector, you gave your parents grief and pain
but left me loneliest, and heartbroken.
You could not open your strong arms to me
45 from your deathbed, or say a thoughtful word,
for me to cherish all my life long
as I weep for you night and day."

Then yoking mules and oxen to their wagons
the people thronged before the city gates.
50 Nine days they labored, bringing countless loads
of firewood to the town. When Dawn that lights
the world of mortals came for the tenth day,
they carried greathearted Hector out at last,
and all in tears placed his dead body high
55 upon its pyre, then cast a torch below.
When the young Dawn with finger tips of rose
made heaven bright, the Trojan people massed
about Prince Hector's ritual fire.
All being gathered and assembled, first
60 they quenched the smoking pyre with tawny wine
wherever flames had licked their way, then friends
and brothers picked his white bones from the char
in sorrow, while the tears rolled down their cheeks.
In a golden urn they put the bones,
65 shrouding the urn with veiling of soft purple.
Then in a grave dug deep they placed it
and heaped it with great stones. The men were quick
to raise the death-mound, while in every quarter
lookouts were posted to ensure against
70 an Achaean surprise attack. When they had finished
raising the barrow, they returned to Ilion,
where all sat down to banquet in his honor
in the hall of Priam king. So they performed
the funeral rites of Hector, tamer of horses.

STUDY QUESTIONS

Hector and Andromache

Recalling

1. What reasons and advice does Andromache give to dissuade Hector from fighting?
2. What are Hector's reasons for wanting to fight?
3. Why does Hector's son cry when he sees his father? What does Hector do? What is Hector's wish for his son?
4. With what thoughts does Hector comfort his wife before he leaves?

Interpreting

5. What considerations and values are pitted against each other in this excerpt? Which set of values is finally placed above all other concerns?

Extending

6. Hector, poised between home and battleground, recognizes his responsibility to both; somehow he must justify his public actions and his private ones as well. In what cases may one's responsibility to the public good be greater than one's responsibility to home and family?

Achilles and Hector

Recalling

1. What are possible courses of action that Hector considers as Achilles approaches him? What course of action does Hector choose?
2. What comparisons does Homer use to describe Achilles in lines 48–57? How is Hector affected by Achilles' appearance?
3. What agreement does Hector attempt to make with Achilles for the burial of their bodies? What is Achilles' response?
4. Describe Hector's death.

Interpreting

5. What are the different reasons Hector and Achilles have for fighting? Which reasons seem more honorable to Homer? Why?
6. How does Homer make Hector appear vulnerable compared to Achilles?
7. What seems to be Homer's attitude toward fate? Consider especially the character of Hector.

Extending

8. Considering the respective behavior of Achilles and Hector as Hector lies dying, which of the two strikes you as a greater, more honorable man? Why? What concept of honor is implied in this excerpt?

Hector's Funeral

Recalling

1. After Hector's death, what vision of the future does Andromache imagine?
2. How long do the Trojans take to bury their dead?
3. Describe the funeral rites performed for Hector.

Interpreting

4. Hector is prepared to die fighting in order to preserve his reputation; nevertheless, he is commemorated by his people and by Homer as the man he was in peacetime: "Hector, tamer of horses." What does this representation of Hector suggest about Homer's attitude toward war and toward the concepts of honor and reputation?

Extending

5. What value can you see in the elaborate funeral rituals practiced by the Greeks and the Trojans?

VIEWPOINT

In describing the characterization of Hector in the *Iliad*, the scholar W. A. Camps writes,

What leaves us with our strongest impression about Hector is his experience, what happens to him in the story. It is a tragic experience in the classic sense of the term. . . . The pathos [the quality in something that arouses pity or sympathy] of Hector's experience is enhanced . . . by a memorable scene with his wife and baby son which fixes in our minds the cause for which he is fighting and makes us feel for him throughout the story as typically human as well as heroic.

1. In terms of what you know about Hector, how would you characterize his experience? What, in your own words, is the "pathos" of his experience?
2. In what ways is Hector both heroic and typically human?

LITERARY FOCUS

The Epic

An **epic** is a long narrative poem written in a lofty style that tells a story about courageous characters who hold high positions in society and whose actions are important to the history of their nation. The heroes of epics appear larger than life; even their faults are frequently only exaggerated virtues. Divine or supernatural forces protect and advise epic heroes and intervene in human affairs.

Early epics—*Gilgamesh* (the most ancient of epics, from the Sumerian civilization in about 2000 B.C.), the *Iliad,* the *Odyssey,* and *Beowulf* (page 9)—were subject to change, as they were told orally. When written literature became established, however, the oral traditions of the past disappeared and epics assumed fixed form. The first western literary epic was Virgil's *Aeneid* (page 718). Other poems of immense importance to the epic tradition are Dante's *Divine Comedy* (page 738) and Milton's *Paradise Lost* (page 230).

Thinking About the Epic

1. Could Hector qualify as the hero of the *Iliad*? Why or why not?
2. What epic qualities are embodied in Hector as well as in Achilles?

The Epithet and Homeric Simile

An **epithet** is an adjective or adjective phrase describing a characteristic of a person or a thing.

Homer's epithets are often compound, such as "rosy-fingered dawn" or "swift-footed Achilles." Epithets used frequently enough become part of a name.

Since the epic poet was constrained by the meter of his poem, it was helpful for him to be able to use an epithet plus a proper name as a building block of regular meter. When referring to a character, the poet would have at hand a stock of epithets that he knew from experience would satisfy certain metrical demands.

The **Homeric simile,** or epic simile, is longer and more elaborate than a conventional simile. It expands the comparison with a detailed and somewhat lengthy description that extends over several lines of verse. For example, at the beginning of the excerpt from Book 22, a Homeric simile describes Hector as he waits for Achilles to strike. Hector is standing firm,

> The way a serpent, fed on poisonous herbs,
> coiled at his lair upon a mountainside,
> with all his length of hate awaits a man
> and eyes him evilly.

Thinking About the Epithet and Homeric Simile

1. Find four epithets in the excerpt from Book 22. How would the meaning of the passage change if the epithets were omitted?
2. Find three Homeric similes in the excerpt from Book 22. Explain who or what is being compared, and explain what details expand the comparison into a Homeric simile.

Aesop   c. 620–560 B.C.

Ancient Greece was rich not only in epics and in mythology but in folktales and folksongs as well. One common type of folktale was the fable, a brief story with characters who are usually animals and occasionally people or inanimate objects. The characters in a fable always talk and act like human beings, and most fables lead to a moral in the form of a proverb that teaches the lesson of the tale. The best-known Greek fables are attributed to Aesop [ē′səp], who, according to popular legend, was a widely traveled slave who lived around 600 B.C. As with Homer, not much is known of Aesop's life.

Many have written fables since Aesop, including the seventeenth-century Frenchman La Fontaine and the eighteenth-century Englishman John Gay. From the Victorian Age, Rudyard Kipling's *Jungle Books* and *Just So Stories* are variants of animal fables.

Aesop

The Town Mouse and the Country Mouse

Translated by Joseph Jacobs

Now you must know that a town mouse once upon a time went on a visit to his cousin in the country. He was rough and ready, this cousin, but he loved his town friend and made him heartily welcome. Beans and bacon, cheese and bread, were all he had to offer, but he offered them freely. The town mouse rather turned up his long nose at this country fare, and said: "I cannot understand, Cousin, how you can put up with such poor food as this, but of course you cannot expect anything better in the country; come you with me and I will show you how to live. When you have been in town a week you will wonder how you could ever have stood a country life."

No sooner said than done: the two mice set off for the town and arrived at the town mouse's residence late at night. "You will want some refreshment after our long journey," said the polite town mouse, and took his friend into the grand dining room. There they found the remains of a fine feast, and soon the two mice were eating up jellies and cakes and all that was nice. Suddenly they heard growling and barking. "What is that?" said the country mouse. "It is only the dogs of the house," answered the other. "Only!" said the country mouse. "I do not like that music at my dinner." Just at that moment the door flew open, in came two huge mastiffs,[1] and the two mice had to scamper down and run off. "Good-by, Cousin," said the country mouse. "What! going so soon?" said the other. "Yes," he replied.

Better beans and bacon in peace than jellies and cakes in fear.

---

1. **mastiffs:** very large dogs.

The Fox and the Grapes

Translated by Joseph Jacobs

One hot summer's day a fox was strolling through an orchard till he came to a bunch of grapes just ripening on a vine which had been trained over a lofty branch. "Just the thing to quench my thirst," quoth he. Drawing back a few paces, he took a run and a jump, and just missed the bunch. Turning round again with a one, two, three, he jumped up, but with no greater success. Again and again he tried after the tempting morsel, but at last had to give it up, and walked away with his nose in the air, saying: "I am sure they are sour."

It is easy to despise what you cannot get.

The Goatherd and the Wild Goats

Translated by Will Nickless

A goatherd, driving his animals from their pasture at sunset, found that some wild goats had mingled with them, and shut them up together with his own goats for the night. In the morning it snowed very hard, so that he could not take the herd from the fold to their usual feeding-place. He gave his goats just enough food to keep them alive, but fed the strangers handsomely, in the hope of enticing them to stay with his flock.

When the thaw set in he led them all out to feed, and the wild goats scampered away as fast as they could to the mountains. The goatherd accused them of being very ungrateful for leaving him, when during the blizzard he had taken more care of them than he had of his own goats. One of the wild goats turned about and called back: "That is the very reason why we are leaving you. As you treated us much better than the goats you have had so long, it is clear that if others came after us, you would prefer them to ourselves."

STUDY QUESTIONS

Recalling

1. What kind of meal does the Country Mouse serve to his cousin, and what does the Town Mouse think of his cousin's meal? Why does the Country Mouse leave the city so quickly?
2. In "The Fox and the Grapes" why does the fox want the grapes? How does he try to reach them? How hard does he try to reach them?
3. In "The Goatherd and the Wild Goats" how much does the goatherd feed his own goats? The new goats? What do the wild goats do as soon as the thaw sets in? Why?

Interpreting

4. Do you think the two cousins in "The Town Mouse and the Country Mouse" understand each other? Which way of life does Aesop seem to find more attractive?
5. Explain how the moral of "The Fox and the Grapes" is illustrated by the fable.
6. The morals for "The Town Mouse and the Country Mouse" and "The Fox and the Grapes" are short and direct; write a moral for "The Goatherd and the Wild Goats."

VIEWPOINT

When La Fontaine, a French fabulist, or fable writer, of the seventeenth century, said that a fable is "a picture in which each one of us may find his own portrait," he implied that fables hold up a mirror to human behavior. In Aesop's time, as in La Fontaine's, it was safer to criticize by disguising one's characters in animal clothing. Perhaps the fabulists also recognized that people are more ready to learn from the mistakes of others.

■ Is the behavior depicted by Aesop's fables typical today, or has human nature changed?

LITERARY FOCUS

The Fable

A **fable** is a short tale that teaches a moral, or lesson. Fables frequently use animals and plants as well as people as characters. Fables, which may be written in verse or prose, satirize human weaknesses. While some have a pointed moral at the end, others require the reader to draw the moral. Popular fables have become proverbial in many languages; for example, in English "The Fox and the Grapes" has evolved into the proverbial expression *sour grapes.*

Thinking About the Fable

■ How effectively do these three fables satirize human weaknesses? Can you think of any modern-day situations to which you could apply the morals from "The Town Mouse and the Country Mouse" and "The Fox and the Grapes"?

COMPOSITION

Comparing and Contrasting the Epic and the Fable

■ What are the differences and similarities between the epic and the fable in style and in intent? Discuss their narrative techniques and the way description is used in the epic and in the fable. Consider what the storytellers of the epic and the fable wanted to convey to their audiences. *For help with this assignment, refer to Lesson 2 in the Writing About Literature Handbook at the back of this book.*

Writing a Fable

■ Write a fable using only animal characters to illustrate the lesson to be found in the following proverbial expression: *It's like looking for a needle in a haystack.*

Sappho   c. 610–580 B.C.

Sappho is considered one of the world's greatest women poets, even though only fragments of her work have survived. Little is known about her life: She was of noble birth, born in the late seventh century B.C., and wrote most of her poems in the early part of the sixth century. She was married and had a daughter named Cleis, and she had three brothers, one of whom she gave some poetic advice on the topics of money and love. Sappho gathered around her a group of young women whom she instructed in the cultural values and social ways of their noble class.

Sappho's poems are personal, revealing her feelings and her private emotional life in a frank and simple manner. Her concerns were love, the joy of children, nature, and the world around her. Her poems were often sung and accompanied by music and dance; try reading them aloud, listening to the music in the words and visualizing the images.

Sappho

Four Fragments

Translated by Willis Barnstone (1 and 4)
and William Ellery Leonard (2 and 3)

1

Hesperus,[1] you bring home all the bright dawn
    disperses,
bring home the sheep,
bring home the goat, bring the child home to
    its mother.

2

Off in the twilight hung the low full moon,
And all the women stood before it grave,
As round an altar. Thus at holy times
The Cretan[2] damsels dance melodiously
With delicate feet about the sacrifice,
Trampling the tender bloom of the soft grass.

3

Round about me hum the winds of autumn,
Cool between the apple boughs: and slumber,
Flowing from the quivering leaves to
    earthward,
        Spreads as a river.

4

I could not hope
to touch the sky
with my two arms.

---

1. **Hesperus** [hes′pər əs]: evening star, actually the planet Venus.
2. **Cretan:** from the island of Crete in the Mediterranean Sea, southeast of Greece.

Pindar *c. 522–443 B.C.*

Unlike the personal lyrical simplicity of Sappho's poetry, Pindar's poetry is public and complex. Pindar was born at Thebes (a leading city-state of ancient Greece, northwest of Athens) to an ancient aristocratic family, whose values he later glorified in his poetry. He studied in Athens, where, by the age of twenty, he had already won recognition as a poet. Pindar studied with both the finest poets and the greatest musicians. He incorporated much music into his poetry, which was performed and accompanied by solo and choral voices and by flute, lyre, or cymbals. Pindar's odes are poems that celebrate state and religious occasions or glorify the winners of athletic competitions or the heroes of wars. They are dignified, imaginative, and intellectual in tone.

Athletic competitions were an essential part of Greek religious festivals and mourning rituals. The Greeks believed that the games, held in honor of the gods, pleased the spirits of the dead. Tradition required that winners receive valuable prizes and their deeds be honored in songs. Pindar wrote fourteen odes to honor winners of Olympian games. These were the most important of the Greek competitions, given in honor of Zeus, the king of the gods. "Olympia 11" commemorates a boxing match: In 476 B.C. the winner of the boys' boxing match was Agesidamos of Locris, a city in what is now southern Italy.

Pindar

Olympia 11

Translated by Richmond Lattimore

There is a time when men need most favoring
gales; there is a time for water from the sky,
rain, child of cloud.
But if by endeavor a man win fairly, soft-spoken songs
5 are given, to be a beginning of men's
speech to come and a true seal on great achievements.

Abundant is such praise laid up for victories
Olympian.[1] My lips have good will
to marshal these words; yet only
by God's grace does a man blossom in the wise turning
10   of his thought.
Son of Archestratos, know
that for the sake, Agesidamos, of your boxing

I shall enchant in strain of song a glory upon
your olive wreath of gold
15 and bespeak the race of the West Wind Lokrians.
There acclaim him; I warrant you,
Muses, you will visit no gathering cold to strangers
nor lost to lovely things
but deep to the heart in wisdom, and spearmen also.
    No thing, neither devious fox
20 nor loud lion, may change the nature born in his blood.

---

1. **Olympian:** referring to games of ancient Greece that took place
   in Olympia.

Sappho

STUDY QUESTIONS

Recalling
1. In Fragment 1 what does Hesperus, the evening star, bring home?
2. In Fragment 2 what image does Sappho use to relate nature and religion?
3. In Fragment 3 what is sleep compared to?

Interpreting
4. What universal sentiment does Fragment 4 express?
5. What are the underlying sentiments in Fragments 1–3?

COMPOSITION

Analyzing the Poet's Techniques
■ Sappho's poetry is fresh, spontaneous, and exquisite. Analyze the poetic techniques Sappho uses in the four fragments. Look at her choice of vocabulary, her selection of sounds (which are different in Greek, of course, but are translated as poetically as possible), her use of adjectives and other modifiers, and her imagery.

Composing a Poetic Fragment
■ Compose a very short poem in the manner of Sappho's fragments. Express a sentiment in a very few lines, using no more than two images.

Pindar

STUDY QUESTIONS

Recalling
1. What reason does Pindar give for wanting to praise the athlete?
2. To whom does the poet turn for help in writing his song of praise? Why?
3. What does the poet say about the fox and the lion in the last stanza?

Interpreting
4. What does Pindar observe about the innate nature of all things? How does this belief apply to the athlete and the poet, both of whom strive for greatness and immortality?

Extending
5. In what ways are artists and athletes alike?

COMPOSITION

Paraphrasing a Poem
■ Rewrite this ode in your own words. Write in prose, using paragraphs instead of stanzas. Stay close to the original meaning of the poem, keeping in mind Pindar's lofty tone and his purpose: to celebrate excellence in athletics and art.

Writing a Research Report
■ Imagine that Agesidamos has been transported to our time. He is curious about modern-day Olympic Games, and he asks you to describe them: When and where do they take place? Are they still given in honor of the gods? Who participates in them, and where do the participants come from? How popular are the games today? How are the winners rewarded? Finally, he asks your impression of the Olympics. Do the necessary research, and compose a report that will answer Agesidamos' questions.

Opposite page: Detail, statue by Greek sculptor Polyclitus, fifth century B.C.

Sophocles   *496?–406 B.C.*

The glory of ancient Greece survives in its drama as well as in its epics, folktales, and lyric poetry. The fifth century B.C. was the most important period of Greek drama, when the most famous Greek dramatists—Aeschylus, Sophocles, and Euripides—were writing. Beloved and revered as a playwright in his own time, Sophocles [sof′ə klēz′] is one of the greatest tragic dramatists of all time. He lived in Athens during the most glorious period of Greek history, the Classical Period. An ideal Greek citizen who participated in all forms of public life, Sophocles served as commissioner of public affairs, and in 440 B.C., when he was about fifty-five, he fought as a general in the war against the people of Samos, an island in the Aegean Sea.

However, Sophocles' lasting influence on western culture is seen in his plays, of which he is said to have written 125. Only seven have survived, and the most famous are his tragedies *Oedipus Rex, Electra,* and *Antigone* [an tig′ə nē]. More than twenty of his plays won first prize at the annual dramatic competition in Athens, and many more won second prize. Today Sophocles' plays are performed around the world, from summer festivals where they are presented in modern Greek in the ancient theater at Epidaurus to experimental productions in English in off-Broadway playhouses.

Greek drama began in the seventh century B.C. as a part of religious rituals surrounding birth and death. Soon drama contests were held in honor of the god Dionysus, and by 534 B.C. the first contest for tragedy was held in Athens. Originally consisting of the chorus and a single actor, Greek drama gradually added more actors as the subject matter became less ritualistic. Sophocles is credited with introducing a third actor to the stage and initiating the use of painted sets.

Theatergoing for the Greeks was more than entertainment. Considered part of a citizen's education and supported by the state, Greek drama allowed mass participation in the tragedy and comedy of human experience (as many as forty thousand people attended a performance at a time). The plays, which took place during the day or for several days at a time during a festival, were presented in outdoor auditoriums. The circular orchestra where the chorus sang and danced had a background called the *skene* (from which the English word *scene* evolved). The acoustics were excellent; voices deflected by the stone sides of the auditorium could be heard everywhere without amplification.

Introducing **Antigone**

For the subject matter of his plays, Sophocles drew upon **legends**, or tales handed down for generations among the people of a certain region. The plots of *Antigone* and *Oedipus Rex* are based on the legends of the city Thebes. Sophocles knew that his audiences were familiar with these legends. For instance, those who came to see the tragedy of *Antigone* already knew that Oedipus [ed′ə pəs] was abandoned by his parents on a hillside at birth. This action was an attempt to escape the prophecy that Oedipus, as king of Thebes, would kill his father and marry his mother. After being sheltered by a shepherd and reaching maturity, Oedipus consults the oracle at Delphi [del′fī]. (The Greeks believed that the god Apollo conveyed his wisdom through the oracle, or prophet, a woman named Pythia. Cities as well as individuals sought the advice of the oracle.) When the oracle repeats the prophecy told to his parents, Oedipus attempts to prevent the tragic events by leaving the couple he believes to be his parents. Traveling to Thebes, he kills a man on the road. When he reaches the city, he is questioned by the Sphinx, a monster who sits at the gates of Thebes and kills passers-by who cannot solve her riddle. By correctly answering the riddle Oedipus saves Thebes and marries its recently widowed queen, with whom he has two sons and two daughters. When the city is in the grip of a plague, an oracle predicts that there will be no relief until the murderer of the previous king has been revealed. At this point Oedipus learns not only that he has murdered the king but also that the king was his father. Oedipus blinds himself and leaves Thebes in exile.

Upon Oedipus' death, his sons, Eteocles and Polyneices, agree to rule Thebes in alternate years; when Eteocles' year ends, however, he refuses to allow Polyneices to take over. Thereupon Polyneices gathers an army and attacks Thebes. In the ensuing battle the brothers kill each other. Their uncle, Creon, who succeeds them as king, buries Eteocles with full honors while proclaiming that Polyneices, as an enemy of the city, shall be denied burial.

The daughters of Oedipus, Antigone and Ismene, are therefore faced with the choice of denying a brother burial rites, thus condemning him to eternal unrest, or of disobeying the command of their uncle and king. *Antigone* opens with Antigone's decision to bury Polyneices.

Key Ideas in *Antigone*

As you read Antigone, look for references to each of the following ideas. You will thus grasp the play's important themes.

* The laws of the state versus the laws of tradition
* The rights and social position of women
* The consequences of uncompromising pride

Teiresias.   Ismene and Antigone.   Creon.

Sophocles

Antigone

Translated by Dudley Fitts and Robert Fitzgerald

CHARACTERS

ANTIGONE [an tig′ə nē]: daughter of Oedipus, former king of Thebes; she has vowed to give her brother Polyneices an honorable burial

ISMENE: Antigone's younger sister; she is unable to break the law in order to help Antigone bury their brother

CREON [krē′on]: the new king of Thebes, uncle of Antigone, Ismene, and Polyneices; he decrees that Polyneices' body must not be buried

EURYDICE [yoo rid′ə sē]: wife of Creon

HAIMON: son of Creon, engaged to Antigone

TEIRESIAS [tī rē′sē əs]: a blind prophet who predicts the consequences of Creon's orders

A SENTRY serving Creon

CHORUS, made up of about fifteen citizens of Thebes

GUARDS

SERVANTS

Scene. Before the palace of CREON, *king of Thebes. A central double door, and two lateral doors. A platform extends the length of the façade, and from this platform three steps lead down into the* "orchestra," *or chorus-ground.*

Time. Dawn of the day after the repulse of the Argive army[1] from the assault on Thebes.

Prologue

[ANTIGONE *and* ISMENE *enter from the central door of the palace.*]

ANTIGONE. Ismene, dear sister,
    You would think that we had already suffered enough
    For the curse on Oedipus:
    I cannot imagine any grief
5   That you and I have not gone through. And now—
    Have they told you of the new decree of our King Creon?

ISMENE. I have heard nothing: I know
    That two sisters lost two brothers, a double death
    In a single hour; and I know that the Argive army
10   Fled in the night; but beyond this, nothing.

ANTIGONE. I thought so. And that is why I wanted you
    To come out here with me. There is something we must do.

ISMENE. Why do you speak so strangely?

ANTIGONE. Listen, Ismene:
15   Creon buried our brother Eteocles
    With military honors, gave him a soldier's funeral,
    And it was right that he should: but Polyneices,
    Who fought as bravely and died as miserably—
    They say that Creon has sworn
20   No one shall bury him, no one mourn for him,
    But his body must lie in the fields, a sweet treasure
    For carrion birds[2] to find as they search for food.
    That is what they say, and our good Creon is coming here
    To announce it publicly: and the penalty—
    Stoning to death in the public square!
25   There it is,
    And now you can prove what you are:
    A true sister, or a traitor to your family.

ISMENE. Antigone, you are mad! What could I possibly do?

---

1. **Argive army:** soldiers from Argos who, under the leadership of Polyneices, attacked Thebes.
2. **carrion birds:** birds of prey.

ANTIGONE. You must decide whether you will help me or not.

30 **ISMENE.** I do not understand you. Help you in what?

ANTIGONE. Ismene, I am going to bury him. Will you come?

ISMENE. Bury him! You have just said the new law forbids it.

ANTIGONE. He is my brother. And he is your brother, too.

ISMENE. But think of the danger! Think what Creon will do!

35 **ANTIGONE.** Creon is not strong enough to stand in my way.

   ISMENE. Ah sister!
   Oedipus died, everyone hating him
   For what his own search brought to light, his eyes
   Ripped out by his own hand: and Iocaste died,
40   His mother and wife at once: she twisted the cords
   That strangled her life; and our two brothers died,
   Each killed by the other's sword. And we are left:
   But oh, Antigone,
   Think how much more terrible than these
45   Our own death would be if we should go against Creon
   And do what he has forbidden! We are only women.
   We cannot fight with men, Antigone!
   The law is strong, we must give in to the law
   In this thing, and in worse. I beg the dead
50   To forgive me, but I am helpless: I must yield
   To those in authority. And I think it is dangerous business
   To be always meddling.

   ANTIGONE.   If that is what you think,
   I should not want you, even if you asked to come.
   You have made your choice, you can be what you want to be.
55   But I will bury him: and if I must die,
   I say that this crime is holy: I shall lie down
   With him in death, and I shall be as dear
   To him as he to me.
               It is the dead,
   Not the living, who make the longest demands:
   We die forever . . .
60   You may do as you like,
   Since apparently the laws of the gods mean nothing to you.

   ISMENE. They mean a great deal to me: but I have no strength
   To break laws that were made for the public good.

ANTIGONE. That must be your excuse, I suppose. But as for me,
   I will bury the brother I love.

65 **ISMENE.**   Antigone,
   I am so afraid for you!

ANTIGONE.   You need not be:
You have yourself to consider, after all.

ISMENE. But no one must hear of this, you must tell no one!
I will keep it a secret, I promise!

ANTIGONE.   Oh tell it! Tell everyone!
70 Think how they'll hate you when it all comes out
If they learn that you knew about it all the time!

ISMENE. So fiery! You should be cold with fear.

ANTIGONE. Perhaps. But I am doing only what I must.

ISMENE. But can you do it? I say that you cannot.

75 **ANTIGONE.** Very well: when my strength gives out, I shall do no more.

ISMENE. Impossible things should not be tried at all.

ANTIGONE. Go away, Ismene:
I shall be hating you soon, and the dead will, too.
For your words are hateful. Leave me my foolish plan:
80 I am not afraid of the danger: if it means death,
It will not be the worst of deaths—death without honor.

ISMENE. Go then, if you feel that you must.
You are unwise,
But a loyal friend indeed to those who love you.

[*Exit into the palace.* ANTIGONE *goes off, left. Enter the* CHORUS.]

Parados[3]

CHORUS. Now the long blade of the sun, lying   [*Strophe 1*]
Level east to west, touches with glory
Thebes of the Seven Gates. Open, unlidded
Eye of golden day! O marching light
5 Across the eddy and rush of Dirce's stream,[4]
Striking the white shields of the enemy
Thrown headlong backward from the blaze of morning!

CHORAGOS.[5] Polyneices their commander
Roused them with windy phrases,
10 He the wild eagle screaming

---

3. **Parados** [par'ə däs']: song chanted as the chorus entered the stage. Facing
one direction, the chorus chanted the **Strophe** [strō'fē], and the other direction,
the **Antistrophe** [an tis'trə fē].
4. **Dirce's** [dər'sēz] **stream:** Dirce, a queen of Thebes, was murdered and
thrown into the stream that thereafter bore her name.
5. **Choragos** [kôr ā'gəs]: chorus leader.

Insults above our land,
His wings their shields of snow,
His crest their marshaled helms.

CHORUS. Against our seven gates in a yawning ring   [Antistrophe 1]
15   The famished spears came onward in the night;
But before his jaws were sated with our blood,
Or pinefire took the garland of our towers,
He was thrown back; and as he turned, great Thebes—
No tender victim for his noisy power—
20   Rose like a dragon behind him, shouting war.

CHORAGOS. For God hates utterly
The bray of bragging tongues;
And when he beheld their smiling,
Their swagger of golden helms,
25   The frown of his thunder blasted
Their first man from our walls.

CHORUS. We heard his shout of triumph high in the air   [Strophe 2]
Turn to a scream; far out in a flaming arc
He fell with his windy torch, and the earth struck him.
30   And others storming in fury no less than his
Found shock of death in the dusty joy of battle.

CHORAGOS. Seven captains at seven gates
Yielded their clanging arms to the god
That bends the battle line and breaks it.
35   These two only, brothers in blood,
Face to face in matchless rage,
Mirroring each the other's death,
Clashed in long combat.

CHORUS. But now in the beautiful morning of victory   [Antistrophe 2]
40   Let Thebes of the many chariots sing for joy!
With hearts for dancing we'll take leave of war:
Our temples shall be sweet with hymns of praise,
And the long night shall echo with our chorus.

Scene I

CHORAGOS. But now at last our new king is coming:
Creon of Thebes. Menoikeus' son.
In this auspicious dawn of his reign
What are the new complexities
5   That shifting fate has woven for him?
What is his counsel? Why has he summoned
The old men to hear him?

[Enter CREON *from the palace, center. He addresses the* CHORUS *from the top step.]*

CREON. Gentlemen: I have the honor to inform you that our ship of state, which recent storms have threatened to destroy, has
10 come safely to harbor at last, guided by the merciful wisdom of Heaven. I have summoned you here this morning because I know that I can depend upon you: your devotion to King Laios⁶ was absolute; you never hesitated in your duty to our late ruler Oedipus; and when Oedipus died, your loyalty was transferred to his
15 children. Unfortunately, as you know, his two sons, the princes Eteocles and Polyneices, have killed each other in battle; and I, as the next in blood, have succeeded to the full power of the throne.

I am aware, of course, that no ruler can expect complete loy-
20 alty from his subjects until he has been tested in office. Nevertheless, I say to you at the very outset that I have nothing but contempt for the kind of governor who is afraid, for whatever reason, to follow the course that he knows is best for the state; and as for the man who sets private friendship above the public
25 welfare—I have no use for him, either. I call God to witness that if I saw my country headed for ruin, I should not be afraid to speak out plainly; and I need hardly remind you that I would never have any dealings with an enemy of the people. No one values friendship more highly than I; but we must remember that
30 friends made at the risk of wrecking our ship are not real friends at all.

These are my principles, at any rate, and that is why I have made the following decisions concerning the sons of Oedipus: Eteocles, who died as a man should die, fighting for his country,
35 is to be buried with full military honors, with all the ceremony that is usual when the greatest heroes die; but his brother Polyneices, who broke his exile to come back with fire and sword against his native city and the shrines of his fathers' gods, whose one idea was to spill the blood of his blood and sell his own
40 people into slavery—Polyneices, I say, is to have no burial; no man is to touch him or say the least prayer for him; he shall lie on the plain, unburied; and the birds and the scavenging dogs can do with him whatever they like.

This is my command, and you can see the wisdom behind it.
45 As long as I am king, no traitor is going to be honored with the loyal man. But whoever shows by word and deed that he is on the side of the state—he shall have my respect while he is living, and my reverence when he is dead.

CHORAGOS. If that is your will, Creon son of Menoikeus,
50 You have the right to enforce it: we are yours.

---

6. **King Laios** [lā′əs]: father of Oedipus and previous king of Thebes.

CREON. That is my will. Take care that you do your part.

CHORAGOS. We are old men: let the younger ones carry it out.

CREON. I do not mean that: The sentries have been appointed.

CHORAGOS. Then what is it that you would have us do?

55 CREON. You will give no support to whoever breaks this law.

CHORAGOS. Only a crazy man is in love with death!

CREON. And death it is; yet money talks, and the wisest
Have sometimes been known to count a few coins too many.

[*Enter* SENTRY *from left.*]

SENTRY. I'll not say that I'm out of breath from running, King, be-
60 cause every time I stopped to think about what I have to tell
you, I felt like going back. And all the time a voice kept saying,
"You fool, don't you know you're walking straight into trouble?";
and then another voice: "Yes, but if you let somebody else get
the news to Creon first, it will be even worse than that for you!"
65 But good sense won out, at least I hope it was good sense, and
here I am with a story that makes no sense at all; but I'll tell it
anyhow, because, as they say, what's going to happen's going to
happen, and—

CREON. Come to the point. What have you to say?

70 SENTRY. I did not do it. I did not see who did it. You must not
punish me for what someone else has done.

CREON. A comprehensive defense! More effective, perhaps,
If I knew its purpose. Come: what is it?

SENTRY. A dreadful thing . . . I don't know how to put it—

CREON. Out with it!

75 SENTRY.   Well, then;
The dead man—
                    Polyneices—

[*Pause. The* SENTRY *is overcome, fumbles for words.* CREON *waits
impassively.*]

                              out there—
                                        someone—
New dust on the slimy flesh! [*Pause. No sign from* CREON.]
Someone has given it burial that way, and
Gone—[*Long pause.* CREON *finally speaks with deadly control.*]

CREON. And the man who dared do this?

80 SENTRY.   I swear I
Do not know! You must believe me!

Listen:
The ground was dry, not a sign of digging, no,
Not a wheeltrack in the dust, no trace of anyone.
It was when they relieved us this morning; and one of them,
The corporal, pointed to it.

85   There it was,
The strangest—

                    Look:
The body, just mounded over with light dust: you see?
Not buried really, but as if they'd covered it
Just enough for the ghost's peace. And no sign
90   Of dogs or any wild animal that had been there.

And then what a scene there was! Every man of us
Accusing the other: we all proved the other man did it,
We all had proof that we could not have done it.
We were ready to take hot iron in our hands,
95   Walk through fire, swear by all the gods,
It was not I!
I do not know who it was, but it was not I!

[CREON's *rage has been mounting steadily, but the* SENTRY *is
too intent upon his story to notice it.*]

And then, when this came to nothing, someone said
A thing that silenced us and made us stare
100   Down at the ground: You had to be told the news,
And one of us had to do it! We threw the dice,
And the bad luck fell to me. So here I am,
No happier to be here than you are to have me:
Nobody likes the man who brings bad news.

CHORAGOS. I have been wondering, King: can it be that the gods
105   have done this?

CREON [*furiously*]. Stop!
Must you doddering wrecks
Go out of your heads entirely? "The gods!"
Intolerable!
110   The gods favor this corpse? Why? How had he served them?
Tried to loot their temples, burn their images,
Yes, and the whole state, and its laws with it!
Is it your senile opinion that the gods love to honor bad men?
A pious thought!—
                    No, from the very beginning
115   There have been those who have whispered together,
Stiff-necked anarchists, putting their heads together,
Scheming against me in alleys. These are the men,
And they have bribed my own guard to do this thing.

[*Sententiously*] Money!
120 There's nothing in the world so demoralizing as money.
Down go your cities,
Homes gone, men gone, honest hearts corrupted,
Crookedness of all kinds, and all for money!

[*To* SENTRY] But you—!
I swear by God and by the throne of God,
125 The man who has done this thing shall pay for it!
Find that man, bring him to me, or your death
Will be the least of your problems: I'll string you up
Alive, and there will be certain ways to make you
Discover your employer before you die;
And the process may teach you a lesson you seem to have
130   missed:
The dearest profit is sometimes all too dear:
That depends on the source. Do you understand me?
A fortune won is often misfortune.

SENTRY. King, may I speak?

CREON.   Your very voice distresses me.

135 SENTRY. Are you sure that it is my voice, and not your conscience?

CREON. By God, he wants to analyze me now!

SENTRY. It is not what I say, but what has been done, that hurts you.

CREON. You talk too much.

SENTRY.   Maybe; but I've done nothing.

CREON. Sold your soul for some silver: that's all you've done.

140 SENTRY. How dreadful it is when the right judge judges wrong!

CREON. Your figures of speech
May entertain you now; but unless you bring me the man,
You will get little profit from them in the end.

[*Exit* CREON *into the palace.*]

SENTRY. "Bring me the man"—!
145 I'd like nothing better than bringing him the man!
But bring him or not, you have seen the last of me here.
At any rate, I am safe! [*Exit* SENTRY.]

Ode I[7]

CHORUS. Numberless are the world's wonders, but none   [*Strophe 1*]
More wonderful than man; the storm-gray sea

---

7. **Ode:** song of the chorus to separate scenes.

Yields to his prows, the huge crests bear him high;
Earth, holy and inexhaustible, is graven
5 With shining furrows where his plows have gone
Year after year, the timeless labor of stallions.

The lightboned birds and beasts that cling to cover,   [*Antistrophe 1*]
The lithe fish lighting their reaches of dim water,
All are taken, tamed in the net of his mind;
10 The lion on the hill, the wild horse windy-maned,
Resign to him; and his blunt yoke has broken
The sultry shoulders of the mountain bull.

Words also, and thought as rapid as air,   [*Strophe 2*]
He fashions to his good use; statecraft is his,
15 And his the skill that deflects the arrows of snow,
The spears of winter rain: from every wind
He has made himself secure—from all but one:
In the late wind of death he cannot stand.

O clear intelligence, force beyond all measure!   [*Antistrophe 2*]
20 O fate of man, working both good and evil!
When the laws are kept, how proudly his city stands!
When the laws are broken, what of his city then?
Never may the anarchic man find rest at my hearth,
Never be it said that my thoughts are his thoughts.

Scene II

[*Reenter* SENTRY, *leading* ANTIGONE.]

CHORAGOS. What does this mean? Surely this captive woman
  Is the princess, Antigone. Why should she be taken?

SENTRY. Here is the one who did it! We caught her
  In the very act of burying him.—Where is Creon?

CHORAGOS. Just coming from the house.

[*Enter* CREON, *center.*]

5 CREON.   What has happened?
  Why have you come back so soon?

SENTRY [*expansively*].   O King,
  A man should never be too sure of anything:
  I would have sworn
  That you'd not see me here again; your anger
10 Frightened me so, and the things you threatened me with;
  But how could I tell then
  That I'd be able to solve the case so soon?

No dice-throwing this time; I was only too glad to come!

Here is this woman. She is the guilty one:

15   We found her trying to bury him.
        Take her, then; question her; judge her as you will.
        I am through with the whole thing now, and glad of it.

    CREON. But this is Antigone! Why have you brought her here?

    SENTRY. She was burying him, I tell you!

    CREON [*severely*].   Is this the truth?

20 **SENTRY.** I saw her with my own eyes. Can I say more?

    CREON. The details: Come, tell me quickly!

    SENTRY.   It was like this:
        After those terrible threats of yours, King,
        We went back and brushed the dust away from the body.
        The flesh was soft by now, and stinking,
25   So we sat on a hill to windward and kept guard.
        No napping this time! We kept each other awake.
        But nothing happened until the white round sun
        Whirled in the center of the round sky over us:
        Then, suddenly,
30   A storm of dust roared up from the earth, and the sky
        Went out, the plain vanished with all its trees
        In the stinging dark. We closed our eyes and endured it.

The whirlwind lasted a long time, but it passed;
And then we looked, and there was Antigone!
35   I have seen
A mother bird come back to a stripped nest, heard
Her crying bitterly a broken note or two
For the young ones stolen. Just so, when this girl
Found the bare corpse, and all her love's work wasted,
40   She wept, and cried on heaven to damn the hands
That had done this thing.

                              And then she brought more dust
And sprinkled wine three times for her brother's ghost.

We ran and took her at once. She was not afraid.
Not even when we charged her with what she had done.
She denied nothing.
45   And this was a comfort to me,
And some uneasiness: for it is a good thing
To escape from death, but it is no great pleasure
To bring death to a friend.
                              Yet I always say
There is nothing so comfortable as your own safe skin!
50 CREON [*slowly, dangerously*]. And you, Antigone,
You with your head hanging—do you confess this thing?

ANTIGONE. I do. I deny nothing.

CREON [*to* SENTRY].   You may go. [*Exit* SENTRY.]
[*To* ANTIGONE] Tell me, tell me briefly:
Had you heard my proclamation touching this matter?

55 ANTIGONE. It was public. Could I help hearing it?

CREON. And yet you dared defy the law.

ANTIGONE.   I dared.
It was not God's proclamation. That final justice
That rules the world below makes no such laws.

Your edict, King, was strong,
60   But all your strength is weakness itself against
The immortal unrecorded laws of God.
They are not merely now: they were, and shall be,
Operative forever, beyond man utterly.

I knew I must die, even without your decree:
65   I am only mortal. And if I must die
Now, before it is my time to die,
Surely this is no hardship: can anyone
Living, as I live, with evil all about me,
Think death less than a friend? This death of mine
70   Is of no importance; but if I had left my brother

Lying in death unburied, I should have suffered.
Now I do not.
                        You smile at me. Ah Creon.
Think me a fool, if you like; but it may well be
That a fool convicts me of folly.

75 **CHORAGOS.** Like father, like daughter: both headstrong, deaf to
     reason!
She has never learned to yield.

CREON.   She has much to learn.
The inflexible heart breaks first, the toughest iron
Cracks first, and the wildest horses bend their necks
At the pull of the smallest curb.
                                    Pride? In a slave?
80 This girl is guilty of a double insolence,
Breaking the given laws and boasting of it.
Who is the man here,
She or I, if this crime goes unpunished?
Sister's child, or more than sister's child,
85 Or closer yet in blood—she and her sister
Win bitter death for this!
                [*To servants*] Go, some of you,
Arrest Ismene. I accuse her equally.
Bring her: You will find her sniffling in the house there.
Her mind's a traitor: crimes kept in the dark
90 Cry for light, and the guardian brain shudders;
But how much worse than this
Is brazen boasting of barefaced anarchy!

ANTIGONE. Creon, what more do you want than my death?

CREON.   Nothing.
That gives me everything.

ANTIGONE.   Then I beg you: kill me.
95 This talking is a great weariness: your words
Are distasteful to me, and I am sure that mine
Seem so to you. And yet they should not seem so:
I should have praise and honor for what I have done.
All these men here would praise me
100 Were their lips not frozen shut with fear of you.
[*Bitterly*] Ah the good fortune of kings,
Licensed to say and do whatever they please!

CREON. You are alone here in that opinion.

ANTIGONE. No, they are with me. But they keep their tongues in
     leash.

105 **CREON.** Maybe. But you are guilty, and they are not.

ANTIGONE. There is no guilt in reverence for the dead.

CREON. But Eteocles—was he not your brother too?

ANTIGONE. My brother too.

CREON.   And you insult his memory?

ANTIGONE [*softly*]. The dead man would not say that I insult it.

110 **CREON.** He would: for you honor a traitor as much as him.

ANTIGONE. His own brother, traitor or not, and equal in blood.

CREON. He made war on his country. Eteocles defended it.

ANTIGONE. Nevertheless, there are honors due all the dead.

CREON. But not the same for the wicked as for the just.

115 **ANTIGONE.** Ah Creon, Creon.
    Which of us can say what the gods hold wicked?

CREON. An enemy is an enemy, even dead.

ANTIGONE. It is my nature to join in love, not hate.

CREON [*finally losing patience*]. Go join them, then; if you must
    have your love,
120 Find it in hell!

CHORAGOS. But see, Ismene comes:

[*Enter* ISMENE, *guarded.*]

Those tears are sisterly, the cloud
That shadows her eyes rains down gentle sorrow.

CREON. You too, Ismene,
125 Snake in my ordered house, sucking my blood
Stealthily—and all the time I never knew
That these two sisters were aiming at my throne!
                                        Ismene,
Do you confess your share in this crime, or deny it?
Answer me.

130 **ISMENE.** Yes, if she will let me say so. I am guilty.

ANTIGONE [*coldly*]. No, Ismene. You have no right to say so.
You would not help me, and I will not have you help me.

ISMENE. But now I know what you meant; and I am here
To join you, to take my share of punishment.

135 **ANTIGONE.** The dead man and the gods who rule the dead
Know whose act this was. Words are not friends.

ISMENE. Do you refuse me, Antigone? I want to die with you:

I too have a duty that I must discharge to the dead.

ANTIGONE. You shall not lessen my death by sharing it.

140 ISMENE. What do I care for life when you are dead?

ANTIGONE. Ask Creon. You're always hanging on his opinions.

ISMENE. You are laughing at me. Why, Antigone?

ANTIGONE. It's a joyless laughter, Ismene.

ISMENE.   But can I do nothing?

ANTIGONE. Yes. Save yourself. I shall not envy you.
145   There are those who will praise you; I shall have honor, too.

ISMENE. But we are equally guilty!

ANTIGONE.   No more, Ismene.
    You are alive, but I belong to death.

CREON [*to the* CHORUS]. Gentlemen, I beg you to observe these
        girls:
    One has just now lost her mind; the other,
150   It seems, has never had a mind at all.

ISMENE. Grief teaches the steadiest minds to waver, King.

CREON. Yours certainly did, when you assumed guilt with the guilty!

ISMENE. But how could I go on living without her?

CREON.   You are.
    She is already dead.

ISMENE.   But your own son's bride!

155 CREON. There are places enough for him to push his plow.
    I want no wicked women for my sons!

ISMENE. O dearest Haimon, how your father wrongs you!

CREON. I've had enough of your childish talk of marriage!

CHORAGOS. Do you really intend to steal this girl from your son?

CREON. No: death will do that for me.

160 CHORAGOS.   Then she must die?

CREON [*ironically*]. You dazzle me.
                            —But enough of this talk!
    [*To* GUARDS] You, there, take them away and guard them well:
    For they are but women, and even brave men run
    When they see death coming.

[ISMENE, ANTIGONE, *and* GUARDS *leave.*]

Ode II

CHORUS. Fortunate is the man who has never tasted God's   *[Strophe 1]*
    vengeance!
  Where once the anger of heaven has struck, that house is
    shaken
  Forever: damnation rises behind each child
  Like a wave cresting out of the black northeast,
5 When the long darkness under sea roars up
  And bursts drumming death upon the windwhipped sand.

  I have seen this gathering sorrow from time long past   *[Antistrophe 1]*
  Loom upon Odeipus' children: generation from generation
  Takes the compulsive rage of the enemy god.
10 So lately this last flower of Oedipus' line
  Drank the sunlight! but now a passionate word
  And a handful of dust have closed up all its beauty.

    What mortal arrogance   *[Strophe 2]*
    Transcends the wrath of Zeus?
15 Sleep cannot lull him, nor the effortless long months
  Of the timeless gods: but he is young forever,
  And his house is the shining day of high Olympos.
    All that is and shall be,
    And all the past, is his.
20 No pride on earth is free of the curse of heaven.

    The straying dreams of men   *[Antistrophe 2]*
    May bring them ghosts of joy:
  But as they drowse, the waking embers burn them;
  Or they walk with fixed eyes, as blind men walk.
25 But the ancient wisdom speaks for our own time:
    Fate works most for woe
    With folly's fairest show.
  Man's little pleasure is the spring of sorrow.

Scene III

CHORAGOS. But here is Haimon, King, the last of all your sons.
  Is it grief for Antigone that brings him here,
  And bitterness at being robbed of his bride?

[*Enter* HAIMON.]

CREON. We shall soon see, and no need of diviners.
                           —Son,
5 You have heard my final judgment on that girl:
  Have you come here hating me, or have you come
  With deference and with love, whatever I do?

HAIMON. I am your son, Father. You are my guide.
You make things clear for me, and I obey you.
10 No marriage means more to me than your continuing wisdom.

CREON. Good. That is the way to behave: subordinate
Everything else, my son, to your father's will.
This is what a man prays for, that he may get
Sons attentive and dutiful in his house,
15 Each one hating his father's enemies,
Honoring his father's friends. But if his sons
Fail him, if they turn out unprofitably,
What has he fathered but trouble for himself
And amusement for the malicious?

                                    So you are right
20 Not to lose your head over this woman.
Your pleasure with her would soon grow cold, Haimon.
Of all the people in this city, only she
Has had contempt for my law and broken it.

Do you want me to show myself weak before the people?
25 Or to break my sworn word? No, and I will not.
The woman dies.
I suppose she'll plead "family ties." Well, let her.
If I permit my own family to rebel,
How shall I earn the world's obedience?
30 Show me the man who keeps his house in hand,
He's fit for public authority.

                                    I'll have no dealings
With lawbreakers, critics of the government:
Whoever is chosen to govern should be obeyed—
Must be obeyed, in all things, great and small,
35 Just and unjust! O Haimon,
The man who knows how to obey, and that man only,
Knows how to give commands when the time comes.
You can depend on him, no matter how fast
The spears come: He's a good soldier, he'll stick it out.

40 Anarchy, anarchy! Show me a greater evil!
This is why cities tumble and the great houses rain down,
This is what scatters armies!

No, no: Good lives are made so by discipline.
We keep the laws then, and the lawmakers,
45 And no woman shall defeat us. If we must lose,
Let's lose to a man, at least! Is a woman stronger than we?

CHORAGOS. Unless time has rusted my wits,
What you say, King, is said with point and dignity.

HAIMON [*boyishly earnest*]. Father:
50 Reason is God's crowning gift to man, and you are right

To warn me against losing mine. I cannot say—
I hope that I shall never want to say!—that you
Have reasoned badly. Yet there are other men
Who can reason, too; and their opinions might be helpful.

55 You are not in a position to know everything
That people say or do, or what they feel:
Your temper terrifies them—everyone
Will tell you only what you like to hear.
But I, at any rate, can listen; and I have heard them
60 Muttering and whispering in the dark about this girl.
They say no woman has ever, so unreasonably,
Died so shameful a death for a generous act:
"She covered her brother's body. Is this indecent?
She kept him from dogs and vultures. Is this a crime?
65 Death?—She should have all the honor that we can give her!"

This is the way they talk out there in the city.

You must believe me:
Nothing is closer to me than your happiness.
What could be closer? Must not any son
70 Value his father's fortune as his father does his?
I beg you, do not be unchangeable:
Do not believe that you alone can be right.
The man who thinks that,
The man who maintains that only he has the power
75 To reason correctly, the gift to speak, the soul—
A man like that, when you know him, turns out empty.

It is not reason never to yield to reason!

In flood time you can see how some trees bend,
And because they bend, even their twigs are safe,
80 While stubborn trees are torn up, roots and all.
And the same thing happens in sailing:
Make your sheet[8] fast, never slacken—and over you go,
Head over heels and under: and there's your voyage.
Forget you are angry! Let yourself be moved!
85 I know I am young; but please let me say this:
The ideal condition
Would be, I admit, that men should be right by instinct;
But since we are all too likely to go astray,
The reasonable thing is to learn from those who can teach.

90 **CHORAGOS.** You will do well to listen to him, King,
If what he says is sensible. And you, Haimon,
Must listen to your father—both speak well.

---

8. **sheet:** rope attached to the lower corner of a sail by which the sail is moved.

CREON. You consider it right for a man of my years and experience
To go to school to a boy?

HAIMON.   It is not right
95   If I am wrong. But if I am young, and right,
What does my age matter?

CREON. You think it right to stand up for an anarchist?

HAIMON. Not at all. I pay no respect to criminals.

CREON. Then she is not a criminal?

100 HAIMON. The city would deny it, to a man.

CREON. And the city proposes to teach me how to rule?

HAIMON. Ah. Who is it that's talking like a boy now?

CREON. My voice is the one voice giving orders in this city!

HAIMON. It is no city if it takes orders from one voice.

CREON. The state is the King!

105 HAIMON.   Yes, if the state is a desert.
    [*Pause*]

CREON. This boy, it seems, has sold out to a woman.

HAIMON. If you are a woman: My concern is only for you.

CREON. So? Your "concern"! In a public brawl with your father!

HAIMON. How about you, in a public brawl with justice?

110 CREON. With justice, when all that I do is within my rights?

HAIMON. You have no right to trample on God's right.

CREON [*completely out of control*]. Fool, adolescent fool! Taken in by a woman!

HAIMON. You'll never see me taken in by anything vile.

CREON. Every word you say is for her!

HAIMON [*quietly, darkly*].   And for you.
115   And for me. And for the gods under the earth.

CREON. You'll never marry her while she lives.

HAIMON. Then she must die—But her death will cause another.

CREON. Another?
Have you lost your senses? Is this an open threat?

120 HAIMON. There is no threat in speaking to emptiness.

CREON. I swear you'll regret this superior tone of yours!
You are the empty one!

HAIMON.   If you were not my father,
I'd say you were perverse.

CREON. You girlstruck fool, don't play at words with me!

HAIMON. I am sorry. You prefer silence.

125 CREON.   Now, by God—!
I swear, by all the gods in heaven above us,
You'll watch it, I swear you shall!
                    [*To the* SERVANTS] Bring her out!
Bring the woman out! Let her die before his eyes!
Here, this instant, with her bridegroom beside her!

130 HAIMON. Not here, no; she will not die here, King.
And you will never see my face again.
Go on raving as long as you've a friend to endure you. [*Exit*
    HAIMON.]

CHORAGOS. Gone, gone.
Creon, a young man in a rage is dangerous!

135 CREON. Let him do, or dream to do, more than a man can.
He shall not save these girls from death.

CHORAGOS.   These girls?
You have sentenced them both?

CREON.   No, you are right.
I will not kill the one whose hands are clean.

CHORAGOS. But Antigone?

CREON [*somberly*].   I will carry her far away
140   Out there in the wilderness and lock her
Living in a vault of stone. She shall have food,
As the custom is, to absolve the state of her death.
And there let her pray to the gods of hell:
They are her only gods:
145   Perhaps they will show her an escape from death,
Or she may learn,
                    though late,
That pity shown the dead is pity in vain. [*Exit* CREON.]

Ode III

CHORUS. Love, unconquerable   [*Strophe*]
    Waster of rich men, keeper

Of warm lights and all-night vigil
In the soft face of a girl;
5   Sea-wanderer, forest-visitor!
Even the pure Immortals cannot escape you,
And mortal man, in his one day's dusk,
Trembles before your glory.

Surely you swerve upon ruin   [Antistrophe]
10 The just man's consenting heart,
As here you have made bright anger
Strike between father and son—
And none has conquered but love!
A girl's glance working the will of Heaven:
15 Pleasure to her alone who mocks us,
Merciless Aphrodite.[9]

Scene IV

CHORAGOS [as ANTIGONE *enters, guarded*]. But I can no longer
      stand in awe of this,
   Nor, seeing what I see, keep back my tears.
   Here is Antigone, passing to that chamber
   Where all find sleep at last.

5 ANTIGONE. Look upon me, friends, and pity me
   Turning back at the night's edge to say
   Good-by to the sun that shines for me no longer;
   Now sleepy death
   Summons me down to Acheron,[10] that cold shore:
10 There is no bridesong there, nor any music.

   CHORUS. Yet not unpraised, not without a kind of honor,
   You walk at last into the underworld;
   Untouched by sickness, broken by no sword.
   What woman has ever found your way to death?

15 ANTIGONE. How often I have heard the story of Niobe,[11]
   Tantalos' wretched daughter, how the stone
   Clung fast about her, ivy-close: and they say
   The rain falls endlessly
   And sifting soft snow; her tears are never done.
20 I feel the loneliness of her death in mine.

   CHORUS. But she was born of Heaven, and you
   Are woman, woman-born. If her death is yours,

----

9. **Aphrodite** [af′rə dī′tē]: Greek goddess of love.
10. **Acheron** [ak′ə ron′]: in Greek mythology, one of the rivers that the soul crosses to reach Hades.
11. **Niobe** [nī′ō bē′]: Because she boasted excessively about her children, the gods punished Niobe by killing them all and by turning her into a column of stone which weeps continuously.

A mortal woman's, is this not for you
Glory in our world and in the world beyond?

25 ANTIGONE. You laugh at me. Ah, friends, friends,
Can you not wait until I am dead? O Thebes,
O men many-charioted, in love with fortune,
Dear springs of Dirce, sacred Theban grove,
Be witnesses for me, denied all pity,
30 Unjustly judged! and think a word of love
For her whose path turns
Under dark earth, where there are no more tears.

CHORUS. You have passed beyond human daring and come at last
Into a place of stone where justice sits.
35 I cannot tell
What shape of your father's guilt appears in this.

ANTIGONE. You have touched it at last: that bridal bed
Unspeakable, horror of son and mother mingling:
Their crime, infection of all our family!
40 O Oedipus, father and brother!
Your marriage strikes from the grave to murder mine.
I have been a stranger here in my own land:
All my life
The blasphemy of my birth has followed me.

45 CHORUS. Reverence is a virtue, but strength
Lives in established law: That must prevail.
You have made your choice,
Your death is the doing of your conscious hand.

ANTIGONE. Then let me go, since all your words are bitter,
50 And the very light of the sun is cold to me.
Lead me to my vigil, where I must have
Neither love nor lamentation; no song, but silence.

[CREON interrupts impatiently.]

CREON. If dirges and planned lamentations could put off death,
Men would be singing forever.
[To the SERVANTS] Take her, go!
55 You know your orders: take her to the vault
And leave her alone there. And if she lives or dies,
That's her affair, not ours: Our hands are clean.

ANTIGONE. O tomb, vaulted bride-bed in eternal rock,
Soon I shall be with my own again
60 Where Persephone[12] welcomes the thin ghosts underground:
And I shall see my father again, and you, Mother,
And dearest Polyneices—

---

12. **Persephone** [pər sef′ə nē]: goddess of vegetation and death; wife of Hades.

<blockquote>
dearest indeed

To me, since it was my hand
That washed him clean and poured the ritual wine:
65 And my reward is death before my time!
</blockquote>

And yet, as men's hearts know, I have done no wrong,
I have not sinned before God. Or if I have,
I shall know the truth in death. But if the guilt
Lies upon Creon who judged me, then, I pray,
May his punishment equal my own.

70 **CHORAGOS.**   O passionate heart,
Unyielding, tormented still by the same winds!

CREON. Her guards shall have good cause to regret their delaying.

ANTIGONE. Ah! That voice is like the voice of death!

CREON. I can give you no reason to think you are mistaken.

75 **ANTIGONE.** Thebes, and you my fathers' gods,
And rulers of Thebes, you see me now, the last
Unhappy daughter of a line of kings.
Your kings, led away to death. You will remember
What things I suffer, and at what men's hands,
80 Because I would not transgress the laws of heaven.
[*To the* GUARDS, *simply*] Come: let us wait no longer.
[*Exit* ANTIGONE, *left, guarded.*]

Ode IV

CHORUS. All Danae's[13] beauty was locked away   [*Strophe 1*]
In a brazen cell where the sunlight could not come:
A small room, still as any grave, enclosed her.
Yet she was a princess, too,
5 And Zeus in a rain of gold poured love upon her.
O child, child,
No power in wealth or war
Or tough sea-blackened ships
Can prevail against untiring destiny!

10 And Dryas' son[14] also, that furious king,   [*Antistrophe 1*]
Bore the god's prisoning anger for his pride:
Sealed up by Dionysos in deaf stone,
His madness died among echoes,
So at the last he learned what dreadful power
15 His tongue had mocked:

---

13. **Danae** [dan′ā ē′]: a princess imprisoned by her father.
14. **Dryas' son:** Lycurgus, a king who, according to one legend, was imprisoned in stone by the gods for attacking Dionysos.

For he had profaned the revels.
And fired the wrath of the nine
Implacable Sisters[15] that love the sound of the flute.

20 And old men tell a half-remembered tale[16]   [Strophe 2]
Of horror done where a dark ledge splits the sea
And a double surf beats on the gray shores:
How a king's new woman, sick
With hatred for the queen he had imprisoned,
25 Ripped out his two sons' eyes with her bloody hands
While grinning Ares[17] watched the shuttle plunge
Four times: four blind wounds crying for revenge,

Crying, tears and blood mingled—piteously born,   [Antistrophe 2]
Those sons whose mother was of heavenly birth!
Her father was the god of the North Wind
30 And she was cradled by gales,
She raced with young colts on the glittering hills
And walked untrammeled in the open light;
But in her marriage deathless Fate found means
To build a tomb like yours for all her joy.

Scene V

[*Enter blind* TEIRESIAS, *led by a boy. The opening speeches of* TEIRESIAS *should be in singsong contrast to the realistic lines of* CREON.]

TEIRESIAS. This is the way the blind man comes, Princes, Princes,
  Lock-step, two heads lit by the eyes of one.

CREON. What new thing have you to tell us, old Teiresias?

TEIRESIAS. I have much to tell you: Listen to the prophet, Creon.

5 **CREON.** I am not aware that I have ever failed to listen.

TEIRESIAS. Then you have done wisely, King, and ruled well.

CREON. I admit my debt to you. But what have you to say?

TEIRESIAS. This, Creon: You stand once more on the edge of fate.

CREON. What do you mean? Your words are a kind of dread.

10 **TEIRESIAS.** Listen, Creon:
  I was sitting in my chair of augury,[18] at the place
  Where the birds gather about me. They were all a-chatter,

---

15. **nine Implacable Sisters:** the Muses, goddesses who inspire creativity in the arts and sciences.
16. **a half-remembered tale:** an ancient myth about Phineas of Thrace.
17. **Ares** [ār'ēz]: god of war and instigator of violence and suffering.
18. **augury:** practice of predicting signs and omens.

As is their habit, when suddenly I heard
A strange note in their jangling, a scream, a
15   Whirring fury: I knew that they were fighting,
Tearing each other, dying
In a whirlwind of wings clashing. And I was afraid.
I began the rites of burned-offering at the altar.
But Hephaestos[19] failed me: Instead of bright flame.
20   There was only the sputtering slime of the fat thighflesh
Melting: The entrails dissolved in gray smoke,
The bare bone burst from the welter. And no blaze!

This was a sign from heaven. My boy described it,
Seeing for me as I see for others.

25   I tell you, Creon, you yourself have brought
This new calamity upon us. Our hearths and altars
Are stained with the corruption of dogs and carrion birds
That glut themselves on the corpse of Oedipus' son.
The gods are deaf when we pray to them, their fire
30   Recoils from our offering, their birds of omen
Have no cry of comfort, for they are gorged
With the thick blood of the dead.
                       O my son,
These are no trifles! Think: all men make mistakes,
But a good man yields when he knows his course is wrong,
35   And repairs the evil. The only crime is pride.
Give in to the dead man, then: Do not fight with a corpse—
What glory is it to kill a man who is dead?
Think, I beg you:
It is for your own good that I speak as I do.
40   You should be able to yield for your own good.

CREON. It seems that prophets have made me their especial
    province.
All my life long
I have been a kind of butt for the dull arrows
Of doddering fortunetellers!
                   No, Teiresias:
45   If your birds—if the great eagles of God himself
Should carry him stinking bit by bit to heaven,
I would not yield. I am not afraid of pollution:
No man can defile the gods.
                 Do what you will,
Go into business, make money, speculate
50   In India gold or that synthetic gold from Sardis,[20]
Get rich otherwise than by my consent to bury him.
Teiresias, it is a sorry thing when a wise man

---

19. **Hephaestos** [hi fes′təs]: god of fire and divine blacksmith.
20. **Sardis** [sär′dis]: capital of ancient Lydia in Asia Minor.

Sells his wisdom, lets out his words for hire!

TEIRESIAS. Ah Creon! Is there no man left in the world—

55 **CREON.** To do what—Come, let's have the aphorism!

TEIRESIAS. No man who knows that wisdom outweighs any wealth?

CREON. As surely as bribes are baser than any baseness.

TEIRESIAS. You are sick, Creon! You are deathly sick!

CREON. As you say: It is not my place to challenge a prophet.

60 **TEIRESIAS.** Yet you have said my prophecy is for sale.

CREON. The generation of prophets has always loved gold.

TEIRESIAS. The generation of kings has always loved brass.

CREON. You forget yourself! You are speaking to your king.

TEIRESIAS. I know it. You are a king because of me.

65 **CREON.** You have a certain skill; but you have sold out.

TEIRESIAS. King, you will drive me to words that—

CREON. Say them, say them!
Only remember: I will not pay you for them.

TEIRESIAS. No, you will find them too costly.

CREON. No doubt. Speak:
Whatever you say, you will not change my will.

70 **TEIRESIAS.** Then take this, and take it to heart!
The time is not far off when you shall pay back
Corpse for corpse, flesh of your own flesh.
You have thrust the child of this world into living night,
You have kept from the gods below the child that is theirs:
75 The one in a grave before her death, the other,
Dead, denied the grave. This is your crime:
And the Furies[21] and the dark gods of hell
Are swift with terrible punishment for you.

Do you want to buy me now, Creon?
Not many days,
80 And your house will be full of men and women weeping,
And curses will be hurled at you from far
Cities grieving for sons unburied, left to rot
Before the walls of Thebes.

These are my arrows, Creon: They are all for you.

---

21. **the Furies:** three hideous, avenging spirits that pursue and punish those
who have committed crimes, particularly against kinship and society.

85   [*To* BOY] But come, child: Lead me home.
     Let him waste his fine anger upon younger men.
     Maybe he will learn at last
     To control a wiser tongue in a better head. [*Exit* TEIRESIAS.]

CHORAGOS. The old man has gone, King, but his words
90   Remain to plague us. I am old, too,
     But I cannot remember that he was ever false.

CREON. That is true . . . It troubles me.
     Oh it is hard to give in! But it is worse
     To risk everything for stubborn pride.

CHORAGOS. Creon: Take my advice.

95 **CREON.**   What shall I do?

CHORAGOS. Go quickly: free Antigone from her vault
     And build a tomb for the body of Polyneices.

CREON. You would have me do this?

CHORAGOS.   Creon, yes!
     And it must be done at once: God moves
100   Swiftly to cancel the folly of stubborn men.

CREON. It is hard to deny the heart! But I
     Will do it: I will not fight with destiny.

CHORAGOS. You must go yourself, you cannot leave it to others.

CREON. I will go.
                    —Bring axes, servants:
105 Come with me to the tomb. I buried her, I
     Will set her free.
                    Oh quickly!
     My mind misgives—
     The laws of the gods are mighty, and a man must serve them
     To the last day of his life! [*Exit* CREON.]

Paean[22]

CHORAGOS. God of many names   [*Strophe 1*]

CHORUS.   O Iacchos[23]
                                        son
     of Kadmeian Semele
                    O born of the Thunderer!
     Guardian of the West
                    Regent
     of Eleusis' plain[24]
                    O Prince of maenad Thebes[25]
5   and the Dragon Field[26] by rippling Ismenos:[27]

CHORAGOS. God of many names   [*Antistrophe 1*]

CHORUS.   the flames of torches
     flares on our hills
                    the nymphs of Iacchos
     dance at the spring of Castalia:[28]

     from the vine-close mountain
                         come ah come in ivy:
10   *Evohe evohe!*[29] sings through the streets of Thebes

CHORAGOS. God of many names   [*Strophe 2*]
CHORUS.   Iacchos of Thebes
     heavenly child
                    of Semele, bride of the Thunderer!

---

22. **Paean** [pē′ɔn]: hymn of praise, this one to Dionysos, at whose festival the play was performed.
23. **Iacchos** [ī′ɔ kus]: the god Dionysos, son of **the Thunderer** Zeus, and **Kadmeian Semele** [kad mē′ɔn sem′ɔ lē], whose father was King Kadmos, founder of Thebes.
24. **Eleusis'** [ē l͞oo′sis] **plain:** site of mysterious rites, over which Dionysos, under the name Iacchos, presided.
25. **maenad** [mē′nad] **Thebes:** the city of Thebes referred to here as a maenad, or priestess of Dionysos.
26. **Dragon Field:** field where King Kadmos was said to have planted dragon teeth, from which grew a race of warriors.
27. **Ismenos** [is mē′nɔs]: small river near Thebes.
28. **Castalia:** fountain on Mount Parnasos sacred to the Muses.
29. *Evohe evohe!* [ē vō′ē]: a cry of joy.

The shadow of plague is upon us:

come

with clement feet

oh come from Parnasos[30]

down the long slopes

15 across the lamenting water.

CHORAGOS. Io[31] Fire! Chorister of the throbbing stars!   [*Antistrophe 2*]
O purest among the voices of the night!
Thou son of God, blaze for us!

CHORUS. Come with choric rapture of circling Maenads
Who cry *Io Iacche!*

20 *God of many names!*

Exodos[32]

[*Enter* MESSENGER, *left.*]

MESSENGER. Men of the line of Kadmos, you who live
Near Amphion's[33] citadel:

I cannot say

Of any condition of human life "This is fixed,
This is clearly good, or bad." Fate raises up,
5 And fate casts down the happy and unhappy alike:
No man can foretell his fate.

Take the case of Creon:

Creon was happy once, as I count happiness:
Victorious in battle, sole governor of the land,
Fortunate father of children nobly born.
10 And now it has all gone from him! Who can say
That a man is still alive when his life's joy fails?
He is a walking dead man. Grant him rich.
Let him live like a king in his great house:
If his pleasure is gone, I would not give
15 So much as the shadow of smoke for all he owns.

CHORAGOS. Your words hint at sorrow; what is your news for us?

MESSENGER. They are dead. The living are guilty of their death.

CHORAGOS. Who is guilty? Who is dead? Speak!

MESSENGER.   Haimon.
Haimon is dead; and the hand that killed him
Is his own hand.

---

30. **Parnasos:** mountain sacred to Dionysos.
31. **Io!** [ĭ′ō]: Hail! Greetings!
32. **Exodos:** exit or final scene, opposite of the *Parados.*
33. **Amphion** [am fī′on]: ruler of ancient Thebes.

20 **CHORAGOS.**   His father's? or his own?

MESSENGER. His own, driven mad by the murder his father had
    done.

CHORAGOS. Teiresias, Teiresias, how clearly you saw it all!

MESSENGER. This is my news; you must draw what conclusions you can
    from it.

CHORAGOS. But look: Eurydice, our queen:
25   Has she overheard us?

   [Enter EURYDICE *from the palace, center.]*

EURYDICE. I have heard something, friends:
   As I was unlocking the gate of Pallas'[34] shrine,
   For I needed her help today, I heard a voice
   Telling of some new sorrow. And I fainted
30   There at the temple with all my maidens about me.
   But speak again; whatever it is, I can bear it:
   Grief and I are no strangers.

MESSENGER.   Dearest lady,
   I will tell you plainly all that I have seen.
   I shall not try to comfort you: What is the use,
35   Since comfort could lie only in what is not true?
   The truth is always best.

               I went with Creon
   To the outer plain where Polyneices was lying,
   No friend to pity him, his body shredded by dogs.
   We made our prayers in that place to Hecate[35]
40   And Pluto,[36] that they would be merciful. And we bathed
   The corpse with holy water, and we brought
   Fresh-broken branches to burn what was left of it,
   And upon the urn we heaped up a towering barrow
   Of the earth of his own land.

               When we were done, we ran
45   To the vault where Antigone lay on her couch of stone.
   One of the servants had gone ahead,
   And while he was yet far off he heard a voice
   Grieving within the chamber, and he came back
   And told Creon. And as the king went closer,
50   The air was full of wailing, the words lost,
   And he begged us to make all haste. "Am I a prophet?"
   He said weeping. "And must I walk this road,
   The saddest of all that I have gone before?
   My son's voice calls me on. Oh quickly, quickly!

---

34. **Pallas:** Pallas Athena, goddess of wisdom and war.
35. **Hecate** [hek′ə tē]: goddess connected with death and the Underworld.
36. **Pluto:** god of the Underworld.

55 Look through the crevice there, and tell me
If it is Haimon, or some deception of the gods!"

We obeyed; and in the cavern's farthest corner
We saw her lying:
She had made a noose of her fine linen veil
60 And hanged herself. Haimon lay beside her,
His arms about her waist, lamenting her,
His love lost under ground, crying out
That his father had stolen her away from him.

When Creon saw him the tears rushed to his eyes
65 And he called to him: "What have you done, child? Speak to me.
What are you thinking that makes your eyes so strange?
O my son, my son. I come to you on my knees!"
But Haimon spat in his face. He said not a word,
Staring—
      And suddenly drew his sword
70 And lunged. Creon shrank back, the blade missed; and the boy,
Desperate against himself, drove it half its length
Into his own side and fell. And as he died
He gathered Antigone close in his arms again,
Choking, his blood bright red on her white cheek.
75 And now he lies dead with the dead, and she is his
At last, his bride in the houses of the dead.

[*Exit* EURYDICE *into the palace.*]

CHORAGOS. She has left us without a word. What can this mean?

MESSENGER. It troubles me, too; yet she knows what is best,
Her grief is too great for public lamentation,
80 And doubtless she has gone to her chamber to weep
For her dead son, leading her maidens in his dirge.

CHORAGOS. It may be so; but I fear this deep silence. [*Pause*]

MESSENGER. I will see what she is doing. I will go in. [*Exit*
MESSENGER *into the palace.*]

[*Enter* CREON *with attendants, bearing* HAIMON'S *body.*]

CHORAGOS. But here is the king himself; oh look at him,
85 Bearing his own damnation in his arms.

CREON. Nothing you say can touch me any more.
My own blind heart has brought me
From darkness to final darkness. Here you see
The father murdering, the murdered son—
90 And all my civic wisdom!

Haimon my son, so young, so young to die,
I was the fool, not you; and you died for me.

CHORAGOS. That is the truth: but you were late in learning it.

CREON. This truth is hard to bear. Surely a god
95 Has crushed me beneath the hugest weight of heaven.
And driven me headlong a barbaric way
To trample out the thing I held most dear.

The pains that men will take to come to pain!

[*Enter* MESSENGER *from the palace.*]

MESSENGER. The burden you carry in your hands is heavy.
100 But it is not all: You will find more in your house.

CREON. What burden worse than this shall I find there?

MESSENGER. The queen is dead.

CREON. O port of death, deaf world,
Is there no pity for me? And you, angel of evil,
105 I was dead, and your words are death again.
Is it true, boy? Can it be true?
Is my wife dead? Has death bred death?

MESSENGER. You can see for yourself.

[*The doors are opened, and the body of* EURYDICE *is disclosed within.*]

CREON. Oh pity!
110 All true, all true, and more than I can bear!
O my wife, my son!

MESSENGER. She stood before the altar, and her heart
Welcomed the knife her own hand guided,
And a great cry burst from her lips for Megareus[37] dead,
115 And for Haimon dead, her sons; and her last breath
Was a curse for their father, the murderer of her sons.
And she fell, and the dark flowed in through her closing eyes.

CREON. O God, I am sick with fear.
Are there no swords here? Has no one a blow for me?

120 **MESSENGER.** Her curse is upon you for the deaths of both.

CREON. It is right that it should be. I alone am guilty.
I know it, and I say it. Lead me in
Quickly, friends.
I have neither life nor substance. Lead me in.

125 **CHORAGOS.** You are right, if there can be right in so much wrong.
The briefest way is best in a world of sorrow.

---

37. **Megareus** [meg′ə rōos]: only brother of Haimon, and son of Creon and Eurydice. He died in the battle for Thebes.

CREON. Let it come,
Let death come quickly, and be kind to me.
I would not ever see the sun again.

130 CHORAGOS. All that will come when it will; but we, meanwhile,
Have much to do. Leave the future to itself.

CREON. All my heart was in that prayer!

CHORAGOS. Then do not pray anymore: the sky is deaf.

CREON. Lead me away. I have been rash and foolish.
135 I have killed my son and my wife.
I look for comfort; my comfort lies here dead.
Whatever my hands have touched has come to nothing.
Fate has brought all my pride to a thought of dust.

[As CREON *is being led into the house, the* CHORAGOS *advances and speaks directly to the audience.*]

CHORAGOS. There is no happiness where there is no wisdom;
140 No wisdom but in submission to the gods.
Big words are always punished,
And proud men in old age learn to be wise.

STUDY QUESTIONS

Prologue Through Ode II

Recalling

1. In lines 14–25 of the Prologue, what kind of funeral does Antigone say Creon has given Eteocles? What has Creon sworn for Polyneices? What penalty must those who disobey Creon face?
2. In lines 26–31 of the Prologue, what does Antigone ask Ismene to do? In lines 36–52 what reason does Ismene give for not helping her sister?
3. In Scene I how does Creon explain his decision regarding Polyneices? What does the Sentry tell him? How does Creon react?
4. What opinion about Creon's decree do Choragos and the Chorus have in Scene I and in the Ode between Scenes I and II?
5. In Scene II, lines 56–63, what does Antigone say about Creon's decree?
6. What do we learn about Antigone's plans for marriage?

Interpreting

7. What basic conflict is represented by the debate between Antigone and Ismene in the Prologue? What would you say is Antigone's error?
8. Although convinced that he is correct, what might Creon actually be overlooking? What mistakes might he be making?

Extending

9. If you had to choose sides between Antigone and Creon now, could you? Why or why not?

Scene III Through Exodos

Recalling

1. What are Creon's arguments in his first long speech to Haimon (Scene III, lines 11–46)?
2. What two metaphors in lines 80–83 of Scene III does Haimon use to persuade Creon to be reasonable?
3. What form of punishment does Creon announce that he has planned for Antigone in Scene IV, lines 55–57?

4. In Scene V, lines 32–40, what specific advice and caution does Teiresias give Creon? What does Creon decide to do?
5. In two or three sentences describe the final outcome of the play?

Interpreting
6. What, according to the blind prophet Teiresias, is Creon's central weakness? How has this weakness affected Creon's actions and attitudes?
7. How does Creon change by the end of the play?

Extending
8. Overall, which character moves you more—Antigone or Creon? Why?

LITERARY FOCUS

Tragedy and the Tragic Hero
According to the Greek philosopher Aristotle, the function of tragedy is to arouse in the audience the emotions of fear and pity in order to produce a **catharsis,** or cleansing, of these emotions. The audience feels fear that misfortunes may befall the hero. The audience feels pity because the hero's fortunes gradually decline as a consequence of a **tragic flaw,** an error that causes the hero to commit a tragic deed and to suffer a reversal. The tragic situation in which the hero is eventually caught arises from a combination of elements in his own character and of fate, or the will of the gods. The tragic hero's courage in the face of an overpowering challenge is astonishing and praiseworthy and thus wins the sympathy of the audience.

Thinking About Tragedy and the Tragic Hero
■ Compare Antigone and Creon as classic tragic figures. What misfortunes does each suffer? What tragic flaw does each display? How does fate affect each?

VOCABULARY

Sentence Completions
Each of the following sentences contains a blank with four possible words for completing the sentence. The words are from *Antigone.* Choose the word that completes each sentence correctly and that uses the word *as the word is used in the selection.* Write the number of each item and the letter of your choice on a separate sheet.

1. Because of the extreme heat and the jagged, rocky terrain, our journey to the ancient ruins did not have a(n) _____ start.
   (a) lateral   (c) headlong
   (b) guarded   (d) auspicious
2. Our guide, who had grown up here, announced _____ that among the ruins the temperature was always lower.
   (a) furiously   (c) sententiously
   (b) miserably   (d) piteously
3. Awed by the rough, still landscape and eerie silence, we walked along quietly and _____ .
   (a) impassively   (c) bitterly
   (b) expansively   (d) stealthily
4. At the gate to the imposing ruins, I felt that to enter would be to _____ a timeless law.
   (a) distress   (c) absolve
   (b) trample   (d) transgress
5. I sensed at once that awesome festivals were once performed here for _____ gods.
   (a) implacable   (c) straying
   (b) untrammeled   (d) lamenting

COMPOSITION

Writing About a Quotation
■ Creon admits, "My own blind heart has brought me / From darkness to final darkness." Analyze Creon's statement. First explain in what sense he is blind. Then show the significance of Creon's statement in the play as a whole by comparing his "blindness" with the "vision" of Antigone, Haimon, and Teiresias (who is physically blind). *For help with this assignment, see Lesson 5 in the Writing About Literature Handbook at the back of this book.*

Composing a Dramatic Scene
■ Imagine a situation involving two characters who come into conflict. Both characters are unyielding. Describe a brief scene in which the two characters have a disagreement. If you like, write some dialogue for the scene and act it out with a classmate.

COMPARING WRITERS

■ Compare Homer's epic and Sophocles' drama in terms of description: For example, which work uses more description? How does its presence or absence affect the work? Are the descriptions realistic or fanciful?

ANCIENT ROME

Colosseum, amphitheater of Rome, built between A.D. 72 and 82.

About 1000 B.C. the Etruscans—a people of sailors, traders, farmers, cattle herders, and horse tamers—settled in what we now call Italy. They were attracted by warm weather and rich soil; they found tin, iron, clay, and timber. They became, like the Greeks across the Adriatic Sea, a civilized people.

Beyond these facts, the history of Italy becomes shrouded in legend. Supposedly, a Trojan warrior named Aeneas fled the burning city of Troy. He led his followers across the Mediterranean to Africa and then northward to Italy, where he was destined to re-establish the glory of Troy and build a great city. Later legends tell of two boys, Romulus and Remus, sons of Mars, who were set adrift on the Tiber River by a wicked uncle, cast ashore in 753 B.C., nursed by a she-wolf, and raised by shepherds. Romulus is said to have killed his brother and then founded the village that the Etruscans developed into a city-state called Roma. The first kings of Roma were Etruscan, and they did much to start the city on its road to success—draining swamp land, building the Forum (a meeting place), and raising the walls that still distinguish the city.

In 509 B.C., however, Rome took an extraordinary step. Breaking its political connections, Rome gave up the tradition of having a king and created a republican form of government. Two consuls replaced the king; citizens participated in assemblies; heads of families formed a senate. During the first years of the Republic, two social classes were at odds. These were the patricians, descendants of the founding fathers, and the plebeians, the poorer residents or commoners. By 367 B.C., however, new laws allowed for greater political equality. Indeed, during this period the Romans produced a legal code, the Twelve Tables, which began the sophisticated legal system that western civilization has inherited.

The Expansion of Rome

From before the Punic Wars with Carthage in 264 B.C. on into the fifth century A.D., the growth and decline of Rome was staggering. Expanding in all directions, Rome became the vital, brutal, sometimes orderly, sometimes chaotic, center of the world. The spectacle and drama of these years have given rise to thousands of novels, histories, plays, poems, and films. Shakespeare immortalized some of the events in two of his most popular plays, *Julius Caesar* and *Antony and Cleopatra.* In the eighteenth century the Englishman Edward Gibbon produced his monumental history *The Decline and Fall of the Roman Empire.* More recently George Bernard Shaw set his play *Androcles and the Lion* in Ancient Rome.

Scenes of Ancient Rome have become part of our common heritage. From the time of the Punic Wars with Carthage, we envision scenes of African elephants in the snow-filled mountain passes of

Europe as Hannibal, the Carthaginian military genius, tries to sack Rome from the rear. That scene is replaced by the Roman general Scipio leading his legions across the sands of Africa to attack Carthage and defeat Hannibal himself. Perhaps the most vivid scenes are those of the life of Julius Caesar (102–44 B.C.): Caesar building a bridge across the Rhine River in what is now Germany, Caesar looking out across the marshy land that is now London, Caesar writing in his *Commentaries* that "all Gaul is divided into three parts." We think of Caesar counseling the young Egyptian queen Cleopatra; finally, we think of Caesar the world-conqueror assassinated in Rome.

After Caesar, Octavian declared himself Caesar Augustus ("revered and majestic one") and began the Augustan Age, the golden age of Rome. The Republic became a memory, but Augustus and his successors gave the world peace for the next two hundred years. Dramatic changes set in around A.D. 180. Barbarian forces began a series of wars on Rome, especially in its far-flung provinces. By 410 the Visigoths were able to march on Rome itself and sack it. By 476 the western part of the Roman Empire had ceased to be. The eastern part, the Byzantine Empire, was able to remain alive for another thousand years. As we watch the history of Rome unfold, we realize that we are seeing scene after scene of war, with Rome acquiring more and more power and land. We see Rome arriving in foreign lands with fire and sword and then staying to bring its civilization to the conquered masses. That civilization began as a stern and hard way of life; later it became more luxurious, more cosmopolitan, more self-destructive.

Life in Ancient Rome

Roman life began with a commitment to deities who were thought to inhabit everything in nature. To the early Romans religion was a contract: If people fulfilled their religious obligations, the gods would help them. Thus ritual became important and dominated public and private life.

In public life the focal unit was the army; after victories, commanders made majestic offerings to the gods. The army was highly trained, strictly disciplined; it was, after all, the means of controlling the world. In private life the family was the center. Children were taught obedience and respect for their parents and devotion to the gods. The early Romans produced men who were vigorous, moral, and authoritarian. As the poet Virgil said: "We carry our children to the streams and harden them in the bitter, icy water; as boys they spend wakeful nights over the chase and tire out the whirlwind; but in manhood, unwearied by toil and trained to poverty, they subdue the soil with their plows and shake towns in war."

As Rome evolved, the Roman character changed, as did the

quality of Roman society. With exposure to the advanced culture of Greece and with the enormous wealth won from conquered lands, Romans began to demand finer things and expect luxuries—statues, paintings, silks, jewelry, gold. Once devoted to the useful, Romans became addicted to the decorative and the wasteful. The Colosseum, the huge amphitheater, was used for gladiatorial games; the Circus Maximus saw chariot races; temples, public baths, pools, and gymnasiums made Rome a city of pleasure for the rich, though many Romans remained miserably poor, living in tenements that were firetraps. All the well-built roads of the empire did indeed lead to Rome. However, internally and externally, Rome had over-extended itself.

Roman Literature

Latin literature may be said to begin about 250 B.C. with the translation of Greek works—Homer's *Odyssey,* for example—into Latin. The poet Graeus Naevius (270–201 B.C.) was the first to produce Latin literature that did not lean on a Greek model, and so we can formally date the birth of Latin literature with him. However, if we recall the influence of the comedies of Plautus (254–184 B.C.) and Terence (195–159 B.C.) on English drama, we can say that Latin literature began with these two playwrights.

The comedies of Plautus and Terence burst upon the world with a new attitude toward drama—pure entertainment. The comedies of Aristophanes were entertaining, of course, but they were also designed to criticize, to satirize, to make a point. Plautus and Terence do not dwell on ideas or great themes; they rely on fun and on innately hilarious situations involving such stock comic characters as the tricky servant, the fake, the boaster.

Cato the Elder (234–149 B.C.) wrote the first Latin history of Rome and also developed the art of public speaking, oratory. This major form of Latin literature was later practiced brilliantly by Cicero (106–43 B.C.).

Poetry in the Augustan Age is one of the glories of world literature. Catullus (84–54 B.C.) produced intense love lyrics. Lucretius (94–55 B.C.), in *De Rerum Natura* ("On the Nature of Things"), set forth the philosophy of Epicurus, which was based on finding individual happiness. The greatest poet of the age was Virgil, whose *Aeneid* stands as a monument to Roman civilization. Virgil also wrote pastoral poems, the *Eclogues* and *Georgics,* that are as lyrical and charming as the *Aeneid* is grand. Virgil's friend Horace (65–8 B.C.) produced lyric masterpieces in his *Odes,* and Ovid (43 B.C.–A.D. 17) is remembered for his *Metamorphoses,* which still endures today as an entertaining reference work to both Greek and Roman mythology.

Virgil   *70–19 B.C.*

Rome's greatest poet, Publius Vergilius Maro (known to us as Virgil), was born near the village of Andes in northern Italy. At the age of seventeen, Virgil went to study oratory and philosophy in Rome, where he became friends with men who were to play important roles in the development of the Roman Empire. Although he himself did not participate in military or political affairs, he was throughout his life close to those in power.

Virgil's first collection, ten pastoral poems called the *Eclogues,* was followed by the *Georgics,* a poetic account of the countryside and rural life that he loved. When he was forty, at the peak of his career, Virgil began work on the *Aeneid* [i nē′id], in which he sought to express Rome's greatness and destiny by glorifying its legendary origins. Nine years later, with the *Aeneid* almost completed, he contracted a fever while returning from a trip to Greece. Protesting that the poem still needed three years of revision, Virgil requested before he died that the manuscript be burned. Emperor Augustus denied the request and published the *Aeneid* posthumously.

Unlike the *Iliad* and the *Odyssey,* which Homer composed in the tradition of oral storytelling, the *Aeneid* is a consciously literary work, written to be read as well as heard. On the other hand, the *Aeneid* resembles the *Iliad* in having a hero who fights battles and the *Odyssey* in having a hero who undertakes long journeys. Furthermore, Virgil imitated Homer's meter, use of epithets, and portrayal of the gods as manipulative. The *Aeneid* fuses elements of the Homeric epics to create the story of Aeneas, the legendary Trojan prince who escapes from Troy when it is destroyed by the Greeks. Directed by the gods to found a new city that will eventually rule the world, Aeneas sets off with his aged father and young son. He eventually lands on the North African coast, where he is welcomed by the queen of Carthage, Dido, who falls in love with him as he tells her and her court about the fall of Troy. Despite his love for Dido, Aeneas continues his search and finally founds the city that will fulfill his and his people's destiny. The following excerpt tells of how the Greeks destroyed Troy and of Aeneas' departure from Troy.

The Trojan Horse, print after a painting by Henri Motte.

Virgil

from the **Aeneid**

Translated by C. Day Lewis

CHARACTERS

Greeks

ACHILLES: leader of the Myrmidons, greatest of the Greek warriors
ULYSSES [ū lis′ēz]: Latin name for Odysseus, Greek leader and hero of the Trojan War

Trojans

AENEAS [i nē′əs]: Trojan warrior who tells the story in first person
ANCHISES: Aeneas' father
ASCANIUS: son of Aeneas and Creusa
CASSANDRA: Trojan princess whose prophecies are not believed
CREUSA: Aeneas' wife
LAOCOON [lā ok′ō on′]: Trojan priest
PRIAM: Troy's king

Goddesses

ATHENA: Greek goddess of war and wisdom
JUNO: queen of the gods and enemy of the Trojans
MINERVA: Roman goddess of wisdom, identified with the Greek goddess Athena

from Book II

All fell silent now, and their faces were all attention
When from his place of honor Aeneas began to speak:

O queen, the griefs you bid me reopen are inexpressible—
The tale of Troy, a rich and a most tragic empire
Erased by the Greeks; most piteous events I saw with my own
5   eyes
And played no minor part in. What Myrmidon or Thessalian,[1]
What soldier of fell Ulysses[2] could talk about such events
And keep from tears? Besides, the dewy night drops fast
From heaven, and the declining stars invite to sleep.
10 But if you want so much to know what happened to us
And hear in brief a recital of Troy's last agony,
Although the memory makes me shudder, and shrink from its
    sadness,
I will attempt it.

               Broken in war and foiled by fate,
With so many years[3] already slipping away, the Greek staff
15 Constructed a horse, employing the craft of the goddess Athena[4]—
It was high as a hill, and its ribs were made from planks of
    pinewood—
To pay for their safe return to Greece, they pretended: this
    rumor
Got round. But, choosing warriors by lot, they secretly
Put them in on the blind side of the horse, until its vast
20 And cavernous belly was crammed with a party of armed men.

In sight of Troy there's an island, a well-known island, Tenedos—
Rich and powerful it was, while Priam's empire[5] stood;
Now, little but a bay, a roadstead unsafe for shipping.
Thither the Greeks sailed out, and hid on its desolate coast.
25 This was evacuation, we thought—they had sailed for Greece.
So all Troy threw off the chains of her long anguish.
We opened the gates, we enjoyed visiting the Greek camp,
Viewing the derelict positions on the abandoned beaches.
Here the Dolopes[6] camped; there, ferocious Achilles:

---

1. **Myrmidon** [mur′mə don′] **or Thessalian** [the sā′lē ən]: Greek soldiers from armies of Thessaly in northern Greece; the Myrmidons were led by the great warrior Achilles.
2. **Ulysses** [ū lis′ēz]: Latin form of Odysseus, Greek leader and hero of the Trojan War; described here as **fell**, cruel or savage.
3. **so many years:** It is the tenth and last year of the Trojan War.
4. **Athena:** Greek goddess of wisdom and war.
5. **Priam's empire:** Troy, of which Priam was king.
6. **Dolopes** [dō′lə pēz]: Greeks from Dolopians, a region bordering Thessaly on the southwest.

30 Here was beached their navy, and here the battle raged.
Some of us gaped at the gift—so deadly—the Greeks had left for
Minerva,[7] and its stupendous bulk. Thymoetes[8] first,
Either from treachery or because Troy's fate now was sealed,
Urged that the horse be brought through the walls and placed in
our citadel.
35 But Capys[9] and all those of sounder views recommended
Hurling it into the sea or setting fire to it, as some
Booby-trap of the Greeks and not to be trusted—or else
Boring holes in its belly to see what might be inside it.
So the rank and file were violently torn between contraries.
40 Then out in front of them all, hundreds straggling behind him,
In a great temper Laocoon[10] came tearing down from the citadel,
Crying from far:

Citizens, are you all stark mad?
Do you really believe our foes are gone? Do you imagine
Any Greek gift is guileless? Is that your idea of Ulysses?
45 This thing of wood conceals Greek soldiers, or else it is
A mechanism designed against our walls—to pry into
Our homes and to bear down on the city; sure, some trick
Is there. No, you must never feel safe with the horse, Trojans.
Whatever it is, I distrust the Greeks, even when they are
generous.
He spoke: he put forth his strength, and spun his huge great
50   spear
At the flank of the monster, right into its belly's rounded frame.
The spear stuck quivering; the hollow womb of the creature
Grunted at the concussion and rumbled hollowly.
If destiny, if our own will had not been so contrary,
Laocoon would have made us rip open that cache of Greek
55   troops—
There'd still be a Troy—O topless towers, you'd be standing
now! . . .

"Bring the horse to Minerva's shrine! Pray for her goodwill!"
All of our people shouted.

---

7. **Minerva:** Roman goddess of wisdom, identified with the Greek goddess
Athena.
8. **Thymoetes** [thī mē′tēz]: Trojan elder and adviser of Priam.
9. **Capys** [kap′is]: Trojan suspicious of the wooden horse; he later fled from
Troy with Aeneas.
10. **Laocoon** [lā ok′ō on′]: After warning the Trojans against the wooden horse,
Laocoon, a Trojan priest, was killed with his two sons by two enormous sea
serpents.

We cut into our walls,[11] laid open the heart of the city.
60 Everyone set about the task: we inserted rollers
Under its hooves, put hawsers of hemp around its neck,
And strained. The disastrous engine[12] was jockeyed over our walls,
An army in its womb. Boys and unmarried maidens
Escorted it, singing psalms, joyfully gripping the traces.
65 The menace mounts, comes trundling into the city center.
O, my country! O Ilium,[13] home of the gods! O Troy town,
Famous through war! Four times the monster stopped, just where
    the entrance
Was, and every time the accouterments[14] clanged in its belly.
Yet we persevered, with never a thought—we were madly
    blind—
70 Until we had lodged the ominous thing in our holy place.
Then, to cap all, Cassandra[15] opened her mouth for prophecy—
She whom her god had doomed to be never believed by the
    Trojans.
But we poor fools, whose very last day it was, festooned
The shrines of the gods with holiday foliage all over the city.

75 So now the sky rolled round, and night raced up from the ocean
Voluminously shrouding the earth and heaven's vault
And the villainous scheme of the Greeks. Not a sound from the
    Trojans, supine
Along the walls, tired out, in the embrace of sleep.
And now the main Greek army was moving from Tenedos
80 In fleet formation, under the favoring silences
Of a quiet moon, toward the coast they knew so well.
Their leading galley had signaled with flame: Sinon, protected
By fate's injustice, stealthily unlocked the wooden horse
And let the Greeks out from its belly. The horse disgorged, the
    men
85 Burst reveling forth from its hollow flank into the fresh air—
Thessander and Sthenelus in the lead, with Ulysses the terrible,
Sliding down a rope they had lowered—Acamas, Thoas,
Neoptolemus son of Peleus, Machaon and Menelaus,
And Epeus—the man who had actually built the clever
    contraption.

---

11. **We . . . walls:** The Trojans had been convinced by Sinon [sī′nən], a
pretended Greek deserter, that if they could succeed in getting the huge horse
into their city, Troy would rule Europe.
12. **engine:** here, evil contrivance.
13. **Ilium** [il′ē əm]: another name for Troy.
14. **accouterments** [ə ko͞o′tər mənts]: arms and armor.
15. **Cassandra:** Trojan princess, sister of Hector; when she rejected the love of
Apollo, he punished her by giving her the gift of prophecy with the curse that
she would never be believed.

90 They broke out over a city drowned in drunken sleep;
They killed the sentries and then threw open the gates, admitting
Their main body, and joined in the prearranged plan of attack. . . .

The Trojan Hector, bloodied and mutilated after being killed by the Greek Achilles, appears to Aeneas in a dream. He advises Aeneas to take his family and flee because the fall of Troy is inevitable and imminent. Awakening to find Troy in flames, Aeneas arms himself and rushes out to fight. Following the Greek soldiers to Priam's palace, he witnesses the destruction of the palace and the murder of Priam on his own altar by Pyrrhus, Achilles' son. Before he dies, Priam reminds Aeneas of his father, to whose house he now returns in an effort to save his family.

When I reached the door of my father's house, the ancestral
Home, my father Anchises, whom first I looked for, wishing
95 To get him away first to the safety of the hills—Anchises
Flatly refused to prolong his life, now Troy was finished,
Or to endure exile. He said:

O you, whose blood
Is in the prime, who are strong enough to stand on your own
feet,
Do you try for escape!
100 But as for me, if the gods had meant me to go on living,
They'd have preserved this place. Enough, more than enough
To have seen Troy ruined once and once have survived her
capture.
Bid me farewell and leave, O leave this body of mine
Where it is! I shall find death in action. The foe will slay me
For pity, or spoils. And to bury me—that will not cost them
105 much.
For years now I have been lingering, obnoxious to heaven and
useless
To mankind, ever since the ruler of gods and men
Blasted me with the searing breath of his levin-flash.[16]

So he went on saying. We could not shift him, although
110 We implored him with floods of tears—I, and my wife Creusa,
Ascanius[17] and the whole household—not to ruin everything,
Not to add his weight to the doom which was heavy upon us.
He refused: obstinately he clung to his house and his purpose.
Once again I am moved to fight, yearning for death in my misery,
115 Since neither luck nor forethought offered a way out now.

---

16. **levin-flash:** lightning-flash.
17. **Ascanius** [as kā′nē əs]: son of Aeneas and Creusa.

"Father," I said, "did you really think I could run away
And leave you? Did so shameful a notion escape your lips?
If it's the will of heaven that nothing be left of our city,
And if your mind's made up that you and your family
120 Shall perish, as well as Troy, a door to that death is wide open:
Pyrrhus is coming, all bathed in Priam's blood; he loves
Butchering sons in front of their fathers, fathers at the altar.
Was it for this, dear mother, you fetched me through fire and
        steel,
That I should witness the enemy right in our house, witness
125 Ascanius and my father and my Creusa beside them
Lying slaughtered here in one another's blood?
To arms, my men! To arms! Their last hour calls the conquered.
Send me back to the Greeks! Let me go back and renew
The fight! It must never be said we died unavenged this day!"

130 My sword was at my side again; I was fitting my left arm
Through the strap of my shield, and on my way out of the house,
When Creusa clung to me at the door, gripping my ankles,
Holding little Ascanius up to his father, and crying:

If it's deathwards you go, take us with you! O take us, and
        come what may!

135 But if your experience tells you that something is to be gained by
Fighting, protect this house first! Think what you're leaving
        us to—
Ascanius, your father, and me who loved to be called your wife
        once!

Loudly she cried these words, and filled the house with her crying.
Just then a miracle happened, a wonderful miracle.
140 Imagine it!—our hands and our sad eyes were upon
Ascanius, when we beheld a feathery tongue of flame
Luminously alight on his head, licking the soft curls
With fire that harmed them not, and playing about his temples.
Anxious, in great alarm, his mother and I hurried to
145 Beat out, put out with water, that holy blaze on his hair.
But father Anchises, greatly heartened, lifted his eyes up,
Stretched up his hands to heaven, with words of prayer, saying:

O god omnipotent, if any prayers can sway you,
Give ear to mine. One thing I ask: if by our goodness
150 We have deserved it, grant your aid, confirm this omen!

The old man had hardly spoken when from our left hand came
A sudden crash of thunder, and a shooting star slid down

The sky's dark face, drawing a trail of light behind it.
We watched that star as it glided high over the palace roof,
155 And blazing a path, buried its brightness deep in the woods of
Ida;[18] when it was gone, it left in its wake a long furrow
Of light, and a sulphurous smoke spread widely over the terrain.
That did convince my father. He drew himself upright,
Addressed the gods above, and worshipped the heaven-sent star:
No more, no more lingering! I follow, I'm there, where you guide
160   me!
Gods of our fathers, guard this family, guard my grandson!
This sign is yours, and Troy is still in your heavenly keeping.
Yea, I consent. I refuse no longer, my son, to go with you.

He had spoken; and now more clearly over the town the fire's roar
165 Was heard, and nearer rolled the tide of its conflagration.
"Quick, then, dear father," I said, "climb onto my back, and I will
Carry you on my shoulders—that's a burden will not be
    burdensome.
However things turn out, at least we shall share one danger,
One way of safety, both of us. Let little Ascanius walk
170 Beside me, and Creusa follow my steps at a distance.
And you, servants, pay careful attention to what I shall tell you.
As you go out of the city, you come to a mound with an ancient
Temple of Ceres[19] upon it, secluded; nearby, an old cypress
Stands, which for many years our fathers preserved in reverence.
175 Let this be our rendezvous: we'll get there by different routes.
Do you, my father, carry the sacred relics and home-gods:
Sinful for me to touch them, when I have just withdrawn
From battle, with blood on my hands, until in running water
I am purified.

180 With these words, I laid the pelt of a tawny lion
For covering over my broad shoulders and bowed neck;
Then stooped to lift my burden: Ascanius twined his fingers
In mine, hurrying to keep up with his father's longer stride.
My wife came on behind. We fared on, hugging the shadows.

185 I, who just now had faced the enemy volleys, the Greeks'
Concentrated attack, without turning a hair—I was scared by
Every breeze, alarmed by every sound, so strung up
Was I with anxiety for my burden and my companion.

---

18. **Ida** [ī′dä]: mountain in a region near Troy, from which Zeus, the king of the gods, often watched and directed the progress of the Trojan War.
19. **Ceres** [sē′rēz]: Roman goddess of grain and harvest; associated with the Greek goddess Demeter.

And now I was nearing the gates and thinking that we had made it,
190 When on a sudden there came to my ears the sound of many
Footsteps—or so it seemed. Then, peering into the gloom,
My father exclaimed:
                    Run! They're upon us! Run, Aeneas!
I can see the shine of their shields and the bronze accoutrements winking.

Well, I panicked. My wits were fuddled, were snatched away
195 By some malignant prompting. For even as I darted off
Into byways, off my course among streets I knew not—O god,
The anguish of it!—my wife Creusa, fate took her—did she
Stop there? or lose her way? Did she sink down in exhaustion?
We never knew. We never set eyes on her again.
200 I did not look back for the lost one, I did not give her a thought
Until we had reached the mound, the ancient, hallowed place
Of Ceres. Here at last, when all were assembled, one was
Missing, one had denied husband and son her company.
I was out of my mind. What mortal, what god did I not curse?
205 In all the city's ruin what bitterer thing did I see?
Commending Ascanius, Anchises and the Teucrian[20] home-gods
To my friends' care, and hiding them deep in the hollow vale,
I put on my shining armor, I made for the city once more.
To reconstruct those events, to retrace our path through Troy
210 And expose my life to its perils again—that was my purpose.

For a start, I returned to the shadowed gate in the city wall
By which I had sallied forth, noting my tracks and following them
Back through the night, straining my eyes to scan them. Everywhere
Dread and the sheer silence reduced my courage to nothing.
215 Next, I went home, in case—just on the chance that she might have
Gone there. The Greeks had broken in, the whole house was occupied.
That instant, gluttonous fire was fanned by the draught right up to
The roof top; flames burst out there, the blast of the heat roared skywards.
I went on, to revisit Priam's house and the citadel.
220 Here, in the empty colonnades of Juno's[21] sanctuary,
Phoenix[22] and fell Ulysses were engaged on the duty allotted them,
Guarding the loot. To this point from all over Troy had plunder,
Salvaged from burning shrines, been brought: tables of gods,
Solid gold bowls and looted vestments were being piled up here
225 In heaps. Children and frightened mothers were standing about
In a long queue.

---

20. **Teucrian** [too′krē ən]: another name for *Trojan,* from Teucer, first king of
Troy.
21. **Juno:** queen of the gods and enemy of the Trojans; she is a most appropriate
guardian for the triumphant Greeks.
22. **Phoenix** [fē′niks]: Greek warrior and foster father of Achilles.

I dared (you will hardly believe it) to call out loud through the gloom
And fill the streets with shouting: sadly I cried "Creusa!"—
Called to her over and over again, but it was no good.

230 As I roamed on that endless, frenzied search through the city buildings,
There appeared before my eyes a piteous phantom, yes,
The very ghost of Creusa—a figure larger than life.
I was appalled: my hair stood on end, and my voice stuck
In my throat. It was she who spoke then, and thus relieved my pain:

235 Darling husband, it's madness of you to indulge your grief
Like this. These happenings are part of the divine
Purpose. It was not written that you should bring Creusa
Away with you; the great ruler of heaven does not allow it.
For you, long exile is destined, broad tracts of sea to be furrowed;
240 Then you will reach Hesperia,[23] where Lydian Tiber[24] flows
Gently through a land in good heart, and good men live.
There, your affairs will prosper; a kingdom, a royal bride
Await you. No more tears now for your heart's love, Creusa:
I shall not see the proud halls of the Myrmidons or Dolopes,
245 Nor work as a slave for Greek women—I, who am Dardan[25]
And daughter-in-law to the goddess Venus.[26]
No, the great Mother of the gods is going to keep me here.
Good-by, Aeneas. Cherish our love in the son it gave us.

With these words, though I wept and had so much to say
250 To her, she left me, fading out into thin air.
Three times I tried to put my arms round her neck, and three times
The phantom slipped my hands, my vain embrace: it was like
Grasping a wisp of wind or the wings of a fleeting dream.
So in the end I went back to my friends, the night being over.
255 I was astonished to find, when I got there, a great number
Of new arrivals come in, both women and men, a sorry
Concourse of refugees assembled for exile. From all sides
They'd rendezvous'd, their minds made up, their belongings ready
For me to lead them wherever I wished across the sea.
260 And now was the dawn star rising over the ridges of Ida,
Bringing another day. The Greeks were holding the gates of
The city in force. Troy was beyond all hope of aid.
I accepted defeat, picked up my father and made for the mountains.

---

23. **Hesperia** [hes pēr′ē ä]: land of the evening or land in the west; Italy.
24. **Lydian Tiber:** Tiber River, second longest in Italy. It bordered a territory
settled by people from ancient Lydia and was therefore often called *Lydian.*
25. **Dardan** [där′dən]: Trojan, that is, one of the race of Trojans begun by
Dardanus, founder of Troy.
26. **Venus:** Roman goddess of love, counterpart of the Greek goddess Aphrodite;
mother of Aeneas.

STUDY QUESTIONS

Recalling

1. Describe in detail how the Greeks used the wooden horse to defeat Troy.
2. List all the Trojan opinions in favor of and opposed to letting the wooden horse into Troy.
3. What two courses of action are open to Aeneas when he returns to his home? What decision does he finally make? What event sways him at the last moment?
4. What and whom does Aeneas take with him from Troy? Who is left behind? Why?

Interpreting

5. Why does the Greek strategy involving the wooden horse work?
6. How does fate influence Aeneas' departure?

Extending

7. When Aeneas again prepares to fight the Greeks on the night of Troy's fall, his wife, Creusa, begs him to consider first her and their young son, Ascanius. Compare this scene with the scene in the *Iliad* where Andromache pleads with Hector. What values and feelings do the two scenes have in common? How do they differ?

VIEWPOINT

The classics scholar Wendell Clausen argues that we are moved by the *Aeneid* in part because

> its larger structure . . . enlists our sympathy on the side of loneliness, suffering, and defeat. For it is the paradox of the *Aeneid,* the surprise of its greatness, that a poem which celebrates the achievement of an exemplary hero and the founding of Rome itself should be a long history of defeat and loss. Aeneas finally wins—for that is his fate—but he wins at a terrible cost. . . .

1. As Aeneas tells of the fall of Troy, do you feel sympathy for him? Why or why not?

2. Does your feeling change with the knowledge that Aeneas himself will live to found Rome?
3. Referring to particular details, tell how this selection supports the theme of ultimate victory through defeat and terrible loss.

VOCABULARY

Word Origins

Many words come to English from Latin, the language of the Romans who occupied Britain and, later, of the medieval church. Using a good dictionary, look up the following words from the translation of the *Aeneid,* and explain their origins. Also explain their meanings *as they are used in the selection.*

1. derelict
2. ferocious
3. concussion
4. voluminously
5. supine
6. obnoxious
7. obstinately
8. luminously
9. omnipotent
10. conflagration
11. malignant
12. sanctuary

COMPOSITION

Writing About Theme

Show how Virgil illuminates his theme in the excerpt from the *Aeneid.* First write a sentence that states the excerpt's theme. Then explain how Virgil develops that theme through characterization, setting, events, point of view, and tone. *For help with this assignment, see Lesson 6 in the Writing About Literature Handbook at the back of this book.*

Writing a First-Person Narrative

Tell a story from the point of view of one of the soldiers inside the wooden horse when it is dragged into Troy. Imagine that soldier's feelings as the Trojans debate whether to destory the horse or to take it into Troy. Describe the atmosphere inside the horse as the soldiers feel the Trojans pulling them into the city, where the surprise attack will occur.

Ovid   43 B.C.–A.D. 17

Born in the later years of the Augustan Empire into a wealthy landowning family, Publius Ovidius Naso (Ovid) studied law and rhetoric in Rome, where he later did considerable public service. Preferring society and poetry to politics and law, however, Ovid delighted the Roman socialites with his brilliant and forthright love poetry. The *Amores* and the *Art of Love* provided advice and described strategies for lovers' intrigues. The *Heroides,* fictitious love letters from legendary women, revealed Ovid's sensitivity to women's feelings and his sympathetic understanding of love. Ovid's auspicious career came to an abrupt halt in A.D. 8, when, for reasons that remain obscure, Emperor Augustus exiled him to the remote town of Tomis on the Black Sea.

At the time of his exile, Ovid was completing the *Metamorphoses* [met′ə môr′fə sēz], his great poem based on the Greek and Roman myths. He continued to write poetry, including some efforts to persuade Augustus to pardon him. In these he failed; he died in exile at the age of sixty without ever seeing his beloved Rome again.

Ovid said of himself at the end of the *Metamorphoses,* "I shall be read, and through all centuries, / If prophecies of bards are ever to be truthful, / I shall be living, always." The prophecy was correct: The *Metamorphoses* has been a source of inspiration for poets and painters from the Middle Ages to the present; Chaucer, Dante, Shakespeare, Milton, Dryden, and, more recently, modern poets such as Yeats and Eliot all acknowledge Ovid's influence. A poem of nearly twelve thousand lines, the *Metamorphoses* is a collection of stories about all kinds of transformations, or metamorphoses, that occur in the myths. These stories begin with the transformation of chaos into an ordered universe and end with Ovid's fanciful transformation of Julius Caesar into a blazing star. One of the most touching metamorphoses occurs in the story of Daedalus, which follows. Daedalus [ded′əl əs] is the legendary craftsman and architect who has been held prisoner with his son, Icarus, on the island of Crete in the Mediterranean. They are prisoners of King Minos, who wants to prevent them from revealing the secret of the labyrinth, or maze, that Daedalus had built for the king.

Ovid

from the **Metamorphoses**

Translated by Rolphe Humphries

from **Book 8, The Story of Daedalus and Icarus**

Homesick for homeland, Daedalus hated Crete
And his long exile there, but the sea held him.
"Though Minos blocks escape by land or water,"
Daedalus said, "surely the sky is open,
5 And that's the way we'll go. Minos' dominion
Does not include the air." He turned his thinking
Toward unknown arts, changing the laws of nature.
He laid out feathers in order, first the smallest,
A little larger next it, and so continued,
10 The way that panpipes[1] rise in gradual sequence.
He fastened them with twine and wax, at middle,
At bottom, so, and bent them, gently curving,
So that they looked like wings of birds, most surely.
And Icarus, his son, stood by and watched him,
15 Not knowing he was dealing with his downfall,
Stood by and watched and raised his shiny face
To let a feather, light as down, fall on it,
Or stuck his thumb into the yellow wax,

---

1. **panpipes:** primitive musical instruments consisting of a series of
reeds or pipes of increasing length.

Fooling around, the way a boy will, always,
20 Whenever a father tries to get some work done.
Still, it was done at last, and the father hovered,
Poised, in the moving air, and taught his son:
"I warn you, Icarus, fly a middle course:
Don't go too low, or water will weigh the wings down;
25 Don't go too high, or the sun's fire will burn them.
Keep to the middle way. And one more thing,
No fancy steering by star or constellation,
Follow my lead!" That was the flying lesson.
And now to fit the wings to the boy's shoulders.
30 Between the work and warning the father found
His cheeks were wet with tears, and his hands trembled.
He kissed his son (*Good-by,* if he had known it),
Rose on his wings, flew on ahead, as fearful
As any bird launching the little nestlings
35 Out of high nest into thin air. *Keep on,*
Keep on, he signals, *follow me!* He guides him
In flight—O fatal art!—and the wings move
And the father looks back to see the son's wings moving.
Far off, far down, some fisherman is watching
40 As the rod dips and trembles over the water,
Some shepherd rests his weight upon his crook,
Some plowman on the handles of the plowshare,
And all look up, in absolute amazement,
At those airborne above. They must be gods!
45 They were over Samos,[2] Juno's[3] sacred island,
Delos and Paros toward the left, Lebinthus
Visible to the right, and another island,
Calymne, rich in honey. And the boy
Thought *This is wonderful!* and left his father,
50 Soared higher, higher, drawn to the vast heaven,
Nearer the sun, and the wax that held the wings
Melted in that fierce heat, and the bare arms
Beat up and down in air, and lacking oarage
Took hold of nothing. *Father!* he cried, and *Father!*
55 Until the blue sea hushed him, the dark water
Men call the Icarian now. And Daedalus,
Father no more, called "Icarus, where are you!
Where are you, Icarus? Tell me where to find you!"
And saw the wings on the waves and cursed his talents,
60 Buried the body in a tomb, and the land
Was named for Icarus.[4]

---

2. **Samos** [sā′mos], **Delos** [dē′los], **Paros** [pār′os], **Lebinthus** [leb in′thəs],
Calymne [kə lim′nē]: islands in the Aegean Sea.
3. **Juno's**: referring to the Roman queen of the gods.
4. **land . . . Icarus**: the Aegean island of Icaria.

STUDY QUESTIONS

Recalling

1. Why must Daedalus change the laws of nature? What means does he employ for his escape?
2. What warning does Daedalus give his son? What simile in lines 32–35 describes Daedalus' paternal feelings?
3. What does Icarus do in disobedience of his father? Why? What are the consequences of his disobedience?

Interpreting

4. What two transformations occur in this story?
5. What moral can be drawn from Daedalus' advice to "fly a middle course"?

Extending

6. The fisherman, the shepherd, and the plowman, seeing Daedalus and Icarus flying, think they must be gods. In what ways is Daedalus like a god? What price does he pay for these gifts? What does the myth imply about human pride and humility?

LITERARY FOCUS

Greek Mythology

A **myth** is an anonymous traditional story with its roots in cultural folk beliefs that rely on the supernatural to explain the mysteries of the world. While not attempting to be rational or scientific, myths do help us to grapple with our perceptions of humankind and the world. All mythologies revolve around ideas of cosmic creation, supernatural power, birth, death, and humanity's existence in the universe.

Greek mythology collects stories told by the ancient Greeks about their gods, ancestors, and legendary heroes. Reflecting the high-spirited and beauty-loving character of their creators, the Greek myths glorify the best in human beings. Although the gods, who are represented mainly as powerful and immortal men and women, may be capricious, they are seldom downright evil. Like mortals, they are susceptible to emotions and are capable of being flattered or enraged.

In their gallery of mythological characters and stories, the Greeks left a heritage that has been a source of artistic inspiration to succeeding generations. The first people influenced by the Greek myths were the Romans, who adopted the Greek gods and goddesses, changing many of their names.

Thinking About Greek Mythology

How does the myth of Daedalus reflect at the same time the classical admiration for spectacular human achievement and a wholesome respect for moderation in all things?

COMPOSITION

Applying a Statement About Literature

Ovid has been called a master storyteller. Show how that evaluation of Ovid applies to "Daedalus and Icarus." First explain what a master storyteller must be. Then show Ovid's mastery in this particular story. You might consider the plot (including the "hints" Ovid drops about its conclusion and the buildup to the climax) and the characters (including qualities that make Daedalus and Icarus seem human). *For help with this assignment, refer to Lesson 9 in the Writing About Literature Handbook at the back of this book.*

Writing Drama

Write a dramatic sketch about a person who has the opportunity to do something new. Examine the conflict that arises between being safe and taking a risk. How does one choose?

COMPARING WRITERS

Both Virgil and Ovid are concerned with the place and purpose of humanity in the universe and with overconfidence. How does each view the consequences of too much confidence? How do the contexts of their stories differ?

Key to Illustrations appears on page 922.

EUROPE
THE MEDIEVAL PERIOD

500–1500

The great civilizations of Ancient Greece and Rome are usually taken as the starting points of western culture. Although these civilizations encompassed vast territories, their intellectual, political, and creative centers were two cities—Athens and Rome. Following the collapse of the Roman Empire in the fifth century, however, western civilization took a radically different course.

Over the continent of Europe, new nations began to emerge, each with a distinctive culture. Many different cities established themselves; no single one maintained absolute control. A variety of vernacular languages began to develop. These were the languages actually spoken by the people of a particular region—such as French, German, Spanish, and Italian—rather than Latin, which had been the language of literature and learning. As the vernacular languages flourished, they produced their own literatures. Western civilization entered the period we now call the Middle Ages.

The Middle Ages comprise roughly the thousand years between 500 and 1500, during which Greco-Roman culture fused with the Christian religion. Beginning with the fall of Rome and ending with the turmoil of the Protestant Reformation, the medieval centuries were shaped by the Christian Church and the political and socio-economic structures of feudalism and divine monarchy.

Castle and Cathedral

With the fall of Rome, Christianity became the unifying force in western civilization. As no fixed national boundaries existed for at least another century, a traveler could still cross the whole of Europe with the sense that it was a single domain; and, throughout the Middle Ages, the western world regarded itself as a Christian kingdom—"Christendom."

The power and authority of the pope in Rome, the power of the papacy, came to represent the highest earthly authority. The papacy took part, directly and indirectly, in virtually every political and social event throughout Europe. When, for example, in 962 the German King Otto first established rule over several European countries, he had the pope crown him the head of the Holy Roman Empire. This attempt at a unification of Europe was never successful enough to be called a real empire; nevertheless, Otto needed the sanction of the Church to give his rule legitimacy as "holy" successor to the original Roman Empire, and he saw himself as *rex et sacerdos,* both "king and priest."

Wars and treaties, laws and trials, marriages and funerals, taxes and inheritances were all

Detail from an illuminated medieval manuscript depicting the siege of Jerusalem during the Crusades.

overseen and authorized in one way or another by the Church. Communities of monks became havens of culture and learning. Latin, the official language of the Church, remained the language of education, scholarship, and law. From the grand scale of cathedrals to the miniature scale of illustrated manuscripts, Christianity permeated the arts and crafts of the time. Its beliefs and philosophy inspired music, art, architecture, and literature.

The principal economic, political, and social system in medieval Europe was *feudalism.* According to the feudal system, land was owned by overlords and worked by serfs, who were legally bound to it. Vassals, or tenants, could hold land and gain the overlord's protection if they pledged allegiance to him and served in his army.

In the Middle Ages these lords of Christendom, with their armies of armored knights on armored horses, were called on for a special kind of war—the Crusades—in which Christian

soldiers tried to reclaim the Holy Land from the Moslems. The first Crusade was organized in 1095 at the request of Pope Urban II. About 30,000 soldiers rode toward Palestine under papal and royal banners and in 1099 captured Jerusalem.

Although subsequent Crusades were far less successful, legends sprang up around them. Minstrels told of knightly heroes and their triumphant exploits. Christianity united in story and song with the spirit of *chivalry*—the code of life that defined the qualities of knighthood, such as honor, courage, loyalty, and willingness to defend the weak and protect women. Chivalry was never in fact as glorious as the epic poems and romances make it seem, but like the Church it was an ordering factor during a time of frequent war and chaos.

Life in the Middle Ages

One of the most moving examples of what life was like in the Middle Ages may be that of the stonemason. During this period artisans labored with great effort and marvelous skill over long periods of time to build the cathedrals that still grace the European landscape. These artisans, however, never signed their work. It never occurred to them to assert their individuality in this way; they remain anonymous. They symbolize the medieval spirit because they labored for God's honor and glory.

Page from an illuminated manuscript of Dante's *Divine Comedy,* fourteenth century.

Europe in the Middle Ages was mostly rural, though it was also dotted with castles, monasteries, bell towers, and magnificent cathedrals. A few cities were famed for a court or a university, but in most cases, towns huddled outside castle walls, seeking protection and providing housing for serfs and storekeepers. In the towns living conditions were poor: Streets were no wider than footpaths; sanitation was inadequate; disease was rampant. In twenty years, beginning in 1334, a plague called the Black Death struck down nearly three quarters of the European population. The common people struggled, and the nobility enjoyed the fruits of those struggles, for feudalism allowed for very little social mobility.

Christianity defined the way of life. Not only priests but poets, soldiers, kings, and emperors were absorbed by the activities of the Church. Scholars, theologians, and teachers such as Pierre Abelard (1079–1142) in France and Thomas Aquinas (1225?–1274) in Italy were among the best known and most respected men of their time. Almost all people looked heavenward in the Middle Ages. From towers across the land, bells rang out the hours—a constant reminder of duty and devotion.

Literature in Medieval Europe

Latin, the language of ancient Rome, remained during the Middle Ages the language of the Church, of monasteries, and of schools. Scholars thought, read, and wrote in Latin; literature was composed in Latin. Simultaneously, however, vernaculars—French, German, Spanish, and Italian—were evolving into literary languages.

The first truly French medieval literature was stimulated by the emperor Charlemagne (A.D. 742–814), who established a vibrant court life and attracted artists, scholars, musicians, and poets. Poems called *chansons de geste*—songs about the deeds of heroes—became popular and were sung in public squares and in castle halls. The greatest of the *chansons de geste* is the *Song of Roland (Chanson de Roland),* an epic poem concerning a Christian hero who is killed in action but whose heroism inspires Charlemagne himself. Other national epics were written about the same time: the *Nibelungenlied (Song of the Niebelungs)* in Germany and *El Cid* in Spain. France also became the center of the ideal of chivalry and of the chivalric tradition in literature. Provençal (southern French) culture developed an extraordinary body of lyric poetry: Traveling poets called *troubadours* wrote and sang their poems in praise of fair ladies and idealized love.

Among those writing in German, chivalry produced one of the supreme works of medieval literature, Wolfram von Eschenbach's *Parzival,* the story of a perfect knight. The German lyric poets of this time were, like the troubadours, masters of the love song. The finest of these poet-singers, or *minnesingers,* was Walter von der Vogelweide, noted for his *minnelieder* (songs of idealized courtly love). In Spain the same interest in chivalry inspired poets to compose *cantares de gesta* in the eleventh century.

In Italy Latin was so pervasive that the vernacular was slower to develop than elsewhere in Europe. Latin literature persisted into the thirteenth century. Yet in its full flowering the Italian vernacular language produced the masterpiece of the Middle Ages, Dante's *Divine Comedy,* in which all of the intellectual, theological, and literary currents of the Middle Ages were blended into one grand vision. Like the ringing of cathedral bells, the *Divine Comedy* celebrated the particularly medieval blend of religious devotion and consummate artistic skill.

Dante *1265–1321*

Of all medieval literature Dante's epic poem, *The Divine Comedy,* is the best known and the most dearly loved. Few other poems of any time have had so much influence or have been the subject of such thorough study. The modern poet T. S. Eliot said, "Dante and Shakespeare divide the world between them; there is no third."

Born in Florence, Dante Alighieri received a traditional medieval education, spending some time at the University of Bologna and studying copiously on his own as well. As was customary, he was betrothed at the age of twelve to Gemma Donati, with whom he later had at least three children. However, when Dante was nine, he met the true love of his life, Beatrice Portinari, who would become the poet's lifelong inspiration.

Active in civil affairs as well as in letters, Dante fought at the battle of Campaldino in 1289. In 1295 he held public office and in 1300 served as an ambassador for Florence. During the same year, as one of the priors, or religious officials, of Florence, he was obliged to exile one of his best friends, the poet Guido Cavalcanti, for inciting a street riot—an exile that caused Guido's death. After further serving his city, Dante was himself exiled when a rival faction took power. He never returned to Florence, and for the next twenty years he moved all over Italy, spending time in Verona, particularly with Bartolommeo della Scala and his son Can Grande, who became his great friend and patron. In 1321 Dante died and was buried in Ravenna, where his remains still rest.

Dante's minor works alone would have assured him a place in literary history. His first work, *La Vita Nuova,* completed around 1293, tells of his great love for Beatrice in a series of poems with prose introductions. Beatrice is represented alternately as an ideal woman—an angel sent by God to comfort men—and as a very lovely, desirable human woman. *Il Convivio* and *De Monarchia,* written in order to inform and to persuade fellow Florentines of the virtues of knowledge and restraint of power, are works in which logic and reason prevail.

Introducing **The Divine Comedy**

Dante's supreme work and the masterpiece of the Middle Ages is his *Commedia*. Dante called his work *The Comedy* because it had a happy ending, not because it was humorous. The word *divine* was not added to the title until the sixteenth century. The poem, which begins in misery and ends in happiness, is divided into three parts of thirty-three cantos each—*Inferno* (Hell), *Purgatorio* (Purgatory), and *Paradiso* (Paradise). The poem is composed in the Italian vernacular in *terza rima*, a difficult verse form of three-line stanzas in which the first and third lines rhyme and the second line rhymes with the first line of the following stanza. The translation of a portion of Dante's work, which begins on the following page, is not in terza rima.

In a letter to Can Grande, Dante explained that the first meaning of *The Divine Comedy* was the literal one: The cantos tell the story, according to the beliefs of medieval Christianity, of the state of souls after death, brought to that point by choices made during life. *The Divine Comedy* may also be read on other levels; on an allegorical level its purpose is to turn the living to the path of salvation.

In the *Inferno* the damned souls occupy nine circles and are divided into three main groups: those lacking self-restraint; those committing violence against themselves, others, nature, or God; and those guilty of all types of fraudulence. Purgatory is divided into nine levels of the penitent and Paradise into nine heavens of the virtuous. *The Divine Comedy* ends with the vision of a human's attainable unity with God, which is the final destination of the entire journey of the soul.

Dante makes himself the central character who undertakes the soul's long and arduous journey. As his guide he takes Virgil, the poet he most loved, who was regarded in the Middle Ages as a magician of sorts. Since Virgil is not a Christian, he must abandon Dante at the end of the journey through Purgatory. Thereafter, it is Beatrice herself, who had sent Virgil to bring Dante to her, who becomes Dante's guide.

Dante's journey begins on the night before Good Friday in 1300, when he finds himself lost in a dark wood. As Dante struggles to find his way out, he meets three terrifying animals who refuse to let him leave the wood. Just as he is about to give up hope of ever escaping, Dante meets the poet Virgil, who leads him from the forest.

Dante

from **The Divine Comedy**

Translated by John Ciardi

from **Canto I, Virgil**

Midway in our life's journey, I went astray
    from the straight road and woke to find myself
    alone in a dark wood. How shall I say

what wood that was! I never saw so drear,
5   so rank, so arduous a wilderness!
    Its very memory gives a shape to fear.

Death could scarce be more bitter than that place!
    But since it came to good, I will recount
    all that I found revealed there by God's grace.

10 How I came to it I cannot rightly say,
    so drugged and loose with sleep had I become
    when I first wandered there from the True Way.

But at the far end of that valley of evil
    whose maze had sapped my very heart with fear
15 I found myself before a little hill

and lifted up my eyes. Its shoulders glowed
    already with the sweet rays of that planet[1]
    whose virtue leads men straight on every road,

and the shining strengthened me against the fright
20 whose agony had wracked the lake of my heart
    through all the terrors of that piteous night.

Just as a swimmer, who with his last breath
    flounders ashore from perilous seas, might turn
    to memorize the wide water of his death—

25 so did I turn, my soul still fugitive
    from death's surviving image, to stare down
    that pass that none had ever left alive.

And there I lay to rest from my heart's race
    till calm and breath returned to me. Then rose
30 and pushed up that dead slope at such a pace

---

1. **that planet:** The sun, which symbolizes God, was considered
a planet in medieval astronomy.

each footfall rose above the last. And lo!
   almost at the beginning of the rise
   I faced a spotted Leopard,[2] all tremor and flow

and gaudy pelt. And it would not pass, but stood
35   so blocking my every turn that time and again
   I was on the verge of turning back to the wood.

This fell at the first widening of the dawn
   as the sun was climbing Aries[3] with those stars
   that rode with him to light the new creation.

40 Thus the holy hour and the sweet season
   of commemoration did much to arm my fear
   of that bright murderous beast with their good omen.

Yet not so much but what I shook with dread
   at sight of a great Lion that broke upon me
45   raging with hunger, its enormous head

held high as if to strike a mortal terror
   into the very air. And down his track,
   a She-Wolf drove upon me, a starved horror

ravening and wasted beyond all belief.
50   She seemed a rack for avarice, gaunt and craving.
   Oh many the souls she has brought to endless grief!

She brought such heaviness upon my spirit
   at sight of her savagery and desperation,
   I died from every hope of that high summit.

55 And like a miser—eager in acquisition
   but desperate in self-reproach when Fortune's wheel
   turns to the hour of his loss—all tears and attrition

I wavered back; and still the beast pursued,
   forcing herself against me bit by bit
60   till I slid back into the sunless wood.

And as I fell to my soul's ruin, a presence
   gathered before me on the discolored air,
   the figure of one who seemed hoarse from long silence.

---

2. **Leopard:** along with the Lion and the She-Wolf, one of three beasts
representing types of worldliness and sin: the Leopard represents
malice and greed; the Lion, violence and pride; and the She-Wolf,
self-indulgence.
3. **Aries:** the first sign of the zodiac, here representing spring, the Easter
season, and rebirth.

At sight of him in that friendless waste I cried:
65   "Have pity on me, whatever thing you are,
      whether shade or living man." And it replied:

"Not man, though man I once was, and my blood
    was Lombard, both my parents Mantuan.[4]
    I was born, though late, *sub Julio*,[5] and bred

70 in Rome under Augustus in the noon
    of the false and lying gods. I was a poet
    and sang of old Anchises' noble son[6]

who came to Rome after the burning of Troy.
    But you—why do *you* return to these distresses
75   instead of climbing that shining Mount of Joy

which is the seat and first cause of man's bliss?"
    "And are you then that Virgil and that fountain
    of purest speech?" My voice grew tremulous:

"Glory and light of poets! now may that zeal
80   and love's apprenticeship that I poured out
    on your heroic verses serve me well!

For you are my true master and first author,
    the sole maker from whom I drew the breath
    of that sweet style whose measures have brought me honor.

85 See there, immortal sage, the beast I flee.
    For my soul's salvation, I beg you, guard me from her,
    for she has struck a mortal tremor through me."

And he replied, seeing my soul in tears:
    "He must go by another way who would escape
90   this wilderness, for that mad beast that fleers[7]

before you there, suffers no man to pass.
    She tracks down all, kills all, and knows no glut,
    but, feeding, she grows hungrier than she was. . . .

Therefore, for your own good, I think it well

95 you follow me and I will be your guide
    and lead you forth through an eternal place.[8]
    There you shall see the ancient spirits tried

---

4. **Lombard . . . Mantuan:** Virgil was born in Mantua, a city in the
region of Lombardy in northern Italy.
5. *sub Julio:* during the reign of Julius Caesar (100?–44 B.C.).
6. **Anchises'** [an kē′sēz] **. . . son:** Aeneas, hero of Virgil's *Aeneid.*
7. **fleers:** sneers at.
8. **an eternal place:** Hell.

in endless pain, and hear their lamentation
    as each bemoans the second death of souls.
100 Next you shall see upon a burning mountain[9]

souls in fire and yet content in fire,
    knowing that whensoever it may be
    they yet will mount into the blessed choir.

To which, if it is still your wish to climb,
105 a worthier spirit shall be sent to guide you.
    With her shall I leave you, for the King of Time,

who reigns on high, forbids me to come there[10]
    since, living, I rebelled against his law.
    He rules the waters and the land and air

110 and there holds court, his city and his throne.
    Oh blessed are they he chooses!" And I to him:
    "Poet, by that God to you unknown,

lead me this way. Beyond this present ill
    and worse to dread, lead me to Peter's gate[11]
115 and be my guide through the sad halls of Hell."

And he then: "Follow." And he moved ahead
    in silence, and I followed where he led.

---

9. **a burning mountain:** Purgatory, where souls may be redeemed.
10. **forbids . . . there:** Because Virgil lived before the Christian Era, he missed salvation through Christ, which, according to Dante's theology, was necessary for entry into Heaven.
11. **Peter's gate:** the gate of Purgatory.

Dante and Beatrice depicted in an illustration from a thirteenth-century manuscript of *The Divine Comedy*.

from **Canto III, The Gate of Hell**

Dante, after spending a whole day trying to climb the mountain, gets discouraged and makes excuses to Virgil. Virgil then explains that Saint Lucy and the Virgin Mary sent Beatrice to Purgatory to beg him to go to Dante's rescue. Thus encouraged, Dante prepares to follow Virgil without further complaint. The poets then arrive at the Gate of Hell, upon which they read an ominous inscription.

I AM THE WAY INTO THE CITY OF WOE.
I AM THE WAY TO A FORSAKEN PEOPLE.
I AM THE WAY INTO ETERNAL SORROW.

SACRED JUSTICE MOVED MY ARCHITECT.
5   I WAS RAISED HERE BY DIVINE OMNIPOTENCE,
PRIMORDIAL LOVE AND ULTIMATE INTELLECT.

ONLY THOSE ELEMENTS TIME CANNOT WEAR[12]
WERE MADE BEFORE ME, AND BEYOND TIME I STAND.[13]
ABANDON ALL HOPE YE WHO ENTER HERE.[14]

10 These mysteries I read cut into stone
        above a gate. And turning I said: "Master,
        what is the meaning of this harsh inscription?"

And he then as initiate to novice:
        "Here must you put by all division of spirit
15   and gather your soul against all cowardice.

This is the place I told you to expect.
        Here you shall pass among the fallen people,
        souls who have lost the good of intellect."

So saying, he put forth his hand to me,
20   and with a gentle and encouraging smile
        he led me through the gate of mystery.

Here sighs and cries and wails coiled and recoiled
        on the starless air, spilling my soul to tears.
        A confusion of tongues and monstrous accents toiled

---

12. **ELEMENTS . . . WEAR:** the highest heavens, the first matter created, and the angels.
13. **BEYOND . . . STAND:** Just punishment for sins is endless.
14. **ABANDON . . . HERE:** For the soul entering Hell there is no return. Dante is naturally fearful; however, since he is still alive, he is entering not Hell itself but the vision of Hell and may escape if he keeps his faith.

25 in pain and anger. Voices hoarse and shrill
    and sounds of blows, all intermingled, raised
    tumult and pandemonium that still

whirls on the air forever dirty with it
    as if a whirlwind sucked at sand. And I,
30   holding my head in horror, cried: "Sweet Spirit,

what souls are these who run through this black haze?"
    And he to me: "These are the nearly soulless
    whose lives concluded neither blame nor praise.

They are mixed here with that despicable corps
35   of angels who were neither for God nor Satan,
    but only for themselves. The High Creator

scourged them from Heaven for its perfect beauty,
    and Hell will not recieve them since the wicked
    might feel some glory over them." And I:

40 "Master, what gnaws at them so hideously
    their lamentation stuns the very air?"
    "They have no hope of death," he answered me,

"and in their blind and unattaining state
    their miserable lives have sunk so low
45   that they must envy every other fate.

No word of them survives their living season.
    Mercy and Justice[15] deny them even a name.
    Let us not speak of them: look, and pass on."

from Canto XXVI, Ulysses

    From here on Dante, guided by Virgil, proceeds to descend through the various levels of Hell. Despite the difficulties they encounter along the way, they eventually arrive in the Eighth Circle. With Virgil's instruction and encouragement, Dante overcomes the barriers to their passage, and the travelers enter the eighth chasm of the Eighth Circle, where evil counselors wrapped in tall flames are punished. Here the poets talk to Ulysses (the Latin form of Odysseus) *and Diomede, the Greeks responsible for the treachery of the wooden horse.*

As many fireflies as the peasant sees
    when he rests on a hill and looks into the valley
    (where he tills or gathers grapes or prunes his trees)

---

15. **Mercy and Justice:** Heaven and Hell.

in that sweet season when the face of him
5   who lights the world rides north, and at the hour
     when the fly yields to the gnat and the air grows dim—

such myriads of flames I saw shine through
     the gloom of the eighth abyss when I arrived
     at the rim from which its bed comes into view. . . .

10   I stood on the bridge, and leaned out from the edge;
     so far, that but for a jut of rock I held to
     I should have been sent hurtling from the ledge

without being pushed. And seeing me so intent,
     my Guide said: "There are souls within those flames;
15   each sinner swathes himself in his own torment."

"Master," I said, "your words make me more sure,
     but I had seen already that it was so
     and meant to ask what spirit must endure

the pains of that great flame which splits away
20   in two great horns, as if it rose from the pyre
     where Eteocles and Polynices lay?"[16]

He answered me: "Forever round this path
     Ulysses and Diomede[17] move in such dress,
     united in pain as once they were in wrath;

25   there they lament the ambush of the Horse
     which was the door through which the noble seed
     of the Romans issued from its holy source;

there they mourn that for Achilles slain
     sweet Deidamia weeps even in death;
30   there they recall the Palladium in their pain."

"Master," I cried, "I pray you and repray
     till my prayer becomes a thousand—if these souls
     can still speak from the fire, oh let me stay

---

16. **pyre . . . lay:** Sons of Oedipus, the brothers Eteocles and Polynices killed
each other in combat over who would rule Thebes. According to one version of
the legend, their mutual hatred was so great that even the flames of their funeral
pyre drew apart.
17. **Ulysses and Diomede:** in the war against Troy, Greek heroes who are being
punished for their joint guilt in three acts considered evil by Dante: devising the
stratagem of the Wooden Horse by which Troy was destroyed; coercing Achilles
into going to Troy, thus causing his love, Deidamia, to die of grief; and stealing
the Palladium, the sacred statue of Pallas Athena, on which the safety of Troy
depended.

until the flame draws near! Do not deny me:
35   You see how fervently I long for it!"
        And he to me: "Since what you ask is worthy,

it shall be. But be still and let me speak;
        for I know your mind already, and they perhaps
        might scorn your manner of speaking, since they were Greek."[18]

40 And when the flame had come where time and place
        seemed fitting to my Guide, I heard him say
        these words to it: "O you two souls who pace

together in one flame!—if my days above
        won favor in your eyes, if I have earned
45   however much or little of your love

in writing my High Verses, do not pass by,
        but let one of you be pleased to tell where he,
        having disappeared from the known world, went to die."

As if it fought the wind, the greater prong[19]
50   of the ancient flame began to quiver and hum;
        then moving its tip as if it were the tongue

that spoke, gave out a voice above the roar.
        "When I left Circe,"[20] it said, "who more than a year
        detained me near Gaeta[21] long before

55 Aeneas came and gave the place that name,
        not fondness for my son, nor reverence
        for my aged father, nor Penelope's[22] claim

to the joys of love, could drive out of my mind
        the lust to experience the far-flung world
60   and the failings and felicities of mankind.

I put out on the high and open sea
        with a single ship and only those few souls
        who stayed true when the rest deserted me.

As far as Morocco and as far as Spain
65   I saw both shores; and I saw Sardinia
        and the other islands of the open main.

---

18. **since they were Greek:** The Greek heroes might have more respect for
Virgil, whose poetry commemorates their fame, than for Dante, who, as an
Italian, is a descendant of Aeneas and the conquered Trojans.
19. **the greater prong:** As both warrior and leader, Ulysses bore a greater guilt.
20. **Circe** [ser′sē]: enchantress who detained Ulysses on her island.
21. **Gaeta** [gä ä′tə]: coastal town in southeastern Italy, named for Aeneas' nurse.
22. **Penelope:** Ulysses' faithful wife.

I and my men were stiff and slow with age
    when we sailed at last into the narrow pass
    where, warning all men back from further voyage,

70 Hercules' Pillars[23] rose upon our sight.
    Already I had left Ceuta[24] on the left;
    Seville[25] now sank behind me on the right.

'Shipmates,' I said, 'who through a hundred thousand
    perils have reached the West, do not deny
75 to the brief remaining watch our senses stand

experience of the world beyond the sun.
    Greeks! You were not born to live like brutes,
    but to press on toward manhood and recognition!'

With this brief exhortation I made my crew
80 so eager for the voyage I could hardly
    have held them back from it when I was through;

and turning our stern toward morning, our bow toward night,
    we bore southwest out of the world of man;
    we made wings of our oars for our fool's flight.

85 That night we raised the other pole ahead[26]
    with all its stars, and ours had so declined
    it did not rise out of its ocean bed.

Five times since we had dipped our bending oars
    beyond the world, the light beneath the moon
90 had waxed and waned, when dead upon our course

we sighted, dark in space, a peak so tall[27]
    I doubted any man had seen the like.
    Our cheers were hardly sounded, when a squall

broke hard upon our bow from the new land:
95 three times it sucked the ship and the sea about
    as it pleased Another to order and command.

At the fourth, the poop rose and the bow went down
    till the sea closed over us and the light was gone."

---

23. **Hercules' Pillars:** now called the straits of Gibraltar, once presumed to
be the western limit beyond which no one could navigate.
24. **Ceuta** [sōō′tä]: town on the African coast opposite Gibraltar.
25. **Seville:** region of southwestern Spain. With Seville and Ceuta behind
them, the sailors had passed into the Atlantic Ocean.
26. **raised . . . ahead:** had sailed south across the equator.
27. **a peak so tall:** the Mount of Purgatory, sighted after five months' sailing.

STUDY QUESTIONS

Recalling

1. In Canto I what three beasts does Dante encounter? How does he behave when he meets each? Which one threatens him most?
2. How does Dante come to recognize Virgil? What is Dante's reaction to Virgil's presence?
3. What does Dante ask of Virgil?
4. How far will Virgil be able to take Dante? Why will Dante later need "a worthier spirit" to take him further?
5. Where does Dante ask Virgil to lead him?
6. What does the inscription at the Gate of Hell mean, according to the "Master"?
7. What is the fault of those souls Dante first encounters after passing through the Gate of Hell? What is their fate?
8. Who are the sinners who share the dual flame? Who responds to Dante's questions?
9. How did Ulysses die, according to his own retelling of the story in Canto XXVI?

Interpreting

10. Given the description of the She-Wolf, why might Dante be fearful of her?
11. Considering the nature of their sin, why is the punishment accorded those souls just within the Gate of Hell appropriate?
12. What did Ulysses hope to achieve by his voyage? Would he have made the voyage if he had foreseen its end?

VIEWPOINT

Literary critic Erich Auerbach argues that Dante's vision of reality, in which the individual is important, provides a link between the medieval (God-centered) and the Renaissance (human-centered) views of the world.

In the history of modern European culture, there is, indeed, a constant . . . which is first discernible in Dante; namely, the idea (whatever its basis may be) that individual destiny is not meaningless, but is necessarily tragic and significant. . . .

■ How does *The Divine Comedy* embody a belief that individual destiny is important? Do these selections from Dante's work imply a tragic view of human destiny? Explain your answer.

LITERARY FOCUS

Allegory

Allegory is a form of extended metaphor in which the events, objects, and persons in a narrative represent moral qualities or specific abstract ideas, such as love, fear, and virtue. In Dante's allegory every element corresponds first to a literal reality; the allegorical reality then expresses a significance that is separate and coherent in itself.

For example, on the literal level Dante is the poet going on a journey, guided by Virgil, the poet of Rome. Beatrice is the beautiful woman adored by Dante. On the allegorical level, however, Dante represents the mortal soul experiencing after death the consequences of choices made in life. Virgil represents human reason and moral wisdom, and Beatrice at the end of the poem is an image of Christian wisdom illuminated by grace. Although *The Divine Comedy* is completely understandable on the literal level, Dante's purpose in writing it—to teach people the consequences of worldly actions in the hereafter—can best be appreciated through recognition of his masterful use of allegory.

Thinking About Allegory

■ As *The Divine Comedy* begins, Dante recounts being lost in a dark wood and is trying to climb up a hill toward the light. What do you think is the allegorical significance of this beginning?

COMPOSITION

Writing a Comparison/Contrast

■ In Canto XXVI ancient Greek values are juxtaposed against medieval Christian values. First define and then compare and contrast the values represented by Ulysses and by Dante, as you understand them. What is important to each? What kind of immortality does each seek? *For help with this assignment, refer to Lesson 2 in the Writing About Literature Handbook at the back of this book.*

Writing a Narrative

■ Compose a narrative in which you meet a favorite historical person who asks to spend the afternoon with you. First decide what you are going to do. Then describe your activities and the reactions of the person with you.

Troubadours and Minnesingers

Among the most beautiful, haunting, and puzzling of all medieval poetry are the love lyrics of the Provençal troubadours of southern France, many of whom remain anonymous. This poetry followed the highly stylized formal convention now called *courtly love poetry*. In courtly love poetry the lady is described as the perfection of womanhood. She is always married and therefore unattainable to the poet, who lives in hope of a word or smile from her. The poet always assumes the voice of an unworthy admirer, and, although stung by her cruelty, he can never give up the love for this woman, which exalts him and makes him capable of the noblest deeds. Certain images and concepts recur in this formalized poetry—the wound of love, the danger from the lady's eyes (whose very light arouses love), the lady's cruelty, the need for mercy, and the ecstasy of love. With such rigid conventions, the poems sometimes degenerate into strings of clichés; however, in the best examples the nature of love is explored.

By the mid-twelfth century in Germany the minnesingers [min′i sing′ərz], or singers of love, were imitating the Provençal poets. The German poets, however, transformed the conventions of courtly love by making the praise of the lady formal and short; what was now more important was the analysis of the lover's feelings. One of the most important minnesingers was Walther von der Vogelweide (c. 1170–c. 1228). Walther so altered the conventions of courtly love in his poems that the lady needed the love song to glorify her, to so endow her with beauty that the whole courtly world would admire her. In one poem Walther says, "her life receives glory from my life: and if I should perish, she is dead."

It is important to remember that the love lyrics of the troubadours and minnesingers are but a part of an elaborate tradition that included music, dramatized actions, and vocal inflections, all familiar to the specialized medieval audience who attended the performances of courtly love poetry. Aside from the lyrics, all else is lost to the modern reader, who is in a position analogous to that of a planetary alien who discovers a scrap of paper containing a few lines of a popular rock song. Therefore, when reading courtly love poetry, use your imagination to supply the appropriate settings and coloration that would complete the atmosphere of courtly love.

Opposite page, detail depicting the sense of hearing from The Lady and the Unicorn Tapestry, late fifteenth century.

The Intimations Kill Me

Translated by Paul Blackburn

The intimations kill me
that my lady gives me
when her handsome eyes
are bright and full of love.

5 If I fail the closeness
and have no part of her
the intimations kill me / that my lady gives me
I shall go before her
hands folded like a beggar
10 the intimations kill me / that my lady gives me
to request that she
make consolation for me,
a soft kiss at least.
The intimations kill me / that my lady gives me
15 when her handsome eyes / are bright and full of love.

Her body's white as snow is
fallen upon ice
the intimations kill me / that my lady gives me
and her color is so fresh
20   as, in May, a rose
the intimations kill me / that my lady gives me.
Above her face the ashen gold
of hair that pleases me
is softer and more lovely
25   than my words can say.
The intimations kill me / that my lady gives me
when her handsome eyes / are bright and full of love.

God has made no other
as beautiful as she is
30 the intimations kill me / that my lady gives me
nor will make another
and besides I love her
the intimations kill me / that my lady gives me
I love her for her straight and slender
35   body while I live,
and I shall die, believe it,
if I cannot have her love.

The intimations kill me
that my lady gives me
40 when her handsome eyes
are bright and full of love.

Walther von der Vogelweide

The Oracle of Straw

Translated by Ian G. Colvin

I sat in a despairful mood,
   And said I wanted to be free,
And would have left my servitude,
   Had not a comfort hindered me.
5 Comfort, alas, it cannot rightly be;
     So small and frail it is, I fear
     You will deride me when you hear.
But none can hope without credulity.

A wisp of straw has cheered my heart;
10   It says much Luck to me is due.
So with one straw I'll make a start,
   As often I see children do.
See if she loves, and listen too!
     "She loves, loves not, a win, a balk,
15   She loves," I hold a single stalk!
This comforts me—for I take hope anew.

She is unto my heart so dear,
   That though I often may perceive
How many nobles court her near,
20   I view their throng and do not grieve.
She would not (this I do believe)
     Bring me from happiness to woe,
     And I would have these gazers know;
It is their own conceit doth them deceive.

STUDY QUESTIONS

The Intimations Kill Me

Recalling
1. What does the poet request from his lady?
2. What are the lady's attributes of beauty?
3. What will be the poet's fate if he is rejected?

Interpreting
4. What do you learn about the lady's personality from the poet's description?
5. To what extent can the poet be taken seriously about his love? Will he indeed die if he cannot have the lady's love? Why does he say this?

Extending
6. Strong emotions like love can affect our perceptions of a person. How do you think the poet would describe the lady if he was not in love with her? Create such a description based on the details the poet provides.

The Oracle of Straw

Recalling
1. In the first stanza what does the poet say that he wanted?
2. According to the second stanza, what has cheered the poet's heart? Why?
3. For what two reasons does the poet not grieve about the many nobles that court his beloved?

Interpreting
4. In the first stanza how does the poet make his "comfort" appear negligible? Is it indeed great or small?
5. What is a modern equivalent of the wisp of straw? Is the poet sensible in using the laws of probability to help him in his decision?

Extending
6. How does the poet's source of assurance differ from that of the nobles? In what way does this contribute to your understanding of the poem?

COMPOSITION

Writing a Comparison/Contrast
■ Compare and contrast the poet's point of view toward his lady in each of these poems. Consider in each case the pose that the lover takes in talking about his lady. Also consider the role of the woman, the extent of her physical description, and her individuality. Finally, tell which of the two poems you prefer, and give reasons for your preference. *For help with this assignment, refer to Lesson 2 in the Writing About Literature Handbook at the back of this book.*

Writing a Poem
■ Write a poem in which you express a strong interest or desire for something. Address the poem to an imagined sympathetic friend with a similar interest.

COMPARING ENGLISH AND WESTERN WRITERS

■ Compare the medieval Scottish and English ballads on pages 39–40 with the lyrics of the medieval troubadours and minnesingers here. What differences can you see in content and in form? Which poems do you think appear more spontaneous? Which poems show characteristics of folk origins, and which poems are pure artifice?

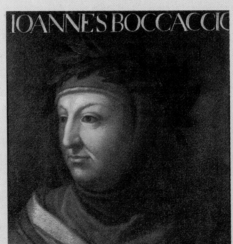

Key to Illustrations appears on page 922.

EUROPE
THE RENAISSANCE
1350–1600

The Renaissance is a period of about 250 years in western civilization that marks the end of what we call the Middle Ages. It is the era of European culture that saw the death of feudalism and the growth of nationalism. It witnessed the end of the unilateral power of the medieval church and the beginning of the modern nation-state. Yet the word *renaissance* is French for "*re*birth," and in examining the Renaissance we must first consider what, precisely, was reborn.

First, many of the ideas and attitudes of classical Greece and Rome were reborn (see page 649). Ancient manuscripts were rediscovered and salvaged, and they became models for Renaissance writers. Second, an interest in the physical world itself was reborn. The medieval European had been deeply concerned with preparing for the afterlife. The Renaissance European, while still aware of spiritual concerns, was also fascinated by the realities of this world— how objects really looked, how nature really functioned, how things really worked. This interest gave rise to the third rebirth—interest in the sciences and humanities, indeed, in all learning. Scholarship in medieval monasteries had been overwhelmingly concerned with one subject—Christianity—and written in one language—Latin, the language of the Church. In contrast, the Renaissance European explored many subjects and

Detail, Ferdinand Magellan's ship *Victoria*, map by Belgian geographer Abraham Ortelius, 1590.

often wrote in the vernacular, or language of the people—Italian, French, Spanish, German.

This development brings us to the most important rebirth of all, the revival of an interest in human nature itself. For the Renaissance was an age of great confidence in the powers and capabilities of human beings, an age that applauded human diversity and believed the world could be improved through human efforts.

A Time of Action, Invention, and Discovery

When European Christians returned from the Crusades to the Holy Land (1096–c.1300), they brought back the wealth and learning of other civilizations. At the same time the cities of Italy were granted special trade privileges for assisting the Crusaders, and consequently they became great commercial centers. In the 1200s Marco Polo, a Venetian merchant, traveled as far as the court of Kubla Khan, in Beijing, China. The book he wrote upon his return brought to European attention the fabulous wealth of the Orient. All of these events ushered in a commercial revolution that spurred the collapse of feudalism throughout Europe.

Nationalism flourished, characterized by strong monarchs who unified their countries and promoted national trade interests. We see the new nationalism in the Hundred Years' War

(1338–1453), in which unified French forces sought to end forever English feudal claims to French soil. Joan of Arc, a courageous peasant girl who led the French in many important battles, became a symbol of French patriotism. We see the new nationalism in the strength of the English monarchy under Henry VII, who in 1485 ended the War of the Roses (a civil war between two branches of the royal family, the House of York and the House of Lancaster). We see it in the campaign of Spain's King Ferdinand and Queen Isabella to cast out the Moors from their country.

Another antimedieval movement, the Protestant Reformation, swept northern Europe and Britain in the 1500s. Led by the German monk Martin Luther and the French-born theologian John Calvin, Protestants "protested" the authority of the Church in Rome and sought to reform what they saw as its abuses. Yet many rulers who championed Protestantism had

more worldly concerns. National feeling had given birth to a violent dislike of any foreign influence, including that of the pope. When Henry VIII broke with the Church of Rome, which would not give him permission for his divorce (1534), he was only doing what many of the English people desired.

National interests also prompted Queen Isabella of Spain to finance an expedition that resulted in one of the most significant events of the Renaissance. Christopher Columbus sailed west in search of a trade route to the East. He never reached the East Indies, but he did discover the New World, ripe for European commercial expansion. Soon not only Spain but Portugal, France, Holland, and England were setting up colonies in the Americas.

Columbus' expedition in 1492 spurred a host of discoveries by European explorers and scientists. In 1498 Vasco da Gama, sailing for Portugal, found an alternate route to the Orient around Africa's Cape of Good Hope. In 1519 Ferdinand Magellan, sailing for Spain, began a voyage that would prove forever that the world was round. In 1543 the Polish cleric Nicolaus Copernicus took this knowledge one step further by proposing that the earth revolved around the sun, a theory that was considered heresy at the time but was proved in the early 1600s by the Italian scientist Galileo.

By far the most important

Detail, oracle of Delphi, ceiling of the Sistine Chapel, Michelangelo, 1508–1512.

technological advance of the Renaissance, however, was the breakthrough in printing. John Gutenberg, a German, began printing with movable type in 1447. By 1500 there were over a thousand printers in Europe, spreading the new ideas of the Renaissance.

Art in the Renaissance

Florence in Italy was the center of the early Renaissance, for the city's artists were nurtured by the wealthy Medici family. Later, Renaissance popes brought the spirit of the times to Rome. Pope Nicholas founded the Vatican library and filled it with classical manuscripts. In 1508 Pope Julius II commissioned the Florentine artist Michelangelo Buonarroti to paint the ceiling of the Sistine Chapel in the Vatican. A brilliant painter and sculptor, well-versed in human anatomy, Michelangelo displays in his timeless works the characteristic Renaissance belief in the dignity of humanity. Such artists as Raphael and Leonardo da Vinci blended religious vision, scientific accuracy, and human warmth in their works. Da Vinci—a painter, sculptor, inventor, architect, and scientist—was a true "Renaissance man," someone who is skilled in many different arts and sciences. Da Vinci studied everything from canals to human anatomy. Above all he is remembered for his paintings, especially *The Last Supper* and *Mona Lisa.*

Literature in the Renaissance

The Renaissance is generally considered to have begun in Italy. Spurred by their new-found wealth and by the recent vernacular masterpiece of Dante, *The Divine Comedy* (see page 738), the fourteenth-century Italians began a revival of learning that would eventually reach Europe's farthest corners.

The Italian writer Petrarch—sometimes called the father of the Renaissance—gave the first impetus to the new scholarship by reconciling pagan classical cultures with Christianity. Petrarch insisted that human beings were rational creatures with an innate dignity. His rediscovery of manuscripts by Ovid, Cicero, and other ancient Romans brought to attention works that might otherwise be unknown to us today. His friend Giovanni Boccaccio also unearthed ancient texts and, using them as models, elevated vernacular prose to the stature of classical literature. Another important prose writer, Niccolò Machiavelli, wrote *The Prince* (1513), a realistic guide to the new breed of European ruler.

The spirit of the Renaissance soon flowered throughout Europe. In Holland Desiderius Erasmus took up the ideas of the Italians, stressing the possibilities of human reason in works such as the satirical *In Praise of Folly* (1509). France also absorbed Renaissance ideas from her neighbors. Among many notable French writers of the period are François Rabelais, a popular satirist, and Michel de Montaigne, who introduced a new literary form—the essay (see page 275).

Another new prose form destined for enormous popularity, the novel, was pioneered by Spain's Miguel de Cervantes with his masterpiece, *Don Quixote.* Spanish literature came late to the Renaissance (*Don Quixote* was published in the early 1600s), in part because of the political and religious turmoil that troubled Spain at the time. England too arrived late on the scene: Its cultural flowering took place from about 1560 to 1625, during the reigns of Elizabeth I and James I (see page 83).

The Renaissance ultimately affected every country—and every succeeding age as well. Even after its historical end, its ideas and attitudes, its energy and way of thinking about human nature, remain alive.

Petrarch   1304–1374

The Italian poet Francesco Petrarca, or Petrarch, the founder of the Renaissance, was a devout Christian who sought all his life to reconcile his faith in Christianity with his love and admiration of classical culture. The son of an exiled Florentine, Petrarch spent his early years in France. Although he preferred to write poetry and to study Greek and Latin, he studied law at his father's insistence and became a prominent diplomatic figure in Europe.

Petrarch's Italian poetry is pervaded by the conflict between the ambiguous attractions of mortal beauty on the one hand and a sense of worldly sinfulness and vanity on the other. The poems are dominated by the figure of Laura, the object and image of Petrarch's poetic love. Laura is a central figure in Sonnet 169, one of 366 poems in Petrarch's *Canzoniere,* or *Book of Songs* (1366). Sonnet 169 is typical of the complaint poems common in the Renaissance, poems in which the speaker laments the failure of his beloved to return his affections.

Petrarch

Sonnet 169

Translated by Anthony Mortimer

Rapt in the one fond thought that makes me stray
from other men and walk this world alone,
sometimes I have escaped myself and flown
to seek the very one that I should flee;

5 so fair and fell I see her passing by
that the soul trembles to take flight again,
so many armèd sighs are in her train,
this lovely foe to Love himself and me!

And yet, upon that high and clouded brow
10 I seem to see a ray of pity shine,
shedding some light across the grieving heart:

so I call back my soul, and when I vow
at last to tell her of my hidden pain,
I have so much to say I dare not start.

STUDY QUESTIONS

Recalling

1. According to the first stanza, how has being "rapt" in his "one fond thought" made the speaker behave toward others? What has he sometimes done to escape his isolation?
2. According to the second stanza, what happens to the speaker's "soul"? Why?
3. What does the speaker seem to see on "that high and clouded brow"?
4. In the last stanza what does the speaker vow? Why can he not keep that vow?

Interpreting

5. What is the "one fond thought" in which the speaker is "rapt"? Who is the "very one" that he should flee?
6. To whose brow do lines 9–11 refer? What does the "light" in line 11 represent for the speaker?
7. In your own words explain the conflict in the speaker expressed in the first eight lines, the decision he makes in the final six lines, and the event or action that prompts his decision. What is the ironical outcome of his decision?

LITERARY FOCUS

Petrarchan Sonnet and Conceit

Dante (page 736) and later Petrarch perfected the sonnet form now called Petrarchan, or Italian, in order to distinguish it from the Shakespearean or English sonnet (page 90).

The **Petrarchan sonnet** is divided into an octave and a sestet. The octave consists of eight lines that follow the rhyme scheme *abbaabba;* the sestet, or remaining six lines, generally has a rhyme sequence of *cdecde* or *cdccdc.* (Sonnet 169 in translation comes close to but does not exactly follow that rhyme scheme.) The structure of the Petrarchan sonnet usually follows the stanza divisions: the octave presents a situation or raises a question that is resolved or answered in the sestet. Because of these restrictions in length, rhythm, rhyme, and structure, the sonnet poses a challenge to the artistry of the poet.

The literary term **conceit** has come to mean a poetic metaphor in which the poet draws an inventive parallel between two elements having little or nothing in common. The **Petrarchan conceit** was introduced by Petrarch in his love sonnets to capture the qualities of the suffering lover and his beloved. The military imagery in lines 7 and 8 of Sonnet 169 —"armèd sighs" and "this lovely foe"—is a typical Petrarchan conceit.

Thinking About the Petrarchan Sonnet and Conceit

1. Indicate the octave and the sestet in Sonnet 169. Why do you think Petrarch further divided the octave and the sestet?
2. Find an example of a Petrarchan conceit in the first three lines of the sestet. What two things are being compared?

COMPOSITION

Writing a Comparison/Contrast

■ Compare and contrast the content and themes of Dante (page 736) and Petrarch in a brief essay. First compare the characteristics of Beatrice and Laura and the relationship each has to the poet. Then consider what each poet reveals about his spiritual beliefs through his portrait of and relationship to his beloved. *For help with this assignment, refer to Lesson 2 in the Writing About Literature Handbook at the back of this book.*

Writing a Letter of Advice

■ Imagine that the speaker in Sonnet 169 is a friend of yours. He has decided he is too preoccupied with being in love, and has written to you for advice. In your response, recommend three or four new activities or hobbies to your friend and explain why they will take his mind off love.

COMPARING ENGLISH AND WESTERN WRITERS

Compare Petrarch's Sonnet 169 to the poetry of one or more Elizabethan writers on pages 81–102. Your comparison should consider the following questions:

1. Which poems are love poems? Are these concerned merely with describing human love, or do they extend this topic into a general comment about human nature or into an expression of spiritual faith? Explain your answers.
2. Which poems are Petrarchan sonnets, and which are Shakespearean? How does the subject matter of each sonnet reflect the stanza breaks? (For a full discussion of the Shakespearean sonnet form, see page 90.)

Boccaccio   *1313–1375*

The first great writer of prose in the modern vernacular, Giovanni Boccaccio [bō kä′chē ō′], an Italian, was born possibly in Paris, possibly in Florence, the child of a French woman and an Italian merchant. Boccaccio took an early delight in writing stories and poems, but his father, wishing his son to become a businessman like himself, sent him to study business and later church law in Naples. While these studies were not at all to Boccaccio's liking, living in Naples gave him the chance to attend the court of Robert of Naples, active patron of writers and artists. With encouragement from Robert, Boccaccio greatly pleased the court with his poetry and stories and became a popular figure among the many beautiful women of Naples. Unfortunately, this pleasant life came to an end when financial reverses forced Boccaccio to return to Florence in 1340.

Ten years later he met Petrarch, whom he had long admired. Under Petrarch's influence Boccaccio embraced a more religious life and turned from writing worldly tales in the Italian vernacular to Latin and scholarship. He was instrumental in producing a Latin translation of Homer from Greek fragments and also in restoring many manuscripts of Roman classics. Never adept at managing his finances, Boccaccio spent his later years in poverty and ill health. Petrarch's death in 1374 was a great blow to him, and he died the following year.

Boccaccio's Italian stories and poetry stand as perhaps the most authentic representation of the Renaissance, for they exude Renaissance confidence in human ability and delight in the diversity of human experience. Boccaccio's masterpiece, the *Decameron* (written between 1348 and 1358), is a collection of one hundred stories that successfully blend the comic and the tragic and succeed in raising vernacular prose to the stature of classical literature. The stories are set in a historical framework: Retiring to the countryside to escape plague-stricken Florence in 1348, ten young people, invented by Boccaccio, amuse themselves by telling stories with topics determined each day by a presiding "king" or "queen." While Boccaccio varies the tone of the stories according to their subjects, his overriding theme asserts that a truly noble individual must accept the consequences of his actions and confine his desire to what is humanly possible. Yet, in true Renaissance spirit, Boccaccio insists that what is humanly possible is frequently a great deal, that a human being can often overcome his fortune or even learn to exploit it.

"Federigo's Falcon," one of the hundred stories of the *Decameron*, is a good example of Boccaccio's narrative artistry as well as his understanding and sympathy for human aspirations and emotions.

Giovanni Boccaccio

from **The Decameron**

Translated by Richard Aldington

Federigo's Falcon

Fifth Day, Ninth Tale

Filomena had ceased speaking, and the queen, seeing that nobody was left to speak except Dioneo (who had his privilege) and herself, began cheerfully as follows:

It is now my turn to speak, dearest ladies, and I shall gladly do so with a tale similar in part to the one before, not only that you may know the power of your beauty over the gentle heart but because you may learn yourselves to be givers of rewards when fitting, without allowing fortune always to dispense them, since fortune most often bestows them, not discreetly but lavishly.

You must know then that Coppo di Borghese Domenichi, who was and perhaps still is one of our fellow citizens, a man of great and revered authority in our days both from his manners and his virtues (far more than from nobility of blood), a most excellent person worthy of eternal fame, and in the fullness of his years, delighted often to speak of past matters with his neighbors and other men. And this he could do better and more orderly and with a better memory and more ornate speech than anyone else.

Among other excellent things, he was wont to say that in the past there was in Florence[1] a young man named Federigo, the son of Messer Filippo Alberighi, renowned above all other young gentlemen of Tuscany for his prowess in arms and his courtesy. Now, as most often happens to gentlemen, he fell in love with a lady named Monna Giovanna, in her time held to be one of the gayest and most beautiful women ever known in Florence. To win her love, he went to jousts and tourneys,[2] made and gave feasts, and spent his money without stint. But she, no less chaste than beautiful, cared nothing for the things he did for her nor for him who did them.

Now as Federigo was spending far beyond his means and getting nothing in, as easily happens, his wealth failed and he remained poor with nothing but a little farm, on whose produce he lived very penuriously, and one falcon which was among the best in the world. More in love than ever, but thinking he would never be able to live in the town anymore as he desired, he went to Campi where his farm was. There he spent his time hawking,[3] asked nothing of anybody, and patiently endured his poverty.

Now while Federigo was in this extremity if happened one day that Monna Giovanna's husband fell ill, and seeing death come upon him, made his will. He was a very rich man and left his estate to a son who was already growing up. And then, since he had greatly loved Monna Giovanna, he made her his heir in case his son should die without legitimate children; and so died.

Monna Giovanna was now a widow, and as is customary with our women, she went with her son to spend the year in a country house she had near Federigo's farm. Now the boy happened to strike up a friendship with Federigo, and delighted in dogs and hawks. He often saw Federigo's falcon fly, and took such great

---

1. **Florence:** largest city in Tuscany, a region in north-central Italy.

2. **jousts and tourneys:** tilting matches between two rival knights at festivals.
3. **hawking:** hunting with trained hawks.

Greenland Falcon, George Stubbs, 1780.

delight in it that he very much wanted to have it, but did not dare ask for it, since he saw how much Federigo prized it.

While matters were in this state, the boy fell ill. His mother was very much grieved, as he was her only child and she loved him extremely. She spent the day beside him, trying to help him, and often asked him if there was anything he wanted, begging him to say so, for if it were possible to have it, she would try to get it for him. After she had many times made this offer, the boy said:

"Mother, if you can get me Federigo's fal-con, I think I should soon be better."

The lady paused a little at this, and began to think what she should do. She knew that Federigo had loved her for a long time, and yet had never had one glance from her, and she said to herself:

"How can I send or go and ask for this fal-con, which is, from what I hear, the best that ever flew, and moreover his support in life? How can I be so thoughtless as to take this away from a gentleman who has no other pleas-ure left in life?"

Although she knew she was certain to have

the bird for the asking, she remained in embarrassed thought, not knowing what to say, and did not answer her son. But at length love for her child got the upper hand and she determined that to please him in whatever way it might be, she would not send, but go herself for it and bring it back to him. So she replied:

"Be comforted, my child, and try to get better somehow. I promise you that tomorrow morning I will go for it, and bring it to you."

The child was so delighted that he became a little better that same day. And on the morrow the lady took another woman to accompany her and as if walking for exercise went to Federigo's cottage, and asked for him. Since it was not the weather for it, he had not been hawking for some days and was in his garden employed in certain work there. When he heard that Monna Giovanna was asking for him at the door, he was greatly astonished and ran there happily. When she saw him coming, she got up to greet him with womanly charm, and when Federigo had courteously saluted her, she said:

"How do you do, Federigo? I have come here to make amends for the damage you have suffered through me by loving me more than was needed. And in token of this, I intend to dine today familiarly with you and my companion here."

"Madonna,"[4] replied Federigo humbly. "I do not remember ever to have suffered any damage through you, but received so much good that if I was ever worth anything it was owing to your worth and the love I bore it. Your generous visit to me is so precious to me that I could spend again all that I have spent, but you have come to a poor host."

So saying, he modestly took her into his house and from there to his garden. Since there was nobody else to remain in her company, he said:

"Madonna, since there is nobody else, this good woman, the wife of this workman, will keep you company while I go to set the table."

---

4. **Madonna:** Italian for "my lady."

Now, although his poverty was extreme, he had never before realized what necessity he had fallen into by his foolish extravagance in spending his wealth. But he repented of it that morning when he could find nothing with which to do honor to the lady, for love of whom he had entertained vast numbers of men in the past. In his anguish he cursed himself and his fortune and ran up and down like a man out his senses, unable to find money or anything to pawn. The hour was late and his desire to honor the lady extreme, yet he would not apply to anyone else, even to his own workman; when suddenly his eye fell upon his falcon, perched on a bar in the sitting room. Having no one to whom he could appeal, he took the bird, and finding it plump, decided it would be food worthy such a lady. So, without further thought, he wrung its neck, made his little maid servant quickly pluck and prepare it, and put it on a spit to roast. He spread the table with the whitest napery, of which he had some left, and returned to the lady in the garden with a cheerful face, saying that the meal he had been able to prepare for her was ready.

The lady and her companion arose and went to table, and there together with Federigo, who served it with the greatest devotion, they ate the good falcon, not knowing what it was. They left the table and spent some time in cheerful conversation, and the lady, thinking the time had now come to say what she had come for, spoke fairly to Federigo as follows:

"Federigo, when you remember your former life and my chastity, which no doubt you considered harshness and cruelty, I have no doubt that you will be surprised at my presumption when you hear what I have come here for chiefly. But if you had children, through whom you could know the power of parental love, I am certain that you would to some extent excuse me.

"But as you have no child, I have one, and I cannot escape the common laws of mothers. Compelled by their power, I have come to ask you—against my will and against all good manners and duty—for a gift which I know is something especially dear to you and reasonably so, because I know your straitened fortune has left you no other pleasure, no other recreation, no other consolation. This gift is your falcon, which has so fascinated my child that if I do not take it to him, I am afraid his present illness will grow so much worse that I may lose him. Therefore I beg you, not by the love you bear me (which holds you to nothing), but by your own nobleness, which has shown itself so much greater in all courteous usage than is wont in other men, that you will be pleased to give it me so that through this gift I may be able to say that I have saved my child's life and thus be ever under an obligation to you."

When Federigo heard the lady's request and knew that he could not serve her because he had given her the bird to eat, he began to weep in her presence, for he could not speak a word. The lady at first thought that his grief came from having to part with his good falcon, rather than from anything else, and she was almost on the point of retraction. But she remained firm and waited for Federigo's reply after his lamentation. And he said:

"Madonna, ever since it has pleased God that I should set my love upon you, I have felt that fortune has been contrary to me in many things, and have grieved for it. But they are all light in comparison with what she has done to me now, and I shall never be at peace with her again when I reflect that you came to my poor house, which you never deigned to visit when it was rich, and asked me for a little gift, and fortune has so acted that I cannot give it to you. Why this cannot be, I will briefly tell you.

"When I heard that you in your graciousness desired to dine with me and I thought of your excellence and your worthiness, I thought it right and fitting to honor you with the best food I could obtain: so, remembering the falcon you ask me for and its value, I thought it a meal worthy of you, and today you had it roasted on the dish and set forth as best I could. But now I see that you wanted the bird in another form, it is such a grief to me that I cannot serve you that I think I shall never be at peace again."

And after saying this he showed her the feathers and the feet and the beak of the bird in proof. When the lady heard and saw all this she first blamed him for having killed such a falcon to make a meal for a woman, and then she inwardly commended his greatness of soul which no poverty could or would be able to abate. But, having lost all hope of obtaining the falcon and thus perhaps the health of her son, she departed sadly and returned to the child. Now, either from disappointment at not having the falcon or because his sickness must inevitably have led to it, the child died not many days later, to the mother's extreme grief.

Although she spent some time in tears and bitterness, yet, since she had been left very rich and was still young, her brothers often urged her to marry again. She did not want to do so, but as they kept on pressing her, she remembered the worthiness of Federigo and his last act of generosity, in killing such a falcon to do her honor.

"I will gladly submit to marriage when you please," she said to her brothers, "but if you want me to take a husband, I will take no man but Federigo degli Alberighi."

At this her brothers laughed at her, saying:

"Why, what are you talking about, you fool? Why do you want a man who hasn't a penny in the world?"

But she replied:

"Brothers, I know it is as you say, but I would rather have a man who needs money than money which needs a man."

Seeing her determination, the brothers, who knew Federigo's good qualities, did as she wanted and gave her with all her wealth to him, in spite of his poverty. Federigo, finding that he had such a woman, whom he loved so much, with all her wealth to boot, as his wife, was more prudent with his money in the future, and ended his days happily with her.

STUDY QUESTIONS

Recalling

1. What caused Federigo to spend his money "without stint"? What was Monna Giovanna's reaction to his behavior?
2. Where did Federigo go after he lost his wealth? How did he occupy his time there?
3. In what financial circumstances was Monna Giovanna left after the death of her husband?
4. Why does Monna Giovanna want to obtain the falcon for her son? What does she realize about the falcon's place in Federigo's life?
5. Why does Federigo serve Monna Giovanna the falcon when she comes to visit? What does he do when she tells him why she wanted the falcon?
6. What does he say has been "contrary" to him in many things?
7. In what financial state is Monna Giovanna left after the death of her son? Who urges her to remarry? What does she remember about Federigo that prompts her to choose him as her new husband?

Interpreting

8. How do Monna Giovanna's feelings for Federigo change throughout the story, from her reactions to his lavish expenditures to her decision to marry him? What causes her feelings to change?
9. Is Federigo in any way responsible for his own eventual happiness? Explain.
10. Explain how the story illustrates the "moral" of giving rewards when they are deserved, as stated by Filomena in the second paragraph.
11. What Renaissance ideas or beliefs does the story illustrate?

Extending

12. What do you think is the role of chance in the achievement of happiness? To what extent are we responsible for our happiness?

LITERARY FOCUS

Narrative

A **narrative** is writing that tells a story, moving from event to event, usually in chronological order. Unlike drama and lyric poetry, which are direct presentations of actions or emotions, a narrative requires a narrator, or storyteller. Starting with the ancient oral epics, narrative has slowly developed into the novel, the dominant form of literature in the West for the past two centuries.

In presenting a fictional narrative, the author generally seeks to give his story a ring of truth that will help the reader accept the tale. In the *Decameron* Boccaccio does this by using a frame story. A **frame story** is a story within which another story unfolds. Boccaccio's frame story is factual—plague actually did strike Florence in 1348, forcing many residents to flee the city. By placing his narrators in this historical context, Boccaccio gradually eases the reader into accepting his fictional tales.

Boccaccio's narrative skill goes beyond realistic plot devices, however, A keen observer of human behavior, Boccaccio uses internal discussions, called **interior monologues,** and comments by the narrator that explain his characters' personalities or reveal their thoughts. It is Boccaccio's combination of action and insight that sets his narratives apart from the stories of the classical and medieval ages and places him at the beginning of the modern tradition.

Thinking About Narrative

1. "Federigo's Falcon" actually has two narrators in addition to Boccaccio himself. Identify these two narrators and explain the function of each.
2. Indicate three passages where Boccaccio explains Monna Giovanna's personality or reveals her thought.

COMPOSITION

Analyzing Characterization

▪ Write a brief essay analyzing Boccaccio's characterization of either Monna Giovanna or Federigo. Begin with a statement about the character's personality. Then show how Boccaccio develops that personality through direct and indirect characterization (see page 32). State and explain your opinion of whether or not the character resembles a real human being.

Writing a Modern Version of a Story

▪ Write an updated version of "Federigo's Falcon." In your frame story make clear why ten young narrators have left an American city (of your choice) and are now telling stories to pass the time. In your story within the frame story, use the same basic plot and themes that Boccaccio uses, but substitute modern names, actions, and settings.

Cervantes   *1547–1616*

The Spaniard Miguel de Cervantes [mē gel′ dä sər vän′tēz] created the best-known and best-loved knight who ever lived in the pages of a book, Don Quixote de la Mancha [don′ kē hō′tē dä lä män′chä]. Cervantes was born near Madrid to a family of minor nobility who moved from place to place in near poverty for most of Cervantes' childhood. In 1571, when he was twenty-four, Cervantes fought under Don John of Austria and was wounded at the Battle of Lepanto—"the battle of the century"—which drove the Turks from the eastern Mediterranean. On his journey back to Spain, Cervantes was captured by pirates, and he spent the next five years as a slave in North Africa. He made several futile efforts to escape, until at length he was ransomed and returned to Spain, where he found his family in severe financial difficulties. Cervantes never emerged from these financial misfortunes, and even the immediate success of *Don Quixote* did little to relieve his burdens. He died in poverty in 1616, the same year that England lost its greatest writer, William Shakespeare.

Author of the greatest work in Spanish literature, Cervantes showed only indifferent talent in the traditional literary forms of his time. He wrote a quantity of insignificant poetry, moderately good prose stories, and twenty or thirty plays, most of which have been lost. Yet *Don Quixote* was an instant best seller and has become an enduring classic. It is generally considered the world's first great novel.

Published in Madrid early in 1605, Part I of *Don Quixote* went through sixteen editions in Cervantes' lifetime and was translated into French and English. Along with Part II, which appeared in 1615, it became the world's most frequently published novel. It was widely imitated by many early English novelists who spurred the eighteenth-century vogue for **picaresque novels,** loosely strung satiric novels that recount episodes in the lives of adventurers or lovable rogues.

Yet *Don Quixote* is far more than a picaresque novel. Although it sets out to satirize the long and complicated medieval romances of chivalry, its title character soon transcends his role as a caricature. Along with his faithful squire, Sancho Panza, Don Quixote rides forth, carrying the improbable banner of right into a world full of probable wrongs. Cervantes allows the reader to decide whether it is better to accept life's injustices and appear sane or to attempt to battle life's various "windmills" and be considered crazy.

Miguel de Cervantes

from **Don Quixote**

Translated by Samuel Putnam

Chapter 1

Which treats of the station in life and the pursuits of the famous gentleman, Don Quixote de la Mancha.

In a village of La Mancha,[1] the name of which I have no desire to recall, there lived not so long ago one of those gentlemen who always have a lance in the rack, an ancient buckler, a skinny nag, and a greyhound for the chase. A stew with more beef than mutton in it, chopped meat for his evening meal, scraps for a Saturday, lentils on Friday, and a young pigeon as a special delicacy for Sunday went to account for three quarters of his income. The rest of it he laid out on a broadcloth greatcoat and velvet stocking for feast days, with slippers to match, while the other days of the week he cut a figure in a suit of the finest homespun. Living with him were a housekeeper in her forties, a niece who was not yet twenty, and a lad of the field and market place who saddled his horse for him and wielded the pruning knife.

This gentleman of ours was close on to fifty, of a robust constitution but with little flesh on his bones and a face that was lean and gaunt. He was noted for his early rising, being very fond of the hunt. They will try to tell you that his surname was Quijada or Quesada—there is some difference of opinion among those who have written on the subject—but according to the most likely conjectures we are to understand that it was really Quejana. But all this means very little so far as our story is concerned, providing that in the telling of it we do not depart one iota from the truth.

You may know, then, that the aforesaid gen-

tleman, on those occasions when he was at leisure, which was most of the year around, was in the habit of reading books of chivalry[2] with such pleasure and devotion as to lead him almost wholly to forget the life of a hunter and even the administration of his estate. So great was his curiosity and infatuation in this regard that he even sold many acres of tillable land in order to be able to buy and read the books that he loved, and he would carry home with him as many of them as he could obtain.

Of all those that he thus devoured, none pleased him so well as the ones that had been composed by the famous Feliciano de Silva, whose lucid prose style and involved conceits were as precious to him as pearls; especially when he came to read those tales of love and amorous challenges that are to be met with in many places, such a passage as the following, for example: "The reason of the unreason that afflicts my reason, in such a manner weakens my reason that I with reason lament me of your comeliness." And he was similarly affected when his eyes fell upon such lines as these: ". . . the high heaven of your divinity divinely fortifies you with the stars and renders you deserving of that desert your greatness doth deserve."

The poor fellow used to lie awake nights in an effort to disentangle the meaning and make sense out of passages such as these, although Aristotle[3] himself would not have been able to understand them, even if he had been resurrected for that sole purpose. He was not at ease in his mind over those wounds that Don

---

1. **La Mancha:** in Cervantes' time a poor and backward region of south-central Spain.

2. **books of chivalry:** medieval stories of knighthood and courtly love. Cervantes refers to many authors, characters, and events from such books.
3. **Aristotle:** Greek philosopher (384–322 B.C.).

Belianís gave and received; for no matter how great the surgeons who treated him, the poor fellow must have been left with his face and his entire body covered with marks and scars. Nevertheless, he was grateful to the author for closing the book with the promise of an interminable adventure to come; many a time he was tempted to take up his pen and literally finish the tale as had been promised, and he undoubtedly would have done so, and would have succeeded at it very well, if his thoughts had not been constantly occupied with other things of greater moment.

He often talked it over with the village curate, who was a learned man, a graduate of Sigüenza,[4] and they would hold long discussions as to who had been the better knight, Palmerin of England or Amadis of Gaul; but Master Nicholas, the barber of the same village, was in the habit of saying that no one could come up to the Knight of Phoebus, and that if anyone *could* compare with him it was Don Galaor, brother of Amadis of Gaul, for Galaor was ready for anything—he was none of your finical knights who went around whimpering as his brother did, and in point of valor he did not lag behind him.

In short, our gentleman became so immersed in his reading that he spent whole nights from sundown to sunup and his days from dawn to dusk in poring over his books, until, finally, from so little sleeping and so much reading, his brain dried up and he went completely out of his mind. He had filled his imagination with everything that he had read, with enchantments, knightly encounters, battles, challenges, wounds, with tales of love and its torments, and all sorts of impossible things, and as a result had come to believe that all these fictitious happenings were true; they were more real to him than anything else in the world. He would remark that the Cid Ruy Díaz had been a very good knight, but there was no comparison between him and the

Knight of the Flaming Sword, who with a single backward stroke had cut in half two fierce and monstrous giants. He preferred Bernardo del Carpio, who at Roncesvalles had slain Roland despite the charm the latter bore, availing himself of the stratagem which Hercules employed when he strangled Antaeus, the son of Earth, in his arms.

He had much good to say for Morgante who, though he belonged to the haughty, overbearing race of giants, was of an affable disposition and well brought up. But, above all, he cherished an admiration for Rinaldo of Montalbán, especially as he beheld him sallying forth from his castle to rob all those that crossed his path, or when he thought of him overseas stealing the image of Mohammed which, so the story has it, was all of gold. And he would have liked very well to have had his fill of kicking that traitor Galalón, a privilege for which he would have given his housekeeper with his niece thrown into the bargain.

At last, when his wits were gone beyond repair, he came to conceive the strangest idea that ever occurred to any madman in this world. It now appeared to him fitting and necessary, in order to win a greater amount of honor for himself and serve his country at the same time, to become a knight errant[5] and roam the world on horseback, in a suit of armor; he would go in quest of adventures, by way of putting into practice all that he had read in his books; he would right every manner of wrong, placing himself in situations of the greatest peril such as would redound to the eternal glory of his name. As a reward for his valor and the might of his arm, the poor fellow could already see himself crowned Emperor of Trebizond at the very least; and so, carried away by the strange pleasure that he found in such thoughts as these, he at once set about putting his plan into effect.

The first thing he did was to burnish up some old pieces of armor, left him by his great-

---

4. **Sigüenza** [sē gwen′zä]: insignificant center of learning.

5. **knight errant:** wandering knight in search of adventures to add to his reputation.

grandfather, which for ages had lain in a corner, moldering and forgotten. He polished and adjusted them as best he could, and then he noticed that one very important thing was lacking: there was no closed helmet, but only a morion, or visorless headpiece, with turned-up brim of the kind foot soldiers wore. His ingenuity, however, enabled him to remedy this, and he proceeded to fashion out of cardboard a kind of half-helmet, which, when attached to the morion, gave the appearance of a whole one. True, when he went to see if it was strong enough to withstand a good slashing blow, he was somewhat disappointed; for when he drew his sword and gave it a couple of thrusts, he succeeded only in undoing a whole week's labor. The ease with which he had hewed it to bits disturbed him no little, and he decided to make it over. This time he placed a few strips of iron on the inside, and then, convinced that it was strong enough, refrained from putting it to any further test; instead, he adopted it then and there as the finest helmet ever made.

After this, he went out to have a look at his nag; and although the animal had more *cuartos,* or cracks, in its hoof than there are quarters in a real,[6] and more blemishes than Gonela's[7] steed which *tantum pellis et ossa fuit,*[8] it nonetheless looked to its master like a far better horse than Alexander's Bucephalus or the Babieca of the Cid. He spent all of four days in trying to think up a name for his mount; for—so he told himself—seeing that it belonged to so famous and worthy a knight, there was no reason why it should not have a name of equal renown. The kind of name he wanted was one that would at once indicate what the nag had been before it came to belong to a knight errant and what its present status was; for it stood to reason that, when the master's worldly condition changed, his

6. **real** [rä äl′]: old Spanish coin. There were eight quarters in a real.
7. **Gonela's:** referring to a court jester in Italy in the fifteenth century.
8. *tantum pellis et ossa fuit* [tän′tōōm pel′ is et′ ô′sä fōō′it]: Latin for "was just skin and bones."

horse also ought to have a famous, high-sounding appellation, one suited to the new order of things and the new profession that it was to follow.

After he in his memory and imagination had made up, struck out, and discarded many names, now adding to and now subtracting from the list, he finally hit upon "Rocinante,"[9] a name that impressed him as being sonorous and at the same time indicative of what the steed had been when it was but a hack, whereas now it was nothing other than the first and foremost of all the hacks in the world.

Having found a name for his horse that pleased his fancy, he then desired to do as much for himself, and this required another week, and by the end of that period he had made up his mind that he was henceforth to be known as Don Quixote,[10] which, as has been stated, has led the authors of this veracious history to assume that his real name must undoubtedly have been Quijada, and not Quesada as others would have it. But remembering that the valiant Amadis was not content to call himself that and nothing more, but added the name of his kingdom and fatherland that he might make it famous also, and thus came to take the name Amadis of Gaul, so our good knight chose to add his place of origin and become "Don Quixote de la Mancha"; for by this means, as he saw it, he was making very plain his lineage and was conferring honor upon his country by taking its name as his own.

And so, having polished up his armor and made the morion over into a closed helmet, and having given himself and his horse a name, he naturally found but one thing lacking still: he must seek out a lady of whom he could become enamored; for a knight errant without a ladylove was like a tree without leaves or fruit, a body without a soul.

"If," he said to himself, "as a punishment for my sins or by a stroke of fortune I should come upon some giant hereabouts, a thing that very commonly happens to knights errant, and if I should slay him in a hand-to-hand encounter or perhaps cut him in two, or, finally, if I should vanquish and subdue him, would it not be well to have someone to whom I may send him as a present, in order that he, if he is living, may come in, fall upon his knees in front of my sweet lady, and say in a humble and submissive tone of voice, 'I, lady, am the giant Caraculiambro, lord of the island Malindrania, who has been overcome in single combat by that knight who never can be praised enough, Don Quixote de la Mancha, the same who sent me to present myself before your Grace that your Highness may dispose of me as you see fit'?"

Oh, how our good knight reveled in this speech, and more than ever when he came to think of the name that he should give his lady! As the story goes, there was a very good-looking farm girl who lived near by, with whom he had once been smitten, although it is generally believed that she never knew or suspected it. Her name was Aldonza Lorenzo, and it seemed to him that she was the one upon whom he should bestow the title of mistress of his thoughts. For her he wished a name that should not be incongruous with his own and that would convey the suggestion of a princess or a great lady; and accordingly, he resolved to call her "Dulcinea[11] del Toboso," she being a native of that place. A musical name to his ears, out of the ordinary and significant, like the others he had chosen for himself and his appurtenances.

from **Chapter 2**
Which treats of the first sally that the ingenious Don Quixote made from his native heath.

Having, then, made all these preparations, he did not wish to lose any time in putting his plan into effect, for he could not but blame himself for what the world was losing by his delay, so many were the wrongs that were to

---

9. **Rocinante:** literally, a worn-out horse of little worth, originating from *rocín*, a nag.
10. **Quixote:** a piece of armor that protects the thigh.

11. **Dulcinea** [dool′sē nā′ə]: a name meaning "the sweet or pleasing one."

be righted, the grievances to be redressed, the abuses to be done away with, and the duties to be performed. Accordingly, without informing anyone of his intention and without letting anyone see him, he set out one morning before daybreak on one of those very hot days in July. Donning all his armor, mounting Rocinante, adjusting his ill-contrived helmet, bracing his shield on his arm, and taking up his lance, he sallied forth by the back gate of his stable yard into the open countryside. It was with great contentment and joy that he saw how easily he had made a beginning toward the fulfillment of his desire.

No sooner was he out on the plain, however, than a terrible thought assailed him, one that all but caused him to abandon the enterprise he had undertaken. This occurred when he suddenly remembered that he had never formally been dubbed a knight, and so, in accordance with the law of knighthood, was not permitted to bear arms against one who had a right to that title. And even if he had been, as a novice knight he would have had to wear white armor, without any device on his shield, until he should have earned one by his exploits. These thoughts led him to waver in his purpose, but, madness prevailing over reason, he resolved to have himself knighted by the first person he met, as many others had done if what he had read in those books that he had at home was true. And so far as white armor was concerned, he would scour his own the first chance that offered until it shone whiter than any ermine. With this he became more tranquil and continued on his way, letting his horse take whatever path it chose, for he believed that therein lay the very essence of adventures. . . .

As his adventures continue, Don Quixote encounters a bewildered innkeeper and persuades the man to "knight" him. He also breaks his "helmet" in the course of his exploits. His travels are cut short by his friends, who trick him into returning home, where he is treated like a madman and not permitted to read his "dangerous" books about chivalry.

from **Chapter 7**

Of the second sally of our good knight, Don Quixote de la Mancha.

. . . He remained at home very tranquilly for a couple of weeks, without giving sign of any desire to repeat his former madness. During that time he had most pleasant conversations with his two old friends, the curate and the barber, on the point he had raised to the effect that what the world needed most was knights errant and a revival of chivalry. The curate would occasionally contradict him and again would give in, for it was only by means of this artifice that he could carry on a conversation with him at all.

In the meanwhile Don Quixote was bringing his powers of persuasion to bear upon a farmer who lived near by, a good man—if this title may be applied to one who is poor—but with very few wits in his head. The short of it is, by pleas and promises, he got the hapless rustic to agree to ride forth with him and serve him as his squire. Among other things, Don Quixote told him that he ought to be more than willing to go, because no telling what adventure might occur which would win them an island, and then he (the farmer) would be left to be the governor of it. As a result of these and other similar assurances, Sancho Panza forsook his wife and children and consented to take upon himself the duties of squire to his neighbor.

Next, Don Quixote set out to raise some money, and by selling this thing and pawning that and getting the worst of the bargain always, he finally scraped together a reasonable amount. He also asked a friend of his for the loan of a buckler and patched up his broken helmet as well as he could. He advised his squire, Sancho, of the day and hour when they were to take the road and told him to see to laying in a supply of those things that were most necessary, and, above all, not to forget the saddlebags. Sancho replied that he would see to all this and added that he was also thinking of taking along with him a very good ass that he had, as he was not much used to going on foot.

With regard to the ass, Don Quixote had to do a little thinking, trying to recall if any knight errant had ever had a squire thus asininely mounted. He could not think of any, but nevertheless he decided to take Sancho with the intention of providing him with a nobler steed as soon as occasion offered; he had but to appropriate the horse of the first discourteous knight he met. Having furnished himself with shirts and all the other things that the innkeeper had recommended, he and Panza rode forth one night unseen by anyone and without taking leave of wife and children, housekeeper or niece. They went so far that by the time morning came they were safe from discovery had a hunt been started for them.

Mounted on his ass, Sancho Panza rode along like a patriarch, with saddlebags and flask, his mind set upon becoming governor of that island that his master had promised him. Don Quixote determined to take the same route and road over the Campo de Montiel that he had followed on his first journey; but he was not so uncomfortable this time, for it was early morning and the sun's rays fell upon them slantingly and accordingly did not tire them too much.

"Look, Sir Knight errant," said Sancho, "your Grace should not forget that island you promised me; for no matter how big it is, I'll be able to govern it right enough."

"I would have you know, friend Sancho Panza," replied Don Quixote, "that among the knights errant of old it was a very common custom to make their squires governors of the islands or the kingdoms that they won, and I am resolved that in my case so pleasing a usage shall not fall into desuetude. I even mean to go them one better; for they very often, perhaps most of the time, waited until their squires were old men who had had their fill of serving their masters during bad days and worse nights, whereupon they would give them the title of count, or marquis at most, of some valley or province more or less. But if you live and I live, it well may be that within

a week I shall win some kingdom with others dependent upon it, and it will be the easiest thing in the world to crown you king of one of them. You need not marvel at this, for all sorts of unforeseen things happen to knights like me, and I may readily be able to give you even more than I have promised."

"In that case," said Sancho Panza, "if by one of those miracles of which your Grace was speaking I should become king, I would certainly send for Juana Gutiérrez,[12] my old lady, to come and be my queen, and the young ones could be infantes."[13]

"There is no doubt about it," Don Quixote assured him.

"Well, I doubt it," said Sancho, "for I think that even if God were to rain kingdoms upon the earth, no crown would sit well on the head of Mari Gutiérrez, for I am telling you, sir, as a queen she is not worth two maravedis.[14] She would do better as a countess, God help her."

"Leave everything to God, Sancho," said Don Quixote, "and he will give you whatever is most fitting; but I trust you will not be so pusillanimous as to be content with anything less than the title of viceroy."

"That I will not," said Sancho Panza, "especially seeing that I have in your Grace so illustrious a master who can give me all that is suitable to me and all that I can manage."

from Chapter 8
Of the good fortune which the valorous Don Quixote had in the terrifying and never-before-imagined adventure of the windmills, along with other events that deserve to be suitably recorded.

At this point they caught sight of thirty or forty windmills which were standing on the plain there, and no sooner had Don Quixote laid eyes upon them than he turned to his squire and said, "Fortune is guiding our affairs

---

12. **Juana Gutiérrez** [hwä′nä gōō tē är′ez]: Sancho's wife, also referred to as Mari Gutiérrez and other names.
13. **infantes** [ēn fän′täs]: Spanish princes and princesses.
14. **maravedis** [mä rä vä dēs′]: copper coins of little value.

better than we could have wished; for you see there before you, friend Sancho Panza, some thirty or more lawless giants with whom I mean to do battle. I shall deprive them of their lives, and with the spoils from this encounter we shall begin to enrich ourselves; for this is righteous warfare, and it is a great service to God to remove so accursed a breed from the face of the earth.

"What giants?" said Sancho Panza.

"Those that you see there," replied his master, "those with the long arms, some of which are as much as two leagues in length."

"But look, your Grace, those are not giants but windmills, and what appear to be arms are their wings which, when whirled in the breeze, cause the millstone to go."

"It is plain to be seen," said Don Quixote, "that you have had little experience in this matter of adventures. If you are afraid, go off to one side and say your prayers while I am engaging them in fierce, unequal combat."

Saying this, he gave spurs to his steed Rocinante, without paying any heed to Sancho's warning that these were truly windmills and not giants that he was riding forth to attack. Nor even when he was close upon them did he perceive what they really were, but shouted at the top of his lungs, "Do not seek to flee, cowards and vile creatures that you are, for it is but a single knight with whom you have to deal!"

At that moment a little wind came up and the big wings began turning.

"Though you flourish as many arms as did the giant Briareus," said Don Quixote when he perceived this, "you still shall have to answer to me."

He thereupon commended himself with all his heart to his lady Dulcinea, beseeching her to succor him in this peril; and, being well covered with his shield and with his lance at rest, he bore down upon them at a full gallop and fell upon the first mill that stood in his way, giving a thrust at the wing, which was whirling at such a speed that his lance was broken into bits and both horse and horseman went rolling over the plain, very much bat-

tered indeed. Sancho upon his donkey came hurrying to his master's assistance as fast as he could, but when he reached the spot, the knight was unable to move, so great was the shock with which he and Rocinante had hit the ground.

"God help us!" exclaimed Sancho, "did I not tell your Grace to look well, that those were nothing but windmills, a fact which no one could fail to see unless he had other mills of the same sort in his head?"

"Be quiet, friend Sancho," said Don Quixote. "Such are the fortunes of war, which more than any other are subject to constant change. What is more, when I come to think of it, I am sure that this must be the work of that magician Frestón, the one who robbed me of my study and my books, and who has thus changed the giants into windmills in order to deprive me of the glory of overcoming them, so great is the enmity that he bears me; but in the end his evil arts shall not prevail against this trusty sword of mine."

"May God's will be done," was Sancho Panza's response. And with the aid of his squire the knight was once more mounted on Rocinante, who stood there with one shoulder half out of joint. And so, speaking of the adventure that had just befallen them, they continued along the Puerto Lápice highway; for there, Don Quixote said, they could not fail to find many and varied adventures, this being a much-traveled thoroughfare. The only thing was, the knight was exceedingly downcast over the loss of his lance.

"I remember," he said to his squire, "having read of a Spanish knight by the name of Diego Pérez de Vargas, who, having broken his sword in battle, tore from an oak a heavy bough or branch and with it did such feats of valor that day, and pounded so many Moors,[15] that he came to be known as Machuca, and he and his descendants from that day forth have been called Vargas y Machuca.[16] I tell you this because I, too, intend to provide myself with just

such a bough as the one he wielded, and with it I propose to do such exploits that you shall deem yourself fortunate to have been found worthy to come with me and behold and witness things that are almost beyond belief."

"God's will be done," said Sancho. "I believe everything that your Grace says; but straighten yourself up in the saddle a little, for you seem to be slipping down on one side, owing, no doubt, to the shaking up that you received in your fall."

"Ah, that is the truth," replied Don Quixote, "and if I do not speak of my sufferings, it is for the reason that it is not permitted knights errant to complain of any wound whatsoever, even though their bowels may be dropping out."

"If that is the way it is," said Sancho, "I have nothing more to say; but, God knows, it would suit me better if your Grace did complain when something hurts him. I can assure you that I mean to do so, over the least little thing that ails me—that is, unless the same rule applies to squires as well."

Don Quixote laughed long and heartily over Sancho's simplicity, telling him that he might complain as much as he liked and where and when he liked, whether he had good cause or not; for he had read nothing to the contrary in the ordinances of chivalry. Sancho then called his master's attention to the fact that it was time to eat. The knight replied that he himself had no need of food at the moment, but his squire might eat whenever he chose. Having been granted this permission, Sancho seated himself as best he could upon his beast, and, taking out from his saddlebags the provisions that he had stored there, he rode along leisurely behind his master, munching his victuals and taking a good, hearty swig now and then at the leather flask in a manner that might well have caused the biggest-bellied tavernkeeper of Málaga to envy him. Between draughts he gave not so much as a thought to any promise that his master might have made him, nor did he look upon it as any hardship, but rather as good sport, to go in quest of adventures however hazardous they might be.

---

15. **Moors:** Moslems of North Africa who invaded Spain.
16. **Machuca** [mä chōō′kä]: the Hammerer.

STUDY QUESTIONS

Recalling

1. What physical description of Don Quixote is provided in the second paragraph of Chapter 1? What does he read in his leisure time?
2. What strange idea does Don Quixote conceive when his wits are "gone beyond repair"? What does he plan to "right"?
3. What does Don Quixote wear on his journey? What does he rename his horse, and why? What does he call himself?
4. Whom does Don Quixote choose as his lady? Why does he believe he needs a lady? What name does he give her?
5. How is Sancho Panza described in the second paragraph of Chapter 7? For what reason does he agree to accompany Don Quixote?
6. In Chapter 8 identify three phrases that Don Quixote uses to describe the windmills.
7. What does Sancho Panza exclaim after Don Quixote falls to the ground? How does Don Quixote explain the windmills after his fall?

Interpreting

8. What aspects of Don Quixote's character are mildly mocked in the first chapter? What else does the chapter criticize?
9. Compare Don Quixote and Sancho Panza with respect to their stations in life, their motives in sallying forth, and their general attitudes toward life.
10. What might the windmills represent?
11. What virtues does Don Quixote possess? What does the fact that he is considered mad suggest about his society?

Extending

12. What parallels can you draw between Don Quixote's time and today's society?

VIEWPOINT

Joseph Wood Krutch, a noted literary critic, explains the value of the developing relationship between Don Quixote and Sancho Panza:

Conceived at first as no more than a simple-minded foil to his extravagant master, the latter [Sancho Panza] grows wiser in one kind of wisdom as the Don grows wiser in another until, though the one is mad and the other a clown, they have come to represent the two types of human wisdom—

that which knows how things really are and that which knows how they ought to be.

—*Five Masters*

■ Explain in your own words the two types of wisdom Krutch is talking about. Do you agree that Don Quixote and Sancho Panza each represents one of these types of wisdom? Support your answer using evidence from the selection.

LITERARY FOCUS

Caricature

A **caricature** is a humorous picture that exaggerates or distorts certain qualities of a person in order to create a ridiculous effect. In literature caricature is frequently associated with satire or parody. Its true intent is not to criticize just one individual but rather to ridicule a societal group or a social practice. The ultimate aim of caricature is to ridicule in order to correct a weakness.

Thinking About Caricature

1. In what sense is Don Quixote a caricature? What things is Cervantes parodying or satirizing in Don Quixote's character?
2. In what sense is Don Quixote not a caricature?

VOCABULARY STUDY

Words from Fictional Names

From the famous fictional character Don Quixote comes the English word *quixotic*, which means "idealistic but impractical." Using a good dictionary, explain the meanings and origins of the following words.

1. babbitt
2. braggadocio
3. chanticleer
4. ignoramus
5. knickerbocker
6. malapropism
7. pantaloons
8. ragamuffin
9. scrooge
10. yahoo

COMPARING ENGLISH AND WESTERN WRITERS

■ Just as Shakespeare is frequently named the greatest writer in English, Cervantes is often cited as the most famous writer in Spanish. What do these two authors have in common that would warrant such evaluations? Consider especially the understanding of human nature that each author displays.

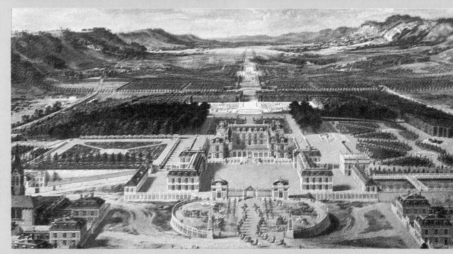

Key to Illustrations appears on page 922.

THE SEVENTEENTH AND EIGHTEENTH CENTURIES

1600–1800

Politically, spiritually, and artistically, the beginning of the seventeenth century marked the end of the Renaissance. The death of Elizabeth I in 1603 and of Shakespeare and Cervantes in 1616 signaled the passing of an age of extraordinary human accomplishment. From our modern perspective, it seems as if Europe needed to stop and take stock, consolidating what it had created.

One force continued into the seventeenth century: Religion and religious conflict played dominant and unsettling roles in Europe. Wars were waged for religious ends, and the greatest writer of the age, John Milton, composed his major work, *Paradise Lost,* to "justify the ways of God to men." Yet also characteristic of the new century was a fiery determination to discover and settle new lands across the oceans. By the middle of the seventeenth century, European colonists had established themselves in the New World, and a new chapter of western civilization had begun.

The eighteenth century is sometimes called the **Classical,** or **Neoclassical, Age** because its artists emulated the beauty and proportion of ancient Greek

and Roman art. They created works of balance and harmony, though they were also capable of sparkling wit and bristling satire, like that of England's Alexander Pope and Jonathan Swift.

The time is also called the **Age of Reason,** or the **Enlightenment,** a period when people believed in the possibilities of the light of reason to improve the world. In France the leaders of the Enlightenment, known as the *philosophes,* were inspired by the learning and the creations of the Renaissance. The greatest of these brilliant thinkers and writers gave still another name to the eighteenth century—the **Age of Voltaire.**

Politics and Power

Religious conflict in seventeenth century Europe took its most violent form in the Thirty Years' War (1618–1648), actually a series of wars fought over a number of political and religious issues. Beginning in Germany as a conflict between Catholics and Protestants, the war eventually involved France, Spain, and Sweden. The Peace of Westphalia in 1648 ended the struggle by allowing the head of each state the right to determine the state's religion, with certain other freedoms being granted to the citizens. The overall effect was the official establishment of religious toleration in Europe.

During the seventeenth century France emerged as the leading political and cultural power

Detail, *King Louis XIV of France,* Charles Le Brun (1619–1690).

in Europe under the absolute monarchies of the first three rulers in the Bourbon dynasty— Henry IV, Louis XIII, and Louis XIV. Louis XIV was the so-called Sun King, whose dazzling reign (1643–1715) produced a magnificent flowering of French culture. The most effective political figure of the age, however, was Cardinal Richelieu [rish′ə lōō′], who, as chief minister to Louis XIII from 1624 to 1642, made himself one of the most powerful men in Europe. Richelieu was largely successful in his two primary goals—to ensure absolute power for the monarchy and to make France the strongest continental power.

Nevertheless, in the eighteenth century the structure of the French monarchy and all of French society began to weaken. While rulers and aristocrats continued to live luxuriously at such locations as the splendid royal palace at Versailles [vər sī′], peasants in the countryside and commoners in Paris labored and starved and worried—and

waited. As the gap between rich and poor increased, it became apparent even to some in power that a great change was imminent. On his deathbed in 1774, Louis XV warned of "the deluge" to come. Fifteen years later, in 1789, it arrived—the culminating event of the eighteenth century, the turbulent French Revolution. The Revolution changed drastically not only France, but all of Europe. In an age of order, it was the ultimate disorder. It altered the relationships among the classes, leading especially to the downfall of the upper class and the rise of the middle class. It propelled changes in attitudes toward science, religion, nature, literature, art, and every aspect of culture as Europe plunged into the nineteenth century.

The Literature of Order and Light

In the course of western civilization, literature has often flourished where political power was great and the sense of national pride and security was strong. For example, stable and prosperous Elizabethan England produced, in Shakespeare and his contemporaries, the finest dramatists since the ancient Greeks. Another towering national drama arose in seventeenth-century France, where monarchy thrived. During this time several great French playwrights dedicated themselves to purifying the language and melding medi-

Eighteenth-century artist's conception of Voltaire and Rousseau walking to the temple of glory and immortality.

eval drama with classical elements. Dignity and nobility were exalted in the plays of Pierre Corneille [kôr nā′] (1606–1684) and Jean Baptiste Racine [ra sēn′] (1639–1699). Laughter and satire flowed from the pen of the master of French comedy, Molière [mōl yãr′] (1622–1673).

French prose became a sophisticated tool in the hands of the mathematician-philosophers Blaise Pascal [pas kal′] (1623–1662) and René Descartes [dā kärt′] (1596–1650). During the eighteenth century philosophical and historical writings dominated French literature. Working in the tradition of the essayist Montaigne (see page 275), the historian Montesquieu [mon′təs kyōō′] (1689–1755) wrote witty, philosophical essays to entertain and instruct his sophisticated readers.

The dominant literary figure of eighteenth-century France, however, was Voltaire [vol tãr′] (1694–1778), a writer who combined the philosophical acuteness of Pascal and Descartes with the wit of Montaigne and Montesquieu. It is Voltaire—poet, playwright, novelist, philosopher, scientist, essayist, historian—who stands as the

culmination of the Enlightenment spirit. His long life and many writings manifest his strong sense of morality, his vision of a balance between liberty and order, his faith in experiment and scientific progress, and, above all, his belief in human possibilities.

The most remarkable literary project of the eighteenth century was the *Encyclopedia,* edited and organized by Denis Diderot [dē′də rō′] and published from 1751 to 1765. This enormous undertaking attempted to record the vast body of knowledge that had accumulated since the Renaissance. The *Encyclopedia* can be considered the literary symbol of its time: Its goal was to put all the world's knowledge in *rational order.* It

is helpful to remember that at the same time Samuel Johnson (see page 291) was working on the great Age of Reason undertaking of English letters. His exceptional *Dictionary* was published in 1755.

Throughout the seventeenth and eighteenth centuries the dominant literary and artistic mode was **classicism,** a style that strove to recreate the order and harmony of the civilizations of ancient Greece and Rome. In hopes of resurrecting the grandeur of the past, the writers of the seventeenth and eighteenth centuries insisted on balance, purity of form, and above all clarity of thought through the exercise of logic and reason. The age embraces the grandeur of Milton's poetry and the refreshing directness of Addison and Steele's prose (see page 268). It encompasses the hilarious comedy of Molière and the subtle wit of Voltaire's philosophical fiction. Yet in all its manifestations, the literature of the seventeenth and eighteenth centuries expressed hope in the ability of humankind to improve, even to perfect, itself. The tools for that formidable task were the sense of order and the light of reason.

Molière   *1622–1673*

The great comic playwright Molière took to task all that was false, affected, and excessive in his society. So inventive was Molière as a dramatist that present-day comedy has found little to improve upon in his work.

Born in Paris into an affluent bourgeois, or middle-class, family, Jean Baptiste Poquelin, who later took the stage name Molière, received a solid education from the liberal and scholarly Jesuits. He studied law for a time, but his early fascination with the theater led him to establish his own acting troupe at the age of twenty-one. With no experience, he soon went bankrupt and joined a company of traveling actors. Becoming director of the group in 1650, Molière wandered through France, learning the vast repertoire of tragedy and comedy and observing a great deal about human nature. Returning to Paris in 1658, Molière gained favor at the court of Louis XIV, the Sun King. For the next fifteen years he managed his company, acted leading roles, directed, and found time to write twenty-nine plays. Among Molière's greatest works are *Tartuffe, or The Imposter* (1664), *The Misanthrope* (1666), *The Miser* (1668), and *The Imaginary Invalid* (1673). On February 17, 1673, during the final scene of a performance of *The Imaginary Invalid,* Molière, long ailing, suffered a hemorrhage on stage; he finished the performance and died shortly thereafter.

The basis of Molière's comedy is realism, which portrays human nature on stage with all the little quirks, graces, flaws, and inconsistencies that can be observed in real life. Yet to gain dramatic effectiveness, Molière simplifies psychology, creating universal types and exaggerating the dominant characteristics of those whose behavior he exposes. Knowing that he could not openly attack the settled opinions of either noble or bourgeois audiences, Molière flattered his spectators by praising the common sense of the average individual while mocking stereotypical characters such as the miser. In several plays, including *The Flying Doctor,* he attacks the pretensions of physicians and of the learned, suggesting that nature may be the better and wiser healer.

Gorgibus, Sganarelle, Lucile, and Sabine, in a recent production of *The Flying Doctor*.

Molière

The Flying Doctor

Translated by Albert Bermel

CHARACTERS

GORGIBUS: respectable, comfortable, but simple-minded citizen

LUCILE: Gorgibus' daughter

SABINE [sa bēn′]: Gorbigus' niece

VALÈRE [va lär′]: young man in love with Lucile

SGANARELLE [sga′nə rel′]: servant to Valère

GROS-RENÉ [grō′rə nā′]: servant to Gorgibus

A LAWYER

A street in a small French town.

[VALÈRE, *a young man, is talking to* SABINE, *a young woman, in front of the house of* GORGIBUS, *her uncle.*]

VALÈRE. Sabine, what do you advise me to do?

SABINE: We'll have to work fast. My uncle is determined to make Lucile marry this rich man, Villebrequin, and he's pushed the preparations so far that the marriage would have taken place today if my cousin were not in love with you. But she is—she has told me so—and since my greedy uncle is forcing our hand, we've come up with a device for putting off the wedding. Lucile is pretending to be ill, and the old man, who'll believe almost anything, has sent me for a doctor. If you have a friend we can trust, I'll take him to my uncle and he can suggest that Lucile is not getting nearly enough fresh air. The old boy will then let her live in the pavilion[1] at the end of our garden, and you can meet her secretly, marry her, and leave my uncle to take out his anger on Villebrequin.

VALÈRE. But where can I find a doctor who will

---

1. **pavilion:** summer house.

be sympathetic to me and risk his reputation? Frankly, I can't think of a single one.

SABINE. I was wondering if you could disguise your valet? It'll be easy for him to fool the old man.

VALÈRE. If you knew my valet as I do—He's so dense he'll ruin everything. Still, I can't think of anybody else. I'll try to find him. [SABINE *leaves.*] Where can I start to look for the half-wit? [SGANARELLE *comes in, playing intently with a yo-yo.*] Sganarelle, my dear boy, I'm delighted to see you. I need you for an important assignment. But I don't know what you can do—

SGANARELLE. Don't worry, Master, I can do anything. I can handle any assignment, especially important ones. Give me a difficult job. Ask me to find out what time it is. Or to check on the price of butter at the market. Or to water your horse. You'll soon see what I can do.

VALÈRE. This is more complicated. I want you to impersonate a doctor.

SGANARELLE. A doctor! You know I'll do anything you want, Master, but when it comes to impersonating a doctor, I couldn't do it if I tried—wouldn't know how to start. I think you're making fun of me.

VALÈRE. If you care to try, I'll give you one hundred francs.[2]

SGANARELLE. One hundred whole francs, just for pretending to be a doctor? No, Master, it's impossible. You see I don't have the brains for it. I'm not subtle enough; I'm not even bright. So that's settled. I impersonate a doctor. Where?

VALÈRE. You know Gorgibus? His daughter is lying in there ill—No, it's no use; you'll only confuse matters.

SGANARELLE. I bet I can confuse matters as well as all the doctors in this town put together. Or

kill patients as easily. You know the old saying, "After you're dead, the doctor comes." When I take a hand there'll be a new saying: "After the doctor comes, you're dead." Now I think it over, though, it's not that easy to play a doctor. What if something goes wrong?

VALÈRE. What can go wrong? Gorgibus is a simple man, not to say stupid, and you can dazzle him by talking about Hippocrates and Galen.[3] Put on a bold front.

SGANARELLE. In other words, talk about philosophy and mathematics and the like. Leave it to me, Master; if he's a fool, as you say, I think I can swing it. All I need is a doctor's cloak and a few instructions. And also my license to practice, or to put it another way, those hundred francs. [*They go out together.*]

[GORGIBUS *enters with his fat valet,* GROS-RENÉ.]

GORGIBUS. Hurry away and find a doctor. My daughter's sick. Hurry.

GROS-RENÉ. The trouble is you're trying to marry her off to an old man when she wants a young man; that's the only thing making her sick. Don't you see any connection between the appetite and the illness?

GORGIBUS. I can see that the illness will delay the wedding. Get a move on.

GROS-RENÉ. All this running about and my stomach's crying out for a new inner lining of food and now I have to wait for it. I need the doctor for myself as much as for your daughter. I'm in a desperate state. [*He lumbers off.*]

[SABINE *comes in with* SGANARELLE *behind her.*]

SABINE. Uncle, I have good news. I've brought a remarkably skilled doctor with me, a man who has traveled across the world and knows the medical secrets of Asia and Africa. He'll certainly be able to cure Lucile. As luck would

---

2. **francs:** A franc is the French monetary unit, now worth about twenty cents.

3. **Hippocrates** [hi pok′ra tēz] (460–370 B.C.) **and Galen** [gā′lən] (A.D. 130–200): Ancient Greek physicians.

have it, somebody pointed him out to me and I knew you'd want to meet him. He's so clever that I wish I were ill myself so that he could cure me.

GORGIBUS. Where is he?

SABINE. Standing right behind me. [*She moves away.*] There he is.

GORGIBUS. Thank you so much for coming, Doctor. I'll take you straight to my daughter, who is unwell. I'm putting all my trust in you.

SGANARELLE. Hippocrates has said—and Galen has confirmed it with many persuasive arguments—that when a girl is not in good health she must be sick. You are right to put your trust in me, for I am the greatest, the most brilliant, the most doctoral physician in the vegetable, mineral, and animal kingdoms.

GORGIBUS. I'm overjoyed to hear it.

SGANARELLE. No ordinary physician am I, no common medico. In my opinion, all others are quacks. I have peculiar talents. I have secrets. *Salamalec* and *shalom aleichem. Nil nisi bonum? Si, Signor. Nein, mein Herr. Para siempre.*[4] But let us begin. [*He takes* GORGIBUS' *pulse.*]

SABINE. He's not the patient. His daughter is. She may be up by now. I'll bring her out. [*She goes into the house and brings* LUCILE *back with her.*]

SGANARELLE. How do you do, Mademoiselle? So you are sick?

LUCILE. Yes, Doctor.

SGANARELLE. That is a striking sign that you are not well. Do you feel pains in your head, in your kidneys?

LUCILE. Yes, Doctor.

SGANARELLE. Very good. As one great physician has said in regard to the nature of animal life—

well—he said many things. We must attribute this to the interconnections between the humors and the vapors.[5] For example, since melancholy is the natural enemy of joy, and since the bile that spreads through the body makes us turn yellow, and since there is nothing more inimical to good health than sickness, we may conclude with that great man that your daughter is indisposed. Let me write you a prescription.

GORGIBUS. Quick! A table, paper, some ink—

SGANARELLE. Is there anybody here who knows how to write?

GORGIBUS. Don't you?

SGANARELLE. I have so many things to think of I forget half of them. Now it's obvious to me that your daughter needs fresh air and open prospects.

GORGIBUS. We have a very beautiful garden and a pavilion with some rooms that look out on it. If you agree, I can have her stay there.

SGANARELLE. Let us examine this dwelling. [*They start to go out. The* LAWYER *appears.*]

LAWYER. Monsieur Gorgibus—

GORGIBUS. Your servant, Monsieur.

LAWYER. I hear that your daughter is sick. May I offer my services, as a friend of the family?

GORGIBUS. I have the most scholarly doctor you ever met looking into this.

LAWYER. Really? I wonder if I might be able to meet him, however briefly?

[GORGIBUS *beckons to* SGANARELLE. LUCILE *and* SABINE *have moved offstage.*]

GORGIBUS. Doctor, I would like you to meet one of my dear friends, who is a lawyer and would like the privilege of conversing with you.

SGANARELLE. I wish I could spare the time,

---

4. *Salamalec . . . siempre:* series of unconnected phrases in Arabic, Hebrew, Latin, Italian, German, and Spanish.

5. **the humors and the vapors:** body fluids and gases once thought to control health and disposition.

Monsieur, but I dare not neglect my patients. Please forgive me.

[*He tries to go. The* LAWYER *holds his sleeve.*]

LAWYER. My friend Gorgibus has intimated, Monsieur, that your learning and abilities are formidable, and I am honored to make your acquaintance. I therefore take the liberty of saluting you in your noble work, and trust that it may resolve itself well. Those who excel in any branch of knowledge are worthy of all praise, but particularly those who practice medicine, not only because of its utility, but because it contains within itself other branches of knowledge, all of which render a perfect familiarity with it almost impossible to achieve. As Hippocrates so well observes in his first aphorism, "Life is short, art is long, opportunity fleeting, experiment perilous, judgment difficult: *Vita brevis, ars vero longa, occasio autem praeceps, experimentum periculosum, judicium difficile.*"[6]

SGANARELLE. [*Confidentially to* GORGIBUS.] Ficile, bicile, uptus, downtus, inandaboutus, wrigglo, gigolo.[7]

LAWYER. You are not one of those doctors who apply themselves to so-called rational or dogmatic medicine, and I am sure that you conduct your work with unusual success. Experience is the great teacher: *experientia magistra rerum.* The first men who practiced medicine were so esteemed that their daily cures earned them the status of gods on earth. One must not condemn a doctor who does not restore his patients to health, for healing may not be effected by his remedies and wisdom alone. Ovid[8] remarks, "Sometimes the ill is stronger than art and learning combined." Monsieur, I will not detain you longer. I have enjoyed this dialogue and am more impressed than before with your percipience and breadth of knowledge. I take my leave, hoping that I may have the pleasure of conversing with you further at your leisure. I am sure that your time is precious, and . . .

[*He goes off, walking backwards, still talking, waving good-bye.*]

GORGIBUS. How did he strike you?

SGANARELLE. He's moderately well informed. If I had more time I could engage him in a spirited discussion on some sublime and elevated topic. However, I must go. What is this?

[GORGIBUS *is tucking some money into his hand.*]

GORGIBUS. Believe me, Doctor, I know how much I owe you.

SGANARELLE. You must be joking, Monsieur Gorgibus. I am no mercenary. [*He takes the money.*] Thank you very much.

[GORGIBUS *goes off, and* SGANARELLE *drops his doctor's cloak and hat at the edge of the stage, just as* VALÈRE *reappears.*]

VALÈRE. Sganarelle, how did it go? I've been worried. I was looking for you. Did you ruin the plan?

SGANARELLE. Marvel of marvels. I played the part so well that Gorgibus thought I knew what I was talking about—and paid me. I looked at his home and told him that his daughter needed air, and he's moved her into the little house at the far end of his garden. You can visit her at your pleasure.

VALÈRE. You've made me very happy, Sganarelle. I'm going to her now. [*He rushes away.*]

SGANARELLE. That Gorgibus is a bigger dimwit than I am to let me get away with a trick like that. Save me—here he comes again. I'll have to talk fast.

[GORGIBUS *returns.*]

GORGIBUS. Good morning, Monsieur.

---

6. *Vita brevis . . . difficile:* translation in Latin of what the lawyer has just said.
7. *Ficile . . . gigolo:* Sganarelle's response to the lawyer is a series of nonsense words with Latin-sounding endings.
8. *Ovid* (43 B.C.–A.D. 17): classical Roman poet famous for his writings about love.

SGANARELLE. Monsieur, you see before you a poor lad in despair. Have you come across a doctor who arrived in town a short while ago and cures people miraculously?

GORGIBUS. Yes, I've met him. He just left my house.

SGANARELLE. I am his brother. We are identical twins and people sometimes take one of us for the other.

GORGIBUS. Heaven help me if I didn't nearly make the same mistake. What is your name?

SGANARELLE. Narcissus, Monsieur, at your service. I should explain that once, when I was in his study, I accidentally knocked over two containers perched on the edge of his table. He flew into such a rage that he threw me out and swore he never wanted to see me again. So here I am now, a poor boy without means or connections.

GORGIBUS. Don't worry; I'll put in a good word for you. I'm a friend of his; I promise to bring you together again. As soon as I see him, I'll speak to him about it.

SGANARELLE. I am very much obliged to you, Monsieur.

[He goes out and reappears in the cloak and hat, playing the doctor again and talking to himself.]

When patients refuse to follow their doctor's advice and abandon themselves to debauchery and—

GORGIBUS. Doctor, your humble servant. May I ask a favor of you?

SGANARELLE: What can I do for you, Monsieur Gorgibus?

GORGIBUS. I just happened to meet your brother, who is quite distressed—

SGANARELLE. He's a rascal, Monsieur Gorgibus.

GORGIBUS. But he truly regrets that he made you so angry, and—

SGANARELLE. He's a scoundrel, Monsieur Gorgibus.

GORGIBUS. But surely, Doctor, you're not going to give the poor boy up?

SGANARELLE. Not another word about him. The impudence of the rogue, seeking you out to intercede for him! I implore you not to mention him to me.

GORGIBUS. In God's name, Doctor, and out of respect for me, too, have pity on him. I'll do anything for you in return. I promised—

SGANARELLE. You plead so insistently that, even though I swore a violent oath never to forgive him—well, I'll shake your hand on it; I forgive him. You can be assured that I am doing myself a great injury and that I would not have consented to this for any other man. Good-bye, Monsieur Gorgibus.

GORGIBUS. Thank you, Doctor, thank you. I'll go off and look for the boy to tell him the glad news.

[*He walks off.* SGANARELLE *takes off the doctor's cloak and hat.* VALÈRE *appears.*]

VALÈRE. I never thought Sganarelle would do his duty so magnificently. Ah, my dear boy, I don't know how to repay you. I'm so happy I—

SGANARELLE. It's easy for you to talk. Gorgibus just ran into me without my doctor's outfit, and if I hadn't come up with a quick story we'd have been sunk. Here he comes again. Disappear.

[VALÈRE *runs away.* GORGIBUS *returns.*]

GORGIBUS. Narcissus, I've been looking everywhere for you. I spoke to your brother and he forgives you. But to be safe, I want to see the two of you patch up your quarrel in front of me. Wait here in my house, and I'll find him.

SGANARELLE. I don't think you'll find him, Monsieur. Anyhow, I wouldn't dare to wait; I'm terrified of him.

GORGIBUS. [*Pushing* SGANARELLE *inside.*] Yes, you will stay. I'm locking you in. Don't be afraid of your brother. I promise you that he's not angry now.

[*He slams the door and locks it, then goes off to look for the doctor.*]

SGANARELLE. [*At the upstairs window.*] Serves me right; I trapped myself and there's no way out. The weather in my future looks threatening, and if there's a storm I'm afraid I'll feel a rain of blows on my back. Or else they'll brand me across the shoulders with a whip—not exactly the brand of medicine any doctor ever prescribed. Yes, I'm in trouble. But why give up when we've come this far? Let's go the limit. I can still make a bid for freedom and prove that Sganarelle is the king of swindlers.

[*He holds his nose, closes his eyes, and jumps to the ground, just as* GROS-RENÉ *comes back. Then he darts away, picking up*

the cloak and hat. GROS-RENÉ *stands staring.*]

GROS-RENÉ. A flying man! What a laugh! I'll wait around and see if there's another one.

[GORGIBUS *reenters with* SGANARELLE *following him in the doctor's outfit.*]

GORGIBUS. Can't find that doctor. Where the devil has he hidden himself?

[*He turns and* SGANARELLE *walks into him.*]

There you are. Now, Doctor, I know you said you forgive your brother, but that's not enough. I won't be satisfied until I see you embrace him. He's waiting here in my house.

SGANARELLE. You are joking, Monsieur Gorgibus. Have I not extended myself enough already? I wish never to see him again.

GORGIBUS. Please, Doctor, for me.

SGANARELLE. I cannot refuse when you ask me like that. Tell him to come down.

[*As* GORGIBUS *goes into the house,* SGANARELLE *drops the clothes, clambers swiftly up to the window again, and scrambles inside.*]

GORGIBUS. [*At the window.*] Your brother is waiting for you downstairs, Narcissus. He said he'd do what I asked.

SGANARELLE. [*At the window.*] Couldn't you please make him come up here? I beg of you— let me see him in private to ask his forgiveness, because if I go down there he'll show me up and say nasty things to me in front of everybody.

GORGIBUS. All right. Let me tell him.

[*He leaves the window, and* SGANARELLE *leaps out, swiftly puts on his outfit again, and stands waiting for* GORGIBUS *outside the door.*]

Doctor, he's so ashamed of himself he wants to beg your forgiveness in private, upstairs. Here's the key. Please don't refuse me.

SGANARELLE. There is nothing I would not do

for you, Monsieur Gorgibus. You will hear how I deal with him.

[*He walks into the house and soon appears at the window.* GORGIBUS *has his ear cocked at the door below.* SGANARELLE *alternates his voice, playing the characters one at a time.*]

SGANARELLE. So there you are, you scoundrel! —Brother, listen to me, please. I'm sorry I knocked those containers over— —You clumsy ox! —It wasn't my fault, I swear it. —Not your fault, you bumpkin? I'll teach you to destroy my work. —Brother, no, please— —I'll teach you to trade on Monsieur Gorgibus' good nature. How dare you ask him to ask me to forgive you! —Brother, I'm sorry, but— —Silence, you dog! —I never wanted to hurt you or— —Silence, I say—

GROS-RENÉ. What exactly do you think is going on up there?

GORGIBUS. It's the doctor and his brother, Narcissus. They had a little disagreement, but now they're making it up.

GROS-RENÉ. Doctor and his brother? But there's only one man.

SGANARELLE. [*At the window.*] Yes, you scoundrel, I'll thump some good behavior into you. [*Pretends to strike a blow.*] Ah, he's lowering his eyes; he knows what he's done wrong, the jailbird. And now this hypocrite wants to play the good apostle—

GROS-RENÉ. Just for fun, tell him to let his brother appear at the window.

GORGIBUS. I will. [*To* SGANARELLE.] Doctor, let me see your brother for a moment.

SGANARELLE. He is not fit to be seen by an honest gentleman like yourself. Besides, I cannot bear to have him next to me.

GORGIBUS. Please don't say no, after all you've done for me.

SGANARELLE. Monsieur Gorgibus, you have such power over me that I must grant whatever you wish. Show yourself, beast!

[*He appears at the window as Narcissus.*]

Monsieur Gorgibus, I thank you for your kindness.

[*He reappears as the doctor.*]

Well, Monsieur, did you take a good look at that image of impurity?

GROS-RENÉ. There's only one man there, Monsieur. We can prove it. Tell them to stand by the window together.

GORGIBUS. Doctor, I want to see you at the window embracing your brother, and then I'll be satisfied.

SGANARELLE. To any other man in the world I would return a swift and negative answer, but to you, Monsieur Gorgibus, I will yield, although not without much pain to myself. But first I want this knave to beg your pardon for all the trouble he has caused you.

[*He comes back as Narcissus.*]

Yes, Monsieur Gorgibus, I beg your pardon for having bothered you, and I promise you, brother, in front of Monsieur Gorgibus there, that I'll be so good from now on that you'll never be angry with me again. Please let bygones be bygones.

[*He embraces the cloak and hat.*]

GORGIBUS. There they are, the two of them together.

GROS-RENÉ. The man's a magician.

[*He hides;* SGANARELLE *comes out of the house, dressed as the doctor.*]

SGANARELLE. Here is your key, Monsieur. I have left my brother inside because I am ashamed of him. One does not wish to be seen in his company now that one has some reputation in this town. You may release him whenever you think fit. Good-bye, Monsieur.

[*He strides off, then as* GORGIBUS *goes into the house he wheels, dropping the cloak and hat, and climbs back through the window.*]

GORGIBUS. [*Upstairs.*] There you are, my boy, you're free. I am pleased that your brother forgave you, although I think he was rather hard on you.

SGANARELLE. Monsieur, I cannot thank you enough. A brother's blessing on you. I will remember you all my life.

[*While they are upstairs,* GROS-RENÉ *has picked up the cloak and hat, and stands waiting for them. They come out of the door.*]

GROS-RENÉ. Well, where do you think your doctor is now?

GORGIBUS. Gone, of course.

GROS-RENÉ. He's right here, under my arm. And by the way, while this fellow was getting in and out of the cloak, the hat, and the window, Valère ran off with your daughter and married her.

GORGIBUS. I'm ruined! I'll have you strung up, you dog, you knave! Yes, you deserve every name your brother called you—What am I saying?

SGANARELLE. You don't really want to string me up, do you, Monsieur? Please listen for one second. It's true that I was having a game with you while my master was with Mademoiselle Lucile. But in serving him I haven't done you any harm. He's a most suitable partner for her, by rank and by income. Believe me, if you make a row about this you'll only bring more confusion on your head. As for that porker there, let him get lost and take Villebrequin with him. Here come our loving couple.

[VALÈRE *enters contritely with* LUCILE. *They kneel to* GORGIBUS.]

VALÈRE. We apologize to you.

GORGIBUS. Well, perhaps it's lucky that I was tricked by Sganarelle; he's brought me a fine son-in-law. Let's go out to celebrate the marriage and drink a toast to the health of all the company.

[*They dance off in couples:* VALÈRE *with* LUCILE, GORGIBUS *with* GROS-RENÉ, *and* SGANARELLE *with* SABINE.]

STUDY QUESTIONS

Recalling

1. Why does Valère need advice, and what advice does Sabine give him?
2. Who is Sganarelle, and what does Valère think of him? Relate Sganarelle's conflicting opinions about his ability to impersonate a doctor.
3. Describe how Sganarelle deceives Gorgibus into believing that he is a doctor.
4. After his initial success what further trick does Sganarelle play on Gorgibus, and why?
5. Explain how Sganarelle is finally found out. What arguments does he then use to convince Gorgibus to condone the marriage?

Interpreting

6. What various character traits does Sganarelle reveal? Does he disprove Valère's opinion of him? Explain.
7. What aspects of the medical profession does Molière mock in this play, and how does he mock them?
8. Which characters represent exaggerations or stereotypes? What elements of society and human nature does Molière ridicule through these characters?
9. What makes *The Flying Doctor* funny? What truths about life might it make an audience remember?

Extending

10. What sorts of weaknesses and wrongs might lend themselves especially well to ridicule? Suggest one specific present-day problem that might be effectively satirized, and give two or three reasons for your choice.

VIEWPOINT

In his introduction to an English translation of Molière's comedies, Professor F. C. Green observes:

> The author [of comedy] must seize and fix the universal and eternal truth which lies at the roots of human conduct. This Molière achieved. He does more than just reflect life: he interprets its hidden significance.

■ What, in your opinion, is the "hidden significance" of Sganarelle's triumph over Gorgibus?

LITERARY FOCUS

Farce

Farce is a type of comedy that relies largely on improbable situations, broad characters, and slapstick action. The object of farce is to provoke the spectator to laugh through surprise and exaggeration. Farce usually includes broad physical "gags," such as pratfalls, fast action, and exaggerated facial expressions. The situations in farce often involve mistaken identity; characters frequently wear outrageous disguises that would fool no one in real life. The characters in a farce are simple and straightforward; generally they are either tricksters or fools.

Molière is a master of the art of farce. He uses the devices of farce for two purposes: to amuse his audience and, more important, to make his audience reflect on the absurdities of extreme social custom and human behavior.

Thinking About Farce

■ Identify three farcical elements in the situation, characters, and action of *The Flying Doctor*. Explain how these elements are both amusing and thought-provoking.

VOCABULARY

Antonyms

Antonyms are words that have opposite, or nearly opposite, meanings. *Gently* and *harshly* are antonyms. The words in capitals below are from *The Flying Doctor*. Choose the word that is most *nearly* the opposite of each word in capitals *as the word is used in the play*. Write the number of each item and the letter of your choice on a separate sheet.

1. CREDULOUS: (a) gullible (b) dangerous (c) skeptical (d) unimaginative
2. INIMICAL: (a) amazing (b) hostile (c) unbeatable (d) helpful
3. FORMIDABLE: (a) slight (b) formal (c) lovely (d) considerable
4. DOGMATIC: (a) traditional (b) feline (c) worldly (d) improvised
5. PERCIPIENCE: (a) keenness (b) dullness (c) wit (d) confusion
6. SUBLIME: (a) boring (b) low (c) intellectual (d) temperamental
7. MERCENARY: (a) volunteer (b) hostage (c) messenger (d) demigod
8. IMPUDENCE: (a) weakness (b) putridness (c) timidity (d) arrogance
9. INTERCEDE: (a) withdraw (b) separate (c) mix (d) forget
10. CONTRITELY: (a) sadly (b) clumsily (c) generously (d) defiantly

COMPOSITION

Writing a Comparison/Contrast

■ Compare and contrast Cervantes' use of humor in *Don Quixote* (page 765) with Molière's use of humor in *The Flying Doctor*. First point out the major similarities and differences between the comic circumstances created by each author. Then compare and contrast the satiric purposes to which both authors put humor. *For help with this assignment, refer to Lesson 2 in the Writing About Literature Handbook at the back of this book.*

Writing a Drama Review

■ Imagine that you have just attended the opening night performance of *The Flying Doctor*. Write a review of the play, either positive or negative. Your review should concentrate on evaluating the effectiveness of the farcical moments and the leading characters. End by telling your readers whether or not they should see the play, and why.

Voltaire   *1694–1778*

Voltaire came to epitomize the entire intellectual life of the eighteenth century. Poet, historian, and philosopher, he ceaselessly questioned the basis of belief; mocker of falsehood, superstition, and tyranny, he valued human reason above everything else.

Born in Paris as François Marie Arouet, Voltaire received an excellent education and gained early success with his witty and satirical verses. Charged with writing some poetry that was too political, he was exiled from Paris and later imprisoned in the Bastille, the huge French state prison. After leaving prison Voltaire moved to England for three years, associating with the leading writers of the Enlightenment—Swift and Pope (pages 258, 276). Impressed with England's parliamentary government and widespread religious tolerance, Voltaire resolved to show his countrymen that their political system was repressive and backward.

Returning to France, Voltaire soon regained his popularity. He studied history, science, mathematics, and philosophy and wrote poems, tragedies, short stories, and philosophical journals. Upon the death of his friend Madame de Chatelet, Voltaire joined the court of his longtime admirer Frederick the Great of Prussia. He eventually settled back in France in the small town of Ferney near the Swiss border, to which he could flee whenever he was hounded by French censors. The great, the wise, and the oppressed all made pilgrimages to Ferney. At eighty-four Voltaire attended the opening of his newest tragedy in Paris, where he was hailed as "the king Voltaire" with a huge ovation, and his statue was crowned on the stage with a laurel wreath. He died shortly after this triumph.

Voltaire was one of the leading *philosophes* of the period. Although the word literally means "philosophers," the eighteenth-century *philosophes* were diverse and individualistic thinkers who wanted to bring to their age the light of knowledge and rationality. All of Voltaire's work aimed at replacing a society based on blind obedience and superstition with one founded on reason. A tireless author, he wrote letters, poems, dramas, stories (which he called "philosophical poems"), and essays; he revolutionized historical writing by basing broad philosophical interpretations on careful research. Some of his best-known works are the *Philosophical Letters,* which record his impressions of England, and his novella *Candide.* Throughout his works the same ideas recur: the role of chance, the evil of extremism, the pettiness and blindness of ignorance. As a storyteller, Voltaire avoids excess and commentary, choosing only those details that express character. Mixing indignation and irony with subtle humor, "Jeannot and Colin" exemplifies Voltaire's art.

Voltaire

Jeannot and Colin[1]

Translated by R. Bruce Boswell

Many trustworthy persons have seen Jeannot and Colin when they went to school at Issoire in Auvergne,[2] a town famous all over the world for its college and its kettles. Jeannot was the son of a dealer in mules, a man of considerable reputation; Colin owed his existence to a worthy husbandman who dwelt in the outskirts of the town, and cultivated his farm with the help of four mules, and who, after paying tolls and tallage, scutage and salt-duty, poundage, poll-tax, and tithes,[3] did not find himself particularly well off at the end of the year.

Jeannot and Colin were very handsome lads for natives of Auvergne; they were much attached to each other, and had little secrets together and private understandings, such as old comrades always recall with pleasure when they afterwards meet in a wider world.

Their schooldays were drawing near their end, when a tailor one day brought Jeannot a velvet coat of three colors with a waistcoat of Lyons[4] silk to match in excellent taste; this suit of clothes was accompanied by a letter addressed to Monsieur de la Jeannotière. Colin admired the coat, and was not at all jealous; but Jeannot assumed an air of superiority which distressed Colin. From that moment Jeannot paid no more heed to his lessons, but was always looking at his reflection in the glass, and despised everybody but himself. Some time afterwards a footman arrived posthaste, bringing a second letter, addressed this time to His Lordship the Marquis de la Jeannotière; it contained an order from his father for the young nobleman, his son, to be sent to Paris. As Jeannot mounted the chaise to drive off, he stretched out his hand to Colin with a patronizing smile befitting his rank. Colin felt his own insignificance, and wept. So Jeannot departed in all his glory.

Readers who like to know all about things may be informed that Monsieur Jeannot, the father, had rapidly gained immense wealth in business. You ask how those great fortunes are made? It all depends upon luck. Monsieur Jeannotière had a comely person, and so had his wife; moreover her complexion was fresh and blooming. They had gone to Paris to prosecute a lawsuit which was ruining them, when Fortune, who lifts up and casts down human beings, at her pleasure, presented them with an introduction to the wife of an army-hospital contractor, a man of great talent, who could boast of having killed more soldiers in one year than the cannon had destroyed in ten. Jeannot took the lady's fancy, and Jeannot's wife captivated the gentleman. Jeannot soon became a partner in the business, and entered into other speculations. When one is in the current of the stream it is only necessary to let oneself drift, and so an immense fortune may sometimes be made without any trouble. The beggars who watch you from the bank, as you glide along in full sail, open their eyes in astonishment; they wonder how you have managed to get on; they envy you at all events, and write pamphlets against you which you never read. That was what happened to Jeannot senior, who was soon styled Monsieur de la Jeannotière, and, after buying a marquisate[5] at the end of six months, he took the young nobleman his son away from school, to launch him into the fashionable world of Paris.

Colin, always affectionately disposed, wrote

---

1. **Jeannot** [zhə nō′] **and Colin** [kō lan′]
2. **Auvergne** [ō vārn′]: region of south-central France.
3. **tolls . . . tithes:** various civil and church taxes.
4. **Lyons** [lē ōn′]: French city known for its fine silk.

5. **marquisate** [mär′kwi zit]: title of a marquis, a nobleman ranking below a duke and above a count.

a kind letter to his old schoolfellow in order to offer his congratulations. The little marquis sent him no answer, which grieved Colin sorely.

The first thing that his father and mother did for the young gentleman was to get him a tutor. This tutor, who was a man of distinguished manners and profound ignorance, could teach his pupil nothing. The marquis wished his son to learn Latin, but the marchioness[6] would not hear of it. They consulted the opinion of a certain author who had obtained considerable celebrity at that time from some popular works which he had written. He was invited to dinner, and the master of the house began by saying:

"Sir, as you know Latin, and are conversant with the manners of the Court—"

"I, sir! Latin! I don't know a word of it," answered the man of wit; "and it is just as well for me that I don't, for one can speak one's own language better, when the attention is not divided between it and foreign tongues. Look at all our ladies; they are far more charming in conversation than men, their letters are written with a hundred times more grace of expression. They owe that superiority over us to nothing else but their ignorance of Latin."

"There now! Was I not right?" said the lady. "I want my son to be a man of wit, and to make way in the world. You see that if he were to learn Latin, it would be his ruin. Tell me, if you please, are plays and operas performed in Latin? Are the proceedings in court conducted in Latin, when one has a lawsuit on hand? Do people talk of love in Latin?"

The marquis, confounded by these arguments, passed sentence, and it was decided that the young nobleman should not waste his time in studying Cicero, Horace, and Virgil.[7]

"But what is he to learn then? For still, I suppose, he will have to know something. Might he not be taught a little geography?"

"What good will that do him?" answered the tutor. "When my lord marquis goes to visit his country-seat, will not his postillions know the roads? There will be no fear of their going astray. One does not want a sextant[8] in order to travel, and it is quite possible to make a journey between Paris and Auvergne without knowing anything about the latitude and longitude of either."

"Very true," replied the father; "but I have heard people speak of a noble science, which is, I think, called *astronomy.*"

"Bless my soul!" rejoined the tutor. "Do we regulate our behavior in this world by the stars? Why should my lord marquis wear himself out in calculating an eclipse, when he will find it predicted correctly to a second in the almanac, which will moreover inform him of all the movable feasts,[9] the age of the moon, and that of all the princesses in Europe?"

The marchioness was quite of the tutor's opinion, the little marquis was in a state of the highest delight, and his father was very undecided.

"What then is my son to be taught?" said he.

"To make himself agreeable," answered the friend whom they had consulted; "for, if he knows the way to please, he will know everything worth knowing; it is an art which he will learn from her ladyship, his mother, without the least trouble to either of them."

The marchioness, at these words, smiled graciously upon the courtly ignoramus, and said:

"It is easy to see, sir, that you are a most accomplished gentleman; my son will owe all his education to you. I imagine, however, that it will not be a bad thing for him to know a little history."

"Nay, madame—what good would that do him?" he answered. "Assuredly the only entertaining and useful history is that of the passing

---

6. **marchioness** [mär′shə nes′]: wife of the marquis.
7. **Cicero** (106–43 B.C.), **Horace** (65–8 B.C.), **and Virgil** (70–19 B.C.): three of the greatest classical Roman writers.

8. **sextant:** navigational instrument.
9. **movable feasts:** religious holidays that fall on different dates from year to year; for example, Easter.

hour. All ancient histories, as one of our clever writers has observed, are admitted to be nothing but fables; and for us moderns it is an inextricable chaos. What does it matter to the young gentleman, your son, if Charlemagne[10] instituted the twelve Paladins of France,[11] or if his successor had an impediment in his speech?"[12]

"Nothing was ever said more wisely!" exclaimed the tutor. "The minds of children are smothered under a mass of useless knowledge; but of all sciences that which seems to me the most absurd, and the one best adapted to extinguish every spark of genius, is geometry. That ridiculous science is concerned with surfaces, lines, and points which have no existence in nature. In imagination a hundred thousand curved lines may be made to pass between a circle and a straight line which touches it, although in reality you could not insert so much as a straw. Geometry, indeed, is nothing more than a bad joke."

The marquis and his lady did not understand much of the meaning of what the tutor was saying; but they were quite of his way of thinking.

"A nobleman like his lordship," he continued, "should not dry up his brain with such unprofitable studies. If, some day, he should require one of those sublime geometricians to draw a plan of his estates, he can have them measured for his money. If he should wish to trace out the antiquity of his lineage, which goes back to the most remote ages, all he will have to do will be to send some learned Benedictine.[13] It is the same with all the other arts. A young lord born under a lucky star is neither a painter, nor a musician, nor an architect, nor a sculptor; but he may make all these arts flourish by encouraging them with his generous approval. Doubtless it is much better to patronize than to practice them. It will be quite enough if my lord the young marquis has taste; it is the part of artists to work for him, and thus there is a great deal of truth in the remark that people of quality (that is, if they are very rich) know everything without learning anything, because, in point of fact and in the long run, they are masters of all the knowledge which they can command and pay for."

The agreeable ignoramus then took part in the conversation, and said:

"You have well remarked, madame, that the great end of man's existence is to succeed in society. Is it, forsooth, any aid to the attainment of this success to have devoted oneself to the sciences? Does anyone ever think in select company of talking about geometry? Is a well-bred gentleman ever asked what star rises today with the sun? Does anyone at the supper table ever want to know if Clodion the Long-Haired[14] crossed the Rhine?"

"No, indeed!" exclaimed the Marchioness de la Jeannotière, whose charms had been her passport into the world of fashion; "and my son must not stifle his genius by studying all that trash. But, after all, what is he to be taught? For it is a good thing that a young lord should be able to shine when occasion offers, as my noble husband has said. I remember once hearing an abbé remark that the most entertaining science was something the name of which I have forgotten—it begins with a *b*."

"With a *b*, madame? It was not botany, was it?"

"No, it certainly was not botany that he mentioned; it began, as I tell you, with a *b*, and ended in *onry*."

"Ah, madame, I understand! It was blazonry or heraldry.[15] That is indeed a most profound science; but it has ceased to be fashionable

---

10. **Charlemagne** [shär′lə mān] (742–814): Charles the Great, king of France from 768 and emperor of the Holy Roman Empire from 800 to 814.

11. **twelve . . . France:** the legendary twelve peers of the court of Charlemagne.

12. **successor . . . speech:** referring to Louis II (846–879), known as the Stammerer, great-grandson of Charlemagne and king of France from 877 to 879.

13. **Benedictine:** monk of the order of St. Benedict.

14. **Clodion the Long-Haired:** legendary fifth-century chief of the Franks, a Germanic tribe living on the banks of the Rhine River.

15. **blazonry or heraldry:** art of describing coats of arms.

since the custom has died out of having one's coat of arms painted on the carriage doors; it was the most useful thing imaginable in a well-ordered state. Besides, that line of study would be endless, for at the present day there is not a barber who is without his armorial bearings, and you know that whatever becomes common loses its attraction."

Finally, after all the pros and cons of the different sciences had been examined and discussed, it was decided that the young marquis should learn dancing.

Dame Nature, who disposes everything at her own will and pleasure, had given him a talent which soon developed itself with prodigious success; it was that of singing street-ballads in a charming style. His youthful grace accompanying this superlative gift, caused him to be regarded as a young man of the highest promise. He was a favorite with the ladies, and, having his head crammed with songs, he had no lack of mistresses to whom to address his verses. He stole the line, "Bacchus[16] with the Loves at play," from one ballad; and made it rhyme with "night and day" taken out of another, while a third furnished him with "charms" and "alarms." But inasmuch as there were always some feet more or less than were wanted in his verses, he had them corrected at the rate of twenty sovereigns[17] a song. And The Literary Year placed him in the same rank with such sonneteers as La Fare, Chaulieu, Hamilton, Sarrasin, and Voiture.[18]

Her ladyship the marchioness then believed that she was indeed the mother of a genius, and gave a supper to all the wits of Paris. The young man's head was soon turned upside down, he acquired the art of talking without knowing the meaning of what he said, and perfected himself in the habit of being fit for nothing. When his father saw him so eloquent, he keenly regretted that he had not had him taught Latin, or he would have purchased some high appointment for him in the Law. His mother, who was of more heroic sentiments, took upon herself to solicit a regiment for her son. He squandered his money freely, while his parents drained their purses and credit to a lower and lower ebb by living in the grandest style.

A young widow of good position in their neighborhood, who had only a moderate income, was well enough disposed to make some effort to prevent the great wealth of the Marquis and Marchioness de la Jeannotière from going altogether, by marrying the young marquis and so appropriating what remained. She enticed him to her house, allowed him to see that she was not quite indifferent to him, led him on by degrees, enchanted him, and made him her devoted slave without the least difficulty. She would give him at one time commendation and at another time counsel; she became his father's and mother's best friend. An old neighbor proposed marriage; the parents, dazzled with the splendor of the alliance, joyfully fell in with the scheme, and gave their only son to their most intimate lady friend. The young marquis was thus about to wed a woman whom he adored, and by whom he was beloved in return. The friends of the family congratulated him, the marriage settlement was on the point of being signed, the bridal dress and the epithalamium[19] were both well under way.

One morning our young gentleman was on his knees before the charmer whom fond affection and esteem were so soon to make his own; they were tasting in animated and tender converse the first fruits of future happiness; they were settling how they should lead a life of perfect bliss, when one of his lady mother's footmen presented himself, scared out of his wits.

"Here's fine news which may surprise you!"

---

16. **Bacchus** [bak′əs]: in Roman mythology the god of revelry.

17. **sovereigns:** French gold coins.

18. **La Fare** [lä fär′], **Chaulieu** [shō lyœ′], **Hamilton, Sarrasin** [sär ä zan′], **and Voiture** [vwä tūr′]: minor French poets of the seventeenth century.

19. **epithalamium** [ep′ə thə lā′mē əm]: song composed in honor of a bride and groom.

said he; "the bailiffs are in the house of my lord and lady, removing the furniture. All has been seized by the creditors. They talk of personal arrest, and I am going to do what I can to get my wages paid."

"Let us see what has happened," said the marquis, "and discover the meaning of all this."

"Yes," said the widow, "go and punish those rascals—go, quick!"

He hurried homewards, he arrived at the house, his father was already in prison, all the servants had fled, each in a different direction, carrying off whatever they could lay their hands upon. His mother was alone, helpless, forlorn, and bathed in tears; she had nothing left her but the remembrance of her former prosperity, her beauty, her faults, and her foolish extravagance.

After the son had condoled with his mother for a long time, he said at last:

"Let us not despair; this young widow loves me to distraction; she is even more generous than she is wealthy, I can assure you; I will fly to her for succor, and bring her to you."

So he returns to his mistress, and finds her conversing in private with a fascinating young officer.

"What! Is that you, my Lord de la Jeannotière? What business have you with me? How can you leave your mother by herself in this way? Go, and stay with the poor woman, and tell her that she shall always have my good wishes. I am in want of a waiting-woman now, and will gladly give her the preference."

"My lad," said the officer, "you seem pretty tall and straight; if you would like to enter my company, I will make it worth your while to enlist."

The marquis, stupefied with astonishment, and secretly enraged, went off in search of his former tutor, confided to him all his troubles, and asked his advice. He proposed that he should become, like himself, a tutor of the young.

"Alas! I know nothing; you have taught me nothing whatever, and you are the primary cause of all my unhappiness." And as he spoke he began to sob.

Painting by Antoine Watteau (1684–1721).

"Write novels," said a wit who was present; "it is an excellent resource to fall back upon at Paris."

The young man, in more desperate straits than ever, hastened to the house of his mother's father confessor; he was a Theatine monk[20] of the very highest reputation, who directed the souls of none but ladies of the first rank in society. As soon as he saw him, the reverend gentleman rushed to meet him.

"Good gracious! My lord marquis, where is your carriage? How is your honored mother, the marchioness?"

The unfortunate young fellow related the disaster that had befallen his family. As he explained the matter further the Theatine assumed a graver air, one of less concern and more self-importance.

"My son, herein you may see the hand of Providence; riches serve only to corrupt the heart. The Almighty has shown special favor then to your mother in reducing her to beggary. Yes, sir, so much the better!—she is now sure of her salvation."

"But, father, in the meantime are there no means of obtaining some succor in this world?"

"Farewell, my son! There is a lady of the Court waiting for me."

The marquis felt ready to faint. He was treated after much the same manner by all his friends, and learned to know the world better in half a day than in all the rest of his life.

As he was plunged in overwhelming despair, he saw an old-fashioned traveling chaise, more like a covered tumbril[21] than anything else, and furnished with leather curtains, followed by four enormous wagons all heavily laden. In the chaise was a young man in rustic attire; his round and rubicund face had an air of kindness and good temper. His little wife, whose sunburnt countenance had a pleasing if not a refined expression, was jolted about as she sat beside him. The vehicle did not go quite so fast as a dandy's chariot, the traveler had plenty of time to look at the marquis, as he stood motionless, absorbed in his grief.

"Oh! good Heavens!" he exclaimed; "I believe that is Jeannot there!"

Hearing that name the marquis raised his eyes—the chaise stopped.

" 'Tis Jeannot himself! Yes, it is Jeannot!"

The plump little man with one leap sprang to the ground, and ran to embrace his old companion. Jeannot recognized Colin; signs of sorrow and shame covered his countenance.

"You have forsaken your old friend," said Colin; "but be you as grand a lord as you like, I shall never cease to love you."

Jeannot, confounded and cut to the heart, told him with sobs something of his history.

"Come into the inn where I am lodging, and tell me the rest," said Colin; "kiss my little wife, and let us go and dine together."

They went, all three of them, on foot, and the baggage followed.

"What in the world is all this paraphernalia? Does it belong to you?"

"Yes, it is all mine and my wife's; we are just come from the country. I am at the head of a large tin, iron, and copper factory, and have married the daughter of a rich tradesman and general provider of all useful commodities for great folks and small. We work hard, and God gives us his blessing. We are satisfied with our condition in life, and are quite happy. We will help our friend Jeannot. Give up being a marquis; all the grandeur in the world is not equal in value to a good friend. You will return with me into the country; I will teach you my trade, it is not a difficult one to learn; I will give you a share in the business, and we will live together with light hearts in that corner of the earth where we were born."

Jeannot, overcome by this kindness, felt himself divided between sorrow and joy, tenderness and shame; and he said within himself:

"All my fashionable friends have proved false to me, and Colin, whom I despised, is the only one who comes to my succor. What a lesson!"

---

20. **Theatine monk:** member of a religious order established in Italy in the sixteenth century.
21. **tumbril:** farm wagon.

Colin's generosity developed in Jeannot's heart the germ of that good disposition which the world had not yet choked. He felt that he could not desert his father and mother.

"We will take care of your mother," said Colin; "and as for the good man your father, who is in prison—I know something of business matters—his creditors, when they see that he has nothing more, will agree to a moderate composition. I will see to all that myself."

Colin was as good as his word, and succeeded in effecting the father's release from prison. Jeannot returned to his old home with his parents, who resumed their former occupation. He married Colin's sister, who, being like her brother in disposition, rendered her husband very happy. And so Jeannot the father, and Jeannotte the mother, and Jeannot the son came to see that vanity is no true source of happiness.

STUDY QUESTIONS

Recalling

1. How does Jeannot's father gain his wealth?
2. Relate the tutor's opinion of four of the subjects considered for Jeannot's education.
3. What does Jeannot finally study? How does he become successful?
4. What happens to Jeannot's family just before his wedding? How do the widow, tutor, priest, and officer respond to this turn of events? How does Colin respond?
5. According to the last sentence in the story, what have Jeannot and his family come to see?

Interpreting

6. What values does Voltaire ridicule in the tutor's dismissal of serious education?
7. What does the story imply about the relationship between wealth and merit? What does it imply about the relationship between wealth and happiness?
8. What do you think Voltaire means by the term *vanity* in the last sentence? Explain how the Jeannot family's rise and fall demonstrates the dangers of vanity.
9. Contrast Colin's response to Jeannot's misfortune to the responses of the widow, officer, tutor, and priest. What points does Voltaire make about "high society" and about friendship?

Extending

10. If you were a modern-day Voltaire, what specific aspects of today's society would you satirize?

COMPOSITION

Writing About Literature and Its Period

■ Write an essay showing how Voltaire's "Jeannot and Colin" exemplifies the Age of Enlightenment (see page 776). First identify some of the major characteristics of the Enlightenment. Then, using specific examples from the story, show how Voltaire's satirical portrayal of the changing fortunes of the Jeannot family demonstrates these characteristics. *For help with this assignment, refer to Lesson 10 in the Writing About Literature Handbook at the back of this book.*

Writing a Satirical Sketch

■ Write a sketch or an outline for a story that satirizes some aspect of society today. Describe in detail the settings you would use and the characters who would embody your criticisms. Be as thorough and fair-minded in your satire as you can be.

COMPARING ENGLISH AND WESTERN WRITERS

■ Compare Pope's satire in *The Rape of the Lock* (page 277) with Molière's in *The Flying Doctor* and Voltaire's in "Jeannot and Colin." Which author seems to you most subtle? Which would you choose to write a satire against something you wished to criticize? Why? Remember that satire is constructive in that it is meant not simply to ridicule but also to instruct and to correct.

Key to Illustrations appears on page 923.

EUROPE
THE NINETEENTH CENTURY

1800—1900

The eighteenth century and much of what it stood for came to an explosive end with the French Revolution in 1789. The Revolution changed much more than a nation's government: It changed all of Europe's way of thinking. It thrust the entire continent into a turbulent century of wars, rejection of tradition, industrial revolution, and assertion of individual rights.

In social and in literary terms, we can grasp the changeable nineteenth century by dividing it into three overlapping movements: Romanticism, Realism, and the beginnings of Modernism. The French Revolution, the rise and fall of Napoleon Bonaparte, and the drastically altered relationship of the social classes accompanied the flowering of Romanticism, led by Goethe in Germany and Hugo in France. Toward the middle of the century, the Industrial Revolution—with its technological marvels, redistribution of wealth, growth of cities, and vast social problems—contributed to the Realistic movement, capped by the achievements of Tolstoy in Russia and Flaubert in France. Then, as the century entered its last decades with a spirit of experimentation, the seeds of Modernism began to sprout in the French Symbolist poets Baudelaire, Rimbaud, and Verlaine.

The Consecration of the Emperor Napoleon and the Coronation of the Empress Josephine, Jacques Louis David, 1806–1807.

The nineteenth century, however, was born out of the eighteenth. To see how and why, we must first go back to Jean-Jacques Rousseau.

Rousseau

Although he lived during the eighteenth century, Rousseau (1712–1778) exerted a profound influence on the politics, thought, and art of the nineteenth century. In fact, Rousseau's entire life and all his writings opposed the century in which he lived, with its emphasis on classical balance, elegance, restraint, and, above all, reason. In his *Confessions*, his novels, and his essays, Rousseau showed himself to be a great individualist and social critic. Rousseau created two revolutionary ideas: respect for humanity in its natural state and the theory of "the social contract."

For Rousseau the fulfillment of human life was endangered not only by government but by civilization itself. Existence in a natural, untamed state, he argued, was healthier and truer to what it means to be fully human. A person would only develop as a genuine individual, Rousseau believed, without the distortions imposed by so-called civilized society. This concept of individualism and freedom from social restraints would be a major theme in Romantic literature.

Then, according to Rousseau, government must have its beginning and its validity in the ability of individuals to organize *themselves*. People ought to set up a government as a contract between the governing and the governed. We can imagine how unpleasant the idea of the social contract was to the Bourbon kings of France, with their notions of divine-right monarchy. The social contract is now accepted as the basic theory of democratic government, and there is little doubt that Rousseau's ideas helped inspire the French Revolution.

The French Revolution and Napoleon Bonaparte

In Paris, on July 14, 1789, a furious crowd stormed the Bastille, a fortress prison that symbolized royal oppression. This uprising marked the beginning of the French Revolution, a violent decade during which thousands lost their lives at the guillotine. The Revolution was the violent result of a combination of old inequalities and injustices, new ideas about freedom and

the limits of government, and internal economic problems.

At first the revolutionaries formed a National Assembly to rectify injustices and draw up a constitution. However, while moderates worked toward a constitutional monarchy, radical groups like the Jacobins demanded a republic. Eventually, in 1792, the radicals seized power and beheaded King Louis XVI. A strongly centralized republic was created under Robespierre and Danton, and with it a powerful Committee of Public Safety to watch over internal security. Thus began the Reign of Terror, during which many people were guillotined simply because they were suspected of disloyalty. After Robespierre himself was beheaded in 1794, reaction set in. Political clubs were disbanded, riots were suppressed, and a conservative regime framed a new constitution providing for a republican government headed by a Directory.

Amid this turmoil, an obscure corporal from Corsica named Napoleon Bonaparte had risen in the ranks of the French Army and in public opinion. Armies under his command conquered Italy and Austria. Returning to Paris, he boldly took control in a brief, bloodless *coup d'état*. He abolished the Directory and made himself first consul. "The little corporal" became a dictator.

Napoleon strengthened the central administration, set up the Bank of France, reorganized

Portrait of Ludwig van Beethoven.

the education system, and founded the Imperial University. His Napoleonic Code remains the basis of French law. Moreover, by 1812 his empire in Europe reached from Norway to southern Italy, from Austria to Spain.

Yet Emperor Napoleon sought to expand farther. In 1812 he raised an army of 600,000 and marched toward Russia. Russia at this time was ruled by Czar (Emperor) Alexander I, once Napoleon's ally and a shrewd and powerful leader. When Napoleon arrived at the gates of Moscow, he found the city silent and deserted. Those who remained set fire to the city, and Napoleon soon stood among ruins. He had no choice but to return to France through the bitter Russian winter. As the frost-bitten, half-starved troops trudged homeward, swarms of Russian Cossacks cut the French flanks to ribbons. Of the original 600,000 soldiers in Napoleon's Grand Army, over 500,000 died, were captured, or deserted. The dramatic events of this campaign are celebrated in Victor Hugo's poem "Russia 1812" (page 814) and in the titanic novel *War and Peace* by Leo Tolstoy.

Several more years of political maneuvering and military defeats forced Napoleon's abdication. He retired to the island of Elba, near Italy, but less than a year later, he raised one more army, only to meet final defeat near the Belgian town of Waterloo at the hands of the British

Duke of Wellington. Exiled to the barren island of St. Helena, Napoleon died in 1821.

Throughout the remainder of the nineteenth century, Europe saw the continued opposition of those who favored monarchies and those who wanted greater national self-determination, giving rise, for example, to a series of revolutions in 1848. The Franco-Prussian War of 1870–1871 marked the decline of France and the rise of Germany; it led to the formation of the alliances that participated in World War I.

Napoleon shaped the life of his time more than any other person. He moved from unknown soldier to hero to tyrant to exile. Perhaps the image of Napoleon can best be summed up, however, by an event not from military history but from musical history. Ludwig van Beethoven, the great German Romantic composer and ardent individualist, at first dedicated his Third Symphony, the "Eroica" (Heroic), to Napoleon. Yet

when Beethoven found out that Napoleon had declared himself emperor, he violently scratched out Napoleon's name from the manuscript. Napoleon may have changed the map of Europe, but Romanticism changed the spirit of the age.

The Industrial Revolution and Everyday Life

From 1830 to 1870, the effects of the Industrial Revolution began to be felt in Europe. People were generally healthier, more vigorous, and—because of the manufactured clothing that had become available—better dressed. Pottery, made more efficiently, aided sanitation. Medical advances reduced disease.

However, with the introduction of the factory system and the leap in urban population came new poverty and hardship. Children were sent to work in thousands of factories; housing grew cramped; and gloomy factory sites darkened city skylines. In political and social terms, the "working class" became a well-defined division of society.

Yet the Industrial Revolution also led to new methods of transportation, communication, and production. Inventions and improvements drew Europe closer together. By 1830 the steamboat was a familiar site on European rivers. Railway lines were laid in France in 1830, in Germany in 1832, and in Russia in 1860. By 1900 most ships on the seas were steamships.

Detail, *La Gare St. Lazare,* Claude Monet, 1877.

As early as 1816, underground cables carried telegraphic messages short distances; cables reaching long distances under water were perfected in the 1850s, when England and France, and then Ireland and Newfoundland, were linked. Experiments with the telephone began in the United States around 1837, and European inventors continued to try to develop a commercially successful telephone in the following decades. It was not until 1874, however, that American Alexander Graham Bell found the answer. By 1877 in Germany, eight hundred villages were linked by telephone.

After 1870 steel and steam became the kings of industrial and economic growth. Steel girders permitted the construction of high buildings, and steam eased transportation and increased factory power. In 1880 Thomas Edison put a practical incandescent lamp on the market, and by the 1890s electric power had become feasible. As the nineteenth century drew to a close, Europe, like metropolitan England, began to become what it is today: a land that in addition to its natural beauty is characterized by cosmopolitan and multifaceted cities—among them Paris, Rome, and Moscow.

Nineteenth-Century European Literature

Romanticism. Of all literary movements, the Romantic move-

ment is the most difficult to define. In fact, one scholarly book identifies over eleven thousand different definitions of *Romanticism.* Romantic artists did not flourish at exactly the same time in different countries, but they did share some general characteristics.

Romantics asserted the importance of emotion over reason. They stressed the individual personality over social and artistic conformity. Usually reacting against the balance and restraint of the classical-oriented eighteenth century, they focused on personal experience—rather than on sets of rules and traditions—as the best guide to truth and happiness.

Romantics went to nature as a source of inspiration: They worshiped what was natural and believed that nature was to be imitated, not altered or ordered. They expressed a passionate nationalism, or love of country. That nationalism, however, did not stop them from yearning for faraway picturesque places.

One of the most significant elements in the Romantic spirit was, and still is, idealism. Romantic artists of all times possess a deep-rooted belief in a noble and heroic way of life that is possible for everyone who lives to the fullest. The Romantic spirit often sees the real world as a reflection of an ideal world and life itself as a constant striving for the infinite.

Germany was the center of European Romanticism. There, a golden age of literature had begun at the end of the eighteenth century under the towering leadership of the philosopher, scientist, poet, and dramatist Johann Wolfgang von Goethe, author of *Faust.* Emphasizing the power of imagination over reason, Germany created a new vision in aesthetics and philosophy, centering on the self, the individual person. After Goethe, the greatest figures with this new Romantic world view were the philosopher Friedrich Schlegel and the lyric poet Heinrich Heine.

Foremost among the French Romantics was Victor Hugo, best known for his massive novels *Les Misérables* and *The Hunchback of Notre Dame.* Hugo's poetry and verse dramas were also extremely influential, with their emphasis on lyricism, love of nature, and heroic vision. A different type of heroism, but no less Romantic, was offered by the French novelist and although no less Romantic, was offered by the French novelist

Faust in His Study, Rembrandt (1606–1669).

and playwright Alexander Dumas, author of *The Three Musketeers* and *The Count of Monte Cristo.*

Romanticism in Italy is best represented by Alessandro Manzoni's novel *The Betrothed,* considered by some the best Italian novel ever written. Russia, too, made its contribution. The summit of Russian Romanticism—in fact the summit of Russian poetry—was attained by Alexander Pushkin, whose historical drama *Boris Godunov* and poetic novel *Eugene Onegin* are landmark works.

In England Romanticism produced many of the greatest works in our language. (See pages 318–401.) From *The Prelude* of William Wordsworth to the "Ode to Autumn" of John Keats, from the exotic "Kubla Khan" of Samuel Taylor Coleridge to the satiric *Don Juan* of Lord Byron—English Romantic poetry remains one of Romanticism's finest achievements.

Realism. From the idealism and emotional display of Romanticism, the swing to Realism seems to have been a natural reaction. Realist writers wanted to tell the unadorned truth of life as they saw it: harsh, hard, sometimes joyful, but usually filled with work and pain and disillusion. They stripped away the lovely masks of the Romantics and sought to get to the heart of the human condition.

The greatest Realist achievements are the century's novels. This is not at all surprising when we think of the capacity of the novel for wealth of everyday details, vast panoramas of people and places, and complex life stories. In England the novels of Charles Dickens (see page 428), William Makepeace Thackeray, and George Eliot remain unmatched both for their characterizations and their compassion. The French novels of Honoré de Balzac, of Stendhal, and especially of Gustave Flaubert pointed the way toward the modern novel. In Russia, Tolstoy's *Anna Karenina* and *War and Peace* and Dostoevsky's *Crime and Punishment* and *Brothers Karamazov* still amaze readers with their sweep, their detail, and their fascinating characters. With these giants stand three writers who specialized in shorter forms: the great Russian dramatist and short story writer Anton Chekhov; the master of the novella Ivan Turgenev; and the French storyteller Guy de Maupassant.

Early Modernism. Toward the end of the century, many writers began boldly to experiment, especially in poetry. Their "new" works, however, were in many ways actually a continuation of Romanticism. This was the case with the most significant movement of the time— French Symbolism.

For the Symbolists poetry should be personal, emotional, individual—just as it had been for the Romantics. It must, however, avoid sentimentality and direct statement; it should strive for greater subtlety. Above all it should celebrate the imagination and the way the imagination interacts with the real world. Charles Baudelaire, Arthur Rimbaud, Paul Verlaine, and Stéphane Mallarmé all produced Symbolist poems that had a profound influence on modern writing.

THE ROMANTIC AGE

Johann Wolfgang von Goethe
1749–1832

When he met Goethe in 1808, Napoleon exclaimed, "Voilà un homme!" (Behold a man!) Poet, playwright, scientist, philosopher, and statesman, Johann Wolfgang von Goethe [yō′hän vôlf′gäng′ von gur′tə] was indeed remarkable. He was born in Frankfurt in what is now West Germany, the son of a wealthy lawyer who supervised his son's education in art, literature, and language. Goethe wrote his first important poetry while studying law. As a student he met Johann Gottfried von Herder, a leader of the *Sturm und Drang* (Storm and Stress) literary movement, a forerunner to German Romanticism that emphasized nature and the emotions. Under Herder's influence, Goethe's style became less formal, more personal, and lyrical.

Goethe practiced law in Frankfurt until his novel *The Sorrows of Young Werther* (1774) became a best seller and made him a hero to young people throughout Europe. The book is a melancholy work about hopeless love and nature's destructive beauty. At the invitation of the duke of Weimar, Goethe moved to that city and became a counselor to the duke. In his new role Goethe studied science and technology, including anatomy, optics, geology, and botany. In 1786 he traveled to Italy for a two-year stay that inspired an admiration for the classical tradition of the Renaissance. When he returned to Weimar, he withdrew from political and social activity to concentrate on writing. His topics included folklore, natural science, philosophy, Oriental literature, and international events. He also composed short stories, plays, and poetry. Goethe once called all his writing "the fragments of a great confession," and he devoted his later years to autobiographical work such as the four volumes of *Poetry and Truth* (1811–1833). Goethe died calling for "more light, more light!"

Goethe's work is massive in quantity and diversity, but his masterwork is *Faust,* a reader's play in verse. In twelve thousand lines *Faust* combines dramatic, epic, and lyrical elements and demonstrates Goethe's interest in theology, mythology, philosophy, economics, science, aesthetics, and music. Goethe worked on *Faust* from 1773, when he was twenty-four, until 1831, a year before his death. According to a legend that Goethe knew from his childhood, Faust is a scholar who trades his immortal soul to Mephistopheles [mef′ə stof′ə lēz′], the devil, in return for complete knowledge and experience. Goethe's version transforms the traditional ending, in which Faust is carried away by demons, into one of salvation. Goethe's Faust is redeemed by his dedication to perfection, a redemption available to all who devote themselves to selfless striving for fulfillment. Faust states a theme of the work and a summary of Goethe's life: "It is restless action makes the man."

Johann Wolfgang von Goethe

from **Faust**

Translated by Louis MacNeice

The Prologue in Heaven

The Lord and the heavenly hosts[1] enter, with Mephistopheles following. After three archangels step forward to praise the Lord and his creations, Mephistopheles speaks.

MEPHISTOPHELES. Since you, O Lord, once more approach and ask
    If business down with us be light or heavy—
    And in the past you've usually welcomed me—
    That's why you see me also at your levee.[2]
5   Excuse me, I can't manage lofty words—
    Not though your whole court jeer and find me low;
    My pathos certainly would make you laugh
    Had you not left off laughing long ago.
    Your suns and worlds mean nothing much to me;
10   How men torment themselves, that's all I see.
    The little god of the world,[3] one can't reshape, reshade him;
    He is as strange today as that first day you made him.
    His life would be not so bad, not quite,
    Had you not granted him a gleam of Heaven's light;
15   He calls it Reason, uses it not the least
    Except to be more beastly than any beast.
    He seems to me—if your Honor does not mind—
    Like a grasshopper—the long-legged kind—
    That's always in flight and leaps as it flies along
20   And then in the grass strikes up its same old song.
    I could only wish he confined himself to the grass!
    He thrusts his nose into every filth, alas.

LORD. Mephistopheles, have you no other news?
    Do you always come here to accuse?
25   Is nothing ever right in your eyes on earth?

MEPHISTOPHELES. No, Lord! I find things there as downright bad as ever.
    I am sorry for men's days of dread and dearth;
    Poor things, *my* wish to plague 'em isn't fervent.

LORD. Do you know Faust?

MEPHISTOPHELES.   The Doctor?

---

1. **HOSTS:** multitudes; here, all the angels and saints.
2. **levee:** monarch's first reception of subjects in the morning.
3. **little . . . world:** man, who was created in God's image and who was given dominion over earthly creatures.

LORD.   Aye, my servant.

30 **MEPHISTOPHELES.** Indeed! He serves you oddly enough, I think.
      The fool has no earthly habits in meat and drink.
      The ferment in him drives him wide and far,
      That he is mad he too has almost guessed;
      He demands of heaven each fairest star
35   And of earth each highest joy and best,
      And all that is new and all that is far
      Can bring no calm to the deep-sea swell of his breast.

      LORD. Now he may serve me only gropingly,
        Soon I shall lead him into the light.
40   The gardener knows when the sapling first turns green
        That flowers and fruit will make the future bright.

      MEPHISTOPHELES. What do you wager? You will lose him yet,
        Provided *you* give *me* permission
        To steer him gently the course I set.

45 **LORD.** So long as he walks the earth alive,
      So long you may try what enters your head;
      Men make mistakes as long as they strive.

      MEPHISTOPHELES. I thank you for that; as regards the dead,
        The dead have never taken my fancy.
50   I favor cheeks that are full and rosy-red;
        No corpse is welcome to my house;
        I work as the cat does with the mouse.

      LORD. Very well; you have my full permission.
        Divert this soul from its primal source[4]
55   And carry it, if you can seize it,
        Down with you upon your course—
        And stand ashamed when you must needs admit;
        A good man with his groping intuitions
        Still knows the path that is true and fit.

60 **MEPHISTOPHELES.** All right—but it won't last for long.
      I'm not afraid my bet will turn out wrong.
      And, if my aim prove true and strong,
      Allow me to triumph wholeheartedly.
      Dust shall be eaten—and greedily—
65   Like my cousin the Snake[5] renowned in tale and song.

      LORD. That too you are free to give a trial;
        I have never hated the likes of you.
        Of all the spirits of denial
        The joker is the last that I eschew.

      ———————

      4. **primal source:** origin; here, God and heaven.
      5. **the Snake:** serpent that tempted Eve in the Garden of Eden.

70   Man finds relaxation too attractive—
       Too fond too soon of unconditional rest;
       Which is why I am pleased to give him a companion
       Who lures and thrusts and must, as devil, be active.
       But ye, true sons of Heaven, it is your duty
75   To take your joy in the living wealth of beauty.
       The changing Essence which ever works and lives
       Wall you around with love, serene, secure!
       And that which floats in flickering appearance
       Fix ye it firm in thoughts that must endure. . . .

       [*Heaven closes.*]

80 **MEPHISTOPHELES** [*alone*]. I like to see the Old One now and then
       And try to keep relations on the level.
       It's really decent of so great a person
       To talk so humanely even to the Devil.

       After "The Prologue in Heaven," the actual poem begins with a scene called "Night." Faust contemplates the limits of human understanding and concludes that complete knowledge is possible only after death. He considers suicide but is distracted by the life-affirming bells of Easter morning. Rushing outside, Faust is temporarily encouraged by the activity of the common people, but later, while the sun sets, he again gives in to despair. Back in his study, Faust is confronted by Mephistopheles. He resists the demon's temptations at first. Then as his despair deepens, he curses all things that humanity strives for—family, love, fame, wealth, hope, and faith. Mephistopheles, delighted that Faust is now more open to his temptation, returns.

The Pact with the Devil

MEPHISTOPHELES. Stop playing with your grief which battens[6]
       Like a vulture on your life, your mind!
       The worst of company would make you feel
       That you are a man among mankind,
5   Not that it's really my proposition
       To shove you among the common men;
       Though I'm not one of the Upper Ten,[7]
       If you would like a coalition
       With me for your career through life,
10   I am quite ready to fit in,
       I'm yours before you can say knife.
       I am your comrade;
       If you so crave,
       I am your servant, I am your slave.

---

6. **battens:** grows fat.
7. **Upper Ten:** ten most powerful spirits.

15   FAUST. And what have I to undertake in return?

    MEPHISTOPHELES. Oh it's early days to discuss what that is.

    FAUST. No, no, the devil is an egoist
      And ready to do nothing gratis[8]
      Which is to benefit a stranger.
20   Tell me your terms and don't prevaricate!
      A servant like you in the house is a danger.

    MEPHISTOPHELES. I will bind myself to your service in this world,
      To be at your beck and never rest nor slack;
      When we meet again on the other side,
25   In the same coin you shall pay me back.

    FAUST. The other side gives me little trouble;
      First batter this present world to rubble,
      Then the other may rise—if that's the plan.
      This earth is where my springs of joy have started,
30   And this sun shines on me when brokenhearted;
      If I can first from them be parted,
      Then let happen what will and can! . . .

    MEPHISTOPHELES. With such an outlook you can risk it.
      Sign on the line! In these next days you will get
35   Ravishing samples of my arts;
      I am giving you what never man saw yet.

    FAUST. Poor devil, can *you* give anything ever?
      Was a human spirit in its high endeavor
      Even once understood by one of your breed?
40   Have you got food which fails to feed?
      Or red gold which, never at rest,
      Like mercury runs away through the hand?
      A game at which one never wins?
      A girl who, even when on my breast,
45   Pledges herself to my neighbor with her eyes?
      The divine and lovely delight of honor
      Which falls like a falling star and dies?
      Show me the fruits which, before they are plucked, decay
      And the trees which day after day renew their green!

50 MEPHISTOPHELES. Such a commission doesn't alarm me,
      I have such treasures to purvey.
      But, my good friend, the time draws on when we
      Should be glad to feast at our ease on something good.

    FAUST. If ever I stretch myself on a bed of ease,
55   Then I am finished! Is that understood?
      If ever your flatteries can coax me

---

8. **gratis:** Latin for "free of charge."

To be pleased with myself, if ever you cast
A spell of pleasure that can hoax me—
Then let *that* day be my last!
60 That's my wager!

MEPHISTOPHELES. Done!

FAUST. Let's shake!
If ever I say to the passing moment
"Linger a while! Thou art so fair!"
Then you may cast me into fetters,
I will gladly perish then and there! . . .

65 **MEPHISTOPHELES.** Think what you're saying, we shall not forget it.

FAUST. And you are fully within your rights;
I have made no mad or outrageous claim.
If I stay as I am, I am a slave—
Whether yours or another's, it's all the same.

70 **MEPHISTOPHELES.** I shall this very day at the College Banquet[9]
Enter your service with no more ado,
But just one point—As a life-and-death insurance
I must trouble you for a line or two.

FAUST. So you, you pedant, you too like things in writing?
75 Have you never known a man? Or a man's word? Never?
Is it not enough that my word of mouth
Puts all my days in bond for ever?* . . .
What do you, evil spirit, require?
Bronze, marble, parchment, paper?
80 Quill or chisel or pencil of slate?
You may choose whichever you desire.

MEPHISTOPHELES. How can you so exaggerate
With such a hectic rhetoric?
Any little snippet is quite good—
85 And you sign it with one little drop of blood.

FAUST. If that is enough and is some use,
One may as well pander to your fad.

MEPHISTOPHELES. Blood is a very special juice.

FAUST. Only do not fear that I shall break this contract.
90 What I promise is nothing more
Than what all my powers are striving for. . . .
Let us cast ourselves into the torrent of time,
Into the whirl of eventfulness,
Where disappointment and success,
95 Pleasure and pain may chop and change

---

9. **College Banquet:** dinner to celebrate the awarding of a doctoral degree.

As chop and change they will and can;
It is restless action makes the man. . . .

MEPHISTOPHELES. You are in the end . . . what you are.
You can put on full-bottomed wigs with a million locks,
100 You can put on stilts[10] instead of your socks,
You remain forever what you are.

FAUST. I feel my endeavors have not been worth a pin
When I raked together the treasures of the human mind,
If at the end I but sit down to find
105 No new force welling up within.
I have not a hair's breadth more of height,
I am no nearer the Infinite.

MEPHISTOPHELES. My very good sir, you look at things
Just in the way that people do;
110 We must be cleverer than that
Or the joys of life will escape from you. . . .
So good-by to thinking! On your toes!
The world's before us. Quick! Here goes!
I tell you, a chap who's intellectual
115 Is like a beast on a blasted heath
Driven in circles by a demon
While a fine green meadow lies round beneath.

FAUST. How do we start?

MEPHISTOPHELES.   We just say go—and skip.
120 But please get ready for this pleasure trip. [*Exit* FAUST.]
Only look down on knowledge and reason,
The highest gifts that men can prize,
Only allow the spirit of lies
To confirm you in magic and illusion,
125 And then I have you body and soul.
Fate has given this man a spirit
Which is always pressing onward, beyond control,
And whose mad striving overleaps
All joys of the earth between pole and pole.
130 Him shall I drag through the wilds of life
And through the flats of meaninglessness,
I shall make him flounder and gape and stick
And to tease his insatiableness
Hang meat and drink in the air before his watering lips;
135 In vain he will pray to slake his inner thirst,
And even had he not sold himself to the devil
He would be equally accursed.

---

10. **full-bottomed . . . stilts:** large curled wigs and elevated shoes worn
by actors in the seventeenth century.

STUDY QUESTIONS

Recalling

1. About what part of creation does Mephistopheles say, "that's all I see"?
2. In the prologue what wager do God and Mephistopheles make regarding Faust?
3. What permission does the Lord give Mephistopheles? What reason does the Lord give for sending humanity the devil as "a companion"?
4. What promise does Mephistopheles make Faust? What does he ask in return? According to Faust, when will he lose the wager?
5. Explain how Mephistopheles describes Faust's spirit in his final speech. What does he say he is planning to do with Faust?

Interpreting

6. Explain the relationship between the Lord and Mephistopheles in the prologue. Find two examples of the Lord's control over the devil.
7. What statements by the Lord and Faust reflect Goethe's belief that "restless action" gives life meaning? Explain how these statements suggest an outcome to Faust's wager.

VIEWPOINT

Writing about freedom, a concept that is central to much of his work, Goethe said:

Let a man but declare himself free, straightway he will feel himself limited. But let him be bold enough to declare himself limited, and he will experience a sense of freedom.

■ In what way does Faust declare himself free, and how does this actually limit him? What must he do to find true freedom?

VOCABULARY

Analogies

An **analogy** is a comparison. Analogy items appear on vocabulary tests as double comparisons between two pairs of words. You may be given the first pair and asked to find or complete a second pair of words that has the same relationship as the first pair. See the following example:

SMILE : GRIN :: laugh : chuckle

Here both pairs of words are synonyms.

Each numbered item below begins with two related words in capital letters, the first of which is from *Faust*. First decide how the two capitalized words relate to each other. Then choose the pair with the relationship most like the relationship between the pair in capital letters. Write the number of each item and the letter of your choice on a separate sheet.

1. FRENZY : TURMOIL : :
   (a) action : consequence
   (b) excitement : agitation
   (c) hope : loss
   (d) warmth : coolness

2. PATHOS : PATHETIC : :
   (a) minuscule : titanic
   (b) strength : power
   (c) humility : humble
   (d) stature : rank

3. TORRENT : TRICKLE : :
   (a) gust : wind
   (b) tornado : breeze
   (c) monsoon : hurricane
   (d) breath : sigh

4. TENACITY : STUBBORN : :
   (a) tradition : radical
   (b) exultation : aggressive
   (c) beauty : charismatic
   (d) ambition : farsighted

5. INSATIABLENESS : FOOD : :
   (a) boredom : exercise
   (b) studiousness : books
   (c) brilliance : dull
   (d) activity : apathy

Heinrich Heine   *1797–1856*

Although he was a poet of the Romantic Age, Heinrich Heine [hīn′riкн hī′nə] maintained a wit and cynicism that set his work apart from that of many other Romantic authors. He was born in Düsseldorf in western Germany. A wealthy uncle agreed to support him in the study of law, but Heine was more interested in history and literature. He did eventually receive a law degree, but his studies were conducted at three different universities and were interrupted often by travel, by work as a journalist, and by his literary ambitions. Heine's first published poetry was inspired by his admiration for his uncle's daughter Amalie; many of his early poems were later collected in *Book of Songs* (1827).

Heine was a member of the "Young Germans," a controversial group of radical authors whose work—like Heine's *Germany, A Winter's Tale* (1844)—criticized the lack of freedom through most of Germany. Heine, whose admiration for Napoleon approached hero worship, traveled to Paris as a journalist in 1831. To inspire a lasting peace between Germany and France and to spread his vision of a common European culture, he wrote extensively on culture, politics, travel, literature, philosophy, and poetry. Heine remained in Paris for the rest of his life; in 1848 a nervous disease confined him to his bed. He remained in his "mattress grave" for ten years, during which he produced some of his finest poetry.

One of Heine's most famous works is the four-volume *Travel Pictures* (1826–1831), a mixture of fiction with nonfiction, of vivid travel sketches with satire on German culture and politics. Heine's lyric poetry, however, is his most celebrated and influential achievement. Many of his lyrics have been set to music by such composers as Schubert, Schumann, Mendelssohn, and Brahms. The poems are bittersweet in their combination of simple fairy-tale moods and exotic dreams with Heine's characteristic irony. The best known of all his poems is "The Lorelei." The Lorelei is a cliff rising above dangerous rapids on the River Rhine in western Germany. According to a popular legend, a siren, or a beautiful female spirit, sang an enticing song from the cliff, thereby blinding sailors to the peril of the rapids.

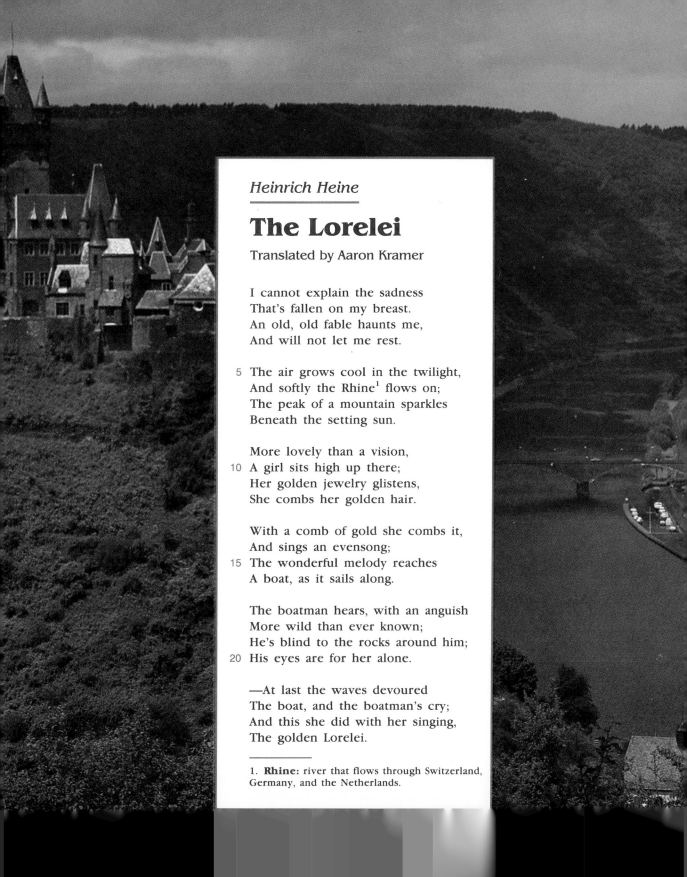

Heinrich Heine

The Lorelei

Translated by Aaron Kramer

I cannot explain the sadness
That's fallen on my breast.
An old, old fable haunts me,
And will not let me rest.

5 The air grows cool in the twilight,
And softly the Rhine[1] flows on;
The peak of a mountain sparkles
Beneath the setting sun.

More lovely than a vision,
10 A girl sits high up there;
Her golden jewelry glistens,
She combs her golden hair.

With a comb of gold she combs it,
And sings an evensong;
15 The wonderful melody reaches
A boat, as it sails along.

The boatman hears, with an anguish
More wild than ever known;
He's blind to the rocks around him;
20 His eyes are for her alone.

—At last the waves devoured
The boat, and the boatman's cry;
And this she did with her singing,
The golden Lorelei.

---

1. **Rhine:** river that flows through Switzerland, Germany, and the Netherlands.

STUDY QUESTIONS

Recalling

1. Give two details of the speaker's mood in the first stanza.
2. Find three details of time and place in the second stanza.
3. Describe the girl and her actions in the third and fourth stanzas.
4. According to the last two stanzas, what effect does the girl have on the boatman?

Interpreting

5. Find at least four words that Heine uses to create a fairy-tale atmosphere.
6. Why do you think the poet does not describe in detail what happens to the boatman? In what sense is the ending of the poem ironic?

Extending

7. Compare the first stanza of "The Lorelei" with the following lines from Samuel Taylor Coleridge's *Rime of the Ancient Mariner* (page 343):

Since then, at an uncertain hour,
That agony returns:
And till my ghastly tale is told,
This heart within me burns.

What function does the telling of a story have for each speaker?

LITERARY FOCUS

Translation

All the selections in Part Two ("Western Literature") of this book are English translations of works originally written in other languages—Greek, Latin, Italian, French, Spanish, German, and Russian. The general elegance of style, beauty of expression, and power of communication in these selections prove that successful translations are possible.

The difficulty in translation, however, lies in avoiding the two extremes of being too literal or too liberal. Literal translations render the work word for word but ignore subtleties of language—idiom, connotation, and imagery. As a result, every word is translated, but the spirit of the original work is damaged. On the other hand, liberal translations attempt to communicate only the essential spirit and meaning of a work and, therefore, often neglect the original language. The best

translations must fall—as the Italian critic Benedetto Croce said—somewhere between "faithful ugliness and faithless beauty."

To see the difference that can exist between two translations of the same poem, compare the translation of "The Lorelei" that follows with the translation on page 811.

I cannot tell why this imagined
　Sorrow has fallen on me;
The ghost of an unburied legend
　That will not let me be.

5 The air is cool and twilight
　Flows down the quiet Rhine;
A mountain alone in the high light
　Catches the faltering shine.

One rosy peak half gleaming
10　Reveals, enthroned in air,
A goddess, lost in dreaming,
　Who combs her golden hair.

With a golden comb she is combing
　Her hair, as she sings a song;
15 Heard and reheard through the gloaming,
　It hurries the night along.

The boatman has heard what has bound him
　In throes of a strange, wild love.
He is blind to the reefs that surround him
20　Who sees but the vision above.

And lo, the wild waters are springing—
　The boat and the boatman are gone . . .
Then silence. And this with her singing,
　The Lorelei has done.

Translated by Louis Untermeyer

Thinking About Translations

1. Compare the first and second stanzas of the two translations of "The Lorelei." Explain how a difference in wording affects the mood of each translation.
2. Compare the third and fourth stanzas of the two translations. Which description of the woman do you think is more effective? Why?
3. Reread the fifth and sixth stanzas of the two translations. Compare the meaning and mood of the two versions of the boatman's story.

Victor Hugo *1802–1885*

Victor Hugo was the acknowledged leader of the Romantic movement in France. A man of great mental, spiritual, and physical power, Hugo was regarded—even in his own time—only in superlatives: as a genius, as the greatest Frenchman ever, as the most significant writer since Shakespeare. Innumerable stories circulated about his boundless strength, energy, and enthusiasm. For example, it was said that he ate unpeeled oranges whole and that his beard blunted the barber's razor.

Hugo was born in Besançon, in eastern France, the third son of an army officer who served under Napoleon. At fifteen young Victor received recognition for his poetry from the Académie Française, a prestigious organization of French writers and scholars. At seventeen he wrote and published a literary magazine with his older brothers. Hugo wrote poetry, plays, and novels. Because of the académie's recognition, his first collected poems, *Odes* (1822), brought him a pension from the French government. His play *Hernani* (1830) avoided common dramatic conventions and as a result is often considered the beginning of French Romanticism. His most famous novels, *The Hunchback of Notre Dame* (1831) and *Les Misérables* (1862) won him fame in England and America. In fact, installments of *Les Misérables* were eagerly awaited by a divided America during the Civil War.

After his eldest daughter and her husband were drowned in 1843, Hugo did not publish anything for ten years. During this time he was elected to the National Assembly, where he fought for liberal reforms like free education and wider voting rights. When President Louis Napoleon declared himself Emperor Napoleon III in 1851, Hugo left France and refused to return until democracy was restored. Napoleon III was overthrown in 1870, and Hugo returned to France, a triumphant champion of freedom.

In France Hugo is revered as a poet; he has been called the greatest painter and musician of the French language. "Russia 1812," an excerpt from "The Expiation," is from Hugo's 1853 collection, *The Chastisements*. Memorized by every French schoolchild today, "Russia 1812" expresses Hugo's admiration for the courage and daring of Napoleon. Having led his troops across Russia to capture Moscow, Napoleon met only devastation. The Russians had burned the city and its environs. In a desperate retreat Napoleon led his troops back across frozen plains in the face of a brutal Russian winter.

Painting illustrating Napoleon's retreat from Moscow in 1812.

Victor Hugo

Russia 1812

Translated by Robert Lowell

The snow fell, and its power was multiplied.
For the first time the Eagle[1] bowed its head—
dark days! Slowly the Emperor returned—
behind him Moscow! Its onion domes[2] still burned.
5 The snow rained down in blizzards—rained and froze.
Past each white waste a further white waste rose.
None recognized the captains or the flags.
Yesterday the Grand Army, today its dregs!
No one could tell the vanguard from the flanks.
10 The snow! The hurt men struggled from the ranks,
hid in the bellies of dead horses, in stacks
of shattered caissons.[3] By the bivouacs,[4]
one saw the picket dying at his post,
still standing in his saddle, white with frost,
15 the stone lips frozen to the bugle's mouth!
Bullets and grapeshot mingled with the snow,
that hailed . . . The Guard, surprised at shivering, march
in a dream now; ice rimes[5] the gray mustache.

---

1. **Eagle:** nickname for Napoleon and emblem of his army.
2. **onion domes:** onion-shaped spires of Russian architecture.
3. **caissons** [kā′sənz]: chests for holding ammunition.
4. **bivouacs** [biv′o͞owaks′]: temporary field camps.
5. **rimes:** covers with frost.

The snow falls, always snow! The driving mire
20 submerges; men, trapped in that white empire,
have no more bread and march on barefoot—gaps!
They were no longer living men and troops,
but a dream drifting in a fog, a mystery,
mourners parading under the black sky.
25 The solitude, vast, terrible to the eye,
was like a mute avenger everywhere,
as snowfall, floating through the quiet air,
buried the huge army in a huge shroud.
Could anyone leave this kingdom? A crowd—
30 each man, obsessed with dying, was alone.
Men slept—and died! The beaten mob sludged on,
ditching the guns to burn their carriages.
Two foes. The North, the Czar. The North was worse.
In hollows where the snow was piling up,
35 one saw whole regiments fallen asleep.
Attila's dawn, Cannaes of Hannibal![6]
The army marching to its funeral!
Litters, wounded, the dead, deserters—swarms,
crushing the bridges down to cross a stream.
40 They went to sleep ten thousand, woke up four.
Ney,[7] bringing up the former army's rear,
hacked his horse loose from three disputing Cossacks[8] . . .
All night, the *qui vive?*[9] The alert! Attacks;
retreats! White ghosts would wrench away our guns,
45 or we would see dim, terrible squadrons,
circles of steel, whirlpools of savages,
rush sabering through the camp like dervishes.
And in this way, whole armies died at night.

The Emperor was there, standing—he saw.
50 This oak already trembling from the axe,
watched his glories drop from him branch by branch:
chiefs, soldiers. Each one had his turn and chance—
they died! Some lived. These still believed his star,
and kept their watch. They loved the man of war,
55 this small man with his hands behind his back,
whose shadow, moving to and fro, was black
behind the lighted tent. Still believing, they

---

6. **Attila's . . . Hannibal:** referring to defeats that altered the course
of history. The Romans defeated Attila and the Huns in A.D. 451.
Hannibal, a Carthaginian general, defeated the Roman forces at Cannae
in 216 B.C., but it was his last victory before his ultimate defeat.
7. **Ney** [nā]: French marshal in charge of the rear guard during the
retreat from Moscow.
8. **Cossacks:** Russian cavalrymen.
9. *qui vive?* [kē vēv]: French for "Who goes there?"

accused their destiny of *lèse-majesté.*[10]
His misfortune had mounted on their back.
60 The man of glory shook. Cold stupefied
him, then suddenly he felt terrified.
Being without belief, he turned to God:
"God of armies, is this the end?" he cried.
And then at last the expiation came,
65 as he heard some one call him by his name,
some one half-lost in shadow, who said, "No,
Napoleon." Napoleon understood,
restless, bareheaded, leaden, as he stood
before his butchered legions in the snow.

---

10. *lèse-majesté* [lez′mä zhes tā′]: French for "high treason."

STUDY QUESTIONS

Recalling

1. Give at least three words or phrases used to describe the snow.
2. From lines 1–32 find at least four specific examples of the effect of the weather on Napoleon's troops.
3. What are Napoleon's two foes? Which is worse? Based on lines 34–48, explain why.
4. Name two things to which Napoleon is compared in the poem. According to lines 49–59, what do his soldiers think of Napoleon?
5. What question does Napoleon ask at the end of the poem? Why? What answer does he get?

Interpreting

6. Why does Hugo call Napoleon's army at this time the "dregs"?
7. Find at least three images of death in the poem. Explain the metaphor in lines 49–51.
8. Who do you think answers Napoleon's cry at the end of the poem? Why do you think the answer is an "expiation"? What do you think Napoleon understands at the end?

Extending

9. Why do you think that many of Napoleon's soldiers continued to believe in him during the grim retreat from Moscow? Why do you think Hugo, who admired Napoleon, chose to write about such a defeat?

COMPOSITION

Developing a Thesis Statement

◼ Develop a thesis statement about Hugo's use of imagery to picture the destruction of war. Then in a brief essay defend your thesis with examples from the poem. To do this, use several images from the poem, and discuss their effectiveness. *For help with this assignment, refer to Lesson 1 in the Writing About Literature Handbook at the back of this book.*

Writing a Letter

◼ Imagine that you are a soldier in Napoleon's army during the retreat from Moscow. Write a letter home in which you describe the humiliation of the retreat, the hardship of the march, and your current feelings for Napoleon.

COMPARING ENGLISH AND WESTERN WRITERS

◼ Compare one English Romantic poet (see pages 326–390) and one western Romantic poet. Expand on at least two of the following statements about Romanticism by citing examples. (1) Both English and western Romantic poets regarded humanity as part of nature. (2) They glorified instinct, emotion, and imagination. (3) They admired individualism. (4) They often drew on recent national history for subject matter.

Leo Tolstoy *1828–1910*

Count Leo Tolstoy is one of the best known Russian novelists in addition to being a moral and social reformer. He was born on his family estate near Moscow. His parents died when he was still a boy, and Tolstoy was raised by relatives. He rarely applied himself to his studies whether at home with tutors or after he entered college. He inherited the family estate, left school to manage it, and became bored after a year. He then traveled to Moscow and St. Petersburg to sample wealthy society, but the debts that he accumulated forced him to return home. Still with little direction he enlisted in the army and fought in the Crimean War in 1854. Throughout these early years Tolstoy looked for spiritual awareness, blamed himself for his life style, and tried unsuccessfully to change. As he became increasingly disillusioned with the repression of the czarist regime, the insincerity of the court, and the brutality of war, Tolstoy withdrew to the estate to launch a successful social experiment. He founded a school for the children of his serfs, peasants attached to his estate, and was among the first to practice the innovative theory that education should respond to the needs of individual students.

In 1862 Tolstoy married Sonya Behrs, the daughter of an old family friend, and they raised a large family on the estate. Tolstoy had published his first story ten years earlier, but in the years that followed his marriage, he wrote two of the world's greatest novels, *War and Peace* (1865–1869) and *Anna Karenina* (1875–1877). In 1879 his constant spiritual search brought him to a dramatic conversion. He began to preach the rejection of all property, of any form of violence, of religious and civil authority; he maintained that the only law was the human conscience. He gave up liquor and tobacco and became a vegetarian. He temporarily deserted fiction and wrote books and essays on social and religious issues. These works were often moralistic and preaching in tone, but they helped to make Tolstoy a kind of spiritual leader to a large group of "believers." Only his wife's vigilant efforts prevented him from giving away his land and the copyrights to his books. At the age of eighty-two, Tolstoy died in a railway station, just days after fleeing from home in an effort to escape his possessions and be closer to God.

Although Tolstoy gave up fiction in favor of more moral writing, his great novels have probably inspired more social reform than his nonfiction. *War and Peace* describes Russian life during Napoleon's invasion in 1812 and is one of the world's strongest condemnations of war. *Anna Karenina,* the tragic story of an unhappy woman and a doomed love, demonstrates the evils of urban society and urges a return to rural simplicity. The story "How Much Land Does a Man Need?" shows Tolstoy's concern with the evils of private property.

Leo Tolstoy

How Much Land Does a Man Need?

Translated by Louise and Aylmer Maude

1

An elder sister came to visit her younger sister in the country. The elder was married to a shopkeeper in town, the younger to a peasant in the village. As the sisters sat over their tea talking, the elder began to boast of the advantages of town life, saying how comfortably they lived there, how well they dressed, what fine clothes her children wore, what good things they ate and drank, and how she went to the theater, promenades, and entertainments.

The younger sister was piqued, and in turn disparaged the life of a shopkeeper, and stood up for that of a peasant.

"I wouldn't change my way of life for yours," said she. "We may live roughly, but at least we're free from worry. You live in better style than we do, but though you often earn more than you need, you're very likely to lose all you have. You know the proverb, 'Loss and gain are brothers twain.' It often happens that people who're wealthy one day are begging their bread the next. Our way is safer. Though a peasant's life is not a rich one, it's long. We'll never grow rich, but we'll always have enough to eat."

The elder sister said sneeringly:

"Enough? Yes, if you like to share with the pigs and the calves! What do you know of elegance or manners! However much your good man may slave, you'll die as you live—in a dung heap—and your children the same."

"Well, what of that?" replied the younger sister. "Of course our work is rough and hard. But on the other hand, it's sure, and we need not bow to anyone. But you, in your towns, are surrounded by temptations; today all may be right, but tomorrow the Evil One may tempt your husband with cards, wine, or women, and all will go to ruin. Don't such things happen often enough?"

Pahom, the master of the house, was lying on the top of the stove and he listened to the women's chatter.

"It is perfectly true," thought he. "Busy as we are from childhood tilling mother earth, we peasants have no time to let any nonsense settle in our heads. Our only trouble is that we haven't land enough. If I had plenty of land, I shouldn't fear the Devil himself!"

The women finished their tea, chatted a while about dress, and then cleared away the tea things and lay down to sleep.

But the Devil had been sitting behind the stove and had heard all that had been said. He was pleased that the peasant's wife had led her husband into boasting and that he had said that if he had plenty of land he would not fear the Devil himself.

"All right," thought the Devil. "We'll have a tussle. I'll give you land enough; and by means of the land I'll get you into my power."

2

Close to the village there lived a lady, a small landowner who had an estate of about three hundred acres. She had always lived on good terms with the peasants until she engaged as her manager an old soldier, who took to burdening the people with fines. However careful Pahom tried to be, it happened again and again that now a horse of his got among the lady's oats, now a cow strayed into her garden, now his calves found their way into her meadows—and he always had to pay a fine.

Pahom paid up, but grumbled, and, going home in a temper, was rough with his family. All through that summer Pahom had much trouble because of this manager, and he was actually glad when winter came and the cattle had to be stabled. Though he grudged the fodder when they could no longer graze on the pasture land, at least he was free from anxiety about them.

In the winter the news got about that the lady was going to sell her land and that the keeper of the inn on the high road was bargaining for it. When the peasants heard this they were very much alarmed.

"Well," thought they, "if the innkeeper gets the land, he'll worry us with fines worse than the lady's manager. We all depend on that estate."

So the peasants went on behalf of their village council and asked the lady not to sell the land to the innkeeper, offering her a better price for it themselves. The lady agreed to let them have it. Then the peasants tried to arrange for the village council to buy the whole estate, so that it might be held by them all in common. They met twice to discuss it, but could not settle the matter; the Evil One sowed discord among them and they could not agree. So they decided to buy the land individually, each according to his means; and the lady agreed to this plan as she had to the other.

Presently Pahom heard that a neighbor of his was buying fifty acres, and that the lady had consented to accept one half in cash and to wait a year for the other half. Pahom felt envious.

"Look at that," thought he, "the land is all being sold, and I'll get none of it." So he spoke to his wife.

"Other people are buying," said he, "and we must also buy twenty acres or so. Life is becoming impossible. That manager is simply crushing us with his fines."

So they put their heads together and considered how they could manage to buy it. They had one hundred rubles[1] laid by. They sold a colt and one half of their bees, hired out one of their sons as a farm hand and took his wages in advance, borrowed the rest from a brother-in-law, and so scraped together half the purchase money.

Having done this, Pahom chose a farm of forty acres, some of it wooded, and went to the lady to bargain for it. They came to an agreement, and he shook hands with her upon it and paid her a deposit in advance. Then they went to town and signed the deeds, he paying half the price down, and undertaking to pay the remainder within two years.

So now Pahom had land of his own. He borrowed seed and sowed it on the land he had bought. The harvest was a good one, and within a year he had managed to pay off his debts both to the lady and to his brother-in-law. So he became a landowner, plowing and sowing his own land, making hay on his own land, cutting his own trees, and feeding his cattle on his own pasture. When he went out to plow his fields, or to look at his growing corn, or at his grass meadows, his heart would fill with joy. The grass that grew and the flowers that bloomed there seemed to him unlike any that grew elsewhere. Formerly, when he had passed by that land, it had appeared the same as any other land, but now it seemed quite different.

3

So Pahom was well contented, and everything would have been right if the neighboring peasants would only not have trespassed on his wheatfields and meadows. He appealed to them most civilly, but they still went on: now the herdsmen would let the village cows stray into his meadows, then horses from the night pasture would get among his corn. Pahom turned them out again and again, and forgave their owners, and for a long time he forbore to prosecute anyone. But at last he lost patience and complained to the District Court. He knew it was the peasants' want of land, and no evil intent on their part, that caused the trouble, but he thought:

"I can't go on overlooking it, or they'll destroy all I have. They must be taught a lesson."

So he had them up, gave them one lesson, and then another, and two or three of the peasants were fined. After a time Pahom's

---

1. **rubles** [r͞oo′bəlz]: Russian money.

neighbors began to bear him a grudge for this, and would now and then let their cattle on to his land on purpose. One peasant even got into Pahom's wood at night and cut down five young lime trees for their bark. Pahom, passing through the wood one day, noticed something white. He came nearer and saw the stripped trunks lying on the ground, and close by stood the stumps where the trees had been. Pahom was furious.

"If he'd only cut one here and there it would have been bad enough," thought Pahom, "but the rascal has actually cut down a whole clump. If I could only find out who did this, I'd get even with him."

He racked his brains as to who it could be. Finally he decided: "It must be Simon—no one else could have done it." So he went to Simon's homestead to have a look around, but he found nothing and only had an angry scene. However, he now felt more certain than ever that Simon had done it, and he lodged a complaint. Simon was summoned. The case was tried, and retried, and at the end of it all Simon was acquitted, there being no evidence against him. Pahom felt still more aggrieved, and let his anger loose upon the Elders and the Judges.

"You let thieves grease your palms," said he. "If you were honest folk yourselves you wouldn't let a thief go free."

So Pahom quarreled with the judges and with his neighbors. Threats to burn his hut began to be uttered. So though Pahom had more land, his place in the community was much worse than before.

About this time a rumor got about that many people were moving to new parts.

"There's no need for me to leave my land," thought Pahom. "But some of the others may leave our village and then there'd be more room for us. I'd take over their land myself and make my estates somewhat bigger. I could then live more at ease. As it is, I'm still too cramped to be comfortable."

One day Pahom was sitting at home when a peasant, passing through the village, happened to drop in. He was allowed to stay the night, and supper was given him. Pahom had a talk with this peasant and asked him where he came from. The stranger answered that he came from beyond the Volga,[2] where he had been working. One word led to another, and the man went on to say that many people were settling in those parts. He told how some people from his village had settled there. They had joined the community there and had had twenty-five acres per man granted them. The land was so good, he said, that the rye sown on it grew as high as a horse, and so thick that five cuts of a sickle made a sheaf. One peasant, he said, had brought nothing with him but his bare hands, and now he had six horses and two cows of his own.

Pahom's heart kindled with desire.

"Why should I suffer in this narrow hole, if one can live so well elsewhere?" he thought. "I'll sell my land and my homestead here, and with the money I'll start afresh over there and get everything new. In this crowded place one is always having trouble. But I must first go and find out all about it myself."

Toward summer he got ready and started out. He went down the Volga on a steamer to Samara, then walked another three hundred miles on foot, and at last reached the place. It was just as the stranger had said. The peasants had plenty of land: every man had twenty-five acres of communal land given him for his use, and anyone who had money could buy, besides, at a ruble and a half an acre, as much good freehold land as he wanted.

Having found out all he wished to know, Pahom returned home as autumn came on, and began selling off his belongings. He sold his land at a profit, sold his homestead and all his cattle, and withdrew from membership in the village. He only waited till the spring, and then started with his family for the new settlement.

4

As soon as Pahom and his family reached their new abode, he applied for admission into

---

2. **Volga:** river in European Russia.

the council of a large village. He stood treat[3] to the Elders and obtained the necessary documents. Five shares of communal land were given him for his own and his sons' use: that is to say—125 acres (not all together, but in different fields) besides the use of the communal pasture. Pahom put up the buildings he needed and bought cattle. Of the communal land alone he had three times as much as at his former home, and the land was good wheat land. He was ten times better off than he had been. He had plenty of arable land and pasturage, and could keep as many head of cattle as he liked.

At first, in the bustle of building and settling down, Pahom was pleased with it all, but when he got used to it he began to think that even here he hadn't enough land. The first year he sowed wheat on his share of the communal land and had a good crop. He wanted to go on sowing wheat, but had not enough communal land for the purpose, and what he had already used was not available, for in those parts wheat is sown only on virgin soil or on fallow land. It is sown for one or two years, and then the land lies fallow till it is again overgrown with steppe grass. There were many who wanted such land, and there was not enough for all, so that people quarreled about it. Those who were better off wanted it for growing wheat, and those who were poor wanted it to let to dealers, so that they might raise money to pay their taxes. Pahom wanted to sow more wheat, so he rented land from a dealer for a year. He sowed much wheat and had a fine crop, but the land was too far from the village—the wheat had to be carted more than ten miles. After a time Pahom noticed that some peasant dealers were living on separate farms and were growing wealthy, and he thought:

"If I were to buy some freehold land and have a homestead on it, it would be a different thing altogether. Then it would all be fine and close together."

The question of buying freehold land recurred to him again and again.

He went on in the same way for three years, renting land and sowing wheat. The seasons turned out well and the crops were good, so that he began to lay by money. He might have gone on living contentedly, but he grew tired of having to rent other people's land every year and having to scramble for it. Wherever there was good land to be had, the peasants would rush for it and it was taken up at once, so that unless you were sharp about it, you got none. It happened in the third year that he and a dealer together rented a piece of pasture land from some peasants, and they had already plowed it up, when there was some dispute and the peasants went to law about it, and things fell out so that the labor was all lost.

"If it were my own land," thought Pahom, "I should be independent, and there wouldn't be all this unpleasantness."

So Pahom began looking out for land which he could buy, and he came across a peasant who had bought thirteen hundred acres, but having got into difficulties was willing to sell again cheap. Pahom bargained and haggled with him, and at last they settled the price at fifteen hundred rubles, part in cash and part to be paid later. They had all but clinched the matter when a passing dealer happened to stop at Pahom's one day to get feed for his horses. He drank tea with Pahom, and they had a talk. The dealer said that he was just returning from the land of the Bashkirs,[4] far away, where he had bought thirteen thousand acres of land, all for a thousand rubles. Pahom questioned him further, and the dealer said:

"All one has to do is to make friends with the chiefs. I gave away about one hundred rubles' worth of silk robes and carpets, besides a case of tea, and I gave wine to those who would drink it; and I got the land for less than three kopecks[5] an acre." And he showed Pahom the title deed, saying:

---

3. **stood treat:** negotiated a deal.

4. **Bashkirs** [bäsh′kərz]: nomads of region in Russia between the Volga and the Ural Mountains.
5. **kopecks** [kō′peks]: Russian money; one hundred kopecks equal one ruble.

"The land lies near a river, and the whole steppe is virgin soil."

Pahom plied him with questions, and the dealer said:

"There's more land there than you could cover if you walked a year, and it all belongs to the Bashkirs. They're as simple as sheep, and land can be got almost for nothing."

"There, now," thought Pahom, "with my one thousand rubles, why should I get only thirteen hundred acres, and saddle myself with a debt besides? If I take it out there, I can get more than ten times as much for my money."

5

Pahom inquired how to get to the place, and as soon as the grain dealer had left him, he prepared to go there himself. He left his wife to look after the homestead, and started on his journey, taking his hired man with him. They stopped at a town on their way and bought a case of tea, some wine, and other presents, as the grain dealer had advised.

On and on they went until they had gone more than three hundred miles, and on the seventh day they came to a place where the Bashkirs had pitched their round tents. It was all just as the dealer had said. The people lived on the steppe,[6] by a river, in felt-covered tents. They neither tilled the ground nor ate bread. Their cattle and horses grazed in herds on the steppe. The colts were tethered behind the tents, and the mares were driven to them twice a day. The mares were milked, and from the milk kumiss[7] was made. It was the women who prepared the kumiss, and they also made cheese. As far as the men were concerned, drinking kumiss and tea, eating mutton, and playing on their pipes was all they cared about. They were all stout and merry, and all the summer long they never thought of doing any work. They were quite ignorant, and knew no Russian, but were good-natured enough.

As soon as they saw Pahom, they came out of their tents and gathered around the visitor. An interpreter was found, and Pahom told them he had come about some land. The Bashkirs seemed very glad; they took Pahom and led him into one of the best tents, where they made him sit on some down cushions placed on a carpet, while they sat around him. They gave him some tea and kumiss, and had a sheep killed, and gave him mutton to eat. Pahom took presents out of his cart and distributed them among the Bashkirs, and divided the tea amongst them. The Bashkirs were delighted. They talked a great deal among themselves and then told the interpreter what to say.

"They wish to tell you," said the interpreter, "that they like you and that it's our custom to do all we can to please a guest and to repay him for his gifts. You have given us presents, now tell us which of the things we possess please you best, that we may present them to you."

"What pleases me best here," answered Pahom, "is your land. Our land is crowded and the soil is worn out, but you have plenty of land, and it is good land. I never saw the likes of it."

The interpreter told the Bashkirs what Pahom had said. They talked among themselves for a while. Pahom could not understand what they were saying, but saw that they were much amused and heard them shout and laugh. Then they were silent and looked at Pahom while the interpreter said:

"They wish me to tell you that in return for your presents they will gladly give you as much land as you want. You have only to point it out with your hand and it is yours."

The Bashkirs talked again for a while and began to dispute. Pahom asked what they were disputing about, and the interpreter told him that some of them thought they ought to ask their chief about the land and not act in his absence, while others thought there was no need to wait for his return.

6. **steppe** [step]: vast Russian plains.
7. **kumiss** [ko͞o′mis]: fermented drink.

6

While the Bashkirs were disputing, a man in a large fox-fur cap appeared on the scene. They all became silent and rose to their feet. The interpreter said: "This is our chief himself."

Pahom immediately fetched the best dressing gown and five pounds of tea, and offered these to the chief. The chief accepted them and seated himself in the place of honor. The Bashkirs at once began telling him something. The chief listened for a while, then made a sign with his head for them to be silent, and addressing himself to Pahom, said in Russian:

"Well, so be it. Choose whatever piece of land you like; we have plenty of it."

"How can I take as much as I like?" thought Pahom. "I must get a deed to make it secure, or else they may say: 'It is yours,' and afterward may take it away again."

"Thank you for your kind words," he said aloud. "You have much land, and I only want a little. But I should like to be sure which portion is mine. Could it not be measured and made over to me? Life and death are in God's hands. You good people give it to me, but your children might wish to take it back again."

"You are quite right," said the chief. "We will make it over to you."

"I heard that a dealer had been here," continued Pahom, "and that you gave him a little land, too, and signed title deeds to that effect. I should like to have it done in the same way."

The chief understood.

"Yes," replied he, "that can be done quite easily. We have a scribe, and we will go to town with you and have the deed properly sealed."

And what will be the price?" asked Pahom.

"Our price is always the same: one thousand rubles a day."

Pahom did not understand.

"A day? What measure is that? How many acres would that be?"

"We do not know how to reckon it out," said the chief. "We sell it by the day. As much as you can go around on your feet in a day is yours, and the price is one thousand rubles a day."

Pahom was surprised.

"But in a day you can get around a large tract of land," he said.

The chief laughed.

"It will all be yours!" said he. "But there is one condition: If you don't return on the same day to the spot whence you started, your money is lost."

"But how am I to mark the way that I have gone?"

"Why, we shall go to any spot you like and stay there. You must start from that spot and make your round, taking a spade with you. Wherever you think necessary, make a mark. At every turning, dig a hole and pile up the turf; then afterward we will go around with a plow from hole to hole. You may make as large a circuit as you please, but before the sun sets you must return to the place you started from. All the land you cover will be yours."

Pahom was delighted. It was decided to start early next morning. They talked a while, and after drinking some more kumiss and eating some more mutton, they had tea again, and then the night came on. They gave Pahom a feather bed to sleep on, and the Bashkirs dispersed for the night, promising to assemble the next morning at daybreak and ride out before sunrise to the appointed spot.

7

Pahom lay on the feather bed, but could not sleep. He kept thinking about the land.

"What a large tract I'll mark off!" thought he, "I can easily do thirty-five miles in a day. The days are long now, and within a circuit of thirty-five miles what a lot of land there will be! I'll sell the poorer land or let it to peasants, but I'll pick out the best and farm it myself. I'll buy two ox teams and hire two more laborers. About a hundred and fifty acres shall be plowland, and I'll pasture cattle on the rest."

Pahom lay awake all night and dozed off only just before dawn. Hardly were his eyes closed when he had a dream. He thought he was lying in that same tent and heard somebody chuckling outside. He wondered who it could be, and rose and went out, and he saw the Bashkir chief sitting in front of the tent holding his sides and rolling about with laughter. Going nearer to the chief, Pahom asked: "What are you laughing at?" But he saw that it was no longer the chief but the grain dealer who had recently stopped at his house and had told him about the land. Just as Pahom was going to ask: "Have you been here long?" he saw that it was not the dealer, but the peasant who had come up from the Volga long ago, to Pahom's old home. Then he saw that it was not the peasant either, but the Devil himself with hoofs and horns, sitting there and chuckling, and before him lay a man, prostrate on the ground, barefooted, with only trousers and a shirt on. And Pahom dreamed that he looked more attentively to see what sort of man it was lying there, and he saw that the man was dead, and that it was himself. Horror-struck, he awoke.

"What things one dreams about!" thought he.

Looking around he saw through the open door that the dawn was breaking.

"It's time to wake them up," thought he. "We ought to be starting."

He got up, roused his man (who was sleeping in his cart), bade him harness, and went to call the Bashkirs.

"It's time to go to the steppe to measure the land," he said.

The Bashkirs rose and assembled, and the chief came, too. Then they began drinking kumiss again, and offered Pahom some tea, but he would not wait.

"If we are to go, let's go. It's high time," said he.

8

The Bashkirs got ready and they all started; some mounted on horses and some in carts. Pahom drove in his own small cart with his servant and took a spade with him. When they reached the steppe, the red dawn was beginning to kindle. They ascended a hillock (called by the Bashkirs a *shikhan*) and, dismounting from their carts and their horses, gathered in one spot. The chief came to Pahom and, stretching out his arm toward the plain:

"See," said he, "all this, as far as your eye can reach, is ours. You may have any part of it you like."

Pahom's eyes glistened; it was all virgin soil, as flat as the palm of your hand, as black as the seed of a poppy, and in the hollows different kinds of grasses grew breast-high.

The chief took off his fox-fur cap, placed it on the ground, and said:

"This will be the mark. Start from here, and return here again. All the land you go around shall be yours."

Pahom took out his money and put it on the cap. Then he took off his outer coat, remaining in his sleeveless undercoat. He unfastened his girdle and tied it tight below his stomach, put a little bag of bread into the breast of his coat, and, tying a flask of water to his girdle, he drew up the tops of his boots, took the spade from his man, and stood ready to start. He considered for some moments which way he had better go—it was tempting everywhere.

"No matter," he concluded, "I'll go toward the rising sun."

He turned his face to the east, stretched himself, and waited for the sun to appear above the rim.

"I must lose no time," he thought, "and it's easier walking while it's still cool."

The sun's rays had hardly flashed above the horizon when Pahom, carrying the spade over his shoulder, went down into the steppe.

Pahom started walking neither slowly nor quickly. After having gone a thousand yards he stopped, dug a hole, and placed pieces of turf one on another to make it more visible. Then he went on; and now that he had walked off his stiffness he quickened his pace. After a while he dug another hole.

Pahom looked back. The hillock could be distinctly seen in the sunlight, with the people on it, and the glittering iron rims of the cart-wheels. At a rough guess Pahom concluded that he had walked three miles. It was growing warmer; he took off his undercoat, slung it across his shoulder, and went on again. It had grown quite warm now; he looked at the sun—it was time to think of breakfast.

"The first shift is done, but there are four in a day, and it's too soon yet to turn. But I'll just take off my boots," said he to himself.

He sat down, took off his boots, stuck them into his girdle, and went on. It was easy walking now.

"I'll go on for another three miles," thought he, "and then turn to the left. This spot is so fine that it would be a pity to lose it. The further one goes, the better the land seems."

He went straight on for a while, and when he looked around, the hillock was scarcely visible and the people on it looked like black ants, and he could just see something glistening there in the sun.

"Ah," thought Pahom, "I have gone far enough in this direction; it's time to turn. Besides, I'm in a regular sweat, and very thirsty."

He stopped, dug a large hole, and heaped up pieces of turf. Next he untied his flask, had a drink, and then turned sharply to the left. He went on and on; the grass was high, and it was very hot.

Pahom began to grow tired: he looked at the sun and saw that it was noon.

"Well," he thought, "I must have a rest."

He sat down, and ate some bread and drank some water; but he did not lie down, thinking that if he did he might fall asleep. After sitting a little while, he went on again. At first he walked easily; the food had strengthened him; but it had become terribly hot and he felt sleepy. Still he went on, thinking: "An hour to suffer, a lifetime to live."

He went a long way in this direction also, and was about to turn to the left again, when he perceived a damp hollow: "It would be a pity to leave that out," he thought. "Flax would do well there." So he went on past the hollow and dug a hole on the other side of it before he made a sharp turn. Pahom looked toward the hillock. The heat made the air hazy: it seemed to be quivering, and through the haze the people on the hillock could scarcely be seen.

"Ah," thought Pahom, "I have made the sides too long; I must make this one shorter." And he went along the third side, stepping faster. He looked at the sun: it was nearly halfway to the horizon, and he had not yet done two miles of the third side of the square. He was still ten miles from the goal.

"No," he thought, "though it will make my land lopsided, I must hurry back in a straight line now. I might go too far, and as it is I have a great deal of land."

So Pahom hurriedly dug a hole and turned straight toward the hillock.

9

Pahom went straight toward the hillock, but he now walked with difficulty. He was exhausted from the heat, his bare feet were cut and bruised, and his legs began to fail. He longed to rest, but it was impossible if he meant to get back before sunset. The sun waits for no man, and it was sinking lower and lower.

"Oh, Lord," he thought, "if only I have not blundered trying for too much! What if I am too late?"

He looked toward the hillock and at the sun. He was still far from his goal, and the sun was already near the rim of the sky.

Pahom walked on and on; it was very hard walking, but he went quicker and quicker. He pressed on, but was still far from the place. He began running, threw away his coat, his boots, his flask, and his cap, and kept only the spade which he used as a support.

"What am I to do?" he thought again. "I've grasped too much and ruined the whole affair. I can't get there before the sun sets."

And this fear made him still more breathless. Pahom kept on running; his soaking shirt and trousers stuck to him, and his mouth was parched. His breast was working like a blacksmith's bellows, his heart was beating like a hammer, and his legs were giving way as if they did not belong to him. Pahom was seized with terror lest he should die of the strain.

Though afraid of death, he could not stop.

"After having run all that way they will call me a fool if I stop now," thought he.

And he ran on and on, and drew near and heard the Bashkirs yelling and shouting to him, and their cries inflamed his heart still more. He gathered his last strength and ran on.

The sun was close to the rim of the sky and, cloaked in mist, looked large, and red as blood. Now, yes, now, it was about to set! The sun was quite low, but he was also quite near his goal. Pahom could already see the people on the hillock waving their arms to make him hurry. He could see the fox-fur cap on the ground and the money in it, and the chief sitting on the ground holding his sides. And Pahom remembered his dream.

"There's plenty of land," thought he, "but will God let me live on it? I have lost my life, I have lost my life! Never will I reach that spot!"

Pahom looked at the sun, which had reached the earth: one side of it had already disappeared. With all his remaining strength he rushed on, bending his body forward so that his legs could hardly follow fast enough to keep him from falling. Just as he reached the hillock it suddenly grew dark. He looked up—the sun had already set!

He gave a cry: "All my labor has been in vain," thought he, and was about to stop, but he heard the Bashkirs still shouting and remembered that though to him, from below, the sun seemed to have set, they on the hillock could still see it. He took a long breath and ran up the hillock. It was still light there. He reached the top and saw the cap. Before it sat the chief, laughing and holding his sides. Again Pahom remembered his dream, and he uttered a cry: his legs gave way beneath him, he fell forward and reached the cap with his hands.

"Ah, that's a fine fellow!" exclaimed the chief. "He has gained much land!"

Pahom's servant came running up and tried to raise him, but he saw that blood was flowing from his mouth. Pahom was dead.

The Bashkirs clicked their tongues to show their pity.

His servant picked up the spade and dug a grave long enough for Pahom to lie in, and buried him in it.

Six feet from his head to his heels was all he needed.

STUDY QUESTIONS

Recalling
1. What does each sister say about life in the country? What does Pahom say about land? What does the devil say in response?
2. What reason does Pahom give for becoming dissatisfied with each piece of land he has?
3. Explain the Bashkirs' custom for measuring land. Briefly tell what happens to Pahom when he tries to claim his land from the Bashkirs.

Interpreting
4. How does the argument between the two sisters foreshadow the remainder of the story?
5. Contrast Pahom's attitude about land with that of the Bashkirs. Who receives more happiness from land? Why?
6. How much land does Pahom want? Explain the irony of the title.

Extending
7. This story was Tolstoy's retelling of a Russian folktale. What similarities can you see between the story and fables by Aesop (page 671)? What is the story's moral?

VIEWPOINT

Marc Slonim, an authority on Russian literature, comments on Tolstoy:

It was not enough for him to be a writer; he wanted to be, and became, a preacher, a philosopher, the founder of a new religion, a critic of society, and a fighter for the renovation of mankind.

◼ Which of these aspects of Tolstoy's personality are evident in "How Much Land Does A Man Need"? Support your answer with specific examples from the story.

COMPOSITION

Writing About Theme
◼ Write an essay about the theme of "How Much Land Does a Man Need?" First identify the theme. Then show how Tolstoy illuminates this theme through (a) plot, (b) characterization, (c) setting, (d) point of view, and (e) tone. *For help with this assignment, refer to Lesson 6 in the Writing About Literature Handbook at the back of this book.*

Writing from Different Points of View
◼ In a brief essay answer the question that Tolstoy asks in the story's title, "How Much Land Does a Man Need?" Answer the question four times, once from each of the following points of view: (a) Pahom's, (b) the Bashkirs', (c) Tolstoy's, and (d) your own.

Anton Chekhov   *1860–1904*

Anton Chekhov's plays revolutionized theater throughout the world; his short stories are models of concise storytelling. Chekhov was born in Taganrog in southern Russia. His grandfather was a serf who bought the family's freedom; his father had an unsuccessful small grocery business. Chekhov studied medicine at Moscow University while also providing the main financial support for his parents and five siblings. He did this by writing sketches and short stories rapidly and for as many magazines as possible. After graduation in 1884, he practiced as a physician for a while, but medicine became a secondary concern as he devoted himself increasingly to his literary career. His interest in science, however, influenced the style of his plays and short stories. As a scientist Chekhov viewed the world objectively without self-deception; as a writer he was untouched by Romanticism. He expressed his philosophy of objectivity in a letter to a friend: "To a chemist, nothing on earth is unclean. A writer must be as objective as a chemist, he must lay aside his personal subjective standpoint and must understand that muck heaps play a very respectable part in a landscape."

As a result of his objectivity, Chekhov is classified as a Realist, but, while picturing the "muck heaps," he retained a love of life and of humanity. Although the themes of his great plays include pettiness, loneliness, disappointment, and loss, his work always celebrates human dignity and searches for glimmers of hope. He said, "In addition to life as it is, the audience must feel life as it should be." In *The Seagull* (1896), for example, Chekhov uses the seagull as a symbol for human potential. His characters suffer not from great tragic flaws but from an inability to accept responsibility for their own deeds. Like *The Seagull, Uncle Vanya* (1899), *The Three Sisters* (1901), and *The Cherry Orchard* (1904) contain little plot; the drama lies in human relationships and psychological insights.

Chekhov's short stories are Realistic also. His heroes are ordinary people struggling with recognizable problems. They often appear foolish and usually cause their own difficulties, but Chekhov's attitude toward them is always warm and tinged with humor. "Other People's Misfortune" is about the sale of a family estate. The plot is inconsequential, but it allows Chekhov to examine people's emotions at a crucial point in their lives.

Anton Chekhov

Other People's Misfortune

Translated by Avrahm Yarmolinsky

It was not later than six o'clock in the morning when Stepan Kovalyov, a young man fresh from law school, got into a carriage with his bride, and they were soon rolling along a country road. Neither he nor his young wife had ever risen so early, and the magnificence of the still summer morning struck them as something out of a fairy tale. The earth, clothed in green, sprinkled with diamond dew, seemed beautiful and happy. The sunlight lay in bright patches on the forest, shimmered on the sparkling river, and there was a freshness in the extraordinarily transparent azure air that made it seem as if all of God's world had just emerged from a bath, and so was refreshed and invigorated.

For the Kovalyovs, as they admitted afterwards, this was the happiest morning of their honeymoon, and indeed of their whole life together. They chatted without stopping, laughed boisterously for no reason, and carried on in such an unrestrained fashion that in the end they were ashamed before the coachman.

Happiness was smiling upon their present and upon their future as well: they were on their way to buy an estate—a small "romantic nook," for which they had been planning since their wedding day. The future held out the brightest prospect for them both. He had visions of a zemstvo[1] post, scientific farming, all the labors and pleasures associated with country life, of which he had heard and read so much; she was captivated by purely romantic aspects: excursions on the lake, dark alleys, fragrant nights. . . .

What with the laughter and the talk, they did not notice that they had covered the eight-een versts[2] to the estate of aulic councilor[3] Mikhailov that they were going to look over. There was a stream just below the hill on which the house stood, almost hidden by a birch grove. The red roof was barely visible through the thick foliage, and the clayey slope was studded with saplings.

"Not a bad view!" said Kovalyov, as they were fording the watercourse. "A house on a hill, a stream at the foot of it! Devilishly nice! But, Verochka, these stairs aren't any good . . . they spoil the view, they are ugly. . . . If we buy the estate, we must certainly replace them with a cast-iron flight of stairs."

Verochka too liked the view. Shaking with vivacious laughter, she ran up the steps, her husband after her, and the two of them, breathless, disheveled, walked into the grove. The first person they caught sight of at the house was a big, hairy peasant, sleepy and sullen. He sat on the porch, cleaning a child's boot.

"Is Mr. Mikhailov in?" Kovalyov asked him. "Go tell him that people who want to buy the estate have come to look at it."

The peasant stared at the Kovalyov couple with vacant amazement and trudged off slowly, not to the mansion, but to the kitchen, which was a structure apart from the house. Immediately faces appeared in the kitchen windows, one more sleepy and astonished than the other.

"Buyers have arrived!" the whisper was heard. "Lord, it's your will. Mikhalkovo's being sold. Look, what a young couple!"

A dog barked somewhere, and there was a shriek like that of a cat when her tail is stepped on. The alarm of the servants soon infected the chickens, the geese, the turkeys that

---

1. **zemstvo** [zyēm′stvô]: local administrative council in czarist Russia.

2. **versts:** Russian measurement of distance. One verst is approximately two thirds of a mile.
3. **aulic** [ô′lik] **councilor:** adviser to the royal court.

had been wandering about. Presently a fellow who looked like a flunkey emerged from the kitchen; he screwed up his eyes at the Kovalyovs and, putting on his jacket as he went, ran toward the house. All this excitement seemed ridiculous to the Kovalyovs and they could hardly keep from laughing.

"What funny faces!" said Kovalyov, exchanging glances with his wife. "They look at us as if we were savages."

Finally, there emerged from the house a little man with a shaven, wizened face and tousled hair. He scraped his feet, which were thrust into torn, embroidered slippers, as he bowed, smiled sourly, and stared at the unbidden guests.

"Mr. Mikhailov?" Kovalyov began, raising his hat. "Permit me to introduce myself. . . . My wife and I read the notice of the Land Bank to the effect that your estate is for sale, and we have come to look it over. Perhaps we'll buy it. . . . Be so good as to show it to us."

Mikhailov became embarrassed, produced another forced smile, and blinked his eyes. In his confusion he mussed up his hair even more, and his shaven face assumed such a ludicrously sheepish and stunned expression that Kovalyov and his Verochka exchanged glances again and could not suppress smiles.

"Pleased to meet you . . ." he mumbled. "I'm at your service. . . . Did you have a long trip?"

"We're coming from Konkovo. We have a summer cottage there."

"So . . . a summer cottage . . . Wonderful! Excuse us, excuse us! We've just gotten up, and we haven't quite tidied the place."

Mikhailov, smiling sourly and rubbing his hands, led the visitors to the back of the house. Kovalyov put on his glasses and with the air of a knowledgeable tourist seeing the sights began to examine the estate. He started with the house. It was a stone structure built in a heavy, old-fashioned style, with armorial bearings, lions, and peeling plaster. The roof was badly in need of a coat of paint, the windowpanes were iridescent with age, grass was growing in the cracks between the steps. Everything was dilapidated and unkempt, but the prospective buyers liked the house on the whole. It had a poetic, modest, good-natured air, like an aged maiden aunt. In front, a few steps from the main entrance, a pond sparkled in the sun. Two ducks and a toy boat were floating on it. The pond was surrounded by birches of uniform height and thickness.

"Aha, you have a pond, too!" said Kovalyov, narrowing his eyes in the sun. "That's nice. Are there crucian[4] in it?"

"Yes, sir . . . There used to be carp there, too, but when we stopped cleaning the pond, all the carp died."

"Too bad," said Kovalyov, in a professorial manner. "A pond should be cleaned as often as possible, all the more so that the silt and water plants are excellent fertilizer for the fields. You know what, Vera? When we buy this estate, we'll build a summer house on piles in the pond with a bridge. I saw a summer house like that at Prince Afontov's place."

"We can have tea in the summer house," Verochka murmured sweetly.

"Of course . . . And what is that tower with a spire?"

"That's a guest house," Mikhailov replied.

"It looks out of place, somehow. We'll pull it down. Generally speaking, a good deal will have to be torn down here. A great deal!"

Suddenly a woman's weeping was distinctly heard. The Kovalyovs looked toward the house, but at that very moment one of the windows banged and two large tear-stained eyes flashed briefly behind the iridescent panes. Apparently, the woman who was crying grew ashamed of her tears, and, shutting the window, hid behind the curtain.

"Won't you look at the garden and the outbuildings?" Mikhailov started talking rapidly, wrinkling his lined face more noticeably and more sourly than ever. "Let's go . . . The most important thing, you know, is not the house, but . . . the grounds, and the rest. . . ."

---

4. **crucian:** fish of the carp family.

The Kovalyovs went to look at the stables and the outbuildings. The newly-fledged lawyer walked around each building, looked at it, sniffed at it and made a show of his knowledge of agronomy. He inquired about the acreage of the estate, the number of head of cattle, scolded Russia for the destruction of her forests, reproved Mikhailov for the large amount of manure he wasted, and so forth. He talked away and from time to time glanced at his Verochka, and she kept her loving eyes riveted on him and was thinking: "How clever this man of mine is!"

During the inspection of the barn, the sound of crying was heard again.

"Please tell me, who is that crying?" asked Verochka.

Mikhailov waved his hand and turned aside.

"Strange," murmured Verochka, when the sobs turned into ceaseless hysterical weeping. "It's as though someone were being beaten or murdered."

"It's my wife, the Lord help her," said Mikhailov.

"But why is she crying?"

"A weak woman, Madam. She cannot bear to see her homestead sold."

"Why are you selling it, then?" asked Verochka.

"We're not selling it, it's the bank. . . ."

"Strange, why do you allow it?"

Mikhailov cast an astonished glance at Verochka's pink face and shrugged his shoulders.

"We must pay interest on the mortgage," he said. "Twenty-one hundred rubles every year. And where are we to get it? And that makes her cry. Women are weak, you know. It grieves her to lose her home, she is sorry for me, for the children . . . and she is ashamed before the servants. Near the pond you were pleased to observe," he said, turning to Kovalyov, "that this had to be torn down, that should be built, and for her it's like a knife in her heart."

Passing the house on the way back, Vera saw in the window the close-cropped head of a high school boy and two little girls—obviously Mikhailov's children. What did they think about, looking at the purchasers? Verochka seemed to understand their thoughts. . . . When she got into the carriage to drive back, the fresh morning and the dreams of a romantic nook had lost all charm for her.

"This is all very disagreeable!" she said to her husband. "Really, why not give them the twenty-one hundred? Let them live on their estate."

"How clever you are!" Kovalyov laughed. "Of course, I'm sorry for them, but it's their own fault. Who forced them to mortgage the estate? Why have they neglected it so? We really oughtn't to be sorry for them. If one were to work this estate intelligently, introduce scientific farming . . . raise livestock, one could make a very good thing of it here . . . But these wasters—they've done nothing. . . . He is probably a drunkard and a gambler—did you see his mug?—and she is a woman of fashion and a spendthrift. I know those characters!"

"How do you know them, Styopa?"[5]

"I know! He complains that he can't pay the interest on the mortgage. How is it that he can't scrape two thousand together? If you were to introduce scientific farming . . . use fertilizer and raise livestock . . . if you take account of the climatic and economic conditions, you can make a living on a couple of acres!"

Styopa kept chatting all the way to the house; his wife listened to him and believed every word he said, but her former mood had vanished. She could not stop thinking of Mikhailov's forced smile and the two eyes big with tears of which she had caught a glimpse.

When, later on, jaunty Styopa attended the auction and purchased the estate with her dowry, she was distressed. . . . Her imagination did not stop picturing Mikhailov and his family getting into a carriage and leaving their old home with tears. And the gloomier and more touching the pictures that her imagination painted, the jauntier Styopa became. With the utmost aplomb he talked about scientific

---

5. **Styopa** [styô′pə]: affectionate form of Stepan.

farming, ordered books and periodicals on agronomy, made fun of Mikhailov. His agricultural planning always ended in the boldest, most shameful bragging. . . .

"You'll see," he would say. "I am no Mikhailov, I'll show you how to farm. Yes!"

When the Kovalyovs moved to deserted Mikhalkovo, the first thing that Verochka noticed was a few intimate traces left behind by the former occupants: a program of lessons written in a childish hand, a headless doll, a penciled scribble on the wall: "Natasha is a fool," a titmouse coming for its customary crumbs, and the like. There was much repainting and repapering to be done, there was much to be torn down, in order to erase the memory of other people's misfortune.

STUDY QUESTIONS

Recalling

1. Give three reasons for the Kovalyovs' happiness at the beginning of the story.
2. List three things that the Kovalyovs plan to change when they buy the estate. Give three examples of Mikhailov's mismanagement of the estate.
3. What reason does Mikhailov give for his wife's crying? How does her crying affect Verochka's mood?
4. What does Verochka suggest to her husband that they do instead of buying the estate? Summarize her husband's reaction.
5. Name three traces of the Mikhailovs that linger in the house after they are gone. What does Chekhov say is the purpose of repainting and repapering?

Interpreting

6. Describe the mood at the beginning of the story, and give at least four details that create it. At what point in the story does the mood begin to change? Give at least four details that help to change the mood.
7. Contrast Kovalyov's position in life with Mikhailov's. What do the differences suggest about life?

Extending

8. What effect does the Mikhailov family's misfortune have on the Kovalyovs? In general, what effect do other people's misfortunes have on a person's life?

VIEWPOINT

After Chekhov's death Leo Tolstoy praised him as an incomparable artist and then said:

He was unreservedly candid, and that is a great quality; he wrote about what he saw and how he saw it. . . . And because of that unreserved candor he created new, to my mind, completely new, forms of writing for the whole world, the like of which I have never met anywhere!

■ Find two examples of Chekhov's candor in this story, and tell why each is effective.

COMPOSITION

Writing About the Total Effect

■ What is the total effect of "Other People's Misfortune"? Answer this question in a brief essay. First describe the impact that Chekhov's story had on you. Then explain how Chekhov uses each of the following elements to achieve this effect: (a) plot, (b) characterization, (c) setting, (d) point of view, (e) theme, (f) tone, and (g) symbolism. *For help with this assignment, refer to Lesson 8 in the Writing About Literature Handbook at the back of this book.*

Writing a Description

■ Imagine that you move into a new home and, like Verochka, find traces of the former owners. Describe an object that has been left behind by a former inhabitant of the house. Use specific details that give clues about who the person was and what happened to him or her.

Guy de Maupassant   *1850–1893*

Guy de Maupassant [gē də mō′pə sänt′] ranks among the world's greatest writers of short stories. Although he was the child of affluent parents, Maupassant grew up among the children of peasants and sailors who lived near his mother's estate in northern France. When he went away to school, he spent Sundays with Gustave Flaubert [goos tav′ flō bär′], the great French novelist who was his mother's childhood friend. Flaubert encouraged the young Maupassant in his literary efforts and suggested that he write poetry first to practice clarity and conciseness. After serving in the Franco-Prussian War of 1870, Maupassant became a government clerk but devoted his free time to writing. Flaubert introduced him to the leading writers of his time including the great Émile Zola at whose gatherings he participated in discussions about artistic and literary theories. Maupassant himself wrote furiously and produced over three hundred short stories in all.

Maupassant's works show the influence of Flaubert's and Zola's literary theories. Through Flaubert Maupassant adopted **Realism**, the literary movement that seeks to report life as exactly as possible. He also attended to Zola's theory of **Naturalism**, an extreme form of Realism that usually concentrates on lower economic classes and applies scientific studies of humanity to characterization. Maupassant demonstrates his debt to Flaubert and Zola in his lack of emotion and romance, in his insightful observation and accurate description of common people, in his search for the precise word and the perfect phrase. In spite of these major influences, however, the terse, ironic view of life expressed in many of his stories—including "A Piece of String"—is original and entirely his own.

Guy de Maupassant

A Piece of String

Translated by Raymond R. Canon

Along all the roads around Goderville the peasants and their wives were coming toward the burgh because it was market day. The men were proceeding with slow steps, the whole body bent forward at each movement of their long twisted legs, deformed by their hard work, by the weight on the plow which, at the same time, raised the left shoulder and swerved the figure, by the reaping of the wheat which made the knees spread to make a firm "purchase,"[1] by all the slow and painful labors of the country. Their blouses, blue, "stiff-starched," shining as if varnished, ornamented with a little design in white at the neck and wrists, puffed about their bony bodies, seemed like balloons ready to carry them off. From each of them a head, two arms, and two feet protruded.

Some led a cow or a calf by a cord, and their wives, walking behind the animal, whipped its haunches with a leafy branch to hasten its progress. They carried large baskets on their arms from which, in some cases, chickens and, in others, ducks thrust out their heads. And they walked with a quicker, livelier step than their husbands. Their spare straight figures were wrapped in a scanty little shawl, pinned over their flat bosoms, and their heads were enveloped in a white cloth glued to the hair and surmounted by a cap.

Then a wagon passed at the jerky trot of a nag, shaking strangely, two men seated side by side and a woman in the bottom of the vehicle, the latter holding on to the sides to lessen the hard jolts.

In the public square of Goderville there was a crowd, a throng of human beings and animals mixed together. The horns of the cattle, the tall hats with long nap of the rich peasant, and the headgear of the peasant women rose above the surface of the assembly. And the clamorous, shrill, screaming voices made a continuous and savage din which sometimes was dominated by the robust lungs of some countryman's laugh, or the long lowing of a cow tied to the wall of a house.

All that smacked of the stable, the dairy and the dirt heap, hay and sweat, giving forth that unpleasant odor, human and animal, peculiar to the people of the field.

Maître[2] Hauchecome, of Breaute, had just arrived at Goderville, and he was directing his steps toward the public square, when he perceived upon the ground a little piece of string. Maître Hauchecome, economical like a true Norman,[3] thought that everything useful ought to be picked up, and he bent painfully, for he suffered from rheumatism. He took the bit of thin cord from the ground and began to roll it carefully when he noticed Maître Malandain, the harness-maker, on the threshold of his door, looking at him. They had heretofore had business together on the subject of a halter,

---

1. **"purchase"**: position of the body appropriate for moving a large weight.

2. **Maître** [mātr]: French for "Master."
3. **Norman:** native of Normandy in northern France.

and they were on bad terms, being both good haters. Maître Hauchecome was seized with a sort of shame to be seen thus by his enemy, picking a bit of string out of the dirt. He concealed his "find" quickly under his blouse, then in his trousers' pocket; then he pretended to be still looking on the ground for something which he did not find, and he went toward the market, his head forward, bent double by his pains.

He was soon lost in the noisy and slowly moving crowd, which was busy with interminable bargainings. The peasants milked, went and came, perplexed, always in fear of being cheated, not daring to decide, watching the vendor's eye, ever trying to find the trick in the man and the flaw in the beast.

The women, having placed their great baskets at their feet, had taken out the poultry which lay upon the ground, tied together by the feet, with terrified eyes and scarlet crests.

They heard offers, stated their prices with a dry air and impassive face, or perhaps, suddenly deciding on some proposed reduction, shouted to the customer who was slowly going away: "All right, Maître Authirne, I'll give it to you for that."

Then little by little the square was deserted, and the Angelus[4] ringing at noon, those who had stayed too long, scattered to their shops.

At Jourdain's the great room was full of people eating, as the big court was full of vehicles of all kinds, carts, gigs, wagons, dump carts, yellow with dirt, mended and patched, raising their shafts to the sky like two arms, or perhaps with their shafts in the ground and their backs in the air.

Just opposite the diners seated at the table, the immense fireplace, filled with bright flames, cast a lively heat on the backs of the row on the right. Three spits were turning on which were chickens, pigeons, and legs of mutton; and an appetizing odor of roast beef and gravy dripping over the nicely browned skin rose from the hearth, increased the jovialness, and made everybody's mouth water.

All the aristocracy of the plow ate there, at Maître Jourdain's, tavern keeper and horse dealer, a rascal who had money.

The dishes were passed and emptied, as were the jugs of yellow cider. Everyone told his affairs, his purchases, and sales. They discussed the crops. The weather was favorable for the green things but not for the wheat.

Suddenly the drum beat in the court, before the house. Everybody rose except a few indifferent persons, and ran to the door, or to the windows, their mouths still full and napkins in their hands.

After the public crier had ceased his drumbeating, he called out in a jerky voice, speaking his phrases irregularly:

"It is hereby made known to the inhabitants of Goderville, and in general to all persons present at the market, that there was lost this morning, on the road to Benzeville, between nine and ten o'clock, a black leather pocketbook containing five hundred francs[5] and some business papers. The finder is requested to return same with all haste to the mayor's office or to Maître Fortune Houlbreque of Manneville, there will be twenty francs reward."

Then the man went away. The heavy roll of the drum and the crier's voice were again heard at a distance.

Then they began to talk of this event discussing the chances that Maître Houlbreque had of finding or not finding his pocketbook.

And the meal concluded. They were finishing their coffee when a chief of the gendarmes[6] appeared upon the threshold.

He inquired:

"Is Maître Hauchecome, of Breaute, here?"

Maître Hauchecome, seated at the other end of the table, replied:

---

4. **Angelus:** prayer recited in the morning, at noon, and at night; the church bells that ring to announce the prayer.

5. **five hundred francs:** French currency worth about one hundred dollars when the story was written.
6. **gendarmes** [zhän′därm]: armed police.

"Here I am."

And the officer resumed:

"Maître Hauchecome, will you have the goodness to accompany me to the mayor's office? The mayor would like to talk to you."

The peasant, surprised and disturbed, swallowed at a draught his tiny glass of brandy, rose, and, even more bent than in the morning, for the first steps after each rest were specially difficult, set out, repeating: "Here I am, here I am."

The mayor was awaiting him, seated on an armchair. He was the notary of the vicinity, a stout, serious man, with pompous phrases.

"Maître Hauchecome," said he, "you were seen this morning to pick up, on the road to Benzeville, the pocketbook lost by Maître Houlbreque, of Manneville."

The countryman, astounded, looked at the mayor, already terrified, by this suspicion resting on him without his knowing why.

"Me? Me? Me pick up the pocketbook?"

"Yes, you, yourself."

"Word of honor, I never heard of it."

"But you were seen."

"I was seen, me? Who says he saw me?"

"Monsieur Malandain, the harnessmaker."

The old man remembered, understood, and flushed with anger.

"Ah, he saw me, the clodhopper, he saw me pick up this string, here, M'sieu',[7] the Mayor." And rummaging in his pocket he drew out the little piece of string.

But the mayor, incredulous, shook his head.

"You will not make me believe, Maître Hauchecome, that Monsieur Malandain, who is a man worthy of credence, mistook this cord for a pocketbook."

The peasant, furious, lifted his hand, spat at one side to attest his honor, repeating:

"It is nevertheless the truth of the good God, the sacred truth, M'sieu' the Mayor. I repeat it on my soul and my salvation."

The mayor resumed:

---

7. **M'sieu'** [mə syœ′]: short form of "monsieur," French for "mister" or "sir."

"After picking up the object, you stood like a stilt, looking a long while in the mud to see if any piece of money had fallen out."

The good, old man choked with indignation and fear.

"How anyone can tell—how anyone can tell—such lies to take away an honest man's reputation! How can anyone—"

There was no use in his protesting, nobody believed him. He was confronted with Monsieur Malandain, who repeated and maintained his affirmation. They abused each other for an hour. At his own request, Maître Hauchecome was searched, nothing was found on him.

Finally the mayor, very much perplexed, discharged him with the warning that he would consult the public prosecutor and ask for further orders.

The news had spread. As he left the mayor's office, the old man was surrounded and questioned with a serious or bantering curiosity, in which there was no indignation. He began to tell the story of the string. No one believed him. They laughed at him.

He went along, stopping his friends, beginning endlessly his statement and his protestations, showing his pockets turned inside out, to prove that he had nothing.

They said:

"Old rascal, get out!"

And he grew angry, becoming exasperated, hot, and distressed at not being believed, not knowing what to do and always repeating himself.

Night came. He must depart. He started on his way with three neighbors to whom he pointed out the place where he had picked up the bit of string; and all along the road he spoke of his adventure.

In the evening he took a turn in the village of Breaute, in order to tell it to everybody. He only met with incredulity.

It made him ill at night.

The next day about one o'clock in the afternoon, Marius Paumelle, a hired man in the employ of Maître Breton, husbandman at Ymanville, returned the pocketbook and its contents to Maître Houlbreque of Manneville.

This man claimed to have found the object in the road; but not knowing how to read, he had carried it to the house and given it to his employer.

The news spread through the neighborhood. Maître Hauchecome was informed of it. He immediately went the circuit and began to recount his story completed by the happy climax. He was in triumph.

"What grieved me so much was not the thing itself, as the lying. There is nothing so shameful as to be placed under a cloud on account of a lie."

He talked of his adventure all day long, he told it on the highway to people who were passing by, in the wineshop to people who were drinking there, and to persons coming out of church the following Sunday. He stopped strangers to tell them about it. He was calm now, and yet something disturbed him without his knowing exactly what it was. People had the air of joking while they listened. They did not seem convinced. He seemed to feel that remarks were being made behind his back.

On Tuesday of the next week he went to the market at Goderville, urged solely by the necessity he felt of discussing the case.

Malandain, standing at his door, began to laugh on seeing him pass. Why?

He approached a farmer from Crequetot, who did not let him finish, and giving him a thump in the stomach said to his face:

"You big rascal."

Then he turned his back on him.

Maître Hauchecome was confused, why was he called a big rascal?

When he was seated at the table, in Jourdain's tavern he commenced to explain "the affair."

A horse dealer from Monvilliers called to him:

"Come, come, old sharper, that's an old trick; I know all about your piece of string!"

Hauchecome stammered:

"But since the pocketbook was found."

But the other man replied:

"Shut up, papa, there is one that finds, and there is one that reports. At any rate you are mixed with it."

The peasant stood choking. He understood. They accused him of having had the pocketbook returned by a confederate, by an accomplice.

He tried to protest. All the table began to laugh.

He could not finish his dinner and went away, in the midst of jeers.

He went home ashamed and indignant, choking with anger and confusion, the more dejected that he was capable with his Norman cunning of doing what they had accused him of, and ever boasting of it as of a good turn. His innocence to him, in a confused way, was impossible to prove, as his sharpness was known. And he was stricken to the heart by the injustice of the suspicion.

Then he began to recount the adventures again, prolonging his history every day, adding each time, new reasons, more energetic protestations, more solemn oaths which he imagined and prepared in his hours of solitude, his whole mind given up to the story of the string. He was believed so much the less as his defense was more complicated and his arguing more subtle.

"Those are lying excuses," they said behind his back.

He felt it, consumed his heart over it, and wore himself out with useless efforts. He wasted away before their very eyes.

The wags now made him tell about the string to amuse them, as they make a soldier who has been on a campaign tell about his battles. His mind, touched to the depth, began to weaken.

Toward the end of December he took to his bed.

He died in the first days of January, and in the delirium of his death struggles he kept claiming his innocence, reiterating:

"A piece of string, a piece of string—look—here it is, M'sieu' the Mayor."

STUDY QUESTIONS

Recalling

1. Give five details that demonstrate the bustling activity of the market at Goderville.
2. Why does Hauchecome pick up the string? Why does he hide it?
3. What is Hauchecome accused of? What evidence is offered against him?
4. What happens to convince Hauchecome that he should be considered innocent? What is the reaction of the townspeople?
5. What finally happens to Hauchecome? What are his final words in the story?

Interpreting

6. Why do you think Maupassant begins the story with a detailed description of the peasants and the market?
7. In what sense is Hauchecome responsible for what happens to him? In what sense is he an innocent victim?

Extending

8. What aspects of human nature do you think Maupassant was trying to illustrate with this story? Do you agree with his depiction of human nature? Why or why not?

LITERARY FOCUS

Realism

We use the word *realism* in its broadest sense to determine whether events, characters, and settings in fiction are lifelike or improbable. More specifically, however, **Realism** began in France, England, and America as a nineteenth-century reaction to Romanticism. It is a literary movement that seeks to report life as exactly as possible. Realistic authors write about common working people and recognizable situations. They report life as they see it without moral judgment or sentimentality. The beginnings of Realism can be traced in France to Honoré de Balzac and Gustave Flaubert, in England to George Eliot and Charles Dickens, and in America to Hamlin Garland and Jack London.

Thinking About Realism

1. Explain how Hauchecome qualifies as a Realistic character. In what sense is the setting of the story Realistic? Give examples.
2. In what sense does Maupassant avoid moral judgment and sentimentality in "A Piece of String"?

VOCABULARY

Sentence Completions

Each of the following sentences contains a blank with four possible words for completing the sentence. The words are from "A Piece of String." Choose the word that completes each sentence most logically and that uses the word *as the word is used in the selection.* Write the number of each item and the letter of your choice on a separate sheet.

1. The interior of the old house was decorated with beautifully _____ moldings.
   (a) deformed   (c) puffed
   (b) ornamented   (d) spare

2. The night was pierced by the distant, _____ cries of the peacock.
   (a) scanty   (c) jerky
   (b) shrill   (d) robust

3. Weary and lost in thought, all of us assembled in the room wore _____ expressions.
   (a) perplexed   (c) impassive
   (b) patched   (d) pompous

4. After an hour of waiting, my sister grew _____ and began to pace across the room.
   (a) incredulous   (c) livelier
   (b) exasperated   (d) astounded

5. The music she played was slow and rather wistful and did not help to dispel the _____ mood of the evening.
   (a) indignant   (c) confused
   (b) impossible   (d) solemn

COMPARING WRITERS

1. Compare at least two of the following stories: "How Much Land Does a Man Need?" "Other People's Misfortune," and "A Piece of String." Give specific examples from each story to explain which story you consider more qualified to be considered Realistic.
2. "How Much Land Does a Man Need?" and "Other People's Misfortune" are Russian; "A Piece of String" is French. Compare at least two of these stories. Explain how each has events and settings that seem peculiar to the culture of its writer. Then explain how each has characters and themes that are universal.

Charles Baudelaire   *1821–1867*

Charles Baudelaire [shärl bōd′əl ār′] profoundly influenced the direction of modern poetry in his native France and in Britain and America. Baudelaire, who was born in Paris, was a rebellious and moody child. As a student he was a cynical, insolent loner. When he inherited a small property, he established himself in the colorful Latin Quarter of Paris. There he mingled with actors and artists, and he turned to writing. His first two books were works of art criticism. Baudelaire knew English and as a result was familiar with writers generally unknown in France. In 1846 he discovered the American writer Edgar Allan Poe (1809–1849), in whose works he found the themes, images, and the very words that he had himself dreamed of writing. Baudelaire translated Poe, who subsequently became better known in France than in the United States and who had a greater impact on French poetry than on American.

A **symbol** is a concrete object, person, or situation that represents something beyond its literal meaning. According to Baudelaire, the "visible universe is nothing but a storehouse of images and of signs" that represent the spiritual world. He called these symbols "correspondences" between the two worlds and asserted the duty of the artist to express them. These theories helped to establish the Symbolist movement in poetry. **Symbolist poems** are richly musical works built around vivid symbols whose larger meanings are implied but not directly stated. Baudelaire's major work is *Flowers of Evil* (1857), a collection of poems that so enraged the French public and censors with its concept of evil that Baudelaire and his publisher were both fined. Today, however, the work is universally considered a masterpiece because of its control of language, careful plotting of effects (a lesson learned from Poe), and sensitivity to the human spirit. "The Sun" is taken from the second section of *Flowers of Evil,* entitled "Pictures of Paris." The poem relates the external world of a Parisian landscape to the inner world of a poet.

Charles Baudelaire

The Sun

Translated by C. F. MacIntyre

Along the old slums where the ruined shutters
hang, where secret vices find a shelter,
when the harsh sun's darts with redoubled heat
fall on town and field, on the roofs and the wheat,
5 I practice my fantastic fencing alone,
stumbling on words as if on paving stones,
sniffing in every corner for chance rhymes,
colliding with verses dreamed at other times.

This foster-father, enemy of chlorosis,[1]
10 wakens in the fields both poems and roses;
he turns to vapor the troubles of our lives,
and fills with honey the brains and the beehives.
It is he restores the cripples, bids them be
gay and fresh as young girls; it is he
15 commands the harvest to multiply and mature
in the deathless heart which would always be in flower.

Shining on the cities, he exalts,
like a poet, all he sees, despite its faults,
and enters like a king, without noise or vassals,[2]
20 all the hospitals and all the castles.

---

1. **chlorosis** [klôr ō′sis]: lack of green color in plants, caused by
insufficient sunlight.
2. **vassals:** subjects to a lord or king.

STUDY QUESTIONS

Recalling

1. Name three activities of the speaker in the first stanza. What is the sun doing?
2. Identify at least five activities of the "foster-father" in the second and third stanzas.

Interpreting

3. Describe the poem's speaker. Explain the term "fantastic fencing."

4. Why does the speaker use the label "foster-father"? What qualities does the "foster-father" share with a poet and with a king?
5. Give examples from the poem of images of ruin and rebirth. What message is implied in the way the poem mixes these images?
6. What relationship between the sun and poetry is presented in each stanza? What does the poem imply about the creation and effect of poetry?

Arthur Rimbaud   *1854–1891*

Arthur Rimbaud [är toor′ ram bō′] composed his greatest poetry in five stormy years between the ages of fifteen and twenty. He was born in Charleville, a small town in northeastern France. He was raised piously and strictly. At school he demonstrated insight and originality and, encouraged by a teacher, began to write at the age of ten. Between the ages of fifteen and seventeen he left home three times for Paris or Belgium. Once he was arrested and sent home; the other times he almost starved and begged his way back. Throughout this time Rimbaud wrote poetry. In 1871 he sent his poems to the poet Paul Verlaine in Paris. Verlaine, thinking the seventeen-year-old an older man, invited him to Paris. Verlaine took Rimbaud as his protégé; they traveled together and became close friends. The relationship, however, was turbulent and ended in 1873 when Verlaine shot Rimbaud and went to prison for two years. At the age of twenty, Rimbaud gave up writing and disappeared; even Verlaine believed him dead. He spent the remaining years of his life as a longshoreman in the southern French port of Marseilles, a soldier in the Dutch army in the Far East, a member of a touring circus in Scandinavia, a quarry boss in Cyprus, and a gunrunner in Ethiopia. He died at the age of thirty-seven.

Rimbaud described his poetic theory as "the systematic derangement of all the senses." He lived his life in a manner calculated to achieve an intensity of experience that he believed necessary to understand the spiritual world. To express incommunicable truth, he broke the rules of language and syntax; to evoke spiritual sensations he used language almost as a chant or incantation. *A Season in Hell* (1873) is an account of his relationship with Verlaine, the only work that he himself published. His other collections were published later by Verlaine. The verse and prose poems collected in *Illuminations* (1886) established him as a leading Symbolist poet. In "The Gypsy Poet" Rimbaud pictures himself as a vagabond, wandering, observing, dreaming, and searching for rhymes.

Arthur Rimbaud

The Gypsy Poet

Translated by Brian Hill

Fists probing my torn pockets, off I'd wander,
My overcoat more holes than cloth and I
Poetry's bondslave under the open sky;
Oh lord, what splendid dreams of love I'd squander!
5 Torn were my only trousers at the knees;
As inn-sign in the sky, the Great Bear[1] shone
And stars, like twinkling silk, smiled down upon
Tom Thumb,[2] the dreamer, shelling rhymes like peas.

I'd listen from the roadside on those fine
10 September nights while dew-drops' heady wine
Moistened my brow; fantastic shadows pressed
About me as in search of rhymes I'd tug
The laces of my worn-out boots and hug
One foot just like a lyre[3] against my chest.

---

1. **Great Bear:** Ursa Major, a northern constellation of stars.
2. **Tom Thumb:** character in folklore whose name refers to his tiny size;
also the name of an American dwarf who toured internationally with P. T.
Barnum's circus during the nineteenth century.
3. **lyre:** stringed instrument like a harp.

STUDY QUESTIONS

Recalling

1. Give three examples of the speaker's poverty.
2. What relationship does the speaker claim to poetry? Name three activities of the speaker in the poem.
3. Find two examples of nature in the poem. What does the speaker say about each?

Interpreting

4. What do you think is the speaker's attitude toward poverty? What is the speaker's image of himself?
5. What is the relationship between nature and the speaker's poetry?
6. Find at least two symbols in the poem, and explain their meaning.

Extending

7. Like Baudelaire in "The Sun," Rimbaud hints at a poetic theory in "The Gypsy Poet." Compare and contrast their creative theories as implied in the poems.

Paul Verlaine   *1844–1896*

Out of the fragments of a broken life, Paul Verlaine created poetry of exceptional loveliness and musicality and of haunting sadness. He was born in Metz, France, and went to school in Paris. Work as a municipal clerk allowed him time for creative efforts. Verlaine's life alternated between periods of self-indulgence and excess and periods of repentance and reform. In one attempt at rehabilitation, in 1870, he married. One year later, however, he met the young poet Arthur Rimbaud and joined him in his wanderings. The stormy friendship of the two poets collapsed disastrously when Verlaine shot and wounded Rimbaud—an action that cost Verlaine two years in prison. Upon his release he converted to Catholicism in yet another attempt to rebuild his life. In later years he lived in England and worked as a teacher of French.

Like the other Symbolists, Verlaine believed that poetry should suggest rather than state its meaning, evoke a mood rather than create a picture. Like Baudelaire, he sought to reveal symbols of the spiritual world, the secret "correspondences" between the spiritual and tangible worlds. In addition, he believed that poetry should yield to "music above all." In poems such as "Autumn Song," Verlaine achieves a vague, misty effect and a music that is quiet but poignant.

Paul Verlaine

Autumn Song

Translated by C. F. MacIntyre

With long sobs
the violin-throbs
 of autumn wound
my heart with languorous
5 and monotonous
 sound.

Choking and pale
when I mind the tale
 the hours keep,
10 my memory strays
down other days
 and I weep;

and I let me go
where ill winds blow,
15 now here, now there,
harried and sped
even as a dead
 leaf, anywhere.

STUDY QUESTIONS

Recalling

1. To what two things does the speaker compare the sound of autumn in the first stanza?
2. In the second stanza what causes the speaker to weep?
3. In the third stanza to what does the speaker compare himself? Why?

Interpreting

4. What mood does the speaker identify with autumn in the first stanza? What words, images, and sounds in the first stanza create this mood?
5. What is "the tale the hours keep"? Explain how it affects the speaker's mood.
6. Why has the speaker become a wanderer?
7. Explain why "Autumn Song" is an appropriate title for the poem.

Extending

8. Do you agree with the speaker's reaction to the passing of time and the actions that result? Why or why not?

LITERARY FOCUS

French Symbolist Poetry

Symbolist poems are richly musical works built around vivid symbols whose larger meanings are implied but not directly stated. A **symbol** is a concrete object, person, or situation that represents something beyond its literal meaning. A reaction to Realism, the Symbolist movement arose in France during the last half of the nineteenth century with Baudelaire, Rimbaud, and Verlaine and continued into the twentieth century with poets such as Rilke and Valéry.

The Symbolists considered the proper function of art to be the evocation of experience, not the mere description of reality. For example, in "The Sun" Baudelaire evokes the warmth of the sun and its effect on our physical and spiritual lives. The Symbolists saw the emotions as the proper subject of art. The poet's emotions, however, are fleeting and inexpressible. Therefore, the Symbolists sought to create a system of symbols to suggest any thought or feeling. The meaning of the symbols, however, is only implied, and the reader is free to interpret them personally. For example,

in "The Sun" Baudelaire compares a poet to any person "stumbling" through life, dreaming and searching for meaning.

Thinking About Symbolist Poetry

■ Explain how "Autumn Song" expresses experience through symbols and sounds. In what sense is the poem deliberately vague? Give examples from the poem.

COMPOSITION

Writing a Comparison/Contrast

■ Compare and contrast Verlaine's poem with John Keats's "To Autumn" (page 389). To do so, discuss similarities and differences in the two poems and the relative success of each poem in evoking autumn. You may want to consider the following: (a) sound techniques, (b) sensory images, and (c) word choice. *For help with this assignment, refer to Lesson 2 in the Writing About Literature Handbook at the back of this book.*

Writing a Description

■ Write a description in prose or poetry of a season that you either love or dread. To do this, use images that suggest your feelings about the season.

COMPARING ENGLISH AND WESTERN WRITERS

1. The Symbolist movement began in France but strongly influenced British and Irish writing well into the twentieth century. Compare at least one poem by Baudelaire, Rimbaud, or Verlaine with a poem by William Butler Yeats (page 531) or T. S. Eliot (page 541). To what extent is the sound of each poem responsible for its mood? What musical techniques does each poem employ?
2. Symbolist poems merely suggest the meanings of their symbols and enable the reader to form personal interpretations. Compare at least one poem by Baudelaire, Rimbaud, or Verlaine with a poem by Yeats or Eliot. Cite the central symbols in each poem. In what sense are meanings merely suggested? To what extent must the reader supply the meaning of each poem?

Key to Illustrations appears on page 923.

EUROPE
THE TWENTIETH CENTURY

1900—Present

"It was the best of times, it was the worst of times. . . ." As Charles Dickens reminds us in *A Tale of Two Cities,* every age seems both a pinnacle and an abyss to those who live through it. The twentieth century, however, seems to lay special claim to this distinction.

Two world wars, numerous revolutions and local wars, the threat of nuclear destruction—these and other facts of modern life have created a frightening new image of humanity, capable of global destruction. Yet we have also seen a tremendous expansion in our knowledge, our ability to improve our physical circumstances, and our concern for the alleviation of suffering. In short, we find ourselves simultaneously capable of doing more good *and* more harm than at any previous age in history.

Literature mirrors its time, and twentieth-century writers provide no easy answers. They do not offer, as earlier writers did, a coherent vision of life, a logical order that overarches and explains the contradictions of our time. Our writers reflect the fragmentation of the age or retreat into private literary worlds, perhaps in self-protection. Yet these authors do offer delight along with many moments of insight and solace. Perhaps now more than ever we can recognize how much we need what literature has to offer.

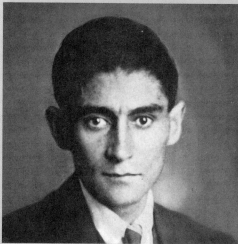

The Peace Conference at Versailles, France, 1919.

The Great War and Its Aftermath

Europe began the twentieth century in peace, riding a wave of scientific progress. The peace, however, was uneasy, threatened by German militarism and fragile alliances. Furthermore, new technology—the radio, the automobile, the X-ray—did little to ease the pressing problems of the poor in Europe's crowded, dirty cities. By the end of the nineteenth century, the religion of progress had come to include the idea that the poor need not accept their lot unquestioningly. As the new century began, the old Europe—a world of privilege, elegance, and tradition—was dying; it would be swept away forever by World War I.

The "war to end all wars" began in 1914 with the assassination of Archduke Franz Ferdinand, heir to the Austrian throne. Germany, an ally of Austria, used this event as a pretext for war in hopes of expanding its territory, especially in Africa, where England, France, Belgium, and Holland were growing rich from their colonies. German troops invaded Belgium, and in response, England and France declared war on Germany.

Victory for England, France, and their allies came after four long years of warfare. For most soldiers the war consisted of endless days and nights in muddy, rat-infested trenches, a deadly tedium broken only by bursts of artillery and short, futile runs into machine-gun fire. Personal heroism counted for little in this first modern war, in which tanks and machine guns mowed down men with horrifying ease.

The entrance of the United States into the conflict in 1917 helped break the stalemate and win the war for the Allies. When the fighting finally stopped in 1918, Europe had lost a whole generation of its young men; millions had died on both sides, and many more were physically and psychologically scarred by the conflict. The peacemaking process was devastating in its own way: The harsh terms of the 1919 treaty of Versailles [ver sī'] antagonized many Germans, planting a seed that would produce its own harvest in World War II.

World War I also delivered the death blow to czarist (imperial) Russia, long plagued by food shortages and government mismanagement. Uprisings during the early 1900s had brought Russia to the brink of revolution, and World War I sent it over that brink. In the Revolution of 1917 the czar was overthrown and replaced by a western-oriented government that was itself replaced by a Communist regime led by a revolutionary intellectual named Nikolai Lenin. Lenin espoused the ideology of nineteenth-century German political economist Karl Marx, proclaiming a classless society in which all property belonged to the state. The new government executed the czar and his family and killed or imprisoned many members of the upper and middle classes. After Lenin's death Joseph Stalin emerged as the head of the increasingly repressive Russian state. The people themselves were theoretically in power, since the state was structured on a series of councils, or soviets. However, Stalin expanded and solidified his personal power through bloody purges.

World War II and the Modern World

A different form of totalitarianism developed west of Russia. After the war economic woes in Italy and Germany contributed to the rise of fascism, government based on dictatorship and the rule of force. One fascist, Benito Mussolini, came to power in Italy in 1922 by manipulating the public and brutalizing his opponents. One of Mussolini's chief admirers was Adolf Hitler, an Austrian whose

Political Drama, Robert Delaunay, collage, 1914.

National Socialist German Workers party, or Nazis, exploited the miseries of postwar Germany. Hitler's fanatical oratory appealed to many Germans by blaming their economic ills on Communists, foreigners, and Jews.

By 1934 Hitler was firmly in control of Germany, and he began a campaign of racial "purification," which consisted mainly of exterminating Jews. Hitler also built up military power to avenge Germany's defeat in World War I. He allied himself with Mussolini and with Japan, then fighting for territory in China. In 1937 Hitler and Mussolini supported the fascist General Francisco Franco in his rebellion against the Spanish republic. The Spanish civil war became a proving ground for the global conflict that was to follow.

When the war in Spain ended in a victory for Franco, Hitler moved on the rest of Europe, invading Austria and annexing part of Czechoslovakia in 1938. England and France went to war when German troops invaded Poland in September 1939. Germany struck decisively at city after city. When France fell in 1940, Hitler prepared for his invasion of Britain with massive air attacks. However, the Royal Air Force successfully defended Britain, and Hitler overreached himself by invading Russia in 1941. In December 1941, when the Japanese extended the war to the Pacific by

attacking the U.S. naval base at Pearl Harbor, the United States entered the war. Drained by fighting on several fronts, Germany finally succumbed to the combined strength of the Allies in May 1945. The war in the Pacific ended in August 1945, when the United States dropped atomic bombs on the Japanese cities of Hiroshima and Nagasaki.

The alliance between the Soviet Union and the western democracies crumbled soon after the war. Europe was divided into eastern and western spheres of influence. In the late 1940s and early 1950s a new type of struggle developed between the United States and the Soviet Union, a "cold war" in which the two superpowers engaged in verbal confrontations while building up huge arsenals of nuclear weapons.

The postwar period saw the end of colonialism and the dramatic economic recovery of the democracies of western Europe and Japan. In 1958 the countries of western Europe formed the

Common Market in order to cooperate with one another in developing economic policy. Such coordination became especially important in the troubled 1970s and 1980s, when inflation, unemployment, and energy shortages stalled economic growth.

The countries of western Europe were also drawn closer together by technology. In a world canopied by nuclear weapons and tied together by television, computers, and satellites, the nations of western Europe have found that the age-old differences that once divided them are far less important than the common ground they share.

Twentieth-Century Western Literature

During the first half of our century, artists tried to make sense of the upheavals that tore the world apart. Nothing had prepared people for the horrors of World War I or for the spiritual desolation that followed it. After the war many artistic and intellectual movements sprang up reflecting the feeling that people in the twentieth century had become alienated—cut off from the past, out of touch with old systems of belief, and divided even within their own minds and personalities.

One movement, for example, was called Dada; it deliberately trivialized itself by taking its name from the French word for "hobbyhorse." Dada was based on the premise that since life

Sigmund Freud in his consulting room in Vienna.

had no meaning, art should not have any meaning either. Similarly, surrealist artists created works that patched together unrelated images in dreamlike jumbles. The most influential intellectual current of the time, however, was undoubtedly Freudian psychology. Austrian doctor Sigmund Freud (1856–1939) formulated a group of theories about the working of the human mind that changed the modern outlook on life and continues to encourage a redefinition of human nature.

Writers living through the decades after World War II have had to take into account such diverse phenomena as television, nuclear arms, space travel, and computers, all of which have complicated human life within a very short time. Ironically, while mass communication has made it possible to reach more and more people, modern writers tend to write for smaller and smaller audiences, in contrast to the great writers of the past—Homer, Shakespeare, Dickens, Tolstoy—whose works reached a huge and diverse audience. Our writers demand that *readers participate* with them in creating the experience of literature—a demand that makes modern literature challenging, courageous, and exciting.

In Russia the Revolution of 1917 inspired a great burst of literary creativity, but by the late 1920s Stalin's government had begun to stifle free expression. Soviet censors prevented

poet Boris Pasternak (1890–1960) from publishing his novel *Dr. Zhivago* in Russia and forced him to refuse the Nobel Prize. His fellow poet Anna Akhmatova [ak ma′tō və] (1888–1966) also came under attack. Many Russian writers have since left their homeland for more liberal societies, among them novelists Vladimir Nabokov [nä bô′kôf] (1899–1977) and Aleksandr Solzhenitsyn [sōl′zhə nēt′sin] (born 1918). However, some Russian writers, like poet Yevgeny Yevtushenko [yev′too shen′kō] (born 1933), have stayed in Russia hoping and working for an easing of restrictions.

Spanish literature before the civil war was dominated by the critic-philosophers Miguel de Unamuno [oo′nə moo′nō] (1864–1936) and José Ortega y Gasset [ôr tä′ga ē′ ga set′] (1883–1955). Later, the Franco dictatorship engaged in brutal repression. Franco's soldiers murdered poet and dramatist Federico García Lorca (1899–1936), and Spain's

most influential poet, Nobel Prize winner Juan Ramón Jiménez [hēmä′neth] (1881–1958) exiled himself to protest Franco's policies.

In Italy during the fascist years Luigi Pirandello [pir′ən del′ō] (1867–1936) pioneered writing about the uncertain and contradictory aspects of experience and became Europe's most innovative playwright. Today the novelist Italo Calvino (born 1923) performs similarly inventive feats with fiction. Between Pirandello and Calvino, Italian literature flourished with the work of such writers as novelists Ignazio Silone [sē lō′nä] (1900–1978), Alberto Moravia [mō ra′vē ə] (born 1907), and Giorgio Bassani (born 1916), poet Eugenio Montale [mon ta′lä] (1896–1981), and historian and philosopher Benedetto Croce [krō′chä] (1866–1952).

Despite the agonies of two wars, German writers have produced a rich and varied body of work. Rainer Maria Rilke [ril′kə] (1875–1926), the greatest German poet of the century, was strongly influenced by the French Symbolists. His contemporaries include two of the towering figures in twentieth-century fiction, Franz Kafka (1883–1924) and Thomas Mann (1875–1955). Playwright Bertolt Brecht [brekt] (1898–1956) turned modern drama away from Realism and used the theater to express political and social concerns. In contrast, novelist Hermann Hesse [hes′ə]

A scene from Samuel Beckett's *Waiting for Godot.*

(1877–1962) searched in his popular fiction for a "pure life" apart from politics. In the postwar period novelists Günter Grass (born 1927) and Heinrich Böll (born 1917) and dramatists Rolf Hochhuth [hōk′hoōt] (born 1931) and Peter Weiss (born 1916) have portrayed the special experience of postwar Germany: doubt and guilt, complacency and prosperity, continuing questions.

Modern French literature has emphasized intellectual rather than political upheavals. The longstanding tradition of brilliant French criticism was carried forward by poet Paul Valéry [va lā rē′] (1871–1945) and the versatile writer of fiction and nonfiction, André Maurois [mô rwa′] (1885–1967). The novelist Marcel Proust [proōst] (1871–1922) wrote one of the most influential works of the century—*Remembrance of Things Past* (published in 1927), a series of novels that revolutionized the portrayal of time and human psychology. His fellow novelist André Gide [zhēd] (1869–1951) wrote works questioning conventional

ideas about truth and reality. Between the world wars the French theater also experienced a renaissance in the poetic dramas of Jean Giraudoux [zhē′rō doō′] (1882–1944), Jean Cocteau [kok tō′] (1891–1963), and Jean Anouilh [ôn′oō ē′] (born 1910). After World War II Jean-Paul Sartre [sart] (1905–1982) and Albert Camus [ka moō′] (1913–1960) dramatized in novels and plays the philosophy of existentialism [eg′zis ten′shə liz′əm], which holds that truth is a matter of human experience and that people create and define themselves by their own actions.

The period after the war also

saw the rise of a new type of drama in France called the Theater of the Absurd, which questioned not only the meaning of life but also the ability of the theater to portray life. These doubts are memorably and often comically expressed by Eugene Ionesco [yə nes′kō] (born 1912) and Samuel Beckett (born 1906), an Irishman who lives and writes in France, and who may well be the most influential writer of the postwar period. Beckett's great dramas *Waiting for Godot* and *Endgame,* as well as his novels and poetry, portray life and art approaching dead ends, yet with a bleak humor and beauty that touch audiences.

Like Beckett, many western writers throughout our century question the very basis of literature, but they continue to write. The literature they produce is diverse, difficult, fragmented, and highly personal. It provides passing moments of insight, not the coherent visions of Dante, Shakespeare, or Tolstoy. Yet perhaps it is out of such moments that, eventually, a new vision can be created.

POETRY

Rainer Maria Rilke *1875–1926*

Rainer [rī'nər] Maria Rilke [ril'kə], the celebrated German lyric poet, is considered one of the guiding influences of modern poetry. He was born in Prague in what is now Czechoslovakia. Rilke's childhood was unhappy; he later described it as a "primer of horror." His father claimed to be an aristocrat even though he came from peasant stock; his mother, who wore only black, was a snobbish woman who abandoned her family when Rilke was only ten years old. Young Rilke was sent to military and business schools, none of which suited his artistic temperament, and later attended the universities of Prague, Munich, and Berlin.

In 1901 Rilke married a sculptor, but the marriage could not accommodate the careers of two artists, and the couple separated after a year. The young poet traveled widely throughout Europe, associating with writers and artists wherever he went. In Paris he served as secretary to the famous sculptor Auguste Rodin [rō dan']. Influenced by Rodin's ideas about art, Rilke became convinced that the artist could achieve perfection through hard work and careful craftsmanship rather than through inspiration, as the Romantics believed. Rilke later shared his theories about art in his influential *Letters to a Young Poet* (published in 1929). Plagued by leukemia in his later years, Rilke withdrew from public life and lived in a medieval tower in Switzerland. While picking flowers he was pricked by a thorn and developed a fatal case of blood poisoning.

Rilke's poetry evolved considerably over time. His early poems, represented in his *Book of Hours* (1905), are neo-Romantic—that is, sentimental and overstated. As his writing matured, it became increasingly complex, unpredictable, and searching. Rilke sought external symbols of his internal visions and became a leader in the Symbolist movement, which had begun in the nineteenth century. His concerns include love, death, childhood fears, and the search for God. Spiritual questions haunted his work more and more as the years passed; his *Duino Elegies* (1912–1920) and *Sonnets to Orpheus* (1923) are intensely mystical. The isolation and self-examination in his work have come to be characteristic of much modern poetry. In addition, Rilke's innovative use of language has had a profound effect on modern literature. Master of the nuance, he writes poems that shimmer with multiple meanings, rich images, and musical effects.

While working with Rodin, Rilke developed his idea of the *ding-Gedict,* or "object poem," which aims to capture in poetry the vital, changeable essence of an object or creature. He once said, "If a thing is to speak to you, you must for a certain time regard it as the only thing that exists." In each of the following poems, Rilke devotes such attention to an animal, capturing its essence.

Rainer Maria Rilke

The Gazelle

Translated by C. F. MacIntyre

Dorcas Gazelle[1]

Enchanted one: how shall two chosen words
achieve the harmony of the pure rhyme
which in you like a signal comes and goes?
From your forehead the leafy lyre[2] climbs,

5 and all your being moves in sure accord,[3]
like those love-lyrics whose words softly flow:
rose petals laid upon the closed eyelids
of one grown weary, who no longer reads

but shuts his eyes to see you—swiftly brought,
10 as though each leg were charged with leaps but not
fired, as long as the neck holds the head

quiet to listen: as when in a green place
a bather in the woods is interrupted . . .
with the lake's shine on her averted face.

---

1. **Dorcas** [dôr′kəs] **Gazelle:** light-brown gazelle less
than two feet high.
2. **lyre:** small, stringed musical instrument resembling a
harp.
3. **accord:** harmony.

Rainer Maria Rilke

The Panther

Translated by C. F. MacIntyre

Jardin des Plantes,[1] Paris

His sight from ever gazing through the bars
has grown so blunt that it sees nothing more.
It seems to him that thousands of bars are
before him, and behind them nothing merely.

5 The easy motion of his supple stride,
which turns about the very smallest circle,
is like a dance of strength about a center
in which a mighty will stands stupefied.

Only sometimes when the pupil's film
10 soundlessly opens . . . then one image fills
and glides through the quiet tension of the limbs
into the heart and ceases and is still.

---

1. **Jardin des Plantes** [zhär dan′ dā plänt]: famous botanical and zoological gardens in Paris.

STUDY QUESTIONS

The Gazelle

Recalling

1. With what two words does Rilke begin his description of the gazelle? What sort of "harmony" does he see in the gazelle?
2. In line 6 to what does Rilke compare the gazelle's movement?
3. How does Rilke describe the gazelle's legs in lines 10–11? In lines 11–14 what image does Rilke use to describe the way the gazelle holds its head?

Interpreting

4. Where in the poem does Rilke use images of motion? Where does he use images of stillness? What impression of the gazelle does he create by mixing these images?

5. Find two references to music and two to poetry in "The Gazelle." Why might these references to arts be appropriate in describing a gazelle?
6. In what ways is the poem musical? What effect does Rilke create by making lines 4–14 into a single sentence?
7. What qualities does this poem present as the "essence" of the gazelle? What might the gazelle come to symbolize in the poem?

Extending

8. Why might a creature like a gazelle be "enchanted" in a way that human beings are not?

The Panther

Recalling

1. According to line 1 why has the panther's sight grown "blunt"? What does he seem to see, according to lines 3–4?

2. In what terms does Rilke describe the panther's motion in lines 5–6? To what does he compare this motion in lines 7–8?
3. According to lines 9–12 what does "one image" do "sometimes"?

Interpreting

4. Describe in your own words the actual situation of the panther in the poem.
5. What contrasting images does the second stanza apply to the panther? Why are these images appropriate to this particular panther?
6. Describe the panther's state of mind at the end of the poem. How does the "one image" change the panther? Is he better or worse off at the end of the poem than at the beginning? Why?
7. How does the poet feel about the panther, and how do you know? In what ways might this panther resemble a poet writing a poem?

Extending

8. What similar responses might people and animals have to the lack of freedom? How might people differ from animals in their response to captivity?

VOCABULARY

Analogies

An **analogy** is a comparison. Analogy items appear on vocabulary tests as double comparisons between two pairs of words. You may be given the first pair of words and asked to find or complete a second pair that has the same or a similar relationship as the first pair. For example, you would complete the analogy POUND : OUNCE : : _____ : _____ with the pair FOOT : INCH, since the first word in each pair represents a whole and the second word a part.

Each of the items in the next column begins with two related words in capital letters; the first capitalized word in each pair comes from the translation of one of Rilke's poems.

1. LYRE : STRING : :
   (a) harp : violin   (c) music : poetry
   (b) floor : board   (d) window : door
2. PETALS : STEM : :
   (a) leaves : branch   (c) stem : stern
   (b) fruit : vegetable (d) gazelle : panther
3. BLUNT : SHARP : :
   (a) boring :   (c) false :
       imaginative   ambiguous
   (b) rounded : curved   (d) durable : old
4. STUPEFIED : DULLED : :
   (a) intense : moderate (c) ignorant : wise
   (b) excited : afraid   (d) friendly : hostile
5. SOUNDLESSLY : QUIETLY : :
   (a) softly : loudly   (c) gently : kindly
   (b) dazzlingly : brightly (d) rapidly : quickly

COMPOSITION

Writing a Comparison/Contrast

Compare and contrast Rilke's two object poems, "The Gazelle" and "The Panther." First make a general statement about the two poems. Then point out the similarities between them, both in their content and Rilke's use of literary techniques such as imagery and sound effects. Go on to identify the differences in the two poems' content and form. End by explaining the different aspects of life that seem to be presented in the two poems. *For help with this assignment, refer to Lesson 2 in the Writing About Literature Handbook at the back of this book.*

Writing Two Poems About Motion

Write two poems describing the motion of two different animals or people. Choose subjects that present a definite contrast: for example, a hummingbird and a bear, or a ballerina and a tap dancer. In each poem use several different images to convey the distinct qualities of your subject's motion.

Paul Valéry   *1871–1945*

Paul Valéry [vä lā rē′] is known chiefly as the last of the great French Symbolist poets—an ironic fame, since for much of his life he refused to write any poetry at all. He was born in Sête, a Mediterranean fishing port where his father worked as a customs officer. Valéry originally intended to become a naval officer, but his poor skills in mathematics thwarted this ambition.

In his early twenties Valéry came to know the poetry of Stéphane Mallarmé, the French Symbolist poet, and befriended André Gide, another Symbolist. Between 1888 and 1891 Valéry wrote and published poetry in Symbolist magazines. However, emotional and artistic frustrations led him to abandon poetry altogether in 1892. He claimed that he was giving up all emotional interests in favor of the "Idol of the Intellect." Fascinated with the workings of the mind, Valéry began recording his thoughts as he woke every morning, and he continued to keep this record for the next fifty years. He served as secretary to the administrator of a news agency, devoting his spare time to philosophy and mathematics.

Two decades after Valéry renounced poetry, his friend Gide persuaded him to publish some of his early work. Writing an introductory poem rekindled Valéry's interest in poetry. When this poem, "La Jeune Parque" ("The Young Goddess of Fate") was finally published in 1917, Valéry became an overnight literary celebrity. However, he wrote little additional poetry and continued to insist that poetry was of little consequence to him.

Valéry was also a critic and essayist and frequently wrote about architecture, dance, and relationships among the various arts. Like Rilke (page 852) he believed that the poet should "calculate" his poems carefully, and he compared the career of the poet-artist to that of the engineer.

Valéry fills his poems with allusions to classical works, and he often takes his imagery from the natural world. Despite his fascination with the processes of pure reason, his poems are highly sensuous. These various traits mesh in "Helen," a dramatic monologue spoken by the legendary Helen of Troy, a character in Homer's *Iliad*. According to legend, Helen, fathered by the god Zeus and married to a Greek king, was abducted from Greece by the Trojan prince Paris. This abduction set off the long Trojan War, after which Helen returned to Greece with her husband. The sixteenth-century English poet Christopher Marlowe (see page 94) said that Helen's was "the face that launched a thousand ships." In the following poem Helen reflects on the war that was fought over her.

Paul Valéry

Helen

Translated by David Paul

Azure,[1] it is I! . . . come from the grottoes of death[2]
To hear the wave breaking on the resounding steps,
And again I can see the galleys in the dawns
Resurrected out of shadow on lines of golden oars.

5   My hands in their loneliness evoke those monarchs
Whose salt beards used to beguile my pure fingers;
I would weep. They would sing their cloudy triumphs,
And the gulfs glided by on the poops of their barks.[3]

I hear the deep conches and the military
10   Clarions ringing in cadence to the flying oars;
The clear song of the rowers enchains the tumult,

And the Gods, up-raised on the heroic prows
With their archaic smiles assaulted by the foam,
Stretch out towards me their fond and sculptured arms.

----

1. **Azure:** sky or heaven.
2. **grottoes of death:** The dead were often buried in cavelike crypts.
3. **poops . . . barks:** decks at the backs of their ships.

STUDY QUESTIONS

Recalling

1. According to lines 1–2, from where has Helen come, and what has she come to hear? What can she see "again"?
2. What emotion does Helen ascribe to her hands in line 5? What did Helen used to do when she was with the monarchs? What did they do?
3. What does Helen hear in lines 9–11? What does she see on the prows of the ships, and what do these figures do?

Interpreting

4. To whom is Helen speaking? Is she alive or dead? How do you know?

5. Where does Valéry use images of war? Where does he use images of love or beauty? Why might such images be mixed in the story of Helen of Troy?
6. Compare and contrast Helen's attitude toward the kings who fought for her with her feeling for the Gods.
7. What seems to be Helen's overall mood? What sounds and images help to evoke Helen's mood?
8. What aspects of human life might Valéry be symbolizing in Helen as she is portrayed here?

Extending

9. What are the joys and sorrows of revisiting a place that was once important to you?

Boris Pasternak   *1890–1960*

Perhaps the best-known writer of postrevolutionary Russia, Boris Pasternak has for fifty years been a poet without honor in his own country—at least as far as the Soviet government is concerned. He was born to an aristocratic, cultivated family in czarist Russia, with a well-known painter for a father and a pianist for a mother. Expecting to become a composer, the young Pasternak studied law and philosophy as well as music. After a trip to Italy in 1913, he expanded his interests to literature and began to write poetry.

When a leg injury prevented him from fighting in World War I, Pasternak went to the Ural Mountains to work in a factory. He returned to Moscow in 1917 and developed a reputation as a leading poet in the heady aftermath of the Russian Revolution. At first the Revolution sparked a great flurry of experimentation among poets, who hoped the new regime would create a better future. However, Pasternak refused to produce propaganda in the vein of "socialist realism" advocated by the government; he preferred instead to write searching, intellectual, and apolitical poetry. In retaliation, Soviet officials prevented his poems from being published during the 1930s and 1940s, and Pasternak was forced to translate the works of others. His most famous encounter with government censorship occurred over his novel *Dr. Zhivago* (1957), which presented a mixed view of the 1917 Revolution. The novel was rejected for publication by Soviet censors and was subsequently smuggled into the West, where it became a best seller in many languages. When the Nobel Committee honored Pasternak with the Nobel Prize for Literature for this work in 1958, the Soviet government pressured him into refusing the award.

Despite the worldwide success of *Dr. Zhivago,* Pasternak is celebrated primarily as a poet. His poems often have religious overtones; like much nineteenth-century Russian literature, these poems return repeatedly to the ideas of faith, love, art, and human destiny. Pasternak's poems are marked by their use of many varied allusions as well as by their fresh imagery and fine coordination of sound and meaning. Pasternak's poetry has often been compared to Impressionist painting in that the perceiver must tie a number of seemingly disconnected parts into a unified whole. Like the bits of glass in a kaleidoscope, the images in the following poem, "My Pictures Swing," interact to create bright patterns of color and motion.

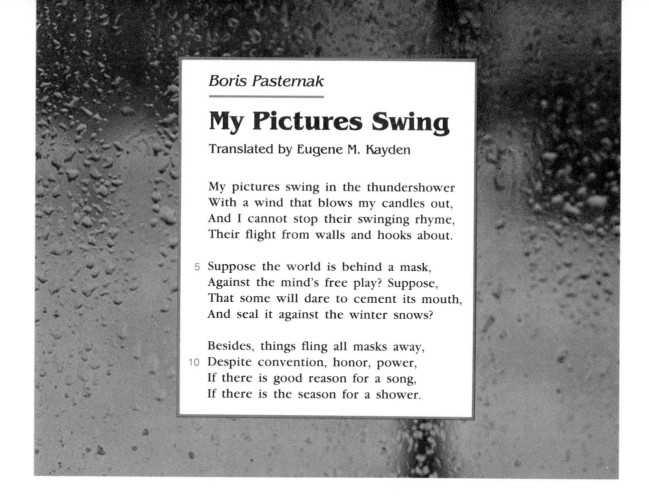

Boris Pasternak

My Pictures Swing

Translated by Eugene M. Kayden

My pictures swing in the thundershower
With a wind that blows my candles out,
And I cannot stop their swinging rhyme,
Their flight from walls and hooks about.

5 Suppose the world is behind a mask,
Against the mind's free play? Suppose,
That some will dare to cement its mouth,
And seal it against the winter snows?

Besides, things fling all masks away,
10 Despite convention, honor, power,
If there is good reason for a song,
If there is the season for a shower.

STUDY QUESTIONS

Recalling

1. When do the speaker's pictures swing?
2. What two things does the speaker suppose in the second stanza?
3. What happens to all masks, according to line 9, and despite what forces does it happen?

Interpreting

4. Does the fact that his pictures swing disturb or please the speaker? How do you know?
5. What might the speaker mean in his reference to "a mask" in line 5? In what way might such a mask hinder "the mind's free play"?
6. What force might the thundershower symbolize? In what sense is this force opposed to "convention, honor, power"? According to the poem, which side will win, and why?

Extending

7. What larger comment might Pasternak have been making about the events in his own country?

VIEWPOINT

Russian critic Andrei Sinyavsky observes the way Pasternak's poetry fuses seemingly disconnected elements:

> In Pasternak's poetry one must not separate man from his environment nor living feelings from dead matter. . . . Reality is depicted as a single unity in the blending of different components and in the intersecting of boundaries and contours.
>
> —*For Freedom of Imagination*

■ Show how the first two stanzas of "My Pictures Swing" introduce different components into the poem. How does the last stanza tie these different components together? What single idea unifies the poem?

Anna Akhmatova   *1888–1966*

Anna Andreyevna Gorenko was born in Odessa, Russia, where her father served as a naval officer. She assumed her grandmother's name, Akhmatova [äk mä′tō və], in her early twenties when she began to publish poetry. In 1910 she married fellow poet Nikolai Gumilev, and the couple joined up with another poet, Osip Mandelstam, to found a literary movement known as Acmeism. The Acmeists' aim was to avoid the obscurity and vagueness of the then-popular Symbolist movement. Akhmatova's group demanded that words be used according to their exact denotative meanings, rather than for their connotative associations and musical qualities.

Akhmatova published five volumes of poetry between 1912 and 1921. She bitterly opposed the 1917 Revolution and was expelled from the Union of Soviet Writers and labeled "dangerous and subversive." The rest of her long life was checkered with periods of silence. From 1922 to 1940 she was prevented from publishing any of her poetry. During World War II she received permission to publish in Leningrad, but the Communist party silenced her again by denouncing her work in 1946. In 1956 she published a few poems, but her work was condemned anew in the following year. Toward the end of her life her poems were published widely in Soviet periodicals. Despite this erratic pattern of publication and censorship, Akhmatova's poems became popular with the Russian people, and today her work is internationally known. She has twice been nominated for the Nobel Prize for Literature.

Akhmatova's work is personal rather than social or political in its concerns; her poems consist almost entirely of love lyrics, many of them unhappy in tone. Akhmatova's early poems are simple and sentimental, emotional and sensuous, while her later poems are admirable for their compression, precision, striking word pictures, and unusual rhythmic patterns. Despite her Acmeist determination to avoid suggested meanings, Akhmatova's work occasionally touches on religious, even mystical, themes, and her love lyrics sometimes capture the emotional atmosphere of her native Russia. She wrote the lyric poem "Now Nobody Will Want to Listen to Songs . . . " in 1917, the year of the Russian Revolution.

Anna Akhmatova

Now Nobody Will Want to Listen to Songs . . .

Translated by Stanley Kunitz

Now nobody will want to listen to songs,
the bitter days foretold come over the hill.
I tell you, song, the world has no more marvels,
do not shatter my heart, learn to be still.

5 Not long ago, as free as any swallow,
you rode the mornings out, you braved their dangers.
Now you must wander as a hungry beggar,
desperately knocking at the doors of strangers.

STUDY QUESTIONS

Recalling

1. What has "come over the hill" according to line 2? What does the world lack now, according to line 3?
2. What "you" is the poet addressing? What request does she make in line 4?
3. What two things did "you" once do? What things must "you" do now?

Interpreting

4. Contrast the present and past as the poet portrays them. What might cause this change?
5. What does Akhmatova mean when she refers to her "song"? What does her song not seem to know that the poet knows, and what power does her song seem to have over her?
6. Given Akhmatova's later difficulties with the government, how might the last two lines of the poem be prophetic?

Extending

7. In what senses does art have an independent life of its own, apart from its creator? Why can art often be more powerful than the individual who created it?

COMPOSITION

Writing About Personification

■ Discuss Akhmatova's use of personification in "Now Nobody Will Want to Listen to Songs . . . ." First, using examples from the poem, show how she attributes human qualities to a nonhuman thing. Then explain why you think she used such personification to express her ideas and feelings about the effect of public events upon her work. Finally indicate whether you think her use of personification increases or diminishes the impact of the poem.

Personifying Present and Past

■ Write a poem of two stanzas in which you personify the present and the past as two different people. Describe the appearance, behavior, and character of each of these people, choosing attributes that indicate your attitude toward present and past. Your poem may be serious or comic in tone, but it should create a definite contrast between present and past. For example, the past might be a shy and retiring fellow, while the present is gregarious and self-confident.

Federico García Lorca   *1899–1936*

Federico García Lorca is the most celebrated Spanish author in this century. Both the content of his writing and his tragic, early death have earned him the title Poet of Blood.

Born near Granada, Spain, García Lorca was the eldest son of a wealthy landowning farmer. Although he studied law at the University of Granada, he abandoned his legal studies for classes in music, art, and literature. His talents proved diverse: He loved to compose and perform music and held a show of his paintings in Barcelona. However, it was with his writing that García Lorca gained his lasting fame. While at the university he began to give recitations of his poetry and thus developed a reputation as an important poet even before any of his work was published. "Verse is made to be recited," he argued, "because in a book it is dead." These readings introduced García Lorca to other prominent Spanish artists, including painter Salvador Dali [dä′lē] and filmmaker Luis Bunuel [b$\overline{oo}$n wel′].

García Lorca's poetry combines local and universal elements. He was fascinated with the *cante jondo,* or "deep song," of the Gypsies from his native region of Andalusia in southern Spain. He used the landscapes and musical rhythms of these regional songs to express his thoughts about such universal subjects as love, poverty, freedom, honor, violence, and death. His best-known collection of poetry is *Gypsy Ballads* (1928). In García Lorca's poems passion often seethes just below a graceful, musical surface. His images vibrate with energy and often change form unexpectedly. Influenced by Dali and other surrealist artists, who put together disconnected objects in their paintings, García Lorca often juxtaposed seemingly unrelated images or ideas in his poetry.

García Lorca was also deeply involved in drama. He founded an experimental theater and worked almost exclusively as a playwright during the last five years of his life. He wrote a number of comedies, but his best-known plays are the tragedies *Blood Wedding* (1933), *Yerma* (1934), and *The House of Bernarda Alba* (1936).

Although García Lorca was apolitical, his associations with liberals made the supporters of fascist Francisco Franco regard him as a threat. His books were banned and then burned in a public square in Granada. When the Spanish civil war broke out, García Lorca went into hiding but was caught by the Francoists. He was forced to dig his own grave and was then shot to death. As a result García Lorca became a martyr and a symbol for generations of Spaniards.

García Lorca's poem "The Guitar" borrows from the people and landscape of his native region and from the music of Spanish Gypsy songs. Although the poem seems intensely personal, it also expresses a potent, universal emotion in a gripping manner.

Federico García Lorca

The Guitar

Translated by Elizabeth du Gué Trapier

Now begins the cry
Of the guitar,
Breaking the vaults
Of dawn.
5 Now begins the cry
Of the guitar.
Useless
To still it.
Impossible
10 To still it.
It weeps monotonously
As weeps the water,
As weeps the wind
Over snow.
15 Impossible
To still it.
It weeps
For distant things,
Warm southern sands
20 Desiring white camelias.
It mourns the arrow without a target,
The evening without morning.
And the first bird dead
Upon a branch.
25 O guitar!
A wounded heart,
Wounded by five swords.[1]

---

1. **five swords:** the fingers of the guitar player.

STUDY QUESTIONS

Recalling

1. What is both useless and impossible?
2. How does the guitar weep, according to lines 11–14? What kinds of things does it weep for? What three things does it mourn?
3. What does Lorca call the guitar in line 26?

Interpreting

4. Describe the sound of a guitar. Why might Lorca refer to that sound as "weeping"? In what ways does the poem re-create the impression of a guitar being played?
5. What extra dimensions does Lorca give the guitar by comparing it to the wind and water? By saying that it weeps, desires, and mourns?
6. What might the guitar symbolize in the poem?

LITERARY FOCUS

Tone

The **tone** of a poem is the attitude the speaker expresses toward the poem's subject matter and audience. Just as our tone of voice reveals the intensity and nature of our feelings, the tone of a poem may be casual, fervent, amused, indifferent, sad, exhilarated, angry, or bewildered.

Many individual elements affect the tone of a poem: the poet's choice and arrangement of words, line length, rhythm, rhyme, imagery, and figurative language. For example, one word of slang can slice through and undercut an otherwise elegant, solemn tone. The *Oh* at the beginning of a line can signal that strong emotion will follow. A plodding rhythm can express exhaustion and defeat; a tripping rhythm suggests exhilaration. Repetition often adds a musical but melancholy quality to the tone of a poem. The image of a cozy fire can add a note of comfort to a poem's tone; the image of a dark forest can add a sense of foreboding.

Thinking About Tone

1. Describe the tone of "The Guitar." Using examples, show how García Lorca's choice and arrangement of words, line length, sound effects, and imagery work together to create this tone.
2. Is the tone of "The Guitar" uniform, or does it change throughout?

George Seferis   *1900–1971*

The life of George Seferis [Georgio Sepheriades] was marked by the same wandering that he often portrays in his poems. Born to Greek parents in Smyrna, which is now in Turkey, Seferis [sə fer′ēs] left his home to study first in Athens and later at the University of Paris. In 1925 he returned to Greece to enter the diplomatic corps but was forced into exile when the Germans invaded his country during World War II. He later served Greece as the ambassador to a number of countries, including Lebanon, Syria, Jordan, Iraq, and Britain. He also served at the United Nations before retiring from public life in 1962. During his varied career he found time to teach international law at Athens University.

Seferis' writing career was also international. A member of the group of poets known as the Generation of the '30s, Seferis translated a number of foreign works and played a central role in introducing T. S. Eliot (page 541) and other modern poets to his countrymen. In 1963 he was awarded the Nobel Prize for Literature, becoming the first Greek to receive this award.

Seferis began writing poems at the age of fourteen. His first volume of poems, *Strophe* (1931), illustrates his ability to fuse contemporary concerns with the literary traditions of Ancient Greece. Seferis often combines everyday speech with the rhythms of classical literature. In addition, his subjects—loneliness, upheaval, and dislocation—are distinctly modern, but he dramatizes them with speakers who recall ancient landscapes and events.

Like Odysseus of Homer's *Odyssey,* the central characters of Seferis' poems are tormented wanderers. Eternal exiles, they journey in search of a homeland and a lost, glorious past. "The Return of the Exile" is one of Seferis' most memorable "wanderer" poems.

George Seferis

The Return of the Exile

Translated by Rex Warner

"Old friend, what are you looking for?
After those many years abroad you come
With images you tended
Under foreign skies
5 Far away from your own land."

"I look for my old garden;
The trees come only to my waist,
The hills seem low as terraces;
Yet when I was a child
10 I played there on the grass
Underneath great shadows
And used to run across the slopes
For hours and hours, breathless."

"My old friend, rest a little.
15 You will soon get used to it.
Together we will climb
The hill paths that you know;
Together we will sit and rest
Underneath the plane trees' dome;[1]
20 Little by little they'll come back to you,
Your garden and your slopes."

"I look for my old house,
The house with the tall windows
Darkened by the ivy,
25 And for that ancient column
The landmark of the sailor.

---

1. **plane trees' dome:** Plane trees, known as sycamore trees in America, are popular shade trees.

How can I get into this hutch?[2]
The roof's below my shoulders
And however far I look
30 I see men on their knees;
You'd say that they were praying."

"My old friend, can't you hear me?
You will soon get used to it.
Here is your house in front of you,
35 And at this door will soon come knocking
Your friends and your relations
To give you a fine welcome."

"Why is your voice so far away?
Raise your head a little higher
40 That I may grasp the words you say,
For as you speak you seem to grow
Shorter still and shorter
As though you were sinking down into
    the ground."

"My old friend, just think a little.
45 You will soon get used to it;
Your homesickness has built for you
A nonexistent land with laws
Outside the earth and man."

"Now I hear nothing—not a sound.
50 My last friend too has sunk and gone.
How strange it is, this leveling
All around from time to time:
They pass and mow here
Thousands of scythe-bearing[3] chariots."

---

2. **hutch:** hut or small shack.
3. **scythe-bearing** [sīth]: carrying a scythe, an implement with a long curved blade attached to a handle, used for mowing or harvesting. The Grim Reaper, a personification of death, is usually portrayed carrying a scythe.

Yevgeny Yevtushenko   *born 1933*

Yevgeny Yevtushenko [yev gen′ē yev′too shen′kō] is one of the best-known poets writing in Russia during the postwar era. He won international celebrity as a daring young poet, a reputation that was based partly on his work and partly on his own flair for the dramatic.

A descendant of exiles sent to Siberia, Yevtushenko was born in Zima, Russia. As a young boy he loved sports, and his dream was to become a soccer player. However, after publishing his first poem in a sports magazine, he began to focus on a literary career, completing his studies at the Gorki Literary Institute in Moscow.

Yevtushenko's first book was published in 1952, when he was only nineteen; he first won national recognition three years later with *Third Snow.* He became known for his dramatic public readings of his poetry; he toured western Europe, Africa, and the United States as well as the Soviet Union, drawing huge audiences wherever he went. In 1961 he published "Babi Yar," an emotional poem that caused a sensation by attacking Soviet anti-Semitism; "The Heirs of Stalin" published in 1963 warned of continued Stalinist repression and persecution and further fueled his international reputation. His works were translated into English as well as other languages. When his *Precocious Autobiography,* which hinted at poor conditions in the Soviet Union, was published in France in 1963, it was officially condemned by the Soviet Union. Because of these events, many have come to view Yevtushenko as a poet of nonconformism and liberation, a courageous opponent of the Soviet government. However, his critics maintain that Yevtushenko, who is a member of the Communist party, remains essentially a poet of the regime.

Yevtushenko's poems are simple and straightforward. His diction is direct, brash, and spiced with slang. His lyrics, especially his love poems, are particularly popular with Russia's young people. Yevtushenko frequently takes up the subjects of liberation and the search for an authentic self. He deals with both the struggles of the masses and the struggles of the solitary person, simultaneously celebrating the union among all human beings and the uniqueness of each individual. As in "People," his works often paint a panoramic view of the world, depicting a variety of people and problems.

Yevgeny Yevtushenko

People

Translated by Robin Milner-Gulland

No people are uninteresting.
Their fate is like the chronicle of planets.

Nothing in them is not particular,
and planet is dissimilar from planet.

5 And if a man lived in obscurity
making his friends in that obscurity
obscurity is not uninteresting.

To each his world is private,
and in that world one excellent minute.

10 And in that world one tragic minute.
These are private.

In any man who dies there dies with him
his first snow and kiss and fight.
It goes with him.

15 They are left books and bridges
and painted canvas and machinery.

Whose fate is to survive.
But what has gone is also not nothing:

by the rule of the game something has gone.
20 Not people die but worlds die in them.

Whom we knew as faulty, the earth's creatures.
Of whom, essentially, what did we know?

Brother of a brother? Friend of friends?
Lover of lover?

25 We who knew our fathers
in everything, in nothing.

They perish. They cannot be brought back.
The secret worlds are not regenerated.

And every time again and again
30 I make my lament against destruction.

STUDY QUESTIONS

The Return of the Exile

Recalling

1. What specific things is the wanderer, or exile, seeking, and what specific things does he find instead?
2. What sentence does the friend repeat to the wanderer in the third, sixth, and eighth stanzas? In lines 46–48 what does he say the wanderer's "homesickness" has done?
3. According to the wanderer, what seems to be happening to the other people, including his friend, at the end of the poem?

Interpreting

4. Summarize the overall change that seems to have come over the homeland, as viewed by the wanderer. How might lines 46–48 explain these apparent changes?
5. Does the wanderer "get used to" these changes? How do you know? What do you think is actually happening to him at the end of the poem?
6. What additional, forbidding meaning might be suggested in the low hutch, the men sinking into the ground, and the scythe-bearing chariots? In this case, what extra meaning might "coming home" have?
7. What does the poem seem to be saying about the relationship between wandering and staying at home? What does it seem to say about the relationship between the past and the present?

Extending

8. Do you think it is possible to "go home again"? Why or why not? What might be the dangers in idealizing a place?

People

Recalling

1. To what does the speaker compare the fate of people in line 2? In lines 9–10 what terms sum up each person's life?
2. When a man dies, what things die with him according to lines 12–13? What cannot be "regenerated," according to line 28?
3. What "lament" does the speaker make "again and again"?

Interpreting

4. According to the poem, in what ways are people unique? In what ways are they similar? Which aspect of life does the poem emphasize more?
5. What is the speaker saying about each life by comparing it to planets and worlds? By comparing it to one minute?
6. Explain the paradox in lines 25–26. What does the speaker mean, and do you agree with him?
7. In what sense is "People" both a celebration and a lament?

Extending

8. In what sense might the privacy of each life be sad? In what sense might such privacy be comforting?

COMPOSITION

Writing About Characters

■ Discuss Seferis' use of two characters, whom we meet only through dialogue. Begin by describing each speaker and pointing out the main differences between them, especially in their attitudes toward the wanderer's home. Then explain the view of life that each speaker expresses.

Writing a Poem in Dialogue

■ Write a "conversation poem" in which two speakers describe the same thing in very different ways, as Seferis' speakers do in "The Return of the Exile." For example, you might present a conversation between an old person and a young person about the same historical event, or between a poet and a scientist about a natural feature. In your poem write dialogue for your two speakers that makes the differences between their personalities and points of view very clear.

Nobel Prize–Winning Poets

Odysseus Elytis, Eugenio Montale, and Czeslaw Milosz

The Nobel Prize for Literature is one of five Nobel Prizes given each year in a variety of fields to individuals whose work is thought to benefit humanity. The prizes were inaugurated by Swedish scientist Alfred Nobel and have been awarded every year since 1901. The winner of the Nobel Prize for Literature is chosen each year by the Swedish Academy of Letters. W. B. Yeats (page 531), T. S. Eliot (page 541), George Bernard Shaw (page 458), and George Seferis (page 864) have all won the Nobel Prize for Literature.

Odysseus Elytis [ə lē′təs] of Greece, Eugenio Montale [mōn tä′lā] of Italy, and Czeslaw Milosz [ches′wa mē′wəsh] of Poland are three contemporary European poets who have won the Nobel Prize for Literature in recent years. All three write poems that are highly representative of their homelands. They draw on the landscapes, histories, and mythologies of their native countries. Yet each speaks not simply for himself and his countrymen; each has developed a voice that speaks for all people everywhere. Each poet has fought in a world war, encountered oppression, and witnessed human suffering. Not surprisingly, each writes about liberty, justice, and the search for values that might work in a troubled modern world.

Odysseus Elytis.

Odysseus Elytis (born 1911) is the youngest of the group of poets known as the Generation of the '30s—a group that included his fellow Nobel laureate, George Seferis (page 864). Elytis, whose actual surname is Alepoudelis, was born on the Greek island of Crete, where his father was a wealthy soap manufacturer. Educated on the mainland, Elytis often returned to the beautiful Greek islands for vacations, and their landscapes figure vividly in his poems. During World War II he joined the fight against Mussolini's fascists in Albania, one of Greece's neighbors in the Balkans. After the war he studied in Paris and then returned to Greece, where he worked in radio and theater in addition to writing poetry.

Elytis is an intuitive poet who often incorporates widely diverging images within a classical Greek literary framework. Upon awarding him the Nobel Prize for Literature in 1979, the Swedish Academy of Letters said that Elytis' poetry is "not only very personal but also represents the traditions of the Greek people. . . . [It] depicts with sensual strength and intellectual clearsightedness modern man's struggle for freedom and creativeness." Marked by imagination, Elytis' poems often use metamorphosis; that is, they turn one thing into another. For example, a girl might change into a flower or an idea into a human being. Elytis' colorful poems are word tapestries weaving together emotion and intellect, past and present, pleasure and pain.

Eugenio Montale.

In awarding the 1975 Nobel Prize to Eugenio Montale (1896–1981), the Swedish Academy described him as "one of the most important poets of the contemporary West." Montale was born and raised in Genoa, Italy. Despite his father's urgings that he take over the family business, Montale originally planned to become an opera singer and then turned to writing at the University of Genoa. After graduating he served as director of the Vieusseux Library in Florence until he lost his position because of his opposition to Mussolini. After World War II he moved to Milan and worked for a newspaper.

Montale's poems depict a troubled, barren world in which people have lost the power to mold their own lives. He refers frequently to the landscapes of his childhood but also uses symbols that translate specific times and places into universal aspects of experience. Montale expands the boundaries of his poems by combining the details of the real world with dreams and fantasies. Like T. S. Eliot (page 541), to whom he is often compared and whose work he translated into Italian, Montale often mixes everyday speech with literary and historical allusions. Montale writes often of the loneliness, exhaustion, and uncertainty of modern life but also leavens his poems with irony and subtle humor.

Czeslaw Milosz.

Although he is now a citizen of the United States, Czeslaw Milosz (born 1911) is still considered one of Poland's major poets. Born in Lithuania, he traveled widely as a child with his engineer father. He began to write poetry while studying law and eventually helped to form a literary circle known as the Catastrophic School because its members predicted worldwide doom. He lived in Warsaw, Poland, during World War II, publishing through the underground press, but eventually was forced to flee to Paris. There he wrote and published *The Captive Mind,* a prose piece that describes the effects of Communism on creativity. In 1960 he came to the University of California in Berkeley, where he now lives and works.

When Milosz received the 1980 Nobel Prize for Literature, the Swedish Academy described his poems as "captivating and arresting." According to the academy, Milosz "voices man's exposed condition in a world of severe conflicts." Milosz himself has said that poetry should capture the "consciousness of an epoch." In other words, it should translate the poet's private pain into larger, universal themes. Milosz draws from many sources for his poems, blending classical and modern events, secular and Christian concerns, eastern and western culture. His language is similarly kaleidoscopic, sprinkled with Old Russian, Lithuanian, and Latin words. Like Elytis and Montale, Milosz finds much inspiration in the landscapes of his childhood. He too returns to topics such as exile, loss, separation, and doubt in his poetry. Yet he lightens these characteristically modern subjects with the equally modern saving graces of irony and humor.

Odysseus Elytis

Drinking the Corinthian Sun

Translated by Kimon Friar

Drinking the Corinthian sun
Reading the marble ruins
Striding over vineyard seas
Aiming with my harpoon
5 At votive[1] fish that elude me
I found those leaves that the psalm[2] of the sun memorizes
The living land that desire rejoices
To open

I drink water, cut fruit
10 Plunge my hands through the wind's foliage
Lemon trees quicken the pollen of summer days
Green birds cut through my dreams
And I leave, my eyes filled
With a boundless gaze where the world becomes
15 Beautiful again from the beginning according to the heart's
        measure.

---

1. **votive:** offered in fulfillment of a vow.
2. **psalm** [säm]: sacred poem or hymn.

STUDY QUESTIONS

Recalling
1. Relate at least five things that the speaker does in the poem.
2. Identify at least seven sense images in the poem.
3. What fills the speaker's eyes as he leaves, and in what terms does he describe the world in lines 14–15?

Interpreting
4. In what senses does the speaker "drink" the Corinthian sun? What is the effect of this and the other sense images in the poem?

5. What different elements does Elytis combine in the image the "wind's foliage"? Find three other examples in which he mixes different elements together (for example, different time periods, the spiritual and the physical, the animal and the human, one sense and another).
6. What picture of the relationship between humans and nature do such combinations create? What feeling about life do they create?
7. What might the speaker mean by "the living land"? How does one "open" this land?

Extending
8. In what different ways can nature "nourish" human beings?

Eugenio Montale

The Arno at Rovezzano

Translated by G. Singh

Big rivers are the image of time,
cruel and impersonal. Seen
from a bridge they declare their inexorable
nullity.[1] Only the hesitant
5 bend of some marshy reed-bed,
some mirror gleaming amid
brushwood and moss can reveal
that the water becomes aware of itself like us
before turning into vortex[2] and plunder.
10 So much time has passed,
yet nothing has changed since when
I'd sing to you on the phone
"toi qui fais l'endormie"[3]
amid immoderate peals of laughter.
15 Your house was a lamp seen from
the train. It leans over the Arno
like the Judas tree[4] which wanted to protect it.
Perhaps it's still there, or there
only in ruins. Full of insects,
20 you would tell me, and quite uninhabitable.
Other comforts are our lot now, other
discomforts.

---

1. **inexorable** [in ek′sər ə bəl] **nullity:** unrelenting
nothingness.
2. **vortex:** whirlpool.
3. **"toi qui fais l'endormie"** [twa kē fā lan dôr mē′]: "you
who pretend to sleep."
4. **Judas tree:** flowering tree so-named because Judas, the
apostle who betrayed Jesus, is said to have hanged himself on
such a tree.

Czeslaw Milosz

Encounter

Translated by Czeslaw Milosz and Lillian Vallee

We were riding through frozen fields in a wagon at dawn.
A red wing[1] rose in the darkness.

And suddenly a hare ran across the road.
One of us pointed to it with his hand.

5 That was long ago. Today neither of them is alive,
Not the hare, nor the man who made the gesture.

O my love, where are they, where are they going
The flash of a hand, streak of movement, rustle of pebbles.
I ask not out of sorrow, but in wonder.

---

1. **red wing:** European thrush with red flank and wing feathers.

STUDY QUESTIONS

The Arno at Rovezzano

Recalling

1. According to line 1, of what are big rivers the image? What two additional adjectives does the speaker assign to "Big rivers"? What do such rivers "declare" when seen from a bridge?
2. In contrast, what does the water do in lines 4–8? Into what does it then turn?
3. In lines 15–17 to what two things does the speaker compare the house of his friend? What various pictures of its present condition does he paint in lines 18–20?
4. What two things are the "lot" of the speaker and his friend now?

Interpreting

5. Contrast the two pictures of water presented by the speaker in lines 1–4 and in lines 4–9. What two aspects of time do these contrasting pictures suggest?
6. What double-edged meaning does the image

of the Judas tree in line 17 suggest? What might this double meaning imply about the speaker's relationship with his friend?
7. What do the past and present images of the friend's house imply about the relationship between the speaker and his friend then and now? What do lines 21–22 suggest about their present relationship?
8. What does the poem seem to say about the effect of time on things and people? How do people change over time? How do they remain the same?

Extending

9. Why do you think the image of a river is often used to suggest the passage of time? What other images might suggest this phenomenon?

Encounter

Recalling

1. What event does the speaker describe in lines 1–4? When did it happen?
2. What has since happened to the man and the hare?

3. What questions does the speaker ask in line 7, and what are his feelings, according to line 9?

Interpreting

4. What feeling is conveyed by the image of the "frozen fields . . . at dawn"? What impression of or idea about life is suggested by "The flash of a hand, streak of movement, rustle of pebbles"? What might these things come to symbolize for the speaker?
5. Why do you think the speaker equates the hare and the man in line 6?
6. Why might the speaker be relating this event after so long? What do you think causes his "wonder"?
7. What "encounters" occur in the poem? What larger questions about existence is the speaker actually posing?

Extending

8. Why might seemingly insignificant moments in our lives take on great importance?

VOCABULARY

Antonyms

Antonyms are words that have opposite or nearly opposite meanings. *Delicious* and *foul* are antonyms. The words in capitals are from the translations of "Drinking the Corinthian Sun," "The Arno at Rovezzano," and "Encounter." On a separate sheet write the letter of the word that is *most nearly the opposite* of each word in capitals, *as the word is used in the selection.*

1. VOTIVE: (a) noisy (b) dangerous (c) swift (d) random
2. ELUDE: (a) escape (b) appear (c) join (d) separate
3. FOLIAGE: (a) desert (b) shrubbery (c) forest (d) street
4. BOUNDLESS: (a) empty (b) short (c) restricted (d) infinite
5. INEXORABLE: (a) avoidable (b) important (c) permanent (d) inexcusable
6. NULLITY: (a) dullness (b) nothingness (c) evenness (d) richness
7. VORTEX: (a) whirlpool (b) calm (c) cone (d) mud
8. PLUNDER: (a) mistake (b) overflow (c) restoration (d) abundance

9. IMMODERATE: (a) clumsy (b) fantastic (c) mediocre (d) slight
10. RUSTLE: (a) sigh (b) roar (c) whisper (d) murmur

COMPOSITION

Writing a Comparison/Contrast

■ Compare and contrast Milosz's "Encounter" with Montale's "Arno at Rovezzano." Discuss in particular how the two works portray time and nature in relation to human beings. Begin by pointing out the similarities between the form and content of the two poems, and then explain their differences. End by indicating which poem you prefer, and why. *For help with this assignment, refer to Lesson 2 in the Writing About Literature Handbook at the back of this book.*

Writing a Poem About Nature

■ Write a very brief poem in which you describe a natural scene in terms that express an intense feeling of identification with nature. As Elytis does in "Drinking the Corinthian Sun," choose images that combine several different senses and that convey a powerful emotional response to nature.

COMPARING ENGLISH AND WESTERN WRITERS

1. Choose one English and one European poet of the twentieth century, and compare the subject matter of their poems. Do they focus primarily on personal or social concerns? As products of the twentieth century, what do these works have in common?
2. Compare the uses of imagery in the works of several twentieth-century English and European poets. In particular, which group of poets seems more likely to combine unrelated images in a single work? Cite specific examples.
3. What attitude toward time is expressed in the works of twentieth-century English and European poets? What attitude toward nature is expressed? Use examples from at least two English and two European writers.
4. Which poets, English or European, take a more hopeful view of human affairs and the future of humanity? Cite specific examples from the poems presented in this book.

PROSE

Luigi Pirandello   *1867–1936*

Outside Italy Luigi Pirandello [lo͞o ē′jē pir′ən del′ō] may be his country's best-known modern author, and he is its most famous playwright. In fact, his plays, more than half of which are dramatizations of his own short stories, won for him the Nobel Prize for Literature in 1934. Pirandello's work—novels and poems as well as plays and short stories—is recognizable for the atmosphere of mystery and tension that he creates.

Pirandello was born in Sicily to a wealthy family. He studied in Rome and received a degree in philosophy from the University of Bonn in Germany. He taught for a while at a girls' high school in Rome. His wrote verse, essays, and novels, but his many volumes of short stories have established him as a master of that genre. He turned to playwrighting reluctantly when he was asked to dramatize one of the stories. His plays include *Six Characters in Search of an Author* (1918) and *Henry IV* (1922). He invented "grotesco," his own grotesque form of theatrical expressionism, a theatrical style that sacrifices realism in order to give expression to psychological experience. In 1925 Pirandello founded his own theater company, which then toured Europe.

A conflict between reality and illusion rages throughout Pirandello's plays, novels, and short stories. His characters often deceive themselves in an effort to avoid troublesome facts. Self-awareness is painful, and the characters survive by perpetuating illusions and ignoring reality. The tone is often mysterious or ironic, and when characters are forced to accept the truth, it becomes tragic.

"War" is a short story that also shows Pirandello's skill with dramatic dialogue. Like much of his work, it shows the ways people struggle to cope with unpleasant reality. Pirandello's own son was a prisoner of war during World War I, and Pirandello knew intimately the anguish he treats in this story.

Luigi Pirandello

War

Translated by Samuel Putnam

The passengers who had left Rome by the night express had to stop until dawn at the small station of Fabriano in order to continue their journey by the small old-fashioned "local" joining the main line with Sulmona.

At dawn, in a stuffy and smoky second-class carriage in which five people had already spent the night, a bulky woman in deep mourning was hoisted in—almost like a shapeless bundle. Behind her—puffing and moaning—followed her husband, a tiny man, thin and weakly, his face death-white, his eyes small and bright and looking shy and uneasy.

Having at last taken a seat, he politely thanked the passengers who had helped his wife and who had made room for her. Then he turned round to the woman trying to pull down the collar of her coat and politely inquired:

"Are you all right, dear?"

The wife, instead of answering, pulled up her collar again to her eyes, so as to hide her face.

"Nasty world," muttered the husband with a sad smile.

And he felt it his duty to explain to his traveling companions that the poor woman was to be pitied, for the war was taking away from her her only son. He was a boy of twenty to whom both had devoted their entire life, even breaking up their home at Sulmona to follow him to Rome, where he had to go as a student. Then they had allowed him to volunteer for war, with an assurance, however, that at least for six months he would not be sent to the front. And now, all of a sudden, they had received a wire that he was due to leave in three days' time and asking them to go and see him off.

The woman under the big coat was twisting and wriggling, at times growling like a wild an-

imal, feeling certain that all those explanations would not have aroused even a shadow of sympathy from those people who—most likely—were in the same plight as herself. One of them, who had been listening with particular attention, said:

"You should thank God that your son is only leaving now for the front. Mine has been sent there the first day of the war. He has already come back twice wounded and been sent back again to the front."

"What about me? I have two sons and three nephews at the front," said another passenger.

"Maybe, but in our case it is our *only* son," ventured the husband.

"What difference can it make? You may spoil your only son with excessive attentions, but you cannot love him more than you would all your other children if you had any. Paternal love is not like bread that can be broken into pieces and split among the children in equal shares. A father gives *all* his love to each one of his children without discrimination, whether it be one or ten, and if I am suffering now for my two sons, I am not suffering half for each of them but double. . . ."

"True . . . true . . ." sighed the embarrassed husband, "but suppose (of course, we all hope it will never be your case) a father has two sons at the front and he loses one of them, there is still one left to console him . . . while . . ."

"Yes," answered the other, getting cross, "a son left to console him but also a son left for whom he must survive, while in the case of the father of an only son, if the son dies, the father can die, too, and put an end to his distress. Which of the two positions is the worse? Don't you see how my case would be worse than yours?"

"Nonsense," interrupted another traveler, a

fat, red-faced man with bloodshot eyes of the palest gray.

He was panting. From his bulging eyes seemed to spurt inner violence of an uncontrolled vitality which his weakened body could hardly contain.

"Nonsense," he repeated, trying to cover his mouth with his hand so as to hide the two missing front teeth. "Nonsense. Do we give life to our children for our own benefit?"

The other travelers stared at him in distress. The one who had had his son at the front since the first day of the war sighed: "You are right. Our children do not belong to us, they belong to the Country. . . ."

"Bosh," retorted the fat traveler. "Do we think of the Country when we give life to our children? Our sons are born because . . . well, because they must be born and when they come to life they take our own life with them. This is the truth. We belong to them but they never belong to us. And when they reach twenty, they are exactly what we were at their age. We, too, had a father and mother, but there were so many other things as well—girls, cigarettes, illusions, new ties—and the Country, of course, whose call we would have answered, when we were twenty, even if father and mother had said no. Now, at our age, the love of our Country is still great, of course, but stronger than it is the love for our children. Is there any one of us here who wouldn't gladly take his son's place at the front if he could?"

There was a silence all round, everybody nodding as to approve.

"Why, then," continued the fat man, "shouldn't we consider the feelings of our children when they are twenty? Isn't it natural that at their age they should consider the love for their Country (I am speaking of decent boys, of course) even greater than the love for us? Isn't it natural that it should be so, as after all they must look upon us as upon old boys who cannot move any more and must stay at home? If Country exists, if Country is a natural necessity like bread, of which each of us must eat in order not to die of hunger, somebody must go to defend it. And our sons go, when they are twenty, and they don't want tears, because if they die, they die inflamed and happy (I am speaking, of course, of decent boys). Now, if one dies young and happy, without having the ugly sides of life, the boredom of it, the pettiness, the bitterness of disillusion . . . what more can we ask for him? Everyone should stop crying: everyone should laugh, as I do . . . or at least thank God—as I do—because my son, before dying, sent me a message saying that he was dying satisfied at having ended his life in the best way he could have wished. That is why, as you see, I do not even wear mourning. . . ."

He shook his light fawn coat as to show it. His livid lip over his missing teeth was trembling, his eyes were watery and motionless and soon after, he ended with a shrill laugh which might well have been a sob.

"Quite so . . . quite so . . ." agreed the others.

The woman who, bundled in a corner under her coat, had been sitting and listening had—for the last three months—tried to find in the words of her husband and her friends something to console her in her deep sorrow, something that might show her how a mother should resign herself to send her son not even to death but to a probable danger of life. Yet not a word had she found among the many which had been said . . . and her grief had been greater in seeing that nobody—as she thought—could share her feelings.

But now the words of the traveler amazed and almost stunned her. She suddenly realized that it wasn't the others who were wrong and could not understand her but herself who could not rise up to the same height of those fathers and mothers willing to resign themselves, without crying, not only to the departure of their sons but even to their death.

She lifted her head, she bent over from her corner trying to listen with great attention to the details which the fat man was giving to his companions about the way his son had fallen as a hero, for his King and his Country, happy and without regrets. It seemed to her that she had stumbled into a world she had never dreamed of, a world so far unknown to her, and she was so pleased to hear everyone joining in congratulating that brave father who could so stoically speak of his child's death.

Then suddenly, just as if she had heard nothing of what had been said and almost as if waking up from a dream, she turned to the old man, asking him:

"Then . . . is your son really dead?"

Everybody stared at her. The old man, too, turned to look at her, fixing his great, bulging, horribly watery light gray eyes deep in her face. For some little time he tried to answer, but words failed him. He looked and looked at her, almost as if only then—at that silly, incongruous question—he had suddenly realized at last that his son was really dead . . . gone forever . . . forever. His face contracted, became horribly distorted, then he snatched in haste a handkerchief from his pocket and, to the amazement of everyone, broke into harrowing, heart-rending, uncontrollable sobs.

STUDY QUESTIONS

Recalling

1. Where are the tiny man and his grieving wife going? Give two examples of the woman's behavior from the beginning of the story.
2. Summarize the arguments of the two fathers who have sons at the front.
3. What reason does the father who lost his son give for not wearing mourning?
4. What is the man's reaction when the woman asks if his son is really dead?

Interpreting

5. Explain the following statement, and tell why the man who lost his son makes it: "We belong to them but they never belong to us."
6. What does the grieving mother think at first of the man's reason for not mourning his son? As a result, what does she think of herself?
7. Why does the man break down? Does his crying affect the strength of his earlier remarks?
8. What do you think is the theme of the story?

LITERARY FOCUS

Dialogue

Dialogue is conversation between characters in any form of writing. Dialogue helps to develop character; it indirectly informs the reader of characters' thoughts and opinions. Dialogue also enables an author to present an interplay of ideas among a number of characters.

What a character says must be appropriate to that character's personality, background, and intelligence. In addition, dialogue must sound like natural speech and still be free of the flaws of everyday conversation.

Thinking About Dialogue

1. What does their dialogue reveal about the personalities of the two men who have sons at the front? Is their dialogue natural? Explain.
2. In what sense does the dialogue in "War" provide an interplay of ideas?

COMPOSITION

Developing a Thesis Statement

Develop a thesis statement about "War," and write a brief essay to defend your thesis. First clearly state your thesis. Then use examples from the story to explain and defend it. You may want to consider one of the following for your thesis: (a) Pirandello's attitude toward war, (b) the attitudes about children, (c) the use of dialogue, or (d) the conflict between illusion and reality. *For help with this assignment, refer to Lesson 1 in the Writing About Literature Handbook at the back of this book.*

Writing Dialogue

Imagine three strangers who begin a conversation while riding on a train. They realize that they agree about some ideas and disagree about others. First describe each character. Then write a brief dialogue in which the three strangers come to know one another.

Thomas Mann   *1875–1955*

A major concern of Thomas Mann's life and of his fiction was the place of the artist in society. Mann [män] saw a conflict between the artist's role as a commentator about society and the necessity of living within that society. His early life was marked by this struggle. Born of a wealthy merchant family in Lübeck, Germany, Mann cultivated his artistic interests in a commercial environment. He supported himself as an editorial assistant and as an insurance salesperson before devoting his full-time energies to writing. Mann won the Nobel Prize for Literature in 1929. Four years later the conflict between art and society became a crisis. Adolf Hitler and the Nazis came to power in 1933. Mann, whose writing expressed his liberal philosophy, sensed a growing rift between himself and the German rulers. He left Germany for Switzerland and eventually for the United States. Later his books were banned in his own country, and Mann was stripped of his German citizenship.

The conflict between art and society also dominates Mann's fiction, in which material deterioration often contrasts with cultural refinement. His first novel, *Buddenbrooks* (1900), focuses on the decline of a wealthy merchant family much like his own. *Death in Venice* (1912) illustrates Mann's interest in Freudian psychology. To explain the main character's behavior, Mann recorded his exterior actions in minute detail and steeped them in symbolic significance. Mann usually worked slowly and deliberately, and he spent twelve years on his novel *The Magic Mountain* (1924), a portrait of a decaying Europe after World War I. *Joseph and His Brothers* (1933–1943) is a four-volume novel that is based on the biblical story.

Like Mann's best fiction, "The Infant Prodigy" concerns the artist's role in society. In the story Mann goes beyond the glitter of a young musician's fame to show us the core of his personality; he goes beyond the applause of adoring audiences to expose the artist's isolation from his society.

Thomas Mann

The Infant Prodigy

Translated by H. T. Lowe-Porter

The infant prodigy entered. The hall became quiet.

It became quiet and then the audience began to clap, because somewhere at the side a leader of mobs, a born organizer, clapped first. The audience had heard nothing yet, but they applauded; for a mighty publicity organization had heralded the prodigy and people were already hypnotized, whether they knew it or not.

The prodigy came from behind a splendid screen embroidered with Empire[1] garlands and great conventionalized flowers, and climbed nimbly up the steps to the platform, diving into the applause as into a bath; a little chilly and shivering, but yet as though into a friendly element. He advanced to the edge of the platform and smiled as though he were about to be photographed; he made a shy, charming gesture of greeting, like a little girl.

He was dressed entirely in white silk, which the audience found enchanting. The little white jacket was fancifully cut, with a sash underneath it, and even his shoes were made of white silk. But against the white socks his bare little legs stood out quite brown; for he was a Greek boy.

He was called Bibi Saccellaphylaccas. And such indeed was his name. No one knew what Bibi was the pet name for, nobody but the impresario,[2] and he regarded it as a trade secret. Bibi had smooth black hair reaching to his shoulders; it was parted on the side and fastened back from the narrow domed forehead by a little silk bow. His was the most harmless childish countenance in the world, with an unfinished nose and guileless mouth. The area beneath his pitch-black mouselike eyes was already a little tired and visibly lined. He looked as though he were nine years old but was really eight and given out for seven. It was hard to tell whether to believe this or not. Probably everybody knew better and still believed it, as happens about so many things. The average man thinks that a little falseness goes with beauty. Where should we get any excitement out of our daily life if we were not willing to pretend a bit? And the average man is quite right, in his average brains!

The prodigy kept on bowing until the applause died down, then he went up to the grand piano, and the audience cast a last look at its programs. First came a *Marche solennelle,*[3] then a *Rêverie,*[4] and then *Le Hibou et les moineaux*[5]—all by Bibi Saccellaphylaccas. The whole program was by him, they were all his compositions. He could not score them, of course, but he had them all in his extraordinary little head and they possessed real artistic significance, or so it said, seriously and objectively, in the program. The program sounded as though the impresario had wrested these concessions from his critical nature after a hard struggle.

The prodigy sat down upon the revolving stool and felt with his feet for the pedals, which were raised by means of a clever device so that Bibi could reach them. It was Bibi's own piano, he took it everywhere with him. It rested upon wooden trestles and its polish was

1. **Empire** [om pēr']: French style of decoration developed in the early nineteenth century during the first French Empire under Napoleon Bonaparte.
2. **impresario** [im'prə sär'ē ō]: organizer or manager of live entertainments.

3. **Marche solennelle** [märsh sô lə nel']: French for "solemn march."
4. **Rêverie** [re ver ē']: brief, quiet musical composition.
5. **Le Hibou et les moineaux** [lə ē bōō'ā lā mwa nō']: French for "The Owl and the Sparrows."

somewhat marred by the constant transportation—but all that only made things more interesting.

Bibi put his silk-shod feet on the pedals; then he made an artful little face, looked straight ahead of him, and lifted his right hand. It was a brown, childish little hand; but the wrist was strong and unlike a child's, with well-developed bones.

Bibi made his face for the audience because he was aware that he had to entertain them a little. But he had his own private enjoyment in the thing too, an enjoyment which he could never convey to anybody. It was that prickling delight, that secret shudder of bliss, which ran through him every time he sat at an open piano—it would always be with him. And here was the keyboard again, these seven black and white octaves, among which he had so often lost himself in abysmal and thrilling adventures—and yet it always looked as clean and untouched as a newly washed blackboard. This was the realm of music that lay before him. It lay spread out like an inviting ocean, where he might plunge in and blissfully swim, where he might let himself be borne and carried away, where he might go under in night and storm, yet keep the mastery: control, ordain—he held his right hand poised in the air.

A breathless stillness reigned in the room— the tense moment before the first note came. . . . How would it begin? It began so. And Bibi, with his index finger, fetched the first note out of the piano, a quite unexpectedly powerful first note in the middle register, like a trumpet blast. Others followed, an introduction developed—the audience relaxed.

The concert was held in the palatial hall of a fashionable first-class hotel. The walls were covered with mirrors framed in gilded arabesques,[6] between frescoes[7] of the rosy and fleshly school. Ornamental columns supported a ceiling that displayed a whole universe of electric bulbs, in clusters darting a brilliance far brighter than day and filling the whole space with thin, vibrating golden light. Not a seat was unoccupied, people were standing in the side aisles and at the back. The front seats cost twelve marks;[8] for the impresario believed that anything worth having was worth paying for. And they were occupied by the best society, for it was in the upper classes, of course, that the greatest enthusiasm was felt. There were even some children, with their legs hanging down demurely from their chairs and their shining eyes staring at their gifted little white-clad contemporary.

Down in front on the left side sat the prodigy's mother, an extremely obese woman with a powdered double chin and a feather on her head. Beside her was the impresario, a man of oriental appearance with large gold buttons on his conspicuous cuffs. The princess was in the middle of the front row—a wrinkled, shriveled little old princess but still a patron of the arts, especially everything full of sensibility. She sat in a deep, velvet-upholstered arm chair, and a Persian carpet was spread before her feet. She held her hands folded over her gray striped-silk breast, put her head on one side, and presented a picture of elegant composure as she sat looking up at the performing prodigy. Next to her sat her lady-in-waiting, in a green striped-silk gown. Being only a lady-in-waiting she had to sit up very straight in her chair.

Bibi ended in a grand climax. With what power this wee manikin[9] belabored the key-board! The audience could scarcely trust its ears. The march theme, and infectious, swinging tune, broke out once more, fully harmonized, bold and showy; with every note Bibi flung himself back from the waist as though he were marching in a triumphal procession. He ended *fortissimo*,[10] bent over, slipped sideways off the stool, and stood with a smile awaiting the applause.

And the applause burst forth, unanimously, enthusiastically; the child made his demure little maidenly curtsy and people in the front seats thought: "Look what slim little hips he has! Clap, clap! Hurrah, bravo, little chap, Saccophylax or whatever your name is! Wait, let me take off my gloves—what a little devil of a chap he is!"

Bibi had to come out three times from behind the screen before they would stop. Some latecomers entered the hall and moved about looking for seats. Then the concert continued. Bibi's *Rêverie* murmured its numbers, consisting almost entirely of *arpeggios*,[11] above which a bar of melody rose now and then, weak-winged. Then came *Le Hibou et les moineaux*. This piece was brilliantly successful, it made a strong impression; it was an effective childhood fantasy, remarkably well envisaged. The bass represented the owl, sitting morosely rolling his filmy eyes; while in the treble the impudent, half-frightened sparrows chirped. Bibi received an ovation when he finished, he was called out four times. A hotel page with shiny buttons carried up three great laurel wreaths onto the stage and proffered them from one side while Bibi nodded and expressed his thanks. Even the princess shared in the applause, daintily and noiselessly pressing her palms together.

Ah, the knowing little creature understood how to make people clap! He stopped behind the screen, they had to wait for him; lingered a little on the steps of the platform, admired

---

6. **arabesques** [arʹə besksʹ]: elaborate designs of intertwined patterns.
7. **frescoes**: paintings done directly on plaster.
8. **marks**: German monetary unit. The value of one mark at the time of the story was approximately twenty-five cents.
9. **manikin**: little man.

10. *fortissimo* [fôr tēsʹē mōʹ]: a musical direction, Italian for "very loud."
11. *arpeggios* [är pejʹē ōzʹ]: notes of a musical chord played in succession instead of together.

the long streamers on the wreaths—although actually such things bored him stiff by now. He bowed with the utmost charm, he gave the audience plenty of time to rave itself out, because applause is valuable and must not be cut short. *"Le Hibou* is my drawing card," he thought—this expression he had learned from the impresario. "Now I will play the fantasy, it is a lot better than *Le Hibou,* of course, especially the C-sharp passage. But you idiots dote on the *Hibou,* though it is the first and the silliest thing I wrote." He continued to bow and smile.

Next came a *Méditation*[12] and then an *Étude*[13]—the program was quite comprehensive. The *Méditation* was very like the *Rêverie*—which was nothing against it—and the *Étude* displayed all of Bibi's virtuosity, which naturally fell a little short of his inventiveness. And then the *Fantaisie.*[14] This was his favorite; he varied it a little each time, giving himself free rein and sometimes surprising even himself, on good evenings, by his own inventiveness.

He sat and played, so little, so white and shining, against the great black grand piano, elect and alone, above that confused sea of faces, above the heavy, insensitive mass soul, upon which he was laboring to work with his individual, differentiated soul. His lock of soft black hair with the white silk bow had fallen over his forehead, his trained and bony little wrists pounded away, the muscles stood out visibly on his brown childish cheeks.

Sitting there he sometimes had moments of oblivion and solitude, when the gaze of his strange little mouselike eyes with the big rings beneath them would lose itself and stare through the painted stage into space that was peopled with strange vague life. Then out of the corner of his eye he would give a quick look back into the hall and be once more with his audience.

"Joy and pain, the heights and the depths—that is my *Fantaisie,*" he thought lovingly. "Listen, here is the C-sharp passage." He lingered over the approach, wondering if they would notice anything. But no, of course not, how should they? And he cast his eyes up prettily at the ceiling so that at least they might have something to look at.

All these people sat there in their regular rows, looking at the prodigy and thinking all sorts of things in their regular brains. An old gentleman with a white beard, a seal ring[15] on his finger and a bulbous swelling on his bald spot, a growth if you like, was thinking to himself: "Really, one ought to be ashamed." He had never got any further than "Ah, thou dearest Augustin" on the piano, and here he sat now, a gray old man, looking on while this little hop-o'-my-thumb performed miracles. Yes, yes, it is a gift of God, we must remember that. God grants His gifts, or He withholds them, and there is no shame in being an ordinary man. Like with the Christ Child.—Before a child one may kneel without feeling ashamed. Strange that thoughts like these should be so satisfying—he would even say so sweet, if it was not too silly for a tough old man like him to use the word. That was how he felt, anyhow.

Art . . . the businessman with the parrot-nose was thinking. "Yes, it adds something cheerful to life, a little good white silk and a little tumty-ti-ti-tum. Really he does not play so badly. Fully fifty seats, twelve marks apiece, that makes six hundred marks—and everything else besides. Take off the rent of the hall, the lighting and the programs, you must have fully a thousand marks profit. That is worthwhile."

That was Chopin[16] he was just playing, thought the piano teacher, a lady with a pointed nose; she was of an age when the understanding sharpens as the hopes decay. "But not very original—I will say that afterwards, it

---

12. *Méditation* [mā dē tä syōn']: short musical piece.
13. *Étude* [ā tōod']: solo musical piece intended to demonstrate a special technique.
14. *Fantaisie* [fän tā zē']: improvisational musical piece.

15. **seal ring:** ring with an embossed design to make imprints on wax.
16. **Chopin** [shō'pan]: Frederick Chopin (1810–1849), Polish-born French composer and pianist.

sounds well. And his hand position is entirely amateur. One must be able to lay a coin on the back of the hand—I would use a ruler on him."

Then there was a young girl, at that self-conscious and chlorotic[17] time of life when the most ineffable ideas come into the mind. She was thinking to herself: "What is it he is playing? It is expressive of passion, yet he is a child. If he kissed me it would be as though my little brother kissed me—no kiss at all. Is there such a thing as passion all by itself, without any earthly object, a sort of child's play of passion? What nonsense! If I were to say such things aloud they would just be at me with some more cod-liver oil. Such is life."

An officer was leaning against a column. He looked on at Bibi's success and thought: "Yes, you are something and I am something, each in his own way." So he clapped his heels together and paid to the prodigy the respect which he felt to be due to all the powers that be.

Then there was a critic, an elderly man in a shiny black coat and turned-up trousers splashed with mud. He sat in his free seat and thought: "Look at him, this young beggar of a Bibi. As an individual he has still to develop, but as a type he is already quite complete, the artist *par excellence*.[18] He has in himself all the artist's exaltation and his utter worthlessness, his charlatanry and his sacred fire, his burning contempt and his secret raptures. Of course I can't write all that, it is too good. Of course, I should have been an artist myself if I had not seen through the whole business so clearly."

Then the prodigy stopped playing and a perfect storm arose in the hall. He had to come out again and again from behind his screen. The man with the shiny buttons carried up more wreaths: four laurel wreaths, a lyre[19] made of violets, a bouquet of roses. He had not arms enough to convey all these tributes, the impresario himself mounted the stage to help him. He hung a laurel wreath round Bibi's neck, he tenderly stroked the black hair—and suddenly as though overcome he bent down and gave the prodigy a kiss, a resounding kiss, square on the mouth. And then the storm became a hurricane. That kiss ran through the room like an electric shock, it went direct to people's marrow and made them shiver down their backs. They were carried away by a helpless compulsion of sheer noise. Loud shouts mingled with the hysterical clapping of hands. Some of Bibi's commonplace little friends down there waved their handkerchiefs. But the critic thought: "Of course that kiss had to come—it's a good old gag. Yes, good Lord, if only one did not see through everything quite so clearly—"

And so the concert drew to a close. It began at half past seven and finished at half past eight. The platform was laden with wreaths and two little pots of flowers stood on the lamp stands of the piano. Bibi played as his last number his *Rhapsodie grecque*,[20] which turned into the Greek national hymn at the end. His fellow-countrymen in the audience would gladly have sung it with him if the company had not been so august. They made up for it with a powerful noise and hullabaloo, a hot-blooded national demonstration. And the aging critic was thinking: "Yes, the hymn had to come too. They have to exploit every vein—publicity cannot afford to neglect any means to its end. I think I'll critize that as inartistic. But perhaps I am wrong, perhaps that is the most artistic thing of all. What is the artist? A jack-in-the-box. Criticism is on a higher plane. But I can't say that." And away he went in his muddy trousers.

After being called out nine or ten times the prodigy did not come any more from behind the screen but went to his mother and the impresario down in the hall. The audience stood about among the chairs and applauded and

---

17. **chlorotic** [klō rot′ik]: referring to a type of anemia that affects adolescent girls.

18. *par excellence* [pär ek′sə läns′]: beyond comparison.

19. **lyre**: small, stringed musical instrument similar to a harp.

20. *Rhapsodie grecque* [räp′sō dē′grek′]: French for "Greek Rhapsody"; a rhapsody is a musical piece of free, irregular form.

pressed forward to see Bibi close at hand. Some of them wanted to see the princess too. Two dense circles formed, one round the prodigy, the other round the princess, and you could actually not tell which of them was receiving more homage. But the court lady was commanded to go over to Bibi; she smoothed down his silk jacket a bit to make it look suitable for a court function, led him by the arm to the princess, and solemnly indicated to him that he was to kiss the royal hand. "How do you do it, child?" asked the princess. "Does it come into your head of itself when you sit down?" "Oui, madame," answered Bibi. To himself he thought: "Oh, what a stupid old princess!" Then he turned round shyly and uncourtierlike and went back to his family.

Outside in the cloak room there was a crowd. People held up their numbers and received with open arms furs, shawls, and galoshes. Somewhere among her acquaintances the piano teacher stood making her critique. "He is not very original," she said audibly and looked about her.

In front of one of the great mirrors an elegant young lady was being arrayed in her evening cloak and fur shoes by her brothers, two lieutenants. She was exquisitely beautiful, with her steel-blue eyes and her clean-cut, well-bred face. A really noble dame. When she was ready she stood waiting for her brothers. "Don't stand so long in front of the glass, Adolf," she said softly to one of them, who could not tear himself away from the sight of his simple, good-looking young features. But Lieutenant Adolf thinks: What cheek! He would button his overcoat in front of the glass, just the same. Then they went out on the street where the arc lights[21] gleamed cloudily through the white mist. Lieutenant Adolf struck up a little dance on the frozen snow to keep warm, with his hands in his slanting overcoat pockets and his collar turned up.

A girl with untidy hair and swinging arms, accompanied by a gloomy-faced youth, came out just behind them. A child! she thought. A charming child. But in there he was an awe-inspiring . . . and aloud in a toneless voice she said: "We are all infant prodigies, we artists."

"Well, bless my soul!" thought the old gentleman who had never got further than Augustin on the piano, and whose boil was now concealed by a top hat. "What does all that mean? She sounds very oracular."[22] But the gloomy youth understood. He nodded his head slowly.

Then they were silent and the untidy-haired girl gazed after the brothers and sister. She rather despised them, but she looked after them until they had turned the corner.

---

21. **arc lights:** high-intensity light produced by an electric arc and used to illuminate outdoor nighttime events.
22. **oracular** [ô rak′yə lər]: with wise but mysterious meaning.

STUDY QUESTIONS

Recalling

1. Describe Bibi and the scene as he enters the concert hall.
2. Describe Bibi's enjoyment of his music. Give two examples of his attitude toward the audience.
3. Give at least three examples of opinions about Bibi and his music from individuals in the audience.

Interpreting

4. What aspects of his concert does Bibi enjoy, and which does he dislike? What does the critic dislike about the concert? What theme about artists is implied?
5. Explain how Bibi's talent makes the audience feel about him. How does it make them feel about themselves?
6. What is significant in the way the crowd surrounds the princess as well as Bibi after the concert?

7. What does the girl with untidy hair mean when she says, "We are all infant prodigies, we artists"? Why does she despise the two brothers and their sister?

Extending
8. To what extent do you think today's artists (or entertainers) and audiences share the attitudes of Bibi and his audience?

VIEWPOINT

In a letter to his friend, conductor Bruno Walter, Thomas Mann wrote:

Music as well as the other arts . . . is in a crisis which sometimes threatens its very life.

—*Letters of Thomas Mann*

■ Based on "The Infant Prodigy," what kind of crisis do you think threatens music and art?

LITERARY FOCUS

Irony
Irony is a broad term used to talk about a contrast between appearance and reality. **Situational irony** exists when what is expected to happen is not what actually comes to pass. For example, near the end of Shakespeare's *Macbeth*, Macbeth is secure in the prediction that he is safe until Birnam Wood marches to his castle at Dunsinane. Situational irony occurs when his enemies hack down Birnam's trees for use as camouflage. **Verbal irony** exists when words that appear to be saying one thing are really saying something quite different. For example, when in Shakespeare's *Julius Caesar* Marc Antony calls Brutus "an honorable man," he actually means the opposite.

Thinking About Irony
1. In what sense does irony exist in the difference between Bibi's public and private personalities? In the difference between the thoughts of the audience and their actions?
2. Review the words of dialogue and interior monologue in "The Infant Prodigy." Find two examples of verbal irony.

VOCABULARY

Antonyms
Antonyms are words that have opposite or nearly opposite meanings. *Traditional* and *innovative* are antonyms. The words in capital letters are from "The Infant Prodigy." Choose the word that is *most nearly the opposite* of each word in capital letters, *as the word is used in the selection.* Write the number of each item and the letter of your choice on a separate sheet.

1. HERALDED: (a) denounced (b) applauded (c) invented (d) cherished
2. NIMBLY: (a) agilely (b) gracefully (c) silently (d) awkwardly
3. MARRED: (a) flawless (b) contained (c) wedded (d) blemished
4. DEMURELY: (a) outrageously (b) singularly (c) modestly (d) tragically
5. MOROSELY: (a) gloomily (b) mournfully (c) cheerfully (d) naturally

COMPOSITION

Citing Evidence
■ In "The Infant Prodigy" Mann uses a few well-chosen details of description to create sympathy for some characters and dislike for others. For example, he wants the reader to sympathize with the girl with untidy hair and to dislike Bibi's mother. Cite evidence from the story—both verbatim and in paraphrase—to demonstrate Mann's use of descriptive detail. *For help with this assignment, refer to Lesson 3 in the Writing About Literature Handbook at the back of this book.*

Writing a Music Review
■ Write a brief review of a musical performance. Comment on a performance that you have seen live or one that you know from film, television, or recording. In your first paragraph describe the musician and the type of music. In your second paragraph write about your favorable impressions of the music and the style of performance. Write a third paragraph in which you record your unfavorable impressions.

Juan Ramón Jiménez   *1881–1958*

Juan Ramón Jiménez [hwän rä môn′ hē mä′neth] wrote poetry, poetic criticism, and lyrical nonfiction, and he is widely considered to be one of Spain's major poetic voices in the twentieth century. A tireless worker and a perfectionist, Jiménez authored more than thirty volumes of poems, and he devoted his life to revising and reworking them. He summed up his approach when he said that "a poem is never finished, only abandoned."

Jiménez was born in the small town of Moguer in southwestern Spain; his family were wealthy wine growers. After planning a career in law, he came to prefer painting and writing. Jiménez was extremely sensitive and was always in poor health. When the woman he loved went to school in the United States, Jiménez followed and married her. Together they returned to Spain, where, with his wife's help, Jiménez withdrew from most public activity and worked in a soundproof room. During the Spanish civil war Jiménez and his wife exiled themselves to Puerto Rico, where he continued to paint and to write poetry and criticism. In 1956, two days before his wife's death, Jiménez received the Nobel Prize for Literature.

Much of Jiménez's poetic career was devoted to achieving what he called "naked poetry," poems that are pure, simple, and objective. His best poems are fragile, refined melodies that are bathed in a gentle melancholy. They reflect a preoccupation with beauty, love, solitude, nature, and death. Jiménez's prose work *Platero and I* is a collection of poetic essays—prose poems—that reflect the isolation from everyday life that he felt as an artist. Platero is a donkey that accompanies the narrator through the small-town world of turn-of-the-century Moguer. The essays, which are more lyrical than expository, take a whimsical, ironic look at the people, landscape, and heartbeat of a little town that could represent many. Although prose, this work is reminiscent of Jiménez's poetry in its simple but poetic language and imagery and in its sensitive insights.

Juan Ramón Jiménez

from **Platero and I**

Translated by Eloïse Roach

Platero

Platero is a small donkey, a soft, hairy donkey: so soft to the touch that he might be said to be made of cotton, with no bones. Only the jet mirrors of his eyes are hard like two black crystal scarabs.

I turn him loose, and he goes to the meadow, and, with his nose, he gently caresses the little flowers of rose and blue and gold. . . . I call him softly, "Platero?" and he comes to me at a gay little trot that is like laughter of a vague, idyllic, tinkling sound.

He eats whatever I give him. He likes mandarin oranges, amber-hued muscatel grapes, purple figs tipped with crystalline drops of honey.

He is as loving and tender as a child, but strong and sturdy as a rock. When on Sundays I ride him through the lanes in the outskirts of the town, slow-moving countrymen, dressed in their Sunday clean, watch him a while, speculatively:

"He is like steel," they say.

Steel, yes. Steel and moon silver at the same time.

Twilight Games

At dusk, when, stiff with cold, Platero and I enter the purple darkness of the miserable by-street that fronts the dry river bed, the children of the poor are playing at make-believe, frightening one another, playing beggars. One throws a sack over his head, another says he is blind, another limps. . . .

Later, with that fickleness of childhood, since they at least wear shoes and clothes, and since their mothers—though only they know how—have fed them, they become princes and princesses.

"My father has a silver clock."

"Mine has a horse."

"Mine a gun."

Clock to rouse him at daybreak; gun that cannot kill hunger; horse to take him to misery. . . .

Then the children join hands, dancing in a circle. In the darkness a little girl with fragile voice like a thread of liquid crystal in the shadow sings proudly like a princess:

> "I am the young widow
> Of great Count Oré. . . ."

Aye, aye! Sing, dream, children of the poor! Soon, at the awakening of your youth, spring, like a beggar disguised as winter, will frighten you.

"Let us go, Platero."

Eclipse

We unwittingly put our hands in our pockets, and on our brows we felt the fine touch of a cool shadow, as when entering a thick pine forest. The chickens began going up their perch, one by one. All around, the countryside darkened its greenness, as if the purple veil of the main altar were spread over it. The distant sea was visible as a white vision, and a few stars shone palely. How the whiteness of the roofs took on a changed whiteness! Those of us who were on the roofs called to each other more or less wittily, small dark creatures in the confining silence of the eclipse.

We tried looking at the sun through all sorts of things: opera glasses, telescopes, bottles, smoked glass; and from all angles: the dormer window, the ladder in the yard, the granary window; through the scarlet and blue panes of the skylight. . . .

On hiding, the sun, which a moment before

made everything twice, thrice, a hundred times greater and better with its complexities of light and gold, now leaves all things, without the long transition of twilight, lonely and poverty-stricken as though one had exchanged gold for silver first and then silver for copper. The town resembles a musty and valueless copper cent. How gloomy and unimportant the streets, the squares, the tower, the mountain roads.

Down in the yard Platero appears less real, different and diminished, a different donkey. . . .

Fear

Large, round, pure, the moon comes with us. In the sleepy meadows we see shadowy forms like black goats among the blackberry bushes. At our passing, someone hides noiselessly. A huge almond tree, snowy with blooms and moonlight, its top enveloped in a white cloud, shadows the road shot with March stars. A penetrating smell of oranges. Dampness and silence. The witches' glen. . . .

"Platero, it is . . . cold!"

Platero—I do not know whether spurred on by his fear or by mine—trots, enters the creek bed, steps on the moon and breaks it into pieces. It is as if a swarm of clear crystal roses were entangled at his feet, trying to hold him. . . .

And Platero trots uphill, shortening his croup as if someone were after him, already sensing the soft warmth—which seems unattainable—of the approaching town.

STUDY QUESTIONS

Recalling

1. Based on "Platero," describe the donkey's appearance, and find at least three things to which the narrator compares him.
2. What are the three "twilight games" that the children play?
3. What is the reaction of the people to the eclipse? To what three metals does the narrator compare the sun's light?
4. What causes the narrator to become afraid? What is Platero's reaction to the fear?

Interpreting

5. According to "Platero," what apparently opposite qualities does the donkey possess?
6. What is the narrator's attitude toward the poor children in "Twilight Games"? What does he predict for them?
7. Explain how the use of detail in "Eclipse" provides a vivid picture of the event.
8. Explain the fear that the narrator feels in "Fear." What happens when Platero "steps on the moon and breaks it into pieces"?
9. In what ways are these essays like poetry? In what ways are they unlike poetry?

COMPOSITION

Writing About Nonfiction

■ In a brief essay discuss Jiménez's purpose in writing *Platero and I*. First explain what you think is the purpose of the essays, the effect that Jiménez wanted them to have. Then cite with examples the particular techniques that he uses to accomplish that purpose. You may want to consider the following: (a) narration, (b) description, (c) figurative language, and (d) tone. *For help with this assignment, refer to Lesson 4 in the Writing About Literature Handbook at the back of this book.*

Writing a Prose Poem

■ In the manner of Jiménez, write a poetic essay that describes an object and hints at emotions that the object awakens. To do so, describe an object in prose, but choose words and images carefully to reveal the feelings associated with the object. You may choose any object for the description, but you may want to consider one of the following: (a) a hamburger, (b) a catcher's mitt (or other piece of sports equipment), (c) a lawnmower, (d) a favorite item of clothing, or (e) a caterpillar.

Franz Kafka   *1883–1924*

Franz Kafka's [fränts käf′kə] fiction presents the most unusual events as completely commonplace. For example, in "The Metamorphosis" a young man wakes to discover his own transformation into an insect. Kafka's world is full of such occurrences, nightmares that capture what he saw as the particular anxiety of modern life. His characters— ordinary, rational beings—must cope with a world they no longer understand. They struggle unsuccessfully with the unknown, trying to make sense of events that are incomprehensible. Kafka's puzzling view of the world defies classification but contains elements of surrealism and existentialism. The nightmare vision, the illogical combination of events, and the seemingly realistic, detailed style create a verbal equivalent of surrealist art. Yet the fiction also pictures an existential world without meaningful order or pattern, a world in which human beings must live according to rules they cannot understand.

Franz Kafka was born in Prague, in what is now Czechoslovakia, to an affluent German-speaking Jewish family. He wrote part time while working as an insurance lawyer. Because his father disapproved of his literary interests and because of his own doubts about his talents, he published only a few works during his life and intended the rest to be destroyed after his death. A friend disobeyed instructions and published the remainder of the work after Kafka died of tuberculosis at forty-one.

Kafka's work is a series of variations on a recurring topic: the estrangement of the individual from society. In *The Trial* (1925) a man is arrested, tried, and executed for a crime he never understands. In *The Castle* (1926) a man struggles to enter the fortress home of a supreme authority. The atmosphere is one of futility, loneliness, and alienation. Meaning exists on different levels and is suggested through symbolism, descriptive detail, and concrete imagery. Like all Kafka's fiction, "First Sorrow" presents a puzzle for both hero and reader.

Franz Kafka

First Sorrow

Translated by Willa and Edwin Muir

A trapeze artist—this art, practiced high in the vaulted domes of the great variety theaters, is admittedly one of the most difficult humanity can achieve—had so arranged his life that, as long as he kept working in the same building, he never came down from his trapeze by night or day, at first only from a desire to perfect his skill, but later because custom was too strong for him. All his needs, very modest needs at that, were supplied by relays of attendants who watched from below and sent up and hauled down again in specially constructed containers whatever he required. This way of living caused no particular inconvenience to the theatrical people, except that, when other turns were on the stage, his being still up aloft, which could not be dissembled, proved somewhat distracting, as also the fact that, although at such times he mostly kept very still, he drew a stray glance here and there from the public. Yet the management overlooked this, because he was an extraordinary and unique artist. And of course they recognized that this mode of life was no mere prank, and that only in this way could he really keep himself in constant practice and his art at the pitch of its perfection.

Besides, it was quite healthful up there, and when in the warmer seasons of the year the side windows all around the dome of the theater were thrown open and sun and fresh air came pouring irresistibly into the dusky vault, it was even beautiful. True, his social life was somewhat limited, only sometimes a fellow acrobat swarmed up the ladder to him, and then they both sat on the trapeze, leaning left and right against the supporting ropes, and chatted, or builders' workmen repairing the roof exchanged a few words with him through an open window, or the fireman, inspecting the emergency lighting in the top gallery, called over to him something that sounded respectful but could hardly be made out. Otherwise nothing disturbed his seclusion; occasionally, perhaps, some theater hand straying through the empty theater of an afternoon gazed thoughtfully up into the great height of the roof, almost beyond eyeshot, where the trapeze artist, unaware that he was being observed, practiced his art or rested.

The trapeze artist could have gone on living peacefully like that, had it not been for the inevitable journeys from place to place, which he found extremely trying. Of course his manager saw to it that his sufferings were not prolonged one moment more than necessary; for town travel, racing automobiles were used, which whirled him, by night if possible or in the earliest hours of the morning, through the empty streets at breakneck speed, too slow all the same for the trapeze artist's impatience; for railways journeys, a whole compartment was reserved, in which the trapeze artist, as a possible though wretched alternative to his usual way of living, could pass the time up on the luggage rack; in the next town on their circuit, long before he arrived, the trapeze was already slung up in the theater and all the doors leading to the stage were flung wide open, all corridors kept free—yet the manager never knew a happy moment until the trapeze artist set his foot on the rope ladder and in a twinkling, at long last, hung aloft on his trapeze.

Despite so many journeys having been successfully arranged by the manager, each new one embarrassed him again, for the journeys, apart from everything else, got on the nerves of the artist a great deal.

Once when they were again traveling together, the trapeze artist lying on the luggage rack dreaming, the manager leaning back in the opposite window seat reading a book, the trapeze artist addressed his companion in a low voice. The manager was immediately all attention. The trapeze artist, biting his lips, said that he must always in future have two trapezes for his performance instead of only one, two trapezes opposite each other. The manager at once agreed. But the trapeze artist, as if to show that the manager's consent counted for as little as his refusal, said that never again would he perform on only one trapeze, in no circumstances whatever. The very idea that it might happen at all seemed to make him shudder. The manager, watchfully feeling his way, once more emphasized his entire agreement, two trapezes were better than one, besides it would be an advantage to have a second bar, more variety could be introduced into the performance. At that the trapeze artist suddenly burst into tears. Deeply distressed, the manager sprang to his feet and asked what was the matter, then getting no answer climbed up on the seat and caressed him, cheek to cheek, so that his own face was bedabbled by the trapeze artist's tears. Yet it took much questioning and soothing endearment until the trapeze artist sobbed: "Only the one bar in my hands—how can I go on living!" That made it somewhat easier for the manager to comfort him; he promised to wire from the very next station for a second trapeze to be installed in the first town on their circuit; reproached himself for having let the artist work so long on only one trapeze; and thanked and praised him warmly for having at last brought the mistake to his notice. And so he succeeded in reassuring the trapeze artist, little by little, and was able to go back to his corner. But he himself was far from reassured, with deep uneasiness he kept glancing secretly at the trapeze artist over the top of his book. Once such ideas began to torment him, would they ever quite leave him alone? Would they not rather increase in urgency? Would they not threaten his very existence? And indeed the manager believed he could see, during the apparently peaceful sleep which had succeeded the fit of tears, the first furrows of care engraving themselves upon the trapeze artist's smooth, childlike forehead.

STUDY QUESTIONS

Recalling

1. Why did the trapeze artist stay on his trapeze night and day? Why did the management permit him to do so?
2. Briefly describe the trapeze artist's manner of traveling.
3. What tearful request does the trapeze artist make of his manager? What is the manager's reaction?
4. What thought worries the manager at the end of the story?

Interpreting

5. In what sense do the trapeze artist's way of life and his request to the manager represent modern life in general? Explain.
6. What is the significance of the story's title?
7. Explain the significance of the story's last four sentences.

LITERARY FOCUS

Existentialism

Existentialism [eg′zis ten′shə liz′əm] is a modern European philosophy that is concerned with the nature of life, or existence. It developed as a highly pragmatic response to the alienation and confusion that defines the modern age. Existentialists consider life empty of any meaning, purpose, or value other than that which individuals give to their own lives. Existentialists believe that people must cope with the indifference of the world around them and define themselves entirely through their own actions. Although Kafka's fiction is not purely existential, his work influenced Jean-Paul Sartre and Albert Camus, leaders of the existentialist movement in France.

Thinking About Existentialism

■ Explain how the events of "First Sorrow" suggest an existentialist view of life.

Hermann Hesse   *1887–1962*

Young people across Europe and America have been responding to Hermann Hesse's [hes′ə] voice for more than fifty years. After World War I Thomas Mann wrote of Hesse's novel *Demian* (1919) that it "struck the nerve of the times and called forth grateful rapture from a whole youthful generation who believed that an interpreter of their innermost life had risen from their own midst—whereas it was a man already thirty-two years old." Hesse was able to appeal to that and succeeding generations of young people by exploring issues that concern them: identity, self-realization, and individuality.

Hermann Hesse was born in Calw, in southern Germany's Black Forest. His parents were Protestant missionaries who spent many years in India. Hesse, who was expected to follow his parents into their vocation, worked instead as a bookseller, a job which he hoped would lead to a writing career. His early writings were successful and won him a following. Hesse angered many of his faithful readers, however, with a series of pacifist essays during World War I. After the war he moved to Switzerland and surrendered his German citizenship.

Demian was the first novel to express the new man that Hesse felt he had become after the war. The novel teaches that people have a "divine duty" to be themselves and that the only way to improve the human condition is for each individual to improve from within. *Demian* and the novels that followed sought a balance between what Hesse saw as conflicting poles in life—order and chaos, reason and antireason, the mind and the senses. Oriental philosophy, which he had absorbed through his family's missionary work, became an influence in novels such as *Siddhartha* (1920) and *Steppenwolf* (1927). Each novel presents one person's journey in search of self-awareness and fulfillment.

Like all of Hesse's work, "The Jackdaw" contains different levels of meaning. (The title refers to a European black bird smaller than a crow.) On the surface the mood of the story is light, but careful reading uncovers a serious, perhaps somber undertone.

Hermann Hesse

The Jackdaw

Translated by Rika Lesser

It has been a long time since, as a returning visitor to Baden[1] to take the cure, I have gone there with the expectation of being surprised. The day will come when the last stretch of the Goldwand will be built over, the lovely spa park converted into factories, but I will not live to see this. And yet on this visit, on the ugly, lopsided bridge to Ennetbaden, a wonderful and charming surprise awaited me. I am in the habit of allowing myself a few moments of sheer pleasure each day when I stand on this bridge—it lies but a few steps from the spa hotel—and feed the gulls with some small pieces of bread. They are not at the bridge at all hours of the day, and when they are there one cannot talk to them. There are times when they sit in long rows on the roof of the city baths building, guarding the bridge and waiting for one of the passers-by to stop, take some bread out of his pocket, and throw it to them. When someone tosses a bit of bread up into the air, the youthful and acrobatic gulls like to hover over the head of the bread-thrower as long as they can; one can watch each one and try to make sure that each gull will get its turn. Then one is besieged by a deafening roaring and flashing, a whirling and clattering swarm of feverish life; beleaguered and wooed, one stands amid a white-gray winged cloud, out of which, without pause, short, shrill shrieks shoot. But there are always a number of more prudent and less athletic gulls who keep their distance from the tumult and who leisurely cruise down below the bridge and over the streaming waters of the river Limmat, where it is calm and where some piece of bread, having escaped the clutches of the vying acrobats up above, is always sure to fall. At other times of day, there are no gulls here at all. Perhaps they have all gone on an outing together, a school or a club excursion; perhaps they have found an especially rich feeding place farther down the Limmat; in any event, they have all disappeared together. And then there are other hours when, to be sure, the whole flock of gulls is at hand, but they are not sitting on the rooftops or thronging over the head of the feeder; rather, they are swarming and raising a din importantly and excitedly just above the surface of the water a bit downstream. No amount of waving or bread-tossing will help, they don't give a hoot, busy as they are with their bird games, and perhaps their human games: gathering the tribes together, brawling, voting, trading stocks, who knows what else. And even with baskets full of the most delectable morsels you would not be able to draw them away from their uproarious and important transactions and games.

This time when I got to the bridge, seated on the railing was a black bird, a jackdaw of extremely small stature, and when it did not fly away at my nearer approach, I stalked it, more and more slowly inching closer to it, one small step after the other. It showed neither fear nor suspicion, only attentiveness and curiosity; it let me get within a half step of it, surveyed me with its blithe bird eyes, and tilted its powdery gray head to one side, as if to say: "Come now, old man, you certainly do stare!" Indeed, I was staring. This jackdaw was accustomed to having dealings with humans, you could talk to it, and a few people who knew him had already come by and greeted him, saying: "Salut,[2] Jakob." I tried to find out more

---

1. **Baden** [bäd′ən]: town and spa, or health resort with hot springs baths, on the Limmat River in northern Switzerland.

2. **Salut** [sä lū′]: French for "hello."

about him, and since that time I've collected quite a bit of information, all of it contradictory. The main questions remain unanswered: where the bird made its home and how it came to be on intimate terms with human beings. One person told me the bird was tamed and that he belonged to a woman in Ennetbaden. Another said that he roamed freely, wherever it suited him, and sometimes he'd fly into a room through an open window, peck at something edible, or pluck to shreds some knitted garment left lying around. A man from one of the French-speaking cantons,[3] obviously a bird specialist, asserted that this jackdaw belonged to a very rare species, which, as far as he knew, could be found only in the mountains of Fribourg,[4] where it lived in the rocky cliffs.

After that, I would meet the jackdaw Jakob almost every day; now by myself, now with my wife, I would greet him and talk to him. One day my wife was wearing a pair of shoes whose uppers had a pattern cut out of the leather, allowing a bit of stocking to shine through the holes. These shoes, and especially the little islands of hose, interested Jakob a great deal; he alit on the ground, and with sparkling eyes he took aim and pecked at them with gusto. Many a time he would sit on my arm or my shoulder and peck at my coat, my collar, my cheek, and my neck, or tear at the brim of my hat. He did not care for bread; still, he would get jealous and sometimes downright angry if you shared it with the gulls in his presence. He accepted and adeptly picked walnuts or peanuts from the hand of the giver. But best of all he liked to peck, pluck, pulverize, and destroy any little thing—a crumpled ball of paper, a cigar stub, a little piece of cardboard or material; he'd put one of his feet on it and rashly and impatiently hack away at it with his beak. And time and again one perceives that he does all this not for his sake alone but on behalf of the onlookers, some of whom always and many of whom

often gather around him. For them he hops about on the ground or back and forth on the railing of the bridge, enjoying the crowd; he flutters onto the head or shoulder of one of the members of the audience, alights again on the ground, studies our shoes, and forcefully pecks at them. He takes pleasure in pecking and plucking, tearing and destroying, he does all this with roguish delight; but the members of the audience must also participate, they must admire, laugh, cry out, feel flattered by his show of friendliness, and then again show fear when he pecks at their stockings, hats, and hands.

He has no fear of the gulls, who are twice as large and many times stronger than he; sometimes he flies on high right in their midst. And they let him be. For one thing, he who scarcely touches bread is neither a rival nor a spoilsport; for another, I suppose that they, too, consider him a phenomenon, something rare, enigmatic, and a little bit uncanny. He is alone, belongs to no tribe, follows no customs, obeys no commands, no laws; he has left the tribe of jackdaws, where once he was one among many, and has turned toward the human tribe, which looks on him with astonishment and brings him offerings, and which he serves as a buffoon or a tightrope walker when it suits him; he makes fun of them and yet cannot get enough of their admiration. Between the bright gulls and the motley humans he sits, black, impudent, and alone, the only one of his kind; by destiny or by choice, he has no tribe and no homeland. Audacious and sharp-eyed, he sits watching over the traffic on the bridge, pleased that only a few people rush past inattentive, that the majority stop for a while, often a long while; because of him they remain standing, and gaze at him in astonishment, racking their brains over him, calling him Jakob, and only reluctantly deciding to walk on. He does not take people more seriously than a jackdaw should, and yet he seems unable to do without them.

When I found myself alone with him—and this happened only rarely—I could talk to him

---

3. **French-speaking cantons** [kan'tənz]: Cantons are states in Switzerland; they are grouped according to the three official languages, French, German, and Italian.
4. **Fribourg** [frē bŏŏr']: canton in western Switzerland.

a little in a bird language which as a boy and youth I had partly learned from years of intimate discourse with our pet parrot and had partly invented on my own; it consisted of a brief melodic series of notes uttered in a guttural tone. I would bend down toward Jakob and talk things over with him in a fraternal way in my half-bird dialect; he would throw back his lovely head; he enjoyed both listening and thinking his own thoughts. But unexpectedly the rogue and the sprite would come to the fore in him again; he would alight on my shoulder, dig in his claws, and rapping like a woodpecker he would hammer his beak into my neck or cheek, until it was too much for me and I would shrug myself free, whereupon he would return to the railing, amused and ready for new games. But at the same time he would survey the footpath in both directions with hasty glances, to see if more of the tribe of humans were on the march and whether there were any new conquests to be made. He understood his position to a tee, his hold on us great clumsy animals, his uniqueness and chosenness in the midst of a strange ungainly people, and he enjoyed it enormously, tightrope walker and actor, when he found himself in the thick of a crowd of admiring, moved, or laughing giants. In me, at least, he had gained favor, and those times when I came to pay him a visit and did not find him I was disappointed and sad. My interest in him was a good deal stronger than in the majority of my fellow human beings. And much as I esteemed the gulls and loved their beautiful, wild, fervent expressions of life, when I stood in their fluttering midst, they were not individuals; they were a flock, a band, and even if I looked back to examine one of them more closely as an individual, never again would I recognize him once he had escaped my field of vision.

I have never learned where and by what means Jakob was estranged from his tribe and the safe harbor of his anonymity, whether he himself had chosen this extraordinary destiny— as tragic as it was radiant—or whether he had been forced to do so. The latter is more plausible. Presumably he was quite young when perhaps he fell wounded or unfledged from the nest, was found and taken in by people, cared for and raised. And yet our imagination is not always satisfied with the most plausible explanation, it also likes to play with the remote and the sensational, and so I have conceived of two further possibilities beyond the probable one. It is conceivable, or rather, imaginable that this Jakob was a genius who from an early age felt himself to be very different, striving for an abnormal degree of individuality, dreaming of accomplishments, achievements, and honors which were unknown in jackdaw life and the jackdaw tribe, and thus he became an outsider and loner who, like the young man in Schiller's poem,[5] shunned the coarse company of his companions and wandered about by himself until through some lucky chance the world opened for him a door to the realm of beauty, art, and fame, about which all young geniuses have dreamed since time out of mind.

The other fable I've made up about Jakob is this: Jakob was a ne'er-do-well, a mischief-maker, a little rascal, which in no way rules out his being a genius. With his impudent attacks and pranks, he had at first bewildered and at times delighted his father and mother, siblings and relatives, and finally the whole of his community or colony. From early on, he was considered to be a little devil and a sly fellow, then he became more and more impertinent, and in the end he had so provoked his father's household against him, as well as the neighbors, the tribe, and the government, that he was solemnly excommunicated and, like the scapegoat, driven out into the wilderness. But before he languished away and perished, he came into contact with human beings. Having conquered his natural fear of the clumsy giants, he drew closer to them and joined them, enchanting them with his cheerful disposition and his uniqueness—of which he himself had

---

5. **Schiller's poem:** refers to "The Lay of the Bell," a poem by the German poet Johann von Schiller (1759–1805).

long been aware. And so he found his way into the city and the world of human beings, and in it a place for himself as a joker, an actor, a main attraction, and a wunderkind.[6] He became what he is today: the darling of a large public, a much sought-after *charmeur*[7]—particularly of elderly ladies and gentlemen, as much a friend to humans as one contemptuous of them, an artist soliloquizing at the podium, an envoy from a strange world—one unknown to clumsy giants, a buffoon for some, a dark admonition for others, laughed at, applauded, loved, admired, pitied, a drama for all, an enigma for the contemplative.

We the contemplative—for doubtless there are many others besides myself—turn our thoughts and conjectures, our impulse to understand the fabulous, not solely toward Jakob's enigmatic lineage and past. His appearance, which so stimulates our imagination, compels us to devote some thought to his fu-

ture as well. And we do this with some hesitation, with a feeling of resistance and sadness; for the presumable and probable end of our darling will be a violent one. No matter how much we may want to imagine a quiet and natural death for him, something on the order of his dying in the warm room and good care of that legendary lady in Ennetbaden to whom he supposedly "belongs," all probability speaks against it. A creature that has emerged from the freedom of the wild, from a secure place in a community and a tribe, and has fallen into the company of human beings and into civilization, no matter how adeptly he may adapt to the foreign surroundings, no matter how aware he may be of the advantages his unique situation provides, such a creature cannot completely escape the countless dangers concealed in this very situation. The mere thought of all these imaginable dangers—from electric current to being locked up in a room with a cat or dog, or being captured and tormented by cruel little boys—makes one shudder.

There are reports of peoples in olden times who every year chose or drew lots for a king.

---

6. **wunderkind** [voon′dər kint′]: "wonder child," or child prodigy.
7. ***charmeur*** [shär mœr′]: French for "charmer."

Then a handsome, nameless, and poor youth, a slave perhaps, would suddenly be clad in splendid robes and raised to the position of king; he would be given a palace or a majestic tent-of-state, servants ready to serve, lovely girls, kitchen, cellar, stable, and orchestra; the whole fairy tale of kingship, power, riches, and pomp would become reality for the chosen one. And so the new ruler would live amidst pomp and circumstance for days, weeks, months, until a year had elapsed. Then he would be tied and bound, taken to the place of execution, and slaughtered.

And it is of this story, which I read once decades ago and whose authenticity I have neither occasion nor desire to verify, this glittering and gruesome story—beautiful as a fairy tale and steeped in death, that I must sometimes think when I observe Jakob, pecking peanuts from ladies' hands, rebuking an overly clumsy child with a blow from his beak, taking an interest in and somewhat patronizingly listening to my parrotlike chatter, or plucking up a paper ball before an enraptured audience, holding it fast with one of his clawed feet—while his capricious head and his bristling gray headfeathers simultaneously appear to express anger and delight.

STUDY QUESTIONS

Recalling

1. Describe the behavior of the two types of gulls near the bridge. In what ways is the jackdaw different from either type?
2. What three explanations does the narrator offer for how the jackdaw became separated from his flock?
3. What activities does the jackdaw share with humans? Find two conflicting emotions toward humans that the narrator gives to the jackdaw.
4. Relate briefly and in your own words the story of the poor youth made king.

Interpreting

5. Why does the narrator call the jackdaw's separation from its flock "tragic" and "radiant"?
6. Based on the type of human the bird represents, explain the symbolism of the jackdaw.
7. Explain the significance of the story of the poor youth made king.

Extending

8. Why do you think authors often choose to disguise their observations on human nature by writing about animals? In answering, consider also the fables by Aesop (page 671).

VIEWPOINT

Hesse's popularity among young people caused many youth to seek his advice. One critic reveals Hesse's reaction to these requests:

> . . . he did not want to be a counselor, a physician, or a leader, and if there was anything he ever intended to teach, it was that young people should become themselves.
>
> —A. Otten, *Hesse Companion*

■ Does "The Jackdaw" exemplify Hesse's refusal to be a leader? According to the story what pressures do people who "become themselves" face?

COMPOSITION

Writing a Comparison/Contrast

■ Compare and contrast Hesse's "Jackdaw" and Thomas Mann's "Infant Prodigy." Point out similarities and differences in their content and in their techniques. You may wish to consider plot, character, setting, theme, and symbolism. *For help with this assignment, refer to Lesson 2 in the Writing About Literature Handbook at the back of this book.*

Writing a Fable

■ Write a brief fable in which an animal character symbolizes a human trait. To do this, choose (1) a facet of human nature about which you would like to write and (2) an animal that is an appropriate symbol of this human trait. In creating your fable, illustrate the personality of the animal character, and show its relationships with other animals.

Albert Camus   *1913–1960*

In the essay *The Myth of Sisyphus* [sis'ə fəs] (1942), Albert Camus [ka m$\overline{oo}$'] demonstrates his existentialist philosophy. Sisyphus is a mythological character who was condemned by the gods to roll a huge boulder up a mountain only to have to begin anew when the boulder rolled down again. Condemned to this absurdity forever, Sisyphus symbolizes Camus's view of life as a ceaseless replay of meaningless existence. Camus refused to be included with French author Jean-Paul Sartre among the existentialists but is usually ranked as one of their strongest voices. One area of disagreement between him and many other existentialists is Camus's optimism. While others denied any hope, Camus gradually came to believe in the possibility of honesty and dignity in a world without order or purpose. Even Sisyphus could attain happiness by being honest with himself and by accepting what he could not change.

Camus was born in Algeria—at the time a French colony—in North Africa. His parents were poor; his mother was deaf. Camus studied philosophy in college and worked as a journalist and as an actor. During World War II he edited a resistance newspaper for the underground movement against the German occupation of France. His essays, novels, and plays won him the Nobel Prize for Literature in 1957, three years before he died in an automobile accident.

Camus's novels show the development of his philosophy. *The Stranger* (1946) illustrates the isolation and alienation of the individual; it also deals with human freedom and its attendant burden of responsibility. *The Plague* (1947) displays Camus's compassion and his call for human solidarity in the face of life's absurdity. *The Fall* (1957), his most pessimistic novel, presents humanity as the source of its own suffering. "The Guest" is one of Camus's later stories. Beyond the plot lies Camus's ever-present question: Why?

Albert Camus

The Guest

Translated by Justin O'Brien

The schoolmaster was watching the two men climb toward him. One was on horseback, the other on foot. They had not yet tackled the abrupt rise leading to the schoolhouse built on the hillside. They were toiling onward, making slow progress in the snow, among the stones on the vast expanse of the high, deserted plateau. From time to time the horse stumbled. Without hearing anything yet, he could see the breath issuing from the horse's nostrils. One of the men, at least, knew the region. They were following the trail although it had disappeared days ago under a layer of dirty white snow. The schoolmaster calculated that it would take them half an hour to get onto the hill. It was cold; he went back into the school to get a sweater.

He crossed the empty, frigid classroom. On the blackboard the four rivers of France, drawn with four different colored chalks, had been flowing toward their estuaries for the past three days. Snow had suddenly fallen in mid-October after eight months of drought without the transition of rain, and the twenty pupils, more or less, who lived in the villages scattered over the pleateau had stopped coming. With fair weather they would return. Daru now heated only the single room that was his lodging, adjoining the classroom and giving also onto the plateau to the east. Like the class windows, his window looked to the south too. On that side the school was a few kilometers from the point where the plateau began to slope toward the south. In clear weather could be seen the purple mass of the mountain range where the gap opened onto the desert.

Somewhat warmed, Daru returned to the window from which he had first seen the two men. They were no longer visible. Hence they must have tackled the rise. The sky was not so dark, for the snow had stopped falling during the night. The morning had opened with a dirty light which had scarcely become brighter as the ceiling of clouds lifted. At two in the afternoon it seemed as if the day were merely beginning. But still this was better than those three days when the thick snow was falling amid unbroken darkness with little gusts of wind that rattled the double door of the classroom. Then Daru had spent long hours in his room, leaving it only to go to the shed and feed the chickens or get some coal. Fortunately the delivery truck from Tadjid, the nearest village to the north, had brought his supplies two days before the blizzard. It would return in forty-eight hours.

Besides, he had enough to resist a siege, for the little room was cluttered with bags of wheat that the administration left as a stock to distribute to those of his pupils whose families had suffered from the drought. Actually they had all been victims because they were all poor. Every day Daru would distribute a ration to the children. They had missed it, he knew, during these bad days. Possibly one of the fathers or big brothers would come this afternoon and he could supply them with grain. It was just a matter of carrying them over to the next harvest. Now shiploads of wheat were arriving from France and the worst was over. But it would be hard to forget that poverty, that army of ragged ghosts wandering in the sunlight, the plateaus burned to a cinder month after month, the earth shriveled up little by little, literally scorched, every stone bursting into dust under one's foot. The sheep had died then by thousands and even a few men, here and there, sometimes without anyone's knowing.

In contrast with such poverty, he who lived almost like a monk in his remote schoolhouse, nonetheless satisfied with the little he had and with the rough life, had felt like a lord with his whitewashed walls, his narrow couch, his un-painted shelves, his well, and his weekly pro-vision of water and food. And suddenly this snow, without warning, without the foretaste of rain. This is the way the region was, cruel to live in, even without men—who didn't help matters either. But Daru had been born here. Everywhere else, he felt exiled.

He stepped out onto the terrace in front of the schoolhouse. The two men were now half-way up the slope. He recognized the horseman as Balducci, the old gendarme[1] he had known for a long time. Balducci was holding on the end of a rope an Arab who was walking behind him with hands bound and head lowered. The gendarme waved a greeting to which Daru did not reply, lost as he was in contemplation of the Arab dressed in a faded blue jellaba,[2] his feet in sandals but covered with socks of heavy raw wool, his head surmounted by a narrow, short *chèche*.[3] They were approaching. Bal-ducci was holding back his horse in order not to hurt the Arab, and the group was advancing slowly.

Within earshot, Balducci shouted: "One hour to do the three kilometers from El Ameur!" Daru did not answer. Short and square in his thick sweater, he watched them climb. Not once had the Arab raised his head. "Hello," said Daru when they got up onto the terrace. "Come in and warm up." Balducci painfully got down from his horse without letting go the rope. From under his bristling mustache he smiled at the schoolmaster. His little dark eyes, deep-set under a tanned forehead, and his mouth surrounded with wrinkles made him look attentive and studious. Daru took the bri-dle, led the horse to the shed, and came back to the two men, who were now waiting for him in the school. He led them into his room. "I am going to heat up the classroom," he said.

---

1. **gendarme** [zhän′därm]: armed policeman in French-speaking countries.
2. **jellaba** [jə lä′bə]: loose-fitting hooded garment worn by men in North Africa.
3. **chèche** [shäsh′yä]: cylindrical tasseled cap worn by Arabs.

"We'll be more comfortable there." When he entered the room again, Balducci was on the couch. He had undone the rope tying him to the Arab, who had squatted near the stove. His hands still bound, the *chèche* pushed back on his head, he was looking toward the window. At first Daru noticed only his huge lips, fat, smooth, almost Negroid; yet his nose was straight, his eyes were dark and full of fever. The *chèche* revealed an obstinate forehead and, under the weathered skin now rather discol-ored by the cold, the whole face had a restless and rebellious look that struck Daru when the Arab, turning his face toward him, looked him straight in the eyes. "Go into the other room," said the schoolmaster, "and I'll make you some mint tea." "Thanks," Balducci said. "What a chore! How I long for retirement." And ad-dressing his prisoner in Arabic: "Come on, you." The Arab got up and, slowly, holding his bound wrists in front of him, went into the classroom.

With the tea, Daru brought a chair. But Bal-ducci was already enthroned on the nearest pupil's desk and the Arab had squatted against the teacher's platform facing the stove, which stood between the desk and the window. When he held out the glass of tea to the pris-oner, Daru hesitated at the sight of his bound hands. "He might perhaps be untied." "Sure," said Balducci. "That was for the trip." He started to get to his feet. But Daru, setting the glass on the floor, had knelt beside the Arab. Without saying anything, the Arab watched him with his feverish eyes. Once his hands were free, he rubbed his swollen wrists against each other, took the glass of tea, and sucked up the burning liquid in swift little sips.

"Good," said Daru. "And where are you headed?"

Balducci withdrew his mustache from the tea. "Here, son."

"Odd pupils! And you're spending the night?"

"No. I'm going back to El Ameur. And you will deliver this fellow to Tinguit. He is ex-pected at police headquarters."

Balducci was looking at Daru with a friendly little smile.

"What's this story?" asked the schoolmaster. "Are you pulling my leg?"

"No, son. Those are the orders."

"The orders? I'm not . . ." Daru hesitated, not wanting to hurt the old Corsican.[4] "I mean, that's not my job."

"What! What's the meaning of that? In wartime people do all kinds of jobs."

"Then I'll wait for the declaration of war!" Balducci nodded.

"O.K. But the orders exist and they concern you too. Things are brewing, it appears. There is talk of a forthcoming revolt. We are mobilized, in a way."

Daru still had his obstinate look.

"Listen, son," Balducci said. "I like you and you must understand. There's only a dozen of us at El Ameur to patrol throughout the whole territory of a small department and I must get back in a hurry. I was told to hand this guy over to you and return without delay. He couldn't be kept there. His village was beginning to stir; they wanted to take him back. You must take him to Tinguit tomorrow before the day is over. Twenty kilometers shouldn't faze a husky fellow like you. After that, all will be over. You'll come back to your pupils and your comfortable life."

Behind the wall the horse could be heard snorting and pawing the earth. Daru was looking out the window. Decidedly, the weather was clearing and the light was increasing over the snowy plateau. When all the snow was melted, the sun would take over again and once more would burn the fields of stone. For days, still, the unchanging sky would shed its dry light on the solitary expanse where nothing had any connection with man.

"After all," he said, turning around toward Balducci, "what did he do?" And, before the gendarme had opened his mouth, he asked: "Does he speak French?"

"No, not a word. We had been looking for him for a month, but they were hiding him. He killed his cousin."

"Is he against us?"

"I don't think so. But you can never be sure."

"Why did he kill?"

"A family squabble, I think. One owed the other grain, it seems. It's not at all clear. In short, he killed his cousin with a billhook.[5] You know, like a sheep, *kreezk!*"

Balducci made the gesture of drawing a blade across his throat and the Arab, his attention attracted, watched him with a sort of anxiety. Daru felt a sudden wrath against the man, against all men with their rotten spite, their tireless hates, their blood lust.

But the kettle was singing on the stove. He served Balducci more tea, hesitated, then served the Arab again, who, a second time, drank avidly. His raised arms made the jellaba fall open and the schoolmaster saw his thin, muscular chest.

"Thanks, kid," Balducci said. "And now, I'm off."

He got up and went toward the Arab, taking a small rope from his pocket.

"What are you doing?" Daru asked dryly.

Balducci, disconcerted, showed him the rope.

"Don't bother."

The old gendarme hesitated. "It's up to you. Of course, you are armed?"

"I have my shotgun."

"Where?"

"In the trunk."

"You ought to have it near your bed."

"Why? I have nothing to fear."

"You're crazy, son. If there's an uprising, no one is safe, we're all in the same boat."

"I'll defend myself. I'll have time to see them coming."

Balducci began to laugh, then suddenly the mustache covered the white teeth.

---

4. **Corsican:** person from Corsica, a French island in the Mediterranean.

5. **billhook:** hook-shaped instrument used for pruning or cutting.

"You'll have time? O.K. That's just what I was saying. You have always been a little cracked. That's why I like you, my son was like that."

At the same time he took out his revolver and put it on the desk.

"Keep it: I don't need two weapons from here to El Ameur."

The revolver shone against the black paint of the table. When the gendarme turned toward him, the schoolmaster caught the smell of leather and horseflesh.

"Listen, Balducci," Daru said suddenly, "every bit of this disgusts me, and first of all your fellow here. But I won't hand him over. Fight, yes, if I have to. But not that."

The old gendarme stood in front of him and looked at him severely.

"You're being a fool," he said slowly. "I don't like it either. You don't get used to putting a rope on a man even after years of it, and you're even ashamed—yes, ashamed. But you can't let them have their way."

"I won't hand him over," Daru said again.

"It's an order, son, and I repeat it."

"That's right. Repeat to them what I've said to you: I won't hand him over."

Balducci made a visible effort to reflect. He looked at the Arab and at Daru. At last he decided.

"No, I won't tell them anything. If you want to drop us, go ahead; I'll not denounce you. I have an order to deliver the prisoner and I'm doing so. And now you'll just sign this paper for me."

"There's no need. I'll not deny that you left him with me."

"Don't be mean with me. I know you'll tell the truth. You're from hereabouts and you are a man. But you must sign, that's the rule."

Daru opened his drawer, took out a little square bottle of purple ink, the red wooden penholder with the "sergeant-major" pen he used for making models of penmanship, and signed. The gendarme carefully folded the paper and put it into his wallet. Then he moved toward the door.

"I'll see you off," Daru said.

"No," said Balducci. "There's no use being polite. You insulted me."

He looked at the Arab, motionless in the same spot, sniffed peevishly, and turned away toward the door. "Good-by, son," he said. The door shut behind him. Balducci appeared suddenly outside the window and then disappeared. His footsteps were muffled by the snow. The horse stirred on the other side of the wall and several chickens fluttered in fright. A moment later Balducci reappeared outside the window leading the horse by the bridle. He walked toward the little rise without turning around and disappeared from sight with the horse following him. A big stone could be heard bouncing down. Daru walked back toward the prisoner, who, without stirring, never took his eyes off him. "Wait," the schoolmaster said in Arabic and went toward the bedroom. As he was going through the door, he had a second thought, went to the desk, took the revolver, and stuck it in his pocket. Then, without looking back, he went into his room.

For some time he lay on his couch watching the sky gradually close over, listening to the silence. It was this silence that had seemed painful to him during the first days here, after the war. He had requested a post in the little town at the base of the foothills separating the upper plateaus from the desert. There, rocky walls, green and black to the north, pink and lavender to the south, marked the frontier of eternal summer. He had been named to a post farther north, on the plateau itself. In the beginning, the solitude and the silence had been hard for him on these wastelands peopled only by stones. Occasionally, furrows suggested cultivation, but they had been dug to uncover a certain kind of stone good for building. The only plowing here was to harvest rocks. Elsewhere a thin layer of soil accumulated in the hollows would be scraped out to enrich paltry village gardens. This is the way it was: bare rock covered three quarters of the region. Towns sprang up, flourished, then disappeared;

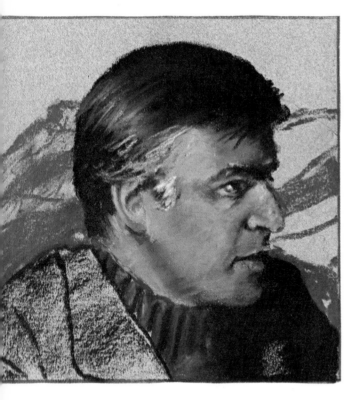

men came by, loved one another or fought bitterly, then died. No one in this desert, neither he nor his guest, mattered. And yet, outside this desert neither of them, Daru knew, could have really lived.

When he got up, no noise came from the classroom. He was amazed at the unmixed joy he derived from the mere thought that the Arab might have fled and that he would be alone with no decision to make. But the prisoner was there. He had merely stretched out between the stove and the desk. With eyes open, he was staring at the ceiling. In that position, his thick lips were particularly noticeable, giving him a pouting look. "Come," said Daru. The Arab got up and followed him. In the bedroom, the schoolmaster pointed to a chair near the table under the window. The Arab sat down without taking his eyes off Daru.

"Are you hungry?"

"Yes," the prisoner said.

Daru set the table for two. He took flour and oil, shaped a cake in a frying pan, and lighted the little stove that functioned on bottled gas. While the cake was cooking, he went out to the shed to get cheese, eggs, dates, and condensed milk. When the cake was done he set it on the windowsill to cool, heated some condensed milk diluted with water, and beat up the eggs into an omelet. In one of his motions he knocked against the revolver stuck in his right pocket. He set the bowl down, went into the classroom, and put the revolver in his desk drawer. When he came back to the room, night was falling. He put on the light and served the Arab. "Eat," he said. The Arab took a piece of the cake, lifted it eagerly to his mouth, and stopped short.

"And you?" he asked.

"After you, I'll eat too."

The thick lips opened slightly. The Arab hesitated, then bit into the cake determinedly.

The meal over, the Arab looked at the schoolmaster. "Are you the judge?"

"No, I'm simply keeping you until tomorrow."

"Why do you eat with me?"

"I'm hungry."

The Arab fell silent. Daru got up and went out. He brought back a folding bed from the shed, set it up between the table and the stove, perpendicular to his own bed. From a large suitcase which, upright in a corner, served as a shelf for papers, he took two blankets and arranged them on the camp bed. Then he stopped, felt useless, and sat down on his bed. There was nothing more to do or to get ready. He had to look at this man. He looked at him, therefore, trying to imagine his face bursting with rage. He couldn't do so. He could see nothing but the dark yet shining eyes and the animal mouth.

"Why did you kill him?" he asked in a voice whose hostile tone surprised him.

The Arab looked away.

"He ran away. I ran after him."

He raised his eyes to Daru again and they were full of a sort of woeful interrogation. "Now what will they do to me?"

"Are you afraid?"

He stiffened, turning his eyes away.

"Are you sorry?"

The Arab stared at him open-mouthed. Obiously he did not understand. Daru's annoyance was growing. At the same time he felt awkward and self-conscious with his big body wedged between the two beds.

"Lie down there," he said impatiently. "That's your bed."

The Arab didn't move. He called to Daru: "Tell me!"

The schoolmaster looked at him.

"Is the gendarme coming back tomorrow?"

"I don't know."

"Are you coming with us?"

"I don't know. Why?"

The prisoner got up and stretched out on top of the blankets, his feet toward the window. The light from the electric bulb shone straight into his eyes and he closed them at once.

"Why?" Daru repeated, standing beside the bed.

The Arab opened his eyes under the blinding light and looked at him, trying not to blink. "Come with us," he said.

In the middle of the night. Daru was still not asleep. He had gone to bed after undressing completely; he generally slept naked. But when he suddenly realized that he had nothing on, he hesitated. He felt vulnerable and the temptation came to him to put his clothes back on. Then he shrugged his shoulders; after all, he wasn't a child and, if need be, he could break his adversary in two. From his bed he could observe him, lying on his back, still motionless with his eyes closed under the harsh light. When Daru turned out the light, the darkness seemed to coagulate all of a sudden. Little by little, the night came back to life in the window where the starless sky was stirring gently. The schoolmaster soon made out the body lying at his feet. The Arab still did not move, but his eyes seemed open. A faint wind was prowling around the schoolhouse. Perhaps it would drive away the clouds and the sun would reappear.

During the night the wind increased. The hens fluttered a little and then were silent. The Arab turned over on his side with his back to Daru, who thought he heard him moan. Then he listened to his guest's breathing become heavier and more regular. He listened to that breath so close to him and mused without being able to go to sleep. In this room where he had been sleeping alone for a year, this presence bothered him. But it bothered him also by imposing on him a sort of brotherhood he knew well but refused to accept in the present circumstances. Men who share the same rooms, soldiers or prisoners, develop a strange alliance as if, having cast off their armor with their clothing, they fraternized every evening, over and above their differences, in the ancient community of dream and fatigue. But Daru shook himself; he didn't like such musings, and it was essential to sleep.

A little later, however, when the Arab stirred slightly, the schoolmaster was still not asleep. When the prisoner made a second move, he stiffened, on the alert. The Arab was lifting himself slowly on his arms with almost the motion of a sleepwalker. Seated upright in bed, he waited motionless without turning his head toward Daru, as if he were listening attentively. Daru did not stir; it had just occurred to him that the revolver was still in the drawer of his desk. It was better to act at once. Yet he continued to observe the prisoner, who, with the same slithery motion, put his feet on the ground, waited again, then began to stand up slowly. Daru was about to call out to him when the Arab began to walk, in a quite natural but extraordinarily silent way. He was heading toward the door at the end of the room that opened into the shed. He lifted the latch with precaution and went out, pushing the door behind him but without shutting it. Daru had not stirred. "He is running away," he merely thought. "Good riddance!" Yet he listened attentively. The hens were not fluttering; the guest must be on the plateau. A faint sound of water reached him, and he didn't know what it was until the Arab again stood framed in the doorway, closed the door carefully, and came back to bed without a sound. Then Daru turned his back on him and fell asleep. Still later he seemed, from the depths of his sleep, to hear furtive steps around the schoolhouse. "I'm dreaming! I'm dreaming!" he repeated to himself. And he went on sleeping.

When he awoke, the sky was clear; the loose window let in a cold, pure air. The Arab was asleep, hunched up under the blankets now, his mouth open, utterly relaxed. But when Daru shook him, he started dreadfully, staring at Daru with wild eyes as if he had never seen him and such a frightened expression that the schoolmaster stepped back. "Don't be afraid. It's me. You must eat." The Arab nodded his head and said yes. Calm had returned to his face, but his expression was vacant and listless.

The coffee was ready. They drank it seated together on the folding bed as they munched their pieces of the cake. Then Daru led the Arab under the shed and showed him the faucet where he washed. He went back into the room, folded the blankets and the bed, made his own bed and put the room in order. Then he went through the classroom and out onto the terrace. The sun was already rising in the blue sky; a soft, bright light was bathing the deserted plateau. On the ridge the snow was melting in spots. The stones were about to reappear. Crouched on the edge of the plateau, the schoolmaster looked at the deserted expanse. He thought of Balducci. He had hurt him, for he had sent him off in a way as if he didn't want to be associated with him. He could still hear the gendarme's farewell and, without knowing why, he felt strangely empty and vulnerable. At that moment, from the other side of the schoolhouse, the prisoner coughed. Daru listened to him almost despite himself and then, furious, threw a pebble that whistled through the air before sinking into the snow. That man's stupid crime revolted him, but to hand him over was contrary to honor. Merely thinking of it made him smart with humiliation. And he cursed at one and the same time his own people who had sent him this Arab and the Arab too who had dared to kill and not managed to get away. Daru got up, walked in a circle on the terrace, waited motionless, and then went back into the schoolhouse.

The Arab, leaning over the cement floor of the shed, was washing his teeth with two fingers. Daru looked at him and said: "Come." He went back into the room ahead of the prisoner. He slipped a hunting jacket on over his sweater and put on walking shoes. Standing, he waited until the Arab had put on his *chèche* and sandals. They went into the classroom and the schoolmaster pointed to the exit, saying: "Go ahead." The fellow didn't budge. "I'm coming," said Daru. The Arab went out. Daru went back into the room and made a package of pieces of rusk, dates, and sugar. In the classroom, before going out, he hesitated a second in front of his desk, then crossed the threshold and locked the door. "That's the way," he said. He started toward the east, followed by the prisoner. But, a short distance from the schoolhouse, he thought he heard a slight sound behind them. He retraced his steps and examined the surroundings of the house; there was no one there. The Arab watched him without seeming to understand. "Come on," said Daru.

They walked for an hour and rested beside a sharp peak of limestone. The snow was melting faster and faster and the sun was drinking up the puddles at once, rapidly cleaning the plateau, which gradually dried and vibrated like the air itself. When they resumed walking, the ground rang under their feet. From time to time a bird rent the space in front of them with a joyful cry. Daru breathed in deeply the fresh morning light. He felt a sort of rapture before the vast familiar expanse, now almost entirely yellow under its dome of blue sky. They walked an hour more, descending toward the south. They reached a level height made up of crumbly rocks. From there on, the plateau sloped down, eastward, toward a low plain where there were a few spindly trees and, to the south, toward outcroppings of rock that gave the landscape a chaotic look.

Daru surveyed the two directions. There was nothing but the sky on the horizon. Not a man could be seen. He turned toward the Arab, who was looking at him blankly. Daru held out the package to him. "Take it," he said. "There are dates, bread, and sugar. You can hold out for two days. Here are a thousand francs too." The Arab took the package and the money but kept his full hands at chest level as if he didn't know what to do with what was being given him. "Now look," the schoolmaster said as he pointed in the direction of the east, "there's the way to Tinguit. You have a two-hour walk. At Tinguit you'll find the administration and the police. They are expecting you." The Arab looked toward the east, still holding the package and the money against his chest. Daru took his elbow and turned him rather roughly toward the south. At the foot of the height on which they stood could be seen a faint path. "That's the trail across the plateau. In a day's walk from here you'll find pasture lands and the first nomads. They'll take you in and shelter you according to their law." The Arab had now turned toward Daru and a sort of panic was visible in his expression. "Listen," he said. Daru shook his head: "No, be quiet. Now I'm leaving you." He turned his back on him, took two long steps in the direction of the school, looked hesitantly at the motionless Arab, and started off again. For a few minutes he heard nothing but his own step resounding on the cold ground and did not turn his head. A moment later, however, he turned around. The Arab was still there on the edge of the hill, his arms hanging now, and he was looking at the schoolmaster. Daru felt something rise in his throat. But he swore with impatience, waved vaguely, and started off again. He had already gone some distance when he again stopped and looked. There was no longer anyone on the hill.

Daru hesitated. The sun was now rather high in the sky and was beginning to beat down on his head. The schoolmaster retraced his steps, at first somewhat uncertainly, then with decision. When he reached the little hill, he was bathed in sweat. He climbed it as fast as he could and stopped, out of breath, at the top. The rock fields to the south stood out sharply against the blue sky, but on the plain to the east a steamy heat was already rising. And in that slight haze, Daru, with heavy heart, made out the Arab walking slowly on the road to prison.

A little later, standing before the window of the classroom, the schoolmaster was watching the clear light bathing the whole surface of the plateau, but he hardly saw it. Behind him on the blackboard, among the winding French rivers, sprawled the clumsily chalked-up words he had just read: "You handed over our brother. You will pay for this." Daru looked at the sky, the plateau, and, beyond, the invisible lands stretching all the way to the sea. In this vast landscape he had loved so much, he was alone.

STUDY QUESTIONS

Recalling

1. Describe the school and the two visitors.
2. What order is the schoolmaster given? Why? What is his reaction?
3. How does Daru finally discharge his duty? What does he find when he returns to the school?

Interpreting

4. Why is Balducci insulted by Daru's response to the order?
5. Why do you think Daru treats the prisoner the way he does both at home and on the trail?
6. Explain why the prisoner is frightened by the choice Daru gives him. Why do you think he chooses as he does? In what sense is Daru responsible for the message he finds on the blackboard?
7. Why do you think Daru returns to the classroom with a heavy heart? Explain the significance of the story's last sentence.

VIEWPOINT

"The Guest" was collected in *The Exile and the Kingdom.* One critic says the topic of the entire collection is

exile and the longing all [people] have to find a country which will give them a home. . . .

—A. Padovano, *The Estranged God*

Explain how each of the story's three main characters is an exile, or an outsider.

COMPOSITION

Writing About Theme

Write a brief essay on one existentialist theme, as it is presented in "The Guest." First identify the theme that Camus conveys in the story. Then show how Camus illuminates this theme through (a) plot, (b) characterization, (c) setting, (d) point of view, and (e) tone. You may wish to consider the following existentialist beliefs as you identify Camus's theme: (a) Individuals are isolated from society; (b) life is absurd; (c) responsibility is a terrible burden; or (d) dignity is possible even in a meaningless world. *For help with this assignment, refer to Lesson 6 in the Writing About Literature Handbook at the back of this book.*

Writing a Dialogue

Write a dialogue between Daru and Balducci that occurs after the end of "The Guest." Imagine that Daru has gone to Balducci for protection from the rebels who threatened him. Record his request for help and Balducci's reply. Answer the following questions in your dialogue: (a) What right has Daru to ask for help? (b) What reasons does Balducci have for refusing? (c) Does Balducci finally help? (d) Why or why not?

Alberto Moravia   *born 1907*

"Our character is formed by the things we are constrained to do, not by those things we do of our own accord." With these words Alberto Moravia, the best-known contemporary Italian novelist, explained how his literary career developed from an enforced captivity in his youth. Moravia was born in Rome. At the age of nine, he developed tuberculosis and was bedridden for most of the next ten years. With the help of governesses, he learned to read English, French, and German in addition to his native Italian. He took refuge in books and as a result passed equivalency tests for a high school diploma. At sixteen Moravia entered a sanitorium; at the same time he began to write a novel. *The Time of Indifference* (1929) was published six years later, and it made Moravia, at the age of twenty-two, one of the most celebrated authors in Europe. Fame brought him work as a film critic, a magazine editor, and a lecturer; he was a foreign correspondent in Paris, London, the United States, and Mexico. He has written stories, novels, poems, essays, plays, and screenplays. Film versions of his fiction—such as the novel *Two Women* (1957)— have been made by Italy's most famous and respected directors.

The Time of Indifference shocked Rome with its portrayal of the Italian middle class. A picture of human despair and alienation in an absurd world, it was an early existentialist novel written before that term was coined. A frequent Moravia topic is the decline of the Italian middle class. Many of his stories are about adolescents or inexperienced adults who must struggle with a dehumanized world. Moravia is a master of plot and concise description. Setting is often deftly used to reflect character. The style is smooth: Phrases and images are apt; sentences flow rhythmically and with ease. The easy style of "Doubles" leads readers along effortlessly until they are faced with a harsh conclusion.

Alberto Moravia

Doubles

Translated by Angus Davidson

One day recently I came to a decision. I picked out an advertisement in which a "good room, sunny, bathroom; friendly atmosphere" was offered at an address a very long way from my own; I got into my car and went there. I live in a turning off the Via Cassia, almost in the country; the room of the advertisement was in a turning off the Via Appia[1] Nuova: so great a distance seemed to me a safe guarantee of independence, secrecy and, above all, dissimilarity.

I myself did not know precisely what I wanted to do. Was I to embark seriously on a double life, with two homes, one near the Via Cassia and one near the Via Appia? I was a student, with my family in the provinces, and it would be easy to make each landlady believe that I had to spend fifteen days out of thirty in the country. Or was I, on the other hand, merely to take a look at the double life, but without—for the moment, anyhow—practicing it? To sound out its possibilities, to get the taste of it?

Yes, that was it; because I did not desire a double life with the object of giving vent to some unavowable instinct; I did not aspire, let us say, to be a faithful fiancé on the Via Cassia and a Don Juan[2] on the Via Appia. No, I had nothing to hide or to give vent to in secret; I merely wished to duplicate myself, that is, to become two people instead of one—and indeed by doing the most innocent and normal things. The double life, in fact, was for me not a means but an end.

I found the house of the advertisement in a turning off the Via Appia that very much resembled the street in which I lived near the Via Cassia: two rows of modern buildings, the surface of the road uneven and full of holes and hummocks and, at the far end, a strip of blue sky above a strip of green countryside. Moreover the building itself was like the one in which I lived: the same eight-story façade riddled with windows and balconies, the same marble entrance-hall, the same lift-shaft, the same staircase, the same balustrade. I reflected that this, after all, was not so very strange: the building had probably been constructed with

1. **Via Cassia** [vē′ə kä′sē ə] . . . **Via Appia** [vē′ə ä′pē ə]: *Via* is Italian for "street." These streets lead out of Rome to the northwest and southeast, respectively.

2. **Don Juan:** refers to the legendary Spanish nobleman.

the same materials, at the same period, perhaps even by the same firm and according to the plans of the same engineer. I reached the fourth floor. I could hardly believe my eyes when I saw that the nameplate bore the name of my Via Cassia landlady: "Longo." Then I reflected that this was not an entirely improbable coincidence: Longo was not an uncommon name; in the telephone directory there was a page and a half of Longos. I rang the bell.

As I waited I was conscious of the same secret feeling of expectation that I had experienced when I rang at the door of Signora Longo No. 1, near the Via Cassia. Moreover this feeling of expectation had not been falsified, for the door had been opened by the lady's daughter, Elena, with whom I had lost no time in forming a mildly amorous relationship. And now the door opened and a gentle voice said: "Yes, what is it?"

I looked up. Elena was fair, this one was dark; Elena's face bore all the signs of health, with its blue eyes, pink cheeks and scarlet mouth; this girl, on the other hand, had a delicate, pale, almost wasted face with two enormous dark, shining eyes. But the welcome was the same: discreet, reticent, even shy, but not indifferent—the usual welcome of a girl who finds herself confronted by a young man of her own age.

I explained what I wanted. She at once showed me into the sitting-room, announced that she would go and tell her mother, and disappeared. I looked round: in the home of Signora Longo No. 1 the predominant style was sham Renaissance; here it was sham Louis XVI;[3] but I felt that this dissimilarity was only apparent and that, like the two Longo daughters, these two styles of decoration had, as far as concerned me, the same "intention." What this "intention" might be, I could not have said; but that it was the same, I was certain. I sat down and then almost shuddered as I recalled

that Elena, too, had said, that day: "I'll go and tell Mother."

Soon the mother appeared. The same phenomenon was again repeated with regard to her as had formerly occurred in the case of Signora Longo No. 1: I did not see her. I was indeed aware that I had in front of me something mellifluous, homely, provincial, calculating and authoritative; but I failed to see what kind of a face and figure Signora Longo No. 2 had, just as, even now, I did not know what Signora Longo No. 1 looked like. Of course we all know that there are people who may even have an intense, though concealed, life, but who nevertheless make no more effect than a damp stain on a wall.

Anyhow, the following dialogue took place between us. "You are a student?"

"Yes, I'm studying literature."

"And your family, where are they?"

"At Ancona."[4]

"A fine city, Ancona. I have a cousin at Ancona. Are you an only son?"

"Yes."

"I'm afraid you must be terribly spoiled, then. You only children . . . For example, my Elena . . ."

I gave a start. "Who is Elena?"

"My daughter."

"Excuse me. You were saying?"

"Ah yes, I was saying that, alas, Elena too is an only child."

"Why alas?"

"I should have liked so much to have a son. I always let the room to young men like you. Then I can partly deceive myself into thinking I have a son."

"I knew that too"; the remark escaped me.

"What?"

"I knew that you wanted so much to have a son and, not having one, that you let the room to young men like me."

"Excuse me, but how did you come to know that?"

"Well, I guessed it, when you told me that

---

3. **sham Renaissance . . . sham Louis XVI:** furniture imitating, respectively, the ornate style of the Italian Renaissance and the simpler French style of the eighteenth century.

4. **Ancona** [än cō′nə]: city on the east coast of Italy.

Elena is an only daughter and when I saw you sigh."

"You're very intuitive, there's no denying it. Anyhow, don't worry: here you'll be like one of the family, but at the same time you'll be free, perfectly free. Would you like to see the room?"

"Thank you, yes."

We went out into the passage; there was a door open, and at the far end of a long, narrow room, facing the window, Elena No. 2 was sitting at her desk. Her mother, as we went past, said: "Elena, let me introduce Signor . . . What is your name? Excuse me."

"Fabiani."

"Signor Fabiani, who is very soon coming to stay with us here."

Elena jumped up and at once came towards us, as though she were merely waiting to be called. We shook hands, and I noticed that, during my conversation with her mother, Elena had changed her clothes. When she had opened the door to me, she had been wearing a little green dress, rather shabby; now she had put on a red blouse and a gray skirt, both of which looked new. She followed us, and we went into the room, all three of us.

"The room is both light and quiet; on fine days you can see the Castelli Romani;[5] this is the bathroom; all the furniture is new; this way, by this door, you can go in and out without anyone noticing." Signora Longo No. 2 went backwards and forwards, opening the windows, displaying drawers and cupboards, exactly as Signora Longo No. 1 had formerly done. And, as then, Elena stood aside looking at us; and I, instead of looking at the furniture and the landscape, looked at Elena. Then the repeated ringing of the telephone bell was heard, and her mother said she was going to answer it and went out, leaving us alone.

I was standing near the door; Elena was at the other end of the room, near the window. We looked at one another, exactly as, in anal-ogous circumstances (but that time it had been the front door bell) in the Longo No. 1 home, I and the other Elena had looked at one another. And in that moment, as with the other Elena, I realized that the girl was begging me to take the room and that I was promising her that I would do so. I felt that I had fallen on my feet; or rather that, just as the materials used, the plan adopted, the engineer and the firm entrusted with the job had brought it about that the building in which I found myself at the moment was in every respect similar to the one in which I lived near the Via Cassia; so, in the same way, an incommensurable number of forces was bringing it about that I should behave with Elena No. 2 in precisely the same way as I had behaved with Elena No. 1. Then, suddenly, an idea occurred to me: *this* was the double life, not that entirely different life that I had pictured. A life, that is, whose principal quality was not so much to change by changing its place and its circumstances, as to remain substantially identical. The feeling of duplication at which I had aimed was, fundamentally, just this: to acquire the consciousness, in doing something, that I had done it already and that anyhow it was impossible for me not to do it in precisely that way and no other.

This reflection lasted no more than a second. Then Signora Longo came back into the room, saying: "Wrong number."

There was nothing left for me but to go away. I told Signora Longo that I would give her my answer next day, I shook hands with Elena who left her hand in mine perhaps a moment longer than was necessary (as the other Elena had done); then I went down to the ground floor in the lift that was so like the one in the building near Via Cassia, even to the rude words scrawled on the glossy wood with the point of a nail.

I returned home. Scarcely had I thrown myself down on my bed, tired after so many adventures, when there was a knock at my door and Elena's voice said: "Telephone."

As I went out to take the call, Elena followed me and, while I was telephoning, took

---

5. **Castelli Romani** [kä stel′ē rō mä′nē]: small hill towns south of Rome.

my hand and played with my fingers. At the other end of the line I heard the voice of the other Elena say: "Signor Fabiani?"

"Yes?"

"My mother asks me to tell you that there's no need for you to give her an answer. There was someone under consideration before you, and my mother has decided to let this other person have the room."

I inquired at once, hurriedly: "Who is this someone?"

"A student called Mariani."

"Ah, a student. And what's he like? Dark, fair, tall, short—what's he like?"

"You're rather strange, aren't you? He's more or less like you, neither dark nor fair, neither tall nor short, so-so. But why d'you want to know?"

"Thank you, I'm sorry, good-bye." I hung up the receiver: Elena came close to me and said in a whisper: "Who was that woman? What is there between you and her?"

I should have liked to reply: "That woman was you. Between me and her there is exactly what there is between you and me. Or rather, the student Mariani, who is so like me, does with her what I should have been able to do, and so there's no need for me to take the room off the Via Appia since he will see to doing everything for me. And all of us, if we want to, can live not merely two lives at the same time but millions; all that's necessary is for us to be aware that we're identical with millions of other people in the world." But I thought she would not understand me and so I answered her with a lie of some kind and went back to my room and threw myself down on the bed again. It occurred to me that at that very moment an infinite number of other people like me were throwing themselves on their beds and, strange to say, this thought comforted me, and, still thinking that I was doing something that so many others were doing, I fell asleep.

STUDY QUESTIONS

Recalling
1. What reason does the narrator give for wanting a double life? In what manner does he seek another life?
2. Find at least six similarities between the two apartments and the two Longo families.
3. What does the narrator realize about a double life before he leaves the second apartment?
4. What prevents him from renting the second apartment? What is his reaction?

Interpreting
5. What is the difference between a double life as means and a double life as end?
6. Why are the two apartments and the two families very similar?
7. Why do you think the narrator is "comforted" at the end of the story?

Extending
8. Do you think the narrator can legitimately find comfort in his discovery at the end of the story? Why or why not?

COMPOSITION

Writing About Setting
■ Write an essay on the setting of "Doubles." First describe the time and place and the mood they create. Then explain how the setting reflects the narrator's personality. Finally tell how the setting adds to the story's theme.

Writing a Plot Outline
■ Write the plot outline of a story in which a character actually does live a double life. Do not write the story, but write at least two sentences to answer each of the following questions: (a) What are the character's dominant personality traits? (b) Why does the character want to live a double life? (c) What form does the double life take? (d) What are the advantages and disadvantages of a double life? (e) What is the final result of living a double life?

Alberto Moravia 913

Heinrich Böll *born 1917*

World War II created a vacuum of ideals in Germany. The Nazis replaced religion and morality with their own chauvinistic principles, which collapsed with their regime. The country, particularly its younger generation who had known nothing else, was left without ideals on which to rebuild. Heinrich Böll sought to fill that vacuum with hope and a simple morality to lift people out of their negativity and despair. In short stories and in novels such as *The Clowns* (1963) and *Safety Net* (1982), he satirizes greed, stupidity, pretentiousness, and arrogance, and reminds readers of their potential to rise above such evils.

Born and raised in Cologne, in what is now West Germany, Böll was an unwilling recruit in the Hitler youth movement. Later he was pressed into military service, was wounded four times, and was held as a prisoner of war. His war stories, however, are not set on battlefields. They are about the effects of the war and take place on crowded trains, in hospitals, and in ruined cities. Böll's postwar fiction deals with a nation's recovery from war and with war's enormous moral and social cost.

Another typical Böll subject is the struggle to be a private individual in an impersonal society. He sees self-delusion as a complication in this struggle; people refuse to admit their lack of effectiveness and lack of accomplishment. Much of Böll's fiction resembles parables with characters and situations that embody moral issues. He often exposes the absurdity of an unacceptable situation by carrying it to a ridiculous extreme. Böll's style is marked by concrete detail and everyday language. His ability to tell an interesting story in simple prose has been traced to the influence of American authors such as Ernest Hemingway. Böll's storytelling skill is demonstrated in "The Thrower-Away," a story that will leave readers with more questions than answers.

Heinrich Böll

The Thrower-Away

Translated by Leila Vennewitz

For the last few weeks I have been trying to avoid people who might ask me what I do for a living. If I really had to put a name to my occupation, I would be forced to utter a word which would alarm people. So I prefer the abstract method of putting down my confession on paper.

Until recently I would have been prepared at any time to make an oral confession. I almost insisted. I called myself an inventor, a scholar, even a student, and, in the melodramatic mood of incipient intoxication, an unrecognized genius. I basked in the cheerful fame which a frayed collar can radiate; arrogantly, as if it were mine by right, I exacted reluctant credit from suspicious shopkeepers who watched margarine, ersatz[1] coffee and cheap tobacco disappear into my pockets; I reveled in my unkempt appearance, and at breakfast, lunch and dinner I drank the nectar of Bohemian life: the bliss of knowing one is not conforming.

But for the past few weeks I have been boarding the streetcar every morning just before 7:30 at the corner of the Roonstrasse;[2] like everyone else I meekly hold out my season ticket to the conductor. I have on a gray double-breasted suit, a striped shirt, a dark-green tie, I carry my sandwiches in a flat aluminum box and hold the morning paper, lightly rolled, in my hand. I look like a citizen who has managed to avoid introspection. After the third stop I get up to offer my seat to one of the elderly working women who have got on at the housing settlement. Having sacrificed my seat on the altar of social compassion, I continue to read the newspaper standing up, now and again letting myself be heard in the capacity of arbitrator when morning irritation is inclined to make people unjust. I correct the worst political and historical errors (by explaining, for instance, that there is a certain difference between SA[3] and USA); as soon as anyone puts a cigarette to his lips I discreetly hold my lighter in front of his nose and, with the aid of the tiny but dependable flame, light his morning cigarette for him. Thus I complete the picture of a well-groomed fellow-citizen who is still young enough for people to say he "has nice manners."

I seem to have been successful in donning the mask which makes it impossible to ask me about my occupation. I am evidently taken for an educated businessman dealing in attractively packaged and agreeably smelling articles such as coffee, tea or spices, or in valuable small objects which are pleasing to the eye such as jewelry or watches; a man who practices his profession in a nice old-fashioned office with dark oil paintings of merchant forebears hanging on the walls, who phones his wife about ten, who knows how to imbue his apparently impassive voice with that hint of tenderness which betrays affection and concern. Since I also participate in the usual jokes and do not refrain from laughing when every morning at the Lohengrinstrasse[4] the clerk from City Hall shouts out "When does the next swan leave?" since I do not withhold my comments concerning either the events of the day or the re-

---

1. **ersatz** [er′zäts]: artificial.
2. **Roonstrasse** [rōōn′shträ sə]: Roon street. *Strasse* is German for "street."

3. **SA**: Societe Anonyme [sō sē ā tā′ ä nō nēm′]: French for "anonymous society," a commercial term similar to "incorporated" in English.
4. **Lohengrinstrasse** [lō′ən grin′ shträ′ sə]: street named for the opera *Lohengrin* by German composer Richard Wagner (1813–1883). The hero of the opera travels in a boat drawn by a swan.

sults of the football pools, I am obviously regarded as someone who, although prosperous (as can be seen from his suit material), has an attitude toward life which is deeply rooted in the principles of democracy. An air of integrity encases me the way the glass coffin encased Snow White.

When a passing truck provides the streetcar window with a background for a moment, I check up on the expression on my face: isn't it perhaps rather too pensive, almost verging on the sorrowful? I assiduously erase the remnants of brooding and do my best to give my face the expression I want it to wear: neither reserved nor familiar, neither superficial nor profound.

My camouflage seems to be successful, for when I get out at the Marienplatz[5] and dive into the maze of streets in the Old Town, where there is no lack of nice old-fashioned offices, where notaries and lawyers abound, no one suspects that I pass through a rear entrance into the UBIA building—a firm that can boast of supporting 350 people and of insuring the lives of 400,000. The commissionaire[6] greets me with a smile at the delivery entrance, I walk past him, go down to the basement, and start in on my work, which has to be completed by the time the employees come pouring into the offices at 8:30. The activity that I pursue every morning between 8 and 8:30 in the basement of this respected establishment is devoted entirely to destruction. I throw away.

It took me years to invent my profession, to endow it with mathematical plausibility. I wrote treatises; graphs and charts covered—and still cover—the walls of my apartment. For years I climbed along abscissas and up ordinates,[7] wallowed in theories, and savored the glacial ecstasy of solving formulas. Yet since

practicing my profession and seeing my theories come to life, I am filled with a sense of sadness such as may come over a general who finds himself obliged to descend from the heights of strategy to the plains of tactics.

I enter my workroom, exchange my jacket for a gray smock, and immediately set to work. I open the mailbags which the commissionaire has already picked up earlier from the main post office, and I empty them into the two wooden bins which, constructed according to my design, hang to the right and left on the wall over my worktable. This way I only need to stretch out my hands, somewhat like a swimmer, and begin swiftly to sort the mail.

First I separate the circulars from the letters, a purely routine job, since a glance at the postage suffices. At this stage a knowledge of the postal tariff renders hesitation unnecessary. After years of practice I am able to complete this phase within half an hour, and by this time it is half past eight and I can hear the footsteps of the employees pouring into the offices overhead. I ring for the commissionaire, who takes the sorted letters to the various departments. It never fails to sadden me, the sight of the commissionaire carrying off in a metal tray the size of a briefcase the remains of what had once filled three mailbags. I might feel triumphant, for this, the vindication of my theory of throwing away, has for years been the objective of my private research; but, strangely enough, I do not feel triumphant. To have been right is by no means always a reason for rejoicing.

After the departure of the commissionaire there remains the task of examining the huge pile of printed matter to make sure it contains no letter masquerading behind the wrong postage, no bill mailed as a circular. This work is almost always superfluous, for the probity of the mailing public is nothing short of astounding. I must admit that here my calculations were incorrect: I had overestimated the number of postal defrauders.

Rarely has a post card, a letter or a bill sent as printed matter escaped my notice; about half past nine I ring for the commissionaire, who

5. **Marienplatz** [mä rēn′pläts]: "Marien Place." *Platz* is German for "place."
6. **commissionaire** [kə mish′ə när′]: one who sweeps and cleans and does errands.
7. **abscissas . . . ordinates:** horizontal and vertical lines on a graph.

takes the remaining objects of my careful scrutiny to the departments.

The time has now come when I require some refreshment. The commissionaire's wife brings me my coffee, I take my sandwich out of the flat aluminum box, sit down for my break, and chat with the commissionaire's wife about her children. Is Alfred doing somewhat better in arithmetic? Has Gertrude been able to catch up in spelling? Alfred is not doing any better in arithmetic, whereas Gertrude has been able to catch up in spelling. Have the tomatoes ripened properly, are the rabbits plump, and was the experiment with the melons successful? The tomatoes have not ripened properly, but the rabbits are plump, while the experiment with the melons is still undecided. Serious problems, such as whether one should stock up on potatoes or not, matters of education, such as whether one should enlighten one's children or be enlightened by them, are the subjects of our intense consideration.

Just before eleven the commissionaire's wife leaves, and usually she asks me to let her have some travel folders. She is collecting them, and I smile at her enthusiasm, for I have retained tender memories of travel folders. As a child I also collected travel folders, I used to fish them out of my father's waste-paper basket. Even as a boy it bothered me that my father would take mail from the mailman and throw it into the waste-paper basket without looking at it. This action wounded my innate propensity for economy: there was something that had been designed, set up, printed, put in an envelope, and stamped, that had passed through the mysterious channels by which the postal service actually causes our mail to arrive at our addresses; it was weighted with the sweat of the draftsman, the writer, the printer, the office boy who had stuck on the stamps; on various levels and in various tariffs it had cost money: all this only to end—without being deemed worthy of so much as a glance—in a waste-paper basket?

At the age of eleven I had already adopted the habit of taking out of the waste-paper bas-

Dovecote (boxlike shelter for doves or pigeons) construction, Joseph Cornell, 1954–1956.

ket, as soon as my father had left for the office, whatever had been thrown away. I would study it, sort it, and put it away in a chest which I used to keep toys in. Thus by the time I was twelve I already possessed an imposing collection of wine-merchants' catalogues, as well as prospectuses on naturopathy[8] and natural history. My collection of travel folders assumed the dimensions of a geographical encyclopedia; Dalmatia was as familiar to me as the Norwegian fjords, Scotland as close as Zakopane, the

8. **naturopathy** [nā′chə rop′ə thē]: method of medical treatment that depends on natural healing agents such as diet and exercise.

forests of Bohemia soothed me while the waves of the Atlantic disquieted me; hinges were offered me, houses and buttons, political parties asked for my vote, charities for my money; lotteries promised me riches, religious sects poverty. I leave it to the reader's imagination to picture what my collection was like when at the age of seventeen, suddenly bored with it all, I offered my collection to a junk dealer who paid me 7 marks and 60 pfennigs[9] for it.

Having finished school, I embarked in my father's footsteps and set my foot on the first rung of the civil service ladder. With the 7 marks and 60 pfennigs I bought a package of squared paper and three colored crayons, and my attempt to gain a foothold in the civil service turned into a laborious detour, for a happy thrower-away was slumbering in me while I filled the role of an unhappy junior clerk. All my free time was devoted to intricate calculations.

Stop-watch, pencil, slide-rule, squared paper, these were the props of my obsession; I calculated how long it took to open a circular of small, medium or large size, with or without pictures, give it a quick glance, satisfy oneself of its uselessness, and then throw it in the waste-paper basket, a process requiring a minimum of five seconds and a maximum of twenty-five; if the circular is at all attractive, either the text or the pictures, several minutes, often a quarter of an hour, must be allowed for this. By conducting bogus negotiations with printing firms, I also worked out the minimum production costs for circulars. Indefatigably I checked the results of my studies and adjusted them (it did not occur to me until two years later that the time of the cleaning-women who have to empty the waste-paper baskets had to be included in my calculations); I applied the results of my research to firms with ten, twenty, a hundred or more employees; and I arrived at results which an expert on economics would not have hesitated to describe as alarming.

Obeying my sense of loyalty, I began by offering my results to my superiors; although I had reckoned with the possibility of ingratitude, I was nevertheless shocked at the extent of that ingratitude. I was accused of neglecting my duties, suspected of nihilism,[10] pronounced "a mental case," and discharged. To the great sorrow of my kind parents, I abandoned my promising career, began new ones, broke these off too, forsook the warmth of the parental hearth, and, as I have already said, eked out my existence as an unrecognized genius. I took pleasure in the humiliation of vainly peddling my invention, and spent years in a blissful state of being antisocial, so consistently that my punch-card in the central files which had long ago been punched with the symbol for "mental case" was now stamped with the confidential symbol for "antisocial."

In view of these circumstances, it can readily be imagined what a shock it was when the obviousness of my results at last became obvious to someone else—the manager of UBIA, how deeply humiliated I was to have to wear a dark-green tie, yet I must continue to go around in disguise as I am terrified of being found out. I try anxiously to give my face the proper expression when I laugh at the Lohengrin joke, since there is no greater vanity than that of the wags who populate the streetcar every morning. Sometimes, too, I am afraid the streetcar may be full of people who the previous day have done work which I am about to destroy that very morning: printers, typesetters, draftsmen, writers who compose the wording of advertisements, commercial artists, envelope stuffers, packers, apprentices of all kinds. From 8 to 8:30 every morning I ruthlessly destroy the products of respected paper mills, worthy

9. **marks . . . pfennigs** [pfe′nigz]: German currency. There are one hundred pfennigs in a mark, which was worth approximately twenty-five cents at the time the story was written.

10. **nihilism** [nī′ə liz′əm]: rejection of established institutions and ideals.

printing establishments, brilliant commercial artists, the texts of talented writers; coated paper, glossy paper, copperplate, I take it all, just as it comes from the mailbag, and without the faintest sentimentality tie it up into handy bundles for the waste-paper dealer. In the space of one hour I destroy the output of 200 work-hours and save UBIA a further 100 hours, so that altogether (here I must lapse into my own jargon) I achieve a concentrate of 1:300.

When the commissionaire's wife leaves with the empty coffeepot and the travel folders, I knock off. I wash my hands, exchange my smock for my jacket, pick up the morning paper, and leave the UBIA building by the rear entrance. I stroll through the town and wonder how I can escape from tactics and get back into strategy. That which intoxicated me as a formula, I find disappointing, since it can be performed so easily. Strategy translated into action can be carried out by hacks. I shall probably establish schools for throwers-away. I may possibly also attempt to have throwers-away placed in post offices, perhaps even in printing establishments; an enormous amount of energy, valuable commodities, and intelligence could be utilized as well as postage saved; it might even be feasible to conceive, compose, and set brochures up in type but not print them. These are all problems still requiring a lot of study.

However, the mere throwing away of mail as such has almost ceased to interest me; any improvements on that level can be worked out by means of the basic formula. For a long time now I have been devoting my attention to calculations concerning wrapping paper and the process of wrapping: this is virgin territory where nothing has been done, here one can strive to spare humanity those unprofitable efforts under the burden of which it is groaning. Every day billions of throwing-away movements are made, energies are dissipated which, could they but be utilized, would suffice to change the face of the earth. It would be a great advantage if one were permitted to undertake experiments in department stores; should one dispense with the wrapping process

altogether, or should one post an expert thrower-away right next to the wrapping table who unwraps what has just been wrapped and immediately ties the wrapping paper into bundles for the waste-paper dealer? These are problems meriting some thought. In any case it has struck me that in many shops the customers implore the clerk not to wrap the purchased article, but that they have to submit to having it wrapped. Clinics for nervous diseases are rapidly filling with patients who complain of an attack of nerves whenever they unwrap a bottle of perfume or a box of chocolates, or open a packet of cigarettes, and at the moment I am making an intensive study of a young man from my neighborhood who earned his living as a book reviewer but at times was unable to practice his profession because he found it impossible to undo the twisted wire tied around the parcel, and even when he did find himself equal to this physical exertion, he was incapable of penetrating the massive layer of gummed paper with which the corrugated paper is stuck together. The man appears deeply disturbed and has now gone over to reviewing the books unread and placing the parcels on his bookshelves without unwrapping them. I leave it to the reader's imagination to depict for himself the effect of such a case on our intellectual life.

While walking through the town between eleven and one I observe all sorts of details: I spend some time unobtrusively in the department stores, hovering around the wrapping tables; I stand in front of tobacco shops and pharmacies and note down minor statistics; now and again I even purchase something, so as to allow the senseless procedure to be performed on myself and to discover how much effort is required actually to take possession of the article one wishes to own.

So between eleven and one in my impeccable suit I complete the picture of a man who is sufficiently prosperous to afford a bit of leisure—who at about one o'clock enters a sophisticated little restaurant, casually chooses the most expensive meal, and scribbles some hieroglyphics[11] on his beer coaster which could equally well be stock quotations or flights of poetry; who knows how to praise or decry the quality of the meat with arguments which betray the connoisseur to even the most blasé waiter; who, when it comes to choosing dessert, hesitates with a knowing air between cake, ice cream and cheese; and who finishes off his scribblings with a flourish which proves that they were stock quotations after all.

Shocked at the results of my calculations I leave the little restaurant. My expression becomes more and more thoughtful while I search for a small café where I can pass the time till three o'clock and read the evening paper. At three I re-enter the UBIA building by the rear door to take care of the afternoon mail, which consists almost exclusively of circulars. It is a matter of scarcely fifteen minutes to pick out the ten or twelve letters; I don't even have to wash my hands after it, I just brush them off, take the letters to the commissionaire, leave the building, and at the Marienplatz board the streetcar, glad that on the way home I do not need to laugh at the Lohengrin joke. When the dark tarpaulin of a passing truck makes a background for the streetcar window, I can see my face: it is relaxed; that is to say pensive, almost brooding, and I relish the fact that I do not have to put on any other face, for at this hour none of my morning fellow-travelers has finished work. I get out at the Roonstrasse, buy some fresh rolls, a piece of cheese or sausage, some ground coffee, and walk up to my little apartment, the walls of which are hung with graphs and charts, with hectic curves: between the abscissas and ordinates I capture the lines of a fever going up and up; not a single one of my curves goes down, not a single one of my formulas has the power to soothe me. I groan under the burden of my vision of economics, and while the water is boiling for the coffee I place my slide-rule, my notes, pencil and paper in readiness.

My apartment is sparsely furnished, it looks more like a laboratory. I drink my coffee standing up and hastily swallow a sandwich, the epicure[12] I was at noon is now a thing of the past. Wash hands, light a cigarette, then I set my stop-watch and unwrap the nerve tonic I bought that morning on my stroll through the town: outer wrapping paper, cellophane covering, carton, inside wrapping paper, directions for use secured by a rubber band: thirty-seven seconds. The nervous energy consumed in unwrapping exceeds the nervous energy which the tonic promises to impart to me, but there may be subjective reasons for this which I shall disregard in my calculations. One thing is certain: the wrapping is worth more than the contents, and the cost of the twenty-five yellow tablets is out of all proportion to their value. But these are considerations verging on the moral aspect, and I would prefer to keep away from morality altogether. My field of speculation is one of pure economics.

Numerous articles are waiting to be unwrapped by me, many slips of paper are waiting to be evaluated; green, red, blue ink, everything is ready. It is usually late by the time I get to bed, and as I fall asleep I am haunted by my formulas, whole worlds of useless paper roll over me; some formulas explode like dynamite, the noise of the explosion sounds like a burst of laughter: it is my own, my laughter at the Lohengrin joke originating in my fear of the clerk from City Hall. Perhaps he has access to the punch-card file, has picked out my card, discovered that it contains not only the symbol for "mental case" but the second, more dangerous one for "antisocial." There is nothing more difficult to fill than a tiny hole like that in a punch-card; perhaps my laughter at the Lohengrin joke is the price I have to pay for my anonymity. I would not like to admit face to face what I find easier to do in writing: that I am a thrower-away.

---

11. **hieroglyphics** [hī'ər ə glif'iks]: picture writing; here, doodling.

12. **epicure:** person with a refined taste for good food and drink.

STUDY QUESTIONS

Recalling

1. What reason does the narrator give for writing the story?
2. Find at least five examples of the narrator's "camouflage" in the morning. Briefly outline his work day.
3. What innovations does the narrator foresee for his career?
4. What reason does the narrator give for being classified as "antisocial"? Briefly describe his life outside the office.

Interpreting

5. What is the narrator's attitude toward his career? Why do you think he feels this way?
6. Contrast the narrator's real personality with his "camouflage." Why is "camouflage" necessary?
7. In what ways is the story critical of society? In what ways is it critical of the narrator?
8. Explain how Böll uses humor in the story to express serious ideas.

Extending

9. Create two or three new job titles that, like "thrower-away," are made necessary by modern life.

VOCABULARY

Synonyms

A **synonym** is a word that has the same or nearly the same meaning as another word. *Generous* and *unselfish* are synonyms. The words in capitals are from "The Thrower-Away." Choose the word that is *nearest* the meaning of each word in capitals, *as the word is used in the selection*. Write the number of each item and the letter of your choice on a separate sheet.

1. INCIPIENT: (a) beginning (b) concluding (c) insistent (d) painful
2. RADIATE: (a) tingle (b) send out (c) absorb (d) develop
3. UNKEMPT: (a) wholesome (b) unloved (c) angry (d) untidy
4. DISCREETLY: (a) cautiously (b) awkwardly (c) proudly (d) abruptly
5. IMBUE: (a) distract (b) fill (c) paint (d) deceive

COMPOSITION

Writing About Literature and Its Period

■ Write an essay showing how Heinrich Böll exemplifies modern European literature. State at least three characteristics of the modern period in Europe. Then for each characteristic give examples from "The Thrower-Away." *For help with this assignment, refer to Lesson 10 in the Writing About Literature Handbook at the back of this book.*

Writing a Monologue

■ While criticizing his society, the narrator of "The Thrower-Away" unintentionally reveals a great deal about himself. Write a brief monologue in which a character unintentionally reveals his or her own personality while offering opinions on some other topic. You may want to consider one of the following topics: (a) junk mail, (b) collecting unusual objects, (c) career "camouflage," or (d) laughing at stale jokes.

COMPARING ENGLISH AND WESTERN WRITERS

1. One frequent topic of modern fiction is the difficulty of meaningful human communication. Compare the manner in which this problem is treated in English and western fiction. What obstacles to communication between people does a given story present? What hope does that story offer for a solution to the difficulty? Cite examples from at least one modern English story (see pages 579–637) and one modern western story (see pages 875–920).
2. Much modern English fiction is psychological and is concerned with inner states of characters. On the other hand, a great deal of modern western fiction is philosophical and deals with the very meaning of life. Demonstrate this difference between English and western fiction by citing examples from at least one English and one western short story in this book.
3. Modern literature created innovations in content and technique to respond to rapidly changing times. Demonstrate this point by comparing innovations in at least one English and one western short story in this book. For each story identify an innovation of content or technique, and cite specific examples. Then tell what world event inspired the innovation.

**Key to Illustrations on
Pages 648–649.**

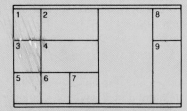

1. Detail, *The Fox and the Grapes*,
engraving, 1879.
2. Detail, *The Colosseum, Rome*,
J. M.W. Turner (1775–1851).
3. Sophocles (496?–406 B.C.),
Roman marble copy of a Greek
original.
4. Detail, women weaving and
folding cloth, design on Athenian
flask, c. 560 B.C.
5. Ruins of small temple at Delphi.
6. Ovid (43 B.C.–A.D. 17?).
7. Detail, Roman mosaic
portraying musicians and their
instruments.
8. Homer, detail of statue from
Herculaneum, ancient city in
southern Italy.
9. Arch of Titus, Rome, A.D. 81.

**Key to Illustrations on
Pages 732–733.**

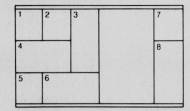

1. Detail, medieval marketplace,
fifteenth-century French
manuscript.
2. Detail, singer and two
musicians, Italian manuscript.
3. Reims Cathedral, France,
c. 1290.
4. Detail, *The Effects of Good
Government*, Ambrogio
Lorenzetti, 1340.
5. Detail, thirteenth-century
miniature depicting Dante
composing the *Divine Comedy*.
6. Detail, interior of a bakery,
fifteenth-century Italian
manuscript.
7. Detail, embarkation of Cheva-
liers du Saint-Esprit on a Crusade,
fourteenth-century miniature.
8. Bishop's tower at the walled
city of Carcassonne, France.

**Key to Illustrations on
Pages 752–753.**

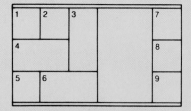

1. Detail, *View of Toledo*, El
Greco, early 1600s.
2. Giovanni Boccaccio
(1313–1375).
3. Vasco da Gama (1469?–1524),
sixteenth-century manuscript.
4. Chenonceaux Castle, France,
mid-sixteenth century.
5. Miguel de Cervantes
(1547–1616).
6. Detail, *Christopher Columbus
at the Royal Court of Spain*,
American lithograph, 1892.
7. The dome of St. Peter's
Cathedral, Rome, Michelangelo,
1546–1564.
8. Francesco Petrarch
(1304–1374).
9. Sixteenth-century Italian
ceramic plate showing an incident
from the campaign of the Roman
general Scipio.

Key to Illustrations on Pages 774–775.

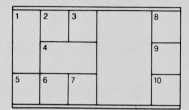

1. Engraving showing French costume, c. 1786.
2. Detail, *Boy Sharpening a Pencil*, Jean-Baptiste-Simeon Chardin (1699–1779).
3. Detail, French etching showing the storming of the Bastille, 1817.
4. Detail, painting of Versailles, Pierre Patel, 1668.
5. Detail, *The Little Street*, Johannes Vermeer, 1658.
6. Parade helmet made for Louis XIV, c. 1700.
7. Voltaire (1694–1778).
8. Molière in the role of Sganarelle, period French engraving.
9. Palace of Versailles.
10. Detail, *A Young Girl Reading*, Jean-Honoré Fragonard, c. 1776.

Key to Illustrations on Pages 796–797.

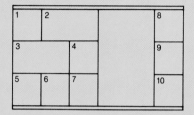

1. Anton Chekhov (1860–1904).
2. Detail, *The Battle of Waterloo*, Sir William Allen, nineteenth century.
3. Detail, *On the Boulevard*, Vladimir Makovsky, 1887.
4. Detail, *The Orchestra of the Opera*, Edgar Degas, 1868–1870.
5. Detail, *Breton Women*, Paul Gauguin, 1894.
6. Guy de Maupassant (1850–1893).
7. Example of art nouveau ceramics, late nineteenth century.
8. Portrait of Johann Wolfgang von Goethe (1749–1832), J. K. Stieler, 1828.
9. Detail, *The Haymarket at Cologne*, German engraving, mid-nineteenth century.
10. Detail, *Wheatfield with Reaper*, Vincent van Gogh, 1889.

Key to Illustrations on Pages 846–847.

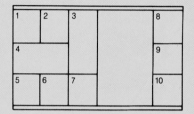

1. Thomas Mann (1875–1955).
2. Silver teapot exemplifying Bauhaus design, Germany, 1920s.
3. *Family Group*, Henry Moore, 1948–1949.
4. Notre Dame du Haut (chapel), Le Corbusier, Ronchamp, France, 1955.
5. Detail, *The Musician*, Louis Marcoussis, 1914.
6. Albert Camus (1913–1960).
7. Wassily Chair, first tubular chair designed by Marcel Breuer, 1925.
8. Detail, *Harlequin*, Pablo Picasso, 1901.
9. Franz Kafka (1883–1924).
10. The Georges Pompidou Center, Plateau Beauborg, Paris, France.

WRITING ABOUT LITERATURE HANDBOOK
Revising and Editing Checklist

The lessons in this handbook will help you think about literature in ways that you may be asked to when you are given essay assignments. If you can think clearly about literature, you will be on your way to writing clear analyses of literature.

The lessons will show you how to approach writing as a process. For each essay assignment they will advise you on prewriting steps to follow, and they will suggest how you can proceed from paragraph to paragraph. Each lesson will also remind you to revise and edit your first draft into a more polished final draft. Here are specific guidelines to follow as you review your first draft.

1. Read your writing aloud. Your ear has been responding to words longer than you have been writing.
2. Use the following checklist to revise your writing. If you can answer "yes" to each question on the list, you will submit an essay that your audience will find interesting and logical.

  I. Organization
     a. Does your thesis statement in the introductory paragraph relate directly to the assignment?
     b. Are the ideas mentioned in the thesis statement then taken up in the following paragraphs with a topic sentence for each?
     c. Is there clear movement from paragraph to paragraph by means of transitions?
     d. Does the final paragraph offer a restatement of the thesis statement along with additional insights?
 II. Content
     a. Does the essay as a whole adequately answer the question posed in the assignment?
     b. Is each idea adequately developed with supporting details from the literature rather than simply stated and restated in different ways without evidence?
III. Grammar, Usage, Mechanics
     a. Is each sentence complete (no fragments, no run-ons)?
     b. Have you avoided errors in the use of verbs (especially, subject-verb agreement), pronouns, and modifiers?
     c. Have you correctly capitalized and punctuated all sentences?
     d. Are all words spelled correctly?
IV. Word Choice, Style
     a. Have you used words that are appropriate for your audience and your purpose?
     b. Have you avoided slang and cliches unless (and this should be rare) you are using them for a very special purpose or effect?
     c. Have you eliminated wordiness and vagueness?
     d. Have you varied sentence length and structure while checking for parallelism?

LESSON 1: *Developing a Thesis Statement*

The thesis statement of a composition states the topic of your composition and explains your purpose in writing about it. The thesis statement, which usually appears in the introductory paragraph, expresses the thesis, or proposition, that you will defend. For example, after reading James Joyce's "Araby" (page 593 in this book) you may want to write about the boy's attitudes toward the fair. "Appearance and reality," then, is your *topic*. What you will say about the topic is the *thesis*, and you will state the thesis in a *thesis statement*. Note that a thesis statement may contain more than one main clause and may even, at times, be two sentences long.

> *Example:* The boy in "Araby" initially expects the fair to be exotic and ablaze; when he reaches his goal of attending the fair, he confronts disappointment and darkness.

A thesis statement is *not* merely a fact; it is an opinion or interpretation based on the facts of the literary selection. In other words, "'Araby' centers around a Dublin fair" would not qualify as a thesis statement. The sentence is not a thesis statement because it does not state a position or opinion based on the facts of the work.

The purpose of the thesis statement is to introduce the subject of the composition to your audience and to explain the nature of the paragraphs that follow. Each of those paragraphs will have its own topic sentence and will support the opening thesis statement.

CONCEPTS TO REMEMBER

1. A thesis statement is much more detailed and specific than a general topic. The topic is often just a single word or phrase. The thesis statement is one or more complete sentences that express your position and indicate the plan you will follow in the composition as a whole. Here are examples:

Beowulf
   ■ *General Topic:* Loyalty to lord and king
   ■ *Thesis Statement:* In excerpts from *Beowulf*, we can see the dominant role that loyalty to lord and king played in the life of Anglo-Saxon nobles.

The thesis statement should narrow and focus the general topic so that you can write a coherent composition with the limits of three to five paragraphs.

2. It is very important that you believe in your thesis. Your composition will lack conviction and your thesis statement will not convince your audience if you yourself do not believe in it. You must look for a topic and then generate a thesis in which you are genuinely interested. Although your observations and analysis may not involve a radically new interpretation, you should nevertheless point out *something of interest to you*.

TYPICAL ESSAY QUESTION

The most challenging essay question may be the kind that asks you to create a thesis statement and to go on to support the thesis statement. Such an assignment may be worded as follows:

> Develop a thesis statement about a piece of literature, and in a brief essay defend your thesis with examples from the work.

PREWRITING

Assuming you have read a work carefully, ask yourself some or all of the following questions or other, similar questions. These questions will help you identify which aspect of the work you want to write about and then to create a thesis statement that will focus your area of concern narrowly enough so that you can handle the topic within a brief essay.

1. What is the most intriguing literary element or aspect of the work?

   a. *Plot:* What is notable about the conflicts in this selection? What prepares you for the climax? What elements of foreshadowing are present?
   b. *Characters:* Do any of the characters experience interesting growth or change? Would a compare/contrast approach produce significant insights?
   c. *Setting:* How is the setting a reflection of the characters or another element of the work?

d. *Point of View:* Why is the point of view appropriate for the selection?

e. *Theme:* Why is the theme intriguing? How is it made clear throughout the work?

f. *Symbol:* What is the purpose of any symbol that the author has used?

g. *Irony:* What type of irony (verbal, dramatic, situational) does the author use? What effect does it have on your understanding of theme, characters, and so on?

h. *Tone:* How does the author achieve his or her tone in this work?

i. *Purpose:* What is the author's purpose? What techniques does the author use to achieve that purpose?

j. *Total Effect:* What is the total impact of the work? How is it achieved?

2. Why is this element or aspect of the work interesting? Is it central to understanding the work? Do other elements or aspects of the work support the one you plan to write about?

3. Can you support your idea about the element you have selected? What support can you find in the text itself? What evidence can you find in secondary sources, such as the author's biography or critics' writings? (See Lesson 3: Citing Evidence for more information about primary and secondary sources.)

4. What are some of the arguments against your thesis statement? How would you go about responding to these arguments?

The following example shows a thesis statement generated for the epic poem *Beowulf.*

Example: In the epic poem *Beowulf* the monster Grendel and the fire-breathing dragon are symbols of absolute evil, and Beowulf's heroic battles with the two monsters represent the eternal, universal, and predestined struggle between good and evil.

WRITING AN ESSAY PARAGRAPH BY PARAGRAPH

1. Begin the introductory paragraph with the thesis statement. Fill out the introductory paragraph with definitions of terms or clarification of your thesis statement.

2. In the following paragraphs give at least two specific examples from *Beowulf* to support the thesis statement.

3. In your concluding paragraph repeat your thesis statement in different words, and indicate that the preceding paragraphs have shown that the thesis statement is defensible.

WRITING A ONE–PARAGRAPH ANSWER

All the preceding advice on structure applies as well to written responses that are only one paragraph long. If you are limited to one paragraph, begin with a strong topic sentence. Each of your following sentences should develop one aspect of the topic sentence. You will not have as much room for supporting details as in a five-paragraph essay, but you nevertheless must give evidence to support the topic sentence. For example, using the thesis statement from Prewriting Step 4 as a topic sentence, you can devote a few sentences to description of the evil nature of the monsters and a few sentences to evidence that Beowulf symbolizes strength and goodness. You may include support to show that the battles and Beowulf's death are predestined. You can conclude this one-paragraph response with a **clincher** sentence, which sums up the evidence you have presented.

REVISING AND EDITING

See page 925 for detailed reminders about improving your writing.

ASSIGNMENTS

1. Write the composition that will support the thesis statement supplied here for *Beowulf.*

2. Do one of the assignments called "Developing a Thesis Statement" that appear after the folk ballads (page 41) or after the selections by Christopher Marlowe and Sir Walter Raleigh (page 97), Samuel Johnson (page 294), William Hazlitt (page 395), and Joseph Conrad (page 588).

LESSON 2: *Writing a Comparison/Contrast*

As you identify similarities and differences between two works of literature, you are examining the properties of each work in order to define its meaning. A comparison/contrast analysis of two works clarifies your understanding of how each author has approached the subject, what the meaning or theme is, and how each author feels about the subject.

CONCEPTS TO REMEMBER

1. *To compare* in this lesson means "to examine two or more literary works for the purpose of noting similarities." *To contrast* means "to examine two or more literary works for the purpose of noting differences."
2. In stories and novels you can compare and contrast these elements: plot, characters, settings, points of view, tones, themes, symbols, and irony.
3. In poetry you can compare and contrast these elements: speakers, sound devices, rhythm, rhyme, imagery, and figurative speech.

TYPICAL ESSAY QUESTION

When you are asked to compare and contrast two literary works, you will often have to answer an essay assignment like this one:

Select two pieces of literature that you have read. Compare and contrast the two by pointing out similarities and differences in content and literary techniques.

PREWRITING

1. Use the following questions and others like them to compare and contrast two stories.

   a. What plot elements in each are similar?
   b. How are the characters similar or different? Do the characters change, or do they remain the same throughout the story?
   c. From what point of view is each story told?
   d. What is the setting of each piece? In what period does it take place? Under what social conditions?
   e. The tone of each piece may be serious, comic, straightforward, ironic, angry, etc. Are the tones of the two pieces alike or different?

   f. What theme is each author expressing?
   g. What symbols are used? How?
   h. How is irony used in each piece?
   i. What is the total impact of each piece?

2. Use the following questions and others like them to compare and contrast two poems.

   a. Does each poem focus on the actions of a character? On a place? On a thing? On an event?
   b. Does each poem focus on an idea? A feeling?
   c. What is your emotional response to each?
   d. On what does each poem cause you to reflect?
   e. Who is the speaker in each poem?
   f. What sound devices are used in each?
   g. What kind of rhyme and rhythm is used?
   h. How does each poem use imagery to appeal to your five senses?
   i. What figures of speech are used in the poem?

3. Prepare a chart (see the opposite page) on which to record your answers to the questions in Prewriting Step 1 or Step 2 and to any other questions you have devised.

WRITING PARAGRAPH BY PARAGRAPH

1. Begin your introductory paragraph with a thesis statement that restates the main points of the assignment. State the major similarities and differences in meaning and technique.

   Example: The two Scottish folk ballads, "Sir Patrick Spens" and "The Wife of Usher's Well" tell different stories that, however, share common techniques and a common theme.

2. Use one of the following options for organizing the body of the essay.

   Option A
   Introductory paragraph
   Next paragraph: Tell about one selection.
   Next paragraph: Tell about the second one.
   Next paragraph: Discuss similarities and differences based on two preceding paragraphs.
   Concluding paragraph

SIMILARITIES AND DIFFERENCES IN POEMS
SELECTION: (1) "Sir Patrick Spens" and (2) "The Wife of Usher's Well"

	SPEAKER AND TONE	FOCUS	SOUND	THEME OR MEANING
SELECTION 1	Speaker tells story directly to audience *Tone:* Foreboding, sad, somber	*Events:* Knight recommends Sir Patrick as the man to sail the king's ship. Shipwreck and drowning of all hands	*Rhythm:* ballad stanza *Rhyme:* Follows ballad rhyme scheme, *abcb* *Alliteration:* "A loud lauch lauched he" *Repetition of words and phrases:* "Half owre, half owre to Aberdour"	Death at sea as a result of the captain's ignoring his premonition to carry out his duty; loyalty both of captain and his men
SELECTION 2	Speaker tells story directly to audience *Tone:* Sad, but not ominous	Drowning at sea of the three sons Visitation by ghosts of three sons to comfort mother and to say good-by to life	*Rhythm:* ballad stanza *Rhyme:* Follows ballad rhyme scheme, *abcb* *Alliteration:* "And a wealthy wife was she" *Repetition of phrases and words:* "They hadna' been a week from her, a week but barely ane."	*Disaster:* Death at sea; loyalty and love of mother and sons

Option B
Introductory paragraph
Next paragraph: Discuss the similarities in meaning and elements in each selection.
Next paragraph: Discuss the differences in meaning and elements in each selection.
Concluding paragraph

3. In the concluding paragraph use different words to remind readers of your thesis. Focus on whether the two selections are more alike or more different.

REVISING AND EDITING
See page 925 for detailed reminders about improving your writing.

ASSIGNMENTS
1. Use the chart for "Sir Patrick Spens" and "The Wife of Usher's Well" to write a comparison/contrast for the two folk ballads.
2. Do one of the "Writing a Comparison/ Contrast" assignments that follow the selections by Geoffrey Chaucer (page 63), Edmund Spenser (page 93), Robert Browning (page 425), William Butler Yeats (page 540), John Galsworthy (page 591), Aesop (page 673), Dante (page 747), the Troubadours (page 751), Petrarch (page 757), Molière (page 787), Paul Verlaine (page 845), Rainer Maria Rilke (page 855), Eugenio Montale and Czeslaw Milosz (page 874), and Hermann Hesse (page 898).

LESSON 3: *Citing Evidence*

Whether you write one paragraph or an entire essay of literary analysis, you must provide details—evidence—to support the generalization you have made in your topic sentence or thesis statement. The following sample paragraph is effective because it includes numerous details providing proof of the opinion stated in the topic sentence.

Sample

In the Prologue to *The Canterbury Tales,* Chaucer's portraits of the pilgrims not only tell us much about life and customs in medieval England but also show that human nature is the same, whatever the period. For example, his detailed descriptions of dress, which tell us much about daily life, include the heroic Knight's ". . . fustian tunic, stained and dark / With smudges where his armor had left mark"; the Yeoman's ". . . coat and hood of green . . . A hunting-horn, well-slung and burnished clean, / That dangled from a baldric of bright green"; and the Woman from Bath's wimple, cloak, and hose of "the finest scarlet red." Chaucer helps us understand customs by showing us people at work: the Reeve, an overseer who was "Feared like the plague"; the Plowman, a hard-working farmer who did "as the gospel bade him." Demonstrating human nature, Chaucer shows us the Miller, who was a "wrangler and buffoon" and "a masterhand at stealing grain," and the Merchant, who worked hard concealing the fact that he was in debt. Chaucer's satiric and witty descriptions make the people of this long-ago period come alive.

CONCEPTS TO REMEMBER

Evidence may be in the form of a paraphrase or in the form of a direct quotation.

1. A **paraphrase** is a restatement in your own words of the sense of a piece of writing. When you paraphrase, you should indicate the source either within the context of your paraphrase or in a footnote or endnote that you refer your reader to by placing a raised numeral at the end of your paraphrase.

Paraphrase

Pilgrims to Canterbury traveled as a group from London and may have passed the time by telling stories to one another as they journeyed. In one famous fictional account of such a pilgrimage, the pilgrims actually competed to see who would tell the most entertaining story.[1]

2. When you use a **direct quotation,** you use precisely the same words and the same word order as your source.

Direct Quotation

One of literature's classic monsters, Grendel, attacks the warriors at Herot:

He slipped through the door and there in silence
Snatched up thirty men, smashed them
Unknowing in their beds and ran out with their bodies,
The blood dripping behind him, back
To his lair, delighted with his night's slaughter.

TYPICAL ESSAY QUESTION

You should always cite evidence in support of your thesis statement. Some essay questions make a particular point of reminding you to do so. The following essay assignment is an example.

Write a brief essay in which you give your opinion or make a generalization about a particular piece of literature. First clearly state your opinion. Then support it with examples.

PREWRITING

1. Gather material in support of your thesis by reading and rereading the piece of literature.
2. Prepare a chart on which you can list (on the left) the arguments you will present in support of your thesis. In the middle column add exact quotations that defend each argument you list. In the right-hand column, offer a paraphrase of the quotation. The chart on the opposite page served as preparation for the sample paragraph near the beginning of this lesson.

USING FOOTNOTES OR ENDNOTES AND BIBLIOGRAPHY ENTRIES

A **footnote** or **endnote** gives source information for a statement in your composition. It tells

CITING EVIDENCE

SELECTION: Prologue to *The Canterbury Tales*

THESIS: In the Prologue to *The Canterbury Tales,* Chaucer's portraits of the pilgrims not only tell us much about life and customs in medieval England but also show that human nature is the same, whatever the period.

ARGUMENT	SUPPORTING QUOTATION	SUPPORTING PARAPHRASE
Descriptions of dress	*Knight:* "He wore a fustian tunic, stained and dark / With smudges where his armor had left mark."	The Knight was dressed simply in a heavy cotton tunic stained by his armor.
	Yeoman: "This Yeoman wore a coat and hood of green, / And peacock-feathered arrows, bright and keen / And neatly sheathed, hung at his belt the while . . . And in his hand he bore a mighty bow. . . A medal of St. Christopher he wore / Of shining silver on his breast, and bore / A hunting-horn, well-slung and burnished clean, / That dangled from a baldric of bright green."	Yeoman was dressed in the costume of a forester—rather Robin Hood–like and very clean and neat. His arrows in a quiver hung from a belt; a horn, from a shoulder strap
	Woman from Bath: "Her hose were of the finest scarlet red / And gartered tight; her shoes were soft and new. / . . . she sat / Well wimpled up, and on her head a hat / As broad as is a buckler or a shield; / She had a flowing mantle that concealed / Large hips, her heels spurred sharply under that."	She wore a long hood topped by a hat that looked like a shield, bright red stockings, long cloak, and spurs on her new shoes.
Descriptions of work customs	*Reeve:* "His master's sheep, his animals and hens, / Pigs, horses, dairies, stores and cattle pens / Were wholly trusted to his government. . . . No bailiff, serf, or herdsman dared to kick, / He knew their dodges, knew their every trick; / Feared like the plague he was, by those beneath."	The overseer who managed the estate for the landowner, keeping all accounts
	Plowman: "He was an honest worker, good and true, . . . / And, as the gospel bade him, so did he."	A hard-working farmer who tried to follow the teachings of the Bible
Examples of human nature	*Miller:* "A wrangler and buffoon, he had a store / Of tavern stories, filthy in the main. / His was a master-hand at stealing grain.	A boorish fellow who told off-color jokes and was very clever at stealing grain.
	Merchant: "This estimable Merchant so had set / His wits to work, none knew he was in debt, / He was so stately in negotiation, / Loan, bargain and commercial obligation."	The merchant pursued his business in such a way as to keep people from suspecting that he was in debt.

who wrote the source, its title, where it was published, by whom, and when.

A **bibliography** is an alphabetical arrangement by last name of the authors of all the sources used in writing a composition. The bibliography appears at the end of the composition.

ASSIGNMENT

Do one of the assignments called "Citing Evidence" that appear after the selections by Geoffrey Chaucer (p. 71), Samuel Pepys (page 247), James Boswell (page 301), James Joyce (page 597), and Thomas Mann (page 886).

LESSON 4: *Writing About Nonfiction*

Essays, biographies, autobiographies, diaries, and journals are all types of nonfiction. You can analyze all kinds of nonfiction, whether book length or just a few paragraphs long, in the same way. You can discuss the author's purpose in writing the piece and demonstrate with specific examples from the work how the author achieved that purpose.

CONCEPTS TO REMEMBER
1. The **purpose** of a piece of nonfiction is the central idea, or general statement about life, that the author wishes to make.
2. To communicate the purpose, the author uses various techniques such as sensory details, facts, statistics, examples, and opinions.

TYPICAL ESSAY QUESTION
When you are asked to write about a piece of nonfiction, you are often answering an assignment such as the following:

Select a piece of nonfiction that you have read. An author always has a purpose in writing nonfiction. To accomplish this purpose, the author may use various techniques such as sensory details, facts, statistics, examples, and opinions.

What is the purpose of the piece of nonfiction you have read? Cite with examples the particular techniques that the author uses to accomplish the purpose of the piece.

PREWRITING
1. To determine the author's purpose in writing a work of nonfiction, ask yourself the following questions:
   a. What, if anything, does the title suggest about the author's opinion of the subject of the essay, diary, or journal or about the person in a biography or autobiography?
   b. What opinion about life in general is suggested by the experiences that the author relates?
   c. What opinion about the subject or about people in general is suggested by details (including sensory details, facts, statistics, examples, and opinions)?

   d. What ideas about the world in general are suggested by details of setting?
   e. What tone, or attitude, toward the subject is revealed by the author's style?

2. Based on your answers to the preceding questions, prepare a statement of the author's purpose, and, on a chart like the one on the opposite page, record the techniques that the author uses to achieve that purpose. The fill-in chart represents an analysis of the essay "Of Ambition" by Sir Francis Bacon (page 191).

WRITING PARAGRAPH BY PARAGRAPH
1. Begin the introductory paragraph with a thesis statement. It should specify the author's purpose and the techniques used to accomplish it.

   Example: In his essay "Of Ambition" Sir Francis Bacon uses sensory detail, facts, examples, and opinion to advise rulers on when to employ ambitious men and how to protect themselves against the dangers of thwarted or unbridled ambition.

2. In each of the body paragraphs, show how the author uses one technique to make the purpose clear.
3. In the concluding paragraph restate in other words the thesis statement from the introductory paragraph. Here you might include briefly your own reaction to the author's efforts.

REVISING AND EDITING
See page 925 for detailed reminders about improving your writing.

ASSIGNMENTS
1. Use the chart for "Of Ambition" (Prewriting Step 2) to write an essay in which you discuss the author's purpose and the techniques he used to achieve that purpose.
2. Do one of the assignments called "Writing About Nonfiction" that follow the selections by Joseph Addison and Sir Richard Steele (page 275) and George Orwell (page 623), or select another piece of literature from this book, and write an essay in which you discuss the author's purpose and the techniques used to achieve that purpose.

PURPOSE AND TECHNIQUES

SELECTION: "Of Ambition"

PURPOSE: To state his opinion that ambitious men can be valuable to rulers but that they can also be very dangerous and, therefore, should be curbed.

SENSORY DETAILS	FACTS	STATISTICS
"But then there must be some middle counselors to keep things steady; for without ballast the ship will roll too much."	". . . choler; which is a humor that maketh men active, earnest, full of alacrity and stirring . . ." ("fact" in Bacon's day)	NONE

EXAMPLES	OPINION
Examples of when to use ambitious men: "Good commanders in the wars must be taken, be they never so ambitious. . . ." "There is also great use of ambitious men in being screens to princes in matters of danger and envy. . . ." "There is use also of ambitious men in pulling down the greatness of any subject that overtops: as Tiberius used Macro in the pulling down of Sejanus." *Examples of how to protect against the dangers of ambition:* "It is counted by some a weakness in princes to have favorites; but it is of all others the best remedy against ambitious great ones." "Another means to curb them is to balance them by others as proud as they."	*Opinions on the value and danger of ambition:* "So ambitious men, if they find the way open for their rising, and still get forward, they are rather busy than dangerous; but if they be checked in their desires, they become secretly discontent, and look upon men and matters with an evil eye, and are best pleased when things go backward; which is the worst property in a servant of a prince or state." ". . . it is good not to use such natures at all." "He that seeketh to be eminent amongst able men hath a great task; but that is ever good for the public. But he that plots to be the only figure amongst ciphers is the decay of a whole age." "Generally, let princes and states choose such ministers as are more sensible of duty than of rising; and such as love business rather upon conscience than upon bravery: and let them discern a busy nature from a willing mind."

LESSON 5: *Writing About a Quotation or a Symbol*

Why does a quotation from a piece of literature stand out? In some fiction, poetry, nonfiction, or drama, a single line can at times sum up the meaning so vividly that the line itself comes to represent the entire work. In the same way, a symbol can create a vivid impression in the reader's mind. Just as a quotation can summarize an idea or opinion in a dramatic way, so a symbol may represent the message that the writer wishes to communicate. Because quotations and symbols express the writer's meaning so clearly and concisely, you should learn how to analyze them and relate them to a work as a whole.

CONCEPTS TO REMEMBER

1. A powerful quotation may have vivid adjectives and strong action verbs. It may use strong parallel structure that gives dramatic rhythm to a sentence. It may use metaphorical language. It may appeal strongly to the reader's emotions or sense. It may have a universal meaning. It may use clever word play or state a paradox. It may occupy a prominent position in the work.
2. A **symbol** is something that stands for itself but also for something larger than itself. It may be a person, an animal, an inanimate object, or an action. A writer often uses a concrete object to express an abstract idea, a quality, or a belief. A symbol may also appeal to a reader's emotions and can provide a dramatic way to express an idea, communicate a message, or clarify meaning.

TYPICAL ESSAY QUESTION

When you are asked to write about a quotation or a symbol, you may find an essay question such as this:

Identify a quotation [or symbol] from a piece of literature. Explain the specific meaning of the quotation [or symbol] in the work as a whole, explaining how it relates to a theme or main idea of the work.

PREWRITING

For a quotation
1. Identify a quotation from a given work of literature. Ask yourself the following questions if you need help in selecting a quotation:

a. Is there a sentence that has already gained fame?
b. Is there a sentence with strong parallel structure, emotional appeal, or notable simplicity?
c. Does the work begin or end with a particularly impressive statement?

For example, in considering Act I, Scene i, of Shakespeare's tragedy *Macbeth,* you might choose the line "Fair is foul, and foul is fair." The witches' observation is, like so many of Shakespeare's lines, quite well known. It is a good choice to write about because it contains strong parallelism, contradiction, alliteration: in addition, it commands a prominent position—the *end* of a scene.

2. Explain in your own words the meaning of the quotation. That is, translate any figurative language, and fill in any information your reader may need in order to understand the quotation. Make sure you explain, when, where, and why the statement was made. For example, if you were working with the quotation "Fair is foul, and foul is fair," you could explain that in this scene, which introduces the play, the witches foreshadow the difference between appearance and reality. Macbeth, we will see, is not the loyal subject he appears to be, for ambition has cast aside his reason.

For a symbol
1. Identify a symbol from a piece of literature. Look for a concrete object that seems to stand for something abstract above and beyond its concrete meaning. Ask yourself the following questions if you need help in selecting a symbol.

a. Does the title of the selection alert you to symbolism? For example, titles such as "A Poison Tree" (page 314), "Sailing to Byzantium" (page 612), and "The New Dress" (page 538) might alert you to an object or place with symbolic meaning.
b. Has the author given particular emphasis to one object or other detail, and thereby perhaps raised it to the level of a symbol? For example, in *Macbeth,* Act IV, Scene iv, unnatural weather—perhaps an eclipse—accompanies the murder of Duncan.

c. Does the object seem to be representative of something *of another kind*? Remember that you would not say that an ant symbolizes all insects; an ant is merely representative of certain types of insects. However, you might say that an ant is symbolic of dogged, hard work. An ant is an insect, while hard work is an action, *something of another kind.*

2. Explain the meaning of the symbol. That is, tell what abstract idea, quality, or belief is called to mind by the given person, animal, object, or action. For example, the unnatural weather seems to symbolize the unnatural human behavior that hungry ambition has caused.

For both a quotation and a symbol
3. Identify a main idea or theme of the piece of literature by asking yourself questions such as the following. Remember that a main idea or theme should be stated in a complete sentence as a *general* truth.

   a. What ideas about life does the selection's *title* suggest?
   b. What do the particular *events* and *conflicts* reveal about life in general?
   c. What might these particular *people* or *characters* with these personality traits tell us about life in general?
   d. What view of the world do the *setting* and its details offer us?

For example, answers to these questions should help you see the following main ideas:

> Appearances do not always reflect the truth; an honest face may mask a traitor.
> —Witches, Act I, Scene i

> The natural order can mirror any upset in the proper order of human society.
> —Ross, Act II, Scene iv

4. Once you have identified the main idea or theme of the work, make notes on how the quotation or symbol relates to the work as a whole. Ask the following questions:

   a. Does the quotation or symbol *summarize* the theme or main idea?
   b. Does the quotation or symbol *illustrate* the theme or main idea?

WRITING PARAGRAPH BY PARAGRAPH

1. Begin your introductory paragraph with a thesis statement that tells what quotation or symbol you are going to write about and that identifies a theme or main idea of the literary work.

Examples
For a quotation: The final comment of the witches in Act I, Scene i, of Shakespeare's tragedy *Macbeth,* "Fair is foul, and foul is fair," introduces the audience to the dominant theme of appearance versus reality.

For a symbol: As described in Act II, Scene iv, of *Macbeth,* the unnatural weather that accompanies the murder of Duncan symbolizes the disruption of the proper order of human society. The play as a whole underscores the chaos that results from meddling with that order.

2. In the next paragraph tell the specific meaning of the quotation or the symbol. Explain, if necessary, how you arrived at your understanding.
3. In the next paragraph explain in what way the quotation or symbol fits into the literary work.
4. In your concluding paragraph you might tell how the analysis of the quotation or symbol has helped you to understand better the nature of the piece as a whole.

REVISING AND EDITING

See page 925 for detailed reminders about improving your writing.

ASSIGNMENTS

1. Using the information in this lesson, write an essay explaining the significance of the quotation from *Macbeth,* Act I, Scene i, or the symbol from Act II, Scene iv.
2. Do one of the assignments called "Writing About a Quotation" or "Writing About a Symbol" that appear after the pieces by John Donne (page 212), John Dryden (page 240), William Blake (page 315), Samuel Taylor Coleridge (page 363), Alfred, Lord Tennyson (page 419), Rupert Brooke (page 552), Louis MacNeice (page 557), Geoffrey Hill (page 578), D. H. Lawrence (page 610), and Sophocles (page 713), or select another piece of literature from this book, and write about a symbol or a quotation within the work.

LESSON 6: *Writing About Theme*

Authors usually have an underlying central idea, or **theme,** in mind when they write a literary work. A theme is more than just the specific topic or subject of the work. Whether the work is a novel, short story, poem, or play, its theme expresses an opinion or raises a question about human nature or the meaning of human experience. You may or may not agree with the theme, but if the selection is well-written, it will provide a new and moving insight into the human condition, and you will be able to write about that. For example, one subject in *Beowulf* is the battle with Grendel. The theme might be stated as "The forces of good will triumph over the forces of evil."

CONCEPTS TO REMEMBER

1. Most pieces of literature have only one theme, although the theme can be worded in several ways. Some works, however, may contain several themes; such is the case with a long, complex novel.
2. Sometimes the theme may be clearly stated. Usually, however, the theme is implied or suggested through other elements. The author uses characterization, setting, events, point of view, and tone to develop the theme.

TYPICAL ESSAY QUESTION

When you are asked to write about the theme of a selection, you are often answering an essay assignment such as the following:

Identify the theme of a work of literature. Show how the author illuminates this theme through characterization, setting, events, point of view, and tone.

PREWRITING

1. Identify the subject of a selection that you have read. The selection may have more than one subject, but select only one. For example, the subject of "The Pardoner's Tale" (page 65) is three friends' secret plot to kill one another in order to keep the whole pile of gold coins they have found.
2. Keeping the subject in mind, ask yourself the following questions so that you can get beyond the subject of the selection to its theme.

a. What do various characters (or the main character) think, say, and do about the subject?
b. What are the character's key traits? Does the character change at all?
c. How do the time, place, clothing, and other details of setting serve as a suitable background for the work's subject?
d. What do the events and conflicts have to do with the subject matter?
e. What do the selection's climax and resolution have to do with the selection's subject matter?
f. From whose point of view is the story told, and how does this point of view affect you?
g. What tone does the writer use, and how does that tone affect your reaction?

3. Prepare a chart to record your answers to the questions in Prewriting Step 2. The chart on the opposite page is a sample prepared for "The Pardoner's Tale."
4. Examine the completed chart, and try to develop a statement of the theme of the selection. For example, for "The Pardoner's Tale" you might state the theme as follows: Greed can lead to destruction.

WRITING PARAGRAPH BY PARAGRAPH

1. Begin your introductory paragraph with a thesis statement that restates the main ideas of the assignment. Indicate what the theme of the selection is, being certain to state the theme in terms of a generalization about human nature or experience. Then show how the theme is illuminated through the other elements of the selection.

   Example: The theme of "The Pardoner's Tale" is that greed can lead to destruction. All the elements in the story—particularly, the characterization of the old man, the setting, and the ironic tone—contribute to the effective presentation of this moral lesson.

2. In the next paragraph focus on how the characters, setting, and events reveal the generalization you feel the selection makes about life. Support your ideas with details from the work.

EVENTS ILLUMINATING THEME

SELECTION: "The Pardoner's Tale"

SUBJECT OF STORY: Three friends secretly plot to kill one another in order to keep all the gold they have found.

CHARACTERIZATION	SETTING	EVENTS
Old man's traits: Very, very old and wise; he wants to die but cannot; might represent the Devil or Death	*Time:* Fourteenth century; Black Plague killing thousands *Place:* An English village and road leading to another village	*Events and Conflicts:* Rioters want to challenge "Death." When they find gold, they forget their vow and decide to share the wealth. One goes off for provisions, leaving the other two, who plot to stab him; the one who has gone off likewise plans to eliminate the remaining two. *Climax:* Upon his return the other two stab him according to plan. *Resolution:* The remaining two celebrate and drink the poisoned wine; they die an agonizing death.

POINT OF VIEW	TONE	
Omniscient: Narrator tells about all events and what characters think and feel; uses Publican to explain the setting (description of Black Death)	Author uses all three types of irony: *Verbal*—Publican says death is a "privy thief." Rioters think they are going off to fight a real person; *Situational*—Merrymaking as death is all around; *Dramatic*—Readers know that two are secretly plotting to kill the third, while the third is secretly plotting to kill the other two.	

3. In the next paragraph focus on how the point of view helps to illustrate the theme.
4. In the next paragraph focus on how the tone clarifies the theme.
5. In the concluding paragraph restate your thesis statement. Explain whether the elements of the selection led you to understand a theme new to you, or whether they helped renew an awareness that you had.

REVISING AND EDITING

See page 925 for detailed reminders about improving your writing.

ASSIGNMENTS

1. Use the chart for "The Pardoner's Tale" to write about theme. How do characterization, setting, events, point of view, and tone show that greed can lead to destruction?
2. Choose one of the assignments called "Writing About Theme" that follow the selections by John Milton (page 38), Sean O'Faolain (page 630), Virgil (page 727), Leo Tolstoy (page 827), and Albert Camus (page 908), or select another piece of literature from this book, and show how all the other elements illuminate its theme.

LESSON 7: Writing About Poetry

Poetry has much in common with both music and art. Musicians use techniques such as rhythm and sound to capture a mood or convey feeling; artists use color and line to create a beautiful painting. In the same way, poets use various literary techniques to convey the sense, or meaning, of a poem and to convey mood and feeling. These techniques include choice of the speaker, sound, imagery, and figurative language. You should learn to think about all these techniques so that when you write an essay about a poem you will be able to show the connection between the techniques of the poem and its meaning.

CONCEPTS TO REMEMBER

1. The **speaker** of the poem is the voice of the poem. Sometimes the speaker is the poet himself or herself; sometimes the speaker is a character or thing created by the poet.
2. Among the sound devices that a poet may use are **onomatopoeia** (a word or phrase that actually imitates or suggests the sound of what it describes); **alliteration** (the repetition of initial consonant sounds); **consonance** (the repetition of similar consonant sounds preceded by different accented vowels); **assonance** (the repetition of vowel sounds).
3. Other aspects of sound in poetry are **rhyme** (the repetition at regular intervals of similar or identical sounds) and **rhythm** (the pattern created by arranging stressed and unstressed syllables).
4. A poem's images may appeal to one or more senses.
5. The most common kinds of figurative language available to a poet are metaphor, simile, and personification. (**Metaphor** is a figure of speech in which two unlike things are compared without the use of *like* or *as*; **simile** is a comparison using *like* or *as*; **personification** is a figure of speech in which an animal, object, or idea is described as having human form or characteristics.)

TYPICAL ESSAY QUESTION

When you are asked to write about poetry, you are often answering an assignment such as the following:

Select a poem that you have read. What is the meaning of the poem? What techniques does the poet use to reveal this meaning? Techniques include the selection of speaker, sound, imagery, and figurative language.

PREWRITING

1. Use the following questions to help you determine the meaning of the poem.

   a. Does the poem focus on the actions of a character?
   b. Does the poem describe something?
   c. Does the poem focus on an idea? A feeling?
   d. What emotional response does the poem seem to call up in you?
   e. After your immediate emotional response to the poem, on what does the poem cause you to reflect?

2. Prepare a chart on which to record your statement of the meaning of the poem. The chart opposite represents an analysis of John Donne's Sonnet 10 (page 210), which begins, "Death, be not proud. . . ." Each column deals with one of the poetic techniques.

WRITING PARAGRAPH BY PARAGRAPH

1. Begin your introductory paragraph with a thesis statement, which should restate the main points of the assignment. Indicate that the various techniques used by the poet all serve to enhance and present effectively the underlying meaning of the poem.

   Example: In Sonnet 10 by John Donne, the poet uses the speaker, sound devices, imagery, and figurative language as he admonishes death not to be proud of its dreadful reputation; in the end, the speaker argues, eternal life will triumph over death.

2. In each of the following paragraphs, discuss one or two of the techniques that the poet uses to underscore the poem's meaning—choice of speaker, sound devices, imagery, and figurative language. Show how each technique enhances the meaning, which you have discussed in your introductory paragraph.

THE MEANING AND TECHNIQUES OF A POEM
SELECTION: Sonnet 10
MEANING: Eternal life triumphs over death.

SELECTION OF SPEAKER	SOUND	IMAGERY	FIGURATIVE LANGUAGE
Narrator cautions Death. Proud speaker ("nor yet canst thou kill me")	*Rhythm:* generally iambic pentameter—i.e., very natural human speech *Alliteration* ("*D*ie not, poor *D*eath"; "*M*uch pleasure, then from thee *m*uch *m*ore *m*ust flow.") and *assonance* ("slave to fate") give richness and smoothness to speaker's words.	Images paint a picture of limitations of death: men dying willingly, death as slave, death as dwelling with "poison, war, and sickness."	*Personification:* Narrator speaks to Death as if it were a person; attributes human quality of pride to be a state or Death as if it were a person; attributes human quality of pride to a state or condition.

3. In the next paragraph discuss further the meaning of the poem.
4. In the concluding paragraph restate your thesis statement. You might here go into greater detail than you have earlier on the emotional impact of the poem on you—now that you have analyzed the elements used to create emotion in the poem.

REVISING AND EDITING

See page 925 for detailed reminders about improving your writing.

ASSIGNMENTS

1. Use the chart for Sonnet 10 to write an essay about poetry. What is the meaning of the poem? What techniques are used to reveal this meaning?

2. Do one of the assignments called "Writing About Poetry" that follow the selections by Andrew Marvell (page 215), John Keats (page 388), Elizabeth Barrett Browning (page 427), Thomas Hardy (page 443), Dylan Thomas (page 569), and Ted Hughes (page 574).

LESSON 8: *Writing About the Total Effect*

A theatrical director combines elements such as lighting, sets, costume, makeup, stage movement, timing, and music to help an audience understand and be moved by the meaning of a play. Similarly, writers use a variety of elements in creating a literary work. These elements include plot, characters, setting, point of view, tone, theme, symbol, and irony. A skillful writer combines these elements to create a total effect, or impact, on the reader. We can analyze this impact by studying the contribution of each element to the whole. Often you will see that, as in a play, one element dominates. However, all the elements are woven together to support that key element. In this way the author—or director—creates a unified effect.

CONCEPTS TO REMEMBER

Review the lessons dealing with writing about the various literary elements individually. Review the definitions and important concepts in each lesson.

TYPICAL ESSAY QUESTION

When you are asked to write about the total effect of a selection, you are often answering an essay question such as the following:

Select a piece of literature that you have read. What is the total effect of the piece—that is, what is its impact on the reader? How does the author use the following literary elements to achieve this effect: plot, character, setting, point of view, tone, theme, symbol, and irony?

PREWRITING

1. Ask yourself the following questions as you reflect on the piece of literature:

    a. What is the impact of the work? Specifically, does the work irritate you, delight you, sadden you? Does it surprise you, or does it support an opinion or impression you already had? Does the work remind you of something else or contrast greatly with something else?
    b. Which literary element dominates?
    c. How do the other literary elements support or relate to the dominant element?

2. Prepare a chart on which to record your answers to the questions in Step 1. The chart should have columns for the question, the answer, and the details that support your answer. For the excerpt from *Le Morte d'Arthur* on page 73, a chart might look like the one on the opposite page.

WRITING PARAGRAPH BY PARAGRAPH

1. Begin the introductory paragraph with a thesis statement. The thesis statement should express the total effect of the work on the reader and note that all the key literary elements work together to create this impact.

    Example: The dominant literary element in *Le Morte d'Arthur* is its theme, but all the elements are woven together to create the total effect that enchants the reader. The reader is transported into the life of a medieval court, with its pageantry, magic, and romantic code of honor and chivalry.

2. In the next paragraph focus on the dominant literary element, and show by the inclusion of details how it contributes to the total effect.
3. In the following paragraphs discuss additional literary elements, and show by the inclusion of details how each element supports or relates to the dominant element.
4. In the concluding paragraph remind your audience that the elements mentioned in the preceding paragraphs work together to produce the total impact on the reader.

REVISING AND EDITING

See page 925 for detailed reminders about improving your writing.

ASSIGNMENTS

1. Use the chart for *Le Morte d'Arthur* to write about the total effect of the work.
2. Do the assignment called "Writing About Total Effect" that appears after the selections by William Shakespeare (page 189), George Bernard Shaw (page 530), and Anton Chekhov (page 832), or write about another piece of literature from this book.

	ANALYSIS OF THE TOTAL EFFECT	
	SELECTION: *Le Morte d'Arthur*	
QUESTION	**ANSWER**	**DETAILS**
A. WHAT IS THE IMPACT OF THE WORK?	Reader is transported into a romantic medieval world where magic flourishes.	*Setting:* "He found there a brilliantly decorated pavilion. . . . A multicolored shield hung from a tree, and resting against it was a spear."
		Magic: "That is the magic sword Excalibur . . . and it will be given to you by the Lady of the Lake, who is now crossing the water in her bark."
B. WHAT IS THE DOMINANT LITERARY ELEMENT?	*Theme:* The romantic ideals of loyalty, honor, respect for women, and skill in battle guide the behavior of a knight and are important in medieval feudal society.	*Loyalty:* "One of Arthur's knights should avenge [Sir Myles'] death."
		Honor: "King Pellinore is already tired. . . . To win would bring you no honor, to lose would be to increase your shame."
		Respect for women: "You must address her courteously. . . ."
		Skill in battle: "Arthur's knights rejoiced in the boldness of their king."
C. HOW DO THE OTHER ELEMENTS SUPPORT THE STORY?	*Plot:* The death of Sir Myles sets in motion the pursuit of revenge.	"[Arthur] decided to avenge Sir Gryfflette secretly. . . ."
	Characters: Each character plays a specific role in presenting the values of a medieval court. Merlin also controls the events; Pellinore provides motive for revenge by killing Sir Myles; Gryfflette illustrates loyalty.	*Merlin:* "Merlin adroitly put him to sleep with a magic spell." *King Pellinore:* ". . . it would seem that no knight can pass this well without your challenging him." *Gryfflette:* ". . . still I mean to joust with you."
	Setting: Details of setting describe medieval England.	". . . they found King Pellinore seated outside his pavilion." "She comes from her castle, which is hewn in the rock. . . ."
	Tone: Air of a fairy tale or ballad; imparts feeling of predestined events.	"King Arthur," she replied, "Excalibur shall be yours, if you consent now to granting me whatever gift I shall ask of you in my own time."
	Symbol: Excalibur, the magic sword, is the symbol of Arthur's power.	". . . the hand grasped a finely jeweled sword and scabbard."
	Irony: There is a bit of situational irony in that Arthur's knights cheer him when actually Merlin prevented Arthur from making a possibly fatal mistake and continues to teach him how to be king.	"I cast a spell over him; had he done so [seen us], you would not have escaped so lightly."

LESSON 9: *Applying a Statement About Literature*

Sometimes a statement about life or literature in general can provide deep insight into a particular work of literature. The statement seems to penetrate to the heart of a situation or illuminate the essential meaning of a literary work. It is your task to explain precisely why the general statement fits the specific piece of literature so well.

TYPICAL ESSAY QUESTION

A common essay question involves giving you a statement, asking you to explain the meaning of the statement, and then requesting you to show how the statement relates to a work you select or to a work specified in the essay question.

Example: Contemplation of the timeless beauty of nature can inspire a dreamlike enchantment that temporarily transcends mortal cares or pain. Explain this statement, and show how it applies to "Ode to a Nightingale" by John Keats.

PREWRITING

1. To make sure you understand the general statement and can do the first part of the assignment, paraphrase the statement and define any key terms.

   Example: People may observe something so overwhelmingly beautiful in nature that they find themselves in a dreamlike trance. They are caught up in the eternal quality of nature and find a joy and peace in which they forget their problems—at least for a while.

2. Prepare a chart that helps you focus on the essay assignment and the piece of literature. The left column will contain questions to help you connect the essay assignment to specific literary elements in the work. In the middle column jot down quotations or other specifics from the work as answers to the questions. Cite specifics from *throughout* the work; remember that giving only one specific is not sufficient evidence to prove a point. In the right column explain more fully the relationship of evidence from the middle column to the essay question and to the particular piece of lit-

erature. The chart on the opposite page was filled in after rereading Keats's "Ode to a Nightingale" (page 383).

WRITING PARAGRAPH BY PARAGRAPH

1. Begin the introductory paragraph with a thesis statement that ties the given statement to a specific work.

   Example: The events, setting, point of view, and poetic techniques in John Keats's "Ode to a Nightingale" illustrate that contemplation of the timeless beauty of nature can inspire a dreamlike enchantment, which, in turn, can temporarily transcend mortal cares or pain.

   The rest of this paragraph might offer a quick summary of the work or a generalization about its main idea or theme.

2. In each of the following paragraphs, discuss how the given statement about the work connects with a specific literary element in the work. Be sure to cite examples.

3. In the concluding paragraph emphasize that the evidence presented from the work demonstrates the applicability of the statement to this particular piece of literature.

REVISING AND EDITING

See page 925 for detailed reminders about improving your writing.

ASSIGNMENTS

1. Use the preceding chart to write a well-developed essay about the application of the following statement to John Keats's "Ode to a Nightingale": Contemplation of the timeless beauty of nature can inspire a dreamlike enchantment that temporarily transcends mortal cares or pain.

2. Do one of the assignments called "Applying a Statement About Literature" that follow the selections by A. E. Housman (page 447), Ovid (page 731), and Voltaire (page 795). Or select another piece of literature from this book, and find a statement that applies to it. Then explain what the statement means and how it relates to the piece.

APPLICATION OF GENERAL STATEMENT TO SPECIFIC WORK

SELECTION: "Ode to a Nightingale"

GENERAL STATEMENT: Contemplation of the timeless beauty of nature can inspire a dreamlike enchantment that temporarily transcends mortal cares or pain.

LITERARY ASPECT	EVIDENCE FROM WORK	RELATIONSHIP OF EVIDENCE AND STATEMENT
WHAT *EVENTS* IN THE WORK DOES THE STATEMENT BRING TO MIND?	A nightingale sings ". . . of summer in full-throated ease." Poet imagines himself flying "on the viewless wings of Poesy" to be with the nightingale and "forget / What thou among the leaves hast never known, / The weariness, the fever, and the fret. . . ." When the nightingale flies off, "thy plaintive anthem fades / Past the near meadows, over the still stream. . . ." The poet wonders, "Was it a vision, or a waking dream? / Fled is that music:—Do I wake or sleep?"	The beautiful song of the nightingale enchants the poet. He wants to be with the bird and *imagines* himself flying to the woods at night, to a world free of pain. When the nightingale flies away, he is not sure whether what he heard and saw is a dream or real.
WHAT DETAILS ABOUT *SETTING* DOES THE STATEMENT BRING TO MIND?	"Here, where men sit and hear each other groan; Where palsy shakes a few, sad last gray hairs, Where youth grows pale, and specter-thin, and dies; Where but to think is to be full of sorrow And leaden-eyed despairs. . . ."	The situation the speaker is in is one of "mortal cares or pain."
WHAT DOES THE *POINT OF VIEW* (OR, IF THE WORK IS A POEM, THE SPEAKER) HAVE TO DO WITH THE STATEMENT?	*Speaker addresses the nightingale:* "Thou wast not born for death, immortal Bird!" *Views bird as immortal:* "The voice I hear this passing night was heard / In ancient days by emperor and clown. . . ." *Wants to die:* "now more than ever seems it rich to die. . . ." *Changes mind:* "Still wouldst thou sing, and I have ears in vain— / To thy high requiem become a sod."	The poet speaks to the bird, reflecting on the *timelessness* of its beautiful song. At first, the speaker wishes to die with its music in his ears, but he realizes that if he dies, he will no longer hear its song.
IF THE WORK IS A POEM, WHAT *POETIC TECHNIQUES* HAVE TO DO WITH THE STATEMENT?	*Imagery:* "Through verduous glooms and winding mossy ways"; "what soft incense hangs upon the boughs"; "The coming musk-rose, full of dewy wine." *Alliteration:* "Fast fading violets covered up in leaves"	The poet uses appeals especially to sight and smell to create a vivid picture of the woods *where he imagines himself to be with the nightingale*. Hearing the nightingale's song affected the poet so much that with poetic techniques he creates a song as lovely and as immortal as that of the nightingale he celebrates.

LESSON 10: *Writing About Literature and Its Period*

Researchers who study a particular period often turn to the great literature, fiction or nonfiction, of the time. Works of great writers reflect—indeed, sometimes create—the religious, economic, social, and political developments of the period in which they wrote.

CONCEPTS TO REMEMBER

1. You learn about a period through literature (a primary source) or through analyses of the period such as history textbooks (secondary sources). Make sure that you look carefully at a literary work and do not "read more into" it than is really there. Some pieces of literature could have been created during any period; they do not specifically reflect one particular time.

2. When thinking about literature and its period, you must remember to pay particular attention to the writer's tone, or attitude. In order to understand how the work relates to the period, you must determine whether the author is being satiric, supportive, optimistic, or pessimistic—to mention just a few possible tones.

TYPICAL ESSAY QUESTION

When you are asked to write about literature and its period, you are often answering an essay question like this one:

Write an essay showing how an author exemplifies a given literary period. State each characteristic of the period, and for each give examples from the work under discussion.

PREWRITING

1. Identify the literary or historical period during which the piece of literature was created. List the major characteristics of the period.

2. Ask yourself the following questions or similar ones as you read or reread a piece of literature:

   a. *Social Customs* What manners and customs of the time does the work present? What seems to be the author's attitude toward them? What does the work say or imply about interpersonal relations?

   b. *Economy* What attitude does the author seem to have toward the economic conditions of the age (toward trade and working conditions, toward agrarian or industrial pressures)?

   c. *Politics* What is the author's reaction to the political situation? Specifically, what does the author seem to think about the ruling powers? The laws? Other political systems?

   d. *Religion and Philosophy* Does the work present religious beliefs accepted during the period in question? Do scenes take place within traditional religious institutions? How are religious people characterized? What seems to be the author's attitude toward the human ability to do good or evil? What seems to be the author's attitude toward the interaction of humans and nature?

3. Prepare a chart that will help you to focus on the most important parts of the essay question. At the top of the chart, identify and define the period. In the left column list ideas about the period that you have been able to determine based on either secondary sources or on answers to the questions in Prewriting Step 2. In the right column cite specifics, including direct quotations from the work, for each of the generalizations on the left. Such a chart for *The Rape of the Lock* by Alexander Pope might look like the one on the opposite page.

WRITING PARAGRAPH BY PARAGRAPH

1. Begin the introductory paragraph with a thesis statement that will define the period. The thesis statement should also indicate that the work being analyzed exemplifies key characteristics of that period.

   Example: The Rape of the Lock by Alexander Pope is a classic example of the cutting and witty satire that deflated the vanity, silliness, and triviality that marked court life during the Age of Reason.

2. In each of the following paragraphs, discuss one or more of the major characteristics of the period, and cite examples from the work that illustrate that particular characteristic.

LITERATURE AND ITS PERIOD

SELECTION: *The Rape of the Lock*

PERIOD: The Age of Reason—a period during which reason and common sense were accepted as the only tests of truth. Neoclassicism became popular, as writers modeled their works on the classics of ancient Greece and Rome. It was also the age of satire, as writers in both prose and poetry mocked the social institutions of the time.

CHARACTERISTICS OF THE PERIOD	EXAMPLES FROM THE WORK
Social Customs The social life of drawing-room society was the target of much of the satire written during this period. The extravagant social intrigues of that society and the rising middle class offered plenty of material for the satirists' pens.	"Hither our nymphs and heroes did resort, To taste awhile the pleasures of a court; In various talk the cheerful hours they passed, Of, who was bitt, or who capotted last: This speaks the glory of the British Queen, And that describes a charming Indian screen; A third interprets motions, looks, and eyes; At every word a reputation dies." —Canto I, lines 70–78
Economics While England was still largely agrarian, it was beginning to build foreign trade and an empire. The birth of the Industrial Revolution was well under way.	"When hungry judges soon the sentence sign, And wretches hang that jury men may dine; When merchants from th' Exchange return in peace. . ." —Canto I, lines 83–85
Politics Under the British constitution, there was a combination of rule by monarchy, aristocracy, and democracy. The king or queen traditionally had the right to choose the ministers. The functions of government were the keeping of order, the protection of property, the conduct of commercial, financial, and foreign affairs, with the direction of whatever warlike operations these might unfortunately involve.	"Here Britain's statesmen oft the fall foredoom Of foreign tyrants, and of nymphs at home; Here thou, great Anna! whom three realms obey, Dost sometimes counsel take—and sometimes tea." —Canto I, lines 67–70
Religion and Philosophy The Church of England was restored to power. Philosophers believed that God regulated nature; they often compared nature to a clock. Great thinkers such as John Locke, Addison and Steele, and others formulated ideals of human dignity and worth.	"With such a prize no mortal must be blessed, So Heaven decrees! with Heaven who can contest?" —Canto II, lines 156–157

3. In the concluding paragraph reiterate that this author and the specific work being studied exemplify key characteristics of the particular literary period.

REVISING AND EDITING

See page 925 for detailed reminders about improving your work.

ASSIGNMENTS

1. Write a well-developed essay in which you identify the Age of Reason and show how Pope's *Rape of the Lock* exemplifies key characteristics of that period.

2. Do one of the assignments called "Writing About Literature and Its Period" that follow the selections by William Wordsworth (page 338), Charles Dickens (page 432), Charles Tomlinson (page 573), Voltaire (page 795), and Heinrich Böll (page 921), or select another piece of literature from this book, and show how that piece exemplifies its literary period.

HANDBOOK OF LITERARY TERMS

ALLITERATION *The repetition of identical consonant sounds, usually at the beginnings of words.* Notice the repeated *f* sounds in these lines from *Beowulf*:

> The in*f*amous killer *f*ought
> *F*or his *f*reedom, wanting no *f*lesh but retreat.

> See pages 20, 362.
> See also ASSONANCE,
> CONSONANCE.

ALLUSION *A short reference to a person, a place, an event, or another work of literature.* The reference, which the reader is expected to know, serves as a shorthand reference to a larger picture or idea, thereby adding to the meaning of a work. For example, Shakespeare's allusion to Mars, the Roman war god, in Sonnet 55 adds strength to the speaker's claims of his friend's immortality.

> See pages 228, 236, 546.

ANALOGY *A comparison made between two things to show the similarities between them.* An analogy explains something unfamiliar by comparing it to something familiar. For example, to explain the difference between Elizabethan poets and poets of his generation, Keats in his letter to John Hamilton Reynolds explains the difference between emperors of great lands and petty officials. According to Keats, the Elizabethans, like the Emperors, have much greater vision and scope.

> See also SIMILE, METAPHOR.

ANAPEST *A poetic foot consisting of two unstressed syllables followed by a stressed syllable (˘ ˘ ´).*

> See also FOOT.

ANECDOTE *A short account of a true event in someone's life.* Anecdotes are used to illustrate or raise a point, to explain an idea, to describe personality. For example, in his *Life of Samuel Johnson* Boswell gives many anecdotes to display Johnson's traits. Boswell demonstrates Johnson's wit by quoting a comment Johnson makes upon learning that Boswell is from Scotland: "That, Sir, I find, is what a very great many of your countrymen cannot help."

> See also
> CHARACTERIZATION.

ANTAGONIST *A person or force that opposes the protagonist in a story or drama.* In "The Guest" by Ca-

mus, Balducci, the Arab, and the customs of society are the antagonists that oppose Daru's search for peace.

> See PLOT, CONFLICT.

APHORISM *A short, pointed statement expressing a wise or clever observation about life.* For example:

> Fools rush in where angels fear to tread.
> —Alexander Pope

APOSTROPHE *A figure of speech in which a poet directly addresses an inanimate object, idea, or absent person.* For example, the speaker addresses the wind in Shelley's "Dirge":

> Rough wind, that moanest loud
> Grief too sad for song. . .

> See page 378.
> See also PERSONIFICATION.

ASIDE *In a play a character's comment that is heard by the audience but not by the other characters.* An aside reveals what the character is thinking and feeling. The dramatist indicates an aside in the script with stage directions. For example, after King Duncan has proclaimed his son Malcolm as heir to the throne, Macbeth reveals in an aside his reaction to the news:

> MACBETH: [Aside.] The Prince of Cumberland! That
> is a step
> On which I must fall down, or else o'erleap
> For in my way it lies. . . .

> See page 108.
> See also SOLILOQUY.

ASSONANCE *The repetition of similar vowel sounds in a line of poetry.* For example, the *i* sound is repeated in this line from *The Rime of the Ancient Mariner*:

> 'Twas n*i*ght, calm n*i*ght, the moon was h*i*gh . . .

> See page 362.
> See also ALLITERATION,
> CONSONANCE.

ATMOSPHERE *The prevailing mood of a work of literature.* An author creates atmosphere through his or her choice of setting and tone. For example, Conrad's jungle setting and serious tone work together to create a tense and suspenseful atmosphere in "The Lagoon."

> See pages 189, 630.

AUGUSTAN AGE *A name given to the eighteenth century in England. Augustan* refers to Emperor Augustus of Rome, under whose reign great literature by such writers as Virgil and Ovid thrived. England's Augustan Age—also a time when great literature flourished—is often divided into two periods: the **Age of Pope** and, after 1750, the **Age of Johnson.** The periods are named after the most prominent writers of the time, Alexander Pope and Samuel Johnson. Augustan writing reflects a rationality and control reminiscent of classical art and literature.

> See page 254.
> See also AGE OF REASON, CLASSICISM, NEOCLASSICISM.

AUTOBIOGRAPHY *The story of a person's life written by that person.* A **diary** is a form of autobiography, recording the day-by-day events in a person's life. Samuel Pepys's *Diary* is a famous example of the diary form.

> See page 301.
> See also BIOGRAPHY, DIARY, JOURNAL.

BALLAD STANZA *Four lines of poetry, usually found in a folk ballad, with a rhyme scheme of abcb.* There are usually four accented syllables in the first and third lines and three in the second and fourth lines, as in this example from the folk ballad "Sir Patrick Spens":

> O wha is this has don this deid,
>   And told the king o' me,
> To send us out at this time o' the yeir,
>   To sail upon the sea!

> See page 41.

BIOGRAPHY *A factual account of a person's life and character written by someone other than the subject.* Boswell's *Life of Samuel Johnson* is a famous example.

> See page 301.
> See also AUTOBIOGRAPHY, DIARY, JOURNAL.

BLANK VERSE *Poetry written in unrhymed iambic pentameter.* Blank verse attempts to sound like spoken English, so every line need not be perfectly regular. For example, Shakespeare's *Macbeth* is written in blank verse:

> And that / which should / accom / pany / old age,

> As hon / or, love, / obe / dience, troops / of
>   friends . . .

> —*Macbeth,* Act V, Scene ii

> See page 129.
> See also METER, FOOT, SCANSION.

CAESURA *The pause or break in a line of poetry, usually near the middle of the line.* For example:

> Vomiting fire and smoke, / / the dragon
> Burned down their homes. / / They watched in horror.

> —*Beowulf*

> See page 20.

CARICATURE *A humorous picture that exaggerates or distorts certain qualities of a person in order to create a ridiculous effect.* As is also true with satire, the intent of caricature is not to criticize just one individual but rather to ridicule a societal group or social practice. Cervantes' *Don Quixote* is an example of a literary caricature.

> See page 773.

CHARACTER *A person in a literary work.* Characters who reveal only one personality trait are considered **flat.** The Porter in Shakespeare's *Macbeth* is a flat character whose purpose in the drama is to provide comic relief after the murder of King Duncan. Characters who show a variety of traits, often complex and contradictory, are called **round.** Macbeth, for example, is a round character who exhibits conflicting behavior and attitudes as he considers the murder of Duncan.

A **static character** remains primarily the same throughout a work, as does the Porter in *Macbeth.* A **dynamic character** changes during the course of a narrative because of the influence of events or other people. In contrast to the Porter, Macbeth is a character who struggles with complex emotions and evolves from a loyal soldier to a ruthless killer.

> See page 189.
> See also CHARACTERIZATION.

CHARACTERIZATION *The personality of a character and the method that an author uses to reveal this personality.* Through **direct characterization** the writer directly states facts about a character's personality. For example, in "The Infant Prodigy" Mann tells us that "Bibi made his face for the audience because he was aware that he had to entertain them a little." With **indirect characterization** the writer reveals a character's personality indirectly through the character's physical appearance, words, thoughts, and actions, or through what other characters say about that character. Most frequently the reader must infer the personality from these suggestions. For instance, the sensitivity of the narrator in O'Faolain's "Sugawn Chair" is revealed through his thoughts.

> See pages 62–63, 588, 610.
> See also CHARACTER.

CHORUS *In drama one or more characters who comment on the action.* In Greek drama, such as *Antigone,* the chorus is made up of a number of people who move and sing together. The chorus often sets the mood of the story with its poetic songs.

> See page 678.

CLASSICISM *A style that reflects the principles and concerns of the literature of Ancient Greece and Rome.* In the eighteenth century the movement to imitate the balanced, orderly rationality of the ancients was called **neoclassicism.**

> See pages 253–255.
> See also AGE OF REASON,
> AUGUSTAN AGE,
> NEOCLASSICISM.

CLIMAX *The point of highest tension or excitement in a narrative.* In a tragedy the climax is usually in the middle of the play, when an event that will lead to the downfall of the tragic hero takes place. In Shakespeare's *Macbeth* the climax occurs in Act III with the banquet scene.

> See pages 188, 597.
> See also PLOT.

COLLOQUIAL LANGUAGE *The everyday language we use in our conversation.*

> See also LITERAL
> LANGUAGE,
> DIALECT.

COMEDY OF IDEAS *A play that presents complex and often controversial themes within the framework of entertaining plots, appealing and unpredictable characters, and witty dialogue.* Shaw's *Pygmalion* is a comedy of ideas.

> See page 459.

CONCEIT *An elaborate simile or metaphor that compares two significantly different things.* There are two basic kinds of conceit: The Petrarchan conceit and the metaphysical conceit. Petrach introduced the **Petrar-**

chan conceit in his sonnets to capture the qualities of the suffering lover and his beloved. The comparison may serve as the controlling idea for the entire poem. For example, Shakespeare's Sonnet 18 is based on the speaker's comparison of his love to a summer's day.

The **metaphysical conceit** generally presents a more elaborate and intellectual comparison than the Petrarchan conceit. One of the most famous of the metaphysical conceits was conceived by Donne in his "Valediction: Forbidding Mourning," where he compares the souls of two lovers to a compass:

> If they be two, they are two so
>   As stiff twin compasses are two;
> Thy soul, the fixed foot, makes no show
>   To move, but doth, if th' other do.

> See pages 209, 757.

CONFLICT *The struggle between two opposing forces, the center of a plot.* Conflict can be **internal,** within a person, or external. Macbeth's attempts to reach a decision to kill Duncan, for example, create an internal conflict. **External** conflict exists when a character struggles against some outside force, such as another person, nature, society, or fate. In Lessing's "Mild Attack of Locusts," for example, the story's external conflict pits the farmers against nature.

> See pages 188, 591, 908.
> See also PLOT.

CONNOTATION *All the suggested meanings and associations that a word brings to mind beyond its denotation, or literal meaning.* For example, in Tennyson's "Ulysses," Ulysses belittles his chores as king when he uses the words *mete* and *dole,* words that connote penny-pinching activities:

> It little profits an idle king,
> By this still hearth, among these barren crags,
> Matched with an aged wife, I mete and dole
> Unequal laws unto a savage race.

> See page 569.
> See also DENOTATION,
> DICTION.

CONSONANCE *The repetition of consonant sounds within the words in a line of poetry.* For example the *l* sound is repeated several times in these lines from *The Rime of the Ancient Mariner*:

> With his crue*l* bow he *l*aid fu*ll l*ow
> The harm*l*ess A*l*batross.

> See page 363.
> See also ASSONANCE,
> ALLITERATION.

COUPLET *Two consecutive lines of poetry that rhyme.* For example, these two lines from Blake's poem "The Tiger" are a couplet:

Tiger! Tiger! burning bright
In the forests of the night . . .

See also HEROIC COUPLET.

DACTYL *A poetic foot consisting of one stressed syllable followed by two unstressed syllables ($' \smile \smile$).*

See also FOOT.

DENOTATION *The literal meaning or dictionary definition of a word.*

See page 569.
See also CONNOTATION, DICTION.

DENOUEMENT *The resolution of a story, which occurs as the conflict is resolved and the knot of the plot is untied.*

See page 597.

DESCRIPTION *Writing that creates an impression of a person, place, or thing.* The specific details of description enhance poems, stories, and nonfiction. For example, in *The Canterbury Tales* Chaucer enhances his portrayal of the pilgrims with descriptions of their physical appearance:

There was a Merchant with a forking beard
And motley dress; high on his horse he sat,
Upon his head a Flemish beaver hat
And on his feet daintily buckled boots.

See also EXPOSITION, NARRATION.

DIALECT *A type of speech that differs from the standard form of a language.* The difference occurs mostly in pronunciation but also in vocabulary and grammar. For example, in Shaw's *Pygmalion* Eliza Doolittle speaks a dialect known as cockney.

See page 530.

DIALOGUE *The conversation between characters in drama, fiction, nonfiction, epic, or dramatic poem.* It reveals indirectly a character's thoughts and opinions and allows an author to present an interplay of ideas among a number of characters.

See pages 38, 878.

DIARY *An individual's personal, day-by-day account of impressions and events.* Daily events may also be chronicled in a **journal.** Journals are usually less intimate than diaries. Pepys's *Diary* is a famous example of the diary form.

See page 246.
See also AUTOBIOGRAPHY, BIOGRAPHY, JOURNAL.

DICTION *The choice of words to fit the character, theme, setting, or subject in a poem, story, essay, or play.* Writers choose their words carefully and precisely so that these words express exactly what they intend. The language of Milton's *Paradise Lost,* for example, is elevated to suit the lofty subject of humankind's fall:

Hail, holy Light, offspring of Heaven first-born!
Or of th' Ethernal coeternal beam,
May I express thee unblamed?

See page 569.
See also CONNOTATION, DENOTATION.

DRAMA *Stories written to be performed before an audience.* The dramatist, or playwright, writes two things: dialogue that the actors speak and stage directions that give instructions about scenery, costumes, gestures, movements, and lighting.

See pages 202–203, 255, 652–653.

DRAMATIC CONVENTIONS *Practices that audiences accept on stage as realistic but that differ from real-life behavior.* Quick shifts in time, blank verse, soliloquies, and asides are dramatic conventions.

See page 502.

DRAMATIC MONOLOGUE *A narrative poem in which a character other than the poet delivers a long speech to a silent listener.* A dramatic monologue usually reveals the speaker's personality by presenting the speaker at a crucial point in his or her life, often a moment of conflict. Robert Browning's "My Last Duchess" is an example of a dramatic monologue.

See page 425.

DRAMATIC POETRY *Verse in the form of a monologue by one character or a dialogue between two or more characters.* The dramatic qualities of this type of poetry often result from stressful situations and conflicting emotions. "Sir Patrick Spens," *Macbeth,* and "Ulysses" are all examples of dramatic poetry.

See page 447.
See also LYRIC POETRY, NARRATIVE POETRY.

ELEGY *A serious poem lamenting the death of an individual or group.* Thomas Gray's "Elegy in a Country Churchyard," is an elegy written in elegiac stanzas: four lines of iambic pentameter rhyming *abab*.

See page 307.

END–STOPPED LINE *A line of poetry that ends with a pause both in punctuation and in thought.* For example,

Ne'er saw I, never felt, a calm so deep!
The river glideth at his own sweet will . . .
—Wordsworth, "Composed upon Westminster Bridge"

See also RUN–ON LINE.

EPIC *A long narrative poem in elevated style presenting the adventures of a central hero who possesses superhuman qualities and generally embodies national ideals.* The *Iliad* and *Beowulf* are epics.

See pages 8, 229, 670.
See also MOCK–EPIC,
EPIC CONVENTIONS.

EPIC CONVENTIONS *The elements of an epic or mock-epic.* These conventions include a hero whose bravery allows him to overcome great trials; a major battle scene; a discussion of the hero's weapon; gods who participate in or direct the action; **epic,** or **Homeric, similes.**

See page 287.

EPIGRAM *A brief, well-phrased philosophical saying.* Among the epigrams by Pope is the well-known "To err is human, to forgive divine."

See page 288.

EPIPHANY *A sudden realization, by the reader as well as a character, of the true nature of a person, place, object, or situation.* Epiphany usually occurs near the end of a work. Joyce's "Araby" ends with an epiphany.

See page 597.

EPITAPH *An inscription on a tombstone, or a brief poem composed in memory of someone who has died.* Gray's "Elegy Written in a Country Churchyard" concludes with an epitaph.

EPITHET *An adjective or adjective phrase describing a characteristic of a person or thing.* Epithets like "rosy-fingered dawn" and "swift-footed Achilles" are common to Homer's epics, *The Odyssey* and *The Iliad.*

See page 670.

ESSAY *A short prose composition that deals with a single subject.* Essays may be classified as formal or informal. A **formal essay** is a carefully structured attempt to instruct or persuade. It has a serious tone and presents its argument logically. Bacon's "Of Ambition" is a formal essay.

An **informal essay** aims to entertain or please the reader while exploring a given topic. Its tone is light, its structure somewhat sprawling. Because the informal essay often makes personal references, it is sometimes called the **personal essay.** Steele's "Funeral of Thomas Betterton" is an informal essay.

See page 275.

EXISTENTIALISM *A modern European philosophy that considers life to be empty of any meaning, purpose, or value other than that which individuals give to their own lives.* The work of Albert Camus reflects existentialist thinking.

See page 892.

EXPOSITION *The background information vital to the plot of a story, novel, or play.* For example, in "Goose Fair" Lawrence's exposition quickly reveals the economic strife of the times. The term also refers to the **expository essay,** such as Shaw's Preface to *Pygmalion,* which is intended primarily to present facts and explain ideas.

See pages 188, 597.

FABLE *A short tale that teaches a moral, or lesson.* Animals and plants that act and speak like people are often the characters of fables. Aesop's fables are among the oldest and most famous fables.

See page 673.

FALLING ACTION *The action in a play or story that is the result of the climax.* In Shakespeare's *Macbeth,* for example, falling action in Acts IV and V depicts the disastrous reversal of Macbeth's fortunes.

See pages 188, 597.

FARCE *A type of comedy that relies largely on improbable situations, broad characters, and slapstick action.* Laughter is provoked through surprise and exaggeration. Molière is a master of the art of farce, and his *Flying Doctor* presents many farcical moments.

See page 787.

FIGURATIVE LANGUAGE *Language that is not meant to be interpreted literally.* Authors use language figuratively for descriptive effect. For example, Chaucer is using the word *snow* in its figurative sense:

It positively snowed with meat and drink.

Various **figures of speech** are used to create figurative language. Some of them include **conceit, metaphor, paradox, personification,** and **simile.**

See pages 104, 378.

FIGURE OF SPEECH *A specific device or kind of figurative language, such as a* **simile** *or* **metaphor.**

See pages 104, 378.
See also figurative language.

FLASHBACK *An interruption in a narrative to relate events that have happened earlier.* This technique is used in stream-of-consciousness writing as well as in conventional narratives. For example, much of Conrad's "Lagoon" is told in flashback as the narrator relates Arat's story.

FOLK BALLAD *A story told or sung in verse.* Transmitted orally from generation to generation, folk ballads such as "The Wife of Usher's Well" are examples of popular literary forms. Love, courage, adventure, and disaster are usually the subjects of folk ballads. Their straightforward narrative style relies heavily on dialogue and quick movement from scene to scene.

See pages 38, 41.
See also BALLAD STANZA,
DIALOGUE, NARRATIVE.

FOOT *The basic unit of meter in a line of poetry.* A foot usually consists of one stressed syllable and one or two unstressed syllables. Common poetic feet include the **iamb** (˘ ′), an unstressed syllable followed by a stressed syllable; the **trochee** (′ ˘), a stressed syllable followed by an unstressed syllable; the **anapest** (˘ ˘ ′), two unstressed syllables followed by a stressed syllable; and the **dactyl** (′ ˘ ˘), a stressed syllable followed by two unstressed syllables.

See also METER.

FORESHADOWING *The use of clues by the author to prepare readers for events that will happen in a narrative.*

FRAME STORY *A story that includes the telling of a story within a story; the frame is the outer story.* Boccaccio's "Federigo's Falcon" is a frame story.

See page 763.

FREE VERSE *Poetry without rhyme or regular rhythm.* T. S. Eliot, for example, uses free verse in "The Hollow Men":

Between the idea
And the reality
Between the motion
And the act
Falls the shadow

See pages 194, 453.
See also RHYTHM.

HEROIC COUPLET *A pair of rhymed lines in iambic pentameter.* For example, the following epigram by Pope is a heroic couplet:

˘ ′ / ˘ ′ / ˘ ′ / ˘ ′ / ˘ ′
Be not / the first / by whom / the new / are tried,
˘ ′ / ˘ ′ / ˘ ′ / ˘ ′ / ˘ ′
Nor yet / the last / to lay / the old / aside.

See pages 237, 288.
See also RHYTHM.

HOMERIC SIMILE *A long, detailed comparison of two seemingly unlike things.* This simile, also known as an **epic simile,** gets its name from Homer, the Ancient Greek author of the *Iliad* and the *Odyssey*, both epics. Longer than the conventional simile, the Homeric simile is an elaborate comparison that extends over several lines of verse.

See page 670.

IAMB *A poetic foot consisting of an unstressed syllable followed by a stressed syllable* (˘ ′).

See also IAMBIC
PENTAMETER.

IAMBIC PENTAMETER *A line of poetry composed of five feet, each of which is an iamb, having one unstressed* (˘) *syllable followed by a stressed* (′) *syllable.* Each line of iambic pentameter is ten syllables long. For example:

˘ ′ / ˘ ′ / ˘ ′ / ˘ ′ / ˘ ′
Thy soul / was like / a Star, / and dwelt / apart;
˘ ′ / ˘ ′ / ˘ ′ / ˘ ′ / ˘ ′
Thou hadst / a voice / whose sound / was like / the
′
sea.

—Wordsworth, "London, 1802"

See page 90.
See also BLANK VERSE,
HEROIC COUPLET,
RHYTHM.

IMAGERY *Words or phrases that evoke sensory images in the reader's mind.* Visual imagery is most common, but a writer can also suggest images that convey sound, taste, smell, and touch. For example, these lines from Tennyson's "Splendor Falls on Castle Walls" appeal to the sense of hearing:

Blow, bugle, blow, set the wild echoes flying,
And answer, echoes, answer, dying, dying, dying.

See page 141.
See also DESCRIPTION.

INTERIOR MONOLOGUE *An internal speech by a single speaker provided by the narrator to explain characters' personalities or to reveal their thoughts.* Woolf uses this technique in "The New Dress."

See page 763.

IRONY *The contrast or difference between appearance and reality.* In **verbal irony** the contrast is between what is stated and what is actually meant, as when a person says one thing and means the opposite.

Situational irony exists when what is expected to happen is not what actually comes to pass. For example, in Pirandello's "War" the parent who seems most accepting of his son's death is in reality less resigned to it than the others.

Dramatic irony occurs when events that mean one thing to the character mean something quite different to the reader or audience. Shakespeare's *Macbeth* presents several examples of verbal and dramatic irony.

See pages 189, 886.

JOURNAL *A daily record of events kept by an individual who is a participant in or witness to the events.* We learn much about people and events of history from journals.

See page 246.
See also AUTOBIOGRAPHY,
BIOGRAPHY, DIARY.

KENNING *In Old English poetry a formalized metaphorical phrase used in place of a simple noun.* In *Beowulf,* for example, the sea is referred to as the "whale-road" and the sun, as "heaven's candle."

See page 20.

LEGEND *A traditional tale, handed down from generation to generation, believed to be based on history.* A legend usually celebrates the heroic qualities of a national leader. King Arthur is a legendary hero, and his story, as told by Malory in *Le Morte d'Arthur,* is a legend.

See page 77.
See also MYTH.

LITERARY CRITICISM *The analysis or interpretation of a literary work to enlarge a reader's appreciation or comprehension.* For example, Hazlitt's "Macbeth"

helps readers understand Shakespeare's play. The Viewpoint quotations in this book are also examples of literary criticism.

See page 395.

LYRIC POETRY *Verse in which a speaker expresses personal thoughts and feelings.* Lyric poems are usually short and can take many forms. For example, the ode and the sonnet are two types of lyric.

See pages 84, 447, 651.
See also NARRATIVE
POETRY, DRAMATIC
POETRY.

METAPHOR *A figure of speech that compares one thing with another, seemingly different thing.* Many metaphors are implied. Notice how Chaucer draws a similarity between a person and a fish in this metaphor from *The Canterbury Tales:*

And that a monk uncloistered is a mere
Fish out of water, flapping on the pier

See pages 104, 378.

METAPHYSICAL POETRY *Highly intellectual verse filled with complex and far-fetched metaphors.* Metaphysical poets wrote both love lyrics and meditative poems that displayed their wit and learning. Donne's "Valediction: Forbidding Mourning" is an intellectual exploration of the concept of death.

See page 206.
See also CONCEIT.

METER *The predictable and regular alternation between stressed and unstressed syllables that gives poetry its rhythm.* Notice the pattern of unstressed and stressed syllables that forms the meter in these lines from Wordsworth's "Slumber Did My Spirit Steal":

She seemed / a thing / that could / not feel
The touch / of earth / ly fears

See pages 90, 419.
See also FOOT, RHYTHM.

MIDDLE ENGLISH *The language spoken in and around London in the 1300s.* Chaucer wrote *The Canterbury Tales* in Middle English.

See page 70.

MOCK–EPIC *An imitation epic, or long narrative poem, that makes fun of a society that cannot live up to the standards of the classical heroic epic.* Pope's *Rape of the Lock* makes the trivial subject of cutting a lock of hair appear ridiculous by using elevated language to describe this mundane event.

> See page 287.
> See also EPIC
> CONVENTIONS.

MODERN ENGLISH *The English spoken and written for the last four hundred years.*

> See page 104.
> See also OLD ENGLISH,
> MIDDLE ENGLISH.

MOOD *The emotional feeling or atmosphere in a work of literature, sometimes created by descriptions of the setting.* Pirandello makes clear the tenseness of the characters in "War," for example, through descriptive details of the setting as well as the words and actions of the characters.

> See page 189.

MOTIVATION *The reasons characters in a literary work behave as they do.* For fictional characters to appear true to life, their motivation must seem plausible to readers. Sometimes the author will state directly why a character behaves in a certain way. Many times the author merely implies the motivation, and readers must deduce it from their knowledge of the character. The motives of the trapeze artist in Kafka's "First Sorrow," for example, have to be determined by the reader from the events of the story.

> See page 63.
> See also CHARACTER.

MYTH *An anonymous traditional story with its roots in cultural or national folk beliefs that rely on the supernatural to explain the mysteries of the world.* Every country and literature has its collection of myths, or mythology. Greek mythology collects stories told by the Ancient Greeks about their gods, ancestors, and legendary heroes, as well as explanations of human nature and events that are difficult to rationalize. For example, the Ancient Greeks used myth to explain the existence of evil. Their myth of Pandora's box tells how the curiosity of Pandora, the first mortal woman, led her to open a box into which the god Zeus had put all human miseries and evils, thus allowing them to escape into the world.

> See pages 77, 731.
> See also LEGEND.

NARRATIVE *Writing that tells a story, moving from event to event, usually in chronological order.* A narrative requires a **narrator,** or storyteller. Since its beginning in ancient oral epics, the narrative has slowly evolved into the novel, the dominant form of literature for the past two centuries.

> See page 763.
> See also NOVEL.

NARRATIVE HOOK *The point in a story, novel, or play at which the author catches the reader's attention by presenting an interesting problem or situation that begins the conflict.* For example, in Mansfield's "Singing Lesson" the conflict begins when Miss Meadows reads the letter she has received from her fiancé.

> See page 597.
> See also PLOT.

NARRATIVE POEM *A poem that tells a story.* The **epic** is an example of a long narrative poem, while the **folk ballad** is a short narrative poem.

> See page 447.
> See also DRAMATIC POEM,
> LYRIC POEM.

NARRATOR *The person who tells a story.* The son narrates the story about his parents in "The Sugawn Chair."

> See also POINT OF VIEW.

NATURALISM *A literary movement that usually concentrates on portraying lower economic classes and applies scientific studies of humanity to characterization.* Naturalism was an outgrowth of **Realism.** The naturalist uses a "facts-only" approach, heavy in detail. While the subject matter of naturalistic writing is often depressing, the purpose generally is to highlight ills so they can be corrected. In "A Piece of String" Maupassant displays the naturalist's lack of idealism and accurate observation of common people.

> See page 833.
> See also ROMANTICISM.

NEOCLASSICISM *A literary movement of the seventeenth and eighteenth centuries that revived the rationality, orderliness, and control characteristic of classical literature.*

> See page 216.
> See also AGE OF REASON,
> AUGUSTAN AGE,
> CLASSICISM.

NOVEL *A book-length work of prose fiction, usually with a complicated plot and numerous characters.* Types of novel include the following: **picaresque,** a loose series of episodes recounting the adventures of wanderers and lovable rogues; **sentimental,** a highly emotional tale of romance and tears; **gothic,** a tale of mystery and suspense; **philosophical,** a story that raises profound questions about life and humankind; **psychological,** a story that probes the complexity of the characters' thinking, behavior, and motivation; **realistic,** a story that focuses objectively on ordinary life; **naturalistic,** a story of characters trapped by overwhelming forces of nature or society; **social criticism,** a story that exposes evils in society for the purpose of correction; and **stream-of-consciousness,** a story told through the free-flowing thoughts of the main character.

See pages 255, 432.
See also REALISM,
NATURALISM, STREAM-OF-
CONSCIOUSNESS.

OCTAVE *An eight-line poem or stanza.*

See also SONNET.

ODE *A long lyric poem, serious and dignified in subject, tone, and style, usually written to celebrate an event or honor a person.* Dryden, Shelley, and Keats are famous for their odes.

See pages 237, 388.

OLD ENGLISH *The language spoken by the Germanic tribes of Angles, Saxons, and Jutes who invaded Britain in the fifth century.* Old English is sometimes called Anglo-Saxon. The epic *Beowulf* was originally told in Old English.

See page 24.

ONOMATOPOEIA *The use of words with sounds that imitate or suggest their meanings.* For example, Hopkins uses onomatopoeia in this line from "God's Grandeur":

It gathers to a greatness, like the ooze of oil.

See page 363.

ORAL TRADITION *The process of passing stories, songs, tales, or myths by word of mouth from one generation to another.* Homer's great epics, the *Iliad* and *Odyssey,* and the Anglo-Saxon epic *Beowulf* all developed through the oral tradition.

See pages 41, 654.

OTTAVA RIMA *An Italian stanzaic form consisting of eight lines of iambic pentameter, rhyming abababcc.* The nearly two thousand stanzas that make up Lord Byron's *Don Juan* are in this form.

See page 369.

PARADOX *A statement or situation that at first seems impossible or self-contradictory but may be true in fact or in a figurative sense.* Auden's poem "Musée des Beaux Arts" is based on the paradox that when suffering and death occur life continues untroubled.

See page 561.

PARALLELISM *The use of repeated phrases or sentences that are alike in structure or meaning.* Parallelism gives emphasis to thoughts, especially in poetry and persuasive writing. For example, Tennyson uses parallelism in this line from "Ulysses":

To strive, to seek, to find, and not to yield.

See also PERSUASION.

PARODY *A humorous imitation of another, usually serious, work.* A parody can ridicule or criticize the other work by imitating or exaggerating its plot, character, style, or theme. In *Gulliver's Travels* Swift uses parody to ridicule British politics and society.

See page 259.

PERSONIFICATION *A figure of speech in which human qualities are given to objects, animals, or ideas.* For example, in *The Canterbury Tales* Chaucer personifies the wind (Zephyrus) by saying that it has breath:

When also Zephyrus with his sweet breath
Exhales an air in every grove and heath

See page 378.
See also METAPHOR.

PERSUASION *A kind of writing that attempts to sway the reader to think or act in a particular way.* Swift's *Gulliver's Travels,* while entertaining and satiric, attempts to persuade readers to accept a particular line of thinking.

PLOT *The sequence of events in a short story, novel, or play, each event causing or leading to the next.* The events are related to the conflict, the struggle which the main character undergoes. Usually a plot begins with **exposition,** which introduces characters, settings, and situations. The **narrative hook** draws readers into the story and is the point at which the **conflict** begins. Events that contribute to the conflict are called the **rising action,** which leads to the **climax,** or point of highest dramatic tension. The **falling action** presents the results of the climax and ends with the **resolution,** or final outcome.

See pages 188, 432.

POINT OF VIEW *The relationship of the storyteller to the story.* In a story with **first-person** point of view, the story is told by one of the characters, referred to as "I." Böll's "Thrower-Away" is told by a first-person narrator.

In a story with **limited third-person** point of view, the narrator tells the story from the limited viewpoint of only one character, speaking of the character as *he* or *she*. Galsworthy uses this point of view in "The Japanese Quince," showing all the action through Mr. Nilson's eyes.

In a story with an **omniscient** point of view, the author is a narrator who reveals the thoughts and feelings of all the characters. An omniscient narrator uses the third person—*he* or *she*—and stands completely outside the story. Lawrence's "Goose Fair" has an omniscient narrator.

> See pages 588, 602.
> See also SHORT STORY.

PROTAGONIST *The central character of a story, novel, play, or dramatic poem.* The action usually revolves around the protagonist, who generally receives the reader's sympathies. The young boy who narrates Joyce's "Araby" is also the story's protagonist.

> See also PLOT,
> ANTAGONIST.

QUATRAIN *A stanza or poem with four lines.*

> See page 90.
> See also SONNET.

REALISM *A literary movement that seeks to report life as exactly as possible.* Realism began as a reaction to the Romantic emphasis on the strange and the idealistic. The realistic writer is more objective than subjective and often writes about ordinary people and situations. Dickens' *Oliver Twist* is a realistic novel.

> See page 838.
> See also NATURALISM.

REFRAIN *In a poem a line or lines repeated at regular intervals.*

> See page 41.
> See also VILLANELLE.

REPETITION *The repeating of sounds, letters, words, or lines, which helps give poetry its meaning, form, and sound.* Common forms of repetition are **alliteration, assonance, consonance, refrain,** and **rhyme.**

RESOLUTION *The part of the plot that ends the falling action by telling or implying the final outcome.* For instance, in Mansfield's "Singing Lesson" the resolution occurs when Miss Meadows receives the telegram from Basil.

> See pages 188, 597.
> See also PLOT.

RHYME *The repetition of similar or identical vowels and succeeding consonants in words of a poem.* When the rhyme occurs at the ends of lines, it is called **end rhyme:**

> The world is too much with us; late and soon,
> Getting and spending, we lay waste our powers;
> Little we see in Nature that is ours;
> We have given our hearts away, a sordid boon!

> —Wordsworth, "The World Is Too Much with Us"

When the rhyme occurs within the line it is called **internal rhyme:**

> At length did cross an Albatross, . . .

> —Coleridge, *The Rime of the Ancient Mariner*

> See page 362.

RHYTHM *The pattern created by arranging stressed and unstressed syllables, particularly in poetry.* Notice the regular pattern of stressed and unstressed syllables in the following lines from *Macbeth:*

> Double, double, toil and trouble;
> Fire burn and caldron bubble.

> See page 419.
> See also METER, SPRUNG
> RHYTHM.

RISING ACTION *The action in a play or story that leads to the climax.* For example, in Shakespeare's *Macbeth* rising action in Act II leads to the climax that takes place in Act III.

> See pages 188, 597.
> See also PLOT.

ROMANTICISM *A literary movement of the late eighteenth and early nineteenth centuries.* Romantic literature generally exhibits some of the following characteristics: a profound love of nature; a focus on the self and the individual; a fascination with the supernatural, the mysterious, the gothic; a yearning for the picturesque and the exotic; a deep-rooted idealism; and a passionate nationalism, or love of country.

Romantic writing can be diverse, ranging from Wordsworth's nature poems to Cervantes' idealistic *Don Quixote.*

> See pages 321–323.
> See also CLASSICISM.

RUN–ON LINE *A line of poetry that has no pause at the end and flows into the next line.* Poets can vary rhythm by using run-on lines occasionally, as in these lines from "Composed Upon Westminster Bridge":

This City now doth, like a garment, wear
The beauty of the morning

> See also END–STOPPED LINE.

SATIRE *A kind of writing that uses humor and wit to ridicule or criticize individuals or societies.* Satire may take the form of poetry, fiction, or nonfiction. Some satires are gentle, poking good-natured fun; others are harsh and bitter. Consistent in all satires is the desire to correct some ill or evil in society. Swift's *Gulliver's Travels* is a famous satire.

> See page 267.

SCANSION *The analysis of a poem to determine its meter.* Scansion is done by marking the stressed (′) and unstressed (˘) syllables in the lines of a poem, as demonstrated below:

Rolled round / in earth's / diur / nal course

With rocks, / and stones, / and trees

—Wordsworth, "A Slumber Did My Spirit Steal"

> See page 954.
> See also FOOT, IAMBIC PENTAMETER.

SESTET *A six-line poem or stanza.*

> See also SONNET.

SETTING *The time and place in which the events of a literary work occur.* In some works the setting helps create an atmosphere, or mood, that can influence the reader as well as the characters. A novel such as Dickens' *Oliver Twist* is set in many places and takes place over a long period of time.

> See pages 189, 432.
> See also ATMOSPHERE.

SHORT STORY *A brief, fictional narrative that usually can be read in one sitting.* The short story generally contains five major elements: plot, characterization, setting, point of view, and theme.

> See page 588.
> See also CHARACTERIZATION, PLOT, POINT OF VIEW, SETTING, THEME.

SIMILE *A figure of speech that states a comparison directly, most often by using the word* like *or* as. For example, in *The Canterbury Tales* Chaucer uses a simile to describe the Monk:

His head was bald and shone like looking-glass.

> See page 104.
> See also ANALOGY, FIGURATIVE LANGUAGE.

SOLILOQUY *The speech of an actor alone on stage, revealing to the audience inner thoughts and feelings.* For example, Macbeth's line "Is this a dagger which I see before me?" begins his famous soliloquy.

> See page 108.
> See also ASIDE.

SONNET *A lyric poem of fourteen lines, usually in iambic pentameter.* There are two basic types of sonnet: the Italian, or Petrarchan, and the English, or Shakespearean. The **Italian, or Petrarchan, sonnet** is divided into two parts in which the first eight lines, or octave, usually follow a rhyme scheme of *abbaabba* or *abababab*. The last six lines, or sestet, may have one of several rhyme combinations—for example, *cdecde* or *cdcdee*. Generally, the octave asks a question or presents a problem, and the sestet answers the question or draws a conclusion. Petrarch's Sonnet 169 is an example of an Italian sonnet.

The **English, or Shakespearean, sonnet** is divided into three quatrains (a group of four lines) followed by a couplet (two lines that rhyme with each other). The rhyme scheme is generally *abab cdcd efef gg*. The main thought of the sonnet is usually presented in the four quatrains, while the couplet draws a conclusion or makes an important point. Shakespeare's sonnets are examples of the English sonnet.

> See pages 90, 757.

SPRUNG RHYTHM *A kind of meter in which each foot contains one stressed syllable, usually the first, and any number of unstressed syllables.* Hopkins created this term for the rhythm in his poems. His combination of syllables often sounds like natural speech. Consider, for example, this line from "Pied Beauty":

He fath / ers-forth whose / beauty is past / change:
Praise / him.

> See page 438.

STAGE DIRECTIONS *Instructions written by the playwright about scenery, costumes, gestures, movements, and lighting for a play.*

> See page 108.

STANZA *A group of lines forming a unit in a poem.* Stanzas usually contain from two to eight lines and often have a definite rhyme scheme.

Common stanzas are the **couplet,** two lines; the **tercet,** three lines; the **quatrain,** four lines; the **sestet,** six lines; the **octave,** eight lines.

See page 90.

STREAM OF CONSCIOUSNESS *A technique of writing that imitates human thought with a continuous flow of thoughts, feelings, images, observations, and memories.* The author seldom speaks directly to the reader but allows characters to reveal themselves through their thoughts. Woolf's "New Dress" is a stream-of-consciousness story.

See page 617.

STRUCTURE *The framework or general plan of a literary work.* The structure is the sequence of thoughts and images that work together to impart meaning.

See pages 338, 626.

STYLE *An author's choice and arrangement of words in any kind of writing.* Style often conveys the author's individuality and theme or purpose.

See pages 203, 236, 573, 626.

SYMBOL *A figure of speech in which a person, object, or situation represents something in addition to its literal meaning.* For instance, a dove is often used to symbolize peace. In his poem "The Sick Rose" Blake uses the rose to symbolize love. **Symbolism** refers to the use of symbols in writing.

See pages 315, 540.
See also SYMBOLIST
POETRY.

SYMBOLIST POETRY *Richly musical verse built around vivid symbols whose larger meanings are implied but not directly stated.* Reacting to Realism, Symbolists saw the emotions as the proper subject of art. The Symbolist movement arose in France in the latter half of the nineteenth century and continued into the twentieth century. Baudelaire, Rimbaud, and Verlaine are all famous French Symbolists.

See page 845.
See also REALISM.

TERZA RIMA *A verse form of three-line stanzas in which the first and third lines rhyme and the second line rhymes with the first line of the following stanza.* Shelley's "Ode to the West Wind" is written in terza rima, as the following stanzas show:

O wild West Wind, thou breath of Autumn's being,
Thou, from whose unseen presence the leaves dead
Are driven, like ghosts from an enchanter fleeing,

Yellow, and black, and pale, and hectic red,
Pestilence-stricken multitudes: O thou,
Who chariotest to their dark wintry bed

THEME *The main idea of a story, poem, novel, or play, usually expressed as a statement about life.* Some works have **stated themes,** which are announced explicitly. Most works have **implied themes** that are revealed indirectly.

See pages 189, 432, 588, 638.

TONE *The attitude the writer expresses toward his or her subject and audience.* The tone of a poem or story may be casual, amused, indifferent, sad, angry, or any of many other possibilities. The tone of "The Panther" by Rilke, for example, combines the emotions of awe and pity for the caged animal.

See page 863.

TRAGEDY *A literary work in which the main character suffers a major downfall.* According to the Greek philosopher Aristotle, the function of tragedy is to arouse the emotions of fear and pity in order to produce a catharsis, or cleansing, of these emotions. The main character, or **tragic hero,** is usually a high-ranking person whose personality is marred by a fatal weakness, or **tragic flaw,** that causes an eventual decline from success to destruction. Macbeth, for example, is a tragic hero whose flaw is his great ambition.

See pages 110, 713.

TROCHEE *A poetic foot consisting of a stressed syllable followed by an unstressed syllable (′ ˘).*

See also FOOT.

VERISIMILITUDE *A sense of reality in a work of literature.* For example, the rambling internal thoughts of the protagonist in "The New Dress" approximate real-life thought processes.

See page 63.

VILLANELLE *A poem of nineteen lines divided into five tercets (three-line stanzas) and a final quatrain, using the rhyme scheme* aba aba aba aba aba abaa. There are only two rhymes in a villanelle, and eight of the nineteen lines are repeated. Lines 6, 12, and 18 repeat line 1; lines 9, 15, and 18 repeat line 3. The villanelle form originated in fifteenth-century France.

See page 566.

GLOSSARY

The following Glossary lists words that are from the selections but may be unfamiliar to you. Although many of the words have several different meanings, they are defined only as they are used in the selections. Some words may be familiar to you in other contexts but may have unusual meanings in the text.

Each Glossary entry contains a pronunciation, a part of speech, and a definition. Some words are used in more than one way in the textbook and therefore have more than one definition and occasionally more than one part of speech. Related words are often combined in one entry: The main form (for example, the verb *afflict*) is defined, and another form (for example, the noun *afflictor*) is run on after the main definition. Adverbs ending in -*ly* are usually run on after the definitions of the adjective form.

Some unusual words or meanings of words are labeled ARCHAIC (old-fashioned), OBSOLETE (no longer in use), RARE, or POETIC. Other special usage labels include COLLOQUIAL, SLANG, CHIEFLY BRITISH, MILITARY, and so on. Occasionally an unfamiliar idiomatic expression is used within a selection; in such cases the main word of the expression is listed, followed by a definition of the idiom.

The following abbreviations are used in this Glossary:

n.	noun	*conj.*	conjunction
v.	verb	*prep.*	preposition
adj.	adjective	*interj.*	interjection
adv.	adverb	*pl.*	plural
pron.	pronoun	*n.pl.*	plural noun

A key to pronunciations may be found in the lower right-hand corner of each right-hand page of the Glossary.

A

abate [ə bāt′] *v.* to lessen; reduce.

abortive [ə bôr′tiv] *adj.* unsuccessful; useless.

absolution [ab′sə lōō′shən] *n.* formal forgiveness for sins.

absolve [ab zolv′, -solv′] *v.* to free from responsibility or blame.

abysmal [ə biz′məl] *adj.* bottomless; immeasurable.

accrue [ə krōō′] *v.* to come as an increase or addition.

acme [ak′mē] *n.* the highest point.

admonish [ad mon′ish] *v.* to caution; warn.

adversary [ad′vər ser′ē] *n.* enemy; opponent.

adversity [ad vur′sə tē] *n.* misfortune; trouble.

advocate [ad′və kit, -kāt′] *n.* a person who pleads the cause of another; lawyer.

afflict [ə flikt′] *v.* to cause pain, distress, or suffering. —**afflictor,** *n.*

affliction [ə flik′shən] *n.* any cause of pain, distress, or suffering.

aggrandizement [ə gran′dīz mənt, -diz mənt] *n.* the act of making greater.

aggregate [ag′rə gāt′] *v.* to collect into a whole; total.

agronomy [ə gron′ə mē] *n.* the science of crop and farmland management.

alacrity [ə lak′rə tē] *n.* readiness; promptness; eagerness.

alien [āl′yən, ā′lē ən] *adj.* foreign; strange.

alliteration [ə lit′ə rā′shən] *n.* repetition of an initial consonant.

amenable [ə mē′nə bəl, ə men′ə-] *adj.* responsive; yielding.

amenity [ə men′ə tē, ə mē′nə-] *n.* courtesy; pleasant manner; polite behavior.

amphibious [am fib′ē əs] *adj.* capable of living on land and in water.

animate [an′ə māt′] *v.* to cause to act; inspire.

annals [an′əlz] *n.pl.* a written, chronological account of events recorded year by year; history.

annihilate [ə nī′ə lāt′] *v.* to destroy; wipe out.

annuity [ə nōō′ə tē, ə nū′-] *n.* an investment that pays a fixed amount of money at regular intervals.

anoint [ə noint′] *v.* to rub oil on.

antiquated [an′tə kwā′tid] *adj.* old-fashioned; outdated.

antiquity [an tik′wə tē] *n.* ancientness.

aphorism [af′ə riz′əm] *n.* a short statement expressing a basic truth or principle; saying.

aplomb [ə plom′, ə plum′] *n.* confidence; assurance.

apostle [ə pos′əl] *n.* one of the twelve disciples of Christ, sent out by him to preach his gospel.

apparition [ap′ə rish′ən] *n.* a ghost.

appellation [ap′ə lā′shən] *n.* a name.

application [ap′lə kā′shən] *n.* steady attention.

apprehension [ap′ri hen′shən] *n.* understanding.

apprise [ə prīz′] *v.* to tell; notify.

approbation [ap′rə bā′shən] *n.* official approval; praise.

appurtenances [ə purt′ən ən səz] *n.pl.* equipment; accessories.

arable [ar′ə bəl] *adj.* (of land) suitable for cultivation.

arbiter [är′bə tər] *n.* a person with complete power to make decisions; judge.

arbitrator [är′bə trā′tər] *n.* a person chosen to settle a dispute.

arbitress [är′bə tris] *n.* a female arbiter.

armorial [är môr′ē əl] *adj.* relating to or bearing a coat of arms, a design representing a family emblem.

arrears [ə rērz′] *n.pl.* unpaid debts or unfinished duties. —**in arrears** behind in paying a debt or fulfilling an obligation.

artifice [är′tə fis] *n.* something skillfully made.

ascension [ə sen′shən] *n.* the act of rising.

asinine [as′ə nīn′] *adj.* like a donkey; stupid, silly, or stubborn. —**asininely,** *adv.*

asperity [as per′ə tē, əs-] *n.* sharpness of temper; harshness.

aspire [əs pīr′] *v.* to seek ambitiously to achieve something.

assay [ə sā′] *v.* to try.

assiduous [ə sij′ōō əs] *adj.* careful and persistent; hardworking. —**assiduously,** *adv.*

assignation [as′ig nā′shən] *n.* an appointment; date; rendezvous.

asunder [ə sun′dər] *adv.* apart in direction or position.

atrophy [at′rə fē] *v.* to waste away.

attribute [at′rə būt′] *n.* a characteristic.

attrition [ə trish′ən] *n.* sorrow for one's sins that comes from shame or fear of punishment.

audacious [ô dā′shəs] *adj.* bold; daring.

audit [ô′dit] *n.* an examination of financial records.

auditor [ô′də tər] *n.* a person who examines financial records.

augment [ôg ment′] *v.* to increase.

auspicious [ôs pish′əs] *adj.* successful; prosperous.

avarice [av′ər is] *n.* greed.

aver [ə vur′] *v.* to state positively; affirm.

avocation [av′ə kā′shən] *n.* OBSOLETE. a distraction.

axiom [ak′sē əm] *n.* an established principle or rule.

B

ballast [bal′əst] *n.* something heavy carried in a ship to make it steady.

balm [bäm] *n.* a sweet-smelling ointment.

bane [bān] *n.* a cause of suffering or destruction.

banter [ban′tər] *v.* to tease; joke.

barren [bar′ən] *adj.* without vegetation.

barrow [bar′ō] *n.* a mound of earth or stones over a grave.

beaker [bē′kər] *n.* a large cup.

beck [bek] *n.* a summoning or commanding gesture.

beleaguer [bi lē′gər] *v.* to surround; torment.

bier [bēr] *n.* a platform for a coffin; a coffin.

bilingual [bī ling′gwəl] *adj.* able to speak two languages.

bilious [bil′yəs] *adj.* bad-tempered; cross.

blasé [blä zā′, blä′zā] *adj.* bored; indifferent.

blear [blēr] *v.* to blur.

✳ **blight** [blīt] *n.* something that damages or destroys.

blunt [blunt] *adj.* perceiving slowly; dull.

bogey [bō′gē] *n.* a cause of excessive fear or anxiety.

bogus [bō′gəs] *adj.* not genuine.

boundless [bound′lis] *adj.* without limits.

brandish [bran′dish] *v.* to wave threateningly.

breach [brēch] *n.* a gap, opening, or break.

bridle [brīd′əl] *v.* to control or restrain, as if with a horse's harness.

buffoon [bə foon′] *n.* a clown; joker.

bulbous [bul′bəs] *adj.* shaped like a bulb; rounded or swollen.

bullion [bool′yən] *n.* gold or silver in the form of bars.

burnish [bur′nish] *v.* to polish.

C

cadence [kād′əns] *n.* a rhythmic pattern of sound or movement.

calligraphy [kə lig′rə fē] *n.* the art of beautiful handwriting.

camouflage [kam′ə fläzh′] *n.* a way of hiding by blending with the background; disguise.

capricious [kə prish′əs, -prē′shəs] *adj.* tending to change suddenly or unpredictably.

casuistry [kazh′oo is trē] *n.* a method for deciding questions of right and wrong by applying moral principles to concrete situations.

causeway [kôz′wā′] *n.* a highway.

cavalcade [kav′əl kād′, kav′əl kād′] *n.* a group of horseback riders moving along together.

censure [sen′shər] *n.* strong disapproval.

certitude [sur′tə tood′, -tūd′] *n.* sureness; certainty of events.

chalice [chal′is] *n.* a cup or goblet, especially one used in Holy Communion.

charlatanry [shär′lə tən rē] *n.* a pretending to have knowledge; fakery; trickery.

chivalry [shiv′əl rē] *n.* the qualities of a perfect knight, such as courtesy, bravery, helpfulness, respect for women.

choleric [kol′ər ik] *adj.* bad-tempered.

chronic [kron′ik] *adj.* constant; always present. —**chronically,** *adv.*

circumscribe [sur′kəm skrīb′] *v.* to encircle; limit; restrict.

citadel [sit′əd əl, -ə del′] *n.* a high fortress for defending a city.

cite [sīt] *v.* to refer to; quote.

civility [si vil′ə tē] *n.* politeness.

clandestine [klan des′tin] *adj.* secret.

clarion [klar′ē ən] *n.* a sound like a trumpet.

cleave [klēv] *v.* to divide; split.

clement [klem′ənt] *adj.* merciful; lenient.

cloy [kloi] *v.* to make weary by too much of anything pleasing; satiate.

coagulate [kō ag′yə lāt′] *v.* to form into a mass; thicken.

coalition [kō ə lish′ən] *n.* an alliance.

✳ **cogitate** [koj′ə tāt′] *v.* to think deeply or seriously.

combustible [kəm bus′tə bəl] *adj.* burning easily.

comely [kum′lē] *adj.* pleasing in appearance; attractive.

commodity [kə mod′ə tē] *n.* a product that is bought and sold.

communal [kə mūn′əl, kom′yən əl] *adj.* shared; public.

compassion [kəm pash′ən] *n.* sympathy for a person's misfortune combined with a desire to help.

complier [kəm plī′ər] *n.* one who agrees or conforms.

composure [kəm pō′zhər] *n.* calmness; self-control.

compulsion [kəm pul′shən] *n.* the act of forcing or being forced.

compulsive [kəm pul′siv] *adj.* able to compel or force.

compulsory [kəm pul′sər ē] *adj.* mandatory; required.

computation [kom′pyə tā′shən] *n.* the act of counting or figuring mathematically; calculation.

concentrate [kon′sən trāt′] *n.* proportional content; strength.

concession [kən sesh′ən] *n.* something granted or yielded.

conchology [kong kol′ə jē] *n.* the study of shells and shellfish.

✳ **conciliate** [kən sil′ē āt′] *v.* to win the friendliness or calm the anger of.

concourse [kon′kôrs, kong′-] *n.* a crowd.

concussion [kən kush′ən] *n.* the shock of a blow or collision.

conduce [kən doos′, -dūs′] *v.* to lead or help bring about a result.

confederate [kən fed′ə rāt′] *v.* to unite; ally; associate.

confiscation [kon′fis kā′shən] *n.* the seizing of private property for public use.

conflagration [kon′flə grā′shən] *n.* a large fire.

conjecture [kən jek′chər] *v.* to guess.

conjunction [kən jungk′shən] *n.* the state of being joined; association; combination.

connoisseur [kon′ə sur′] *n.* an expert.

consequential [kon′sə kwen′shəl] *adj.* RARE. conceited; pompous.

consign [kən sīn′] *v.* to give; deliver.

consort [kon′sort] *n.* a companion; wife or husband.

consummation [kon′sə mā′shən] *n.* fulfillment.

---

at; āpe; cär; end; mē; it; īce; hot; ōld; fôrk; wood; fool; oil; out; up; ūse; turn; ə in ago, taken, pencil, lemon, circus; bat; chin; dear; five; game; hit; hw in white; joke; kit; lid; man; not; singer; pail; ride; sat; shoe; tag; thin; this; very; wet; yes; zoo; zh in treasure; ᴋн in loch, German ach; ɴ in French bon; œ in French feu, German schön

---

contemporary [kən tem′pə rer′ē] *n.* a person of the same age.

contend [kən tend′] *v.* to struggle; compete.

contrite [kən trīt′, kon′trīt] *adj.* sorry or guilty for one's wrongdoing; regretful; repentant. —**contritely,** *adv.*

contrive [kən trīv′] *v.* to construct cleverly.

copious [kō′pē əs] *adj.* **1.** abundant; lavish. **2.** pouring out words; enthusiastically long-winded.

cordial [kôr′jəl] *n.* a sweet liqueur.

covert [kuv′ərt, kō′vərt] *n.* a hidden or protected place; a thick growth of bushes or trees where animals can hide.

croup [krōop] *n.* the rear part of an animal's body; rump.

crystalline [krist′əl in, -īn′] *adj.* clear; transparent.

curfew [kur′fū] *n.* in the Middle Ages, a bell rung to indicate the time to put out lights and retire.

D

dale [dāl] *n.* a valley.

dappled [dap′əld] *adj.* spotted.

dearth [durth] *n.* scarcity; famine.

debauchery [di bô′chər ē] *n.* excessive indulgence in pleasure.

decanter [di kan′tər] *n.* a decorative bottle used for serving liquids.

declaim [di klām′] *v.* to recite or speak in a dramatic or artificial manner.

decree [di krē′] *v.* to make an official order or decision.

decry [di krī′] *v.* to speak out against; express disapproval of.

deem [dēm] *v.* to think; judge; consider.

defer [di fur′] *v.* to put off; delay.

deference [def′ər əns] *n.* respect.

defile [di fīl′] *v.* to stain; disgrace; dishonor.

deign [dān] *v.* to consider something good enough for oneself.

delusive [di lōo′siv] *adj.* misleading.

delve [delv] *v.* ARCHAIC. to dig.

demure [di myoor′] *adj.* proper; reserved; modest. —**demurely,** *adv.*

denounce [di nouns′] *v.* to accuse; criticize.

depict [di pikt′] *v.* to picture; portray.

deprecate [dep′rə kāt′] *v.* to criticize; belittle.

derision [di rizh′ən] *n.* mockery.

dervish [dur′vish] *n.* a member of a Moslem group among whom whirling and other movements are performed as religious exercises.

desolation [des′ə lā′shən] *n.* waste; ruin; destruction.

despoil [di spoil′] *v.* to rob; plunder.

desultory [des′əl tôr′ē] *adj.* not orderly; rambling; disconnected.

devastate [dev′əs tāt′] *v.* to destroy; ruin.

dexterity [deks ter′ə tē] *n.* skill in using one's hands, body, or mind.

didactic [dī dak′tik] *adj.* instructive.

differentiate [dif′ər en′shē āt′] *v.* to perceive as different; distinguish.

diligent [dil′ə jənt] *adj.* careful; persistent; hard-working.

diminution [dim′ə nū′shən,-nōo-] *n.* a lessening; decrease.

dirge [durj] *n.* a slow, mournful piece of music.

discourse [dis kôrs′] *v.* to talk; converse.

discreet [dis krēt′] *adj.* not showy; modest; unobtrusive. —**discreetly,** *adv.*

disinterested [dis in′tris tid, -in′tər is-, -in′tə res′-] *adj.* unconcerned; aloof.

disparage [dis par′ij] *v.* to speak of as having little value; belittle.

disperse [dis purs′] *v.* to scatter; cause to disappear.

disquisition [dis kwə zish′ən] *n.* a long, formal discussion of a topic.

dissemble [di sem′bəl] *v.* to disguise; conceal.

dissipate [dis′ə pāt] *v.* to scatter; disperse.

distracted [dis trak′tid] *adj.* OBSOLETE. crazy; insane.

ditty [dit′ē] *n.* a little song.

divert [di vurt′, dī-] *v.* to turn from a particular course.

dogmatic [dôg mat′ik] *adj.* relating to established beliefs or principles.

doughty [dou′tē] *adj.* brave.

drear [drēr] *adj.* POETIC. dreary; gloomy.

dregs [dregz] *n.pl.* the most unwanted or useless part.

E

ecclesiast [i klē′zē ast] *n.* a clergyman.

edict [ē′dikt] *n.* an official announcement.

effectual [i fek′chōo əl] *adj.* producing a result; effective. —**effectually,** *adv.*

effluence [ef′lōo əns] *n.* something that flows out.

effusion [i fū′zhən] *n.* emotional expression or outpouring.

egregious [i grē′jəs] *adj.* ARCHAIC. extraordinary.

eke [ēk] *v.* to make (a living, etc.) with great difficulty.

elemental [el′ə ment′əl] *adj.* relating to one of the four elements, earth, air, fire, and water.

elocution [el′ə kū′shən] *n.* a style of public speaking. —**elocutionary,** *adj.*

elongate [i lông′gāt] *v.* to lengthen.

elude [i lōod′] *v.* to get away from or avoid skillfully.

elysium [i lizh′əm, i liz′ē əm] *n.* a place of great happiness; paradise.

emanate [em′ə nāt′] *v.* to come out; flow.

embolden [em bōld′ən] *v.* to make bold or courageous.

eminent [em′ə nənt] *adj.* famous; outstanding.

emolument [i mol′yə mənt] *n.* ARCHAIC. benefit.

encumber [en kum′bər] *v.* to hold back; hinder; burden.

enigma [i nig′mə] *n.* a mystery; puzzle. —**enigmatic** [en′ig mat′ik, ē′nig-] *adj.*

entreaty [en trē′tē] *n.* a humble request.

envisage [en viz′ij] *v.* to imagine; picture.

envoy [en′voi, än′-] *n.* a messenger.

equity [ek′wə tē] *n.* LAW. a set of general rules used to supplement specific laws.

estrange [es trānj′] *v.* to separate; keep away.

estuary [es′chōo er′ē] *n.* a place where a river widens and meets an arm of the sea.

etymology [et′ə mol′ə jē] *n.* **1.** the history of a word. **2.** the study of the history of words.

eunuch [ū′nək] *n.* a castrated man.

exaltation [eg′zôl tā′shən, ek′sôl-] *n.* a feeling of great joy or pride; elation.

exasperate [ig zas′pə rāt′] *v.* to annoy greatly; irritate; anger.

exemplify [eg zem′plə fī′] *v.* to give an example of.

exempt [ig zempt′] *v.* to release from a rule or requirement; excuse.

exhortation [eg′zôr tā′shən, ek′sôr-] *n.* an attempt to persuade; strong advice.

exonerate [ig zon′ə rāt′] *v.* to declare free of blame; pardon.

exorbitant [ig zôr′bə tənt] *adj.* higher or greater than is reasonable.

exorciser [ek′sôr sī′zər] *n.* one who frees a person or place from an evil spirit.

expatiate [eks pā′shē āt′] *v.* to speak or write in detail.

expedient [iks pē′dē ənt] *n.* something useful for achieving a purpose.

expiation [eks′pē ā′shən] *n.* an atonement or payment for a wrongdoing.

expletive [eks′plə tiv] *n.* an exclamation or curse.

expound [iks pound′] *v.* to state or explain in detail.

expunge [iks punj′] *v.* to erase.

extort [iks tôrt′] *v.* to take by force or threats.

extremity [iks trem′ə tē] *n.* the farthest part.

F

façade [fə säd′] *n.* the front of a building.

faction [fak′shən] *n.* quarreling between opposing groups. —**factious,** *adj.*

fallow [fal′ō] *n.* land that is plowed but left unplanted for a time. —**fallow,** *adj.*

farthing [fär′thing] *n.* an old British coin worth one-fourth of a penny.

faze [fāz] *v.*COLLOQUIAL. to disturb.

feasible [fē′zə bəl] *adj.* possible.

feign [fān] *v.* to pretend.

felicity [fi lis′ə tē] *n.* 1. happiness. 2. a source of happiness.

ferment [fur′ment] *n.* a state of great excitement or unrest.

fickle [fik′əl] *adj.* changeable.

finical [fin′i kəl] *adj.* overly careful or particular; finicky.

flaccid [flak′sid] *adj.* hanging loosely; limp.

flank [flangk] *n.* the side of a formation of soldiers.

flog [flog, flôg] *v.* to force; drive; urge.

florin [flôr′in, flor′-] *n.* a British coin worth two shillings.

flunkey [flung′kē] also **flunky** *n.* a person who does low, minor jobs; servant.

foliage [fō′lē ij] *n.* the leaves of a plant.

formidable [fôr′mi də bəl] *adj.* impressive.

freehold [frē′hōld′] *adj.* held for life or able to be passed on by inheritance.

frenzy [fren′zē] *n.* a wild outburst of activity.

friar [frī′ər] *n.* a member of any of several religious orders that survive mainly by begging.

G

gable [gā′bəl] *n.* a wall with a triangular top formed by a pointed roof that slopes down on both sides. —**gabled,** *adj.*

gantlet [gônt′lit, gant′-] *n.* a punishment in which two rows of men armed with clubs strike a person who runs between them.

garrulous [gar′ə ləs, gar′yə-] *adj.* talkative.

gelding [gel′ding] *n.* a castrated male horse.

gentry [jen′trē] *n.* people of a high social class.

genuflection [jen′yoo flek′shən] *n.* the bending of the knee, as in worship.

girdle [gurd′əl] *n.* a belt.

glade [glād] *n.* an open area within a forest.

glean [glēn] *v.* to examine or pick over for information.

granary [grā′nər ē, gran′ər ē] *n.* a place for storing grain.

gratuitous [grə tōō′ə təs, -tū′-] *adj.* unjustified; uncalled-for.

grisly [griz′lē] *adj.* horrible; ghastly.

guileless [gīl′lis] *adj.* candid; not sly or crafty.

gumption [gump′shən] *n.* initiative; daring.

guttural [gut′ər əl] *adj.* throaty; rasping.

H

habituate [hə bich′ōō āt′] *v.* to make used to; accustom.

harry [har′ē] *v.* to push along.

hawser [hô′zər] *n.* a heavy rope for moving or anchoring a ship.

heath [hēth] *n.* an area of open, uncultivated land.

herald [her′əld] *v.* to introduce; announce; publicize.

heraldic [he ral′dik] *adj.* relating to coats of arms.

hireling [hīr′ling] *n.* a person hired to perform an unpleasant or criminal act.

homage [hom′ij, om′-] *n.* a sign of honor or respect.

host [hōst] *n.* a crowd; multitude.

hostelry [host′əl rē] *n.* an inn.

hull [hul] *n.* the body of a ship.

I

imbue [im bū′] *v.* to fill; spread through.

imitable [im′ə tə bəl] *adj.* able to be imitated.

immoderate [i mod′ər it] *adj.* exceeding proper limits; excessive; unreasonable.

immutable [i mū′tə bəl] *adj.* unchanging. —**immutably,** *adv.*

impalpable [im pal′pə bəl] *adj.* not able to be touched or detected.

impart [im pärt′] *v.* to give; tell, reveal.

impassive [im pas′iv] *adj.* not showing any feelings.

impeccable [im pek′ə bəl] *adj.* without fault; perfect.

imperious [im pēr′ē əs] *adj.* ruling over harshly; overly proud and scornful.

imperturbable [im′pər tur′bə bəl] *adj.* not able to be upset; showing no feeling; calm.

impetuous [im pech′ōō əs] *adj.* rushing forcefully; violent.

impinge [im pinj′] *v.* to hit sharply; collide.

impious [im′pē əs] *adj.* disrespectful.

implacable [im plak′ə bəl, -plā′kə-] *adj.* without pity; not able to be won over.

impotence [im′pət əns] *n.* weakness; helplessness.

imprecation [im′pri kā′shən] *n.* a curse.

impudence [im′pyə dəns] *n.* sauciness; disrespectfulness.

impute [im pūt′] *v.* to place blame for; charge with.

inadvertency [in′əd vurt′ən sē] *n.* inattentiveness; carelessness.

incantation [in′kan tā′shən] *n.* the chanting of magical spells or charms.

incarnate [in kär′nit, -nāt] *adj.* given human form.

incarnation [in′kär nā′shən] *n.* the taking of human form.

incense [in′sens] *n.* 1. a substance that releases a pleasant smell when burned. 2. a pleasant smell; fragrance.

---

at; āpe; cär; end; mē; it; īce; hot; ōld; fôrk; wood; fōōl; oil; out; up; ūse; turn; ə in ago, taken, pencil, lemon, circus; bat; chin; dear; five; game; hit; hw in white; joke; kit; lid; man; not; singer; pail; ride; sat; shoe; tag; thin; <u>th</u>is; very; wet; yes; zoo; zh in treasure; KH in loch, German ach; N in French bon; œ in French feu, German schön

incessant [in ses′ənt] *adj.* never stopping; constant.

incipient [in sip′ē ənt] *adj.* just beginning.

incommensurable [in′kə men′sər ə bəl, -shər-] *adj.* not measurable or comparable.

incommodious [in′kə mō′dē əs] *adj.* inconvenient; troublesome.

incongruity [in kən grōō′ə tē] *n.* lack of agreement or harmony.

inconsiderable [in′kən sid′ər ə bəl] *adj.* unimportant.

incredulous [in krej′ə ləs] *adj.* unbelieving.

incursion [in kur′zhən] *n.* the act of entering or intruding.

indefatigable [in′di fat′ə gə bəl] *adj.* not able to be made tired; untiring. —**indefatigably,** *adv.*

indignant [in dig′nənt] *adj.* angry because of injustice, meanness, or ingratitude.

✳ **ineffable** [in ef′ə bəl] *adj.* too awesome to be put into words; indescribable.

ineptitude [i nep′tə tōōd, -tūd] *n.* awkwardness; clumsiness.

✳ **inexorable** [i nek′sər ə bəl] *adj.* that cannot be changed or stopped.

inextricable [in eks′tri kə bəl, -iks trik′ə bəl] *adj.* that cannot be untangled or untied.

infamous [in′fə məs] *adj.* having a very bad reputation.

infectious [in fek′shəs] *adj.* spreading easily to others.

infest [in fest′] *v.* to fill; overrun.

ingress [in′gres] *n.* entrance.

inimical [in im′i kəl] *adj.* opposed; unfavorable; harmful.

iniquity [in ik′wə tē] *n.* wickedness.

inquisition [in′kwə zish′ən] *n.* an investigation or harsh questioning, often of those who do not conform.

insatiable [in sā′shə bəl] *adj.* not able to be satisfied. —**insatiableness,** *n.*

inscrutable [in skrōō′tə bəl] *adj.* difficult to understand; mysterious.

inseparable [in sep′ər ə bəl, -sep′rə-] *adj.* not able to be separated.

insolence [in′sə ləns] *n.* disrespectfulness; impertinence.

integrity [in teg′rə tē] *n.* honesty; sincerity; trustworthiness.

inter [in tur′] *v.* to bury.

intercede [in′tər sēd′] *v.* to plead in behalf of another person.

interfuse [in′tər fūz′] *v.* to spread through something; blend.

interminable [in tur′mi nə bəl] *adj.* endless.

intimation [in′tə mā′shən] *n.* a hint; suggestion.

intone [in tōn′] *v.* to say or recite in a singsong way or on a single note; chant.

introspection [in′trə spek′shən] *n.* the act of looking inward; examination of one's own thoughts and feelings.

✳ **intuition** [in′tōō ish′ən, -tū-] *n.* something that is known or understood without the use of conscious thought.

inventory [in′vən tôr′ē] *n.* a list of items.

inverse [in vurs′, in′vurs′] *adj.* opposite; reverse.

inveterate [in vet′ər it] *adj.* fixed as a habit; established.

invoke [in vōk′] *v.* to request solemnly.

iridescent [ir′ə des′ənt] *adj.* showing shifting, rainbowlike colors.

irreducible [ir′i dōō′sə bəl, -dū′-] *adj.* not able to be reduced or lessened.

✳ **irremediable** [ir′i mē′dē ə bəl] *adj.* not able to be remedied or fixed.

J

jackdaw [jak′dô′] *n.* a blackbird like a crow but smaller.

jocund [jok′ənd, jō′kənd] *adj.* cheerful; merry.

L

landed [lan′did] *adj.* possessing land.

languid [lang′gwid] *adj.* lacking liveliness and interest in things.

lateral [lat′ər əl] *adj.* relating to the side.

laudable [lô′də bəl] *adj.* worthy of praise.

lay [lā] *n.* a short poem.

legion [lē′jən] *n.* a large unit of soldiers; army.

lexicon [lek′sə kən, -kon′] *n.* a dictionary.

libellous [lī′bə ləs] also **libelous** *adj.* containing damaging written or printed information about a person.

lichen [lī′kən] *n.* a plant that grows in patches on rocks or other surfaces.

liege [lēj] *adj.* loyal.

ligature [lig′ə choor′, -chər] *n.* something used to tie.

lineage [lin′ē ij] *n.* family descent; ancestry.

listless [list′lis] *adj.* lacking energy and interest in things.

litany [lit′ən ē] *n.* a repetitive reciting or chanting.

lithograph [lith′ə graf′] *v.* to print from a stone or plate that has been treated to attract ink to certain areas and repel it from others.

livid [liv′id] *adj.* discolored; black-and-blue.

lucid [lōō′sid] *adj.* clear; transparent.

lugubrious [loo gōō′brē əs, -gū′-] *adj.* exaggeratedly sad or mournful.

lurid [loor′id] *adj.* pale or grayish; ghastly.

M

malign [mə līn′] *adj.* evil; harmful.

malignant [mə lig′nənt] *adj.* wishing evil; malicious.

mallow [mal′ō] *n.* any of a group of plants, usually having showy flowers and leaves with rounded divisions.

manifest [man′ə fest′] *adj.* clear; obvious. —**manifestly,** *adv.*

manor [man′ər] *n.* an estate or mansion.

mansion [man′shən] *n.* ARCHAIC. a dwelling; residence.

mantle [mant′əl] *n.* a cloak; cape.

mar [mär] *v.* to damage; spoil.

marrow [mar′ō] *n.* the soft, fatty tissue inside bones.

meander [mē an′dər] *v.* to wander; ramble.

mellifluous [me lif′lōō əs] *adj.* sweet; smooth; flowing.

melodious [mi lō′dē əs] *adj.* producing a melody; sweet-sounding.

mercenary [mur′sə ner′ē] *adj.* working only for money, as a soldier in a foreign army. —*n.* a person who works only in order to make money.

metaphysical [met′ə fiz′i kəl] *adj.* supernatural.

mindful [mīnd′fəl] *adj.* paying attention; aware.

ministry [min′is trē] *n.* the representatives of a government.

miscarriage [mis kar′ij] *n.* bad handling; failure.

modulation [moj′ə lā′shən] *n.* regulation of the tone or pitch of the voice.

molder [mōl′dər] *v.* to crumble; decay.

molest [mə lest′] *v.* to annoy; trouble.

molten [mōlt′ən] *adj.* glowing.

morose [mə rōs′] *adj.* bad-tempered and gloomy. —**morosely,** *adv.*

mortification [môr′tə fi kā′shən] *n.* shame; humiliation.

motley [mot′lē] *adj.* made up of many colors or varied elements.

muse [mūz] *v.* to think; ponder.

myriad [mir′ē əd] *n.* an extremely large number.

N

narcissistic [när′si sis′tic] *adj.* self-centered.

nimble [nim′bəl] *adj.* moving quickly and lightly. **—nimbly,** *adv.*

nocturnal [nok turn′əl] *adj.* of or occurring in the night.

nomenclature [nō′mən klā′chər] *n.* a system of names.

notary [nō′tər ē] *n.* an official who declares documents authentic, records statements made under oath, etc.: short for **notary public.**

O

obdurate [ob′dər it, ob′dyər-] *adj.* stubborn; unbending; hardened.

obese [ō bēs′] *adj.* very fat.

oblique [ə blēk′, ō blēk] *adj.* slanting; sloping. **—obliquely,** *adv.*

obliterate [ə blit′e rāt] *v.* to wipe out; erase.

oblivion [ə bliv′ē ən] *n.* forgetfulness.

obsequies [ob′sə kwēz] *n.pl.* funeral rites.

obtuse [əb tōōs′, -tūs′] *adj.* slow in understanding; insensitive.

odious [ō′dē əs] *adj.* disgusting; hateful.

office [ô′fis, of′is] *n.* a religious ceremony.

officious [ə fish′əs] *adj.* impertinent; meddling.

ogle [ō′gəl] *v.* to eye flirtatiously.

opiate [ō′pē it, -āt′] *n.* a medication that relieves pain or brings on sleep or relaxation.

oppressive [ə pres′iv] *adj.* harsh; cruel.

opulence [op′yə ləns] *n.* wealth; luxury.

ordain [ôr dān′] *v.* to order; decree.

ornament [ôr′nə ment′] *v.* to decorate.

P

palatial [pə lā′shəl] *adj.* like a palace; large and stately.

pallor [pal′ər] *n.* paleness.

palpitation [pal′pə tā′shən] *n.* rapid beating.

palsy [pôl′zē] *n.* a condition marked by a shaking or trembling of a part of the body.

paltry [pôl′trē] *adj.* unimportant; worthless.

pandemonium [pan′də mō′nē əm] *n.* wild uproar or confusion.

pander [pan′dər] *v.* to satisfy or exploit someone's desires or weaknesses.

paraphernalia [par′ə fər nāl′yə] *n.pl.* equipment.

parley [pär′lē] *n.* conversation; conference.

partiality [pär′shē al′ə tē, pär shal′-] *n.* a certain fondness or taste.

passion [pash′ən] *n.* suffering or agony.

pathetic [pə thet′ik] *adj.* arousing pity, sadness, or sympathy.

pathos [pā′thos] *n.* a quality that causes a feeling of pity or compassion.

patriarch [pā′trē ärk′] *n.* a father, founder, or leader; respected old man.

pauper [pô′pər] *n.* a very poor person.

pecuniary [pi kū′nē er′ē] *adj.* relating to money.

pedant [ped′ənt] *n.* a person who overemphasizes minor details or points of knowledge. **—pedantic** [pi dan′tik], *adj.*

penitent [pen′ə tənt] *n.* a person who regrets and wants to make up for wrongdoing.

penury [pen′yər ē] *n.* severe poverty.

percipience [pər sip′ē əns] *n.* perception.

peremptory [pə remp′tər ē] *adj.* not permitting argument or delay; commanding. **—peremptorily,** *adv.*

perfidious [pər fid′ē əs] *adj.* not trustworthy; disloyal. **—perfidiousness,** *n.*

pernicious [pər nish′əs] *adj.* RARE. wicked.

perplex [pər plex′] *v.* to puzzle; confuse.

personable [pur′sə nə bəl] *adj.* attractive.

peruse [pə rōōz′] *v.* to study; examine; read carefully.

pestilence [pes′tə ləns] *n.* a highly contagious and dangerous disease; plague.

petulance [pech′ə ləns] *n.* bad temper; crankiness.

philology [fi lol′ə jē] *n.* the study of language.

phonetic [fə net′ik] *adj.* relating to the study of speech sounds.

picket [pik′it] *n.* a soldier or group of soldiers stationed away from the main group to protect it from surprise attack; sentry.

piety [pī′ə tē] *n.* devotion to religion, family, etc.; faithfulness.

pipe [pīp] *n.* a tubelike musical instrument into which air is blown. **—v.** to play on a pipe.

pique [pēk] *v.* to offend; annoy.

plaintive [plān′tiv] *adj.* sad; sorrowful.

plaudits [plô′dits] *n.pl.* praise; applause.

ploy [ploi] *n.* a playful adventure.

plunder [plun′dər] *n.* things taken by force; loot.

podium [pō′dē əm] *n.* a platform for a speaker, orchestra conductor, etc.

polecat [pōl′kat′] *n.* a small animal like a weasel.

pomegranate [pom′gran′it, pom′ə-, pum′-] *n.* a reddish fruit with a thick skin and numerous small seeds, each covered with juicy pulp.

pompous [pom′pəs] *adj.* overly proud and dignified; pretentious.

ponderous [pon′dər əs] *adj.* heavy.

postillion [pōs til′yən, pos-] *n.* a person who rides on one of the horses drawing a carriage.

prate [prāt] *v.* to chatter foolishly.

precedent [pres′ə dənt] *n.* an earlier action, decision, etc., that serves as an example or rule.

precipitate [pri sip′ə tāt′] *v.* to cause; bring on.

precipitation [pri sip′ə tā′shən] *n.* hurriedness.

predestinate [prē des′tə nit, -nāt′] *adj.* having a certain destiny or fate.

prelate [prel′it] *n.* a high-ranking clergyman.

prevarication [pri var′ə kā′shən] *n.* the act of lying or avoiding the truth.

primordial [prī môr′dē əl] *adj.* existing from the earliest times.

probity [prō′bə tē, prob′ə-] *n.* honesty; honorableness.

procurement [prə kyoor′mənt] *n.* the act of getting or obtaining.

prodigious [prə dij′əs] *adj.* enormous.

prodigy [prod′ə jē] *n.* an unusually talented child.

---

at; āpe; cär; end; mē; it; īce; hot; ōld; fôrk; wood; fōōl; oil; out; up; ūse; turn; ə in ago, taken, pencil, lemon, circus; bat; chin; dear; five; game; hit; hw in white; joke; kit; lid; man; not; singer; pail; ride; sat; shoe; tag; thin; this; very; wet; yes; zoo; zh in treasure; KH in loch, German ach; N in French bon; œ in French feu, German schön

profane [prō fān′, prə-] *v.* to treat with disrespect or contempt.

promontory [prom′ən tôr′ē] *n.* a high point of land that juts out into the water.

propagate [prop′ə gāt′] *v.* to spread widely. —**propagator**, *n.*

propensity [prə pen′sə tē] *n.* a tendency; inclination.

propitiate [prə pish′ē āt′] *v.* to win the favor of.

propitious [prə pish′əs] *adj.* favorably inclined; benevolent.

prospectus [prə spek′təs] *n.* a statement describing a proposed work or undertaking.

prostrate [pros′trāt] *adj.* lying flat or with the face down.

protract [prō trakt′] *v.* to draw out; lengthen.

provincial [prə vin′shəl] *adj.* of a province, or division of a country.

proximity [prok sim′ə tē] *n.* nearness.

pullet [pool′it] *n.* a young hen.

pulverize [pul′və rīz′] *v.* to pound into dust.

purvey [pur vā′] *v.* to supply.

R

rabid [rab′id] *adj.* overly enthusiastic or devoted.

radiate [rā′dē āt′] *v.* to send out; spread.

rafter [raf′tər] *n.* a beam that supports a roof.

rally [ral′ē] *v.* to recover; revive.

rapacious [rə pā′shəs] *adj.* taking by force; robbing.

recoil [ri koil′] *v.* to draw back.

redound [ri dound′] *v.* to lead; contribute.

regenerate [ri jen′ə rāt′] *v.* to form again; renew; reestablish.

rend [rend] *v.* to tear; split.

render [ren′dər] *v.* to cause to be; make.

rent [rent] past tense of **rend.**

repast [ri past′] *n.* a meal.

repository [ri poz′ə tôr′ē] *n.* a place in which something is stored.

repudiate [ri pū′dē āt′] *v.* to refuse; reject; disown.

requiem [rek′wē əm, rē′kwē-] *n.* a piece of music sung in honor of the dead.

resurrection [rez′ə rek′shən] *n.* a rising from the dead.

retraction [ri trak′shən] *n.* a taking back or withdrawing.

revel [rev′əl] *n.* a wild, noisy celebration.

rhetoric [ret′ər ik] *n.* showy language.

risible [riz′ə bəl] *adj.* making one laugh; funny.

robust [rō bust′, rō′bust] *adj.* strong and healthy.

rod [rod] *n.* a stick used for punishment, carried as a symbol of authority, etc.

rogue [rōg] *n.* a mischievous person. —**roguish,** *adj.*

rubicund [rōō′bi kənd] *adj.* reddish.

rustic [rus′tik] *n.* a person from the country. —*adj.* relating to the country.

rustle [rus′əl] *n.* a series of soft, fluttering sounds.

S

sacrilegious [sak′rə lij′əs, -lē′jəs] *adj.* showing disrespect toward something sacred.

saffron [saf′rən] *adj.* orange-yellow.

sagacity [sə gas′ə tē] *n.* sound judgment; shrewdness.

salvation [sal vā′shən] *n.* a saving from the punishment for sins; redemption.

sanctity [sangk′tə tē] *n.* sacredness; holiness.

sanctuary [sangk′chōō er′ē] *n.* a holy place, such as a church, temple, or part of a church.

sanguine [sang′gwin] *adj.* having a healthy, reddish complexion and a cheerful manner.

sate [sāt] *v.* to satisfy fully.

scabbard [skab′ərd] *n.* a case for the blade of a sword, etc.

scanty [skan′tē] *adj.* barely enough; small; meager.

scarab [skar′əb] *n.* a stone carved with the form of a beetle, used as a charm in ancient Egypt.

schism [siz′əm, skiz′-] *n.* a division in a church.

scope [skōp] *n.* the range of activity or thought.

scourge [skurj] *n.* a cause of trouble or suffering.

scrupulosity [skrōō′pyə los′ə tē] *n.* strict attention to what is proper or conventional.

sear [sēr] *v.* **1.** to burn. **2.** to dry up; wither.

sect [sekt] *n.* a religious or political group.

secular [sek′yə lər] *adj.* not relating to religion.

sensibility [sen′sə bil′ə tē] *n.* the tendency to be easily hurt or offended.

sensible [sen′sə bəl] *adj.* aware.

sententious [sen ten′shəs] *adj.* fond of using trite phrases or maxims. —**sententiously,** *adv.*

sepulcher [sep′əl kər] *n.* a grave or tomb.

sequestered [si kwes′tərd] *adj.* isolated; secluded.

sere [sēr] *adj.* POETIC. withered.

serf [surf] *n.* in the feudal system, a slavelike laborer bound to the land of a lord.

servile [sur′vil, -vīl] *adj.* lacking self-respect; timid and obedient. —**servilely,** *adv.*

shire [shīr] *n.* a county or region in England.

shrivel [shriv′əl] *v.* to shrink; wrinkle up; wither.

shrill [shril] *adj.* high-pitched and piercing.

sickle [sik′əl] *n.* a tool with a curved blade and short handle used for cutting grass, etc.

signal [sig′nəl] *adj.* noticeable; remarkable.

signification [sig′nə fi kā′shən] *n.* OBSOLETE. a sign; symbol.

sinew [sin′ū] *n.* a tough, cordlike tissue that connects a muscle to another part of the body; tendon.

sinuous [sin′ū əs] *adj.* winding.

slack [slak] *v.* to be careless or lazy.

slander [slan′dər] *n.* the spreading of false and harmful statements about a person.

slavish [slā′vish] *adj.* like a slave; overly humble and obedient.

slough [sluf] *v.* to shed; get rid of.

solemn [sol′əm] *adj.* serious; sacred.

solicitous [sə lis′ə təs] *adj.* full of concern.

sonorous [sə nôr′əs, son′ər əs] *adj.* impressive sounding.

spare [spār] *adj.* thin.

specter [spek′tər] *n.* a ghost.

splay [splā] *v.* to spread out.

sprightly [sprīt′lē] *adj.* lively.

staff [staf] *n.* a stick carried for support.

stagnant [stag′nənt] *adj.* not moving or flowing.

stave [stāv] *n.* a stick.

stealthy [stel′thē] *adj.* secret; sly; sneaky. —**stealthily,** *adv.*

stile [stīl] *n.* a set of steps leading over a wall or fence.

stint [stint] *n.* a holding back or limiting.

straiten [strāt′ən] *v.* to cause to be in distress or need, especially financially.

stratagem [strat′ə jəm] *n.* a clever plan or trick for achieving something.

strife [strīf] *n.* struggle; conflict.

stupefy [stōō′pə fī′, stū′-] *v.* to make dull; stun.

sublime [səb līm′] *adj.* noble; lofty.

submissive [səb mis′iv] *adj.* giving in easily to the power or control of another.

subsistence [səb sis′təns] *n.* means of living; livelihood.

succor [suk′ər] *v.* to help.

suffuse [sə fūz′] *v.* to spread over and fill with light or a liquid. —**suffusion,** *n.*

sullen [sul′ən] *adj.* gloomy; dull.

sulphurous [sul′fər əs, sul fūr′əs] *adj.* fiery; hellish.

sultry [sul′trē] *adj.* hot; fiery; passionate.

sundry [sun′drē] *adj.* various.

superfluous [soo pur′floo əs] *adj.* unnecessary; extra.

supine [soo pīn′] *adj.* lying on one's back.

supplant [sə plant′] *v.* to replace.

supple [sup′əl] *adj.* able to bend easily; limber; flexible.

surmise [sər mīz′, sur′mīz] *n.* a guess.

susceptible [sə sep′tə bəl] *adj.* easily affected or influenced; sensitive.

swain [swān] *n.* a country person.

swathe [swoth, swāth] *v.* to wrap; surround.

swound [swound] *n.* a swoon; faint.

symmetry [sim′ə trē] *n.* the matching of parts or opposite sides; balanced proportions.

syndicate [sin′di kit] *n.* a business that sells articles, etc., to be published at the same time to a number of newspapers or magazines.

syntax [sin′taks] *n.* the arrangement of words in sentences.

T

tally [tal′ē] *n.* something used for recording accounts.

tariff [tar′if] *n.* a list of taxes or prices.

tarry [tar′ē] *v.* to leave slowly; stay; linger.

tee [tē] *n.* the letter *t.* —**to a tee** exactly.

teem [tēm] *v.* to be full.

temerity [tə mer′ə tē] *n.* foolhardy boldness; recklessness.

temperate [tem′pər it, -prit] *adj.* not extreme; mild.

tenacity [ti nas′ə tē] *n.* persistence; stubbornness.

tenor [ten′ər] *n.* a continuing course or tendency.

terrestrial [tə res′trē əl] *adj.* earthly.

throes [thrōz] *n.pl.* a condition of pain or struggle.

titillation [tit′ə lā′shən] *n.* a reaction; feeling; thrill.

tome [tōm] *n.* a book, especially a large one.

torrent [tôr′ənt, tor′-] *n.* a rapid, violent stream.

tortuous [tôr′choo əs] *adj.* twisting; winding.

trace [trās] *n.* a strap or chain connecting an animal's harness to a vehicle being pulled.

transgress [trans gres′, tranz-] *v.* to violate; break.

tremulous [trem′yə ləs] *adj.* trembling; throbbing.

trepidation [trep′ə dā′shən] *n.* a shaking or trembling.

trestle [tres′əl] *n.* a framework for supporting something.

trick [trik] *v.* to ornament.

tumult [too′məlt, tū′-] *n.* violent motion; confusion.

turbid [tur′bid] *adj.* muddy; confusing.

U

unallayed [un′ə lād′] *adj.* not lessened or quieted.

unassailable [un′ə sā′lə bəl] *adj.* not able to be attacked or questioned.

unburnished [un bur′nisht] *adj.* unpolished.

unconditional [un′kən dish′ən əl] *adj.* unlimited; absolute.

unfledged [un flejd′] *adj.* not yet having all its feathers.

unkempt [un kempt′] *adj.* not well groomed; messy.

unravished [un rav′isht] *adj.* not violated.

unslaked [un slākt′] *adj.* not satisfied or quenched.

untrammeled [un tram′əld] *adj.* not restrained or tied up.

V

vacillate [vas′ə lāt′] *v.* to be unable to decide; hesitate.

valance [val′əns, vā′ləns] *n.* a decorative strip of wood or other material.

valediction [val′ə dik′shən] *n.* a farewell.

vanguard [van′gärd′] *n.* the front part of a moving army.

vantage [van′tij] **ground** a position giving an advantage.

velocity [vi los′ə tē] *n.* speed.

vend [vend] *v.* to sell.

venomous [ven′ə məs] *adj.* poisonous.

veracious [və rā′shəs] *adj.* honest; accurate.

verbatim [vər bā′tim] *adj.* word-for-word.

verisimilitude [ver′ə si mil′ə tood′, -tūd′] *n.* something having the appearance of truth or reality.

verity [ver′ə tē] *n.* truth.

vermin [vur′min] *n.* a small, harmful or disgusting animal.

vessel [ves′əl] *n.* a ship or boat.

vexatious [vek sā′shəs] *adj.* annoying; disturbing.

vicissitude [vi sis′ə tood′, -tūd′] *n.* changeableness.

victuals [vit′əlz] *n.pl.* food.

vie [vī] **vied, vying** *v.* to compete.

vigilance [vij′ə ləns] *n.* watchfulness; alertness.

vilify [vil′ə fī′] *v.* to say harmful and false things about.

vindication [vin′də kā′shən] *n.* the act of defending.

virtuosity [vur′choo os′ə tē] *n.* great skill in music, art, acting, etc.

visage [viz′ij] *n.* a person's face.

vivacious [vi vā′shəs, vī-] *adj.* lively; animated.

vociferous [vō sif′ər əs] *adj.* shouting forcefully.

voluble [vol′yə bəl] *adj.* speaking easily and rapidly; talkative.

voracious [vô rā′shəs, və-] *adj.* wanting large amounts of food; ravenous.

vouchsafe [vouch sāf′] *v.* to be nice enough to give.

W

warden [wôrd′ən] *n.* a person in charge of something.

weal [wēl] *n.* well-being.

wend [wend] *v.* ARCHAIC. to travel.

whet [hwet, wet] *v.* to sharpen.

wile [wīl] *n.* a trick.

wizened [wiz′ənd] *adj.* dried out; shriveled.

wrangler [rang′glər] *n.* a quarrelsome person.

wrest [rest] *v.* to take by force; wring.

Z

zealous [zel′əs] *adj.* extremely enthusiastic or devoted.

zenith [zē′nith] *n.* the point in the sky directly above the observer.

zephyr [zef′ər] *n.* a breeze.

---

at; āpe; cär; end; mē; it; īce; hot; ōld; fôrk; wood; fōōl; oil; out; up; ūse; turn; ə in ago, taken, pencil, lemon, circus; bat; chin; dear; five; game; hit; hw in white; joke; kit; lid; man; not; singer; pail; ride; sat; shoe; tag; thin; this; very; wet; yes; zoo; zh in treasure; KH in loch, German ach; N in French bon; œ in French feu, German schön

Index of Titles by Theme

Index of Titles by Genre

SHORT STORY

SONG

Index of Skills

Page numbers in boldface italics indicate entries in the Writing About Literature Handbook.
Page numbers in italics indicate entries in the Handbook of Literary Terms.

LITERARY SKILLS

Acmeism, 860
Age of Classicism, 253
Age of Elegance, 253
Age of Johnson, 254, 289, *947*
Age of Pope, 254, *947*
Age of Reason, 253, 776–777
Allegory, 747
Alliteration, 20, 362, **938**, *946*
Alliterative verse, 20
Allusion, 228, 236, 546, *946*
Analogy, *946*
Anapest, *946, 951*
Anecdote, *946*
Anglo-Saxon, 5, 26–27
Antagonist, *946*
Aphorism, *946*
Apostrophe, 378, *946*
Aside, 108, *946*
Assonance, 362, **938**, *946*
Atmosphere, 189, 630, *946*
Audience, 196
Augustan Age, 254, 716, *947*
Autobiography, 301, 416, *947*

Ballad stanza, 41, *947*
Bibliography, **930**
Biography, 301, *947*
Blank verse, 129, 229, 236, *947*

Caesura, 20, *947*
Caricature, 773, *947*
Catharsis, 713
Cavaliers, 202, 216, 221, 224
Chansons de geste, 735
Character, 62–63, 189, 420, 428, 610, 716, 778, *947*
  complex, 610
  dynamic, 189, 610, *947*
  flat, 189, 610, *947*
  round, 62–63, 189, 610, *947*
  static, 189, 610, *947*
  stock, 716
Characterization, 62–63, 78, 588, 598, 610, *947–948*
  direct, 63, 610, 947
  indirect, 63, 598, 610, *947–948*
  in short story, 588, 610
Chivalry, 33–34, 734
Chorus, *948*
Classical Age, 775
Classicism, 253–255, 777, *948*

Climax, 188, 597, *948, 954*
Colloquial language, *948*
Comedy, 202, 459, *948*
  of ideas, 459
  of manners, 202
  satiric, 202
Conceit, 209, 757, *948*
  metaphysical, *948*
  Petrarchan, 757, *948*
Conflict, 188, 591, 908, *948, 954*
  external, 188, 591, 908, *948*
  internal, 188, 591, 908, *948*
Connotation, 569, *948*
Consonance, **938**, *948*
Couplet, 90, 237, 288, *949, 951*
  heroic, 237, 288, *951*
  rhymed, 90
Courtly love poetry, 748

Dactyl, *949, 951*
Dada, 849–850
Denotation, 569, *949*
Denouement, *949*
Description, *949*
Details, 28, 63, 78
Dialect, *949*
Dialogue, 38, 878, *949*
Diary, 247, *947, 949*
Diction, 569, 573, 626, *949*
Dirge, 107
Drama, 108–109, 196, 202, 323, 678, *949*
  closet, 323
  Elizabethan, 108–109
  Greek, 678
  melodrama, 323
  Restoration, 202
  sound in, 196
Dramatic age, 650, 652–653
Dramatic conventions, 108, 502, *949*
Dramatic monologue, 420, 425, 856, *949*
Droll, the, 202

Elegy, 307, 652, *950*
Endnote, **930**
End-stopped line, *950*
Enlightenment, 776–777
Epic, 5, 8, 229, 236, 287, 670, *950, 953*
Epic age, 650–651
Epigram, 288, *950*
Epiphany, 597, *950*
Epitaph, 306, *950*
Epithet, 670, *950*
Essay, 190, 268, 275, 391, *950*
  expository, *950*
  familiar, 396
  formal, 275, *950*
  informal, 275, *950*

Exemplum, 65
Existentialism, 851, 892, 899, *950*
Exposition, 188, 597, *950, 954*

Fable, 671, 673, *950*
Falling action, 188, 597, *950, 954*
Farce, 787, *950*
Figurative language, 104, 378, *950–951*
Figure of speech, 104, 378, *951*
Flashback, *951*
Folk ballad, 35, 38, 41, 444, *951, 953*
Foot, 90, *951*
Footnote, **930**
Foreshadowing, *951*
Frame story, 43, 763, *951*
Free verse, 194, 453, *951*

Georgian poetry, 547, 548

Hero, 110, 365, 713, *957*
  Byronic, 365
  tragic, 110, 713, *957*
Homeric (epic) simile, 670, *950, 951*

Iamb, 90, *951*
Iambic pentameter, 90, 129, *951*
Imagery, 141, 863, *951–952*
Imaginative reading, 448
Implication, 316
Inference, 316
Interior monologue, 763, *952*
Interludes, 85
Irish National Theater, 454
Irish Renaissance, 531
Irony, 189, 886, *952*
  dramatic, 189, *952*
  situational, 886, *952*
  verbal, 189, 886, *952*

Journal, 247, *952*

Kenning, 20, *952*

Legend, 77, 679, *952*
Literary criticism, 203, 395, 400, *952*
Lyric age, 650–652

Madrigal, 107
Masque, 85
Metaphor, 104, 378, **938**, *952*
Metaphysical poetry, 202, 206, *952*
Meter, 90, 419, *952*
Middle English, 26, 42, 70–71, *952*
Minnelieder, 735
Minnesingers, 735, 748
Miracle play, 35
Mock-epic, 287, *952*
Modern English, 26–27, 71, 104, *953*
Modernism, 453–455, 801

Mood, 189, 630, *953*
Morality play, 35
Motivation, 63, 610, *953*
Mystery play, 35
Myth, 77, 731, *953*

Narrative, 763, *953*
Narrative hook, 597, *953, 954*
Narrator, 579, 602, 763, *953*
Naturalism, 833, *953*
Neoclassical Age, 775, *953*
Neoclassicism, 216, 254, 302, 327, *953*
Novel, 255, 323, 432, 555, 764, *953–954*
   adventure, 323
   gothic, 255, 323, 555, *954*
   historical, 323, 555
   of manners, 255, 323
   naturalistic, *954*
   philosophical, *954*
   picaresque, 255, 764, *953*
   psychological, *954*
   realistic, *954*
   of sentiment, 255, *953*
   of social criticism, *954*

Object poem, 852
Octave, 90, 757, *954*
Ode, 388, 652, *954*
Old English, 5, 26–27, *954*
Onomatopoeia, 363, **938,** *954*
Oral tradition, 5, 20, 38, 41, 654, *954*
Oratory, 716
Ottava rima, 369, *954*

Paradox, 561, *954*
Parallelism, *954*
Parody, 259, *954*
Pentameter, 90
Personification, 378, **938,** *954*
Persuasion, *954*
Philosophes, 788
Plot, 188, 432, 588, 597, *954*
   in drama, 188
   in novel, 432
   in short story, 588, 597
Poetry, 84, 248, 447, 573, 650, *949, 952, 953*
   dramatic, 447, *949*
   lyric, 84, 447, 650, *952*
   modern, 573
   narrative, 447, *953*
   sound in, 248
Point of view, 315, 588, 602, *955*
   first-person, 602, *955*
   limited third-person, 602, *955*
   omniscient, 602, *955*
   in short story, 588, 602
Pre-Raphaelites, 405
Prose, sound in, 644
Protagonist, *955*
Psalms, 194
Purpose, **932**

Quatrain, 90, 566, *955*

Realism, 406, 453, 801, 833, 838, *955*
   psychological, 453
Refrain, 41, *955*
Renaissance, 83–84, 753–755
Repetition, 863, *955*
Resolution, 188, 597, *954, 955*
Restoration comedy, 202
Rhyme, 90, 362, **938,** *955*
   end, 90, 362, *955*
   internal, 362, *955*
Rhymed couplet, 90
Rhythm, 419, 438, 863, **938,** *955*
   sprung, 438, *956*
Rising action, 188, 597, *954*
Romance, 35
Romanticism, 321–323, 326–327, 364–365, 372, 800–801, *955*
Runes, 26
Run-on line, *956*

Satire, 202, 267, *956*
Scansion, *956*
Scop, 5, 20
Sensibility, 269
Sestet, 90, 757, *956*
Setting, 189, 432, 630, *956*
Short story, 455, 588, *956*
Simile, 104, 670, **938,** *950, 951, 956*
   Homeric (epic), 670, *950, 951*
Situational irony, 886
Soliloquy, 108, *956*
Song, 5, 105, 107, 308, 444, 671, 735, 748
   Elizabethan, 105, 107, 444
Sonnet, 90, 757, *956*
   English (Shakespearean), 90, *956*
   Italian (Petrarchan), 90, 757, *956*
Sons of Ben, 202, 216
Speaker, **938**
Stage directions, 196, *956*
Stanza, 41, 90, 307, *947, 957*
   ballad, 41, *947*
   elegiac, 307
Stream of consciousness, 611, 617, *954, 957*
Structure, 338, 626, *957*
Sturm und Drang, 802
Style, 236, 626, *957*
Subject, 626
Subplot, 432
Surrealism, 862, 890
Symbol, 540, 839, **934,** *957*
Symbolism, 315, 540, 801, 839, 843, 845, 860
Symbolist poetry, 801, 839, 845, *957*

Tercet, 566
Terza rima, 737, *957*
Theater of the Absurd, 624, 851

Theme, 189, 432, 588, 638, **936,** *957*
   implied, 638, *957*
   stated, 638, *957*
Thesis statement, **926**
Tone, 630, 863, **944,** *957*
Total effect, 188–189, 529, **940**
Tragedy, 110, 255, 713, *957*
   classical, 255
   Elizabethan, 110
   sentimental, 255
Tragic flaw, 110, 713, *957*
Tragic hero, 110, 713, *957*
Tragicomedy, 202
Translation, 812
Tribe of Ben, 202, 216
Trochee, *951, 957*
Troubadours, 735

Verbal irony, 886
Verisimilitude, 63, *957*
Vernacular, 194, 735
Villanelle, 566, *957*

Word choice, 569, 863

COMPOSITION SKILLS

Page numbers in boldface italics indicate entries in the Writing About Literature Handbook.

ANALYTICAL

Character, writing about, 27, 77, 617, 868
Characterization, analyzing, 763
Comparison, writing a, 93
Comparison/contrast, writing a, 425, 540, 591, 747, 751, 757, 787, 845, 855, 874, 898, **928**
Details, writing about significant, 643
Epic and fable, comparing and contrasting the, 673
Evidence, citing, 247, 301, 597, 886, **930**
   and documenting, 247
Folk ballad, supporting a thesis about a, 41
Images, analyzing use of, 107
Irony, writing about, 287
Literature, applying a statement about, 447, 731, **942**
Literature, supporting an opinion about, 71
Literature, writing about your reaction to, 626
Literature and its period, writing about, 338, 432, 573, 795, 921, **944**
Medieval literature, comparing and contrasting, 63
Nonfiction, writing about, 193, 275, 623, 889, **932**
Personification, writing about, 861
Play's ending, writing about a, 530

Index of Authors and Titles